Whitelaw Reid

Ohio in the War

Her Statesmen, her Generals, and Soldiers - Vol. II

Whitelaw Reid

Ohio in the War
Her Statesmen, her Generals, and Soldiers - Vol. II

ISBN/EAN: 9783337133849

Printed in Europe, USA, Canada, Australia, Japan

Cover: Foto ©ninafisch / pixelio.de

More available books at **www.hansebooks.com**

OHIO IN THE WAR:

HER STATESMEN,

HER

GENERALS, AND SOLDIERS.

BY WHITELAW REID.

IN TWO VOLUMES.

VOLUME II:

THE HISTORY OF HER REGIMENTS,

AND

OTHER MILITARY ORGANIZATIONS.

"The real heroes of this war are the great, brave, patient, nameless PEOPLE."—GUROWSKI.

PUBLISHERS:
MOORE, WILSTACH & BALDWIN,
25 WEST FOURTH STREET, CINCINNATI.
NEW YORK: 60 WALKER STREET.
1868.

CONTENTS.

LIST OF ILLUSTRATIONS.

PART III.

THE HISTORY OF OHIO REGIMENTS,

AND

OTHER MILITARY ORGANIZATIONS.

INTRODUCTORY.

THE REGIMENTS AND SOLDIERS OF OHIO.

AT the close of the War against the Rebellion, the State of Ohio had in the National service two hundred regiments of all arms.* In the course of the war she furnished two hundred and thirty regiments, besides twenty-six independent batteries of artillery, five independent companies of cavalry, several companies of sharp-shooters, large parts of five regiments credited to the West Virginia contingent, two credited to the Kentucky contingent, two transferred to "United States Colored Troops," and a large proportion of the rank and file for the Fifty-Fourth and Fifty-Fifth Massachusetts.

Of these organizations, twenty-three were infantry regiments furnished for three months at the outbreak of the war, being an excess of nearly one-half over the quota allotted to the State.† One hundred and ninety-one were infantry regiments afterward furnished in obedience to the several calls of the President—one hundred and seventeen for three years, twenty-seven for one year, two for six months. three for three months, and forty-two for a hundred days. Thirteen were cavalry and three were artillery regiments for three years. And of these three-years' troops from Ohio, over twenty thousand re-enlisted as veterans at the end of their long term of service—to fight till the war should ebb out in Victory.

In these various organizations, as original members or as recruits, the State furnished to the National service the magnificent army of three hundred and ten thousand six hundred and fifty-four soldiers.‡ The older, larger, and

* Rep. Adj. Gen. of Ohio for 1865, p. 67.

† The quota was only thirteen regiments. The Government would not then accept more, and so the State put them in the field on her own account. The Government finally paid them.

‡ In this statement I follow throughout the figures of the United States Provost-Marshal-General in his final report to the War Department (Vol. I, pp. 160 to 164). Nearly all the States have industriously reckoned up larger totals—obtained by counting those who paid commutation money as so many soldiers actually furnished, by treating the veteran re-enlistments as so many new troops, by enumerating their citizens enlisted in the organizations of other States, their sailors, etc. Much may be plausibly said in favor of counting most of these different classes; but, on the whole, it seems to me fairer to reject them, and to accept the figures on which the War Department acted in apportioning the quotas and enforcing the draft. This gives a less imposing appearance to the statement of our troops, but it is perfectly free from any possibility of being charged with the unwise exaggeration to which a morbid State pride has sometimes led. The Adjutant-General of Ohio, however, in his report for 1864, reckoning most of the classes we have rejected, had swelled the number of troops furnished by the State (up to December 1, 1864) to 346,326.—Report, p. 47.

more populous commonwealth of Pennsylvania gave not quite twenty-eight thousand more, while Illinois fell forty-eight thousand behind, Indiana a hundred and sixteen thousand, Kentucky two hundred and thirty-five thousand, and Massachusetts a hundred and sixty-four thousand. Thus Ohio more than maintained in the army the rank among her sisters to which her population pointed. Let us not fail to add—in no spirit of detraction to other States, but with the honest pride which the facts entitle us to entertain—that Ohio furnished, from first to last, more troops than the Government ever required of her; that, at the end of the war, with a thousand men in the camps of the State that were never mustered, she still had a credit on the rolls of the War Department for four thousand three hundred and thirty-two soldiers beyond the aggregate of all quotas ever assigned her;* and that, besides all these, six thousand four hundred and seventy-nine of her citizens had paid the commutation in lieu of personal service; while Indiana was behind her quotas five thousand four hundred and twenty-five men, Kentucky twenty-four thousand nine hundred and nineteen, Pennsylvania fifty-thousand three hundred and sixty, and New York sixty-one thousand one hundred and eighty-nine.† So nobly through all those years of trial and death did she keep the promise of the memorable dispatch from her first war Governor: "If Kentucky refuses to fill her quota, Ohio will fill it for her."

The great army thus put into the field by the State that, half a century ago, was a wilderness, was enlisted, under the different calls of the President, as follows:

Under the call of	Ohio furnished	Her quota being
April 15, 1861, for 75,000 men	12,357	10,153‡
July 22, 1861, for 500,000 men	84,116	67,365
July 2, 1862, for 300,000 men	58,325	36,858
August 4, 1862, for 300,000 for nine months		36,858
June 15, 1863, for militia	2,736	......
October 17, 1863, for 500,000	32,837	51,465
March 14, 1864, for 200,000 men	29,931	20,595
April 22, 1864, for one-hundred days' militia	36,254	30,000
July 18, 1864, for 500,000 men	30,823	27,001
December 19, 1864, for 300,000 men	23,275	26,027
Totals	310,654	306,322

The period of service of these troops ranged from that of the National Guards for a hundred days to that of the veteran volunteers for five years.

* Furthermore, she was to have been credited on the next call, had another been needed, with thirteen thousand and twenty-two years of service not hitherto credited to her on any of her quotas—for no reason, save that it had been voluntarily offered when the Government had not been calling for it.—Provost-Marshal-General's Report, Vol. 1, p. 164.

† The States of Illinois and Massachusetts, which, having been included in the previous comparison, ought to appear in this one, had also more than filled their quotas, and had handsome credits.

‡ No credit was here given, it will be seen, for the extra ten regiments raised for the three-months' service in April and May, 1861, which the Government refused to accept.

Reduced to the department standard, they represent not quite two hundred and forty thousand three-years' soldiers.

Even this does not present the full sum of the contributions of men from Ohio to the National armies. The State was credited with one thousand and seventy-six men furnished to the gun-boat service on the Western waters, and, before the department began to give credit for these naval enlistments, there had been two thousand three hundred and sixty-seven of them. Furthermore, there were five thousand and ninety-two negro soldiers from Ohio, either credited to other States or to the "United States Colored Troops," besides some complete white regiments and large numbers of recruits raised in Ohio, but, in the varying exigencies of the department, credited elsewhere.

Altogether, reckoning the sum of these various numbers, we may safely conclude that the army of the State, from the outbreak of the war to its close, swelled to the noble proportions of a third of a million of men.

Of these, nearly all were volunteers. Only eight thousand seven hundred and fifty had to be raised in Ohio by the draft throughout the war. But the volunteers received from the people of the State, independent of Government pay and premiums, over twenty-three and a half million dollars of local bounties.

Their service was deadly. Eleven thousand two hundred and thirty-seven of them were killed or mortally wounded in action, of whom six thousand five hundred and sixty-three were left dead on the field of battle. Thirteen thousand three hundred and fifty-four died, before the expiration of their terms of enlistment, of diseases contracted in the service. Thirty-seven Ohio soldiers out of every thousand fell dead or mortally wounded in battle; forty-seven more died in the hospitals; seventy-one more were honorably discharged, unable longer to do the duty of soldiers, by reason of wounds or sickness incurred in the Country's service. Let us not, in the fullness of our just pride, conceal the darker side of the picture: forty-four out of every thousand deserted.*

They fought on well-nigh every battle-field of the war. Within forty-eight hours after the telegraphic call, two Ohio regiments were on their way to the rescue of the imperiled capital in the spring of 1861. An Ohio brigade, in good order, covered the retreat from the first Bull Run. Ohio troops formed

* It should be remembered that many of these desertions were not such in intention, and that, after a stolen visit to their families, the men went back to the service. The number of desertions in Ohio troops, however, was small compared with that in the troops in many States. We have said that in Ohio it was 44 to the thousand. In New York it was 89 to the thousand, in Pennsylvania 58, in New Jersey 107, in New Hampshire 112, in Connecticut 117, in Kansas 117, in Kentucky 87, in Indiana 37, and in Illinois 51.

The battle mortality compares as follows in some of the States:

In Ohio 37 to the thousand, in Indiana 30, in Illinois 35, in Kentucky 25, in New York 36, in Pennsylvania 31, in Massachusetts 47. These figures show what troops got into the places in battle where they lost the most.

The mortality from disease, in the troops from the same States, compares as follows:

In Ohio 47 to the thousand, in Indiana 69, in Illinois 78, in New York 43, in Pennsylvania 34, and in Massachusetts 63. Supposing exposure to be equal, these figures would show which States had a population possessing the highest vitality, and therefore the lowest mortality.

the bulk of the army that saved West Virginia; the bulk of the army that saved Kentucky; a large share of the army that took Fort Donelson; a part of the army at Island No. 10; a great part of the army that, from Stone River, and Chickamauga, and Mission Ridge, and Kenesaw, and Atlanta, swept down to the sea and back through the Carolinas to the Old Dominion. They fought at Pea Ridge. They charged at Wagner. They campaigned against the Indians along the base of the Rocky Mountains. They helped to redeem North Carolina. They were in the siege of Vicksburg, the siege of Charleston, the siege of Richmond, the siege of Mobile. At Pittsburg Landing, at Antietam, at Gettysburg, at Corinth, in the Wilderness, before Nashville, at Five Forks, and Appomattox C. H., their bones, reposing on the fields they won, are a perpetually-binding pledge that no flag shall ever wave over these graves of our soldiers but the flag they fought to maintain.

"The real heroes of this war are the great, brave, patient, nameless PEOPLE." It is to their service through these varied scenes that we now gladly turn. The Victory was not won through Generalship—it is a libel on the word to say that Generalship delayed for four years the success of twenty-five millions over ten millions, or required a million men in the closing campaigns to defeat a hundred thousand—it was won by the sacrifices, the heroism, the sufferings, the death of the men in the ranks. Their story we now seek to tell. It will be less picturesque, less attractive, fuller of dry details, fruitless fighting, tedious marches, labor, and waiting, and weariness. Even such was the life they led for us; and its record, we are firmly persuaded, will never cease to be cherished by their grateful countrymen.

As it is possible that this second volume of *Ohio in the War* may fall into the hands of some who may not have access to Vol. I, the following explanations are here reproduced from the Preface to the work:

(1.) At the beginning of Vol. II is presented a table, showing at a glance the leading facts concerning the formation, service, losses, recruits, commanders, and muster-out of all the important volunteer organizations of the State.

(2.) Prefixed to the sketch of the history of each regiment, battery, or company, is an exhaustive Roster of its officers, from which the main facts in their military career may be traced. The basis of these Rosters is the record on the rolls of the State Adjutant-General at Columbus, and the Volunteer Register for Ohio, in the War Department at Washington. Both these are necessarily more or less inaccurate. Every effort has been made to correct them, and great numbers of changes have been made. We scarcely dare to hope that the Rosters, as here presented, are entirely free from errors; but we know them to be incomparably better than any others now in existence.

(3.) Aside from the information given in the Rosters, Vol. II is devoted to the Men in the Ranks. Special mention is not therefore habitually made, even of the commanders of regiments. Concerning very many of them, however, full information may be found in the Lives of the Generals in Vol. I; where also the reader must look for the History of the State during the War, and for many incidents illustrative of the heroism of private soldiers.

THE MILITARY ORGANIZATIONS OF OHIO IN THE FIELD* DURING THE WAR,

WITH THE LEADING FACTS, IN THEIR HISTORY.

INFANTRY.

REGIMENT.	TERM OF ENLISTM'T.	ORIGINAL STRENGTH.	STRENGTH AT MUSTER OUT.	COMMANDANT AT ENTRY INTO SERVICE.	COMMANDANT AT MUSTER OUT.	LEFT STATE.	MUSTERED OUT.	WHERE MUSTERED OUT.	WHERE PAID AND DISCHARGED.	STATUS OF FIRST COMMANDANT.
1st	3 years	1001	474	Col. B. F. Smith	Lt.Col. E.B. Langdon	Nov. 5, 1861	Aug. 15, 1864	By com. at Atlanta	Camp Chase	Appointed Col. 128th O. V. I.
2d	Do.	913	383	" L. A. Harris	Col. A. G. McCook	Sept. 17, "	Oct. 10, "	Columbus	Camp Chase	Resigned December 24, 1862.
3d	Do.	910	310	" I. H. Marrow	" O. A. Lawson	Jan. 20, 1862	June 23, "	Camp Dennison	Camp Dennison	Resigned February 4, 1862.
4th	Do.	1004	177	" Lorin Andrews	" L. W. Carpenter	June 20, 1861	July 12, 1865	Jeffersonville, Ind.	Tod Barracks	Died of disease October, 1861.
5th	Do.	941	322	" S. H. Dunning	" Robt. Kirkup	" 14, "	" 26, "	Louisville, Ky	Camp Dennison	Resigned August 2, 1862.
6th	Do.	931	525	" W. K. Bosley	" N. L. Anderson	June 30, "	June 23, 1864	Camp Dennison	Camp Dennison	Hon. disch'd Aug. 19, 1862—since dead.
7th	Do.	1086	240	" E. B. Tyler	Lt.Col. S. McClelland	" 26, "	July 8, "	Camp Cleveland	Camp Cleveland	App. Brigadier-General of volunteers.
8th	Do.	905	72	" H. G. Depuy	" F. Sawyer	July 9, "	" 13, "	Camp Cleveland	Camp Cleveland	Resigned November 9, 1861.
9th	Do.	971	400	" Rob't L. McCook	" F. Schroeder	June 16, "	June 7, "	Camp Dennison	Camp Dennison	App. Brig. Gen.—killed by guerrillas.
10th	Do.	958	310	" W. H. Lytle	Col. J. W. Burke	" 24, "	" 17, "	Camp Dennison	Camp Dennison	App. Brig. Gen.—killed at Chickam'ga.
11th	Do.	887	312	" C. A. De Villiers	" Ogden Street	July 7, "	" 21, "	Camp Dennison	Camp Dennison	Cashiered April 23, 1862.
12th	Do.	937	482	" John W. Lowe	" Carr B. White	" 6, "	July 11, "	Columbus	Camp Chase	Killed at Carnifex Ferry.
13th	Do.	900	142	" Wm. Sooy Smith	Lt.Col. D. Jarvis, jr.	June 30, "	Dec. 5, 1865	San Antonio, Texas	Camp Chase	App. Brig. Gen. of vols. May 13, 1862.
14th	Do.	996	504	" J. B. Steedman	Col. Geo. P. Este	Aug. 25, "	July 11, "	Louisville, Ky	Camp Cleveland	App. Major-General of volunteers.
15th	Do.	938	502	" M. R. Dickey	" Frank Askew	Oct. 4, "	Nov. 21, "	San Antonio, Texas	Camp Chase	Resigned October 24, 1862.
16th	Do.	923	477	" J. F. De Courcey	Lt.Col. P. Kershner	Jan. 12, 1862	Oct. 31, 1864	Morganza, La	Camp Chase	Hon. discharged March 3, 1864.
17th	Do.	852	620	" John M. Connell	" B. Showers	Sept. 30, 1861	July 16, 1865	Louisville, Ky	Tod Barracks	Resigned November 12, 1863.
18th	Do.	921	831	" T. R. Stanley	Col. C. H. Grosvenor	Nov. 6, "	Oct. 9, "	Augusta, Ga	Camp Chase	Mustered out at expiration of service.
19th	Do.	996	478	" Sam. Beatty	" James M. Nash	" 16, "	" 21, "	San Antonio, Texas	Camp Chase	App. Brigadier General of volunteers.
20th	Do.	916	411	" Chas. Whittlesey	" Harrison Wilson	Oct. 21, "	July 15, "	Louisville, Ky	Camp Chase	Resigned April 19, 1862.
21st	Do.	849	378	" Jesse S. Norton	" A. McMahan	" 2, "	" 25, "	Louisville, Ky	Columbus	Resigned December 20, 1862.
22d	Do.	850	133	" C. J. Wright	" Oliver Wood	Nov. 5, "	Nov. 18, 1864	Columbus	Columbus	Resigned Sept. 9, 1862. [volunteers.
23d	Do.	927	732	" W. S. Rosecrans	" Jas. M. Comly	July 25, "	July 26, 1865	Cumberland, Md.	Camp Cleveland	App. Brig. Gen Reg. Army & Maj. Gen.
24th	Do.	923	310	" Jacob Ammen	" A.T.M. Cockerill	" 26, "	June 24, 1864	Columbus	Camp Chase	App. Brigadier-General of vols.
25th	Do.	940	352	" J. A. Jones	Lt.Col. E. C. Culp	" 29, "	" 18, 1866	Columbus	Tod Barracks	Resigned May 16, 1862.
26th	Do.	914	249	" E. P. Fyffe	" Wm. Clark	" 25, "	Oct. 21, 1865	Victoria, Texas	Camp Chase	Transferred to Vet. Reserve Corps.
27th	Do.	898	474	" J. W. Fuller	Col. I. N. Gilruth	Aug. 20, "	July 11, "	Louisville, Ky	Camp Dennison	App. Brig. Gen. & Bvt. Maj. Gen. vols.
28th	Do.	1002	194	" A. Moor	" Gottfried Becker	July 31, "	" 23, "	Wheeling, W. Va.	Camp Chase	Mustered out; app. Brig. Gen. vols.
29th	Do.	968	496	" L. P. Buckley	" J. Schoonover	Jan. 17, 1862	" 22, "	Louisville, Ky	Camp Cleveland	Resigned January 26, 1863.
30th	Do.	796	282	" Hugh Ewing	" Theo. Jones	Aug. 30, 1861	Aug. 13, "	Little Rock, Ark.	Camp Chase	App. Brig. Gen. & Bvt. Maj. Gen. vols.
31st	Do.	970	719	" M. B. Walker	Lt.Col. M. B. W. Harmon	Sept. 31, "	July 20, "	Louisville, Ky	Camp Chase	App. Brevet Brig. Gen. of vols.
32d	Do.	884	766	" Thomas H. Ford	Col. J. J. Hibbitts	" 15, "	" 20, "	Louisville, Ky	Tod Barracks	Dismissed November 18, 1862. [River.
33d	Do.	839	368	" J. W. Sill	" Jos. Hinson	" 13, "	" 12, "	Louisville, Ky	Camp Dennison	App. Brig. Gen. vols.—killed at Stone
34th†	Do.	953		" A. S. Piatt	" F. E. Franklin	" 15, "				App. Brig. Gen. of volunteers.
35th	Do.	812	510	" F. Vanderveer	Lt.Col. H. V. N. Boynton	" 26, "	Aug. 26, 1864	Chattanooga, Ga.	Camp Chase	App. Brig. Gen. & Bvt. Maj. Gen. vols.
36th	Do.	850	959	" George Crook	Lt.Col. W. S. Wilson	" 10, "	July 27, 1865	Wheeling, W. Va.	Tod Barracks	App. Maj. Gen. of volunteers.
37th	Do.	867	416	" Edw. Siber	" L. Von Blessingh	Oct. 8, "	Aug. 12, "	Little Rock, Ark.	Camp Cleveland	Resigned March 23, 1864.
38th	Do.	968	697	" E. D. Bradley	" Wm. Irving	" 1, "	July 12, "	Louisville, Ky	Camp Cleveland	Resigned February 8, 1862.
39th	Do.	977	773	" John Groesbeck	Col. Dan Weber	Aug. 18, "	" 9, "	Louisville, Ky	Camp Dennison	Resigned July 8, 1862.

* There were in addition to those represented in this tabular statement, twenty-three three months' organizations, of which no systematic record was kept in the State Adjutant General's office. All that can appear of their service will be found, with some of the Rosters, in the succeeding pages, in connection with the first twenty-three regiments organized for three years' service.

† Consolidated with 36th O. V. I.

THE MILITARY ORGANIZATIONS OF OHIO—CONTINUED.

REGIMENT.	TERM OF ENLISTM'T.	ORIGINAL STRENGTH.	STRENGTH AT MUSTER OUT.	COMMANDANT AT ENTRY INTO SERVICE.	COMMANDANT AT MUSTER OUT.	LEFT STATE.	MUSTERED OUT.	WHERE MUSTERED OUT.	WHERE PAID AND DISCHARGED.	STATUS OF FIRST COMMANDANT.
40th*	3 years	890		Col. J. Cranor	Col. Jacob E. Taylor.	Dec. 11, 1861		Victoria, Texas	Camp Chase	Resigned February 5, 1863.
41st	Do.	889	293	" W. B. Hazen	" E. S. Holloway	Nov. 13, "	Nov. 26, 1865	Camp Chase	Camp Chase	App. Major-General of volunteers.
42d	Do.	941		" J. A. Garfield	" L. A. Sheldon	Dec. 15, "	Dec. 2, 1864	Camp Chase	Camp Chase	App. Major-General of volunteers.
43d	Do.	925	817	" J. L. Kirby Smith	" Horace Park	Feb. 21, 1862	July 13, 1865	Louisville, Ky	Columbus	Killed at Corinth October 4, 1862.
44th	Do.	925		" S. A. Gilbert	Changed to 8th Cav.	Oct. 14, 1861	" 30, "	Clarksburg, Va	Camp Dennison	Resigned for disability.
45th	Do.	916	436	" B. P. Runkle	Lt.Col. J. H. Humphrey	Aug. 20, 1862	June 15, "	Camp Harker, Tenn	Columbus	App. Bvt. Brig. Gen. of volunteers.
46th	Do.	865	308	" T. Worthington.	Lt.Col. E. N. Upton.	Feb. 18, "	July 22, "	Louisville, Ky	Columbus	Dismissed September 16, 1863. Rest'd
47th	Do.	830	277	" F. Poschner	Col. Thos. T. Taylor.	Aug. 28, 1861	Aug. 11, "	Little Rock, Ark	Camp Dennison	Resigned July 17, 1862.
48th	Do.	938	267	" P. J. Sullivan	Lt.Col. J. R. Lynch	Feb. 17, 1862	May 9, 1866	Galveston, Texas	Tod Barracks	Resigned August 17, 1863.
49th	Do.	866	293	" W. H. Gibson	Lt.Col. J. R. Bartlett	Sept. 21, 1861	Nov. 30, 1865	Victoria, Texas	Camp Chase	Mustered out at expiration of service.
50th	Do.	971	684	" Jonah R. Taylor.	Col. S. A. Strickland.	" 1, 1862	June 26, "	Salisbury, N. C.	Camp Dennison	Resigned October 16, 1862.
51st	Do.	965	669	" Stanl'y Matthews	" Chas. H. Woods.	Nov. 3, 1861	Oct. 3, "	Victoria, Texas	Camp Chase	Resigned April 14, 1863.
52d	Do.	978	437	" Dan. McCook	Lt.Col. C. W. Clancey	Aug. 25, 1862	June 3, "	Washington, D. C.	Columbus	App. Brig. Gen. vols.- died of w'nds.
53d	Do.	869	416	" J. J. Appler	Col. Wells S. Jones	Feb. 16, "	Aug. 11, "	Little Rock, Ark	Camp Dennison	Mustered out April 18, 1862.
54th	Do.	700	256	" T. K. Smith	Lt.Col. I. T. Moore.	" 17, "	" 15, "	Little Rock, Ark	Camp Dennison	App. Brigadier-General of volunteers.
55th	Do.	946	378	" John C. Lee	" E. H. Powers	Jan. 25, "	July 11, "	Louisville, Ky	Camp Cleveland	Res. May 8, '63; app. Brev. Brig. Gen.
56th	Do.	866	263	" Peter Kinney	" H. E. Jones	Feb. 12, "	March —, 1866	New Orleans, La	Tod Barracks	Resigned April 2, 1862.
57th	Do.	937	243	" Wm. Mungen	Col. Sam'l R. Mott	" 18, "	Aug. 14, 1865	Little Rock, Ark	Tod Barracks	Resigned April 16, 1863.
58th	Do.	873	361	" V. Bausenwein	Lt.Col. W. S. Friesner	" 11, "	Jan. 14, "	Vicksburg, Miss	Camp Chase	Dismissed and restored.
59th	Do.	609	176	" Jas. P. Fyffe	" G. A. Frambers	Oct. 1, 1861	Oct. 31, 1864	Nashville, Tenn	Camp Chase	Resigned Oct. 6, 1863; since deceased.
60th	1 year.	867		" W. H. Trimble		April 27, 1864	" 10, 1862	Chicago, Ill	Camp Chase	Mustered out at expiration of service.
60th	3 years		563	Lt. Col. J. N. McElroy	Maj. H. R. Stevens	" —, "	July 25, 1865	Delany House, D. C.	Camp Chase	Discharged on disability by wounds.
61st†	Do.	875		Col. N. Schleich		May 27, 1862				Resigned September 23, 1862.
62d‡	Do.	936		" F. B. Pond		Jan. 17, "				Mustered out at expiration of service.
63d	Do.	901	561	" J. W. Sprague		Feb. 18, "	July 8, 1865	Louisville, Ky	Camp Dennison	App. Brig. Gen. vol. & Bvt. Maj. Gen.
64th	Do.	890	258	" John Ferguson	Col. Sam'l M. Wolff	Dec. 10, 1861	Dec. 3, "	Victoria, Texas	Camp Chase	Dismissed.
65th	Do.	909	141	" C. G. Harker	Lt. Col. Orlow Smith.	" 18, "	" 16, "	San Antonio, Texas	Camp Chase	App. Brig. Gen. vols.; killed in bat.
66th	Do.	921	439	" Chas. Candy	" J. T. Mitchell, jr	Jan. 17, 1862	July 15, "	Louisville, Ky	Tod Barracks	Mustered out at expiration service.
67th	Do.	1025	570	" O. Burstenbinder	Col. A. C. Voris	" 19, "	Dec. 7, "	City Point, Va	Camp Chase	Dismissed July 19, 1862.
68th	Do.	990	514	" S. H. Steedman	Lt.Col. A. C. Crockett	Feb. 7, "	July 10, "	Louisville, Ky	Camp Cleveland	Mustered out July 5, 1862.
69th	Do.	900	536	" L. D. Campbell	" J. H. Brigham	April 19, "	" 17, "	Louisville, Ky	Camp Dennison	Resigned Aug. 9, 1862.
70th	Do.	941	335	" J. R. Cockerill	" H. L. Phillips.	Feb. 17, "	Aug. 14, "	Little Rock, Ark	Camp Dennison	Resigned April 13, 1864.
71st	Do.	879	377	" Rodney Mason	" Jas. H. Hart	" 10, "	Nov. 30, "	San Antonio, Texas	Camp Chase	Cashiered, restored and hon. dis.
72d	Do.	1010	319	" R. P. Buckland	Col. Chas. G. Eaton	" 15, "	Sept. 11, "	Vicksburg, Miss	Camp Chase	App. Brig. Gen. vols. vols.
73d	Do.	891	454	" Orland Smith	Lt.Col. T. W. Higgins.	Jan. 24, "	July 20, "	Louisville, Ky	Camp Dennison	Res. Feb. 17, 1864; app. Bvt. Brig. Gen.
74th	Do.	970	457	" Granville Moody.	Col. R. P. Findley	April 20, "	" 10, "	Louisville, Ky	Camp Dennison	Res. May 16, '63; app. Bv. Brig. Gen. vols.
75th	Do.	921		" N. C. McLean	" A. L. Harris	Jan. 23, "	Nov. & Dec. 1864	Columbus	Columbus	App. Brigadier General volunteers.
76th	Do.	929	433	" Chas. R. Woods.	" Edward Briggs	Feb. 9, "	July 15, 1865	Louisville, Ky	Camp Chase	App. Major-General volunteers.
77th	Do.	910	411	" J. Hildebrand	" Wm. E. Stevens.	" 17, "	March 8, 1866	Brownsville, Texas.	Tod Barracks	Died April 18, 1863.
78th	Do.	908	521	" M. D. Leggett	" G. F. Wiles	" 11, "	July 11, 1865	Louisville, Ky	Tod Barracks	App. Major-General volunteers.
79th	Do.	859	531	" H. G. Kennett	" A. W. Doane	Sept. 3, "	June 9, "	Washington, D. C.	Camp Dennison	Res. Aug. 1864; ap. Bt. Brig. Gen. vols.
80th	Do.	919	325	" E. R. Eckley	Lt.Col. T. C. Morris	Feb. 20, "	Aug. 15, "	Little Rock, Ark	Tod Barracks	Resigned February 14, 1864.
81st	Do.	950	588	" Thomas Morton.	" W. H. Hill	Sept. —, 1861	July 13, "	Louisville, Ky	Camp Dennison ?	Resigned July 30, 1864.
82d	Do.	931	727	" James Cantwell.	Col. S. J. McGroarty.	Jan. 25, 1862	" 24, "	Louisville, Ky	Tod Barracks	Killed in battle August 29, 1862.
83d	Do.	1010		" F. W. Moore	" F. W. Moore	Sept. 3, "	" 21, "	Galveston, Texas	Camp Dennison	App. Bvt. Brig. Gen. volunteers.
84th†	3 months	1021		" Wm. Lawrence	" W. Lawrence	June 11, "				
85th§	Do.	871		" C. W. B. Allison.	" C. W. B. Allison.	" 10, "				
86th	Do.	958		" B. Burns	" B. Burns	" 16, "	Sept. 25, 1862	Camp Delaware	Camp Delaware	Mustered out of service.
86th	6 months	977		" W. C. Lemert	" W. C. Lemert	Aug. 8, 1863	Feb. 10, 1864	Cleveland	Camp Cleveland	Mustered out of service.
87th	Do.	1024		" H. B. Banning	" H. B. Banning	June 12, 1862	Sept. 20, 1862	Camp Chase	Camp Chase	App. Bvt. Brig. Gen. volunteers.
88th**	Do.	620		" E. A. Bratton	" Peter Zinn			Camp Chase	Camp Chase	
88th††	3 months	1022	1017	" Geo. W. Neff	" Geo. W. Neff		July 3, 1865	Camp Chase	Camp Chase	App. Bvt. Brig. Gen. volunteers.
89th	Do.	993	418	" J. G. Marshall	Lt.Col. W. H. Glenn.	Sept. 3, 1862	June 7, "	Washington, D. C.	Camp Dennison	Dismissed October 7, 1862.
90th	Do.	963	457	" Isaac N. Ross	Col. Sam. N. Yeoman	Aug. 29, "	" 13, "	Camp Harker, Tenn	Camp Dennison	Resigned April 14, 1862.

91st	3 years	951	741	Col. John A. Turley	Col. B. F. Coates	Sept. 13, 1862	June 24, 1865	Cumberland, Md.	Camp Dennison	Discharged for wounds Nov. 4, 1864
92d	Do.	905	488	" N. H. Van Vorhes	Lt. Col. J. C. Morrow	Oct. 7, "	" 10, "	Washington, D. C.	Camp Chase	Resigned March 22, 1863.
93d	Do.	967	376	" Chas. Anderson	" Dan. Bowman	Aug. 23, "	" 8, "	Camp Harker, Tenn.	Camp Dennison	Resg. for wounds February 24, 1863.
94th	Do.	1010	418	" J. W. Frizzell	" R. P. Hutchins	" 28, "	" 6, "	Washington, D. C.	Camp Chase	Resg. for wounds February 22, 1863.
95th	Do.	1017	359	" W. L. McMillen	Maj. W. R. Warnock	" 20, "	Aug. 19, "	Louisville, Ky.	Tod Barracks	App. Brigadier-General volunteers.
96th	Do.	1014	427	" J. W. Vance	Lt. Col. A. H. Brown	Sept. 1, "	July 7, "	Mobile, Ala.	Camp Chase	Killed in action April 8, 1864.
97th	Do.	964	371	" John Q. Lane	Col. John Q. Lane	" 7, "	June 12, "	Nashville, Tenn.	Tod Barracks	App. Bvt. Brig. Gen. volunteers.
98th	Do.	985	401	" George Webster	" John S. Pearce	Aug. 23, "	June 3, "	Washington, D. C.	Camp Cleveland	Killed at Perryville, October 8, 1862.
99th ::	Do.	1020		" A. Langworthy		" 31, "				Discharged November 4, 1862.
100th	Do.	1014	526	" John C. Groom	Lt. Col. F. Rundell	Sept. 9, "	June 20, 1865	Greensboro', N. C.	Camp Cleveland	Resigned May 13, 1863.
101st	Do.	980	339	" Leander Stem	" B. D. McDanald	" 4, "	" 12, "	Camp Harker, Tenn.	Camp Cleveland	Killed Dec. 26, 1862, at Stone River.
102d	Do.	1061	631	" Wm. Given	" John Huston	" 4, "	" 30, "	Nashville, Tenn.	Tod Barracks	Mustered out; since deceased.
103d	Do.	975	185	" J. S. Casement	Col. P. C. Hayes	" 3, "	" 22, "	Greensboro', N. C.	Camp Cleveland	Resigned April 30, 1865.
104th	Do.	1017	640	" J. W. Reilly	" Oscar W. Sterl	" 1, "	" 17, "	Greensboro', N. C.	Camp Cleveland	App. Brigadier-General volunteers.
105th	Do.	1009	427	" A. S. Hall	Lt. Col. G. T. Perkins	Aug. 21, "	" 3, "	Washington, D. C.	Camp Cleveland	Died July 10, 1863.
106th	Do.	700	520	Lt. Col. G. Tafel	" G. Tafel	Sept. 4, "	" 29, "	Nashville, Tenn.	Camp Dennison	Mustered out at expiration of service.
107th	Do.	850	491	Col. S. Meyer	" J. S. Cooper	" 25, "	July 10, "	Charleston, S. C.	Camp Cleveland	Resigned February 8, 1864.
108th	Do.	625	412	Lt. Col. G. T. Limberg	Col. Jos. Good	" —, "	June 9, "	Washington, D. C.	Camp Dennison	Discharged May 16, 1864.
110th	Do.	797	627	Col. J. W. Keifer	" Otho H. Binkley	Oct. 19, "	" 25, "	Washington, D. C.	Tod Barracks	App. Bvt. Major-General volunteers.
111th	Do.	1011	557	" John R. Bond	Lt. Col. T. C. Norris	Sept. 11, "	" 27, "	Salisbury, N. C.	Camp Cleveland	Honorably discharged Oct. 8, 1862.
113th	Do.	819	526	" J. A. Wilcox	Col. Toland Jones	Dec. 27, "	July 6, "	Louisville, Ky.	Tod Barracks	Resigned April 29, 1863.
114th	Do.	940	393	" J. Cradlebaugh	" John H. Kelley	Dec. 1, "	" 31, "	Houston, Texas	Tod Barracks	Resigned September 20, 1863.
115th	Do.	972	696	" J. A. Lucy	" Thos. C. Boone	Nov. —, "	June 23, "	Murfreesboro', Ten.	Camp Cleveland	Discharged July 6, 1864.
116th	Do.	897	590	" J. Washburn	Lt. Col. W. B. Teters	Sept. 1, "	" 14, "	Richmond, Va.	Camp Dennison	Mustered out at expiration of service.
117th ;;	Do.	795		" C. G. Hawley		Oct. 2, "	Aug. 1, "	Camp Dennison	Camp Dennison	See 1st Ohio Heavy Artillery.
118th	Do.	908	530	" S. R. Mott	Lt. Col. Ed. Sowers	Sept. —, "	June 24, "	Salisbury, N. C.	Camp Cleveland	Resigned February 10, 1864.
120th §§	Do.	949		" Dan'l French		Oct. 25, "				Resigned February 18, 1863.
121st	Do.	943	391	" W. P. Reed	Lt. Col. A. B. Robinson	Sept. 15, "	June 8, 1865	Washington, D. C.	Camp Chase	Resigned February 4, 1863.
122d	Do.	936	585	" W. H. Hall	" C. M. Cornyn	Oct. 23, "	" 26, "	Washington, D. C.	Tod Barracks	Resigned February 3, 1865.
123d	Do.	959	662	" Wm. T. Wilson	" H. Kellogg	" 16, "	" 12, "	Camp Chase	Camp Chase	Mustered out at expiration of service.
124th	Do.	847	431	" O. H. Payne	Col. Jas. Pickands	Jan. 1, 1863	July 9, "	Nashville, Tenn.	Camp Cleveland	Resigned.
125th	Do.	911	360	" E. Opdycke	" J. Bruff	" 3, "	Sept. 25, "	Camp Irwin, Texas	Camp Chase	App. Brig. Gen. vols. and Bvt. Maj. Gen. vols.
126th	Do.	889	597	" B. F. Smith	" B. F. Smith	Sept. 16, 1862	June 25, "	Washington, D. C.	Tod Barracks	Belongs to regular army.
127th ¶	Do.	830				Nov. 18, 1863				
128th	Do.	1025	985	Col. C. W. Hill	Col. C. W. Hill	Dec. 26, "	July 17, 1865	Camp Chase	Camp Chase	Must. out; app. Bvt. Brig. Gen. vols.
129th	6 months	926		" H. D. John	" H. D. John	Aug. 10, "	March 11, 1864	Camp Cleveland	Camp Cleveland	Mustered out at expiration of service.

OHIO NATIONAL GUARD.

130th	100 days	840	797	Col. C. B. Phillips	Col. C. B. Phillips	June 4, 1864	Sept. 22, 1864	Toledo	Toledo	Mustered out at expiration of service.
131st	Do.	871	865	" John G. Lowe	" John G. Lowe	May 15, "	Aug. 25, "	Columbus	Camp Chase	Do. do.
132d	Do.	816	803	" Joel Haines	" Joel Haines	" 22, "	Sept. 10, "	Columbus	Camp Chase	Do. do.
133d	Do.	917	857	" G. L. Innis	" G. L. Innis	" 6, "	Aug. 20, "	Columbus	Camp Chase	Do. do.
134th	Do.	867	867	" J. B. Armstrong	" J. B. Armstrong	" 7, "	" 31, "	Columbus	Camp Chase	Do. do.
135th	Do.	850	658	" Andrew Legg	" Andrew Legg	" 11, "	Sept. 1, "	Columbus	Camp Chase	Do. do.
136th	Do.	869	663	" W. S. Irwin	" W. S. Irwin	" 13, "	Aug. 30, "	Columbus	Camp Chase	Do. do.
137th	Do.	935	800	" Len. A. Harris	" Len. A. Harris	" 12, "	" 21, "	Camp Dennison	Camp Dennison	Do. do.
138th	Do.	843	804	" S. S. Fisher	" S. S. Fisher	" 14, "	Sept. 1, "	Camp Dennison	Camp Dennison	Do. do.
139th	Do.	773	661	Lt. Col. Lloyd Wayne	Lt. Col. Lloyd Wayne	" 20, "	Aug. 26, "	Camp Chase	Camp Dennison	Do. do.
140th	Do.	858	855	Col. R. B. Wilson	Col. R. B. Wilson	" 10, "	Sept. 3, "	Gallipolis	Gallipolis	Do. do.
141st	Do.	866	860	" A. L. Jaynes	" A. L. Jaynes	" 21, "	" 3, "	Gallipolis	Gallipolis	Do. do.
142d	Do.	845	845	" W. C. Cooper	" W. C. Cooper	" 14, "	" 2, "	Camp Chase	Camp Chase	Do. do.
143d	Do.	856	856	" W. H. Vodrey	" W. H. Vodrey	" 15, "	" 12, "	Camp Chase	Camp Chase	Do. do.
144th	Do.	831	831	" S. H. Hunt	" S. H. Hunt	" 11, "	Aug. 31, "	Camp Chase	Camp Chase	Do. do.
145th	Do.	870	832	" H. C. Ashwell	" H. C. Ashwell	" 10, "	" 23, "	Camp Chase	Camp Chase	Do. do.
146th	Do.	882	822	" H. Crampton	" H. Crampton	" 17, "	Sept. 7, "	Camp Dennison	Camp Dennison	Do. do.

* Consolidated with 51st O. V. I. † Consolidated with 82d O. V. I. ‡ Consolidated with 67th O. V. I.

‖ This regiment served about four months at Cumberland, Md., and New Creek, Va. § Only a battalion, which was retained on duty at Camp Chase, Ohio.

** This organization was made the nucleus for a three years' organization of same number. †† Mostly on duty at Camp Chase. :: Consolidated with 50th O. V. I.

;; Consolidated with 1st Ohio Heavy Artillery. §§ Consolidated with 114th O. V. I. ¶ Fifth U. S. Colored Troops.

THE MILITARY ORGANIZATIONS OF OHIO—CONTINUED.

REGIMENT.	TERM OF ENLISTM'T.	ORIGINAL STRENGTH.	STRENGTH AT MUSTER OUT.	COMMANDANT AT ENTRY INTO SERVICE.	COMMANDANT AT MUSTER OUT.	LEFT STATE.	MUSTERED OUT.	WHERE MUSTERED OUT.	WHERE PAID AND DISCHARGED.	STATUS OF FIRST COMMANDANT.
147th	100 days	852	787	Col. B. F. Rosson	Col. B. F. Rosson	May 20, 1864	Aug. 30, 1864	Camp Dennison	Camp Dennison	Mustered out at expiration of service.
148th	Do.	823	775	" T. W. Moore	" T. W. Moore	" 23, "	Sept. 14, "	Marietta	Marietta	Do. do.
149th	Do.	858	755	" Allison L. Brown	" Allison L. Brown	" 11, "	Aug. 30, "	Camp Dennison	Camp Dennison	Do. do.
150th	Do.	929	907	" W. H. Hayward	" W. H. Hayward	" 5, "	" 23, "	Camp Cleveland	Camp Cleveland	Do. do.
151st	Do.	850	816	" J. M. C. Marble	" J. M. C. Marble	" 14, "	" 27, "	Camp Chase	Camp Chase	Do. do.
152d	Do.	860	821	" David Putnam	" David Putnam	" 12, "	Sept. 2, "	Camp Dennison	Camp Dennison	Do. do.
153d	Do.	909	753	" I. Stough	" I. Stough	" 12, "	" 2, "	Camp Chase	Camp Chase	Do. do.
154th	Do.	842	743	" R. Stevenson	" R. Stevenson	" 12, "	" 1, "	Camp Dennison	Camp Dennison	Do. do.
155th	Do.	838	785	" H. H. Sage	" H. H. Sage	" 9, "	Aug. 27, "	Camp Dennison	Camp Dennison	Do. do.
156th	Do.	877	841	" Caleb Marker	" Caleb Marker	July 18, "	Sept. 1, "	Camp Dennison	Camp Dennison	Do. do.
157th	Do.	859	809	" G. W. McCook	" G. W. McCook	May 17, "	" 2, "	Camp Chase	Camp Chase	Do. do.
159th	Do.	874	847	" Lyman J. Jackson	" Lyman J. Jackson	" 11, "	Aug. 24, "	Zanesville	Zanesville	Do. do.
160th	Do.	856	806	" Cyrus Reasoner	" Cyrus Reasoner	" 13, "	Sept. 7, "	Zanesville	Zanesville	Do. do.
161st	Do.	855	831	" O. P. Taylor	" O. P. Taylor	" 9, "	" 2, "	Camp Chase	Camp Chase	Do. do.
162d	Do.	853	849	" E. Ball	" E. Ball	June —, "	" 4, "	Camp Chase	Camp Chase	Do. do.
163d	Do.	839	774	" Hiram Miller	" Hiram Miller	May 13, "	" 10, "	Camp Chase	Camp Chase	Do. do.
164th	Do.	865	831	" J. C. Lee	" J. C. Lee	" 14, "	Aug. 27, "	Camp Cleveland	Camp Cleveland	Do. do.
165th	Do.	598	591	Lt.Col. A. Bohlander	Lt.Col. A. Bohlander	" 25, "	" 31, "	Camp Dennison	Camp Dennison	Do. do.
166th	Do.	940	960	Col. H. G. Blake	Col. H. G. Blake	" 15, "	Sept. 9, "	Camp Cleveland	Camp Cleveland	Do. do.
167th	Do.	793	765	" Thomas Moore	" Thomas Moore	" 18, "	" 8, "	Camp Dennison	Camp Dennison	Do. do.
168th	Do.	851	767	" C. Garis	" C. Garis	June 9, "	" 6, "	Camp Dennison	Camp Dennison	Do. do.
169th	Do.	945	873	" Nat. Haynes	" Nat. Haynes	May 19, "	" 4, "	Camp Cleveland	Camp Cleveland	Do. do.
170th	Do.	851	788	" Miles J. Saunders	" M. J. Saunders	" 17, "	" 10, "	Camp Chase	Camp Chase	Do. do.
171st	Do.	898	898	" Joel F. Asper	" Joel F. Asper	" 9, "	Aug. 20, "	Sandusky	Sandusky	Do. do.
172d	Do.	851	845	" John Ferguson	" John Ferguson		" 24, "	Nashville, Tenn.	Gallipolis	Do. do.
173d	1 year	1017	884	" John R. Hurd	" John R. Hurd	Sept. 18, 1864	June 28, 1865	Camp Dennison	Camp Dennison	Do. do.
174th	Do.	952	782	" J. S. Jones	" J. S. Jones	" 23, "	" 28, "	Charlotte, N. C.	Columbus	App. Brigadier-General volunteers.
175th	Do.	957	582	Lt.Col. Dan. McCoy	Lt.Col. Dan. McCoy	Oct. 11, "	" 27, "	Nashville, Tenn.	Camp Dennison	Do. do.
176th	Do.	941	760	Col. E. C. Mason	Col. E. C. Mason	Sept. 21, "	" 4, "	Nashville, Tenn.	Tod Barracks	Do. do.
177th	Do.	1020	766	" A. T. Wilcox	" A. T. Wilcox	Oct. 9, "	" 24, "	Greensboro', N. C.	Camp Cleveland	Mustered out at expiration of service.
178th	Do.	937	769	" Joab A. Stafford	" Joab A. Stafford	Sept. 29, "	" 29, "	Charlotte, N. C.	Tod Barracks	Do. do.
179th	Do.	949	764	" H. H. Sage	" H. H. Sage	" 28, "	" 18, "	Nashville, Tenn.	Tod Barracks	Do. do.
180th	Do.	917	746	" Willard Warner	Lt.Col. John T. Wood	Oct. 15, "	July 12, "	Charlotte, N. C.	Tod Barracks	App. Bvt. Brig. Gen. volunteers.
181st	Do.	1007	850	" John O'Dowd	" J. E. Hudson	" 24, "	" 14, "	Salisbury, N. C.	Camp Dennison	Honorably discharged May 27, 1865.
182d	Do.	971	771	" Lewis Butler	Col. Lewis Butler	Nov. 1, "	" 7, "	Nashville, Tenn.	Camp Chase	Mustered out at expiration of service.
183d	Do.	1007	793	" George W. Hoge	" George W. Hoge	" 19, "	" 7, "	Washington, D. C.	Camp Chase	App. Bvt. Brigadier-General vols.
184th	Do.	985	861	" H. S. Commager	" H. S. Commager	Feb. 21, 1865	Sept. 20, "	Nashville, Tenn.	Camp Chase	App. Brig. Gen.; died at New Orleans.
185th	Do.	1006	859	" J. E. Cummins	" J. E. Cummins	" 27, "	Sept. 26, "	Lexington, Ky.	Camp Chase	Mustered out at expiration of service.
186th	Do.	991	851	" T. F. Wilds	" T. F. Wilds	March 2, "	Sept. 18, "	Nashville, Tenn.	Camp Chase	App. Bvt. Brig. Gen. volunteers.
187th	Do.	998	835	" A. R. Z. Dawson	" A. R. Z. Dawson	" 3, "	Jan. 20, 1866	Macon, Ga.	Camp Chase	Do. do.
188th	Do.	1001	919	" J. E. Taylor	" J. E. Taylor	" 4, "	Sept. 21, 1865	Nashville, Tenn.	Camp Chase	Do. do.
189th	Do.	1008	939	" H. D. Kingsbury	" H. D. Kingsbury	" 7, "	" 28, "	Nashville, Tenn.	Camp Chase	Do. do.
191st	Do.	1009	871	" R. L. Kimberly	" R. L. Kimberly	" 10, "	Aug. 27, "	Winchester, Va.	Camp Chase	App. Brigadier-General volunteers.
192d	Do.	1011	894	" F. W. Butterfield	" F. W. Butterfield	" 12, "	Sept. 1, "	Winchester, Va.	Camp Chase	Mustered out at expiration of service.
193d	Do.	997	842	" E. Powell	" E. Powell	" 14, "	Aug. 4, "	Winchester, Va.	Camp Chase	App. Bvt. Brig. Gen. volunteers.
194th	Do.	990	785	" A. G. McCook	" A. G. McCook	" 14, "	Oct. 24, "	Washington, D. C.	Camp Chase	Do. do.
195th	Do.	981	759	" H. B. Banning	" H. B. Banning	" 22, "	Dec. 18, "	Washington, D. C.	Camp Chase	App. Bvt. Major-General volunteers.
196th	Do.	984	792	" R. P. Kennedy	" R. P. Kennedy	" 25, "	Sept. 11, "	Baltimore, Md.	Camp Chase	App. Bvt. Brig. Gen. volunteers.
197th	Do.	1006	853	" Benton Halstead	" Benton Halstead	April 25, "	July 31, "	Camp Bradford, Md.	Tod Barracks	Mustered out at expiration of service.

CAVALRY.

REGIMENT.	TERM OF ENLISTM'T.	ORIGINAL STRENGTH.	STRENGTH AT MUSTER OUT.	COMMANDANT AT ENTRY INTO SERVICE.	COMMANDANT AT MUSTER OUT.	LEFT STATE.	MUSTERED OUT.	WHERE MUSTERED OUT.	WHERE PAID AND DISCHARGED.	STATUS OF FIRST COMMANDANT.
1st	3 years	1039	733	Col. O. P. Ransom	Col. B. B. Eggleston.	Dec. 9, 1861	Sept. 13, 1865	Hilton Head, S. C.	Camp Chase	Resigned.
2d	Do.	1177	757	" C. Doubleday	" Dudley Seward	Jan. —, 1862	" 11, "	Bent'n Barr'cks, Mo	Camp Chase	Resigned June 16, 1862.
3d	Do.	1115	881	" Lewis Zahn	" H. N. Howland	Feb. 10, "	Aug. 4, "	Edgefield, Tenn	Tod Barracks	Honorably discharged January, 1863.
4th	Do.	823	746	" John Kennett	Lt. Col. J. Thompson.	Dec. 6, "	July 15, "	Nashville, Tenn	Camp Dennison	Resigned January 23, 1863.
5th	Do.	1074		" W. H. H. Taylor.	" T. T. Heath	Feb. 26, "	Oct. 30, "	Salisbury, N. C.	Camp Dennison	Resigned August 11, 1863.
6th	Do.	778	652	" W. R. Lloyd	" F. C. Loveland	May 13, "	Aug. 7, "	Petersburg, Va	Camp Cleveland	Resigned April 2, 1863.
7th	Do.	1201	840	" Israel Garrard	Col. Israel Garrard	Nov. —, 1863	July 4, "	Nashville, Tenn	Camp Dennison	App. Brevet Brig. Gen. of vols.
8th	Do.	1096	886	" Alpheus S. Moore	" Wesley Owens	April 26, 1861	" 30, "	Clarksburg, Va	Camp Dennison	Resigned January 4, 1865.
9th	Do.	1087	1001	" W. D. Hamilton.	Lt. Col. Wm. Stough.	" 23, 1863	" 20, "	Lexington, N. C.	Camp Chase	App. Brevet Brig. Gen. of vols.
10th	Do.	1084	881	" Chas. C. Smith	Col. T. W. Sanderson	Feb. 27, "	" 24, "	Lexington, N. C.	Camp Cleveland	Honorably discharged Jan. 13, 1863.
11th	Do.	814	436	Lt. Col. W. O. Collins	Lt. Col. T. S. Mackey	" —, 1862	" 14, 1866	Ft. L'venw'th, K'ns	Tod Barracks	Mustered out April 1, 1865.
12th	Do.	1218	729	Col. R. W. Ratliff	" J. F. Herrick	Nov. 24, 1863	Nov. 14, 1865	Nashville, Tenn	Camp Chase	Mustered out at expiration of service.
13th	Do.	1038	884	" S. R. Clarke	" R. H. Wheeler	May 11, 1864	Aug. 10, "	Petersburg, Va	Tod Barracks	Mustered out at expiration of service.

LIGHT ARTILLERY.

BATTERIES.	TERM OF ENLISTM'T.	ORIGINAL STRENGTH.	STRENGTH AT MUSTER OUT.	COMMANDANT AT ENTRY INTO SERVICE.	COMMANDANT AT MUSTER OUT.	LEFT STATE.	MUSTERED OUT.	WHERE MUSTERED OUT.	WHERE PAID AND DISCHARGED.	STATUS OF FIRST COMMANDANT.
1st Reg	3 years	1800		Col. JAS. BARNETT	Col. JAS. BARNETT	Fall of 1861	July 31, 1865			Mustered out at expiration of service.
A	Do.		134	Capt. C. S. Cotter	Capt. Louis Herker	Sept. 25, "	" 31, "	Camp Cleveland	Camp Cleveland	
B	Do.		111	" W. A. Standart.	" N. A. Baldwin	Oct. 8, "	" 22, 1866	Camp Cleveland	Camp Cleveland	
C	Do.		133	" D. Kenney	" M. B. Gary	" 1, "	June 15, 1865	Camp Cleveland	Camp Cleveland	
D	Do.		99	" G. J. Cockerill	Lt. H. C. Lloyd	Nov. 1, "	July 15, "	Camp Cleveland	Camp Cleveland	
E	Do.			" A. J. Conkle	Capt. E. B. Belding	Dec. —, "	" 22, "	Camp Dennison	Camp Dennison	
F	Do.		143	" D. T. Cockerill	" W. R. Pease	" 3, "	" 25, "	Camp Dennison	Camp Dennison	
G	Do.		104	" Jos. Bartlett	" A. C. Marshall	Feb. 10, 1862	Aug. 31, "	Camp Chase	Camp Chase	
H	Do.		123	" L. F. Huntingt'n	" S. D. Dorsey	June 20, "	June 14, "	Camp Cleveland	Camp Cleveland	
I	Do.		92	" H. F. Hyman	" Aubert Dilger	Jan. 26, "	July 24, "	Camp Dennison	Camp Dennison	
K	Do.			" W. L. De Beck	" Louis Heckman	Feb. —, "	" 17, "			
L	Do.		96	" L. N. Robinson.	" T. C. Gibbs	Jan. 20, "	" 4, "	Columbus	Tod Barracks	
M	Do.			" F. Schultz	" C. W. Scoville	" —, "	Oct. —, 1864	Camp Dennison	Camp Dennison	

HEAVY ARTILLERY.

REGIMENT.	TERM OF ENLISTM'T.	ORIGINAL STRENGTH.	STRENGTH AT MUSTER OUT.	COMMANDANT AT ENTRY INTO SERVICE.	COMMANDANT AT MUSTER OUT.	LEFT STATE.	MUSTERED OUT.	WHERE MUSTERED OUT.	WHERE PAID AND DISCHARGED.	STATUS OF FIRST COMMANDANT.
1st reg.	3 years	1764	1279	Col. C. G. Hawley		Fall of 1863	July 25, 1865	Knoxville, Tenn	Camp Dennison	Mustered out at expiration of service.
2d reg.	Do.	1786	1492	" H. G. Gibson		Fall of "	Aug. 23, "	Nashville, Tenn	Camp Chase	App. Bvt. Brig. Gen. volunteers.

THE MILITARY ORGANIZATIONS OF OHIO—CONTINUED.

OHIO INDEPENDENT BATTERIES.

BATTERIES.	TERM OF ENLISTM'T.	ORIGINAL STRENGTH.	STRENGTH AT MUSTER OUT.	COMMANDANT AT ENTRY INTO SERVICE.	COMMANDANT AT MUSTER OUT.	LEFT STATE.	MUSTERED OUT.	WHERE MUSTERED OUT.	WHERE PAID AND DISCHARGED.	STATUS OF FIRST COMMANDANT.
1st	3 years		142	Capt. J. R. McMullen	Capt. G. P. Kirtland.	July —, 1861	June 26, 1865	Columbus	Tod Barracks	
2d	Do.		145	" Thos. J. Carlin.	" August's Beach	Aug. 15, "	July 21, "	Columbus	Tod Barracks	
3d	Do.		123	" W. S. Williams.	" John Sullivan	Feb. —, 1862	Aug. 1, "	Camp Cleveland	Camp Taylor	
4th *	Do.			" Lewis Hoffman.		Aug. 18, 1861	" 29, 1864	Cincinnati	Cincinnati	
5th	Do.		108	" A. Hickenlooper	Capt. A. Hickenlooper	Oct. 11, "	July 31, 1865	Camp Dennison	Camp Dennison	App. Bvt. Brigadier-General.
6th	Do.		97	" C. Bradley	" A. C. Baldwin	Dec. 15, "	Sept. 1, "	Camp Chase	Camp Chase	
7th	Do.		129	" S. A. Burnap	" H. P. M'Naughton	March 18, 1862	Aug. 11, "	Camp Dennison	Camp Dennison	
8th	Do.		160	" L. Markgraff	" J. F. Putnam	" 22, "	" 9, "	Camp Dennison	Camp Dennison	
9th	Do.		138	" H. S. Wetmore.	" H. B. York	Dec. 11, 1861	July 25, "	Camp Cleveland	Cleveland	
10th	Do.		169	" H. B. White	" J. R. Crain	March 3, 1862	" 17, "	Camp Dennison	Camp Dennison	
11th	Do.			" A. G. A. Constable	" F. E. Armstrong	Oct. 27, 1861	Nov. 5, 1864	Columbus	Camp Chase	
12th	Do.		142	" A. C. Johnston.	" Alfred Noecker.	May 17, 1862	July 12, 1865	Columbus	Camp Chase	
13th †	Do.									
14th	Do.		140	Capt. J. B. Burrows	Capt. W. C. Myers	Feb. 5, 1862	Aug. 8, 1865	Camp Dennison	Camp Dennison	
15th	Do.			" E. Spear, jr.	" James Burdick.	" 16, "	June 20, "	Columbus	Tod Barracks	
16th	Do.		97	" J. A. Mitchell	" R. P. Twist	Sept. 5, 1861	Aug. 2, "	Camp Chase	Camp Chase	
17th	Do.		148	" A. A. Blount	" C. S. Rice	" 3, 1862	" 16, "	Camp Chase	Camp Chase	
18th	Do.			" C. C. Aleshire	Lieut. J. McCafferty.	Oct. 10, "	June 29, "	Camp Dennison	Camp Dennison	
19th	Do.		115	" Jos. C. Shields	Capt. F. Wilson	July —, "	" 29, "	Camp Cleveland	Camp Cleveland	
20th	Do.		139	" L. Smithwright	" Wm. Backus	Dec. 31, "	July 19, "	Camp Cleveland	Camp Cleveland	
21st	Do.		83	" J. W. Patterson	" Jas. N. Walley	May 8, 1863	" 21, "	Camp Cleveland	Camp Cleveland	
22d	Do.		142	" H. M. Neil	" A. B. Alger	Aug. 12, "	" 13, "	Camp Chase	Camp Chase	
23d ‡	Do.		111							
24th	Do.			Capt. John L. Hill	Capt. John L. Hill	Sept. 22, 1864	June 24, 1865	Camp Dennison	Camp Dennison	
25th	Do.			" Julius L. Hadley	Lieut. E. F. Webster.	Feb. 17, 1863	Dec. 12, "	Columbus	Camp Chase	
26th	Do.		111	" Theo. D. Yost	" O. S. Lee	Dec. 22, "	Sept. 2, "	Tod Barracks	Tod Barracks	

*Consolidated with Tenth Ohio Battery.

† After battle of Pittsburg Landing this number was dropped.

‡ Detached from Second Kentucky Infantry; one of the wrongly named Ohio regiments.

[A considerable number of irregular organizations, regiments credited to other services, etc., were sent from Ohio, which are not presented in the above table; sketches of their career however, will be found at the close of the volume.

1st REGIMENT OHIO VOLUNTEER INFANTRY.

ROSTER, THREE MONTHS' SERVICE.

RANK.	NAME.	DATE OF RANK.	COM. ISSUED.	REMARKS.
Colonel	ALEX. M. McCOOK	April 17, 1861	April 17, 1861	
Lt. Colonel	EDWIN A. PARROTT	" 17, "	" 17, "	
Major	J. G. HUGHES	" 17, "	" 17, "	
Surgeon	WM. L. McMILLEN	" 16, "	" 16, "	
Ass't Surgeon	ALBERT WILSON	" 18, "	" 18, "	
Captain	J. A. Stafford	" 17, "	" 17, "	
Do.	P. Dister	" 17, "	" 17, "	
Do.	Walter B. Pease	" 17, "	" 17, "	
Do.	T. S. Paddock	" 17, "	" 17, "	
Do.	John Kell	" 17, "	" 17, "	
Do.	George B. Beily	" 17, "	" 17, "	
Do.	J. C. Hazlett	" 17, "	" 17, "	
Do.	Wm. McLaughlin	" 17, "	" 17, "	
Do.	J. P. Bruck	" 17, "	" 17, "	
Do.	Jeremiah Ensworth	July 8, "	July 8, "	
Do.	George D. McKinney	" 8, "	" 8, "	
1st Lieutenant	T. M. Hunter	April 17, "	April 17, "	
Do.	L. Kuhlman	" 17, "	" 17, "	
Do.	J. Winder	" 17, "	" 17, "	
Do.	P. O'Connell	" 17, "	" 17, "	
Do.	J. Ensworth	" 17, "	" 17, "	
Do.	P. S. Turner	" 17, "	" 17, "	Resigned July 12, 1861.
Do.	W. H. Rayner	" 17, "	" 17, "	
Do.	J. R. Eckert	" 17, "	" 17, "	
Do.	A. McElvain	" 17, "	" 17, "	
Do.	M. Klein	" 17, "	" 17, "	
Do.	J. E. Hampson	" 17, "	" 17, "	
Do.	James Steele	" 17, "	" 17, "	
2d Lieutenant	E. Rickets	" 17, "	" 17, "	
Do.	J. Hand	" 17, "	" 17, "	
Do.	Wm. W. Woodward	" 17, "	" 17, "	
Do.	J. Fitch	" 17, "	" 17, "	
Do.	J. M. Richards	" 17, "	" 17, "	
Do.	O. C. Maxwell	" 17, "	" 17, "	
Do.	A. Kinney	" 17, "	" 17, "	
Do.	F. Fracker	" 17, "	" 17, "	
Do.	T. E. Douglass	" 17, "	" 17, "	
Do.	I. Bruck	" 17, "	" 17, "	
Do.	J. M. Frazer	" 17, "	" 17, "	

ROSTER, THREE YEARS' SERVICE.

RANK.	NAME.	DATE OF RANK.	COM. ISSUED.	REMARKS.
Colonel	BENJ. F. SMITH	Oct. 12, 1861	Oct. 12, 1861	Col. to J'e 2,'62; rep. for duty as Capt. in R.A.
Do.	EDWIN A. PARROTT	Feb. 4, 1862	Feb. 4, 1862	Honorably discharged February 15, 1864.
Lt. Colonel	EDWIN A. PARROTT	Aug. 17, 1861	Jan. 16, 1862	Promoted to Colonel.
Do.	E. BASSETT LANGDON	Feb. 4, 1862	Feb. 4, "	Wounded at Mission Ridge; must'd out with regiment.
Major	E. BASSETT LANGDON	Aug. 6, 1861	Aug. 6, 1861	Promoted February 4, 1862.
Do.	JOAB A. STAFFORD	Feb. 4, 1862	Feb. 4, 1862	Mustered out with 5th comp'y August 17, 1864.
Surgeon	ROBERT FLETCHER	Oct. 21, 1861	Jan. 11, "	Promoted by President November 13, 1863.
Do.	J. CULLEN BARR	Nov. 13, 1863	Feb. 20, 1864	Mustered out September, 1864.
Ass't Surgeon	A. WILSON	Aug. 27, 1861	Jan. 11, 1862	Promoted to Surgeon; assigned to 113th O.V.I.
Do.	J. CULLEN BARR	" 21, 1862	Aug. 29, "	Promoted to Surgeon.
Do.	A. J. BROCKETT	April 22, 1864	April 22, 1864	Mustered out September, 1864.
Chaplain	GEORGE H. FULLERTON	Oct. 11, 1861	Jan. 16, 1862	Resigned October, 1861.
Captain	Joab A. Stafford	Aug. 1, "	" 14, "	Promoted.
Do.	George A. Pomeroy	" 5, "	" 14, "	Resigned March 8, 1863.
Do.	Louis Kuhlman	" 17, "	" 14, "	Mustered out at expiration of service.
Do.	Gates P. Thruston	" 17, "	" 14, "	Resigned March 25, 1863.
Do.	James B. Hampson	" 17, "	" 14, "	Mustered out for promotion December 10, '63.
Do.	Alexander T. Snodgrass	" 20, "	" 14, "	Mustered out.
Do.	Nicholas Trapp	" 30, "	" 14, "	Mustered out 1864.
Do.	Patrick O'Connell	" 17, "	" 14, "	Mustered out.
Do.	Thomas J. Lawton	" 31, "	" 14, "	Resigned May 15, 1862.
Do.	Benjamin F. Prentiss	Oct. 7, "	" 14, "	Resigned May 17, 1864.
Do.	Emanuel T. Hooker	Feb. 28, 1862	Feb. 28, "	Mustered out in 1864.
Do.	George L. Hayward	Dec. 10, "	Dec. 31, "	Mustered out in 1863 for promotion.
Do.	Henry Dornbusch	March 23, "	April 17, 1863	Mustered out in 1864.
Do.	James E. Jones	" 23, "	March 30, "	Mustered out in 1864.
Do.	William L. Patterson	May 15, 1863	May 29, "	Mustered out in 1864.
Do.	Samuel W. Davies	" 17, "	" 29, "	Mustered out in 1864.
Do.	Solomon Homan	July 8, 1864	July 8, 1864	Mustered out in 1864.
1st Lieutenant	Emanuel T. Hooker	Aug. 1, 1861	Jan. 16, 1862	Promoted February 28, 1862.
Do.	Silas R. Ewing	" 10, "	" 16, "	Resigned May 22, '62; discharged June 21,'63.
Do.	Henry Dornbusch	" 17, "	" 16, "	Promoted to Captain.
Do.	Wm. L. Patterson	" 17, "	" 16, "	Promoted to Captain.

RANK.	NAME.	DATE OF RANK.		COM. ISSUED.		REMARKS.
1st Lieutenant	John Allen Campbell........	Aug.	20, 1861	Jan.	16, 186[illegible]	Res. Dec. 21,'62; promoted by Pres. Oct. 27,'62.
Do.	James Hill........................	"	23, "	"	16, "	Resigned October 17, 1863.
Do.	James W. Powell..............	"	21, "	"	16, "	Resigned June 19, 1862.
Do.	S. Barnett Paddock..........	Sept.	5, "	"	16, "	Resigned December 15, 1862.
Do.	James E. Jones................	Aug.	17, "	"	16, "	Promoted to Captain.
Do.	George L. Hayward..........	"	17, "	"	16, "	Promoted to Captain.
Do.	Wm. A. Owesney..............	Oct.	7, "	"	16, "	Resigned June 21, 1862.
Do.	John Parrott.....................	"	19, "	"	16, "	Resigned October 18, 1862.
Do.	James M. Wyley...............	Feb.	28, 1862	Feb.	28, "	Resigned December 21, 1862.
Do.	Wm. M. Carpenter...........	May	26, "	June	21, "	Resigned as 2d Lieutenant April 10, 1863.
Do.	Alexander Johnson...........	June	19, "	Nov.	19, "	Resigned March 17, 1863.
Do.	Samuel W. Davies............	Oct.	18, "	"	25, "	Promoted to Captain.
Do.	Dennis Regan....................	June	24, "	Dec.	12, "	Mustered out, 1865.
Do.	Anton Kuhlman................	Oct.	27, "	"	26, "	Resigned January 31, 1863.
Do.	George P. Leonhard..........	Dec.	15, "	"	26, "	Mustered out.
Do.	Alexander Varian, jr........	"	10, "	"	31, "	Killed.
Do.	George Grove....................	"	21, "	March	24, 1863	Commission revoked.
Do.	Thomas W. Boyer.............	Jan.	31, 1863	April	22, "	Mustered out.
Do.	R. B. Chappell..................	March	17, "	"	22, "	Promoted
Do.	John W. Jackson..............	"	23, "	"	22, "	Killed September 19, 1863.
Do.	Edward J. Collins.............	"	25, "	"	22, "	Mustered out.
Do.	Charles N. Winner...........	April	1, "	"	22, "	Mustered out.
Do.	Solomon Homan................	March	23, "	"	22, "	Promoted to Captain.
Do.	George Grove....................	May	15, "	May	29, "	Killed.
Do.	Sylvanus Dickson.............	Nov.	15, "	Jan.	16, "	Killed.
Do.	Dennis Denny....................	July	8, 1864	July	8, 1864	Mustered out.
Do.	O. S. Ward.........................	"	8, "	"	8, "	Mustered out.
Do.	G. Hallenburg....................	"	8, "	"	8, "	Mustered out March 11, 1865.
Do.	Anton Kuhlman.................	"	8, "	"	8, "	Mustered out.
Do.	Francis M. Wareham........	"	8, "	"	8, "	Mustered out September 14, 1865.
Do.	Joseph Morrow..................	"	8, "	"	8, "	Mustered out.
2d Lieutenant	James M. Wyley...............	Aug.	1, 1861	Jan.	16, 1862	Promoted February 28, 1862.
Do.	Frank Smith......................	"	10, "	"	16, "	Resigned May 25, 1862; discharged June 21, '63.
Do.	Anton Kuhlman.................	"	17, "	"	16, "	Promoted October 27, 1862.
Do.	Samuel W. Davies............	"	17, "	"	16, "	Promoted October 18, 1862.
Do.	Wm. M. Carpenter...........	"	17, "	"	16, "	Promoted May 26, 1862; resigned April 10, 1863.
Do.	Dennis Regan....................	"	17, "	"	16, "	Promoted June 24, 1862.
Do.	John J. Patton..................	"	26, "	"	16, "	Resigned June 16, 1862.
Do.	David E. Roatch...............	Sept.	1, "	"	16, "	Resigned May 28, 1862.
Do.	Alexander Johnson...........	"	5, "	"	16, "	Promoted June 19, 1862.
Do.	J. H. Prentiss....................	Oct.	5, "	"	16, "	Resigned November 26, 1862.
Do.	George P. Leonhard..........	March	1, 1862	March	20, "	Promoted December 15, 1862.
Do.	Alexander Varian, jr........	May	26, "	June	24, "	Promoted December 10, 1862.
Do.	George Grove....................	June	21, "	Oct.	22, "	Promoted.
Do.	Dennis Denny....................	"	16, "	"	22, "	Promoted.
Do.	John W. Jackson..............	May	28, "	"	22, "	Promoted.
Do.	Robert B. Chappell...........	June	19, "	"	22, "	Promoted to 1st Lieutenant.
Do.	Thomas W. Boyer.............	Oct.	18, "	Nov.	25, "	Promoted to 1st Lieutenant.
Do.	S. S. Dixon........................	June	21, "	Dec.	26, "	Promoted to 1st Lieutenant.
Do.	Solomon Homan................	Oct.	27, "	"	26, "	Promoted to 1st Lieutenant.
Do.	George McCracken............	Nov.	26, "	Jan.	26, 1863	Resigned July 28, 1864.
Do.	Williard C. Prentiss..........	Dec.	10, "	Feb.	10, "	Resigned June 10, 1863.
Do.	Charles Young..................	"	13, "	March	21, "	Honorably discharged June 14, 1864.
Do.	Daniel J. Deardorff...........	"	21, "	"	21, "	Commission revoked.
Do.	Christopher Wollenhaupt.	March	23, "	April	22, "	Killed at Mission Ridge.
Do.	O. S. Ward.........................	Jan.	31, "	"	22, "	Promoted to 1st Lieutenant.
Do.	G. Hallenburg....................	March	17, "	"	22, "	Promoted to 1st Lieutenant.
Do.	Anton Kuhlman.................	May	6, "	May	6, "	Promoted to 1st Lieutenant.
Do.	Thomas H. Teaff...............	Sept.	16, 1864	Sept.	16, 1864	Mustered out.

FIRST OHIO VOLUNTEER INFANTRY.

THE FIRST OHIO was organized under President Lincoln's first call for troops in April, 1861. Its nucleus was found in some of the old militia companies, and its ranks were largely filled by young men of the best social and pecuniary advantages from South-Western Ohio. So prompt was its response to the cry of danger from the Capital, that within sixty hours after the telegraph brought the President's call, the cars were bearing the regiment to Washington. It met, however, with vexatious delays on the route, and did not arrive on the Potomac till the danger was averted. Its earliest action was that at Vienna, whither General Schenck's brigade, to which it was attached, in careful obedience to General Scott's orders, and with his approval, was moving by rail. The Rebels were found much sooner than General Scott had expected. They fired into the train; but the First, followed by the rest of the brigade, hastily debarked, formed on the side of the track, and made so handsome a resistance, that they were presently able to retire unmolested, and with comparatively small loss. In the battle of Bull Run the First had little active share, but it and the rest of the brigade were kept in excellent order through all the disaster, and they rendered incalculable service in covering the retreat. Its losses were slight. The term of service of the regiment having now expired, it was sent home and mustered out.

In August, 1861, the regiment began to be reorganized for three years' service, but the reorganization was not completed until October. Its place of rendezvous was at Camp Corwin, near Dayton. October 31st it left Dayton and reached Cincinnati; November 4th received its arms, and on the 5th left on the steamer Telegraph No. 3 for Louisville. Arriving at midnight, it went into Camp York, near that city. On the 8th of November, at half past one P. M., it embarked for West Point, at the mouth of Salt River. On the 15th of November the regiment marched *via* Elizabethtown, reaching Camp Nevin on the 16th, where it reported to General A. M. McCook, then in command of the Second Division of the Army of the Cumberland. Soon after it was brigaded with the First Kentucky or Louisville Legion, Sixth Indiana, First Battalion Fifteenth United States Infantry, and battalions of the Sixteenth and Nineteenth Infantry, forming the Fourth Brigade of the Second Division. On December 10th the regiment marched to Bacon Creek, and on the 17th to Green River. During the last four miles the march was made under the inspiration of music from Willich's guns at Munfordsville. As the regiment marched into camp that evening the dead and wounded of the Thirty-Second Indiana were being brought in from the field. It remained in camp, at Green River, from December 17th until February 14, 1862, during which time it was thoroughly drilled and prepared for the field. On the morning of the 14th orders were received for the troops to march to West Point, Kentucky, there to take steamers and join the forces under General Grant, then moving on Fort Henry. Reaching Upton Station, the regiment bivouacked in the snow until the morning of the 16th, when news was received of the fall of Fort Henry. This intelligence caused a retrograde movement to Green River. On February 17th the regiment began its march to Nashville; arriving March 3d, it went into camp late at night five miles out on the Franklin Turnpike. This march at night will long be remembered, for it was pitch dark, and rain, snow, and sleet were falling thick and fast. The men had neither tents, blankets, nor shelter of any kind, and, encamping in an open field on the icy ground, they suffered terribly. On the 16th of March the regiment marched with its division to Duck River, opposite Columbia, reaching there on the 21st. Awaiting the completion of a bridge over Duck River, it went into camp. It crossed Duck River March 31st, and moved toward Savannah.

At half past nine A. M., April 6th, heavy cannonading was heard in the direction of Shiloh, which caused a double-quick movement forward. The troops marched thirteen miles from half past one to half past four P. M., and arrived at Savannah at half past seven P. M., and at Pittsburg Landing at daylight the next morning.

At six A. M., the regiment moved to the front and formed in line of battle, occupying a position on the left of its brigade and to the right of General Crittenden's division. After fighting until about noon, charging and driving the enemy steadily, and recapturing General Sherman's head-quarters' camp, the regiment retired to replenish its ammunition boxes, leaving a part of the Fifth Brigade as its relief. Ammunition being procured, the First returned to the field and participated in the general charge on the enemy's lines.

Colonel Gibson's brigade being menaced by the enemy on its left flank, the First Ohio and Nineteenth Regulars went to its relief, arriving just in time to repulse a vigorous attack from the Rebels. This closed the terrible battle. The First Ohio was commanded by Colonel B. F. Smith, a regular army officer, whose soldierly qualities and experience undoubtedly saved the regiment from great loss. Other regiments occupying the same position suffered terribly. Captains Hooker and Kuhlman were severely wounded. Its loss in this battle was sixty men and officers killed and wounded. It was ordered back to the Landing, where it bivouacked that night in the rain and mud.

The regiment participated in the tedious movement on Corinth, having occasional skirmishes. On the 27th of May six companies of the regiment, under Major Bassett Langdon, had a brisk fight at Bridge Creek. The enemy's pickets were driven in, and the ground held. On the 30th of May Corinth was entered by the National forces.

The First did not participate in the pursuit of the enemy, but remained in and about Corinth, doing picket and guard duty, until the 10th of June, when it received marching orders and started for Nashville, passing through Iuka, Tuscumbia, Florence, and Huntsville. At Huntsville the cars were taken, and the regiment reached Boiling Fork, a tributary of the Elk River, on the 7th of July.

On the 14th of July the regiment went by rail to Tullahoma to repel an anticipated attack on that point. It returned to Cowan's Station on the 18th. On the 10th of August General J. W. Sill took command of the brigade, and on the 24th the regiment, with its brigade and division, marched for Pelham, where it joined the forces under General A. M. McCook. On the 28th of August the regiment marched to Altamont, on the Cumberland Mountains, and on the 29th and 30th reconnoissances were made down the main road toward Sequatchie Valley. On the afternoon of the 30th it marched toward Nashville, passing through Manchester, Murfreesboro', and Lavergne, arriving in the vicinity of Nashville on the 7th of September.

The march was resumed September 10th at seven P. M., passing through Nashville and across the Cumberland River at three o'clock the next morning.

The regiment had now fairly commenced its march, in company with General Buell's army, in pursuit of Bragg's Rebel army, then on its way to Louisville. The race was won by the National forces, and Louisville reached September 26th. It is needless to describe the arduous march or the sufferings of the men on this memorable occasion. The extremely hot weather, the dusty roads, and the almost total absence of drinking water, either for the men or animals, occasioned the most intense suffering and the loss of many valuable lives.

But little rest was allowed at Louisville. October 1st the march was resumed, the First, with its brigade, moving out on the Frankfort Turnpike. Shelbyville was reached on the 2d, and Frankfort October 6th. This column of National troops was under the command of General J. W. Sill.

On the 9th, at Dog-Walk, a brisk fight was had with the enemy, in which the First Ohio took a prominent part, with the loss of eight or ten men. Lieutenant Anton Kuhlman was wounded severely. The march was very arduous, and at times perilous, as it was in the power of the Rebel army to mass and overwhelm the National forces. During most of the time the enemy hung on the flanks of the National forces, and annoyed them in every possible way.

A junction with the main army under General Buell was effected on the 11th of October, two days after the battle of Perryville, and the First went into camp on the battle-field.

On October 13th the regiment took up the line of march and reached Danville on the 14th, and passing through, continued on to Crab Orchard, where it went into camp for four days on Logan's Creek, near Hall's Gap. This completed the pursuit of Bragg's forces, and the National army, after a few days' rest, turned the head of its column toward Nashville, whence it had started. This place was reached November 16th. The First passed on and went into camp nine miles out on the Murfreesboro' Turnpike, near the State Insane Asylum. In this little march some skirmishing was had with the Rebel cavalry, then in considerable force on all the roads in the vicinity of Nashville.

On the retrograde march through Kentucky General Buell, commanding the Army of the Ohio, had been superseded by General William S. Rosecrans. General Rosecrans immediately reorganized the whole army; a new name was given to it—Army of the Cumberland—and a general change in its structure was made. General J. W. Sill, commanding the division in which the First was brigaded, was superseded by General R. W. Johnson. The name of the corps and division was changed to the Fourteenth Army Corps, Second Division, right wing of Army of the Cumberland.

On December 26, 1862, General Rosecrans having completed his arrangements, the movement on Bragg's army at Murfreesboro' commenced. The First Ohio moved out on the Nolinsville Turnpike with the right wing, about noon of the 26th, in the midst of a drenching rainstorm, and reached Nolin Creek at four o'clock P. M. During this march almost constant skirmishing was had with Hardee's Rebel corps. This continued to the vicinity of Murfreesboro', which was reached on the 30th, in the midst of the still driving and drenching rain.

On December 31st the Battle of Stone River commenced. The First Ohio, at daylight, was stationed on the right, with R. W. Johnson's Second Division. The pickets were driven in at six o'clock. The First was immediately formed in line of battle and stationed across an open field behind a fence, and formed the right of Johnson's front line. Within five minutes the enemy's skirmishers advanced, but were quickly repulsed. Following their skirmishers, the enemy advanced in force, but were promptly checked. This action lasted half an hour, when another heavy force made its appearance on the right and rear of the First, compelling the regiment to fall back. In effecting this it encountered the Louisville Legion, which formed the second line, at a time when it was making a change of front to meet the onset on its flank. This created some confusion in both regiments. Order was partially restored, however, and the fight continued, but the entire National right wing was so hardly pressed that it was forced back on the center, creating for a time much confusion. After several ineffectual attempts at a stand, it finally reached the line of the Nashville and Chattanooga Railroad. At this point it was re-enforced, the enemy held in check, and finally driven back. After hard fighting, a line of battle was re-established and maintained until the close of the action.

When the First was driven from its line it was broken into squads, several of which skirmished with the enemy, and did good service in checking his onset. One under Lieutenant Darnbursch, of Company B, repulsed an attack from the enemy's cavalry. Before reaching the Nashville Railroad the bulk of the regiment was rallied by Major J. A. Stafford (commanding the regiment) and formed on the right of the Sixth Ohio, where it fought gallantly until driven back. During the 1st, 2d, and 3d of January there was considerable maneuvering by the enemy, and some skirmishing. On the 2d of January a heavy attack was made on the left of the National lines. In this attack the 1st Ohio did not participate.

On January 4th it was ascertained that the enemy had evacuated Murfreesboro', and on the 6th the First passed through that place and went into camp four miles out on the Shelbyville Turnpike. While lying at Murfreesboro' the army was reorganized, and the First Ohio was placed in the Second Division of the Twentieth Army Corps.

On June 24, 1863, the movement on Tullahoma commenced. The enemy was encountered on the first day's march, at Liberty Gap, twelve miles from Murfreesboro'. The First was not actively engaged in this affair, being held in reserve, but was under a heavy artillery fire. June 26th, at eight P. M., the regiment was withdrawn from the picket line, leaving its fires burning, and made a night march of five miles through rain and deep mud to Millersburg. The march on Tullahoma was one of the most severe the regiment had ever experienced, the rain falling constantly, and the roads being rendered almost impassable from the mud and broken-down vehicles.

Manchester, Tennessee, was reached June 29th. At this place all the extra baggage of the army, including the knapsacks of the men, were sent back to Murfreesboro'.

On July 1st the regiment passed through Manchester, and arrived at Tullahoma at one o'clock that night. At this place extensive Rebel camps were found—tents still standing—artillery, shells, etc., lying at the depot. On the 2d these shells by accident exploded, killing two members of the First, and wounding several others.

On August 16th the line of March was resumed, passing through Estell Springs, Winchester, Salem, across Smoky Mountain, through White and Paint Rock Gaps, and encamping at Bellefonte, on the Memphis and Charleston Railroad, on the 22d.

On August 30th the Chickamauga campaign was initiated, and the First Ohio moved to Stevenson, Alabama. It crossed the Tennessee at Caperton's Ferry on the 31st of August. September 2d it ascended the Sand or Raccoon Mountains, and marched across them to Winston's Gap. September 9th it crossed the Lookout range of mountains—a march of twenty-three miles.

On the afternoon of the 13th of September the troops were recalled from Broomtown Valley. They recrossed the Lookout range, and moving down the valley, again ascended Lookout on the 16th, passing along its crest and descending at Catletts' Gap, near Pond Springs, having marched twenty-six miles in one day. September 18th the First Ohio was placed on picket near the right of the National lines. There was constant firing between the pickets during this day. At nine o'clock A. M. of the 19th the regiment was relieved from picket-duty and marched to the support of General Thomas. After a march of ten miles, frequently stopping to form line of battle, the regiment reported to General Thomas, was placed in line of battle with the Second Division, and directed to recover the ground from which General Baird's division had just been driven with great slaughter. The position of the First was in the front line on the right of the Fourth Brigade. While forming its line and preparing for a charge, it was subjected to heavy firing. Two men were torn from its ranks by round shot.

The charge was made and the enemy driven from the captured position, leaving in our hands all the artillery that had been captured from Terrill in the morning, with the addition of two guns belonging to the enemy. The enemy was steadily driven for a mile and a half, and to a point far beyond the ground occupied by Baird in the morning. At this point the regiment halted, and the brigade commanders formed a line of battle, which was quickly assailed by the enemy in a determined effort to recover their losses. The attack was handsomely repulsed, and two more pieces of artillery captured.

Additional re-enforcements were brought up by the enemy, and about sunset he was observed massing troops in front for another attack. Before this time orders had been received by the brigade commanders to fall back to the main National lines, which were not acted on because of some misunderstanding respecting the picket-lines. About dusk the enemy came up in great force, crushing back the right brigade and seriously shaking the center, the left of which, composed of the Fifteenth Ohio Volunteer Infantry, fell back in confusion. This compelled the First Ohio (which joined the Fifteenth on the left, at an angle of about one hundred and twenty degrees) to change its position in order to confront the enemy. In performing this movement the First was compelled to fall back about one hundred and fifty yards, where it re-formed its lines. A most terrific fight ensued in the gathering darkness, added to which the smoke from the first discharge made it impossible to see anything in front but the flash of the enemy's guns. A Rebel battery which had been brought close up to the front of the National lines lost every horse and every man by the murderous fire poured into it. Such a contest could not last long, and the fight soon ceased, the enemy having fallen back. The division (National) now received orders and fell back to a point where it had left its knapsacks, and laid down for the night.

Early on the following morning rude breastworks were thrown up in front of the National lines. The First occupied the second line of intrenchments. At eight o'clock the enemy attacked the left of the National lines, and extended his attack around the line. The National skirmishers were rapidly driven in, and the enemy appeared in force in front, but unable to withstand the withering fire by which he was received, fell back almost immediately, and could not afterward be brought to close work.

About one o'clock P. M. a heavy Rebel force which had passed around the National left wing, was observed driving some scattering soldiers through an open woods almost in the immediate rear of the National lines. The First Ohio and the Louisville Legion were quickly "about-faced." Advancing to the edge of the timber through which the National lines ran, they delivered a volley and charged. The Rebels instantly gave way and fled. The First was then ordered back to its position in line.

At sunset orders were received from General Thomas to fall back upon Mission Ridge. The Rebels at this time were swarming over the intrenchments thrown up by Reynolds's command, which had fallen back in obedience to orders. These works were to the immediate right of the position occupied by the First Ohio. The broad open field in front of the regiment was crossed under fire, but with slight loss. General Steedman and his command were met at this point, having also fallen back. Pausing to form the troops, the National forces marched to Rossville unpursued by the enemy.

The loss of the regiment in killed and wounded was, in this battle, one hundred and twenty, a majority of whom fell in the terrific fight of Saturday evening. Lieutenant John W. Jackson, a resident of New Lisbon, Ohio, was killed in this action. He was a gallant and meritorious officer, and was greatly lamented by his fellow-soldiers. A gallant soldier, Sergeant Burgtorf, was also killed. Among the wounded were Captain Darnbursch, Lieutenant Grove, and Lieutenant Hallenburg. The last named fell into the hands of the enemy.

September 21st, at daylight, a line of battle was formed and breastworks thrown up. The day was spent awaiting an attack from the enemy, but he did not appear. At half past twelve on the morning of the 22d, the National forces withdrew and marched into Chattanooga. In forming the lines around the city the First Ohio was placed on the left of the Chattanooga road, its right resting at the bridge over Chattanooga Creek, where it lay for one hour and a half under the fire of two Rebel batteries without being able to return a shot. The loss of the regiment from this cannonading was one killed and five wounded. This position was occupied by the First Ohio until the night of the 25th of September, fighting the enemy by day and building earthworks by night. It then fell back to the second line of works, and for the first time in eight days the men were allowed to throw off their accouterments and rest in comparative safety.

From the beginning of March, 1863, up to and including the battle of Chickamauga, and the operations around Chattanooga, Lieutenant-Colonel Bassett Langdon was in command of the First Ohio.

About the 20th of October the Twentieth Army Corps was consolidated with the Fourth Corps, and the First Ohio was brigaded under General Hazen, in the Third Division of that corps.

On the 20th of October the First Ohio had formed part of the important expedition down the Tennessee River to Brown's Ferry, which resulted in the surprise and capture of the ridge commanding the ferry, and the roads between Lookout Valley and the Raccoon Mountains, thus enabling supplies to reach Chattanooga. In this affair Surgeon J. C. Barr received a flesh wound in the arm while crossing the river under the fire of the enemy.

On November 23, 1863, the battle of Orchard Knob was fought—really the opening of the battle of Mission Ridge. About noon of that day the First Ohio, consolidated with the Twenty-Third Kentucky, the whole under command of Lieutenant-Colonel Bassett Langdon, was formed in column doubled on the center, to the right of Hazen's brigade. It immediately advanced on the enemy, driving in his pickets and attacking his rifle-pits on the knob. The pits and one hundred and fifty prisoners were captured, and the Rebels driven into their intrenchments at the foot of Mission Ridge. That night was spent in reversing the captured rifle-pits and constructing other defensive works. This position was held until the afternoon of the 25th.

At half past three of the 25th of November the First Ohio was placed in the front line on the right of the brigade and division. At the signal of three guns the forces moved off and were saluted by the enemy's batteries on the crest of the ridge, some thirty or forty in number. The space to be traversed was about one mile, mostly open ground. The movement was performed in quick time to within three hundred yards, when the troops charged on the double-quick, and the Rebels were fairly lifted out of their works almost without firing a shot.

The National forces, in obedience to orders, took possession of the abandoned works and sought to protect themselves within them. While occupying this position the First Ohio suffered severely, and it became apparent that the only safe course left was to make a dash at the top of the ridge. Lieutenant-Colonel Langdon was the first to see the necessity. Getting his regiment in line, and rising to the height of the occasion, he pointed with his sword to the summit of the ridge and moved on. The whole command caught the inspiration and mounted the almost perpendicular sides of the hill with an energy superhuman. The enemy was amazed at the audacity of the movement, but contested the fight with stubbornness.

The intensity of the Rebel fire was such that five color-bearers of the First Ohio were either killed or wounded. The last one, Captain Trapp, of Company G, was wounded twice within twenty paces of the crest of the hill, while gallantly heading the regiment. At this time the regiment had assumed the shape of a letter A. The nature of the ground being such as to protect the head of the regiment from the Rebel fire in its front, it was halted to gather strength for the final charge. A few minutes sufficed to effect this, and the first and second lines moved up in mass, breaking over and carrying the enemy's works and the crest of the hill. While directing the movement, at the head of the column and within about twenty paces of the crest, Lieutenant-Colonel Langdon was shot in the face, the ball coming out at the back of the neck. The shock of the ball disabled him for a few minutes, but he recovered his feet and charged with his men to within ten paces of the works, when loss of blood compelled him to retire, not, however, without witnessing the capture of the Rebel works. Major Stafford, of the First, was wounded at the foot of the hill, but accompanied his regiment to the top, and carried the flag into the works on the crest. Lieutenant Christopher Wollenhaupt and Sergeant-Major Ogden Wheeler were killed near the crest of the ridge. The entire loss of the regiment was five officers and seventy-eight men killed and wounded.

On November 28, 1863, the First started with other regiments and marched to the relief of General Burnside at Knoxville. On this march and during the East Tennessee campaign, the men suffered intensely from cold, scanty rations, and ragged clothing. January 17, 1864, the regiment had a brisk engagement with the enemy at Dandridge, losing some men. During this campaign the First volunteered three different times to re-enlist as veterans, but on each occasion was prevented from doing so by apprehension of attack and other causes. On one of these occasions the men had actually marched six miles on their way homeward.

On May 4, 1864, the First Ohio started with Sherman's forces on the Atlanta campaign.

On the 10th of May, at Buzzard's Roost it had a skirmish, in which Lieutenant Darnbursch and six men were wounded, and three killed. May 14th it had another engagement near Resaca, with a loss of two killed and sixteen wounded. Among the severely wounded was Captain Louis Kuhlman, of Company D. The next day it suffered a loss of four killed and twelve wounded. May 17th, near Adairsville, a sharp skirmish was had with the enemy. Loss, two killed and two wounded. Among the latter was Lieutenant George McCracken, of Company H. May 27th, at Burnt Hickory, the regiment lost two officers, Lieutenants Dickson and Grove, and eight men killed, and two officers and seventy-one men wounded. June 17th, at Kenesaw, eight men were wounded. At the crossing of Chattahoochie River two men were killed. After this affair the regiment did not meet with any notable encounters. Almost immediately thereafter it commenced to be mustered out by companies—the last one on the 14th of October, 1864.

During its term of service the First Ohio was engaged in twenty-four battles and skirmishes, and had five hundred and twenty-seven officers and men killed and wounded. It saw its initial battle at Pittsburg Landing, and closed its career in front of Atlanta. It marched about two thousand five hundred miles, and was transported by car and steamboat nine hundred and fifty miles.

2d REGIMENT OHIO VOLUNTEER INFANTRY.

ROSTER, THREE MONTHS' SERVICE.

RANK.	NAME.	DATE OF RANK.			COM. ISSUED.			REMARKS.
Colonel	LEWIS WILSON	April	17,	1861	April	17,	1861	
Lt. Colonel	RODNEY MASON	"	17,	"	"	17,	"	
Major	AUGUSTUS C. PARRY	"	17,	"	"	17,	"	
Surgeon	CLARK M. MCDERMONT	"	18,	"	"	18,	"	Resigned July 13, 1861.
As't Surgeon	JAMES D. WEBB	"	18,	"	"	18,	"	
Captain	George M. Finch	"	17,	"	"	17,	"	
Do.	Henry Thrall	"	17,	"	"	17,	"	
Do.	A. O. Mitchell	"	17,	"	"	17,	"	
Do.	James G. Baldwin	"	17,	"	"	17,	"	
Do.	Charles Hallenhoff	"	17,	"	"	17,	"	
Do.	E. C. Mason	"	17,	"	"	17,	"	Resigned.
Do.	J. Q. Black	"	17,	"	"	17,	"	
Do.	A. G. McCook	"	17,	"	"	17,	"	
Do.	L. A. Harris	"	17,	"	"	17,	"	
Do.	W. Baldeon.	"	17,	"	"	17,	"	
Do.	David King	June	29,	"	June	29,	"	
1st Lieutenant	E. D. Sanders	April	17,	"	April	17,	"	
Do.	Albert G. Toother	"	17,	"	"	17,	"	
Do.	J. R. Jones	"	17,	"	"	17,	"	
Do.	J. E. Biggs	"	17,	"	"	17,	"	
Do.	Benj. Russ	"	17,	"	"	17,	"	
Do.	David King	"	17,	"	"	17,	"	Promoted to Captain.
Do.	J. E. Taylor	"	17,	"	"	17,	"	
Do.	Y. A. Gamble	"	17,	"	"	17,	"	
Do.	W. A. Smith	"	17,	"	"	17,	"	
Do.	T. T. Brand	"	17,	"	"	17,	"	
Do.	A. S. Berryhill	June	25,	"	June	25,	"	
Do.	Howard D. John	"	29,	"	"	29,	"	
2d Lieutenant	F. S. Wallace	April	27,	"	April	17,	"	
Do.	T. C. Platt	"	17,	"	"	17,	"	
Do.	H. H. Thatcher	"	17,	"	"	17,	"	
Do.	G. V. S. Askew	"	17,	"	"	17,	"	
Do.	Jacob Waldman	"	17,	"	"	17,	"	
Do.	John G. Clark	"	17,	"	"	17,	"	
Do.	M. McCoy	"	17,	"	"	17,	"	
Do.	Arthur Carnahan	"	17,	"	"	17,	"	
Do.	John Herrell	"	17,	"	"	17,	"	
Do.	Alexander Berryhill	"	17,	"	"	17,	"	Promoted to First Lieutenant.
Do.	Henry Ashton	June	25,	"	June	25,	"	

ROSTER, THREE YEARS' SERVICE.

RANK.	NAME.	DATE OF RANK.			COM. ISSUED.			REMARKS.
Colonel	LEONARD A. HARRIS	Aug.	6,	1861	Dec.	13,	1861	Resigned December 4, 1862.
Do.	JOHN KELL	Dec.	24,	1862	"	24,	1862	Killed at Murfreesboro' December 31, 1862.
Do.	ANSON G. McCOOK	"	31,	"	Jan.	19,	1863	Mustered out with regiment.
Lt. Colonel	JOHN KELL	Aug.	6,	1861	Dec.	13,	1861	Promoted to Colonel December 24, 1862.
Do.	ANSON G. MCCOOK	Dec.	24,	1862	"	24,	1862	Promoted December 31, 1862.
Do.	O. C. MAXWELL	"	31,	"	"	31,	"	Hon. Disch'd on acc't of wounds Feb. 1, 1864.
Do.	WILLIAM T. BEATTY	March	3,	1864	March	3,	1861	
Major	ANSON G. MCCOOK	Aug.	6,	1861	Dec.	13,	1861	Promoted December 21, 1862.
Do.	O. C. MAXWELL	Dec.	24,	1862	"	24,	1862	Promoted December 31, 1862.
Do.	WILLIAM T. BEATTY	"	31,	"	Feb.	26,	1863	Promoted to Lieutenant-Colonel.
Do.	JAMES F. SARRATT	March	3,	1864	March	3,	1864	Mustered out October 10, 1864.
Surgeon	D. E. WADE	Aug.	27,	1861	Dec.	13,	1861	Resigned January 23, 1862.
Do.	B. F. MILLER	Feb.	28,	1862	Feb.	28,	1862	Mustered out October 10, 1864.
Ass't Surgeon	B. F. MILLER	Aug.	27,	1861	Dec.	13,	1861	Promoted February 28, 1862.
Do.	THOMAS J. SHANNON	Feb.	28,	1862	Feb.	28,	1862	Appointed Surgeon of the 116th O. V. I.
Do.	W. A. CARMICHAEL	Aug.	22,	"	Aug.	29,	1862	Mustered out October 10, 1864.
Do.	A. S. COMBS	"	11,	1863	"	11,	1863	Refused to muster; commission returned.
Chaplain	MAXWELL P. GADDIS	Dec.	13,	1861	Dec.	13,	1861	Resigned February 10, 1863.
Captain	Wm. T. Beatty	July	27,	"	"	13,	"	Promoted December 31, 1862.
Do.	Alexander S. Berryhill	Aug.	1,	"	"	13,	"	Killed at Chaplin Hill October 8, 1862.
Do.	Wm. A. Smith	"	19,	"	"	13,	"	Dismissed September 1, 1862.
Do.	John Herrell	"	20,	"	"	13,	"	Killed at Chaplin Hill October 8, 1862.
Do.	O. C. Maxwell	"	31,	"	"	13,	"	Promoted December 24, 1862, to Major.
Do.	James F. Sarratt	Sept.	5,	"	"	13,	"	Promoted to Major.
Do.	John C. Hazlett	Aug.	1,	"	Jan.	28,	1862	Died June 7, 1863; from w'nds rec'd Dec. 31, '62.
Do.	Milton McCoy	"	15,	"	"	28,	"	Resigned March 1, 1863.
Do.	George D. McKinney	Sept.	1,	"	"	28,	"	Discharged October 24, 1863; Restored January 19, 1864.
Do.	David Mitchell	"	20,	"	"	28,	"	Mustered out October 10, 1864.
Do.	James Ambrose	Oct.	8,	1862	Nov.	30,	"	Mustered out October 10, 1864.
Do.	Jacob Fottrell	"	8,	"	"	30,	"	Killed at Resaca, Ga., May 14, 1864.
Do.	Wm. S. B. Randall	Dec.	31,	"	Feb.	26,	1863	Mustered out October 10, 1864.
Do.	John T. Gallagher	"	31,	"	"	26,	"	Mustered out October 10, 1864.
Do.	James Warnock	Oct.	2,	"	Jan.	23,	"	Mustered out October 10, 1864.

RANK.	NAME.	DATE OF RANK.	COM. ISSUED.	REMARKS.
Captain	James E. Murdoch, jr.	March 1, 1863	March 13, 1863	Resigned November 7, 1863.
Do.	H. Lee Anderson	July 12, "	Aug. 1, "	Mustered out.
Do.	James W. Glasener	Jan. 1, 1864	Feb. 4, 1864	Resigned.
Do.	George A. Hollister	" 1, "	" 4, "	Resigned March 30, 1864.
Do.	Jerome A. Fisher	March 19, "	March 19, "	Mustered out.
Do.	Jacob A. Leonard	May 9, "	May 9, "	Mustered out.
Do.	John B. Emory	Sept. 30, "	Sept. 30, "	Transferred to 18th Ohio Volunteer Infantry.
1st Lieutenant	Wm. S. B. Randall	July 27, 1861	Dec. 13, 1861	Promoted December 31, 1862, to Captain.
Do.	James Ambrose	Aug. 1, "	" 13, "	Promoted October 8, 1862, to Captain.
Do.	James Warnock	" 19, "	" 13, "	Promoted October 2, 1862, to Captain.
Do.	Jacob Fottrell	" 20, "	" 13, "	Promoted October 8, 1862, to Captain.
Do.	John A. Allen	" 31, "	" 13, "	Resigned March 3, 1862.
Do.	James W. Glasener	Sept. 5, "	" 13, "	Promoted to Captain.
Do.	George Todd	Jan. 9, 1862	Jan. 9, 1862	Declined.
Do.	Henry Lee Anderson	Aug. 9, 1861	" 28, "	Promoted to Captain.
Do.	George A. Vandegrift	Oct. 25, "	13, "	Resigned April 25, 1863.
Do.	George A. Hollister	Jan. 9, 1862	Jan. 9, "	Promoted to Captain.
Do.	A. W. Plummer	Aug. 15, 1861	" 28, "	Resigned September 17, 1862.
Do.	David Clingman	Sept. 1, "	" 28, "	Resigned December 8, 1861.
Do.	J. R. D. Clendenning	" 20, "	" 28, "	Resigned December 7, 1861.
Do.	William Thacker	Dec. 8, "	March 20, "	Resigned as Second Lieutenant August 9, 1862.
Do.	John F. Gallagher	March 3, 1862	" 20, "	Promoted December 31, 1862, to Captain.
Do.	Richard S. Chambers	Dec. 8, 1861	Nov. 30, "	Killed in action December 31, 1863.
Do.	Lafayette Van Horn	Sept. 17, 1862	" 30, "	Died Jan. 12, 1863; from wounds rec'd Dec. 31, '62.
Do.	John F. Horr	Oct. 8, "	" 30, "	Resigned October 23, 1863.
Do.	Jerome A. Fisher	" 8, "	" 30, "	Promoted to Captain.
Do.	George W. Landrum	" 2, "	Feb. 12, 1863	Killed at Chickamauga September 21, 1863.
Do.	Jacob A. Leonard	Dec. 31, "	" 26, "	Promoted to Captain.
Do.	James E. Murdoch, jr.	" 31, "	" 26, "	Promoted March 1, 1863.
Do.	John Thomas	March 1, 1863	April 7, "	Killed at Peachtree Creek, Ga., July 20, 1864.
Do.	Thomas Dyall	June 12, "	" 22, "	Resigned October 21, 1863.
Do.	Ira H. Bird	April 28, "	June 15, "	Mustered out October 10, 1864.
Do.	Andrew J. Tetor	July 12, "	Aug. 1, "	Mustered out March 25, 1865.
Do.	Malachi Krebs	Jan. 1, 1864	Feb. 4, 1864	Mustered out October 10, 1864.
Do.	Jacob C. Staley	" 1, "	" 4, "	Mustered out October 10, 1864.
Do.	George W. Stoddard	" 1, "	" 4, "	Mustered out October 10, 1864.
Do.	Henry Purlier	" 1, "	" 4, "	Mustered out March 12, 1865.
Do.	Julius F. Williams	" 1, "	" 4, "	Mustered out October 10, 1864.
Do.	B. F. Brady	" 1, "	" 4, "	Mustered out October 10, 1864.
Do.	John B. Emory	March 19, "	March 19, "	Promoted to command detachment.
2d Lieutenant	William Thacker	July 27, 1861	Dec. 13, 1861	Promoted December 8, 1861; Resigned August 9, 1862.
Do.	John F. Horr	Aug. 1, "	" 13, "	Promoted October 8, 1862.
Do.	George W. Landrum	" 19, "	" 13, "	Promoted October 2, 1862, to First Lieutenant.
Do.	Jerome A. Fisher	" 20, "	" 13, "	Promoted October 8, 1862, to First Lieutenant.
Do.	Ira H. Bird	" 21, "	" 13, "	Promoted to First Lieutenant.
Do.	John F. Gallagher	" 31, "	" 13, "	Promoted March 2, 1862, to First Lieutenant.
Do.	Lafayette Van Horn	Sept. 5, "	" 13, "	Promoted Sept. 17, 1862, to First Lieutenant.
Do.	Thomas McCary	Aug. 1, "	Jan. 28, 1862	Resigned July 17, 1862.
Do.	James E. Murdoch, jr.	" 15, "	" 28, "	Promoted December 31, 1862.
Do.	Richard S. Chambers	Sept. 1, "	" 28, "	Promoted December 8, 1861.
Do.	Thomas S. Dyall	" 20, "	" 28, "	Promoted to First Lieutenant.
Do.	James A. Suter	Dec. 8, 1862	March 20, "	Declined.
Do.	Jacob A. Leonard	March 3, "	" 20, "	Promoted Dec. 31, 1862, to First Lieutenant.
Do.	John W. Thomas	July 27, "	Nov. 30, "	Promoted March 1, 1862, to First Lieutenant.
Do.	George W. Stoddard	Oct. 8, "	Dec. 24, "	Promoted to First Lieutenant.
Do.	Henry Purlier	" 8, "	" 24, "	Promoted to First Lieutenant.
Do.	Malachi Krebs	Sept. 17, "	" 24, "	Promoted to First Lieutenant.
Do.	Jacob C. Staley	" 14, "	" 24, "	Promoted to First Lieutenant.
Do.	Daniel W. De Witt	" 15, "	" 24, "	Resigned April 3, 1863.
Do.	John F. Davis	Oct. 2, "	Feb. 11, 1863	Resigned July 24, 1863.
Do.	Julius F. Williams	Dec. 31, "	" 11, "	Promoted to First Lieutenant.
Do.	Andrew J. Tetor	" 31, "	April 7, "	Promoted to First Lieutenant.
Do.	John B. Emory	April 3, 1863	" 22, "	Promoted to First Lieutenant.
Do.	Aaron McCune	Jan. 12, "	" 22, "	Mustered out December 19, 1864.
Do.	William Pittinger	April 28, "	June 16, "	Never mustered.
Do.	Horace Abbott	July 12, "	Aug. 1, "	Never mustered.
Do.	A. W. Henry	" 24, "	" 10, "	Never mustered.
Do.	B. F. Brady	Jan. 1, "	Jan. 15, "	Promoted to First Lieutenant.

SECOND OHIO VOLUNTEER INFANTRY.

THE SECOND OHIO was organized at Camp Dennison, in August and September, 1861. Before this period it had served in the three months' campaign, and participated in the first "flurry" of the war around Washington City. In the organization for three years, the majority of the field, line, and staff had seen service in different capacities in the three months' service, many of them participating in the first eastern campaign of the regiment, including its honorable service at the first Bull Run.

In September, 1861, the regiment, with a full complement of officers and over nine hundred men, crossed the Ohio River, and by direction of General O. M. Mitchel, then in command at Cincinnati, moved by the way of Paris and Mount Sterling, to Olympian Springs, in Eastern Kentucky. As it was the first regiment of National soldiers ever seen in that section of the State, both officers and men resolved to do their very best, by good conduct and courteous treatment, to show the citizens that the Yankees were not so bad as they had been represented. The result was, that the regiment left behind it a fair name, which is yet adverted to in the section of country in which they were encamped.

At Olympian Springs the Second was engaged in scouting and intercepting the numerous bands from Central Kentucky on their way to join the Rebel army in the South, induced thereto by Buckner and John C. Breckinridge.

On the 22d of October the regiment made a forced night march of nearly thirty miles, surprised, at West Liberty, and totally defeated a band of Rebels under Jack May, inflicting some loss to the enemy in killed and wounded, and coming off scathless. Subsequently joining the command of General Nelson, it participated in a movement toward Prestonburg, causing its evacuation by the enemy. The Second also assisted in the repulse of the Rebels at Ivy Mountain, quite a spirited affair, in which it suffered the loss of one man killed and one officer, (Captain Berryhill), and seven men wounded. The enemy was pursued to Piketon, Kentucky, and with the balance of the force the regiment marched down the Big Sandy to Louisa, Kentucky; thence to Louisville by water.

At Louisville the regiment was brigaded with other troops under the command of Colonel Joshua W. Sill, attached to the division of General O. M. Mitchel.

The winter months of 1861-2 were spent in cantonments at Bacon Creek, where they perfected themselves in drill and discipline, preparatory to entering upon the arduous work before them. In the month of February, 1862, the division moved in the advance of the Army of the Ohio, Major-General D. C. Buell commanding, on Bowling Green, Gallatin, and Nashville, occupying the last-named place.

When, in March, the main body of General Buell's army marched to the assistance of General Grant at Pittsburg Landing, General O. M. Mitchel's division, to which the Second Ohio was attached, moved on Murfreesboro', Shelbyville, Fayetteville, and Huntsville. The regiment on this march was engaged in several small affairs with the enemy on the line of the Memphis and Charleston Railroad, the most considerable of which, at Widow's Creek, near Bridgeport, resulted in the dispersion of a force placed to dispute the passage of the creek, and the capture of their camp equipage. The Second Ohio was also with the column that first occupied Bridgeport, and destroyed the railroad bridge at that point across the Tennessee River.

When General Bragg, by his invasion of Kentucky, caused our forces to fall back on Louisville, the Second Ohio, then stationed at Battle Creek, Tennessee, moved across the mountains *via* Manchester, Murfreesboro', Nashville, Bowling Green, Green River, and Louisville, under command of Lieutenant-Colonel Kell, Colonel Harris being in command of the brigade. In the re-organization of the army at Louisville, the regiment was assigned to Rosseau's division in General McCook's left wing, and with two divisions of that command participated in the well-contested battle of Perryville or Chaplin Hills, fought on the 8th of October, 1862, losing in the action nearly forty per cent. of all engaged. Captains Berryhill and Herrel, and twenty-seven enlisted men, were killed; and Captains Beatty, Maxwell, and McCoy, and eighty-seven enlisted men, wounded. With the army, the Second Ohio continued in pursuit of the enemy up to Crab Orchard. Finding it impracticable to pursue the fleeing Confederates further, or supposing so, at least, General Buell turned the head of his column toward Nashville again, reaching that city on the 26th of February, 1862. On the march, however, General Buell had been superseded in the command of the army, by General Wm. S. Rosecrans. On the 30th of October, 1862, the new order of things commenced. The new chief took hold of matters energetically, the name of the department was changed, and the army itself rebaptized as the "Army of the Cumberland." The new General took personal command at Bowling Green, on the 1st day of November, and established his head-quarters, temporarily, at that point. The Rebel army was still making its difficult way over the rugged mountains of East Tennessee, with a wide detour, *via* Chattanooga, toward Murfreesboro'. General Breckinridge was at Murfreesboro' with a strong division, and Nashville itself was invested by a large force of enterprising Rebel cavalry. That city was held by a fine division of troops under General Negley, and was considered safe in their hands. The Rebels could not concentrate for its assault before General Rosecrans could move to its relief. General Rosecrans, therefore, contented himself with keeping his communications open with Nashville, and entered energetically into the important work of perfecting the re-organization of his command, and repairing the railroad and bridges, over which the whole subsistence of the army would necessarily have to be transported. As a prudent General, he did not wish to arrive at his terminus or base without the certainty of being able to subsist his men steadily, and without greater interruption than the ordinary casualties of war, and wear and tear of railroad machinery. Lines of couriers connecting with Nashville and the various camps were established; maps of the country were collected from every source; and business of every kind pertaining to the campaign was thoroughly systematized and rapidly dispatched. Discontent in the army was almost overwhelming, but the General found a way to correct it. Impartiality was his text, and he adhered to it strictly. Furloughs, resignations, and sick-leaves were summarily stopped, and every officer required to rigidly enforce the "rules and regulations," and to shape his exertions and labor with an eye and aim singly to the good of the service. Working to this end, and to this purpose, as one man, the object was attained, and the "Army of the Cumberland" marched into Nashville a thoroughly organized and effective "machine" with which to operate against the Herculean efforts of the Rebel hosts in their front.

The division to which the regiment was attached had in the meantime been assigned to the Fourteenth Army Corps, General Geo. H. Thomas, in which command it remained up to Atlanta, and participated in all the marches and battles of that distinguished corps.

On the 31st of December, 1862, in the battle of Stone River, the Second Ohio was closely engaged, and suffered serious loss. Its Colonel, John Kell, was killed at the head of the regiment; Major Maxwell was slightly wounded; Captain Hazlett, Lieutenants Chambers and Van Horn, and seven enlisted men, were also killed, and a large number of men wounded. In this action the regiment, with the assistance of Guenther's Battery H, Fourth Artillery, captured the colors of the Thirty-Second regiment Arkansas volunteers.

Murfreesboro' was occupied until the spring of 1863, when a forward movement was made by the Army of the Cumberland. The month of June found General Rosecrans on the "war-path" toward Tullahoma and Shelbyville, where the Rebel General Bragg had strongly fortified his lines. The advance of the National forces was not very vigorously contested; but several quite spirited affairs occurred, in one of which, at Hoover's Gap, the Second suffered the loss of one man killed and two wounded.

Chickamauga was the next battle-ground. In this hotly-contested engagement the regiment lost Lieutenant Geo. Landrum (detached on General Thomas' staff) killed, Lieutenant-Colonel Maxwell (then in command) wounded, Major Beatty, Adjutant John Thomas, Captains Randall and Gallagher, and Lieutenants Tetor and Purlier captured. Aggregate loss in this engagement, one hundred and eighty-three officers and men, killed, wounded, and missing.

After falling back into the intrenchments at Chattanooga, they remained in that prison-house until the 24th of November, 1862, when the brigade to which the Second was attached was sent to the assistance of General Hooker, on Lookout Mountain, in his celebrated battle above the clouds. In the night engagement the regiment lost four enlisted men killed, and Captain James Warnock, Lieutenant John Emory, and nine enlisted men were wounded. In the battle of Mission Ridge, which occurred on the succeeding day, the regiment made its way to the crest with slight loss, and captured the colors of the Thirty-Eighth Alabama volunteers. The Second, with its brigade, pursued the enemy to Ringgold, Georgia, at which place a halt was made.

In the reconnoissance to Buzzard's Roost, in February, 1864, the Second was in the advance, and developed the strength of the enemy's position before Dalton.

In the following May the regiment formed a portion of Sherman's force for the Atlanta campaign, and on the 14th of that month, at Resaca, suffered heavily in an attempt to carry by assault the enemy's intrenched position. In this action Captain Jacob Fottrell and twelve enlisted men were killed, and Captains Staley and Mitchel, and twenty-seven enlisted men wounded.

The Second Ohio then moved with the division through Georgia to the Chattahoochie River, and took part in the battle at Peachtree Creek, July 21, 1864, where First Lieutenant and Adjutant John W. Thomas (acting on the staff of the brigade commander) was killed—the last man of the regiment to offer up his life for the cause.

The regiment remained in front of Atlanta until August 1, 1864, when orders were received to march to Chattanooga, preparatory to final discharge. After several unsuccessful chases after the Rebel General Wheeler, within the space of four weeks, the regiment was finally sent to Columbus, Ohio, where, after thirty-eight months of active service, it was honorably discharged and mustered out of the United States service.

It is impossible, owing to the loss of official papers, to give the exact casualties of the regiment. When mustered in, it was nearly up to the maximum strength. It received about one hundred and fifty recruits; thirty-three enlisted as veterans, and about three hundred and fifty were mustered out. The number of men and officers killed in battle was one hundred and eleven; wounded, (including those wounded more than once), four hundred and twenty-five.

The nucleus of this regiment, like that of the Sixth and others raised in Cincinnati, was found in one of the independent peace organizations of the city. It was commanded through part of its career by Colonel L. A. Harris (late mayor of Cincinnati), and a native of that city.

3d REGIMENT OHIO VOLUNTEER INFANTRY.

ROSTER, THREE MONTHS' SERVICE.

RANK.	NAME.	DATE OF RANK.	COM. ISSUED.	REMARKS.
Colonel	ISAAC H. MARROW	April 27, 1861	April 27, 1861	
Lt. Colonel	JOHN BEATTY	" 27, "	" 27, "	
Major	J. WARREN KEIFER	" 27, "	" 27, "	
Surgeon	ROBERT R. M. MEANS	" 29, "	" 29, "	
Asst. Surgeon	H. H. SEYS	May 2, "	May 2, "	
Captain	O. A. Lawson	" 3, "	" 3, "	
Do.	J. H. Wing	April 19, "	April 19, "	
Do.	Joseph M. Dana	" 27, "	" 27, "	
Do.	James Cornelius Vananda	" 19, "	" 19, "	
Do.	Ephraim P. Abbott	" 19, "	" 19, "	
Do.	W. Clement Rossman	" 23, "	" 23, "	
Do.	Owen T. Turney	" 22, "	" 22, "	
Do.	Leonidas McDougal	" 19, "	" 19, "	
Do.	David Colvin Rose	" 30, "	" 30, "	
Do.	Henry Cope	Nov. 1, 1860	Nov. 1, 1860	
1st. Lieutenant	E. D. House	May 3, 1861	May 3, 1861	
Do.	W. H. Sage	April 19, "	April 19, "	
Do.	Nelson H. Van Vorhes	" 26, "	" 26, "	
Do.	Joel E. Thompson	" 19, "	" 19, "	
Do.	George Egan	" 19, "	" 19, "	
Do.	Jerome Buckingham	" 23, "	" 23, "	
Do.	James Mara	" 22, "	" 22, "	
Do.	Leroy S. Bell	" 19, "	" 19, "	
Do.	John McNeil	" 30, "	" 30, "	
Do.	Asa H. Batton	Nov. 1, 1860	Nov. 1, 1860	
2d Lieutenant	William A. Swayze	May 3, 1861	May 3, 1861	
Do.	W. L. Patterson	April 19, "	April 19, "	
Do.	A. M. Goodspeed	" 30, "	" 30, "	
Do.	Azel Babb Smith	" 19, "	" 19, "	
Do.	John R. Johnson	" 19, "	" 19, "	
Do.	James Smith Wilson	" 23, "	" 23, "	
Do.	E. T. McGill	" 22, "	" 22, "	
Do.	Francis P. Dale	" 19, "	" 19, "	
Do.	James St. John	" 30, "	" 30, "	
Do.	James F. Smith	Nov. 1, 1860	Nov. 1, 1860	
Do.	John Nelson	Aug. 14, 1861	Aug. 14, 1861	

ROSTER, THREE YEARS' SERVICE.

RANK.	NAME.	DATE OF RANK.	COM. ISSUED.	REMARKS.
Colonel	ISAAC H. MARROW	June 12, 1861	June 12, 1861	Resigned Feb'ry 4, 1862.
Do.	JOHN BEATTY	Feb'ry 12, 1862	Feb'ry 12, 1862	Appointed Brig. Gen. Vols., Nov. 29, 1862.
Do.	ORRIS A. LAWSON	Nov. 29, "	April 9, 1863	Mustered out June 21, 1861.
Lt. Colonel	JOHN BEATTY	June 12, 1861	June 12, 1861	Promoted and appointed Col. 110 O. V. I.
Do.	J. WARREN KEIFER	Feb'ry 12, 1862	Feb'ry 12, 1862	Resigned September 30, 1862.
Do.	ORRIS A. LAWSON	Sept. 16, "	Sept. 22, "	Promoted.
Do.	JAMES H. WING	Nov. 29, "	April 9, 1863	Mustered out June 21, 1861.
Major	J. WARREN KEIFER	June 12, 1861	June 12, 1861	Promoted.
Do.	ORRIS A. LAWSON	Feb'ry 12, 1862	Feb'ry 12, 1862	Promoted.
Do.	JAMES H. WING	Sept. 16, "	Sept. 22, "	Promoted.
Do.	JAMES C. VANANDA	Nov. 29, "	April 9, 1863	Mustered out June 21, 1864.
Surgeon	R. R. McMEANS	June 12, 1861	June 12, 1861	Died October 30, 1862.
Do.	WILLIAM L. PECK	Nov. 7, 1862	Dec. 2, 1862	Mustered out June 21, 1864.
Asst. Surgeon	H. H. SEYS	June 12, 1861	June 12, 1861	Mustered out July 3, 1861.
Do.	F. C. CLASON	Aug. 21, 1862	Aug. 29, 1862	Honorably discharged August 19, 1863.
Do.	T. J. EATON	July 5, "	Feb'ry 10, 1863	Commissioned returned.
Do.	J. N. KINSMAN	Sept. 1, 1863	Sept. 1, "	Declined. Returned commission.
Do.	WESLEY H. RACE	Oct. 6, "	Oct. 6, "	Mustered out June 21, 1864.
Chaplain	E. A. STRONG	June 27, 1861	Aug. 3, 1861	Mustered out June 21, 1864.
Captain	Orris A. Lawson	" 11, "	June 11, "	Promoted.
Do.	James H. Wing	" 11, "	" 11, "	Promoted.
Do.	Joseph M. Dana	" 11, "	" 11, "	Resigned December 9, 1861.
Do.	James C. Vananda	" 11, "	" 11, "	Promoted.
Do.	Ephraim P. Abbott	" 11, "	" 11, "	Resigned September 5, 1862
Do.	William Clement Rossman	" 11, "	" 11, "	Mustered out June 21, 1864
Do.	Leonidas McDogal	" 11, "	" 20, "	Killed October 8, 1862.
Do.	Henry E. Cunard	" 11, "	" 20, "	Killed October 8, 1862.
Do.	Asa H. Batton	" 11, "	" 20, "	Resigned April 9, 1862.
Do.	Philip Fithian	" 20, "	" 20, "	Resigned August 4, 1862.
Do.	John G. Mitchell	Dec. 21, "	Dec. 21, "	Appointed Lt. Col. 113th O. V. I. Sept. 3, 1862.
Do.	Elitha D. House	Feb'ry 28, 1862	Feb'ry 28, 1862	Resigned November 12, 1862.
Do.	Wesley L. Patterson	April 8, "	May 1, "	Resigned February 18, 1863.
Do.	Leroy S. Bell	Aug. 4, "	Aug. 28, "	Mustered out June 21, 1864.
Do.	Charles Byron	Sept. 3, "	Sept. 9, "	Mustered out December 16, 1861.
Do.	James M. Imbra	" 5, "	" 16, "	Mustered out June 21, 1864.

RANK.	NAME.	DATE OF RANK.	COM. ISSUED.	REMARKS.
Captain	James St. John	Sept. 16, 1862	Oct. 5, 1862	Killed October 8, 1862.
Do.	William A. Swayze	Nov. 12, "	Nov. 24, "	Mustered out June 21, 1864.
Do.	Edward M. Driscoll	Oct. 8, "	Dec. 2, "	Mustered out December 19, 1864.
Do.	Benj. C. G. Reed	" 8, "	" 2, "	Mustered out August 12, 1864.
Do.	A. K. Taylor	" 8, "	" 25, "	Mustered out June 21, 1864.
Do.	John B. McRoberts	Feb'ry 18, 1863	Feb'ry 26, 1863	Mustered out June 20, 1864.
Do.	John D. Whiting	Jan. 1, "	Jan. 10, "	Mustered out May 30, 1865.
1st Lieutenant	Elitha D. House	June 11, 1861	June 11, 1861	Promoted.
Do.	Wesley L. Patterson	" 11, "	" 11, "	Promoted.
Do.	Carl A. Cranston	" 11, "	" 11, "	Resigned October —, 1861.
Do.	Joel E. Thomson	" 11, "	" 11, "	Resigned March 12, 1862.
Do.	Charles Allen	" 11, "	" 11, "	Appointed Captain and C. S., Feb'ry —, 1863.
Do.	Jerome B. Ebort	" 11, "	" 11, "	Resigned February 8, 1862
Do.	Leroy S. B[illegible]	" 11, "	" 11, "	Promoted.
Do.	James St. John	" 11, "	" 11, "	Promoted.
Do.	James M. Imbra	" 11, "	" 11, "	Promoted.
Do.	John Ritchie	" 20, "	" 20, "	Resigned March 29, 1862.
Do.	John G. Mitchell	Aug. 1, "	Aug. 1, "	Promoted.
Do.	A. K. Taylor	" 3, "	" 3, "	Promoted.
Do.	Silas Pruden	Dec. 21, "	Dec. 21, "	Resigned June 20, 1862.
Do.	Lyne S. Sullivan	Jan. 9, 1862	Jan. 9, 1862	Declined.
Do.	Stephen D. Carpenter	" 11, "	" 11, "	Mustered out March 12, 1865.
Do.	William A. Swayze	Feb'ry 28, "	Feb'ry 28, "	Promoted.
Do.	James S. Wilson	" 28, "	" 28, "	Mustered out June 21, 1864.
Do.	Frank P. Dale	March 12, "	March 20, "	Resigned August 9, 1862.
Do.	Edward M. Driscoll	" 29, "	May 1, "	Promoted.
Do.	Calvin L. Starr	April 9, "	" 1, "	Killed October 8, 1862.
Do.	Charles Byron	June 30, "	June 30, "	Promoted.
Do.	John B. McRoberts	Aug. 4, "	Aug. 28, "	Promoted.
Do.	Benj. C. G. Reed	Dec. 21, 1861	Sept. 8, "	Promoted.
Do.	John D. Whiting	Aug. 19, 1862	" 8, "	Promoted.
Do.	Abraham Wolback	Sept. 3, "	" 9, "	Mustered out June 21, 1864.
Do.	John Richey	" 5, "	" 16, "	Mustered out December 19, 1861.
Do.	Samuel B. Piper	" 18, "	Oct. 5, "	Mustered out March 27, 1865.
Do.	Joel G. Blue	Oct. 8, "	Dec. 2, "	Mustered out January 5, 1864.
Do.	Kimball C. Wells	" 8, "	" 26, "	Mustered out June 21, 1864.
Do.	David J. Kissinger	" 8, "	" 26, "	Mustered out June 21, 1865.
Do.	Thos. B. Stevenson	" 8, "	" 26, "	Mustered out August 12, 1864.
Do.	William A. Curry	Nov. 12, "	" 26, "	Died in rebel prison September 29, 1864.
Do.	Oliver P. Barnes	Feb'ry 18, 1863	Feb'ry 26, 1863	Mustered out March 12, 1865.
Do.	John C. Roney	Jan. 1, "	Jan. 10, "	Mustered out March 12, 1865.
2d Lieutenant	William A. Swayze	June 11, 1861	June 11, 1861	Promoted.
Do.	Wilbur H. Sage	" 11, "	" 11, "	Resigned September 6, 1861.
Do.	Silas Pruden	" 11, "	" 11, "	Promoted.
Do.	Stephen D. Carpenter	" 11, "	" 11, "	Promoted.
Do.	Richard B. Johnson	" 11, "	" 11, "	Resigned August 23, 1861.
Do.	James S. Wilson	" 11, "	" 11, "	Promoted.
Do.	Frank P. Dale	" 11, "	" 11, "	Promoted.
Do.	Joseph D. More	" 11, "	" 11, "	Killed at Elkwater, Virginia.
Do.	Calvin L. Starr	" 11, "	" 11, "	Promoted.
Do.	Edward M. Driscoll	" 20, "	" 20, "	Promoted.
Do.	John B. McRoberts	July 31, "	Sept. 7, "	Promoted.
Do.	Benj. C. G. Reed	Aug. 23, "	" 7, "	Promoted.
Do.	Charles Byron	Dec. 21, "	Dec. 21, "	Promoted.
Do.	John D. Whiting	Jan. 11, 1862	Jan. 11, 1862	Promoted.
Do.	Joel G. Blue	" 21, "	" 21, "	Promoted.
Do.	Charles Hivling	Feb'ry 28, "	Feb'ry 28, "	Commission returned.
Do.	Samuel B. Piper	" 28, "	March 20, "	Promoted.
Do.	Kimball C. Wells	March 12, "	May 1, "	Promoted.
Do.	George W. Fish	Feb'ry 28, "	" 1, "	Mustered out June 21, 1864.
Do.	Thomas B. Stevenson	April 9, "	June 3, "	Promoted.
Do.	David J. Kissinger	June 30, "	July 22 "	Promoted.
Do.	Albert G. Brush	March 29, "	Aug. 25, "	Resigned November 21, 1862.
Do.	Oliver P. Barnes	Aug. 4, "	" 28, "	Promoted.
Do.	William A. Curry	Dec. 21, "	Sept. 8, "	Promoted.
Do.	John C. Roney	Aug. 19, "	" 18, "	Promoted.
Do.	Charles A. Maxwell	Sept. 16, "	Oct. 5, "	Mustered out June 21, 1864.
Do.	George W. Bailey	Oct. 8, "	Dec. 10, "	Mustered out June 21, 1864.
Do.	John W. Elim	" 8, "	" 25, "	Mustered out June 21, 1864.
Do.	David H. Harris	Nov. 12, "	" 26, "	Mustered out June 21, 1864.
Do.	Charles Trownsell	Oct. 8, "	Jan. 26, 1863	Mustered out December 19, 1864.
Do.	Edwin Reid	" 8, "	" 27, "	Mustered out June 21, 1864.
Do.	James Murdock	Nov. 24, "	" 27, "	Mustered out June 21, 1864.
Do.	Michael D. King	Feb'ry 18, 1863	Feb'ry 26, "	Mustered out March 27, 1865.
Do.	George L. Wells	Jan. 1, "	July 9, "	Mustered out June 21, 1864.

THIRD OHIO VOLUNTEER INFANTRY.

LIKE a majority of the regiments raised under President Lincoln's first proclamation, the Third Ohio Volunteer Infantry served under two separate terms of enlistment, April 16, 1861, and May 3, 1861, the first for three months and the latter for three years.

The regiment was organized in the suburbs of Columbus, Ohio, at "Camp Jackson," the organization being completed by the 21st of April, and the most rigid drill being at once instituted. On the 27th of April it was mustered into the United States service. An election by ballot was held for field officers, which resulted in the choice of Isaac Marrow, of Columbus, Ohio, for Colonel; John Beatty, of Morrow county, for Lieutenant-Colonel; and J. Warren Keifer, of Clark county, for Major.

On the 28th of April, the right wing of the regiment was sent to Camp Dennison, with orders to break ground and prepare a suitable camping place for the regiment. A newly-planted cornfield on the west side of the railroad was selected, and, without blankets, tents, or other covering, this detachment of the regiment passed its first night of field service.

On the 30th the remainder of the regiment arrived, bringing with it lumber and tools, with which the men soon constructed comfortable quarters. Throughout the month of May the regiment lay in this camp, and during that time was subjected to the most thorough discipline and drill—that is, so far as drill could be carried by soldiers devoid of arms or uniforms. Near the last of May the men were supplied with an assortment of old arms, flint-locks altered to percussion, and a small lot of blouses and gray pants.

Before orders for the field arrived, a considerable portion of the three months' term had expired; and volunteers for three years being called for, the Third re-enlisted with alacrity and enthusiasm. Recruiting parties were sent out, and on the 12th day of June, 1861, the regiment re-organized by re-electing their officers with great unanimity.

On the 20th of January, 1862, the regiment was supplied with arms and uniforms, and ordered to proceed to Grafton, Virginia, then the seat of war. It was an event at that early day to witness the transportation of a regiment of men in war's full panoply, and the people along the line of railway by which the regiment moved (*via* Columbus and Xenia, and Central Ohio) assembled in crowds at every station, and bid the soldier boys God speed with tearful eyes and earnest prayers.

The regiment arrived at Bellair on the 22d of June, in time to claim the honor of being the first three years' regiment to leave the State. Crossing the Ohio River to the town of Benwood, it was supplied with the first instalment of ammunition. Grafton was reached on the 23d, where the regiment at once reported to Major-General McClellan. In the absence of tents, the men were assigned quarters in deserted houses at Fetterman, a little village two miles north of Grafton. Two days only were spent here, when the regiment proceeded by rail to Clarksburg, where camp equipage was supplied, and every preparation made for an active campaign.

At this date (25th June, 1861) the Third Ohio was brigaded with the Fourth and Ninth Ohio and Loomis' Michigan Battery, Brigadier-General Schleich, of Fairfield county, commanding.

From Clarksburg the Third Ohio advanced with the army, nothing of interest occurring until the 5th of July, when the regiment lay at Buckhannon, Virginia. A scouting party of fifty men, under Captain O. A. Lawson, of company A, was sent out by General Schleich to reconnoiter the road leading to the Rebel position at Rich Mountain. Proceeding cautiously, the little band, upon approaching Middle Fork bridge, discovered that it was occupied by the enemy. A gallant, but unsuccessful, effort was made to dislodge the Rebels. In this, its first drawing of blood, the detachment lost one man killed and five wounded. Gathering up the wounded, the party returned to camp. In the hurry of the search, the dead soldier was not found; but a few days later, upon the general advance of the army, the body of private Johns was found and decently interred by his comrades. He was the first man of the Third Ohio to die in battle.

At the battle of Rich Mountain the Third was in the division which was to advance directly on the enemy's works, but as the fight occurred in the rear of the fortifications, the regiment was not engaged. The pursuit of the flying enemy carried the Third Ohio and its division to Beverly on the 12th of July; thence to Huttonsville and Cheat Mountain Summit, where the pursuit was abandoned, and the troops commenced fortifying the passes of the Alleghanies.

The Third Ohio returned to the foot of Cheat Mountain, where the greater part of it was engaged in erecting a line of telegraph from Huttonsville to the post of Cheat Mountain Summit.

On the 4th of August the regiment marched to Elkwater Creek, and, in company with the Fifteenth Indiana Infantry and Loomis' Battery, commenced a series of fortifications extending entirely across the valley. The common routine of camp life, varied by labor on the works, and an occasional scout, occupied the time of the regiment until the 11th of September, when the Rebels, under General Robert E. Lee, attacked the position, making their appearance on the Huntersville road, driving in the National pickets as they advanced. The Third Ohio, with the Fifteenth and Seventh Indiana, and a section of Loomis' Battery, were in position at Elkwater Junction, and contested the Rebel advance in several sharp skirmishes; in one of which, Colonel John A. Washington, of Mount Vernon, Va., was killed. He was at the time one of General Lee's staff officers. In all the subsequent movements of that period, resulting in the repulse of the Rebel army and its retirement to Mingo Flats, the Third Ohio took an active part.

On the 3d of October two companies of the Third Ohio, under Captain McDougall, scouted the country as far as Marshall, and on the 6th the regiment made a reconnoissance to Big Springs, but found only deserted camps, the Rebels having given up the campaign. With this reconnoissance ended the first campaign of the Third Ohio Volunteer Infantry. It was a campaign of peculiar hardship to the then new soldier, filled as it was with hard marches through the almost impenetrable mud, amid driving rain-storms, severe drilling, and some fighting.

Proceeding to Clarksburg, the regiment enjoyed the first visit of the ever-welcome paymaster. From there it went to Parkersburg by rail, and took steamers at the wharf of that place for Cincinnati, November 28. The regiment was cordially received at the Queen City, was reviewed on the main landing, and thereafter re-embarked for Louisville, Kentucky. Arriving at the last named city, it marched at once to Camp Jenkins, four miles distant from the city. At this place the Army of the Ohio was organized, and the Third Ohio assigned to the Third Division, General O. M. Mitchel commanding.

On the 7th of December the regiment, with its division, marched for Elizabethtown, Kentucky, and on the 17th of the same month went into winter-quarters at Bacon Creek, or Camp Jefferson, as it was styled. During its stay here it was subjected to the severest discipline, under the eye of General Mitchel. Some important changes occurred among the staff officers. Colonel Isaac H. Marrow found it necessary to resign, which, of course, caused a regular promotion among the officers.

On the 22d of February, 1862, in that inclement season, the Third Ohio broke camp and, marching by roads tramped into mire by the passage of artillery trains, entered Bowling Green just as the flying Rebels left it, and reached the bank of the Tennessee River, opposite Nashville, some twelve hours in advance of troops under General Nelson, who, approaching by water, were really the first to enter the city.

From Nashville the Third Ohio marched southward with General Mitchel's column—the distinguished Third Division. It took an active part in all the events of that stirring and brilliant campaign, including the capture of Murfreesboro', and the occupation of Shelbyville and Fayetteville, Tennessee. It was also a participant in the sudden descent of the Nationals on Huntsville, the pursuit down the railroad to Decatur, in which was saved the splendid bridge across the Tennessee, and the enemy was so closely pressed through Tuscumbia to Iuka that the National morning gun could be heard by their comrades on the battle-field before Corinth. In the battle of Bridgeport the Third Ohio acted well its part. Led in person by the impetuous Mitchel, it charged and drove the enemy across the bridge.

Then followed a long and monotonous season of "masterly inactivity," by which the greater part of the summer of 1862 was consumed—during which the Rebels were allowed to perfect their preparations for a struggle compared with which all their former attempts were but child's-play. Huntsville continued to be the rendezvous of the regiment, and the base from which detachments were sent out on scouting, foraging, and other duty.

During the month of August the Army of the Ohio was concentrating opposite and in the vicinity of the then Rebel stronghold of Chattanooga, and for that purpose the posts in Western Alabama were abandoned, and the National troops moved nearer the point where the Rebels were preparing to cross the river.

In the latter part of August, 1862, it will be recollected that General Bragg, with the Rebel army, made a bold push toward Louisville, Kentucky, hoping thereby to compel the evacuation by the National armies of all their posts south of the Tennessee River, including Nashville itself. On the 23d of that month, the Third Ohio, with other troops, evacuated Huntsville and marched to Decherd Station. The race between Buell and Bragg had fairly opened. On the 27th of August it became necessary that a detachment from the Third Ohio should go to Stevenson by rail to bring off some sick men and hospital stores. In returning, the train was fired into by a force of Rebels, and several seriously wounded.

The march from Decherd to Louisville was severe in the extreme. The weather was intensely warm, and the roads dry and covered inches thick with stifling dust. The water-courses were dried up, and what water there was to be had was often very filthy and loathsome All these disabilities, combined with scant rations, and the necessity of thus apparently abandoning Tennessee and Alabama, made the march one of peculiar hardship and toil to the soldier Almost every day the Rebels were within striking distance, and the army eager for battle, but Shelbyville, Murfreesboro', and Nashville were reached and no stand made. Bowling Green was occupied and evacuated; at Green River the army waited almost within sound of the battle in which Wilder and his gallant little band were allowed to be overpowered. Thus the northward march continued until, on the morning of September 25, the Third Ohio again entered the city of Louisville.

While lying at Louisville, Lieutenant Colonel J. Warren Keifer left the regiment to accept the position of Colonel of the One Hundred and Tenth Ohio.

After a few days of rest the National forces again resumed their movements. The first encounter of any importance was at Perryville, Kentucky. In this ill-starred affair the Third Ohio bore an honorable part. It was in Colonel Lytle's brigade, and in the beginning of the action took its position in an open field on the right of the Perryville road, protected only by a rail fence. The Rebel attack was fierce and deadly, but notwithstanding their exposure, the Third stood its ground, and returned volley for volley, until more than one-third of its number had fallen, dead or wounded.

In the opening of the battle, color-sergeant Wm. V. McCoubrie stood a little in advance of the color-guard, bearing the regimental standard proudly aloft. His exposed and marked position instantly brought upon him a fierce fire from the enemy, and the gallant fellow was killed. Five others shared the same fate, until a sixth rushed forward and caught the colors ere they touched the ground. This last gallant hero was a beardless boy of seventeen, named David C. Walker, of company C, who successfully carried the flag through the remainder of the action, and was rewarded for his bravery by being made color-sergeant on the battle-field by Colonel Beatty.

Before the close of the battle the regiment was ordered to withdraw to the second line, which command it executed in good order, though sorely pressed by the enemy. It remained in its last position until night put an end to the unequal conflict. While in line, General Rousseau rode up to the regiment and thanked it in the name of the army for its gallant conduct. He said: "You stood in that withering fire like men of iron." The valor of the Third Ohio is fully attested when it is stated that its loss in this battle was two hundred and fifteen officers and men killed and wounded. Among the killed were Captain McDougall, of Company A; Captain E. Cunard, of Company I; Lieutenant J. St. John, of Company I, Aide-de-Camp to Colonel Lytle; and Lieutenant Starr, of Company K.

In the further and fruitless pursuit of Bragg's army to and beyond Crab Orchard, Kentucky, the Third Ohio joined. Then, ill-clad and dispirited, the regiment and army turned their weary steps westward, and once more marched along the same beaten roads to Nashville, Tennessee. At least, the army had not lost territory, but its retention had been secured at a most bitter cost of valuable lives and time.

The Third Ohio lay at New Market, Kentucky, for a time, waiting for a supply of clothing, and the camp equipage of the regiment, which had been left at Louisville. Receiving both, it resumed the march with buoyancy, greatly encouraged by the removal of General Buell from the command of the army, and the accession of General Wm. S. Rosecrans.

On the 30th of November, 1862, the Third Ohio again entered Nashville, and went into camp on the south side of the city. In the meantime General Rosecrans had completely re-organized his army, and had placed the regiment in the Reserve Division, General Rousseau commanding. With the rest of the army, it remained quietly in camp until the advance upon Murfreesboro' was made. The battle of Stone River ensued. In this bloody affair the brigade to which the Third Ohio belonged was commanded by its Colonel, John Beatty, the command of the regiment devolving upon Lieutenant-Colonel Lawson.

The Third occupied a position upon the right center and became engaged early in the day. As the right wing of the army was forced back, the center, which was partially engaged, changed front, to accommodate itself to the changes made on the right. Maneuvering among the thick cedars in the face of a vigilant enemy, was difficult, but the Third Ohio preserved its line until, upon reaching the edge of an open cotton field, the whole tide of battle seemed to roll down from the right and launch itself upon the center. It then began to give ground, stubbornly, delivering its fire steadily and effectively, though receiving two volleys for one. At last, orders came to fall back upon the new line which had been formed under cover of the artillery. In its new position the regiment was exposed to a galling fire, and lost heavily. During this day it was not again actively engaged, but during the afternoon was exposed to a heavy artillery fire.

Early in the second day of the battle, the Third Ohio was posted on the extreme left of the National line, and employed in guarding a crossing of Stone River. The first day and night of the new year (1863) were spent at this ford. On Friday morning the regiment was relieved, and returned to the center just in time to receive a share of the fierce cannonade opened by the Rebels on that day. On Saturday morning (the 3d of January) the regiment took a position in the front, and its skirmish line was briskly engaged for the most part of the forenoon. In the afternoon the regiment was withdrawn, with others, to make preparations to charge the woods in front of the National center, from which the Rebel sharpshooters kept up a galling fire. The charge was made at dark, the Third Ohio moving down between the railroad and 'pike on the double-quick. It captured the Rebel pickets and first line of breastworks, and held the position under a heavy fire until it was ordered to retire. This proved to be the last of the battle of Stone River, as during the night the Rebel army retreated hastily on Shelbyville and Tullahoma.

Another long interval of rest now occurred, and for three months the Third Ohio lay in camp at Murfreesboro', relieving the monotony of camp life in building fortifications, going on an occasional scout, etc. While lying here a series of promotions occurred among the officers, in consequence of the appointment of Colonel Beatty, (for gallant conduct at the battle of Stone River and other actions), to Brigadier-General of Volunteers.

Now comes a sad epoch in the history of this regiment. Early in April, 1863, the Third was detached from the army proper, and in company with the Fifty-First and Seventy-Third Indiana, Eightieth Illinois Infantry regiments, and two companies of the First Alabama Cavalry, was dispatched under the command of the Colonel of the Fifty-First Indiana, on a raid into Northern Georgia, with the intention of destroying the iron works near Rome, in that State, as well as its extensive foundries and arsenals.

On the 8th of April the Third left Murfreesboro' and proceeded to Nashville; thence by water down the Cumberland to Palmyra, Tennessee, where part of the expedition landed and scoured the country between there and Fort Henry, gathering horses and mules, while the remainder went around by water. At Fort Henry the command was re-united, and proceeded to Eastport, Mississippi. From thence it went by land to Tuscumbia, Alabama. At this point a great embarrassment was felt in the scarcity of horses. About two hundred men were compelled to remain at Tuscumbia for that reason. Every effort was made to remedy this defect, but to little avail. It was the forerunner and cause of the subsequent failure of the expedition.

On the 27th of April, 1863, the regiment left Tuscumbia for Russelville, Alabama. Being poorly mounted on unbroken and unshod mules, its progress was necessarily slow. No resistance was met with until after having passed Russelville; in the afternoon the advance was fired into by a party of Rebels who, being well mounted, made good their escape. On the 28th and 29th the command moved through Moulton, and eastward, keeping detachments of the best mounted men scouring the country for horses and mules, and destroying large trains loaded with bacon for the Rebel army.

On the 30th of April, while crossing Sand Mountain, the command was overtaken and attacked by General Roddy, in command of a large cavalry force. After a running fight of ten miles, the raiding party turned and gave battle. The Third Ohio was placed on the left, as a support to the Howitzer Battery. The Rebels dismounted, formed their lines, and opened fire, running their artillery within three hundred yards of the National front. A desperate fight ensued.

After the Rebel force had been tested, the Colonel commanding ordered a charge, which was executed in fine style. The Third Ohio alone captured the Rebel battery of twelve pounders, with its caisson and ammunition, and the enemy was completely routed. The march was resumed, and no further trouble from Roddy's command was anticipated. The Rebel General Forrest, however, happened to be near at hand, and came up shortly after the fight. He at once saw his advantage, possessing, as he did, fresh men and animals, and commenced a vigorous pursuit with his combined force. Toward night, the Third Ohio being in the rear of the column, was overtaken and attacked. A severe fight ensued, which the regiment was compelled to maintain against large odds for a time, but the whole National force soon came to the rescue, and again the enemy was badly beaten. The fight lasted until after dark, and under cover of the darkness the raiders again took the road, and making an ambush at the crossing of Black River, succeeded in checking their pursuers. Instantly taking the road again, they marched all night, reaching Gadsden unmolested. At this place the raiders found large stores of flour and five thousand stand of rifles, all of which they destroyed.

The raiders then marched up the right bank of the Coosa River, in the direction of Rome. The long and harrassing marches began to tell upon their broken-down animals, and at a point eleven miles above Gadsden the enemy, strongly reinforced, and bent upon crushing the expedition, again overtook the raiders. A third battle ensued, in which Colonel Hathaway, of the Seventy-Third Indiana, and his Adjutant, were killed, and the Third Ohio lost a large number of men. The fight was, as usual, continued until after dark, and again the National troops drew off and took the road. The prospect, however, was beginning to look very dark. Two hundred and fifty of the best mounted men were selected from the command, and sent forward with orders to enter and destroy Rome if possible, while the remainder of the command would make its way to the same point in the shortest possible time.

The Rome Mountain Iron Works, one of the most extensive and valuable establishments of the kind in the so-called Confederacy, was reached and burned. Arrived on the banks of the Catoosa River, the ferry-boats could not be found, which compelled the command to go up the river four miles to a ford, which proved so deep that most of the ammunition became damaged, thus placing the Nationals in a bad condition for battle. At daylight Cedar Bluff was reached. The morning of May 3d dawned upon a brigade of extempore troopers badly situated. Their horses were ridden down, their ammunition was almost completely destroyed, and the enemy, strongly reinforced, was dashing after them. Rome was still twenty-two miles away. Would it ever be reached?

General Forrest and his Rebel cavalry came up and immediately sent in a demand for surrender. The Colonel commanding refused to entertain it, but upon learning the condition of the ammunition, a council of war was held, the pet scheme of the commander was abandoned, and terms of surrender agreed upon. Thus, after a brief but gallant career, the "Provisional Brigade" laid down its arms, and the Third Ohio became prisoners of war.

It was immediately marched to Rome, where the terms of the surrender were shamelessly violated by the Rebels, the men being searched and stripped of everything valuable, leaving numbers of them half naked. From Rome the regiment proceeded to Atlanta, where it remained a few days; thence, *via* Knoxville, to Richmond, Virginia, where it was quartered in the open air on Belle Isle, and remained there until the 15th of May, at which time the men were paroled, but the officers of the regiment, including the Chaplain and Surgeons, were incarcerated in Libby prison.

An exchange being ordered, the Third Ohio was included in its provisions. The men marched to City Point, where boats had been provided, and they were taken to Annapolis, Maryland. After a brief stay at Annapolis, the regiment was transferred to Camp Chase, Ohio, there to await exchange. It remained in Ohio until August 1, 1863, engaged in quelling local trouble, such as the Holmes county rebellion, and other outcrops of the Rebel sympathizing element. The regiment also took an active part in the pursuit and capture of John Morgan and his Rebel raiders, being among the number that finally captured him.

A detachment of fifty men of the Third Ohio accompanied the Twenty-Second Ohio Battery into Maryland during Lee's second invasion, and performed valuable service on that occasion.

On the 1st of August, 1863, the Third Ohio received orders to report to General Gordon Granger, at Nashville, for duty. Reaching that place, it was again armed and equipped, and ordered to rejoin its old brigade, under General John Beatty, then on duty at Stevenson, Alabama. Elated with the prospect of once more meeting their old companions, the regiment marched at once, but arrived at Stevenson too late to rejoin their command, as it had already crossed the Tennessee, and had marched to a point beyond Chattanooga.

Reporting at Stevenson, the regiment was temporarily attached to the Reserve Corps, and with it proceeded to Bridgeport, where it guarded pontoons and escorted trains to Chattanooga until after the battle of Chickamauga, when the pontoons were raised and the south side road to Chattanooga abandoned.

The Third Ohio then went to Battle Creek. Thence against Wheeler's cavalry raid, to Anderson's Gap, Tennessee. Thence down Sequatchie Valley to Looney Creek, where it remained some time, repairing the roads and facilitating the passage of trains to Chattanooga.

On the 18th of November, 1863, the Third Ohio marched for Kelly's Ferry on the Tennessee River, where, being still without its officers, it remained until after the battle of Mission Ridge. The river being clear at Kelly's Ford, the post was abandoned, and the regiment proceeded to Chattanooga, where it performed garrison duty until the 9th of June, 1864, when it received orders to report at Camp Dennison, Ohio, its term of service having expired.

The officers of the Third Ohio being retained in prison for such a length of time, no effort was made at the proper time to re-enlist the regiment as Veterans, and, therefore, at the end of their first three years' term, 23d of June, 1864, the men were mustered out of service.

After a brief visit to their homes, the great majority of the men and officers re-enlisted in other regiments "for the war," and performed gallant service up to the end of the strife. Many of them laid down their lives a willing sacrifice to their country's need.

4th REGIMENT OHIO VOLUNTEER INFANTRY.

ROSTER, THREE MONTHS' SERVICE.

RANK.	NAME.	DATE OF RANK.	COM. ISSUED.	REMARKS.
Colonel	LORIN ANDREWS	April 26, 1861	April 26, 1861	
Lt. Colonel	JAMES CANTWELL	" 26, "	" 26, "	
Major	JAMES H. GODMAN	" 26, "	" 25, "	
Surgeon	H. H. MCABEE	May 2, "	May 2, "	
Ass't Surgeon	J. T. CANTWELL	" 1, "	" 1, "	
Captain	James C. Irvine	April 27, "	April 27, "	
Do.	H. B. Banning	" 20, "	" 20, "	
Do.	James M. Crawford	" 16, "	" 16, "	
Do.	George Weaver	" 18, "	" 18, "	
Do.	James McMillen	" 19, "	" 19, "	
Do.	James Wallace	" 21, "	" 21, "	
Do.	J. S. Robinson	" 19, "	" 19, "	
Do.	E. B. Olmstead	" 27, "	" 27, "	
Do.	E. Powell	" 21, "	" 21, "	
Do.	A. H. Brown	" 22, "	" 22, "	
1st Lieutenant	L. W. Carpenter	" 27, "	" 27, "	
Do.	W. C. Cooper	" 20, "	" 20, "	
Do.	John S. Jones	" 16, "	" 16, "	
Do.	Gordan A. Stewart	" 18, "	" 18, "	
Do.	Jacob Shultz	" 19, "	" 19, "	
Do.	Percy S. Sowers	" 21, "	" 21, "	
Do.	Peter Grubb	" 19, "	" 19, "	
Do.	Wm. S. Straub	" 27, "	" 27, "	
Do.	N. W. Scott	" 21, "	" 21, "	
Do.	M. J. Lafever	" 22, "	" 22, "	
2d Lieutenant	F. A. Coates	" 27, "	" 27, "	
Do.	George Rogers	" 20, "	" 20, "	
Do.	Byron W. Dolbear	" 16, "	" 16, "	
Do.	D. Timmons	" 18, "	" 18, "	
Do.	R. B. Spink	" 19, "	" 19, "	
Do.	G. F. Laird	" 21, "	" 21, "	
Do.	Wm. Surgeson	" 19, "	" 19, "	
Do.	J. R. Prichard	" 23, "	" 23, "	
Do.	Wm. Constant	" 21, "	" 21, "	
Do.	Wm. H. Garrett	" 22, "	" 22, "	
Do.	Richard B. Treat	May 20, "	May 20, "	

ROSTER, THREE YEARS' SERVICE

BANK.	NAME.	DATE OF BANK.	COM. ISSUED.	REMARKS.
Colonel	LORIN ANDREWS	June 5, 1861	July 5, 1861	Died Oct. 4, 1861. [Nov. 29, 1862
Do.	JOHN S. MASON	Oct. 3, "	Oct. 3, "	Appointed Brigadier-General by President,
Do.	JAMES H. GODMAN	Nov. 29, 1862	April 9, 1863	Honorably discharged July 28, 1863.
Do.	LEO'D W. CARPENTER	July 28, 1863	Aug. 19, "	Mustered out.
Lt. Colonel	JAMES CANTWELL	June 5, 1861	June 5, 1861	Appointed Colonel 82d Regiment O. V. I.
Do.	JAMES H. GODMAN	Jan. 9, 1862	Jan. 9, 1862	Promoted to Colonel November 29, 1862.
Do.	LEONARD W. CARPENTER	Nov. 29, "	April 9, 1863	Promoted to Colonel. [tained.
Do.	GORDON A. STEWART	July 28, 1863	Aug. 19, "	Mustered out as Major July 28, 1863, to be re-
Do.	FRANK J. SPALTER	Aug. 29, 1864	" 29, 1861	Remained in command of Fourth Battalion.
Do.	CHARLES C. CALLAHAN	Dec. 9, "	Dec. 9, "	[ary 23, 1865.
Do.	SEWELL W. DEWITT	May 31, 1865	May 31, 1865	Absent from regiment with leave since Janu-
Major	JAMES H. GODMAN	June 5, 1861	June 5, 1861	Promoted to Lieutenant-Colonel Jan. 9, 1862.
Do.	GEORGE WEAVER	Jan. 9, 1862	Jan. 9, 1862	Resigned November 6, 1862.
Do.	LEONARD W. CARPENTER	Nov. 6, "	Dec. 26, "	Promoted to Lieutenant-Colonel.
Do.	GORDON A. STEWART	" 29, "	April 9, 1863	Mustered out. [Captain.
Do.	PETER GRUBB	July 28, 1863	Aug. 29, "	Mustered out July 28, 1863, to be retained as
Do.	FRANK J. SPALTER	June 25, 1864	July 25, 1864	Killed at battle of Wilderness, 1864.
Surgeon	H. H. MCABEE			Honorably discharged, September 16, 1863.
Do.	T. W. MORRISON	Sept. 16, 1863	Nov. 7, 1863	Mustered out.
Ass't Surgeon	ALBERT LONGWELL	Aug. 21, 1861	Aug. 21, 1861	Resigned October 27, 1862.
Do.	T. W. MORRISON	July 31, 1862	July 31, 1862	Promoted to Surgeon.
Do.	JOHN B. LAIRD	Nov. 20, "	Feb. 13, 1863	Resigned July 11, 1864.
Do.	W. D. WILSON	Jan. 15, 1864	Jan. 18, 1864	Commission returned.
Do.	BARZELLIA GRAY	April 22, "	April 22, "	Mustered out with regiment.
Chaplain	LORENZO WARNER	June 15, 1861	Aug. 26, 1861	Resigned March 17, 1863.
Do.	DANIEL G. STRONG	March 25, 1863	May 6, 1863	Mustered out.
Captain	L. W. Carpenter	June 4, 1861	June 4, 1861	Promoted November 6, 1862, to Captain.
Do.	H. B. Banning	" 4, "	" 4, "	Appointed Colonel 87th Regim't, June 25, 1862.
Do.	James M. Crawford	" 4, "	" 4, "	Honorably discharged, August 31, 1862.
Do.	George Weaver	" 4, "	" 4, "	Promoted January 9, 1862, to Major.
Do.	James McMillen	" 4, "	" 4, "	Deceased.
Do.	James Wallace	" 4, "	" 4, "	Died January 6, 1863.
Do.	J. S. Robinson	" 4, "	" 4, "	Appointed Major 82d Regiment O. V. I.
Do.	E. B. Olmstead	" 4, "	" 4, "	Honorably discharged October 17, 1862.
Do.	Eugene Powell	" 4, "	" 4, "	Appointed Major 66th Regiment O. V. I.
Do.	A. H. Brown	" 4, "	" 4, "	Resigned June 11, 1862.
Do.	Gordon A. Stewart	Jan. 9, 1862	Jan. 9, 1862	Promoted November 29, 1862, to Major.
Do.	Peter Grubb	" 9, "	" 9, "	Mustered out.
Do.	William Constant	" 9, "	" 9, "	Resigned November 22, 1862. [Oct. 15, 1862
Do.	Foster A. Coates	June 11, "	Sept. 12, "	Honorably discharged as First Lieutenant
Do.	John S. Jones	" 28, "	" 12, "	Mustered out.
Do.	George F. Laird	" 29, "	" 12, "	Mustered out.
Do.	James Ferguson	Nov. 22, "	Dec. 11, "	Deceased.
Do.	John Green	June 11, "	" 26, "	Promoted by the President April 17, 1863.
Do.	William S. Straub	Aug. 31 "	" 26, "	Mustered out.

RANK.	NAME.	DATE OF RANK	COM. ISSUED.	REMARKS.
Captain	Daniel Timmons	Oct. 17, 1862	Dec. 26, 1862	Mustered out.
Do.	Israel Underwood	Nov. 6, "	" 26 "	Declined Promotion.
Do.	Byron W. Dolbear	" 6, "	Jan. 20, 1863	Deceased.
Do.	Samuel L. Brearley	Jan. 10, 1863	Feb. 10, "	Mustered out.
Do.	William Wallace	April 29, "	May 18, "	Declined promotion.
Do.	William M. Camp	March 1, "	" 18, "	Mustered out.
Do.	J. R. Prichard	April 1, "	" 23, "	Mustered out.
Do.	Byron W. Evans	" 1, "	June 17, "	Died in prison.
Do.	Charles C. Calahan	June 4, 1864	" 25, 1864	Promoted.
Do.	Sewell W. Dewitt	" 25, "	" 25, "	Promoted.
Do.	George C. Denniston	" 25, "	" 25, "	Mustered out March 2, 1865.
Do.	Lewis Rounds	Dec. 9, "	Dec. 9, "	Mustered out July 12, 1865.
Do.	Asa T. Freeman	March 29, 1865	March 29, 1865	Mustered out.
Do.	Lucian P. Abbott	May 31, "	May 31, "	Mustered out.
Do.	Jeremiah J. Garman	" 31, "	" 31, "	Mustered out.
1st Lieutenant	Foster A. Coates	June 4, 1861	June 4, 1861	Promoted June 11, 1862; honorably discharged Oct. 15, 1862.
Do.	John Green	" 4, "	" 4, "	Promoted June 11, 1862, to Captain.
Do.	John S. Jones	" 4, "	" 4, "	Promoted June 25, 1862, to Captain.
Do.	Gordon A. Stewart	" 4, "	" 4, "	Promoted January 9, 1862, to Captain.
Do.	Jacob Shultz	" 4, "	" 4, "	Resigned June 21, 1862.
Do.	G. F. Laird	" 4, "	" 4, "	Promoted June 29, 1862.
Do.	Peter Grubb	" 4, "	" 4, "	Promoted January 9, 1862.
Do.	Wm. S. Straub	" 4, "	" 4, "	Promoted August 31, 1862.
Do.	William Constant	" 4, "	" 4, "	Promoted January 9, 1862.
Do.	Bradford R. Durfee	" 4, "	" 4, "	Appointed Lieutenant-Colonel of 82d regiment O. V. I.
Do.	Wm. H. Garrett	Aug. 9, "	Aug. 9, "	Resigned December 7, 1862.
Do.	Daniel Timmons	Jan. 9, 1862	Jan. 9, 1862	Promoted October 17, 1862.
Do.	Israel Underwood	" 9, "	" 9, "	Resigned April 29, 1863.
Do.	A. W. Lippett	" 9 "	" 9, "	Died December 26, 1862.
Do.	James Ferguson	" 9, "	" 9, "	Promoted to Captain.
Do.	Byron W. Dolbear	" 9, "	" 9, "	Promoted Nov. 6, 1862.
Do.	William M. Camp	June 21, "	Sept. 12, "	Promoted to Captain.
Do.	Samuel L. Brearley	" 31, "	" 12, "	Promoted to Captain.
Do.	George Lester		" 12, "	Mustered out.
Do.	Lemuel Jeffries	" 25, "	" 12, "	Resigned January 7, 1867.
Do.	Reason Beall Spink	Nov. 22, "	Dec. 11, "	Resigned March 23, 1863.
Do.	J. R. Prichard	June 11, "	" 28, "	Promoted to Captain.
Do.	William T. Patton	Aug. 31, "	" 26, "	Mustered out.
Do.	Theodore H. Dickerson	Oct. 17, "	" 26, "	Mustered out.
Do.	Byron W. Evans	Nov. 6, "	" 26, "	Promoted to Captain.
Do.	William Welch	Dec. 7, "	" 26, "	Promoted to Captain.
Do.	Byron Thomas	Dec. 26, "	Feb. 16, 1863	Honorably discharged August 12, 1863.
Do.	William Wallace	Nov. 6, "	" 10, "	Mustered out.
Do.	Joseph H. Carr	Jan. 7, 1863	" 10, "	Honorably discharged November 3, 1863.
Do.	Andrew M. Anderson	March 21, "	July 20, "	Mustered out.
Do.	George Orville Hill	Jan. 10, "	May 18, "	Honorably discharged November 28, 1863.
Do.	C. L. Pettibone	April 29, "	" 28, "	
Do.	George Brophy	March 1, "	July 20, "	Mustered out.
Do.	John Dunlap	April 1, "	" 20, "	Commission revoked.
Do.	Frank J. Spalter	Jan. 1, "	" 20, "	Made Major of Fourth Battalion.
Do.	George W. Cruikshank	June 7, 1864	" 25, 1864	Killed August 25, 1864.
Do.	Lewis Rounds	July 25, "	" 25, "	Commission revoked.
Do.	Frank R. Saiter	" 25, "	" 25, "	Declined promotion; mustered out.
Do.	Ranson E. Braman	" 25, "	" 25, "	Declined promotion.
Do.	Asa T. Freeman	Aug. 9, "	Aug. 9, "	Promoted to Captain.
Do.	Lucian P. Abbott	Sept. 8, "	Sept. 8, "	Promoted to Captain.
Do.	Jeremiah J. Garman	Nov. 3, "	Nov. 3, "	Promoted to Captain.
Do.	Hiram Lynn	Jan. 18, 1865	Jan. 18, 1865	Resigned.
Do.	Gerrard Welch	May 31, "	May 31, "	
Do.	John W. Hendershott	June 6, "	June 6, "	
2d Lieutenant	Israel Underwood	" 4, 1861	June 4, "	Promoted January 9, '62, to First Lieutenant.
Do.	A. W. Lippett	" 4, "	" 4, "	Promoted January 9, '62, to First Lieutenant.
Do.	Byron W. Dolbear	" 4, "	" 4, "	Promoted January 9, '62, to First Lieutenant.
Do.	Daniel Timmons	" 4, "	" 4, "	Promoted January 9, '62, to First Lieutenant.
Do.	Henry Cutter	" 4, "	" 4, "	Resigned June 21, 1862.
Do.	Samuel L. Brearley	" 4, "	" 4, "	Promoted June 11, 1862, to First Lieutenant.
Do.	W. F. Surgeson	" 4, "	" 4, "	Resigned November 7, 1862.
Do.	J. R. Prichard	" 4, "	" 4, "	Promoted June 11, 1862, to First Lieutenant.
Do.	James Ferguson	" 4, "	" 4, "	Promoted January 9, '62, to First Lieutenant.
Do.	Wm. H. Garrett	" 4, "	" 4, "	Promoted August 9, 1861, to First Lieutenant.
Do.	William M. Camp	Aug. 9, "	Aug. 9, "	Promoted June 21, 1862, to First Lieutenant.
Do.	Algernon Gilliam	" 9, "	" 9, "	Resigned June 21, 1862.
Do.	Lemuel Jeffries	Dec. 20, "	Dec. 20, "	Promoted June 25, 1862, to First Lieutenant.
Do.	Isaiah Larkins	Jan. 9, 1862	Jan. 9, 1862	Resigned October 31, 1862.
Do.	William T. Patten	" 9, "	" 9, "	Promoted August 31, '62, to First Lieutenant.
Do.	George Lester	" 9, "	" 9, "	Promoted to First Lieutenant.
Do.	Theodore H. Dickerson	" 9, "	Sept. 12, "	Promoted October 17, '62, to First Lieutenant.
Do.	Byron W. Evans	June 11, "	" 12, "	Promoted Nov. 6, '62, to First Lieutenant.
Do.	William Welch	" 13, "	" 12, "	Promoted Dec. 7, 1862, to First Lieutenant.
Do.	Byron Thomas	" 21, "	" 12, "	Promoted Dec. 26, 1862, to First Lieutenant.
Do.	William Brighton	" 25, "	" 12, "	Killed December 13, 1862.
Do.	Reason Beall Spink	" 29, "	" 12, "	Promoted Nov. 22, 1862, to First Lieutenant.
Do.	William Wallace	" 21, "	" 12, "	Promoted Nov. 6, 1862, to First Lieutenant.
Do.	C. L. Pettibone	Nov. 22, "	Dec. 11, "	Promoted to First Lieutenant.
Do.	Andrew M. Anderson	Oct. 31, "	" 26, "	Promoted to First Lieutenant.
Do.	Joseph H. Carr	June 11, "	" 31, "	Promoted Jan. 7, 1863, to First Lieutenant.
Do.	Samuel J. Shoub	Aug. 31, "	Feb. 10, 1863	Killed July 3, 1863.
Do.	Watson McCollough	Oct. 17, "	Dec. 31, 1862	Died March 29, 1863.
Do.	Frank J. Spalter	Nov. 6, "	" 31, "	Promoted to First Lieutenant.
Do.	George Orville Hill	Dec. 7, "	" 31, "	Promoted to First Lieutenant.
Do.	George Brophy	" 26, "	Feb. 16, 1863	Promoted to First Lieutenant.
Do.	John Dunlap	Nov. 6, "	March 30, "	Promoted to First Lieutenant.
Do.	William F. Lynch	Jan. 7, "	" 30, "	Resigned.
Do.	William A. McDermott	Dec. 13, "	April 29, "	Mustered out.
Do.	John R. Knapp, jr	June 10, 1863	May 18, "	Mustered out.
Do.	Addison H. Edgar	March 29, "	" 25, "	Killed July 2, 1863.
Do.	John G. Evans	April 29, "	" 24, "	Promoted to First Lieutenant.
Do.	William W. Williams	March 24, "	July 20, "	Mustered out.
Do.	Joseph Watkins	Jan. 1, "	" 20, "	Mustered out.
Do.	Albert H. Perry	March 1, "	" 20, "	Mustered out.
Do.	Joseph L. Dickleman	April 1, "	Aug. 25, "	Mustered out.
Do.	Lucian Abbott	Jan. 20, "	Jan. 20, "	Transferred from 8th O. V. I.; promoted.

FOURTH OHIO VOLUNTEER INFANTRY.

THE FOURTH OHIO was organized at Camp Jackson, Columbus, on the 25th day of April, 1861, and, acting under the old militia law of the State, the men proceeded to choose their officers by ballot. Lorin Andrews, the well-known and highly-honored President of Kenyon College, who had volunteered as a private, (and who was among the first prominent citizens of the State who hastened to tender their services to the Government in any capacity in which they might be needed), thus became the Colonel of the regiment. Its ranks were filled by two companies from Mount Vernon, two from Delaware, two from Kenton, two from Marion, one from Canton, and one from Wooster.

On the 2d of May the regiment moved to Camp Dennison, and on the 4th of the same month was mustered into the three months' service by Captain Gordon Granger, United States Army. A few days thereafter the President's call for three years' men was made public, whereupon the majority of the regiment signified their willingness to enter the service for that period, and it was mustered in for three years, dating from the 5th of June, 1861.

On the 20th of June the regiment left Camp Dennison for Western Virginia, arriving at Grafton on the 23d. Moving through Clarksburg and Buckhannon, it arrived at Rich Mountain on the 9th of July, but did not participate actively in that engagement, being held as a support for the skirmishers. On the 12th of July the regiment joined in the pursuit of the enemy, going to Beverly, Virginia, where it went into camp and rested for a day. On the 13th, six companies of the regiment, under Colonel Andrews, moved with the main column of General McClellan's forces to Huttonsville. The other four companies, under Lieutenant-Colonel Cantwell, remained at Beverly, in charge of six hundred Rebel prisoners until they were paroled. On the 14th the six companies moved to the summit of Cheat Mountain, but on the 16th returned to Beverly, where they remained until the 23d, when they took the cars for New Creek, arriving there July 28. On the 7th of August they marched to Pendleton, Maryland.

On the 7th of September three companies of the regiment, A, F, and K, under Major J. H. Godman, had a skirmish with the Rebels at Petersburg, Virginia, and captured a large quantity of provisions, animals, and some prisoners, and brought the results of their enterprise back to Pendleton. Lieutenant-Colonel Cantwell, with six companies of the regiment, moved on Romney, leaving Pendleton on the 24th of September, and, after a brisk engagement, drove the Rebels from that place. The loss of the regiment in this action was thirty-two men wounded.

Colonel Andrews having died at his home in Gambier, Ohio, of camp fever, on the 4th of October his successor was appointed in the person of John S. Mason, a Captain in the United States Regular Infantry. Colonel Mason assumed command on the 14th of October.

On the 25th of October the regiment marched to New Creek, Virginia, where it joined General Kelly's command, and on the next day moved on Romney. The Rebels were again driven from that place, all his baggage, two pieces of artillery, and a number of prisoners captured. Romney was occupied until January 7, 1862, when the regiment under Colonel Mason moved on the Rebels at Blue Gap, sixteen miles from Romney, surprised and drove them from a fortified position, capturing all the camp equipage and two pieces of artillery.

Romney was evacuated on the 10th of January, and the regiment transferred to Patterson's

Creek, on the north branch of the Potomac; and thence, on February 9, to Pawpaw Tunnel on the Baltimore and Ohio Railroad. On the 1st of March the regiment moved toward Winchester, under Brigadier-General Lander, but hearing of his death the next day, it returned to Pawpaw Tunnel, and remained there until the 7th of March. On that day it took the cars for Martinsburg, and arrived there on the 9th. On the 11th it moved toward Winchester, to find on its arrival that the enemy had evacuated the place on the day previous.

Making Winchester its base, detachments from the regiment were sent out in different directions, until the night of the 23d of March, when the regiment was re-assembled at Winchester, and on the 24th it started in pursuit of Stonewall Jackson, who had been defeated at Kernstown the day previous. The enemy was pursued as far as Strasburg, where the regiment remained until the night of the 30th of March. It then moved to Edenburg, in the Valley. On the 17th of April the regiment again moved to New Market, skirmishing by the way. On the 27th it moved to Moor's farm, five miles from Harrisonburg, where it remained in camp until the 5th of May, when it again returned to New Market.

On the 12th of May the Fourth Ohio Infantry marched *via* Luray, Front Royal, Chester Gap, Warrenton, and Catlett's Station, for Fredericksburg, Virginia, to join McDowell's Corps, arriving there on the 22d of May. The next day the regiment was ordered back to the Valley *via* Manassas Junction. It reached Front Royal on the 30th, drove the enemy from that place, and captured a large quantity of ammunition, supplies, and a number of prisoners. On the 3d of June it moved toward Luray, and reached that place on the 7th. From Luray a forced march was made by the brigade for Port Republic, reaching there in time to cover the retreat of the National forces.

After marching and counter-marching around Luray and Front Royal until the 29th of June, the regiment went by rail to Alexandria, from whence they embarked for the Peninsula, arriving at Harrison's Landing on the 1st of July. It remained at this Point until the 15th of August, and was the last regiment to leave Harrison's Landing on its evacuation by the Army of the Potomac. It marched *via* Charles City C. H., Williamsburg, and Yorktown to Newport News, and on the 24th of August embarked for Aquia Creek and Alexandria, reaching the latter place on the 27th of August. On the 29th the regiment marched to Centerville, and on the 1st of September returned to Fairfax C. H. On the 2d it marched to Fort Gaines, District of Columbia, and from thence to Harper's Ferry *via* the Baltimore and Ohio Railroad. On the 1st of October the regiment marched to Leesburg *via* Waterford, returning to Harper's Ferry on the 2d. On the 4th it marched to Halltown, coming back to Harper's Ferry on the 6th. October 30th the regiment broke camp and crossed the Shenandoah; November 1st marched to Gregory's Gap; thence through Smucker's and Ashby's Gap to Rectortown and Piedmont; thence to Salem, Warrenton, and Falmouth, Virginia, where it remained in camp until the 12th of December, at which time, under command of Colonel Mason, it crossed the Rapidan into Fredericksburg, and was thrown to the front as skirmishers, and held that position until the next day, 13th of December, when the desperate charge was made through the streets of Fredericksburg. It received the first fire of the Rebel artillery on the right of the National line. The loss of the Fourth Ohio in this disastrous affair was very severe; five officers and forty-three enlisted men, out of one hundred and fifteen engaged, were either killed or wounded. The regiment crossed the river in the night, with the rest of the National forces, and went into its old camp near Falmouth.

Colonel Mason was made Brigadier-General for his conduct at Fredericksburg.

The regiment continued in camp at Falmouth until the 28th of April, when it participated in Hooker's remarkable movement on Chancellorsville. On the 3d of May the battery engaged the enemy, and captured one stand of colors and over one hundred prisoners, among whom were nine commissioned officers. It lost in killed and wounded, seventy-eight out of three hundred and fifty-two engaged. On the 6th of May the regiment moved back to their old camp at Falmouth.

On the 14th of June the line of march was resumed toward Pennsylvania, in consequence of the Rebel army under Lee having invaded that State. Gainesville, Virginia, was reached on the 20th, where a halt was made until the 25th. The next day the Potomac was crossed at Edward's Ferry, and passing through Frederick, Uniontown was reached on the 29th, and Gettysburg, Pennsylvania, on the 1st of July, where the regiment took part in that great battle. It was one of the three regiments that drove the Rebels from Cemetery Hill, after they had driven a part of the Eleventh Corps from the field, and had gained possession of two of our batteries. Generals Hancock, Howard, Gibbon, and other prominent Generals witnessed this charge, and gave it their highest commendation. The Fourth Ohio lost in this engagement three commissioned officers and thirty-four enlisted men killed and wounded.

After the battle the regiment, with its brigade and division, marched in pursuit of the flying Rebels, passing through Frederick City; and thence, through Crampton's Gap of the South Mountain, crossing the Potomac River at Harper's Ferry, July 18th, marching through Snucker's Gap, Woodbury, Bloomfield, and Upperville, to Markham and Manassas Gap; thence to Salem and White Plains, Warrenton Junction, Elk Run, Kelly's Ford on the Rappahannock, returning to Elk Run on the 1st of August. Here it remained until the 16th of August, and then moved to Bealton Station, and took cars for Alexandria, Virginia. On the 20th of August the regiment embarked for New York, arriving in that city on the 22d. The riotous spirit prevailing there having subsided, the troops were removed, and on the 26th of August the Fourth Ohio moved to Jamaica, Long Island, near the city, in order that they might be on hand in case of further outbreak.

On the 6th of September the regiment took passage at New York City for Alexandria, Virginia, arriving there on the 11th. Again a series of marches commenced, embracing Fairfax C. H., Bristoe Station, Bealton, Brandy Station, Cedar Mountain, and Robinson's Run, arriving at the last named place on the 17th of September, and remaining until October 6th. It then moved to Culpepper C. H.; thence to Bealton Station; thence to Auburn; thence to Bristoe Station, where it had a skirmish with the enemy. After this another series of marches in a circle was gone through with, until, on the 26th of September, the regiment crossed the Rapidan at Germania Ford, and on the 27th, at Robinson's Cross Roads, it had a brisk skirmish with the enemy, with a loss of twenty-eight men killed and wounded. On the 1st of December the regiment went into winter-quarters near Stevensburg, Virginia.

On the 6th of February the regiment moved to Morton's Ford, on the Rapidan, crossed the river, had a skirmish with the enemy, and lost seventeen men wounded. Recrossed the river on the 7th, and returned to camp near Stevensburg, Virginia, where it remained until the latter part of August. It then moved with the forces of General Grant, participating in the skirmishes and engagements of that arduous campaign, until in the early part of September, the term of enlistment of the main part of the regiment having expired, it was mustered out of the service as a regiment. Those who had re-enlisted as veterans were retained and organized into a battalion, called the Fourth Ohio Battalion. This remainder of the Fourth was placed on duty in and around Washington City, and continued in that locality until the final muster out during the closing scenes of the war.

The movements of the regiment have thus been briefly noted. A few points, bearing on its relations to other regiments and to commanding officers may be added.

The Fourth was first brigaded with the Ninth Ohio, and How's Battery, Fourth United States Artillery, July, 1861, Colonel Robt. McCook commanding. This brigade was General McClellan's advance guard during his Western Virginia campaign. In January, 1862, a new brigade was formed, consisting of the Fourth and Eighth Ohio Infantry, Clark's Battery Fourth United States Artillery, Damm's First Virginia Battery, Robinson's and Huntington's First Ohio Batteries, known as the Artillery Brigade of Lander's Division, commanded by Colonel J. S. Mason. After General Lander's death, in March, 1862, General Shields assumed command of the Division. When the division was reorganized, the Fourth and Eighth Ohio, Fourteenth Indiana, and Seventh Virginia Volunteers constituted the First Brigade of Shield's Division, Colonel N. Kimball of the Fourteenth Indiana commanding.

General Shields was relieved from his command in June, 1862, and Kimball's Brigade ordered to join the Army of the Potomac, then on the Peninsula. After arriving there, it was assigned to the Second Army Corps as an independent brigade. In September, 1862, the Third Division of the Second Army Corps was organized under General French, of which General Kimball's brigade constituted the First Brigade. General Kimball retained command until he was wounded at Fredericksburg. Colonel Mason, of the Fourth, succeeded him. General Mason was relieved in January, 1863, when Colonel Brooks, of the Fifty-Third Pennsylvania Volunteers, was assigned. In April, 1863, Colonel S. S. Carroll, of the Eighth Ohio, relieved Colonel Brooks, and retained command of the brigade up to its muster out.

The Fourth Ohio Infantry marched one thousand nine hundred and seventy-five miles, and traveled by railroad and transport two thousand two hundred and seventy-nine miles, making an aggregate of four thousand two hundred and fifty-four miles traveled. Throughout its career the Fourth maintained its reputation for discipline, efficiency in drill, and good conduct on the field of battle.

5th REGIMENT OHIO VOLUNTEER INFANTRY.*

ROSTER, THREE YEARS' SERVICE.

RANK.	NAME.	DATE OF RANK.	COM. ISSUED.	REMARKS.
Colonel	SAMUEL H. DUNNING	June 11, 1861	July 15, 1861	Resigned August 2, 1862.
Do.	JOHN H. PATRICK	Aug. 2, 1862	Sept. 1, 1862	Killed.
Do.	ROBERT KIRKUP	July 21, 1865	July 20, 1865	Mustered out with regiment.
Lt. Colonel	JOHN H. PATRICK	June 11, 1861	" 15, 1861	Promoted to Colonel August 2, 1862.
Do.	HARRY G. ARMSTRONG	Aug. 2, 1862	Sept. 1, 1862	Mustered out by order of War Dep. Jan. 8,'63.
Do.	HARRY G. ARMSTRONG	Jan. 8, 1863	Jan. 19, 1863	Reinstated; revoked Feb. 17, '63, S. O.71, W.D.
Do.	R. L. KILPATRICK	" 8, "	April 8, "	Honorably discharged August 17, 1864.
Do.	ROBERT KIRKUP	Sept. 26, 1864	Sept. 26, 1864	Promoted to Colonel.
Do.	KREWSON YERKES	July 20, 1865	July 20, 1865	Mustered out with regiment.
Major	WILLIAM GASKILL	June 11, 1861	" 15, 1861	Resigned January 27, 1862.
Do.	HARRY G. ARMSTRONG	Feb. 8, 1862	Feb. 8, 1862	Resigned.
Do.	HARRY G. ARMSTRONG	June 4, "	June 5, "	Recommissioned by order War Department; promoted.
Do.	JOHN COLLINS	Aug. 2, "	Sept. 1, "	Resigned March 29, 1863.
Do.	HENRY E. SYMMES	March 29, 1863	April 8, 1863	Deceased; wounds received in battle.
Do.	KREWSON YERKES	Feb. 23, 1865	Feb. 23, 1865	Promoted to Lieutenant-Colonel.
Do.	JOSEPH PLAISTED	July 20, "	July 26, "	Mustered out.
Surgeon	A. BALL	June 11, 1861	Oct. 23, 1861	Mustered out.
Do.	A. E. JENNER	Aug. 26, 1864	Aug. 26, 1864	Mustered out with regiment.
Ass't Surgeon	CURTIS J. BELLOWS	" 3 1861	" 3, 1861	Dismissed Sept 10, 1862.
Do.	WILLIAM F. TIBBALS	July 7, 1862	July 23, 1862	Resigned September 27, 1864.
Do.	O. G. FIELD	Jan. 6, '63	Feb. 10, 1863	Resigned October 15, 1863.
Do.	J. D. JUNKIN	Nov. 3, 1864	Nov. 3, 1864	Mustered out with regiment.
Chaplain	S. L. YOURTEE	June 11, 1861	Aug. 31, 1861	Mustered out.
Captain	Theophilus Gaines	May 28, 1861	July 15, 1861	Commissioned by the President of U. S.
Do.	Robert M. Hays	June 4, "	" 15, "	Resigned May 26, 1862.
Do.	Alonzo C. Horton	" 5, "	" 15, "	Resigned August 21, 1861.
Do.	George B. Whitcom	" 6, "	" 15, "	Killed at Winchester, Va., March 23, 1862.
Do.	John Collins	" 6, "	" 15, "	Promoted August 2, 1862, to Major.
Do.	Charles H. Jackson	" 7, "	" 15, "	Resigned December 5, 1862.
Do.	Jacob A. Remley	" 8, "	" 15, "	Resigned April 26, 1862.
Do.	John F. Fletcher	" 8, "	" 15, "	Dismissed April 27, 1863.
Do.	R. L. Kilpatrick	" 8, "	" 15, "	Promoted Jan. 8, 1863, to Lieutenant-Colonel.
Do.	Henry E. Symmes	" 11, "	" 15, "	Promoted March 29, 1863, to Major.
Do.	Waldo C. Booth	Sept. 14, "	Sept. 28, "	Resigned November 15, 1861.
Do.	Frederick W. Moore	Jan. 9, 1862	Jan. 9, 1862	Void; having resigned before appointed.
Do.	Theophilus A. Startzman	March 19,	March 20, "	Honorably discharged January 23, 1863.
Do.	Frederick W. Moore	April 27, "	April 23, "	Resigned July 23, 1862.
Do.	Lewis C. Robinson	" 26, "	May 29, "	Resigned March 29, 1863.
Do.	Thomas W. Hefferman	May 26, "	June 21, "	Mustered out August 13, 1862.
Do.	Jacob A. Remley	July 23, "	July 31, "	Resigned April 30, 1864.
Do.	J. D. McDonald	Aug. 31, "	Oct. 15, "	Resigned April 4, 1864.
Do.	Robert Kirkup	" 2, "	" 15, "	Promoted to Lieutenant-Colonel.
Do.	James Kinkaid	Dec. 5, "	Dec. 26, "	Deceased.
Do.	Thomas W. Hefferman	Jan. 23, 1863	Feb. 17, 1863	Commission returned.
Do.	Austin J. Shirer	May 29, 1863	April 8, "	Mustered out.
Do.	William M. Dick	Jan. 8, 1863	" 8, "	Died May 24, 1863.
Do.	William V. Seeley	March 29, "	" 8, "	Resigned May 23, 1863.
Do.	R. Egbert Fisher	May 23, "	Aug. 25, "	Resigned July 5, 1864.
Do.	Krewson Yerkes	" 24, "	" 25, "	Promoted to Major.
Do.	Morgan S. Shaw	" 25, "	" 25, "	Mustered out.
Do.	Benjamin Jelleff, Jr.	" 26, "	" 25, "	Resigned January 30, 1864.
Do.	Joseph M. Jackaway	" 27, "	" 25, "	Resigned February 27, 1864.
Do.	John M. Paver	March 3, 1864	March 3, 1864	Declined promotion.
Do.	William H. Thomas	" 10, "	" 10, "	Declined promotion.
Do.	Edward R. Anthony	" 10, "	" 10, "	Mustered out.
Do.	James L. Thompson	" 10, "	" 10, "	Mustered out.
Do.	Charles Friebborn	May 9, "	May 9, "	Resigned April 9, 1865.
Do.	Stephen Coddington	" 9, "	" 9, "	
Do.	Hiram R. Treher	" 25, "	" 25, "	Deserted; dismissed.
Do.	Joseph Plaisted	Sept. 26, "	Sept. 26, "	Promoted to Major.
Do.	Wilson B. Gaither	Feb. 23, 1865	Feb. 23, 1865	Mustered out with regiment.
Do.	Henry C. Koogle	" 23, "	" 23, "	Returned commission; declined promotion.
Do.	Jeremiah Robinson	" 23, "	" 23, "	Cashiered July 19, 1865.
Do.	Alexander Mott	" 23, "	" 23, "	Mustered out with regiment.
Do.	Morton Barringer	" 21, "	" 23, "	Mustered out with regiment.
Do.	Henry A. Fortman	" 23, "	" 23, "	Died of diarrhea September 28, 1864.
Do.	Thomas W. Scott	May 11, "	May 11, "	Mustered out with regiment.
Do.	Charles B. Jacobs	" 11, "	" 11, "	Mustered out with regiment.
Do.	Henry C. Koogle	June 16, "	June 16, "	Mustered out with regiment.
Do.	Herman Belmer	July 20, "	July 20, "	Mustered out with regiment.
Do.	Joseph L. Gaul	" 20, "	" 20, "	Mustered out with regiment.
1st Lieutenant	Robert B. Bromwell	May 28, 1861	" 15, 1861	Resigned January 22, 1862.
Do.	Robert S. Logan	June 4, "	" 15, "	Resigned March 11, 1862.
Do.	Waldo C. Booth	" 5, "	" 15, "	Promoted September 14, 1861, to Captain.
Do.	Lewis C. Robinson	" 6, "	" 15, "	Promoted April 26, 1862, to Captain.
Do.	Joseph Rudolph	" 6, "	" 15, "	Resigned March 11, 1862.
Do.	C. C. Whitson	" 6, "	" 21, "	Transferred to Invalid Corps June 16, 1863.
Do.	Thomas W. Hefferman	" 7, "	" 15, "	Promoted May 26, 1862, to Captain
Do.	George N. C. Frazier	" 8, "	" 15, "	Resigned December 27, 1861.
Do.	George H. Whitcamp	" 8, "	" 15, "	Resigned April 26, 1862.
Do.	J. C. McDonald	" 11, "	" 15, "	Promoted August 13, 1862, to Captain.
Do.	T. G. Swartzman	" 11, "	" 15, "	Promoted March 19, 1862, to Captain.
Do.	Frederick W. Moore	Sept. 4, "	Sept. 28, "	Res'd Jan. 2, '62; disability removed March 13, 1862.
Do.	Robert Kirkup	Jan. 9, 1862	Jan. 9, 1862	Promoted August 2, 1862, to Captain.
Do.	Dolin F. McKenzie	" 9, "	" 9, "	Resigned October 3, 1862.

* The Roster of three months' service is not on record.

RANK.	NAME.	DATE OF RANK.	COM. ISSUED.	REMARKS.
First Lieutenant	James Kinkaid	Jan. 22, 1862	March 20, 1862	Promoted December 5, 1862, to Captain.
Do.	Charles W. Smith	Feb. 8, "	" 20, "	Resigned January 9, 1862.
Do.	Wm. M. Dick	March 19, "	" 20, "	Promoted January 8, 1863, to Captain.
Do.	Wm. M. Neely	" 11, "	May 1, "	Promoted March 29, 1863, to Captain.
Do.	Hugh Marshall	" 11, "	" 1, "	Resigned February 11, 1863.
Do.	Austin J. Shirer	April 26, "	" 29, "	Promoted May 29, 1862, to Captain.
Do.	John M. Paver	" 26, "	" 29, "	Promoted to Captain.
Do.	James Timmons	May 26, "	June 24, "	Resigned April 7, 1863.
Do.	R. Egbert Fisher	June 9, "	July 10, "	Promoted to Captain.
Do.	Alexander L. Little	Aug. 13, "	Oct. 15, "	Resigned April 4, 1863.
Do.	George Sharp	" 2, "	" 15, "	Resigned.
Do.	Krewson Yerkes	Oct. 3, "	Dec. 26, "	Promoted to Captain.
Do.	Frederick Fairfax	Dec. 5, "	" 26, "	Died May 3, 1863.
Do.	Wm. H. Thomas	Feb. 11, 1863	Feb. 25, 1863	Mustered out June 28, 1864.
Do.	Morgan S. Shaw	Jan. 8, "	April 8, "	Promoted to Captain.
Do.	Henry C. Brinkman	May 29, "	" 8, "	Deceased July 3, 1863.
Do.	Benjamin Jelleff, jr	" 29, "	" 8, "	Promoted to Captain.
Do.	Edward R. Anthony	April 4, "	Jan. 10, "	Promoted to Captain.
Do.	James L. Thompson	Jan. 3, "	Aug. 25, "	Promoted to Captain.
Do.	Charles Friedeborn	May 23, "	" 25, "	Promoted to Captain.
Do.	Charles S. Jessup	" 24, "	" 25, "	Resigned January 31, 1864.
Do.	Stephen Coddington	" 25, "	" 25, "	Promoted to Captain.
Do.	Hiram R. Treber	" 27, "	" 25, "	Deserted; dismissed.
Do.	Lewis B. Stevens	" 27, "	" 25, "	Resigned April 4, 1864.
Do.	James Clark	" 27, "	" 25, "	Resigned.
Do.	Edward L. Quinton	March 3, 1864	March 3, 1864	Promoted to Captain.
Do.	Joseph Plaisted	" 3, "	" 3, "	Promoted to Captain.
Do.	John B. Heal	" 3, "	" 3, "	Resigned July 13, 1864.
Do.	Wilson B. Gaither	" 3, "	" 3, "	Promoted to Captain.
Do.	Henry C. Koogle	" 10, "	" 10, "	Promoted to Captain.
Do.	Jeremiah Robinson	" 10, "	" 10, "	Promoted to Captain.
Do.	Alexander Mott	" 10, "	" 10, "	Promoted to Captain.
Do.	Edward L. Quinton	May 9, "	May 9, "	Declined; commission returned.
Do.	Martin Barringer	" 25, "	" 25, "	Promoted to Captain.
Do.	Henry A. Fortman	" 25, "	" 25, "	Promoted to Captain.
Do.	Thomas W. Scott	" 25, "	" 25, "	Promoted to Captain.
Do.	Charles B. Jacobs	Feb. 23, 1865	Feb. 23, 1865	Promoted to Captain.
Do.	Herman Behmer	" 23, "	" 23, "	Promoted to Captain.
Do.	Joseph L. Gaul	" 23, "	" 23, "	Promoted to Captain.
Do.	Peter A. Cozine	" 23, "	" 23, "	Cashiered July 17, 1865.
Do.	George Heintzelberger	" 23, "	" 23, "	Discharged.
Do.	Joseph Grunkeymeyer	" 23, "	" 23, "	Mustered out with regiment.
Do.	Albert M. Towsley	" 23, "	" 23, "	Mustered out with regiment.
Do.	Stephen Mosier	" 23, "	" 23, "	Mustered out.
Do.	Herman Strickler	" 23, "	" 23, "	Mustered out with regiment.
Do.	Thomas Hussey	May 11, "	May 11, "	Mustered out with regiment.
Do.	Matthias Schwab	" 11, "	" 11, "	Mustered out with regiment.
Do.	James Richey	July 20, "	July 20, "	
Do.	Michael Ward	" 20, "	" 20, "	
Do.	Andrew J. Barr	" 20, "	" 20, "	
Do.	Christian Knauft	" 20, "	" 20, "	Mustered out with regiment.
Do.	Donald McLeod	" 20, "	" 20, "	Mustered out with regiment.
Do.	Benjamin E. Ford	" 20, "	" 20, "	Mustered out with regiment.
2d Lieutenant	James Kinkaid	May 28, 1861	" 15, 1861	Promoted Jan. 22, 1862, to First Lieutenant.
Do.	Robert Kirkup	June 4, "	" 15, "	Promoted January 9, '62, to First Lieutenant.
Do.	Frederick W. Moore	" 5, "	" 15, "	Promoted Sept. 4, 1861, to First Lieutenant.
Do.	William M. Dick	" 5, "	" 15, "	Promoted March 19, 1862, to First Lieutenant.
Do.	Harry G. Armstrong	" 6, "	" 15, "	Promoted to majority.
Do.	Charles W. Smith	" 6, "	" 15, "	Promoted Feb. 8, 1862, to First Lieutenant.
Do.	William M. Neely	" 7, "	" 15, "	Promoted March 11, 1862, to First Lieutenant.
Do.	Robert H. Barrett	" 8, "	" 15, "	Resigned.
Do.	Hugh Marshall	" 8, "	" 15, "	Promoted March 11, 1862, to First Lieutenant.
Do.	John M. Paver	" 11, "	" 15, "	Promoted April 26, 1862, to First Lieutenant.
Do.	Austin J. Shirer	Sept. 7, "	Sept. 16, "	Promoted April 26, 1862, to First Lieutenant.
Do.	Augustus J. Moonert	" 24, "	" 28, "	Resigned May 26, 1862.
Do.	James Timmons	" 28, "	" 28, "	Promoted May 26, 1862, to First Lieutenant.
Do.	P. M. McCann	Jan. 9, 1862	Jan. 9, 1862	Resigned July 9, 1862.
Do.	Alexander L. Little	" 22, "	March 20, "	Promoted August 13, '62, to First Lieutenant.
Do.	R. Egbert Fisher	Feb. 8, "	" 20, "	Promoted June 9, 1862, to First Lieutenant.
Do.	George Sharp	March 19, "	" 20, "	Promoted August 2, 1862, to First Lieutenant.
Do.	Robert Graham	" 11, "	May 29, "	Killed June 9, 1862.
Do.	Krewson Yerkes	" 11, "	" 29, "	Promoted Oct. 3, 1862, to First Lieutenant.
Do.	Frederick Fairfax	April 26, "	" 29, "	Promoted Dec. 5, 1862, to First Lieutenant.
Do.	Joseph W. Jackaway	" 26, "	" 29, "	Promoted to First Lieutenant.
Do.	William H. Thomas	May 26, "	June 24, "	Promoted Feb. 11, '63, to First Lieutenant.
Do.	Morgan S. Shaw	July 10, "	July 10, "	Promoted Jan. 8, 1863, to First Lieutenant.
Do.	Henry Brinkman	" 10, "	" 10, "	Promoted March 29, 1863, to First Lieutenant.
Do.	Joseph Miller	June 9, "	" 10, "	Resigned June 11, 1863.
Do.	Ephriam B. Stout	Aug. 9, "	Sept. 9, "	Failed to report.
Do.	Charles A. Walker	" 2, "	Oct. 15, "	Killed December 29, 1862.
Do.	Benjamin Jelleff, jr	" 13, "	" 15, "	Promoted March 29, 1863, to First Lieutenant.
Do.	Edward R. Anthony	Oct. 3, "	Dec. 23, "	Promoted to First Lieutenant.
Do.	Charles Friedeborn	Dec. 5, "	" 26, "	Promoted to First Lieutenant.
Do.	James L. Thompson	" 29, "	Jan. 20, 1863	Promoted to First Lieutenant.
Do.	Charles S. Jessup	Jan. 20, 1863	" 20, "	Promoted to First Lieutenant.
Do.	Hiram R. Treber	....	....	Promoted to First Lieutenant.
Do.	Stephen Coddington	Jan. 8, 1863	April 8, 1863	Promoted to First Lieutenant.
Do.	Wm. P. Jackson	March 29, "	" 8, "	Deceased May 3, 1863.
Do.	Edward L. Quinton	" 29, "	" 29, "	Promoted to First Lieutenant.
Do.	Joseph Plaisted	May 3, "	Aug. 25, "	Promoted to First Lieutenant.
Do.	A. Lemoin	June 11, "	" 25, "	Refused to muster.
Do.	Harvey Woodward	" 10, "	" 25, "	Refused to muster.
Do.	Wilson B. Gaither	July 3, "	" 25, "	Promoted to First Lieutenant.
Do.	Henry C. Koogle	May 23, "	" 25, "	Promoted to First Lieutenant.
Do.	Jeremiah Robinson	" 25, "	" 25, "	Promoted to First Lieutenant.
Do.	Philip Nunn	" 26, "	" 25, "	Refused to muster.
Do.	Martin Barringer	March 25, "	" 25, "	Promoted to First Lieutenant.
Do.	John B. Heal	" 27, "	" 25, "	Promoted to First Lieutenant.
Do.	Charles B. Jacobs	" 25, 1861	May 25, 1864	Promoted to First Lieutenant.
Do.	Herman Behmer	Sept. 26, "	Sept. 26, "	Promoted to First Lieutenant.
Do.	Joseph L. Gaul	" 26, "	" 26, "	Promoted to First Lieutenant.
Do.	Peter A. Cozine	" 26, "	" 26, "	Promoted to First Lieutenant.

FIFTH OHIO VOLUNTEER INFANTRY.

THIS was originally one of the three-months' organizations, and was made up of young men from Cincinnati and the vicinity. It went into Camp Harrison, near Cincinnati, April 20, 1861, and was mustered into the United States service May 8th. On the 23d of May it was sent to Camp Dennison. Before, however, the regiment was completely equipped, the call for the three-years' troops was issued, and on the 20th of June the Fifth Ohio, by unanimous consent of the men, was mustered for three years. On July 10, 1861, the regiment left Camp Dennison and went by rail to Bellair, where it crossed the Ohio River to Benwood, Virginia, and from thence to Grafton and Clarksburg, Virginia.

On the afternoon of the 13th of July orders were received to move, but the cars were not ready until the night of the 14th, when the regiment was taken to Oakland, Virginia. It marched from that place on the same day, under Brigadier-General Charles W. Hill. This was the first march of the regiment, and was especially severe, on account of their total inexperience. Its route lay up and over a spur of the Alleghany Mountains. After failing in this attempt to intercept the flying Rebel forces of General Garnet's defeated army, the regiment returned to Oakland. The first death in the regiment occurred at this place, a private being accidentally shot by one of his comrades.

Parkersburg was the next camping place, where the regiment lay until the 5th of August, most of the time engaged in guard-duty and drill.

On August 5th the regiment again took up the line of march for Buckhannon. It lay here until the 3d of November. Near this place, at French Creek, companies A, B, and C had an engagement with a band of Rebels, killing six or seven of them, and losing one man killed. From thence it went to New Creek, on the Baltimore and Ohio Railroad. On the 7th of November it was at Romney, Virginia. The duties at this place were very arduous, companies being sent out daily on scouts. The picket-force alone amounted to nearly one thousand men, portions of whom were stationed six and seven miles from camp.

While at Romney General Kelly, then in command of the National forces, was disabled by the wound he had received at Philippi, and was superseded by Colonel S. H. Dunning, of the Fifth Ohio. Learning that a force of Rebels, fifteen hundred strong, was stationed at Blue's Gap, sixteen miles from Romney, Colonel Dunning determined, if possible, to surprise and capture it. Selecting the night of the 6th of January, 1862, he started at midnight, during a driving snow-storm, and, reaching the enemy's outpost picket-line, captured it, and moved on until within a mile of the Rebel camp. At this point the expedition was discovered by the Rebel pickets, who fled to the main body and gave the alarm. The National troops pushed on and up the steep mountain side, the men being compelled to drag themselves up by the aid of the underbrush and roots. Arriving at the top, the men opened fire and charged the enemy, driving him out of his intrenchments, killing twenty, capturing a number of prisoners and two pieces of cannon. The residence of Colonel Blue, his outhouses, and mill were burned to the ground. This was the commencement of the reputation of the Fifth Ohio for bravery and thoroughness in dealing with Rebels. The Rebel papers of that day contained notices and anathemas against the regiment, headed, as they said, "by a butcher," and advising the Rebel commanders to show the members of it no quarter.

The Fifth returned to its camp at Romney the same day of the fight, having marched thirty-four miles and dispersed and defeated fifteen hundred Rebels inside of fourteen hours.

On January 10, 1862, the regiment left Romney and fell back to Patterson Creek. General Lander was now in command. Thence the Fifth went to New Creek, and remained there up to the 3d of February; then returned to Patterson Creek. From this date until the 13th of February it was engaged in a series of arduous marches and counter-marches, often camping in the snow without tents or blankets, and suffering intensely from the fierce winds of that wild country.

On the 13th of February the Fifth and Eighth Ohio, with a force of cavalry, made a reconnoissance on Bloomery Furnace, the whole under command of General Lander. The cavalry, led by General Lander, had a skirmish with a body of Rebels, killing and wounding a number, and taking some thirty prisoners, including a Colonel, Major, Adjutant, and twelve officers of the line.

The regiment returned to camp at Pawpaw on the 14th of February. At this place, on the 2d of March, General Lander died, and was succeeded in the command by Colonel Nathan Kimball, of the Fourteenth Indiana.

From this time until the latter part of March nothing of material interest occurred. On the 18th of March the command, under General Shields, made a reconnoissance to Strasburg, the Fifth Ohio in the advance. Some shots were exchanged with a force of Rebels, but no casualties occurred. The enemy was followed to a point seven miles beyond Mount Jackson, when the command returned and marched to Winchester, reaching that place on the evening of the 20th of March.

On Saturday, the 22d of March, the long-roll was sounded and the whole force ordered out. The Fifth went through Winchester on the double-quick, cheering, and eager for the fight. Some slight cannonading occurred that afternoon, during which General Shields was wounded in the arm. The Fifth performed picket-duty on the Romney Road that night, to prevent surprise from that direction.

On the morning of the 23d of March the Fifth marched out to Kernstown, four miles from Winchester, and took position in support of Daum's Indiana battery. At nine o'clock A. M. the battle of Winchester was opened. The Fifth continued in support of Daum's battery until late in the afternoon, when companies A, B, C, D, and E, under command of Colonel Kilpatrick, moved up, under orders, and passing through a clump of underbrush emerged into an open field, where it received the first fire of the enemy. This little band, although faced by overwhelming numbers, returned the Rebel fire with interest. The Eighty-Fourth Pennsylvania, on its right, attempted to follow, but quailed and fell back in disorder. Colonel Murray, of that regiment, in attempting to rally them, lost his life. The Fifth Ohio poured its volleys into the enemy at short range, and stubbornly maintained its position until re-enforcements came up. It then advanced and drove the enemy in disorder. In this fierce encounter five of the color-bearers of the regiment were shot down in succession. Captain George B. Whitcom, of Cincinnati, was one of these, and lost his life while waving the colors over his head. A bullet struck him just above the eye, and buried itself in his brain.

When the Eighty-Fourth Pennsylvania fell back in confusion General Sullivan, commanding the brigade, exclaimed that the army was whipped; but on looking again he observed the Fifth Ohio still fighting, and exclaimed: "No, thank God; the brave Fifth Ohio is still standing its ground, and holding the Rebels." The Fourteenth Indiana moved forward at this critical moment, and the tide was turned. The enemy, beaten at all points, turned and fled. The darkness of the night alone prevented the most vigorous pursuit. The loss of the Fifth Ohio was forty-seven killed and wounded. The entire loss of the National force did not exceed five hundred. The Rebel loss was believed to be more than double that number. The regimental colors were perforated with forty-eight bullet holes, and the State flag with ten.

The dead were buried and the wounded properly disposed of, and again, on the 24th of March, the regiment resumed the march. The first camping-place was five miles beyond Strasburg. On the 1st of April the regiment passed on through Woodstock, again encamped near Edinburg, near the bank of the Shenandoah River. The progress of the National force was checked at this point by the burning of a bridge which spanned the river, and by Ashby's cavalry, which had taken position on the opposite side. Shots were exchanged, but no damage resulted. A few days thereafter a dash was made by the Fifth Ohio and some Vermont cavalry into Mount Jackson, but the enemy had flown. After making sundry marches up and down the valley the regiment went into camp at New Market, Colonel S. H. Dunning in command of the brigade. It remained at New Market two weeks, drilling, reviewing, etc.

On May 3d marching orders were received, and an advance was made to Harrisonburg. General Banks's force was falling back. General Shields's force now also fell back about eight miles and took a position in which the General declared he could easily whip Jackson, but that renowned Rebel kept out of the way. Before leaving Harrisonburg (on the 7th of May) the Fifth Ohio was presented with a beautiful stand of colors, sent to them by the City Council of Cincinnati, as a token of the appreciation of the people of Cincinnati for its bravery and efficiency in the battle of Winchester.

Marching was resumed on the 12th of May, and continued until Falmouth was reached, a distance of one hundred and fifty miles. After lying here until the 25th of May the regiment marched to Front Royal, where, halting a few hours, it again pushed on through the driving rain and muddy roads. The night of the 3d of June found the regiment on the banks of the Shenandoah, having marched two hundred and eighty-five miles to no purpose, and with scarcely half-rations. The same history was repeated until, on the 8th of June, the regiment reached Port Republic. The next morning the battle was opened. This was a hot and well-contested affair, and the regiment conducted itself with its usual bravery and dash. After firing a couple of volleys it was ordered to charge on a fence behind which a couple of Rebel regiments were hid. The charge was a success, the Rebels fleeing before them into the woods, where they rallied. Again the Fifth charged, and captured one piece of artillery. Immediately thereafter it marched to the left and repulsed a charge made by the enemy on a battery. The Rebels were too strong, however, and retreat became necessary. The order was finally given, and the Fifth was designated to cover the movement, in doing which it lost one hundred and eighty-five men taken prisoners. The total loss of the regiment was two hundred and forty-four in killed, wounded, and prisoners.

Many incidents of personal valor and cunning occurred in this affair. Lieutenant Kirkup, of Cincinnati, who had been taken prisoner, escaped from his guard, but had not proceeded far when he came in contact with two Rebels. He claimed them as prisoners—they yielded, and conducted him safely out of the mountains. The colors were saved by the Color-Corporals, Brinkman and Shaw, by wrapping them around their persons, swimming the Shenandoah, and joining General Fremont's command four days thereafter.

The retreat was continued until the evening of the 10th, when a halt was made near Luray, where it was allowed to rest until the 21st of June. It then marched through Thoroughfare Gap to Bristow Station, reaching that point about five P. M. of the 24th.

From the 24th of June the regiment was on the march every day for five successive weeks; those days of sullen gloom and confusion, when the enemy, under Jackson, was worrying them with his swift and uncertain movements. In these marches they traversed a distance of more than five hundred miles, and when at last they were halted at Alexandria, the men were nearly naked, without shelter, and completely worn out. After being recruited in health, on the 25th of July they went by rail to Warrenton, Virginia, where they remained until the 31st; thence marched to Little Washington, arriving on the 1st of August. While at this place General Tyler took leave of the brigade, and of the Fifth in particular, as they were mutually endeared to each other by reason of "floods and perils" together. The successor of General Tyler took command in the person of General Geary, of Mexican fame.

On the 9th of August, 1862, then lying at Culpepper C. H., the Fifth made a forced march of eight miles, to reach the battle-field of Cedar Mountain, in which engagement they participated under command of Colonel J. H. Patrick. Re-enforcements failing to arrive in season, overwhelming numbers forced the troops to fall back. The loss of the Fifth in this battle was eighteen killed, thirteen commissioned officers and eighty-nine men wounded, and two missing, out of two hundred and seventy-five with which they entered the battle. In this engagement Lieutenant-Colonel H. G. Armstrong was so badly wounded as to disable him from further field-service. Then came the retrogade movements of Pope's army; those fierce, sanguinary battles, fighting over almost the whole territory from Cedar Mountain to the intrenchments around Washington City. In all this the Fifth bore a brave and bloody part. After a brief respite it joined the forces in pursuit of the Rebel army.

Passing through Frederick City, Middletown, and Boonsboro', the field of Antietam was reached on the night of the 16th of September. At daylight the regiment marched on the battle-field. The Twenty-Eighth Pennsylvania had the right, followed by the Fifth Ohio, in command of Major John Collins, Colonel Patrick being sick. The Fifth Ohio proceeded in column, by company, until within the range of the enemy's fire. About fifty yards in front was a belt of woods, occupied by the Rebels. The regiment advanced to the edge and opened fire, and in a short time drove the Rebels into a cornfield, where it followed and engaged them in a fierce hand-to-hand conflict, many of the men using the butts of their guns. The conflict here was terrible, but the enemy was at last compelled to give way, contesting every foot of the ground as they did so. They were driven from the field into an open plain, and from thence into and through a woods about a quarter of a mile distant. The pursuit was stopped, and the position held.

Fresh bodies of Rebels were continually coming up, and it became apparent that without re-enforcements the Fifth Ohio and its brigade could not hold out much longer, for its whole strength did not exceed five hundred men. Two regiments were sent to its assistance; but, after firing a few volleys, they broke and ran in great confusion. These flying regiments were posted on the left, and their retreat made it necessary for the brigade to fall back to prevent its being outflanked. The advancing Rebels were soon met by a portion of Franklin's command, who again drove them beyond the woods. Night coming on closed the battle, the National forces occupying the whole battle-field, having driven the Rebels, with great loss, half a mile beyond their original lines.

During the time the Fifth Ohio was engaged in the battle its cartridge-boxes were emptied three times, making about one hundred shots per man. On the outer edge of the cornfield mentioned above lay a row of dead Rebels on their faces, as though they had been dragged there and laid in order. In the open field near no less than three hundred dead and wounded Rebels were lying.

In this battle the Fifth Ohio lost fifty-four men killed and wounded out of one hundred and eighty, the number with which it entered the conflict.

After various marches and counter-marches the Fifth went into camp at Dumfries, Virginia, on the 16th of December, 1862. On the 27th the garrison was attacked by General Stuart's Rebel cavalry. The engagement lasted from one P. M. until after dark, when the Rebels retreated, leaving many dead on the field. Colonel Patrick led the Fifth in this affair. Lieutenants Walker and Leforce, of company G, were killed, three wounded, and five made prisoners.

The regiment lay at Dumfries through the months of January, February, March, and part of April. On the 20th of April, 1863, it joined the general advance of Major-General Hooker's army, skirmishing as it marched, and crossed the Rapidan on the 29th. On the 1st of May the regiment entered the battle of Chancellorsville, under command of Lieutenant-Colonel Kilpatrick. In this bloody battle the Fifth performed a distinguished part—now fighting behind intrenchments thrown up at night in the face of the enemy; again, making fruitless efforts to arrest the retreating tide of the Eleventh Corps, which had given way on the second day; at another time retiring to the trenches for rest, to be aroused at midnight by the artillery, which (by reason of the bright moonlight) could be rendered as effective by night as by day; buffeting the pitiless rain and northern blasts of the fourth day; now breasting the iron hail, and, finally, abandoning their position near Chancellor House only when all our forces to the right, left, and rear, except one regiment, had retired.

Their next great battle was that of Gettysburg. The cannonading commenced early in the morning of the 2d of July. The Fifth lay in the woods in front of the town nearly all of that day, and did not suffer much until about four P. M., when the shells began to fall thickly around, several of the men being wounded while lying on the ground. At sundown they moved to the extreme right, and acted as pickets till midnight, when they returned to their old position in the woods; on the 3d they were engaged from daylight until eleven A. M. About four P. M. the enemy, with parked artillery, began a terrific cannonade. The Fifth being in direct range of this fire, the shot and shell crashed terribly among the trees of the orchard in which they were lying. The men lay on their arms that night. On the morning of the 4th of July it was definitely ascertained that victory had crowned our arms, and that the Rebels were in full retreat for Richmond, leaving thousands of their dead and wounded in our hands. Lieutenant Brinkman, one of the heroes of Port Republic, was killed in this engagement. The Fifth participated in the fruitless pursuit that followed.

In August, 1863, the regiment was sent from Alexandria, Virginia, to New York City, just after the great mob there. It remained in New York until September 8th; then returned to Alexandria, and after a series of marches around Washington, Manassas Junction, etc., embarked on the 28th of September *via* the Baltimore and Ohio Railroad for Benwood, Virginia, where it arrived on the 30th. Thence it went by rail through Ohio to Indianapolis, Indiana, avoiding Cincinnati, the home of nearly all the men, where they had not been for two and a half years. A perfect ovation accompanied them through Ohio and Indiana—"their deeds had gone before them." At Louisville they took the cars for Nashville; from thence they were rushed down to Murfreesboro' (which place was menaced by the enemy), arriving there on the 6th of October. They found the trenches filled with the people, and the enemy in the town. The Fifth, with others, drove the enemy out and re-instated the citizens.

In the grand advance of Rosecrans's army toward Chattanooga the Fifth formed a part, and and on the 14th of November, 1863, had the honor of opening the battle above the clouds, on Lookout Mountain, under the lead of General Hooker.

On the 14th of January, 1864, the Fifth was at Bridgeport, Alabama, doing post-duty in connection with the Seventh. It was with Sherman in his grand march toward Atlanta, and participated in the conflicts which marked his progress. At or near Dalton, Georgia, they lost their brave Colonel, J. H. Patrick, who fell while leading the Fifth in a charge against the enemy, and died amid the shouts of victory. A few days thereafter, the time of the regiment (three years) having expired, they were ordered to the rear, in charge of prisoners. Notwithstanding their hard and almost continual service; notwithstanding they were literally shattered to pieces, this brave band of heroes resolved to "go in for the war." This gave them the privilege of a short furlough home. Before the term expired most, if not all, "the boys" were back "to the front," bravely and zealously following the lead of General Sherman in his "march to the sea," participating in all the hardships of the campaign, and always on hand when fighting was to be done. From Savannah to Goldsboro' they waded through the swamps, driving the enemy; then came that great flood of sunlight, Lee's surrender; the triumphant march up through the Rebel States and Richmond; thence to Washington, joining in the grand review; thence to the Queen City of the West, their home; and at last the muster-out at Louisville, 26th July, 1865, and the final payment and discharge at Camp Dennison.

This gallant regiment, during its term of service, took part in twenty-eight different engagements, the principal of which were: Winchester, Port Republic, McDowell, Cedar Mountain, Dumfries, South Mountain, Antietam, Chancellorsville, Gettysburg, Lookout Mountain, Dallas, Kenesaw Mountain, Peachtree Creek, Atlanta, and Savannah.

During its term of service the regiment traveled one thousand three hundred and seventy-five miles on foot and nine hundred and ninety-three on cars, and was engaged in six pitched battles, besides a great number of reconnoissances and skirmishes, and sustained a loss in the aggregate of five hundred men, killed, wounded, and taken prisoners.

To show the fierceness of the contest around and in the vicinity of Washington at the commencement of Pope's campaign, we give the following passages, copied from a diary kept by an officer of the Fifth Ohio:

"On the afternoon of the 25th of July, having first loaded the camp equipage, we were once more on the move. We arrived at Warrenton late at night. General Pope, who was now in command of the Army of Virginia, had his head-quarters here, and was concentrating his forces. We left Warrenton on the 31st of July, arriving near Little Washington the next day. The Twenty-Eighth Pennsylvania, consisting of fifteen companies and Knapp's Battery, were now added to our brigade, and Brigadier-General Geary placed in command. We were now assigned to, and formed part of, Major-General Banks's corps. We again pulled up stakes on the 5th of August, passing through Sperryville the same day, arriving at Culpepper C. H. on the night of the 7th. We remained in camp on the 8th under orders to turn out at a moment's notice. During the day, reports came into camp that our troops, in considerable numbers, were drawn up in order of battle, and that Banks's corps was intended for the reserve.

"The next morning about eight o'clock, we passed through Culpepper, all in fine spirits at the prospect of a fight. . . . We kept on, and it now became apparent that instead of the reserve, we had become the advance, and if any fighting was to be done we would have a hand in it. Three miles further, and within five miles of the Rapidan, we turned into a field under cover of a hill. Our cavalry made a reconnoissance, and were fired upon by the enemy. A sharp fire was kept up for some time, and our cavalry withdrew.

"The Rebels could now be seen maneuvering in our front, and shortly after opened fire with a piece of artillery. Their fire remained unanswered for some time. Finally, a battery was put in position near the brow of the hill, and opened fire upon them. The shot from this battery all fell short, while those of the rebels all overreached. Knapp's Battery of Parrott guns was afterward put in position and opened fire with better success, forcing the Rebel battery to change its position. . . . The infantry was assigned its position. The Second Division, General Augur, occupied the left of the road leading to the Rapidan; the First Division the right of the road. The whole line, with the exception of the left-center, was heavily timbered. This position was assigned our brigade composed of the Fifth, Seventh, Twenty-Ninth, and Sixty-Sixth Ohio.

"The brigade was formed in two lines—Seventh and Sixty-Sixth, and Fifth and Twenty-Ninth—and was stationed to the right and in rear of Knapp's Battery. The Rebel infantry having made their appearance in our front, the first line—the Seventh and Sixty-Sixth—was ordered forward. The infantry fire now opened, and soon after the Fifth and Twenty-Ninth were ordered up. The ground in front of us was rolling, and, advancing about one hundred yards, we ascended the brow of a hill, when the enemy opened upon us with canister and grape. We moved on, reserving our fire for closer range, and then opened upon them, advancing as we did so. As we advanced, we observed a large body of Rebels on our left flank, and the regiment changed front to attack them, thus leaving those who were before in front, on our right flank.

"Simultaneous with our change of front a fire was opened upon us from the rear of our right flank, our forces on the right having fallen back, and we were thus subject to three fires. The General had ordered a retreat, but it never reached the men, or was not heard by them. We maintained our position, subject to this cross-fire, until driven from it, which was not until one-half of the brigade had fallen killed or wounded.

"Our regiment went into the fight with two hundred and seventy-five men, and lost one hundred and twenty-five killed and wounded. Among the number wounded were eleven line officers, the Major and Adjutant. We fell back about two miles in confusion, there not being sufficient officers left to re-form the men. The Rebels did not follow, but remained in possession of the field."

6th REGIMENT OHIO VOLUNTEER INFANTRY.

ROSTER, THREE MONTHS' SERVICE.

RANK.	NAME.	DATE OF RANK.	COM. ISSUED.	REMARKS.
Colonel	W. K. BOSLEY	April 20, 1861	April 20, 1861	
Lt. Colonel	ELIPHALET LORING	" 20, "	" 20, "	
Major	ALEX. C. CHRISTOPHER	" 20, "	" 20, "	
Surgeon	STARLING LOVING	May 2, "	May 2, "	
Ass't Surgeon	F. W. AMES	" 2, "	" 2, "	
Captain	Marcus Aurelius Westcott	April 20, "	April 20, "	
Do.	Julian White	" 20, "	" 20, "	
Do.	John C. Lane	" 20, "	" 20, "	
Do.	Frank H. Ehrman	" 20, "	" 20, "	
Do.	Samuel Carrick Erwin	" 20, "	" 20, "	
Do.	George S. Smith	" 20, "	" 20, "	
Do.	Anthony O. Russell	" 20, "	" 20, "	
Do.	Henry H. Tinker	" 20, "	" 20, "	
Do.	James Bense	" 20, "	" 20, "	
Do.	Julius C. Guthrie	" 20, "	" 20, "	
1st Lieutenant	John Wilber Wilson	" 20, "	" 20, "	
Do.	James Willis Wilmington	" 20, "	" 20, "	
Do.	John A. Asbury	" 20, "	" 20, "	
Do.	John C. Parker	" 20, "	" 20, "	
Do.	John F. Hoy	" 20, "	" 20, "	
Do.	Charles H. Brutton	" 20, "	" 20, "	
Do.	Wm. S. Getty	" 20, "	" 20, "	
Do.	John W. Morgan	" 20, "	" 20, "	
Do.	Richard Southgate	" 20, "	" 20, "	
Do.	Frank M. Hulburd	" 20, "	" 20, "	
Do.	Nicholas L. Anderson	" 20, "	" 20, "	
Do.	Edward M. Shoemaker	" 20, "	" 20, "	
2d Lieutenant	Henry McAlpin	" 20, "	" 20, "	
Do.	Thomas S. Royse	" 20, "	" 20, "	
Do.	Charles H. Titus	" 20, "	" 20, "	
Do.	Ezekiel H. Tatem	" 20, "	" 20, "	
Do.	Louis S. Worthington	" 20, "	" 20, "	
Do.	Charles H. Heron	" 20, "	" 20, "	
Do.	Jules J. Montagnier	" 20, "	" 20, "	
Do.	Edgar M. Johnson	" 20. "	" 30, "	
Do.	Charles F. Porter	" 20, "	" 20, "	
Do.	Augustus B. Billerbeck	" 20, "	" 20, "	

ROSTER, THREE YEARS' SERVICE.

RANK.	NAME.	DATE OF RANK.	COM. ISSUED.	REMARKS.
Colonel	W. K. BOSLEY	June 12, 1861	June 12, 1861	Honorably discharged August 19, 1862.
Do.	NICHOL'S L. ANDERSON	Aug. 19, 1862	Oct. 8, 1862	Mustered out with regiment.
Lt. Colonel	NICHOLAS L. ANDERSON	June 12, 1861	June 12, 1861	Promoted to Colonel.
Do.	ALEX'R C. CHRISTOPHER	Aug. 19, 1862	Oct. 8, 1862	Mustered out with regiment.
Major	ALEX'R C. CHRISTOPHER	June 12, 1861	June 12, 1861	Promoted to Lieutenant-Colonel.
Do.	ANTHONY O. RUSSELL	Aug. 19, 1862	Nov. 18, 1862	Resigned February 20, 1862.
Do.	SAMUEL C. ERWIN	Feb. 20, 1863	April 19, 1863	Killed in action November 25, 1862.
Do.	JAMES BENSE	Nov. 25, "	Jan. 20, 1864	Mustered out with regiment.
Surgeon	STARLING LOVING	June 18, 1861	June 18, 1862	Resigned October 20, 1861.
Do.	A. H. STEPHENS	Oc'. 20, "	July 7, 1862	Mustered out with regiment.
Ass't Surgeon	F. W. AMES	June 18, 1861	June 18, 1861	Resigned June 12, 1863.
Do.	WM. W. FOUNTAIN	May 6, 1863	May 6, 1863	Resigned August 8, 1863.
Do.	ISRAEL BIDELL	Aug. 11, "	Aug. 11, 1863	Mustered out with regiment.
Captain	Marcus A. Westcott	June 12, 1861	June 12, 1861	Resigned March 9, 1863.
Do.	Joseph A. Andrews	" 12, "	" 12, "	Resigned April 22, 1862.
Do.	James Willis Wilmington	" 12, "	" 12, "	Resigned July 6, 1862.
Do.	Ezekiel H. Tatem	" 12, "	" 12, "	Killed by railroad July 19, 1862.
Do.	Samuel C. Erwin	" 12, "	" 12, "	Promoted to Major.
Do.	Charles H. Brutton	" 12, "	" 12, "	Resigned January 11, 1862.
Do.	Anthony O. Russell	" 12, "	" 12, "	Promoted to Major. [with regiment.
Do.	Henry H. Tinker	" 12, "	" 12, "	Wounded at Chickamauga; mustered out
Do.	James Bense	" 12, "	" 12, "	Promoted to Major.
Do.	Charles M. Clark	" 12, "	" 12, "	Resigned September 8, 1862.
Do.	Henry McAlpin	April 22, 1862	May 9, 1862	Died of wounds rec'd at Stone River Jan. 10, '63.
Do.	Wm. S. Getty	July 6, "	Nov. 8, "	Resigned February 21, 1863.
Do.	Richard Southgate	Sept. 8, "	" 18, "	Mustered out with regiment.
Do.	Charles B. Russell	Aug. 19, "	" 18, "	Mustered out with regiment.
Do.	James M. Donovan	July 19, "	Dec. 18, "	Mustered out with regiment.
Do.	Jules J. Montagnier	Jan. 10, 1863	Jan. 19, 1863	W'nded and disch'd Feb. 19, '64. [with reg.
Do.	Justin M. Thatcher	" 14, "	Feb. 13, "	Wounded at Mission Ridge; mustered out
Do.	Wm. S. Getty	March 1, "	April 7, "	Mustered out with reg't; wounded at Resaca.
Do.	Wm. E. Sheridan	" 9, "	" 10, "	Served in S. C. since Jan. 26, '62; m. o. with r.
Do.	Charles Gilman	Feb. 20, "	" 7, "	Honorably discharged December 21, 1863.
Do.	Benjamin F. West	April 1, 1864	" 1, 1864	Mustered out with regiment. [reg't.
Do	Frank S. Schehler	" 1, "	" 1, "	Wounded at Stone River; mustered out with

RANK.	NAME.	DATE OF RANK.	COM. ISSUED.	REMARKS.
Captain	Henry C. Choate..............	May 9, 1864	May 9, 1864	Mustered out with regiment.
1st Lieutenant	Henry McAlpin..................	July 12, 1861	July 12, 1861	Promoted to Captain.
Do.	Charles B. Russell............	" 12, "	" 12, "	Promoted to Captain. [Oct. 12, 1862.
Do.	Frank H. Ehrman............	" 12, "	" 12, "	Promoted by President Sept. 25, '62; hon. dis.
Do.	John C. Parker................	" 12, "	" 12, "	Resigned February 14, 1862.
Do.	John F. Hoy......................	" 12, "	" 12, "	Resigned February 14, 1862.
Do.	Charles Heron..................	" 12, "	" 12, "	Resigned August 1, 1862.
Do.	Edward M. Shoemaker......	" 12, "	" 12, "	Resigned October 22, 1863.
Do.	Wm. S. Getty....................	" 12, "	" 12, "	Promoted to Captain.
Do.	John W. Morgan................	" 12, "	" 12, "	Resigned September 11, 1862.
Do.	Richard Southgate............	" 12, "	" 12, "	Promoted to Captain.
Do.	Augustus B. Billerbeck.....	" 12, "	" 12, "	Resigned October 26, 1861.
Do.	James M. Donovan............	Aug. 3, "	Sept. 7, "	Promoted July 19, 1862. [regiment.
Do.	Charles C. Peck................	Dec. 12, "	Dec. 12, "	Detached at own request; mustered out with
Do.	Justin M. Thatcher...........	" 20, "	" 20, "	Promoted to Captain.
Do.	Benjamin J. West.............	Feb. 28, 1862	Feb. 28, 1862	Promoted to Captain. [regiment.
Do.	George W. Morris.............	" 14, "	March 20, "	Detached at own request; mustered out with
Do.	Charles Gilman.................	April 22, "	May 9, "	Promoted to Captain.
Do.	Jules J. Montagnier..........	July 6, "	Nov. 8, "	Promoted to Captain.
Do.	Benjamin F. West.............	Aug. 19, "	" 18, "	Promoted to Captain.
Do.	Wm. E. Sheridan..............	Sept. 8, "	" 18, "	Promoted to Captain.
Do.	Albert G. Williams...........	Aug. 1, "	" 18, "	Killed December 31, 1862.
Do.	James K. Reynolds...........	Nov. 20, "	" 20, "	Detached at own request.
Do.	Frank S. Scheiffer............	July 19, "	Dec. 16, "	Promoted to Captain.
Do.	Everett S. Throop.............	Dec. 31, "	Jan. 19, 1863	
Do.	Henry C. Choate...............	Jan. 10, 1863	" 19, "	Promoted to Captain.
Do.	John R. Kestner...............	" 28, "	Feb. 3, "	Mustered out with regiment.
Do.	James F. Irwin.................	" 14, "	" 3, "	Honorably discharged January 29, 1864.
Do.	J. Burt Holmes................	Feb. 20, "	April 7, "	Mustered out with regiment.
Do.	Joseph L. Antram............	March 9, "	" 10, "	Resigned October 29, 1863.
Do.	Jesse C. La Bille..............	Oct. 22, "	Jan. 10, 1864	Mustered out with regiment.
Do.	John F. Meline.................	" 29, "	" 10, "	Mustered out with regiment.
Do.	George F. Lewis...............	April 1, 1864	April 1, "	Mustered out with regiment.
Do.	J. F. Graham....................	" 1, "	" 1, "	Mustered out with regiment.
Do.	George W. Cormany..........	" 1, "	" 1, "	Mustered out with regiment.
Do.	Leonard Boyce..................	May 9, "	May 9, "	Mustered out with regiment.
2d Lieutenant	James M. Donovan............	June 12, 1861	June 12, 1861	Promoted to 1st Lieutenant.
Do.	Thomas S. Royse..............	" 12, "	" 12, "	Resigned April 14, 1864.
Do.	Charles Gilman.................	" 12, "	" 12, "	Promoted April 22, 1862, to 1st Lieutenant.
Do.	Thomas H. Baylan............	" 12, "	" 12, "	Resigned February 15, 1862.
Do.	George W. Morris.............	" 12, "	" 12, "	Promoted February 14, 1862, to 1st Lieutenant.
Do.	Frank S. Scheiffer............	" 12, "	" 12, "	Promoted July 19, 1862, to 1st Lieutenant.
Do.	Jules J. Montagnier..........	" 12, "	" 12, "	Promoted July 6, 1862, to 1st Lieutenant.
Do.	Solomon Bidwell..............	" 12, "	" 12, "	Accidentally killed at Elkwater, Va.
Do.	Benjamin F. West.............	" 12, "	" 12, "	Promoted February 28, 1862, to 1st Lieutenant.
Do.	Justin M. Thatcher...........	" 12, "	" 12, "	Promoted.
Do.	Wm. P. Anderson..............	Aug. 3, "	Aug. 3, "	Appointed by President September 19, 1862.
Do.	Wm. E. Sheridan..............	Dec. 12, 1862	Dec. 12, 1862	Promoted September 8, to 1st Lieutenant.
Do.	Edward M. Gettier............	" 20, "	" 20, "	Dismissed March 1, 1863.
Do.	Henry C. Choate...............	Feb. 28, "	Feb. 28, "	Promoted to 1st Lieutenant.
Do.	Henry Ges........................	" 15, "	March 20, "	Resigned September 11, 1862.
Do.	Edmund B. Warren...........	April 14, "	May 1, "	Resigned July 11, 1862.
Do.	Albert G. Williams...........	" 22, "	June 3, "	Promoted August 1, 1862, to 1st Lieutenant
Do.	Walter Lawrence..............	July 11, "	Oct. 25, "	Resigned January 22, 1862.
Do.	James F. Irwin.................	" 6, "	Nov. 8, "	Promoted to 1st Lieutenant.
Do.	J. Burt Holmes................	Sept. 11. "	" 18, "	Promoted to 1st Lieutenant.
Do.	J. L. Antram.....................	Aug. 19, "	" 18, "	Promoted to 1st Lieutenant.
Do.	O. H. Foster.....................	" 1, "	" 18, "	Killed December 31, 1863.
Do.	John R. Kestner...............	Sept. 8, "	" 18, "	Promoted to 1st Lieutenant.
Do.	John F. Meline.................	" 19, "	" 18, "	Promoted to 1st Lieutenant.
Do.	Jesse La Bille..................	July 19, "	Dec. 16, "	Promoted to 1st Lieutenant.
Do.	George T. Lewis...............	Dec. 31, "	Jan. 19, 1863	Promoted to 1st Lieutenant.
Do.	J. F. Graham....................	Jan. 10, 1863	" 19, "	Promoted to 1st Lieutenant.
Do.	G. W. Cormany.................	" 14, "	Feb. 3, "	Promoted to 1st Lieutenant.
Do.	Leonard Boyce..................	" 28, "	" 3, "	Promoted to 1st Lieutenant.
Do.	Josiah W. Slanker.............	" 22, "	Jan. 12, "	
Do.	Wesley B. McLane............	Feb. 20, "	April 3, "	Resigned —— 25, 1863.
Do.	Wm. R. Glenn..................	March 9, "	" 10, "	
Do.	W. R. Goodnough.............	" 1, "	" 22, "	Mustered out with regiment.
Do.	Wm. C. Perkins................	June 10, "	July 25, "	
Do.	F. Mellen.........................	Oct. 25, "	Dec. 4, "	
Do.	Wm. R. Gleeson...............	" 29, "	Jan. 10, 1864	Mustered out with regiment.

SIXTH OHIO VOLUNTEER INFANTRY.

THE nucleus of this regiment was an independent military organization of the city of Cincinnati, known as the Guthrie Gray Battalion, from which the regiment was first organized in April, 1861, and mustered into the three months' service, about eight hundred strong, upon the 18th of the same month, at Camp Harrison, Ohio, by Captain Gordon Granger, United States Army, afterward Major-General Volunteers. Shortly after muster-in it was transferred to Camp Dennison.

Under the call for three hundred thousand men, the regiment was reorganized for the three years' service, recruited to the maximum, and mustered in June 18, 1861, by Captain Walker, United States Army, with an aggregate of one thousand and sixteen.

Immediately after the muster-in and equipment, the regiment was ordered to Western Virginia. Leaving Camp Dennison on the 30th of June, 1861, it traveled by rail to Grafton, West Virginia, where it arrived on the 2d of July, and reported for duty to Brigadier-General Morris, then in command of that district. On July 4th it marched to Philippi, and thence, on July 6th, to Laurel Hill, then fortified and held by the Rebels under General Garnet.

The regiment took part in the operations before that place, and in the subsequent pursuit of the Rebels, ending in the affair of Carrick's Ford, July 10th.

On the 20th of July it marched to Beverly, went into camp there, and remained till August, when it was ordered to Elkwater, and went into camp at the foot of Cheat Mountain. Colonel Bosley was left in command of the post at Beverly, and Lieutenant-Colonel Anderson took command of the regiment.

Here it remained, making several reconnoissances to the front, among the defiles of the mountains, holding the fortifications with the rest of the division then under the command of Brigadier-General J. J. Reynolds, against the advance of General Lee, with some skirmishing, but no serious fighting. During the advance of General Lee, an advance picket post from the Sixth, consisting of Captain Bense, Lieutenants Scheiffer and Gilman, with forty men from company I, were cut off from the main army and taken prisoners. They were exchanged in the fall of 1862, and joined the regiment near Nashville, Tennessee.

Upon the 19th of November, 1861, the camp at Elkwater was broken up; and leaving the Second Virginia Infantry in the works, the regiment marched through Beverly, Buckhannon, and Clarksburg, to Parkersburg, and thence moved by steamer to Louisville, where it joined the Army of the Ohio, then concentrating at that point under General Buell.

In the organization of the Army of the Ohio, the Sixth was placed in the Fifteenth Brigade, Colonel M. S. Hascall, Seventeenth Indiana Volunteers, commanding, and in the Fourth Division, Brigadier-General William Nelson commanding.

The division marched to Camp Wickliffe, some sixty miles south of Louisville, and went into a camp of instruction for the winter, where it remained, drilling daily, until February 14, 1862, when the camp was broken up, and the division marched to West Point and there embarked on steamers, and sailed down the Ohio River, with the intention of re-enforcing General Grant, who was at that time besieging Fort Donelson. When the fleet reached Evansville the news of the surrender of Fort Donelson was received; and, after cruising up and down the Ohio for several days, the fleet proceeded to Smithland, and then up the Cumberland River to Nashville.

On the 25th of February, 1862, first of all the Army of the Ohio, the Fourth Division reached Nashville; the remainder of the army, marching across the country from Louisville, arrived later. The Sixth Ohio was the first of the division to march through the town; and their regimental flag was the first National flag hoisted over the State house in that city. The Fourth Division went into camp on the Murfreesboro' 'pike; and while here, the Sixth was assigned to the Tenth Brigade, Colonel Ammen, Twenty-Fourth Ohio Volunteers, commanding. On the 17th of March the Army of the Ohio moved southward from Nashville, the Fourth Division taking the advance. Crossing Duck River at Columbia, Tennessee, and going into camp at Savannah, Tennessee, April 5, 1862. The next morning the battle of Pittsburg Landing opened, and the division marched across the country Sunday afternoon to the field. The Tenth Brigade, composed of the Ninety-Fourth Ohio, Thirty-Sixth Indiana, and Sixth Ohio, was the advance; and these were the first troops of Buell's army that crossed the river at Pittsburg Landing. The crossing was effected under fire, and the two regiments first mentioned, with the right wing of the Sixth, were thrown into line just in time to repel the last charge the Rebels made upon the National left that day. The next morning the division advanced at daylight, and was soon actively engaged with the enemy. The Sixth was held in reserve, supporting Captain Terrill's Battery of the Fifth United States Artillery, and, except the companies on the skirmish line, was not actively engaged with the enemy, although under a heavy artillery fire during the entire engagement. The army camped upon the field of battle till May 24th, when the advance against Corinth commenced. Colonel Bosley joined the regiment from sick-leave while in camp on the battle-ground, but shortly returned to Cincinnati on renewed sick-leave.

The Sixth bore its part in all the operations before Corinth, and in the subsequent pursuit of the Rebels for sixty miles south of that place, when the Fourth Division returned, marching through Iuka, Mississippi; Tuscumbia, and Florence, Alabama, to Athens, Alabama, where they went into camp till July 17, 1862, when the entire division was ordered to Murfreesboro', Tennessee. Remaining at this point but a week, they were ordered to McMinnville, Tennessee, where they went into camp. While at McMinnville the Sixth was detailed as provost guards, and was quartered in the town. General Nelson being relieved from the command of the division, General Ammen succeeded him, and Colonel Grose, of the Thirty-Sixth Indiana, took command of the brigade.

Upon the 17th of August the movement of the Army of the Ohio, from its advanced position in Tennessee to Louisville commenced, and the Sixth marched with its division, *via* Nashville, Gallatin, Bowling Green, and West Point, to Louisville. The army reached the latter place on the 26th of September, 1862; and in the reorganization of the Army of the Ohio the Sixth was placed in the Third Brigade, Colonel Grose commanding; Second Division, Brigadier-General W. S. Smith commanding; of the Fourteenth Army Corps, Major-General T. S. Crittenden commanding. The Sixth, in its place in the brigade and division, marched across the State of Kentucky, in pursuit of Bragg, to within thirty-five miles of Cumberland Gap. It went into camp near Nashville, November 23d, and while here, General Smith was relieved from command, and Brigadier-General J. W. Palmer succeeded him.

The regiment marched with its brigade in the advance upon Murfreesboro', which commenced December 26, 1862, taking its share of all skirmish and picket duty. On Wednesday, December 31st the division was heavily engaged; the regiment losing, out of three hundred and eighty-three officers and men, one hundred and fifty-two killed, wounded, and prisoners. Only six of these were prisoners, taken when the brigade was driven back from its first line. On Friday the regiment was again actively engaged, losing, however but seven killed and wounded. The regiment went into camp in front of Murfreesboro', and afterward moved out on the McMinnville road to Cripple Creek, eight miles from town. While in camp at these places, several reconnoissances were made to the front, as far as to Woodbury and Shelbyville. In the movement against Tullahoma, which commenced June 24, 1863, the regiment had hard marching, but no fighting; and after the evacuation of that point and the retreat of the Rebels to Chattanooga, it went into camp at Manchester on July 7th, and remained till August 16th, when the campaign against Chattanooga commenced.

The Sixth was assigned, temporarily, during this advance, to the Second Brigade, under Brigadier-General Hazen, and with this brigade crossed the two ranges of the Cumberland Mountains into East Tennessee; then was ordered back, and joined the Third Brigade again at the crossing of the Tennessee, below Chattanooga. The brigade marched up the south bank of the river, over Lookout Mountains, past the town of Chattanooga, and out to Rossville and Gordon's Mills. In the battle of Chickamauga, on the 19th and 20th of September, the regiment was actively engaged, losing, out of three hundred and eighty-four officers and men, one hundred and twenty-five killed, wounded, and missing. Colonel Anderson was wounded on the 19th, and the regiment was under the command of Major Erwin until October, when Lieutenant-Colonel Christopher joined the regiment from recruiting service, and remained in command till January 18, 1864.

After the army fell back to Chattanooga, the Twentieth and Twenty-First Corps were consolidated as the Fourth Corps, under Major-General Gordon Granger, and the regiment became a part of the Second Brigade, Brigadier-General Hazen's; Third Division, Brigadier-General T. J. Wood's, of that Corps. The shutting up of the army in Chattanooga, after the battle of Chickamauga, and the scarcity of rations, consequent upon the partial severance of the lines of communication, was a severe test of the endurance of both officers and men. The affair of October 25th, known as the battle of Brown's Ferry, was fought by picked men from the brigades of Generals Hazen and Turchin, of whom the Sixth furnished its due proportion. This battle relieved the pressure as to supplies, and enabled the army to hold Chattanooga. When active operations commenced in front of Chattanooga, the Fourth Army Corps occupied the center, and this regiment was in the advance on Orchard's Knob, November 23d, and in the charge up Mission Ridge, on November 25th. Although actively engaged in skirmishing on the morning of the 25th, when Major Erwin was killed, and in the first line of battle in the charge on the afternoon of the same day, the regiment lost, out of two hundred and sixty-five officers and men, only thirty-three killed, wounded, and missing.

On the 28th the regiment, with its division, marched to the relief of Knoxville, Tennessee, then threatened by Longstreet, and reached that town and went into camp near it on the 7th of December. On the 16th of December the regiment marched north to Blair's Cross Roads, and then to Morristown, Dandridge, Rutledge, and other points, seldom camping more than one week in a place the entire winter, till February 14th, when the division marched south of Knoxville and went into camp at Lenoir; afterward, northward to Morristown, Rutledge, and New Market again, until April 6th, when the division was ordered to Cleveland to join the main army. The campaign of East Tennessee was the most severe service the regiment ever saw. From November 28th till February 14th the troops were without their baggage, both officers and men living in shelter tents, and subsisting, for the most part, off the country already twice passed over.

The regiment went into camp near Cleveland on the 12th of April, and when the campaign against Atlanta opened it was left, with another regiment, to do garrison duty in the town, they having the shortest time to serve of any regiments in the division. Upon the 17th of May it was ordered to join the main army, and accordingly marched to Kingston, Georgia, and reported to General Thomas, who ordered it back to Resaca, to guard the railroad bridge over the Oostenaula at that point, where it remained till June 6th, when it was released from duty and ordered home to be mustered out of the service.

The regiment arrived at Cincinnati on June 15th, and after the public reception given by the citizens, went into quarters at Camp Dennison, where it was mustered out of the service June 23, 1864, with an aggregate of thirty officers and four hundred and ninety-five enlisted men. Several of the non-commissioned officers held commissions, but could not be mustered in, as the companies in which the vacancies occurred were below the minimum.

A SCENE ON LOOKOUT MOUNTAIN.

The Sixth carried to the close of its service a beautiful stand of colors, which had been presented by the ladies of Cincinnati in December, 1862, and a regimental banner received at the same time from the City Council. The pledges which Colonel Anderson made for the regiment on the occasion of these presentations were, within three weeks, fully redeemed by the part borne by the Sixth in that deadly conflict in the cedars of Stone River, where its percentage of killed and wounded is claimed to have been heavier than that of any other regiment engaged, with the exception of the 21st Illinois.

Colonel Anderson was three times wounded—slightly, by a spent ball at Pittsburg Landing; painfully, by a flesh wound through the thigh on the first day of Stone River, which, without leaving the field, he had bound up, remaining on active duty till the battle was over; and severely, in the left arm, at Chickamauga. Many of the Sixth, after their muster-out, re-enlisted in Hancock's Corps.

During the term of service the regiment marched, in round numbers, three thousand two hundred and fifty miles; traveled by steamboat and railroad, two thousand six hundred and fifty miles, making a total of five thousand nine hundred miles. The regiment was in four pitched battles, losing a total of three hundred and twenty five killed, wounded, and missing. And in addition it shared in some half dozen skirmishes and lesser engagements. A large number of enlisted men, at least seventy-five, received commissions in other regiments, and *eleven* of these were in the *regular army*. It was in the front from the time it was first ordered to the field till May 2, 1864; and a remarkable feature of the regiment was its uniformly healthy condition, the reports showing but sixteen deaths by disease during the entire three years; and, including officers and enlisted men, there were at least two hundred who never lost a day's duty. As there were a large number of men possessing a business education in the ranks, the details for duty in the Quartermaster's and Adjutant-General's departments of the army were unusually large; at one time over two hundred men being on duty in these departments; so that, notwithstanding the excellent health, there were never, after the first year's service, more than five hundred officers and enlisted men present for duty at any one time; and the regiment went into action, usually, with from three hundred and fifty to four hundred men. It was in a good state of discipline from first to last; and in the personal neatness of the men, cleanliness of its camp, and condition of arms and accouterments, it was fully equal to the majority of volunteer regiments. The men were always cheerful, willing, and obedient, and were at all times ready for duty.

The record does not show much hard fighting, but it *does show* that which, in the judgment of experienced minds, tests the true qualities of a soldier—marching and duty of the most severe kind. Deeds of heroism and endurance belong to all the regiments of the Army of the Republic; and comparisons are, generally, as unjust as they are unnecessary. It is sufficient to say, that both officers and men enjoyed the fullest confidence of their brigade, division, and corps commanders, and earned a reputation in the Army of the Ohio, and in the Army of the Cumberland, with which their native city may be well satisfied.

7th REGIMENT OHIO VOLUNTEER INFANTRY.

ROSTER, THREE MONTHS' SERVICE.

RANK.	NAME.	DATE OF RANK.	COM. ISSUED.	REMARKS.
Colonel	ERASTUS B. TYLER	May 7, 1861	May 7, 1861	
Lt. Colonel	WM. R. CREIGHTON	" 7, "	" 7, "	
Major	JOHN S. CASEMENT	" 7, "	" 7, "	
Surgeon	HENRY K. CUSHING	" 2, "	" 2, "	
As't Surgeon.	F. SALTER	" 2, "	" 2, "	
Captain	Wm. R. Creighton	April 19, "	April 15, "	Promoted to Lieutenant-Colonel.
Do.	Charles A. DeVilliers	" 22, "	" 22, "	Resigned.
Do.	Giles W. Shurtliff	" 22, "	" 22, "	
Do.	John N. Dever	" 22, "	" 22, "	
Do.	John W. Sprague	" 23, "	" 23, "	
Do.	John Morris	" 23, "	" 23, "	
Do.	Fred A. Seymour	" 23, "	" 23, "	
Do.	Joel F. Asper	" 24, "	" 24, "	
Do.	W. R. Sterling	" 24, "	" 24, "	
Do.	John J. Wiseman	" 20, "	" 20, "	
Do.	Wm. Stedman	May 14, "	May 14, "	
Do.	Orrin J. Crane	" 14, "	" 14, "	
Do.	James T. Sterling	" 15, "	" 15, "	
1st Lieutenant	Orrin J. Crane	April 19, "	April 19, "	Promoted to Captain
Do.	James T. Sterling	" 22, "	" 22, "	Promoted to Captain.
Do.	H. Kinaston	" 22, "	" 22, "	Resigned.
Do.	Benj. F. Gill	" 22, "	" 22, "	
Do.	Ralph Lockwood	" 23, "	" 23, "	
Do.	John B. Rouse	" 23, "	" 23, "	
Do.	W. H. Robinson	" 23, "	" 23, "	
Do.	George L. Wood	" 24, "	" 24, "	
Do.	Samuel McClelland	" 24, "	" 24, "	
Do.	John F. Schute	" 20, "	" 20, "	
Do.	Albert C. Burgess	May 14, "	May 14, "	
Do.	Thomas T. Sweeney	" 14, "	" 14, "	
Do.	Judson N. Cross	April 29, "	April 29, "	
2d Lieutenant	Albert C. Burgess	" 20, "	" 29, "	Promoted to 1st Lieutenant.
Do.	Thomas T. Sweeney	" 22, "	" 22, "	Promoted to 1st Lieutenant.
Do.	Stephen Cole	" 22, "	" 22, "	
Do.	Andrew F. Williams	" 22, "	" 22, "	
Do.	Arthur T. Wilcox	" 23, "	" 23, "	
Do.	Isaac N. Wilcox	" 23, "	" 23, "	
Do.	Elliott S. Quay	" 23, "	" 23, "	
Do.	James B. Cleveland	" 24, "	" 24, "	
Do.	Edward T. Fitch	" 21, "	" 21, "	
Do.	Oscar W. Sterl	" 20, "	" 20, "	
Do.	Dudley A. Kimball	May 14, "	May 14, "	
Do.	Ephraim H. Baker	April 29, "	April 29, "	

ROSTER, THREE YEARS' SERVICE.

RANK.	NAME.	DATE OF RANK.	COM. ISSUED.	REMARKS.
Colonel	ERASTUS B. TYLER	June 19, 1861	July 25, 1861	Appointed Brigadier-General May 20, 1862.
Do.	WM. R. CREIGHTON	May 20, 1862	June 10, 1862	Killed at Mission Ridge, November 27, 1863.
Lt. Colonel	WM. R. CREIGHTON	June 19, 1861	July 19, 1861	Promoted May 20, 1862.
Do.	JOEL F. ASPER	May 20, 1862	June 10, 1862	Resigned as Captain.
Do.	ORRIN J. CRANE	Nov. 2, "	Dec. 4, "	Revoked.
Do.	ORRIN J. CRANE	March 2, 1863	March 12, 1863	Killed at Mission Ridge November 27, 1863.
Do.	SAMUEL McCLELLAND	Dec. 1, "	Dec. 27, "	Mustered out with regiment.
Major	JOHN S. CASEMENT	June 19, "	July 25, 1862	Resigned May 25, 1863.
Do.	ORRIN J. CRANE	May 25, 1862	Oct. 6, 1862	Promoted to Lieutenant-Colonel.
Do.	FREDERICK A. SEYMOUR	March 2, 1863	June 22, 1863	Revoked.
Do.	FREDERICK A. SEYMOUR	Aug. 13, "	Aug. 13, "	Resigned March 29, 1864.
Surgeon	F. SALTER	" 10, 1861	Sept. 7, 1861	Resigned November 2, 1862.
Do.	CURTISS J. BELLOWS	Dec. 1, 1862	Dec. 4, 1862	Mustered out with regiment.
Ass't Surgeon	CHARLES E. DENIG	Sept. 9, 1861	Sept. 9, 1861	Resigned November 1, 1862.
Do.	ELIZAR HITCHCOCK	Nov. 11, 1862	Nov. 20, 1862	Resigned June 2, 1863.
Do.	WM. E. THOMPSON	March 12, 1863	March 12, 1863	Declined; returned commission.
Do.	JOHN C. FERGUSON	April 14, "	April 14, "	Mustered out with regiment.
Do.	N. BELDING	June 29, "	June 29, "	Declined; returned commission.
Do.	DAVID WILLIAMS	July 18, "	July 18, "	Promoted to Surgeon 56th regiment O. V. I.
Chaplain	D. C. WRIGHT	Jan. 11, 1862	Jan. 11, 1862	Resigned January 9, 1863.
Captain	J. F. Asper	June 3, 1861	July 25, 1861	Promoted; resigned May 19, 1862.
Do.	Orrin J. Crane	" 13, "	" 25, "	Mustered out for promotion May 21, 1862.
Do.	Frederick J. Seymour	" 14, "	" 25, "	Resigned.
Do.	Giles W. Shurtliff	" 17, "	" 25, "	Resigned March 18, 1863.
Do.	John N. Dyer	" 17, "	" 25, "	Killed at Battle of Cross Lanes Aug. 26, 1861.
Do.	John W. Sprague	" 17, "	" 25, "	Appointed Colonel 63d O. V. I.
Do.	Wm. R. Sterling	" 17, "	" 25, "	Mustered out July 6, 1861.
Do.	John F. Schulte	" 17, "	" 25, "	Died from wounds received August 22, 1861.

RANK.	NAME.	DATE OF RANK.	COM. ISSUED.	REMARKS.
Captain	James T. Sterling	June 18, 1861	July 25, 1861	Discharged and app'ted Lieut. Col. Sept. 1, '62
Do.	Dercourt B. Clayton	" 19, "	" 25, "	Resigned August 18, 1861.
Do.	George L. Wood	Nov. 25, "	Nov. 25, "	Honorably dis. Nov. 12, 1862, acct. of wounds.
Do.	Albert C. Burgess	" 25, "	" 25, "	Resigned July 9, 1862.
Do.	Judson N. Cross	" 25, "	" 25, "	Honorably discharged February 9, 1863.
Do.	Charles A. Weed	Feb. 5, 1862	Feb. 5, 1862	Resigned February 19, 1863.
Do.	Samuel McClelland	May 20, "	June 10, "	Promoted to Major.
Do.	Arthur T. Wilcox	July 9, "	Dec. 4, "	Mustered out July 6, 1864.
Do.	Joseph B. Molyneaux	Sept. 1, "	" 4, "	Mustered out as 1st Lieutenant Dec. 31, 1863
Do.	A. H. Day	Nov. 2, "	" 4, "	Resigned January 18, 1863.
Do.	Mervin Clark	Sept. 1, 1862	May 25, 1863	Mustered out July 6, 1864.
Do.	Marcus S. Hopkins	March 18, 1863	June 26, "	Revoked.
Do.	Wm. A. Howe	Nov. 12, 1862	May 25, "	Mustered out July 6, 1864.
Do.	E. J. Kreiger	Feb. 9, 1863	Feb. 25, "	Mustered out July 6, 1864.
Do.	L. R. Davis	" 19, "	" 25, "	Mustered out December 19, 1864.
Do.	Wm. D. Braden	March 8, "	May 25, "	Mustered out July 6, 1864.
Do.	Stephen P. Loomis	" 19, 1864	March 19, 1864	Declined promotion.
Do.	George A. McKay	" 19, "	" 19, "	Mustered out July 6, 1864.
Do.	Harlow N. Spencer	" 19, "	" 19, "	Mustered out July 6, 1864.
Do.	Christian Nesper	" 13, "	" 19, "	Mustered out July 6, 1864.
Do.	George D. Lockwood	June 7, "	June 7, "	Mustered out July 6, 1864.
Do.	Seymour S. Reed	Nov. 2, 1862	Dec. 4, 1862	Resigned January 18, 1863.
1st Lieutenant	George L. Wood	June 3, 1861	July 25, 1861	Promoted to Captain.
Do.	Albert C. Burgess	" 13, "	" 25, "	Promoted to Captain.
Do.	Wm. H. Robinson	" 14, "	" 25, "	Died.
Do.	Judson N. Cross	" 17, "	" 25, "	Promoted to Captain.
Do.	Charles A. Weed	" 17, "	" 25, "	Promoted to Captain.
Do.	Arthur T. Wilcox	" 17, "	" 25, "	Promoted to Captain.
Do.	Samuel McClelland	" 17, "	" 25, "	Promoted to Captain.
Do.	C. T. Nitchelm	" 17, "	" 25, "	Resigned April 13, 1862.
Do.	Joseph B. Molyneaux	" 18, "	" 25, "	Promoted to Captain.
Do.	John B. Rouse	" 19, "	" 25, "	Resigned August 8, 1861.
Do.	Louis G. DeForrest	" 19, "	" 25, "	Resigned March 1, 1862.
Do.	John Morris	" 19, "	" 25, "	Resigned December 5, 1861.
Do.	Joshua G. Willis	Oct. 31, "	Oct. 31, "	Resigned July 23, 1862.
Do.	Halbert B. Case	Nov. 25, "	Nov. 25, "	Resigned January 30, 1862.
Do.	Ralph Lockwood	" 25, "	" 25, "	Honorably discharged November 12, 1862.
Do.	E. Hudson Baker	" 25, "	" 25, "	Resigned July 25, 1862.
Do.	Elliott S. Quay	" 30, "	" 30, "	Promoted by President.
Do.	Oscar W. Sterl	Feb. 5, 1862	Feb. 5, 1862	Resigned April 14, 1862.
Do.	Henry Z. Eaton	" 20, "	" 20, "	Resigned November 6, 1862.
Do.	Dudley A. Kimball	March 1, "	March 20, "	Resigned April 13, 1862.
Do.	A. H. Day	April 1, "	April 10, "	Honorably discharged November 12, 1862.
Do.	Frank Payne	March 1, "	May 1, "	Resigned June 10, 1862.
Do.	E. J. Kreiger	April 13, "	" 1, "	Promoted to Captain.
Do.	Wm. B. Sheppard	" 14, "	" 9, "	Resigned March 23, 1863.
Do.	Seymour S. Reed	May 20, "	June 10, "	Mustered out November 1, 1862.
Do.	Leicester King	June 10, "	Dec. 4, "	Dismissed December 22, 1863.
Do.	Marcus S. Hopkins	July 25, "	" 4, "	Resigned July 2, 1863.
Do.	Mervin Clark	" 23, "	" 4, "	Promoted to Captain.
Do.	Wm. A. Howe	Nov. 12, "	" 4, "	Promoted to Captain.
Do.	L. R. Davis	" 2, "	" 4, "	Promoted to Captain.
Do.	Wm. D. Braden	July 9, "	" 4, "	Promoted to Captain.
Do.	Stephen T. Loomis	Sept. 1, "	" 4, "	Declined promotion.
Do.	Henry W. Lincoln	Nov. 6, "	" 4, "	Honorably discharged January 7, 1863.
Do.	George D. Lockwood	" 2, "	" 4, "	Promoted to Captain.
Do.	Morris Baxter	Dec. 1, "	Jan. 10, 1864	Killed November 27, 1863.
Do.	George A. McKay	Jan. 1, 1863	May 25, 1863	Promoted to Captain.
Do.	Charles A. Brooks	May 23, "	" 25, "	Killed.
Do.	Harlow N. Spencer	Nov. 1, "	Jan. 26, 1864	Promoted to Captain.
Do.	Christian Nesper	" 1, "	" 26, "	Promoted to Captain.
Do.	Edward H. Bohn	" 1, "	" 26, "	Mustered out July 6, 1864.
Do.	Henry M. Dean	" 1, "	" 26, "	Mustered out July 6, 1864.
Do.	Dwight H. Brown	" 1, "	" 26, "	Mustered out July 6, 1864.
Do.	George C. Ketchum	March 30, 1864	March 30, "	Mustered out July 6, 1864.
2d Lieutenant	Halbert B. Case	June 3, 1861	July 25, 1861	Promoted to 1st Lieutenant.
Do.	E. Hudson Baker	" 17, "	" 25, "	Promoted to 1st Lieutenant.
Do.	Andrew J. Williams	" 17, "	" 25, "	Resigned September 6, 1861.
Do.	Ralph Lockwood	" 17, "	" 25, "	Promoted to 1st Lieutenant.
Do.	Edward F. Fitch	" 17, "	" 25, "	Resigned November 28, 1861.
Do.	Oscar W. Sterl	" 17, "	" 25, "	Promoted to 1st Lieutenant.
Do.	Henry Z. Eaton	" 17, "	" 25, "	Promoted February 20, 1862, to 1st Lieutenant.
Do.	Dudley A. Kimball	" 19, "	" 25, "	Promoted March 1, 1862, to 1st Lieutenant.
Do.	A. H. Day	" 19, "	" 25, "	Promoted April 1, 1862, to 1st Lieutenant.
Do.	Elliott S. Quay	" 19, "	" 25, "	Promoted to 1st Lieutenant.
Do.	Ezra H. Witler	Oct. 1, "	Oct. 9, "	Resigned April 13, 1862.
Do.	Wm. B. Sheppard	Nov. 25, "	Nov. 25, "	Promoted April 14, 1862, to 1st Lieutenant.
Do.	Frank Payne	" 25, "	" 25, "	Promoted March 1, 1862, to 1st Lieutenant.
Do.	Seymour S. Reed	Dec. 12, "	Dec. 12, "	Promoted May 20, 1862, to 1st Lieutenant.
Do.	Leicester King	" 17, "	" 17, "	Promoted to 1st Lieutenant.
Do.	James P. Brisbine	" 20, "	" 20, "	Killed Aug. 9, 1862, at battle Cedar Mountain.
Do.	Marcus S. Hopkins	Feb. 5, 1862	Feb. 5, 1862	Promoted to 1st Lieutenant.
Do.	Mervin Clark	" 20, "	" 20, "	Promoted to 1st Lieutenant.
Do.	Frank Johnson	April 1, "	April 10, "	Killed Aug. 9, 1862, at battle Cedar Mountain.
Do.	Wm. A. Howe	" 13, "	May 1, "	Promoted to 1st Lieutenant.
Do.	L. R. Davis	" 13, "	" 1, "	Promoted to 1st Lieutenant.
Do.	Joseph H. Ross	March 1, "	" 1, "	Killed Aug. 9, 1862, at battle Cedar Mountain.
Do.	Wm. D. Braden	April 14, "	June 7, "	Promoted to 1st Lieutenant.
Do.	Stephen T. Loomis	May 20, "	" 30, "	Promoted to 1st Lieutenant.
Do.	Harlow N. Spencer	Aug. 21, "	Sept. 5, "	Promoted to 1st Lieutenant.
Do.	George D. Lockwood	" 9, "	Oct. 6, "	Promoted to 1st Lieutenant.
Do.	Henry W. Lincoln	" 9, "	" 6, "	Honorably discharged January 7, 1863.
Do.	George A. McKay	Nov. 7, "	Nov. 9, "	Promoted to 1st Lieutenant.
Do.	Wm. H. Howk	June 10, "	Dec. 4, "	Died June 21, 1863.
Do.	Christian Nesper	July 25, "	" 4, "	Promoted to 1st Lieutenant.
Do.	Joseph Crayne	" 23, "	" 4, "	Mustered out July 6, 1864.
Do.	Isaac C. Jones	Nov. 6, "	" 8, "	Mustered out July 6, 1864.
Do.	Edward H. Bohn	" 2, "	Jan. 13, 1863	Mustered out July 6, 1864.
Do.	Morris Baxter	" 12, "	" 7, "	Mustered out July 6, 1864.
Do.	Henry M. Dean	Sept. 1, "	Feb. 25, "	Promoted to 1st Lieutenant.
Do.	Dwight H. Brown	Jan. 7, 1863	May 25, "	Promoted to 1st Lieutenant.

SEVENTH OHIO VOLUNTEER INFANTRY.

THIS organization may be termed one of the representative regiments of Ohio. The first Rebel gun fired on Fort Sumter was the signal for its assemblage. Its echo had scarcely died out in the North ere the seventy-five thousand men first called for by President Lincoln were in camp, eager to be led against the rebellious foe; and among these enthusiastic patriots were those composing the Seventh Ohio. Its ranks were filled by the sturdy citizens of Northern Ohio. The city of Cleveland furnished three companies, Oberlin one, Warren one, Painesville one, Youngstown one, Norwalk one, and Franklin one, all of whom rendezvoused at Camp Taylor, near Cleveland; and on the 30th of April, 1861, they were mustered into the service of the United States as the Seventh Ohio Volunteer Infantry.

On a beautiful Sunday morning, early in May, this regiment, more than a thousand strong, marched into Cleveland, and down Euclid street to the railroad depot, where the cars were in readiness to transport them to Camp Dennison, near Cincinnati. It was there, in that then wretched camp, that the men of the Seventh Ohio experienced their first real practice of field service. The grounds were in their original state, cut up by baggage wagons, whose wheels had sunk deep into the miry mud, and left great fissures, filled with thick, gummy water, mixed with soil, through which the men were compelled to march, and on which, at night, they were expected to repose. The regiment was composed of men of high culture—ministers of the gospel, students of theology and law, merchants, bankers, mechanics and farmers—all used to the refinements of pleasant homes. But they made light of their surroundings, and went immediately to work building huts in which to bivouac for the night. Before dark, a sufficient number were erected to shelter the whole command.

In those early days of the war the men of the regiments selected their own officers, by ballot, a "democratic" way of "doing up the military" not tolerated in the latter and iron days of the rebellion. After the regiment had become settled in their new quarters, and somewhat accustomed to camp life, an election for field officers was held. E. B. Tyler, of Ravenna, Ohio, was chosen Colonel; Wm. R. Creighton, of Cleveland, Lieutenant-Colonel; John S. Casement, of Painesville, Major.

The organization of the Seventh Ohio Volunteer Infantry being completed, the drill and discipline of the regiment was next in order. This important and indispensable duty was performed with intelligence and thoroughness by its officers, having in view, as they had, the stern ordeal through which their men would be called upon to pass. By the time the regiment had mastered the manual of arms, and become somewhat familiar with the regimental and battalion movements, the second call of President Lincoln for three hundred thousand men, to serve for three years, was issued. The regiment entered the three years' service almost to a man, and the citizen's dress, which they had hitherto worn, gave place to the army blue.

The men were allowed to visit their homes on a six days' furlough, at the expiration of which time they were promptly in camp, and were duly mustered into the service of the United

States for three years. The privilege of sharing in the opening campaign in Western Virginia was allotted to this regiment, and on the 26th of June, 1861, it started for that field.

The men went out of their camp with cheers and shouts of exultation, that at last they were to meet and combat the Rebels. On the following day the regiment reached Benwood, Virginia, and for the first time set foot on Rebel soil. Here the men were furnished with ammunition. Various rumors were afloat respecting the movements of the enemy. Bridges had been destroyed and trains of cars fired into.

The regiment was marched along the line of the Baltimore and Ohio Railroad to Clarksburg, where tents were provided and transportation furnished, to enable the regiment to operate independently of lines of railroad. The first tented camp was formed at this place, and the regiment quietly settled down to the respective duties of its position. After being a few days in camp, Captain Schulte, commanding one of the companies, presented the regiment with a beautiful stand of colors in behalf of the "Social Turn Verein" of Cleveland. This present was received with all the honors, the regiment going into line with presented arms.

The 29th of June, 1861, will ever mark a memorable era in the annals of the Seventh Ohio. It was the first march the men had made with the shoulder knapsack and all the accouterments of the soldier. The day was oppressively hot, and before one mile had been laboriously overcome, many valuable and useful articles, supposed to be absolutely indispensable, had become an intolerable burden; and at three miles, when a halt was ordered, the men went deliberately to work reducing their baggage. Blankets, dress uniforms, books, under-clothing, and every article that could possibly be dispensed with, were emptied on the ground, and left there. One of the most useful articles, canteens, had not been supplied, and the men suffered dreadfully for the means of quenching their thirst.

The rising of the morning sun revealed to the men their destination. Twenty-three miles had been made, and the little town of Weston reached. The object of the march was accomplished, which was to receive sixty-five thousand dollars in gold, that had been deposited in the bank at Weston by the Virginia State Government, to defray the expense of erecting a large lunatic asylum at that place. No opposition was made. The money was secured, and the regiment went into camp.

On the 4th of July the people of Weston—or the Union portion of the town—gave a fine dinner to the regiment. Before the men had fully recovered from the fatigue of the march, and ere the blisters on their feet had healed, news came that the Rebels were in force near Glenville, twenty-eight miles distant, and had surrounded a detachment of the Seventeenth Ohio, who occupied that place. The Seventh was called upon to march to the relief of this beleaguered force. After a day's hard marching, Glenville was reached, but the Rebels had fled.

At Glenville the army rations gave out, which rendered it necessary to abandon the opposing theory and adopt confiscation. The consciences of the officers and men were somewhat sensitive at first, but hunger soon dissipated all qualmish scruples, and taking supplies became a solemn duty with all. No organized enemy appeared at this place, though hostile demonstrations were occasionally made by bushwhackers. One man of the regiment was wounded while on picket duty, and an officer had his horse shot from under him. The time was principally occupied in drilling, scouting and confiscating.

The plan of the campaign was that the Seventh Ohio should open up communication with General Cox, who at that time was making his way up the Kanawha Valley. Situated as the Seventh was, in the midst of an enemy's country, far away from any base of supply, and in a mountainous district, this duty was a most difficult one to perform. By hard marching, encamping respectively at Bulltown, Salt Lake and Flatwood, the regiment reached Sutton, at which place, as a precautionary measure, it threw up fortifications on a bluff overhanging the town, which afterward proved of service to other regiments. Owing to the nature of the country, and want of knowledge of its peculiarities, the regiment felt its way cautiously, sometimes remaining a week in camp, to enable scouting parties to go forward and explore the way, and gain all possible information of the movements of the enemy. Passing on from Sutton, the regiment reached Cross Lanes on the 15th of August, having encamped, in its route, at Birch Mountain and Summerville. The time passed at Cross Lanes was occupied in drilling, scouting and doing guard and picket duty. Prior to this time an officer and two men had been captured by Rebel cavalry, and a scouting party had been attacked, one of whom was killed and three wounded.

Just after tattoo, on the evening of the 21st of August, a dispatch was received from General Cox, ordering the Seventh to join him, without delay, at Gauley Bridge. The long roll was sounded; the men sprang to their places in line, and in an hour's time the regiment was on its march to fulfill the order.

While the Seventh Ohio was encamped at Twenty-mile Creek, near General Cox's position, it was ascertained that General Floyd, with four thousand men, was preparing to cross the Gauley River at Cross Lanes, the place the regiment had so recently left. A countermarch was immediately ordered, and the regiment returned in the direction of their old camp. When within six miles of Cross Lanes (August 24th), the pickets of the enemy were encountered. The further advance of the regiment was made with great precaution, to guard against surprise, but no enemy in force was discovered. During the night the regiment bivouacked in the vicinity of its old camping ground. The entire regiment was ordered on picket duty, each company to occupy designated positions, with instructions to fall back under cover of each other if attacked by a force they could not repel.

The firing of the pickets at daybreak aroused the men to arms. In a few minutes the enemy was seen approaching in line of battle. The companies of the Seventh Ohio, acting independently of each other, took position on neighboring hills, and, though pressed against by overwhelming numbers, tenaciously held their positions, until, at last, they were forced to retreat, leaving the field and the dead and wounded in possession of the enemy. The loss of the regiment in this unfortunate affair was one hundred and twenty—killed, wounded, and prisoners. The regiment became scattered, one-half finding its way back to Gauley, the remainder coming into the National lines near Charleston, several miles down the river.

While at Gauley, the regiment was presented with a beautiful stand of colors by Professor N. E. Peck, of Oberlin College, in behalf the people of the Western Reserve.

After the battle of Carnifex Ferry, the forces under General Cox advanced to Dogwood Gap, with the view of intercepting the retreat of General Floyd; but the movement was unsuccessful, and the expedition returned to the old camp at Gauley.

On the 16th of October, Colonel Dyer was placed in command at Charleston, and the Seventh Ohio was ordered thither, where it remained until the 1st of November. At that date the enemy was again threatening the force at Gauley. The Seventh Ohio was ordered to join General Benham's forces, then stationed at Loup Creek. The plan was for this force to make its way to the rear of Floyd, and thus entrap him. General Benham's disobedience of orders led to the failure of the plan, Floyd making good his escape. A hot pursuit was made, but the only success was the capture of Colonel Cragan and several of his men. The incessant and heavy rains, and consequent deep mud, coupled with the necessary exposure of the men, rendered this march one of extreme severity and suffering.

The Seventh was now returned, by steamer, to Charleston, November 17, 1861.

The campaign in Western Virginia for the winter having ended, the Seventh was ordered to join the army under General Lander, who then occupied Romney, in Central Virginia. Accordingly, the regiment, on the 10th of December, 1861, took steamer at Charleston, and, passing down the Kanawha to the Ohio River, landed at Parkersburg, where it took rail for Green Spring River. From thence, after a march of sixteen miles, it found itself in an entirely new field, and much nearer the enemy.

A large force under General Jackson, forming the left wing of the Rebel army, was in camp at Winchester. Jackson anticipated and thwarted the movement that was about to be made against him from different points, by attacking the National forces separately and unexpectedly. When Jackson advanced on Romney, in mid-winter, General Lander withdrew the National forces to Patterson Creek, a small place on the Baltimore and Ohio Railroad, a short distance from Cumberland. The retreat began at night, in the midst of a severe rain-storm, and ended by pitching tents in a mudhole. This camp was the most wretched and illy chosen the men had ever occupied, and dire were the maledictions uttered against those who had committed the foolish blunder. And yet the men did not suffer from ill health or epidemics.

Jackson entered and occupied Romney the day after the National forces had withdrawn. Lander's force remained in camp at Patterson's Creek nearly a month, Jackson still occupying Romney. On the 5th of February, 1862, a move was made to entrap Jackson's force. With this design, the Seventh Ohio was sent by rail to French's Store, and from thence a distance of twenty miles, to a point on the road between Romney and Winchester, with the hope of intercepting the retreat of Jackson, which had been anticipated. The point was reached, but the enemy had escaped. This march was one of intense suffering to the men. It was begun on a cold winter night, and by noon on the day following the men were almost exhausted, when the return march was ordered. The regiment returned to within eight miles of the Baltimore and Ohio Railroad, where it bivouacked on the Heights of Hampshire, and remained there ten days. This was in the middle of winter. The winds were boisterous, the snow was ten inches deep, and the cold intense. The regiment was without tents, and hardly averaged a blanket for every two men; was on short rations, and had no cooking utensils. The only protection from the cold that could be obtained was a sort of hut ingeniously formed of rails and brush, which, together with huge bonfires, kept the men from freezing, although it did not shield them from suffering.

From Hampshire Heights the regiment advanced east to Pawpaw Station, near which it encamped, and remained until the opening of spring. It was here that the army met with a great loss, in the death of General Lander, a noble, brave and earnest patriot. All the troops in the vicinity were assembled to do honor to the departed hero. The Seventh Ohio escorted his remains to the railroad cars to be conveyed to Washington.

General Shields succeeded General Lander in the command of the division. About the 7th of March the spring campaign opened, and the whole division advanced *via* Martinsburg to a point four miles north of Winchester. General Banks had already occupied Winchester without a battle, as Jackson hastily withdrew on the approach of the National troops. Shields' division made a reconnoissance to Strasburg, twenty-two miles distant. A few rounds of artillery were fired; but the enemy making but little opposition, the division returned from whence it started, marching the whole distance in a little more than four hours. This move served to draw out Jackson, who had concentrated his forces at a point four miles distant from Winchester. The Rebel artillery opened on the National advance (March 23, 1862), as a challenge to a general engagement. This was really the commencement of the first battle of Winchester.

Shields' division was immediately called out, and advanced to the front, eager for the fight. The morning was consumed in skirmishing and reconnoitering, the two armies gradually approaching each other. By three o'clock in the afternoon the whole line became furiously engaged, and continued so until dark, at which time the battle ended. The Seventh Ohio performed an important part in this battle, and added to its reputation for efficiency. Its loss was fourteen killed, fifty-one wounded, and several prisoners. Colonel E. B. Tyler, its commander, received from the Secretary of War a commission as Brigadier-General of Volunteers, Lieutenant-Colonel Creighton succeeding him in command of the regiment.

General Shields' division moved up the Shenandoah to Harrisonburg, but finding no suitable ground for encampment, it fell back a few miles, and took a strong position near New Market. Remaining here a few days, an order was received from the War Department to join the forces of General McDowell, then stationed at Fredericksburg. On this march no tents were allowed the men, and only six baggage wagons to a regiment.

The division began its march on the 12th of May, and nine days thereafter reached its destination, a distance of one hundred and thirty-two miles. This long and weary march almost utterly exhausted the men; and, foot-sore, ragged and dirty, they threw themselves on the ground in an improvised camp, and rested until the next day. In the morning of the day following, President Lincoln and other Government officials arrived from Washington, and a review was ordered. Mr. Lincoln having expressed a desire to see the men who had whipped Jackson and driven him out of the Shenandoah Valley, Shields' division was ordered out with the rest, and went through with another day of exhaustive duty.

Having received heavy reinforcements from Richmond, Jackson re-entered the Shenandoah Valley, left open by the withdrawal of Shields' division, meeting with but slight opposition from General Banks, who then occupied a portion of the Valley. Jackson made a direct march toward Washington. This bold raid necessitated the abandonment of the move on Richmond. Shields' division was immediately ordered to march back to the Valley and intercept Jackson in his retreat, and, if possible, capture him and his army. The troops at Fredericksburg were put in motion, and a large force under General Fremont moved forward from another direction in pursuit of Jackson. That enterprising Rebel General, aware of the great efforts being made to entrap him, made a hasty retreat up the Valley, and a hotly-contested race ensued. This pursuit was continued until Jackson made a stand at Cross Keys, where he engaged Fremont in a battle which resulted against him.

By this time the Third and Fourth Brigades of Shields' division had, by forced marches, reached a point opposite Port Republic. The advance, under Colonel Carroll, was driven back and prevented from occupying the town or destroying the bridge across the Shenandoah, as directed. By the time General Tyler came up the Rebel General had arranged a heavy force to meet him. At five o'clock the next morning Jackson commenced the assault, and was promptly met by the National forces, with a resistance that would have been creditable to an army of ten thousand men. The Seventh, in connection with the Fifth Ohio, bore the brunt of the fight, and became the rallying center of the battle. These two regiments fought splendidly and effectively. General Tyler, seeing the terrible odds against him, and the extent of the enemy's lines, determined to handle his inadequate force with extreme caution, and met the wily Stonewall with his own favorite tactics of strategy and cunning. Taking advantage of a wheat field near the enemy's center, he extended his lines from hill to river, and double-quicked the Fifth and Seventh from point to point along the line, under cover of some standing wheat, halting at intermediate points to deliver a galling fire. This was kept up for five long hours; and, with less than three thousand muskets, the National forces repelled Jackson, with fourteen thousand veteran Rebel troops.

General Tyler ordered a retreat, with the Seventh Ohio as the rear guard. That regiment performed this perilous duty with great gallantry, coming off the field in line, loading as they marched, at intervals halting and firing by the rear rank into the advancing columns of Jackson. The National forces retreated toward Washington, while Jackson's army shortly after fell back on the main Rebel army near Richmond.

By the 28th of June, Shields' division had reached Alexandria, on the Potomac, and on the same day embarked for the Peninsula as a reinforcement to General McClellan, then operating against Richmond. The Third and Fourth Brigades of this division having been greatly reduced, both by forced marches and losses in battle, the War Department decided to send only the First and Second Brigades. The other two were ordered to disembark and go into camp near Alexandria, where it remained until the latter part of July, when it joined the forces of General Banks, at Little Washington. While lying at that place, General Tyler was ordered to report to Washington, and the Seventh Ohio lost their old and loved commander.

General Geary succeeded General Tyler in the command of the brigade. The ever-memorable campaign of 1862 was about opening. General John Pope assumed command of the Army of Virginia. On the morning of August 9th, General Banks' corps, to which the Seventh Ohio belonged, reached Culpepper, having marched all of the previous night. After an hour's rest it marched five miles further, near to Cedar Mountain, a point then held by Stonewall Jackson. The Rebels were in high spirits over their successes on the Peninsula, and seemed determined to make an attack on the National Capital. A great portion of the day was spent in reconnoitering. About three o'clock P. M. the battle was opened by General Banks' corps.

It had not advanced far when it was ascertained that the Rebels had greatly the advantage, in being protected by thick woods, while the National force was obliged to pass through an open field, every part of which was in full range of the enemy's guns. With steady ranks the National column marched boldly up to the woods where the opposing force was concealed. The action became general along the whole line. The Seventh Ohio was advanced to the front, and became at once engaged in a fierce hand-to-hand struggle. The shades of evening closed in on this bloody scene, when the National forces retired a short distance and bivouacked for the night.

Of three hundred men engaged in the Seventh Ohio, only one hundred escaped unhurt. No decided advantage was gained by either side in this hard-fought battle. General Lee's whole army approached, and the National forces were compelled to fall back on Washington. Then commenced a season of hardship and trial. For over a month the men were constantly engaged in marching and fighting. On the 17th of September the National army reached Antietam. Although on the field during the battle, the Seventh was not in the front line, and, therefore, its loss was comparatively slight.

Shortly after the battle of Antietam, the brigade to which the Seventh was attached went into camp on Bolivar Heights. While at this point, about two hundred recruits joined the regiment, which had, by its losses in battle, been reduced from one thousand men to less than three hundred.

On the 10th of December the brigade broke camp, and marched toward Fredericksburg to join the grand army under General Hooker. Before reaching its destination, counter-orders were received to encamp at Dumfries. Both armies went into winter-quarters, and all was quiet. But the force at Dumfries was not allowed to remain undisturbed. In the latter part of December, on a bleak, cold day, Stuart's cavalry, with two pieces of artillery, suddenly appeared before Dumfries, evidently with the intention of surprising and capturing its garrison. No sooner had the pickets signaled the approach of the enemy, than every man of the Seventh was under arms, ready to repel the enemy. The contest was brief. The enemy was driven off with considerable loss.

The quiet of the camp was not again disturbed until April 20th, 1863, when, in obedience to orders, the brigade marched toward Chancellorsville, with eight days' rations. The march occupied ten days. The day after the arrival of the Seventh the battle of Chancellorsville opened. The Seventh was ordered to support a battery, and latterly a line of skirmishers that had been thrown forward. The skirmishers soon fell back to the main body, but the Seventh continued to advance until it was ordered to retreat. Early on the following morning it occupied a line of rifle-pits exposed to a terrible cross-fire from the enemy. About noon it was ordered back to its former position. While here, the rest of the National forces had withdrawn, leaving the Seventh, with two other regiments, to cover the retreat. Its conduct in this hazardous and responsible position, and its gallant action in the battle, reflected the highest honor on not only the regiment, but the State from whence it came. The loss of the Seventh Ohio in this battle was fourteen men killed and seventy wounded.

An interim of a few days ensued, during which both armies were engaged in reorganizing their forces and recuperating their strength. Then came the race for Maryland and Pennsylvania. On the 1st of June, 1863, the Seventh, after a tedious and hard march, reached Gettysburg, Pennsylvania, and took its position on the left of the National lines. During the battle, the regiment was ordered from point to point, where and when reinforcements were most needed. Its loss was small, owing to the protection of breastworks, of which it availed itself in the hottest part of the battle. It lost but one man killed and seventeen wounded.

Troops were now dispatched to New York to quell the riots; and, among other regiments sent, was the Seventh Ohio. Taking steamers at Alexandria, it, with two others of the same brigade, landed on Governor's Island, in New York Harbor, on the 26th of August, and went into camp.

About the 1st of September, 1863, the draft being over in New York, the Seventh returned to and occupied the old camp on the Rapidan, and remained there until the latter part of the month. At that time, the Twelfth Army Corps, to which it was attached, together with the Eleventh Corps, were ordered to the Western Department. These two corps were afterward consolidated, forming the Twentieth Corps, under the command of General Jos. Hooker. Its route was through Washington City, *via* the Baltimore and Ohio Railroad, through Columbus, Indianapolis, Louisville, Nashville, to Wartrace, Tennessee, where it was ordered to construct winter-quarters. Before, however, these quarters were fully completed, the brigade to which the Seventh belonged was ordered to Bridgeport, Alabama.

It had been determined by General Grant, who was then in command of the department, to drive the Rebels from their stronghold on Lookout Mountain, and for that purpose nearly all the troops in his command were concentrated at or near Bridgeport. The Seventh Ohio was ordered to leave its comfortable winter-quarters, and joined the troops at Bridgeport. It was not brought under fire until it arrived at the foot of the mountain, at a point where the formation of the ground was such as to shield the men from the fire of the enemy. The guns on the top of the mountain could not be depressed sufficiently to take effect. In order, therefore, to harass the National troops as much as possible, the Rebels shot off the tops of the trees, that they might fall on their heads as they toiled up the slope. This lofty and rugged mountain, with the enemy intrenched upon its summit, would have presented an obstacle seemingly insurmountable to an army less disciplined, or one in want of patriotic zeal to inspire it. Moving further up, the assaulting force was exposed to a severe musketry fire. A heavy fog soon enveloped the whole mountain, and the firing ceased. At early dawn the enemy had disappeared, and the Stars and Stripes were planted upon the highest pinnacle of the mountain.

The National army, fully alive to their great victory, swarmed down the mountain, across the plains of Chattanooga, and up the sides of Mission Ridge, in pursuit of the enemy, but only to meet with a feeble resistance. The enemy fled, pursued hotly through the day, which was crowned with the capture of two thousand prisoners. The troops were in high spirits, and rent the air with their jubilant cheers. The pursuit was continued until the 27th of November, when the enemy posted himself in a strong position, called Taylor's Ridge, just beyond Ringgold, in order to prevent the National forces from passing through Thompson's Gap. Geary's brigade was ordered to storm the heights. It formed in two columns, on the railroad, half a mile north of the Gap, the Seventh Ohio occupying the right of the rear column.

The assault commenced. Just as the steep declivity was reached, the advance was halted to return the enemy's fire. The rear column passed over it, and entered a gorge that was directly in front. At this point the gallant Creighton shouted to his regiment: "Boys, we are ordered to take that hill; I want to see you walk right up to it!" And up they went, in the face of a merciless fire in front, on right and left. Only one commissioned officer of the Seventh Ohio was left uninjured. It was a fearful repulse, and all that was left the shattered remnant was to fall back to the foot of the hill.

The loss of the regiment was very severe. Nineteen were killed and sixty-one wounded. No positive advantage was gained, and the army fell back and encamped at Chattanooga. This gallant charge cost the Seventh Ohio dearly. Two of its best and bravest officers went down before the fearful storm of bullets. The fiery Creighton and the unflinching Crane were killed, together with a score of noble and daring comrades. At this inauspicious time the question of re-enlisting was presented to the members of the Seventh Ohio. Is it to be wondered that the proposition was not favorably considered by these war-worn soldiers?

This brings the history of the Seventh Ohio up to the 1st of January, 1864, at which time it was again in its old camp at Bridgeport, Alabama. Here it spent the winter in comparative quiet, with the exception of a few slight skirmishes, in which a few prisoners were captured. On the 3d of May, the regiment left Bridgeport, under orders, and, passing in the vicinity of Lookout Mountain, Ringgold, and Taylor's Ridge, it reached Rocky Face Ridge on the 8th of May. At this place the enemy was found intrenched, but he was soon routed by Hooker's corps. At Resaca the enemy again made a stand, and were again driven, and pursued until the

11th of June, with but slight loss to either side. This was the last service performed by the Seventh Ohio as a regiment. It was ordered home to be mustered out. The recruits, whose term of service had not yet ended, were consolidated with the Fifth Ohio, and participated, with that gallant regiment, in the brilliant and successful march of Sherman, through Georgia and South Carolina, to the sea.

The Seventh proceeded by rail to Nashville; thence by steamer to Cincinnati. There the Fifth Ohio was met; and, as the citizens of Cincinnati were about to tender that regiment a reception, the Seventh was invited to participate. The long and intimate relations between these two regiments—the one representing the northern and the other the southern portion of the State—made it doubly pleasant thus to meet and spend a few hours in social intercourse, at the close of these long years of hardship and trial spent in the service of their country.

On Saturday, June 24, 1864, the regiment took its departure for Cleveland, and on the 8th of July, 1864, was there mustered out of the service.

The Seventh had served a little more than three years. During that time, eighteen hundred men had served with it; and now, save some sixty new recruits transferred to the Veteran Corps, only two hundred and forty able-bodied men remained to bring home their unsullied colors, pierced through by the shot and shell of more than a score of battles. The regiment performed an important part in the war. Enlisting, as it did, at the very outset of the rebellion, it was kept well in the van during most of its service, and was present at most of the severely-contested battles of the war. Its losses were severe in both officers and men; yet in all the trying scenes through which it passed, it was ever the same brave, ready, and enduring body of soldiers.

8th REGIMENT OHIO VOLUNTEER INFANTRY.

ROSTER, THREE MONTHS' SERVICE.

RANK.	NAME.	DATE OF RANK.	COM. ISSUED.	REMARKS.
Colonel	HERMIN G. DEPUY	May 4, 1861	May 4, 1861	
Lt. Colonel	FREEMAN E. FRANKLIN	" 4, "	" 4, "	
Major	HENRY F. WILSON	" 4, "	" 4, "	
Surgeon	BENJ. TAPPAN	" 2, "	" 2, "	
Ass't Surgeon	S. SEXTON	" 2, "	" 2, "	
Captain	Ezra W. Clapp, jr	" 6, "	May 6, "	
Do.	Wm. Kinney	April 18, "	April 18, "	
Do.	Francis W. Butterfield	" 20, "	" 20, "	
Do.	Franklin Sawyer	" 20, "	" 20, "	
Do.	James E. Gregg	" 8, "	" 8, "	
Do.	Geo. M. Tillottson	" 19, "	" 19, "	
Do.	Wm. E. Hays	" 22, "	" 22, "	
Do.	Wm. W. Starr	" 22, "	" 22, "	
Do.	Elizur G. Johnson	" 5, "	" 5, "	
Do.	Wilbur F. Pierce	" 23, "	" 23, "	
1st Lieutenant	Benj. F. Ogle	May 6, "	May 6, "	
Do.	Wm. Delany	April 18, "	April 18, "	
Do.	Enoch W. Memman	" 20, "	" 20, "	
Do.	Horace Kellogg	" 20, "	" 20, "	
Do.	John Bixby	" 8, "	" 8, "	
Do.	Chas. M. Fouke	" 19, "	" 19, "	
Do.	Edward D. Dickinson	" 22, "	" 22, "	
Do.	Charles A. Park	" 22, "	" 22, "	
Do.	Lewis Breckinridge	" 5, "	" 5, "	
Do.	Henry W. Fritzs	" 23, "	" 23, "	
2d Lieutenant	Chas. W. Barnes	May 6, "	May 6, "	
Do.	Christopher Keary	April 18, "	April 18, "	
Do.	David Lewis	" 20, "	" 20, "	
Do.	Daniel C. Daggatt	" 20, "	" 20, "	
Do.	Alfred S. Craig	" 9, "	" 9, "	
Do.	Everton J. Conger	" 19, "	" 19, "	
Do.	Creighton Thompson	" 22, "	" 22, "	
Do.	Harry C. Landon	" 22, "	" 22, "	
Do.	David W. Houghton	" 5, "	" 5, "	
Do.	Otis Shaw, jr	" 23, "	" 23, "	

ROSTER, THREE YEARS' SERVICE.

RANK.	NAME.	DATE OF RANK.	COM. ISSUED.	REMARKS.
Colonel	HERMIN G. DEPUY	July 8, 1861	July 8, 1861	Resigned November 9, 1861.
Do.	S. S. CARROLL	Dec. 7, "	Dec. 7, "	Wounded at bat. of Spottsylvania; mustered out with regt.
Lt. Colonel	CHARLES A. PARK	July 8, "	July 8, "	Resigned November 4, 1861.
Do.	CHARLES A. DEVILLIERS	June 26, "	June 26, "	Elected Colonel Eleventh Regiment.
Do.	FRANKLIN SAWYER	Nov. 25, "	Nov. 25, "	Mustered out with regiment.
Major	FRANKLIN SAWYER	July 8, "	July 8, "	Promoted to Lieutenant-Colonel.
Do.	ALBERT H. WINSLOW	Nov. 25, "	Nov. 25, "	Mustered out with regiment.
Surgeon	W. H. LAMME	Sept. 7, "	Sept. 7, "	Resigned November 26, 1861.
Do.	THOMAS MCEBRIGHT	Nov. 27, "	Dec. 3, "	Resigned January 2, 1863.
Do.	J. L. BRENTON	March 5, "	March 5, "	Mustered out with regiment.
Ass't Surgeon	S. SEXTON	July 8, "	Jan. 11, 1862	Resigned October 23, 1862.
Do.	FREEMAN A. TUTTLE	Dec. 13, 1862	" 10, 1863	
Do.	J. S. POLLOCK	Aug. 11, 1863	Aug. 11, "	Mustered out with regiment.
Chaplain	LYMAN N. FREEMAN	July 9, 1861	July 9, 1861	Honorably discharged November 27, 1862.
Do.	ALEX MILLER	Feb. 9, 1863	Feb. 9, 1863	Resigned July 8, 1861.
Captain	Albert H. Winslow	June 4, 1861	June 4, 1861	Promoted to Major.
Do.	Francis W. Butterfield	" 5, "	" 5, "	Promoted.
Do.	Wilbur F. Pierce	" 5, "	" 5, "	Mustered out with regiment.
Do.	Elizur G. Johnson	" 9, "	" 9, "	Not mustered in.
Do.	Oran H. Kelsea	" 10, "	" 10, "	Resigned March 11, 1862.
Do.	James E. Gregg	" 17, "	" 17, "	Mustered out with regiment.
Do.	Wm. Kinney	" 18, "	" 18, "	Mustered out with regiment.
Do.	George M. Tillottson	" 18, "	" 18, "	Died March 4, 1863
Do.	Franklin Sawyer	" 18, "	" 18, "	Promoted to Major.
Do.	William E. Haynes	" 18, "	" 18, "	Mustered out for promotion, Nov. 3, 1862
Do.	Daniel C. Daggatt	July 9, "	July 9, "	Resigned February 6, 1862.
Do.	Richard Allen		Aug. 30, "	Resigned December 13, 1862.
Do.	Benjamin F. Ogle	Nov. 25, 1861	Nov. 25, "	Resigned November 27, 1862.
Do.	John Reed	Feb. 6, 1862	March 20, 1862	Cashiered February 1, 1865.
Do.	Willis W. Miller	March 11, "	April 11, "	Honorably discharged January 8, 1861
Do.	George S. Smith	Nov. 27, "	Dec. 31, "	Honorably discharged August 4, 1863.
Do.	David Lewis	Jan. 15, 1863	Feb. 16, 1863	Mustered out with regiment.
Do.	Azor H. Nickerson	" 20, "	" 16, "	Honorably discharged November 20, 1863.
Do.	Alfred S. Craig	March 4, "	April 7, "	Missing after battle of Wilderness.
Do.	Edward D. Dickinson	" 3, 1861	March 3, 1864	Declined promotion.
Do.	James K. O'Riley	" 3, "	" 3, "	Mustered out with regiment.
Do.	John G. Reed	" 3, "	" 3, "	
Do.	Wm. W. Witherell	April 22, "	April 22, "	Mustered out with regiment.

RANK.	NAME.	DATE OF RANK.	COM. ISSUED.	REMARKS.
1st Lieutenant	Benj. F. Ogle	June 4, 1861	June 4, 1861	Promoted to Captain.
Do.	David Lewis	" 5, "	" 5, "	Promoted to Captain.
Do.	Henry W. Fritzs	" 5, "	" 5, "	Resigned June 16, 1862.
Do.	Lewis Breckinridge	" 9, "	" 9, "	Not mustered in.
Do.	Chas. A. Park	" 10, "	" 10, "	Promoted to Captain.
Do.	Wm. Delany	" 18, "	" 18, "	Died Sept. 23, 1862; wounded at Antietam Sept. 17, 1862.
Do.	Willis W. Miller	" 17, "	" 17, "	Promoted to Captain March 11, 1862.
Do.	Chas. M. Fouke	" 18, "	" 18, "	Honorably discharged January 7, 1863.
Do.	Edward D. Dickinson	" 18, "	" 18, "	Mustered out with regiment.
Do.	Daniel C. Daggatt	" 18, "	" 18, "	Promoted to Captain.
Do.	Philo W. Chase	" 28, "	" 28, "	Resigned April 26, 1862.
Do.	James R. Swigert	July 6, "	July 6, "	Detached as Aide-de-Camp to Gen. Kimball.
Do.	John Reed	" 9, "	" 9, "	Promoted to Captain.
Do.	Wm. M. Pearce	Aug. 30, "	Aug. 30, "	Resigned April 29, 1862.
Do.	G. Shillito Smith	Nov. 25, "	Nov. 25, "	Promoted to Captain.
Do.	Chas. W. Barnes	Feb. 6, 1862	March 20, 1862	Died Oct. 7, 1862; wounded at Antietam, Sept. 17, 1862.
Do.	Alfred P. Craig	March 11, "	April 10, "	Promoted to Captain.
Do.	Azor H. Nickerson	April 29, "	June 3, "	Promoted to Captain.
Do.	Elijah Hayden	" 26, "	Oct. 15, "	Died July 3, 1863.
Do.	Creighton Thompson	June 16, "	" 15, "	Mustered out Aug. 31, '62; resigned Feb. 10, '63.
Do.	James K. O'Riley	Sept. 23, "	" 15, "	Promoted to Captain.
Do.	John G. Reed	Oct. 7, "	" 15, "	Promoted to Captain.
Do.	Herman Ruess	" 1, "	" 15, "	Dismissed as 2d Lieutenant October 17, 1862.
Do.	Wm. W. Witherell	" 17, "	Feb. 16, 1863	Promoted to Captain.
Do.	Jacob P. Hysung	Feb. 11, 1863	" 16, "	Mustered out with regiment.
Do.	Henry A. Farnum	Jan. 7, "	" 16, "	Mustered out with regiment.
Do.	David R. Wallace	" 20, "	" 16, "	Revoked.
Do.	Finney R. Loomis	" 15, "	" 16, "	Mustered out with regiment.
Do.	John W. Depuy	March 4, "	April 7, "	Mustered out with regiment.
Do.	Thomas F. Galway	Jan. 20, "	June 23, "	Mustered out with regiment.
Do.	Chas. Mannahan	March 3, 1864	March 3, 1864	
Do.	John W. Travis	" 3, "	" 3, "	Mustered out with regiment.
Do.	Thomas H. Thornbaugh	" 3, "	" 3, "	Mustered out with regiment.
Do.	Oramel G. Daniels	" 3, "	" 3, "	Mustered out with regiment.
Do.	Stephen Strange	" 3, "	" 3, "	Mustered out with regiment.
2d Lieutenant	Chas. W. Barnes	June 4, 1861	June 4, 1861	Promoted February 6, 1862.
Do.	Jacob P. Hysung	" 5, "	" 5, "	Promoted.
Do.	Otis Shaw, jr	" 5, "	" 5, "	Resigned June 11, 1862.
Do.	David W. Hougaton	" 9, "	" 9, "	Not mustered in.
Do.	Philo W. Chase	" 10, "	" 10, "	Promoted to 1st Lieutenant.
Do.	Alfred P. Craig	" 17, "	" 17, "	Promoted to 1st Lieutenant March 11, 1862.
Do.	John Lantry	" 18, "	" 18, "	Killed at Antietam September 17, 1862.
Do.	Anthony S. Sutton	" 18, "	" 18, "	Resigned February 22, 1862.
Do.	Edward W. Cook	" 18, "	" 18, "	
Do.	Creighton Thompson	" 18, "	" 18, "	Promoted June 16, 1862, to 1st Lieutenant.
Do.	Chas. W. Wright	" 28, "	" 28, "	Resigned March 11, 1862.
Do.	Herman Ruess	July 8, "	July 8, "	Promoted Oct. 1, 1862; discharged Oct. 17, '62
Do.	Azor H. Nickerson	....	Aug. 30, "	Promoted April 29, 1862.
Do.	John G. Reed	Feb. 27, 1862	March 20, 1862	Promoted to 1st Lieutenant.
Do.	Elijah Hayden	March 11, "	April 10, "	Promoted to 1st Lieutenant.
Do.	Wm. W. Witherell	" 11, "	" 10, "	Promoted to 1st Lieutenant.
Do.	Henry A. Farnum	Feb. 6, "	May 1, "	Promoted to 1st Lieutenant.
Do.	David R. Wallace	April 29, "	June 3, "	Dismissed March 23, 1863.
Do.	Horace H. Bills	" 26, "	Aug. 1, "	Killed September 17, 1862.
Do.	John W. Depuy	Sept. 1, "	Oct. 15, "	Promoted to 1st Lieutenant.
Do.	Finney R. Loomis	June 11, "	" 15, "	Promoted to 1st Lieutenant.
Do.	Thomas F. Galaway	Sept. 7, "	" 15, "	Promoted to 1st Lieutenant.
Do.	Chas. Mannahan	Oct. 9, "	" 15, "	Promoted to 1st Lieutenant.
Do.	Robert L. McConnell	June 16, "	" 15, "	Honorably discharged December 9, 1863.
Do.	Jno. N. Travis	Nov. 7, "	Nov. 7, "	Promoted to 1st Lieutenant.
Do.	Thomas H. Thornbaugh	Jan. 7, 1863	Feb. 16, 1863	Promoted to 1st Lieutenant.
Do.	Oramel G. Daniels	Oct. 17, "	" 16, "	Promoted to 1st Lieutenant.
Do.	Stephen Strange	Jan. 20, "	" 16, "	Promoted to 1st Lieutenant.
Do.	David S. Koons	" 15, "	" 16, "	Mustered out with regiment.
Do.	Lester V. McKisson	March 4, "	April 7, "	Mustered out with regiment.
Do.	Lucien Abbott	Jan. 20, "	Jan. 23, "	Transferred to Fourth Battalion.

EIGHTH OHIO VOLUNTEER INFANTRY.

THE EIGHTH OHIO VOLUNTEER INFANTRY was originally organized as a three months' regiment, under the first call of the President, most of the companies having been enlisted between the 16th and 22d days of April, 1861, and all of them arriving at Camp Taylor, Cleveland, as early as April 29th.

On the 2d of May, all the companies having been mustered into the service, the regiment was ordered to Camp Dennison, where it arrived on the 3d, during a drenching rain, and many of the men, for the first time in their lives, slept in the open air, with only a soldier's blanket for floor, roof, walls, and bedclothes.

The regimental organization was here completed by the appointment of the field and staff officers.

Instructions in the "drill" now commenced, and vigorous efforts were put forth to fit the regiment for service; but it soon became evident that the troops at this camp would not be sent to the field as three months' men, and an effort was made to re-enlist the regiment for three years. To this every company responded except company I, and the regiment of nine companies was mustered into the service for three years on the 22d, 25th, and 26th of June.

In the following September company I joined the regiment at Grafton, Virginia.

On the ninth day of July, 1861, the regiment left Camp Dennison for Grafton, Virginia, and on the 12th arrived at West Union, Preston county, Virginia, on the summit of the Alleghany Mountains where they are crossed by the Great Western Turnpike, and along which Garnett's Rebel army was then being rapidly driven by McClellan's troops.

For some weeks after this the regiment was stationed at various places among the mountains and along the Baltimore and Ohio Railroad, during which time it suffered severely from typhoid fever, which the men believed to have been contracted at a camp which they will long remember as "Maggotty Hollow." At one time over three hundred were in hospital, and some thirty-four deaths resulted from the fever in a short space of time.

On the 24th of September the regiment participated in an attack on Romney. At the "Hanging Rock" it was exposed to a severe fire, and lost several men in killed, and a number wounded. The regiment again participated in an attack on Romney, October 24th; which, being evacuated by the enemy, was occupied by the troops under General Kelley until the 12th of January, 1862. From this place the regiment participated in a brisk and successful attack on Blue's Gap. General Lander assumed command of the department and removed the troops to Patterson's Creek in January, and in February to Pawpaw Tunnel. On the 14th of February the Eighth participated in a brisk fight at Bloomey Gap, in which Colonel Baldwin, with his staff and part of his command were captured. The gallant Lander died on the 2d of March, and shortly after the division moved to the Shenandoah Valley, where General Shields took command. The enemy having evacuated Winchester, Shields followed them up the Valley, and on the 18th and 19th of March fought sharply at Cedar Creek and Strasburg. In these actions the Eighth acted as skirmishers, and established at once a reputation for that kind of duty, which it maintained throughout its term of service.

On the 22d the outposts at Winchester were attacked by Ashby, and in a brisk battle General Shields was severely wounded. The next day the battle of Winchester was fought. But few of the troops had ever been under fire, and none of them, as then organized, in any serious engagements. Colonel Kimball commanded, and made his arrangements to whip Stonewall Jackson, who had arrived during the night. The battle was one of the most severe of the war. Jackson, toward evening, attempted to turn our right flank, but was met by Tyler's brigade in front, when Colonel Kimball threw several regiments on his right flank, and after a desperate fight, which in some instances was hand to hand, the enemy was routed and driven furiously from the field.

The Eighth was deployed as skirmishers, both the evening before and on the morning of this engagement. Toward evening the right wing was withdrawn from the skirmish line and participated in the charge on the enemy's right flank. The killed and wounded of the Eighth amounted to over one-fourth the number engaged. The companies engaged were C, E, D, and H. The loss in the other companies was two killed and eight wounded.

During the months of March and April the regiment followed the enemy up the Valley, skirmishing with him at Woodstock, Mount Jackson, Edinburgh, and New Market. At the latter place Colonel Kimball received his commission as Brigadier-General, and became commander of the brigade in which the Eighth was. On the 12th of May the regiment started for Fredericksburg to join McDowell's corps, where it arrived on the 22d, and on the 23d was reviewed by President Lincoln. On the 25th, Jackson having driven General Banks out of the Valley, the division was ordered back to the Valley, and on the 30th reached and recaptured Front Royal. The Eighth skirmished from Rectortown, a distance of eighteen miles. Among the prisoners captured was the famous Belle Boyd.

From Front Royal, Shield's division marched up the South Branch of the Shenandoah, while Fremont's artillery could be heard as he pushed Jackson rapidly up the North Branch.

Shield's division was now broken up, and Kimball's and Terry's brigades ordered to the Peninsula, arriving at Harrison's Landing on the 1st of July. On the 3d and 4th of July the Eighth was thrown out toward the Chickahominy swamps, having on each day a brisk skirmish, losing seven severely wounded.

The army remained at Harrison's until the 16th of August, during which time it participated in a reconnoissance to Malvern Hill, and was while here united to the Second Corps, then commanded by Sumner. The Eighth was with Kimball's brigade, in French's division. With this corps it continued to act during the remainder of its service.

When the army retreated the Second Corps acted as rear guard until the army crossed the Chickahominy, and from thence marched by Yorktown to Newport News, when it was embarked in transports and taken to Alexandria, arriving on the 28th. On the 30th the roar of battle between Lee and Pope could be distinctly heard, and at noon the corps commenced a rapid march to the front, but only arrived at Centerville in time to witness the massing, at that place, of Pope's army. The next day the march toward Chain Bridge commenced, the Second Corps being on the left flank. The Eighth in this march was only once under fire, and that at Germantown, a few miles north of Fairfax C. H.

The Potomac was crossed at Chain Bridge, and the march through Maryland commenced, which ended in the battles of South Mountain and Antietam. The corps came up as a supporting line at South Mountain, but was not actively engaged, but crossed the mountain and skirmished with the enemy at Boonsboro' and Reedyville. Near this place the whole army was massed by the morning of the 16th of September, and a furious artillery duel commenced. One of the first of the enemy's shots killed W. W. Farmer, a color-sergeant of the Eighth. This cannonade lasted all day. The next day the battle of Antietam was fought. The Second Corps crossed the river and occupied the center of the line. Hooker had been engaged on the right for several hours, when French's and Sedgwick's divisions advanced—Sedgwick on the right—and met the enemy in strong position on a ridge. In the advance, Kimball's brigade formed the third line, Morris and Max Weber's preceding. They struck the Rebel line and were driven back; when Kimball advanced at a double-quick, carrying the line handsomely, and holding it for four hours, and until firing ceased in front. During this time Sedgwick was driven back on the right, which made it necessary for the Fourteenth Indiana and Eighth Ohio to change front; which was done most gallantly, and saved the brigade from rout. General Sumner pronounced Kimball's the "Gibraltar Brigade."

The regiment moved with its corps to Bolivar Heights, from whence, on the 1st of October, it participated in a reconnoissance to Leesburg. From this place the regiment moved with the army to Falmouth, participating in skirmishes at Hulltown, Snicker's Gap, United States Ford, etc.

In the terrible battle of Fredericksburg, on the 13th of December, the Eighth formed the right wing of the forlorn hope; the Fourth Ohio and First Delaware forming the left. The Eighth passed up Hanover street by the left flank, in order to deploy to form line with the other regiments which marched out lower down. Before the regiment cleared the street the Rebel fire struck the head of the column, killing and wounding twenty-eight; the other regiments also lost heavily, but the line was formed, and the enemy's outposts driven in to the foot of the hill on which were his main works. Here the line was to halt, seeking cover, for the main line to advance, but no line could reach it; column after column, for hours, was broken and driven back by the terrible shower of missiles passing over this line, which at dusk was withdrawn. In this battle the killed and wounded numbered thirty-seven.

The army remained in camp until the 28th of April, 1863, when it crossed the river and fought the battle of Chancellorsville. In this battle the regiment was almost constantly under fire for four days, but its loss was only two killed and eleven wounded. The brigade was at this time and subsequently commanded by General Carroll.

No further active service was had until the Gettysburg campaign. In that battle the regiment bore a conspicuous part. On the afternoon of the 2d of July it was thrown forward beyond the Emmetsburg road, to take and hold a knoll, from which the Rebel sharpshooters were annoying our lines. This position it captured by a charge at the double-quick, and held until the final close of the battle, a period of twenty-six hours. It was three times attacked by superior numbers, and once by three regiments, which were gallantly repelled, broken, and nearly all, with three stands of colors, captured. A change of front was then effected, and the fire of the regiment poured into the flank of the immense mass of troops marching upon General Hay's division. The regiment lost one hundred and two, killed and wounded.

During the pursuit of Lee across the Potomac, the regiment was engaged in several skirmishes, and after the enemy's escape, marched with the army to the Rapidan.

On the 15th of August the regiment was sent to New York City to help quell the riots then threatening that city. The trip was made by water, and this, with the sojourn in Brooklyn, forms a pleasant episode in the history of the soldiers of the Eighth.

Returning again to the field, it joined the army at Culpepper, and proceeded to Robinson River, looking the enemy in the face again. On the 10th of October, Lee having turned our right, a rapid march was made back to Centerville. On the route the regiment was engaged in the battles of Auburn and Bristow, October 14th, having two men wounded.

On the 27th, 28th, and 29th of November the regiment participated in the battles of Robinson's Cross Roads, Locust Grove, and Mine Run, acting mainly as skirmishers, in which several men were killed and wounded.

On February 6, 1864, crossed the Rapidan and fought the battle of Morton's Ford. In this battle several officers and men were wounded.

On the evening of the 3d of May the vast army was in motion, and the great campaign opened. The Second Corps crossed the Rapidan at Germania Ford, and moved rapidly through the Wilderness by the old Chancellorsville battle-field to "Todd's tavern," occupying the extreme left of the line. On the evening of the 5th the right of the line was furiously engaged, and the Second Corps moved to its support. At a point known as the "cross roads," the Fourteenth Indiana, Eighth Ohio, and Seventh Virginia, under the command of Colonel Coons, (Fourteenth Indiana), retook a section of a battery which had been lost by the Sixth Corps.

During the entire day of the 6th the regiment was engaged. In the morning, in a terrible fight in the dense undergrowth, a heavy loss was sustained. On the 7th, 8th, and 9th continued skirmishing was going on as the enemy was closely followed to Spottsylvania C. H. On the 10th a very strong work of the Rebels was charged, in which another severe loss was sustained, and Sergeant Conlan, who had gallantly carried the regimental colors in over thirty engagements, was wounded. On the morning of the 12th, in the splendid charge of Hancock on the enemy's right, the regiment again lost heavily. The regiment was engaged throughout the day, and for the next two days was almost constantly under fire, until the movement to Guiney. The loss in these several engagements was over sixty in killed and wounded.

In the numerous skirmishes from Spottsylvania to Petersburg, and in the battles of North Anna, Cold Harbor, and in front of Petersburg, the regiment was engaged. At North Anna a difficult duty of taking and holding a ford was assigned the regiment and gallantly executed.

On the 25th of June, its term of service having expired, the regiment was relieved from duty, being then in the trenches before Petersburg with only seventy-two officers and men for duty, and returned to Ohio to be mustered out of service.

On the route home it was frequently greeted with tokens of respect; especially at Zanesville, where a collation was provided; and at Cleveland, where it arrived on the morning of the 3d of July, and was cordially received by the mayor and military committee.

The regiment was formally mustered out on the 13th of July, 1864, by Captain Douglass.

9th REGIMENT OHIO VOLUNTEER INFANTRY.

ROSTER, THREE MONTHS' SERVICE.

RANK.	NAME.	DATE OF RANK.	COM. ISSUED.	REMARKS.
Colonel	ROBERT L. McCOOK	April 23, 1861	April 28, 1861	
Lt. Colonel	CHARLES SONDERSHOFF	" 23, "	" 23, "	
Major	FRANK LINK	" 23, "	" 23, "	
Surgeon	CHARLES E. BOYLE	May 2, "	May 2, "	
Ass't Surgeon	RUDOLPH WIRTH	" 2, "	" 2, "	
Captain	Charles Joseph	April 23, "	April 23, "	
Do.	Wm. Margedant	" 23, "	" 23, "	
Do.	Henry Broderson	" 23, "	" 23, "	
Do.	Frederick Schroeder	" 23, "	" 23, "	
Do.	Lewis C. Frintz	" 23, "	" 23, "	
Do.	Gustavus Kæmmerling	" 23, "	" 23, "	
Do.	F. Lammers	" 23, "	" 23, "	
Do.	F. Congelin	" 23, "	" 23, "	
Do.	John Jansen	" 23, "	" 23, "	
Do.	George Sommers	" 23, "	" 23, "	
1st Lieutenant	Louis Heuser	" 23, "	" 23, "	
Do.	Gebhart King	" 23, "	" 23, "	
Do.	George H. Harries	" 23, "	" 23, "	
Do.	Ernest Rubenow	" 23, "	" 23, "	
Do.	Gustavus F. Nopper	" 23, "	" 23, "	
Do.	B. Benz	" 23, "	" 23, "	
Do.	K. Jahn	" 23, "	" 23, "	
Do.	Maurice Pohlman	" 23, "	" 23, "	
Do.	Nathan Levi	" 23, "	" 23, "	
Do.	Lucas Schwenk	" 23, "	" 23, "	
Do.	Augustus Willich	" 23, "	" 23, "	
2d Lieutenant	Ferdinand Mueller	" 23, "	" 23, "	
Do.	Jacob Mueller	" 23, "	" 23, "	
Do.	Joseph Haider	" 23, "	" 23, "	
Do.	C. Lœwenstein	" 23, "	" 23, "	
Do.	Martin Bruner	" 23, "	" 23, "	
Do.	Charles Munn	" 23, "	" 23, "	
Do.	Henry Hunger	" 23, "	" 23, "	
Do.	Adolphus Kuehne	" 23, "	" 23, "	
Do.	Jacob Gluckowski	" 23, "	" 23, "	
Do.	Theodore Hafner	" 23, "	" 23, "	

ROSTER, THREE YEARS' SERVICE.

RANK.	NAME.	DATE OF RANK.	COM. ISSUED.	REMARKS.
Colonel	ROBERT L. McCOOK	May 28, 1861	May 28, 1861	Promoted to Brigadier-General by President.
Do.	GUST'S KÆMMERLING.	" 6, 1862	" 20, 1862	Discharged; revoked by President.
Lt. Colonel	CHARLES SONDERSHOFF	" 28, 1861	" 28, 1861	Resigned March 8, 1862.
Do.	GUSTAVUS KÆMMERLING	March 8, 1862	April 10, 1862	Promoted to Colonel.
Do.	CHARLES JOSEPH	Aug. 6, "	Nov. 30, "	Resigned May 10, 1863.
Do.	FREDERICK SCHRŒDER	Jan. 1, 1864	Feb. 6, 1864	Mustered out June 7, 1864.
Major	FRANK LINK	May 28, 1861		Declined.
Do.	AUGUSTUS WILLICH	" 28, "		Appointed Colonel 32d Indiana Regiment.
Do.	GUSTAVUS KÆMMERLING	Nov. 1, "	Feb. 18, 1862	Promoted to Lieutenant-Colonel.
Do.	CHARLES JOSEPH	March 8, 1862	June 24, "	Promoted to Lieutenant-Colonel.
Do.	FREDERICK SCHRŒDER	Aug. 6, "	Nov. 30, "	Promoted to Lieutenant-Colonel.
Do.	BARTHOLOMEW BENZ	Jan. 1, 1864	Feb. 6, 1864	Mustered out June 7, 1864.
Surgeon	CHARLES E. BOYLE	May 28, 1861	May 28, 1861	Resigned April 29, 1863.
Do.	CONRAD SŒLLHEIM	April 29, 1863	" 19, 1863	Mustered out June 7, 1864.
Ass't Surgeon	CONRAD SŒLLHEIM	Oct. 23, 1861	Oct. 23, 1861	Promoted to Surgeon.
Do.	JAMES DAVENPORT	Aug. 21, "	Aug. 21, "	Died March 29, 1863.
Do.	A. M. BEEBS	July 24, 1863	July 24, 1863	Mustered out June 7, 1864.
Chaplain	WM. STÆNGEL	Aug. 6, 1861	Aug. 24, 1861	Transferred to Captaincy of company C.
Do.	JOSEPH A. FUCHSHUBER	Feb. 18, 1862	Feb. 19, 1862	Resigned June 9, 1863.
Captain	Charles Joseph	May 28, 1861	May 28, 1861	Promoted to Major.
Do.	Wm. Margedant	" 28, "	" 28, "	Declined promotion.
Do.	Henry Broderson	" 28, "	" 28, "	Resigned October 22, 1861.
Do.	Frederick Schrœder	" 28, "	" 28, "	Promoted to Major.
Do.	Lewis C. Frintz	" 28, "	" 28, "	Declined promotion.
Do.	Gustavus Kæmmerling	" 28, "	" 28, "	Promoted to Major.
Do.	F. Lammers	" 28, "	" 28, "	Declined promotion.
Do.	F. Congelin	" 28, "	" 28, "	Declined promotion.
Do.	John Jansen	" 28, "	" 28, "	Died October 28, 1863.
Do.	George Sommers	" 28, "	" 28, "	Resigned June 13, 1861, W. Dept.
Do.	Ferdinand Mueller	" 28, "	" 28, "	Killed in action, September 26, 1863.
Do.	Bartholomew Benz	" 28, "	" 28, "	Promoted to Major.
Do.	Gustav Richter	" 28, "	" 28, "	Killed in action, September 20, 1863.
Do.	Jacob Gluckowski	" 28, "	" 28, "	Mustered out June 7, 1864.
Do.	B. Edliff Thœuson	June 28, "	Sept. 9, "	Mustered out June 7, 1864.
Do.	Geo. H. Harries	Jan. 9, 1862	Jan. 9, 1862	Revoked.
Do.	Louis Heuser	Nov. 1, 1861	Feb. 18, "	Mustered out June 7, 1864.

RANK.	NAME.	DATE OF RANK.	COM. ISSUED.	REMARKS.
Captain	Wm. Stengel	Sept. 6, 1861	Feb. 18, 1862	Cashiered August 28, 1862.
Do.	Ernest Rubenow	March 8, "	June 24, "	Canceled.
Do.	Chas. B. Gentsch	May 30, "	Nov. 30, "	Mustered out June 7, 1864.
Do.	Gustavus F. Nepper	Sept. 28, "	" 30, "	Mustered out June 7, 1864.
Do.	Maurice Pohlman	Aug. 28, "	April 22, 1863	Mustered out June 7, 1864.
Do.	Adam Shoemaker	Feb. 1, 1864	Feb. 6, 1864	Mustered out June 7, 1864.
Do.	Herman Luetkenhaus	Jan. 1, "	" 6, "	Declined.
Do.	George H. Harries	" 1, "	" 6, "	Mustered out June 7, 1864.
Do.	Joseph Græff	March 21, "	March 21, "	Mustered out as 1st Lieutenant June 7, 1864.
1st Lieutenant	Louis Heuser	May 28, 1861	May 28, 1861	Promoted to Captain.
Do.	Gebhart King	" 28, "	" 28, "	Declined promotion.
Do.	George H. Harris	" 28, "	" 28, "	Adjutant promoted.
Do.	Ernest Rubenow	" 28, "	" 28, "	Resigned July 13, 1862.
Do.	Gustavus F. Nepper	" 28, "	" 28, "	Promoted to Captain.
Do.	B. Benz	" 28, "	" 28, "	Promoted to Captain.
Do.	Chas. John	" 28, "	" 28, "	Resigned October 31, 1861.
Do.	Maurice Pohlman	" 28, "	" 28, "	Promoted to Captain.
Do.	Augustus Willich	" 28, "	" 28, "	Declined promotion.
Do.	Lucas Schwenk	" 28, "	" 28, "	Declined promotion.
Do.	Herman Luetkenhaus	" 28, "	" 28, "	Promoted to Captain.
Do.	William Henbig	" 28, "	" 28, "	Resigned July 5, 1862.
Do.	Theodore Hafner	" 28, "	" 28, "	Resigned July 5, 1862.
Do.	Jacob Mueller	" 28, "	" 28, "	Resigned September 23, 1861.
Do.	Joseph Haider	Jan. 9, 1862	Jan. 9, 1862	Resigned July 18, 1862.
Do.	Theodore Lammers	" 27, "	" 27, "	Died of wounds October 9, 1863.
Do.	Frederick Bertsch	Feb. 5, "	Feb. 5, "	Declined commission.
Do.	Adam Shoemaker	Nov. 1, 1861	" 18, "	Promoted to Captain.
Do.	Joseph Græff	Feb. 18, 1862	" 18, "	Promoted to Captain.
Do.	Nicholas Willig	Sept. 29, 1861	" 18, "	Resigned February 7, 1862.
Do.	Martin Bruner	Feb. 7, 1862	June 21, "	Mustered out June 7, 1864.
Do.	Charles B. Gentsch	March 8, "	" 21, "	Promoted to Captain.
Do.	Charles Dolezich	July 24, "	Nov. 30, "	Mustered out June 7, 1864.
Do.	Henry Luedke	Sept. 1, "	" 30, "	Killed in action September 22, 1863.
Do.	Richard Schneider	July 21, "	" 30, "	Mustered out June 7, 1864.
Do.	John Mangold	" 21, "	" 30, "	Dismissed January 15, 1863.
Do.	Herman Poenitz	Feb. 1, 1864	Feb. 6, 1864	Mustered out June 7, 1864.
Do.	Louis Grove	" 1, "	" 6, "	Mustered out June 7, 1864.
Do.	Herman Grosskordt	Aug. 28, 1862	April 22, 1863	Mustered out June 7, 1864.
Do.	Henry Spæth	Feb. 1, 1864	Feb. 6, 1864	Mustered out June 7, 1864.
Do.	Alexander Heilbrunn	" 1, "	" 6, "	Mustered out June 7, 1864.
2d Lieutenant	Frederick Mueller	May 28, 1861	May 21, 1861	Declined promotion.
Do.	Jacob Mueller	" 28, "	" 21, "	Declined promotion.
Do.	Joseph Haider	" 28, "	" 21, "	Promoted to 1st Lieutenant.
Do.	Charles Liewenstein	" 28, "	" 21, "	Declined promotion.
Do.	Martin Bruner	" 28, "	" 21, "	Promoted to 1st Lieutenant February 7, 1862.
Do.	Joseph Græff	" 28, "	" 21, "	Promoted to 1st Lieutenant February.
Do.	Henry Hunger	" 28, "	" 21, "	Declined commission.
Do.	Adolphus Kuehne	" 28, "	" 21, "	Resigned.
Do.	Jacob Gluckowski	" 28, "	" 21, "	Declined commission.
Do.	Theodore Hafner	" 28, "	" 21, "	Declined commission; resigned July 5, 1862.
Do.	Charles B. Gentsch	" 28, "	" 21, "	Promoted to 1st Lieutenant.
Do.	Frederick Bertsch	" 28, "	" 21, "	Promoted; declined commission.
Do.	Daniel Wagner	" 28, "	" 21, "	Resigned July 5, 1862.
Do.	John Baumgærtner	" 28, "	" 21, "	Resigned July 5, 1862.
Do.	Louis Fricker	" 28, "	" 21, "	Resigned May 10, 1862.
Do.	Theodore Lammers	" 28, "	" 21, "	Promoted to 1st Lieutenant.
Do.	Max Polacheck }	Jan. 9, 1862	Jan. 9, 1862	{ Colonel refused to recognize; ordered them
Do.	John Vertessy }	" 9, "	" 9, "	{ from regiment.
Do.	Henry Luetke	Sept. 6, 1861	Feb. 13, "	Promoted to 1st Lieutenant.
Do.	Andrew Jenny	" 29, "	" 13, "	Mustered out June 7, 1864.
Do.	Herman Grosskordt	" 29, "	" 13, "	Promoted to 1st Lieutenant.
Do.	Herman Poenitz	July 25, 1862	Nov. 30, "	Promoted to 1st Lieutenant.
Do.	Louis Grove	" 21, "	" 30, "	Promoted to 1st Lieutenant.
Do.	Raymond Herman	Sept. 1, "	" 30, "	Killed in action September 19, 1863.
Do.	Frederick Stemmer	" 28, "	" 30, "	Mustered out June 7, 1864.
Do.	Alex Heilbrunn	July 24, "	" 30, "	Promoted to 1st Lieutenant.
Do.	Frederick Oberkline	" 21, "	" 30, "	Resigned May 8, 1863.
Do.	Henry Blandowski	March 1, "	" 30, "	Resigned November 16, 1862.
Do.	Henry Spæth	Sept. 1, "	" 30, "	Promoted to 1st Lieutenant.
Do.	Theodore Racek	Nov. 16, "	April 22, "	Mustered out June 7, 1864.
Do.	Louis Kusser	Aug. 28, "	" 22, "	Dismissed March 21, 1864.
Do.	George Hartung	May 8, 1863	May 29, "	Mustered out June 7, 1864.

NINTH OHIO VOLUNTEER INFANTRY.

WHEN the news of the fall of Sumter reached Cincinnati, the Germans immediately held a meeting at Turner Hall, for the purpose of raising a German regiment. The assembly was addressed by Judge J. B. Stallo, Colonel A. Moor, Colonel Robert L. McCook and others. Two hundred men were soon enrolled, and three days later there were fifteen hundred ready to be mustered into the service; but, as the companies were not allowed to exceed ninety-eight men, many were rejected and compelled, reluctantly, to return to their homes.

On the 22d of April, 1861, the regiment was mustered into the three months' service, by Captain Gordon Granger, United States Army, at Camp Harrison, near Cincinnati, and May 18th it marched to Camp Dennison. Here the regiment was reorganized and mustered into the service for three years, and was the first three years' organization from the State of Ohio. In consideration of this the ladies of Columbus presented a very fine bass-drum to the regiment. It was mustered in with one thousand and thirty-five officers and men, exclusive of the band, which consisted of twenty-four musicians.

On the 16th of June the Ninth left the State, and on the 20th entered Western Virginia, with the first of General McClellan's re-enforcements for Morris's command. The regiment marched from Webster to Philippi, a distance of fifteen miles, in three hours, and thence moved to Buckhannon, and met the enemy's outposts at Middle Fork Bridge. They were soon routed, and the troops advanced to Rich Mountain, where the Ninth was engaged, and sustained its first loss—one killed and two wounded. The advance continued across Rich Mountain into Tygart's Valley, through Beverly and Huttonsville to Cheat Mountain. From here the regiment was ordered back to Beverly, and thence *via* Webster and Oakland across the Alleghanies to New Creek, on the Potomac, arriving July 27th.

Here the regiment performed very heavy guard duty, one company being detached as an outpost at Cumberland, Maryland, and another at an important railroad bridge across the Potomac, three miles beyond New Creek. About this time the Ninth was brigaded with the Fourth and Eighth Ohio Volunteer Infantry and Howe's battery of the Fourth United States artillery. On the 22d of August five companies of the Ninth were sent back to Huttonsville and Elkwater, where they had hardly arrived when with other troops they were ordered to Frenchtown. The march was continued to Bulltown, where they joined the other half of the regiment, which had left New Creek on the 27th of August, and reached Bulltown, *via* Clarksburg and Weston, on September 2d. Upon the concentration of the forces at Sutton, the regiment moved to that point, and was assigned to the Second Brigade, consisting of the Ninth, Twenty-Eighth, and Forty-Seventh Ohio Volunteer Infantry, and a Company of Chicago Dragoons. On the 7th of September the army broke camp, and on the morning of the 10th drove the Rebel cavalry out of the village of Summerville, and at three o'clock P. M., arrived in front of the fortifications near Carnifex Ferry. In the engagement which ensued, the Ninth lost two killed and eight wounded. The army followed the retreating Rebels and occupied Big Sewell Mountain;

but, on account of the difficulty in transporting supplies, the troops fell back to a point about six miles east of Gauley Bridge, and the Second Brigade encamped on the right bank of New River, at Camp Anderson. During the month of October there were frequent skirmishes with the Rebels, who had their sharpshooters and masked battery posted among the rocky hills on the opposite side of the river, and in these little engagements the Ninth lost a few killed and wounded.

The Ninth left Camp Anderson November 24th, and proceeded to Louisville, Kentucky, arriving December 2d. It camped at Jeffersonville, Indiana, for a few days, and then moved to Lebanon, Kentucky, where the Ninth, together with the Thirty-Fifth Ohio Infantry and Second Minnesota, formed the Third Brigade, First Division, Army of the Ohio. On the 1st of January, 1862, the division moved toward Columbia, and from there advanced to Camp Hamilton, twelve miles from Zollicoffer's intrenchments, arriving January 17th. The regiment participated in the battle of Mill Springs, and made a decisive charge, completely routing the Rebels. Ever after the battle of Mill Springs the Ninth Ohio and the Second Minnesota were attached to each other by the strongest friendship. Perfect harmony of feeling existed between them, and each was always watchful for the honor of the other. On the 10th of February the division marched *via* Crab Orchard, Danville, Lebanon, and Bardstown, to Louisville. The patriotic ladies of Louisville presented to the Ninth Ohio, Second Minnesota, Tenth Indiana, and Fourth Kentucky, each a beautiful National flag, as a reward for their gallantry at Mill Springs. Immediately after the presentation, the division embarked on steamers, and was conveyed down the Ohio and up the Cumberland to Nashville, Tennessee; arriving March 2d.

About the middle of March the Army of the Ohio left Nashville for Pittsburg Landing, but as Thomas's division was held in reserve, the Ninth did not arrive on the battle-field until the 8th of April. In the advance on Corinth the regiment performed its full share of duty in the trenches, and on the picket line. After the evacuation of Corinth, it joined the pursuit of the Rebels, but soon returned and camped near the town. On the 22d of June the Ninth marched *via* Iuka to Tuscumbia, Alabama, and while in camp there received an elegant regimental flag, presented by the Council of Cincinnati in the name of the city. On the 27th of July the camp was broken up, and the command moved toward Decherd, Tennessee. It was on this march that General Robert L. McCook, commanding Third Brigade, First Division, was ambuscaded and shot by a party of guerrillas; and the command of the Third Brigade devolved upon Brigadier-General James B. Steedman.

The division concentrated at Decherd, and after enjoying a few days rest joined the general movement of the Army of the Ohio northward. After enduring many hardships, occasioned by forced marches, excessive heat, and scarcity of water, the army reached Louisville, September 27th. On the 3d of October a forward movement commenced, and on the 8th, Steedman's brigade rested nearly all day within hearing of the guns at Perryville. Late in the evening it was ordered to the field, and for about an hour was exposed to a heavy fire from the Rebel batteries; but, as they were badly managed and did not have correct range, the loss was small. The Ninth followed the retreating Rebels as far as Crab Orchard, and from there marched *via* Lancaster, Danville, and Lebanon, to Bowling Green.

Steedman's brigade now consisted of the Ninth and Thirty-Fifth Ohio, the Second Minnesota, the Eighty-Seventh Indiana, and the Eleventh Regulars, and Battery I, Fourth United States Artillery. It was posted at South Tunnel, and assigned the duty of cleaning out the tunnel, in order to open railroad communication with Nashville. The men worked hard and continually, day and night, from the 8th to the 26th of November, when the tunnel was opened and trains were able to run through. The brigade was next ordered to Pilot Knob, to guard the railroad and the fords of the Cumberland, opposite, and below Saundersville. It moved to Gallatin, Tennessee, December 26th, and during the battle of Murfreesboro' guarded the fords of the Cumberland, that connected with the Lebanon Pike. After scouting the country up the Cumberland as far as Hartsville, the brigade marched to Nashville, January 14th, 1863, and was engaged in scouting and reconnoitering from the Murfreesboro' Pike to Franklin, and as far south as Chaplin Hills, until March 6th, when tents were pitched at Triune.

Here the Ninth was engaged in erecting strong works, and was frequently instructed in brigade and division drill. It occasionally joined scouting and foraging expeditions, and its efficiency was greatly increased by a supply of Springfield rifled muskets. This improvement was mainly due to the efforts of Governor Tod and Quartermaster-General Wright, of Ohio. Another cause of gratification to the boys of the Ninth, was the arrival in camp of a newly recruited regimental band. Comfortable huts were erected for their accommodation as soon as it was known they were coming, and their arrival was greeted with hearty shouts of welcome.

On the 24th of June the troops again advanced. The weather had been very favorable and the roads were in excellent condition; but on the morning of the 24th a heavy rain set in, and continued for seventeen consecutive days. The Ninth participated in the movement on Hoover's Gap and Fairfield, and on the evening of the 29th led a heavy reconnoitering party within six miles of Tullahoma. Upon the evacuation of Tullahoma the army followed the Rebels over continuous mountain ranges to the banks of the Tennessee. The regiment in the Third Division (General Brannon's,) of the Fourteenth Corps (General Thomas's,) crossed the river at Battle Creek on rafts; marched over Sand and Raccoon Mountains through Lookout Valley by way of Trenton Gap, over Lookout Mountain and down to McLemon's Cove, arriving September 10th. Two days later the division moved to the support of two advanced divisions, toward Dry Gap. On the 17th, the division marched with the bulk of the Fourteenth Corps, down the Chickamauga toward Gordon's Mills, and thence toward Rossville. As rapidly as possible, and without rest or interruption, the troops pushed on during the whole night preceding the battle. The fences on both sides of the road were on fire, and the blinding smoke greatly increased the hardships of that night's march. The leading brigade of the division became engaged about daylight, and the Third Brigade soon after. It was commanded by Colonel Van Derveer, who succeeded General Steedman.

At the beginning of the action the regiment was in charge of an ammunition train in the rear, and did not come up until the battle was raging. Passing the place where the Regular Brigade of Baird's division lost its guns, the Ninth pressed forward and boldly charged for the captured guns. They were posted nearly a quarter of a mile off, and were well protected by the Rebel fire, and by a cross-fire of our own guns; but without faltering, the regiment dashed on, drove the Rebels back and recaptured the battery. It did not stop to rest here, but joined the brigade in time to assist in repelling Longstreet's forces. On the second day of the battle the regiment participated in the famous bayonet charge of Van Derveer's brigade; and in the afternoon, while holding the hill on which the right of General Thomas's corps rested, it once more drove the Rebels back at the point of the bayonet. When nightfall closed the struggle, the supply of ammunition was completely exhausted, and the men had been compelled to gather cartridges from the boxes of the dead and wounded. The loss of the Ninth in the two days' battle was equal to one-third the loss of the entire brigade. The regiment went into action about five hundred strong, and lost in killed, wounded, and missing, eleven officers and two hundred and thirty-seven enlisted men.

The army occupied Chattanooga, and for some time the Ninth, in common with other regiments, suffered from want of sufficient rations. In the reorganization of the army under Thomas, Van Derveer's brigade was assigned to General Baird's command, and denominated Second Brigade, Third Division, Army of the Cumberland.

In the assault on Mission Ridge, Baird's division was on the left, near to Tunnel Hill. The open ground between the timber and the foot of the ridge was crossed by the troops on the double-quick, under a heavy fire of musketry and artillery, and the ascent began. After wonderful exertions the summit was reached, and the Rebels routed. As the National troops were resting after their labors, the Rebel forces on Tunnel Hill moved against a battery of five guns, which Van Derveer's brigade had captured. The Ninth Ohio and One Hundred and First Indiana immediately formed, and though greatly outnumbered by the Rebels, repulsed them three times, when they abandoned the attack. In this engagement the regiment lost two killed and twelve wounded.

On the 30th of December the Ninth started in charge of a battery and provision train for Calhoun, and returned to Chattanooga, January 8th, 1864. It moved to Ringgold, Georgia, and participated in a heavy skirmish at Crow's Valley, February 25th. During the months of March and April the Ninth remained encamped at Ringgold, and on the 5th of May joined the grand forward movement under General Sherman. It participated in the battle of Resaca, May 15th, and on the 20th entered on its last march against the enemy, moving from Kingston to the Etowah River.

As the regiment's term of service expired May 27th, 1864, it was ordered to Ohio for muster out. Up to the last moment it stood within range of the enemy's guns, and from the very outer picket line it was relieved by General Thomas, in person, and started for Cincinnati. All along the road stood their fellow-soldiers who cheered most heartily as the regiment moved away; and not any less hearty were the farewells returned by the boys of the Ninth Ohio. The regiment received an enthusiastic reception at Cincinnati, and was mustered out of the service at Camp Dennison on the 7th of June, 1864.

10th REGIMENT OHIO VOLUNTEER INFANTRY.

ROSTER, THREE MONTHS' SERVICE.

RANK.	NAME.	DATE OF RANK.	COM. ISSUED.	REMARKS.
Colonel	WM. H. LYTLE	May 6, 1861	May 6, 1861	
Lt. Colonel	HERMAN J. KORFF	" 6, "	" 6, "	
Major	JOSEPH W. BURKE	" 6, "	" 6, "	
Surgeon	C. S. MUSCROFT	" 2, "	" 2, "	
Ass't Surgeon	JOHN B. RICE	" 2, "	" 2, "	
Captain	John O'Dowd	April 19, "	April 19, "	
Do.	Emil Seip	" 22, "	" 22, "	
Do.	Oliver C. Pier	" 19 "	" 19, "	
Do.	Robert M. Moore	" 21, "	" 24, "	
Do.	Stephen J. McGroarty	" 18, "	" 18, "	
Do.	Christian Amies	" 18, "	" 18, "	
Do.	James P. Sedam	" 25, "	" 25, "	
Do.	Thomas G. Tiernan	" 27, "	" 27, "	
Do.	Wm. M. Ward	May 1, "	May 1, "	
Do.	Henry Robinson	April 12, "	April 12, "	
1st Lieutenant	John Fanning	" 19, "	" 19, "	
Do.	George Schlafemaker	" 22, "	" 22, "	
Do.	John E. Hudson	" 19, "	" 19, "	
Do.	Philip C. Marmion	" 21, "	" 24, "	
Do.	James M. Fitzgerald	May 1, "	May 1, "	
Do.	Conrad Frederick	April 18, "	April 18, "	
Do.	Isaac J. Carter	" 25, "	" 25, "	
Do.	Thomas McMullen	" 28, "	" 28, "	
Do.	Chas. C. Cramsey	May 1, "	May 1, "	
Do.	Samuel S. G. Peterson	April 12, "	April 12, "	
2d Lieutenant	John Cranley	" 19, "	" 19, "	
Do.	Rudolphus Labanas	" 22, "	" 22, "	
Do.	James F. Hickey	" 19, "	" 19, "	
Do.	John S. Mulroy	" 24, "	" 24, "	
Do.	John C. Sullivan	" 18, "	" 18, "	
Do.	Sebastian Eustachi	" 18, "	" 18, "	
Do.	Wm. H. Steele	" 25, "	" 25, "	
Do.	Joseph Conley	" 28, "	" 28, "	
Do.	Nicholas Lacy	May 1, "	May 1, "	
Do.	John Dailey	April 12, "	April 12, "	

ROSTER, THREE YEARS' SERVICE.

RANK.	NAME.	DATE OF RANK.	COM. ISSUED.	REMARKS.
Colonel	WM. H. LYTLE	June 4, 1861	June 4, 1861	Appointed Brig. Gen. by President Nov. 29, '62.
Do.	JOSEPH W. BURKE	Jan. 20, 1863	Feb. 16, 1863	Mustered out June 17, 1864.
Lt. Colonel	HERMAN J. KORFF	June 4, 1861	June 4, 1861	Discharged December 12, 1861; order revoked.
Do.	JOSEPH W. BURKE	Jan. 9, 1862	Jan. 9, 1862	Promoted to Colonel January 20, 1862.
Do.	ROBERT M. MOORE	" 20, 1863	Feb. 16, 1863	Resigned March 15, 1863.
Do.	WM. W. WARD	March 15, "	March 24, "	Mustered out June 17, 1864.
Major	JOSEPH W. BURKE	June 4, 1861	June 4, 1861	Promoted to Lieutenant-Colonel.
Do.	ROBERT M. MOORE	Jan. 9, 1862	Jan. 9, 1862	Promoted to Lieutenant-Colonel.
Do.	JOHN E. HUDSON	" 20, 1863	" 26, 1863	Mustered out June 17, 1864.
Surgeon	HOMER C. SHAW	June 9, "	June 23, "	Mustered out June 17, 1864.
Do.	C. S. MUSCROFT			Resigned June 9, 1863.
Ass't Surgeon	JOHN D. RICE	June 6, 1861	Nov. 9, 1861	Appointed Surgeon Seventy-Second Regiment.
Do.	HOMER C. SHAW	Nov. 25, "	Dec. 4, "	Promoted to Surgeon.
Do.	F. E. POWERS	Sept. 1, 1862	Sept. 6, 1862	Resigned May 8, 1863.
Do.	JOSEPH H. VANDAMAN	May 9, 1863	June 29, 1863	Resigned May 23, 1864.
Chaplain	T. O. HIGGINS	June 3, 1861	" 3, 1861	Mustered out June 17, 1864.
Captain	John O'Dowd	" 3, "	" 3, "	Resigned July 13, 1862.
Do.	Emil Seip	" 3, "	" 3, "	Resigned December 12, 1861.
Do.	John E. Hudson	" 3, "	" 3, "	Promoted to Major.
Do.	Robert M. Moore	" 3, "	" 3, "	Promoted to Major.
Do.	Stephen McGroarty	" 3, "	" 3, "	Appointed Colonel Fiftieth O. V. I.
Do.	Christian Amies	" 3, "	" 3, "	Mustered out June 17, 1864.
Do.	James P. Sedam	" 3, "	" 3, "	Resigned July, 1861.
Do.	Thomas G. Tiernan	" 3, "	" 3, "	Discharged December 12, 1861.
Do.	Wm. M. Ward	" 3, "	" 3, "	Promoted to Lieutenant-Colonel.
Do.	Henry Robinson	" 3, "	" 3, "	Resigned November 8, 1861.
Do.	Wm. H. Steele	Dec. 21, "	Dec. 21, "	Resigned October 19, 1862.
Do.	John Bentley	" 21, "	" 21, "	Resigned March 15, 1863.
Do.	Chas. F. Nickel	" 21, "	" 21, "	Died November 3, 1862.
Do.	Philip C. Marmion	Jan. 9, 1862	Jan. 9, 1862	Mustered out June 17, 1864.
Do.	John Fanning	" 28, "	" 28, "	Mustered out June 17, 1864.
Do.	James T. Hickey	Dec. 12, 1861	June 24, "	Mustered out June 17, 1864.
Do.	James M. Fitzgerald	July 13, 1862	Oct. 20, "	Deceased November 17, 1863.
Do.	John Sullivan	Oct. 19, "	Dec. 27, "	Resigned May 12, 1863.
Do.	Thomas J. Kelley	Nov. 3, "	" 27, "	Mustered out June 17, 1864.
Do.	Wm. Margadant	Jan. 20, 1863	March 11, 1863	General Rosecrans's staff.
Do.	Daniel O'Connor	March 15, "	May 5, "	Mustered out June 17, 1864.
Do.	Rudolph Seebaum	" 15, "	" 11, "	Mustered out June 17, 1864.

RANK.	NAME.	DATE OF RANK.	COM. ISSUED.	REMARKS.
Captain	Luke H. Murdock	May 12, 1863	May 22, 1863	Mustered out June 17, 1864.
Do.	Chas. C. Cramsey	Nov. 17, "	Jan. 10, 1864	Mustered out June 17, 1864.
1st Lieutenant	John Fanning	June 3, 1861	June 3, 1861	Promoted to Captain.
Do.	Geo. Schaefenbaker	" 3, "	" 3, "	Resigned September 16, 1861.
Do.	James F. Hickey	" 3, "	" 3, "	Promoted to Captain.
Do.	Philip C. Marmion	" 3, "	" 3, "	Promoted to Captain.
Do.	James M. Fitzgerald	" 3, "	" 3, "	Promoted to Captain.
Do.	Conrad Frederick	" 3, "	" 3, "	Resigned.
Do.	Wm. H. Steele	" 3, "	" 3, "	Promoted to Captain December 12, 1861.
Do.	Thomas McMullin	" 3, "	" 3, "	Resigned December 24, 1861.
Do.	Chas. C. Cramsey	" 3, "	" 3, "	Promoted to Captain.
Do.	John Bentley	" 3, "	" 3, "	Promoted to Captain.
Do.	John Stiles	Dec. 21, "	Dec. 21, "	Resigned August 12, 1862.
Do.	Henry D. Page	" 21, "	" 21, "	Resigned February 6, 1862.
Do.	John S. Mulroy	Jan. 9, 1862	Jan. 9, 1862	Killed October 8, 1862.
Do.	Joseph Holan	" 9, "	" 9, "	Resigned January 12, 1862.
Do.	John Sullivan	" 9, "	" 9, "	Promoted to Captain.
Do.	James A. Grover	" 28, "	" 28, "	Mustered out for promotion May 1, 1863.
Do.	Thomas Burnes	" 28, "	" 28, "	Resigned June 4, 1862.
Do.	Nicholas Lacy	Feb. 28, "	Feb. 28, "	Resigned April 30, 1863.
Do.	Rudolph Seebaum	" 28, "	" 28, "	Promoted to Captain.
Do.	George C. Mueller	Jan. 12, "	March 20, "	Discharged May 2. Sec. War.
Do.	Thomas J. Kelley	Dec. 12, "	June 24, "	Promoted to Captain.
Do.	Nicholas Knox	June 4, "	" 24, "	Resigned August 12.
Do.	Wm. Lambert	May 2, "	" 24, "	Resigned July 30, 1862.
Do.	Daniel O'Connor	" 2, "	Dec. 27, "	Promoted to Captain.
Do.	Luke H. Murdock	June 4, "	" 27, "	Promoted to Captain.
Do.	Wm. Ostendorff	July 13, "	Jan. 26, 1863	Resigned April 13, 1863.
Do.	Alfred Pirtle	Aug. 12, "	Dec. 27, 1862	Honorably discharged April 7, 1864.
Do.	Luke Murrin	Oct. 8, "	" 27, "	Mustered out June 17, 1864.
Do.	Thomas Patterson	" 19, "	" 27, "	Mustered out June 17, 1864.
Do.	Eugene R. Eaton	Nov. 3, "	" 27, "	Mustered out June 17, 1864.
Do.	Timothy McNeff	" 17, "	Jan. 10, 1864	Mustered out June 17, 1864.
Do.	Dominick J. Burke	Jan. 20, 1863	March 10, 1863	Mustered out June 17, 1864.
Do.	Joseph Donahoe	April 13, "	May 22, "	Mustered out June 17, 1864.
Do.	Daniel Toohey	" 30, "	" 22, "	Mustered out June 17, 1864.
Do.	Granville McSheeney	May 1, "	" 22, "	Mustered out June 17, 1864.
Do.	Daniel O'Neil	March 15, "	" 22, "	Mustered out June 17, 1864.
Do.	Chas. Weber	May 12, "	" 22, "	Mustered out June 17, 1864.
2d Lieutenant	John Cranley	June 3, 1861	June 3, 1861	Resigned November 20, 1861.
Do.	Francis Darr	" 3, "	" 3, "	Appointed in regular army.
Do.	Joseph Hoban	" 3, "	" 3, "	Promoted to 1st Lieutenant.
Do.	John Mulroy	" 3, "	" 3, "	Promoted to 1st Lieutenant.
Do.	John Sullivan	" 3, "	" 3, "	Promoted to 1st Lieutenant.
Do.	Sebastian Eustachi	" 3, "	" 3, "	Died in West Virginia.
Do.	James A. Grover	" 3, "	" 3, "	Adjutant promoted.
Do.	Joseph Connelley	" 3, "	" 3, "	Resigned January 1, 1862.
Do.	Nicholas Lacy	" 3, "	" 3, "	Promoted to 1st Lieutenant February 28, 1862.
Do.	John Stiles	" 3, "	" 3, "	Promoted to 1st Lieutenant.
Do.	Thomas Burnes	" 4, "	Aug. 12, "	Promoted to 1st Lieutenant.
Do.	Rudolph Seebaum	" 4, "	" 12, "	Promoted to 1st Lieutenant February 28, 1862.
Do.	George C. Mueller	Aug. 7, "	" 22, "	Promoted to 1st Lieutenant.
Do.	Wm. Lambert	Dec. 21, "	Dec. 21, "	Promoted to 1st Lieutenant May 2, 1863.
Do.	Nicholas Knox	" 21, "	" 21, "	Prom. 1st Lieut. June 4, '62, res'g'd Aug. 12, '62.
Do.	Thomas J. Kelley	Jan. 9, 1862	Jan. 14, 1862	Promoted to 1st Lieutenant December 12, 1861.
Do.	Daniel O'Connor	" 9, "	" 14, "	Promoted to 1st Lieutenant.
Do.	Luke H. Murdock	" 9, "	" 14, "	Promoted to 1st Lieutenant.
Do.	Bushrod Birch	" 9, "	" 14, "	Promoted to 1st Lieutenant.
Do.	Alfred Pirtle	" 28, "	" 28, "	Promoted to 1st Lieutenant.
Do.	Luke Murrin	Feb. 28, "	March 20, "	Promoted to 1st Lieutenant October 8, 1862.
Do.	Thomas Patterson	Jan. 12, "	May 1, "	Promoted to 1st Lieutenant.
Do.	Eugene R. Eaton	Feb. 28, "	" 1, "	Promoted to 1st Lieutenant.
Do.	William Porter	July 9, "	Oct. 7, "	Killed October 8, 1862, at Perryville.
Do.	Dominick Burke	Dec. 1, "	Jan. 26, 1863	Promoted to 1st Lieutenant.
Do.	Daniel O'Neil	May 2, "	Oct. 7, 1862	Promoted to 1st Lieutenant.
Do.	Joseph Donahoe	" 2, "	" 7, "	Promoted to 1st Lieutenant.
Do.	Daniel Toohey	Jan. 4, "	" 7, "	Promoted to 1st Lieutenant.
Do.	Timothy McNeff	Aug. 12, "	" 7, "	Promoted to 1st Lieutenant.
Do.	Granville McSheeney	" 12, "	" 7, "	Promoted to 1st Lieutenant.
Do.	Chas. Weber	Nov. 3, "	" 7, "	Promoted to 1st Lieutenant.
Do.	Wm. Harmon	Jan. 20, 1863	March 10, 1863	Mustered out June 17, 1864.
Do.	James Toley	" 1, "	May 22, "	Mustered out June 17, 1864.
Do.	Wm. Thiede	" 1, "	" 22, "	Mustered out June 17, 1864.
Do.	John Mulloy	" 1, "	" 22, "	Dismissed June 2, 1864.
Do.	Thomas Downey	" 1, "	" 22, "	Mustered out June 17, 1864.
Do.	Isaac Sheidler	May 1, "	" 22, "	Mustered out June 17, 1864.
Do.	Peter Gepner	March 15, "	" 22, "	Mustered out June 17, 1864.
Do.	Nicholas Walter	April 13, "	" 22, "	Mustered out June 17, 1864.
Do.	M. Reidlinger	May 12, "	" 22, "	Mustered out June 17, 1864.

TENTH OHIO VOLUNTEER INFANTRY.

AFTER the fall of Sumter, the city of Cincinnati promptly responded to the call for volunteers, by sending several regiments of infantry, of which the Tenth was one, to Camp Harrison. It was mustered into the service on the 7th of May, 1861, by Captain Gordon Granger, United States Army, and a few days after it marched to Camp Dennison, Ohio, a distance of seventeen miles, in three hours and three-quarters. During the short period of its instruction at Camp Dennison, the regiment rapidly acquired a knowledge of its military duties. In its ranks were many old soldiers, who had studied the art of war, and were not unfamiliar with scenes of actual combat. Some had served in European armies, and not a few had been through the Mexican war. It was at this time that the regiment was inspected by General McClellan, who expressed his admiration of it in very high terms.

The Tenth was a three-months' regiment, and already half of its time had expired; and as it became evident that troops were needed for a longer term of service, the Tenth, almost as a whole, volunteered for three years; and on the 3d of June it was mustered into the service as a three-years' regiment. Immediately after this, the ladies of Cincinnati presented a magnificent stand of colors to the regiment. The presentation took place at Camp Dennison. Judge Storer made the presentation speech, to which the lamented Lytle responded in eloquent terms, causing shout after shout to burst from the ranks.

At last marching orders came, and by the 24th of June the regiment had crossed the Ohio, and reported to General McClellan at Grafton, West Virginia, where it bivouacked a week, when it was ordered to Clarksburg, and thence to Buckhannon, where the army was being concentrated. Just as McClellan's columns had taken up the line of march, a courier arrived with the intelligence that five companies of the Seventeenth Ohio, stationed at Glenville, about forty miles distant, had been surrounded by a large force of Rebels under Wise. The Tenth was immediately sent to the assistance of the garrison, and arrived the afternoon of the next day, and found that Colonel Tyler, of the Seventh Ohio Infantry, had anticipated orders and rescued the besieged companies. Two months' marching and countermarching, and scouting in the mountains of Virginia, inured the regiment to the hardships of campaigning.

When General Rosecrans assumed command of the army his first move was to the right of his front of operations, on the Gauley and New Rivers, the Tenth leading the advance of the army. Information having been received that Floyd was intrenching himself at Carnifex Ferry, the column moved to attack him, and, after four days' marching, reached the Gauley River. Company C deployed as skirmishers, and first struck the enemy, and drove them back on their camp, which was carried by the bayonet, and everything in it captured, including a fine drove of cattle. The Tenth was ordered to move forward and reconnoiter the enemy's position. The regiment advanced through a dense wood; and, just as it gained the crest of the hill, the Rebels opened with shot, shell, and musketry. The regiment fixed bayonets, and advanced to the charge by the flank, no other formation being possible. The head of the column reached the ditch, when the whole Rebel line delivered a volley and the advance was checked. Fitzgibbon, the color-bearer, had his right hand shot off at the wrist, but immediately picked up the colors with the left hand, and, while advancing thus, was mortally wounded, exclaiming as he fell: "*Never mind me, boys. Save the flag!*" Each company was sadly shattered as it came over the hill; and at last, slowly and reluctantly, they fell back. The line was re-formed, and a brisk fire kept up, to prevent the enemy from capturing the wounded. The next morning the Rebels were in full retreat, having abandoned their camp equipage and a large quantity of ammunition, stores, and supplies.

After a short rest at Cross Lanes the regiment was again in motion. Cox had driven Wise from the Kanawha Valley to Sewell Mountain, where Floyd followed. To prevent their capture, Lee retired from Cheat Mountain and came to their assistance. In this part of the campaign the Tenth took an active share. In falling back from Sewell to Gauley, the roads were very muddy, and the column was much delayed by the trains. The Tenth was placed in charge of the train, and after that there was no more delay. The regiment served with General Rosecrans in every skirmish and battle in the campaign of Western Virginia, closing with the pursuit of Floyd from Cotton Mountain. On the 2d of November, 1862, the regiment reached Cincinnati, on its way to Kentucky, and received an enthusiastic welcome. The "heroes of Carnifex" were everywhere greeted with applause, and the streets through which the column passed were so thronged that it was with difficulty it moved to its rendezvous. The column halted and wheeled into line on Broadway, its center resting opposite the residence of Colonel Lytle, who, though suffering from a wound, had risen from his bed to accompany the regiment in its triumphal march through the city.

The regiment remained a week in Cincinnati, and, upon arriving in Kentucky, was brigaded with the Third and Thirteenth Ohio, Fifteenth Kentucky, and Loomis's battery, forming the Seventeenth Brigade of Buell's army, and was a part of the Third Division (Mitchel's). The regiment moved through Kentucky and Tennessee to Northern Alabama, sharing in all the splendid achievements of General Mitchel. After three months' severe service the regiment was designated as the garrison for the city of Huntsville, and Lieutenant-Colonel Burke became Provost-Marshal of Middle Tennessee and Northern Alabama. It is a remarkable circumstance, that during the time the regiment performed the duty of provost guard, not a single case of outrage occurred, and the government of the city was more secure than when under civil rule, facts held in grateful remembrance by the citizens of Huntsville. When General Mitchel was ordered to Washington, that portion of the regiment on duty was assembled, and the General took leave of them in an appropriate address, speaking in the highest terms of the efficiency and discipline of the regiment, and expressing the warmest friendship for Colonel Lytle and Lieutenant-Colonel Burke.

The command of the division devolved upon General Rousseau, and under him Lytle's brigade commenced the long march to Kentucky after Bragg, and, in common with the whole army, endured all the privations incident to the movement. On the 2d of October, 1862, the regiment received an accession of sixty recruits, and the day after marched with the division, in McCook's corps, to meet Bragg's army. On the 8th of October the corps marched from Macksville toward Perryville, Lytle's brigade in the advance, and the Tenth leading. Upon reaching the field the regiment was deployed as skirmishers, and, after advancing some distance, was withdrawn and placed as a support to Loomis's battery. When Loomis had exhausted his ammunition, and retired to replenish, the Tenth moved to the crest of the eminence. This position was held till the regiment was exposed on both flanks. It drove the enemy from the front by a charge, but in retiring, which it was forced to do, its track was marked by the dead of the regiment. Company formation was impossible, and the men crowded toward the colors. Being aware of the loss the regiment must sustain if it retired in disorder, Colonel Burke seized a bugle and sounded a halt, formed and dressed the lines, deployed the flank companies as skirmishers to cover the retreat, and then retired to the new lines, having but two hundred and sixty-three men out of five hundred and twenty-eight.

When General Rosecrans assumed command of the army, in general orders the Tenth was announced as head-quarters and provost guard of the Army of the Cumberland. The regiment relieved the Fifteenth United States Infantry, and entered upon its new duties, furnishing guards for head-quarters, taking charge of prisoners, preventing straggling during engagements, and during the battle of Stone River it protected the line of communication, and for its efficiency was specially mentioned in General Rosecrans's report. The three bridges on which the army crossed Stewart's Creek were left in charge of Colonel Burke and eight companies, companies A and C having accompanied General Rosecrans to the front. In the early part of the engagement the Rebel cavalry captured several trains, but Colonel Burke sent out parties and succeeded in recapturing every wagon, and in bringing them within reach of his guns. The little band intrenched themselves, and calmly awaited the approach of Wheeler, who advanced cautiously toward Stewart's Creek; and, meeting an obstinate resistance from Colonel Burke's skirmishers, he proceeded to Lavergne, where a great part of the large army train was parked. During Wheeler's march to Lavergne the little handful of troops at Stewart's Creek were deployed as skirmishers, and engaged in arresting crowds of fugitives from the battle-field; and in less than two hours over three thousand men were stopped, re-assured, and returned to their regiments. Cannonading was heard in the direction of Lavergne, where Colonel Innes, Michigan Engineers, commanded. Thomas Reilly, a citizen, dashed through the Rebel lines, bearing dispatches to Burke from Innes, asking assistance. Four companies of cavalry and two pieces of artillery, which had reported to Colonel Burke, were sent to Innes; but the officer in command, seeing the vast number of Rebels besieging the garrison, refused to charge through to its assistance, and the artillery officer returned and reported the facts to Colonel Burke. The Rebels had made several furious assaults on Innes's gallant little band, and he again appealed for assistance. Colonel Burke abandoned Stewart's Creek, leaving a few men to guard the bridges, and with seven small companies marched against the three thousand Rebel cavalry surrounding Innes. A mile from Lavergne the Rebel force was struck, coolly rifling the train preparatory to burning it. The Rebel troopers did not fire a shot, but rode off to the main body bearing the intelligence of the arrival of re-enforcements, and Wheeler quickly withdrew. A courier was dispatched to General Rosecrans with the report of Wheeler's retreat, and General Rosecrans replied:

"Lieutenant-Colonel Burke, Tenth Ohio Infantry:

"The General commanding has received your dispatch, and is highly gratified with your conduct. By command of General Rosecrans. FRANK BOND, Lt. and A. D. C."

At head-quarters the regiment soon regained its spirit, and increased in numbers, and its appearance and discipline were subjects of comment among its comrades. General Rosecrans's wife presented the members of the "Roll of Honor" with their ribbons, and pinned them herself on the breasts of the veterans. The city of Cincinnati presented the regiment with an elegant National standard, in appreciation of its gallantry and daring. The Tenth followed Rosecrans to the Tennessee River, and was present at Chickamauga, where it was again officially noticed for its efficiency in the performance of its duties.

When General Thomas assumed command of the army, he retained the regiment as head-quarters' guard, and with him it was present at Mission Ridge, Buzzard's Roost, Rocky Face Ridge, Resaca, and as far in the Atlanta campaign as Kingston.

The regiment's term of service having nearly expired, a day was fixed for its departure, and it was drawn up in line in front of General Thomas's head-quarters. The General, contrary to his usual custom, spoke a few words of parting cheer, and kindly eulogized the regiment for its bearing on all occasions. The Chief of Staff, General W. D. Whipple, addressed the regiment a very complimentary letter, expressing his great regret that the army was going to lose the "glorious old Tenth Ohio." The boys gave "three times three" for General Thomas, the same for the Army of the Cumberland; and, concluding with three cheers for the cause of the Union, filed off on their way to their long absent homes and friends. At Cincinnati the friends of the regiment greeted it with a cordial welcome; and though it did not return bearing the trophies and spoils of war, it bore that which was far better, an unsullied fame. Its ranks were thinned and its banners were blood-stained and torn; and of the thousand brave hearts that beat the day they pledged their lives for the protection of their colors, but few remained to tell of Lytle and the Tenth Ohio.

11th REGIMENT OHIO VOLUNTEER INFANTRY.

ROSTER, THREE MONTHS' SERVICE.

RANK.	NAME.	DATE OF RANK.	COM. ISSUED.	REMARKS.
Colonel	JAMES F. HARRISON	April 25, 1861	April 25, 1861	
Lt. Colonel	JOSEPH W. FRIZELL	" 29, "	" 29, "	
Major	AUGUSTUS H. COLEMAN	" 29, "	" 29, "	
Captain	Calvin J. Childs	" 15, "	" 15, "	
Do.	Thos. L. P. Defriese	" 22, "	" 22, "	
Do.	Robert A. Knox	" 24, "	" 24, "	
Do.	John V. Curtis	" 21, "	" 24, "	
Do.	John C. Langston	" 19, "	" 19, "	
Do.	Stephen Johnson	" 18, "	" 18, "	
Do.	Michael P. Nolan	" 20, "	" 20, "	
Do.	John C. Drury	" 20, "	" 20, "	
Do.	Jonathan Cranor	" 20, "	" 20, "	
Do.	John M. Newkirk	" 23, "	" 23, "	
1st Lieutenant	George W. Hatfield	" 15, "	" 15, "	
Do.	Samuel Alward	" 22, "	" 22, "	
Do.	Charles Calkins	" 20, "	" 20, "	
Do.	Henry S. Ravenscroft	" 20, "	" 20, "	
Do.	Jackson Shade	" 19, "	" 19, "	
Do.	Isaac S. Clark	" 18, "	" 18, "	
Do.	Samuel B. Smith	" 20, "	" 20, "	
Do.	Cornelius N. Hoagland	" 24, "	" 24, "	
Do.	James B. Cerviston	" 20, "	" 20, "	
Do.	Henry Angle	" 23, "	" 23, "	
Do.	Ira B. Gibbs	May 21, "	May 21, "	
2d Lieutenant	Thomas L. Stewart	April 15, "	April 15, "	
Do.	John D. Shannon	" 22, "	" 22, "	
Do.	Thos. J. McDowell	" 20, "	" 20, "	
Do.	Jarvis S. Rogers	" 20, "	" 20, "	
Do.	Hiram Moore	" 22, "	" 22, "	
Do.	Solomon Teverbaugh	" 18, "	" 18, "	
Do.	Robert Patterson	" 20, "	" 20, "	
Do.	Jerome B. Weller	" 24, "	" 24, "	
Do.	Thomas F. Cooper	" 20, "	" 20, "	
Do.	Wesley Gorsuch	" 23, "	" 23, "	
Do.	Wm. H. H. Gahagan	May 21, "	May 21, "	
Do.	J. H. Horton	" 22, "	" 22, "	

ROSTER, THREE YEARS' SERVICE.

RANK.	NAME.	DATE OF RANK.	COM. ISSUED.	REMARKS.
Colonel	CHAS. A. DEVILLIERS	July 6, 1861	July 6, 1861	Dismissed from service April 23, 1862.
Do.	AUGUSTUS H. COLEMAN	April 23, 1862	Sept. 17, 1862	Killed September 17, 1862.
Do.	PHILANDER P. LANE	Sept. 17, "	Oct. 9, "	Resigned October 26, 1863.
Do.	OGDEN STREET	Oct. 26, 1863	Jan. 10, 1864	Mustered out.
Lt. Colonel	JOSEPH W. FRIZELL	July 6, 1861	July 6, 1861	Resigned December 21, 1861.
Do.	AUGUSTUS H. COLEMAN	Jan. 9, 1862	Jan. 9, 1862	Killed September 17, 1862.
Do.	OGDEN STREET	Sept. 17, "	Nov. 12, "	Promoted to Colonel.
Do.	D. CLINTON STUBBS	Feb. 23, 1865	Feb. 23, 1865	Mustered out as Captain June 11, 1865.
Major	AUGUSTUS H. COLEMAN	July 6, 1861	July 6, 1861	Promoted to Colonel January 9, 1862.
Do.	LYMAN J. JACKSON	Jan. 9, 1862	Feb. 5, 1862	Resigned October 1, 1862.
Do.	ASA HIGGINS	Oct. 1, "	Nov. 12, "	Mustered out.
Surgeon	J. FRANK GABRIEL	July 7, 1861	July 7, 1861	Resigned September 25, 1862.
Do.	JOHN MCCURDY	Oct. 26, 1862	Nov. 10, 1863	Mustered out.
Ass't Surgeon	HENRY Z. GILL	July 7, 1861	Oct. 23, 1861	Resigned July 11, 1862.
Do.	S. HUDSON	" 11, 1862	July 23, 1862	Resigned October 1, 1862.
Do.	A. C. MCNUTT	" 9, "	" 22, "	Resigned February 8, 1863.
Do.	N. H. SIDWELL	Dec. 2, "	Jan. 24, 1863	Mustered out.
Do.	A. B. HARTMAN	Aug. 11, 1863	Aug. 11, "	Mustered out.
Chaplain	GEORGE W. DUBOIS	July 10, 1861	Oct. 23, 1861	Resigned January 18, 1862.
Do.	WM. W. LYLE	Jan. 31, 1862	Feb. 12, 1863	Mustered out with regiment.
Captain	Calvin J. Childs	June 14, 1861	June 14, 1861	Resigned May 1, 1862.
Do.	Stephen Johnson	" 14, "	" 14, "	Resigned September 20, 1861.
Do.	John C. Drury	" 17, "	" 17, "	Resigned December 28, 1861.
Do.	Thos. L. P. Defriese	" 18, "	" 18, "	Resigned October 8, 1861.
Do.	John V. Curtis	" 19, "	" 19, "	Resigned April 18, 1862.
Do.	Ogden Street	July 7, "	Oct. 23, "	Promoted to Lieutenant-Colonel Sept. 17, '62.
Do.	Philander P. Lane	" 7, "	" 23, "	Promoted to Colonel September 17, 1863.
Do.	Asa Higgins	" 23, "	July 29, "	Promoted to Major October 1, 1862.
Do.	Alexander Duncan	Aug. 26, "	Sept. 21, "	Mustered out.
Do.	Solomon Teverbaugh	Nov. 12, "	Nov. 12, "	Mustered out.
Do.	Wm. S. Douglas	Dec. 19, "	Jan. 10, 1862	Resigned September 30, 1862.
Do.	George W. Hatfield	Jan. 9, 1862	" 9, "	Resigned June 7, 1863.
Do.	Henry L. Seymour	April 18, "	June 3, "	Resigned November 20, 1862.
Do.	Jerome B. Weller	May 1, "	" 3, "	Resigned April 18, 1863.
Do.	Joseph P. Staley	Aug. 9, "	Oct. 2, "	Resigned June 31, 1863.
Do.	Lewis G. Brown	" 2, "	" 3, "	Mustered out.
Do.	Emmor H. Price	Sept. 17, "	Nov. 12, "	Mustered out.

RANK.	NAME.	DATE OF RANK.			COM. ISSUED.			REMARKS.
Captain	George Johnson	Sept.	17,	1862	Nov.	12,	1862	Resigned December 16, 1863.
Do.	Andrew H. Chapman	Oct.	1,	"	Dec.	30,	"	Resigned February 12, 1864.
Do.	David M. Layman	Nov.	20,	"	Feb.	10,	1863	Mustered out June 21, 1864.
Do.	D. K. Curtiss	April	18,	1863	Aug.	25,	"	Killed in action November 25, 1863.
Do.	E. C. Jordan	June	7,	"	"	25,	"	Mustered out June 21, 1864.
Do.	Robert C. Morris	"	21,	"	"	25,	"	Mustered out June 21, 1864.
Do.	D. Clinton Stubbs	"	29,	1864	Nov.	12,	1864	Promoted to Lieutenant-Colonel.
Do.	Francis M. Ogden	Feb.	23,	1865	Feb.	23,	1865	Mustered out as 1st Lieutenant June 11, 1865.
Do.	Francis M. Wilmington	"	23,	"	"	23,	"	Mustered out as 1st Lieutenant June 11, 1865.
Do.	John W. Green	"	23,	"	"	23,	"	
Do.	David W. Maurice	"	23,	"	"	23,	"	
1st Lieutenant	Solomon Teverbaugh	June	14,	1861	June	14,	1861	Promoted to Captain.
Do.	Cornelius N. Hoagland	"	17,	"	"	17,	"	Resigned November 12, 1861.
Do.	H. L. Seymour	"	19,	"	"	19,	"	Promoted April 18, 1862.
Do.	George W. Hatfield	"	20,	"	"	20,	"	Promoted January 9, 1862.
Do.	J. D. Shannon	"	20,	"	"	20,	"	Resigned August 11, 1861.
Do.	Emmor H. Price	July	7,	"	Oct.	23,	"	Promoted September 17, 1862.
Do.	George P. Darron	"	7,	"	July	7,	"	Resigned November 2, 1861.
Do.	Charles B. Lindsley	"	23,	"	"	29,	"	Resigned April 10, 1862.
Do.	John E. Alexander	Aug.	28,	"	Sept.	21,	"	Deceased.
Do.	Wm. S. Douglas	Oct.	3,	"	Jan.	10,	1862	Promoted December 19, 1861.
Do.	Newton S. McAbee	Nov.	12,	"	Nov.	12,	1861	Resigned June 5, 1862.
Do.	John W. McAbee	"	29,	"	"	29,	"	Mustered out June 21, 1864.
Do.	Silas Roney	Dec.	19,	"	Jan.	2,	"	Resigned May, 1862.
Do.	Jerome B. Weller	"	21,	"	Dec.	21,	"	Promoted May 1, 1862, to Captain.
Do.	C. J. Cottingham	"	26,	"	"	26,	"	Resigned June 16, 1862.
Do.	Joshua H. Horton	"	26,	"	"	26,	"	Resigned June 6, 1862.
Do.	George Johnson	Jan.	9,	1862	Jan.	9,	1862	Promoted September 17, 1862, to Captain.
Do.	Andrew H. Chapman	April	10,	"	May	1,	"	Promoted October 1, 1862, to Captain.
Do.	David M. Layman	"	18,	"	June	3,	"	Promoted November 20, 1862 to Captain.
Do.	E. C. Jordan	May	1,	"	"	3,	"	Promoted to Captain.
Do.	Wm. Crumbaugh	June	5,	"	"	24,	"	Declined promotion.
Do.	D. K. Curtiss	May	1,	"	"	21,	"	Promoted to Captain.
Do.	Theodore Cox	June	5,	"	Sept.	6,	"	Mustered out June 21, 1864.
Do.	Francis W. Anderton	Aug.	9,	"	Oct.	2,	"	Resigned March 17, 1863.
Do.	George E. Peck	"	20,	"	"	3,	"	Died of wounds November 26, 1863.
Do.	Robert C. Morris	June	16,	"	Nov.	12,	"	Promoted to Captain.
Do.	P. A. Arthur	Sept.	17,	"	"	12,	"	Mustered out June 21, 1864.
Do.	Chas. P. Achuff	"	17,	"	"	12,	"	Resigned April 29, 1863
Do.	Chas. J. McClure	June	5,	"	Dec.	30,	"	Resigned February 22, 1864.
Do.	Wm. K. Young	Oct.	1,	"	"	30,	"	Resigned May 22, 1863.
Do.	Martin L. Edwards	Nov.	20,	"	Feb.	10,	1863	Mustered out June 21, 1864.
Do.	Thomas L. Stewart	May	17,	"	July	20,	"	Mustered out June 21, 1864.
Do.	George S. Swain	April	29,	"	Aug.	25,	"	Mustered out June 21, 1864.
Do.	John Roney	May	22,	"	"	25,	"	Mustered out June 21, 1861.
Do.	Cyrenius Longley	April	18,	"	"	25,	"	Mustered out June 21, 1864.
Do.	John C. Keifibar	June	7,	"	"	25,	"	Mustered out June 21, 1864.
Do.	Milton H. Wilson	"	21,	"	"	25,	"	Mustered out June 20, 1864.
Do.	Francis M. Ogden	"	29,	1864	Nov.	12,	1864	Promoted to Captain.
Do.	Francis M. Wilmington	"	29,	"	"	12,	"	Promoted to Captain.
Do.	John W. Green	"	29,	"	"	12,	"	Promoted to Captain.
Do.	Mark Kirby	Feb.	23,	1865	Feb.	23,	1865	Mustered out as 1st Lieutenant May 15, 1865.
Do.	Don Carlos Sherman	"	23,	"	"	23,	"	Mustered out with regiment.
Do.	Wm. W. Cromer	"	23,	"	"	23,	"	Mustered out June 11, 1865.
Do.	Charles Abbott	"	23,	"	"	23,	"	Mustered out with regiment.
2d Lieutenant	John W. LaRue	June	14,	1861	June	14,	1861	Resigned September 6, 1861.
Do.	Joshua H. Horton	"	14,	"	"	14,	"	Promoted December 26, 1861.
Do.	Jerome B. Weller	"	17,	"	"	17,	"	Promoted December 21, 1861.
Do.	C. J. Cottingham	"	18,	"	"	18,	"	Promoted December 26, 1861.
Do.	W. H. H. Gahagan	"	19,	"	"	19,	"	Promoted October 28, 1861.
Do.	Henry M. Wilson	July	7,	"	Oct.	23,	"	Resigned November 8, 1861.
Do.	Geo. Johnson	"	7,	"	"	23,	"	Promoted January 9, 1862.
Do.	Andrew H. Chapman	"	23,	"	July	29,	"	Promoted April 10, 1862.
Do.	D. K. Curtiss	Sept.	2,	"	Sept.	21,	"	Promoted May 1, 1862.
Do.	James M. Elliott	Dec.	19,	"	Jan.	2,	"	Resigned June 3, 1862.
Do.	Joseph P. Staley	"	26,	"	Dec.	26,	"	Resigned June 19, 1862.
Do.	Smith Williams	"	26,	"	"	26,	"	Resigned April 10, 1862.
Do.	Wm. Crumbaugh	"	26,	"	"	26,	"	Promoted June 5, 1862, to 1st Lieutenant.
Do.	David M. Layman	"	26,	"	"	26,	"	Promoted April 18, 1862, to 1st Lieutenant.
Do.	E. C. Jordan	Jan.	9,	1862	Jan.	9,	1862	Promoted May 1, 1862, to 1st Lieutenant.
Do.	Robert C. Morris	"	9,	"	"	9,	"	Promoted June 16, 1862, to 1st Lieutenant.
Do.	P. A. Arthur	April	10,	"	May	1,	"	Promoted Sept. 17, 1862, to First Lieutenant.
Do.	Chas. J. McClure	"	18,	"	June	3,	"	Promoted June 5, 1862, to First Lieutenant.
Do.	Wm. M. Culbertson	May	1,	"	"	3,	"	Dismissed November 19, 1862.
Do.	Charles P. Achuff	April	10,	"	"	3,	"	Promoted Sept. 17, 1862, to 1st Lieutenant.
Do.	Wm. K. Young	June	19,	"	"	24,	"	Promoted October 1, 1862, to 1st Lieutenant.
Do.	Samuel A. Collins	"	3,	"	"	24,	"	Honorably discharged September 15, 1863.
Do.	M. L. Edwards	May	1,	"	"	24,	"	Promoted Nov. 20, 1862, to 1st Lieutenant.
Do.	Thos. L. Stewart	Aug.	9,	"	Oct.	2,	"	Promoted to 1st Lieutenant.
Do.	Cyrenius Longley	Sept.	7,	"	"	3,	"	Promoted to 1st Lieutenant.
Do.	Alfred L. Conklin	June	16,	"	Nov.	10,	"	Dismissed November 24, 1863.
Do.	Jesse G. Buckingham	Nov.	29,	"	"	24,	"	Resigned May 25, 1863.
Do.	Thos. M. Mitchell	"	19,	"	Jan.	21,	1863	Died January 9, 1863.
Do.	John Roney	Oct.	1,	"	"	21,	"	Promoted to 1st Lieutenant.
Do.	Lucius H. Hollabird	June	5,	"	Feb.	10,	"	Promoted to 1st Lieutenant.
Do.	Joseph Pearson	Sept.	17,	"	"	10,	"	Mustered out June 21, 1864.
Do.	John C. Keifibar	Oct.	1,	"	"	10,	"	Promoted to 1st Lieutenant.
Do.	George S. Swain	Nov.	20,	"	"	10,	"	Promoted to 1st Lieutenant.
Do.	Louis Gibbs	April	29,	1863	Aug.	25,	"	Mustered out.
Do.	J. S. Morrison	May	22,	"	"	25,	"	Mustered out.
Do.	George S. Hardinbrook	"	5,	"	June	16,	"	Mustered out June 21, 1864.
Do.	John W. Green	March	17,	"	July	20,	"	Not mustered.
Do.	Francis M. Wilmington	April	18,	"	Aug.	25,	"	Not mustered.
Do.	Isaac McKenzie	June	7,	"	"	25,	"	Mustered out.
Do.	T. L. Winslow	"	25,	"	"	25,	"	Mustered out.
Do.	Mark Kirby	"	29,	"	Nov.	12,	1864	
Do.	David W. Maurice	"	29,	"	"	12,	"	Mustered out June 11, 1865.
Do.	Corbly Kinney	March	1,	1865	March	1,	1865	
Do.	Porter Livian	"	1,	"	"	1,	"	
Do.	John T. Selman	"	1,	"	"	1,	"	
Do.	John T. Hunt	"	1,	"	"	1,	"	

ELEVENTH OHIO VOLUNTEER INFANTRY.

THIS regiment was raised in the counties of Miami, Clinton, Hamilton, Montgomery, and Columbiana, and mustered into the service for three months, at Camp Dennison, in April, 1861. The regiment was reorganized and mustered into the service for three years on the 20th of June, 1861, and on the 7th of July was ordered to the Kanawha Valley.

It arrived at Point Pleasant on the 11th, and formed a part of the celebrated Kanawha Division, commanded by General J. D. Cox. On the 26th of July General Cox began his movement up the Kanawha, but on reaching the Pocotaligo River, it was found that the Rebels had burned the bridge. Captain Lane, of the Eleventh, with his company, composed principally of mechanics, rebuilt the bridge in less than twenty-four hours, with no tools but a few axes and two or three augers, and the army proceeded with but little delay. During the fall and early part of the winter the regiment remained in the vicinity of Gauley Bridge, never idle, but continually on a reconnoissance, a raid, or a scout, and was actively engaged at Cotton Hill and Sewell Mountain.

On the 1st of December, 1861, the regiment fell back from Gauley Bridge to Point Pleasant, and went into winter-quarters. While here nothing occurred to break the monotony of camp life. A regimental church was organized, which was kept up until the regiment was mustered out. Members were received either upon presenting a certificate of membership in some church at home, or upon profession of belief in God and the Holy Spirit, and of faith in Jesus Christ.

On the 16th of April, 1862, the regiment left Point Pleasant, and proceeded by way of Winfield to Gauley Bridge. In the campaign of the Kanawha, the regiment accompanied General Cox as far as Raleigh, where it was ordered to remain until further orders. Floyd, on his retreat from Cotton Mountain, had completely blockaded the road from Shady Springs to Pack's Ferry, at New River, a distance of sixteen miles. Two companies (G and K) of the Eleventh were detailed to open and guard the road. One-half of the men were under arms while the other half were at work with spades and axes; and, after great labor, on the evening of the fifth day they reached the ferry, having cleared the road and rendered it available for artillery and supply trains. In a short time two boats were built out of the timber in a barn near by, with the use of one auger and a few axes, and by joining the two boats, they formed a ferry-boat one hundred and forty feet long, and communication was thus opened between the two wings of the Kanawha army. In the latter part of July the regiment returned to Gauley Bridge, and company C was ordered to Summerville to re-enforce a detachment of the Ninth Virginia, stationed there, and remained until the regiment moved to Washington City.

On the 18th of August the Eleventh, with the greater portion of the Kanawha Division, moved to Parkersburg, and proceeded thence, by the Baltimore and Ohio Railroad, to Washington, District of Columbia, encamping near Alexandria. On the 27th of August the Eleventh Ohio, under General Scammon, was ordered to Manassas Junction, demonstrations being made in that direction by a Rebel force. Upon arriving at Fairfax Station it was found that the Rebels had taken possession of the fortifications at Manassas, and that Taylor's brigade of New Jersey troops was falling back. The regiment crossed Bull Run, formed in line near to the railroad, and checked a flanking movement of the enemy. Companies E and F, of the

Eleventh, were placed in a position guarding the approaches to the railroad and a ford, and the remainder of the regiment went into action. The National forces only numbered three thousand, and it was impossible to contend successfully against the combined forces of Ewell and Fitzhugh Lee; so that at three o'clock orders were given to fall back to Fairfax. The regiment acted as rear guard in the retreat, and its cool and determined bravery did much toward securing the safety of the whole column. At Fairfax the troops "formed square," the station building, in which the wounded were placed, being in the center.

After resting until half-past ten the columns were re-formed, cautiously and secretly, and by twelve o'clock on the 28th the Eleventh reached the vicinity of the defenses around Washington.

On the 29th of August the entire Kanawha Division moved to the front, and the Eleventh was posted at Fort Munson, on Munson's Hill. On the 6th of September the regiment moved toward Maryland, and on the 11th halted near Ridgeville, and the next day reached the Rebel picket-line in the vicinity of Frederick City. The Rebels were posted on the banks of the Monocacy, holding the bridge across the stream. Three attacking columns were formed, with the Eleventh in the advance of the center, and advanced against the Rebels. The center column gained the bridge and drove the enemy from it. A charge was ordered, but the line was thrown into some confusion, and the Rebels rallied and captured two pieces of artillery. General Cox called to Colonel Coleman: "Will the Eleventh recover those guns?" With a loud cheer the regiment dashed at the Rebels, drove them from the guns, and still pressed on cheering and charging, advancing into the city, and only halting when the enemy was completely routed. That night the Kanawha Division bivouacked near the city, and by the evening of the next day advanced to Catoctin Creek, near Middletown, the Eleventh being posted near the bridge.

Next morning the division crossed the creek and moved toward Turner's Gap, in South Mountain. After proceeding a short distance the division moved to the left and struck the old Sharpsburg road, and upon reaching a narrow gorge, concealed by timber and undergrowth, the Eleventh formed in line of battle. When the order came to charge, the Eleventh moved along the edge of a strip of woods, and by adroitness and bravery drove back a strong force of the Rebels attempting a flank movement. The regiment was exposed to a galling fire from sharpshooters, but not a man flinched. One old man, Nathan Whittaker, of company E, who had two sons in the regiment, exhibited wonderful bravery in standing a pace or two in advance, and coolly loading and firing as if at a target, while the enemy's bullets were falling like hail all around him. About noon there was a lull in the battle-storm, but about three o'clock the entire National line advanced, fighting desperately. The Eleventh was ordered to charge across an open field on the left of the road, against a force of the enemy protected by a stone wall. They met the enemy in almost a hand-to-hand fight; muskets were clubbed and bayonets crossed over the low stone wall, but finally the enemy was driven from their position into the undergrowth. The Rebels retreated toward Sharpsburg during the night, and at an early hour next morning the National army was in pursuit.

The night before the battle of Antietam the Kanawha Division, under General Crook, moved into position near the lower bridge, which crosses the Antietam on the Rorheback farm, the Eleventh being posted a little above the bridge on a rough, wooded slope. At ten o'clock A. M., on the 17th of September, an assault was ordered upon the bridge, but they were met with such a heavy fire from the bluffs opposite that they were compelled to retire. At this juncture an order was received from General McClellan to carry the bridge at all hazards. The Eleventh was to lead the storming party, and while advancing steadily and determinedly Colonel Coleman fell mortally wounded. The regiment wavered an instant and then pressed on, gained the bridge, crossed it, scaled the bluffs, and drove the Rebels from their position.

On the morning of the 8th of October the division commanded by General Crook moved to Hagerstown. The men suffered greatly from the heat and dust, and though accustomed to forced marches, this was one of the most severe the regiment ever endured. The troops moved on to the Potomac at Hancock, and there took the Baltimore and Ohio Railroad for Clarksburg. At

Clarksburg the regiment suffered greatly for the want of clothing. In addition to this they were without blankets and tents, and this, too, when they were among the mountains of Virginia, exposed to the storms of November. In this condition the division took up the line of march, and was distributed at different points along the Kanawha and Gauley Rivers, the Eleventh being assigned to Summerville, which was to be held as an outpost of the forces in the Kanawha Valley. Here the regiment erected comfortable winter-quarters, and rapidly recovered from the effects of its severe campaign. A small portion of the regiment was mounted and was employed in guarding the fords of the Gauley, while the remainder fortified the position at Summerville. During their stay here the Eleventh, forming a junction with the Second Virginia Cavalry at a designated point, engaged in a successful expedition into the Greenbrier country. While on the march the men were exposed to many hardships and suffered greatly from the inclemency of the weather, several being temporarily disabled by being frost-bitten.

On the 24th of January, 1863, the regiment marched for Loup Creek Landing, and there embarked on steamer T. J. Patton. On arriving at Gallipolis the fleet was increased to ten steamers, under command of General Crook, and proceeded to Nashville, Tennessee. On the 22d of February the entire division moved to Carthage, on the Tennessee River, occupied the heights north-east of the town and fortified the position. On the 24th of March the regiment went on a scout to Rome, and returned next day with a Captain, twenty-eight privates, a wagon-train and about seventy horses and mules, belonging to Forrest's cavalry, as the fruits of the expedition. On the 13th of April the Eleventh, with other regiments, under command of Colonel Lane, made a reconnoissance toward McMinnville, and met the enemy strongly posted with artillery and cavalry. After making a careful disposition of the force Colonel Lane sent a request for artillery. Meanwhile the Rebels had made several dashes at the line, but were repulsed. No artillery arrived; but General Spear was sent out by General Crook and ordered the troops back to Carthage. On the 23d of April the Eleventh and Eighty-Ninth Regiments marched, with three days' rations, to join General Reynolds, moving from Murfreesboro' against Wheeler and Forrest's cavalry. The enemy retired, and nothing was accomplished except the destruction of some supplies; after which both forces returned to their former stations. The regiment marched to Murfreesboro', arriving on the 27th of June, and was assigned to the Third Division (General Reynolds commanding), Fourteenth Army Corps (General Geo. H. Thomas commanding).

On the 24th of June Reynolds's division moved out the Manchester road and engaged the enemy at Hoover's Gap. The Eleventh was under arms all night, and after the enemy was driven back it pressed on and led the advance into Manchester, capturing a number of Rebels. The entire brigade bivouacked south-west of the town. On the morning of the 29th the brigade, with the Eleventh in the advance, moved on the Tullahoma road. The enemy was met about noon, but was soon driven back. The next day the march was continued, and on the 1st of July Crook's brigade entered Tullahoma. The regiment pursued the Rebels, and finally halted near Big Springs, and within two miles of Decherd Station, on the Nashville and Chattanooga Railroad. At this point General Crook was appointed to the command of a cavalry brigade, and General J. B. Turchin assumed command of the Second Brigade. On the 2d of August the brigade moved to University and on to Blue Springs and Jasper, and crossed the Tennessee River at Shell Mound on the 1st of September. The troops were soon again on the march, and on the 5th Reynolds's division took possession of Trenton. From here the regiment moved through Cooper's Gap into McLemore's Cove, and continued to gradually close in upon the Rebels. On the 17th the Rebels made an assault on the position held by the Eleventh at Catlett's Gap and were repulsed.

During the forenoon of the 18th the regiment, in common with other regiments, changed position several times in order to bewilder the enemy, and at night the whole corps moved, and soon after daylight went into line of battle near Gordon's Mill, the Eleventh forming on a wooded slope on the east of the Lafayette and Rossville road. Chaplain Lyle rode to the center of the line, and, with Colonel Lane's consent, addressed the regiment in words of comfort and encouragement, and asked the men to join with him in prayer. Instantly every head was uncovered and every hand clasped devoutly on the gleaming muskets. The old colors, pierced and rent on many battle-fields, were drooped, and amid the rattle of musketry the voice of prayer, a strange but glorious sound, was heard. General Reynolds, who was passing during the exercises, halted till their conclusion, and then, grasping the Chaplain cordially by the hand, expressed his delight at being present.

Immediately the regiment was moved to the support of some regiments already hotly engaged, and soon after it moved into the front line. The enemy's sharpshooters annoyed the regiment greatly, and at last the order to charge was given and the Rebels were driven back. In this charge Sergeant Peck, the color-bearer, was wounded, but his brother instantly seized the colors and led the line most gallantly. In the afternoon, when the enemy were pressing the right of Reynolds's division, Turchin's brigade changed front and charged the enemy, driving them back in disorder. The next day the Eleventh took position on a slight elevation behind a rude breastwork of logs and stones. The enemy's fire was so severe that in less than half an hour company D lost one-half of its men killed and wounded. The rude breastwork behind which the regiment sought protection several times caught fire, and at the third time in burned so rapidly that it was necessary to have it extinguished. Company B volunteered for the dangerous work and succeeded in putting out the fire effectually. In the afternoon the enemy succeeded in getting in the rear of Reynolds's division through a gap in the line of battle, and the Eleventh was exposed to a heavy cross-fire. Turchin's brigade was ordered to charge the enemy in the rear, which was done in gallant style. The Rebel ranks were broken and many prisoners and guns captured. In the night the troops withdrew to Rossville, and from there to Chattanooga. On the 24th the regiment formed part of a heavy reconnoitering force, and was engaged in a severe skirmish with the enemy, after which it withdrew and was posted within the line of rifle-pits to the left of Fort Negley.

Later in the month the regiment marched down the river, and co-operating at Brown's Ferry with a force that floated down in pontoons, gained a foothold on Lookout Mountain. On the 23d of November the regiment took position in front of Fort Negley, but next morning was placed in front of Fort Wood, and in the afternoon advanced on Mission Ridge. In the charge the regiment captured one battle-flag and a quantity of artillery and small arms. Sergeant Bull, who was carrying the colors of the Eleventh, was struck several times, but still pressed on until, struck the seventh time, he was unable to rise. Lieutenant Peck seized the colors, planted them on the Rebel ramparts, and almost instantly fell mortally wounded. The regiment pursued the enemy toward Ringgold, and after some severe fighting at Ringgold Gap, returned to Chattanooga. On the 17th of February, 1864, the regiment was paraded in full view of Lookout Mountain and Mission Ridge, and presented by Chaplain Lyle with a stand of colors in the name of the donors, the ladies of Troy, Ohio. The regiment was engaged in a reconnoissance toward Rocky Face Ridge, and advancing as far as Buzzard's Roost, the enemy was found in strong position. By some mistake the Eleventh was ordered to charge up a steep hill held by two brigades and several pieces of artillery. The regiment advanced bravely, but after heroic efforts was compelled to fall back with a loss of one-sixth of its men.

The troops fell back to Ringgold, and on the 26th of March the veterans of the regiment, numbering about two hundred, returned to Ohio for the purpose of recruiting, so that when the regiment should be mustered out the name and organization might still be continued. The regiment remained at Ringgold on garrison duty till the 10th of June, when it proceeded to Cincinnati, Ohio, where it received a hearty welcome.

The regiment was mustered out at Camp Dennison on the 21st of June, 1864.

Two companies, whose time had not yet expired, and the veterans of the regiment, were officially recognized as the Eleventh Ohio Detachment, and were assigned to Baird's division of the Fourteenth Corps. They accompanied Sherman in his wonderful campaign, and after the surrender of the Rebel armies were mustered out. They were commanded by Lieutenant-Colonel D. C. Stubbs, promoted from Sergeant-Major of the old organization.

12th REGIMENT OHIO VOLUNTEER INFANTRY.

ROSTER, THREE MONTHS' SERVICE.

RANK.	NAME.	DATE OF RANK.	COM. ISSUED.	REMARKS.
Colonel	JOHN W. LOWE	May 2, 1861	May 2, 1861	
Lt. Colonel	Jacob Ammen	" 2, "	" 2, "	
Major	Carr B. White	" 2, "	" 2, "	
Surgeon	Wm. W. Holmes	April 19, "	April 19, "	
Ass't Surgeon	C. H. Swain	May 2, "	May 2, "	
Captain	James D. Wallace	April 20, "	April 20, "	
Do.	Robert B. Harlan	" 19, "	" 19, "	
Do.	Watts McMurchy	" 26, "	" 26, "	
Do.	Robert Lytle	May 3, "	May 3, "	
Do.	Albert Galloway	April 22, "	April 23, "	
Do.	Rigdon Williams	" 19, "	" 19, "	
Do.	Joseph L. Hilt	" 21, "	" 24, "	
Do.	Edward M. Carey	May 4, "	May 4, "	
Do.	Wm. Hays	" 4, "	" 4, "	
Do.	James Sloan	April 20, "	April 20, "	
1st Lieutenant	Henry S. Clements	" 20, "	" 20, "	
Do.	Azariah W. Doane	" 19, "	" 19, "	
Do.	Thomas G. Wood	" 26, "	" 26, "	
Do.	Leigh McClung	May 3, "	May 3, "	
Do.	Andrew J. Thorp	April 22, "	April 22, "	
Do.	Daniel W. Pauley	May 14, "	May 14, "	
Do.	Joel H. Deardorf	April 24, "	April 24, "	
Do.	Richard C. Rankin	May 14, "	May 14, "	Resigned July 25, 1861.
Do.	Thomas T. Taylor	" 4, "	" 4, "	
Do.	Benjamin R. A. Jones	April 20, "	April 20, "	
Do.	Jonathan D. Hines	May 2, "	May 2, "	
Do.	Andrew J. Roosa	" 2, "	" 2, "	
2d Lieutenant	John W. Bowser	April 20, "	April 20, "	
Do.	Isaac B. Allen	" 14, "	" 14, "	
Do.	Tirman C. Warren	" 26, "	" 26, "	
Do.	Moses W. Trader	" 19, "	" 19, "	
Do.	Wm. H. Hivling	" 22, "	" 22, "	
Do.	J. Whitcomb Ross	" 19, "	" 19, "	
Do.	Robert Wilson	" 21, "	" 24, "	
Do.	Alexander M. Ridgway	" 4, "	" 4, "	
Do.	Chas F. King	" 4, "	" 4, "	
Do.	Wm. P. Cowne	" 20, "	" 20, "	

ROSTER, THREE YEARS' SERVICE.

RANK.	NAME.	DATE OF RANK.	COM. ISSUED.	REMARKS.
Colonel	JOHN W. LOWE	June 28, 1861	Aug. 31, 1861	Killed at Carnifex Ferry
Do.	CARR B. WHITE	Sept. 10, "	Oct. 1, "	Mustered out July 11, 1864.
Lt. Colonel	Carr B. White	June 28, "	Aug. 31, "	Promoted to Colonel September 10, 1861.
Do.	Jonathan D. Hines	Sept. 10, "	Oct. 1, "	Mustered out July 11, 1864.
Major	Jonathan D. Hines	June 28, "	Aug. 31, "	Promoted to Lieutenant-Colonel Sept. 10, '61.
Do.	James D. Wallace	Sept. 10, "	Oct. 1, "	Resigned April 18, 1862.
Do.	Edward M. Carey	April 14, 1862	June 3, 1862	Dismissed March 7, 1864.
Do.	Rigdon Williams	March 15, 1864	March 15, 1864	Mustered out Feb. 7, 1865.
Surgeon	Wm. W. Holmes			Resigned April 25, 1862.
Do.	Wm. T. Ridenour	May 1, 1862	May 1, 1862	Resigned December 28, 1862.
Do.	N. F. Graham	Dec. 28, "	Feb. 23, 1863	Mustered out July 11, 1864.
Ass't Surgeon	Wm. T. Ridenour	Nov. 9, 1861	Nov. 12, 1861	Promoted to Surgeon May 1, 1862.
Do.	James D. Webb	May 1, 1862	May 1, 1862	Resigned December 8, 1862.
Do.	N. F. Graham	July 13, "	July 23, "	Promoted to Surgeon.
Do.	Horace P. Kay	Jan. 2, 1863	Jan. 2, 1863	Mustered out.
Do.	Silas T. Buck	May 6, "	May 6, "	Mustered out.
Chaplain	Russell D. Van Dusen	Aug. 10, 1861	Dec. 16, 1861	Resigned July 25, 1862.
Do.	Charles L. Allen	July 25, 1862	May 6, 1863	Mustered out.
Captain	James D. Wallace	May 30, 1861	Aug. 31, 1861	Promoted to Major.
Do.	Edward M. Carey	June 4, "	" 31, "	Promoted to Major April 18, 1862.
Do.	James Sloane	" 6, "	" 31, "	Resigned November 21, 1861.
Do.	Wm. B. Smith	" 7, "	" 31, "	Cashiered December 9, 1863.
Do.	Rigdon Williams	" 11, "	" 31, "	Promoted to Major.
Do.	Joseph L. Hilt	" 11, "	" 31, "	Detached at Cumberland, Md., by order of Gen. Sigel, Aug. 30, '62.
Do.	Azariah W. Doane	" 18, "	" 31, "	Resigned October 24, 1861.
Do.	Watts McMurchy	" 18, "	" 31, "	Resigned March 31, 1862.
Do.	Andrew Legg	" 22, "	" 31, "	Resigned June 20, 1862.
Do.	Ferdinand Gunckle	" 28, "	" 31, "	Resigned March 20, 1862.
Do.	Henry S. Clement	Sept. 10, "	Oct. 1, "	Mustered out; appointed Major 79th O. V. I.
Do.	John Curtis	Nov. 9, "	Nov. 9, "	Resigned June 18, 1862.
Do.	Ezra Stevenson	Jan. 9, 1862	Jan. 9, 1862	Resigned June 20, 1862.
Do.	Wm. W. Liggett	March 31, "	April 21, "	Deceased September 21, 1862.
Do.	Daniel W. Pauley	April 18, "	June 3, "	Resigned October 1, 1862.
Do.	Wm. E. Fisher	June 18, "	July 16, "	Resigned October 3, 1862.
Do.	Henry F. Hawkes	" 20, "	" 16, "	Promoted by President.

RANK.	NAME.	DATE OF RANK.	COM. ISSUED.	REMARKS.
Captain	Jonathan C. Wallace	March 20, 1862	July 16, 1862	Declined.
Do.	John Lewis	" 20, "	" 16, "	Resigned December 2, 1862.
Do.	Robert Wilson	" 20, "	Nov. 12, "	Mustered out July 11, 1864.
Do.	Aaron N. Channell	Aug. 30, "	" 12, "	Killed May 9, 1864.
Do.	James W. Ross	Sept. 21, "	" 12, "	Mustered out July 11, 1864.
Do.	Horatio G. Tibballs	Oct. 1, "	Dec. 30, "	Mustered out July 11, 1864.
Do.	Jacob A. Yordy	" 3, "	" 30, "	Mustered out July 11, 1864.
Do.	Jonathan Wallace	Dec. 2, "	" 30, "	Mustered out July 11, 1864.
Do.	Hiram McKay	Nov. 21, "	March 14, 1863	Mustered out July 11, 1864.
Do.	Ashley Brown	Dec. 9, "	Jan. 22, 1864	Mustered out July 11, 1864.
1st Lieutenant	Henry S. Clement	May 30, 1861	Aug. 31, 1861	Promoted to Captain September 10, 1861.
Do.	Wm. W. Liggett	June 4, "	" 31, "	Promoted to Captain March 31, 1862.
Do.	Wm. P. Coune	" 6, "	" 31, "	Resigned October 24, 1861.
Do.	George W. Goode	" 7, "	" 31, "	Died September 25, 1861.
Do.	Daniel W. Pauley	" 11, "	" 31, "	Promoted to Captain April 18, 1862.
Do.	Robert Wilson	" 11, "	" 31, "	Promoted to Captain June 20, 1862.
Do.	Wm. Hivling	" 18, "	" 31, "	Resigned October 9, 1861.
Do.	Alex. M. Ridgway	" 18, "	" 31, "	Resigned March 31, 1862.
Do.	Jonathan C. Wallace	" 22, "	" 31, "	Promoted to Captain December 2, 1862.
Do.	Ashley Brown	" 28, "	" 31, "	Promoted to Captain December 2, 1862.
Do.	Andrew J. Roosa	" 28, "	" 31, "	Resigned October 15, 1861.
Do.	W. H. Roberts	July 2, "	July 2, "	Resigned August 21, 1861.
Do.	Wm. E. Fisher	Sept. 10, "	Oct. 1, "	Promoted to Captain June 18, 1862.
Do.	Henry F. Hawkes	" 26, "	Sept. 26, "	Promoted to Captain June 20, 1862.
Do.	John Lewis	Oct. 3, "	Oct. 23, "	Promoted to Captain June 20, 1862.
Do.	John Wise	Nov. 8, "	Nov. 8, "	Resigned September 30, 1862.
Do.	Aaron N. Channell	Dec. 6, "	Dec. 6, "	Promoted to Captain August 30, 1862.
Do.	Calvin Goddard	Jan. 9, 1862	Jan. 9, 1862	Resigned November 24, 1862.
Do.	James W. Ross	March 31, "	April 21, "	Promoted to Captain September 21, 1862.
Do.	Jacob A. Yordy	" 31, "	" 21, "	Promoted to Captain October 3, 1862.
Do.	Horatio G. Tibballs	April 18, "	June 3, "	Promoted to Captain October 1, 1862.
Do.	Robert H. Shoemaker	June 18, "	July 16, "	Canceled.
Do.	Hiram McKay	" 18, "	" 16, "	Promoted to Captain.
Do.	John C. Campbell	" 20, "	" 16, "	Resigned December 26, 1862.
Do.	John V. O'Connor	" 20, "	" 16, "	Mustered out July 11, 1864.
Do.	Michael B. Mahony	Nov. 24, "	Feb. 2, 1863	Dismissed August 12, 1863.
Do.	Wm. H. Glotfelter	Sept. 30, "	Nov. 12, 1862	Mustered out July 11, 1864.
Do.	John W. Hiltz	June 20, "	" 12, "	Transferred to 23d O. V. I. as Captain.
Do.	Thomas J. Atkinson	Aug. 30, "	" 12, "	Mustered out July 11, 1864.
Do.	Wm. B. Nesbitt	Sept. 21, "	" 12, "	Mustered out July 11, 1864.
Do.	Wm. A. Ludlum	Oct. 1, "	Dec. 30, "	Mustered out July 11, 1864.
Do.	Frank M. Slade	" 3, "	" 30, "	Mustered out July 11, 1864.
Do.	Thomas F. Hill	Dec. 2, "	" 30, "	Mustered out July 11, 1864.
Do.	John Lewis	June 11, "	June 15, "	Revoked.
Do.	Harrison G. Otis	March 21, 1863	May 25, 1863	Transferred to 23d O. V. I. as Captain.
Do.	Abraham King	Aug. 12, "	Jan. 10, 1864	Mustered out March 12, 1865.
2d Lieutenant	Wm. E. Fisher	May 30, 1861	Aug. 31, 1861	Promoted to 1st Lieutenant Sept. 10, 1861.
Do.	John Curtis	June 4, "	" 31, "	Promoted to Captain.
Do.	Ezra Stevenson	" 6, "	" 31, "	Promoted to 1st Lieutenant.
Do.	Moses W. Trader	" 7, "	" 31, "	Cashiered March 20, 1862.
Do.	James W. Ross	" 11, "	" 31, "	Promoted to 1st Lieutenant March 31, 1862.
Do.	Jacob A. Yordy	" 11, "	" 31, "	Promoted to 1st Lieutenant March 31, 1862.
Do.	Wm. H. Miller	" 18, "	" 31, "	Died from wounds rec'd at Peter's Creek, Va.
Do.	Alonzo M. Dimmitt	" 18, "	" 31, "	Resigned April 18, 1862.
Do.	Aaron N. Channell	" 22, "	" 31, "	Promoted to 1st Lieutenant Dec. 6, 1861.
Do.	Horatio G. Tibballs	" 28, "	" 31, "	Promoted to 1st Lieutenant April 18, 1862.
Do.	Robert H. Shoemaker	Oct. 1, "	Oct. 1, "	Promoted to 1st Lieut. June 10, '62; r'd Jy 17, '62
Do.	Hiram McKay	Nov. 9, "	Nov. 9, "	Promoted to 1st Lieutenant March 20, 1862.
Do.	John C. Campbell	Dec. 13, "	Dec. 13, "	Promoted to 1st Lieutenant June 20, 1862.
Do.	John V. O'Connor	Jan. 9, 1862	Jan. 9, 1862	Promoted to 1st Lieutenant June 20, 1862.
Do.	John W. Hiltz	" 9, "	" 9, "	Promoted to 1st Lieutenant June 20, 1862.
Do.	Frederick B. Schnebly	" 9, "	" 9, "	Resigned September 30, 1862.
Do.	Thomas J. Atkinson	March 31, "	May 5, "	Promoted to 1st Lieutenant August 30, 1862.
Do.	Edwin M. Jacoby	" 31, "	" 5, "	Resigned October 3, 1862.
Do.	Wm. H. Glotfelter	April 18, "	June 5, "	Promoted to 1st Lieutenant September 30, '62.
Do.	Wm. B. Nesbitt	" 18, "	July 16, "	Promoted to 1st Lieutenant September 21, '62.
Do.	Wm. A. Ludlum	June 18, "	" 16, "	Promoted to 1st Lieutenant October 1, 1862.
Do.	Andrew C. Miller	" 20, "	" 16, "	Resigned December 9, 1862.
Do.	Wm. Sine	" 20, "	" 16, "	Resigned October 3, 1862.
Do.	Thomas F. Hill	" 20, "	Oct. 13, "	Promoted to 1st Lieutenant December 2, 1862.
Do.	Frank M. Slade	Sept. 21, "	Nov. 12, "	Promoted to 1st Lieutenant October 3, 1862.
Do.	Michael B. Mahony	Oct. 3, "	" 12, "	Promoted to 1st Lieutenant November 24, 1862.
Do.	Harrison G. Otis	Sept. 30, "	" 12, "	Promoted to 1st Lieutenant.
Do.	James H. Palmer	Oct. 3, "	" 12, "	Wounded and prisoner.
Do.	John White	Sept. 30, "	" 12, "	Mustered out July 11, 1864.
Do.	Maurice Watkins	June 20, "	" 25, "	Transferred to 23d O. V. I. as 1st Lieutenant.
Do.	Henry L. Sherwood	Aug. 30, "	Dec. 19, "	Mustered out July 11, 1864.
Do.	Robert B. Wilson	Dec. 9, "	" 29, "	Mustered out July 11, 1864.
Do.	Jonathan H. McMillan	Oct. 1, "	" 21, "	Transferred to 23d O. V. I. as 1st Lieutenant.
Do.	Abraham King	Dec. 2, "	Jan. 12, 1863	Promoted to 1st Lieutenant.
Do.	John M. Busby	Oct. 3, "	" 20, "	Resigned.
Do.	Fenton L. Torrence	Jan. 6, 1863	Feb. 27, "	Killed June 19, 1864.
Do.	Edward R. Grim	Aug. 1, "	May 19, "	Mustered out July 11, 1864.

TWELFTH OHIO VOLUNTEER INFANTRY.

UNDER the call for seventy-five thousand three-months, troops the Twelfth Ohio Infantry was organized at Camp Jackson, Ohio, on the 3d of May, 1861. It moved to Camp Dennison May 6th, and there re-enlisted, was reorganized and mustered into the service for three years on the 28th of June, 1861.

The Twelfth left Camp Dennison for the Kanawha Valley July 6th; arrived at Point Pleasant on the 9th, and on the 14th reached Pocotaligo River. On the 17th of July the regiment fought the battle of Scary Creek, the enemy being strongly posted beyond a ravine. The regiment fought three hours; and after exhausting its ammunition fell back in good order to its camp at the mouth of the Pocotaligo, with a loss of five killed, thirty wounded, and four missing. The regiment entered Charleston, West Virginia, on the 25th, and reached Gauley Bridge on the 29th, where it captured a large quantity of arms and ammunition. Eight companies marched down the Kanawha to Camp Piatt August 13, and from there moved to Clarksburg, West Virginia, and were assigned to General Benham's brigade. Marching south through Weston, Sutton and Summerville, they arrived at Carnifex Ferry September 10th, and engaged in the battle at that place with a loss of two killed and ten wounded. Two days after this they were engaged in a slight skirmish on the Gauley with guerrillas; then marched to Camp Lookout, and from there, on October 10th, moved to Hawk's Nest on New River. In the meantime the two companies left at Gauley Bridge surprised and routed two hundred Rebel cavalry under Jenkins, on the 25th of August. They were engaged in several skirmishes and reconnoissances, and finally joined the other eight companies at Hawk's Nest on the 16th of October. On the 1st of November the Twelfth marched to the mouth of Loop Creek and attempted to flank Floyd, who was threatening Gauley. It soon after engaged in the pursuit of Floyd's forces, and having followed him until near Raleigh, C. H., gave up the chase and returned to Loop Creek. The regiment was transferred to General Cox's brigade December 10th, and moved to Charleston and went into winter-quarters.

On the 3d of May, 1862, the regiment left Charleston and joined Scammon's brigade at the mouth of East River. It skirmished at the narrows of New River, and fell back to Princeton, then to Blue Stone River, and then to the summit of Flat Top Mountain and fortified. From the 20th of May until the 14th of August the regiment scouted the country in every direction, made some heavy marches in the mountains and captured many "bushwhackers." It was ordered to the Army of the Potomac August 15th, and arrived at Alexandria on the 24th.

It met the enemy at Bull Run Bridge August 27th; was severely engaged for six hours against a greatly superior force, and was compelled to fall back to Fairfax Station with a loss of nine killed, sixty-eight wounded, (six mortally) and twelve missing. The regiment returned to Alexandria, rejoined Cox's brigade and marched to Upton Hill. On the 7th of September it advanced into Maryland, and after a sharp skirmish at Monocacy Bridge on the 12th entered Frederick City. On the 14th of September it engaged in the battle of South Mountain, participating in three bayonet charges and capturing three battle flags, a large number of small arms, and over two hundred prisoners, with a loss of sixteen killed, ninety-one wounded, and eight missing. On the 17th the regiment was engaged at Antietam and lost six killed and twenty-nine wounded. After the battle it marched for West Virginia, *via* Hagerstown and Hancock, Maryland; but, on arriving at Hancock, it moved into Pennsylvania to operate against Stuart's cavalry. Stuart having retreated, the Twelfth returned to Hancock, and arrived at Clarksburg, Western Virginia, October 16th. The regiment marched from Clarksburg October 25th, in Crook's division, through Weston, Sutton, and Summerville, endeavoring to gain the rear of the Rebel forces in the Kanawha Valley, and arrived at Gauley Bridge November 14th, the Rebels having retreated before the division arrived.

On the 4th of December the regiment marched to Fayette C. H., West Virginia, and went into winter-quarters. Here it was assigned to the Second Brigade, Third Division, Eighth Army Corps. The brigade under Colonel White repulsed the enemy's attack on Fayette C. H., May 19th, 1863, the regiment losing two killed, nine wounded, and eight missing. It pursued the retreating Rebels to Raleigh C. H., and returned to Fayette C. H. On July 13th the Twelfth marched against the enemy at Piney Creek, but the Rebels retreated and the regiment returned to Fayette C. H. On the 17th the brigade was ordered to Ohio to assist in capturing John Morgan, and after proceeding up the Ohio as far as Blennerhassett's Island and guarding fords for several days, it returned to Fayette C. H. During the months of August and September the regiment was employed in constructing fortifications. On the 4th of November it marched against Lewisburg, but the enemy fled and it again returned to Fayette C. H. On the 9th of December it made another move on Lewisburg as a diversion for General Averill. Bushwhackers were very troublesome on this march, and the regiment lost two killed, two slightly, and two mortally wounded, and two missing. The Twelfth went into winter-quarters at Fayette C. H., and was engaged in holding outposts and in watching the enemy.

On the 3d of May, 1864, the regiment left Fayette C. H., marched to Cloyd's Mountain and there engaged the enemy on the 9th. The fight lasted over an hour, and the regiment lost eleven killed and sixty-eight wounded, in addition to these Surgeon Graham and nineteen men, left on the field in charge of the wounded, fell into the enemy's hands. The Twelfth pursued the fleeing Rebels to New River Bridge, where a heavy artillery fight ensued, in which the enemy was driven back. The regiment crossed New River at Pepper's Ferry, destroyed a number of bridges and a large amount of property belonging to the Virginia and Tennessee Railroad. The Twelfth marched northward, and on the 19th reached Blue Sulphur Springs where it remained until the 31st, when it moved on Staunton. Arriving at Staunton June 8th, it joined the forces under Hunter, marched southward, flanked Lexington, and on the 12th assisted in destroying large quantities of ammunition and in burning the Virginia Military Institute. On the 16th it destroyed the railroad between Liberty and Lynchburg and burned several large bridges. The next day it moved on Lynchburg, and met the enemy in force at Quaker Church, three miles from the city. The Twelfth and Ninety-First Ohio regiments charged the enemy in fine style and drove them back in disorder. The regiment captured a number of prisoners, and lost eight killed and eleven wounded. The next day the regiment was engaged before the enemy's works but withdrew after dark, and on the 19th marched to Liberty. It moved along the Virginia and Tennessee Railroad to Salem, and from there proceeded northward, *via* Catawba Valley, New Castle, Sweet Springs, White Sulphur, Lewisburg and Gauley to Camp Piatt, on the Kanawha, where it arrived June 29th. On this march both men and horses suffered considerably from hunger and thirst.

The regiment was ordered to Columbus, Ohio, July 2d, and was mustered out of the service at that city on the 11th of July, 1864.

During its term of service the regiment moved on foot, by rail and by water, a distance of four thousand and forty-nine miles, and sustained a loss in killed, wounded and missing, of four hundred and fifty-five men.

13th REGIMENT OHIO VOLUNTEER INFANTRY.

ROSTER, THREE MONTHS' SERVICE.

RANK.	NAME.	DATE OF RANK.	COM. ISSUED.	REMARKS.
Colonel	A. SAUNDERS PIATT	April 30, 1861	April 30, 1861	
Lt. Colonel	COLUMBUS B. MASON	" 30, "	" 30, "	
Major	JOSEPH S. HAWKINS	" 30, "	" 30, "	
Captain	Samuel W. Ashmead	" 16, "	" 16, "	
Do.	Francis S. Parker	May 1, "	May 1, "	
Do.	Don. Piatt	April 30, "	April 30, "	
Do.	Benj. P. Runkle	" 19, "	" 19, "	
Do.	Albert F. Beach	" 19, "	" 19, "	
Do.	Jeremiah Slocum	" 29, "	" 29, "	
Do.	Wm. Schneider	" 20, "	" 20, "	
Do.	James McGarr	" 22, "	" 22, "	
Do.	John Castell	" 27, "	" 27, "	
Do.	John A. Corwin	" 20, "	" 20, "	
1st Lieutenant	Isaac R. Gardiner	April 16, 1861	" 16, "	
Do.	Nelson L. Lutz	May 1, "	May 1, "	Resigned June 24, 1861.
Do.	Thos. R. Roberts	April 30, "	April 30, "	
Do.	Elkanan M. Mast	" 19, "	" 19, "	
Do.	Dwight Jarvis, jr.	" 19, "	" 19, "	
Do.	Marcenos C. Lawrence	" 29, "	" 29, "	
Do.	Nicholas Reiter	" 20, "	" 20, "	
Do.	Wm. R. Wallace	" 22, "	" 22, "	
Do.	John Conwell	" 27, "	" 27, "	
Do.	Daniel G. Coleman	" 20, "	" 20, "	
Do.	Reason A. Henderson	" 30, "	" 30, "	
Do.	James A. Leazure	" 30, "	" 30, "	

ROSTER, THREE YEARS' SERVICE.

RANK.	NAME.	DATE OF RANK.	COM. ISSUED.	REMARKS.
Colonel	WM. S. SMITH	June 22, 1861	June 22, 1861	Appointed Brig. Gen. of Vols. May 13, 1862.
Do.	JOSEPH G. HAWKINS	May 13, 1862	July 9, 1862	Killed at Stone River December 31, 1862.
Do.	DWIGHT JARVIS, JR.	Jan. 1, 1863	Jan. 26, 1863	Mustered out.
Lt. Colonel	COLUMBUS B. MASON	June 22, 1861	June 22, 1861	Resigned.
Do.	JOSEPH G. HAWKINS	Oct. 25, "	Oct. 25, "	Promoted to Colonel May 13, 1862.
Do.	BENJ. P. RUNKLE	May 13, 1862	July 9, 1862	Appointed Colonel 45th O. V. I. Aug. 14, 1862.
Do.	WM. SCHNEIDER	Aug. 11, "	Oct. 4, "	Resigned December 24, 1862.
Do.	DWIGHT JARVIS, JR.	Dec. 24, "	Jan. 17, 1863	Promoted to Colonel January 1, 1863.
Do.	ELKANAN M. MAST	Jan. 1, 1863	" 26, "	Killed September 19, 1863.
Major	JOSEPH G. HAWKINS	June 22, 1861	June 22, 1861	Promoted to Lieutenant-Colonel Oct. 25, 1861.
Do.	BENJ. P. RUNKLE	Oct. 25, "	Nov. 1, "	Promoted to Lieutenant-Colonel May 13, 1862.
Do.	THOMAS R. ROBERTS	May 13, 1862	July 9, 1862	Canceled.
Do.	DWIGHT JARVIS, JR.	Aug. 14, "	Oct. 4, "	Promoted to Lieutenant-Colonel Dec. 24, 1862.
Do.	ELKANAN M. MAST	Dec. 24, "	Jan. 17, 1863	Promoted to Lieutenant-Colonel Jan. 1, 1862.
Do.	JOSEPH T. SNYDER	Jan. 1, "	" 26, "	
Surgeon	SAMUEL D. TURNEY	June 26, "	" 11, 1862	Appointed Surgeon of Volunteers April 1, 1863.
Do.	ALLEN JONES	May 18, "	May 19, 1863	Mustered out.
Ass't Surgeon	E. Y. CHASE	Aug. 28, 1861	Aug. 26, 1861	Resigned September 17, 1862.
Do.	J. W. SMITH	Sept. 17, 1862	Feb. 10, 1863	Resigned April 1, 1863.
Do.	JAMES MCCREADY	Jan. 7, 1863	Jan. 7, "	Mustered out.
Do.	JOHN K. MOORE	June 15, "	June 15, "	Mustered out.
Do.	S. M. SEEDS	May 2, 1865	May 2, 1865	Mustered out.
Chaplain	ANTHONY W. SMITH	July 8, 1861	Aug. 26, 1861	Resigned March 30, 1862.
Do.	THOMAS B. VAN HORN	" 10, 1862	July 10, 1862	Mustered out.
Captain	A. F. Beach	May 29, 1861	May 29, 1861	Resigned March 12, 1862.
Do.	Francis S. Parker	" 24, "	" 29, "	Resigned January 30, 1862.
Do.	Benj. P. Runkle	June 1, "	June 1, "	Promoted to Major October 25, 1861.
Do.	Jeremiah Slocum	" 5, "	" 5, "	Resigned December 9, 1861.
Do.	Horatio S. Cosgrove	" 6, "	" 6, "	Mustered out.
Do.	Wm. Schneider	" 7, "	" 7, "	Promoted to Major August 14, 1862.
Do.	James McGarr	" 10, "	" 10, "	Resigned September 15, 1861.
Do.	Isaac R. Gardner	" 12, "	" 12, "	Died May 31, 1862.
Do.	John Castell	" 13, "	" 13, "	Resigned February 3, 1862.
Do.	Thomas R. Roberts	" 21, "	" 21, "	Promoted to Major May 13, '62; re'd J'y 30, '62.
Do.	Dwight Jarvis, jr.	Oct. 25, "	Oct. 25, "	Promoted to Major August 14, 1862.
Do.	Elkanan M. Mast	Nov. 8, "	Nov. 8, "	Promoted to Major December 24, 1862.
Do.	James D. Smith	Jan. 9, 1862	Jan. 9, 1862	Resigned November 28, 1862.
Do.	James B. Douy	Feb. 5, "	Feb. 5, "	Resigned July 28, 1862.
Do.	Ranson R. Henderson	" 19, "	" 19, "	Mustered out September 10, 1862.
Do.	Joseph T. Snider	March 12, "	March 20, "	Promoted to Major June 1, 1863.
Do.	James O. Stonage	" 20, "	May 1, "	Revoked; no vacancy.
Do.	James O. Stonage	May 13, "	July 9, "	Appointed Captain and C. S.
Do.	John Seibert	" 31, "	Oct. 4, "	Mustered out.
Do.	Thos. L. Carnahan	July 28, "	" 4, "	Honorably discharged February 12, 1864.
Do.	Jepthia H. Powell	Aug. 14, "	" 4, "	Resigned.
Do.	Thomas J. Loudon	" 14, "	" 4, "	Drowned, in 1863.
Do.	Frank J. Jones	Jan. 1, 1863	Feb. 11, 1863	Promoted by President May 6, 1863.
Do.	John Murphy	Dec. 25, 1862	" 11, "	Died January 10, 1863.
Do.	Samuel C. Gold	Jan. 1, "	April 9, "	Honorably discharged September 3, 1863.
Do.	Thomas F. Murdock	" 1, "	May 18, "	Killed September 19, 1863.
Do.	John E. Ray	" 10, "	" 18, "	Resigned September 10, 1864.
Do.	Samuel W. McCulloch	May 6, "	" 25, "	Died of wounds May 28, 1864.

RANK.	NAME.	DATE OF RANK.		COM. ISSUED.		REMARKS.
Captain	Thomas B. George	Sept.	30, 1861	Sept.	30, 1864	Resigned September 29, 1864, as 1st Lieut.
Do.	Wm. B. Lambert	"	30, "	"	30, "	Mustered out August 25, 1865.
Do.	Robert K. Seig	"	30, "	"	30, "	Honorably discharged January 26, 1865.
Do.	James Thompson	"	30, "	"	30, "	Mustered out with regiment.
Do.	James H. Scott	Nov.	3, "	Nov.	3, "	Mustered out with regiment.
Do.	John P. Millet	Feb.	10, 1865	Feb.	10, 1865	Resigned May 17, 1865.
Do.	James H. Merrill	May	31, "	May	31, "	Dismissed August 15, 1865.
Do.	Erastus C. Hawkins	Oct.	25, "	Oct.	25, "	Mustered out with regiment.
1st Lieutenant	Dwight Jarvis, jr.	May	29, 1861	May	29, 1861	Promoted to Captain October 25, 1861.
Do.	James B. Dony	"	29, "	"	29, "	Promoted to Captain February 5, 1862.
Do.	Elkanan M. Mast	June	1, "	June	1, "	Promoted to Captain November 8, 1861.
Do.	James D. Smith	"	5, "	"	5, "	Promoted to Captain January 9, 1862.
Do.	George H. Guild	"	6, "	"	6, "	Resigned January 13, 1862.
Do.	Joseph T. Snyder	"	10, "	"	10, "	Promoted to Captain March 12, 1862.
Do.	James D. Stover	"	12, "	"	12, "	Resigned January 3, 1862.
Do.	John Conwell	"	13, "	"	13, "	Resigned October 15, 1861.
Do.	James O. Stonage	"	21, "	"	21, "	Promoted to Captain May 13, 1862.
Do.	John Seibert	"	22, "	"	22, "	Promoted to Captain May 31, 1862.
Do.	Reason R. Henderson	Aug.	1, "	Aug.	29, "	Promoted to Captain February 19, 1862.
Do.	John A. Hunter	Oct.	26, "	Oct.	26, "	Declined.
Do.	L. A. Laizure					Died October 18, 1861.
Do.	Jepthia H. Powell	Nov.	8, "	Nov.	8, "	Promoted to Captain August 14, 1862.
Do.	Thomas J. London	"	8, "	"	8, "	Promoted to Captain August 14, 1862.
Do.	Thomas L. Carnahan	"	9, "	"	9, "	Promoted to Captain July 28, 1862.
Do.	John Murphy	Jan.	9, 1862	Jan.	9, 1862	Died January 8, 1863.
Do.	John Conwell	"	9, "	"	9, "	Honorably discharged September 11, 1862.
Do.	Frank J. Jones	"	21, "	"	21, "	Promoted to Captain January 1, 1863.
Do.	David P. Doherty	Feb.	5, "	Feb.	5, "	Resigned March 15, 1862.
Do.	James W. McConnell	"	19, "	"	19, "	Resigned March 15, 1862.
Do.	Wm. Rains	March	12, "	March	20, "	Resigned May 10, 1862.
Do.	Thomas F. Murdock	"	15, "	April	10, "	Promoted January 1, 1863.
Do.	George H. Guild	"	15, "	"	10, "	Dismissed March 1, 1863.
Do.	Thomas B. George	"	30, "	May	1, "	Revoked.
Do.	Rudolph De Steigner	May	14, "	"	14, "	Resigned December 8, 1862.
Do.	Nathan W. Daniels	"	10, "	"	22, "	Mustered out July 13, 1862.
Do.	Thomas B. George	"	13, "	July	9, "	Promoted to Captain.
Do.	Samuel S. Gold	"	31, "	Oct.	4, "	Promoted to Captain January 1, 1862.
Do.	John E. Ray	July	28, "	"	4, "	Promoted to Captain
Do.	Cyrus S. Bates	Aug.	14, "	Dec.	30, "	Resigned January 19, 1864.
Do.	Charles Lindenberg	"	14, "	"	30, "	Mustered out.
Do.	Wm. B. Lambert.	Dec.	8, "	"	30, "	Promoted to Captain
Do.	S. W. McCulloch	July	13, "	"	30, "	Promoted to Captain.
Do.	Robert K. Seig	Sept.	11, "	"	30, "	Promoted to Captain.
Do.	Thomas J. Stone	Jan.	1, 1863	April	9, 1863	Honorably discharged November 7, 1863.
Do.	Joseph Coe	"	1, "	May	18, "	Resigned February 8, 1864.
Do.	Samuel C. Bosler	March	1, "	"	18, "	Mustered out.
Do.	Frank Bryer	Jan.	1, "	"	18, "	Resigned April 15, 1864.
Do.	Samuel E. Henderson	"	1, "	"	18, "	Mustered out.
Do.	Andrew Smith	"	10, "	"	18, "	Mustered out.
Do.	Richard B. Crawford	July	1, "	Sept.	3, "	Mustered out.
Do.	James H. Scott	Sept.	30, 1864	"	30, 1864	Promoted to Captain.
Do.	John P. Millet	"	30, "	"	30, "	Promoted to Captain.
Do.	James H. Merrill	"	30, "	"	30, "	Promoted to Captain.
Do.	Erastus C. Hawkins	"	30, "	"	30, "	Promoted to Captain.
Do.	James C. Armstrong	Feb.	10, 1865	Feb.	10, 1865	Promoted to Captain.
Do.	Henry S. Leister	"	10, "	"	10, "	Resigned June 18, 1865.
Do.	John G. Clifford	May	31, "	May	31, "	Mustered out with regiment.
Do.	Henry Netchey	Oct.	25, "	Oct.	25, "	Mustered out with regiment.
Do.	M. Sussman	Dec.	5, "	Dec.	5, "	
2d Lieutenant	Halley H. Sage	May	29, 1861	May	29, 1861	Resigned September 6, 1861.
Do.	Joseph H. Powell	June	1, "	June	1, "	Promoted to 1st Lieutenant November 8, 1861.
Do.	Charles P. Cavis	"	5, "	"	5, "	Resigned January 3, 1862.
Do.	John Dauhwuth	"	6, "	"	6, "	Resigned September 24, 1861.
Do.	Howard S. Woodrow	"	10, "	"	10, "	Promoted to 1st Lieutenant U. S. A.
Do.	Sanford F. Timmons	"	13, "	"	13, "	Resigned September 24, 1861.
Do.	John Murphy	"	14, "	"	14, "	Promoted to 1st Lieutenant January 9, 1832.
Do.	Wm. D. W. Mitchell	"	21, "	"	21, "	Resigned November 4, 1861.
Do.	Wm. Rains	"	22, "	"	22, "	Promoted to 1st Lieutenant.
Do.	Frank J. Jones	"	28, "	"	28, "	Promoted to 1st Lieutenant January 21, 1862.
Do.	James W. McConnell	July	10, "	Aug.	26, "	Promoted to 1st Lieutenant.
Do.	David P. Doherty	Oct.	3, "	Oct.	10, "	Promoted to 1st Lieutenant February 5, 1862.
Do.	Thomas F. Murdock	"	15, "	"	15, "	Promoted to 1st Lieutenant March 15, 1862.
Do.	Thomas B. George	"	25, "	"	25, "	Promoted to 1st Lieutenant May 13, 1862.
Do.	Samuel S. Gold	Nov.	8, "	Nov.	8, "	Promoted to 1st Lieutenant May 31, 1862.
Do.	John E. Ray	"	27, "	"	27, "	Promoted to 1st Lieutenant July 28, 1862.
Do.	Henry H. Kendrick	Jan.	9, 1862	Jan.	9, 1862	Resigned March 22, 1862.
Do.	S. W. McCulloch	"	9, "	"	9, "	Promoted to 1st Lieutenant July 13, 1862.
Do.	M. Sussman	"	9, "	"	9, "	Canceled.
Do.	Cyrus S. Bates	Feb.	5, "	Feb.	5, "	Promoted to 1st Lieutenant August 14, 1862.
Do.	Charles Lindenberg	"	19, "	"	19, "	Promoted to 1st Lieutenant August 14, 1862.
Do.	Robert K. Seig	March	31, "	March	31, "	Promoted to 1st Lieutenant September 11, '62.
Do.	Wm. B. Lambert	"	12, "	April	10, "	Promoted to 1st Lieutenant December 8, 1862.
Do.	Joseph Coe	"	15, "	"	10, "	Promoted to 1st Lieutenant January 1, 1863.
Do.	J. K. Guthrie	"	22, "	"	10, "	Resigned December 20, 1862.
Do.	Wm. H. Campbell	"	30, "	May	1, "	Revoked; no vacancy.
Do.	Thomas J. Stone	May	13, "	July	9, "	Promoted to 1st Lieutenant January 1, 1863.
Do.	John Fox	"	31, "	Oct.	4, "	Killed at Stone River December 31, 1863.
Do.	James C. Witaker	July	28, "	"	4, "	Killed at Stone River December 31, 1863.
Do.	Richard B. Crawford	Aug.	12, "	"	24, "	Resigned February 11, 1863.
Do.	Samuel C. Bosler	Sept.	11, "	Dec.	30, "	Promoted to 1st Lieutenant March 1, 1863.
Do.	Frank Bryer	Dec.	8, "	"	30, "	Promoted to 1st Lieutenant January 1, 1863.
Do.	Frank Geiger	Nov.	1, "	Jan.	12, 1863	Discharged on account of wounds.
Do.	Samuel E. Henderson	Dec.	20, "	March	13, "	Promoted to 1st Lieutenant January 1, 1863.
Do.	James Thompson	"	31, "	May	18, "	Promoted to 1st Lieutenant.
Do.	Robert F. Wolfkill	Jan.	1, "	"	18, "	Mustered out.
Do.	Wm. A. Short	Feb.	11, "	"	18, "	Mustered out.
Do.	George H. Dorman	Jan.	1, "	"	18, "	Mustered out.
Do.	Emery Maline	"	1, "	"	18, "	Mustered out.
Do.	Frank Reiger	"	1, "	"	18, "	Resigned February 15, 1864.
Do.	James S. Caskey	March	1, "	"	18, "	Mustered out.
Do.	Daniel M. Rutern	Jan.	1, "	"	18, "	Mustered out.
Do.	Franklin Blackburn	"	1, "	"	18, "	Resigned May 29, 1864.

THIRTEENTH OHIO VOLUNTEER INFANTRY.

THE THIRTEENTH OHIO VOLUNTEER INFANTRY was organized at Camp Jackson, Columbus, about the 20th of April, 1861, under the command of W. S. Smith, an experienced officer of the regular army, as Colonel; C. B. Mason, Lieutenant-Colonel, and J. G. Hawkins, Major. Thursday, May 9th, it moved to Camp Dennison, where it was disciplined, drilled, and prepared for the arduous struggle in which it was to participate.

On the 30th of June the regiment left Camp Dennison, and embarked on the Ohio River for Western Virginia, to re-enforce the column of General McClellan, then operating in that region. On Monday, July 1st, it reached Parkersburg, Virginia, numbering one thousand men, rank and file. On the 14th it left Parkersburg by the Parkersburg Branch Railroad for Oakland, on the Baltimore and Ohio Railroad. From thence it marched to Greenland Gap, in pursuit of a Rebel force, said to be intrenched at that place. Finding no enemy, it retraced its steps to Oakland. From thence to Clarksburg, and through obstructed roads to the town of Sutton, on Elk River, in a valley surrounded on all sides with large hills. The Thirteenth, in company with the National forces to the number of five thousand infantry and artillery, encamped on these hills, the artillery commanding all approaches to the town Frequent scouts were made into the surrounding country, but nothing of importance transpired.

On the 10th of September Colonel Smith led his regiment in the battle of Carnifex Ferry, occupying the extreme left, and made a good record for the command. From this date until November 6th, the regiment was encamped at Gauley Bridge, having frequent skirmishes with the enemy.

On the 6th of November, Benham's brigade, composed of the Tenth, Twelfth, and Thirteenth Ohio regiments, crossed the Kanawha and went into camp at Loup Creek. McMullen's battery having joined the brigade on the 12th, the combined force set out in pursuit of General Floyd. The Thirteenth Ohio held the post of honor, and was preceded by company A as skirmishers. The first brush occurred at Cotton Hill, in which the regiment lost one killed and two wounded. Floyd made good his retreat to Lewisburg, and the National troops halted at Fayetteville. The Rebels having been driven from West Virginia, the principal portion of the troops were withdrawn from that section, and transferred by transports down the Ohio River to Jeffersonville, Indiana, the Thirteenth going into camp near that place, opposite Louisville. On the 11th of December it received orders to join the column under Buell, then about to resume his chase after Bragg's Rebel army. On the 13th the regiment went into camp near Elizabethtown, Kentucky, and remained there until the 26th, when, with the rest of the forces, it moved to Bacon Creek. Here the most rigid drill was instituted, giving confidence to the men and to the regiment as an organization.

On the 10th of February, 1862, the regiment received orders to march, and entered Bowling Green on the evening of the 15th of February, to find it evacuated. On the 22d the regiment took cars on the Louisville and Nashville Railroad, forming the advance of Buell's army on Nashville, and reached Gallatin, forty miles from Nashville, where, under the superintendence of Colonel Scott, Assistant-Secretary of War, an important bridge over the Cumberland, damaged by the enemy in their retreat, was repaired. Reaching Nashville on the 26th, the Thirteenth crossed the Cumberland on the steamer "Lady Jackson," marched through the city, and encamped two miles beyond.

On the 1st of March the Seventeenth Brigade advanced on Lavergne, on the Murfreesboro' Pike, in support of a detachment of National troops that had been attacked by the enemy. The enemy retreated, and the Thirteenth returned to its camp. Tuesday, March 10th, the regiment was detached from Mitchel's division and ordered to report to General Crittenden. On the 19th companies A and G were detached from the regiment to assist the First Michigan to repair bridges on the Alabama and Tennessee Rivers, and on the 2d of April the remainder of the regiment, under command of Lieutenant-Colonel Hawkins, joined the column on the march to re-enforce General Grant, then in anticipation of an attack from the Rebels on Pittsburg Landing. The regiment, after a terrible march, endured in common with the other troops, reached the town of Savannah, on the Tennessee River, on the morning of the 6th of April. It was at once forwarded to the battle-field, and with the Fifth Division, formed on the right of Nelson's command. About eight o'clock the division moved forward to meet the foe. It soon came upon the enemy in position, supported by the famous Washington Battery, of New Orleans. The Thirteenth Ohio, burning to avenge their fallen comrades of the day before, sprang for this battery, and after a desperate struggle, captured it entire, but only to lose it, as the enemy in larger numbers made a charge and retook their pieces. In this affair the Major, Ben. Piatt Runkle, fell, severely wounded, and was reported dead.

About one o'clock, when the last grand advance of the National army was made, another attempt was made by the Thirteenth to capture the Washington (Rebel) Battery. It was successful, and the famed guns were once more the trophies of the regiment. The enemy, foiled in his attempt to sweep the National forces into the Tennessee, retreated, and on the 29th the Thirteenth Ohio, complete once more, joined in the advance on Corinth. The regiment reached the vicinity of Corinth about the 12th of May, where it performed its share on the picket-line and the various affairs with the enemy, until the evacuation of the city on the 31st of May.

The Fourteenth Division, on the morning of 4th June, started with the army of Buell on its advance against Chattanooga. On the 5th it crossed the Tuscumbia River, the Thirteenth Ohio camping at Danville. On the 24th the regiment crossed the Tennessee to Florence, Alabama, and encamped on the right of the Twenty-Fifth, at Shallow Creek, seven miles from the city. On Monday, July 1st, Huntsville, Alabama, was reached, after an excessively fatiguing march. On the 9th it was detached from the division to perform guard duty on the Chattanooga Railroad. It, however, joined the division at Stevenson a few days thereafter, and on the 16th went into camp at that well-known spot, "Battle Creek," familiar to the memory of every soldier of the old organization of the Army of the Ohio. Here they remained until the 21st day of August. During a considerable portion of their sojourn at Battle Creek the troops, from the scarcity of provisions, were placed on half-rations.

On August 20th orders were received to march. Bragg had left Chattanooga, and was well on his way to Louisville, Kentucky, with designs on Indiana and Ohio. Then commenced a march that has made the Army of the Ohio a record as enduring as time. From the 21st of August until the 26th of September, a period of thirty-six days, the National soldiers patiently toiled on after their exultant enemy, enduring the hot rays of the sun, almost unbearable thirst, half-rations, and the stifling dust. What soldier of the Thirteenth Ohio will ever forget this terrible march? On the 26th the troops reached Louisville, having outmarched and passed, on a parallel road, the Rebel army. After a rest until the 1st of October, the pursuit of Bragg was resumed.

On the 8th of October the right wing, under Rousseau and McCook, encountered the enemy at Perryville, and attacked without orders and before the commanding General's preparations were complete. The Thirteenth Ohio, in Crittenden's division, on the right, as well as the other troops in that organization, were not actively engaged. Having repulsed the attack the enemy continued his retreat, and Crittenden's division pursued as far as Mount Vernon, when they halted and rejoined the main column. In this pursuit the regiment penetrated the country watered by the Big Rockcastle River, called by some, "Wild Cat Country," one of the wildest and most mountainous localities in Kentucky.

On the 30th of October General Buell was relieved, and General William S. Rosecrans assigned to the command of the Army of the Ohio. The National troops immediately pushed in pursuit of the enemy, and on Wednesday, the 5th of November, the tents of the Thirteenth Ohio were pitched near Glasgow, Kentucky, having, by forced marches from Mount Vernon, Kentucky, accomplished the distance in twelve days. From this point to within half a mile of Nashville, nothing of great moment occurred, although the regiment was almost continually under arms to repel skirmishers.

On Tuesday, December 2d, the Fifth Division, consisting of three brigades, General Van Cleve commanding, was reviewed by General Rosecrans, who paid a high compliment to the soldierly appearance of the Thirteenth Ohio, reminding them at the same time that he had a lively remembrance of their services in Western Virginia.

Picket duty and foraging, interspersed with an occasional skirmish, were the daily occupations of the regiment until the advance on Murfreesboro', December 26, 1862. In one of the skirmishes near Lavergne, with Wheeler's cavalry, after a severe fight, the Thirteenth lost two men killed and several wounded, and Lieutenant Bates, of company B, captured.

Crittenden's division (in which was the Thirteenth Ohio) held the left wing, Thomas the center, and McCook the right. The grand advance commenced on the morning of the 26th. The Thirteenth Ohio moved with Crittenden's column out on the Nashville and Murfreesboro' Pike toward Lavergne. The enemy slowly fell back, fighting as they retreated. On the morning of the 27th Lavergne was shelled, and the rebels immediately evacuated the place. By order of General Rosecrans, the next day (being Sunday) was observed as a day of rest. On the 29th the advance was sounded and the entire line moved forward, and, after some fighting, reached Stone River in the evening. McCook's column met with more resistance, and did not get up until the next day at noon.

On the morning of Wednesday, December 31st, the Thirteenth Ohio, under Colonel Jos. G. Hawkins, was ordered in from outpost duty, and took position in line with their brigade, (the Fourteenth), constituting the Second Brigade of the Fifth Division, composed of the Forty-Fourth and Eighty-Sixth Indiana, Fifty-Ninth and Thirteenth Ohio, and the Third Wisconsin Battery, under command of Colonel F. P. Fyffe. Receiving orders to cross Stone River and threaten the enemy, the regiment, with the division of Van Cleve, had commenced the advance when the orders were countermanded. The right wing, under McCook, had been driven back, and the center was in danger. The Thirteenth Ohio was at once counter-marched and "double-quicked" back to the Murfreesboro' Pike, where it assisted in the rescue of a train that was about being captured by the enemy's cavalry. About ten o'clock the brigade received orders to form on the right of the First Brigade, with Colonel Hawkins's brigade on its right, (the Second Brigade's right), and advanced down the slope of the Cedar Ridge and across an open field toward the enemy, in the wood beyond. In this advance the Thirteenth Ohio occupied the left of the second line, covering the Thirty-Ninth Ohio, and having the Eighty-Sixth Ohio on its right. Some disorder occurred in the line from the density of the woods on the slope, but on emerging into the open field, the line was "dressed" and advanced regularly across the field. The front line, consisting of the Fifty-Ninth Ohio and Forty-Fourth Indiana, pushed rapidly forward and entered the woods. The Thirteenth Ohio and Eighty-Sixth Indiana were sheltered behind a fence, adjacent to the woods in front, in readiness to support the front line. In a few moments the front line was desperately attacked and driven back over the second line. The Thirteenth Ohio immediately opened on the enemy, and held them in check until it became evident that it was outflanked. At this time Colonel Hawkins was killed, and with him others of the regiment. The command devolved upon Major Dwight Jarvis. The regiment continued fighting the enemy until they had passed around both flanks, when Major Jarvis, after repeated commands and expostulations, induced the men to fall back; but in doing so they became somewhat disordered, and suffered sadly from a Rebel battery, which played upon them in their retreat. Reaching the line of reserves on the border of the woods, the regiment halted, re-formed, and turned on the enemy, driving them back with considerable loss. In this brief struggle of an hour's duration, the Thirteenth Ohio lost one hundred and forty-two officers and men in killed, wounded, and missing. The day following, January 1, 1863, the Thirteenth did not participate in any important movement. January 2d the regiment was on the extreme left of the National lines, on the south bank of Stone River. At three P. M. the Rebels, in three lines of battle, charged the National position, compelling the Thirteenth, with others, to fall back under cover of the artillery on the north bank. The enemy still pushed forward, when thirty-six pieces of National artillery opened with canister and grape, literally mowing down the Rebels, and compelling their instant and speedy retreat from the field. The Thirteenth bivouacked on the north bank of the river that night. The morning of the 3d found Murfreesboro' evacuated, and the enemy in full retreat. The loss of the regiment in this series of battles was thirty-one killed, eighty-five wounded, and sixty-nine missing—total, one hundred and eighty-five.

The regiment did not participate in any movement or engagement of special moment during the long sojourn of the "Army of the Cumberland" at Murfreesboro'. On June 24, 1863, the bugles sounded the advance Southward, and on the 27th of the same month the regiment once more joined the marching column. About August 1st it reached and occupied McMinnville. Rosecrans's movements threatening the envelopment of Bragg, the latter General rapidly retreated from Tullahoma, falling back on Chattanooga. On the morning of the 16th of August, with the entire corps under Crittenden, the organization pushed forward by the Pikeville route. This movement seriously threatening one of the flanks of Bragg's forces, that General again retreated, completely uncovering Chattanooga. On the 9th of September the Thirteenth, with drums beating and banners flying, marched through this celebrated city of imaginary impregnability, and encamped for the night at Rossville, five miles south of Chattanooga.

When the concentration of the army began, previous to the battle of Chickamauga, the Thirteenth, with the remaining troops of Van Cleve's division, took post on the southern spur of Missionary Ridge. On the morning of the 19th of September the battle of Chickamauga opened, and through all the varying fortunes of that and the succeeding day, the Thirteenth preserved unsullied its record, made sacred at Stone River.

The regiment, during this series of battles, was commanded by its Lieutenant-Colonel, the Colonel (Dwight Jarvis) being absent on duty at McMinnville. Colonel Jarvis rejoined the regiment shortly afterward. The Lieutenant-Colonel was killed, and the Major severely wounded, and the skeleton ranks, after the battle of Chattanooga, attested the heavy and mournful loss of rank and file.

The National army fell back into the fortifications at Chattanooga. On the 22d the regiment had a severe skirmish with the enemy on Missionary Ridge, which continued during the entire forenoon of that day. In the afternoon it withdrew from its position to its former place in the intrenchments of Chattanooga. Here it remained until November 23d, when it again moved. General Thomas now commanded the three old corps of the Army of the Cumberland. General Grant directed the onward movement, and the preliminaries toward the expulsion of Bragg from Missionary Ridge were at once commenced. History has already recorded the successful charge that swept the Rebel host down the mountain, across the valley, and converted its retreat into a shameful rout. In this charge the Thirteenth bore itself bravely, and, it is claimed, was the first to plant its colors on the Rebel works, and Sergeant Daniel Ritter, of company A, was the first man of the regiment to scale and enter the fortifications. The losses of the regiment in this affair were severe. On the 28th of November the Thirteenth Ohio, with the Third Division, and another division of the Fourth Corps, to which it had been attached since the reorganization at Chattanooga, advanced to the rescue of Knoxville, then besieged by Longstreet. Upon the approach of the National forces, the enemy retreated, and was pursued as far as Blain's Cross Roads, and Four Corners, near Clinch Mountain. The regiment during these marches suffered severely for the want of shoes and clothing, as well as rations. For a great portion of the time it was compelled to subsist off the country through which it marched. From Blain's Cross-Roads it advanced in pursuit of the enemy to Strawberry Plains, crossed the Holston River and marched to Dandridge, twenty-three miles from the North Carolina line. Here it encountered the enemy, and sharp skirmishing ensued, but no general engagement, the Rebels rapidly getting out of the way of the progressive Yankees. Upon the retreat of the enemy the National forces returned over the most horrible roads and through weather of almost incessant snow and rain to the Plains, and from thence to Knoxville.

Leave of absence was now granted the regiment to enable it to return to Chattanooga, settle its affairs and visit their homes in Ohio; thirty days being granted for that purpose, in consideration of their having enlisted as veterans. The remainder of the regiment—those who did not re-enlist—were transferred to the Fifty-Ninth Ohio, of the same brigade, division and corps to which the original Thirteenth had been attached. The Fifty-Ninth was at this time (January 28, 1864) stationed at Marysville, sixteen miles south-west of Knoxville. At this date, after thirty-four months of marching and fighting, closes the first term of service of the Thirteenth Ohio Volunteer Infantry.

On the 5th of January, 1864, three-fourths of the members of the Thirteenth Ohio re-enlisted for another term of three years' service. Their muster was, however, delayed until the 10th of February. The commissioned officers were Colonel Dwight Jarvis, Captain McCulloch, and Lieutenants Bosler, Henderson, Crawford, Rutern, and George.

The veterans reached Columbus, Ohio, on the 25th of February, were furloughed to their homes, and at the end of thirty days promptly reported for duty at Camp Chase, near Columbus, and returned in a body to Chattanooga. At that place they found that the non-veterans of the regiment had been attached to the Eighty-Sixth Indiana Infantry, on duty at Cleveland, Tennessee. The march was resumed, and in due time the regiment was reunited. From this time until June 21, 1864, when the term of the original organization expired, the veteran and the non-veteran served amicably and efficiently together, both organizations being consolidated into one, and both, therefore, sharing the same dangers and the same glory. The regiment was attached to the Third Brigade (General John S. Beatty), Third Division (General T. J. Wood), and Fourth Corps (Major-General Howard). The Fourth Corps, with the Fourteenth and Twentieth, constituted the Army of the Cumberland, under the command of Major-General Geo. H. Thomas.

On the 1st day of May, 1864, the troops received orders to prepare for the Atlanta campaign, and on the 3d struck tents and advanced against Ringgold, Georgia, which place was occupied without resistance on the 5th. It was ascertained that the enemy in strong force, under General Joe Johnston, held the line between Dalton and Resaca, showing a disposition to dispute the further progress of the National army.

The Thirteenth Ohio went into camp at Catoosa Springs, near Ringgold, and on the 7th of May, after some night skirmishing with the enemy's rear-guard, in which the whole command was engaged, reached and occupied Tunnel Hill. From this point the regiment, with the remaining troops of the corps, pushed forward as near to the top of Rocky Face Ridge as it was possible for troops to go, when the enemy, fearing one of Sherman's flank movements, evacuated their position and fell back toward Resaca. Had General Johnston defended this position with anything like the pertinacity displayed a few days thereafter, the graves of National soldiers would have been more numerous on Rocky Face Ridge than they are to-day.

On the 10th the Fourth Corps relieved the entire front, while the rest of the army, viz.: the Thirteenth, Fourteenth, Fifteenth, Sixteenth, Twentieth, and Twenty-Third Corps, went toward Resaca. Incessant skirmishing followed until the night of the 12th, when the enemy retreated from Dalton, which was occupied by the National forces on the 13th. The Thirteenth passed through the town and beyond in pursuit of the enemy, who, on the 14th, after some hard skirmishing, were driven into the fortifications around Resaca. In all these encounters the regiment performed important services, as is shown from the loss of the division. On the 14th its loss was seventy-one killed and three hundred and eighty-four wounded, including General Willich, commanding the Second Brigade, who fell badly wounded while leading his troops in a charge.

At Resaca, on the 14th, the Fourth Corps formed a junction with the balance of the army and relieved the Twentieth and Twenty-First Army Corps, which passed on to the left to counteract an attempted flank movement of the enemy. On the 15th General Hooker fought the enemy at Resaca; but as the Thirteenth Ohio formed part of the reserve, it was not engaged on that day. That night Johnson retreated and fell back on Calhoun, on the south bank of the Oostenaula River; but on the advance of the victorious legions of Sherman he again retreated, retiring slowly in the direction of Atlanta. Skirmishing was the order of the day, and the Thirteenth performed its full share, and many a Rebel fell under its rifles.

Passing Cassville and Adairsville on the 25th, the Rebel commander determined that Atlanta should be fairly lost, if lost at all, and so drew up his forces around Lost Mountain; and here occurred the battle of that name. On the 27th of May the Third Division, Fourth Corps, passed around the left to strike the enemy's flank, marching about eight miles, supposing the extremity of the Rebel line had been reached and passed. But a sad mistake was made. Instead of striking the enemy on the flank, the Third Division had struck the Rebel center, and encountered breastworks gray with men and bristling with artillery. The division was advancing in three lines of battle through a dense forest, and the first intimation it had of its position was a terrific discharge from the enemy's works, but a few yards in advance. The first line was destroyed under the withering fire. The second line, of which the Thirteenth formed a part, immediately advanced on the double-quick, and with a yell and a volley rushed up to the works. The fire became very warm, but the second line maintained their ground steadily and returned the volleys with interest. From four P. M. until nine at night the efforts of the National forces to take the position were unavailing. The ammunition of the Thirteenth became exhausted. McCulloch was struck by a ball going in at one cheek and out at the other. Thompson had his right arm shattered, and the killed and wounded were lying thickly around. The Major of the Thirteenth (J. T. Snyder), then in command, still rallied the remnant; hearing the men calling for more ammunition, and knowing that unless it was procured his men would be compelled to retreat, with his own hands took from the boxes of the killed and wounded their remaining cartridges and distributed them among the regiment.

General Thomas observing that no impression could be made on the enemy's line, ordered a withdrawal of the forces, which was effected in good order. The Third Division went into the action with four thousand one hundred men and came out at nine that night with barely twenty-five hundred. The loss of the regiment was about fifty killed, wounded, and prisoners.

On the 9th of June the regiment went into camp near Acworth, skirmishing almost all the way with the retreating enemy.

The term of enlistment of the non-veterans of the Thirteenth (officers and men) having expired on the 21st, General Howard issued orders for their transportation to Chattanooga, at which point they were to be paid and discharged. Simultaneously with this order came another, that the veteran Thirteenth should be transferred to the Nineteenth Ohio Volunteer Infantry. This order created considerable feeling in the regiment, and on proper representation to General Thomas it was revoked, and the old and endeared name of "Thirteenth" retained. An order was then issued consolidating the veterans into a battalion of four companies, to be called the Thirteenth Ohio Veteran Volunteer Infantry Battalion, under the command of Major J. T. Snyder. Five enlisted men were breveted as Lieutenants and placed in command of companies until the commissions were received from the Governor of Ohio. Companies A and F were by this consolidation merged into one company, called company A; B, K, and G formed company B; D, I, and C, company C, and H and E, company E. John H. Scott commanded company A, John P. Millet company B, James H. Merrill company C, Erastus C. Hawkins company D.

The entire battalion numbered one hundred and twenty men present for duty, and eighty men on extra and daily duty, and sick in hospital. The battalion had the same position in the brigade as before the change.

On the 10th of June the Thirteenth Battalion joined the advance toward the rugged slopes of Kenesaw, but did not participate in any of the engagements until Kenesaw was reached. General Thomas pushed his forces as far up those terrible heights as it was possible for men to go in the face of such a fire, but all in vain; he was compelled to fall back. The loss of the battalion in the struggle was Shildecker, Muncaster, Gregory, and Miller, of company D, killed; Alexander, of company D, and Wm. H. Clay, of company A, wounded.

The enemy evacuated Kenesaw on the night of the 29th, as General Sherman was again engaged in flanking their position. The battalion accompanied the corps in this flank movement; and when Sherman commenced to draw his lines gradually around the doomed city of Atlanta the battalion was stationed in close proximity to the Rebel lines, busily engaged in throwing up intrenchments preparatory to the siege of the place. Shot and shell day and night came plunging through their camp. Miller, of company C, was killed by a piece of shell, and Brown, of company A, severely wounded in the head by a Minie ball.

On the 29th of August General Sherman commenced another flanking movement from the front of Atlanta, passing to its south side. The movement commenced about ten o'clock at night. The battalion was thrown out on picket to protect the brigade while in the process of withdrawing. To prevent the enemy from discovering the movement at this point of the line, the battalion opened a heavy fire on the Rebels, which was kept up until three o'clock in the morning, when they began to retire. The enemy, discovering their retreat, gave immediate pursuit, and a continuous skirmish was kept up. The battalion succeeded, however, in bringing off all their equipage, and misled the enemy to the full extent desired.

This move necessarily compelled the Rebel General Hood to leave Atlanta to save his communications, and advance southward to Jonesboro' and Lovejoy's Station. At the latter place a desperate fight took place on the 2d of September, in which the Third Division participated; and, after a fierce struggle, failed to drive the enemy from a strong position. The Thirteenth Battalion lost, in killed, Ambrose Andeman, of company A; John Van Godon and George Thorn, of company D. Sergeant Busick, of company B, was wounded. Atlanta fell, and the victorious Sherman took up his quarters within its corporate limits.

The division, to which what was left of the Thirteenth Ohio Volunteer Infantry belonged, was not permitted to remain in Atlanta. It was ordered into camp six miles north of the city, on the battle-ground of the 22d of July, near the spot where the brave McPherson fell. This chance for rest was very grateful to the tired and worn-out troops, as it was the first regular camp enjoyed since the commencement of the campaign in May. Their restless and energetic Commander-in-Chief, General W. T. Sherman, had taxed their energies to the very utmost, and had thereby accomplished the most brilliant results. The duty was light, the battalion only coming in for their share of duty every fifth day; and in the same time half the battalion was detailed for forage duty.

On the 4th of October the camp was struck, under orders to resume the march. It had been announced that the Rebel General Hood, becoming desperate at the continued defeats of the Confederate forces, had turned at bay and was endeavoring, by quick and solid blows and rapid marching, to gain the rear of General Sherman's army and cut his communications with his base of supply. The National troops pushed forward as far as Acworth, on the Georgia Central Railroad, where the army divided, the Fourth and Twenty-Third Corps, under Thomas, continuing after Hood, while General Sherman, with the balance of the troops, halted and prepared for his memorable march to the sea.

The Fourth and Twenty-Third Corps followed Hood into Tennessee, and at Pulaski succeeded in getting ahead of his forces. Nashville was the goal of both armies. The National forces must reach it in time to fortify, else the Confederate army would fight for its possession in the very streets of the city. It was an exciting and closely-contested race, but the National forces came out ahead, not, however, without an obstinate and sanguinary engagement at Franklin, Tennessee. In this engagement the most desperate valor was displayed on both sides, but the sturdy endurance of the National soldiers triumphed, and the march for Nashville was resumed.

In marching from Columbia the Third Division, of which the Thirteenth formed a portion, brought up the rear of the army. Schofield's corps was in the advance, who, with his division, reached Franklin at ten o'clock A. M., and began at once to fortify. The hasty and frail defenses were almost completed when the advance of the Third Division reached the Harpeth River, and was immediately ordered into position above and below the town, along the stream, to prevent a flank movement. The Rebel army under Hood soon made an impetuous attack, and the fight was fairly opened. General Thomas was prepared. The enemy was received by a withering fire of well-posted artillery, which swept the plains on every side. Again and again did Hood precipitate his Rebel hosts on the National lines, but without signal success, until at nightfall he was compelled to withdraw his shattered columns. The struggle at Franklin being over, the National army was again put in rapid march for Nashville. The Thirteenth Battalion reached that city on the 3d of December and took position inside the defenses. The Rebel army was close at hand. It appeared in front of the city on the 4th of December and commenced to fortify. From this date, until the battles of the 15th and 16th, the battalion was actively engaged in skirmishing and picket-firing along the lines.

On the morning of the 15th of December General Thomas took the offensive and began his movements against the enemy. On the evening of the 14th the Third Division was ordered to be ready for action before daylight the next morning, to pass around the enemy's left, and when the advance in front was sounded, to vigorously attack. One regiment in each brigade was ordered to hold the line left by the brigade, and to keep up a continuous fire until the action began. The Thirteenth Battalion occupied the trenches vacated by its brigade, and was, therefore, not engaged in the action of the 15th of December. On the morning of the 16th it left the defenses and joined the brigade in front before Hood's new line of works, thrown up by him during the previous night. About three o'clock P. M., Steedman's negro brigade charged this part of the line, but were repulsed with heavy loss. The Second Brigade was then ordered up and made a charge, but they, too, were compelled to fall back. The Third Brigade was then ordered to prepare for action. The men charged forward with great spirit. The Thirteenth Battalion was among the first troops over the Rebel works, aiding in the capture of a battery of four guns. The work of destruction was quick but desperate. The Confederate army was shattered, and immediately commenced a rapid retreat, the National army following, capturing large numbers of prisoners and much material of war. The retreat soon became a rout, and by the time the pursuing infantry reached the Tennessee all further attempts to reach them, except with cavalry, was entirely useless, as the Rebels were scattered widely over Southern Tennessee and Northern Alabama.

The Thirteenth Battalion stopped at Huntsville, Alabama, and went into camp near that beautiful town, where it remained until the 1st of March, 1865. It was then ordered to East Tennessee. While at Jonesboro', in April, the news of Lee's surrender was received. The battalion was thereafter ordered to Nashville, where it arrived on the 9th day of June, 1865.

On the 16th of June all the troops composing the Fourth Corps were ordered to Texas. The route of the battalion was by cars to Johnsonville, thence by boats down the Cumberland and Ohio Rivers to Cairo, thence down the Mississippi to New Orleans, at which place it arrived on the 27th of June. It remained at New Orleans until the 7th of July, when it embarked for Indianola, Texas, reaching that place on the 10th. From this point the battalion marched to and occupied the village of Green Lake, a settlement about thirty miles from Matagorda Bay. The camp was on the open prairies, where the water was literally horrible and the surrounding country very unhealthy. Agues and fevers were prevalent, and the men suffered intensely. On the 4th of September the battalion broke camp and marched to San Antonio, one hundred and fifteen miles further into the interior. This proved a most happy change. The place was healthy, the air salubrious, water excellent. The men soon began to recover from the miasmatic effects of their Green Lake residence.

The battalion remained at San Antonio until December 5, 1865, at which date it was mustered out of the United States service. It left San Antonio on the 6th of December, and on the 17th of January reached Columbus, Ohio, where its arms and equipments were turned over to the proper authorities, the men were paid off and discharged and embarked for their several homes. Thus ended the service of this gallant and faithful regiment.

14th REGIMENT OHIO VOLUNTEER INFANTRY.

ROSTER, THREE MONTHS' SERVICE.

RANK.	NAME.	DATE OF RANK.	COM. ISSUED.	REMARKS.
Colonel	JAMES B. STEEDMAN	April 24, 1861	April 24, 1861	
Lt. Colonel	GEORGE PEABODY ESTE	" 24, "	" 24, "	
Major	PAUL EDWARDS	" 24, "	" 24, "	
Surgeon	J. A. COONS	May 4, "	May 4, "	
Ass't Surgeon	W. C. DANIELS	" 4, "	" 4, "	
Captain	Seth B. Moe	April 25, "	April 25, "	
Do.	Louis Von Blessing	" 25, "	" 25, "	
Do.	Benj. N. Fisher	" 24, "	" 24, "	
Do.	Sidney S. Sprague	" 24, "	" 24, "	
Do.	Edwin D. Bradley	" 24, "	" 24, "	
Do.	Andrew Crawford	" 24, "	" 24, "	Killed at Laurel Hill.
Do.	John S. Snook	" 24, "	" 24, "	
Do.	F. L. Barber	" 24, "	" 24, "	
Do.	Caleb Dodd	" 24, "	" 24, "	
Do.	George W. Kirk	" 23, "	" 23, "	
Do.	Amon C. Bradley	May 27, "	June 9, "	
Do.	Enoch B. Mann	June 25, "	" 9, "	
1st Lieutenant	Wilbur F. Stopford	April 25, "	April 25, "	
Do.	John A. Chase	" 25, "	" 25, "	
Do.	Edwin J. Evans	" 24, "	" 24, "	
Do.	Wm. Irving	" 24, "	" 24, "	
Do.	Amon C. Bradley	" 24, "	" 24, "	Promoted to Captain.
Do.	John D. Belknap	" 24, "	" 24, "	Killed at Laurel Hill.
Do.	Alfred Russell	" 24, "	" 24, "	
Do.	Thomas M. Ward	" 24, "	" 24, "	
Do.	Denis C. Lahan	" 24, "	" 24, "	
Do.	John F. Wallace	" 23, "	" 23, "	
Do.	David S. Tallerday	May 27, "	June 9, "	
Do.	Edwin D. Bradley	April 29, "	April 29, "	
Do.	Henry D. Kingsbury	" 25, "	" 25, "	
Do.	George E. Welles	" 27, "	" 27, "	
2d Lieutenant	Frank W. Marion	" 25, "	" 25, "	
Do.	Wm. Shultz	" 25, "	" 1, "	
Do.	Edward M. Deuchar	" 24, "	" 24, "	
Do.	Charles Kahlo	" 24, "	" 24, "	
Do.	David S. Tallerday	" 24, "	" 24, "	Promoted to 1st Lieutenant.
Do.	Samuel Pomroy	" 24, "	" 24, "	
Do.	John Crossen	" 24, "	" 24, "	
Do.	R. A. Franks	" 24, "	" 24, "	
Do.	James Manton	" 24, "	" 24, "	
Do.	Samuel Sherman	" 23, "	" 23, "	
Do.	Orrin D. Doughton	May 27, "	July 9, "	

ROSTER, THREE YEARS' SERVICE.

RANK.	NAME.	DATE OF RANK.	COM. ISSUED.	REMARKS.
Colonel	JAMES B. STEEDMAN	Aug. 16, 1861	Aug. 16, 1861	Promoted to Brigadier-General July 17, 1862.
Do.	GEO. PEABODY ESTE	July 17, 1862	Nov. 20, 1862	Mustered out July 7, 1865.
Lt. Colonel	GEORGE PEABODY ESTE	Aug. 6, 1861	Jan. 21, 1861	Promoted to Colonel July 17, 1862.
Do.	PAUL EDWARDS	July 17, 1862	Nov. 20, 1862	Resigned November 26, 1862.
Do.	HENRY D. KINGSBURY	Dec. 27, "	Feb. 16, "	Mustered out November 8, 1864.
Do.	ALBERT MOORE	Nov. 18, 1864	Nov. 18, 1864	Mustered out.
Major	PAUL EDWARDS	Aug. 16, 1861	Jan. 21, 1861	Promoted to Lieutenant-Colonel.
Do.	HENRY D. KINGSBURY	July 17, 1862	Nov. 20, 1862	Promoted to Lieutenant-Colonel.
Do.	JOHN W. WILSON	Jan. 20, 1863	Feb. 16, 1863	Died of wounds September 1, 1864.
Surgeon	W. C. DANIELS	Aug. 16, 1861	Aug. 16, 1861	Resigned November 7, 1862.
Do.	GEORGE E. SLOATE	Nov. 7, 1862	Dec. 17, 1862	Resigned November 3, 1864.
Do.	E. KING NASH	" 10, 1864	Nov. 10, 1864	Mustered out.
Ass't Surgeon	GEORGE E. SLOATE	Sept. 9, 1861	Jan. 21, 1862	Promoted to Surgeon.
Do.	CHARLES E. AMES	Dec. 30, 1862	Dec. 31, "	Promoted to Surgeon.
Do.	CHARLES M. EATON	Aug. 21, "	Feb. 10, 1863	Resigned March 4, 1863.
Do.	E. KING NASH	April 10, 1863	April 10, "	Promoted to Surgeon.
Do.	THOMAS J. CROUSE	July 30, 1864	July 30, 1864	
Chaplain	E. B. KAFFENSPERGER	Sept. 17, 1861	Sept. 18, 1861	Resigned February 14, 1863.
Do.	HORATIO L. SARGENT	May 28, 1864	July 8, 1864	
Captain	Jacob W. Brown	Aug. 15, 1861	Jan. 21, 1862	Resigned.
Do.	George W. Kirk	" 15, "	" 21, "	Mustered out September 12, 1864.
Do.	Henry D. Kingsbury	" 17, "	" 21, "	Promoted to Major.
Do.	John W. Wilson	" 21, "	" 21, "	Promoted to Major.
Do.	Noah W. Ogan	" 25, "	" 21, "	Mustered out September 12, 1864.
Do.	Wm. H. Eckles	" 26, "	" 21, "	Mustered out September 12, 1864.
Do.	John A. Chase	" 28, "	" 21, "	Mustered out September 13, 1864.
Do.	Wilbur F. Stopford	Sept. 1, "	" 21, "	Killed in action September 1, 1864.
Do.	D. Pomroy	" 4, "	" 21, "	Mustered out September 24, 1864.
Do.	James W. McCabe	" 5, "	" 21, "	Resigned.
Do.	Albert Moore	Aug. 16, 1862	Feb. 16, 1863	Promoted to Lieutenant-Colonel.

RANK.	NAME.	DATE OF RANK.	COM. ISSUED.	REMARKS.
Captain	Wm. B. Pugh	Nov. 1, 1862	Nov. 16, 1863	Mustered out.
Do.	David A. Gleason	" 15, "	" 16, "	Honorably discharged January 11, 1865.
Do.	Henry W. Bigelow	Jan. 20, 1863	May 29, "	Mustered out.
Do.	John J. Clarke	Nov. 18, 1864	Nov. 18, 1864	Mustered out.
Do.	Marshall Davis	" 18, "	" 18, "	Detached at own request.
Do.	Wm. B. Steedman	" 18, "	" 18, "	Detached at own request.
Do.	Henry G. Newbert	" 18, "	" 18, "	Transferred January, 1865.
Do.	Joseph B. Newton	" 18, "	" 18, "	Mustered out.
Do.	Henry B. Ferguson	" 18, "	" 18, "	Mustered out September 28, 1864.
Do.	James E. McBride	Jan. 6, 1865	Jan. 6, 1865	Mustered out with regiment.
Do.	Oscar N. Gunn	" 6, "	" 6, "	Mustered out with regiment.
Do.	David Bowker	April 20, "	April 20, "	Mustered out with regiment.
Do.	Joseph Reynolds	" 20, "	" 20, "	
Do.	George W. Eckles	" 20, "	" 20, "	Discharged.
1st Lieutenant	Ezra B. Kirk	Aug. 15, 1861	Jan. 21, 1862	Promoted to Captain and A. Q. M.
Do.	Edward S. Dodd	" 15, "	" 21, "	Mustered out September 27, 1864.
Do.	Albert Moore	" 17, "	" 21, "	Promoted to Captain.
Do.	Seth B. Moe	" 21, "	" 21, "	Promoted by President.
Do.	Daniel H. Nye	" 21, "	" 21, "	Mustered out September 13, 1864.
Do.	David A. Gleason	" 21, "	" 21, "	Promoted to Captain.
Do.	Robert E. Patterson	" 25, "	" 21, "	Resigned March 29, 1862.
Do.	Crawford C. Adams	" 26, "	" 21, "	Resigned January 27, 1864.
Do.	John J. Clark	" 29, "	" 21, "	Promoted to Captain.
Do.	Robert Just	Sept. 1, "	" 21, "	Resigned February 5, 1863.
Do.	Wm. H. Brownell	" 4, "	" 21, "	Resigned September 10, 1864.
Do.	Josiah Farrington	" 5, "	" 21, "	Resigned October 14, 1862.
Do.	Marshall Davis	Nov. 15, "	Feb. 16, 1863	Promoted to Captain.
Do.	Wm. B. Steedman	Dec. 21, 1862	" 16, "	Promoted to Captain.
Do.	James B. Rutlige	Nov. 2, 1861	" 16, "	Resigned September 19, 1863.
Do.	Henry W. Bigelow	Oct. 15, 1862	" 16, "	Promoted to Captain.
Do.	Wm. B. Pugh	....	....	Promoted to Captain November 15, 1862.
Do.	Joseph B. Newton	Feb. 5, 1863	May 29, 1863	Promoted to Captain.
Do.	Henry G. Newbert	Jan. 20, "	" 29, "	Promoted to Captain.
Do.	Henry B. Ferguson	May 9, 1864	" 9, 1864	Promoted to Captain.
Do.	Frank Fleck	" 9, "	" 9, "	Resigned September 24, 1864.
Do.	James E. McBride	Nov. 18, "	Nov. 18, "	Promoted to Captain.
Do.	Wm. T. Bennett	" 18, "	" 18, "	Detached at own request.
Do.	Oscar N. Gunn	" 18, "	" 18, "	Promoted to Captain.
Do.	Henry H. Everhard	" 18, "	" 18, "	Never a member of regiment.
Do.	Charles B. Mitchell	" 18, "	" 18, "	Died of wounds September 28, 1864.
Do.	Andrew J. Morse	" 18, "	" 18, "	On detached duty.
Do.	David Bowker	" 18, "	" 18, "	Promoted to Captain.
Do.	Joseph Reynolds	" 18, "	" 18, "	Promoted to Captain.
Do.	George W. Eckles	" 18, "	" 18, "	Promoted to Captain.
Do.	Henry A. Valentine	" 18, "	" 18, "	Mustered out with regiment.
Do.	Harrison Wood	" 18, "	" 18, "	Mustered out with regiment.
Do.	Sampson A. Hildreth	" 18, "	" 18, "	Discharged.
Do.	Albert Burroughs	Jan. 6, 1865	Jan. 6, 1865	Mustered out with regiment.
Do.	Wm. B. Moats	" 6, "	" 6, "	
Do.	John P. Crawford	" 6, "	" 6, "	Mustered out with regiment.
Do.	Jesse Trapp	" 6, "	" 6, "	Mustered out with regiment.
Do.	John E. Teal	April 20, "	April 20, "	Mustered out with regiment.
Do.	Isaac Bogart	" 20, "	" 20, "	
Do.	Alonzo H. Wood	" 20, "	" 20, "	Promoted.
2d Lieutenant	John M. Hamilton	Aug. 15, 1861	Jan. 21, 1862	Resigned August 11, 1862.
Do.	Wm. B. Pugh	" 17, "	" 21, "	Promoted to 1st Lieutenant.
Do.	Wm. N. Rogers	" 21, "	" 21, "	Resigned February 11, 1862.
Do.	John Dixon	" 25, "	" 21, "	Resigned December 19, 1862.
Do.	Henry B. Ferguson	" 26, "	" 21, "	Promoted to 1st Lieutenant.
Do.	Josia Johnson	" 28, "	" 21, "	Discharged.
Do.	George E. Murray	Sept. 1, "	" 21, "	Resigned November 26, 1862.
Do.	Wm. B. Steedman	" 4, "	" 21, "	Promoted to 1st Lieutenant December 23, '63
Do.	Alexander Walp	" 5, "	" 21, "	Mustered out December 12, 1861.
Do.	James B. Rutlige	" 12, "	" 21, "	Promoted to 1st Lieutenant.
Do.	Marshall Davis	....	....	Promoted to 1st Lieutenant.
Do.	Joseph B. Newton	Nov. 2, 1862	Feb. 16, 1863	Promoted to 1st Lieutenant.
Do.	Frank Fleck	Aug. 16, "	" 16, "	Promoted to 1st Lieutenant.
Do.	Henry G. Newbert	" 14, "	" 16, "	Promoted to 1st Lieutenant.
Do.	Oscar N. Gunn	Dec. 20, "	" 16, "	Promoted to 1st Lieutenant.
Do.	Wm. T. Bennett	Nov. 15, "	" 16, "	Promoted to 1st Lieutenant.
Do.	James McBride	" 1, "	" 16, "	Promoted to 1st Lieutenant.
Do.	Walter B. Kirk	Nov. 28, "	" 16, "	Killed in action.
Do.	N. O. Cobb	Oct. 16, "	" 16, "	Died of wounds September 1, 1864.
Do.	Ebner C. Tillitson	" 16, "	" 16, "	Died at Lookout Mountain September 24, '64.
Do.	John W. Beecher	Jan. 20, 1863	" 16, "	Resigned August 1, 1864.
Do.	Isaac L. Van Meter	Feb. 5, "	" 16, "	Tendered resignation.
Do.	Henry H. Everhard	Oct. 17, "	April 6, 1864	
Do.	Charles B. Mitchell	May 9, 1864	May 9, "	Promoted to 1st Lieutenant.

FOURTEENTH OHIO VOLUNTEER INFANTRY.

THERE are but few of the original records of the three-months' regiments preserved. In fact, the majority had no special record further than the disabilities and sometimes actual sufferings of an illy-appointed encampment.

After the first burst of patriotic indignation had expended itself, and was rendered futile by the want of system, large bodies of men, intended as the nuclei of regiments, lay in camp, often for weeks, awaiting muster into the service, and sometimes actually suffering for food and adequate shelter. These delays disgusted the recruits and damaged the service to an extent almost irretrievable. But, in the face of all these impediments, some regiments filled up immediately and presented themselves to the State ready for immediate service. Among these was the Fourteenth Ohio. It was raised in the Tenth Congressional District of Ohio, in and around Toledo.

The President's Proclamation for seventy-five thousand men was resp·nded to here just as it was in all parts of the State. Nearly one-half who offered their services had to be refused. In less than three days the Fourteenth Ohio was ready for the field, and on the 25th day of April, 1861, (just twelve days after the firing on Fort Sumter), it started from Toledo for Camp Taylor, near Cleveland, where it was thoroughly drilled and its organization completed. On the 18th of May the regiment was transferred from the State to the General Government.

The regiment left Cleveland on the 22d day of May for Columbus, there received their arms and accouterments, and on the same day started for Zanesville, Ohio; arrived at 1 P. M. on the 23d and immediately embarked for Marietta; occupied Camp Putnam until the 27th of May, then was ordered to embark for Parkersburg, Va., at which place it landed without opposition, and for the first time the regimental flag of the Fourteenth was unfurled in the enemy's country. Immediately on its arrival one company was double-quicked along the line of the Baltimore and Ohio Railroad, the bridges of which were being fired by retreating Rebels as a signal of the arrival of National troops in Western Virginia. Four Rebels were taken in the act of firing a bridge and sent to the rear as prisoners—guards were posted along the road to prevent further destruction; and on the 29th the regiment moved forward until Clarksburg was reached, having repaired all the burnt bridges and culverts up to that point. At Clarksburg some important arrests were made, and the trains were put to running for supplies.

On the 2d of June the regiment started by rail for the town of Webster, supplied with rations sufficient for a march to Philippi, a distance of thirteen miles. This march was performed on a dark, dismal, rainy night, to surprise a force of about two thousand Rebel cavalry in camp near that place. The march brought the regiment in front of the town at 5 A. M., when a battery belonging to the force opened on the surprised Rebels. The expedition was not wholly successful, because of a mistake made by a co-operating force of National troops who were to have come from an opposite direction. However, the Rebels were frightened and scattered to the bushes and hills as fast as their horses could carry them, some leaving their clothing and boots behind, and making off almost in the Georgia costume of "a shirt and pair of spurs." A few prisoners, all the Rebel stores, and five wagon loads of arms and munitions fell into the hands of the National force. On the

National side there were but four men wounded, including Colonel Kelly, afterward Major-General. One of the Rebel cavalry had his leg taken off by a cannon ball.

On the next day the Fourteenth, in company with the Sixteenth and Seventeenth Ohio, Sixth and Seventh Indiana, and First Virginia Infantry, went into camp on the hills in the rear of the town of Philippi.

From this camp expeditions were sent out against the guerrilla bands which infested that region; forced marches were made, in which the men suffered terribly, and frequently to no purpose, as at that early period "scares" were very easily raised and the wildest reports implicitly believed. A few men lost their lives on either side, but nothing of consequence was gained by either party. On the 2d of July, 1861, the regiment received its first pay, in gold and Ohio currency.

On the 7th of June the Rebels began to show themselves in force at Laurel Hill, and works were thrown up at Bealington to repel their attacks. Several cavalry charges made by the enemy were handsomely repulsed. On the 12th, General Garnett having suddenly retreated, the National forces moved out of their works, the Fourteenth taking the advance, took possession of a fort vacated by the enemy and pressed on after the retreating column. The Rebels were closely pressed, the road being strewed with trunks, boxes, tents, stalled baggage wagons and "tuckered-out" Rebels. In crossing Carrick's Ford the enemy was obliged to make a stand to save their trains. Taking a strong position they awaited the coming of the National forces. The advance guard of the Fourteenth was under the Rebel guns before they were aware of it. The Rebel flag was flaunted in their faces, and with shouts for Jeff. Davis came a shower of balls from the bluff above and opposite the stream. The Fourteenth closed up to its advanced guard and answered the enemy's first volley before the second had been fired. In twenty minutes, and just as the first regiment of the main column came up for action, the enemy gave way in great confusion, casting off everything that could retard escape. Over thirty well-laden baggage wagons, one battery, three stand of colors, and two hundred and fifty prisoners were the fruits of this victory. The next morning the regiment returned toward Philippi with the prisoners and captured train, fording at least six rivers and creeks swollen by the heavy rains, arriving at Philippi on the 15th of July.

The Fourteenth remained in camp on Laurel Hill until the 22d, when it moved to and crossed the Ohio at Bellaire, and there took cars on the Central Ohio for Toledo and home. The wounded received great attention from the people along the road, and the regiment was tendered ovations and kindnesses without number. It arrived at Toledo on the 25th of July, where it was hailed by the ringing of bells and firing of cannon. After partaking of a sumptuous feast, prepared by the citizens at the Oliver House, the regiment dispersed, and after a few days rest at home the men re-assembled, and again volunteered, in a body, for three years or during the war.

On the 23d of August, 1861, the Fourteenth received orders, and moved from Toledo to Cincinnati on the same day, reaching there in the evening. It was here supplied with arms and accouterments, and on the morning of the 25th crossed the Ohio to Covington, Ky., and took cars for Lexington and Frankfort. A short distance from Frankfort the train was assaulted by some of the "chivalry" of Kentucky, by hurling a volley of stones against the officer's car, breaking its windows and injuring some of its inmates. The train was stopped, two of the rascals captured and taken into Frankfort. Marching up the main street, with the prisoners in the column, one of them was recognized by a citizen of the place, who rushed into the ranks and drew a butcher knife across his throat. Although severely wounded the man did not die, and was placed in hospital. This incident serves to show the intense feeling between the loyal and rebel citizens of Kentucky at that day.

Remaining in Frankfort two days, the regiment moved by cars to Nicholasville, and established a camp of rendezvous, where for three weeks it was engaged in daily drill and was thoroughly disciplined.

Camp Dick Robinson was its next stopping place, and was reached on the evening of October 2d. While there a regiment of loyal East Tennesseeans arrived, having, as the men said, crawled on all fours through the Rebel lines. Among these brave and self-sacrificing loyal mountaineers were the then Tennessee United States Senator, Andrew Johnson, and Horace Maynard, Congressman, on their way to Washington City. Colonel Steedman, of the Fourteenth, invited Johnson to share his tent for the night. The rough attire and begrimmed appearance of Johnson caused "the boys" of the regiment to remark that "Old Jim Steedman" would invite "Andy" to a free use of soap before he would allow him to bunk with him. The East Tennesseeans being without arms, discipline, or drill, a detail was made from the Fourteenth for the purpose of perfecting them in drill.

About this time rumors were rife that the National forces stationed at or near Wild Cat, a desolate region sixty miles south-east of Camp Dick Robinson, were surrounded by the Rebels. The Fourteenth, with Barnet's First Ohio Artillery, started at once for Wild Cat, making forced marches through the deep mud and driving rain, and reached there at 9 A. M. of the 21st of October. On nearing the battle-field the crash of musketry and artillery was heard. This spurred the excited troops, who were going into their first engagement, and they double-quicked to the point of attack. Barnet's artillery was placed in position and the enemy shelled. Five companies of the Thirty-Third Indiana were on a wild knob almost completely surrounded by the Rebels. Under cover of a brisk fire from Barnet's battery, two companies of the Fourteenth, with picks and shovels, crawled through the bushes over a ravine, and reaching the knob fortified it in such manner that the enemy shortly abandoned the siege and retreated toward London, Ky. The Rebels left on the ground about thirty of their number killed and wounded.

The National forces pursued the Rebels under Zollicoffer to a point near London, and then went into camp for some two weeks. Orders were received to march back toward Lancaster, passing through Crab Orchard and Mt. Vernon. The next point was Lebanon, at which place the troops went into winter-quarters.

On the 31st of December the camp at Lebanon was abandoned and the march resumed, taking the route toward Somerset or Mill Springs. At Logan's Cross Roads the Rebels under Zollicoffer were met and defeated. Only one company of the Fourteenth participated in this—Compay C, Captain J. W. Brown, of Toledo.

Following up their success, the National troops pursued and drove the Rebels into their fortifications at Mill Springs. The night of the 19th of January was consumed in cannonading the enemy's works. Early on the morning of the 20th a general assault was ordered and executed, the Rebel works carried, twenty pieces of artillery, all the camp equipage, and one regiment of men captured. The main body of Rebels crossed the Cumberland River in a steamer and escaped, burning the steamer as they left. In the charge which carried the works the Fourteenth was the first regiment to enter. Pushing on after the flying enemy the regiment reached the bank of the river in time to fire into the rear of the retreating column as it was boarding the steamer.

The National forces remained at Mill Springs until the 11th of February. Then, with five days' rations, the line of march was resumed toward Louisville, passing through Stanford, Somerset, Danville, and intermediate places, arriving at Louisville on the 26th. Marching through the city, the Fourteenth was placed on board of transports, and in company with twenty thousand other troops left for Nashville, arriving there on the 4th of March.

Remaining in and around Nashville, building fortifications and perfecting the drill of the men, until the 20th of March, the necessity of re-enforcing General Grant's forces at Pittsburg Landing being apparent, General Buell marched with the greater part of his army, reaching Savannah on the 6th of April. Taking steamers a portion of the troops were landed on the field, at Pittsburg Landing, on the morning of the 7th of April, in time to participate in the engagement of that day, turning the tide of battle in favor of the National army. The Fourteenth did not come up in time to participate.

On the night of the 12th of April the regiment was sent on an expedition to Chickasaw Landing, in the vicinity of which five or six bridges were destroyed, thus preventing the enemy from being re-enforced. In effecting this destruction several severe skirmishes were had.

The regiment was taken back to Pittsburg Landing on a steamer on board of which was

General Sherman, who publicly thanked the men for the service they had performed. The Fourteenth rejoined its brigade, and with the vast army then concentrated under General Halleck, shared in the slow advance on Corinth. The only death in the regiment, during the siege, was that of fifer Frank Callern, of heart disease.

The regiment joined in pursuing the enemy to the vicinity of Booneville, Mississippi, where the chase was abandoned, the National troops returning to Corinth.

On the 23d of June, 1862, the Fourteenth, with other troops, was sent to Iuka, Mississippi, and from there marched to Tuscumbia, Alabama. After doing duty of various kinds, in and around this place, the line of march was resumed toward Nashville, Tennessee, passing through Florence, Fayetteville, Pulaski, etc. On this march General Robert L. McCook was murdered by guerrillas, near Waynesburg, Tennessee. Nashville was reached on the 7th of September. On the 14th marching orders were received for Bowling Green, Kentucky. This march was made in pursuit of Bragg's army, which was then moving on Louisville, Kentucky, which was reached on the 26th day of September, 1862. On this march the Fourteenth Ohio was under the command of Major Paul Edwards, Colonel Steedman having been assigned to General Robert L. McCook's late command, and Lieutenant-Colonel Este being absent on furlough. The march from Nashville to Louisville was one of great hardship, the weather being intensely hot, the roads very dusty, and water almost unattainable.

On the 1st of October the National army, under General Buell, moved out of Louisville and resumed the pursuit of Bragg's Rebel army. Marching by the Bardstown road, the Fourteenth in the advance, Springfield, Kentucky, was reached on the second day and Bardstown on the third. On the 9th day of October the brigade, in which the Fourteenth was acting, was detailed as head-quarter and ammunition train-guard, and for that reason did not participate in the battle of Perryville fought on that day.

General Buell's army moved in pursuit of the Rebels, marching through Danville and Crab Orchard, where the pursuit was abandoned and the National forces commenced a retrogade movement toward Nashville. Gallatin was reached on the 15th of November, where the brigade, in which the Fourteenth Ohio was acting, went into winter-quarters. While at this place the regiment was frequently detailed on scouting duty against the guerrilla (General John Morgan's) cavalry, with which it had several severe skirmishes losing some men. At Rolling Fork, Morgan was badly whipped and driven off, thus preventing a contemplated raid against Louisville. The regiment remained at Gallatin until January 13, 1863, engaged in similar duty. Leaving Gallatin, Nashville was reached on the 15th day of January, and after a day's rest in that city the regiment marched to Murfreesboro', as guard to an ammunition and provision train, returning the same night to Lavergne, where the brigade was engaged in fortifying against the enemy.

On the 3d day of June the regiment and brigade left Lavergne and took up the line of march for Triune, Tennessee, forming a portion of Rosecrans's advance on Tullahoma and Chattanooga. At Triune twenty days were consumed in rigid drill, gaining time to allow the necessary supplies to come up. The march being resumed, Hoover's Gap was reached on the night of the 26th of June, a brisk engagement coming off at that point, in which the Fourteenth participated with its brigade. Thirty men were lost in killed and wounded in this affair. The vicinity of Tullahoma was reached on the evening of the 28th day of June, and the enemy's videttes driven in. That night Captain Neubert's picket detail of the Fourteenth Ohio drove in the enemy's line of pickets, and reached a point so near the town as to enable him to discover that the Rebels were evacuating the place. This important information was immediately sent to head-quarters by Captain Neubert, and caused the advance, early the next morning, of the National forces. Elk River was crossed with great difficulty, that stream being quite deep, with a swift current, and a number of men were drowned. A spur of the Cumberland Mountains was crossed, and the National forces encamped in Sequatchie Valley on the 18th day of August, near Sweden Cove. On the 31st of August the army crossed the Tennessee River by means of rafts, the pontoons not being on hand. On the 19th of September the enemy was discovered in force on Chickamauga

Creek. The Fourteenth Ohio, under command of Lieutenant-Colonel Kingsbury, was immediately deployed in line of battle. The men were not in the best trim to engage in a fatiguing day's work, having marched incessantly all of the previous day and night, but they were ready and willing to perform their whole duty, and did it nobly. The regiment was engaged in hot and close contest with the enemy from nine A. M. to four P. M. Being then relieved, it replenished its ammunition boxes and again entered the fight, continuing in until sundown. That night it fell back one mile and went into camp. The next morning at nine o'clock the regiment again entered the field and had a desperate encounter with a portion of Longstreet's Rebel division. An unfortunate gap being left open by mistake in Thomas's line, the whole National force was compelled to fall back to prevent being overwhelmed. The village of Rossville was its stopping point.

On the 21st of September the regiment, with its brigade and division, was in line of battle all day, but was again compelled to give ground and fall back into hastily-constructed intrenchments near Chattanooga, the enemy following closely. The regiment went into the battle with four hundred and forty-nine men. Out of that number it lost two hundred and thirty-three killed, wounded, and missing. Fourteen enlisted men were captured by the enemy. Of fourteen officers, eight were severely wounded; among them, Captains Albert Moore, company A; H. W. Bigelow, company I; Dan. Pomeroy, company D; W. B. Pugh, company H; J. J. Clark, company C; and Lieutenant James E. McBride, company F. Colonel Croxton, of the Tenth Kentucky, commanding the brigade, was also severely wounded.

To procure rations on one occasion, during the ensuing beleaguerment at Chattanooga, a detail of one hundred men from the Fourteenth, under Captain Neubert, was sent to Stevenson, Alabama, crossing the rugged mountain between that place and Chattanooga. This detail started on a march of eleven days' duration with only one day's rations. After encountering terrible hardships, subsisting on parched corn, leaving along the roads the wrecks of more than half their wagons and the dead bodies of twenty mules, Stevenson was reached; ten wagons out of the sixty they started with were loaded with "hard-tack," and the return journey commenced. After twenty-five days' absence this detail reached Chattanooga (9th of November) and distributed their precious freight among the famished troops.

In the brilliant assault on Mission Ridge the Fourteenth Ohio bore a gallant part, charging and capturing a Rebel battery of three guns, which General Hardee in person was superintending, losing sixteen killed, ninety-one wounded, and three missing.

On the 26th of November the National forces started in pursuit of the Rebel army toward Ringgold, at which point the enemy made a stand on the 28th. General Hooker's forces being in the advance, made a charge on the Rebels, but were driven back. The Fourteenth Corps coming up, formed a line of battle and charged the Rebel position, but the enemy had fled toward Buzzard's Roost. The Fourteenth Ohio returned to Chattanooga on the 29th of November, and was reviewed by General Grant on the 1st of December, 1863.

Of those that were eligible, all but thirty men of the entire regiment re-enlisted for another term of three years. This occurred on the 17th of December. On Christmas-day the mustering of the men commenced, and by working hard all day and through the night the rolls were completed. Marching to Bridgeport on the 31st of December, the Fourteenth Ohio there took the cars and reached Nashville on the 2d day of January, 1864. On this trip the cold was so intense as to freeze the feet of several colored servants belonging to the regiment so badly as to make amputation necessary.

From Nashville the regiment went by cars to Louisville, and thence by boat to Cincinnati, arriving at that city on the morning of the 4th of January. Cars were at once taken for Toledo, the home of the regiment, where it was warmly received by the citizens, and addressed in their behalf by the Hon. M. R. Waite.

On the 6th day of February, the thirty days' furlough having expired, the regiment moved by rail to Cleveland, and there went into camp. Remaining there about a week, it started for Cincinnati and the front, reaching Nashville on the 23d of February and Chattanooga on the 29th.

On the 5th day of March the regiment moved to Ringgold, where it performed hard duty in building corduroy roads between that place and Chattanooga, picketing outposts, etc. On the 9th day of May it moved with its brigade on Dalton, driving in the enemy's videttes to the vicinity of Tunnel Hill, there encountering the enemy in force. At this point commenced that long, fatiguing campaign for the possession of Atlanta, the "Gate City" of the extreme South. The Fourteenth, in all the marches and the almost incessant skirmishes and flanking movements of that campaign, bore an honorable part. It lost heavily in men and officers. While lying in front of Atlanta the regiment lost twenty men killed and wounded.

On the 26th of August a flanking movement was commenced toward Jonesboro', and on the 31st the Atlanta and Western Railroad was struck five miles north of Jonesboro', where two hundred prisoners were captured. On the 1st of September the Third Division of the Fourteenth Army Corps, in which was brigaded the Fourteenth Ohio, continued the movement in the direction of Jonesboro', destroying the track of the railroad as it marched. At half-past four P. M. of that day the Third Division (General Baird) confronted the enemy's works surrounding Jonesboro'.

The Third Brigade, in command of Colonel Este, of the Fourteenth Ohio, of Baird's division, was drawn up in line of battle in the immediate rear of a regular brigade of General Carlin's division, which had just made an unsuccessful charge on the Rebel works in the edge of the woods on the opposite side of a large cornfield. Colonel Este, with his brigade, consisting of the Fourteenth and Thirty-Eighth Ohio, Tenth Kentucky, and Seventy-Fourth Indiana, stood ready for the fight. Colonel Este gave the order: "Battalions, forward!—guide center!" and General Baird waved his hand for the "forward." The lines moved steadily forward amid a shower of balls. A battery opened with grape and cannister, but the brigade moved steadily on. The edge of the timber was gained, and, with a yell and a charge, the Rebel works were gained, and a hand-to-hand conflict ensued. The Rebels belonged to General Pat. Cleburne's division, and contested the ground with great stubbornness and bravery. It was not until many of them were killed with the cold steel that they would surrender. They finally succumbed and were marched to the rear as prisoners. The Fourteenth took nearly as many prisoners as the regiment numbered, a battery of four guns, several stands of colors, and two lines of trenches full of men. All this was not accomplished without sad cost. The brigade lost thirty-three per cent. of its number. One hundred members of the Fourteenth, whose time had expired, went willingly into this fight, some of whom were killed and many wounded.

After the Jonesboro' fight the brigade in which the Fourteenth was acting marched back to Atlanta, leaving the pursuit of the enemy to other troops.

The Fourteenth next followed in pursuit of Hood's troops, on their advance into Tennessee, as far up as Rome, where the chase was abandoned, and the brigade returned to Kingston, Georgia, reaching there on the 6th of November.

It next joined General Sherman's forces at Atlanta, and participated in the "march to the sea." Then came the march through the Carolinas to Goldsboro' and Raleigh.

At Raleigh the surrender of Lee and his army near Richmond was promulgated to the National forces. The surrender of Johnston quickly followed, and then the march up to the Capital of the Nation, where the Grand Armies of the Republic passed in review before the President and Cabinet.

On the 15th of June the Fourteenth Ohio started from Washington by rail for Parkersburg, on the Ohio River, arriving there on the 18th of June. It immediately embarked on boats and was taken to Louisville, Kentucky. Remaining in camp at that place until the 11th day of July, the regiment was mustered out of the service and returned to its home, reaching Toledo on the 13th of July, 1865, after over four years of as honorable and active a career as that of any regiment in the army.

15th REGIMENT OHIO VOLUNTEER INFANTRY.*

ROSTER, THREE YEARS' SERVICE.

RANK.	NAME.	DATE OF RANK.	COM. ISSUED.	REMARKS.
Colonel	MOSES R. DICKEY	Aug. 7, 1861	Aug. 7, 1861	Resigned October 21, 1862.
Do.	WM. WALLACE	Oct. 24, 1862	Nov. 28, 1862	Honorably discharged July 19, 1864.
Do.	FRANK ASKEW	July 22, 1864	July 22, 1864	Mustered out with regiment.
Lt. Colonel	WM. T. WILSON	Aug. 6, 1861	Aug. 7, 1861	Resigned August 11, 1862.
Do.	WM. WALLACE	" 11, 1862	" 26, 1862	Promoted to Colonel October 24, 1862.
Do.	FRANK ASKEW	Oct. 24, "	Nov. 28, "	Promoted to Colonel.
Do.	JOHN McCLENAHAN	July 22, 1864	July 22, 1864	Mustered out with regiment.
Major	WM. WALLACE	Aug. 7, 1861	Aug. 7, 1861	Promoted to Lieutenant-Colonel Aug. 11, 1862.
Do.	JOHN McCLENAHAN	" 11, 1862	" 26, 1862	Promoted to Lieutenant-Colonel.
Do.	ANDREW R. Z. DAWSON	July 22, 1864	July 22, 1864	Mustered out with regiment.
Do.	JOHN N. DUBOIS	Feb. 28, 1865	Feb. 28, 1865	Mustered out with regiment.
Surgeon	ORRIN FERRIS	Sept. 20, 1861	Oct. 21, 1861	Resigned March 15, 1862.
Do.	HENRY SPILLMAN	March 18, 1862	April 4, 1862	
Do.	D. S. HALL	June 2, "	June 2, "	Resigned July 1, 1862.
Do.	HENRY H. SEIS	Aug. 1, "	Dec. 1, "	Resigned August 1, 1864.
Do.	WM. J. KELLY	Sept. 26, 1864	Sept. 26, 1864	Resigned.
Do.	WM. M. CLARK	Oct. 14, "	Oct. 14, "	Mustered out with regiment.
Ass't Surgeon	GEORGE LIGGETT	" 21, 1861	Jan. 28, 1862	Resigned July 13, 1862.
Do.	WM. J. KELLY	July 13, 1862	July 22, "	Promoted to Surgeon.
Do.	DAVID WELSH	Aug. 12, "	Aug. 12, "	Promoted to Surgeon 33d regiment.
Do.	WM. M. CLARK	July 20, 1863	July 20, 1863	Promoted to Surgeon.
Do.	J. B. YOUNG	March 14, 1865	March 14, 1865	Mustered out with regiment.
Chaplain	RICHARD L. GANTER	Sept. 20, 1861	Oct. 21, 1861	Resigned April 15, 1862.
Do.	RANDALL ROSS	July 6, 1863	July 20, 1863	Mustered out with regiment.
Captain	James Cummings	Sept. 9, 1861	Oct. 17, 1861	Died March, 1864.
Do.	John McClenahan	" 10, "	" 17, "	Promoted to Major August 11, 1862.
Do.	Hiram Miller	" 11, "	" 17, "	Resigned July 27, 1862.
Do.	Isaac M. Kirby	" 12, "	" 17, "	Resigned May 4, 1862.
Do.	Frank Askew	" 13, "	" 17, "	Promoted to Lieutenant-Colonel Oct. 24, 1862.
Do.	Amos Glover	" 20, "	" 17, "	Honorably discharged March 17, 1864.
Do.	Andrew R. Z. Dawson	" 11, "	" 17, "	Promoted to Major.
Do.	Abraham C. Cummins	" 12, "	" 17, "	Resigned April 25, 1862.
Do.	T. S. Gilliland	" 21, "	" 17, "	Resigned April 30, 1862.
Do.	Otho S. Holloway	" 23, "	Nov. 29, "	Resigned July 1, 1862.
Do.	David J. Culbertson	Jan. 30, 1862	Jan. 30, 1862	Revoked.
Do.	Cyrus Reasoner	April 25, "	May 9, "	Resigned July 1, 1862.
Do.	Andrew M. Burns	" 30, "	" 10, "	Resigned March 18, 1863.
Do.	Thomas E. Douglas	July 1, "	July 10, "	Transferred to Invalid Corps.
Do.	Chandler W. Carroll	" 1, "	Aug. 12, "	Mustered out.
Do.	David J. Culbertson	May 4, "	" 12, "	Dismissed April 6, 1863.
Do.	Jeremiah M. Dunn	July 27, "	" 12, "	Resigned April 1, 1863.
Do.	Joshua K. Brown	Aug. 11, "	Sept. 19, "	Resigned June 1, 1863.
Do.	Lorenzo Danford	Oct. 24, "	Nov. 28, "	Resigned August 1, 1864.
Do.	George W. Cummins	March 18, 1863	April 7, 1863	Mustered out.
Do.	John G. Byrd	April 1, "	June 3, "	Mustered out.
Do.	Samuel S. Pettit	" 6, "	" 3, "	Resigned April 28, 1864.
Do.	Calvin R. Taft	June 1, "	" 10, "	Mustered out.
Do.	J. R. Updegrove	Nov. 21, "	March 18, 1864	Resigned October 2, 1864.
Do.	Cyrus H. Askew	March 18, 1864	" 18, "	Resigned June 14, 1865.
Do.	Thomas W. Hanson	July 9, "	July 9, "	Killed December 16, 1865.
Do.	Samuel Becktell	" 9, "	" 9, "	Resigned September 1, 1864, as 1st Lieutenant.
Do.	J. N. Dubois	Aug. 11, "	Aug. 11, "	Promoted to Major.
Do.	David N. Geiger	" 11, "	" 11, "	Mustered out with regiment.
Do.	Vesper Dornick	Oct. 12, "	Oct. 12, "	Mustered out with regiment.
Do.	Augustus L. Smith	Nov. 26, "	Nov. 26, "	Declined promotion.
Do.	Alexis Cope	" 27, "	" 27, "	On detached service at muster out of reg't.
Do.	Alexander B. Lord	Jan. 18, 1865	Jan. 18, 1865	Honorably discharged Jan 19, 1865.
Do.	Lucius Doolittle	" 18, "	" 18, "	Mustered out with regiment.
Do.	Julius A. Gleason	" 18, "	" 18, "	Mustered out with regiment.
Do.	Thomas C. Davis	" 18, "	" 18, "	Mustered out with regiment.
Do.	Collin P. Leiter	Feb. 2, "	Feb. 2, "	Commission returned.
Do.	John J. Glover	" 2, "	" 2, "	Mustered out at expiration of service.
Do.	Joseph N. Welker	" 28, "	" 28, "	Declined promotion.
Do.	Reese Pickering	" 28, "	" 28, "	Mustered out with regiment.
Do.	John W. Wilson	March 29, "	March 29, "	Mustered out with regiment.
Do.	David Weh	" 29, "	" 29, "	Mustered out with regiment.
Do.	Jesse L. Grimes	Sept. 4, "	Sept. 4, "	Mustered out with regiment.
1st Lieutenant	Theodore C. Bowles	Aug. 31, 1861	Oct. 21, 1861	Resigned May 17, 1862.
Do.	Cyrus Reasoner	Sept. 9, "	" 17, "	Promoted to Captain April 25, 1862.
Do.	Joshua K. Brown	" 10, "	" 17, "	Promoted to Captain August 11, 1862.
Do.	Jeremiah M. Dunn	" 11, "	" 17, "	Promoted to Captain July 27, 1862.
Do.	Thomas E. Douglas	" 11, "	" 17, "	Promoted to Captain July 1, 1862.
Do.	David J. Culbertson	" 12, "	" 17, "	Promoted to Captain.
Do.	Andrew M. Burns	" 12, "	" 17, "	Promoted to Captain.
Do.	Chandler W. Carroll	" 13, "	" 17, "	Promoted to Captain.
Do.	Calvin R. Taft	" 12, "	" 21, "	Promoted to Captain.
Do.	James B. Welch	" 20, "	" 17, "	Mustered out August 17, 1863.
Do.	Wm. C. Scott	" 21, "	" 17, "	Resigned May 25, 1862.
Do.	Robert H. Cochran	" 23, "	" 17, "	Resigned May 30,'63; mustered out June 16,'63
Do.	Joseph McKee	Nov. 26, "	Nov. 26, "	Resigned November 28, 1862.
Do.	Joseph Goldsmith	Jan. 30, 1862	Jan. 30, 1862	Revoked.
Do.	John R. Clark	April 25, "	May 9, "	Resigned December 19, 1862.
Do.	George W. Cummins	" 30, "	" 10, "	Promoted to Captain.
Do.	John G. Gregg	May 26, "	Jan. 26, "	Resigned July 3, 1862.

* For three months' Roster see page 138.

RANK.	NAME.	DATE OF RANK.	COM. ISSUED.	REMARKS.
1st Lieutenant	Lorenzo Danford	July 1, 1862	Aug. 12, 1862	Promoted to Captain.
Do.	Cyrus H. Askew	" 1, "	" 10, "	Promoted to Captain.
Do.	Joseph Goldsmith	May 4, "	" 12, "	Resigned May 30, 1863.
Do.	John G. Byrd	July 27, "	" 12, "	Promoted to Captain. [May 30, 1863.
Do.	Robert H. Cochran	June 16, "	" 11, "	Reinstated by req. of Maj. Gen. Buell; resig'd
Do.	J. R. Updegrove	May 26, "	Sept. 19, "	Promoted to Captain.
Do.	J. N. Dubois	Aug. 11, "	" 19, "	Promoted to Captain.
Do.	Samuel Hellis	Oct. 24, "	Nov. 28, "	Honorably discharged December 15, 1863.
Do.	Elze Stringer	Dec. 19, "	Dec. 31, "	Resigned March 7, 1863.
Do.	Thomas W. Hanson	Nov. 28, "	April 7, 1863	Promoted to Captain.
Do.	Samuel Becktell	March 7, 1863	" 7, "	Promoted to Captain.
Do.	Samuel S. Pettit	" 18, "	" 7, "	Promoted to Captain.
Do.	Wallace McGrath	April 1, "	June 3, "	Mustered out.
Do.	David N. Geiger	" 6, "	" 3, "	Promoted to Captain.
Do.	David S. Adams	June 11, "	" 11, "	Resigned January 24, 1865.
Do.	Vesper Dorniek	May 30, "	" 10, "	Promoted to Captain.
Do.	Augustus L. Smith	June 11, "	" 10, "	Mustered out.
Do.	Nicholas M. Fowler	Aug. 8, "	Sept. 9, "	Killed September 20, 1863.
Do.	Alexander B. Lord	March 18, 1864	March 18, 1864	Promoted to Captain.
Do.	Alexis Cope	Dec. 15, 1863	Jan. 10, "	Promoted to Captain.
Do.	Lucius Doolittle	March 18, 1864	March 18, "	Promoted to Captain.
Do.	Alonzo J. Gleason	" 18, "	" 18, "	Promoted to Captain.
Do.	Nathaniel Neiland	July 9, "	July 9, "	Honorably discharged Sept. 23, 1864, as 2d Lt.
Do.	Thomas C. Davis	" 9, "	" 9, "	Promoted to Captain.
Do.	Charles J. Rodig	Aug. 11, "	Aug. 11, "	Killed September 16, 1864.
Do.	Collin P. Leiter	" 11, "	" 11, "	Revoked; wounded at Ricket Mills, Ga.
Do.	John J. Glover	Oct. 12, "	Oct. 12, "	Promoted to Captain.
Do.	Oliver Donner	" 12, "	" 12, "	Honorably discharged July 21, 1865.
Do.	Joseph N. Welker	Nov. 26, "	Nov. 26, "	Declined promotion.
Do.	Reese Pickering	Dec. 27, "	Dec. 27, "	Promoted to Captain.
Do.	Andrew J. Gleason	" 27, "	" 27, "	Declined promotion.
Do.	John W. Wilson	Jan. 18, 1865	Jan. 18, 1865	Promoted to Captain.
Do.	Peter G. Gardner	" 18, "	" 18, "	No vacancy at time of promotion.
Do.	Jasper N. Welch	" 18, "	" 18, "	No vacancy at time of promotion.
Do.	James G. Gass	" 18, "	" 18, "	No vacancy at time of promotion.
Do.	David Web	Feb. 2, "	Feb. 2, "	Promoted to Captain.
Do.	Jesse L. Grimes	" 2, "	" 2, "	Promoted to Captain.
Do.	Jacob Boger	" 2, "	" 2, "	Mustered out with regiment.
Do.	Peter G. Gardner	" 2, "	" 2, "	Mustered out with regiment.
Do.	Jasper N. Welch	" 2, "	" 2, "	Mustered out with regiment.
Do.	James G. Gass	" 10, 1865	" 10, 1865	Mustered out with regiment.
Do.	Robert S. McClenahan	" 10, "	" 10, "	Mustered out with regiment.
Do.	Morris Cope	" 28, "	" 28, "	Mustered out with regiment.
Do.	Franklin Armstrong	March 29, "	March 29, "	Mustered out with regiment.
Do.	Vincent T. Trago	June 16, "	June 16, "	Mustered out with regiment.
Do.	Samuel C. McKirahan	" 16, "	" 16, "	Mustered out with regiment.
Do.	Alexander Moore	Sept. 4, "	Sept. 4, "	
2d Lieutenant	Samuel W. Stover	" 9, "	Oct. 17, "	Discharged February 15, 1862.
Do.	John R. Clark	" 10, "	" 17, "	Promoted to 1st Lieutenant.
Do.	John G. Byrd	" 11, "	" 17, "	Promoted to 1st Lieutenant.
Do.	Cyrus H. Askew	" 11, "	" 17, "	Promoted to 1st Lieutenant.
Do.	Samuel Becktell	" 12, "	" 17, "	Promoted to 1st Lieutenant.
Do.	George W. Cummings	" 12, "	" 17, "	Promoted to 1st Lieutenant.
Do.	Lorenzo Danford	" 13, "	" 17, "	Promoted to 1st Lieutenant.
Do.	Nicholas M. Fowler	" 20, "	" 17, "	Promoted to 1st Lieutenant.
Do.	Baldwin D. Challin	" 21, "	" 17, "	Resigned December 18, 1861.
Do.	Vesper Dorn ck	" 23, "	Nov. 20, "	Promoted to 1st Lieutenant. [3, 1862.
Do.	J. G. Gregg	Jan. 9, 1862	Jan. 9, 1862	Promoted to 1st Lieut. May 26, '62; resi'd July
Do.	Elze Stringer	" 30, "	" 30, "	Promoted to 1st Lieutenant.
Do.	J. R. Updegrove	April 25, "	May 10, "	Promoted to 1st Lieutenant.
Do.	J. N. Dubois	" 25, "	" 10, "	Promoted to 1st Lieutenant.
Do.	Lucius Doolittle	" 30, "	" 10, "	Promoted to 1st Lieutenant.
Do.	Samuel S. Pettit	" 30, "	" 10, "	Promoted to 1st Lieutenant.
Do.	Wallace McGrath	May 2?, "	June 28, "	Promoted to 1st Lieutenant.
Do.	Samuel Hellis	July 1, "	July 10, "	Promoted to 1st Lieutenant.
Do.	Augustus Smith	" 1, "	Aug. 12, "	Promoted to 1st Lieutenant.
Do.	Alonzo J. Gleason	Aug. 1, "	" 12, "	Promoted to 1st Lieutenant.
Do.	Walter Hewittson	" 11, "	Sept. 19, "	Resigned August 1, 1863.
Do.	Thomas Hanson	May 28, "	" 19, "	
Do.	Andress E. Smiley	Oct. 21, "	Nov. 28, "	Killed June 24, 1863.
Do.	Alexander B. Lord	March 18, 1863	April 7, 1863	Promoted to 1st Lieutenant.
Do.	David Geiger	Nov. 28, 1862	" 7, "	Promoted to 1st Lieutenant.
Do.	Thomas C. Davis	April 1, 1863	June 3, "	Promoted to 1st Lieutenant.
Do.	Alexis Cope	" 6, "	" 3, "	Promoted to 1st Lieutenant.
Do.	Frank W. Saunders	May 30, "	" 10, "	Died of wounds received at Mission Ridge.
Do.	Nathaniel Neiland	Jan. 1, "	" 10, "	Promoted to 1st Lieutenant.
Do.	Oliver Donner	March 18, 1864	March 18, 1864	Detached at own request.
Do.	John J. Glover	Nov. 21, 1863	" 8, "	Promoted to 1st Lieutenant.
Do.	Andrew L. Hadden	" 21, "	" 8, "	Killed at Kenesaw.
Do.	Charles J. Rodig	" 2, "	" 9, "	Promoted to 1st Lieutenant.
Do.	Joseph N. Welker	March 18, 1864	" 18, "	Promoted to 1st Lieutenant.
Do.	Reese Pickering	" 18, "	" 18, "	Promoted to 1st Lieutenant.
Do.	Collin P. Leiter	Nov. 4, 1863	" 30, "	Promoted to 1st Lieutenant.
Do.	John W. Wilson	July 9, 1864	July 9, "	Promoted to 1st Lieutenant.
Do.	Andrew J. Gleason	" 9, "	" 9, "	Promoted to 1st Lieutenant.
Do.	Peter G. Gardener	" 9, "	" 9, "	Commissions returned on account of not be-
Do.	Jasper N. Welch	" 9, "	" 9, "	ing ranking sergeants at date of issue.
Do.	James G. Gass	Nov. 26, "	Nov. 26, "	
Do.	Robert S. McClenahan	" 26, "	" 26, "	Promoted to 1st Lieutenant.
Do.	Morris Cope	" 26, "	" 26, "	Commission returned; not in line of promot.
Do.	Franklin Armstrong	" 26, "	" 26, "	Promoted to 1st Lieutenant.
Do.	Vincent T. Trago	Feb. 28, 1865	Feb. 28, 1865	Promoted to 1st Lieutenant.
Do.	Alexander Moore	June 16, "	June 16, "	Promoted to 1st Lieutenant.
Do.	George W. Chessell	Nov. 21, "	Nov. 24, "	
Do.	John J. Gregory	" 21, "	" 21, "	
Do.	John A. Green	" 24, "	" 21, "	Mustered out as sergeants with regiment. Complimentary commissions given after muster out.
Do.	Calvin Etzler	" 21, "	" 21, "	
Do.	Henry M. Leedy	" 21, "	" 21, "	
Do.	John Crampton	" 21, "	" 24, "	
Do.	James O. Scott	" 24, "	" 21, "	
Do.	David C. Thurstin	" 24, "	" 21, "	

FIFTEENTH OHIO VOLUNTEER INFANTRY.

THE FIFTEENTH OHIO VOLUNTEER INFANTRY was among the first to respond to the President's call for seventy-five thousand men for three months' service, and on the 4th of May, 1861, the regiment was organized at Camp Jackson, Columbus, Ohio, and four days after moved to Camp Goddard, near Zanesville, Ohio. Here it spent about ten days, engaged in drilling, disciplining, and active preparations for the field. It was then ordered into West Virginia, and crossing the Ohio River at Bellaire, it was employed for some time in guard duty on the Baltimore and Ohio Railroad, advancing as far as Grafton. It was engaged in the rout of the Rebels under General Porterfield at Philippi, on the 13th of June, and afterward took part in the affairs of Laurel Hill and Carrick's Ford. The regiment performed a large amount of marching and guard duty and rendered valuable service to the Government in assisting to stay the progress of the Rebels, who were endeavoring to carry the war into the North. Having served its term of enlistment, it returned to Columbus, Ohio, and was discharged about the 1st of August, having lost but two men—one killed and one died of disease.

The President having issued his call for three hundred thousand men for three years, the soldiers of the Fifteenth felt the importance of a hearty response, and with their patriotism and ardor not lessened, but rather increased by the trials and exposure incident to their three months' campaign, they almost immediately and almost unanimously resolved to re-enlist; and the regiment was reorganized at Camp Mordecai Bartley, near Mansfield, Ohio, and left Camp Bartley for Camp Dennison on the 26th of September, 1861. At this place they received their arms and the remainder of their clothing, camp, and garrison equipage. The regiment was armed with old Springfield and Harper's Ferry muskets altered, except companies A and B, which received Enfield rifles.

The outfit being completed, on the 4th of October the regiment left for the field, its destination being Lexington, Kentucky. It remained in camp at Lexington until the 12th, when it was transported by rail to Louisville, and from there to Camp Nevin near Nolin's Station, Kentucky. At this place it was assigned to the Sixth Brigade, (General R. W. Johnston commanding), Second Division, (General A. McD. McCook commanding), of the Army of the Ohio, then commanded by General W. T. Sherman, subsequently by General Buell. The regiment remained at Camp Nevin until the 9th of December, 1861, when the division marched to Bacon Creek, and on the following day the Sixth Brigade occupied Mumfordsville. On the morning of the 14th the Second Division broke camp, moving in the direction of West Point to embark for Fort Donelson; but upon receiving intelligence of its capture, the division was marched to Bowling Green. Crossing Barren River on the 27th, the command marched for Nashville, Tennessee, which place was reached on the 2d of March. Camping grounds were selected about three miles from the city, and the army rested till the 16th, when the march to Savannah began; which point was reached on the night of April 6th, and on the morning of the 7th the regiment embarked for the battle-field and was engaged from about 12 M. till 4 P. M., when the enemy retreated. In this engagement the regiment lost six men killed and sixty-two wounded.

In the subsequent operations against Corinth the Second Division formed the reserve of the army and did not take the front until the 27th of May. It was continually skirmishing with the enemy until the 30th, when the town was occupied by our forces. On the 10th of June the division marched to Battle Creek, Tennessee, crossing the Tennessee River at Florence, and resting there several days, arrived at Battle Creek on the 18th of July. The regiment was engaged in building a fort at the mouth of Battle Creek, and in the ordinary duties of camp, until the 20th of August, when General McCook's command moved to Altemonte on the Cumberland Mountains, in which direction the invading army under Bragg was marching. From Altemonte the division marched *via* Manchester and Murfreesboro' to Nashville, arriving there on the 8th of September. After halting two or three days the army marched to Bowling Green, and thence by way of West Point to Louisville, arriving on the 25th of September. On the 1st of October the Second Division marched on the Shelbyville Pike in pursuit of the enemy, reaching Shelbyville the second day; remaining in camp a few days the march was resumed to Lawrenceburg, where a skirmish was had with the enemy, in which the regiment was engaged. The division then marched to Perryville, which was reached a few days after the battle of Chaplin Hills, and there joined the main army and marched in pursuit of Bragg as far as Crab Orchard, where it remained several days, and then marched to Nashville, where it arrived on the 7th of November, 1862.

The army was reorganized and thoroughly drilled here, and on the 26th of December advanced upon the enemy's position at Murfreesboro'. In the battle of Stone River the regiment was heavily engaged, losing eighteen killed and eighty-nine wounded. After the occupation of Murfreesboro' by the army under General Rosecrans, the Fifteenth was engaged in drilling, foraging, fortifying, and picket duty, until the 24th of July, when an advance was ordered on Tullahoma and Shelbyville, which places were occupied by our army after the enemy was dislodged from his strong position at Golner's and Liberty Gaps, the latter being carried by the Second Division, and this regiment taking a very prominent part throughout. In this engagement one officer and seven men were killed, and twenty-three wounded. The Second Division was stationed at Tullahoma till the 16th of August, when it was ordered to Bellefonte, Alabama, marching *via* Winchester and Salem, and arriving at its destination on the 22d. Remaining there about a week, the division marched to near Stevenson, Alabama. On the 2d of September the march was resumed in the direction of Rome, Georgia, crossing Lookout Mountain and camping at the eastern foot, near Alpine, on the 10th. After remaining in position for two days the command recrossed Lookout Mountain to Winson's Valley, and on the 11th marched to a position in connection with the main army in Lookout Valley.

The regiment remained in position on the extreme right flank of the army until the morning of the 19th when it marched for the battle-field of Chickamauga, a distance of thirteen miles, and was engaged soon after its arrival. At Chickamauga the regiment lost one officer and nine men killed, two officers and sixty-nine men wounded, and forty men missing. The regiment bore its share in the arduous labors and privations of the seige of Chattanooga, and on the 25th of November participated in the brilliant assault of Mission Ridge, capturing a number of prisoners and some artillery. On the 28th of November the regiment, then belonging to the First Brigade, Third Division, Fourth Army Corps, marched with the corps to the relief of Knoxville, Tennessee, arriving on the 8th of December; on the 20th the command moved to Strawberry Plains by way of Flat Creek.

On the 14th of January, 1864, the greater portion of the regiment having re-enlisted as veterans, it started for Columbus, Ohio, *via* Chattanooga, preparatory to being furloughed. The regiment arrived in Columbus, with three hundred and fifty veterans, on the 10th of February, and the men were furloughed on the 12th. On the 14th of March the regiment assembled at Camp Chase to return to the field, having recruited to upward of nine hundred men. Upon arriving at Nashville, on the 22d, the regiment was ordered to march to Chattanooga, arriving on the 5th of April. On the 8th the regiment moved to Cleveland, Tennessee, meeting with a serious accident near Charleston, Tennessee, by a railroad train being thrown from the track, by which twenty men were more or less injured.

The regiment moved to McDonald's Station on the 20th, and remained there till the opening

THE TENNESSEE AT CHATTANOOGA.

of the spring campaign. At noon, on the 3d of May, the regiment broke camp and marched to Tunnel Hill, where General Sherman's army took position, and was constantly skirmishing with the enemy, this regiment being frequently engaged until the 13th, when the enemy evacuated Rocky Face Ridge and our army took possession of Dalton.

The Fifteenth participated in the subsequent pursuit of the Rebels, in the battle at Resaca and again in the pursuit and engagement near Dallas, where the regiment suffered severely; losing nineteen men killed, three officers and sixty-one men wounded, and nineteen men missing, who were supposed to be either killed or severely wounded. The color-guard, with the exception of one corporal, were all either killed or wounded, but the colors were safely brought off by the surviving member of the guard, Corporal David Hart, of company I. The Rebels having evacuated their works on the 5th of June, the army moved to the vicinity of Acworth, and on the 10th advanced near to Kenesaw Mountain. While skirmishing sharply, on the 14th of June, the regiment lost one officer and one man killed, and five men wounded, all belonging to company A. On the morning of June 18th, the Rebels having withdrawn, a party of three or four men advanced to reconnoiter, and picking up a couple of stragglers they were sent back in charge of Peter Cupp, a private of company H, who, in returning to the regiment, suddenly came upon a Rebel outpost which had been left by accident. Cupp announced the withdrawal to them and ordered them to stack their arms and surrender, which they did, and one captain, one lieutenant and sixteen men of the First Georgia Volunteers, were marched into our lines by private Cupp. While in the vicinity the regiment was engaged in scouting and skirmishing, frequently capturing prisoners.

After crossing the Chattahoochie the regiment moved down the river on the 11th of July, and in connection with the division, drove back the enemy's cavalry and covered the crossing of the Fourteenth Corps. The line was advanced each day until it closed in around the Rebel works before Atlanta. On the night of August 25th, the command to which the regiment belonged withdrew from the works in front and commenced the movement upon the communications in rear of Atlanta, skirmishing with the enemy at Lovejoy's Station. The army withdrew from Lovejoy's Station on the night of September 5th, and reaching Atlanta the 8th, the Fourth Corps encamped near Decatur.

When the army of Hood began its raid upon our communications the regiment marched *via* Marietta and Rome, to the relief of Resaca, October 3d, and from Resaca it marched through Snake Creek Gap, by way of Salesville, Chattanooga, and Pulaski, to Columbia, where it was engaged in a slight skirmish. From Columbia the army moved toward Franklin, passing in view of the camp-fires of a corps of the enemy near Spring Hill, Tennessee. The regiment did not participate in the battle of Franklin, but was assigned the duty of covering the withdrawal of the forces and the retreat to Nashville. At Nashville the regiment formed the extreme left of the army, and when the order came for the left to move forward the regiment advanced rapidly, capturing a fine battery of four brass guns and some thirty prisoners. On the 16th of December the enemy was found entrenched in a strong position on the Franklin Pike, about five miles from the city. The regiment participated in a movement upon these works, capturing prisoners to the number of two commissioned officers and one hundred men. The entire loss sustained by the regiment in the two days of the fight was two officers and one man killed, and two officers and twenty-four men wounded. The most vigorous pursuit was made by our army, but the infantry was unable to overtake the flying enemy, and after following the Rebels to Lexington, Alabama, the corps moved in the direction of Huntsville, and the regiment went into Camp at Bird Springs about the 4th or 5th of January, 1865, and remained till the 15th of March when it was ordered to move into East Tennessee.

It moved by railroad to New Market, Tennessee, and then took up the line of march to Greenville, to assist in preventing the escape of Lee and Johnson, while Grant and Sherman pressed them to a surrender. The Fifteenth arrived at Greenville on the 5th of April, and on the 22d was ordered back to Nashville. On this march the regiment acted as train guard and reached Nashville about the 1st of May, 1865. From this time till the 16th of June, the regiment was in camp near Nashville, Tennessee, when orders were received to move to Texas. With a good degree of cheerfulness the men turned their backs once more upon their homes, went to Johnstonville and thence by boat to New Orleans. Moving down a short distance below the city they bivouacked in the old Jackson Battle Ground till July 5th, when they shipped for Texas. The regiment arrived at Indianola, Texas, July 9th; disembarked, and in order to obtain a sufficient supply of water marched that same night to Green Lake, a distance of about twenty miles. Remaining here just one month, on the 10th of August it marched for San Antonio, a distance of one hundred and fifty miles. The scarcity of water, the extreme heat, the want of suitable rations, together with inadequate transportation all combined, made this one of the most severe marches the regiment ever endured. It reached the Salado, a small stream near San Antonio, on the 21st of August, and remained there until October 20th, when it was designated to perform post duty in the city, and it continued to act in this capacity till November 21st, when it was mustered out and ordered to Columbus, Ohio, for final discharge. The regiment left San Antonio on the 24th of November, and marched to Indianola, proceeding thence by way of New Orleans and Cairo to Columbus, Ohio, where it arrived December 25th, and was finally discharged the service of the United States on the 27th of December, 1865.

The Fifteenth was among the first regiments to be mustered in, and among the last to be mustered out, having been in the service as an organization about four years and eight months. Few regiments present a better record upon battle-fields and marches than the Fifteenth, while in respect to the intelligence and moral character of its officers and soldiers it holds an enviable position.

15th REGIMENT OHIO VOLUNTEER INFANTRY.

ROSTER, THREE MONTHS' SERVICE.

RANK.	NAME.	DATE OF RANK.	COM. ISSUED.	REMARKS.
Colonel	GEO. W. ANDREWS	May 4, 1861	May 4, 1861	
Lt. Colonel	MOSES R. DICKEY	" 4, "	" 4, "	
Major	S. B. WALKER	" 4, "	" 4, "	
Surgeon	ORRIN FERRIS	" 4, "	" 4, "	
Ass't Surgeon	J. N. MOURY	" 4, "	" 4, "	
Captain	R. W. P. Muse	" 17, "	" 17, "	
Do.	Wm. Wallace	" 22, "	" 22, "	
Do.	Wm T. Wilson	" 23, "	" 23, "	
Do.	Abraham C. Cummins	" 18, "	" 18, "	
Do.	Israel D. Clark	" 18, "	" 18, "	
Do.	Abraham Kaga	" 6, "	" 8, "	
Do.	Peter A. Tyler	April 20, "	April 20, "	
Do.	Hiram Miller	May 6, "	May 8, "	
Do.	Isaac M. Kirby	April 20, "	April 20, "	
Do.	W. V. M. Layton	" 20, "	" 20, "	
1st Lieutenant	Victor S. Perry	May 17, "	May 17, "	
Do.	James W. Cark	" 22, "	" 22, "	
Do.	Franklin W. Martin	" 23, "	" 23, "	
Do.	Tilman H. Wiggins	" 18, "	" 18, "	
Do.	Charles B. Smith	" 18, "	" 18, "	
Do.	Warrent Owens	" 6, "	" 6, "	
Do.	Wm. H. Kilmer	April 20, "	April 20, "	
Do.	Andrew R. Z. Dawson	May 6, "	May 6, "	
Do.	David J. Culbertson	April 20, "	April 20, "	
Do.	Samuel R. Mott, jr.	May 6, "	May 8, "	
Do.	Albert Spaulding	" 8, "	" 8, "	
Do.	C. W. Cowan	June 3, "	June 3, "	
2d Lieutenant	Asa C. Cassady	May 17, "	May 17, "	
Do.	Joseph Frazier	" 22, "	" 22, "	
Do.	Henry C. Miner	" 23, "	" 23, "	
Do.	Henry B. Gaylord	" 18, "	" 18, "	
Do.	Ralston Craig	" 18, "	" 18, "	
Do.	Joel F. Skillings	" 6, "	" 6, "	
Do.	Frederick Agerton	April 20, "	April 20, "	
Do.	Rufus L. Avery	May 6, "	May 6, "	
Do.	Samuel Bachtell	April 20, "	April 20, "	
Do.	J. W. Moody	May 6, "	May 6, "	

16th REGIMENT OHIO VOLUNTEER INFANTRY.

ROSTER, THREE MONTHS' SERVICE.

RANK.	NAME.	DATE OF RANK.	COM. ISSUED.	REMARKS.
Colonel	JAMES IRVINE	May 3, 1861	May 3, 1861	
Lt. Colonel	JOHN S. FULTON	" 3, "	" 3, "	
Major	G. W. BAILEY	" 3, "	" 3, "	
Surgeon	J. D. ROBINSON	" 4, "	" 4, "	
Ass't Surgeon	C. E. DENIO	" 4, "	" 4, "	
Captain	J. D. Nicholas	" 4, "	" 4, "	
Do.	Thomas J. Kinney	" 7, "	" 7, "	
Do.	Aquila Wiley	" 4, "	" 4, "	
Do.	Richard W. McClain	April 24, "	April 24, "	
Do.	Philip Kershure	" 23, "	" 23, "	
Do.	Thomas Collier	" 24, "	" 24, "	Resigned.
Do.	James McNulty	" 22, "	" 22, "	
Do.	James W. Moore	" 23, "	" 23, "	
Do.	Miller Moody	" 23, "	" 23, "	
Do.	Milton Mills	May 5, "	May 5, "	
Do.	J. Hunter Odlin	June 3, "	Aug. 28, "	
1st Lieutenant	David W. Marshall	May 4, "	May 4, "	
Do.	Wm. B. McCarty	" 7, "	" 7, "	
Do.	Cushman Cunningham	" 4, "	" 4, "	
Do.	Willis C. Workman	April 24, "	April 24, "	
Do.	Wm. H. Wade	" 23, "	" 23, "	
Do.	Charles T. Espy	" 24, "	" 24, "	
Do.	John A. Irvine	" 22, "	" 22, "	
Do.	Charles H. Moore	" 23, "	" 23, "	
Do.	August W. Loback	" 23, "	" 23, "	
Do.	Wm. Hanoah	May 5, "	May 5, "	
Do.	David W. Marshall	" 18, "	" 18, "	
Do.	Levi M. Rinehart	" 18, "	" 18, "	
2d Lieutenant	James McClintock	" 4, "	" 4, "	
Do.	Samuel L. Wilson	April 22, "	April 22, "	
Do.	Joseph C. Plummer	May 4, "	May 4, "	Discharged on acct. phis. dis. June 18, 1861.
Do.	Albert Shaw	April 21, "	April 21, "	
Do.	Forset Pool	" 23, "	" 23, "	
Do.	Henry C. Hayden	" 24, "	" 21, "	
Do.	Wm. Spangler	" 22, "	" 22, "	
Do.	John T. Rainey	" 23, "	" 23, "	
Do.	James Riddle	" 23, "	" 23, "	
Do.	Wm. Dorsey	May 5, "	May 5, "	
Do.	Hamilton Richeson	June 18, "	Aug. 16, "	

ROSTER, THREE YEARS' SERVICE.

RANK.	NAME.	DATE OF RANK.	COM. ISSUED.	REMARKS.
Colonel	JOHN F. DECOURCEY	Sept. 22, 1861		Honorably discharged March 31, 1864.
Lt. Colonel	GEORGE W. BAILEY	Aug. 9, "		Honorably discharged August 27, 1862.
Do.	PHILIP KESHNER	" 27, 1862		Mustered out October 31, 1864.
Major	PHILIP KESHNER	" 9, 1861		Promoted to Lieutenant-Colonel.
Do.	ROBERT W. P. MUSE	" 27, 1862		Resigned January 13, 1863.
Do.	MILTON MILLS	Jan. 13, 1863	April 23, 1863	Resigned February 12, 1864.
Do.	ELI W. BOTSFORD	March 18, 1864	March 18, 1864	Mustered out October 31, 1864.
Surgeon	BASIL B. BREASHER	Sept. 7, 1861		Mustered out October 31, 1864.
Ass't Surgeon	CHARLES E. DENIO	" 1, "	Sept. 1, 1861	Transferred to Seventh regiment.
Do.	BYRON S. CHASE	Nov. 1, "		Appointed Surg'n Miss. col'd rgt. June 10, '63.
Do.	ISAAC N. ELLSBERRY	Aug. 25, 1862	Feb. 10, 1863	Dismissed August 8, 1863.
Do.	OLIVER POMEROY	July 9, 1863	July 9, "	Resigned March 23, 1864.
Do.	JAMES W. VANDERVOOT	" 13, 1864	" 13, 1864	Mustered out October 31, 1864.
Chaplain	JOSEPH MATTOCK	March 19, 1862	April 4, 1862	Resigned February 18, 1863.
Captain	Milton Mills	Sept. 13, 1861		Promoted to Major.
Do.	Eli W. Botsford	" 19, "		Promoted to Major.
Do.	Wm. Spangler	" 23, "		Died January 19, 1862.
Do.	Robert W. P. Muse	" 27, "		Promoted to Major.
Do.	Samuel Smith	Oct. 6, "		Resigned January 10, 1862.
Do.	Hamilton Richeson	" 12, "	Jan. 15, 1862	Resigned November 16, 1863.
Do.	W. R. Monroe	" 26, "		Died October 7, 1862.
Do.	Addison S. McClure	Nov. 7, "		Honorably discharged June 30, 1864.
Do.	Richard W. Fannyhill	" 28, "		Resigned March 1, 1864.
Do.	George H. Harn	Dec. 1, "		Killed December 29, 1862.
Do.	Wm. P. Vandoorn	Feb. 3, 1862		Mustered out October 31, 1864.
Do.	Joseph Edgar	" 18, "	Feb. 19, 1862	Resigned August 6, 1862.
Do.	Robert W. Leggett	Aug. 6, "		Dismissed March 13, 1863.
Do.	Cushman Cunningham	Oct. 7, "		Resigned August 9, 1863.
Do.	George W. Stein	Aug. 28, "		Mustered out with regiment.
Do.	Absalom Finch	May 9, 1864	May 9, 1864	Mustered out with regiment.
Do.	Wm. M. Ross	Jan. 15, 1863		Mustered out with regiment.
Do.	George J. Jones	May 9, 1864	May 9, 1864	Mustered out with regiment.
Do.	Philip M. Smith	" 9, "	" 9, "	Mustered out with regiment.

RANK.	NAME.	DATE OF RANK.	COM. ISSUED.	REMARKS.
Captain	Silas H. Corns	May 9, 1864	May 9, 1864	Mustered out with regiment.
Do.	Wm. Dorsey	" 25, "	" 25, "	Mustered out with regiment.
Do.	Samuel Lichty	" 25, "	" 25, "	Deceased May 17, 1864, as 1st Lieutenant.
Do.	Wm. Buchanan	July 30, "	July 30, "	Mustered out with regiment.
Do.	Resin H. Voorhes	" 30, "	" 30, "	Mustered out with regiment.
1st Lieutenant	Clavert W. Cowan	Sept. 10, 1861		Resigned.
Do.	Samuel Edge	" 13, "		Mustered out at expiration of service, Sept. 16, 1864.
Do.	George W. Stein	" 19, "		Promoted to Captain.
Do.	Joseph Edgar	" 23, "		Promoted to Captain February 19, 1862.
Do.	Lewis Moore	" 27, "		Resigned.
Do.	Wm P. Vandoorn	Oct. 6, "		Promoted to Captain.
Do.	Wm. M. Ross	" 15, "		Promoted to Captain.
Do.	Absalom Finch	" 16, "		Promoted to Captain.
Do.	Hiram N. Shaffer	Nov. 7, "		Dismissed February 15, 1863.
Do.	Cushman Cunningham	" 25, "		Promoted to Captain.
Do.	Manuel B. De Silva	" 28, "		Dismissed from service July 22, 1863.
Do.	George J. Jones	Dec. 1, "		Promoted to Captain.
Do.	Philip M. Smith	Feb. 3, 1862	Feb. 3, 1862	Promoted to Captain.
Do.	Robert W. Leggett	" 19, "	" 19, "	Promoted to Captain August 6, 1862.
Do.	Silas H. Corns	Aug. 6, "	Nov. 18, "	Promoted to Captain.
Do.	Charles B. Smith	Oct. 7, "	" 18, "	Mustered out with regiment.
Do.	Wm. Dorsey	Nov. 8, "	" 20, "	Promoted to Captain.
Do.	Samuel Lichty	Feb. 15, 1863	May 6, 1863	Promoted to Captain; deceased May 17, 1864.
Do.	Josiah B. Beall	Aug. 28, 1862	" 6, "	Revoked; resigned as 2d Lieutenant.
Do.	Wm. Buchanan	Jan. 15, 1863	" 6, "	Promoted to Captain.
Do.	Resin H. Voorhes	March 8, 1864	March 18, 1864	Promoted to Captain.
Do.	Benj. F. Hackert	May 9, "	May 9, "	Mustered out with regiment.
Do.	John N. Bowling	" 9, "	" 9, "	Mustered out with regiment.
Do.	H. S. Wood	" 9, "	" 9, "	Mustered out with regiment.
Do.	Wm. H. Ruckle	" 9, "	" 9, "	Mustered out with regiment.
Do.	Chas. W. Oldroyd	" 9, "	" 9, "	Mustered out with regiment.
Do.	Anthony W. Somers	" 25, "	" 25, "	Mustered out with regiment.
Do.	Wm. W. Woodland	" 25, "	" 25, "	Mustered out with regiment.
Do.	Madison E. Storrs	July 30, "	July 30, "	Mustered out with regiment.
Do.	George H. Clark	" 30, "	" 30, "	Mustered out with regiment.
2d Lieutenant	Wm. Dorsey	Sept. 13, 1861		Promoted to 1st Lieutenant.
Do.	Isaiah S. Beall	" 19, "		Resigned April 27, 1863.
Do.	Robert W. Leggett	" 23, "		Promoted to 1st Lieutenant February 19, '62
Do.	John Blessing	" 27, "	Jan. 15, 1862	Resigned November 15, 1862.
Do.	George J. Jones	Oct. 4, "		Promoted to 1st Lieutenant.
Do.	Addison S. McClure	" 4, "		Promoted to Captain.
Do.	Hamilton Richeson	" 5, "		Promoted to Captain.
Do.	Philip M. Smith	" 6, "		Promoted to 1st Lieutenant.
Do.	Samuel Lichty	" 15, "		Promoted to 1st Lieutenant.
Do.	Wm. W. Boyd	" 26, "		Resigned October 20, 1862.
Do.	Wm. Lightcap	Nov. 7, "		Dismissed February 15, 1863.
Do.	Resin H. Voorhes	" 28, "		Promoted to 1st Lieutenant.
Do.	Wm. Buchanan	Dec. 1, "		Promoted to 1st Lieutenant.
Do.	B. F. Heckert	Feb. 3, 1862		Promoted to 1st Lieutenant.
Do.	Silas H. Corns	" 19, "		Promoted to 1st Lieutenant.
Do.	John N. Bowling	Aug. 6, "	Nov. 18, 1862	Promoted to 1st Lieutenant.
Do.	H. S. Wood	Oct. 20, "	" 18, "	Promoted to 1st Lieutenant
Do.	Edward O. G. Reed	Nov. 8, "	" 20, "	Resigned July 16, 1863.
Do.	Wm. H. Ruckle	" 15, "	May 6, "	Promoted to 1st Lieutenant.
Do.	Martin H. Norton	Feb. 15, 1863	" 6, "	Deceased August 17, 1863.
Do.	Chas. W. Oldroyd	Aug. 28, 1862	" 6, "	Promoted to 1st Lieutenant.
Do.	Anthony W. Somers	Feb. 15, 1863	" 6, "	Promoted to 1st Lieutenant.
Do.	Wm. W. Woodland	Jan. 15, "	" 6, "	Promoted to 1st Lieutenant.
Do.	Madison E. Storrs	Oct. 5, "	Feb. 26, 1864	Promoted to 1st Lieutenant.
Do.	George H. Clark	March 18, 1864	March 18, "	Promoted to 1st Lieutenant.

SIXTEENTH OHIO VOLUNTEER INFANTRY.

THIS regiment was organized under Colonel John F. DeCourcey, at Camp Tiffin, near Wooster, Ohio, on the 2d day of October, 1861, and was mustered into the service on the same day by Captain Belknap, of the Eighteenth United States Regulars. It reached Camp Dennison November 28th and remained there until the 19th of December, when, receiving its arms, it moved to Lexington, Kentucky. On January 12, 1862, orders were received to report to General S. P. Carter, at Somerset, Kentucky. At this point the regiment was engaged in repairing and building military roads to facilitate the transportation of supplies to General Thomas's forces at Mill Springs.

The battle of Mill Springs was fought and won by General Thomas on the 19th of January. The regiment was ordered up during the fight, but being retarded by a flood in Fishing Creek, did not reach the ground until after the enemy had been routed.

On January 31, 1862, the regiment left Somerset, Kentucky, and marched across the country to London. After a short rest at this point it continued its march to Cumberland Ford, arriving there on the 12th of February. Nothing of interest transpired during its stay.

On March 12th a reconnoissance in force was made toward Cumberland Gap, but with the exception of a slight skirmish with the enemy nothing was accomplished. Another reconnoissance was made on the 22d of March. About this time the regiment was brigaded with the Forty-Second Ohio and Twenty-Second Kentucky, forming the Twenty-Sixth Brigade, Seventh Division, Army of the Ohio, under command of Brigadier-General George W. Morgan.

On April 28th another reconnoissance was made to the top of the Cumberland Mountains in the vicinity of Cumberland Gap. The mountain was climbed in the midst of a heavy fog. Arriving at the top at eight A. M. they met the enemy and a brisk fight ensued, which lasted till the middle of the afternoon. The regiment lost one man killed and two wounded.

The month of May was occupied in preparing for the assault on Cumberland Gap. On June 10th the march was resumed toward the Gap. On the morning of the 17th of June the regiment marched up Powell's Valley to the rear of Cumberland Gap, where it was discovered that the enemy had abandoned that stronghold and retreated toward Knoxville, Tennessee. The Sixteenth was the first regiment to enter the enemy's abandoned intrenchments and raise the National colors. From this time until the 3d of August the troops were engaged in strengthening the position, drilling, and foraging, with frequent skirmishing.

On August 6th the Sixteenth was ordered to relieve the Fourteenth Kentucky, at Tagewell. About ten A. M. of that day two companies (B and E) of the regiment were sent forward as advance pickets. Companies F and D were ordered to the right of the Main Hill Road on the same duty. Companies C and G were held in reserve. At eleven A. M. heavy skirmishing commenced at the front and continued until the enemy appeared on the front and right in force. Companies D and F were compelled to fall back. Companies B and E were cut off from the main force by a Rebel brigade, and most of them captured. Companies C and G were ordered up as a support, but were also overwhelmed and compelled to fall back to a position on the left of the road. They were now re-enforced by stragglers from other companies and held the enemy in check for two hours, when the ammunition was exhausted. They then fell back to the main line, where the National forces were massed. Toward night the National army retreated into the intrenchments, the enemy following to within three miles of the Gap.

On September 8th the Sixteenth Ohio and its brigade were ordered to Manchester, Kentucky, for supplies. On the 19th this force was joined by the remainder of the National troops from the Gap. The supplies having been almost completely exhausted, General Morgan ordered a retreat toward the Ohio River. This retreat was opposed by the enemy, who harrassed the National forces by frequent attacks, and by placing obstructions in the roads, up to Grayson, Kentucky, within twenty-five miles of the Ohio River. The sufferings of the men on this march were very severe, having nothing to eat for several days excepting ears of corn gathered from the fields as they passed. To quench their thirst the men were compelled to drink the water collected in stagnant pools. On the 3d of October the command arrived at Greenupsburg, Kentucky, on the Ohio River, utterly worn out, ragged, shoeless, and covered with the accumulated dust of sixteen days' march. Their appearance was forlorn in the extreme.

Resting until the 21st of October at Portland, Ohio, the regiment then moved to Charleston, Virginia, on the Kanawha River. On November 10th it marched, under orders, to Point Pleasant, Virginia, and there embarked on steamers for Memphis, Tennessee, arriving at that place on the 27th of the same month. On December 20th it moved with Sherman's command on transports to the rear of Vicksburg, Mississippi, and participated, on the 29th, in the disastrous assault on Chickasaw Bayou. In this affair the Sixteenth suffered terribly, losing three hundred and eleven officers and men killed, wounded, and prisoners. After the assault the command of the regiment devolved on Captain E. W. Botsford.

The next service performed by the regiment was in the expedition against Arkansas Post. That post being captured the Sixteenth Ohio, with other troops composing the expedition, were taken back to Young's Point, Louisiana. The regiment remained here until 8th March, and then moved to Milliken's Bend.

On April 6, 1863, the regiment joined General Grant's expedition to the rear of Vicksburg. It was engaged at Thompson's Hill on the 1st of May, and lost nine men killed and wounded. It was also engaged at Champion Hills, or Baker's Creek, on 16th of May, and on the 17th at Black River Bridge. On May 19th it took a prominent part in the disastrous assault on the Rebel works in the rear of Vicksburg. In these several affairs the regiment lost severely in killed and wounded. On the 22d of May it was again engaged in an assault on the Rebel works, losing several men killed and wounded. It remained in the rear of Vicksburg until its fall, July 4, 1863. On the 6th of July it was ordered to Jackson, Mississippi, where it participated in the siege and capture of that place.

The regiment now marched back to Vicksburg, where it was placed on transports with orders to report to the commanding officer at New Orleans, Louisiana. It arrived at Carrollton, six miles above the city, on the 15th of August.

General Banks's expedition to the Teche country was then forming at New Orleans, and the Sixteenth was made a part of it. About the 7th of September the expedition left New Orleans. Starting from Algiers, opposite the city, the regiment moved by railroad to Brashear City, and from thence marched across the country to Opelousas. Returning to New Orleans it joined the expedition under General Washburne to Texas, landing at DeCrow's Point, on Matagorda Peninsula. From thence it went by steamer to Indianola, and from there to Fort Esperanza, opposite DeCrow's Point, on Matagorda Island. From this place it sailed to New Orleans, arriving at that city on the 21st of April, 1864.

The regiment remained in New Orleans only two days, and was then sent up the river to Alexandria to re-enforce General Banks's army, just returned from his disastrous expedition into the Red River country. It arrived at Alexandria April 26th and was immediately sent to the front, where the enemy was met and engaged in several skirmishes. In these the regiment lost some men. Returning to Alexandria five companies were detailed to assist in building a dam across Red River to enable the gunboats to reach the Mississippi River.

About the 15th of May the Sixteenth Ohio, with the rest of the forces under General Banks, commenced the retreat to Morganza, Louisiana, on the Mississippi. Morganza was reached without loss and the regiment went into camp. In this camp it remained, performing garrison-duty, until the 6th of October, when orders were received to proceed to Columbus, Ohio, for final discharge from the service.

This ended the service of the Sixteenth Ohio as an organized regiment, it having failed to re-enlist for the war from the fact that it was feared by the men that the regimental organization would not be preserved.

The regiment reached Columbus, Ohio, on the 14th of October, and was paid and discharged from the service on the 31st of October, 1863.

During its service the Sixteenth traveled by railroad one thousand two hundred and eighty-five miles; by steamboat three thousand six hundred and nineteen miles; by steamship twelve hundred miles, and on foot one thousand six hundred and twenty-one miles. No accident occurred to any one while traveling on the water or by cars. While on the Gulf of Mexico, in November, 1863, off the coast of Texas, in latitude 27°, several of the men of the regiment had their feet frozen during the prevalence of a severe "Norther."

The total number of deaths, from all causes, in the regiment was two hundred and fifty-one. There were killed in battle and died of their wounds two officers and sixty men. There was one death from suicide, and one from accidental shooting. Two men were drowned, one while bathing in the Mississippi River, at Vicksburg; the other while returning from general hospital at New Orleans, to rejoin his regiment at Morganza.

There were one hundred and eighty-five deaths from disease, of which forty-seven occurred with the regiment. The others were in general hospital, or in hospital or other transports, at home on furlough, or in Rebel prisons. The number of wounded who recovered was one hundred and eighty-eight. The largest per cent. sick at any one time occurred while the regiment was in barracks at Camp Dennison in 1861. The most fatal disease was typho-malarial, or camp fever. The most prevalent disease was diarrhea.

There were two cases of small-pox and fifty-nine of varioloid, but no deaths. Of measles there were fifty-two cases and two deaths. There were three cases of typhoid-pneumonia, all of which proved fatal. Two died from diphtheria. The greatest mortality in any one month was in April, 1862, at Cumberland Ford, Kentucky, where there were eight deaths—four from typhoid-malarial fever, two from typhoid-pneumonia, one from congestive measles, and one from hospital gangrene.

On Surgeon's certificate of disability one hundred and eighty-six were discharged, and thirty-eight were transferred to the Veteran Reserve Corps, fifteen of whom were directly from the regiment. Before leaving Morganza the recruits, ninety in number, were transferred to the One Hundred and Fourteenth Ohio to serve out the unexpired term of their enlistment.

The number of officers and men mustered out at the expiration of its term of service was four hundred and seventy-seven, all that was left of one thousand one hundred and ninety-one, the total of original organization and recruits.

17th REGIMENT OHIO VOLUNTEER INFANTRY.

ROSTER, THREE MONTHS' SERVICE

RANK.	NAME.	DATE OF RANK.	COM. ISSUED.	REMARKS.
Colonel	JOHN M. CONNELL	....	....	
Lt. Colonel	FRANCIS B. POND	....	....	
Major	CLEMENT F. STEELE	....	....	
Surgeon	JOHN G. S. KYLE	May 6, 1861	May 6, 1861	
Ass't Surgeon	T. G. CLEVELAND	" 4, "	" 4, "	
Captain	A. H. Giesy	April 22, "	April 22, "	
Do.	Homer Thrall	" 21, "	" 21, "	
Do.	Thomas Acton	" 24, "	" 22, "	
Do.	Charles A. Baker	" 25, "	" 25, "	
Do.	Lyman H. Jackson	" 27, "	" 27, "	
Do.	J. W. Stinchcomb	" 22, "	" 22, "	
Do.	Thomas J. Haynes	May 1, "	May 1, "	
Do.	Wm. H. Floyd	" 17, "	" 17, "	
Do.	Wm. D. Stone	April 23, "	April 23, "	
Do.	Peter Tallman	" 17, "	" 17, "	
1st Lieutenant	Abraham Ogden	" 22, "	" 22, "	
Do.	Henry C. Knoop	" 24, "	" 21, "	
Do.	D. S. Deland	" 22, "	" 22, "	
Do.	Samuel H. Baker	" 25, "	" 25, "	
Do.	W. H. Free	" 27, "	" 27, "	
Do.	John Wiseman	" 22, "	" 22, "	
Do.	Daniel Taylor	May 1, "	May 1, "	
Do.	Amos A. Whisson	April 26, "	April 26, "	
Do.	Preston R. Galloway	" 23, "	" 23, "	
Do.	Frank Askew	" 17, "	" 17, "	
Do.	A. J. Davis	....	....	
Do.	Charles N. Goulding	May 15, "	May 15, "	
2d Lieutenant	Leo Noles	April 22, "	April 22, "	
Do.	Nelson Sinnett	" 24, "	" 24, "	
Do.	O. E. Davis	" 22, "	" 22, "	
Do.	Charles H. Rippey	" 25, "	" 25, "	
Do.	Benj. S. Schirley	" 27, "	" 27, "	
Do.	J. C. Watson	" 22, "	" 22, "	
Do.	George W. Doerty	May 1, "	May 1, "	
Do.	Amos W. Ewing	April 26, "	April 26, "	
Do.	David J. Roop	" 23, "	" 23, "	
Do.	Charles W. Carroll	" 17, "	" 17, "	

ROSTER, THREE YEARS' SERVICE.

RANK.	NAME.	DATE OF RANK.	COM. ISSUED.	REMARKS.
Colonel	J. M. CONNELL	Aug. 16, 1861	Dec. 28, 1861	Resigned November 12, 1863.
Do.	DURBIN WARD	Nov. 13, 1863	" 8, 1863	Mustered out November 8, 1864.
Lt. Colonel	MARSHALL F. MOORE	Aug. 20, 1861	" 28, "	Promoted to Colonel 69th O. V. I. Dec. 31, '63.
Do.	DURBIN WARD	Dec. 31, 1862	Feb. 23, 1863	Promoted to Colonel.
Do.	BENJ. SHOWERS	May 9, 1864	May 9, 1864	Absent when regiment was mustered out.
Major	DURBIN WARD	Aug. 17, 1861	Dec. 28, 1861	Promoted to Lieutenant-Colonel.
Do.	BENJ. F. BUTTERFIELD	Dec. 31, 1862	March 11, 1863	Died of wounds December 15, 1863.
Do.	JAMES W. STINCHCOMB	" 15, 1863	Jan. 5, 1864	Resigned May 2, 1864.
Do.	WILLIS G. CLARK	May 9, 1864	May 9, "	Mustered out with regiment.
Surgeon	WASHINGTON L. SCHENCK	Oct. 2, 1861	Dec. 28, 1861	
Do.	HENRY J. HERRICKS	Dec. 12, "	....	Resigned.
Do.	JONATHAN E. FOWLER	Jan. 9, 1865	Jan. 9, 1865	Resigned May 30, 1865.
Do.	D. D. BENEDICT	June 6, "	June 6, "	Mustered out with regiment.
Ass't Surgeon	E. SINNETT	Sept. 28, 1861	Dec. 28, "	Resigned January 18, 1862.
Do.	HENRY J. HERRICK	Feb. 14, 1862	Sept. 14, 1862	Promoted to Surgeon.
Do.	J. E. FOWLER	Aug. 21, "	" 5, 1863	Promoted to Surgeon.
Do.	D. D. BENEDICT	Feb. 5, 1863	" 5, "	Promoted to Surgeon.
Chaplain	A. T. FULLERTON	Sept. 18, 1861	Sept. 24, 1861	Mustered out.
Do.	JAMES H. GARDNER	Jan. 24, 1863	March 27, 1863	Mustered out May 15, 1865.
Captain	Benj. F. Butterfield	Aug. 27, 1861	Dec. 28, 1861	Promoted to Major.
Do.	James W. Stinchcomb	Sept. 11, "	" 28, "	Promoted to Major.
Do.	Joel Haines	" 12, "	" 28, "	Resigned June 6, 1862.
Do.	Charles H. Ripley	" 16, "	" 28, "	Resigned August 4, 1862.
Do.	Ezra Rickets	" 19, "	" 28, "	Died September 20, 1863.
Do.	Abraham Ogden	" 26, "	" 28, "	Resigned May 6, 1864.
Do.	Bonham H. Fox	" 28, "	" 28, "	Resigned April 25, 1864.
Do.	Amos A. Whisson	Nov. 4, "	" 28, "	Resigned October 27, 1863.
Do.	Daniel M. Rea	" 4, "	" 28, "	Resigned August 16, 1862.
Do.	Benj. B. Getzendanner	" 4, "	" 28, "	Resigned January 1, 1862.
Do.	Benj. Showers	Jan. 9, 1862	Jan. 9, 1862	Promoted to Lieutenant-Colonel.
Do.	Caleb B. Sharp	June 6, "	June 24, "	Died at Corinth July 21, 1862.
Do.	Gilruth M. Webb	Aug. 9, "	Oct. 3, "	Resigned March 2, 1863.
Do.	Willis G. Clark	" 18, "	" 3, "	Promoted to Major.
Do.	Emanuel A. Richards	July 21, "	" 3, "	Resigned May 30, 1862.
Do.	Leo Noles	March 2, 1863	March 11, 1863	Mustered out.
Do.	Henry Arney	Dec. 31, "	" 11, "	Resigned.
Do.	Daniel Sheets	Aug. 30, "	Jan. 23, "	Resigned September 9, 1863.
Do.	John D. Innskeep	Sept. 9, "	Oct. 30, "	Mustered out with regiment.
Do.	Frank Spencer	March 23, 1864	March 23, 1864	Mustered out March 12, 1865.

RANK.	NAME.	DATE OF RANK.			COM. ISSUED.			REMARKS.
Captain	Owen W. Brown................	March	23,	1864	March	23,	1864	Revoked; resigned as 1st Lieutenant.
Do.	Oliver B. Brandt................	"	23,	"	"	23,	"	Mustered out with regiment.
Do.	Daniel Sullivan................	April	1,	"	April	1,	"	Resigned April 21, 1865.
Do.	John L. Ely................	May	9,	"	May	9,	"	Resigned July 5, 1865.
Do.	Theodore C. Stewart........	"	9,	"	"	9,	"	Killed.
Do.	Seth Collins................	"	9,	"	"	9,	"	Resigned July 5, 1865.
Do.	Thomas R. Thatcher........	June	27,	"	June	27,	"	Mustered out July 16, 1865.
Do.	Levi Cornwall................	"	27,	"	"	27,	"	Resigned May 22, 1865.
Do.	James F. Weakley............	April	20,	1865	April	20,	1865	Mustered out with regiment.
Do.	George E. Blair................	"	20,	"	"	20,	"	Mustered out with regiment.
Do.	Augustus Ward................	"	20,	"	"	20,	"	Mustered out with regiment.
Do.	William H. Walker..........	May	18,	"	May	18,	"	Mustered out with regiment.
Do.	John B. Eversole............	"	31,	"	"	31,	"	Mustered out with regiment.
1st Lieutenant	James McDonald............	Aug.	16,	1861	Dec.	28,	1861	Resigned January 22, 1863.
Do.	A. J. Davis................	"	22,	"	"	28,	"	Promoted by President September 23, 1863.
Do.	Benj. Showers................	"	26,	"	"	28,	"	Promoted to Captain.
Do.	Aaron P. Ashbrook..........	Sept.	11,	"	"	28,	"	Resigned November 3, 1862.
Do.	Jacob Humphreys............	"	12,	"	"	28,	"	Died December 21, 1861.
Do.	Gilruth M. Webb............	"	16,	"	"	28,	"	Promoted to Captain August 9, 1862.
Do.	Irvin Linn................	"	19,	"	"	28,	"	Resigned January 25, 1862.
Do.	Leo Noles................	"	26,	"	"	28,	"	Promoted to Captain.
Do.	Perry Crossan................	"	28,	"	"	28,	"	Resigned September 3, 1863.
Do.	Daniel Sheets................	Nov.	4,	"	"	28,	"	Promoted to Captain.
Do.	Frank Spencer................	"	4,	"	"	28,	"	Promoted to Captain.
Do.	Wm. Cook................	"	4,	"	"	28,	"	Resigned November 21, 1861.
Do.	Willis G. Clark................	Jan.	9,	1862	Jan.	9,	1862	Promoted to Captain.
Do.	Henry Arney................	"	9,	"	"	9,	"	Promoted to Captain.
Do.	Owen W. Brown................	Feb.	3,	"	Feb.	3,	"	Promoted to Captain March 18, 1864.
Do.	Joseph H. Pool................	"	5,	"	"	5,	"	Resigned May 2.
Do.	Caleb B. Sharp................	"	5,	"	May	5,	"	Promoted to Captain.
Do.	Oliver B. Brandt................	June	6,	"	June	24,	"	Promoted to Captain.
Do.	Daniel Sullivan................	Aug.	9,	"	Oct.	3,	"	Promoted to Captain.
Do.	John L. Ely................	"	18,	"	"	3,	"	Promoted to Captain.
Do.	Theodore C. Stewart........	Nov.	3,	"	Dec.	30,	"	Promoted to Captain.
Do.	Seth Collins................	Dec.	3,	"	March	11,	1863	Promoted to Captain.
Do.	Samuel H. Hurd................	Nov.	26,	"	"	11,	"	Declined promotion.
Do.	S. Austin Thayer............	March	2,	"	"	11,	"	Resigned November 4, 1863.
Do.	Thomas R. Thatcher........	May	30,	"	Jan.	23,	"	Promoted to Captain.
Do.	Levi Cornwall................	March	23,	1864	March	23,	1864	Promoted to Captain.
Do.	Jacob M. Ruffner............	Sept.	23,	1863	Oct.	30,	1863	Killed.
Do.	James F. Weakley............	March	23,	1864	March	23,	1864	Promoted to Captain.
Do.	Isaiah M. Daniels............	"	23,	"	"	23,	"	Resigned September 21, 1864.
Do.	George E. Blair................	"	23,	"	"	23,	"	Promoted to Captain.
Do.	L. L. Simpson................	"	23,	"	"	23,	"	Honorably discharged July 8, 1864.
Do.	George Rainey................	April	1,	"	April	1,	"	Resigned November 3, 1864.
Do.	Oliver Kibby................	May	9,	"	May	9,	"	Declined promotion.
Do.	Richard Foster................	"	9,	"	"	9,	"	Deceased June 15, 1864.
Do.	Lyman W. Barnes............	"	9,	"	"	9,	"	Killed.
Do.	Augustus Ward................	June	27,	"	June	27,	"	Promoted to Captain.
Do.	Wm. H. Walker................	"	27,	"	"	27,	"	Promoted to Captain.
Do.	John B. Eversole............	"	27,	"	"	27,	"	Promoted to Captain.
Do.	James Strode................	July	25,	"	July	25,	"	Resigned December 31, 1864.
Do.	Edward Champlin............	"	25,	"	"	25,	"	Mustered out with regiment
Do.	James Outcault................	Oct.	6,	"	Oct.	6,	"	Mustered out with regiment.
Do.	Patrick Wilson................	"	6,	"	"	6,	"	Resigned June 12, 1865.
Do.	Joshua Jones................	"	6,	"	"	6,	"	Resigned February 4, 1865.
Do.	Daniel S. Bird................	April	20,	1865	April	20,	1865	Mustered out with regiment.
Do.	Allen Tittler................	"	20,	"	"	20,	"	Mustered out with regiment.
Do.	Joseph James................	"	20,	"	"	20,	"	Mustered out with regiment.
Do.	James E. Larimer............	May	18,	"	May	18,	"	Mustered out with regiment.
Do.	John E. Lane................	"	18,	"	"	18,	"	Mustered out with regiment.
Do.	Malcome D. Lane............	"	31,	"	"	31,	"	Mustered out with regiment.
2d Lieutenant	Henry Arney................	Aug.	26,	1861	Dec.	28,	1861	Promoted to 1st Lieutenant.
Do.	Owen W. Brown................	Sept.	11,	"	"	28,	"	Promoted to 1st Lieutenant.
Do.	Joseph H. Pool................	"	12,	"	"	28,	"	Promoted to 1st Lieutenant.
Do.	Henry Dewar................	"	16,	"	"	28,	"	Resigned June 6, 1862.
Do.	Daniel Sullivan................	"	18,	"	"	28,	"	Promoted to 1st Lieutenant August 9, 1862.
Do.	Theodore Michaels............	"	26,	"	"	28,	"	Resigned July 21, 1862.
Do.	John L. Ely................	"	28,	"	"	28,	"	Promoted to 1st Lieutenant.
Do.	Theodore C. Stewart........	Nov.	4,	"	"	28,	"	Promoted to 1st Lieutenant.
Do.	Wm. H. Eagle................	"	4,	"	"	28,	"	Resigned April 1, 1862.
Do.	Seth Collins................	"	4,	"	"	28,	"	Promoted to 1st Lieutenant.
Do.	S. Austin Thayer............	Jan.	9,	1862	Jan.	9,	1862	Promoted to 1st Lieutenant.
Do.	Wm. H. Pugh................	Feb.	3,	"	Feb.	3,	"	Resigned August 15, 1862.
Do.	Oliver B. Brandt................	"	19,	"	"	19,	"	Promoted to 1st Lieutenant.
Do.	Thomas R. Thatcher........	April	1,	"	May	1,	"	Promoted to 1st Lieutenant.
Do.	John D. Inskeep............	June	6,	"	June	24,	"	Promoted to Captain.
Do.	Emanuel A. Richards........	"	6,	"	July	14,	"	Promoted to 1st Lieutenant.
Do.	Levi Cornwall................	July	21,	"	Oct.	3,	"	Promoted to 1st Lieutenant.
Do.	Jacob M. Ruffner............	Aug.	15,	"	"	3,	"	Promoted to 1st Lieutenant.
Do.	James F. Weakley............	"	9,	"	"	3,	"	Promoted to 1st Lieutenant.
Do.	Isaiah M. Daniels............	"	18,	"	"	3,	"	Promoted to 1st Lieutenant.
Do.	George E. Blair................	Sept.	10,	"	"	3,	"	Promoted to 1st Lieutenant.
Do.	L. L. Simpson................	Nov.	3,	"	Dec.	30,	"	Promoted to 1st Lieutenant.
Do.	George Rainey................	March	2,	"	March	11,	1863	Promoted to 1st Lieutenant.
Do.	Alfred St. John................	Dec.	31,	"	April	7,	"	Resigned March 30, 1864.
Do.	Oliver Kibby................	May	30,	1863	June	23,	"	Promoted to 1st Lieutenant.
Do.	Richard Foster................	Nov.	16,	"	Jan.	9,	1864	Promoted to 1st Lieutenant.
Do.	Lyman W. Barnes............	Dec.	14,	"	March	15,	"	Promoted to 1st Lieutenant.
Do.	Augustus Ward................	March	9,	1861	"	9,	"	Promoted to 1st Lieutenant.
Do.	Wm. H. Walker................	Dec.	14,	1863	"	14,	"	Promoted to 1st Lieutenant.
Do.	John B. Eversole............	"	14,	"	"	14,	"	Promoted to 1st Lieutenant.
Do.	James Strode................	April	11,	1864	April	11,	"	Promoted to 1st Lieutenant.
Do.	Edward Champlin............	"	11,	"	"	11,	"	Promoted to 1st Lieutenant.
Do.	James Outcault................	"	11,	"	"	11,	"	Promoted to 1st Lieutenant.
Do.	Pat. Wilson................	"	13,	"	"	13,	"	Promoted to 1st Lieutenant.
Do.	John Matlock................	May	9,	"	May	9,	"	Promoted to 1st Lieutenant.
Do.	Joshua Jones................	"	9,	"	"	9,	"	Promoted to 1st Lieutenant.
Do.	Daniel S. Bird................	June	27,	"	June	27,	"	Promoted to 1st Lieutenant.
Do.	Allen Tittler................	"	27,	"	"	27,	"	Promoted to 1st Lieutenant.
Do.	Joseph James................	"	27,	"	"	27,	"	Promoted to 1st Lieutenant.

SEVENTEENTH OHIO VOLUNTEER INFANTRY.

THE nucleus of this regiment was an organization of thirty-two men, raised under the militia law of Ohio, at Lancaster, Ohio, commanded by Joseph A. Stafford. Four days after the attack on Sumter, Captain Stafford had filled his company to the required number of one hundred men, and started by cars *via* Zanesville for Columbus, arriving there the next day. They were assigned as company A, First Ohio Volunteer Infantry.

Sergeants Theodore Nichols and A. H. Geisy and private J. W. Stinchcomb were detailed as recruiting officers, with orders to return to Fairfield County and recruit another company. By the 20th of April one hundred and eighty-five men had been recruited, and on the 27th two companies, instead of one, were organized, Sergeant Geisy being elected Captain of one and private Stinchcomb Captain of the other.

The second call of the President on Ohio for twenty-three regiments found these two companies in camp on the Fair Grounds, near Lancaster, Ohio. They were at once made the nucleus of the Seventeenth Regiment Ohio Volunteer Infantry, for the three months' service. In a few days Captain Acton, of Madison County, Captain Haynes, of the same county, Captain Lyman Jackson, of Perry County, Captain Charles A. Baker, of Hocking County, Captain Frank F. Pond, of Morgan County, Captain Stone, of Mercer County, Captain Thrall, of Licking, and Captain Tallman, of Belmont County, each reported with a company, and organized the regiment by electing the field officers.

On the 20th of April the regiment was placed on board the cars at Zanesville for Bellaire, and on arriving at Benwood, on the Ohio River opposite Bellaire, a large fleet of boats were found in waiting to receive troops. On the morning of the 23d, all the troops and baggage being aboard the boats, the fleet steamed down the Ohio River, and arrived at Marietta on Sunday afternoon, where it lay until the next morning, and then started for Parkersburg, and in a few hours were on Virginia soil.

The Seventeenth was at once brigaded with the Ninth and Tenth Ohio, General William S. Rosecrans commanding the brigade. Its first duty was to guard trains to Clarksburg, Virginia, and return. Company F was sent to guard two trains loaded with provisions to Clarksburg, West Virginia, and return. Companies A and B were detailed as guard to General McClellan. Companies I, F, G, and K, were sent down the river on an expedition, under charge of Major Steele, with sealed orders, not to be opened until Blennerhassett's Island was passed. One company was put off at Larue, West Virginia, and the other two proceeded on down to Ripley Landing, and crossed over by land to Ripley, the county seat of Jackson County. Both detachments were to operate against the guerrillas of the different localities. The two Wises, father and son, were operating in that part of Virginia, and made their boasts that they would "annihilate the Yankees on sight." They, however, took good care to keep within safe running distance of the aforesaid "Yankees." O. Jennings Wise had tried "cleaning out" the two companies of the Seventeenth stationed near Ravenswood, but had ignominiously failed. The old Wise, feeling outraged that his son had not brought back with him the two companies of Yankees, swore he would bring them himself. A young lady of the neighborhood of Charleston, Virginia, being advised by a mulatto boy of Wise's intentions, on the evening of the 1st of July started on horseback for Ravenswood, taking the by-roads and cow-paths to reach there. At daybreak next morning she notified Captain Stinchcomb of the impending danger, and before Wise reached Ravenswood a courier had arrived at Parkersburg, and re-enforcements were on the march from Larue, Virginia, Hockingport, and Gallipolis, Ohio. Governor Wise, hearing of these re-enforcements, retired to Ripley in the greatest haste, starting for that place at three o'clock in the morning.

The two companies remained at Ravenswood and garrisoned the place until the 10th of July, when they were ordered to evacuate and report to the regiment at Buckhannon, Virginia, on the 14th of July. The other five companies of the regiment, Colonel Connell commanding, left the railroad at Petroleum and marched across to Buckhannon *via* Glenwood, at which place, on the 4th of July, they were surrounded by about fifteen hundred Rebels, but being well posted, held their position until re-enforced by the Tenth Ohio, Colonel Lytle.

It was intended to have had the Seventeenth Ohio concentrated in time to participate in the battle of Rich Mountain, but, as it was thought a much better work was being performed in Jackson County by breaking up recruiting camps and preventing many from joining the Rebel ranks, it was not done.

Shortly after the regiment was consolidated at Buckhannon, it was ordered on an expedition, in company with several other regiments, Colonel Tyler commanding, to Sutton, Virginia. After a long and very hard march, some days making thirty-three miles, Sutton was occupied and fortified.

On the 3d of August, 1861, the Seventeenth Ohio, having overserved the time some days, started for home, arriving at Zanesville, Ohio, on the 13th of August, and was mustered out on the 15th.

Efforts were immediately made to reorganize the regiment for three years, and on the 30th of August it assembled at Camp Dennison.

The regiment drilled until the 30th of September, when it was ordered to Kentucky, and reported at Camp Dick Robinson on the 2d of October, 1861. From thence it moved to Wild Cat, and was the first regiment to relieve Colonel Garrard, of the First Kentucky. The regiment participated in the Wild Cat fight and lost seven men wounded. It was brigaded with the Thirty-First and Thirty-Eighth Ohio, General Albin Schœpf commanding.

The Seventeenth Ohio also participated in the battle of Mill Springs, resulting in the defeat of General Zollicoffer. From this battle-ground the regiment marched to Louisville, Kentucky, and took boats for Nashville, Tennessee, where it arrived on the 3d of March, 1862. Thence across the country to Shiloh, but being detailed to guard the wagon train through, did not reach the ground in time to take part in the battle. It participated in the siege of Corinth, and was engaged in several severe skirmishes, in one of which company B, with seventy men, penetrated the Rebel lines, drove the Rebel pickets on their reserves, and held the position for two hours, losing two men severely wounded, and four slightly.

Thence the regiment marched to Booneville, Mississippi, in pursuit of the flying enemy; then back *via* Corinth and Iuka to Tuscumbia, Alabama, where it arrived on the 1st of July. From this place they joined and marched with Buell's army to Louisville, Kentucky. It was at the battle of Perryville but did not participate, though under fire in the rear of General Mitchel's command. From Danville and Lebanon, Kentucky, the backward march of the army was commenced, the Seventeenth accompanying.

At the battle of Stone River the brigade to which the regiment was attached was stationed on the extreme right until the 29th of December, when, after night, it marched from Nolinsville to the Murfreesboro' Pike, and next day had a severe skirmish with Wheeler's cavalry at Lavergne, recaptured all the mules Wheeler had taken from our train, and saved about two hundred wagons from being burned. The regiment went into the battle-line on the Stone River field about one o'clock on the 31st of December, and with its brigade charged the Rebel General Hanson's brigade, drove them in confusion, killing their General, and some one hundred and fifty of the rank and file. The loss of the Seventeenth was twenty wounded.

After the long rest at Murfreesboro', General Rosecrans inaugurated the Tullahoma campaign. The Seventeenth moved with its brigade, and at Hoover's Gap, under the command of Lieutenant-Colonel Durbin Ward, charged the Seventeenth Tennessee Rebel regiment, strongly posted in a belt of woods. In making this charge the Seventeenth Ohio was compelled to cross an open field, and receive a full fire directly in its left flank from a Rebel brigade and battery. Yet the regiment went steadily on, drove the Seventeenth Tennessee, and occupied their position. This charge was executed with such coolness and determination as to draw the particular attention of General Thomas.

At the battle of Chickamauga the regiment was on the extreme right of the center, attached to the corps commanded by General Thomas. When General Wood's division was double-quicked out of the line, the gap left exposed the right flank of the regiment, of which the Rebels immediately took advantage, and opened fire both on the right flank and front, causing it to lose heavily, and scattering the men in confusion. Company B, being the only one of the regiment that retreated in a body, was halted about three hundred yards from where they had been driven, gave three cheers, sounded the rally for the Seventeenth Ohio, gathered some two hundred of them together, and charged back on the enemy, but to little purpose, as the Rebels outnumbered them ten to one. Falling back again, now only about one hundred strong, they held a given point, and fought throughout that memorable day, leaving the field with but fifty-two men. The loss of the Seventeenth in this battle in killed and wounded was over two hundred, not counting those with slight flesh wounds. This was the severest fight in which the regiment had participated. The gallant Captain Ricketts fell dead in the early part of the fight, and Lieutenant-Colonel Ward fell about the middle of the afternoon, on the front line, badly wounded. During the siege of Chattanooga the Seventeenth was in several severe skirmishes, and at the Brown's Ferry *coup de main* it won honor along with the brigade to which it was attached. At Mission Ridge, though in the rear line at the start, the regiment was in the front when the top of the hill was gained. In this brilliant charge the brave and gallant Major Butterfield fell mortally wounded, while leading the regiment. Captain Benjamin Showers, next in rank, completed the charge. The regiment captured a Rebel battery and turned the guns on the retreating enemy.

Captain Stinchcomb about this time returned from a leave of absence in Ohio, and being the ranking officer, took command of the regiment. General Bragg's late head-quarters on Mission Ridge was occupied by the regiment for some time.

On the 1st of January, 1864, the subject of re-enlisting as veterans having been agitated, three hundred and ninety-three members of the Seventeenth agreed to embark if necessary in another three years' campaign, and on the 22d of January the regiment started home on furlough. On the 7th of March it returned to the field, with an addition to its ranks of over four hundred men. Colonel Ward, though still suffering from his wound, and compelled through the entire Atlanta campaign to wear his arm in a sling, resumed command of the regiment. It took only a subordinate part in the heavy skirmishing at Rocky Face Ridge, but on the 13th of May bore its full share in the battle of Resaca. An assault having been ordered, it moved forward with Turchin's brigade until, unsupported on either right or left, it could go no further. It still, however, held the position it had gained until the commanding General decided to abandon the attack on the enemy's works at that point. Its loss here was quite heavy.

Skirmishes, that were half battles, continued almost daily; and in those at New Hope Church, Pumpkin Vine Creek, and several other places, the Seventeenth was actively engaged. One of these skirmishes, coming on the 18th of June, was long remembered in the regiment as "Waterloo"—the drenching rain in which they fought having quite as much to do, in their minds, with the name as the anniversary.

At Kenesaw Mountain the regiment suffered less than it had in previous actions of less importance; but the heat was so intense that many men were carried off, prostrated by sun-stroke.

At the battle of Peach Tree Creek, July 20th, the regiment was actively engaged. The heaviest fighting was further to the left, but the Seventeenth lost two officers and several privates.

Moving with Jeff. C. Davis's corps to the rear of Atlanta, the Seventeenth was among the claimants for the honor of having been first to strike the railroad. The next day Hunter's brigade—formerly Turchin's—in which the Seventeenth had been placed throughout the cam paign, sustained Este's, and advanced under a galling fire of musketry and artillery to the assault on Jonesboro'. This ended the campaign.

Colonel Ward's wounded arm having become worse, he feared the effects of exposure through the winter, and now resigned; although he afterward acted as volunteer aid on Schofield's staff at the battle of Nashville.

Lieutenant-Colonel Showers had just escaped from a Rebel prison in time to assume the command, and lead the regiment, with the rest of Sherman's army, "Down to the Sea." The Seventeenth saw very little more fighting which, after its past experience, it could call severe. It followed Sherman through the Carolinas, took part in the battle of Bentonville, passed in review before the President at Washington, and was mustered out at Louisville, Kentucky, in July, 1865.

One-half of the Seventeenth was raised in Fairfield County; three of its companies belonged in the Miami Valley. It was in the service from the beginning of the war. It was always at the front—never doing a single day's service in mere garrison duty. It served under nearly all the most famous commanders—McClellan, Buell, Rosecrans, Thomas, Grant, Halleck, Sherman, and Schofield. It held an honorable place from the first in that noted corps, Thomas's Fourteenth. And it was never driven, save at Chickamauga. Even then it quit the field only under orders, and at nightfall.

18th REGIMENT OHIO VOLUNTEER INFANTRY.

ROSTER, THREE MONTHS' SERVICE.

RANK.	NAME.	DATE OF RANK.	COM. ISSUED.	REMARKS.
Colonel	TIMOTHY R. STANLEY	May 29, 1861	May 29, 1861	
Lt. Colonel	WM. M. BOLLES	" 29, "	" 29, "	
Major	WM. H. BISBEE	" 29, "	" 29, "	
Surgeon	A. S. SWARTZWELDER	" 12, "	" 12, "	
Ass't Surgeon	W. H. DRURY	" 12, "	" 12, "	Resigned.
Do.	THOMAS L. NEAL	June 21, "	June 21, "	
Captain	Henry C. Rogers	April 23, "	April 23, "	
Do.	Frank Buell	" 20, "	" 20, "	
Do.	C. Kingsbury	May 30, "	May 30, "	
Do.	J. W. Caldwell	April 24, "	April 24, "	
Do.	John P. Merrill	" 22, "	" 22, "	
Do.	R. L. Curtiss	" 24, "	" 24, "	
Do.	C. C. Aylshire	" 22, "	" 22, "	
Do.	J. L. Wallace	" 25, "	" 25, "	
Do.	John J. Hoffman	" 30, "	" 30, "	
Do.	John McMahon			
Do.	John Henderson	May 7, "	May 7, "	
Do.	Wm. Bolles	April 22, "	April 22, "	
Do.	Geo. E. Downing	June 28, "	June 28, "	
1st Lieutenant	John V Keepers	April 23, "	April 23, "	
Do.	Dennis O'Leary	" 20, "	" 20, "	
Do.	Geo. E. Downing	May 30, "	May 30, "	Promoted to Captain.
Do.	H. S. Hamilton	April 24, "	April 24, "	
Do.	Hasley C. Burr	" 22, "	" 22, "	
Do.	George Hatch	" 24, "	" 24, "	
Do.	Junius Gates	" 22, "	" 22, "	
Do.	S. W. Ross	" 25, "	" 25, "	
Do.	David Dove	" 30, "	" 30, "	
Do.	Thomas Ross	May 7, "	May 7, "	
Do.	Chas. Kingsbury	April 22, "	April 22, "	
Do.	H. S. Spear	June 28, "	June 28, "	
Do.	Alex. Pearce	" 1, "	" 1, "	Adjutant.
Do.	J. C. Paxton	" 1, "	" 1, "	Quartermaster.
2d Lieutenant	John McMahon	April 23, "	April 23, "	
Do.	Wm. H. Bisbee	" 20, "	" 20, "	
Do.	H. S. Spear	May 30, "	May 30, "	
Do.	Alex. Pearce	April 24, "	April 24, "	
Do.	Warren G. Hubbard	" 22, "	" 22, "	
Do.	Wm. McCain	" 24, "	" 24, "	
Do.	George R. Hibben	" 22, "	" 22, "	
Do.	J. W. Jenkins	" 25, "	" 25, "	
Do.	John Andrews	" 30, "	" 30, "	
Do.	O. H. P. Scott	May 7, "	May 7, "	
Do.	George E. Downing	April 22, "	April 22, "	
Do.	Joshua Mathiot	June 28, "	June 28, "	
Do.	D. B. Caldwell	" 18, "	" 18, "	
Do.	Wallace Hill	July 22, "	July 22, "	
Do.	Silas E. Emmons			

ROSTER, THREE YEARS' SERVICE.

RANK.	NAME.	DATE OF RANK.	COM. ISSUED.	REMARKS.
Colonel	TIMOTHY R. STANLEY	Aug. 6, 1861	Aug. 6, 1861	Mustered out November 9, 1864.
Do.	CHAS. H. GROSVENOR	April 8, 1865	April 8, 1865	On duty as Prov. Marsh. Gen. of Ga. until Oct. 27, 1865.
Lt. Colonel	JOSIAH GIVEN	Aug. 17, 1861	Nov. 2, 1861	Appointed Colonel 74th Regiment.
Do.	CHAS. H. GROSVENOR	March 16, 1863	June 15, 1863	Promoted to Colonel.
Do.	JOHN M. BENEDICT	April 8, 1865	April 8, 1865	Mustered out with regiment.
Major	CHAS. H. GROSVENOR	July 30, 1861	July 30, 1861	Promoted to Lieutenant-Colonel.
Do.	J. M. WELCH	March 16, 1863	March 16, 1863	Mustered out November 9, 1864.
Do.	JOHN M. BENEDICT	Feb. 1, 1865	Feb. 1, 1865	Promoted to Lieutenant-Colonel.
Do.	ROBERT B. CHAPPELL	April 8, "	April 8, "	Mustered out with regiment.
Surgeon	WM. P. JOHNSON	Sept. 24, 1861	Nov. 22, 1861	Mustered out November 9, 1864.
Do.	HORACE P. KAY	Feb. 20, 1865	Feb. 20, 1865	Mustered out with regiment.
Ass't Surgeon	WM. W. MILLS	Sept. 24, 1861	Nov. 22, 1861	Resigned February 28, 1864.
Do.	CHAS. H. FRENCH	Jan. 1, 1863	Jan. 5, 1863	Mustered out November 9, 1864.
Do.	ARTHUR C. NEWELL	May 2, 1865	May 2, 1865	Mustered out October 9, 1865.
Do.	SAMUEL A. BAXTER	May 29, "	" 29, "	Mustered out October 9, 1865.
Chaplain	JOHN DILLON	Sept. 16, 1861	Sept. 25, 1861	Mustered out November 9, 1864.
Captain	Henry R. Miller	Aug. 1, "	Nov. 22, "	Resigned January 19, 1863.
Do.	Asbel Fenton	" 10, "	" 22, "	Died April 14, 1863.
Do.	J. M. Welch	" 26, "	" 22, "	Promoted to Major.
Do.	John Jumper	Sept. 8, "	" 22, "	Resigned October 4, 1863.
Do.	David H. Miles	" 18, "	" 22, "	Resigned September 18, 1862.
Do.	Philip E. Taylor	Oct. 11, "	" 22, "	Died of wounds January 2, 1863.
Do.	George Stivers	" 21, "	" 22, "	Died of wounds January 4, 1863.
Do.	Chas. C. Ross	Nov. 1, "	" 22, "	Mustered out November 9, 1864.
Do	Julius C. Stedman	" 4, "	" 22, "	Resigned May 26, 1863.

RANK.	NAME.	DATE OF RANK.			COM. ISSUED.			REMARKS.
Captain	Wm. L. Edmiston	Nov.	5,	1861	Nov.	22,	1861	Resigned August 30, 1862.
Do.	Ebenezer Grosvenor	Aug.	30,	"	Dec.	9,	1862	Killed December 15, 1864.
Do.	Alexander Pearce	Sept.	18,	"	"	9,	"	Mustered out November 9, 1864.
Do.	Chas. W. McNeill	Jan.	4,	1863	Feb.	18,	1863	Mustered out November 9, 1864.
Do.	J. C. McElroy	"	4,	"	"	18,	"	Mustered out November 9, 1864.
Do.	Geo. W. Dunkle	"	19,	"	March	6,	"	
Do.	Chas. A. Cable	March	26,	"	June	15,	"	Mustered out November 9, 1864.
Do.	Homer C. Jones	April	11,	"	Aug.	1,	"	Mustered out November 9, 1864.
Do.	Amos C. Royston	March	16,	"	June	23,	"	Resigned October 4, 1863.
Do.	Pearly G. Brown	June	10,	"	"	23,	"	Mustered out November 9, 1864.
Do.	John M. Benedict	Oct.	4,	"	Jan.	21,	1864	Promoted to Major.
Do.	George W. Clark	"	4,	"	"	21,	"	Declined promotion.
Do.	David H. Miles	June	8,	1864	June	8,	"	Mustered out November 9, 1864.
Do.	John B. Emory	Sept.	30,	1864	Sept.	30,	"	Honorably discharged March 25, 1865.
Do.	George Collings	Dec.	21,	"	Dec.	21,	"	Absent, per spec'l order, at muster-out of reg't.
Do.	Robert B. Clapp II	"	21,	"	"	21,	"	Promoted to Major.
Do.	Geo. W. Brown	"	21,	"	"	21,	"	Mustered out with regiment.
Do.	Chas. Grant	"	21,	"	"	21,	"	Mustered out with regiment.
Do.	Chas. J. Phillips	Jan.	20,	1865	Jan.	20,	1865	Declined promotion.
Do.	Daniel M. Bates	Feb.	10,	"	Feb.	10,	"	Mustered out with regiment.
Do.	Travis Lynch	"	10,	"	"	10,	"	Mustered out with regiment.
Do.	Milton W. Halsey	March	29,	"	March	29,	"	Mustered out with regiment.
Do.	Nelson McCoy	April	8,	"	April	8,	"	Absent without leave at muster-out of reg't.
Do.	Wm. S. Ware	"	12,	"	"	12,	"	Mustered out with regiment.
Do.	Thomas C. Sheldon	"	12,	"	"	12,	"	Cashiered October 11, 1865.
Do.	Henry Carr	"	12,	"	"	12,	"	Mustered out with regiment.
Do.	James F. H. Cook	May	11,	"	May	11,	"	
1st Lieutenant	Felix McNeill	Aug.	1,	1861	Nov.	22,	1861	Resigned September 26, 1862.
Do.	Geo. W. Dunkle	"	10,	"	"	22,	"	Promoted to Captain.
Do.	John C. Neal	"	7,	"	"	22,	"	Dismissed by order of W. D. June 16, 1862.
Do.	Alex. W. S. Minear	"	26,	"	"	22,	"	Resigned July 9, 1863.
Do.	J. C. McElroy	Sept.	2,	"	"	22,	"	Promoted to Captain.
Do.	Robert R. Danford	"	8,	"	"	22,	"	Resigned January 17, 1862.
Do.	Nelson H. Van Vorhes	"	13,	"	"	22,	"	Resigned August 15, 1862.
Do.	Jacob C. Frost	"	19,	"	"	22,	"	Resigned February 8, 1862.
Do.	Chas. W. McNeill	"	24,	"	"	22,	"	Promoted to Captain.
Do.	Wm. L. Edmiston	"	25,	"	"	22,	"	Promoted to Captain.
Do.	Henn. M. Berkstresser	Oct.	14,	"	"	22,	"	Resigned March 15, 1862.
Do.	Chas. A. Cable	"	24,	"	"	22,	"	Promoted to Captain.
Do.	Ebenezer Grosvenor	Nov.	5,	"	"	22,	"	Promoted to Captain.
Do.	Wm. B. Williams	Feb.	3,	1862	Feb.	3,	1862	Resigned February 8, 1863.
Do.	Alexander Pearce	"	19,	"	"	19,	"	Promoted to Captain.
Do.	Frederick J. Ryan	Sept.	1,	"	Nov.	11,	"	Resigned April 1, 1864.
Do.	Robert Davidson	"	26,	"	Dec.	20,	"	Resigned June 14, 1863.
Do.	Pearly G. Brown	Aug.	30,	"				Promoted to Captain.
Do.	John M. Benedict	Sept.	18,	"				Promoted to Captain.
Do.	Amos C. Royston	"	22,	"	Feb.	6,	1863	Promoted to Captain.
Do.	Homer C. Jones	Feb.	8,	1863	March	6,	"	Promoted to Captain.
Do.	Geo. W. Clark	Jan.	4,	"	Feb.	18,	"	Resigned September 20, 1864.
Do.	John C. Barron	March	26,	"	June	23,	"	Mustered out November 9, 1864.
Do.	Charles G. Baldwin	Jan.	4,	"	"	23,	"	Dismissed April 12, 1864.
Do.	John G. Honnold	Feb.	1,	"	July	20,	"	Mustered out November 9, 1864.
Do.	John H. Acton	Jan.	9,	"	June	23,	"	Discharged March 28, 1864.
Do.	Wm. B. Evans	June	18,	"	July	20,	"	Mustered out November 9, 1864.
Do.	Charles E. Stevens	"	10,	"	Aug.	1,	"	Resigned September 16, 1864.
Do.	Chas. Grant	March	16,	"	"	1,	"	Promoted to Captain.
Do.	Chas. M. Grubb	April	14,	"	"	1,	"	Mustered out November 9, 1864.
Do.	Theodore Ferrel	Aug.	18,	"	"	19,	"	Resigned October 17, 1863.
Do.	David B. Carlin	Oct.	4,	"	Jan.	4,	1864	Resigned February, 1864.
Do.	Sylvanus Bartlett	"	17,	"	Nov.	27,	1863	Mustered out November 9, 1864.
Do.	Charles J. Phillips	April	13,	1864	April	13,	1864	Resigned February 26, 1865.
Do.	David J. Seal right	July	12,	"	July	12,	"	Mustered out November 9, 1864.
Do.	John M. Grosvenor	"	12,	"	"	12,	"	Mustered out November 9, 1864.
Do.	John M. Grosvenor	Nov.	15,	"	Nov.	15,	"	Declined promotion.
Do.	Samuel W. Thomas	Dec.	21,	"	Dec.	21,	"	Killed December 15, 1864.
Do.	Daniel M. Bates	"	21,	"	"	21,	"	Promoted to Captain.
Do.	Travis Lynch	"	21,	"	"	21,	"	Promoted to Captain.
Do.	Nelson McCoy	"	21,	"	"	21,	"	Promoted to Captain.
Do.	Wm. S. Ware	"	21,	"	"	21,	"	Promoted to Captain.
Do.	Thomas C. Sheldon	"	21,	"	"	21,	"	Promoted to Captain.
Do.	Milton W. Halsey	"	21,	"	"	21,	"	Promoted to Captain.
Do.	Daniel Emory	Jan.	20,	1865	Jan.	20,	1865	Mustered out with regiment.
Do.	Henry Carr	"	20,	"	"	20,	"	Promoted to Captain.
Do.	Chas. R. Wilkinson	Feb.	10,	"	Feb.	10,	"	Mustered out with regiment.
Do.	Robert S. King	March	29,	"	March	29,	"	Absent at muster-out of regiment.
Do.	John G. G. Carter	"	29,	"	"	29,	"	Trans'red to Adjutant 18th O.V.I. Sept. 1, 1865.
Do.	D. S. Shellenbarger	"	29,	"	"	29,	"	Mustered out with regiment.
Do.	Jas. G. Irwin	April	8,	"	April	8,	"	Mustered out with regiment.
Do.	Wm. H. Emerick	"	12,	"	"	12,	"	Resigned July 11, 1865.
Do.	Benj. F. Davis	"	12,	"	"	12,	"	Declined promotion.
Do.	John McManus	"	12,	"	"	12,	"	Mustered out with regiment.
Do.	Chas. W. Stanneart	"	12,	"	"	12,	"	Mustered out with regiment.
Do.	Jerome F. Fry	"	12,	"	"	12,	"	Mustered out with regiment.
Do.	Isaac A. Shafer	May	2,	"	May	2,	"	Discharged July 2, 1865.
Do.	James F. H. Cook	"	11,	"	"	11,	"	Mustered out with regiment.
Do.	Wm. H. Holdeness	Sept.	4,	"	Sept.	4,	"	Mustered out with regiment.
2d Lieutenant	James H. Haynes	Aug.	1,	1861	Nov.	22,	"	Resigned November 28, 1862.
Do.	Homer C. Jones	"	10,	"	"	22,	1861	Promoted to 1st Lieutenant.
Do.	Amos C. Royston	"	26,	"	"	22,	"	Promoted to 1st Lieutenant.
Do.	Wm. B. Williams	Sept.	8,	"	"	22,	"	Promoted to 1st Lieutenant.
Do.	Samuel H. Martin	"	19,	"	"	22,	"	Resigned January 8, 1862.
Do.	Wm. W. Blacker	Oct.	14,	"	"	22,	"	Killed December 31, 1862.
Do.	Wm. B. Shirvin	"	21,	"	"	22,	"	Resigned August, 1862.
Do.	John C. Barron	"	21,	"	"	22,	"	Promoted to 1st Lieutenant.
Do.	Wm. H. Baird	Nov.	1,	"	"	22,	"	Resigned September 26, 1862.
Do.	Charles G. Baldwin	"	1,	"	"	22,	"	Promoted to 1st Lieutenant.
Do.	Alexander Pearce	Jan.	21,	1862	Jan.	21,	1862	Promoted to 1st Lieutenant.
Do.	Henry H. Welch	Feb.	3,	"	Feb.	3,	"	Resigned November 30, 1862.
Do.	Chas. B. Saunders	"	19,	"	"	19,	"	Resigned September 30, 1862.
Do.	Chas. M. Grubb	March	15,	"	April	10,	"	Promoted to 1st Lieutenant.
Do.	Chas. E. Stevens	Nov.	29,	"	Nov.	29,	"	Promoted to 1st Lieutenant.
Do.	Edward McLaren	Sept.	26,	"	Dec.	9,	"	Resigned August 5, 1863.

RANK.	NAME.	DATE OF RANK.	COM. ISSUED.	REMARKS.
2d Lieutenant	Chas. Grant	Sept. 20, 1862	Dec. 20, 1863	Promoted to 1st Lieutenant.
Do.	Lorenzo D. Carter	Nov. 30, "	" 31, "	Resigned January 2, 1864.
Do.	Wm. B. Evans	" 28, "	Jan. 23, "	Promoted to 1st Lieutenant.
Do.	David B. Carlin	Sept. 22, "	Feb. 6, "	Promoted to 1st Lieutenant.
Do.	John H. Acton	Dec. 31, "	" 18, "	Promoted to 1st Lieutenant.
Do.	John G. Honnold			Promoted to 1st Lieutenant.
Do.	Theodore Ferrell	June 9, 1863	June 23, "	Promoted to 1st Lieutenant.
Do.	David J. Seabright	April 14, "	Aug. 1, "	Promoted to 1st Lieutenant.
Do.	Chas. J. Phillips	" 18, "	July 20, "	Promoted to 1st Lieutenant.
Do.	Sylvanus Bartlett	Feb. 1, "	" 20, "	Promoted to 1st Lieutenant.
Do.	John M. Grosvenor	" 19, 1861	Feb. 19, 1861	Promoted to 1st Lieutenant.
Do.	Russell S. Carpenter	Nov. 1, 1863	March 9, "	Mustered out November 9, 1864.
Do.	Wm. Quigley	" 27, "	" 9, "	Mustered out November 9, 1864.
Do.	John F. Camp	Dec. 8, "	" 10, "	Mustered out November 9, 1864.
Do.	Travis Lynch	June 8, 1864	June 8, "	Promoted to 1st Lieutenant.
Do.	George Hewitt	July 12, "	July 12, "	Never mustered.
Do.	Daniel M. Bates	" 12, "	" 12, "	Promoted to 1st Lieutenant.
Do.	Daniel Emory	Dec. 21, "	Dec. 21, "	Promoted to 1st Lieutenant.
Do.	Henry Carr	" 21, "	" 21, "	Promoted to 1st Lieutenant.
Do.	Jas. G. Irwin	" 21, "	" 21, "	Promoted to 1st Lieutenant.
Do.	Wm. H. Emerick	" 21, "	" 21, "	Promoted to 1st Lieutenant.
Do.	Robert S. King	" 21, "	" 21, "	Promoted to 1st Lieutenant.
Do.	David A. Piatt	" 21, "	" 21, "	Declined promotion.
Do.	John G. G. Carter	" 21, "	" 21, "	Promoted to 1st Lieutenant.
Do.	D. S. Shellenbarger	" 21, "	" 21, "	Promoted to 1st Lieutenant.
Do.	Benj. F. Davis	Feb. 10, 1865	Feb. 10, 1865	Resigned June 12, 1865.
Do.	John McManus	" 10, "	" 10, "	Promoted to 1st Lieutenant.
Do.	Chas. W. Stanneart	April 8, "	April 8, "	Promoted to 1st Lieutenant.
Do.	Jerome F. Fry	" 8, "	" 8, "	Promoted to 1st Lieutenant.
Do.	Isaac A. Shafer	" 8, "	" 8, "	Promoted to 1st Lieutenant.
Do.	Wm. H. Holdeness	" 8, "	" 8, "	Promoted to 1st Lieutenant.
Do.	James F. H. Cook	" 12, "	" 12, "	Promoted to 1st Lieutenant.
Do.	Jonathan W. Pontius	" 12, "	" 12, "	Mustered out with regiment.
Do.	Wm. A. Davidson	" 12, "	" 12, "	Declined to accept commission.
Do.	David T. Shotts	May 2, "	May 2, "	Declined to accept commission.
Do.	Samuel L. Clark	" 2, "	" 2, "	Resigned July 28, 1865.
Do.	Samuel Charles	" 2, "	" 2, "	Mustered out with regiment.
Do.	David W. Bost	" 2, "	" 2, "	Mustered out with regiment.
Do.	Caleb Richmond	" 2, "	" 2, "	Mustered out with regiment.
Do.	Henry Klabish	" 2, "	" 2, "	Mustered out with regiment.
Do.	Peter Gutherell	" 18, "	" 18, "	Mustered out with regiment.
Do.	James W. Slater	" 31, "	" 31, "	Mustered out with regiment.
Do.	John A. Miller	Sept. 4, "	Sept. 4, "	Declined promotion.
Do.	George P. Jarvis	" 4, "	" 4, "	Mustered out with regiment.
Do.	George W. Kearns	" 4, "	" 4, "	Mustered out with regiment.

EIGHTEENTH OHIO VOLUNTEER INFANTRY.

FIRST ORGANIZATION.

THE organization of this regiment was commenced at Camp Wool, Athens, Ohio, in August, 1861, and completed at Camp Dennison, November 4, 1861. The regiment, nine hundred and thirty strong, left Camp Dennison November 6, 1861, and reported to General W. T. Sherman, at Louisville, the next day. Thence it marched down the river to West Point. On the 15th it reported at Elizabethtown, and was organized into a brigade comprising the Nineteenth Illinois, Eighteenth Ohio, Thirty-Seventh Indiana, and Twenty-Fourth Illinois, under command of Colonel Turchin, Nineteenth Illinois, General O. M. Mitchel's division of the Army of the Ohio. Remaining at Elizabethtown about a month, the division marched thence to Bacon Creek, where, for nearly two months, the command was instructed and drilled under the eye of General Mitchel.

On February 7th General Mitchel commenced in earnest his brilliant progress; he passed General McCook at Green River, encamped on its south bank, and on the 8th marched for Bowling Green, occupied in force by the enemy. On the night of the 9th the regiment for the first time bivouacked, and on the morning of the 10th showed hillocks of men covered with snow. The day the regiment reached the vicinity of Bowling Green, the place was reported deserted by the Rebels, and the bridge and public stores in flames. A difficulty in crossing the river was overcome by the ingenuity of Colonel Stanley, who detailed a number of men, and quickly constructed a bridge. The brigade marched down the bank, and, silently, that snowy night, the crossing was made, and at daylight Colonel Turchin, with his command, marched into Bowling Green. Large quantities of supplies and subsistence were captured, but more had been destroyed.

On February 23d General Mitchel moved for Nashville, sixty-two miles distant, reaching it in three days. Here, as at Bowling Green, the Fourth Ohio Cavalry preceded the infantry, and found the railroad bridge and the fine suspension bridge over the Cumberland River destroyed, but means of crossing were soon found and the City of Nashville was taken. The whole National army, under General Buell, encamped in and around the city.

General Mitchel's command being an independent one, that officer, March 18th, marched for Huntsville, Alabama, taking possession of the country as he passed. This bold and timely movement surprised the Rebels, who fell back as the National troops advanced. The whole country, from Nashville to Huntsville, and the railroad east to Bridgeport and west to Tuscumbia, were taken by a single division of less than seven thousand men. The railroads, bridges, and turnpikes, injured by the Rebels in their flight, were repaired, rendering the campaign very arduous. To the Michigan Engineers mainly belongs the credit of overcoming the difficulties in crossing bridgeless streams. The bridge over Stone River, two hundred and sixty feet long, was rebuilt in eight days, by a detail from the Eighteenth Ohio, with axes only.

On April 10th at midnight the command arrived within ten miles of Huntsville. A council of war was held at General Mitchel's head-quarters, and the plan of the capture of Huntsville decided upon. At three o'clock A. M. the command marched, and was in sight of Huntsville before the citizens were out of their beds. Some three hundred prisoners were captured, seventeen locomotives, one hundred and fifty cars, and large amounts of supplies. The Eighteenth Ohio, with other forces, were detailed to work the railroad and transport troops and supplies.

Tuscumbia was occupied, and Colonel Turchin, the brigade commander, with a small force, including the Eighteenth Ohio, made his head-quarters in the town, although almost surrounded by Rebel troops. Strategy was resorted to to deceive them as to the strength of the National forces. Names of officers from some dozen regiments were entered on the hotel books, whose regiments were supposed to be in camp, but an inspection would have found but six hundred men there. Colonel Stanley was careful not to let any citizens leave. General Buell ordered all west of Decatur evacuated, and the regiment was sent to Athens to guard the railroad.

On May 1st, at daylight, Colonel Stanley's pickets were attacked by Scott's Rebel cavalry, six hundred strong and three pieces of artillery, yet the Rebels were held in check for three hours. Colonel Stanley, learning that the Rebels consisted of three battalions of infantry, ordered a retreat toward Huntsville. While the Eighteenth was yet in Decatur General Mitchel came from Huntsville to Decatur on the cars, and ordered Colonel Stanley to fall back in good order to a point where re-enforcements would be met. General Mitchel came near being captured, as the Rebels sent a small force across to a bridge, setting it on fire, but the General and his train ran over it while burning. At this bridge a spirited fight occurred, in which six Rebels were killed and a number wounded. The regiment lost three killed and several wounded.

On May 31st the Eighteenth joined the brigade at Fayetteville, and marched thence, under General Negley, for Chattanooga. The town was bombarded from the north side of the river, by which it was believed the Rebels were deterred from a contemplated invasion of Kentucky. The distance marched in this movement was two hundred and forty miles, accomplished in twelve days, crossing Cumberland Mountain and Walden's Ridge.

From Fayetteville the regiment marched to Huntsville, thence to Stevenson and Battle Creek, where the Rebels were confronted; the Tennessee River being between the forces. The regiment built fortifications and remained at Battle Creek until July 11th, when it and half of the Twenty-Fourth Illinois, all under command of Colonel Stanley, marched across Cumberland Mountain, arriving at Decherd after midnight of the day in which General Forrest had captured Murfreesboro'. The Eighteenth next moved to Elk River, and along the railroad to Cowan; thence to Tullahoma and Manchester, and guarded the road from Tullahoma to McMinnville.

On August 29, 1862, companies A and I of the Eighteenth Ohio, and D of the Ninth Michigan, under command of Captain Miller, Eighteenth Ohio, were attacked at a stockade, twelve miles from Winchester, by Forrest, who dismounted nine hundred of his men before making the attempt. The Rebels were soon repulsed, losing about one hundred men without the loss of a man on our side. General Thomas complimented them in general orders. The Rebels having retreated a short distance, commenced destroying the railroad. Captain Miller sent a squad after them, but they were so badly whipped that they instantly decamped.

The Eighteenth was the last regiment to leave Manchester with Buell's retreating column. At Nashville the regiment was brigaded with the Sixty-Ninth Ohio, Eleventh Michigan, and Nineteenth Illinois, forming the Twenty-Ninth Brigade, under Colonel Stanley, and with another brigade, under Colonel Miller, was left for the defense of Nashville. Colonel Stanley commanded the brigade from September 10, 1862, until after the battle of Chickamauga.

The division in which the regiment was brigaded was the right of General Thomas's (Fourteenth) corps at the battle of Stone River. On Tuesday, the 30th of December, 1862, the division took post south of the Cedar Woods and drove the Rebel sharpshooters from several points. Early Wednesday the right, under General McCook, gave way and, after a short struggle, in which the Twenty-Ninth Brigade vainly battled with the Rebel masses, it was compelled to do likewise. During this fearful time, at a critical moment, under the lead of General Rousseau, the Eighteenth charged into the woods filled with Rebels, and checked their advance.

Friday found the division on the extreme left. Breckinridge attacked and drove the division, thrown across Stone River, in great confusion. General Rousseau ordered Colonel Stanley to take his brigade across the stream. It was a fearful thing to do, but the order was executed by both brigades. Advancing a little, to closer cover, the men fell upon their faces, and awaited the advancing foe. On came the Rebels, but they were received with a leaden storm which thinned their ranks fearfully, and without giving them a chance to recover, an order to charge was given, which caused them to flee panic-stricken; meantime the artillery was doing its work. The brigade captured four pieces of artillery. In this action of forty minutes Breckinridge acknowledged the loss of one thousand seven hundred men. The Eighteenth lost Captains Fenton, Taylor, and Stivers, Lieutenant Blacker, and thirty-two men killed; Lieutenant-Colonel Given, Captains Welch and Ross, Adjutant Mincar, and one hundred and forty-three men wounded. In June it accompanied the advance on Tullahoma, across Lookout Mountain into McLamore's Cove, and, with Negley's and Baird's divisions, September 11th at Dug Gap, confronted Bragg's army. In this movement, at the foot of Mission Ridge, General Negley directed Colonel Stanley to hold his position. The enemy were pressing, but the brigade kept them at a respectable distance.

In a day or two commenced the march for Chickamauga. The regiment did not get into the thickest of the fight until Sunday, September 20th, but went gallantly through the battle, making several brilliant charges. Colonel Stanley in his report noticed the gallantry and coolness of Captains Grosvenor, McElroy, and Cable, Lieutenants Carlin, Benedict, Clark, Honnold, Grubb, Ryan, Carter, Acton, Ferrel, and Evans. Sergeant-Major George Hewitt and private Joseph Imbody, of company H, are noticed "for their gallantry in rescuing the colors of the regiment when they fell from Lieutenant Carlin's hands, and bringing them safely from the field."

The regiment performed Engineering-duty, and aided in building boats, warehouses, saw-mills, and hospitals at Chattanooga, until October 20th, when it was ordered to Camp Chase to be mustered out of service. On the 9th of November, 1864, it was honorably discharged. Nearly one hundred men had re-enlisted as veterans, and there were enough recruits, whose time was not out, to make it up to two hundred and twenty-five men.

SECOND ORGANIZATION.

Before the Eighteenth Ohio left Chattanooga, Major-General Steedman, then commanding the District of the Etowah, solicited from General Thomas the requisite authority, and received an order to consolidate the detachments of the First, Second, Eighteenth, Twenty-Fourth, and Thirty-Fifth Ohio Regiments, remaining in service in accordance with the requirements of

General Order, No. 86, of April 2, 1863, from War Department; the organization formed to be designated the Eighteenth Ohio, and to be commanded by Lieutenant-Colonel C. H. Grosvenor.

Colonel Grosvenor went energetically to work, and succeeded in getting his command together and ready for the battle of Nashville, which was fought on the 6th of December, 1864. The Eighteenth was in the first line of the brigade, and moved behind Colonel Morgan's line, and, finally, well up to Rains's House, and in the ravines skirting the elevation on which were the Rebels. Colonel Morgan's skirmish-line had been driven back by the terrible fire of the enemy posted behind earthworks. The Eighteenth assaulted and dislodged this force. A cornfield, covered by the enemy in its front, was to be passed over, two heavy picket fences were rapidly thrown down and a desperate charge on the Rebel works made. The palisade defenses were swept away, and nearly one hundred men gained the interior and made short work of driving the Rebels out. Captain Grosvenor led the head of his regiment straight upon the enemy's works, and while in the act of springing over the embankment fell forward dead, struck by three balls. Lieutenant Samuel W. Thomas also fell, instantly killed, while removing palisades. Captain Benedict was wounded, Lieutenant Charles Grant assuming command. The regiment was withdrawn under a hot fire, and re-formed on the left of the Orphan Asylum. That night the regiment slept upon the field. On the 16th, under Captain Benedict, the Eighteenth took part in the bloody and finally successful assault upon Overton Hill. It lost four officers out of seven, and seventy-five men killed and wounded out of less than two hundred. That night, in a drenching rain, without blankets, the men bivouacked in the woods in line of battle.

Attached to General Steedman's command, the Eighteenth followed Hood's defeated forces to Huntsville, and two days later assisted in the capture of Decatur. The pursuit was continued to Tuscumbia. Chattanooga was reached January 10, 1865, and the regiment went into camp. Captain Benedict was promoted to Major, and took command, Lieutenant-Colonel Grosvenor commanding the brigade. The organization of the regiment was now prosecuted with vigor, but the mustering officers were tardy in their movements, and the complete organization was not effected until April. At that time the officers were regularly advanced, but not without much useless controversy with the Governor of Ohio. During the spring several expeditions were made into East Tennessee to capture and disperse bands of Rebel cavalry.

In April the regiment moved to the vicinity of Fort Phelps, where a beautiful model camp was made and the regiment thoroughly drilled. A few bad men had crept into the organization, belonging to that class of miserable skulkers called substitutes, some of whom were guilty of depredations and desertion, but the old and true soldiers fully sustained the record earned by the old Eighteenth on the battle-fields of the Army of the Cumberland. Colonel Grosvenor, brevetted Brigadier-General, was assigned to the command of the Post of Chattanooga in May.

The war had closed, and the men of the Eighteenth amused themselves in decorating their camp. Company head-quarters fairly bloomed with flowers; the streets were macadamized also.

In July the regiment accompanied General Steedman to his new quarters at Augusta, Georgia. General Grosvenor was assigned to duty as Provost-Marshal General of the Department with Major Chappell and Lieutenant Irwin as Aids. Upon Lieutenant Irwin devolved the duty of administering the oath of allegiance to the female Rebels of the city. In performing this duty many rich scenes were witnessed, as it was impossible, under the orders, for any of them to get their letters out of the post-office without a certificate that they had taken the oath. One morning a bright-eyed beauty bustled into the office, and with a look of mingled scorn and disgust demanded to take the oath, at the same time saying: "I take it so I can get my letters, but I hate your Government as bad as ever." Her hand was uplifted, and the words of the oath were upon her lips, when General Grosvenor, who had just entered the room unperceived, seized the paper from Lieutenant Irwin's hand, and turning to the beauty said: "Madam, *you* may not hesitate to lay perjury upon your soul, but I will not let you do so." He tore up the paper and gave orders that in future this woman should not be permitted to take the oath.

On October 9th the order for muster out came, and in a few days the regiment was on its was to Columbus, Ohio, where, October 22, 1865, the men scattered to their homes.

19th REGIMENT OHIO VOLUNTEER INFANTRY.

ROSTER, THREE MONTHS' SERVICE.

RANK.	NAME.	DATE OF RANK.	COM. ISSUED.	REMARKS.
Colonel	SAMUEL BEATTY	May 29, 1861	May 29, 1861	
Lt. Colonel	E. W. HOLLINGSWORTH	" 29, "	" 29, "	
Surgeon	B. B. BRASHEAR	" 13, "	" 13, "	
Ass't Surgeon	FRANCIS D. MORRIS	" 13, "	" 13, "	
Captain	Samuel Beatty	April 24, "	April 24, "	Promoted to Colonel.
Do.	E. W. Hollingsworth	" 24, "	" 21, "	Promoted to Lieutenant-Colonel.
Do.	Norman A. Barrett	May 14, "	May 14, "	
Do.	Robert W. Crane	" 25, "	" 25, "	
Do.	Urwin Bean	" 25, "	" 25, "	
Do.	George E. Paine	" 21, "	" 24, "	
Do.	Lewis P. Buckley	" 22, "	" 22, "	
Do.	Hiram K. Preston	" 22, "	" 22, "	
Do.	Wm. B. Hoyt	" 24, "	" 24, "	
Do.	Andrew J. Konkle	" 23, "	" 23, "	
Do.	Chas. F. Manderson	" 30, "	" 30, "	
Do.	Roswell Shurtliff	June 8, "	June 8, "	
Do.	Alex. Stilwell	May 29, "	May 29, "	
1st Lieutenant	Chas. F. Manderson	April 21, "	April 24, "	Promoted to Captain.
Do.	James C. Richards	" 24, "	" 24, "	
Do.	Henry G. Stratton	May 14, "	May 14, "	
Do.	John J. Hoyt	" 25, "	" 25, "	
Do.	Robert Shearer	" 25, "	" 25, "	
Do.	Harmon J. Clark	" 21, "	" 24, "	
Do.	Andrew J. Fulkerson	" 23, "	" 22, "	
Do.	Alex. Stilwell	" 22, "	" 22, "	Promoted to Captain.
Do.	J. P. Manning	" 24, "	" 24, "	
Do.	Paul T. Kirby	" 23, "	" 23, "	
Do.	James S. Harber	" 30, "	" 30, "	
Do.	W. H. K. Hilliard	" 29, "	" 29, "	
Do.	J. W. Fitch	" 29, "	" 29, "	Adjutant.
2d Lieutenant	Robert H. Rea	April 24, "	April 24, "	
Do.	George T. Perkins	" 24, "	" 21, "	
Do.	Henry G. Walcott	May 14, "	May 14, "	
Do.	Orrin Copp	" 25, "	" 25, "	
Do.	Alex. T. Snodgrass	" 25, "	" 25, "	
Do.	Samuel Hathaway	" 24, "	" 24, "	
Do.	Gilbert S. Carpenter	" 22, "	" 22, "	
Do.	J. Allen Campbell	" 22, "	" 22, "	
Do.	Marshal H. Haskell	" 24, "	" 24, "	
Do.	James Nelson	" 23, "	" 23, "	

ROSTER, THREE YEARS' SERVICE.

RANK.	NAME.	DATE OF RANK.	COM. ISSUED.	REMARKS.
Colonel	SAMUEL BEATTY	Aug. 10, 1861	Dec. 16, 1861	Appointed Brigadier-General Nov. 29, 1862.
Do.	CHAS. F. MANDERSON	March 15, 1863	April 7, 1863	Honorably discharged March 16, 1865.
Do.	JAMES M. NASH	May 31, 1865	May 31, 1865	Mustered out as Lieutenant-Colonel.
Lt. Colonel	E. W. HOLLINGSWORTH	Aug. 6, 1861	Dec. 16, 1861	Resigned January 19, 1863.
Do.	CHAS. F. MANDERSON	Jan. 19, 1863	Feb. 25, 1863	Promoted to Colonel.
Do.	HENRY G. STRATTON	March 15, "	April 7, "	Mustered out February 13, 1865.
Do.	JAMES M. NASH	Feb. 20, 1865	Feb. 20, 1865	Promoted to Colonel.
Do.	SOLOMON FIRESTON	May 31, "	May 31, "	Mustered out as Major.
Major	TIMOTHY D. EDWARDS	Aug. 2, 1861	Dec. 16, 1861	Killed at Pittsburg Landing April 7, 1862.
Do.	CHAS. F. MANDERSON	April 7, 1862	May 1, 1862	Promoted to Lieutenant-Colonel.
Do.	HENRY G. STRATTON	Jan. 19, 1863	Feb. 25, 1863	Promoted to Lieutenant-Colonel.
Do.	WM. H. ALLEN	March 15, "	April 7, "	Resigned July 19, 1863.
Do.	JAMES M. NASH	June 19, "	July 20, "	Promoted to Lieutenant-Colonel.
Do.	SOLOMON FIRESTON	March 29, 1865	March 29, 1865	Promoted to Lieutenant-Colonel.
Do.	LEWIS R. FIX	May 31, "	May 31, "	Mustered out with regiment.
Surgeon	FRED'K. T. HURXTHAL	Oct. 1, 1861	Dec. 16, 1861	Discharged March 14, 1863.
Do.	BENJ. M. TAYLOR	March 14, 1863	March 30, 1863	Mustered ont April 1, 1865.
Do.	A. H. SOWERS	April 8, 1865	April 8, 1865	Mustered out with regiment.
Ass't Surgeon	BENJ. M. TAYLOR	Oct. 3, 1861	Dec. 16, 1861	Promoted to Surgeon.
Do.	NEEMAS COLE	Aug. 20, 1862	Aug. 22, 1862	Declined.
Do.	A. H. SOWERS	July 4, "	Oct. 31, "	Promoted to Surgeon.
Do.	ROBERT MCNEELEY	April 29, 1863	April 29, 1863	Resigned August 22, 1864.
Do.	J. H. BITEMAN	" 8, 1865	" 8, 1865	Died September 25, 1865.
Chaplain	THOMAS MCCLEARY	Oct. 31, 1861	Dec. 16, 1861	Resigned February 18, 1862.
Do.	JOHN B. SMITH	May 1, 1862	Feb. 19, 1864	Mustered out per Special Order Aug. 3, 1865.
Captain	Wm. Rakestraw	Aug. 28, 1861	Dec. 16, 1861	Deceased.
Do.	Paul F. Kirby	" 28, "	" 16, "	Resigned December 2. 1862.
Do.	Chas. F. Manderson	Sept. 1, "	" 16, "	Promoted to Major.
Do.	Henry G. Stratton	" 7, "	" 16, "	Promoted to Major.
Do.	Wm. H. Allen	" 7, "	" 16, "	Promoted to Major.
Do.	Thomas Stackpole	" 10, "	" 16, "	Resigned December 18, 1863.
Do.	Urwin Bean	" 12, "	" 16, "	Killed January 2, 1863.
Do.	James M. Nash	" 13, "	" 16, "	Promoted to Major.
Do.	Franklin E. Stowe	" 15, "	" 16, "	Died April 31, 1862.
Do.	Peter A. Sanbie	Jan. 1, 1862	Feb. 5, 1862	Mustered out February 13, 1865.
Do.	Oscar O. Miller	Feb. 5, "	" 5, "	Mustered out May 27, 1863.
Do.	Charles Brewer	April 7, "	May 1, "	Declined.

RANK.	NAME.	DATE OF RANK.	COM. ISSUED.	REMARKS.
Captain	Solomon Fireston	Aug. 7, 1862	Aug. 22, 1862	Promoted to Major.
Do.	Cyrus Frease	" 30, "	" 22, "	Resigned December 16, 1862.
Do.	J. Ransford Percival	Dec. 2, "	" 22, "	Resigned November 23, 1863.
Do.	Charles Brewer	" 16, "	April 7, 1863	Killed May 29, 1864.
Do.	Carrel Smith	Jan. 2, 1863	" 7, "	Resigned October 4, 1864.
Do.	Uriah W. Irwin	March 15, "	" 7, "	Died December 8, 1863.
Do.	Wm. H. Burke	" 15, "	" 7, "	Dismissed July 24, 1863.
Do.	Joseph J. Agard	June 19, "	July 20, "	Honorably discharged January 27, 1865.
Do.	Aurora C. Keel	July 29, "	Aug. 18, "	Honorably discharged as 1st Lieutenant.
Do.	Wm. A. Knapp	May 27, "	" 18, "	Honorably discharged October 19, 1864.
Do.	Lewis R. Fix	March 15, 1864	March 15, 1864	Promoted to Major.
Do.	Richard L. Walker	July 25, "	July 25, "	Detached at own request.
Do.	Calvin S. Chamberlin	" 25, "	" 25, "	Mustered out with regiment.
Do.	Albert K. Upson	" 25, "	" 25, "	Mustered out with regiment.
Do.	Wm. S. S. Erb	" 25, "	" 25, "	Resigned November 22, 1861.
Do.	Philip Reefy	Dec. 21, "	Dec. 21, "	On detached duty at muster out of regiment.
Do.	Almon K. Raff	" 21, "	" 21, "	Mustered out with regiment.
Do.	Wm. H. Adams	" 21, "	" 21, "	Mustered out with regiment
Do.	Homer C. Reed	Feb. 20, 1865	Feb. 25, 1865	On detached service at muster out of regiment.
Do.	David Bash	" 20, "	" 25, "	Mustered out with regiment.
Do.	Henry M. Fusselman	March 29, "	March 28, "	Mustered out with regiment.
Do.	Joseph Vignos	Nov. 1, "	Nov. 25, "	Mustered out with regiment as Q. M.
1st Lieutenant	Charles Brewer	Aug. 1, 1861	Dec. 16, 1861	Promoted to Captain.
Do.	Solomon Fireston	" 26, "	" 16, "	Promoted to Captain.
Do.	George R. Lentz	" 26, "	" 16, "	Resigned August 1, 1862.
Do.	Oscar O. Miller	Sept. 7, "	" 16, "	Promoted to Captain.
Do.	Cyrus Frease	" 7, "	" 16, "	Promoted to Captain.
Do.	Peter A. Saubie	" 10, "	" 16, "	Promoted to Captain.
Do.	Samuel Lentz	" 12, "	" 16, "	Died February 9, 1862.
Do.	J. Ransford Percival	" 13, "	" 16, "	Promoted to Captain.
Do.	Carrel Smith	" 15, "	" 16, "	Promoted to Captain.
Do.	Wm. H. Burke	" 25, "	" 16, "	Promoted as Q. M.
Do.	Edward S. Myers	Nov. 1, "	" 16, "	Appointed Captain 107th O. V. I. Nov. 11, 1862.
Do.	Uriah W. Irwin	Dec. 12, 1862	Feb. 5, 1862	Promoted to Captain.
Do.	Job D. Bell	Feb. 5, "	" 5, "	Killed January 2, 1863.
Do.	Thomas J. Walton	" 5, "	" 5, "	Mustered out February 13, 1865.
Do.	David W. Hildebrand	April 7, "	May 1, "	Revoked.
Do.	Joseph J. Agard	Feb. 9, "	Aug. 22, "	Promoted to Captain.
Do.	Wm. A. Knapp	April 7, "		Promoted to Captain.
Do.	Aurora C. Keel	" 30, "		Promoted to Captain.
Do.	Lewis R. Fix	Aug. 1, "		Promoted to Captain.
Do.	Daniel Donovan	Nov. 19, "	Dec. 2, 1862	Killed December 31, 1863.
Do.	Wm. A. Sutherland	Dec. 2, "	" 30, "	Appointed A. A. G. May 9, 1864.
Do.	Calvin S. Chamberlin	" 31, "	Feb. 18, 1863	Promoted to Captain.
Do.	Albert K. Upson	Jan. 2, 1863	April 7, "	Promoted to Captain.
Do.	Richard L. Walker	Dec. 16, 1862	" 7, "	Promoted to Captain.
Do.	Wm. S. S. Erb	Jan. 2, 1863	" 7, "	Promoted to Captain.
Do.	J. Steward Kelley	April 2, "	" 2, "	Resigned June 22, 1863.
Do.	Philip Reefy	March 15, "	" 7, "	Promoted to Captain.
Do.	Homer C. Reed	June 23, "	July 20, "	Promoted to Captain.
Do.	Wm. H. Adams	" 19, "	" 20, "	Promoted to Captain.
Do.	Almon K. Raff	May 27, "	Aug. 18, "	Promoted to Captain.
Do.	David Bash	July 29, "	" 18, "	Promoted to Captain.
Do.	Henry M. Fusselman	" 25, 1864	July 25, 1864	Promoted to Captain.
Do.	Joseph Vignos	" 25, "	" 25, "	Promoted to Captain.
Do.	Wesley Upson	" 25, "	" 25, "	
Do.	Wm. F. McHenry	" 25, "	" 25, "	Killed in action August 24, 1864.
Do.	Thomas A. Brierly	" 25, "	" 25, "	Mustered out with regiment.
Do.	Jason Hurd	" 25, "	" 25, "	Mustered out with regiment.
Do.	Christian Felber	Dec. 21, "	Dec. 21, "	Mustered out with regiment.
Do.	John Culbertson	" 21, "	" 21, "	Mustered out with regiment.
Do.	George M. Hull	" 21, "	" 21, "	Mustered out with regiment.
Do.	Joseph H. Penny	" 21, "	" 21, "	Mustered out with regiment.
Do.	Jacob Bidamont	Feb. 20, 1865	Feb. 20, 1865	On detached service at muster out of reg't.
Do.	Alfred W. Stambaugh	" 20, "	" 20, "	Resigned May 31, 1865.
Do.	James G. Bailey	" 20, "	" 20, "	Mustered out with regiment.
Do.	Monroe Ebi	March 29, "	March 29, "	Resigned June 7, 1865.
Do.	Wm. F. Hunt	Sept. 4, "	Sept. 4, "	Mustered out with regiment.
Do.	Philip C. Meek	" 4, "	" 4, "	Mustered out with regiment.
Do.	Wm. M. Carr	Nov. 1, "	Nov. 1, "	Mustered out with regiment.
2d Lieutenant	David W. Hildebrand	Aug. 26, 1861	Dec. 16, 1861	Died July 20, 1862.
Do.	Joseph J. Agard	" 28, "	" 16, "	Promoted to 1st Lieutenant.
Do.	Wm. A. Knapp	Sept. 4, "	" 16, "	Promoted to 1st Lieutenant.
Do.	Job D. Bell	" 7, "	" 16, "	Promoted to 1st Lieutenant.
Do.	Aurora C. Keel	" 7, "	" 16, "	Promoted to 1st Lieutenant.
Do.	Thomas J. Walton	" 10, "	" 16, "	Promoted to 1st Lieutenant.
Do.	Lewis R. Fix	" 12, "	" 16, "	Promoted to 1st Lieutenant.
Do.	Daniel Donovan	" 13, "	" 16, "	Promoted to 1st Lieutenant.
Do.	Ambrose C. Shaffer	" 15, "	" 16, "	Discharged September 15, 1862.
Do.	Wm. A. Sutherland	Aug. 26, "	Feb. 18, 1864	Promoted to 1st Lieutenant.
Do.	James Wilson	Feb. 5, 1862	" 5, "	Resigned December 25, 1862.
Do.	Homer J. Ball	" 19, "	" 19, "	Resigned June 3, 1862.
Do.	Richard L. Walker	July 20, "	Aug. 22, "	Promoted to 1st Lieutenant.
Do.	Albert K. Upson	Feb. 9, "	" 22, "	Promoted to 1st Lieutenant.
Do.	Wm. S. S. Erb	April 7, "	" 22, "	Promoted to 1st Lieutenant.
Do.	Russell Case	Aug. 18, "	Oct. 5, "	Resigned March 26, 1863.
Do.	Philip Reefy	April 30, "	Dec. 2, "	Promoted to 1st Lieutenant.
Do.	Wm. H. Adams	Sept. 15, "	" 2, "	Promoted to 1st Lieutenant.
Do.	Homer C. Reed	June 3, "	" 2, "	Promoted to 1st Lieutenant.
Do.	Calvin F. Chamberlin	Nov. 19, "	" 2, "	Promoted to 1st Lieutenant.
Do.	Almon K. Raff	Dec. 2, "	April 7, 1863	Promoted to 1st Lieutenant.
Do.	Henry M. Fusselman	" 25, "	" 7, "	Promoted to 1st Lieutenant.
Do.	David Bash	" 16, "	" 7, "	Promoted to 1st Lieutenant.
Do.	Wesley Upson	Jan. 2, 1863	" 7, "	Promoted to 1st Lieutenant.
Do.	Jason Hurd	March 26, "	" 7, "	Promoted to 1st Lieutenant.
Do.	Wm. F. McHenry	Jan. 2, "	" 7, "	Promoted to 1st Lieutenant.
Do	Thomas A. Brierly	March 15, "	" 7, "	Promoted to 1st Lieutenant.
Do.	Joseph Vignos	Jan. 1, "	May 6, "	Promoted to 1st Lieutenant.
Do.	Christian Felber	June 19, "	July 20, "	Promoted to 1st Lieutenant.
Do.	John Culbertson	" 23, "	" 20, "	Promoted to 1st Lieutenant.
Do.	Joseph H. Penny	May 27, "	Aug. 18, "	Revoked.
Do.	George J. Swank	July 29, "	" 18, "	Revoked.

RANK.	NAME.	DATE OF RANK.	COM. ISSUED.	REMARKS.
2d Lieutenant	George M. Hull	July 25, 1864	July 25, 1864	Promoted to 1st Lieutenant.
Do.	Joseph H. Penny	" 25, "	" 25, "	Promoted to 1st Lieutenant.
Do.	Jacob Bidamont	" 25, "	" 25, "	Promoted to 1st Lieutenant.
Do.	Alfred W. Stambaugh	" 25, "	" 25, "	Promoted to 1st Lieutenant.
Do.	Frank H. Wheeler	" 25, "	" 25, "	
Do.	James G. Bailey	" 25, "	" 25, "	Promoted to 1st Lieutenant.
Do.	Monroe Ebl	" 25, "	" 25, "	Promoted to 1st Lieutenant.
Do.	J. Stanley Cochran	" 25, "	" 25, "	
Do.	Onesemus P. Shaffer	Feb. 20, 1865	Feb. 20, 1865	Resigned May 19, 1865.
Do.	Wm. M. Carr	" 20, "	" 20, "	Promoted to 1st Lieutenant.
Do.	Wm. F. Hunt	" 20, "	" 20, "	Promoted to 1st Lieutenant.
Do.	Philip C. Meek	" 20, "	" 20, "	Promoted to 1st Lieutenant.
Do.	James M. Linn	Nov. 1, "	Nov. 1, "	Mustered out as Sergeants; complimentary commissions given after the regiment was mustered out.
Do.	Reynolds J. Coroden	" 1, "	" 1, "	
Do.	Asahel Adams	" 1, "	" 1, "	
Do.	Wm. H. Underwood	" 1, "	" 1, "	
Do.	J. David Vestal	" 1, "	" 1, "	
Do.	Alonzo Hines	" 1, "	" 1, "	
Do.	Loreston Lane	" 1, "	" 1, "	
Do.	Hugh Cameron	" 1, "	" 1, "	
Do.	Wm. Bennett	" 1, "	" 1, "	
Do.	Henry C. Nicholson	" 1, "	" 1, "	

NINETEENTH OHIO VOLUNTEER INFANTRY.

THE NINETEENTH INFANTRY was among the organizations which sprang into existence at the sound of the guns at Fort Sumter. It was composed of recruits from seven counties, as follows: company A from Canton, Stark County; company B, Youngstown, Mahoning County; company C, Warren, Trumbull County; company D, Ashtabula; company E, New Lisbon, Columbiana County; company F, Geauga County; company G, Akron, Summit County; company H, New Lisbon, Columbiana County; company I, Ashtabula County; company K, Akron.

By the 15th of May, 1861, these companies were all in quarters at Camp Taylor, near Cleveland. On May 27th they repaired by rail to Columbus and occupied Camp Jackson, where, as was then the custom, an election for officers was held, with the following result: Colonel, Samuel Beatty; Lieutenant-Colonel, Elliott W. Hollingsworth; Major, Lewis P. Buckley. In the afternoon companies A and B were marched to the State Arsenal, were armed and equipped, and at once started in the cars for Bellair. The other eight companies were sent to Camp Goddard, at Zanesville, to perfect themselves in the drill.

Companies A and B continued on duty guarding the ferry at Bellair until June 3d. They were then taken to Glover's Gap and Mannington, where they performed the same duty until the 20th of June. Both companies then joined the regiment at Bellair, where, on June 21st, the Seventeenth, Nineteenth, and Twentieth Ohio regiments of infantry embarked on twelve steamers, and reached Parkersburg on June 23d. While at Parkersburg the Nineteenth, with the Eighth and Tenth Ohio and Thirteenth Indiana, were organized into a brigade, under Brigadier-General Wm. S. Rosecrans.

On June 25th the troops moved by rail to Clarksburg. Here was brought together General McClellan's "Provisional Army of West Virginia." On June 29th the Nineteenth, with the advance, left Clarksburg and made its first real march, reaching Buckhannon on July 2d. Moving from Buckhannon on July 7th, the army reached Roaring Creek, and encamped in front of the fortified Rebel position at Rich Mountain. General Rosecrans said of the part which the Nineteenth Ohio bore in this battle: "Seven companies of the Nineteenth deployed into line and delivered two splendid volleys, when the enemy broke." And subsequently: "The Nineteenth distinguished itself for the cool and handsome manner in which it held its post against a flank attack, and for the manner in which it came into line and delivered its fire near the close of the action." The regiment had but three men slightly wounded.

On July 23d, its term of service having expired, it moved to Webster, on the Baltimore and Ohio Railroad, and thence to Columbus, Ohio, where it arrived on the 27th of July, and by August 5th all the men were at home, receiving the congratulations of friends. In their trip through Ohio, especially at Chillicothe, the regiment received all the attentions that could be bestowed by a patriotic and grateful people.

Many of the officers immediately busied themselves in obtaining recruits for a three years' term of service, and by the 26th of September nine companies had reported with full complements of men, and were mustered into the service.

By November 7th the regiment was in Camp Dennison, fully armed and equipped. On November 16th it moved by rail to Cincinnati, and thence by steamer to Louisville, Kentucky, and was the first regiment to go into Camp Jenkins, five miles from the city. Here it remained, with General Ormsby M. Mitchel as its camp commander, until December 6th, when it was taken by rail to Lebanon, Kentucky. Thence it marched forty miles to Columbia. On this march a teamster, Jacob Clunck, was run over by his team and instantly killed. This was the first death in the Nineteenth Ohio.

The regiment reached Columbia on December 10th, and was brigaded with the Fifty-Ninth Ohio, Second and Ninth Kentucky Infantry, and Haggard's regiment of cavalry, constituting the Eleventh Brigade, General J. T. Boyle commanding. While at Columbia a beautiful silk flag was received by the hands of A. Kitt, Esq., as a present from the ladies of Canton. The flag was received with all the honors, and the presentation address of Mr. Kitt appropriately replied to by Captain Charles F. Manderson. On December 17th the regiment lost Captain Wm. Rakestraw, of company I, who died of diptheria.

On January 17, 1862, the Nineteenth Ohio and Third Kentucky marched to the mouth of Renick's Creek, near Burkesville, on the Cumberland River. On January 16th the command moved up the Cumberland River, through Creelsboro', to Jamestown, and was there joined by the Sixth Ohio Battery of artillery. Position was taken at the mouth of Greasy Creek for the purpose of preventing a junction by river of the forces at Mill Springs, under Zollicoffer, and the enemy at Nashville. The Rebel defeat at Mill Springs, and the evacuation by the enemy of his fortifications at Bowling Green, rendered a force on the upper waters of the Cumberland unnecessary, and February 15th saw the Nineteenth again on the march back to Columbia.

While lying at Columbia disease made sad havoc among the men of the regiment. The measles and typhoid fever prevailed. In a few days over two hundred men were in hospital. Lieutenant S. Lentz, of company E, died of typhoid fever February 9, 1852; also Sergeant Augustus Johns, of the same disease, about the same time.

After making tedious marches to Glasgow and Bowling Green, the march was directed on Nashville, which place was reached on March 10th, and the regiment went into camp five miles out on the Murfreesboro' Turnpike. The march from Camp Green had been one hundred and seventy miles, nearly half of which was made by the men with their shoes in such condition that they might be termed barefooted.

On March 18th the regiment, with its brigade, left Nashville for Savannah, on the Tennessee River, and by Sunday, April 6th, was within fourteen miles of that place. The heavy boom of the cannon was heard, and the men struck out on the double-quick, hoping to reach the field in time to take part in the conflict. It was dark before the regiment was placed on board the boat that was to take it to Pittsburg Landing. On its arrival a sorry sight was presented; the army was driven almost to the river, and thousands of stragglers and wounded men lined the banks.

The dreary rainy night was passed in line of battle on the field. At daylight the sharp rattle of musketry at the front showed that the enemy, flushed with his wonderful success of the first day, had determined to pursue his good fortune. Moving to the right, the men deposited their knapsacks and stripped off all useless weight for the coming fight. General J. T. Boyle, commanding the brigade, said of the Nineteenth: "The Colonel and Captain Manderson (acting Major) held their men steady, and deported themselves, as did their officers and men, with coolness and courage, until the Colonel ordered them back to a position from under the fire of the enemy's battery. This position was held until the guns of the enemy were silenced by the well-directed fire of Captain Bartlett's battery. Major Edwards (acting Lieutenant-Colonel) was shot dead from his horse, and a number of privates were killed and wounded." Privates O. T. Powell and Horace H. Bailey, of company C, and Corporal W. E. Gibson, of company H, were killed. Lieutenant Wm. A. Sutherland, of company H, was severely wounded in the shoulder.

The next ten days were spent by the regiment without tents or camp equipage, in the mud and rain, and the terrible stench of the battle-field. With the baggage, which reached the command on April 11th, came pleasant weather, and the blush of early spring spread itself over the battle-field.

The regiment participated in the approach to and siege of Corinth. During the march on the 31st of April, 1862, Captain Franklin E. Stowe, of company G, died of disease. On May 22d, near Farmington, the regiment had a picket skirmish in which six men were wounded, two of whom subsequently died. On May 29th it entered Corinth with the army, and on the 3d of June marched in pursuit of the enemy, going as far as Brownsboro'. It then returned to Iuka, and there joined General Buell's column, and marched with it to Florence, Alabama, and to Battle Creek, which last place it reached July 14th. On July 21st Lieutenant David W. Hildebrand died of disease.

On August 21st the regiment marched from Battle Creek, with General McCook's division, to Nashville. At that place it joined the concentrated army under General Buell, and with it made that arduous march to Louisville, Kentucky.

On October 1st the regiment marched out of Louisville with Crittenden's division on the Bardstown Turnpike, passing through that place and reaching the vicinity of Perryville on October 8th, in time to witness a portion of that battle, but not to participate. After the battle was ended, the regiment moved with the army in pursuit of the Rebels, and in the vicinity of Crab Orchard had a running skirmish, capturing a Rebel gun with its accouterments.

The Rebel army having retreated from Kentucky by way of Cumberland Gap, the Nineteenth marched through Somerset and Glasgow to Gallatin. After doing provost-duty at Gallatin for two weeks, it joined its division at the Hermitage, and passing through Nashville, went into camp on the Murfreesboro' Turnpike, near the State Lunatic Asylum.

On December 26th the regiment, under command of Major Charles F. Manderson, marched with the army in its advance on Murfreesboro'. December 31st it was thrown across Stone River, on the left, with the view of swinging around into Murfreesboro', but the disaster to McCook's right wing compelled its withdrawal, and recrossing the river it passed to the right, and by a determined resistance aided to check the advance of the Rebels. Under the personal lead of Major-General Rosecrans, Beatty's brigade charged the enemy, drove him about three-fourths of a mile, and held by the position until relieved by Colonel M. B. Walker's brigade.

On January 2d, with the Fourteenth and Twenty-Third Brigades, the regiment crossed Stone River, and received the charge of the Rebel column under Breckinridge. They were forced to retreat, but the pursuing Rebels coming under the range of the massed artillery, were driven back over the river and beyond it, with great slaughter. The Nineteenth Ohio and the Ninth Kentucky were the first to cross Stone River, and with the assistance of men of other regiments captured four pieces of artillery from the famous Washington (Louisiana) Battery. A mile of ground was gained, and had darkness not prevented, they would have gone into Murfreesboro'. Captain Bean, of company E, Lieutenant Bell, of company C, Lieutenant Donovan, of company B, and Sergeant-Major Lyman Tilce were here killed. Lieutenant Sutherland, company H, and Lieutenant Keel, company F, were severely wounded. The regiment entered the battle with four hundred and forty-nine men, and lost in killed, wounded, and missing, two hundred and thirteen, nearly one-half.

Murfreesboro' was occupied January 4, 1863. The regiment went into camp on the Liberty Turnpike. On January 5th Lieutenant-Colonel Hollingsworth having resigned, Major C. F. Manderson was promoted to Lieutenant-Colonel, and Captain H. G. Stratton to Major.

The whole army remained at Murfreesboro' until June 28th, during which time the Nineteenth guarded an ammunition train to Manchester over the worst of roads. Thence it marched to McMinnville, where it remained until August 16th. It then crossed the Cumberland Mountains to Pikeville, in Sequatchie Valley, and with the division passed over Lookout Mountain, and reached Lee & Gordon's Mills on the 13th of September. At Crawfish Springs the regiment had a brisk skirmish in which two men of company D were killed.

On September 18th, at nine o'clock A. M., the Nineteenth was ordered, with the Seventy-Ninth Indiana, supported by the Ninth and Seventeenth Kentucky, to advance upon the enemy. The regiment advanced with a cheer, drove the enemy, and captured a Rebel battery, with some prisoners. The advance of this small force was checked by a large body of the enemy, which forced it back, but not until it had secured and carried off its captures. As they fell back they were mistaken for Rebel troops and fired upon. This fatal mistake caused the loss of a number of men. McCook's division opportunely charged the advancing Rebels and drove them in turn.

On September 20th, the second day of the battle of Chickamauga, the regiment held an important position, and performed its share of hard fighting until nightfall, when the whole army withdrew to Chattanooga. Captain Uriah W. Irwin received a wound in this battle, which caused his death December 8, 1863. Lieutenant W. F. McHenry was also severely wounded. A private of company G received seven wounds during the first day's battle. The aggregate loss of the regiment was one hundred men killed, wounded, and missing.

The Nineteenth remained in Chattanooga during the siege. On November 23d the regiment took part in the advance on Orchard Knob, and lost some twenty men, killed and wounded. On November 25th it participated in that glorious charge on the Rebel works at the foot of Mission Ridge, and seizing the inspiration, climbed, without orders, the precipitous sides of the mountain and aided in driving the Rebels over and down the opposite side. In this charge the regiment lost one man killed and thirteen wounded.

Returning to Chattanooga, it was almost immediately sent with Sherman toward Knoxville. This march was among the severest during the war. The men were ragged and almost shoeless, and left their footprints in blood on the snowy ground. Finding that Longstreet had raised the siege of Knoxville, the forces moved to Strawberry Plains and Flat Creek. At the last-named place, on January 1, 1864, four hundred men of the Nineteenth Ohio re-enlisted as veteran volunteers. On January 4th the regiment left Flat Creek, and by the 16th reached Chattanooga, where the papers being prepared, the three years' regiment was mustered out of, and the veteran Nineteenth Ohio mustered into, the service. The regiment then returned to Ohio, reaching Cleveland on the 16th of February.

On March 17th the veterans were promptly in camp at Cleveland. They returned immediately to the front, reaching Knoxville on the 24th of March. The regiment remained here up to the 9th of April, when it moved to McDonald's Station, Tennessee, and with the Third Brigade, Third Division, Fourth Army Corps, remained quietly in camp, awaiting the return of non-veterans and preparing for the Atlanta campaign.

On May 6th Sherman's entire command entered on the Atlanta campaign. The Nineteenth was sent to Parker's Gap, to hold that pass. On May 20th it rejoined its brigade at Cassville. Moving with the column, the Nineteenth participated in the sharp fight at New Hope Church. Captain Charles Brewer, of company E, was killed, Major Nash lost his left hand, Captain Smith, of company G, was severely wounded in the head, and forty-four men were killed and wounded. The regiment was engaged at Kenesaw, at Peachtree Creek, and at the crossing of the Chattahoochie River, and was under fire almost daily up to the evacuation of Atlanta. It also passed with Sherman around to the right of Atlanta in the affair at Jonesboro'.

On September 2, 1864, the regiment participated in the action at Lovejoy Station. Captain Miller, of company I, was killed; Colonel C. F. Manderson severely wounded in the spine; Captain Agard, of company K, severely wounded in the shoulder. Seventy men were killed and wounded. It captured the enemy's front line of works and held it for three days, and until Sherman's army returned to Atlanta.

The entire loss of the regiment in the Atlanta campaign was: killed, two commissioned officers and twenty-eight men; wounded, six commissioned officers and ninety-six men; missing, thirteen men; total, one hundred and forty-five. Lieutenant Wm. F. McHenry, of company I, was killed in front of Atlanta on the 24th of August, 1864, and Captain Lewis R. Fix, of company B, was severely wounded on the same day.

On October 1st, after General Sherman had started with the main army in his march to the sea, the Nineteenth, forming a part of General George H. Thomas's command, left Atlanta and marched toward Nashville to aid in opposing General Hood.

On October 29th, at the battle of Franklin, the regiment was held in reserve. It reached Nashville the night after the battle of Franklin, and during the investment of that place by the Rebels engaged in frequent sorties, with inconsiderable loss.

The regiment participated in the battle of Nashville with small loss, and then followed in pursuit of Hood's defeated and demoralized army to the Tennessee River.

On January 5, 1865, the regiment was at Huntsville, Alabama, where comfortable quarters were erected, but were only occupied until the 31st, when the command again moved to Nashville, for what purpose it was never ascertained, for on February 6th it was ordered back to Huntsville.

On March 17th Colonel Manderson resigned from physical disability, and Colonel Stratton having resigned some months earlier, Major Nash was made Lieutenant-Colonel, and remained in command of the regiment during the rest of its service.

From Huntsville it was moved into East Tennessee. Marching as far as the Virginia line, it then returned to Nashville on April 25th. On June 16th it formed a part of that column of troops sent to Texas, reaching Green Lake July 14, 1865. It left Green Lake September 11th, and arrived at San Antonio on the 23d. This march was one of the most arduous of all its campaigns. The excessive heat and lack of water caused intense suffering. The march was made over one of the sandy plains of that region.

On October 21st the Nineteenth was mustered out of service at San Antonio, and started on its return home. It reached Columbus, Ohio, on November 22d, and was paid off and discharged at Camp Chase November 25, 1865, after nearly five years of varied and honorable service.

20th REGIMENT OHIO VOLUNTEER INFANTRY.*

ROSTER, THREE YEARS' SERVICE.

RANK.	NAME.	DATE OF RANK.	COM. ISSUED.	REMARKS.
Colonel	CHAS. WHITTLESEY	Aug. 19, 1861	Dec. 16, 1861	Resigned April 19, 1862.
Do.	MANNING F. FORCE	April 19, 1862	May 1, 1862	Appointed Brigadier-General.
Do.	HARRISON WILSON	June 21, 1865	June 21, 1865	Mustered out with regiment.
Do.	JOHN C. FRY	Jan. 7, 1864	Feb. 9, 1864	Resigned October 19, 1864, as Lieut. Col.
Lt. Colonel	MANNING F. FORCE	Aug. 19, 1861	Dec. 16, 1861	Promoted to Colonel.
Do.	JAMES N. MCELROY	April 19, 1862	May 1, 1862	Resigned January 7, 1864.
Do.	JOHN C. FRY	Jan. 7, 1864	Feb. 8, 1864	Resigned October 19, 1864; promoted to Colonel.
Do.	FRANCIS M. SHACKLEE	" 6, 1865	Jan. 6, 1865	Mustered out November 25, 1864.
Do.	HARRISON WILSON	" 11, "	" 11, "	Promoted to Colonel.
Do.	PETER WEATHERBY	June 21, "	June 21, "	Mustered out with regiment.
Major	JAMES N. MCELROY	Sept. 11, 1861	Dec. 16, 1861	Promoted to Lieutenant-Colonel.
Do.	JOHN C. FRY	April 19, 1862	May 1, 1861	Promoted to Lieutenant-Colonel.
Do.	EDWIN C. DOWNS	Jan. 7, 1864	Feb. 8, 1864	Resigned April 1, 1864.
Do.	FRANCIS M. SHACKLEE	April 22, "	April 22, "	Promoted to Lieutenant-Colonel.
Do.	HARRISON WILSON	Jan. 6, 1865	Jan. 6, 1865	Promoted to Lieutenant-Colonel.
Do.	NATHAN BOSTWICK	" 11, "	" 11, "	Mustered out as Captain.
Do.	PETER WEATHERBY	April 1, "	April 1, "	Promoted to Lieutenant-Colonel.
Do.	WM. L. WADDELL	June 21, "	June 21, "	Mustered out as Captain.
Surgeon	EDWARD L. HILL	Sept. 7, 1861	Dec. 16, 1861	Mustered out September 18, 1864.
Do.	H. B. FRICKER	Oct. 12, 1864	Oct. 12, 1864	Mustered out with regiment.
Ass't Surgeon	JOHN G. PURPLE	Sept. 9, 1861	Dec. 16, 1861	Died May 13, 1862.
Do.	H. B. FRICKER	May 13, 1862	May 26, 1862	Promoted to Surgeon.
Do.	J. W. GUTHRIE	Aug. 21, "	Aug. 28, "	Mustered out with regiment.
Chaplain	JAMES KNAPP	Dec. 16, 1861	Dec. 16, 1861	Resigned April 28, 1862.
Do.	J. W. ALDERMAN	July 28, 1862	Aug. 11, 1862	Resigned July 20, 1863.
Captain	John C. Fry	Aug. 18, 1861	Dec. 16, 1861	Promoted to Major.
Do.	Elisha Hyatt	Sept. 3, "	" 16, "	Resigned February 22, 1862.
Do.	George Rogers	" 4, "	" 16, "	Resigned February 16, 1863.
Do.	John N. Cassell	" 4, "	" 16, "	Resigned January 5, 1863.
Do.	James M. McCoy	" 8, "	" 16, "	Resigned November 14, 1862.
Do.	Charles H. McElroy	" 10, "	" 16, "	Appointed Major 96th regiment Aug. 8, 1862.
Do.	Wm. W. Updegraff	" 16, "	" 16, "	Resigned April 25, 1863.
Do.	James Powers	Dec. 5, "	Jan. 22, "	Resigned February 9, 1862.
Do.	Edwin C. Downs	Feb. 19, 1862	Feb. 19, "	Promoted to Major.
Do.	Wm. Rogers	" 9, "	March 6, "	Resigned April 26, 1862.
Do.	Abraham Kaga	Jan. 27, "	Jan. 27, "	Honorably discharged January 6, 1864.
Do.	Peter N. Hitchcock	April 19, "	May 1, "	Declined.
Do.	Benj. A. F. Greer	" 21, "	" 9, "	Mustered out.
Do.	Francis M. Shacklee	Feb. 11, "	" 15, "	Promoted to Major.
Do.	Erastus N. Owens	April 19, "	June 21, "	Declined promotion.
Do.	Wm. Rogers	Sept. 9, "	Sept. 12, "	Resigned December 3, 1862.
Do.	Velorus T. Hills	Aug. 8, "	Oct. 30, "	Honorably discharged March 28, 1864.
Do.	Lyman N. Ayres	Nov. 14, "	Jan. 12, 1863	Mustered out December 18, 1864.
Do.	George L. Mellick	Dec. 3, "	Feb. 10, "	Died October 20, 1863.
Do.	Anderson J. Edwards	Jan. 5, 1863	" 10, "	Resigned April 14, 1863.
Do.	Harrison Wilson	Feb. 16, "	April 8, "	Promoted to Major.
Do.	Henry M. Davis	April 14, "	May 25, "	Mustered out October 18, 1864.
Do.	Wm. H. Jacobs	" 19, "	" 25, "	Mustered out November 5, 1865.
Do.	Nathan Bostwick	Jan. 1, 1864	Jan. 30, 1864	Promoted to Major.
Do.	Wm. D. Neal	April 20, "	April 20, "	Killed in action June 26, 1864.
Do.	Arthur H. Humiston	" 20, "	" 20, "	Mustered out.
Do.	Peter Weatherby	" 20, "	" 20, "	Promoted to Major.
Do.	Wm. M. Waddell	" 22, "	" 22, "	Mustered out as Captain with regiment.
Do.	Reuben M. Colby	July 25, "	July 25, 1864	Mustered out with regiment.
Do.	Henry D. Dwight	Jan. 6, 1865	Jan. 6, 1865	Declined promotion.
Do.	Wm. Rush	" 6, "	" 6, "	Declined promotion.
Do.	Samuel G. Hasler	" 6, "	" 6, "	Declined promotion.
Do.	Caleb Taylor	" 6, "	" 6, "	Declined promotion.
Do.	John W. Manning	" 6, "	" 6, "	Declined promotion.
Do.	John W. Skillen	" 11, "	" 11, "	Declined promotion; mustered out as Q. M.
Do.	Newton R. Persinger	" 11, "	" 11, "	Mustered out with regiment.
Do.	James McCracken	" 11, "	" 11, "	Mustered out with regiment.
Do.	Wm. G. Downs	" 11, "	" 11, "	
Do.	Joshua E. Clark	" 11, "	" 11, "	Mustered out with regiment.
Do.	Joseph Haines	" 11, "	" 11, "	Mustered out with regiment.
Do.	Edmund E. Nutt	" 10, "	" 10, "	Mustered out with regiment.
Do.	Thomas S. Hawley	June 21, "	June 21, "	Mustered out with regiment.
Do.	Wm. L. Barrington	" 21, "	" 21, "	Mustered out with regiment.
1st Lieutenant	James Knapp	Aug. 18, 1861	Dec. 16, 1861	Promoted to Captain.
Do.	Peter N. Hitchcock	" 19, "	" 16, "	Mustered out August 18, 1864.
Do.	Zachariah S. Adkins	" 31, "	" 16, "	Resigned February 28, 1862.
Do.	Wm. Rogers	Sept. 3, "	" 16, "	Promoted to Captain.
Do.	Benj. A. F. Greer	" 4, "	" 16, "	Promoted to Captain.
Do.	George L. Mellick	" 7, "	" 16, "	Promoted to Captain.
Do.	Velorus T. Hills	" 10, "	" 16, "	Promoted to Captain.
Do.	John R. Bond	" 11, "	" 16, "	Promoted to Major 67th regiment.
Do.	David R. Hume	" 16, "	" 16, "	Resigned May 16, 1862.
Do.	Erastus N. Owen	Oct. 11, "	" 16, "	
Do.	Edward C. Downs	Dec. 5, "	Jan. 22, 1862	Promoted to Captain February 19, 1862.
Do.	Anson J. Edwards	" 16, "	Dec. 16, 1861	
Do.	Henry M. Davis	Feb. 19, 1862	Feb. 19, 1862	
Do.	Conrad Garvis	" 28, "	March 6, "	Resigned April 24.
Do.	Lyman N. Ayres	" 22, "	" 6, "	Promoted to Captain.

* For three months' Roster see page 167.

RANK.	NAME.	DATE OF RANK.	COM. ISSUED.	REMARKS.
1st Lieutenant	David R. Rinehart	Jan. 27, 1862	Jan. 27, 1862	Resigned June 28, 1863.
Do.	Wm. H. Jacobs	April 19, "	May 1, "	Promoted to Captain.
Do.	Nathan Bostwick	" 24, "	" 9, "	Promoted to Captain.
Do.	Wm. D. Neil	" 24, "	" 9, "	Resigned May 16, 1862.
Do.	Harrison Wilson	Feb. 15, "	" 15, "	Promoted to Captain.
Do.	Wm. D. Neil	May 16, "	June 3, "	Promoted to Captain.
Do.	Reuben M. Colby	April 19, "	" 24, "	Revoked.
Do.	Arthur N. Humiston	Aug. 8, "	Dec. 10, "	Promoted to Captain.
Do.	Peter Weatherby	Nov. 14, "	Jan. 12, 1863	Promoted to Captain.
Do.	Wm. L. Waddell	Dec. 3, "	Feb. 10, "	Promoted to Captain.
Do.	Reuben M. Colby	Jan. 5, 1863	" 10, "	Promoted to Captain.
Do.	J. B. Walker	" 28, "	April 8, "	Appointed Assistant Adj. Gen. Oct. 10, 1863.
Do.	Henry D. Dwight	Feb. 16, "	" 8, "	Declined promotion; mustered out as Adjt.
Do.	Presley McCafferty	April 14, "	May 25, "	Killed; commission returned.
Do.	Reuben Woodmancy	" 19, "	" 25, "	Honorably discharged November 1, 1864.
Do.	Joshua L. Dunlevy	" 20, "	April 20, 1864	Honorably discharged as 2d Lieutenant.
Do.	Wm. Rush	" 20, "	" 20, "	Mustered out.
Do.	Samuel G. Hasler	" 20, "	" 20, "	Mustered out.
Do.	Wm. H. Nagle	" 20, "	" 20, "	Mustered out with regiment.
Do.	John G. Stevenson	" 20, "	" 20, "	Mustered out December 18, 1864.
Do.	Caleb Taylor	" 20, "	" 20, "	Mustered out.
Do.	Edmund E. Nutt	" 20, "	" 20, "	Promoted to Captain.
Do.	John W. Manning	May 9, "	May 9, "	Mustered out.
Do.	John W. Skillen	" 9, "	" 9, "	Declined promotion; mustered out as Q. M.
Do.	A. B. Godfrey	July 25, "	July 25, "	Deserted.
Do.	Newton R. Persinger	Aug. 19, "	Aug. 19, "	Promoted to Captain.
Do.	Thomas S. Hawley	June 11, 1865	Jan. 11, 1865	Promoted to Captain.
Do.	Wm. L. Barrington	" 11, "	" 11, "	Promoted to Captain.
Do.	Chaney Grimes	" 11, "	" 11, "	Mustered out with regiment.
Do.	C. W. McCracken	" 11, "	" 11, "	Mustered out with regiment.
Do.	Sylus A. Reynolds	" 11, "	" 11, "	Mustered out with regiment.
Do.	Daniel Fitzgerald	" 11, "	" 11, "	Mustered out with regiment.
Do.	Jesse L. Felt	" 11, "	" 11, "	Mustered out with regiment.
Do.	Wm. L. Phillips	" 11, "	" 11, "	Mustered out with regiment.
Do.	Jesse L. Dickensheets	" 11, "	" 11, "	Mustered out with regiment.
Do.	George Thoura	" 11, "	" 11, "	Mustered out with regiment.
Lieutenant	Erastus N. Owen	Aug. 18, 1861	Dec. 16, 1861	Promoted to 1st Lieutenant.
Do.	Lyman N. Ayers	Sept. 3, "	" 16, "	Promoted to 1st Lieutenant February 22, '62.
Do.	Conrad Garvis	" 8, "	" 16, "	Promoted to 1st Lieutenant.
Do.	Henry Sherman	" 10, "	" 16, "	Mustered out March 5, 1862.
Do.	Wm. H. Jacobs	" 10, "	" 16, "	Promoted to 1st Lieutenant.
Do.	Wm. D. Neal	" 16, "	" 16, "	Promoted to 1st Lieutenant April 26, 1862.
Do.	Nathan Bostwick	Oct. 18, "	" 16, "	Promoted to 1st Lieutenant.
Do.	Henry M. Davis	Dec. 5, "	Jan. 22, 1862	Promoted to 1st Lieutenant.
Do.	Reuben M. Colby	" 16, "	Dec. 16, 1861	Promoted to 1st Lieutenant.
Do.	Herman H. Sherwin	Feb. 19, 1862	Feb. 19, 1862	Resigned March 3, 1862.
Do.	Peter Weatherby	" 22, "	March 6, "	Promoted to 1st Lieutenant.
Do.	Robert J. Irwin	" 28, "	" 6, "	Promoted to 1st Lieutenant.
Do.	Seneca Hale	Nov. 26, "	Jan. 27, "	Resigned February 16, 1863.
Do.	Henry O. Dwight	March 5, "	May 1, "	Promoted to 1st Lieutenant.
Do.	Arthur N. Humiston	" 31, "	" 1, "	Promoted to 1st Lieutenant.
Do.	Wm. L. Waddell	Feb. 11, "	" 15, "	Promoted to 1st Lieutenant.
Do.	J. B. Walker	April 19, "	June 3, "	Promoted to 1st Lieutenant.
Do.	Samuel H. Davis	" 24, "	" 3, "	Died April 14, 1863.
Do.	Reuben Woodmancy	May 16, "	" 3, "	Promoted to 1st Lieutenant.
Do.	Presley McCafferty	" 15, "	" 24, "	Promoted to 1st Lieutenant.
Do.	Joshua L. Dunlevy	Aug. 8, "	Dec. 10, "	Honorably discharged April 28, 1863.
Do.	Wm. W. McCracken	Nov. 14, "	Jan. 12, 1863	Honorably discharged August 19, 1863.
Do.	Wm. Rush	Dec. 3, "	Feb. 10, "	Promoted to 1st Lieutenant.
Do.	Russell B. Neil	Jan. 3, "	" 10, "	Appointed 1st Lieutenant.
Do.	Samuel G. Hasler	April 8, 1863	May 25, "	Promoted to 1st Lieutenant.
Do.	Wm. H. Nagle	Feb. 16, "	" 25, "	Promoted to 1st Lieutenant.
Do.	Byron Selby	" 16, "	" 25, "	Killed.
Do.	John G. Stephenson	Jan. 28, "	April 8, "	Promoted to 1st Lieutenant.
Do.	Caleb Taylor	April 14, "	May 25, "	Promoted to 1st Lieutenant.
Do.	Edmund E. Nutt	" 19, "	" 25, "	Promoted to 1st Lieutenant.
Do.	Columbus V. Johnson	June 1, "	June 18, "	Mustered out December 12, 1863
Do.	John W. Manning	Nov. 16, "	April 22, 1864	Promoted to 1st Lieutenant.

TWENTIETH OHIO VOLUNTEER INFANTRY.

THE TWENTIETH OHIO was organized for the three months' service in May, 1861, but beyond its roster, which is given in the proper place, little or nothing of its history or movements need be said in this connection. First-Lieutenant John C. Fry was soon promoted to Captain, and continued in the service, entering the three years' organization with his company, and was made Colonel of the regiment in January, 1864.

The reorganization took place at Camp King, near Covington, Kentucky, on the 21st of October, 1861. Its commander, Colonel Charles Whittlesey, a citizen of Northern Ohio, graduated at West Point, and for some years preceding the war was an eminent engineer and geologist, residing much of the time in the region of Lake Superior. He supervised and carried toward completion the defenses of Cincinnati, which were commenced back of Covington by General O. M. Mitchel. While there, and mainly under the supervision of Lieutenant-Colonel M. F. Force, the members of this regiment were imbued with that thoroughly soldierly spirit which adhered to them through all the vicissitudes of their field-service.

During the winter of 1861 and 1862 the regiment was employed in guarding several batteries in the rear of Covington and Newport. Four companies were sent during the winter into an insurrectionary district near Warsaw, Kentucky, and on the 11th of February, 1862, the entire regiment, with the exception of company K, embarked on the steamers Emma Duncan and Doctor Kane for the Cumberland River.

The Twentieth arrived at Fort Donelson on the evening of the 14th of February, and was under fire to some extent, during the 15th. It marched to the extreme right of the army, was placed in reserve, and was compelled to stand a severe test in seeing crowds of stragglers falling back from the front, and in being forced to hear their wild reports of disaster and defeat; but, notwithstanding these discouragements, the regiment passed through its first battle with no little credit to every man. After the surrender of the Fort the Twentieth was sent North in charge of prisoners, and became scattered all over the land. By the middle of March seven companies had been brought together, and they proceeded up the Tennessee River, on the expedition to Yellow Creek, on the steamer Continental, which General Sherman occupied as head-quarters.

On the 6th of April, while on inspection in camp at Adamsville, the Twentieth heard the booming of the guns at Pittsburg Landing, and at 3 P. M. marched to the field, went into position on the right of the army, and spent a comfortless night standing in the rain. The regiment participated in the next day's battle with considerable loss, and is fully entitled to a share in the glory of the victory. It was commanded during the engagement by Lieutenant-Colonel Force, Colonel Whittlesey being in command of a brigade. During the advance on Corinth the Twentieth remained on duty at Pittsburg Landing. Death and sickness held a perfect carnival in its camp, and it was accustomed to appear on parade with scarcely one hundred men. After the fall of Corinth, the regiment moved to Purdy, and there joining its division, marched to Bolivar, where it was left as a part of the garrison on the 6th of June, 1862. Here the health of the regiment improved greatly, and it was principally employed in expeditions for information or for forage.

On the 30th of August, 1862, the Rebel General, Armstrong, with fifteen regiments marching to destroy railroad communications northward, was held in check the entire day by the Twentieth

Ohio, a portion of the Seventy-Eighth Ohio, and two companies of the Second Illinois Cavalry. The steady fire of the skirmishers from the Twentieth Ohio did much toward restraining the enemy from any attack in line. Late in the afternoon two companies, G and K of the Twentieth, were captured by a cavalry charge, but not until they had emptied many a saddle in repulsing two previous charges. This affair was considered of so much importance that Colonel M. M. Crocker, commanding the post of Bolivar, was promoted to Brigadier-General, to date from the day of the engagement. Colonel Force, Major Fry, Captain Kaga, Adjutant Owen, Lieutenants Ayres, Hills, and Mellick, of the Twentieth, were specially and honorably mentioned in the official report of Colonel Leggett, who commanded the brigade in this battle.

The regiment assisted in driving Price from Iuka, on the 20th of September, and in the engagement between Hurlburt and Price at the crossing of the Hatchie near Metamora, Tennessee, it arrived on the field at 4 P. M., with a wagon train loaded with supplies, having marched twenty-eight miles since 10 o'clock, A. M. The supplies were immediately turned over and the regiment marched in pursuit of the Rebels that same night.

On the 28th of November the regiment marched southward from Lagrange in the Second Brigade of Logan's Division, and on the 4th of December entered Oxford, Mississippi. The regiment advanced as far as Water Valley, Mississippi, and on the capture of Holly Springs returned northward, halting a few days at Abbeville, where, on Christmas and New Year's days, the men regaled themselves on dinners of parched corn. About this time the Seventeenth Army Corps was organized, and Logan's division became the Third Division in the corps. By slow marches the Twentieth reached Memphis on the 28th of January, 1863, and there received an addition of two hundred recruits and drafted men. On the 22d of February the regiment moved down the Mississippi River on the steamer Louisiana, landed at Lake Providence, and a few weeks later marched to the relief of Porter's fleet, blockaded in Steele's Bayou, and after spending three days in the Louisiana swamps returned to its camp. The regiment arrived at Milliken's Bend on the 18th of April, and marched to Hard Times Landing on the Mississippi. It crossed the river, moved through Port Gibson, and pursued the retreating Rebels to Hawkinson's Ferry on the Big Black.

On the 12th of May the Twentieth deployed in advance of the Seventeenth Corps as it approached Raymond, Mississippi, and while resting with arms stacked, was fired upon from a dense thicket beyond a small stream. The regiment immediately formed and advanced across the creek, using the bank on the opposite side as a breastwork. For an hour the struggle was severe, and especially so to the Twentieth, as the regiments on the right withdrew their lines a little distance to the rear, and the flank of the Twentieth was exposed to a raking cross-fire. Every man stood firm until the line again advanced, and the Rebels gave way. The regiment lost in this engagement twelve killed and fifty-two wounded. Private Canavan, of company E, was promoted to a sergeantcy on the field for skillfully managing his company when all the officers and sergeants were struck down. Captain Wilson was decorated with the Seventeenth Corps Medal of Honor, in silver, for gallantry in assembling his skirmishers under the very muzzles of the enemy's guns in the first charge. Lieutenant Weatherby, of company A, being on the extreme right of the skirmish line with his company, and being cut off from his regiment, assembled his company and reported to the Colonel of the nearest regiment, the Eighty-First Illinois, and fought as a part of that regiment till the end of the battle; when, as the company marched to join its regiment, the Eighty-First showed their appreciation of its services by giving three hearty cheers for the "Twentieth Ohio Boys."

The regiment moved on through Clinton, Jackson, Bottom Depot, to Champion Hills, when the regiment was early pushed forward to a strong position in a ravine, under such a fire that it was dangerous for a staff officer to approach with orders. Though the adjoining regiments on each flank were pushed back as the enemy moved up in mass, the Twentieth held its ground without wavering till its ammunition was exhausted; it then fixed bayonets and prepared to maintain its position, but the Sixty-Fifth Ohio came to its assistance from the reserve and the enemy was driven back.

Crossing Big Black the regiment reached the rear of Vicksburg, and acted as support to the assaulting party on the 21st of May. The regiment did its proportion of work in the saps, and mines, and trenches, until the 29th of May; when, with the brigade, it withdrew from the line and accompanied an expedition to the Yazoo Valley. It returned again to Vicksburg on the 4th of June, and was placed in reserve. On the day of its return Colonel Force was ordered to assume command of the Second Brigade, and was afterward promoted to Brigadier-General. Lieutenant Walker, acting Adjutant of the Twentieth, was made Captain and Assistant Adjutant-General on General Force's staff, and Lieutenant H. O. Dwight was appointed Adjutant, and held the position to the close of the war, declining a captaincy when it was offered to him.

It was about this time that several of the Twentieth, who had been transferred to the Fifth United States Heavy Artillery (colored), passed through a severe hand-to-hand action at Milliken's Bend, in which the attacking Rebels were thoroughly defeated by the raw negro troops.

On the 26th of June the regiment, marching with the Second Brigade, withdrew to Titlin, near Black River, in order to observe the movements of Johnston. After the fall of Vicksburg the regiment camped at Bovina Station, on the Mississippi Southern Railroad, but was shortly ordered to join Sherman's army besieging Jackson. It finally returned to Vicksburg, July 30th, and encamped in the outskirts of the city. In the latter part of August, the Twentieth was a part of an expedition to Monroe, on the Ouachita River, and returned to its camp at Vicksburg, September 1st. On the 7th of October the regiment crossed Big Black at Messenger's Ferry, skirmished slightly at Boquecchitto Creek, advanced toward Canton as far as Livingston, thence to Clinton, and then over the old Champion Hills battle-ground to Big Black and Vicksburg.

In January, 1864, two-thirds of the men present re-enlisted, and on the 3d of February the regiment crossed Big Black and joined the celebrated Meridian expedition. In crossing Baker's Creek one of the enemy's batteries opened upon the column. The Twentieth rapidly formed in line, and the battery retired. The regiment was compelled to march in line until late in the afternoon, as the Rebels placed their battery on every hill-top and skirmished briskly along the road. In spite of this the head of the column passed over eighteen miles, and camped at Jackson that night. Passing through Brandon, the troops reached Morton, and from this point to Meridian the Twentieth acted as rear-guard to the whole army the greater portion of the distance. After arriving at Meridian the regiment assisted in destroying ten or fifteen miles of railroad, and then marched to the wagon corral on Chunkey Creek; and, being misdirected by a Rebel, it marched eight miles to advance three. The next day the Rebel's house was burned, in order that he might remember the time he enjoyed the pleasure of misdirecting the Yankees.

On the 20th of February the regiment marched on its return as a part of the convoy for seven hundred wagons. It marched by way of Hillsboro' and Canton, and reached Vicksburg on the 4th of March.

The regiment went North on veteran furlough; and, after spending thirty days at their homes, rendezvoused at Camp Dennison on the 1st of May, and proceeded to Cairo, Illinois, and from there by steamer to Clifton, Tennessee. From this point it marched, *via* Pulaski, Huntsville, Decatur, and Rome, to Acworth, where it joined General Sherman on the 9th of June, after a march of two hundred and fifty miles from Clifton. In the advance from Acworth the Twentieth formed the escort to the wagon-train, but finally joined its brigade, on the 23d, at Bushy Ridge, near Kenesaw Mountain.

On the night of the 26th the Twentieth, with its division, marched to the left of the line, and at eight o'clock next morning moved vigorously and with great noise upon the enemy, the object being to divert the enemy's attention from the general assault made by the other portions of the National line. The division advanced to within easy range of the Rebel works, near Marietta, and was exposed to the concentrated fire of four batteries. Having succeeded to a certain extent in accomplishing their object, the regiment engaged in another demonstration on the Rebel works in front of its camp at three P. M.; and, advancing up a thickly wooded hill till within one hundred yards of the enemy's works, sustained a brisk musketry fire till dark. On the 2d of July the regiment marched with its corps to the mouth of the Nickojack Creek, where the enemy was found intrenched. After the evacuation of the works at Nickojack, the regiment was employed in picketing the river, which was lively business, as the Rebels kept up a constant and accurate fire during the day. On the 16th of July the regiment crossed the Chattahoochie at Rossville, and on the 20th reached the Rebel works before Atlanta.

The regiment took position in the advanced line on the 21st, and on the 22d firing was heard in its rear. The regiment formed in the works; but, as the Rebels advanced, the men leaped the parapet and faced toward the enemy. The Rebels pressed up to and around the regiment, and the bullets came from front, flank, and rear; and, according as the fire was hottest in front or rear, the men of the Twentieth leaped the works and delivered their fire in that direction. Cartridges became scarce, but portions of companies A, F, and D risked their lives and obtained, in the very face of the enemy, five cases of ammunition, which were piled up near the regimental head-quarters; but even this supply was insufficient, and the ammunition of the wounded and dead was distributed, and charges were made to capture Rebels for their cartridges. At four o'clock P. M. many of the men had only two or three cartridges left. The batteries in Atlanta threw shell upon the rear of the brigade, the enemy redoubled their fire in front, and, placing a captured gun within fifty paces of the flank of the Twentieth, raked the regiment with cannister. Orders came to withdraw from the works and form a new line, and the Twentieth slowly retired, the men turning now and then to fire the last cartridge at the enemy. In the new line the Twentieth was placed in reserve, with the exception of a detachment of about one hundred men, who were posted in the works on Force's Hill, and fought desperately until the close of the battle. In this engagement the Twentieth lost forty-four killed, fifty-six wounded, and fifty-four missing. Instances of personal daring were numberless, but Lieutenants Nutt, of company F, and Skillen, of company G, and the following named enlisted men: Crabbe and Casey, of company C; Elder, of company G, and Speeker and Stevenson, of company F, especially distinguished themselves.

The regiment was engaged in changing position and building works until the 24th of August, when it received orders to march as guard to the supply trains of the Army of the Tennessee. Four days later the regiment joined its brigade at Fairburn, and assisted in destroying railroads. In the battle of Jonesboro', on the 31st, the Twentieth was on the left of the Fifteenth Corps, at right-angle to the main line, as "refused flank," and in this position was greatly annoyed by a heavy artillery fire. On the 2d of September the regiment took position on a hill near Lovejoy's Station, where it remained several days, exposed to some annoyance from the enemy's sharp-shooters, and finally settled down in camp near Atlanta, on the East Point Road. On the 5th of October the regiment joined the pursuit of Hood, and, after following as far as Galesville, Alabama, returned and camped at Smyrna Church, about twenty miles from Atlanta, November 5th.

The regiment left Atlanta with Sherman's army, on the 15th of November, for Savannah. It participated in the destruction of the town of Millin, Georgia, and, on reaching Savannah, took position on the right of the Seventeenth Corps. On the 19th of December it was detached from the brigade and sent to the Ogeechee, near King's Bridge, where it was engaged in building wharves on which to land supplies for the army. This work was cut short by the surrender of Savannah, and the regiment rejoined the brigade, December 24th, in camp at the outskirts of the city.

The Twentieth embarked on the steamer Fanny, on the 5th of January, 1865, proceeded to Beaufort, South Carolina, crossed Port Royal Ferry, and advanced until the enemy was found intrenched beyond a rice swamp. The Twentieth deployed as skirmishers, charged the enemy's works in fine style, and the regimental colors were soon waving from the parapet. At dark the troops encamped before the fortifications of Pocotaligo, and, on the morning of the 13th of January, the Twentieth was assigned camping ground beyond the railroad station of Pocotaligo, and remained there until the 30th of January, when it started on the Carolina campaign.

The head of the column struck the enemy, February 13th, near the bridge across the North Edisto at Orangeburg. Two companies of the Twentieth were deployed as skirmishers, and soon the regiment advanced on the double-quick and drove the enemy back to their fortifications, which were concealed by a turn in the road, and from which the Rebels opened fire. The regiment deployed as skirmishers, advanced through the swamp in water icy-cold and waist deep, opened fire on the enemy on the opposite side, stood until late in the afternoon, and was relieved. Next day crossed the river and engaged in destroying the railroad. In this the National loss was less than the enemy's missing, wounded, or killed. Reached Columbia the night the town was destroyed; the next morning marched through its smoking ruins and up the railroad, destroying it as far as Winnsboro'. On the 24th of February was left in rear of the entire army to guard the pontoon train; and, after a wearisome march, entered Cheraw March 3d, and Bennettsville the 6th. The regiment moved on over miserable roads, being frequently compelled to lift the wagons out of the mud, hub-deep, until March 10th, then moved toward Bentonville, where it arrived at five P. M. next day. On the 21st fortified rapidly, expecting an attack, but the enemy withdrew, and on the 24th the regiment entered Goldsboro'. After two weeks' rest the regiment pushed on to Raleigh, and on the 15th of April moved toward Johnston's army. It became known that Johnston had asked terms for a surrender; the men seemed crazy with joy; they shouted, laughed, flung their hats in the air, threw their knapsacks at each other, hugged each other, stood on their heads in the mud, and were fairly mad with delight.

Leaving Raleigh, May 1st, the regiment marched *via* Richmond to Washington; was in the grand review, May 24th; thence was sent to Louisville, Kentucky, and, July 18th, back to Columbus, where it was mustered out of service.

20th REGIMENT OHIO VOLUNTEER INFANTRY.

ROSTER, THREE MONTHS' SERVICE.

RANK.	NAME.	DATE OF RANK.	COM. ISSUED.	REMARKS.
Colonel	THOMAS MORTON	May 23, 1861	May 23, 1861	
Lt. Colonel	J. W. CRUIKSHANK	" 23, "	" 23, "	
Major	C. N. LAMISON	" 23, "	" 23, "	
Surgeon	E. L. HILL	" 13, "	" 13, "	
Ass't Surgeon	C. J. BELLOWS	" 13, "	" 13, "	
Captain	M. H. Nichols	April 20, "	April 20, "	
Do.	Ozro Dodds	" 18, "	" 18, "	
Do.	Thomas Morton	" 22, "	" 22, "	Elected Colonel.
Do.	A. V. Thompson	" 22, "	" 22, "	
Do.	S. R. Mott	" 17, "	" 17, "	
Do.	C. N. Lamison	" 20, "	" 20, "	Elected Major.
Do.	Henry Rigby	" 21, "	" 24, "	
Do.	J. W. Cruikshank	May 13, "	May 13, "	Elected Lieutenant-Colonel.
Do.	David S. Cable	April 23, "	April 23, "	
Do.	Thomas P. Cook	" 25, "	" 25, "	
Do.	A. L. Harris	May 27, "	May 27, "	
Do.	M. Armstrong	" 27, "	" 27, "	
Do.	J. C. Fry	" 27, "	" 27, "	
1st Lieutenant	C. M. Hughes	April 20, "	April 20, "	
Do.	M. D. Whelpley	" 18, "	" 18, "	
Do.	J. W. Sater	" 22, "	" 22, "	
Do.	David Gans	" 22, "	" 22, "	
Do.	E. Arnold	" 17, "	" 17, "	
Do.	M. Armstrong	" 20, "	" 20, "	Promoted to Captain.
Do.	S. E. Adams	" 24, "	" 24, "	Quartermaster May 27, 1861.
Do.	J. C. Fry	May 13, "	May 13, "	Promoted to Captain.
Do.	J. F. Sarratt	April 22, "	April 22, "	
Do.	J. R. McDonald	" 25, "	" 25, "	
Do.	G. A. Taylor	" 27, "	May 27, "	
Do.	J. W. Dunn	" 27, "	" 27, "	
Do.	James Knapp	" 27, "	" 27, "	
2d Lieutenant	T. J. Hustler	" 20, "	April 20, "	
Do.	Frank Evans	" 18, "	" 18, "	
Do.	A. L. Harris	" 22, "	" 22, "	Promoted to 1st Lieutenant.
Do.	Thomas Gray	" 22, "	" 22, "	
Do.	W. W. Watts	" 17, "	" 17, "	
Do.	A. G. Taylor	" 20, "	" 20, "	Promoted to 1st Lieutenant.
Do.	E. A. James	" 21, "	" 24, "	
Do.	James Knapp	May 13, "	May 13, "	
Do.	W. A. O. Measney	April 22, "	April 22, "	
Do.	J. C. McDonald	" 25, "	" 25, "	Resigned June 7, 1861.
Do.	Peter O. Cain	May 27, "	May 27, "	
Do.	J. W. Pepper	" 27, "	" 27, "	
Do.	A. S. Jones	June 17, "	June 17, "	
Do.	John A. Whiteside	May 27, "	May 27, "	
Do.	A. J. Bowers	" 27, "	" 27, "	

21st REGIMENT OHIO VOLUNTEER INFANTRY.

ROSTER, THREE MONTHS' SERVICE.

RANK.	NAME.	DATE OF RANK.	COM. ISSUED.
Colonel	JESSE S. NORTON	May 15, 1861	May 15, 1861
Lt. Colonel	J. M. NEIBLING	" 15, "	" 15, "
Major	A. J. TAYLOR	" 15, "	" 15, "
Surgeon	WM. M. EAMES	" 13, "	" 13, "
Ass't Surgeon	D. S. YOUNG	" 13, "	" 13, "
Captain	James Wilson	April 17, "	April 17, "
Do.	Omer C. Carr	" 26, "	" 26, "
Do.	Asher Cook	" 25, "	" 25, "
Do.	Thomas G. Allen*	May 1, "	May 1, "
Do.	A. V. Rice	" 16, "	" 16, "
Do.	George F. Walker	April 23, "	April 23, "
Do.	R. Henry Lovell	" 26, "	" 26, "
Do.	A. M. Blackman	" 24, "	" 24, "
Do.	Ira K. Seaman	" 25, "	" 25, "
Do.	Samuel A. Strong	" 25, "	" 25, "
Do.	Mattaew Ewing	July 18, "	Aug. 9, "
1st Lieutenant	D. M. Stoughton	April 17, "	April 17, "
Do.	James J. Voorhees	" 26, "	" 26, "
Do.	Arnold McMahan	" 25, "	" 25, "
Do.	Matthew Ewing†	May 1, "	May 1, "
Do.	P. J. Bowman	April 27, "	April 27, "
Do.	Morgan D. Shafer	" 23, "	" 23, "
Do.	Joshua S. Preble	" 26, "	" 26, "
Do.	Matthew H. Chance	" 24, "	" 24, "
Do.	Charles H. Vantine	" 25, "	" 25, "
Do.	John Paul, jr.	" 25, "	" 25, "
Do.	Charles W. Allen	July 18, "	Aug. 9, "
Do.	Frederick R. Miller	April 27, "	" 12, "

NAME.	DATE.	ISSUED.
2d Lieutenants.		
George Foreman	Ap.17,'61	Ap.17,'61
John E. McGowan	" 26, "	" 26, "
Leonard B. Blinn	" 26, "	" 25, "
Guy Pomeroy	May1, "	May1, "
George Matthews	" 16, "	" 16, "
J. E. Stearns	Ap.23, "	Ap.23, "
J. J. A. Thrapp	" 26, "	" 26, "
Jonas Foster	" 21, "	" 21, "
Ira M. Kelsey	" 25, "	" 25, "
James P. Arrants	" 25, "	" 25, "
James F. Pocock	J'y 18, "	Aug9, "
George O. McPherson	Ap.27, "	" 12, "

ROSTER, THREE YEARS' SERVICE.

RANK.	NAME.	DATE OF RANK.	COM. ISSUED.	REMARKS.
Colonel	JESSE S. NORTON	Sept. 11, 1861	Nov. 11, 1861	Resigned December 20, 1862.
Do.	JAMES M. NEIBLING	Dec. 20, 1862	Dec. 30, 1862	Honorably discharged December 6, 1864.
Do.	ARNOLD McMAHAN	July 12, 1865	July 12, 1865	Mustered out as Lieutenant-Colonel.
Lt. Colonel	JAMES M. NEIBLING	Sept. 19, 1861	Nov. 11, 1861	Promoted to Colonel December 20, 1862.
Do.	D. M. STOUGHTON	Dec. 20, "	Dec. 30, "	Died of wounds November 19, 1863.
Do.	ARNOLD McMAHAN	Feb. 29, 1864	Feb. 29, 1864	Promoted to Colonel.
Do.	WM. B. WICKER	July 12, 1865	July 12, 1865	
Major	SAMUEL A. STRONG	Sept. 19, 1861	Nov. 11, 1861	Resigned October 3, 1862.
Do.	D. M. STOUGHTON	Oct. 3, 1862	" 20, 1862	Promoted to Lieutenant-Colonel.
Do.	GEORGE F. WALKER	Dec. 20, "	Dec. 30, "	Resigned June 14, 1863.
Do.	ARNOLD McMAHAN	June 14, 1863	June 24, 1863	Promoted to Lieutenant-Colonel.
Do.	ISAAC CUSAC	Feb. 29, 1864	Feb. 29, 1864	Mustered out.
Do.	JOHN C. MARTIN	July 12, 1865	July 12, 1865	Mustered out as Captain August 3, 1865.
Surgeon	WM. M. EAMES	Sept. 19, 1861	Dec. 20, 1861	Resigned October 3, 1862.
Do.	DANIEL S. YOUNG	Oct. 3, 1862	" 18, 1862	Mustered out with regiment.
Ass't Surgeon	DANIEL S. YOUNG	Sept. 19, "	Nov. 11, "	Promoted to Surgeon October 3, 1862.
Do.	RICHARD GRAY	Aug. 21, "	Sept. 1, "	Mustered out June 5, 1865.
Do.	WM. C. PAYNE	Dec. 18, "	Dec. 18, "	Resigned August 13, 1863.
Captain	D. M. Stoughton	Sept. 19, 1861	Nov. 11, 1861	Promoted to Major October 3, 1862.
Do.	George F. Walker	" 19, "	" 11, "	Promoted to Major.
Do.	Arnold McMahan	" 19, "	" 11, "	Promoted to Major.
Do.	Silas S. Canfield	" 19, "	" 11, "	Mustered out April 1, 1865.
Do.	Isaac Cusac	" 19, "	" 11, "	Promoted to Major.
Do.	Matthew Ewing	" 19, "	" 11, "	Resigned February 20, 1863.
Do.	Milo Caton	" 19, "	" 11, "	Resigned June 5, 1865.
Do.	James P. Arrants	" 19, "	" 11, "	Resigned April 9, 1862.
Do.	H. H. Alban	" 19, "	" 11, "	Honorably discharged March 8, 1865.
Do.	David Gibbs	" 19, "	" 11, "	Resigned January 25, 1862.
Do.	Chas. H. Vantine	Feb. 8, 1862	Feb. 8, 1862	Resigned December 10, 1863.
Do.	John C. Martin	April 9, "	May 1, "	Commission returned.
Do.	Lewis E. Brewster	" 9, "	July 8, "	Resigned May 13, 1863.
Do.	James W. Knaggs	Oct. 3, "	Dec. 30, "	Resigned July 20, 1863; wounded.
Do.	James L. Curry	Dec. 20, "	Feb. 12, 1863	Resigned August 28, 1864.
Do.	Charles W. Allen	Feb. 20, 1863	March 25, "	Resigned October 4, 1864; wounded.
Do.	Wm. B. Wicker	May 13, "	June 15, "	Promoted to Lieutenant-Colonel.
Do.	Edward L. Baird	June 14, "	" 29, "	Declined promotion.
Do.	James Porter	Feb. 29, 1864	Feb. 29, 1864	Declined promotion.
Do.	John C. Martin	" 29, "	" 29, "	Promoted.
Do.	Robert S. Munger	" 29, "	" 29, "	Declined promotion.
Do.	Samuel F. Cheney	" 29, "	" 29, "	Mustered out with regiment.
Do.	Daniel Lewis	" 29, "	" 29, "	Killed July 21, 1864.
Do.	John Patterson	" 29, "	" 29, "	Mustered out December 29, 1864.
Do.	James I. Bumpus	Dec. 30, "	Dec. 30, "	Dismissed January 21, 1865.
Do.	Elihu H. Mason	" 30, "	" 30, "	Discharged as 1st Lieutenant May 15, 1865.
Do.	Thomas Anderson	Jan. 28, 1865	Jan. 28, 1865	Hon. disc'd as 1st Lieut. Jan. 23, '65; wounded.
Do.	John S. Mahoney	May 11, "	May 11, "	Mustered out as 2d Lieutenant May 15, 1865.
Do.	Jacob L. Keller	" 11, "	" 11, "	Mustered out with regiment.
Do.	Wm. Welker	" 18, "	" 18, "	Mustered out as 2d Lieutenant May 15, 1865.
Do.	George Scheets	July 12, "	July 12, "	
Do.	Augustus Besanson	" 12, "	" 12, "	

* Killed at Scary Creek, Virginia.

† Promoted to Captain.

RANK.	NAME.	DATE OF RANK.	COM. ISSUED.	REMARKS.
Captain	Christian B. Sholty	July 12, 1865	July 12, 1865	
Do.	David McClintock	" 12, "	" 12, "	Mustered out as 1st Lieutenant.
Do.	John H. Bolton	" 12, "	" 12, "	
Do.	Robert F. McDonald	" 12, "	" 12, "	
Do.	John W. Pember	" 12, "	" 12, "	
Do.	Squire J. Carlin	" 12, "	" 12, "	
1st Lieutenant	John A. Williams	Sept. 19, 1861	Nov. 11, 1861	Resigned January 8, 1862.
Do.	Wm. Vance	" 19, "	" 11, "	Resigned December 5, 1862.
Do.	James W. Knaggs	" 19, "	" 11, "	Promoted to Captain.
Do.	Wm. B. Wicker	" 19, "	" 11, "	Promoted to Captain.
Do.	James Porter	" 19, "	" 11, "	Mustered out September 20, 1864.
Do.	Matthew H. Chance	" 19, "	" 11, "	Resigned January 21, 1862.
Do.	James L. Curry	" 19, "	" 11, "	Promoted to Captain.
Do.	Lewis E. Brewster	" 19, "	" 11, "	Promoted to Captain.
Do.	John C. Martin	" 19, "	" 11, "	Promoted to Captain.
Do.	Charles H. Vantine	" 19, "	" 11, "	Promoted to Captain.
Do.	Robert S. Munger	" 19, "	" 11, "	Mustered out at expiration of service.
Do.	George O. McPherson	" 19, "	" 11, "	Resigned December 17, 1861.
Do.	George Foreman	Feb. 3, 1862	Feb. 3, 1862	Honorably discharged Sept. 11, '62; reinstated
Do.	Joseph E. Stearns	" 3, "	" 3, "	Revoked. [Nov. 13, '62.
Do.	Amos E. Wood	" 8, "	" 8, "	Died June 13, 1863.
Do.	Enoch B. Wiley	April 9, "	May 1, "	Killed.
Do.	Charles W. Allen	Jan. 21, "	" 1, "	Promoted to Captain.
Do.	Edward L. Baird	Dec. 17, 1861	June 6, "	Mustered out December 27, 1864.
Do.	Samuel F. Cheney	April 9, 1862	July 8, "	Promoted to Captain.
Do.	Daniel Lewis	Nov. 18, "	Feb. 12, 1863	Promoted to Captain.
Do.	Alex. A. Monroe	Dec. 5, "	" 12, "	Resigned May 21, 1863.
Do.	Enoch B. Wiley	Oct. 3, "	Dec. 30, 1862	Killed December 31, 1862.
Do.	John Patterson	Dec. 20, "	" 30, "	Promoted to Captain.
Do.	James I. Bumpus	" 20, "	Feb. 12, 1863	Promoted to Captain.
Do.	Elihu H. Mason	Feb. 20, 1863	April 11, "	Promoted to Captain; discharged.
Do.	Thomas Anderson	May 2, "	May 25, "	Promoted to Captain.
Do.	Thomas B. Lamb	" 13, "	June 15, "	Revoked.
Do.	John W. Berry	June 14, "	" 29, "	Resigned January 6, 1865.
Do.	Robert S. Dillsworth	" 13, "	" 29, "	Killed June 27, 1864.
Do.	Thomas B. Lamb	Feb. 29, 1864	Feb. 29, 1864	Resigned January 8, 1865. [Lieut.
Do.	Ara C. Spafford	" 29, "	" 29, "	Died in prison Oct. 14, '64; not mustered as 1st
Do.	John S. Mahoney	" 29, "	" 29, "	Promoted to Captain.
Do.	Jacob L. Keller	" 29, "	" 29, "	Promoted to Captain.
Do.	Daniel Richards	" 29, "	" 29, "	Discharged January 31, 1865.
Do.	George Cleghorn	Dec. 30, "	Dec. 30, "	Mustered out as 2d Lieutenant Feb. 8, 1865.
Do.	Wilson J. Vance	" 30, "	" 30, "	Resigned April 2, 1864.
Do.	Wilson W. Brown	Jan. 20, 1865	Jan. 20, 1865	Discharged as an enlisted man.
Do.	John R. Porter	" 28, "	" 28, "	Declined promotion.
Do.	John Mercer	" 28, "	" 28, "	Mustered out February 4, 1865, as 2d Lieut.
Do.	Wm. Welker	" 28, "	" 28, "	Promoted to Captain.
Do.	George Scheets	Feb. 15, "	Feb. 15, "	Promoted to Captain.
Do.	George T. Squire	" 15, "	" 15, "	Resigned July 3, 1865.
Do.	Augustus Besanson	" 15, "	" 15, "	Promoted to Captain.
Do.	Christian B. Sholty	" 10, "	" 10, "	Promoted to Captain.
Do.	David McClintock	" 10, "	" 10, "	Promoted to Captain.
Do.	Celestine Chochard	May 11, "	May 11, "	Declined promotion.
Do.	Wm. J. Henry	" 11, "	" 11, "	Declined promotion.
Do.	Earl W. Merry	" 18, "	" 18, "	Discharged; wounded.
Do.	John H. Bolton	" 18, "	" 18, "	Promoted to Captain.
Do.	Christopher Gundy	June 26, "	June 26, "	Declined promotion.
Do.	Robert F. Bonham	July 12, "	July 12, "	Declined promotion.
Do.	Philip Wilch	" 12, "	" 12, "	
Do.	Henry Grahlman	" 12, "	" 12, "	
Do.	Quincy A. Randall	" 12, "	" 12, "	
Do.	Finley Britton	" 12, "	" 12, "	
Do.	Jeremiah E. Millhoof	" 12, "	" 12, "	
Do.	Henry R. Skinner	" 12, "	" 12, "	
Do.	Matthew P. Cullican	" 12, "	" 12, "	
Do.	Oscar A. Clark	" 12, "	" 12, "	Wounded.
Do.	Thomas Crook	" 12, "	" 12, "	
Do.	Joseph Power	" 12, "	" 12, "	
2d Lieutenant	George Foreman	Sept. 19, 1861	Nov. 11, 1861	Promoted to 1st Lieutenant. [Aug. 26, '62.
Do.	Joseph E. Stearns	" 19, "	" 11, "	Appointed A. A. G. by Presid't, rank as Capt
Do.	Enoch B. Wiley	" 19, "	" 11, "	Promoted to 1st Lieutenant.
Do.	John Patterson	" 19, "	" 11, "	Promoted to 1st Lieutenant.
Do.	Simon B. Webber	" 19, "	" 11, "	Resigned.
Do.	Charles W. Allen	" 19, "	" 11, "	Promoted to 1st Lieutenant.
Do.	Joab Squire, jr.	" 19, "	" 11, "	Resigned March 9, 1862.
Do.	Samuel F. Cheney	" 19, "	" 11, "	Promoted to 1st Lieutenant.
Do.	Alex. A. Monroe	" 19, "	" 11, "	Appointed 1st Lieutenant.
Do.	Amos E. Wood	" 19, "	" 11, "	Promoted to 1st Lieutenant.
Do.	Daniel Lewis	Feb. 8, 1862	Feb. 8, 1862	Promoted to 1st Lieutenant.
Do.	James Blakely	" 8, "	" 8, "	Revoked.
Do.	Thomas Anderson	Jan. 21, "	May 1, "	Promoted to 1st Lieutenant.
Do.	James I. Bumpus	Feb. 8, "	June 6, "	Promoted to 1st Lieutenant.
Do.	Wm. A. Prior	May 9, "	" 6, "	Resigned February 15, 1863.
Do.	John W. Berry	April 9, "	July 8, "	Promoted to 1st Lieutenant.
Do.	Thomas B. Lamb	Aug. 26, "	Feb. 12, 1863	Promoted to 1st Lieutenant.
Do.	Ara C. Spafford	Oct. 3, "	" 12, "	Promoted to 1st Lieutenant.
Do.	John S. Mahoney	Dec. 20, "	" 12, "	Promoted to 1st Lieutenant.
Do.	Jacob L. Keller	" 5, "	" 12, "	Promoted to 1st Lieutenant.
Do.	Daniel Richards	Nov. 18, "	" 12, "	Promoted to 1st Lieutenant.
Do.	Robert S. Dillsworth	March 1, "	" 12, "	Promoted to 1st Lieutenant.
Do.	George Cleghorn	Dec. 20, "	" 12, "	Promoted to 1st Lieutenant.
Do.	Robert Buffum	April 24, 1863	April 24, 1863	Resigned April 28, 1864.
Do.	Wilson J. Vance	May 2, "	June 8, "	Promoted to 1st Lieutenant.
Do.	Wilson W. Brown	" 13, "	" 15, "	Promoted to 1st Lieutenant.
Do.	John R. Porter	June 13, "	" 29, "	Mustered out March 31, 1865.
Do.	John Mercer	" 14, "	" 29, "	Promoted to 1st Lieutenant.
Do.	James Blakely	Sept. 14, "	Sept. 14, "	Killed September 20, 1863, at Chickamauga.
Do.	Mark Wood	Feb. 26, 1864	Feb. 26, 1864	Hon. discharged Nov. 3, 1864; wounded.
Do.	Wm. Welker	" 29, "	" 29, "	Promoted to 1st Lieutenant.
Do.	Christian B. Sholty	" 29, "	" 29, "	Promoted to 1st Lieutenant.
Do.	David McClintock	" 29, "	" 29, "	Promoted to 1st Lieutenant.

TWENTY-FIRST OHIO VOLUNTEER INFANTRY.

THE TWENTY-FIRST OHIO was organized at Camp Taylor, near Cleveland, on the 27th of April, 1861. It moved on the 23d of May, passing through Columbus, where it received its arms, to Gallipolis. It went into camp at that place and remained there until the 3d of July, when it moved to Ravenswood, by order of General McClellan, to re-enforce the Seventeenth Ohio, then expecting an attack from O. Jennings Wise, whose forces lay at a little town called Ripley, twelve or fifteen miles from the river.

The National force under Colonel Norton, of the Twenty-First Ohio, disembarked at eleven o'clock at night, made a forced march to Ripley, surprised the Rebels and drove them from the place. The expedition then returned by steamer to Gallipolis. A day or two after this Colonel Norton made a reconnoissance up the Kanawha River, and captured forty prominent Rebel citizens as hostages for the good treatment and safe return of some loyal Virginians captured by the notorious Jenkins. Colonel Norton also led an expedition to Jenkins's farm, just below Guyandotte, consisting of company F, Captain George F. Walker, and company C, Lieutenant A. McMahan, and captured a steamboat load of cattle, horses, corn, etc., for the use of the army, and once more returned to their camp at Gallipolis.

On the 11th of July General Cox took command of the brigade, consisting of the Eleventh, Twelfth, and Twenty-First Ohio, the First and Second Kentucky, Cotter's First Ohio Battery of two guns, and Captain George's cavalry, and marched to Red House, on the Kanawha River. At this place Colonel Norton was ordered to make a reconnoissance for the purpose of discovering the Rebel position. Company F, Captain George F. Walker; company H, Captain A. M. Blackman, and company G, Captain Lovell, with a portion of Captain George's cavalry, started, under command of Colonel Norton, early on Sunday morning, the 14th of July, moving on three different roads, all terminating at a little village on Scarey Creek, where it empties into the Kanawha River. After marching some eight miles the enemy's pickets were encountered in a church, from which they fired and fell back on their main body. Skirmishers were thrown out by Colonel Norton, which developed the enemy in force on the opposite bank of the creek, occupying a strong position, with a full battery.

After developing the strength of the Rebels, the National troops fell back two miles, and at twelve o'clock that night were re-enforced by the remaining companies of the Twenty-First Ohio and part of the Second Kentucky, under Lieutenant-Colonel Enyart; but, lacking artillery, Colonel Norton thought it best to fall back and await the arrival of the main body. On the 15th the main body, under General Cox, arrived, and, on the morning of the 17th, Colonel Lowe was placed in command of a force, consisting of his own regiment; company K, Captain S. A. Strong, and company D, Captain Thomas G. Allen, of the Twenty-First; Captain Cotter's two rifled guns, and a portion of Captain George's cavalry, as an attacking column, and ordered to drive the enemy from his position. The fight opened at great disadvantage to the Nationals, from the fact that their old United States smooth-bore muskets did not carry far enough to reach the enemy, who were stationed in the bed of the creek and protected by its high banks. Colonel Norton seeing the disadvantage, determined to drive the enemy out of the creek with the bayonet, and, as a preliminary movement, sent a flanking force to turn the enemy's left, and divert his attention from the contemplated charge in front. The charge was successfully made by Colonel Norton, with two companies of the Twelfth Ohio under Lieutenant-Colonel White, and two companies of the Twenty-First Ohio, the enemy being lifted out of the creek, and the whole Rebel force driven back. Colonel Norton was severely wounded through the hips in this affair, but remained on the field, hoping to be supported by Colonel Lowe. Three messengers were dispatched to Colonel Lowe, one of whom was killed, but the needed support was not given. In the meantime the enemy received re-enforcements; and, discovering that the National force was not properly supported, again advanced their column, and in turn drove them, capturing Colonel Norton and Lieutenant Brown, of the Twelfth Ohio, who had remained with Colonel Norton and the other wounded.

The loss in this engagement was nine killed, including Captain Allen and Lieutenant Pomeroy, of company D, and seventeen wounded.

On the evening of the battle, Colonel Woodruff, of the Second Kentucky; Colonel De Villiers, of the Eleventh Ohio, and Lieutenant-Colonel George W. Neff, of the First Kentucky, rode up to the battle-ground by a different road from that on which the troops were retreating, and were instantly made prisoners by the Rebels.

The Twenty-First Ohio remained in the field, under command of Lieutenant-Colonel Neibling, until ordered home to be mustered out, which occurred on the 12th of August, 1861, at Columbus, Ohio. It was again reorganized, on the 19th of September, 1861, for the three years' campaign, and mustered into the service at Findlay, Ohio. It received marching orders a few days thereafter, was supplied with arms at Camp Dennison on the 2d of October, and marched the same day for Nicholasville, Kentucky. It remained there ten days, and was then ordered to march to McCormick's Gap to join General Nelson, then in command at that point.

During that campaign no engagement occurred, excepting that at Ivy Mountain, in which the Rebels attempted an ambush, but were foiled and whipped, mainly through a flank movement executed by the Twenty-First Ohio. The Rebels were driven from that line, and the whole command returned to Louisville, reaching that city in November.

The National army was reorganized in the following December, under General Buell, and moved to Bacon Creek and Green River, where it remained in winter-quarters up to late in February. In General O. M. Mitchel's division the Twenty-First marched on Bowling Green, driving the Rebels from that strong position. Then moving direct on Nashville, General Mitchel summoned the city authorities to surrender, which demand was promptly acceded to. Colonel Kennett, of the Fourth Ohio Cavalry, took possession of the city on the 13th of March.

On the 17th General Mitchel's column moved out on the Murfreesboro' turnpike, occupied Murfreesboro' on the 19th, and remained there until the 4th of April, when it moved on Huntsville. At this point the famous expedition under Andrews, a citizen of Kentucky, was sent out to sever the Rebel communication with Richmond, so as to prevent re-enforcements from reaching Beauregard. This was made up from the Twenty-First, Thirty-Third, and Second Ohio, and consisted of twenty-four men. It failed by reason of meeting trains on the road not specified in the time-table in possession of Andrews.

From Fayetteville the command moved, on the morning of the 10th of April, for Huntsville, and reached that place on the morning of the 11th, drove the Rebels out, captured three hundred prisoners, sixteen locomotives, and a large number of freight and passenger cars.

The most vigorous measures were then inaugurated by General Mitchel. Expeditions were sent in every direction, railroad bridges burned, and every precaution taken against surprise. One of these, which consisted of company C, Captain McMahan, and company F, Captain H. H. Alban, of the Twenty-First, and a portion of the Thirty-Third Ohio, all under command of Colonel Oscar F. Moore, of the Thirty-Third, was sent to Stevenson, Alabama, to burn an important bridge spanning the Tennessee River. It was completely successful, and returned to Huntsville.

About the 20th of April Captain Milo Caton, company H, of the Twenty-First Ohio, was sent in charge of Rebel prisoners to Nashville. On his return he was surrounded by Morgan's cavalry, and, after a hard fight, the Captain and his company were obliged to surrender. The whole party were sent to Richmond. Captain Caton remained in Rebel prisons over a year. On the 28th of May the regiment moved to Athens to relieve Colonel Turchin, and remained there up to the 28th of August. While the Twenty-First Ohio was at Athens the nucleus of the First Alabama loyal regiment was formed, mainly through the efforts of Captain McMahan.

The regiment returned from Athens, Alabama, to Nashville, on the 29th of August, 1862, and arrived on the 2d of September. It remained with its division, under the command of Brigadier-General James S. Negley, and was besieged in the city until the 7th of November, when the siege was raised by the approach of the army under General Rosecrans. During the siege the Twenty-First Ohio was engaged in the sallies of Lavergne, White's Creek, Wilson's Bend, and Franklin Pike. At Lavergne the regiment captured a part of the Third Alabama Rifle Regiment, with their colors and camp and garrison equipage, and fifty-four horses.

On the 19th of November General Rosecrans issued a special order, complimenting this regiment for its efficiency on the grand guard around Nashville.

On the 26th of December the Twenty-First Ohio moved with the army against the enemy at Murfreesboro'. Skirmishing continued incessantly until December 31st, when a general battle commenced and continued until January 3d. The Twenty-First Ohio was engaged every day—first in the center, and (January 2d) on the left of the army. In the battle of January 2d, with the Rebels under Breckinridge, the Twenty-First charged across Stone River, the water being waist-deep, and captured three brass field-pieces, the only artillery captured in the battle before Murfreesboro'. After the battle, Captain A. McMahan, of company C, was recommended to the Governor of Ohio for promotion by General James S. Negley, and was soon afterward appointed Major of his regiment. On the 4th of January the Twenty-First entered Murfreesboro', having the advance of its division.

In the battle of Stone River the regiment lost one officer, Lieutenant Enoch B. Wiley, of company C, and forty-six men killed, and Lieutenant J. W. Knaggs and seventy-five men wounded. Seventeen men were captured.

During the occupation of Murfreesboro', from January 4th to June 24th, 1863, the Twenty-First was engaged in several expeditions and skirmishes. On the 24th of June it moved with the army upon the enemy at Tullahoma. The enemy having retired upon Chattanooga, the Twenty-First went into camp with the army at Decherd Station on the 7th of July. On the 16th of August, it crossed the Tennessee River near Stevenson, and dragging its artillery and trains over Lookout Mountain by hand, it found the enemy at Dug Gap, Georgia, on the 11th of September.

Heavy skirmishing continued until the 19th, when the enemy was found in force on the line of Chickamauga Creek. The regiment immediately deployed into line of battle, under command of Lieutenant-Colonel D. M. Stoughton, and opened a brisk fire upon the Rebels, which continued until night. Early the next morning (Sunday, September 20th) the battle was resumed. At eleven o'clock the Twenty-First was posted on Horseshoe Ridge, upon the earnest request of Brigadier-General J. M. Brannon, who retired with his troops to another part of the field soon afterward. Immediately after forming in this new position, the Twenty-First became fully engaged, and a severe contest resulted in the repulse of the enemy, not, however, without severe loss to the Twenty-First. Lieutenant-Colonel Stoughton had an arm fractured and soon after died. The command now devolved upon Major A. McMahan.

The result of the battle, by three o'clock in the afternoon, demonstrated the inability of the National army to meet successfully the immensely superior numbers under command of General Bragg. The National troops were forced back on the right and left; but the Twenty-First, being armed with Colt's revolving rifles, continued to hold its position. The Rebels charged upon the regiment in this position five times without success, retiring each time with severe loss. An hour before sundown a full battery was brought to bear upon it, inflicting severe damage. Under cover of the smoke of this battery the Rebels charged again, but were met with a volley and a counter-charge, and the Twenty-First continued to hold its position.

The scene at this time was horrible. The battery had set fire to the leaves and dry brush, and the dead and wounded were consumed by the fire. To remedy this was out of the question. To detain the Rebels, if possible, was all that could be expected while the troops of McCook's corps, which had been so severely crushed, could effect a retreat. The ammunition was now nearly exhausted, and a further supply could not be found nearer than Chattanooga, nearly a day's march distant. The cartridge-boxes of the dead were searched, and also the hospitals, for any that might be carried there in the cartridge-boxes of the wounded. By economy the regiment continued to fire until dark, when its last shot was expended. At this time the enemy had appeared upon the right and rear, and the regiment, now greatly reduced in numbers, was formed for one more desperate effort to hold the ridge and give time for our shattered columns to effect a retreat. A charge was ordered by Major McMahan, and, though entirely without ammunition, the bayonet was applied with entire success. The enemy was forced back, leaving nine prisoners with the Twenty-First Ohio.

The helpless condition of the regiment was discovered by the enemy in its inability to return their fire. It was now after dark, and, in a second attempt to push back the enemy with the bayonet, the Twenty-First Ohio was overwhelmed, and Major McMahan and one hundred and fifteen of the officers and men of the command were captured. The Twenty-First Ohio expended, in this battle, forty-three thousand five hundred and fifty rounds of Colt's fixed ammunition, and sustained a loss of one officer and fifty men killed, three officers and ninety-eight men wounded, and twelve officers and one hundred and four men captured.

The survivors of the regiment retired with the army to Chattanooga, where it arrived September 22d, and remained until January 1, 1864, when it re-enlisted as a veteran organization, mainly through the efforts of Quartermaster Daniel Lewis, Quartermaster-Sergeant Geo. Sheets, and the non-commissioned officers of the regiment, and returned to Ohio upon veteran furlough. It had in the meantime, however, been present at the battle of Mission Ridge.

The regiment returned to Chattanooga on the 6th of March and moved forward to Ringgold, Georgia, from which point it moved, May 7th, with Sherman's grand army upon the campaign to Atlanta, Georgia. Fighting soon commenced, and the regiment opened its veteran campaign with the battle of Buzzard's Roost, May 9th, and Resaca, May 15th. Moving forward the regiment was present at the battle of New Hope Church, and on the morning of May 28th, while the regiment was moving to a position in reserve, a piece of stray shell fractured the right arm of Colonel James M. Neibling, and the command of the regiment again devolved upon Major A. McMahan, who had just returned from Libby Prison.

The regiment was immediately ordered to the front, and in capturing a ridge which was abandoned without a fight on the evening before, company K sustained a loss of four men killed and two wounded. The position thus captured commanded that of the enemy, and was held by the Twenty-First Ohio until the enemy withdrew.

Skirmishing continued daily until the enemy presented front at Kenesaw Mountain, June 17th. The Twenty-First was engaged at this point every day, holding the front line at Bald Knob, twelve days and nights in succession, at which point Lieutenant Robert S. Dilworth, of company G, and two men were killed and ten men wounded. On the 4th of July the regiment marched through Marietta in pursuit of the enemy, who had retired toward the Chattahoochie River the previous night. Skirmishing continued until the 9th of July, when the regiment was ordered forward to learn the position of the enemy, with orders to attack and drive in his outposts. A severe engagement at Vining's Station was the result. Two regiments of the enemy, the Fourth Mississippi and Fifty-Fourth Louisiana Infantry, were encountered in their rifle-pits. A charge was ordered by Major McMahan, the rifle-pits captured, with seventeen prisoners and thirty-three stand of new English rifles. The enemy was driven into his main works after a desperate struggle, in which the Twenty-First Ohio lost fifteen men killed, and two officers and thirty-seven men wounded, and one officer missing.

The regiment continued to hold the rifle-pits and annoy the enemy in his main works. Corporal William Waltman, of company G, upon this occasion led his company in the charge, and would have been promoted had not his term of enlistment expired before his commission could be obtained. Early in the morning of July 10th the enemy withdrew, and the regiment advanced by daylight to the Chattahoochie River. No other troops besides the Twenty-First Ohio were engaged on this occasion.

Having crossed the river, the regiment again engaged the enemy at Nancy's Creek, July 19th, and continued to engage him until July 20th, when the battle of Peach Tree Creek was fought. In this battle Captain Daniel Lewis, company C, was killed, Sergeant-Major Earll W. Merry was wounded, and had a leg amputated.

On the 22d of July the siege of Atlanta was commenced, and continued until the night of September 1st, when the defense of that city was abandoned by the enemy in consequence of his defeat at Jonesboro', thirty-five miles south of Atlanta. The Twenty-first Ohio during the siege of Atlanta was engaged with the enemy on several occasions, and was under his fire every day.

At the battle of Jonesboro', Georgia, September 1st, which won Atlanta, the regiment was again engaged, and again added new laurels to its character as a fighting regiment. Its loss in this battle was five men killed, thirty men wounded, and one man missing. After the battle of Jonesboro' the Twenty-First returned with the army to Atlanta, and went into camp on the 8th of September. The total loss of the regiment in this campaign, from May 7th to the occupation of Atlanta, September 2d, was two officers and thirty-two men killed, and five officers and one hundred and nineteen men wounded, many of whom subsequently died.

On the 3d of October the regiment moved with the army in pursuit of Hood toward Chattanooga, and arrived at Galesville, Alabama, October 20th. From this point it returned to Atlanta, where it again arrived on the 15th of November. On the 16th it moved with the army in the direction of Savannah, Georgia. On the 4th of December it was engaged with the enemy near Lumpkin Station, on the Augusta and Savannah Railroad. From the 12th to the night of the 20th of December it was engaged with the enemy's outposts before Savannah, and entered the city the following morning at nine o'clock A. M., in advance of its army corps.

During this campaign the regiment destroyed three miles of railroad and captured eight thousand rations for its own use. It also captured forage to supply twenty-one head of horses and mules attached to the regiment during the campaign. Six prisoners of war were also captured. The regiment lost one man wounded, and fourteen men were "bush-whacked" by the enemy.

The regiment moved again from Savannah, Georgia, under command of Lieutenant-Colonel McMahan upon the campaign through North and South Carolina. It was engaged at Rocky Mount, South Carolina, and subsequently at Averysboro', North Carolina, and participated in the battle of Bentonville, North Carolina, on the 19th of March. In this battle it sustained a loss of one man killed and one officer, Captain W. B. Wicker, of company E, and four men wounded, and ten men missing. On this campaign a large amount of railroad was destroyed by this regiment, and it drew its subsistence entirely from the country through which it passed, and also supplied the horses and mules which belonged to it with sufficient forage. Twenty-one Rebel prisoners were captured by the regiment during this campaign.

During the battle on the 19th of March at Bentonville, Lieutenant-Colonel McMahan was assigned to the command of his brigade, and Captain Samuel F. Cheney, of company B, to the command of the Twenty-First Ohio. This was the last hostile meeting of this regiment with the enemy. The Rebels retired rapidly from Goldsboro' through Raleigh, North Carolina, the regiment marching through that city on the 12th of April, 1865, and moved forward to Martha's Vineyard, where it remained until the Confederate forces under General Joseph E. Johnston laid down their arms and dispersed. The regiment then returned to Washington *via* Richmond, Virginia, and was present at the grand review on the 26th day of May, 1865. It then proceeded to Louisville, Kentucky, where it was mustered out of service, and from there returned to Columbus, Ohio, where it was finally discharged and paid on the 28th day of July.

22d REGIMENT OHIO VOLUNTEER INFANTRY.

ROSTER, THREE MONTHS' SERVICE.

RANK.	NAME.	DATE OF RANK.	COM. ISSUED.	REMARKS.
Colonel	WM. E. GILMORE	May 23, 1861	May 23, 1861	
Lt. Colonel	JOHN A. FINLEY	" 23, "	" 23, "	
Major	JULIUS A. PENN	" 23, "	" 23, "	
Surgeon	DOUGLASS DAY	" 13, "	" 13, "	Resigned.
Do.	ISAAC L. CRANE	June 29, "	June 29, "	
Ass't Surgeon	JULIUS R. SCHENCK	" 28, "	" 28, "	
Captain	George F. Reed	May 25, "	May 25, "	
Do.	Erastus E. Guthrie	April 23, "	April 23, "	
Do.	Solomon S. Robinson	" 22, "	" 22, "	
Do.	Jesse D. Appler	" 22, "	" 22, "	
Do.	George W. Hulick	" 25, "	" 25, "	
Do.	John M. Bell	" 20, "	" 20, "	
Do.	George Weikelm	May 25, "	May 25, "	
Do.	Nathan Pickett	" 2, "	" 2, "	
Do.	Farron Olmstead	April 23, "	April 23, "	
Do.	Wm. T. Payne	" 24, "	" 24, "	
1st Lieutenant	Alexander C. Maitland	May 25, "	May 25, "	
Do.	Julius C. Steadman	April 23, "	April 23, "	
Do.	John H. Nugent	" 23, "	" 23, "	
Do.	Oliver Wood	" 22, "	" 22, "	
Do.	Edward Links	" 23, "	" 23, "	
Do.	Charles A. White	" 20, "	" 20, "	
Do.	Benj. L. Tryer	May 25, "	May 25, "	
Do.	Benj. G. Harrison	" 2, "	" 2, "	
Do.	Robert L. McKinley	April 24, "	April 24, "	
Do.	Charles G. McArthur	" 24, "	" 24, "	
Do.	E. M. Hall	June 14, "	June 14, "	
2d Lieutenant	Chas. H. Shultz	May 25, "	May 25, "	
Do.	Horace W. Deshler	April 23, "	April 23, "	
Do.	James R. Blackburn	" 23, "	" 23, "	
Do.	John C. Collins	" 22, "	" 22, "	
Do.	Lowell H. Smith	" 23, "	" 23, "	
Do.	Jerrie Howser	" 20, "	" 20, "	
Do.	Francis M. Mills	May 25, "	May 25, "	
Do.	George W. Rutledge	" 2, "	" 2, "	
Do.	Jackson Woodson	April 23, "	April 23, "	
Do.	Henry W. Rayburn	" 24, "	" 24, "	
Do.	W. H. Brown	May 24, "	May 24, "	

ROSTER, THREE YEARS' SERVICE.

RANK.	NAME.	DATE OF RANK.	COM. ISSUED.	REMARKS.
Colonel	CRAFTS J. WRIGHT	Aug. 3, 1861	Oct. 17, 1861	Resigned September 9, 1862.
Do.	OLIVER WOOD	Sept. 16, "	Nov. 12, 1862	Mustered out.
Lt. Colonel	J. T. ST. JAMES	Aug. 5, "	Aug. 5, "	Died April 8, 1862.
Do.	BENJ. T. WRIGHT	May 1, "	" 5, "	Resigned September 9, 1862.
Do.	HOMER THRALL	Sept. 16, "	Nov. 30, "	Mustered out.
Major	C. W. ANDERSON	" 20, "	Aug. 5, "	Resigned May 9, 1862.
Do.	OLIVER WOOD	May 9, 1862	" 5, "	
Do.	GEORGE R. FRENCH	Sept. 16, "	Nov. 30, "	Mustered out.
Surgeon	JOHN B. BELL	 1861	Aug. 5, "	Resigned February 11, 1862.
Do.	H. E. FOOTE	Feb. 19, 1862	....	Mustered out.
Ass't Surgeon	A. M. BROWN	Aug. 27, 1861	Aug. 5, 1862	Promoted to Surgeon 68th O. V. I.
Do.	W. H. GILMORE	" 21, 1862	" 29, "	Resigned May 24, 1863.
Chaplain	C. E. BABB	Nov. 6, 1861	" 5, "	Resigned May 21, 1862.
Captain	John H. Fox	Aug. 9, "	" 5, "	Resigned May 6, 1862.
Do.	Oliver Wood	" 21, "	" 5, "	Promoted to Major May 9, 1862.
Do.	Benj. F. Wright	" 20, "	" 5, "	Promoted to Major May 1, 1862.
Do.	Homer Thrall	" 21, "	" 5, "	Promoted to Major September 16, 1862.
Do.	Peter O. Cain	Sept. 3, "	" 5, "	Killed June 27, 1862.
Do.	George H. Lemley	Aug. 18, "	" 5, "	Died February 10, 1862.
Do.	Wm. W. Sosman	Sept. 6, "	" 5, "	Honorably discharged September 11, 1862.
Do.	Moses Kline	" 6, "	" 5, "	Mustered out.
Do.	A. J. Hall	" —, "	" 5, "	Died April 11, 1862.
Do.	Thomas C. Mitchell	" 6, "	" 5, "	Resigned February 1, 1862.
Do.	George R. French	Feb. 1, "	" 5, "	Promoted to Major.
Do.	Channing Richards	" 10, "	" 5, "	Resigned September 8, 1862.
Do.	John Craighan	April 30, "	" 5, "	Resigned July 17, 1865.
Do.	Charles W. Miner	May 1, "	" 5, "	Mustered out with regiment.
Do.	John Birch	" 14, "	" 5, "	Mustered out.
Do.	Channing Richards, jr	Aug. 28, "	Oct. 23, "	Mustered out.
Do.	Wm. C. Miller	Sept. 11, 1862	Nov. 30, "	Mustered out.
Do.	Wm. Govett	May 6, "	" 30, "	Mustered out.
Do.	J. T. Campbell	Sept. 16, "	" 30, "	Mustered out.
Do.	Jacob Zwiedler	" 16, "	Dec. 26, "	Resigned as 1st Lieut. March 12, 1863; revoked.
Do.	Wm. Ambrose	June 27, "	" 26, "	Commission returned.

RANK.	NAME.	DATE OF RANK.	COM. ISSUED.	REMARKS.
Captain	W. E. Fay	Sept. 16, 1862	April 28, 1863	Mustered out.
Do.	Wm. E. Lockwood	Jan. 27, "	June 13, "	Mustered out.
1st Lieutenant	Wm. Govett	Aug. 9, 1861	Aug. 5, 1862	Promoted to Captain.
Do.	Charles A. Barton	Sept. 6, "	" 5, "	Resigned April 18, 1862.
Do.	E. F. Smith	Nov. 5, "	" 5, "	Resigned February 11, 1862.
Do.	George V. Asker	Sept. 3, "	" 5, "	Resigned July 14, 1862.
Do.	Daniel Shewman	Oct. 1, "	" 5, "	Mustered out June 25, 1862.
Do.	Pleasant W. Frogge	Aug. 18, "	" 5, "	Resigned February 25, 1861.
Do.	Wm. Ambrose	Sept. 6, "	" 5, "	Dismissed December 21, 1862.
Do.	Jacob Zwiedler	Oct. 3, "	" 5, "	Promoted Sept. 16; resigned March 12, 1863.
Do.	James Evans	Nov. 6, "	" 5, "	Resigned January 18, 1862.
Do.	George R. French	Aug. 23, "	" 5, "	Promoted to Captain.
Do.	E. Kesner	April 18, 1862	" 5, "	Mustered out.
Do.	Channing Richards	Jan. 11, "	" 5, "	Promoted to Captain.
Do.	Robert McGregor	Feb. 10, "	" 5, "	Resigned April 16, 1862.
Do.	James Ferris	Jan. 18, "	" 5, "	Resigned March 16, 1862.
Do.	John Birch	Feb. 1, "	" 5, "	Resigned May 14, 1862.
Do.	W. E. Fay	Aug. 20, 1861	" 5, "	Promoted to Captain.
Do.	Wm. Bradford	" 20, "	" 5, "	Discharged October 6, 1862.
Do.	John S. McClintock	May 6, 1862	Nov. 30, "	Mustered out.
Do.	Martin Beim	Feb. 11, "	" 30, "	Honorably discharged October 21, 1862.
Do.	Edwin E. Thomas	July 14, "	" 30, "	Mustered out.
Do.	Wm. E. Lockwood	June 25, "	" 30, "	Promoted to Captain.
Do.	Edward Walcott	April 16, "	" 30, "	Mustered out.
Do.	James W. Whitehead	March 16, "	" 30, "	Mustered out.
Do.	Larkin H. Moreland	Oct. 6, "	" 30, "	Mustered out.
Do.	Alvis Fisher	May 14, "	Dec. 26, "	Revoked.
Do.	Jacob A. Pritz	June 27, "	" 26, "	Revoked.
Do.	Eugene Armour	Sept. 16, "	" 26, "	Resigned July 11, 1863.
Do.	Daniel J. Hytenger	" 16, "	April 28, "	Mustered out.
Do.	Joseph D. Emory	" 16, "	May 11, "	Mustered out.
Do.	Alvis Fisher	June 27, "	June 3, "	Mustered out.
Do.	Jacob A. Pritz	Jan. 27, "	Jan. 18, 1864	Mustered out.
Do.	Moses H. White	" 1, "	Feb. 1, "	Mustered out.
Do.	John Buxton	Dec. 21, 1861	Dec. 21, "	Mustered out.
2d Lieutenant	J. S. McClintock	Aug. 9, 1861	Aug. 5, 1862	Promoted to 1st Lieutenant May 6, 1862.
Do.	John W. Wallace	Sept. --, "	" 5, "	Resigned January 8, 1862.
Do.	J. S. Delavie	Nov. 5, "	" 5, "	Resigned March 5, 1862.
Do.	A. G. Dinsmore	Sept. 3, "	" 5, "	Resigned April 18, 1862.
Do.	Wm. Sands	Aug. 18, "	" 5, "	Resigned September 3, 1861.
Do.	W. C. Miller	Oct. 31, "	" 5, "	Promoted to Captain.
Do.	Alvis Fisher	" 12, "	" 5, "	Resigned July 1, 1861.
Do.	John Craighan	" 1, "	" 5, "	Promoted to 1st Lieutenant.
Do.	John Birch	Sept. 6, "	" 5, "	Promoted to 1st Lieutenant.
Do.	E. Kesner	Jan. 8, "	" 5, "	Promoted to 1st Lieutenant.
Do.	Martin Beim	May 1, "	" 5, "	Promoted to 1st Lieutenant.
Do.	Thomas J. Roads	Oct. 20, "	" 5, "	Resigned January 17, 1862.
Do.	Robert McGregor	Jan. 26, "	" 5, "	Promoted to 1st Lieutenant.
Do.	J. T. Campbell	Feb. 10, "	" 5, "	Promoted to 1st Lieutenant.
Do.	James Whitehead	March 16, 1862	" 5, "	Promoted to 1st Lieutenant.
Do.	L. Moreland	Feb. 1, "	" 5, "	Promoted to 1st Lieutenant.
Do.	Edward W. Thomas	April 18, "	" 22, "	Promoted to 1st Lieutenant.
Do.	Jacob A. Pritz	" 18, "	Sept. 11, "	Promoted to 1st Lieutenant.
Do.	Wm. E. Lockwood	Oct. 3, 1861	" 17, "	Promoted to 1st Lieutenant.
Do.	Eugene Armour	May 6, 1862	March 30, "	Promoted to 1st Lieutenant.
Do.	John Christie	Feb. 11, "	" 30, "	Resigned August 14, 1863.
Do.	John Buxton	March 16, "	" 30, "	Promoted to 1st Lieutenant.
Do.	John R. Brownell	Oct. 6, "	" 30, "	Mustered out.
Do.	Joseph D. Emory	June 25, "	" 30, "	Promoted to 1st Lieutenant.
Do.	Alexander C. Barr	Sept. 11, "	" 30, "	Mustered out.
Do.	Moses H. White	" 16, 1862	Jan. 20, 1863	Promoted to 1st Lieutenant.
Do.	Thomas A. Pollock	" 16, "	May 11, "	
Do.	Jacob Day	March 12, 1863	April 28, "	Mustered out.
Do.	Henry Digby	Jan. 7, 1864	Jan. 16, 1864	Mustered out.
Do.	Wm. Kramme	May 18, 1865	May 18, 1865	Mustered out.

TWENTY-SECOND OHIO VOLUNTEER INFANTRY.

THE TWENTY-SECOND OHIO VOLUNTEER INFANTRY was one of the offshoots of the appointment of Major-General John C. Fremont to the command of the Western Department. Its place of organization was Benton Barracks, near St. Louis, Missouri. Although officered by Ohio men, and its ranks filled mainly from the counties of the "Buckeye State," it was organized originally under the name of the Thirteenth Missouri Volunteer Infantry, and mustered into the service November 5th, 1861. It started to the field as a Missouri regiment, on the 26th of January, 1862, with the Colonel, three of the other field-officers, and eight of the Captains from Ohio.

On the 26th of January, 1862, the regiment received orders to proceed by rail and transports to Cairo, Illinois, and there report to Brigadier-General Grant, then commanding that district. On its arrival at Cairo it was met by orders to proceed to Smithland, Kentucky, reporting to Colonel Lanman, commanding that post. On its arrival at Smithland, the men had barely time to get camp and garrison equipage to the place selected for their camp, when orders came to prepare three days' rations and march in light order to support a cavalry reconnoissance then in progress toward Fort Henry. This movement was made on the 31st of January. After marching nearly two days the cavalry force was met on its return, and the next morning the regiment started back to Smithland, having carried out the intent of their instructions. This march was the first experience of the regiment in field-service; and, owing to a sudden change of weather from summer to winter, its initiation was quite severe.

Orders were found awaiting the regiment at Smithland, to proceed by transports up the Tennessee River, as a part of the investing force against Fort Henry. It was found, however, on its arrival at Fort Henry that General Grant was already in possession of that fort, and was busily engaged in organizing the army for an attack on Fort Donelson. In the organization of this force the Thirteenth Missouri was brigaded in General C. F. Smith's Division. In the first attack the position of the regiment was near the left of the line, and as the heavy fighting took place on the right they were not exposed to much danger. On the 15th, when General Smith assaulted the enemy's works on the right, the regiment was in position near the center, two miles from the point of assault. Receiving orders to report at once to the left the men dropped their knapsacks, blankets, overcoats, in fact everything but their arms and ammunition, and reported on the "double-quick" to the General. Lanman's brigade had charged, and were now holding the outer works under a storm of grape and canister from the enemy's heavy batteries.

Night found the regiment in a position to support Lanman. During the night orders came directing the regiment to prepare for storming the batteries at day-break of the ensuing morning. The dawn found the regiment in front of Lanman's advanced position. Everything was in readiness, and all ears anxiously waiting to hear the signal to charge given. But the Rebel batteries were silent, eliciting many surmises as to the reason. Presently a sound from the interior of the fort attracted all eyes in that direction—the white flag of surrender was discovered floating from the principal work.

After occupying the fort for a few days orders were received to proceed to Clarksville, thence to Nashville, thence back to Clarksville. From Clarksville the next move was to Pittsburg

Landing, where the regiment arrived on the 20th of March. It lay in camp until the morning of the 6th of April, the day of the commencement of the battle of Shiloh, when it was ordered into line of battle. The numerical force of the regiment at this time was four hundred and fifty officers and men. During the two days of that well-contested battle the regiment was warmly engaged, and lost in killed and wounded eighty-nine officers and men. Early in the first day's fight the gallant Lieutenant-Colonel St. James fell mortally wounded. (About this time several changes occurred in the staff. Major C. W. Anderson resigned, and Captains Wright and Wood were promoted, the first to the position of Lieutenant-Colonel, the latter to that of Major. Surgeon Bell had resigned, and his place filled by Doctor Henry E. Foote, of Cincinnati.)

In the slow and tedious advance on Corinth, succeeding the battle of Shiloh, the regiment was continually in the front, and on the evacuation of Corinth by the enemy marched with the army to Booneville, Mississippi, in pursuit, and then returned to Corinth.

On the 7th of July, 1862, the Secretary of War, recognizing the absurdity of designating the regiment by an erroneous title, issued an order transferring the Thirteenth Missouri Volunteers to the State of Ohio, to be named the Twenty-Second Ohio Volunteer Infantry.

The long sojourn of our troops at Corinth was terminated about the 17th of September, 1862. At that time the Twenty-Second Ohio moved with the army upon Iuka, Mississippi, where the Rebel General Price was in force. Nothing of interest, however, occurred on this expedition, that is, so far as the regiment was concerned.

On the 16th of September, 1862, Colonel Crafts J. Wright and Lieutenant-Colonel Wright tendered their resignations, which were accepted. This left the regiment under the command of Major Wood.

October 3d came before the calm was broken at Corinth. On that memorable day the Rebel Generals Price and Van Dorn appeared before the place, eager to secure the post of Corinth and the vast supplies collected there. The Rebels were confident of an easy victory and the capture of the place. Major-General Rosecrans, commanding the National forces, was perfect master of the situation. He allowed the overconfident Rebels to precipitate themselves completely within the trap he had so ingeniously prepared for them, and although the enemy at one time threatened to "carry off the trap," they were soundly thrashed, and sent reeling into the swamps and bayous of Mississippi. The Twenty-Second did not participate in this sanguinary struggle, having been detailed for post duty. The regiment joined in the pursuit of the Rebels, but, like the whole army engaged in that fruitless race, gained no laurels.

Two months passed away without action. In December, 1862, the Rebel General Forrest made a raid upon the Mobile and Ohio Railroad, one of the channels of communications of Iuka with the outer world. By mistake the Twenty-Second was sent to look after Forrest, supposing the regiment belonged to the Ohio brigade. The error was not rectified before reaching Trenton, at which place it was left as garrison and railroad guard. Again occurred a quiet of two or three months, nothing more exciting occurring than an occasional scout for guerrillas, from which the detachments sent out generally returned successful. Whilst at Trenton a detachment of the Twenty-Second captured the notorious guerrilla chief Colonel Dawson, who afterward died in the Alton (Illinois) penitentiary.

March 11th, 1863, brought orders for the regiment to evacuate the Mobile and Ohio Railroad, and report at Jackson, Tennessee. It was ordered back to Corinth April 29th, and returned to Jackson, Tennessee, May 3d, 1863. May 29th it was ordered to move by rail to Memphis, and on arrival there found preparations being made to move to the vicinity of Vicksburg. On the 1st of June the regiment embarked on transports for Haines's Bluff, on the Yazoo River. It arrived there on the 3d of June, and was engaged in throwing up earthworks until July 16th, when orders were received to report at Helena, Arkansas. General Steele was engaged at this point in organizing the Army of the Arkansas. The Twenty-Second Ohio was made part of this organization, and on the 13th of August, 1863, left Helena with the army for Little Rock. After marching twenty-nine days the National forces entered the Capital of Arkansas with but slight difficulty, the cavalry arm of the expedition bearing the brunt of all opposition.

The occupation of Little Rock occurred on September 10th, 1863, and from that time to October 28th the Twenty-Second remained there, when orders were issued for the regiment to proceed to Brownsville, Arkansas, to aid in guarding the railroad connecting Little Rock and Duvall's Bluff. Nearly one year was consumed in this duty, remaining at Brownsville from October 30th, 1863, until October 26th, 1864. During the whole of this time nothing of importance occurred, with the exception of a few dashes after guerrillas. These outlaws were peculiarly brutal in Arkansas—veritable murderers—real Cain-marked scoundrels, who scrupled at nothing in the way of cruelty and outrage. The Twenty-Second, as a general thing, did not bring in any prisoners when returning from such expeditions. A portion of the time the regiment was on this duty one hundred and sixty of the men were mounted.

In February, 1864, one hundred and five officers and men re-enlisted as veterans. Captains Craighan and Miner, with Lieutenants Whitehead, Pollock, and Buxton, making up the list of officers remaining with the detachment. Beside the veterans there were eighty-nine recruits. On the 26th of October, 1864, the regiment received orders to report at Camp Dennison, Ohio, to complete their record, and be mustered out of the service. The same locomotive which drew the regiment from its first camp of rendezvous at St. Louis, also drew it from Little Rock to Duvall's Bluff, and when the regiment reached the mouth of White River they embarked on the steamer Continental, the same boat that carried them into service.

The regiment arrived in Cincinnati November 7th, 1864, and proceeded at once to Camp Dennison, where, on the 18th of November, it was mustered out of service, completing its term of three years and a few days over.

23d REGIMENT OHIO VOLUNTEER INFANTRY.

ROSTER, THREE YEARS' SERVICE.

RANK.	NAME.	DATE OF RANK.	COM. ISSUED.	REMARKS.
Colonel	W. S. ROSECRANS	June 7, 1861	June 7, 1861	Appointed Brigadier-General.
Do.	E. PARKER SCAMMON.	" 14, "	" 14, "	Appointed Brigadier-General October 15, 1862.
Do.	R. B. HAYES	Oct. 15, 1862	Oct. 24, 1862	Appointed Brigadier-General October 29, 1864.
Do.	JAMES M. COMLY	" 19, 1864	" 19, 1864	Mustered out with regiment.
Lt. Colonel	STANLEY MATHEWS	June 7, 1861	June 7, 1861	Promoted to Colonel of Fifty-First regiment.
Do.	R. B. HAYES	Oct. 23, "	Oct. 24, "	Promoted to Colonel October 15, 1862.
Do.	JAMES M. COMLY	" 15, "	" 24, 1862	Promoted to Colonel.
Do.	RUSSELL HASTINGS	March 8, 1865	March 8, 1865	Mustered out with regiment.
Major	R. B. HAYES	June 7, 1861	June 7, 1861	Promoted to Lieutenant-Colonel.
Do.	JAMES M. COMLY	Oct. 28, "	Oct. 28, "	Promoted to Lieutenant-Colonel.
Do	JAMES P. McILRATH	" 15, "	Nov. 3, 1862	Mustered out.
Do.	HARRY THOMPSON	March 8, 1865	March 8, 1865	Mustered out with regiment.
Surgeon	JOSEPH T. WEBB	July 2, 1861	July 2, 1861	Mustered out with regiment.
Ass't Surgeon	JOHN McCURDY	" 2, "	" 2, "	Mustered out October 26, 1862.
Do.	JOSEPH E. BARRET.	" 4, 1862	" 23, 1862	Promoted to new regiment.
Do.	JAMES McCLURE	April 22, 1864	April 22, 1864	Mustered out with regiment.
Do.	ELMORE Y. KING	March 22, 1865	March 22, 1865	Mustered out with regiment.
Chaplain	AMOS WILSON	July 20, 1861	July 29, 1861	Resigned April 30, 1862.
Do.	ROSWELL G. FRENCH	April 30, 1862	June 21, 1862	Discharged August 31, 1863.
Do.	ANSON P. JONES	June 16, 1865	" 16, 1865	
Captain	J. P. McIlrath	" 1, 1861	July 12, 1861	Promoted to Major.
Do.	G. R. Giddings	" 1, "	" 12, "	Appointed Major U. S. A. [July 29, 1863.
Do.	John W. Skiles	" 1, "	" 12, "	Appointed Major 88th O. V. I. by War Dept.,
Do.	H. S. Lovejoy	" 1, "	" 12, "	Resigned February 14, 1863.
Do.	W. H. Zimmerman	" 1, "	" 12, "	Mustered out.
Do.	Israel Canby	" 1, "	" 12, "	Mustered out.
Do.	W. Slocum	" 1, "	" 12, "	Resigned July 17, 1861.
Do.	J. L. Drake	" 1, "	" 12, "	Resigned September 24, 1862.
Do.	R. B. Moore	" 1, "	" 12, "	Resigned March 23, 1862.
Do.	D. C. Howard	" 1, "	" 12, "	Resigned February 11, 1862.
Do.	Carlos A. Sperry	July 23, "	" 23, "	Mustered out.
Do.	W. J. Woodward	" 23, "	" 23, "	Died November 6, 1861.
Do.	Henry Monroe Haven	Dec. 10, "	Dec. 10, "	Resigned November 30, 1862.
Do.	Abraham A. Hunter	Feb. 11, 1862	March 20, 1862	Killed May 9, 1864.
Do.	Selleck B. Warren	March 23, "	April 14, "	Mustered out.
Do.	Henry G. Hood	Sept. 24, "	Nov. 3, "	Mustered out.
Do.	Wm. S. Rice	Oct. 15, "	" 3, "	Mustered out.
Do.	Martin P. Avery	Nov. 30, "	Dec. 31, "	Honorably discharged April 19, 1864.
Do.	George W. Stevens	Feb. 14, 1863	March 30, 1863	Mustered out.
Do.	Russell Hastings	Aug. 8, "	Aug. 8, "	Promoted to Lieutenant-Colonel.
Do.	DeHaven K. Smith	June 14, 1864	June 14, 1864	Revoked.
Do.	Harry Thompson	" 14, "	" 14, "	Promoted to Major.
Do.	John U. Hatz	July 1, "	July 1, "	Mustered out with regiment.
Do.	Harrison G. Otis	" 1, "	" 1, "	Mustered out with regiment.
Do.	Jonathan H. McMullen	" 1, "	" 1, "	Honorably discharged December 31, 1864.
Do.	John S. Ellen	" 1, "	" 1, "	Honorably discharged November 30, 1864.
Do.	Andrew Y. Austin	" 1, "	" 1, "	Killed in action September 3, 1864.
Do.	Edward A. Abbott	" 1, "	" 1, "	Mustered out with regiment.
Do.	Amos F. Gillis	" 1, "	" 1, "	Killed in action September 3, 1864.
Do.	Wm. McKinley, jr	" 25, "	" 25, "	On detached duty at muster out of regiment.
Do.	Charles W. Atkinson	Sept. 17, "	Sept. 17, "	Mustered out with regiment.
Do.	Wm. E. Sweet	" 17, "	" 17, "	Discharged March 13, 1865.
Do.	Francis M. Kelley	Jan. 11, 1865	Jan. 11, 1865	Mustered out with regiment.
Do.	Leander H. Lane	" 11, "	" 11, "	Mustered out with regiment.
Do.	Maurice Watkins	April 20, "	April 20, "	Mustered out with regiment.
Do.	Wm. C. Lyon	" 20, "	" 20, "	Mustered out.
Do.	Eugene Clark	" 20, "	" 20, "	Mustered out with regiment.
Do.	Charles H. Morgan	May 11, "	March 11, "	Mustered out with regiment.
1st Lieutenant	W. J. Woodward	June 1, 1861	July 12, 1861	Promoted to Captain.
Do.	C. A. Sperry	" 1, "	" 12, "	Promoted to Captain.
Do.	J. Ross McMullin	" 1, "	" 12, "	Resigned July 19, 1861.
Do.	Abraham A. Hunter	" 1, "	" 12, "	Promoted to Captain.
Do.	W. S. Rice	" 1, "	" 12, "	Promoted to Captain.
Do.	Cyrus N. Fisher	" 1, "	" 12, "	Appointed Major Fifty-Fourth O. V. I.
Do.	Henry G. Hood	" 1, "	" 12, "	Promoted to Captain.
Do.	J. P. Cunningham	" 1, "	" 17, "	Resigned July 17, 1861.
Do.	S. B. Warren	" 1, "	" 12, "	Promoted to Captain.
Do.	Fred. H. Baron	" 1, "	" 12, "	Resigned December 26, 1862.
Do.	Charles E. Reichenback	July 17, "	" 17, "	Appointed Captain and A. Q. M.
Do.	John F. Walls	" 23, "	" 23, "	Resigned September 19, 1861.
Do.	Martin P. Avery	" 23, "	" 23, "	Promoted to Captain.
Do.	Henry Richardson	" 23, "	" 23, "	Appointed Captain Fifty-Fourth regiment.
Do.	James Naughton	" 23, "	" 23, "	Honorably Discharged December 12, 1862.
Do.	John E. Jewett	" 23, "	" 23, "	Resigned. [staff, Oct. 27, 1862.
Do.	James L. Bottsford	Jan. 17, 1862	Jan. 17, 1862	Prom. to Capt. A.A.G. Brig. Gen. Scammon's
Do.	W. W. Sheppard	Feb. 8, "	Feb. 8, "	Resigned April 18, 1862. [Oct. 7, 1862.
Do.	R. P. Kennedy	" 9, "	March 14, "	Prom. to Capt. A. A. G. on Gen. Cook's staff,
Do.	George W. Stevens	" 11, "	" 20, "	Promoted to Captain.
Do.	Russell Hastings	March 23, "	April 14, "	Promoted to Captain.
Do.	DeHaven K. Smith	April 18, "	June 24, "	Promoted to Captain.
Do.	Harry Thompson	Sept. 21, "	Nov. 3, "	Promoted to Captain.
Do.	Archie C. Fisk	Oct. 15, "	" 8, "	Promoted to Captain and A. A. G.
Do.	Adam W. Durkee	Nov. 1, "	" 1, "	Resigned December 26, 1862.
Do.	Andrew Y. Austin	Dec. 26, "	Dec. 31, "	Promoted to Captain.
Do.	Benj. F. Cooper	" 26, "	" 31, "	Resigned February 7, 1863.

RANK.	NAME.	DATE OF RANK.	COM. ISSUED.	REMARKS.
1st Lieutenant	George W. Hicks	Nov. 20, 1862	Dec. 31, 1862	Promoted to Colonel 180th N. Y. Volunteers.
Do.	John S. Ellen	Oct. 7, "	Jan. 24, "	Promoted to Captain
Do.	Benj. W. Jackson	Jan. 1, 1863	March 30, 1863	Mustered out.
Do.	Wm. McKinley, jr.	Feb. 7, "	" 30, "	Promoted to Captain.
Do.	Milton B. Deshong	" 14, "	" 30, "	Mustered out.
Do.	Wm. P. Chamberlin	Aug. 8, "	Aug. 8, "	Mustered out.
Do.	Edward A. Abbott	" 8, "	" 8, "	Promoted to Captain.
Do.	Thomas A. Stephens	" 8, "	" 8, "	Mustered out.
Do.	Wm. H. Nessle	" 8, "	" 8, "	Mustered out.
Do.	Amos F. Gillis	June 14, 1864	June 14, 1864	Promoted to Captain.
Do.	John W. Cracraft	" 14, "	" 14, "	Mustered out.
Do.	Maurice Watkins	July 1, "	July 1, "	Promoted to Captain.
Do.	John A. Snyder	" 1, "	" 1, "	Transferred to field and staff October 29, 1864
Do.	Andrew Mahan	" 1, "	" 1, "	Mustered out with regiment.
Do.	Leander H. Lane	" 1, "	" 1, "	Promoted to Captain.
Do.	Benj. Killiam	" 1, "	" 1, "	Mustered out with regiment,
Do.	Charles W. Atkinson	" 1, "	" 1, "	Promoted to Captain.
Do.	Wm. C. Lyon	" 1, "	" 1, "	Promoted to Captain.
Do.	Francis M. Kelley	" 1, "	" 1, "	Promoted to Captain.
Do.	Chas. H. Morgan	" 1, "	" 1, "	Promoted to Captain.
Do.	Eugene Clarke	" 1, "	" 1, "	Promoted to Captain.
Do.	Wm. E. Sweet	" 1, "	" 1, "	Promoted to Captain.
Do.	Cyrus M. Hubbard	" 25, "	" 25, "	Appointed regimental Q. M. May 27, 1866.
Do.	Lyman H. McBride	Sept. 17, "	Sept. 17, "	Resigned July 5, 1865.
Do.	Bri. Hill	" 17, "	" 17, "	Mustered out with regiment.
Do.	Lewis E. Vance	Jan. 11, 1865	Jan. 11, 1865	Mustered out with regiment.
Do.	Albert B. Logan	" 11, "	" 11, "	Mustered out with regiment.
Do.	Frederick Thompson	April 20, "	April 20, "	Mustered out with regiment.
Do.	Charles P. Conant	" 20, "	" 20, "	Mustered out with regiment.
Do.	John N. Bayless	" 20, "	" 20, "	Mustered out with regiment.
Do.	James T. Ogden	May 11, "	May 11, "	Mustered out with regiment.
2d Lieutenant	John F. Walls	June 1, 1861	July 12, 1861	Promoted to 1st Lieutenant.
Do.	W. W. Sheppard	" 1, "	" 12, "	Promoted to 1st Lieutenant.
Do.	Martin P. Avery	" 1, "	" 12, "	Promoted to 1st Lieutenant.
Do.	Henry Richardson	" 1, "	" 12, "	Promoted to 1st Lieutenant.
Do.	James L. Bottsford	" 1, "	" 12, "	Promoted to 1st Lieutenant.
Do.	R. P. Kennedy	" 1, "	" 12, "	Promoted to 1st Lieutenant.
Do.	George W. Stevens	" 1, "	" 12, "	Promoted to 1st Lieutenant.
Do.	DeHaven K. Smith	" 1, "	" 12, "	Promoted to 1st Lieutenant.
Do.	R. Hastings	" 1, "	" 12, "	Promoted to 1st Lieutenant.
Do.	A. C. Fisk	" 1, "	" 12, "	Promoted to 1st Lieutenant.
Do.	Lafayette Hoge	July 23, "	" 23, "	Declined promotion.
Do.	John F. Cutter	" 23, "	" 23, "	Resigned September 22, 1861.
Do.	Adam W. Durkee	" 23, "	" 23, "	Promoted to 1st Lieutenant.
Do.	Harry Thompson	" 22, "	" 23, "	Promoted to 1st Lieutenant.
Do.	Robert Skiles Gardner	Sept. 7, "	Sept. 7, "	Assistant Quartermaster United States Army
Do.	John S. Ellen	" 7, "	" 7, "	Promoted to 1st Lieutenant.
Do.	Benj. F. Cooper	Jan. 17, 1862	Jan. 17, 1862	Promoted to 1st Lieutenant.
Do.	George W. Hicks	Feb. 8, "	Feb. 8, "	Promoted to 1st Lieutenant.
Do.	Andrew Y. Austin	" 9, "	March 14, "	Promoted to 1st Lieutenant.
Do.	George C. Warren	" 11, "	" 20, "	Resigned December 20, 1862.
Do.	Benj. W. Jackson	March 23, "	April 14, "	Promoted to 1st Lieutenant.
Do.	Martin V. Ritter	April 18, "	June 24, "	Resigned February 11, 1863.
Do.	Wm. McKinley, jr.	Sept. 24, "	Nov. 3, "	Promoted to 1st Lieutenant.
Do.	Milton B. Deshong	Oct. 15, "	" 3, "	Promoted to 1st Lieutenant.
Do.	Edward A. Abbott	Dec. 26, "	Dec. 31, "	Promoted to 1st Lieutenant.
Do.	George Seaman	" 26, "	" 31, "	Killed May 9, 1864.
Do.	Wm. H. Nessle	" 26, "	" 31, "	Promoted to 1st Lieutenant.
Do.	W. P. Chamberlin	Nov. 30, "	" 21, "	Promoted to 1st Lieutenant.
Do.	Thos. A. Stephens	Dec. 26, "	" 31, "	Promoted to 1st Lieutenant.
Do.	Amos F. Gillis	" 26, "	Jan. 24, 1863	Promoted to 1st Lieutenant.
Do.	Wm. C. Lyon	Feb. 14, 1863	March 30, "	Promoted to 1st Lieutenant.
Do.	Chas. A. Townslee	Jan. 1, "	" 30, "	Mustered out.
Do.	John W. Cracraft	Feb. 7, "	" 30, "	Promoted to 1st Lieutenant.
Do.	Henry M. Beer	" 14, "	" 30, "	Mustered out.
Do.	Theodore Harris	Aug. 8, "	Aug. 8, "	Declined.
Do.	Orville W. Richards	" 8, "	" 8, "	Commission returned.
Do.	Charles W. Atkinson	" 8, "	" 8, "	Promoted to 1st Lieutenant.
Do.	Chas. H. Morgan	" 8, "	" 8, "	Promoted to 1st Lieutenant.
Do.	Wm. E. Sweet	Jan. 14, 1864	June 14, 1864	Promoted to 1st Lieutenant.
Do.	Leander H. Lane	" 14, "	" 14, "	Promoted to 1st Lieutenant.
Do.	Eugene Clarke	" 14, "	" 14, "	Promoted to 1st Lieutenant.
Do.	Francis M Kelley	" 14, "	" 14, "	Promoted to 1st Lieutenant.
Do.	Benj. Killiam	" 14, "	" 14, "	Promoted to 1st Lieutenant.
Do.	Lewis E. Vance	July 1, "	July 1, "	Promoted to 1st Lieutenant.
Do.	Lyman H. McBride	" 1, "	" 1, "	Promoted to 1st Lieutenant.
Do.	James F. Bowers	" 1, "	" 1, "	Honorably discharged January 13, 1865.
Do.	Chas. H. Moore	" 1, "	" 1, "	Resigned September 23, 1864.
Do.	Bri. Hill	" 1, "	" 1, "	Promoted to 1st Lieutenant.
Do.	Lewis R. Gray	" 1, "	" 1, "	Killed at Winchester July 24, 1864.
Do.	Cyrus M. Hubbard	" 1, "	" 1, "	Promoted to 1st Lieutenant.
Do.	Oliver H. Ferrell	" 1, "	" 1, "	Declined promotion.
Do.	Andrew Sheppard	" 1, "	" 1, "	Mortally wounded.
Do.	Addison A. Udell	" 1, "	" 1, "	Promoted to 1st Lieutenant U. S. col'd reg't.
Do.	Albert B. Logan	Sept. 17, "	Jan. 11, 1865	Promoted to 1st Lieutenant.
Do.	Edward A. Klosterman	" 17, "	" 11, "	Discharged March 22, 1865.
Do.	Frederick Thompson	" 17, "	" 11, "	Promoted to 1st Lieutenant.
Do.	Charles Edward Brigden	" 17, "	" 11, "	Resigned March 10, 1865.
Do.	Charles P. Conant	April 20, "	April 20, "	Promoted to 1st Lieutenant.
Do.	John N. Bayless	" 20, "	" 20, "	Promoted to 1st Lieutenant.
Do.	James T. Ogden	" 20, "	" 20, "	Promoted to 1st Lieutenant.
Do.	James M. Craig	" 20, "	" 20, "	Mustered out with regiment.
Do.	Leonidas H. Inscho	" 20, "	" 20, "	Mustered out with regiment.
Do.	Percival Hawes	" 20, "	" 20, "	Mustered out with regiment.
Do.	Wm. H. McConnell	June 22, "	June 22, "	Mustered out with regiment.
Do.	George W. Holston	" 22, "	" 22, "	Mustered out with regiment.
Do.	Charles A. Willard	" 22, "	" 22, "	Mustered out with regiment.
Do.	Dewitt C. Sperry	" 22, "	" 22, "	Mustered out with regiment.
Do.	John B. Gustin	" 22, "	" 22, "	Resigned July 11, 1865.
Do.	John Martin	" 22, "	" 22, "	
Do.	Wm. A. Stoner	" 22, "	" 22, "	

TWENTY-THIRD OHIO VOLUNTEER INFANTRY.

THIS was one of the first regiments organized at the commencement of the war for the Union, and had for its commander one who, shortly after his entrance into the service, became one of the most distinguished leaders of the National forces. The Twenty-Third was organized at Camp Chase, Ohio, in the month of June, 1861, under Colonel William S. Rosecrans, and was mustered into the United States service for three years on the 11th day of June, 1861. Before leaving for the field Colonel Rosecrans received a commission as Brigadier-General in the regular army of the United States, and Colonel E. P. Scammon succeeded to the command of the Twenty-Third. On the 25th of July, 1861, the regiment was ordered to Clarksburg, West Virginia, where it arrived on the 27th.

It was at once launched into the arena of war, receiving orders on the 28th to proceed to Weston. From this point it operated against the numerous guerrillas infesting the country in that quarter, performing many days and nights of excessively hard duty, marching and countermarching over the rugged spurs of Rich Mountain range, and drenched by the almost continual rains of that season.

For the purpose of operating with greater facility against the scattered bands of the enemy, the regiment had been divided—five companies being placed under command of Lieutenant-Colonel Stanley Mathews as a movable force, to be used exclusively against the guerrillas, and constituting the right wing. The left wing remained at Weston, sending out occasional foraging and scouting expeditions against guerrillas and other disaffected inhabitants of that wild region.

On the 1st of September the two wings of the regiment united at Bulltown, whence, with the main body of General Rosecrans's army, the Twenty-Third marched on Carnifex Ferry, where the Rebels, under General Floyd, were posted in a strong position. The evening of the 10th found the Twenty-Third in line of battle, engaged in sharp skirmishing with the enemy. In the night Floyd abandoned his position and retreated across the Gauley River. Heavy rains rendered the pursuit of the Rebels almost impossible, but it was attempted, and with much success in capturing prisoners. The chase was continued to the enemy's intrenchments at the foot of Big Sewell Mountain. Remaining here but a few days, the Twenty-Third fell back to Camp Ewing, on New River. This camp proved a very unhealthy one, and the ranks of the regiment were rapidly thinned—diarrheas, fevers, etc., proving fatal in many cases.

The winter of 1861 was devoted to recruiting, drill, and discipline. Two companies (F and G) joined a detachment under Major Comly, which, on December 31, 1861, occupied Raleigh C. H. without opposition. Over three hundred stand of arms, twenty-seven prisoners, and a quantity of supplies were captured. Companies A and B were added to this detachment; and, on the 10th of February, Major Comly marched his command from Raleigh C. H. to the mouth of Blue Stone River, a distance of twenty-eight miles, through a snow-storm, driving a regiment of the enemy's infantry and a small force of cavalry, with considerable loss, across the river. The camps, tents, and forage of this force were captured. The detachment received the thanks of General Rosecrans, commanding department, in general orders, for its bravery and efficiency.

On the 17th of April, 1862, orders were received to quit winter-quarters and go into camp.

The command, on the 22d, moved in the direction of Princeton, the Twenty-Third, under command of Lieutenant-Colonel Hayes, being in the advance all the way through. Princeton was reached on the 1st of May, the enemy leaving the town on the approach of our forces, after having doomed it to the flames. From this date until the 8th of May nothing but foraging and skirmishing occurred.

On the morning of the 8th the regiment was attacked by four regiments of the enemy's infantry and six pieces of artillery, under command of the Rebel General Heth. Only nine companies of the Twenty-Third were present and three small companies of cavalry. All of the cavalry except Gillmore's dragoons disappeared after the first fire. The regiment, however, made a determined stand, and, when overwhelmed and forced to retire, did so in good order, fighting as it went. It fell back to East River, being pursued by the enemy to the narrows of New River. Meeting re-enforcements at Adair's farm, after destroying tents, camp, and garrison equipage, on the 18th of May, the command left Princeton and returned to Flat Top Mountain, after having endured excessive hardships and almost starvation, the enemy having cut off all supplies.

The regiment remained at Flat Top Mountain until the 13th of July, when it was ordered to Green Meadows, seven miles from Pack's Ferry, on New River. Orders were received on the 15th of August to march, with all possible dispatch, to Camp Piatt, on the Great Kanawha, where the regiment arrived on the morning of the 18th, and embarked on board transports, having marched one hundred and four miles in a little more than three days. Its officers claim this to be the fastest march on record, as made by any considerable force. Here the Twenty-Third went on board transports to Parkersburg, where it took the cars for Washington City, arriving on the 24th of August. From Washington the regiment marched with General McClellan's army toward Frederick City, from which place the Rebels were driven, with slight loss on both sides. Middletown was reached on the 13th. Here was commenced the battle of South Mountain, culminating in the great battle of Antietam, on the 17th of September, in both of which the Twenty-Third participated.

At South Mountain the regiment, under Lieutenant-Colonel Hayes (General J. D. Cox commanding division), was the first infantry engaged, being the advance of the column on that day. It was ordered at an early hour to advance by an unfrequented road leading up the mountain, and to attack the enemy. Posted behind stone walls, the enemy, in greatly superior force, poured a destructive fire of musketry, grape, and canister into our ranks at very short range and in a very short space of time. Lieutenant-Colonel Hayes, Captain Skiles, and Lieutenants Hood, Ritter, and Smith were each badly wounded (Colonel Hayes's arm broken; Captain Skiles shot through the elbow, arm amputated; Ritter, leg amputated); and over one hundred dead and wounded lay upon the field, out of the three hundred and fifty who went into the action. The command now devolved upon Major Comly, and remained with him from that time forward. The enemy suddenly opened fire from the left, and the regiment changed front on first company. Lieutenant-Colonel Hayes soon after again made his appearance on the field, with his wound half dressed, and fought, against the remonstrances of the whole command, until carried off. Soon after, the remainder of the brigade came up, a gallant charge was made up the hill, and the enemy was dislodged and driven into the woods beyond. In this charge a large number of the enemy were killed with the bayonet. During the remainder of the day the regiment fought with its division. Three bayonet charges were made by the regiment during the day, in each of which the enemy were driven with heavy loss.

During the day the Twenty-Third lost nearly two hundred, of whom almost one-fourth were killed on the field or afterward died of their wounds. Only seven men were unaccounted for at the roll-call after the action. The colors of the regiment were riddled, and the blue field almost completely carried away by shells and bullets.

At Antietam the regiment fought with the Kanawha Division. Near the close of the day a disastrous charge was made by the division (the Twenty-Third occupying the right of the First Brigade), by which the left of the division was exposed to a large force of the enemy, who suddenly emerged from a corn-field in rear of the left. The colors of the regiment were instantly shot down. At the same time a feint was made in the front. A battery in the rear opened fire on the advancing column of the enemy, by which also the National forces sustained more loss than the enemy. After a moment's delay the colors were planted by Major Comly on a new line at right angles with the former front, and, without waiting for any further order, the regiment, at a run, formed a line in the new direction, and opened fire on the enemy, who, for some cause, retired. Little damage was done by the enemy except a few captures from the left. The division soon after withdrew; but, through some inadvertency, no order reached the Twenty-Third, and it remained on the field until Colonel Scammon (commanding the division) came back and ordered it to the rear.

Almost exhausted by several days' hard fighting, the regiment was ordered to support a battery of General Sturgis's division during the night, and was not relieved until the afternoon of the next day.

On the 8th of October the Twenty-Third received orders to return, with the Kanawha Division, to West Virginia. It marched *via* Hagerstown, and arrived there on the 10th. Before embarking, however, on the cars for Clarksburg, information was received of Stuart's raid into Pennsylvania, and, of course, a "double-quick" into that quarter was the result. The report was premature. No enemy was discovered. The regiment returned to Hancock on the 13th of October, having eaten breakfast in Pennsylvania, dinner in Maryland, and supper in Virginia. It arrived at Clarksburg on the 15th of October. Here a change was made in the command of the regiment. Colonel Scammon was appointed Brigadier-General, and Lieutenant-Colonel Hayes appointed Colonel; Major Comly promoted to Lieutenant-Colonel, and Captain McIlrath to Major. The division was ordered to the Kanawha Valley, where it arrived on the 10th of November, having marched the entire distance over nearly the same route as in 1861. On the 18th of November the Twenty-Third went into winter-quarters at the Falls of the Great Kanawha. During the campaign of 1862 it marched about six hundred miles; but now, with the exception of occasional scouting, its duties were light.

On the 15th of March, 1863, the regiment was ordered to Charleston, Virginia, where it lay in camp during March, April, May, June, and part of July, performing little or no duty, with the exception of a few scouts, and an advance as far as Raleigh, Virginia, and its participation in the movements against the Morgan raid in July. In the last-named affair the Twenty-Third performed good service in heading off Morgan's band on the line of the Ohio River, at Buffington Bar, and near Hockingport, picking up a number of the guerrillas as they attempted to cross the Ohio River.

The regiment then returned to Charleston, Virginia, and lay there in camp during the remainder of 1863, and up to April 29, 1864, when a movement was made to a point two miles above Brownstown, on the Kanawha, preparatory to joining the forces gathering under General Crook for a raid on the Virginia and Tennessee Railroad. This expedition was something worthy of their mettle. Their long inaction had not hardened their sinews or made them impervious to fatigue; but, as was their custom, the rank and file of the Twenty-Third entered into the expedition with cheerfulness, and a determination, if possible, to make it signally successful. Without detailing their daily marches, it is sufficient to say that the regiment toiled on over the rugged mountains, up ravines, and through the dense woods, meeting with snows and rains in sufficient volumes to appal the stoutest hearts; but they toiled patiently, occasionally brushing the enemy out of their way, until, on the 9th of May, 1864, the battle of Cloyd Mountain was fought.

In this engagement the Twenty-Third was on the right of the First Brigade. About noon they were ordered to charge the enemy, who occupied the first crest of the mountain, with artillery and infantry, behind rudely-constructed breastworks. The hill itself was thickly wooded, steep and difficult of ascent, and was skirted by a stream of water from two to three feet deep. The approach was through a beautiful meadow five or six hundred yards in width. At the word of command the regiment advanced at double-quick across the meadow, under a very heavy fire of musketry and artillery, to the foot of the mountain, across the stream. The regiment advanced steadily to this point, without returning the fire of the enemy; and, after a short pause, a furious assault was made upon the enemy's works, carrying them, and capturing two pieces of artillery, which were brought off the field by Lieutenant Austin. The enemy fell back to the second crest or ridge of the mountain, where a determined attempt was made to form a line, but, after a short struggle, he was driven from there in full retreat. Re-enforcements arriving on the field, a third attempt was made to make a stand, but unsuccessfully. The struggle at the guns was of the fiercest description. The Rebel artillerymen attempted to reload their pieces when our line was not more than ten paces distant. Private Kosht, company G, a recruit, eighteen years of age, was the first to reach the guns. With a boyish shout he sprang from the ranks, and hung his hat over the muzzle of one of the guns.

In this charge Captain Hunter, company K, and Lieutenant Seaman, commanding company D, were both killed. Captain Rice, company A, was slightly wounded, but rejoined his company before the action was over. Lieutenant Abbott, company I, a valuable officer, was severely wounded, and left in hospital at Dublin Depot.

On the 10th of May there was another affair at New River Bridge, in which artillery was mostly used. The enemy were driven, and the bridge destroyed. The forces marched to Pepper's Ferry, and crossed without opposition—a tediously-slow process, however, as the whole army was crossed in one small ferry-boat, of very limited capacity, with the rain pouring down and dashing in the men's faces all night. The trains crossed at Rocky Ford a short distance above, at the expense of some men and a number of horses drowned.

On May 11th the march was continued to Blacksburg, skirmishing by the way, with two Rebels killed, two of our men wounded, and four of company F captured. On May 12th Salt Pond Mountain was crossed, the Twenty-Third acting as train-guard. The constant rains for several days had put the road in wretched condition. Most of the way it was wide enough for only one team to pass at a time. The animals were much fagged by heavy work and insufficient forage, and many of them dropped dead in the harness, so that loads had to be shifted and a number of wagons abandoned and burned. To add to the confusion a large number of "contrabands," who had joined the column with all sorts of conveyances, and a great many with no conveyance at all, began to lose horses and wagons, which clogged the road, and many of the poor wretches had to walk through the mud and rain, carrying children and supplies, and whatever household goods they were unwilling to leave.

On the morning of the 13th camp was reached at twenty minutes past five, greatly exhausted by the fatigues of the crossing. After an hour's rest the march was resumed, and prosecuted day by day, the troops almost constantly harrassed by the enemy, encountering great obstacles in swollen streams, rocky, muddy roads, and semi-starvation.

At Staunton, June 8th, the Twenty-Third joined General Hunter's command. The first terms of service of the regiment expiring on the 11th, those not re-enlisting as veterans were sent home, also the old colors, which were no longer in condition for service. The depot, railroad, bridges, and some of the public buildings and machine-shops of Staunton were destroyed by fire, and a beautiful stone arch spanning one of the streets where the railway passed, was blown up. Private property was respected.

On June 10th the regiment marched to Brownsburg, twenty-three miles from Staunton, skirmishing nearly all the way. The enemy was driven with ease. Lexington was reached about noon of the 11th, the Rebels burning a bridge at the approach of the National forces, and a pretty sharp artillery duel being kept up, while White's brigade effected a crossing about two miles above the town, compelling the enemy to retire. General Hunter's column came up in great haste just as the town was captured. By General Hunter's orders, the Military Academy, Washington College, and Governor Letcher's residence were burned. Good discipline only secured the execution of this order, which was protested against, formally, by Generals Crook and Averill, and, tacitly, by nearly every officer and man of the command.

On the 14th the Twenty-Third marched twenty-five miles to Buckhannon, thence to within two miles of Lynchburg; and, while moving up the Virginia and Tennessee Railroad, met the enemy and drove them pell-mell for two miles, capturing four pieces of their artillery. It was supposed our forces would immediately push on into Lynchburg after this success, but, after moving about until a short time after dark, they were ordered into camp. One brigade camped so near the enemy in the dark that the men commenced taking rails from the same fence. Some men of Gordon's (Rebel) brigade having exposed themselves, a lively little skirmish sprang up about midnight, but was quelled by withdrawing a short distance from each other.

On the 18th, at two A. M., Crook's command set off on a flanking expedition to the right to cross James River and attack Lynchburg in the rear. The cavalry, at the same time, were sent to the left to make a diversion. The Twenty-Third had not commenced crossing, however, when a messenger came from General Hunter with information that the enemy had received heavy re-enforcements, and was preparing to attack the lines in the center. It, with other forces, marched back rapidly, and soon after received information that the enemy was about to attack in overwhelming force, and that the artillery was in danger. It then moved double-quick to the exposed point, in the advance, led by General Crook in person. The roar of artillery and the crash of shell prevented any orders from being heard, but the command always followed such lead. The attack was soon repulsed, with trifling loss. The troops lay in line of battle at this point until some time after dark, when, finding the enemy heavily re-enforced from Richmond, a skirmish-line was left on the front, while the rest quietly withdrew and commenced the retreat from Lynchburg, marching rapidly toward the town of Liberty. The fighting was all done in a dense thicket where the light of the sun could not be seen. The men had had no sleep for two days and nights, and scarcely anything to eat. In this condition they marched, falling down frequently asleep in the road, it being with the utmost difficulty that they could be kept on their feet. About ten A. M. the regiment rested an hour and twenty minutes, and then pushed on without any more halts. Of the subsequent march, the following extracts from the diary of an officer of the regiment form a fitting record:

"*June* 19.—Marched all day, dragging along very slowly. The men had nothing to eat, the trains having been sent in advance. It is almost incredible that men should have been able to endure so much, but they never faltered, and not a murmur escaped them. Often men would drop out silently, exhausted, but not a word of complaint was spoken. Shortly after dark, at Liberty, had a brisk little fight with the enemy's advance; reached Buford's Gap about ten A. M. of the 20th. General Crook remained here with Hayes's brigade, holding the gap until dark, inviting an attack. The army was, however, too cautious to do more than skirmish. After dark we withdrew, and marched all night to overtake the command in the advance. Reached Salem about nine A. M. Hunter had passed through Salem, and a body of the enemy's cavalry fell upon his train and captured the greater part of his artillery. About the same time Crook was attacked in front and rear, and, after a sharp fight, pushed through, losing nothing. Heavy skirmishing all day, and nothing to eat, and no sleep. Continued the march until about ten P. M., when we reached the foot of North Mountain, and slept.

"At four A. M. next morning (22d) left in the advance, the first time since the retreat commenced. By a mistake a march of eight miles was made for nothing. Thus we toiled on, suffering intensely with exhaustion, want of food, clothing, etc. On the 27th a supply-train was met on Big Sewell Mountain. Men all crazy. Stopped and ate; marched and ate; camped about dark, *and ate all night.* Marched one hundred and eighty miles in the last nine days, fighting nearly all the time, and with very little to eat."

The column reached Charleston July 1st, and remained there refitting and resting until July 10th, when the Twenty-Third embarked for Parkersburg, *en route* for Martinsburg, General Crook's command having been ordered East to meet Early, who had invaded Maryland and Pennsylvania. It reached Martinsburg on the 14th, lay in camp there until the 18th, and then marched to Cabletown, ten miles beyond Harper's Ferry, driving in the enemy's pickets. Still under the immediate command of General Hunter, General Crook being at Snicker's Gap, Hayes's brigade (including the Twenty-Third) was sent, without cavalry and with two sections of a howitzer battery of the oldest and clumsiest pattern, to attack Early's army of twenty thousand or more, in flank, with no other force on this side of the Shenandoah and no possibility of communicating. The enemy had already whipped the First Division, with the whole Sixth Corps to back them, and they lay on the opposite bank of the river at Snicker's Ferry. After pretty heavy skirmishing the Twenty-Third, with the Thirty-Sixth Ohio, were entirely surrounded by two divisions of the enemy's cavalry, but fought their way out and returned to camp. Marching toward Harper's Ferry, on the 22d of July, they joined General Crook at Winchester.

On the 24th a battle was fought at Winchester, in which the National forces were defeated after a well-contested fight from early in the morning until nine o'clock at night. The Twenty-Third Ohio lost in this engagement one hundred and fifty-three men, ten of whom were commissioned officers. General Mulligan and his brother-in-law were killed, and Lieutenant-Colonel Comly and many others wounded.

The forces moved toward Martinsburg early next morning, the enemy following closely. At Martinsburg the enemy's cavalry charged into the town, when General Crook made a sudden advance with his whole force, drove them badly and captured a number of prisoners. He then withdrew, and under cover of the feint of numerous camp-fires, moved off quietly toward the ford at Williamsport, and camped on the south bank of the Potomac.

On the 26th of July a series of marches and countermarches were inaugurated which was kept up until the evening of the 14th of August, when Duvall's brigade had quite a battle with a considerable force of Rebel infantry and artillery. The enemy's artillery gave them such an advantage that they drove our forces back five or six hundred yards, but a charge was made and in turn they were driven back, with the loss of some prisoners and a fine lot of beef cattle. Then followed another dance up and down the Valley, fighting and retreating. At Front Royal Sheridan's cavalry made a saber charge and captured two hundred and sixty of the enemy.

At Halltown, on the 23d of August, the enemy attacked at daylight but did not follow it up. At six P. M. Hayes's brigade, the Twenty-Third and Thirty-Sixth Ohio, with part of the Fifth West Virginia, sallied out and drove in the enemy's skirmish-line, capturing a lot of prisoners from Kershaw's Rebel division. This charge was brilliantly executed, and excited astonishment among the Rebel prisoners. The universal inquiry was: "Who the h——l are 'uns?" On the 23d another sortie was made, and six officers and one hundred prisoners taken, all from Kershaw's (South Carolina) division.

Nothing of importance transpired until the 3d of September at Berryville, where the Twenty-Third was sent out on picket. A general engagement was brought on just before dark, in which was desperate fighting—the most of it after dark. As the Twenty-Third formed line and went into battle, the boys were received with loud cheers. Colonel Hayes, commanding brigade, went out of the line to meet and lead his old regiment. The cannonade was very rapid and continuous, and the exploding shells and the blaze of the discharge from guns and small arms made a diabolic display. At ten o'clock both parties withdrew, apparently satisfied, and the Twenty-Third returned to picket-duty. It lost in this affair Captains Austin and Gillis, both brave and accomplished officers.

After the usual amount of marching and countermarching, from the 4th to the 18th of September, the battle of Opequan was fought on the 19th. General Crook's command was in reserve, but was very soon brought into action and sent to the extreme right of the line to make a flank attack. Hayes's brigade had the extreme right of the infantry. The position was reached under cover of an almost impenetrable growth of cedar, crossing a swampy stream. Here the division was halted and formed—First Brigade (Hayes's) in front, and the Second (Johnson's) in rear. Throwing out a light line of skirmishers the brigade advanced rapidly to the front, driving the enemy's cavalry. The National cavalry at the same time advanced out of the woods on the right. After advancing in this way across two or three open fields, under a scattering fire, the crest of a slight elevation was reached, when the enemy's infantry line came into view, off diagonally to the left front, and he opened a brisk artillery fire.

Moving forward double-quick under this fire, the brigade reached a thick fringe of underbrush, dashing through which it came upon a deep slough, forty or fifty yards wide and nearly waist deep, with soft mud at the bottom, overgrown with a thick bed of moss, nearly strong enough to bear the weight of a man. It seemed impossible to get through it, and the whole line was staggered for a moment. Just then Colonel Hayes plunged in with his horse, and under a shower of bullets and shells, with his horse sometimes down, he rode, waded, and dragged his way through—the first man over. The Twenty-Third was immediately ordered by the right flank and over the slough at the same place. In floundering through this morass men were suffocated and drowned, still the regiment plunged through, and, after a pause long enough to partially re-form the line, charged forward again, yelling and driving the enemy. Sheridan's old cavalry kept close up on the right, having passed around the slough, and every time the enemy was driven from cover charged and captured a large number of prisoners. This plan was followed throughout the battle, by which the cavalry was rendered very effective. In one of these charges Colonel Duvall, the division commander, was wounded and carried from the field, leaving Colonel Hayes in command. He was everywhere exposing himself recklessly as usual. He was the first over the slough; he was in advance of the line half the time afterward; his Adjutant-General was severely wounded; men were dropping all around him, but he rode through it all as if he had a charmed life.

No re-enforcements—no demonstration as promised. Something must be done to stop the murderous concentrated fire that is cutting the force so dreadfully. Selecting some Saxony rifles in the Twenty-Third, pieces of seventy-one caliber with a range of twelve hundred yards, Lieutenant McBride was ordered forward with them to kill the enemy's artillery horses, in plain sight. They moved forward rapidly under cover as much as possible. At the first shot a horse drops; almost immediately another is killed; a panic seems to seize the artillery and they commence limbering up. The infantry take the alarm, and a few commence running from the intrenchments. The whole line rises, and with a tremendous yell the men rush frantically for the breastworks; and thus, without stopping to fire another shot, the enemy ran in utter confusion—that terrible cavalry, which had been hovering like a cloud on the flanks, sweeping down on the Rebels and capturing them by regiments. Eight battle-flags were captured and a large number of prisoners. The "graybacks" soon looked as numerous as the "blue coats." The enemy's artillery in the Star fort was obliged to stop firing and fall back, and the battle was at an end.

About this time the Sixth Corps emerged from the woods in the rear and started forward in magnificent style, lines all well dressed, and everything in striking contrast with the shattered condition of the troops just engaged. Thus ended the battle of Opequan (pronounced O-pee-can). The result was a complete and decisive victory. Lieutenant McBride with his party, sent to kill artillery horses, brought in one hundred and two prisoners, of whom he captured Colonel Edgar and forty-two others himself. The regiment captured about two hundred men. The artillery was captured by the combined force, and therefore the credit does not belong to either in particular.

The battle of North Mountain occurred September 20, 1864. It was more of an impetuous charge than a regular battle. The Twenty-Third, with its companions of the brigade, charged with perfect fury up the whole line of intrenchments, the enemy scarcely making a stand at all, flying in utter rout and terror as Crook's command gained their rear, abandoning gun after gun to their hands. The loss of the regiment was only one killed and one mortally wounded.

From this time forward until October 19th no regular battle was fought. The usual amount of hard marching from point to point in the Valley was gone through with, with occasional skirmishes and one or two "artillery duels" to vary the monotony of camp-life.

On the 19th, however, the battle of Cedar Creek was inaugurated. The Nineteenth and Sixth Corps and the cavalry occupied positions on a parallel line with the enemy's front as he lay in camp, or nearly so. General Crook's First Division (Thoburn's) occupied works about a mile further to the front and on the left of the main line, and the works from their left flank rearward were entirely empty, except that the Ninth Virginia, from the Second Division, occupied a small portion of them about half a mile back, where they had been at work the day before. Crook's Second Division (Duvall's, commanded by Hayes), or as much of it as was left from details for cattle-guards, pickets, etc., occupied a camp about one mile and a quarter in rear of the First Division, and in rear of the Manchester Pike. An independent brigade (Kitching's) occupied a camp to the left and rear of that. The Rebel attacking column crossed the North Fork of the Shenandoah from the left of Fisher's Hill, passed down near the base of the Massanutten Mountain, beyond the picket-line, and recrossed the river at Buxton Ford, well to the rear of Crook's command. From there they passed again toward the front, just outside the National lines, through the darkness and fog, forming a line of battle extending from Thoburn's right to a point about opposite Middletown, beyond the extreme left. (Prisoners reported that this movement was commenced at dark the preceding night.) The night was very dark, and even after daylight a thick fog obscured everything and added to the effect of the enemy's attack. The nearest force of National cavalry on the left was at Front Royal, eight miles distant. The reader will please note this fact particularly. It may be well to state that a feint was made in Custar's front on the extreme right, before the attack, and that a small column of the enemy accompanied by General Early in person, crossed Cedar Creek, on the Winchester Pike, after the left was turned.

General Sheridan was absent in Washington, and, by seniority, the command devolved upon Major-General Wright, commanding Sixth Corps. As soon as the lines were settled into position General Crook discovered the weak point on the left, a ford across the North Fork of the Shenandoah, accessible from the Massanutten Mountain, and which could not be covered by his infantry. He applied immediately for a division of cavalry to cover this ford and picket the front of the mountain. This request was immediately granted. For some unexplained reason the cavalry had not yet been placed there on the nights of the 18th and 19th. It was generally supposed that it was there, and the division officer of the day for the Second Division was instructed that it was there, as was also the corps officer of the day Colonel Brown, of the Thirteenth West Virginia. When the division officer of the day for the Second Division (Colonel Furney, of the Thirty-Fourth Ohio Volunteer Infantry), made the grand rounds, it was reported to him it was suspected that troops were moving through the woods in that direction; and while he was on the picket-line he discovered cavalry there, and supposing it to be National cavalry patrolling, rode out to see what news they had, and was quietly "gobbled up." (He afterward escaped at Mount Jackson and arrived safely in camp.)

Nearly the whole flanking force of the enemy crossed at this ford. With the cavalry in position this would have been simply impossible; and sufficient notice of any such event would have been given to have placed not only the Army of West Virginia, but the whole of Sheridan's army, in the works at the left, to oppose the enemy after he had crossed. The enemy's line, when the attack opened, extended from the front of Crook's First Division all the way round to a point about opposite Middletown, they having gained their position under cover of the fog and darkness, as above stated. To meet this force lying quietly there under cover, waiting for the feint on the right of the line (which was the signal for the attack), General Crook had about four thousand men. If placed in skirmish-line they would not more than cover the front of the enemy's attacking force. The Second Division (Hayes) had but fourteen hundred and forty-five men in camp for duty. This was the situation when, at about half-past four A. M., the enemy advanced in heavy force against the works of the First Division, pushing in rapidly whatever of the picket-line they failed to capture. Although the forces were promptly in line, the enemy had it all their own way, and overwhelmed and overlapped the lines so as to push them back rapidly.

The situation in a few minutes after the attack was about this: Crook's command, overpowered and driven from their advanced position, were forming on the left of the Nineteenth Corps, which corps was just getting into action, the left being hotly engaged, but not so much so as Crook's command yet. The right of the line had not been engaged at all, and was not for some time after. While the line was in this situation the trains were all slowly moving off. A desperate stand was made by the shattered lines of Crook's command to save the head-quarters train of the army, which came last from the right, and it succeeded. Many brave men lost their lives in this—Colonel Thoburn, commanding First Division; Captain Bier, General Crook's Adjutant-General, and others. Colonel Hayes, commanding the First Division, had his horse shot under him, and narrowly escaped with his life. Lieutenant-Colonel Hall, of the Thirteenth Virginia, was killed, but the train was saved.

From this time the whole line fell slowly back, fighting stubbornly, to a new position which had been selected. There they halted, and the enemy seemed content with shelling us

General Crook lay a couple of rods away from the line, in a place which seemed to be more particularly exposed than any other part of the line. Colonel Hayes lay close by, badly bruised from his fall, and grumbling because the troops did not charge the enemy's line, instead of waiting to be charged. Suddenly there is a dust in the rear, on the Winchester Pike; and, almost before they are aware, a young man, in full Major-General's uniform, and riding furiously a magnificent black horse, literally "flecked with foam," reins up and springs off by General Crook's side. There is a perfect roar as everybody recognized—SHERIDAN! He talks with Crook a little while, cutting away at the tops of the weeds with his riding-whip. General Crook speaks a half-dozen sentences that sound a great deal like the crack of the whip; and by that time some of the staff are up. They are sent flying in different directions. Sheridan and Crook lie down and seem to be talking, and all is quiet again, except the vicious shells of the different batteries and the roar of artillery along the line. After awhile Colonel Forsyth comes down in front and shouts to the General: "The Nineteenth Corps is closed up, sir." Sheridan jumps up, gives one more cut with his whip, whirls himself around once, jumps on his horse, and starts up the line. Just as he starts he says to the men: "*We are going to have a good thing on them now, boys!*" And so he rode off, and a long wave of yells rolling up to the right with him. The men took their posts, the line moved forward, and the balance of the day is a household word over a whole nation.

On October 7th the regiment was detailed as train-guard to Martinsburg, and marched to Winchester, where a brigade of the enemy's cavalry was reported to be. On the march the men voted at the Presidential election. It was impossible to take all the votes, as the train required vigilant watching. The votes were collected by the judges of election as the column was in march, from among the wagons, etc. There were seven anti-war votes, the first ever cast in the regiment, principally from among the teamsters. The regiment reached Martinsburg about nine P. M., with the weather very cold, raining, and no wood.

On the 13th of November it returned to Winchester with a supply-train of seven hundred wagons. On the 14th it marched to camp at Kernstown, where the Army of the Shenandoah was lying, and went into camp in a dense thicket. The next day the regiment re-commenced drill and ordinary camp routine, and kept it up until the middle of December, when it was transferred from the extreme left to the extreme right of the line. About the 20th of December Hayes's brigade was ordered to Stephenson's Depot, where it remained on duty until the 29th, when it marched to Martinsburg and went into camp.

On January 1, 1865, it embarked for Cumberland at ten A. M., and arrived at six P. M. Colonel Hayes was promoted to a Brigadier-Generalship, and Lieutenant-Colonel Comly to Colonel, both to date from October 19, 1864.

The regiment reached Grafton on the 12th of January. The post at Beverly had been captured, and the regiment was to operate against the enemy and protect the railroad. From the 13th to the 18th it lay at Grafton, without tents and with insufficient bedding. The weather was very cold. Returning to Cumberland on the 19th, the regiment was there occupied down to March 1st with drill and discipline, and the ordinary camp routine.

Thereafter followed the collapse of the Southern Confederacy and the surrender of their armies. The boys became anxious to get home. The rest of April, May, June, and most of July were spent in restive, inglorious ease. The wished-for order came at last, and the Twenty-Third was mustered out on the 26th of July, 1865, at Cumberland, and took the cars for Camp Taylor, near Cleveland, where the men were paid and discharged.

24th REGIMENT OHIO VOLUNTEER INFANTRY

ROSTER, THREE YEARS' SERVICE.

RANK.	NAME.	DATE OF RANK.	COM. ISSUED.	REMARKS.
Colonel	JACOB AMMEN	Jan. 22, 1861	June 22, 1861	Appointed Brigadier-General of Volunteers.
Do.	FREDERICK C. JONES	May 14, 1862	May 11, 1862	Killed December 31, 1862.
Do.	DAVID J. HIGGINS	Jan. 1, 1863	Jan. 10, 1863	Resigned October 25, 1863.
Do.	A. T. M. COCKERILL	Oct. 23, "	Oct. 31, "	Mustered out June 24, 1864.
Lt. Colonel	J. A. GARFIELD	June 10, 1861	June 10, 1861	Declined.
Do.	SAMUEL A. GILBERT	" 22, "	" 22, "	Appointed Colonel 44th regiment.
Do.	LUCIAN BUTTLES	Oct. 14, "	Oct. 14, "	Resigned November 28, 1861.
Do.	FREDERICK C. JONES	Dec. 18, "	Dec. 18, "	Promoted to Colonel May 14, 1862.
Do.	ALBERT S. HALL	May 14, 1862	June 6, 1862	Appointed Colonel 105th regiment Aug. 11, '62.
Do.	HENRY TERRY	Aug. 11, "	Dec. 30, "	Killed December 31, 1862.
Do.	A. T. M. COCKERILL	Dec. 31, "	Jan. 21, 1863	Promoted to Colonel.
Major	SAMUEL A. GILBERT	June 10, 1861	June 10, 1861	Promoted to Lieutenant-Colonel.
Do.	LUCIAN BUTTLES	" 22, "	" 22, "	Promoted to Lieutenant-Colonel.
Do.	SHELTON STURGESS	Oct. 14, "	Oct. 14, "	Resigned November 28, 1861.
Do.	ALBERT S. HALL	Dec. 20, "	Dec. 20, "	Promoted to Lieutenant-Colonel May 14, 1862.
Do.	HENRY TERRY	May 14, 1862	June 6, 1862	Promoted to Lieutenant-Colonel Aug. 11, 1862.
Do.	ENOCH WELLER	Aug. 11, "	Dec. 30, "	Killed December 31, 1862.
Do.	THOMAS M. MCCLURE	Dec. 31, "	Jan. 24, 1863	Dismissed October 3, 1863.
Do.	WM. B. STURGESS	Oct. 3, 1863	Oct. 31, "	Mustered out June 21, 1864.
Surgeon	DAVID WELSH	July 2, 1861	July 2, 1861	Resigned July 26, 1861.
Do.	J. R. WEEKS	" 26, "	" 26, "	Mustered out with regiment.
Do.	C. M. COOK	April 23, 1863	June 5, 1863	Mustered out June 24, 1864.
Ass't Surgeon	ENOCH PEARCE	July 2, 1861	July 2, 1861	Declined.
Do.	J. M. COOK	" 24, "	" 24, "	Promoted to Surgeon.
Do.	HENRY G. SMITH	Aug. 19, 1862	Aug. 19, 1862	Resigned June 23, 1863.
Do.	E. M. HOBOLAND	July 21, 1863	July 24, 1863	Mustered out June 24, 1864.
Chaplain	WM. G. LEWIS	" 15, 1861	Aug. 7, 1861	Resigned August 17, 1861.
Do.	EDWARD JONES	Dec. 23, "	Dec. 23, "	Cancelled; commission returned.
Do.	WM. H. KNOWLDES	July 2, 1862	July 2, 1862	Resigned August 2, 1862.
Captain	Lyman M. Kellogg	April 23, 1861	April 23, 1861	Resigned July 4, 1861.
Do.	Shelton Sturgess	June 3, "	June 12, "	Promoted to Major.
Do.	David J. Higgins	" 3, "	" 12, "	Promoted to Major.
Do.	Moses J. Patterson	" 3, "	" 12, "	Died September 2, 1861.
Do.	Samuel B. Jackson	" 3, "	" 12, "	Resigned January 23, 1862.
Do.	Albert S. Hall	" 3, "	" 12, "	Promoted to Major.
Do.	Henry Terry	" 3, "	" 12, "	Promoted to Major May 14, 1862.
Do	George Arnold	" 3, "	" 12, "	Res'd Oct. 9,'61; re-inst. Jan. 20,'62; must'd out
Do.	J. B. Hill	" 3, "	" 12, "	Resigned Jan. 22, '62. (for promo. Aug. 26,'63.
Do.	Isaiah Given	" 3, "	" 12, "	Promoted to Lieutenant-Colonel 18th regt.
Do.	Samuel H. Wheeler	July 23, "	July 23, "	Died November 29, 1861.
Do.	Thomas M. McClure	Sept. 28, "	Sept. 28, "	
Do.	Enoch Weller	Oct. 15, "	Oct. 23, "	Promoted to Major.
Do.	A. T. M. Cockerill	Nov. 15, "	Nov. 15, "	Promoted to Major.
Do.	Warrington S. Weston	Dec. 20, "	Dec. 20, "	Resigned July 18, 1862.
Do.	Hyman N. Easton	" 20, "	" 20, "	Resigned.
Do.	Wm. B Sturgess	Jan. 28, 1862	Jan. 28, 1862	Promoted to Major.
Do.	Moses T. Wooster	" 28, "	" 28, "	Resigned August 15, 1862.
Do.	George M. Bacon	Feb. 8, "	Feb. 8, "	
Do.	Lafayette Foster	June 6, "	June 6, "	Resigned June 3, 1862.
Do.	Merrit Emerson	" 3, "	" 24, "	Died January 14, 1863.
Do.	Uzziel Stevens	Aug. 15, "	Dec. 30, "	Mustered out.
Do.	Charles R. Harmon	July 18, "	" 30, "	Killed December 31, 1862.
Do.	Jacob Diehl	Aug. 26, "	" 30, "	Mustered out.
Do.	John W. Brooks	" 11, "	" 30, "	Mustered out June 21, 1864.
Do.	De Witt C. Wadsworth	Dec. 31, "	Jan. 24, 1863	Killed September 20, 1863.
Do.	Henry Y. Graham	" 31, "	" 24, "	Revoked; resigned as 1st Lieut. Oct. 26, 1863.
Do.	Isaac N. Dryden	" 31, "	" 24, "	Killed September 20, 1863.
Do.	B. J. Horton	Jan. 1, 1863	Feb. 18, "	Resigned as 1st Lieutenant August 14, 1864.
Do.	David A. Merrill	" 10, "	June 10, "	Mustered out June 17, 1864.
Do.	Samuel F. Reber	April 21, 1864	April 21, 1861	Mustered out October 13, 1864.
Do.	Burch Fouraker	" 21, "	" 21, "	Resigned October 13, 1864.
Do.	Wm. C. Beck	" 21, "	" 21, "	Mustered out June 22, 1864.
Do.	David Thomas	" 21, "	" 21, "	Mustered out.
Do.	Daniel W. McCoy	" 21, "	" 21, "	Mustered out June 23, 1864.
1st Lieutenant	Moses T. Wooster	" 23, 1861	" 23, 1861	Promoted to Captain.
Do.	Wm. B. Sturgess	July 6, "	July 6, "	Promoted to Captain.
Do.	Samuel H. Wheeler	June 3, "	" 12, "	Promoted to Captain.
Do.	Enoch Weller	" 3, "	" 12, "	Promoted to Captain.
Do.	A. T. M. Cockerill	" 3, "	" 12, "	Promoted to Captain.
Do.	George M. Bacon	" 3, "	" 12, "	Promoted to Captain.
Do.	Warrington S Weston	" 3, "	" 12, "	Promoted to Captain.
Do.	J. Samuel Clock	" 3, "	" 12, "	Resigned October 28, 1861.
Do.	Baptist Bukler	" 3, "	" 12, "	Resigned September 14, 1861.
Do.	Hyman N. Easton	" 3, "	" 12, "	Promoted to Captain.
Do.	James R. Inskeep	" 3, "	" 12, "	Resigned October 14, 1861.
Do.	Wm. M. Vogleson	July 1, "	" 1, "	Declined.
Do.	Lafayette Foster	" 23, "	" 23, "	Resigned June 3, 1863.
Do.	John H. Elbert	Oct. 15, "	Oct. 15, "	Resigned December 30, 1861.
Do.	Henry S. Harding	Nov. 15, "	Nov. 15, "	Resigned January 18, 1862.
Do.	Merrit Emerson	" 15, "	" 15, "	Promoted to Captain June 3, 1862.
Do.	Robert G. Clark	" 15, "	" 15, "	Resigned January 17, 1862.
Do.	De Witt C. Wadsworth	Dec. 20, "	Dec. 20, "	Promoted to Captain December 31, 1862.
Do.	Benj. J. Horton	" 20, "	" 20, "	Promoted to Captain January 1, 1863.
Do.	Henry Y. Graham	" 30, "	" 30, "	Promoted to Captain December 31, 1862.
Do.	Uzziel Stevens	Jan. 9, 1862	Jan. 9, 1862	Promoted to Captain August 15, 1862.

RANK.	NAME.	DATE OF RANK.		COM. ISSUED.		REMARKS.
1st Lieutenant	John Archer	Jan.	9, 1862	Jan.	9, 1862	Honorably discharged May 10, 1863.
Do.	Robert F. Wheeler	"	28, "	"	28, "	Died at Zanesville, Ohio.
Do.	Charles R. Harmon	"	28, "	"	28, "	Promoted to Captain July 18, 1862.
Do.	David O. Williams	"	28, "	"	28, "	Resigned June 3, 1862.
Do.	Paul Spohn	Feb.	8, "	Feb.	8, "	Resigned April 30, 1864.
Do.	Jacob Diehl	May	7, "	May	2[illegible], "	Promoted to Captain August 26, 1862.
Do.	John W. Brooks	June	6, "	June	6, "	Promoted to Captain August 11, 1862.
Do.	James C. Williams	"	3, "	"	21, "	Resigned.
Do.	Isaac N. Dryden	"	3, "	"	24, "	Promoted to Captain December 31, 1862.
Do.	Samuel F. Reber	July	18, "	Dec.	30, "	Promoted to Captain.
Do.	David A. Merrill	Aug.	11, "	"	30, "	Promoted to Captain.
Do.	Burch Foraker	"	15, "	"	30, "	Promoted to Captain.
Do.	Augustus Draeger	"	26, "	"	30, "	Revoked; resigned as 2d Lieut. March 20, '62.
Do.	Wm. C. Beck	Dec.	31, "	Jan.	24, 1863	Promoted to Captain.
Do.	David Thomas	"	31, "	"	24, "	Promoted to Captain.
Do.	Pernett L. Cooper	"	31, "	"	24, "	Resigned March 5, 1864.
Do.	Daniel W. McCoy	May	1, 1863	June	10, "	Promoted to Captain.
Do.	John Sparrow	"	1, "	"	10, "	Resigned June 22, 1863, as 2d Lieutenant.
Do.	Andrew J. Garrison	"	1, "	"	10, "	Mustered out at expiration of service.
Do.	James F. Jaques	"	1, "	"	10, "	Mustered out at expiration of service.
Do.	Wm. A. Dehass	April	21, 1864	April	21, 1864	Mustered out at expiration of service.
Do.	Thomas J. Delong	"	21, "	"	21, "	Mustered out at expiration of service.
Do.	E. Molyneaux	"	21, "	"	21, "	Mustered out at expiration of service.
Do.	George Collings	"	21, "	"	21, "	Transferred to 18th Ohio Volunteer Infantry.
Do.	Charles G. Morehouse	"	21, "	"	21, "	Mustered out.
Do.	Lewis J. Kies	"	21, "	"	21, "	Mustered out.
Do.	George W. Brown	"	21, "	"	21, "	Transferred to 18th Ohio Volunteer Infantry.
2d Lieutenant	Wm. B. Sturges	"	23, 1861	"	23, 1861	Promoted to 1st Lieutenant.
Do.	Henry S. Harding	June	3, "	July	12, "	Transferred to company D.
Do.	De Witt C. Wadsworth	"	3, "	"	12, "	Promoted to 1st Lieutenant.
Do.	Lafayette Foster	"	3, "	"	14, "	Promoted to 1st Lieutenant.
Do.	John H. Elbert	"	3, "	"	12, "	Promoted to 1st Lieutenant.
Do.	Merrit Emerson	"	3, "	"	12, "	Promoted to 1st Lieutenant.
Do.	Robert G. Clark	"	3, "	"	12, "	Promoted to 1st Lieut. (enlisted May 7, '62.
Do.	Jacob Diehl	"	3, "	"	12, "	Promoted to 1st Lieut.; resi'd Sept. 20, '61; re-
Do.	Wm. C. Middleton	"	3, "	"	12, "	Resigned October 22, 1861.
Do.	Gabriel R. Still	"	3, "	"	12, "	Resigned.
Do.	Edgar R. Kellogg	July	6, "	"	6, "	Resigned October 28, 1861.
Do.	Thomas M. McClure	"	23, "	"	23, "	Promoted to 1st Lieutenant.
Do.	Uzziel Stevens	"	23, "	"	23, "	Promoted to 1st Lieutenant.
Do.	Henry S. Harding	"	23, "	"	23, "	Promoted to 1st Lieutenant.
Do.	Earley D. Bissett	Sept.	28, "	Sept.	28, "	Resigned January 3, 1862.
Do.	John Archer	"	28, "	"	28, "	Promoted to 1st Lieutenant.
Do.	Robert F. Wheeler	Oct.	4, "	Oct.	4, "	Promoted to 1st Lieutenant.
Do.	Charles R. Harmon	Nov.	15, "	Nov.	15, "	Promoted to 1st Lieutenant.
Do.	David O. Williams	"	15, "	"	15, "	Promoted to 1st Lieutenant.
Do.	Paul Spohn	"	15, "	"	15, "	Promoted to 1st Lieutenant.
Do.	John W. Brooks	"	15, "	"	15, "	Promoted to 1st Lieutenant June 6, 1862.
Do.	Isaac N. Dryden	"	15, "	"	15, "	Promoted to 1st Lieutenant June 3, 1862.
Do.	Henry Williams	"	15, "	"	15, "	Resigned.
Do.	James C. Williams	Dec.	20, "	Dec.	24, "	Promoted to 1st Lieutenant June 3, 1862.
Do.	James K. Jones	Jan.	9, 1862	Jan.	9, 1862	Resigned April 27, 1862.
Do.	Pernett L. Cooper	"	9, "	"	9, "	Promoted to 1st Lieutenant December 31, 1862.
Do.	Willard J. Stokes	"	28, "	"	28, "	Resigned October 7, 1862.
Do.	Daniel Reynolds	Feb.	8, "	Feb.	8, "	Resigned July 13, 1862.
Do.	Burch Foraker	"	8, "	"	8, "	Promoted to 1st Lieutenant August 15, 1862.
Do.	Samuel F. Reber	"	8, "	"	8, "	Promoted to 1st Lieutenant July 18, 1862.
Do.	Alexander Jolly	"	8, "	"	8, "	Declined.
Do.	Wm. C. Beck	June	6, "	June	6, "	Promoted to 1st Lieutenant December 31, '62.
Do.	Augustus Draeger	"	6, "	"	6, "	Promoted; resigned March 20, 1863.
Do.	David A. Merrill	"	6, "	"	6, "	Promoted August 11, 1862.
Do.	John Marshal	Nov.	18, "	Nov.	19, "	Discharged February 19, 1864.
Do.	Wm. J[illegible]ries	June	3, "	Dec.	31, "	Promoted.
Do.	Thomas J. Delong	July	18, "	"	30, "	Promoted.
Do.	James H. Jaques	Aug.	11, "	"	30, "	Promoted May 1, 1863.
Do.	John Sparrow	"	26, "	"	30, "	Promoted May 1, 1863; resigned Jan. 22, 1863.
Do.	E. Molyneaux	"	15, "	"	30, "	Promoted to 1st Lieutenant.
Do.	Daniel W. McCoy	July	13, "	Jan.	21, 1863	Promoted to 1st Lieutenant May, 1863.
Do.	George Collings	Oct.	7, "	"	24, "	Promoted to 1st Lieutenant.
Do.	Wm. A. Dehass	Dec.	31, "	"	21, "	Resigned April 6, 1864.
Do.	Andrew J. Garrison	"	31, "	"	21, "	Promoted to 1st Lieutenant May 1, 1863.
Do.	Charles G. Morehouse	May	1, 1863	June	10, "	Promoted to 1st Lieutenant.
Do.	Lewis J. Kies	"	1, "	"	10, "	Promoted to 1st Lieutenant.
Do.	Samuel W. Thomas	April	21, 1864	April	21, 1864	Transferred to 18th Ohio Volunteer Infantry.

TWENTY-FOURTH OHIO VOLUNTEER INFANTRY.

THE TWENTY-FOURTH OHIO was organized at Camp Chase, near Columbus, in the latter part of June, 1861. Two companies came from Huron County, one from Zanesville, one from Sandusky and Columbiana Counties, one from Adams County, one from Dayton, one from Trumbull County, one from Highland County, one from Cleveland, and one from Coshocton County.

The regiment left Camp Chase for the field July 26, 1861, and reached Cheat Mountain Summit, Virginia, August 14th, there joining the Fourteenth Indiana, which had been on duty at this mountain-pass some weeks. The enemy was in superior force fifteen miles in front, and almost every day attacked the pickets, giving frequent opportunities for skirmishing, requiring the regiment to be formed for battle promptly during the day and at night, and showing the necessity for strengthening the position by felling trees, preparing abattis, and throwing out heavy pickets to prevent surprise and to be prepared for any emergency. The position being considered important, and enemy in front enterprising, the camp was re-enforced by the Twenty-Fifth Ohio.

The night of September 11th was stormy, with heavy rain. The raw pickets, not yet taught the importance of special vigilance at such times, were careless; and at break of day on the 12th the camp was surrounded by a largely-superior force of Rebel soldiers. Fortunately the abattis on the left of the camp of the Twenty-Fourth proved efficient, caused delay in the movements of the enemy, and gave time to form the troops for battle, which was done promptly. In this, their first engagement, the Twenty-Fourth gave indications of that coolness and discipline for which the regiment was at a later period distinguished. After a combat of three hours the Rebels abandoned the attack and fled, leaving on the field many blankets, arms, etc., losing some prisoners and some killed. The loss of the Twenty-Fourth was only two wounded.

The next engagement in which the Twenty-Fourth took part was at Greenbrier, Virginia, October 3, 1861. It was here exposed to a heavy fire of shell, grape, and canister, but stood firm. Its loss was only two killed and three wounded. The service in the mountains of Virginia was arduous, requiring the greatest vigilance.

On November 18th the regiment marched from Cheat Mountain, under orders for Louisville, Kentucky; reported at that place on the 28th of the same month, and was assigned to duty in the Tenth Brigade, Fourth Division, Army of the Ohio. On February 25th, 1862, it reached Nashville, Tennessee, and remained there in camp until March 17th, when the division took up the line of march for Savannah and Pittsburg Landing.

The bridge over Duck River at Columbia, Tennessee, having been burned by the Rebels, and the stream being very high, the army was detained some days repairing the bridge. Before this was done (the river having fallen) the Fourth Division was ordered to advance. It waded the river March 29th and hurried on to Savannah, on the Tennessee River, which place it reached on Saturday, April 5th, and went into camp. As the swamp on the right bank of the Tennessee was deemed impassable, boats were to be sent to transport the troops to Pittsburg Landing, twelve miles up the river.

On Sunday morning, April 6th, the roar of the artillery at Pittsburg Landing was heard at Savannah. The troops were immediately put in readiness to move. No boats arriving to transport them, at one o'clock P. M. the Tenth Brigade (to which the Twenty-Fourth belonged) started through the swamp, the other brigades of the division following; and, after a hard march through mud and water, reached the opposite bank of the river, were ferried across by the steamboats, and took part in the battle that evening on the extreme left. On April 7th the Twenty-Fourth was engaged all day in the battle, and not only sustained its former reputation, but added new laurels. Major Hall was here severely wounded. The loss was small, considering the desperate nature of the conflict, amounting only to four killed and twenty-eight enlisted men wounded.

The Twenty-Fourth took part in most of the skirmishes between Pittsburg Landing and Corinth, and was one of the first regiments that entered the latter place. It was with the army in the pursuit of the enemy in North Mississippi and North Alabama, and in July was encamped at McMinnvillle, Tennessee.

It left that place September 3d and returned to Louisville, Kentucky, with the army during General Bragg's invasion, having a long, dusty, and greatly-dispiriting march. In October, 1862, it was assigned to the Fourth Division, Twenty-First Army Corps.

It was at the battle of Perryville, but, being on the extreme right, did not take part in the general engagement. It then moved in the pursuit of the retreating army; and, on the abandonment of the chase in the mountains of south-eastern Kentucky, it marched to Nashville.

When, in December, 1862, General Rosecrans advanced from Nashville, the Twenty-Fourth was reduced, by sickness, desertion, and other losses, to thirteen officers and three hundred and forty men. Company A, however, was on detached duty. With this strength it went into the battle of Stone River. Its loss was heavy, the regiment having been assigned an important position, and having held it faithfully. Colonel F. C. Jones, Major H. Terry, and Lieutenant Harmon were killed the first day, and Lieutenant Horton was severely wounded. The command of the regiment devolved on Major Weller, who was killed the second day, Captain A. T. M. Cockerill commanding the remainder of the day. Lieutenants Archer, Diehl, and Draeger were wounded. The loss was—commissioned officers, four killed, four wounded; men, ten killed, sixty-nine wounded (ten of these mortally). In other words, the regiment lost in this battle one-fourth of the entire strength with which it went into it.

Numerous promotions now occurred to fill the sad vacancies thus caused. The Twenty-Fourth was next in the affair at Woodbury, Tennessee, January 24, 1863, but its loss here was small. After a long rest through the spring and summer, it advanced with the army on Tullahoma, and was on duty at Manchester, Tennessee, until the advance on Chattanooga. It was in the engagement at Lookout Mountain; also in the battle of Chickamauga, with a loss of Captains Wadsworth and Dryden killed, together with a large number of men. Colonel D. J. Higgins and Major T. M. McClure were dismissed the service for bad conduct in this action. The regiment was next in the battle of Mission Ridge, and in pursuit of the enemy in the affair at Taylor's Ridge, near Ringgold.

It was now assigned to the Second Division, Fourth Army Corps, and was in an engagement near Dalton, with a loss of two killed and eight wounded. In April, 1864, the Twenty-Fourth was sent to Chattanooga to await orders for mustering out. On the 15th of June it received orders to proceed to Columbus for that purpose; and on the 24th of June it was mustered out and discharged.

Company D, of the Twenty-Fourth, re-enlisted as veteran volunteers, to serve during the war.

The colors of the regiment were presented to the State, to be placed in the archives for preservation, Colonel A. T. M. Cockerill turning them over with a few pertinent remarks. In response Governor Brough said:

"*Colonel, Officers, and Soldiers of the Twenty-Fourth:* I thank you in behalf of the people of the State of Ohio, not only for the colors, but for having borne them so nobly and gallantly as you have throughout the three years' service. They come worn and tattered; but there is not a rent in them that is not honorable, and an emblem of your bravery and gallantry. No regiment that has gone from Ohio has endured hardships with greater cheerfulness or more nobly discharged its duty. Yes, Sir (turning to the Colonel), no matter what the future may bring forth, no regiment can occupy a better position than the one you have had the honor to command I shall place these banners in the archives of the State as historic mementoes worthy of any people. Again, soldiers, I thank you."

These flags were presented to the regiment—the regimental flag by General Jacob Ammen, then its Colonel, and the National colors by the Sixth Ohio, better known as the "Guthrie Grays," of Cincinnati. The flag from the Sixth Ohio bears this inscription: "The Sixth Ohio to the Twenty-Fourth Ohio: Shiloh, April 7, 1862," and was presented to the regiment during the siege of Corinth by the late lamented General Wm. Nelson, then commander of the Fourth Division, Army of the Ohio (to which both the regiments at that time belonged), in behalf of the officers and men of the Sixth.

These flags have passed through the bloody fields of Pittsburg Landing and Stone River, where Colonel Fred. Jones, Lieutenant-Colonel Terry, Major Weller and Captain Harmon sealed their devotion to their country with their heart's blood. They were at the brilliant dash at Woodbury; in the terrible strife at Chickamauga, where Wadsworth and Dryden fell in their Nation's cause. They waved through the fierce struggle for the possession of Lookout Mountain, and the gallant charge on Mission Ridge. They were borne in the murderous assault on Taylor's Ridge at Ringgold; and last, but not least, in the bold reconnoissance of the gallant Palmer, so stubbornly resisted by the enemy at Buzzard's Roost Gap and Rocky Face Ridge. At Stone River the battle-ax was shot from the staff, and two balls passed through the staff. The holes made by twenty-three distinct bullets at Stone River may be seen in the flag itself, together with many more received on other memorable occasions. Three Color-Sergeants of the regiment were killed and seven severely wounded while bravely carrying their standards in the front line of battle. Two of them were killed at Stone River within five minutes of each other, and one at Chickamauga.

25th REGIMENT OHIO VOLUNTEER INFANTRY.

ROSTER, THREE YEARS' SERVICE.

RANK.	NAME.	DATE OF RANK.	COM. ISSUED.	REMARKS
Colonel	JAMES A. JONES	June 12, 1861	June 22, 1861	Resigned May 16, 1862.
Do.	WM. P. RICHARDSON	May 16, 1862	" 21, 1862	Mustered out May 9, 1866.
Do.	NATHAN'L HAUGHTON	" 25, 1866	May 25, 1866	Mustered out as Lieutenant-Colonel.
Lt. Colonel	JAMES A. JONES	June 10, 1861	June 10, 1861	Promoted to Colonel.
Do.	WM. P. RICHARDSON	" 22, "	" 22, "	Promoted to Colonel May 16, 1862.
Do.	GEORGE WEBSTER	May 16, 1862	" 24, 1862	Resigned July 30, 1862.
Do.	JAS. F. CHARLESWORTH	July 30, "	Aug. 16, "	Resigned May 13, 1863.
Do.	JEREMIAH WILLIAMS	May 13, 1863	May 25, 1863	Resigned June 20, 1864.
Do.	NATHANIEL HAUGHTON	July 13, 1864	July 13, 1864	Promoted to Colonel.
Do.	E. C. CULP	May 25, 1866	May 25, 1866	Mustered out as Major.
Major	WM. P. RICHARDSON	June 10, 1861	June 10, 1861	Promoted to Lieutenant-Colonel.
Do.	JOHN COONS	" 22, "	" 22, "	Declined.
Do.	GEORGE WEBSTER	" 28, "	" 28, "	Promoted to Lieutenant-Colonel May 16, 1862.
Do.	JAS. F. CHARLESWORTH	May 16, 1862	" 21, 1862	Promoted to Lieutenant-Colonel July 30, 1862.
Do.	JEREMIAH WILLIAMS	July 30, "	Aug. 16, "	Promoted to Lieutenant-Colonel.
Do.	JOHN W. BOWLUS	May 13, 1863	June 22, 1863	Resigned August 4, 1863.
Do.	NATHANIEL HAUGHTON	Aug. 4, "	Sept. 9, "	Promoted to Lieutenant-Colonel.
Do.	C. R. RANDALL	" 11, 1864	Aug. 16, 1864	Died of wounds November 30, 1864.
Do.	E. C. CULP	Jan. 6, 1865	Jan. 6, 1865	Promoted to Lieutenant-Colonel.
Do.	LUTHER B. MESNARD	May 25, 1866	May 25, 1866	Mustered out as Captain.
Surgeon	DAVID WELSH	July 2, 1861	July 2, 1861	Transferred to Twenty-Fourth Regiment.
Do.	L. G. MYER	" 25, "	Feb. 11, 1862	Mustered out.
Do.	WM. WALTON	Aug. 8, 1864	Aug. 8, 1864	Mustered out with regiment.
Ass't Surgeon	G. R. WEEKS	July 2, 1861	July 2, 1861	Promoted Surgeon Twenty-Fourth Regiment.
Do.	LAWRENCE G. ANDREWS	Sept. 7, "	Feb. 11, 1862	Resigned May 22, 1863.
Do.	WM. T. DEAN	July 13, 1862	July 23, "	Deceased September 17, 1862.
Do.	WM. WALTON	Oct. 7, "	Oct. 9, "	Promoted to Surgeon.
Do.	E. M. WILSON	Aug. 6, 1864	Aug. 8, 1864	Mustered out with regiment.
Captain	James F. Charlesworth	June 4, 1861	July 12, 1861	Promoted to Major May 16, 1862.
Do.	James Washburn	" 4, "	" 12, "	Resigned July 7, 1862.
Do.	Jeremiah Williams	" 4, "	" 12, "	Promoted to Major July 30, 1862.
Do.	Aaron C. Johnson	" 4, "	" 12, "	Transferred to Twelfth Battery O. V. A.
Do.	Moses H. Crowell	" 4, "	" 12, "	Resigned June 2, 1863.
Do.	John F. Oliver	" 4, "	" 12, "	Resigned May 10, 1863.
Do.	Asa Way	" 4, "	" 12, "	Resigned October 20, 1862.
Do.	Lewis R. Green	" 4, "	" 12, "	Deceased September 5, 1862.
Do.	John M. Mosley	" 4, "	" 12, "	Died September 25, 1862.
Do.	Jonathan Brown	" 4, "	" 12, "	Resigned March 20, 1862.
Do.	Wm. Askew	Sept. 25, "	Oct. 16, "	Resigned May 13, 1863.
Do.	John W. Bowlus	May 16, 1862	Aug. 16, 1862	Promoted to Major.
Do.	Chas. B. Jones	July 7, "	" 16, "	Resigned March 24, 1863.
Do.	Nathaniel Haughton	" 30, "	" 16, "	Promoted to Major.
Do.	John D. Merryman	Sept. 5, "	Dec. 30, "	Revoked.
Do.	Arthur Higgins	Oct. 20, "	" 30, "	Resigned May 17, 1863.
Do.	Alfred G. Cornelius	Sept. 5, "	Jan. 15, 1863	Revoked; resigned as 2d Lieut. April 1, 1863.
Do.	Nathaniel J. Manning	March 20, 1863	May 25, "	Mustered out.
Do.	C. R. Randall	" 21, "	" 25, "	Promoted to Major.
Do.	John T. Wood	" 20, "	June 15, "	Resigned September 1, 1864.
Do.	James Madison Barr	Oct. 1, "	Oct. 2, "	Mustered out April 13, 1865.
Do.	Henry H. Mosley	March 15, 1864	March 15, 1864	Commission returned.
Do.	David R. Hunt	" 15, "	" 15, "	On detached duty at muster out of regiment.
Do.	John R. Millman	" 15, "	" 15, "	Mustered out.
Do.	Edward C. Culp	" 17, "	" 17, "	Promoted to Major.
Do.	Luther B. Mesnard	May 25, "	May 25, "	Promoted to Major.
Do.	Israel White	Aug. 11, "	Aug. 11, "	Mustered out with regiment.
Do.	George N. Holcomb	" 11, "	" 11, "	Mustered out with regiment.
Do.	B. McConnaugh	" 11, "	" 11, "	Mustered out with regiment.
Do.	Chas. W. Ferguson	Oct. 17, "	Oct. 17, "	Mustered out with regiment.
Do.	Michael Murray	" 18, "	" 18, "	Mustered out with regiment.
Do.	Wm. M. King	Jan. 6, 1865	Jan. 6, 1865	Honorably discharged April 25, 1865.
Do.	John O. Archibald	Feb. 10, "	Feb. 10, "	Killed.
Do.	Wm. P. Scott	Sept. 4, "	Sept. 4, "	Mustered out with regiment.
Do.	Alex. Mattison	March 25, 1866	March 25, 1866	Mustered out with regiment.
Do.	Elisha Biggerstaff	" 25, "	" 25, "	Mustered out as 1st Lieutenant.
1st Lieutenant	Wm. Askew	June 4, 1861	July 12, 1861	Promoted to Captain.
Do.	Chas. B. Jones	" 4, "	" 12, "	Promoted to Captain July 7, 1862.
Do.	Wm. P. Reichner	" 4, "	" 12, "	Resigned October 31, 1862.
Do.	Darius Durham	" 4, "	" 12, "	Transferred to Twelfth Battery.
Do.	John W. Bowlus	" 4, "	" 12, "	Promoted to Captain May 16, 1862.
Do.	John W. Ross	" 4, "	" 12, "	Resigned April 27, 1862.
Do.	Wesley Chamberlain	" 4, "	" 12, "	Resigned May 6, 1862.
Do.	Francis A. Davis	" 4, "	" 12, "	Honorably discharged September 11, 1862.
Do.	James H. Pettay	" 4, "	" 12, "	Resigned December 21, 1861.
Do.	Nathaniel Haughton	" 4, "	" 12, "	Promoted to Captain July 30, 1863.
Do.	Wm. L. Hoyt	July 1, "	July 1, "	Resigned January 23, 1863.
Do.	Arthur Higgins	Oct. 16, "	Oct. 16, "	Promoted to Captain October 20, 1862.
Do.	John D. Merryman	Jan. 9, 1862	Jan. 9, 1862	Prom. Sept. 15, 1862; hon. disch'd Dec. 30, '62.
Do.	Francis D. Sinclair	" 9, "	" 9, "	Resigned March 12, 1862.
Do.	Nathaniel J. Manning	March 12, "	April 10, "	Promoted to Captain.
Do.	Wm. A. Powell	April 27, "	June 3, "	Declined to accept.
Do.	Benj. W. Blandy	May 6, "	" 3, "	Resigned September 19, 1862.
Do.	James Templeton	April 27, "	July 30, "	Resigned February 1, 1863.
Do.	John T. Wood	May 16, "	Aug. 16, "	Revoked.
Do.	George W. Martin	July 30, "	" 16, "	Honorably discharged October 26, 1863.
Do.	Alex. Sinclair	" 30, "	" 16, "	Killed May 6, 1863

RANK.	NAME.	DATE OF RANK.	COM. ISSUED.	REMARKS.
1st Lieutenant	Edward H. Severance	Sept. 11, 1862	Dec. 18, 1862	Revoked.
Do.	Thomas J. Janney	" 19, "	" 30, "	Resigned July 28, 1863.
Do.	Henry H. Mosley	June 30, "	" 30, "	Mustered out March 20, 1865.
Do.	Wm. A. Whitcraft	Sept. 5, "	" 30, "	Died June, 1863.
Do.	Carrington E. Randall	Oct. 20, "	" 30, "	Promoted to Captain.
Do.	Andrew J. Hale	Jan. 23, 1863	Feb. 20, 1863	Revoked; resigned as 2d Lieutenant.
Do.	David R. Hunt	" 23, "	March 30, "	Promoted to Captain.
Do.	Edward C. Culp	Sept. 11, 1862	April 8, "	Promoted to Captain.
Do.	John H. Milman	Feb. 1, 1863	" 21, "	Promoted to Captain.
Do.	Isaac N. Kirk	March 20, "	Jan. 15, "	Discharged March 25, 1864.
Do.	Israel White	Jan. 1, "	" 15, "	Promoted to Captain.
Do.	George C. Edgerton	May 1, "	May 25, "	Honorably discharged November 20, 1863.
Do.	Lewis E. Wilson	July 1, "	Aug. 1, "	Killed at Gettysburg July 1, 1863.
Do.	Joseph H. Hollis	March 15, 1864	March 15, 1864	Killed at Gettysburg July 1, 1863.
Do.	James A. Driggs	" 15, "	" 15, "	Honorably discharged April 12, 1864.
Do.	George N. Holcomb	" 15, "	" 15, "	Promoted to Captain.
Do.	Charles H. King	" 15, "	" 15, "	Resigned April 20, 1864.
Do.	H. McConnaugh	" 15, "	" 15, "	Promoted to Captain.
Do.	Wm. F. Bloon	" 15, "	" 15, "	Mustered out.
Do.	Wm. Malony	" 15, "	" 15, "	Mustered out.
Do.	Chas. W. Ferguson	" 16, "	" 16, "	Promoted to Captain.
Do.	Michael Murray	April 13, "	April 13, "	Promoted to Captain.
Do.	John O. Archibald	May 25, "	May 25, "	Promoted to Captain.
Do.	Wm. P. Scott	" 25, "	" 25, "	Promoted to Captain.
Do.	John H. Kehn	" 25, "	" 25, "	Resigned July 8, 1865.
Do.	Alex. Mattison	" 25, "	" 25, "	Promoted to Captain.
Do.	Elisha Biggerstaff	" 25, "	" 25, "	Promoted to Captain.
Do.	Oliver W. Williams	Aug. 11, "	Aug. 11, "	Honorably discharged April 26, 1865.
Do.	John C. Livensparger	" 11, "	" 11, "	Mustered out with regiment.
Do.	Hezekiah Thomas	" 11, "	" 11, "	Mustered out with regiment.
Do.	Phineas Gino	" 11, "	" 11, "	Resigned January 18, 1865.
Do.	Solomon Ebersole	" 11, "	" 11, "	Deceased.
Do.	S. T. Hutchinson	Oct. 12, "	Oct. 12, "	Honorably discharged March 27, 1865.
Do.	Maurice S. Bell	" 18, "	" 18, "	Mustered out.
Do.	Austin Haughton	Jan. 6, 1865	Jan. 6, 1865	Deceased.
Do.	Ethan W. Guthrie	Feb. 10, "	Feb. 10, "	Died April 8, 1865.
Do.	Wm. L. Fouts	" 10, "	" 10, "	Mustered out with regiment.
Do.	Peter Triquart	May 18, "	May 18, "	Resigned July 25, 1865.
Do.	Samuel R. Stewart	" 18, "	" 18, "	Resigned July 18, 1865.
Do.	Oliver P. Hershey	" 18, "	" 18, "	Resigned March 26, 1866.
Do.	Thomas H. Ferrall	Sept. 4, "	Sept. 4, "	Captain One Hundred and Fourth U. S. C. T.
Do.	Wm. J. Kyle	" 4, "	" 4, "	Mustered out as Regimental Quartermaster.
Do.	Samuel J. Brooks	" 29, "	" 29, "	Mustered out as 2d Lieutenant.
Do.	John Walton	" 29, "	" 29, "	Mustered out with regiment.
Do.	George W. Iden	" 29, "	" 29, "	Mustered out as 2d Lieutenant.
Do.	Dan. J. Crooks	" 29, "	" 29, "	Mustered out as 2d Lieutenant.
Do.	David McGuckin	" 29, "	" 29, "	Mustered out as 2d Lieutenant.
Do.	B. Volney Howard	June 15, 1866	June 15, 186	Absent at date of muster out.
2d Lieutenant	Arthur Higgins	" 4, 1861	July 12, 1861	Promoted to 1st Lieutenant October 16, 1861.
Do.	John D. Merryman	" 4, "	" 12, "	Promoted to 1st Lieutenant January 9, 1862.
Do.	Francis D. Sinclair	" 4, "	" 12, "	Promoted to 1st Lieutenant January 9, 1862.
Do.	Archibald McClellan	" 4, "	" 12, "	Transferred to Twelfth Battery.
Do.	Andrew J. Hale	" 4, "	" 12, "	Resigned December 21, 1862.
Do.	James Templeton	" 4, "	" 12, "	Promoted to 1st Lieutenant April 27, 1862.
Do.	Benj. W. Blandy	" 4, "	" 12, "	Promoted to 1st Lieutenant May 6, 1862.
Do.	John T. Wood	" 4, "	" 22, "	Promoted; resigned June 30, 1862.
Do.	James L. Bale	" 4, "	" 22, "	Resigned October 6, 1862.
Do.	Harlan Milliken	" 4, "	" 12, "	Resigned October 28, 1861.
Do.	Benj. F. Hawkes	July 2, "	" 12, "	Promoted to Lt. Colonel of 78th regiment.
Do.	Alston C. Archibald	Oct. 1, "	Oct. 16, "	Resigned March 12, 1862.
Do.	Nathaniel J. Manning	Jan. 9, 1862	Jan. 9, 1862	Promoted to 1st Lieutenant March 12, 1862.
Do.	Henry H. Mosley	" 9, "	" 9, "	Promoted to 1st Lieutenant June 30, 1862.
Do.	Thomas J. Janney	" 8, "	" 8, "	Promoted to 1st Lieutenant September 19, '62.
Do.	Carrington E. Randall	March 6, "	March 7, "	Promoted to 1st Lieutenant October 20, 1862.
Do.	Wm. A. Whitcraft	" 12, "	April 8, "	Promoted to 1st Lieutenant September 5, '62.
Do.	Alex. Sinclair	" 12, "	" 10, "	Promoted to 1st Lieutenant July 30, 1862.
Do.	Edward C. Culp	May 6, "	June 3, "	Promoted to 1st Lieutenant September 11, '62.
Do.	Samuel P. Houston	April 17, "	Aug. 16, "	Resigned March 6, 1863.
Do.	Edward H. Severance	May 16, "	" 16, "	Promoted; discharged March 20, 1863.
Do.	John H. Milman	July 30, "	" 16, "	Promoted to 1st Lieutenant.
Do.	Wm. H. Davis	Sept. 11, "	Sept. 20, "	Discharged April 2, 1863.
Do.	Alfred G. Cornelius	" 11, "	Dec. 18, "	Promoted Sept. 5, 1862; resigned April 1, 1863.
Do.	Wm. Malony	Oct. 20, "	" 30, "	Promoted to 1st Lieutenant.
Do.	Isaac N. Kirk	June 30, "	" 30, "	Promoted to 1st Lieutenant.
Do.	Lewis E. Wilson	Sept. 19, "	" 30, "	Killed at Gettysburg July 1, 1863.
Do.	J. M. Perry	" 5, "	" 30, "	Resigned April 18, 1863.
Do.	Alfred A. Lampkin	Jan. 23, 1863	Feb. 20, 1863	Resigned November 7, 1863.
Do.	Israel White	March 6, "	March 30, "	Promoted to 1st Lieutenant
Do.	Joseph H. Hollis	Sept. 11, 1862	April 8, "	Promoted to 1st Lieutenant.
Do.	James A. Driggs	Feb. 1, 1863	" 21, "	Promoted to 1st Lieutenant.
Do.	George N. Holcomb	April 1, "	May 25, "	Promoted to 1st Lieutenant.
Do.	Chas. H. King	Jan. 24, "	" 25, "	Promoted to 1st Lieutenant.
Do.	H. McConnaugh	April 18, "	June 15, "	Promoted to 1st Lieutenant.
Do.	Wm. F. Bloon	June 1, "	" 15, "	Promoted to 1st Lieutenant.
Do.	Michael Murray	" 15, "	" 15, "	Promoted to 1st Lieutenant.
Do.	John O. Archibald	July 30, "	July 30, "	Promoted to 1st Lieutenant.
Do.	Wm. P. Scott	March 16, 1864	March 16, 1864	Promoted to 1st Lieutenant.
Do.	John H. Kehn	Nov. 23, 1863	Jan. 12, "	Promoted to 1st Lieutenant.
Do.	Alex. Mattison	Feb. 15, 1864	March 16, "	Promoted to 1st Lieutenant.
Do.	Elisha Biggerstaff	April 13, "	April 13, "	Promoted to 1st Lieutenant.
Do.	Oliver W. Williams	May 25, "	May 25, "	Promoted to 1st Lieutenant.
Do.	John S. Snyder	" 25, "	" 25, "	Mustered out.
Do.	John C. Livensparger	" 25, "	" 25, "	Promoted to 1st Lieutenant.
Do.	Austin Haughton	Oct. 12, "	Oct. 12, "	Promoted to 1st Lieutenant.
Do.	Ethan W. Guthrie	" 12, "	" 12, "	Promoted to 1st Lieutenant.
Do.	Wm. L. Fouts	" 17, "	" 17, "	Promoted to 1st Lieutenant.
Do.	Peter Triquart	" 17, "	" 17, "	Promoted to 1st Lieutenant.
Do.	Samuel R. Stewart	" 17, "	" 17, "	Promoted to 1st Lieutenant.
Do.	Oliver P. Hershey	" 17, "	" 17, "	Promoted to 1st Lieutenant.
Do.	Wm. McFee	" 18, "	" 18, "	Resigned July 15, 1865.
Do.	Thomas H. Ferrall	Nov. 18, "	Nov. 18, "	Promoted to 1st Lieutenant.
Do.	Wm. J. Kyle	" 18, "	" 18, "	Promoted to 1st Lieutenant.

RANK.	NAME.	DATE OF RANK.	COM. ISSUED.	REMARKS.
2d Lieutenant	Samuel J. Brooks	Feb. 10, 1865	Feb. 10, 1865	Promoted to 1st Lieutenant.
Do.	John Walton	" 10, "	" 10, "	Promoted to 1st Lieutenant.
Do.	George W. Iden	May 18, "	May 18, "	Promoted to 1st Lieutenant.
Do.	Dan. J. Crooks	Sept. 4, "	Sept. 4, "	Promoted to 1st Lieutenant.
Do.	D. Volney Howard	" 4, "	" 4, "	Promoted to 1st Lieutenant.
Do.	David McGuckin	" 4, "	" 4, "	Promoted to 1st Lieutenant.
Do.	John S. Dunn	" 4, "	" 4, "	Mustered out with regiment.
Do.	James R. Smith	" 4, "	" 4, "	
Do.	John M. Rhodes	April 2, 1866	April 2, 1866	
Do.	John Weyer	June 15, "	June 15, "	
Do.	James B. Heathorn	" 15, "	" 15, "	
Do.	Samuel G. Shirk	" 15, "	" 15, "	
Do.	John H. Saunders	" 15, "	" 15, "	
Do.	Francis A. Lumbar	" 15, "	" 15, "	
Do.	Garwood P. Lacy	" 15, "	" 15, "	

TWENTY-FIFTH OHIO VOLUNTEER INFANTRY.

THE TWENTY-FIFTH was composed of men from almost every section of the State, and was organized at Camp Chase on the 28th of June, 1861. On the 29th of July it proceeded to Western Virginia, and was stationed along the Baltimore and Ohio Railroad from Oakland to the Ohio River. Scouting parties were sent out from the different posts, and several gangs of bushwhackers were broken up. The regiment was relieved on the 21st of August, and, after a fatiguing march, reported to General Reynolds at Beverly. After a short halt it marched up Cheat Mountain and encamped on the summit. During the fall and winter the troops at this point suffered severely. They were continually on duty, either in the fort or on the picket-line. Sleet or snow fell almost daily; the men of the Twenty-Fifth were totally unprovided with overcoats, and many of them were without shoes or blankets.

The camp at Cheat Mountain remained comparatively quiet until the morning of the 12th of September, when a wagon-train on its way to the valley for rations was surprised and captured. Companies H and D, of the Twenty-Fifth, were sent immediately in pursuit of the Rebels. Company H soon met them, and, being re-enforced, it drove them to their main supports, when it was discovered that the enemy was present in force, under the command of General Robert E. Lee. Preparations were made for a strenuous defense. Every available man was placed on picket-duty, and for eight days the skirmishing was continuous. At the end of this time troops from the valley succeeded in breaking through the Rebel lines, bringing with them to the summit supplies of provisions, and the Rebel commander, seeing the futility of his efforts, withdrew.

On the 3d of October General Reynolds marched with several Regiments from the summit against the Rebel works at Greenbrier. After several hours' fighting the expedition returned to the summit without having accomplished anything of importance. The Twenty-Fifth was engaged, and was the last regiment to leave the field. On the 25th of November it marched into the valley, and went into winter-quarters at Huttonsville. Several companies, under Captain Washburn, were sent to Elkwater. The duty in the valley was light, and an opportunity was afforded for the men to recover from the exposure on the mountain. On the 11th of December a detachment from the regiment, numbering four hundred and sixty men, under Colonel Jones, participated in an expedition against the enemy at Camp Baldwin. At one o'clock on the morning of the 13th the force was distributed for the attack. Colonel Jones, with his detachment, and with detachments from the Thirty-Second Ohio and Thirteenth Indiana, was to advance to the right and rear

GRAVES OF OHIO SOLDIERS. LIBBY PRISON, RICHMOND, VA.

of the enemy's camp, and there await the attack in front. Owing to a succession of blunders the attack was not made in front at the proper time; and the Rebels having discovered the position of Colonel Jones, he was forced to make an immediate attack or to retire. He chose the former course, and at daylight he advanced his line and at once became engaged. The Rebels were driven in, but being re-enforced, they made a stand, and for three hours the fight raged. Three times the Rebels were driven into their cabins, and were compelled to fire from the windows; but at last the troops under Colonel Jones exhausted their ammunition and were compelled to retire, which they did in perfect order, and without molestation from the enemy. In this engagement the regiment lost nine killed and seventy-five severely wounded. On the return march it traveled sixty miles in twenty-six hours. On the 31st the regiment moved on a raid to Huntersville. It marched one hundred and six miles in five days, penetrated far into the enemy's country, met and dispersed considerable numbers of Rebels, and destroyed large quantities of Confederate stores. At the time this expedition was regarded as one of the greatest feats of the war. While at Huttonsville company D was detached permanently as a battery of artillery, and was armed with Wiard's steel guns. It was afterward known as the Twelfth Ohio Battery.

On the 27th of February, 1862, the Twenty-Fifth marched to Beverly. Here the "smooth-bores" were turned over to the ordnance officer, and the regiment was armed with Vincennes rifles. They were very effective pieces, but proved too heavy, and were gradually exchanged for Springfield rifles. On the 1st of April the regiment moved on the Seneca scout. It crossed Cheat and Alleghany Mountains, passed through Circleville, and arrived at Monterey, having marched one hundred and twenty-five miles through a country entirely new to National troops. At Monterey the regiment was joined by a similar expedition, sent by way of Camp Alleghany. On the 12th General Johnston, who had retired from Monterey upon the advance of the National troops, made an attack on that point, but, after a sharp engagement, he was repulsed; and on the arrival of General Milroy with the remainder of the division, he fell back to McDowell. On the 18th Milroy moved forward to McDowell, and the Rebels retreated to Staunton. The troops remained quietly in camp at McDowell until the 7th of May, when a large Rebel force, under Johnston and Jackson, made its appearance. Heavy forces of skirmishers were thrown out, and a general engagement was delayed until the 8th, when General Schenck, with his brigade, arrived, and the battle of Bull-Pasture Mountain was fought. The Twenty-Fifth opened the battle by a charge, in which the enemy was driven from his position. Re-enforcements were sent forward rapidly on both sides, and the battle assumed a serious character. It continued till after nightfall, and, as darkness settled down upon the mountain, a blazing circle of light from ten thousand muskets still revealed the position of the opposing armies. It was deemed expedient to fall back to Franklin, and the troops were withdrawn gradually. The Twenty-Fifth remained until the last regiment had retired, and then it covered the retreat. Its loss in this engagement was nine killed and fifty-six wounded.

On the 26th of May the regiment accompanied General Fremont on his march from Franklin to Strasburg, and thence up the Shenandoah Valley in pursuit of Jackson, and participated in the battle of Cross Keys, with a loss of eight killed, fifty-four wounded, and two missing. After a short rest at Strasburg the regiment, in July, passed with Sigel's corps into Eastern Virginia, and participated in General Pope's campaign along the lines of the Rappahannock, and from the Rapidan to the plains of Manassas, where, on the 29th and 30th of August, it engaged in the second battle of Bull Run, with a loss of ten killed, seventy-eight wounded, and twenty-two missing. On the evening of the 30th the regiment fell back to Centerville, and on the 3d of September it moved, by way of Fairfax C. H., to Upton Hill, having marched, since the 8th of August, two hundred and twenty miles, having been under fire fourteen successive days on the Rappahannock, and having participated in the second battle of Bull Run. From this time until the spring of 1863 the Twenty-Fifth was engaged in marches and counter-marches, and in building numerous sets of winter-quarters, until at last it settled down quietly near Brooke's Station. Battalion drill was practiced daily, and every effort was made to prepare the troops for the spring campaign.

On the 27th of April, 1863, the army broke camp and started on the Chancellorsville campaign, and on the 30th it encamped around Chancellorsville. Never was a march better conducted, and it is worthy of note that the Twenty-Fifth left Brooke's Station with four hundred and forty-three men and took four hundred and forty-four men into camp at Chancellorsville, one man having joined from hospital, and not one having straggled from the ranks during the march. The regiment was in the Second Brigade of the First Division of the Eleventh Corps. The First Brigade of the division occupied the extreme right, and the Second Brigade was on the immediate left of the first. The picket-line extended along the front, but did not cover the right of the division. Only two or three sentinels were posted on the right, and these but a short distance from the outer regiments. Thus lay on the afternoon of May 2d the right wing of an army of one hundred thousand men. Colonels Richardson and Lee, of the Twenty-Fifth and Fifty-Fifth Ohio, felt the impending danger and quietly sent some tried scouts into the wilderness to the right of the division. They soon returned with the intelligence that the Rebels were massing heavily on the right and rear of the corps, and that there were no pickets between the two armies. The two Ohio Colonels hurried with this intelligence to division head-quarters, but the General commanding told them that their men "were probably scared," and sent them back to their regiments.

An hour afterward and Stonewall Jackson with his veteran troops came down upon the unprepared division. Several regiments in the First Brigade had their guns in stack, and many of the men were eating their supper. The surprise was complete. No solitary picket-shot told of the approaching danger, no rattling skirmish heralded the coming storm; but one solid shot, crashing through the Second Brigade and post division head-quarters, was followed by the thunder of twenty thousand muskets and the deafening roar of artillery. The First Brigade gave way in confusion, the men not stopping to unbuckle their knapsacks, but cutting the straps with their knives. The Twenty-Fifth deployed, changed front, and moved forward some one hundred yards, exposed to a merciless fire, under the disadvantage of having men from other regiments breaking through its ranks. The Fifty-Fifth and Seventy-Fifth Ohio joined the ranks of the Twenty-Fifth, and these three regiments held their position until the broken fragments of the First Brigade had passed to their rear and the enemy had encircled them on three sides, and then they, too, fell back. The next morning the corps was reorganized, and it remained in the trenches until the 5th, when, with the army, it recrossed the river and went into its old camp at Brooke's Station. In this engagement the regiment lost seventeen killed, one hundred and twenty wounded, and thirty-seven missing.

On the 27th of June the regiment started on the Gettysburg campaign, with General Barlow in command of the division and General Ames in command of the brigade. The Eleventh Corps passed over the Bull Run battle-field, crossed the Potomac at Edwards's Ferry, marched through Maryland, and arrived at Emmettsburg on the 29th. On the 1st of July the corps moved toward Gettysburg, with Barlow's division in advance. Upon reaching the town the division was placed in position and became engaged almost immediately, and for a short time drove the enemy before it. The Twenty-Fifth was ordered to support Battery G, of the Fourth United States Artillery, and it took position under a most trying cannonade. Soon a general advance was ordered, and the entire division moved forward, but after fighting obstinately for an hour it fell back to Cemetery Hill. Here the Twenty-Fifth, numbering forty-five men and commanded by a Second-Lieutenant, was deployed as skirmishers on the outskirts of the town, while the remainder of the division was placed behind stone fences. On the 2d and 3d the regiment still occupied the advanced lines and suffered severely from sharp-shooters, and on the morning of the 4th it led the advance into Gettysburg. The majority of the officers had been killed or wounded, and the regiment was commanded by a First-Lieutenant, who had been wounded in the first day's battle. The Twenty-Fifth went into action with two hundred and twenty men, and lost twenty killed, one hundred and thirteen wounded, and fifty missing.

On the afternoon of the 5th the regiment moved in pursuit of the Rebels, marching through Emmettsburg, Frederick City, Middletown, Boonsboro', and Hagerstown. At the latter city the division supported Kilpatrick's cavalry in a lively skirmish, driving the Rebel cavalry and infantry through Hagerstown to their main supports. On the 25th Warrenton Junction was reached, where the regiment remained in camp until the 6th of August, when, with its division, it moved for the Department of the South, and took up quarters on Folly Island. The regiment at this time numbered seventy-two men and was commanded by a Lieutenant. It subsequently removed to Morris Island and took part in the siege of Fort Wagner. After the capture of the fort it went into camp on Folly Island beach and an opportunity was afforded for rest and recuperation.

On the 1st of January, 1864, the regiment re-enlisted, and on the 15th it started for Ohio on veteran furlough. It was furloughed from Camp Taylor, near Cleveland, on the 3d of February, and on the 5th of March it rendezvoused at Camp Chase. Many recruits were added to the regiment and one entirely new company, company B, was consolidated with company C, and the new company was designated company B. On the 16th the regimental flags, which had passed through twenty battles, and under which eighteen color-bearers had been killed or wounded, were presented to Governor Brough for the State archives, and the regiment received a beautiful stand of new colors. The regiment left Camp Chase on the same day and was transported by way of Cleveland, Buffalo, New York, Philadelphia, and Washington, to Camp Grant, Virginia, where it remained a month preparing for the field, and on the 23d of April it embarked at Alexandria on the "Admiral Dupont," and arrived at Hilton Head, South Carolina, on the 26th.

On the 28th it went on duty on the picket-line which formed the inside defenses of the Sea Islands. The posts were reduced to the least possible number, and yet the men were frequently on duty several days in succession. This, together with the malaria from the swamps, produced much sickness, and before cold weather came nearly every member of the regiment had been prostrated. On the 25th of September companies A, K, and G, were ordered to Fort Pulaski, Georgia, where they remained until the 23d of October, when they rejoined the regiment, and the next day it was relieved from the picket-line and was ordered into camp a short distance from Hilton Head for rest. On the 2d of November nearly three hundred recruits joined the regiment, including one entire company, which was designated company D. The Twenty-Fifth now presented a good line; a regular course of drill was inaugurated and sustained until the 26th, when orders were received to prepare for immediate service.

On the 28th of November the regiment left Hilton Head in the Coast Division on an expedition, with the Charleston and Savannah Railroad as the objective point. Several steamers ran aground and it was not until the afternoon of the next day that the troops were landed at Boyd's Neck, on the main land. On the same evening the column moved forward toward Grahamsville, but it became bewildered in the darkness and about midnight encamped near a church. Early the next morning the enemy was discovered. Companies A and B were deployed as skirmishers and the regiment was placed in line. The right wing was ordered to silence the enemy's artillery by a flank movement. This it did and then returned to its place in line. The regiment moved forward steadily in support of its skirmishers. The enemy retreated to his works, and the brigade moved forward to charge the position. The Twenty-Fifth was placed on the extreme right of the second line, the formation being "column by division, right in front." The regiment overtook the first line and deployed in support of a New York regiment. A charge was ordered, but the first line was broken up considerably in crossing a swamp, and could not take the benefit of the advantage gained. The Twenty-Fifth crossed in perfect order, and the sight of a solid front, backed by a well-directed volley, caused the Rebels to give way. The regiment changed front forward on the tenth company, and continued to advance through an almost impenetrable thicket, and under a terrible fire, until within two hundred yards of the enemy's works. A New York regiment was to support the Twenty-Fifth, but instead it moved to the rear, and for several hours the Twenty-Fifth sustained its position, being altogether out of ammunition a portion of the time. At last two regiments came up, and Colonel Haughton, of the Twenty-Fifth, proposed to charge if the Colonel on the right would support him. But that officer declined to advance without orders, and so the troops were compelled to retire to the first line of battle. The Twenty-

Fifth was again almost out of ammunition, but it received a supply in time to check an attempted flank attack. After dark the troops withdrew from the field to the cover of the gunboats. In this engagement the regiment's loss in killed and wounded was one hundred and fifty, and of these sixteen were commissioned officers.

On the morning of the 4th of December the regiment embarked on some small steamers and proceeding some distance up the Coosa River disembarked on the main land, and by a rapid march flanked and captured an entire Rebel battery. One gun and caisson were hauled by hand to Port Royal Ferry, and the others were destroyed. On the 6th the regiment, with the brigade, proceeded on steamers up Broad River and effected a landing on Devereaux Neck. The troops pushed forward rapidly and soon encountered the enemy posted advantageously on the opposite side of a marsh, which extended the whole length of his line. The Twenty-Fifth moved forward and by the aid of the other regiments the works were carried in good style. The enemy retreated in some disorder, but made a gallant stand on the west side of the Charleston and Savannah Pike, but the terrific fire of the Twenty-Fifth again compelled him to fall back, leaving the killed and wounded on the field.

On the 8th a reconnoissance was made and the enemy was found intrenched strongly on the Charleston and Savannah Railroad, with artillery of considerable caliber. The Twenty-Fifth was ordered to cut a road through dense woods to the railroad, in order that the artillery might destroy the trains. A skirmish-line was thrown forward, supported by several regiments, and the Twenty-Fifth followed immediately after, felling the trees in regular backwoodsman style. After clearing the road for about a mile, the troops became actively engaged. Fighting continued, at intervals, during the day, and at night the troops withdrew to a well-fortified camp about two miles east of the railroad. During the day the regiment lost fifty-four men killed and wounded. The approach of the Fifteenth and Seventeenth Corps, of Sherman's army, compelled the Rebels to evacuate their position on the railroad, and a few days after the regiment, with its division, moved up the coast. Skirmishing was frequent and the march was a very severe one. On the 26th of February, 1865, the regiment crossed the Ashley River, and marched into Charleston, quartering in the South Carolina Depot.

On the last day of February the regiment moved by railroad to Goose Creek, twenty miles from Charleston, with the One Hundred and Seventh Ohio and Fifty-Sixth New York, and marched without interruption nearly to the Santee River. Returning, it joined the main portion of the division at Briggin's Church, and the whole column marched down the north side of Cooper River, and crossed the bay into Charleston on the evening of the 10th. The regiment went into quarters in the depot and remained until the 12th, when it crossed the bay and went into camp at Mount Pleasant. On the 2d of April the regiment was placed on a steamer and the next day it disembarked at Georgetown, South Carolina. Several regiments had already arrived, and orders were issued to march on the 5th. The force was commanded by General E. E. Potter, and the expedition was ordered by General Sherman for the purpose of destroying all railroad communication and rolling stock in Central and Eastern South Carolina. The raid was successful, and in addition to the railroads immense quantities of cotton were destroyed. Engagements were fought at Dingle's Mills, Statsburg, Rafting Creek, Boykin's Mills, Swift Creek, and Red Hill. On the 20th of April sixteen locomotives and two hundred and forty-five cars, loaded with ammunition and clothing, were totally destroyed, and the next day the little army marched toward the coast, one hundred and twenty-five miles distant. While encamping on Gevernor Manning's plantation for dinner a staff officer from General Beauregard came to the lines with a flag of truce, and stated that the war had probably closed, as Lee had surrendered to Grant, and Sherman and Johnston had agreed to a cessation of hostilities. Great was the joy in camp, and the remaining one hundred miles to the coast was marched in three days, the last two days each man having issued to him, as a ration, two ears of corn. The troops reached Georgetown on the 25th of April, and on the 28th the regiment was placed on the "W. W. Coit" and taken to Charleston, and from there it went into its old camp at Mount Pleasant.

On the 6th of May the regiment again received marching orders and on the same day it proceeded to Charleston. The next day it moved into the interior, through Summerville, Ridgeville, Branchville, and Orangeburg, to Columbia, where it arrived on the 25th and camped in the grounds of the South Carolina College. Here the regiment performed garrison-duty. In September the counties of Fairfield, Newberry, Edgefield, Lexington, and Richland, were designated as a subdistrict, Lieutenant-Colonel Haughton commanding, and were garrisoned by the Twenty-Fifth. During the fall and winter the duty was arduous in the extreme. The country became infested with bands of outlaws, and several collisions occurred between them and the soldiers. On the 27th of December a private of company C was murdered at Newberry. The murderer is still at large. Several of the soldiers were wounded at different times and many attempts at assassination were made. Bands of outlaws roamed through the country, killing the negroes and committing other depredations, yet receiving such protection from a large mass of the citizens that their arrest was almost impossible. On the 30th of April, 1866, the regiment removed to Summerville and garrisoned the surrounding country; and in May a portion of the regiment was detached for garrison-duty on the Sea Islands. On the 6th of June orders were received for the regiment to proceed to Tod Barracks for muster-out. The next day it left Charleston on the steamer Flambeau, for New York, and from there it was transferred by way of the New York Central Railroad, to Columbus, Ohio, arriving on the 12th. On the 16th the regiment held its last parade in front of the Capitol, the regimental colors were presented to Governor Cox, and on the 18th of June, 1866, after having been in the service over five years, the Twenty-Fifth was mustered out and discharged.

26th REGIMENT OHIO VOLUNTEER INFANTRY.

ROSTER, THREE YEARS' SERVICE.

RANK.	NAME.	DATE OF RANK.	COM. ISSUED.	REMARKS.
Colonel	EDWARD P. FYFFE	June 10, 1861	June 10, 1861	Honorably discharged December 18, 1863.
Lt. Colonel	Ephraim R. Eckley	" 10, "	" 10, "	Appointed Colonel of 80th Ohio Vol. Infantry.
Do.	Wm. H. Young	Jan. 1, 1862	Jan. 8, 1862	Resigned March 28, 1864.
Do.	Wm. Squires	April 2, 1864	April 2, 1864	Resigned November 17, 1864.
Do.	Wm. Clark	Dec. 9, "	Dec. 9, "	Mustered out with regiment.
Major	Christo'r N. Dagenfeld	June 10, 1861	June 10, 1861	Resigned December 4, 1861.
Do.	Wm. H. Squires	Dec. 7, 1862	Dec. 19, 1862	Promoted to Lieutenant-Colonel.
Do.	Norris T. Peatman	April 2, 1864	April 2, 1864	Resigned October 26, 1864.
Do.	James Spence	Feb. 10, 1865	Feb. 10, 1865	Mustered out with regiment.
Surgeon	M. M. Stimmel	July 2, 1861	July 2, 1861	Resigned May 14, 1863; dis'bility rem'd July 9.
Do.	Wm. B. McGavran	May 11, 1863	June 4, 1863	Resigned September 17, 1864.
Do.	David Rush	Sept. 26, 1864	Sept. 26, 1864	Resigned June 20, 1865.
Do.	Lewis Slusser	July 15, 1865	July 15, 1865	Mustered out with regiment.
Ass't Surgeon	Andrew Sabine	" 2, 1861	" 2, 1861	Resigned February 19, 1863.
Do.	Wm. H. Cretcher	March 11, 1863	March 11, 1863	Resigned May 11, 1863.
Do.	Wm. B. McGavran	" 12, "	" 12, "	Promoted to Surgeon.
Do.	D. C. Hall	June 15, "	June 15, "	Declined.
Do.	David Rush	July 20, "	July 20, "	Promoted to Surgeon
Do.	F. W. Inman	Sept. 26, 1864	Sept. 26, 1864	Declined.
Do.	James G. Carr	Oct. 3, "	Oct. 3, "	Absent on sick leave at muster out of regt.
Chaplain	L. H. Long	July 5, 1861	July 8, 1861	Resigned March 4, 1862.
Do.	Emmor Kimber	March 17, 1862	March 17, 1862	Resigned September 29, 1862.
Captain	J. W. C. Smith	June 5, 1861	July 25, 1861	Resigned October 30, 1861.
Do.	Raymond Allston	" 5, "	" 25, "	Resigned October 10, 1861.
Do.	Jesse Meredith	" 5, "	" 25, "	Resigned August 11, 1862.
Do.	Wm. H. Seaton	" 5, "	" 25, "	Resigned December 5, 1862.
Do.	Sylvester M. Hewett	" 5, "	" 25, "	Promoted to Major 32d regiment.
Do.	John Ferguson	July 1, "	" 25, "	Promoted to Major 30th regiment.
Do.	Samuel C. Rook	" 4, "	" 25, "	Resigned March 6, 1863.
Do.	Samuel D. Henderson	" 11, "	" 25, "	Promoted by President April 20, 1863.
Do.	Washington C. Appler	" 20, "	" 25, "	Resigned October 30, 1861.
Do.	Wm. H. Squires	" 22, "	" 25, "	Promoted to Major.
Do.	Norris T. Peatman	" 31, "	" 31, "	Promoted to Major.
Do.	James K. Ewart	" 29, "	Nov. 12, "	Resigned December 2, 1862.
Do.	Samuel H. Ewing	Nov. 8, "	" 12, "	Mustered out.
Do.	John H. James, jr.	Dec. 12, "	Dec. 12, "	Resigned February 12, 1863.
Do.	E. A. Hicks	" 12, "	" 12, "	Resigned July 10, 1862.
Do.	Wm. H. Ross	Aug. 11, 1862	Nov. 25, 1862	Died September 19, 1863.
Do.	Lewis D. Adair	July 10, "	" 25, "	Mustered out.
Do.	James R. Hume	Dec. 2, "	Dec. 19, "	Declined promotion; remained on Brig. Gen. Hascall's staff.
Do.	Wm. Clark	" 5, "	" 19, "	Promoted to Lieutenant-Colonel.
Do.	Alexander Frazier	" 7, "	" 19, "	Mustered out.
Do.	Nathaniel Potter	Feb. 12, 1863	March 6, 1863	Mustered out.
Do.	James R. Warren	Dec. 2, 1862	....	Resigned January 24, 1864.
Do.	Wm. Baldwin	March 6, 1863	April 8, 1863	Mustered out January 28, 1865.
Do.	Samuel H. Hamilton	April 6, "	May 12, "	Discharged June 29, 1864.
Do.	James R. Hume	Sept. 20, "	Dec. 8, 1864	Resigned as 1st Lieutenant January 24, 1864.
Do.	James A. Barr	April 2, 1864	April 2, "	Mustered out January 25, 1865.
Do.	Asahel R. Franklin	" 2, "	" 2, "	Mustered out.
Do.	James Spence	" 2, "	" 2, "	Promoted to Major.
Do.	Morris Renick	Dec. 9, "	Dec. 9, "	Declined promotion.
Do.	Lyman B. Foster	" 9, "	" 9, "	Discharged as 1st Lieutenant July 5, 1865.
Do.	Luther Timberlake	" 9, "	" 9, "	Declined promotion.
Do.	Philip M. Ogan	" 9, "	" 9, "	Mustered out with regiment.
Do.	E. Guy	" 9, "	" 9, "	Resigned March 1, 1865.
Do.	Cyrus Hill	" 9, "	" 9, "	Declined promotion.
Do.	Samuel Platt	Feb. 10, 1865	Feb. 10, 1865	Killed June 4, 1864.
Do.	Justin A. Goodhue	" 10, "	" 10, "	Mustered out February 18, 1865.
Do.	August Spetnagle	" 10, "	" 10, "	Mustered out as Quartermaster.
Do.	Jerry E. Coomer	" 10, "	" 10, "	Resigned June 8, 1865.
Do.	Benj. Crane	" 10, "	" 10, "	Mustered out with regiment.
Do.	John Sharp	" 10, "	" 10, "	Mustered out with regiment.
Do.	Walden Kelly	" 28, "	" 28, "	Mustered out with regiment.
Do.	Charles D. Brusman	" 28, "	" 28, "	Mustered out with regiment,
1st Lieutenant	Norris T. Peatman	June 5, 1861	June 25, 1861	Promoted to Captain.
Do.	Samuel H. Ewing	" 5, "	" 25, "	Promoted to Captain.
Do.	E. E. Hicks	" 5, "	" 25, "	Promoted to Captain.
Do.	Charles H. Bean	" 5, "	" 25, "	Resigned November 29, 1861.
Do.	Henry C. Brumback	" 5, "	" 25, "	Resigned December 27, 1861.
Do.	Peter Dennis	July 1, "	" 25, "	Resigned March 20, 1862.
Do.	Wm. H. Ross	" 4, "	" 25, "	Promoted to Captain.
Do.	Henry Hickborn	" 11, "	" 25, "	Resigned April 1, 1862.
Do.	Lewis D. Adair	" 20, "	" 25, "	Promoted to Captain.
Do.	James R. Hume	" 22, "	" 25, "	Promoted on Brig. Gen. Hascall's staff.
Do.	Francis M. Leiffer	" 21, "	" 25, "	Resigned June 23, 1862.
Do.	John H. James, jr.	June 29, "	" 29, "	Promoted to Captain.
Do.	John L. Watson	Nov. 8, "	Nov. 8, "	Resigned June 16, 1862.
Do.	Andrew J. Kendall	Dec. 12, "	Dec. 12, "	Resigned December 7, 1862.
Do.	Wm. Clark	" 12, "	" 12, "	Promoted to Captain.
Do.	Andrew J. Fletter	" 23, "	" 23, "	Resigned March 20, 1862.
Do.	James E. Gudman	" 23, "	" 23, "	Resigned April 26, 1863.
Do.	Alexander Frazier	March 20, 1862	April 10, 1862	Promoted to Captain.
Do.	David McClelland	" 20, "	" 10, "	Resigned June 18, 1862.
Do.	Charles K. Smith	April 1, "	" 10, "	Resigned June 15, 1862.
Do.	Nathaniel Potter	" 1, "	May 5, "	Promoted to Captain.

RANK.	NAME.	DATE OF RANK.	COM. ISSUED.	REMARKS.
1st Lieutenant	James R. Warren	April 26, 1862	June 3, 1862	Promoted to Captain.
Do.	David McClelland	June 16, "	Aug. 12, "	Killed Dec. 31, 1862, at Stone River, Tenn.
Do.	James A. Barr	" 15, "	Nov. 25, "	Promoted to Captain.
Do.	Wm. Baldwin	July 10, "	" 25, "	Promoted to Captain.
Do.	Asahel R. Franklin	June 16, "	Dec. 19, "	Promoted to Captain.
Do.	Marcus P. Bestow	" 25, "	" 19, "	Resigned February 19, 1863.
Do.	Samuel H. Hamilton	Aug. 11, "	" 19, "	Promoted.
Do.	Wm. M. Este	Dec. 5, "	" 19, "	Resigned April 1, 1863
Do.	James Spence	" 7, "	" 19, "	Promoted to Captain.
Do.	James W. Burbridge	" 7, "	" 19, "	Revoked.
Do.	Francis M. Williams	" 2, "	March 26, 1863	Killed at Chickamauga September 19, 1863.
Do.	Morris Renick	" 7, "	" 6, "	Mustered out with regiment.
Do.	Benj. F. Grafton	" 3, "	" 6, "	Resigned November 8, 1864.
Do.	James G. Morrow	Feb. 19, 1863	" 6, "	Honorably discharged January 14, 1864.
Do.	Lyman B. Foster	" 12, "	" 6, "	Promoted to Captain.
Do.	James W. Burbridge	April 25, "	April 29, "	Killed September 19, 1863.
Do.	Luther Timberlake	" 1, "	" 29, "	Mustered out January 23, 1863.
Do.	Benj. W. Shotwell	" 6, "	May 12, "	Resigned September 13, 1864.
Do.	Wm. M. Young	" 2, 1864	April 2, 1864	Honorably discharged November 15, 1865.
Do.	Philip M. Ogan	" 2, "	" 2, "	Promoted to Captain.
Do.	Wm. B. Johnson	" 2, "	" 2, "	Honorably discharged October 19, 1864.
Do.	W. N. Hoge	" 2, "	" 2, "	Mustered out.
Do.	E. Guy	" 2, "	" 2, "	Promoted to Captain.
Do.	Cyrus Hill	" 2, "	" 2, "	Mustered out January 23, 1865.
Do.	Samuel Platt	" 2, "	" 2, "	Promoted to Captain.
Do.	Justin A. Goodhue	Dec. 9, "	Dec. 9, "	Promoted to Captain.
Do.	August Spetnagle	" 9, "	" 9, "	Promoted to Captain.
Do.	Samuel Milliken	" 9, "	" 9, "	Declined to accept.
Do.	Jerry E. Coomer	" 9, "	" 9, "	Promoted to Captain.
Do.	Benj. Crane	" 9, "	" 9, "	Promoted to Captain.
Do.	Wm. Jones	" 9, "	" 9, "	Declined promotion.
Do.	John Sharp	" 9, "	" 9, "	Promoted to Captain.
Do.	Walden Kelley	" 9, "	" 9, "	Promoted to Captain.
Do.	John H. Ostler	" 9, "	" 9, "	Honorably discharged October 4, 1865.
Do.	Ed. C. Miller	" 9, "	" 9, "	Mustered out with regiment.
Do.	Charles D. Brusman	" 9, "	" 9, "	Promoted to Captain.
Do.	Samuel Chestnut	Feb. 10, 1865	Feb. 10, 1865	Mustered out with regiment.
Do.	E. F. Wilkins	" 10, "	" 10, "	Mustered out with regiment.
Do.	Wm. H. Bevans	" 10, "	" 10, "	
Do.	John D. Shollstall	" 10, "	" 10, "	Mustered out with regiment.
Do.	John M. Stutsman	" 10, "	" 10, "	Mustered out with regiment.
Do.	David Brooks	" 10, "	" 10, "	Mustered out with regiment.
Do.	John F. Raper	" 9, "	" 9, "	Retained in service per Special Order No. 55.
2d Lieutenant	Francis M. Leffler	June 15, 1861	July 25, 1861	Promoted to 1st Lieutenant.
Do.	John L. Watson	" 15, "	" 25, "	Promoted to 1st Lieutenant.
Do.	Wm. Clark	" 15, "	" 25, "	Promoted to 1st Lieutenant.
Do.	Andrew J. Fletter	" 15, "	" 25, "	Promoted to 1st Lieutenant.
Do.	James Godman	" 15, "	" 25, "	Promoted to 1st Lieutenant.
Do.	Alexander Frazier	July 1, "	" 25, "	Promoted to 1st Lieutenant.
Do.	Charles K. Smith	" 1, "	" 25, "	Promoted to 1st Lieutenant; Quartermaster.
Do.	David McClelland	" 4, "	" 25, "	Promoted to 1st Lieutenant.
Do.	Nathaniel Potter	" 11, "	" 25, "	Promoted to 1st Lieutenant.
Do.	Wm. Colvin	" 20, "	" 25, "	Resigned March 15, 1862.
Do.	James R. Warren	" 22, "	" 25, "	Promoted to 1st Lieutenant.
Do.	Marcus P. Bestow	" 31, "	" 31, "	Promoted to 1st Lieutenant.
Do.	Asahel R. Franklin	Nov. 8, "	Nov. 8, "	Promoted to 1st Lieutenant.
Do.	Wm. M. Este	Dec. 17, "	Dec. 17, "	Promoted to 1st Lieutenant.
Do.	Wm. Baldwin	" 23, "	" 23, "	Promoted to 1st Lieutenant.
Do.	Samuel H. Hamilton	" 23, "	" 23, "	Promoted to 1st Lieutenant.
Do.	James W. Burbridge	March 15, 1862	March 28, 1862	Promoted to 1st Lieut. Dec. '62; resigned Dec. 13, 1862
Do.	Wm. M. Young	" 20, "	May 1, "	Promoted to 1st Lieutenant.
Do.	Morris Renick	" 20, "	" 1, "	Promoted to 1st Lieutenant.
Do.	Benj. F. Grafton	April 1, "	" 1, "	Promoted to 1st Lieutenant.
Do.	Francis M. Williams	" 26, "	June 3, "	Promoted to 1st Lieutenant.
Do.	James G. Morrow	June 16, "	Dec. 19, "	Promoted to 1st Lieutenant.
Do.	Lyman B. Foster	" 23, "	" 19, "	Promoted to 1st Lieutenant.
Do.	George H. Louder	July 10, "	" 19, "	Resigned January 25, 1863.
Do.	Luther Timberlake	Aug. 11, "	" 19, "	Promoted to 1st Lieutenant.
Do.	Benj. W. Shotwell	Dec. 5, "	" 19, "	Promoted to 1st Lieutenant.
Do.	Philip M. Ogan	Jan. 25, 1863	Feb. 16, 1863	Promoted to 1st Lieutenant.
Do.	Wm. D. Johnson	Dec. 7, "	March 6, "	Promoted to 1st Lieutenant.
Do.	John W. Ruly	" 31, "	" 6, "	Killed September 20, 1863.
Do.	W. N. Hoge	" 2, "	" 6, "	Promoted to 1st Lieutenant.
Do.	E. Guy	Feb. 19, "	" 6, "	Promoted to 1st Lieutenant.
Do.	Cyrus Hill	" 12, "	" 6, "	Promoted to 1st Lieutenant.
Do.	Samuel Platt	April 1, "	May 12, "	Promoted to 1st Lieutenant.
Do.	Jacob Matthias	" 6, "	" 12, "	Resigned November 6, 1864.
Do.	Justin A. Goodhue	" 6, "	" 12, "	Promoted to 1st Lieutenant.

TWENTY-SIXTH OHIO VOLUNTEER INFANTRY.

THE TWENTY-SIXTH OHIO was organized at Camp Chase, Ohio, in July, 1861, and was recruited from the counties of Butler, Ross, Delaware, Guernsey, Mahoning, Champaign, Scioto, and Madison. As soon as the organization was complete the regiment was ordered to the Upper Kanawha Valley, where it performed its first service. The regiment remained in that valley until the January following, most of the time engaged in severe scouting-duty. In the movement by General Rosecrans on Sewell Mountain, the Twenty-Sixth claims to have led the advance, and to have brought up the rear on the retreat from that point. Although no great battle occurred in which it might have shown its powers, yet, by hardy endurance of fatigue and exposure, and patient forbearance under great privations, its fidelity when duty called, and bearing when danger threatened, established for it a superior reputation.

In January, 1862, Lieutenant-Colonel Eckley was mustered out, to take command of the Eightieth Ohio, and William H. Young, of the Seventy-Ninth, previously Professor of Mathematics and Civil Engineering in the Ohio University, was transferred to fill the vacancy. About the same time the regiment was transferred from the Department of West Virginia to the Department of the Ohio, soon after named the Department of the Cumberland. It was brigaded with the Fifteenth, Seventeenth, and Fiftieth Indiana Regiments, under command of Colonel M. S. Hascall (soon after made Brigadier), and placed in Brigadier-General Thomas J. Wood's division, of which it constituted a part until October, 1863. On the organization of the Army of the Cumberland into corps, at Louisville, in September, 1862, the division was assigned to the Twenty-First Corps, and so remained until October, 1863, when the Twentieth and Twenty-First Corps were consolidated with the Fourth Corps, and the Twenty-Sixth Regiment became a part of the Second Brigade (Wagner's), Second Division (then Sheridan's), of the Fourth Corps.

The regiment formed a part of the column of advance on Nashville, after the capture of Fort Donelson, and shared the forced marches, hardships, and privations of General Buell's army in its advance to Pittsburg Landing to relieve General Grant. While at Nashville General Wood, in the particulars of discipline, drill, and police arrangements, as well as personal cleanliness, commended, in general orders, the Twenty-Sixth Ohio as a model for the other regiments in his division. In the advance from Shiloh, through the swamps of Northern Mississippi, upon Corinth, the Twenty-Sixth occupied the front line, and was among the first to enter the place. During the summer of 1862, while the little and ill-supplied army of General Buell was, by forced marches and counter-marches, holding its line of three hundred miles, the Twenty-Sixth bore its full share of the burdens and hardships of that fruitless campaign. During much of this time Colonel Fyffe was commanding the brigade, leaving the regiment to the command of Lieutenant-Colonel Young. About the last of August, 1862, the Twenty-Sixth, under Lieutenant-Colonel Young, together with the Seventeenth and Fifty-Eighth Indiana, about fourteen hundred strong, all under Colonel Fyffe, had a slight engagement, near McMinnville, Tennessee, with Forrest's brigade of cavalry, numbering about fifteen hundred. Colonel Young led the attack, before which the Rebels soon gave way, leaving in his hands, among other prisoners, General Forrest's body-servant, battle-horse, and private carriage. This horse, a splendid blooded gray, was subsequently ridden by Colonel Young at the battle of Perryville, in command of the Fifty-Sixth Ohio, and was lost at the battle of Stone River. In the memorable forced marches of Buell and Bragg, from the Tennessee to the Ohio, and thence toward Cumberland Gap, in the fall of 1862, the Twenty-Sixth Ohio performed its whole duty. For the greater part of this time the regiment was under the command of Major C. M. Dagenfeld, Colonel Fyffe commanding the brigade, and Lieutenant-Colonel Young the Sixty-Fifth Ohio.

On the 26th of December, 1862, General Rosecrans commenced his advance from Nashville against Murfreesboro'. During this engagement the Twenty-Sixth Ohio, under Major Squires, supported in part by the Fifty-Eighth Indiana, made a gallant and successful charge, storming and driving from a strong position in the village of Lavergne a far larger force of the enemy, that for many hours had held the left wing of the army at bay, and seriously impeded the execution of the movements in progress. Later in the day, Captain Ewing, of this command, with his two companies of skirmishers, charged the enemy's retreating rear-guard, drove them from and extinguished the fire of a burning bridge, to the great advantage of our advancing columns. This gallant deed was thought of sufficient importance to entitle the regiment to especial mention in reports, but the name of a Kentucky regiment was mentioned by mistake as the one that performed this important and gallant service.

At the battle of Stone River the Twenty-Sixth, under Major Squires, was one of several regiments which stood firm against the charge of the Rebels on the 26th, when three-fourths of the National forces on the right had given way and were in full flight; and though for many hours the heavily-massed columns of the enemy were hurled against it, they still stood their ground; and the Twenty-Sixth Ohio formed the apex of that little convex line of battle that all Bragg's victorious army could not break or bend. At this time the command lost one-third of its strength in killed and wounded. Major Squires was presented with an elegant sword from the command, in appreciation of his services in this battle.

About the 1st of January, 1862, Colonel Young returned to duty, and again took command of the regiment, which he retained until his resignation, in March, 1863. Colonel Fyffe, during this time, was in command of the brigade, or "on leave," until December, 1863, when he was honorably discharged on account of disability. He was afterward attached to the Veteran Reserve Corps.

In the advance on Bragg's lines at Tullahoma and Shelbyville the regiment bore a conspicuous and honorable part. In the advance on Chattanooga, in December, 1863, the Twenty-Sixth led the advance of Crittenden's corps (which first entered the place), Colonel Young leading the regiment in skirmish-line over the northern bluff of Lookout Mountain, the subsequent scene of Hooker's memorable battle. At Chickamauga the Twenty-Sixth was in the thickest and bloodiest of the fight, where it acquitted itself with honor. Its loss in killed and wounded was very severe, being nearly three-fifths of the number engaged. Colonel Young's horse and equipments were badly cut up by bullets. Captain Ewing (Acting Major) had his horse killed under him, himself wounded, and was captured. Captain Ross, Lieutenants Williams, Burbridge and Ruly were killed, and Captains Hamilton and Potter, and Lieutenants Platt, Hoge, Morrow, and Shotwell wounded. Company H lost all its officers, and twenty-one out of twenty-four men. There was no surrender by sound men.

At the storming of Mission Ridge by the Army of the Cumberland, the Twenty-Sixth Ohio maintained its good reputation. It occupied nearly the center of the front line of assault (Wagner's brigade, Sheridan's division), and was there called upon to sustain the concentated fire of the Rebel circular line of forty cannon and thousands of muskets. The assault was made in the face of this terrible fire, and the column worked its way slowly and painfully, yet steadily and unfalteringly, up the long and rugged slope of that blazing, smoking, jarring, blood-drenched, and death-laden mountain, fighting its way, step by step; every minute becoming weaker by the exhaustive outlay of strength in so prolonged a struggle, and thinner by the murderous fire of the foe from above, until, with less than half the command, with the entire color-guard disabled, the Colonel, bearing his own colors, spurred his foaming and bleeding horse over the enemy's works, and they threw down their arms, abandoned their guns, and gave themselves to precipitate flight. In this action the Twenty-Sixth captured about fifty prisoners and two cannon. Later in the day the Twenty-Sixth Ohio and Fifteenth Indiana, under command of Colonel Young, captured a six-gun battery the enemy were endeavoring to carry off in their retreat, and flanked and dislodged a strong body of the enemy, who, with two heavy guns, were attempting to hold in check the National forces until their train could be withdrawn. These guns, also, were captured. In token of their appreciation of Colonel Young's gallantry on Lookout Mountain, his command subsequently presented him a magnificent sword and belt. The Twenty-Sixth suffered at this time a loss of about one-fourth of its strength in killed and wounded. Ere its dead were buried on the mountain side of Mission Ridge, the Twenty-Sixth, now reduced, by two years and a half of arduous service, from one thousand to less than two hundred rifles, was on its way with the Fourth Corps to raise the siege of Knoxville. This campaign proved to be the most severe of any yet experienced. They marched barefoot over frozen ground, and bivouacked without shelter, in mid-winter, clad in summer dress, with half rations, on the desolate and dreary hillsides of East Tennessee. Yet even then, with elbows out, pants worn half way to the knees, socks and shirts gone to threads, hungry, and shivering in the bitter cold of January 1, 1864, the Twenty-Sixth, almost to a man, re-enlisted for three years more. The Twenty-Sixth Ohio was the first regiment in the Fourth Corps to re-enlist, and the first to arrive home on veteran furlough.

Returning to the field at the expiration of its furlough, the regiment rejoined the Fourth Corps at Bridgeport, Tennessee.

On the completion of arrangements by General Sherman for his movement on Atlanta, it marched with its corps and participated in that arduous campaign. It was at Resaca, Kenesaw, Peachtree Creek, Jonesboro', and in all the minor engagements of that march, and in each maintained its splendid fighting reputation.

After resting with the army for three weeks at Atlanta, the regiment was again called upon to seek the enemy. The Rebel General Hood, thinking to circumvent and defeat the plans of General Sherman, made his dash at the rear of Atlanta, and marched on Nashville. In the well-contested race that ensued the Twenty-Sixth Ohio bore a part, and again had the honor of contending, under the gallant Thomas, with the Rebel foe.

The battle of Franklin was fought, the enemy checked in his swift march, and the National forces won the race into Nashville, closely followed, however, by the still sanguine Rebel army. A few days of preparation and of rest, varied by sharp skirmishing along the front of the works protecting Nashville, and again the two armies contended with each other in a pitched battle. It was won by the National forces, the Rebels completely demoralized and put to flight. The National army, including the Fourth Corps, pursued the enemy across the Tennessee River, and then, glutted with prisoners and with abandoned Rebel stores, fell back on Huntsville and Nashville.

The Texas campaign was resolved upon. Transports were provided, on which a large force was embarked and taken down the Ohio and Mississippi Rivers to New Orleans, and from thence to Texas. The Twenty-Sixth Ohio formed part of that force, and participated in the severe march across the country from Port Lavaca to San Antonio, a march which will long be remembered by those who participated in it, from its disagreeable associations of intense heat, burning thirst, and the almost unbearable annoyances of mosquitoes, centipedes, and other "inhabitants" of that region.

On the 21st of October, 1865, the regiment was mustered out of the service at Victoria. Immediately thereafter it was sent home to Camp Chase, paid off, and discharged.

27th REGIMENT OHIO VOLUNTEER INFANTRY.

ROSTER, THREE YEARS' SERVICE.

RANK.	NAME.	DATE OF RANK.	COM. ISSUED.	REMARKS.
Colonel	JOHN W. FULLER	Aug. 1, 1861	Aug. 5, 1861	Promoted May 22, 1864, to Brig. Gen. Vols.
Do.	MENDALL CHURCHILL	June 27, 1864	June 27, 1864	Resigned September 15, 1864.
Do.	ISAAC N. GILRUTH	May 31, 1865	May 31, 1865	On leave of absence at muster out of reg't.
Lt. Colonel	HENRY G. KENNETT	July 25, 1861	July 26, 1861	Promoted to Colonel Seventy-Ninth reg't.
Do.	Z. SWIFT SPAULDING	Nov. 2, 1862	Nov. 2, 1862	Resigned February 19, 1864.
Do.	MENDALL CHURCHILL	March 19, 1864	March 19, 1864	Promoted to Colonel.
Do.	EDWIN NICHOLS	June 27, "	June 27, "	Resigned September 24, 1864.
Do.	FRANK LYNCH	Nov. 3, "	Nov. 3, "	Mustered out as Captain May 15, 1865.
Do.	ISAAC N. GILRUTH	May 29, 1865	May 29, 1865	Promoted to Colonel.
Do.	JAMES P. SIMPSON	" 31, "	" 31, "	
Major	Z. SWIFT SPAULDING	July 25, 1861	July 26, 1861	Promoted to Lieutenant-Colonel.
Do.	MENDALL CHURCHILL	Nov. 2, 1862	Dec. 22, 1862	Promoted to Lieutenant-Colonel.
Do.	EDWIN NICHOLS	March 19, 1864	March 19, 1864	Promoted to Lieutenant-Colonel.
Do.	JAMES MORGAN	Nov. 3, "	Nov. 3, "	Mustered out December 31, 1861, as Captain.
Do.	ISAAC N. GILRUTH	Jan. 28, 1865	Jan. 28, 1865	Promoted to Lieutenant-Colonel.
Do.	JAMES P. SIMPSON	May 29, "	May 29, "	Promoted to Lieutenant-Colonel.
Do.	CHAS. H. SMITH	" 31, "	" 31, "	
Surgeon	WM. R. THRALL	Aug. 1, 1861	Aug. 9, 1861	Resigned March 12, 1863.
Do.	JACOB C. DENISE	March 12, 1863	March 30, 1863	Resigned.
Do.	ISAAC YOUNG	Nov. 1, 1864	Nov. 1, 1864	
Ass't Surgeon	JACOB C. DENISE	Aug. 19, 1861	Aug. 19, 1861	Promoted to Surgeon.
Do.	JAMES SPRAGUE	July 24, 1862	July 29, 1862	Resigned April 30, 1864.
Do.	ISAAC YOUNG	May 11, 1863	May 11, 1863	Promoted to Surgeon.
Do.	JOHN L. CHAPEL	April 10, 1865	April 10, 1865	
Chaplain	J. EATON, jr	Aug. 15, 1861	Dec. 6, 1861	Appointed Colonel of a colored regiment.
Captain	Nelson L. Lutz	July 18, "	Aug. 12, "	Resigned March 4, 1864.
Do.	Edwin Nichols	" 19, "	" 5, "	Promoted to Major.
Do.	Wm. W. Culbertson	Aug. 1, "	" 9, "	Resigned March 14, 1861.
Do.	Milton Wells	" 2, "	" 9, "	Resigned March 26, 1862.
Do.	Mendall Churchill	" 6, "	" 9, "	Promoted to Major November 2, 1862.
Do.	J. Stanwood Menkin	" 7, "	" 12, "	Honorably discharged October 1, 1861.
Do.	Norman Tucker	" 10, "	" 16, "	Resigned June 16, 1862.
Do.	Frank Lynch	" 14, "	" 16, "	Promoted to Lieutenant-Colonel.
Do.	Wm. Sayers	" 14, "	" 16, "	Resigned March 31, 1862.
Do.	Wm. Feeny	" 16, "	" 19, "	Mustered out August 20, 1864.
Do.	James H. Hedges	Dec. 7, "	Dec. 7, "	Resigned June 16, 1862.
Do.	J. W. M. Brock	March 26, 1862	April 10, 1862	Resigned September 5, 1861.
Do.	Samuel Thomas	" 31, "	May 1, "	Mustered out.
Do.	James Morgan	June 16, "	July 21, "	Promoted to Major.
Do.	Wm. H. Winters	" 16, "	" 21, "	Resigned October 23, 1862.
Do.	Chas. W. Greene	Nov. 2, "	Dec. 22, "	Resigned September 1, 1864.
Do.	Elisha G. Hamilton	Oct. 23, "	" 22, "	Mortally wounded at Kenesaw Mountain.
Do.	Theodore Sawyer	March 5, 1863	April 8, 1863	Killed at Dallas May 27, 1864.
Do.	James H. Boggis	" 19, 1864	March 19, 1864	Mustered out December, 1864.
Do.	Isaac N. Gilruth	April 13, "	April 13, "	Promoted to Major.
Do.	James P. Simpson	May 9, "	May 9, "	Promoted to Major.
Do.	Zeph. C. Bryan	June 27, "	June 27, "	Died of wounds received at battle of Atlanta.
Do.	Lucius M. Miely	Aug. 11, "	Aug. 11, "	Mustered out as 1st Lieutenant.
Do.	Wm. L. Watt	Sept. 26, "	Sept. 26, "	Mustered out as 1st Lieutenant.
Do.	Jonathan Reese	" 28, "	" 26, "	Resigned September 30, 1864.
Do.	David H. Moore	" 26, "	" 26, "	Declined promotion.
Do.	John M. Weaver	Nov. 3, "	Nov. 3, "	Honorably discharged November 27, 1864.
Do.	Chas. H. Smith	" 3, "	" 3, "	Promoted to Major.
Do.	John H. Cooper	" 3, "	" 3, "	Absent with leave at muster out of regiment.
Do.	Wm. D. Phillips	" 3, "	" 3, "	Mustered out with regiment.
Do.	Frank B. Hazleton	Jan. 28, 1865	Jan. 28, 1865	Declined promotion.
Do.	James Skelton	" 28, "	" 28, "	
Do.	Edward A. Webb	" 28, "	" 28, "	
Do.	Thomas M. Willis	" 28, "	" 28, "	Resigned as Lieutenant April 3, 1865.
Do.	R. H. Worth	" 28, "	" 28, "	Resigned Juge 16, 1865.
Do.	Demetrius McFann	Nov. 2, 1864	May 11, "	Resigned Juno 3, 1865.
Do.	Chas. Chadwick	May 11, 1865	" 11, "	
Do.	Stephen Allison	" 11, "	" 11, "	Mustered out with regiment.
Do.	John A. Evans	" 31, "	" 31, "	Mustered out with regiment.
Do.	Francis M. Washburn	" 31, "	" 31, "	Resigned June 20, 1865.
Do.	Daniel W. Jones	June 6, "	June 6, "	Mustered out with regiment.
Do.	Robert C. Beggadike	" 6, "	" 6, "	Mustered out as 1st Lieutenant.
1st Lieutenant	James H. Hedges	July 18, 1861	Aug. 12, 1861	Promoted to Captain.
Do.	George B. Upham	" 19, "	" 5, "	Resigned February 6, 1862.
Do.	Wm. M. Vogleson	" 24, "	July 24, "	Promoted by President to Capt. and A. A. S.
Do.	Philip B. Cloon	" 27, "	Aug. 9, "	Resigned September 30, 1861.
Do.	Wm. H. Winters	Aug. 1, "	" 9, "	Promoted to Captain Juno 6, 1862.
Do.	J. W. M. Brock	" 2, "	" 9, "	Promoted to Captain.
Do.	Samuel Thomas	" 6, "	" 9, "	Promoted to Captain.
Do.	James Morgan	" 7, "	" 12, "	Promoted to Captain.
Do.	Elisha G. Hamilton	" 10, "	" 16, "	Promoted to Captain.
Do.	Henry A. Webb	" 14, "	" 16, "	Killed October 4, 1862.
Do.	Wm. E. Johnson	" 14, "	" 16, "	Resigned May 17, 1862.
Do.	George McDonough	" 16, "	" 19, "	Resigned March 27, 1862.
Do.	Theodore Sawyer	Dec. 7, "	Dec. 7, "	Promoted to Captain.
Do.	James H. Boggis	" 13, "	" 13, "	Promoted to Captain.
Do.	Albert R. Austin	Feb. 6, 1862	April 10, 1862	Resigned April 27, 1862.
Do.	Matthew Brown	March 26, "	" 10, "	Revoked.
Do.	Chas. W. Greene	" 27, "	" 10, "	Promoted to Captain.
Do.	Isaac N. Gilruth	Feb. 6, "	May 1, "	Promoted to Captain.

RANK.	NAME.	DATE OF RANK.	COM. ISSUED.	REMARKS.
1st Lieutenant	Edward Gibson	March 31, 1862	May 1, 1862	Resigned March 14, 1864.
Do.	James P. Simpson	" 26, "	" 24, "	Promoted to Captain.
Do.	Zeph. C. Bryan	May 17, "	June 24, "	Promoted to Captain.
Do.	Jonathan Reese	June 16, "	July 21, "	Promoted to Captain.
Do.	Lucius M. Miely	" 16, "	" 21, "	Promoted to Captain.
Do.	George W. Young	Oct. 4, "	Dec. 22, "	Mustered out February 5, 1864.
Do.	Wm. L. Watt	" 23, "	" 22, "	Promoted to Captain.
Do.	David H. Moore	Nov. 2, "	" 22, "	Mustered out December 23, 1864.
Do.	Orrin B. Gould	March 5, 1863	March 5, 1863	Mustered out.
Do.	Henry W. Diebolt	Jan. 1, "	June 26, "	Died of wounds received at Dallas May 28, '64.
Do.	Thomas A. Walker	March 19, 1864	March 19, 1864	Appointed Major of colored regiment.
Do.	Wm. E. Ells	April 13, "	April 13, "	Mustered out December 22, 1864.
Do.	John M. Weaver	" 13, "	" 13, "	Promoted to Captain.
Do.	James F. Day	" 13, "	" 13, "	Killed June 16, 1864.
Do.	Chas. H. Smith	May 9, "	May 9, "	Promoted to Captain.
Do.	John H. Cooper	" 9, "	" 9, "	Promoted to Captain.
Do.	Marcus D. L. Faverty	June 27, "	June 27, "	Declined promotion.
Do.	Demetrius McFann	" 27, "	" 27, "	Promoted to Captain.
Do.	Elwood B. Temple	July 13, "	July 13, "	Resigned as 2d Lieutenant October 14, 1864.
Do.	Wm. D. Phillips	" 25, "	" 25, "	Promoted to Captain.
Do.	Frank B. Hazleton	" 25, "	" 25, "	Resigned June 3, 1865.
Do.	James Skelton	Aug. 11, "	Aug. 11, "	Promoted to Captain.
Do.	Edward A. Webb	Sept. 26, "	Sept. 26, "	Promoted to Captain.
Do.	Thomas M. Willis	" 26, "	" 26, "	Promoted to Captain.
Do.	R. H. Worth	" 26, "	" 26, "	Promoted to Captain.
Do.	Chas. Chadwick	Nov. 3, "	Nov. 3, "	Promoted to Captain.
Do.	Stephen Allison	Jan. 28, 1865	Jan. 28, 1865	Promoted to Captain.
Do.	John A. Evans	" 28, "	" 28, "	Promoted to Captain.
Do.	Francis M. Washburn	" 28, "	" 28, "	Promoted to Captain.
Do.	John F. Woodruff	" 28, "	" 28, "	Mustered out with regiment.
Do.	Newton H. Ervin	" 28, "	" 28, "	Mustered out as Regimental Quartermaster.
Do.	John A. Graham	" 28, "	" 28, "	Mustered out with regiment.
Do.	Jonas S. Stukey	" 28, "	" 28, "	Mustered out with regiment.
Do.	Daniel W. Jones	" 28, "	" 28, "	Promoted to Captain.
Do.	Robert C. Beggadike	" 28, "	" 28, "	Promoted to Captain.
Do.	Wm. H. Hamilton	May 11, "	May 11, "	Mustered out with regiment.
Do.	Orlin J. Baldwin	" 31, "	" 21, "	Mustered out with regiment.
Do.	Samuel N. Weeks	" 31, "	" 31, "	Mustered out with regiment.
Do.	Matthew F. Madigan	June 6, "	June 6, "	Mustered out with regiment.
Do.	James Dixon	" 6, "	" 6, "	Mustered out with regiment.
2d Lieutenant	Daniel Blaize	July 18, 1861	Aug. 12, 1861	Resigned October 15, 1861.
Do.	Albert R. Auston	" 19, "	" 5, "	Promoted to 1st Lieutenant.
Do.	Isaac N. Gilruth	" 1, "	" 9, "	Promoted to 1st Lieutenant.
Do.	Matthew Brown	" 2, "	" 9, "	Resigned June 21, 1862.
Do.	Chas. W. Greene	" 6, "	" 9, "	Promoted to 1st Lieutenant.
Do.	Theodore Sawyer	" 7, "	" 12, "	Promoted to 1st Lieutenant.
Do.	Lucius M. Miely	" 10, "	" 16, "	Promoted to 1st Lieutenant.
Do.	Edward Gibson	" 14, "	" 16, "	Promoted to 1st Lieutenant.
Do.	James P. Simpson	" 14, "	" 16, "	Promoted to 1st Lieutenant.
Do.	John Scofe	" 16, "	" 19, "	Resigned June 25, 1862.
Do.	Wm. Wilson	Nov. 25, "	Nov. 25, "	Resigned July 16, 1862.
Do.	Zeph. C. Ryan	Dec. 12, "	Dec. 12, "	Promoted to 1st Lieutenant.
Do.	Jonathan Reese	Feb. 6, 1862	April 10, 1862	Promoted to 1st Lieutenant.
Do.	Chas. F. Moore	March 27, "	" 10, "	Resigned March 19, 1863.
Do.	Henry W. Diebolt	Feb. 6, "	May 1, "	Promoted to 1st Lieutenant.
Do.	Jacob C. Cohen	March 26, "	" 1, "	Resigned July 24, 1863.
Do.	Geo. W. Young	" 31, "	" 1, "	Promoted to 1st Lieutenant.
Do.	David H. Moore	May 17, "	June 24, "	Promoted to 1st Lieutenant.
Do.	Wm. L. Watt	June 21, "	July 21, "	Promoted to 1st Lieutenant.
Do.	Finley C. McGrew	" 23, "	" 21, "	Resigned July 15, 1863.
Do.	Thomas A. Walker	July 16, "	" 21, "	Promoted to Major colored regiment.
Do.	Wm. E. Ells	June 16, "	" 21, "	Promoted to 1st Lieutenant.
Do.	John M. Weaver	Aug. 14, "	Sept. 9, "	Promoted to 1st Lieutenant.
Do.	George S. Spaulding	Oct. 4, "	Dec. 22, "	Resigned April 1, 1864.
Do.	James F. Day	" 23, "	" 22, "	Promoted to 1st Lieutenaut
Do.	Chas. H. Smith	Nov. 2, "	" 22, "	Promoted to 1st Lieutenant.
Do.	John H. Cooper	March 19, 1863	June 10, 1863	Promoted to 1st Lieutenant.
Do.	Marcus D. L. Faverty	Jan. 1, "	" 26, "	Honorably discharged January 5, 1865.
Do.	Demetrius McFann	April 28, 1864	April 28, 1864	Promoted to 1st Lieutenant.
Do.	Elwood B. Temple	May 9, "	May 9, "	Promoted to 1st Lieutenant.
Do.	Wm. D. Phillips	" 9, "	" 9, "	Promoted to 1st Lieutenant.
Do.	Frank B. Hazleton	" 9, "	" 9, "	Promoted to 1st Lieutenant.
Do.	James Skelton	June 27, "	June 27, "	Promoted to 1st Lieutenant.
Do.	Edward A. Webb	" 27, "	" 27, "	Promoted to 1st Lieutenant.
Do.	Thomas M. Willis	" 27, "	" 27, "	Promoted to 1st Lieutenant.
Do.	R. H. Worth	" 27, "	" 37, "	Promoted to 1st Lieutenant.
Do.	Chas. Chadwick	Aug. 29, "	Aug. 29, "	Promoted to 1st Lieutenant.

TWENTY-SEVENTH OHIO VOLUNTEER INFANTRY.

THIS regiment was organized at Camp Chase, Ohio, in August, 1861. The enlisted men who composed it were from all parts of the State, and were, to a great extent, strangers to themselves and to their officers. On the morning of the 20th of August, 1861, the regiment marched out of camp nine hundred and fifty strong, and took the cars for St. Louis, Missouri. On its arrival the regiment encamped near the city, and great efforts were made to perfect the men in drill and discipline. Early in September the regiment moved by steamer to St. Charles, and thence to Mexico, on the St. Joseph Railroad. Soon after this, orders were received to march to the relief of Colonel Mulligan at Lexington. The troops moved rapidly across the country; but, before they could reach the city, the enemy had seized all the boats, and so rendered it impossible to cross the river. The command moved up the north bank of the Missouri and crossed over to Kansas City. While here the regiment was constantly engaged in drilling, and soon became able to maneuver with promptness and precision. In October the command marched to join General Fremont, then moving on Springfield; but, upon the arrival of General Hunter, the regiment was ordered to Sedalia. In December, 1861, the regiment shared in the capture of thirteen hundred recruits, who were endeavoring to join the Rebel General Price. In February, 1862, the regiment was ordered to proceed to St. Louis, where it arrived, after a severe march, on the 20th. The next morning the regiment moved down the river, and landed at Commerce.

In the organization of the Army of the Mississippi, the Twenty-Seventh was assigned to the First Brigade, First Division. In March, the army moved upon New Madrid, the Twenty-Seventh being in the advance. The morning the column neared the town, the regiment drove the enemy's skirmishers back to the main line, and then advanced upon this line through a perfect storm of shells from the forts and gunboats. When the enemy's position had been well ascertained, the regiment moved back out of the range of the Rebel guns and encamped. On the night of March 12th, two companies of the Twenty-Seventh, with a detachment from another regiment, drove in the Rebel pickets and protected the force detailed to place the siege-guns in position. This was effected without loss, and the next day the regiment moved up in support of the battery. The regiment was actively engaged during the remainder of the siege, and, after the surrender of the town, remained in camp about two weeks, constantly engaged in drilling. It then moved to Island No. 10, and assisted in the capture of that place, and a few weeks later moved to the vicinity of Fort Pillow.

The army being ordered to Pittsburg Landing, arrived at Hamburg (near Pittsburg Landing) about the 1st of May, 1862, and moved on Corinth, forming the left of Halleck's army. During the advance, the regiment was frequently engaged in skirmishing, and, during the siege, was repeatedly under fire, and in every instance behaved well. The regiment shared in the pursuit of the Rebels, but soon returned to the vicinity of Corinth, where the summer months were spent quietly in camp. Fuller's brigade, or, [illegible] it was frequently called, the Ohio Brigade, to which the Twenty-Seventh belonged, had occupied Iuka, but, about the middle of September, was again concentrated at Corinth. Hardly had they reached Corinth when General Price attacked the small force left at Iuka, and occupied the place. The Ohio Brigade was a part of the force sent to recapture the town, which it reached on the 19th of September. The fight began at noon, near Barnett's Station, eight miles from Iuka, and it was after four P. M. before the Rebels were forced back to the town. The Ohio Brigade acted as rear-guard on the 19th, and the battle was raging furiously when it reached the field. It was immediately formed for action, and moved to the front on the double-quick, driving the enemy over the crest of a ridge. Darkness put an end to the conflict, and in the morning the enemy was gone. They were followed for ten or twelve miles, and then the troops returned to Rienzi.

In a short time the brigade returned to Corinth, and encamped near the town on the Tuscumbia. The next day (October 3d) the brigade formed in line of battle on the north-east side of town, but after nine o'clock in the evening it moved to the Chewalla Road, and took position on both sides of Battery Robinett, which it sustained during the whole of the next day's fight. During the night of the 3d the hostile lines were resting within range of each other, and the skirmishers were close together. Before daylight the Rebel guns, two hundred yards distant, opened fire with great rapidity. As soon as it was light enough to sight a piece, the guns of Robinett and Williams drove the Rebels from their position. Skirmishers were very active for several hours, those from the Twenty-Seventh using seventy rounds of ammunition, and losing several men. When the right of the National line was forced back to Corinth, Van Dorn made a vigorous attack on the Ohio Brigade, and, after a desperate struggle, was repulsed. In this engagement the brigade lost three hundred men, and more than sixty of these belonged to the Twenty-Seventh. The regiment joined in the pursuit, and after advancing as far as Ripley, with nothing of importance occurring, it returned to Corinth. Here the regiment received two hundred recruits, a very timely re-enforcement, as the Twenty-Seventh was much reduced, some of the companies mustering mere squads.

On the 1st of November the Ohio Brigade marched toward Grand Junction to join Grant's army, and with that army it marched as far south as Oxford, Mississippi. When Forrest crossed the Tennessee River, in December, the brigade was ordered to Jackson, Tennessee, to assist in driving the Rebel raider back. After considerable marching, the brigade encountered Forrest at Parker's Cross Roads, and took an active part in the engagement at that place, capturing seven guns, three hundred and sixty prisoners, and four hundred horses. In this capture the Twenty-Seventh bore an honorable share. The Ohio Brigade followed Forrest to the Tennessee River, marching in the middle of winter, over ice one day and in fathomless mud the next, without tents, without rubber blankets, without proper food, and without ambulances. When the troops reached Corinth one-fifth of the men were bare-footed, and the Surgeon of the Twenty-Seventh reported officially that the deaths resulting from that march equaled the losses of a severe skirmish. When the brigade arrived at Corinth, it was attached to General Dodge's command; and though the garrison was living on half rations, in view of the hardships the Ohio troops had sustained, full supplies were issued to them. Comfortable log huts were built, and quite a rivalry sprang up among the regiments as to whose camp should be the finest. That of the Twenty-Seventh was laid out with great care and taste, and was remarkably neat and clean.

The brigade moved eastward with General Dodge, through Iuka and the Tuscumbia Valley. General Dodge drove the Rebel cavalry from Bear Creek, and followed as far east as Town Creek. After returning from Town Creek the Ohio Brigade was ordered to Memphis, and remained some time, performing garrison duty. During its stay at Memphis the Twenty-Seventh was engaged in several reconnoissances, and one hundred men from the regiment, with detachments from the other regiments of the brigade, were engaged in guarding prisoners of war from Vicksburg to Johnson's Island, Fort Delaware, and other points. In October, 1863, the brigade left Memphis, and moved *via* Corinth to Iuka. In the march from Iuka the Twenty-Seventh was in the advance brigade, and moved from eighteen to twenty miles per day, and encamped at night from six to ten miles in advance of the main column. Communication was held each night by means of rockets. General Dodge finally halted with a large portion of his command at Pulaski, but the Ohio Brigade marched about fifteen miles south and occupied Prospect. Here the troops were employed in building fortifications and bridges. When these works were about completed the Twenty-Seventh re-enlisted as veterans and were furloughed to their homes. Shortly after their return to the field the Ohio Brigade moved against Decatur and captured it. Fortifications were laid out, and the town was soon well intrenched. While at Decatur the Ohio Brigade was discontinued, and the Twenty-Seventh and Thirty-Ninth Ohio, Sixty-Fourth Illinois, and Eighteenth Missouri, constituted the First Brigade (Colonel Fuller commanding) of the Fourth Division, Sixteenth Army Corps.

On the 1st of May, 1864, the Fourth Division moved from Decatur and joined the main army at Chattanooga. When the army approached Resaca, the Twenty-Seventh, with other regiments, was ordered to move upon the railroad north of the town, to damage it as much as possible, and to endeavor to reach the bridge over the Oostenaula. They were succeeding well in their undertaking when they were recalled and fell back to Snake Creek Gap. At Dallas, Georgia, early on the morning of the 27th of May, the pickets were sharply attacked by the Rebels, and driven back to within easy musket range of the main body. The brigade formed in line, and two companies of the Twenty-Seventh advanced on the double-quick to re-enforce the guard. The Rebels were driven back, but Captain Sawyer, commanding the skirmish-line, and his First-Lieutenant, Henry W. Diebolt, were mortally wounded; and these two officers, who had served in the same company and eaten at the same table, were laid side by side that evening, in the little grave-yard just north of Dallas. The regiment was engaged with Hood's corps on the 28th of May, skirmished at Big Shanty in June, and fought at Kenesaw, losing heavily, both in officers and men. On the 4th of July, 1864, the regiment participated in the action at Nicojack Creek, advancing at the head of the division with fixed bayonets, and charging the Rebel works with complete success.

On the 22d of July, before Atlanta, the regiment was engaged in one of its most severe battles, and sustained its heaviest loss. It charged the enemy again and again, and at one time, when threatened on its flanks, changed front to rear, under fire, formed the new line promptly, and again advanced to the charge. Under a clump of pines, two miles south-east of Atlanta, near where they fell, rest the heroes of the Twenty-Seventh who were killed upon that field. The regiment was with the Sixteenth Corps as it moved to the west side of Atlanta, and participated in the skirmish of July 27th, driving back the enemy's cavalry. In August the regiment was sent to Marietta, where it remained till the fall of Atlanta. From the time it left Chattanooga till Atlanta was in our possession, it had lost sixteen officers and two hundred and one men, only six of whom (all enlisted men) were reported "missing." This was a loss of more than half the men present for duty when the regiment left Chattanooga.

The regiment pursued Hood northward, and, after returning, marched with Sherman to the sea, skirmishing near Savannah, with slight loss. It shared in the campaign of the Carolinas, and at the crossing of the Salkehatchie, South Carolina, the Twenty-Seventh literally hewed its way through forest and swamp, with water nearly up to the waist, for more than a mile, and was among the first to find a way to cross the river. At Cheraw, South Carolina, the Twenty-Seventh was the first regiment to enter the town, skirmishing with the Rebel cavalry, driving them through the streets of the town and across the Pedee. Here the regiment captured a fine English twenty-pound gun, which bore the following inscription: "Presented to the *sovereign State of South Carolina*, by one of her citizens residing abroad, in commemoration of the 20th of December, 1860" (the day South Carolina seceded). At Bentonville, North Carolina, Monroe's division, to which the Twenty-Seventh belonged, attacked the enemy's left, and pushed forward so vigorously that the skirmish-line was at General Joe Johnston's head-quarters before they were aware of it. This was the last time the Twenty-Seventh was under fire.

After the surrender of Johnston it moved *via* Richmond to Washington, participated in the review, and then proceeded to Louisville. In July, 1865, the regiment was ordered to Camp Dennison, and there the members of it received their final payment and discharge.

28th REGIMENT OHIO VOLUNTEER INFANTRY.

ROSTER, THREE YEARS' SERVICE.

RANK.	NAME.	DATE OF RANK.	COM. ISSUED.	REMARKS.
Colonel	AUGUST MOOR	June 10, 1861	Oct. 30, 1861	Breveted Brigadier-General; mustered out July 23, 1864.
Do.	GOTTFRIED BECKER	Nov. 27, 1863	Jan. 10, 1864	
Lt. Colonel	GOTTFRIED BECKER	June 10, 1861	Oct. 30, 1861	Resigned September 24, 1862.
Do.	ALEX. BOLENDER	Sept. 24, 1862		Resigned March 17, 1863.
Do.	ALEX. BOLENDER	May 14, 1863	May 14, 1863	Declined.
Do.	GOTTFRIED BECKER	Aug. 5, "	Aug. 5, "	Mustered out July 23, 1864
Do.	ERNEST SCHACHI	March 27, "	Jan. 10, 1864	Declined.
Do.	EDWIN FREY	Dec. 14, 1864	Dec. 14, "	Not mustered out.
Major	RUDOLPH HEINTZ	June 10, 1861	Oct. 30, 1861	Resigned October 9, 1861.
Do.	ALEX. BOLENDER	Oct. 9, "		Promoted to Lieutenant-Colonel Sept. 24, '62.
Do	ERNEST SCHACHI	Sept. 24, "		Killed at battle of Piedmont.
Surgeon	GERHARD SAAL	June 10, "	Oct. 30, 1861	Resigned January 21, 1863.
Do.	CHAS. E. DENIG	Feb. 26, 1863	Feb. 26, 1863	Mustered out July 23, 1864.
Ass't Surgeon	ADOLPH SHOENBEIN	June 10, 1861	Oct. 30, 1861	Resigned April 16, 1863.
Do.	GEORGE P. HACKINBERG	July 4, 1862	July 23, 1862	Resigned February 14, 1863.
Do.	GEORGE CORNELL	April 28, 1863	April 28, 1863	Declined.
Do.	A. E. JENNER	June 29, "	June 29, "	Mustered out July 23, 1864.
Do.	JOSEPH HEBBELL	July 24, "	July 24, "	Mustered out July 23, 1864.
Chaplain	KARL BEYSCHLAG	June 10, "	Oct. 30, 1861	Resigned January 1, 1862.
Captain	Ernest Schachi	" 13, 1861	" 30, "	Promoted to Major.
Do.	Albert Ritter	" 13, "	" 30, "	Transferred to 1st Lieutenancy.
Do.	Matthias Reichings	" 13, "	" 30, "	Resigned March 24, 1863.
Do.	Louis Frey	" 13, "	" 30, "	Resigned July 17, 1862.
Do.	Arthur Forbriger	" 13, "	" 30, "	Resigned June 8, 1862.
Do.	Henry Sommer	" 13, "	" 30, "	Mustered out.
Do.	Tobias Nagle	" 13, "	" 30, "	
Do.	Bernhard Eith	" 13, "	" 30, "	Resigned March, 1862.
Do.	Maurice Wesolowski	" 13, "	" 30, "	Resigned July 25, 1862.
Do.	George Sommer	" 13, "	" 30, "	Resigned March 17, 1862.
Do.	Wm. Ewald	July 27, "	" 30, "	Resigned October 4, 1862.
Do.	Charles Drach	March 1, 1862	March 20, 1862	Declined promotion.
Do.	Matthew Louterbach	" 17, "	May 1, "	Resigned March 24, 1863.
Do.	Augustus Fix	June 3, "	June 24, "	Mustered out July 23, 1864.
Do.	Elwin Frey	March 1, "	" 24, "	Mustered out.
Do.	Louis Frey	July 17, "	Dec. 31, "	Reinstated; mustered out July 23, 1864.
Do.	Frederick Wiesing	" 25, "	" 15, "	Mustered out July 23, 1864.
Do.	Charles Drach	Sept. 24, "	" 15, "	Mustered out July 23, 1864.
Do.	John Amrein	Oct. 1, "	" 15, "	Resigned.
Do.	Arnold Heer	March 24, "	April 8, "	Mustered out December 17, 1864.
Do.	Albert Traub	" 24, "	" 8, "	Mustered out July 23, 1864.
Do.	Samuel Rosenthal	" 19, 1864	March 19, 1864	Declined promotion.
Do.	Herman Koenigsberger	April 22, "	April 22, "	Mustered out.
Do.	Leopold Markbreit	" 22, "	" 22, "	Mustered out as 1st Lieutenant July 23, 1864.
Do.	Edwin Frey	July 7, 1862	Dec. 31, 1862	On detached service at muster out of reg't.
Do.	F. Birk	Nov. 18, 1864	Nov. 18, 1864	Mustered out with regiment.
1st Lieutenant	Charles H. Mayer	June 13, 1861	Oct. 30, 1861	Resigned August 27, 1861.
Do.	Wm. Ewald	" 13, "	" 30, "	Promoted to Captain.
Do.	Augustus Fix	" 13, "	" 30, "	Promoted to Captain.
Do.	Matthew Louterbach	" 12, "	" 30, "	Promoted to Captain.
Do.	Alex. Bolender	" 13, "	" 30, "	Promoted to Captain.
Do.	Ernest Zimmerman	" 13, "	" 30, "	Resigned.
Do.	Edwin Frey	" 13, "	" 30, "	Promoted to Captain.
Do.	Chas. Drach	" 13, "	" 30, "	Promoted to Captain.
Do.	S. Gronewald	" 13, "	" 30, "	Resigned October 21, 1861.
Do.	Philip Wich	" 13, "	" 30, "	Resigned October 21, 1861.
Do.	Charles A. Lucius	July 15, "	" 30, "	Resigned December 27, 1861.
Do.	Albert Ritter	" 27, "	" 30, "	Resigned February 14, 1862.
Do.	Frederick Wiesing	Sept. 13, "	" 30, "	Promoted to Captain.
Do.	Anton Grodzicki	Oct. 23, "	Nov. 20, "	Resigned November 10, 1862.
Do.	John Amrein	" 10, "	" 20, "	Promoted to Captain.
Do.	Carlo Peipho	" 26, "	" 20, "	Appointed Captain 108th reg't July 30, 1862.
Do.	Arnold Heer	Nov. 11, "	" 20, "	Promoted to Captain.
Do.	Frank Schmidt	Jan. 21, 1862	Jan. 21, 1862	Resigned December 26, 1862.
Do.	Albert Traub	March 1, "	March 20, "	Revoked.
Do.	Martin Houser	Feb. 14, "	" 20, "	Resigned April 18, 1862.
Do.	Herman Koenigsberger	March 17, "	May 1, "	Promoted to Captain.
Do.	Gottlieb Hummel	April 18, "	June 3, "	
Do.	Samuel Rosenthal	June 3, "	" 24, "	Declined promotion; mustered out July 23,'64.
Do.	Leopold Markbreit	March 1, "	" 24, "	Promoted to Captain.
Do.	Louis C. Frintz	April 6, "		Mustered out.
Do.	Ferdinand Holzer	July 25, "		Resigned December 31, 1862.
Do.	Conrad Schlicher	Oct. 1, "		Resigned March 17, 1862.
Do.	Herman Guthard	Sept. 24, "		Mustered out July 23, 1861.
Do.	John Lang	March 17, "	Dec. 15, 1862	Mustered out July 23, 1864.
Do.	Louis Weitzel	Dec. 26, "	" 31, "	Resigned April 22, 1863.
Do.	Albert Liomin	" 31, "	" 31, "	Mustered out July 23, 1864.
Do.	Augustus Grieff	Feb. 25, 1863	April 8, 1863	Mustered out July 23, 1861.
Do.	Michael Klein	March 17, "	" 8, "	Mustered out July 23, 1864.
Do.	John J. Schellenbaum	" 24, "	" 8, "	Mustered out.
Do.	Henry Raabe	April 22, 1864	" 22, 1864	Mustered out.
Do.	John Roedell	" 22, 1863	June 11, 1863	Mustered out.
Do.	Henry Oker	" 22, 1864	April 22, 1864	Mustered out.
Do.	Rudolph Guthenstein	" 22, "	" 22, "	Mustered out as 2d Lieutenant July 23, 1864.
Do.	Frederick Hagenbuch	Nov. 18, "	Nov. 18, "	Mustered out with regiment.

RANK.	NAME.	DATE OF RANK.	COM. ISSUED.	REMARKS.
1st Lieutenant	Christian Hildebrand	Nov. 18, 1864	Nov. 18, 1864	Mustered out with regiment.
2d Lieutenant	Albert Traub	June 13, 1861	Oct. 30, 1861	Promoted to 1st Lieutenant.
Do.	Carlo Peipho	" 13, "	" 30, "	Promoted to 1st Lieutenant.
Do.	Arnold Heer	" 13, "	" 30, "	Promoted to 1st Lieutenant.
Do.	John Amrein	" 13, "	" 30, "	Promoted to 1st Lieutenant.
Do.	Martin Houser	" 13, "	" 30, "	Promoted to 1st Lieutenant.
Do.	Emil Wilde	" 13, "	" 30, "	Resigned October 29, 1861.
Do.	Frank Schmidt	" 13, "	" 30, "	Promoted to 1st Lieutenant.
Do.	Anton Grodzicki	" 13, "	" 30, "	Promoted to 1st Lieutenant.
Do.	Herman Koenigsberger	" 13, "	" 30, "	Promoted to 1st Lieutenant.
Do.	Leopold Markbreit	Sept. 13, "	" 30, "	Promoted to 1st Lieutenant.
Do.	Samuel Rosenthal	Oct. 11, "	Nov. 20, "	Promoted to 1st Lieutenant.
Do.	Louis C. Frintz	" 11, "	" 20, "	Promoted to 1st Lieutenant.
Do.	Charles Miller	" 27, "	" 20, "	Resigned April 5, 1862.
Do.	Lucas Schwank	" 27, "	" 20, "	Resigned March 17, 1862.
Do.	John Lang	" 27, "	" 20, "	Promoted to 1st Lieutenant.
Do.	Ferdinand Holzer	Nov. 1, "	" 20, "	Promoted to 1st Lieutenant.
Do.	Gottlieb Hummel	" 11, "	" 20, "	Promoted to 1st Lieutenant.
Do.	Herman Guthard	Jan. 21, 1862	Jan. 21, 1862	Promoted to 1st Lieutenant.
Do.	Augustus Grieff	March 1, "	May 1, "	Revoked.
Do.	Conrad Schleicher	" 1, "	" 1, "	Promoted to 1st Lieutenant.
Do.	Joseph Newbacker	" 17, "	" 1, "	Resigned September 25, 1865.
Do.	Edward Otte	April 15, "	" 1, "	Resigned July 30, 1865.
Do.	Michael Klein	" 18, "	June 3, "	Promoted to 1st Lieutenant.
Do.	James G. Worthington	June 5, "	" 5, "	Died February 6, 1863.
Do.	John Roedell	Aug. 26, "	Sept. 16, "	Promoted to 1st Lieutenant.
Do.	Albert Liomin	April 14, "	Dec. 15, "	Promoted to 1st Lieutenant.
Do.	August Herman	July 25, "	....	Resigned February 21, 1863.
Do.	Louis Weitzell	March 17, "	Dec. 15, 1862	Promoted to 1st Lieutenant.
Do.	Henry Raabe	Sept. 24, "	" 15, "	Promoted to 1st Lieutenant.
Do.	Louis Gerhardt	" 25, "	" 15, "	Resigned March 2, 1863.
Do.	John J. Schellenbaum	July 30, "	" 15, "	Promoted to 1st Lieutenant.
Do.	Henry Uker	Oct. 1, "	" 15, "	Promoted to 1st Lieutenant.
Do.	Rudolph Guthenstein	Dec. 26, "	" 31, "	Promoted to 1st Lieutenant.
Do.	George Kappes	April 22, 1864	April 22, 1864	Mustered out July 23, 1864.
Do.	Wm. Althammer	Feb. 21, 1863	" 8, 1863	Resigned March 11, 1864.
Do.	John Eppinger	March 2, "	" 8, "	Mustered out.
Do.	Jacob Mork	" 24, "	" 8, "	Mustered out.
Do.	Michael Schmitthemer	" 17, "	" 8, "	Mustered out April 28, 1864.
Do.	Ernest Kudell	" 24, "	" 8, "	Mustered out April 28, 1864.
Do.	Charles Woelfer	April 20, 1864	" 20, 1864	Mustered out July 23, 1864.
Do.	Frederick Kuhlman	" 22, "	" 22, "	Killed at battle of Piedmont.
Do.	Jacob Zeeb	" 22, "	" 22, "	Mustered out.
Do.	Frank Birk	" 22, "	" 22, "	Mustered out.
Do.	Frederick Eberhardt	" 22, "	" 22, "	Mustered out.
Do.	John Huser	Nov. 18, "	Nov. 18, "	Mustered out with regiment.
Do.	Christian Tinge	" 18, "	" 18, "	Mustered out with regiment.
Do.	George Siering	Dec. 15, "	Dec. 15, "	
Do.	George Benzing	June 15, 1863	....	Mustered out with regiment.

TWENTY-EIGHTH OHIO VOLUNTEER INFANTRY.

THE TWENTY-EIGHTH OHIO was accepted by the President direct, through the exertion of Hon. John A. Gurley, on the 10th of June, 1861. Owing to the absence of the proper officer, the muster-in was delayed until the 6th of July, when the regiment went to Camp Dennison.

The regiment, thoroughly organized, equipped, and drilled, moved to Point Pleasant, Virginia, July 31st, and to Parkersburg August 10th. Here Colonel Moor was ordered by General Rosecrans to scout the counties of Jackson and Roane, with four hundred picked men, which resulted in relieving the town of Spencer, the Rebels having besieged the home-guards, who had barricaded and fortified the court-house. The remainder of the regiment marched to Clarksburg, and was ordered to Buckhannon on the 16th. Colonel Moor, after accomplishing his mission, arrived at Buckhannon August 23d, and the regiment, as a part of General Rosecrans's army, marched to Bulltown on the 27th, to Sutton September 1st, and started for Summerville on the 7th. At noon on the 10th the Rebels, under Floyd, were found intrenched near Carnifex Ferry, the attack on which commenced in the afternoon and lasted until night-fall. During the night Floyd retreated. The Twenty-Eighth lost three killed and twenty-seven wounded.

On the 14th the regiment crossed Gauley River and marched to Camp Lookout, and, on September 25th, marched to Big Sewell Mountain; remained opposite the fortified position of the Rebels (Lee commanding) until the 6th of October, when, at ten o'clock at night, the retreat commenced over horrid roads. The troops arrived at Camp Anderson (on New River) on the 9th, crossed New River to Fayetteville on the 19th, and returned the same night after some skirmishing. On the 21st the pickets on New River were attacked. Two companies of the regiment, directed to re-enforce the pickets, soon repulsed the Rebels. Company C had one killed and one wounded. On December 6th Camp Anderson was evacuated, and the troops marched to Gauley. The regiment was drilled and instructed thoroughly, and May 2, 1862, was marched to Fayetteville, where General Cox assumed command, and formed the Kanawha Division into four brigades. The Twenty-Eighth, Thirty-Fourth, Thirty-Seventh Regiments, and Simmond's Battery, of Ohio troops, constituting the Second Brigade, Colonel Moor commanding, moved on the Tennessee and Virginia Railroad May 10th, by way of Raleigh, Flat Top Mountain, and Princeton, arriving at French Mill May 14th.

Two companies of the Twenty-Eighth were sent across East River Mountain to reconnoiter, and fell in with a Rebel force at Wolf Creek with commissary stores. Killed three and captured eight prisoners, a number of arms and horses, and burned the wagons and stores.

May 15th Colonel Moor sent five companies of the Twenty-Eighth, four companies of the Thirty-Seventh, and two companies of the Thirty-Fourth Regiments, under command of Lieutenant-Colonel Blessing, up the East River and Wytheville Road, to ascertain the Rebel force at Rocky Gap, with orders to return next day. About nine P. M. General Cox and staff arrived at French Mill, having been attacked and driven from Princeton that afternoon, his force scattering in the woods. Colonel Moor marched with his brigade for Princeton forthwith; the companies under Lieutenant-Colonel Blessing were notified by courier to march direct on Princeton by the Wytheville road and join the brigade in the morning. The brigade arrived at Princeton at six A. M., much fatigued, the enemy having evacuated after burning commissary and quartermaster's stores, and leaving a picket for observation, which retired as our skirmishers became visible.

Learning from our wounded that the Rebels, under General Marshal, were in position one mile west of town, Colonel Moor, with five companies and one Parrott gun, took possession of the cemetery. General Cox, with the rest of the brigade, remained in town, waiting for the First Brigade, under Colonel Scammon, which was falling back also from the Narrows of New River. An artillery duel and some skirmishing ensued, in which the Rebels wasted much ammunition. At ten o'clock A. M. heavy musketry firing was heard, distant about one and a half miles, on the heights of the Wytheville road, the first sign of the detachment ordered to move to Princeton by the Wytheville road. Five companies were ordered to advance to their support, which order, however, was not complied with, and Lieutenant-Colonel Blessing was forced back with a loss of eighteen dead and fifty-six wounded—the Twenty-Eighth having six dead and eleven wounded. In the afternoon the First Brigade arrived, and, during the night, General Cox concluded to fall back on Flat Top Mountain.

At three o'clock A. M. the retrogade movement commenced. At noon, the ten companies under Blessing, driven back the day before, fell in with our column near Blue Stone River, having marched all night by a circuitous route through Black Oak Mountains. The division reached Flat Top without molestation, May 19th.

Up to the 14th of August, companies A, C, D, E, and F had skirmishes on divers expeditions, losing but few men. Receiving orders to proceed to Washington City, the division left Flat Top Mountain August 15th, for the Kanawha and Ohio River *via* Parkersburg, and arrived at Washington August 25th; marched to Fort Albany the 26th; to Fort Buffalo on the 28th. The regiment skirmished with Stuart's cavalry at Falls Church, September 4th.

General McClellan assuming command of the army, the division was attached to the Ninth Corps, under General Reno. Coming up with the Rebels near Frederick City, Maryland, September 13th, Colonel Moor, with the cavalry attached to his brigade, was ordered to force an entrance and drive the Rebels out of the town, which was accomplished after a sharp contest.

On the 14th the battle of South Mountain was fought, and the Kanawha Division bore the brunt of the battle. At Antietam the Twenty-Eighth was the first regiment which forded the creek above the stone bridge, and remained in front of the Ninth Corps in skirmish-line all night. It lost forty-two killed and wounded. On the 8th of October marched with the division to Clear Springs, and, on the 9th, to Hancock, watching Stuart's cavalry, which had recrossed the Potomac. The division was ordered to march for the Kanawha on the 14th. The Twenty-Eighth Regiment, after a tedious march, arrived at Brownstown on the 17th of November. During December expeditions were sent through Wyoming and Logan Counties, capturing many prisoners and horses.

January 8, 1863, the regiment was ordered to Buckhannon. April 28th, General Roberts having assumed command of the troops in the District of Western Virginia, the regiment fell back under him to Clarksburg, before the Rebel General Jones, and advanced on Weston again, May 9th. The command marched to Maryland, opposite New Creek, June 16th. Meanwhile Western Virginia was threatened with another invasion, and the regiment was ordered to march to Beverly, and arrived on the 7th of July. After many marches and skirmishes in the mountains, General Averell arrived with a brigade of cavalry, and, on the 1st of November, the whole force moved south, across Cheat Mountain, through Pocahontas into Greenbrier. On the 5th the advance came in contact with the enemy at Millpoint, who made a hasty retreat to Droop Mountain. On the 6th the infantry forces were ordered to flank and attack the enemy, under General Echols, if possible, in the rear, which was done, and the Rebels routed, stating their loss in killed, wounded, and captured, at eight hundred.

On the 7th our forces marched to Lewisburgh, picking up prisoners, cannon, and other abandoned property. On the 8th Colonel Moor, in charge of the prisoners, captured some arms and four hundred cattle, and was ordered with the infantry and Keeper's battery to return to Beverly; General Averill with the cavalry taking another road. The force reached Beverly on the 12th, marching and bivouacking in snow and ice. On the 8th of December the regiment, with a column under Colonel Moor, in co-operation with General Averill's great raid to Salem, advanced again to threaten Lewisburg, diverting the attention of the Rebels and remaining near Falling Springs until General Averill passed the enemy's rear. On the 13th the regiment marched to Elk Mountain, and found the pass blockaded with rocks and heavy timbers for two miles. At early dawn on the 15th a detail of men was sent up the mountain to remove the blockade, which was accomplished, and at ten o'clock the march was resumed and Beverly reached on the 17th, with little annoyance from bushwackers. April 25th, 1864, the regiment was ordered to join the army of the Shenandoah, collecting under General Sigel at Bunker Hill, where it arrived on the 29th. May 11th Colonel Moor with a force of some two thousand five hundred men, of all arms, was sent to Rude's Hill, near New Market, to feel the enemy; the army under General Sigel was to follow at four the next morning. Moor's advance was attacked near Rude's Hill at three P. M.; a running fight ensued; at New Market, artillery came into play. Prisoners stated that Imboden was there in force. Toward evening Imboden was driven out and New Market was in our possession—Colonel Moor occupying Imboden's camp. The night being very dark and cloudy the enemy made two attacks to regain their first position, but were repulsed handsomely. Early next morning, learning from scouts and other sources that Imboden had joined Breckinridge five miles south of New Market, Colonel Moor made some alterations in his position and was again attacked. After seven A. M., Generals Stahl and Sigel arrived on the field with a cavalry division; other positions were taken, and the battle of New Market was fought amidst heavy thunder-storms. Our army was forced back to Cedar Creek, which was reached on the 17th of May.

On the 26th advanced again on Woodstock, New Market, Harrisburg, and Port Republic. June 5th came up on the Rebels under General Jones near Piedmont, who occupied a strongly intrenched position. Colonel Moor's brigade was ordered to attack, and after a stubborn contest drove the Rebels into their works. At about noon it again was ordered to storm the works. The assault, made in gallant style, was received with so tremendous a fire that it forced four regiments, after losing heavily, to fall back; the Twenty-Eighth remained on the ground and was ordered to lie down and prevent the enemy from making a counter-charge. The regiment kept the Rebels at bay for three-quarters of an hour, when it was recalled and resumed its place in the new line of battle; being highly complimented by General Hunter. Soon after the third charge was made with complete success. One thousand three hundred prisoners were captured and about the same number were killed and wounded. Among the killed was General Jones. The Twenty-Eighth lost thirty-three killed and one hundred and five wounded out of four hundred and eighty-four combatants; two color-bearers were killed and three wounded in quick succession, and the regimental flag was perforated by seventy-two balls and pieces of shell.

On the 6th of June the regiment entered Staunton, and on the 7th made a feint toward Lynchburg, destroying miles of railroad and bridges. Subsistence being scarce, and the forces of Generals Averill and Crook forming a junction with our army, Colonel Moor was ordered, with the Twenty-Eighth Ohio and portions of other regiments, one thousand Rebel prisoners, one hundred and fifty wounded, and hundreds of refugees and contrabands, to march directly across the mountains for the Baltimore and Ohio Railroad, a distance of one hundred and forty-seven miles.

After a very exhausting march the regiment arrived at Webster on the 18th, and was ordered to Camp Morton, Indiana, with the prisoners, where it arrived safely, and was reviewed on the 23d of June by Governor Morton and General Carrington. The term of service expiring in July, the regiment was ordered to Cincinnati, where it received a cordial welcome, and was honorably discharged on the 23d of July, 1864.

The regiment lost while in the field, two officers killed, seven wounded; ninety men killed, one hundred and sixty-two wounded, and one hundred and seventy-three disabled by disease; making a total of four hundred and thirty-four.

29th REGIMENT OHIO VOLUNTEER INFANTRY.

ROSTER, THREE YEARS' SERVICE.

RANK.	NAME.	DATE OF RANK.	COM. ISSUED.	REMARKS.
Colonel	LOUIS P. BUCKLEY	Aug. 27, 1861		Resigned January 26, 1863.
Do.	WM. T. FITCH	Jan. 26, 1863	June 18, 1863	Honorably discharged October 13, 1864.
Do.	JONAS SCHOONOVER	July 12, 1865	July 12, 1865	Mustered out with regiment.
Lt. Colonel	THOMAS CLARK	Nov. 28, 1861		Resigned June 19, 1863.
Do.	EDWARD HAYES	June 19, 1863	Oct. 2, 1863	Discharged November 4, 1864.
Do.	MYRON T. WRIGHT	Jan. 18, 1865	Jan. 18, 1865	Deceased from gun-shot wound.
Do.	JONAS SCHOONOVER	" 28, "	" 28, "	Promoted to Colonel.
Do.	EVERSON J. HULBURT	July 12, "	July 12, "	Mustered out as Major.
Major	JOHN S. CLEMMER	Dec. 31, 1861		Resigned December 12, 1862.
Do.	WM. T. FITCH	" 12, 1862	June 28, 1863	Promoted to Colonel.
Do.	EDWARD HAYES	Jan. 26, 1863	" 18, "	Promoted to Lieutenant-Colonel.
Do.	MYRON T. WRIGHT	" 5, 1864	Jan. 5, 1864	Promoted to Lieutenant-Colonel.
Do.	JONAS SCHOONOVER	" 18, 1865	" 18, 1865	Promoted to Lieutenant-Colonel.
Do.	EVERSON J. HULBURT	April 10, "	April 10, "	Promoted to Lieutenant-Colonel.
Do.	EDWIN B. WOODBURY	July 12, "	July 12, "	Mustered out with regiment as Captain.
Surgeon	A. K. FIFIELD	Aug. 23, 1861		Resigned August 12, 1861.
Do.	EDWARD P. HAINES	" 29, 1861	Aug. 29, 1862	Mustered out with regiment.
Do.	THOMAS B. MISER	July 5, 1865	July 5, 1865	Mustered out with regiment.
Ass't Surgeon	SYLVESTER BURROWES	Oct. 3, 1861		Resigned January 26, 1863.
Do.	CYRUS HOSACK	Aug. 21, 1862	Aug. 22, 1862	Resigned August 7, 1863.
Do.	EDWARD P. HAINES	Jan. 26, 1863	Feb. 27, 1863	Promoted to Surgeon.
Do.	THOMAS B. MISER	Aug. 24, 1864	Aug. 24, 1864	Promoted to Surgeon.
Chaplain	R. H. HULBURT	Sept. 10, 1861	Dec. 12, 1861	Resigned August 4, 1862.
Do.	LYMAN D. AMES	Feb. 18, 1863	Feb. 18, 1863	Resigned June 26, 1865.
Captain	Wm. T. Fitch	Aug. 14, 1861		Promoted to Major.
Do.	Wilber F. Stevens	" 19, "		Discharged September 9, 1864.
Do.	Edward Hayes	" 26, "		Promoted to Major.
Do.	Pulaski C. Hard	Sept. 10, "		Resigned March 15, 1862.
Do.	Horatio Luce	" 13, "		Killed June 9, 1862.
Do.	John F. Morse	" 28, "		Resigned April 13, 1862.
Do.	John S. Clemmer	" 30, "		Promoted to Major.
Do.	Jonas Schoonover	Oct. 15, "		Promoted to Major.
Do.	Russell B. Smith	Nov. 12, "		Promoted; resigned May 13, 1863.
Do.	Alden P. Steele	" 18, "		Resigned April 13, 1862.
Do.	Josiah J. Wright	Dec. 21, "		Honorably discharged October 1, 1862.
Do.	Myron T. Wright	March 13, 1862	March 13, 1862	Promoted to Major.
Do.	David E. Hulburt	April 13, "	May 1, "	Resigned August 29, 1864.
Do.	Eleazor Burridge	" 13, "	" 1, "	Resigned February 3, 1862; re-instated.
Do.	Ebenezer B. Howard	June 9, "	Dec. 23, "	Resigned.
Do.	James Treen	Oct. 1, "	" 31, "	Resigned May 22, 1863.
Do.	Everson J. Hulburt	Dec. 12, "	June 28, 1863	Promoted to Major.
Do.	Rowland H. Baldwin	Feb. 3, 1863	Feb. 18, "	Discharged October 30, 1864.
Do.	Andrew J. Fulkerson	May 25, 1864	May 25, 1864	Declined promotion.
Do.	Oscar F. Gibbs	" 25, "	" 25, "	Declined promotion.
Do.	George W. Dice	" 25, "	" 25, "	Killed June 16, 1864.
Do.	Andrew Wilson	" 25, "	" 25, "	Declined.
Do.	Edwin B. Woodbury	" 25, "	" 25, "	Promoted to Major.
Do.	Chas. W. Kellogg	Oct. 12, "	Oct. 12, "	Mustered out with regiment.
Do.	James B. Storer	" 12, "	" 12, "	Declined promotion.
Do.	C. H. Russell	" 12, "	" 12, "	
Do.	Thomas W. Nash	" 12, "	" 12, "	Mustered out with regiment.
Do.	Wilbur F. Chamberlin	" 12, "	" 12, "	Mustered out with regiment.
Do.	Silas G. Elliott	Jan. 6, 1865	Jan. 6, 1865	Mustered out with regiment.
Do.	Lyman H. McAdams	" 6, "	" 6, "	Mustered out with regiment.
Do.	Wm. H. Wright	" 6, "	" 6, "	Mustered out with regiment.
Do.	Rollin L. Jones	" 6, "	" 6, "	Mustered out with regiment.
Do.	Almer B. Paine	" 28, "	" 28, "	Mustered out with regiment.
Do.	Ulysses S. Hoxter	" 28, "	" 28, "	
Do.	David W. Thomas	April 10, "	April 10, "	Mustered out with regiment.
Do.	Thomas Folger	July 12, "	July 12, "	
1st Lieutenant	Leverett Grover	Aug. 14, 1861		Resigned February 6, 1862.
Do.	Alfred Bishop	" 19, "		Resigned February 11, 1863.
Do.	C. T. Chaffer	" 19, "		Resigned April 13, 1862.
Do.	Benjamin F. Perry	" 26, "		Resigned June 20, 1862.
Do.	Myron T. Wright	Sept. 10, "		Promoted to Captain.
Do.	Theodore C. Winship	" 16, "		Resigned January 26, 1863.
Do.	Hamblin Gregory	" 28, "		Resigned January 21, 1863.
Do.	David E. Hulburt	" 28, "		Promoted to Captain.
Do.	James Treen	" 30, "		Promoted to Captain.
Do.	Andrew J. Fulkerson	Oct. 15, "		Discharged August 15, 1864.
Do.	Oscar F. Gibbs	" 21, "		Declined promotion.
Do.	A. A. Philbrick	Dec. 22, "		Resigned March 13, 1863.
Do.	Wm. S. Crowell	Feb. 28, 1862	Feb. 28, 1862	Resigned April 13, 1862.
Do.	Seth E. Wilson	March 13, "	April 10, "	Resigned April 30, 1862.
Do.	Andrew Wilson	" 13, "	" 10, "	Revoked; discharged October 30, 1864
Do.	William Neil	April 13, "	May 1, "	Resigned January 25, 1863.
Do.	Everson J. Hulburt	" 13, "	" 1, "	Promoted to Captain.
Do.	Ebenezer B. Howard	" 13, "	" 1, "	Promoted to Captain.
Do.	George W. Dice	" 13, "	" 1, "	Promoted to Captain.
Do.	Andrew Wilson	" 30, "	June 3, "	Discharged November 1, 1864.
Do.	Frank P. Stewart	June 20, "	Sept. 10, "	Honorably discharged December 12, 1864.
Do.	Benj. N. Smith	Oct. 1, "	Dec. 30, "	Resigned as 2d Lieutenant March 11, 1864
Do.	Edwin B. Woodbury	Dec. 12, "	Jan. 28, 1863	Promoted to Captain.
Do.	Winthrop H. Grant	May 1, 1863	June 18, "	Killed May 8, 1864
Do.	Chas. W. Kellogg	June 26, "	Feb. 15, "	Promoted to Captain

RANK.	NAME.	DATE OF RANK.	COM. ISSUED.	REMARKS.
1st Lieutenant	James B. Storer	Jan. 26, 1863	Feb. 18, 1863	Honorably discharged November 30, 1864.
Do.	Cary H. Russell	" 24, "	June 10, "	Honorably discharged November 30, 1864.
Do	George Hayward	Feb. 11, "	May 25, "	Killed July 3, 1863.
Do.	James H. Grinnell	May 25, 1864	" 25, 1864	Honorably discharged as 2d Lieutenant.
Do.	Thomas W. Nash	" 25, "	" 25, "	Promoted to Captain.
Do.	E. T. Curtis	" 25, "	" 25, "	Detached at own request.
Do.	Gurley C. Crane	" 25, "	" 25, "	Hon. discharged as 2d Lieut. July 5, 1864.
Do.	Wilbur F. Chamberlin	" 25, "	" 25, "	Promoted to Captain.
Do.	Silas G. Elliott	" 25, "	" 25, "	Promoted to Captain.
Do.	Winthrop H. Grant	" 25, "	" 25, "	Killed May 8, 1864.
Do.	Joel E. Tanner	June 27, "	June 27, "	Promoted to Captain.
Do.	Lyman H. McAdams	July 25, "	July 25, "	Promoted to Captain.
Do.	Almer B. Paine	Jan. 6, 1865	Jan. 6, 1865	Promoted to Captain.
Do.	Ulysses S. Hoxter	" 6, "	" 6, "	Promoted to Captain.
Do.	Joshua Hile	" 6, "	" 6, "	Mustered out with regiment.
Do.	Addison J. Andrews	" 6, "	" 6, "	Mustered out with regiment.
Do.	Stephen Kissinger	" 6, "	" 6, "	Mustered out with regiment.
Do.	Thadeus E. Hoyt	" 6, "	" 6, "	Mustered out with regiment.
Do.	Ralph. Griswold	" 6, "	" 6, "	Mustered out with regiment.
Do.	Benj. F. Manderbach	" 6, "	" 6, "	Mustered out with regiment.
Do.	David W. Thomas	" 6, "	" 6, "	Promoted to Captain.
Do.	Thomas Folger	" 6, "	" 6, "	Promoted to Captain.
Do.	Giles R. Leonard	May 31, "	May 31, "	Mustered out with regiment.
Do.	George McNutt	" 31, "	" 31, "	Mustered out with regiment.
Do.	Marcus F. Roberts	" 31, "	" 31, "	Mustered out with regiment.
Do.	Jacob Buck	July 12, "	July 12, "	
2d Lieutenant	Wm. S. Crowell	Aug. 11, 1861		Promoted to 1st Lieutenant.
Do.	Andrew Wilson	" 19, "		Promoted to 1st Lieutenant.
Do.	Frank P. Stewart	" 26, "		Promoted to 1st Lieutenant.
Do.	James H. Grinnell	Sept. 10, "		Honorably discharged June 14, 1864.
Do.	Ebenezer B. Howard	" 16, "		Promoted to 1st Lieutenant.
Do.	Eleazor Burridge	" 28, "		Promoted to 1st Lieutenant.
Do.	Josiah J. Wright	" 30, "		
Do.	Henry Mack	Oct. 3, "		Resigned May 2, 1862.
Do.	Wm. J. Hall	" 11, "		Resigned February 6, 1862.
Do.	Wm. Neil	Nov. 26, "		Promoted to 1st Lieutenant.
Do.	Wm. P. Williamson	Dec. 21, "		Killed March 23, 1862.
Do.	Everson J. Hulburt	Feb. 28, 1862	Feb. 28, 1862	Promoted to 1st Lieutenant April 13, 1862.
Do.	Seth E. Wilson	" 28, "	" 28, "	Promoted to 1st Lieutenant.
Do.	Edwin B. Woodbury	May 13, "	April 10, "	Promoted to 1st Lieutenant.
Do.	Martin D. Norris	April 13, "	May 1, "	Resigned October 25, 1862.
Do.	Albert Durkee	" 13, "	" 1, "	Resigned July 9, 1862.
Do.	James B. Storer	" 13, "	" 1, "	Promoted to 1st Lieutenant.
Do.	Cary H. Russell	" 13, "	" 1, "	Promoted to 1st Lieutenant.
Do.	Wm. B. Quirk	July 29, "	Sept. 8, "	Resigned October 27, 1862.
Do.	Chas. W. Kellogg	June 30, "	" 10, "	Promoted to 1st Lieutenant.
Do.	John J. Hoyt	Sept. 8, "	Oct. 1, "	Resigned October 27, 1862.
Do.	Wm. Nelson	" 4, "	" 1, "	Resigned October 27, 1862.
Do.	Benj. N. Smith	May 1, "	Nov. 29, "	Promoted to 1st Lieutenant.
Do.	Thomas W. Nash	Oct. 27, "	" 29, "	Promoted to 1st Lieutenant.
Do.	E. T. Curtis	" 27, "	Dec. 18, "	Promoted to 1st Lieutenant.
Do.	Theodore L. Gould	" 27, "	" 30, "	Discharged October 1, 1863.
Do.	J. G. Marsh	Dec. 12, "	Jan. 28, 1863	Killed July 3, 1863.
Do.	Henry N. Ryder	Oct. 25, "	" 28, "	Died September 25, 1863.
Do.	Gurley C. Crane	Jan. 25, "	Feb. 18, "	Honorably discharged July 5, 1864.
Do.	Winthrop H. Grant	" 26, "	" 18, "	Promoted to 1st Lieutenant.
Do.	Wilbur F. Chamberlin	" 24, "	" 18, "	Promoted to 1st Lieutenant.
Do.	Silas G. Elliott	May 1, 1863	June 18, "	Promoted to 1st Lieutenant.

TWENTY-NINTH OHIO VOLUNTEER INFANTRY.

THE TWENTY-NINTH OHIO was organized at Camp Giddings, near Jefferson, Ashtabula County, August 26, 1861, and was one among the first to answer the call of the President for the three years' service. Delays and difficulties that could not be surmounted kept it in camp until the 25th of December, 1861, when orders were received to march into Ashtabula, where cars were ready to transport the regiment to Camp Chase, Columbus.

In camp the regiment remained until the 17th of January, 1862, when it was ordered to Cumberland, Maryland, *via* the Central Ohio and Baltimore and Ohio Railroads. It remained at Cumberland until the fall of 1863. While there it was brigaded with the Fifth, Seventh, and Sixty-Sixth Ohio, and the One Hundred and Tenth Pennsylvania Regiments, commanded by Colonel E. B. Tyler, of the Seventh Ohio. The division was commanded by General Lander until his decease, about the 1st of March, 1862, when he was succeeded by General James Shields.

We have not been successful in procuring, in detail, the facts making up the full history of this regiment, its marches, scouts, privations, and sufferings, but can truthfully say, in general terms, that no regiment from Ohio surpassed it in numerous actions and soldierly bearing.

The regiment participated with the Army of the Potomac, in the battles of Winchester, Virginia, March 23, 1862; Port Republic, June 9, 1862; Cedar Mountain, August 9, 1862; the second Bull Run; Chancellorsville, May 1, 2, and 3, 1863. It was sent to New York City, to aid in enforcing the draft, arriving there on the 1st of September, and leaving on the 8th. It again joined the Potomac army, on the Rapidan River, Virginia; and, with it, on the 25th of September, was transported *via* Washington to Columbus, Indianapolis, and Louisville, to Chattanooga, Tennessee; and with General Joe Hooker, as its corps commander, engaged in the battle of Lookout Mountain, November 24th and 25th, 1863.

In the spring of 1864, (May 4th), the regiment joined the Atlanta campaign at Bridgeport, Alabama, and, under Major-General W. T. Sherman, participated in the battles of Dug Gap, Georgia, May 8, 1864; Resaca, May 18th and 19th; Dallas, May 25th; Pine Knob, June 15th; Kenesaw Mountain, June 27th; Peach Tree Creek, July 20th, and the siege of Atlanta.

The Twenty-Ninth left Atlanta on the 15th of November, and, with the army, marched through Georgia, and arrived within three miles and a half of Savannah on the evening of December 10th. In eleven days thereafter the city of Savannah was occupied by the National troops, December 21, 1864. The regiment remained in Savannah until January 27, 1865, when it accompanied the army through South and North Carolina to Goldsboro' *via* Columbia, Winsboro', Cheraw, and Fayetteville, arriving at Goldsboro' on the 24th of March. It remained in Goldsboro' until the 10th of April, and then marched to Raleigh, North Carolina, arriving there on the 14th. Thence, on the 29th of April, it started for Washington City *via* Richmond, Virginia, and arrived near Alexandria, Virginia, May 17th.

On the 25th the regiment left camp, passed over to Washington, and participated in the grand review. Its next camp was near Bladensburg, Maryland. It remained there until the 10th of June, when it marched into Washington and took the cars for Parkersburg, Virginia; and, on its arrival, was met by transports, and conveyed down the Ohio to Louisville, and went into camp until the 13th of July, when it started for Cleveland *via* Cincinnati, Columbus, etc. On its arrival at Camp Taylor the men were paid off and discharged, July 22 and 23, 1865.

30th REGIMENT OHIO VOLUNTEER INFANTRY.

ROSTER, THREE YEARS' SERVICE.

RANK.	NAME.	DATE OF RANK.	COM. ISSUED.	REMARKS.
Colonel	JOHN GROESBECK	July 24, 1861	July 26, 1861	Transferred to 39th regiment.
Do.	HUGH EWING	Aug. 15, "	Aug. 28, "	Appointed Brig. Gen. Nov. 29, '62, by Pres't.
Do.	THEODORE JONES	Nov. 29, 1862	April 9, 1863	Mustered out with regiment.
Lt. Colonel	THEODORE JONES	Aug. 2, 1861	Aug. 28, 1861	Promoted to Colonel.
Do.	GEORGE H. HILDT	Nov. 29, 1862	April 9, 1863	Resigned September 30, 1864.
Do.	E. W. MUENSCHER	Jan. 6, 1865	Jan. 6, 1865	Declined to accept; mustered out as Captain.
Do.	EMERSON P. BROOKS	Feb. 23, "	Feb. 23, "	Mustered out with regiment.
Major	JOHN FERGUSON	July 31, 1861	Aug. 5, 1861	Appointed Colonel 54th regiment.
Do.	GEORGE H. HILDT	Jan. 28, 1862	Jan. 28, 1862	Promoted to Lieutenant-Colonel.
Do.	D. CUNNINGHAM	Nov. 29, "	April 9, 1863	Resigned September 20, 1863.
Do.	CHAS. TOWNSEND	Sept. 20, 1863	Jan. 26, 1864	Resigned September 22, 1864.
Do.	ELIJAH WARNER	Nov. 3, 1864	Nov. 3, "	Resigned.
Do.	CYRUS A. EARNST	May 31, 1865	May 31, 1865	Mustered out as Captain.
Surgeon	HENRY F. GRIER	Aug. 28, 1861	Aug. 28, 1861	Resigned November 12, 1861. [given
Do.	JOSIAH B. POTTER	Nov. 9, "	Feb. 8, 1862	Acting Med. Director 15th A. C.; no discharge
Ass't Surgeon	C. B. RICHARDS	Aug. 31, "	Nov. 15, 1861	
Do.	D. B. WREN	July 4, "	July 23, 1862	Declined.
Do.	PHILANDER F. BEVERLY	Aug. 5, "	Aug. 12, "	Resigned April 6, 1863.
Do.	O. FISHER	July 20, 1863	July 20, 1863	
Chaplain	HENRY LANGE	Aug. 28, 1861	Aug. 28, 1861	Never reported; dropped from roll Feb. 28, '62.
Captain	Wm. W. Reilly	" 10, "	" 28, "	Resigned March 17, 1862.
Do.	D. Cunningham	" 10, "	" 28, "	Promoted to Major.
Do.	C. Townsend	" 10, "	" 28, "	Promoted to Major.
Do.	John W. Fowler	" 20, "	" 28, "	Mustered out.
Do.	Elijah Warner	" 21, "	" 28, "	Promoted to Major.
Do.	C. J. Gilbleant	" 22, "	" 28, "	Discharged March 18, 1862.
Do.	Wm. H. Harlan	" 22, "	" 28, "	Discharged October 2, 1862.
Do.	Jacob E. Taylor	" 22, "	" 28, "	Promoted to Major 40th regiment.
Do.	George H. Hildt	" 24, "	" 29, "	Promoted to Major.
Do.	Wm. H. Ijams	" 24, "	" 28, "	Resigned July 9, 1863.
Do.	John H. Groce	Nov. 19, "	Nov. 20, "	Killed December 13, 1864.
Do.	John C. Lewis	Jan. 28, 1862	Jan. 28, 1862	Resigned June 28, 1862.
Do.	Thomas Hayes	March 17, "	May 1, "	Killed May 22, 1863.
Do.	John Brown	" 18, "	" 1, "	Honorably discharged January 31, 1863.
Do.	Emory W. Muencher	June 28, "	Aug. 12, "	Promoted to Lieutenant-Colonel.
Do.	Gordan Lofland	Oct. 2, "	Dec. 30, "	Appointed A. A. G. April 23, 1863, by Pres't.
Do.	E. R. Patterson	July 5, 1863	July 10, 1863	Mustered out.
Do.	Aaron B. Chamberlain	April 23, "	May 6, "	Killed.
Do.	Joseph Collins	July 9, "	Aug. 25, "	Mustered out.
Do.	Cyrus A. Earnst	May 22, "	" 25, "	Promoted to Major.
Do.	Emerson P. Brooks	April 23, "	" 25, "	Promoted to Lieutenant-Colonel.
Do.	George E. O'Neal	Feb. 29, 1864	Feb. 29, 1861	Deserted.
Do.	Ezra McConnell	July 25, "	July 25, "	Declined.
Do.	Wm. S. Hatcher	" 25, "	" 25, "	Mustered out as 1st Lieutenant Dec. 29, 1864.
Do.	Wm. B. Todd	Nov. 3, "	Nov. 3, "	Mustered out.
Do.	Benj. Fowler	" 3, "	" 3, "	Mustered out with regiment.
Do.	James D. Bain	" 3, "	" 3, "	Mustered out with regiment.
Do.	Daniel Forney	Jan. 6, 1865	Jan. 6, 1855	Mustered out with regiment.
Do.	Isaac N. Thomas	" 6, "	" 6, "	Discharged July 28, 1865.
Do.	Joseph Dickerson	" 6, "	" 6, "	Mustered out with regiment.
Do.	Samuel Howarth	" 28, "	" 28, "	Mustered out with regiment.
Do.	Joseph Brooks	" 28, "	" 28, "	Mustered out with regiment.
Do.	Cyrus W. Delaney	" 28, "	" 28, "	Mustered out with regiment.
Do.	James W. McIlravy	May 11, "	May 11, "	Mustered out with regiment.
Do.	Theophilus Peasler	" 31, "	" 31, "	
1st Lieutenant	Thomas Hayes	Aug. 14, 1861	Aug. 28, 1861	Promoted to Captain.
Do.	John Brown	" 14, "	" 28, "	Promoted to Captain.
Do.	Wm. W. Olds	" 14, "	" 28, "	Transferred to 42d regiment.
Do.	Emory W. Muencher	" 15, "	" 28, "	Promoted to Captain.
Do.	James Taylor	" 20, "	" 28, "	Resigned September 27, 1862.
Do.	Henry R. Brinkerhoff	" 21, "	" 28, "	Lieutenant-Colonel negro regiment.
Do.	E. R. Patterson	" 22, "	" 28, "	Promoted to Captain.
Do.	George E. O'Neal	" 22, "	" 28, "	Discharged June 21, 1864; promoted.
Do.	John H. Groce	" 23, "	" 28, "	Promoted to Captain.
Do.	John C. Lewis	" 24, "	" 29, "	Promoted to Captain.
Do.	Reese R. Finley	" 24, "	" 28, "	Deceased September 17, 1862.
Do.	Gordan Lofland	" 28, "	" 28, "	Promoted to Captain.
Do.	Emerson P. Brooks	" 30, "	" 30, "	Promoted to Captain.
Do.	Moses B. Gist	Nov. 19, "	Nov. 20, "	Resigned.
Do.	Joseph Collins	Jan. 28, 1862	Jan. 28, 1862	Promoted to Captain.
Do.	Jeremiah Hall	" 28, "	" 28, "	Mustered out.
Do.	Ezra McConnell	March 17, "	May 1, "	Mustered out.
Do.	Wm. Massie	" 18, "	" 1, "	Resigned June 13, 1862.
Do.	Cyrus A. Earnst	June 13, "	Aug. 12, "	Promoted to Captain.
Do.	Charles L. Duffield	Jan. 28, "	" 12, "	Deceased September 17, 1862.
Do.	Henry Hensel	Sept. 17, "	Dec. 30, "	Revoked.
Do.	Hiram J. Davis	" 17, "	" 30, "	Died June 4, 1863.
Do.	Emmitt Headington	" 27, "	" 30, "	Honorably discharged April 25, 1865.
Do.	P. S. Sodan	Oct. 2, "	" 30, "	Revoked.
Do.	Wm. S. Hatcher	Jan. 1, 1863	May 25, 1863	Promoted to Captain.
Do.	Thomas Hunter			Mustered out
Do.	Wm. B. Todd	July 9, 1863	Aug. 25, 1863	Promoted to Captain.
Do.	Henry McIntyre	April 23, "	" 25, "	Killed at Kenesaw.
Do.	Israel P. White	May 22, "	" 25, "	Killed June 17, 1864.
Do.	James H. Odell	June 4, "	" 25, "	Resigned September 21, 1864.

RANK.	NAME.	DATE OF RANK.	COM. ISSUED.	REMARKS.
1st Lieutenant	Benj. Fowler	Feb. 29, 1864	Feb. 29, 1864	Promoted to Captain.
Do.	James D. Bain	" 29, "	" 29, "	Promoted to Captain.
Do.	Daniel Forney	" 29, "	" 29, "	Promoted to Captain.
Do.	Thomas K. White	May 9, "	May 9, "	Killed at Dallas.
Do.	Isaac N. Thomas	" 9, "	" 9, "	Promoted to Captain.
Do.	Joseph Dickerson	July 25, "	July 25, "	Promoted to Captain.
Do.	Samuel Howarth	" 25, "	" 25, "	Promoted to Captain.
Do.	Joseph Brooks	Sept. 26, "	Sept. 26, "	Promoted to Captain.
Do.	Cyrus W. Delaney	Nov. 3, "	Nov. 3, "	Promoted to Captain.
Do.	James W. McIlravy	" 18, "	" 18, "	Promoted to Captain.
Do.	Theophilus Peasler	" 18, "	" 18, "	Promoted to Captain.
Do.	James Trotter	" 18, "	" 18, "	Mustered out with regiment.
Do.	Orris Parrish	" 18, "	" 18, "	Resigned June 14, 1865.
Do.	John McHugh	" 18, "	" 18, "	Mustered out with regiment.
Do.	Oliver P. Demuth	May 11, 1865	May 11, 1865	Mustered out with regiment.
Do.	Franklin Fawatt	" 11, "	" 11, "	Mustered out with regiment.
Do.	Erasmus J. Allton	" 11, "	" 11, "	Mustered out with regiment.
Do.	Hiram Roney	" 11, "	" 11, "	
Do.	Henry C. Gamble	" 11, "	" 11, "	
Do.	John E. Edmonds	" 11, "	" 11, "	Mustered out with regiment.
Do.	Richard L. Albrittain	" 11, "	" 11, "	Mustered out with regiment.
Do.	John A. Hank	" 11, "	" 11, "	
2d Lieutenant	Jeremiah Hall	Aug. 14, 1861	Aug. 14, 1861	Promoted to 1st Lieutenant.
Do.	Ezra McConnell	" 14, "	" 14, "	Promoted to 1st Lieutenant.
Do.	John C. Rickey	" 14. "	" 14, "	Resigned November 1, 1861.
Do.	Wm. Massie	" 20, "	" 14, "	Resigned.
Do.	Henry Hensel	" 2, "	" 14, "	Resigned May 15, 1862.
Do.	P. S. Sodan	" 22, "	" 14, "	Resigned January 13, 1863.
Do.	Edward Greaves	" 22, "	" 14, "	Resigned June 20, 1862.
Do.	Moses B. Gist	" 22, "	" 14, "	Promoted to 1st Lieutenant.
Do.	Joseph Collins	" 24, "	" 29, "	Promoted to 1st Lieutenant.
Do.	Hiram J. Davis	" 24, "	" 28, "	Promoted to 1st Lieutenant September 17, '62.
Do.	Cyrus A. Earnst	Nov. 19, "	Nov. 20, "	Promoted to 1st Lieutenant.
Do.	Wm. B. Todd	Jan. 9, 1862	Jan. 9, 1862	Promoted to 1st Lieutenant.
Do.	Stephen B. Wilson	" 28, "	" 28, "	Deceased September 17, 1862.
Do.	Francis E. Russell	Feb. 8, "	Feb. 8, "	Resigned April 2, 1863.
Do.	Charles L. Duffield	March 17, "	May 1, "	Promoted to 1st Lieutenant.
Do.	Emmitt Headington	" 18, "	" 1, "	Promoted to 1st Lieutenant.
Do.	Israel P. White	June 13, "	Aug. 12, "	Promoted to 1st Lieutenant.
Do.	Aaron Chamberlain	" 28, "	" 12, "	Promoted to 1st Lieutenant.
Do.	Robert Roales	" 20, "	" 12, "	Resigned April 12, 1863.
Do.	Wm. S. Hatcher	Sept. 17, "	Nov. 15, "	Promoted to 1st Lieutenant.
Do.	James H. Odell	" 17, "	Dec. 30, "	Promoted to 1st Lieutenant.
Do.	Henry McIntyre	" 27, "	" 30, "	Promoted to 1st Lieutenant.
Do.	Benj. Fowler	" 17, "	" 30, "	Promoted to 1st Lieutenant.
Do.	James D. Bain	Oct. 2, "	" 30, "	Promoted to 1st Lieutenant.
Do.	Samuel O. Thomas	April 2, 1863	Aug. 25, 1863	Killed.
Do.	Daniel Forney	" 12, "	" 25, "	Promoted to 1st Lieutenant.
Do.	Thomas K. White	" 23, "	" 25, "	Promoted to 1st Lieutenant.
Do.	Thomas J. Evans	June 4, "	" 25, "	Dead.
Do.	Samuel Howerth	July 9, "	" 25, "	Promoted to 1st Lieutenant.
Do.	Joseph Dickerson	April 23, "	" 25, "	Promoted to 1st Lieutenant.
Do.	Isaac N. Thomas	" 23, "	" 25, "	Promoted to 1st Lieutenant.
Do.	Joseph Brooks	June 5, "	" 25, "	Promoted to 1st Lieutenant.
Do.	Cyrus M. Delaney	May 9, 1864	May 9, 1864	Promoted to 1st Lieutenant.

THIRTIETH OHIO VOLUNTEER INFANTRY.

THIS regiment was organized at Camp Chase, Ohio, on the 28th day of August, 1861. It was armed and equipped immediately, and on the 30th was ordered to the field. The next day found the regiment at Benwood, Virginia, and on the 2d of September it reached Clarksburg. Here an attack was expected, and company H was sent out to reconnoiter, but the enemy was not discovered. Late in the evening the Thirtieth marched out the Weston Pike, and on the afternoon of the next day entered Weston, and camped beside the Forty-Seventh Ohio, with which the fortunes of the Thirtieth were afterward closely allied. Here the regiment received its first outfit of camp and garrison equipage. Two wagons were furnished to each company, and even this supply was deemed barely sufficient for transportation. In later years the men considered themselves fortunate if there was one wagon in the regiment; and if by any means the authorities should furnish two, it was a liberality for which the soldier could not be sufficiently grateful.

On the 6th of September the regiment joined General Rosecrans at Sutton Heights. Here companies D, F, G, and I were ordered to remain, and the remainder of the regiment marched with the army toward Summerville. Two companies (C and E) were left at Big Birch Bottoms, and the remainder of the regiment moved on to Carnifex Ferry, where a sharp engagement took place. During the night the enemy withdrew to Sewell Mountain. A considerable amount of arms and camp equipage, and some huge double-edged knives, with which one of the Rebels was to annihilate five of the Yankees, fell into the hands of the National army. A stand of colors, on which was inscribed "Floyd's Brigade! The price of liberty is the blood of the brave!" was secured by the Thirtieth. After ten days' rest the regiment moved to Sewell Mountain, but the condition of the roads rendered further advance impracticable, and the National army fell back to the Falls of the Gauley, arriving on the 8th of October. This position was called Camp Ewing. The enemy took position on Cotton Hill, overlooking Camp Ewing, and annoyed the National troops with artillery. The army advanced upon the Rebels, drove them from their position, and pursued them until twelve miles beyond Fayette C. H. On the 14th of November the regiment entered Fayetteville and quartered in the deserted houses.

In the meantime, the detachment at Sutton was frequently engaged in expeditions against bushwhackers and horse-thieves. Two men of the Thirtieth were killed, and quite a number were wounded from time to time in various skirmishes. On the morning of the 22d of October a scouting party was fired upon, and one man was killed instantly. The skulking murderer could not be found; and, enraged by the loss of their comrade, the soldiers killed, in cold blood, two men who were captured the same day. The officer in charge of the party was accused of complicity in the deed, and for this and other misdemeanors, he was dishonorably dismissed the service, by sentence of a general court-martial.

On the 23d of December the detachment at Sutton joined the regiment at Fayetteville, and on the 25th the regiment held its first dress-parade.

During the winter the regiment worked upon fortifications, which were upon several occasions of signal benefit to the army. Several of the companies were sent to outposts. Company H was sent to the White House, on Loup Creek Road; company A to a church five miles out, on the Raleigh Road, and company B to McCoy's, further out on the same road. The winter, though not unusually severe, was very wet, and consequently there was much sickness in the

Thirtieth. On the 28th of December companies F and K, forming part of a detachment under Major Comly, of the Twenty-Third, started for Raleigh C. H., and on arriving were quartered in deserted houses. These companies returned to Fayetteville on the 10th of March, 1862, at which time the Thirtieth and two sections of McMullen's battery comprised the entire force at that point.

On the 17th of April the regiment broke up winter-quarters and moved to Raleigh. From this point a detachment of one hundred men moved to Richmond's Ferry, on New River. The detachment crossed the river, and was engaged for several days in marching and scouting in Greenbrier County. It returned to Raleigh on the 26th, with some prisoners and horses. On the 5th of May the Thirtieth camped near Princeton, and on the 10th it resumed the march to Giles's C. H. At noon information was received that the troops at Giles's C. H. had been attacked and were falling back. The men unslung knapsacks, pushed forward rapidly, and joined the Twenty-Third at the mouth of the Narrows, having marched twenty miles in five hours, and having carried knapsacks twelve miles of that distance. But the regiment arrived too late. The enemy had closed the gate which led to the country beyond. The next day the regiment encamped at the confluence of the East and New Rivers, and company H was pushed forward up the Narrows, and succeeded in developing the enemy's position, and in drawing the fire of his batteries. This company claims to have been the first in the Thirtieth under artillery fire. For eight days the allowance of rations was one cracker, with a small quantity of sugar, coffee, beans, and rice, to each man.

Early on the morning of the 17th of May the First Brigade of Cox's division, consisting of the Twelfth, Twenty-Third, and Thirtieth Ohio Regiments, and McMullen's battery, fell back to Princeton, where supplies were received. The next day the troops marched out the Raleigh Road, and on the 19th camped on the summit of the Great Flat Top Mountain. They were without tents, but the men stripped the bark from the large chestnut trees, and with that constructed huts which furnished some shelter. This place was called Camp Bark. On the 1st of June two companies of the Thirtieth were sent to Green Meadows, which was occupied as an outpost. The companies at Green Meadows were relieved from time to time. At Flat Top a site was selected for a new camp, and heavy details were made to prepare it. This became one of the most complete camps the regiment ever occupied.

On the 16th of August the Thirtieth started to join the army in Eastern Virginia. At noon on the 19th the regiment reached Brownstown, at that time the head of navigation on the Kanawha, having carried knapsacks and marched ninety-five miles in three days and a half. All were delighted to leave the mountains; and when the band played "Get Out of the Wilderness," as it came down Cotton Hill to the river, the deafening cheers that went up from the column showed that the hit was duly appreciated.

The regiment proceeded on transports to Parkersburg, where it took the cars for the East. On the 23d of August it passed through Washington City, and that night went into camp at Warrenton Junction, Virginia. Three days later the right wing reported at General Pope's head-quarters for guard-duty. The left wing was to follow as soon as it came off picket. General Pope's head-quarters were moved to Centerville, and the left wing of the Thirtieth followed in Robertson's brigade. At the battle of Centerville the left wing was at no time completely engaged with musketry, but it was compelled to lie under a heavy artillery fire. General Robertson, in his official report, says: "It moved forward under a heavy fire from the enemy's batteries, in as good order as if on parade." On the 31st of August the left wing joined the right at General Pope's head-quarters.

On the 3d of September the regiment joined the brigade at Upton Hills. On the 7th it broke camp, marched through Washington City, and at ten o'clock A. M. on the 9th came in view of Frederick City, Maryland. The Thirtieth deployed, moved by the flank above the city, waded the Monocacy, advanced as skirmishers, and, converging into the line of battle, entered the city on the right of the Twentieth and Twenty-Third Ohio. On the 14th of September the regiment arrived at South Mountain, and at nine o'clock A. M. engaged the enemy's skirmishers. A Rebel battery, placed behind a stone fence, opened fire upon the regiment, killing and wounding several men. For several hours the Thirtieth lay under a terrific artillery fire, and at four o'clock P. M. it advanced against the Rebel battery. The enemy's lines advanced at the same time, and a severe engagement ensued, lasting forty-five minutes. The regiment stood its ground bravely, and lost eighteen men killed and forty-eight wounded.

On the evening of the 16th of September the Thirtieth lay down within sight of the Antietam bridge. The next morning the regiment moved to the left and front, crossed the stream, and moved up toward the bridge, which had been carried by the National troops. Upon reaching the bridge it was ordered forward on the double-quick to a stone wall five hundred yards in advance. It was necessary to pass over a field recently plowed in order to reach the wall. When the line had advanced as far as the field the men were almost exhausted, and for want of proper support the left flank of the regiment was unprotected. General A. P. Hill's division came down with crushing weight on the exposed flank. The regiment endeavored to execute a movement by the right flank, in order to avoid the blow, but it was thrown into some confusion, and was compelled to fall back to the river bank. The regiment lost two commissioned officers killed and two wounded, and eight men killed and thirty-seven wounded. The National colors were torn in fourteen places by the enemy's balls, and two color-bearers fell dead on the field. Sergeant White stood up and waved the flag defiantly in the enemy's face until he fell, never to rise again, and Sergeant Carter grasped the flag-staff so firmly in his death agony that it could with difficulty be taken from his hands.

After remaining for a few days near the battle-ground, the regiment moved for West Virginia, and on the 10th of October crossed the Potomac at Hancock. On the same day General Stuart crossed the Potomac on his raid into Pennsylvania. The Thirtieth started in pursuit, but returned to Hancock on the 12th, and continued the journey westward. On the 13th of November General Ewing's brigade was directed to erect winter-quarters below the confluence of the Gauley and Kanawha. The Thirtieth went into camp opposite to Cannelton. Winter-quarters were erected. On the 30th of November the Thirtieth, with another regiment, started on a march into Logan County. It moved *via* Clifton and Brownstown; thence up Len's Creek, crossing it fifty-two times within three miles; thence down Shot Creek to Coal River; thence over Droity and Price Mountains, and through Chapmansville to Logan C. H. The advance charged into the town, killed one Rebel and captured another. The regiment returned with seventeen prisoners and seventy-five horses. On the 4th of December the Thirtieth marched for Brownstown, where it arrived the next day, and was placed on transports. The brigade consisted of the Fourth Virginia, and the Thirtieth, Thirty-Seventh, and Forty-Seventh Ohio, under General Ewing. The Thirtieth occupied the flag-ship. The fleet steamed down the river, and on the 3d of January, 1863, it arrived at Louisville, Kentucky. It moved on down the Ohio and the Mississippi until it reached Helena, Arkansas, where the brigade was assigned as the Second Brigade to the Second Division of the Fifteenth Army Corps.

On the 21st of January the regiment landed at Young's Point, and worked for a time on the canal at that place. In March the Thirtieth moved on an expedition to the relief of some gunboats in Steel's Bayou, and returned to Young's Point March 28th. On the 17th of April a fleet was preparing to run the batteries at Vicksburg—volunteers were called for, and Lieutenant George E. O'Neal, of company G, and Quartermaster A. B. Chamberlain, of the Thirtieth, with a sufficient crew from the regiment, took charge of the Silver Wave and successfully ran the blockade—only one shot striking the boat. On the 29th of April the regiment embarked on the R. B. Hamilton, and with other troops engaged in a demonstration on Haines's Bluff. It returned to Young's Point at one o'clock A. M. on the 2d of May, and on the same morning at six o'clock it embarked and proceeded to Milliken's Bend. After spending a few days at this place and in the vicinity, the regiment returned to Young's Point, arriving at twelve M. on the 3d of May. At three P. M. on the same day the regiment took up the line of march down the river. A short distance below Warrenton it embarked on the Silver Wave, and landed at Grand Gulf at four o'clock P. M. on the 15th of May. That same evening the regiment began its march. It moved by way of Rocky Springs, Raymond, and Champion Hills, and on the 19th of May it was in the rear of Vicksburg, in front of Fort Beauregard, on the Old Grave Yard Road.

On the afternoon of the 20th of May the regiment participated in a demonstration in favor of an assault made on the left. In three hours the regiment fired forty-five thousand rounds of cartridges. On the 22d of May, at ten o'clock A. M., the Thirtieth led an assault on the works in General Sherman's front. The regiment was preceded by a storming party of one hundred men. The flag was placed on the Rebel parapet, and guarded there until night enabled the troops to retire. The three leading companies of the Thirtieth suffered severely, losing forty-seven men killed and wounded. From this time until the surrender of Vicksburg the regiment was engaged in demonstrations against the enemy's works and in fatigue and picket-duty. The casualties of the Thirtieth during the siege were one commissioned officer killed and six wounded, and six men killed and forty-eight wounded. After the surrender of Vicksburg the regiment marched to Jackson, and upon the evacuation of that place by the Rebels it returned as far as Black River and went into camp July 23d.

The regiment, with the army, left Black River on the 26th of September and the next day embarked on transports at Vicksburg and moved up the river, arriving at Memphis on the 2d of October. On the 4th of October the regiment left Memphis and on the 20th of November it camped at Brown's Ferry, ten miles from Chattanooga. On the 24th it was in position in front of Mission Ridge, and on the 25th, in company with a detachment of the Fourth Virginia, it assaulted and carried the outer line of the enemy's works. Later in the day the Thirtieth and Thirty-Seventh Ohio made two unsuccessful assaults on the works on Tunnel Hill; the Thirtieth losing thirty-nine men killed and wounded. On the 26th of November the Rebels evacuated and the regiment joined in the pursuit, returning to Bridgeport, Alabama, on the 19th of December. Here the regiment received supplies. On the 29th of November two days' rations had been issued, and from that time until arriving at Bridgeport the regiment had subsisted off the country; and, in addition to this, one-fourth of the men were without shoes.

On the 26th of December the regiment took up the line of march, and on the 29th went into camp at Bellefonte Station. Here the Thirtieth proceeded to erect quarters, at the same time sending out foraging parties. The regiment moved to Larkin's Ferry, on the Tennessee River, on the 26th of January, 1864, and thence to Cleveland, Tennessee, where a sufficient number of men re-enlisted to make it a veteran regiment. It was one of the largest in the division, numbering three hundred and fifteen men. The regiment was ordered North, and arrived at Columbus, Ohio, on the 8th of April. The next day the men were furloughed. On the 9th of May the regiment re-assembled at Columbus, and on the 10th started for the South, proceeding by way of Cincinnati, Louisville, Nashville, and Chattanooga, to Kingston, Georgia, where it arrived May 20th. On the morning of the 23d the regiment was on the march. It moved through Dallas and Acworth, and on the 19th of June reached the foot of Kenesaw Mountain. During this march the regiment was almost continually under fire. On the 26th of June the Thirtieth, with its division, moved three miles to the right of the former position, and the next day made an assault on the Rebel works. The regiment advanced for a quarter of a mile on the "double-quick" over an open field, then through a low woods, from the further end of which it drove the Rebel skirmishers in gallant style, and still pressed on and formed under a heavy cross-fire of artillery and musketry. As the regiment was unable to harm the enemy by its fire it fell back to the Rebel skirmish-line, and then to the other edge of the woods, where it was sheltered comparatively well. In this attack it lost thirty-five men killed and wounded.

On the afternoon of the 2d of July the regiment was on the march. On the 13th it passed through Marietta, and on the 20th was within two and a half miles of Atlanta. On the 22d of July the enemy assaulted that portion of the line in which the Thirtieth was posted. The line at first gave way, but soon re-formed and repulsed the enemy. In this engagement the regiment lost twenty-seven men killed, wounded, and prisoners. On the 28th of July the enemy attacked the Second and Fourth Divisions of the Fifteenth Corps with great dash and determination, but was repulsed with heavy loss four successive times. The regiment maintained its ground manfully and lost thirty men killed and wounded. The enemy abandoned a stand of colors under the regiment's fire, and one hundred and five dead Rebels were picked up in its immediate front. Private Hayden DeLany, of company B, seized a wagon load of ammunition which was stampeding, drove it under fire in rear of the line, and supplied the troops with cartridges. For bravery in this instance and general good conduct he was appointed a cadet at West Point, and reported there upon the arrival of the regiment at Washington, D. C., in 1865. The regiment was transferred to the First Brigade on the 5th of August, and on the 29th those who were not veterans were mustered out by reason of the expiration of their term of service.

On the night of the 30th of August the regiment went on picket within one mile of Jonesboro', and the next day the Rebels attacked the line of the First Brigade but were repulsed. In this engagement the Thirtieth lost twenty-five killed and wounded. On the 2d of September the enemy evacuated Jonesboro', and the regiment pursued them to Lovejoy's Station. On the 5th it returned, and on the 8th went into camp at East Point. Here some weeks were spent in resting and refitting. On the 5th of October the regiment moved in pursuit of Hood's army into Alabama. It returned and went into camp near Atlanta on the 13th of November. On the 15th of November it was again on the march, and on the 13th of December it was in front of Fort McAllister. The First Brigade occupied the right of the assaulting line. At a given signal all moved forward, pressed on to the crest of the works and engaged the enemy in a hand-to-hand conflict. The Thirtieth, Forty-Seventh, and Seventieth Ohio were specially mentioned in the official report of General Hazen, the division commander. On the 15th of December the regiment moved on an expedition to destroy the Gulf Railroad. It returned to Fort McAllister on the 21st, and remained in camp near the fort during the remainder of the month.

On the 1st of January, 1865, the regiment marched for Savannah, and the next day encamped just outside of the city. On the 14th it moved to Thunderbolt. On the 17th it embarked, and on the 18th it went into camp just outside of the fortifications of Beaufort. On the 26th of January the regiment moved out to Gay's Hill, on the 30th it camped at Pocotaligo Station and waited for the trains to close up. On the 1st of February the Thirtieth was fairly started on the campaign of the Carolinas. The regiment reached Shilling's Bridge, over the North Edisto, on the 12th of February, and effected a crossing about three miles below the bridge. A swamp, a mile in width and waist deep, lay on the Rebel side of the river, and this had to be waded after the main current was crossed. When the troops emerged from the swamp they were subjected to the fire of the enemy's skirmishers, but the National line advanced with a hurrah, drove back the Rebels, and captured many prisoners. The regiment passed through Columbia on the 17th of February, and pushed on, corduroying and skirmishing, until the 20th of March, when it had a sharp engagement with the enemy at Harper's Farm. On the 24th of March the regiment arrived at Goldsboro', marched two miles out the Newbern Road and went into camp and remained until the 10th of April. The Thirtieth arrived at Raleigh on the 14th of April, and remained there until the 29th, when it moved for Washington, D. C., by way of Richmond. The regiment passed through Richmond on the 13th of May, and on the 23d bivouacked at night at the south end of the Long Bridge over the Potomac at Washington. The next morning the column moved at daylight, and after passing in review in front of the White House, the Thirtieth moved out Fourteenth Street and went into camp four miles from the city.

On the 2d of June the regiment left Washington and proceeded to Louisville, Kentucky, and went into camp, June 7th, near the City Water Works. On the 13th it was detailed as the headquarter guard of the Fifteenth Army Corps, and was relieved June 25th, and on the same day embarked for Little Rock, Arkansas, arriving July 5th. Here the time was spent in the ordinary routine of camp life until the 13th of August, when the regiment was mustered out. It embarked immediately for Columbus, Ohio, and arrived August 21st. It was paid and discharged on the 22d, having traveled, as a regiment, during its term of service, a distance of thirteen thousand two hundred miles.

31st REGIMENT OHIO VOLUNTEER INFANTRY.

ROSTER, THREE YEARS' SERVICE.

RANK.	NAME.	DATE OF RANK.	COM. ISSUED.	REMARKS.
Colonel	MOSES B. WALKER	Aug. 10, 1861	Sept. 27, 1861	Mustered out with regiment.
Lt. Colonel	CYRUS GRANT	" 6, "	" 6, "	Resigned February 27, 1862.
Do.	FREDERICK W. LISTER	Feb. 28, 1862	Feb. 28, 1862	Promoted to Colonel Fortieth U. S. C. T.
Do.	MILTON B. W. HARMON	June 20, 1865	June 20, 1865	Mustered out with regiment.
Major	SAMUEL L. LEFFINGWELL	Aug. 3, 1861	Sept. 27, 1861	Mustered out of service.
Do.	FREDERICK W. LISTER	Sept. 28, "	Oct. 24, "	Promoted to Lieutenant-Colonel.
Do.	SAMUEL R. MOTT	Feb. 28, 1862	Feb. 28, 1862	Declined.
Do.	JOHN W. FREE	" 28, "	March 20, "	Honorably discharged December 5, 1864.
Do.	GEORGE T. WALKER	June 20, 1865	June 20, 1865	
Surgeon	JOHN R. ARTER	Sept. 13, 1861	Sept. 27, 1861	Mustered out at expiration of service.
Do.	ELIAS S. CHAPPEL	Oct. 4, 1864	Oct. 4, 1864	Mustered out with regiment.
Ass't Surgeon	J. L. MOUNT	Sept. 15, 1861	Sept. 27, 1861	Resigned January 11, 1863.
Do.	R. W. VARNEY	March 11, 1863	March 11, 1863	Mustered out with regiment.
Do.	ELIAS S. CHAPPEL	Feb. 4, "	Nov. 10, "	Promoted to Surgeon.
Chaplain	L. F. DRAKE	Sept. 21, 1861	Sept. 27, 1861	Resigned April 26, 1862.
Captain	John W. Free	Aug. 7, "	" 27, "	Promoted to Major.
Do.	Wm. M. Bowen	" 9, "	" 27, "	Resigned April 30, 1862.
Do.	Samuel R. Mott	Sept. 3, "	" 27, "	Promoted to Major.
Do.	Lyman J. Jackson	" 4, "	" 27, "	Promoted.
Do.	Wm. R. Free	" 7, "	" 27, "	Honorably discharged December 30, 1863.
Do.	David H. Miller	" 19, "	" 27, "	Resigned November 3, 1862.
Do.	Amos J. Sterling	" 21, "	" 27, "	Mustered out.
Do.	John H. Putnam	" 23, "	" 27, "	Resigned February 1, 1863.
Do.	David C. Rose	" 21, "	" 27, "	Deceased.
Do.	Wm. H. Wade	" 27, "	" 27, "	Mustered out September 19, 1864.
Do.	Samuel Lyons	Jan. 28, 1862	Jan. 28, 1862	Declined promotion.
Do.	John L. Williams	Feb. 8, "	Feb. 8, "	
Do.	Michael Stone	" 28, "	" 28, "	Mustered out March 12, 1865.
Do.	Chas. O. Jeline	March 13, "	March 13, "	On Gen. Morgan's staff at muster out of reg't.
Do.	Henry C. Greiner	April 30, "	June 21, "	Resigned May 14, 1863.
Do.	Edwin C. Denig	Oct. 5, "	Nov. 1, "	Resigned January 11, 1863.
Do.	Milton B. W. Harmon	Nov. 3, "	" 18, "	Promoted to Lieutenant-Colonel.
Do.	James A. Cahill	Jan. 11, 1863	Jan. 17, 1863	Killed June 23, 1864.
Do.	Wm. H. Sutton	" 11, "	" 17, "	Resigned December 8, 1863.
Do.	John H. McCune	Feb. 1, "	Feb. 23, "	Discharged February 24, 1864.
Do.	Abraham V. Barber	May 11, "	June 17, "	Resigned December 15, 1864.
Do.	James J. Donahoe	March 11, 1864	March 11, 1864	Resigned January 30, 1865.
Do.	Eli Wilkins	" 11, "	" 11, "	Mustered out with regiment.
Do.	George T. Walker	Jan. 11, "	" 21, "	Promoted to Major.
Do.	Albert S. Scott	Oct. 12, "	Oct. 12, "	Mustered out with regiment.
Do.	Henry S. Byers	" 12, "	" 12, "	Mustered out with regiment.
Do.	Chas. H. Hood	" 12, "	" 12, "	Mustered out with regiment.
Do.	Alfred P. Alpin	" 12, "	" 12, "	Resigned as 1st Lieutenant May 30, 1865.
Do.	Wm. Carlisle	April 20, 1865	April 20, 1865	Mustered out with regiment.
Do.	Wm. H. McArthur	June 6, "	June 6, "	Mustered out with regiment.
Do.	Emanuel Clark	" 6, "	" 6, "	Mustered out with regiment.
Do.	Columbus L. Williams	" 6, "	" 6, "	Mustered out with regiment.
Do.	Wm. Bennett	" 20, "	" 20, "	Mustered out as 1st Lieutenant.
Do.	Warren Clark	" 20, "	" 20, "	Mustered out as 1st Lieutenant.
1st Lieutenant	Henry S. Babbitt	Aug. 6, 1861	Sept. 27, 1861	Resigned October 1, 1862.
Do.	Samuel Lyons	" 7, "	" 27, "	Discharged August 19, 1862.
Do.	John L. Williams	" 9, "	" 27, "	Promoted to Captain.
Do.	Edwin C. Denig	" 10, "	" 27, "	Promoted to Captain by President.
Do.	Michael Stone	Sept. 3, "	" 27, "	Promoted to Captain.
Do.	Henry C. Greiner	" 4, "	" 27, "	Promoted to Captain.
Do.	Oliver Eckles	" 7, "	" 27, "	Resigned June 6, 1862.
Do.	John M. Hills	" 9, "	" 27, "	Discharged April 27, 1863.
Do.	W. H. Sutton	" 19, "	" 27, "	Promoted to Captain.
Do.	James A. Cahill	" 21, "	" 27, "	Promoted to Captain.
Do.	John H. McCune	" 23, "	" 27, "	Promoted to Captain.
Do.	George P. Stiles	" 24, "	" 27, "	Mustered out September 24, 1864.
Do.	Isaac P. Primrose	Jan. 28, 1862	Jan. 28, 1862	Resigned November 7, 1862.
Do.	James K. Rochester	Feb. 8, "	Feb. 8, "	Killed November 25, 1863.
Do.	Abraham V. Barber	" 28, "	" 28, "	Promoted to Captain.
Do.	Thomas W. Beacham	April 30, "	June 21, "	Revoked.
Do.	James J. Donahoe	June 6, "	Aug. 27, "	Promoted to Captain.
Do.	James W. Martin	Aug. 19, "	Oct. 17, "	Discharged February 15, 1864.
Do.	Milton B. W. Harmon	Oct. 1, "	" 17, "	Promoted to Captain.
Do.	John S. Harbaugh	Nov. 2, "	Nov. 18, "	Resigned
Do.	James T. Hayden	" 7, "	March 30, 1863	Resigned September 22, 1864.
Do.	George M. Morris	Oct. 5, 1863	Nov. 28 "	Resigned October 2, 1864.
Do.	Eli Wilkins	June 11, "	June 17, "	Promoted to Captain.
Do.	Silas Daw	Feb. 1, "	Feb. 23, "	Discharged August 29, 1864.
Do.	Albert S. Scott	Jan. 11, "	June 17, "	Promoted to Captain.
Do.	John J. Martin	May 11, "	" 17, "	Revoked.
Do.	Henry S. Byers	July 1, "	July 27, "	Promoted to Captain.
Do.	Charles H. Hood	Oct. 1, "	Dec. 3, "	Promoted to Captain.
Do.	Alfred P. Alpin	April 29, "	Jan. 10, 1864	Promoted to Captain.
Do.	Wm. Carlisle	March 11, 1861	March 11, "	Promoted to Captain.
Do.	Wm. H. McArthur	" 11, "	" 11, "	Promoted to Captain.
Do.	Emanuel Clark	" 11, "	" 11, "	Promoted to Captain.
Do.	Columbus L. Williams	" 21, "	" 21, "	Promoted to Captain.
Do.	Wm. W. Spurrier	Oct. 12, "	Oct. 12, "	
Do.	Joseph Taylor	" 12, "	" 12, "	Mustered out with regiment.
Do.	Samuel Southard	" 12, "	" 12, "	Mustered out with regiment.

RANK.	NAME.	DATE OF RANK.	COM. ISSUED.	REMARKS.
1st Lieutenant	Wm. Bennett	Oct. 12, 1864	Oct. 12, 1864	Promoted to Captain.
Do.	Warren Clark	" 12, "	" 12, "	Promoted to Captain.
Do.	J. J. Miller	" 12, "	" 12, "	Mustered out with regiment.
Do.	Henry Roether	April 20, 1865	April 20, 1865	Mustered out as Adjutant.
Do.	James A. North	" 20, "	" 20, "	
Do.	Alex. F. Kirkpatrick	" 20, "	" 20, "	Mustered out with regiment.
Do.	Benj. Brown	June 6, "	June 6, "	Mustered out as Captain.
Do.	Samuel W. Batt	" 6, "	" 6, "	Mustered out with regiment.
Do.	Harrison Allspaugh	" 6, "	" 6, "	
Do.	Hamilton H. Henry	" 6, "	" 6, "	Mustered out as 2d Lieutenant.
Do.	John Stollsmith	" 20, "	" 20, "	
2d Lieutenant	Isaac P. Primrose	Aug. 7, 1861	Sept. 27, 1861	Promoted to 1st Lieutenant.
Do.	James K. Rochester	" 9, "	" 27, "	Promoted to 1st Lieutenant.
Do.	Abraham V. Barber	Sept. 3, "	" 27, "	Promoted to 1st Lieutenant; revoked.
Do.	James E. Howe	" 7, "	" 27, "	Resigned July 13, 1862.
Do.	Thomas W. Beacham	" 19, "	" 27, "	Discharged June 27, 1863.
Do.	John Hartshorn	" 21, "	" 27, "	Resigned February 12, 1863.
Do.	Edward Ewing	" 23, "	" 27, "	Mustered out May 10, 1862.
Do.	Geo. W. Reed	" 24, "	" 27, "	Resigned March 11, 1862.
Do.	James W. Martin	" 24, "	" 27, "	Promoted to 1st Lieutenant.
Do.	Geo. W. Morris	" 27, "	" 27, "	Promoted to 1st Lieutenant.
Do.	Milton B. W. Harmon	Jan. 28, 1862	Jan. 28, 1862	Promoted to 1st Lieutenant.
Do.	J. W. Lidey	Feb. 19, "	Feb. 19, "	Resigned January 8, 1863.
Do.	James J. Donahoe	March 14, "	April 10, "	Promoted to 1st Lieutenant.
Do.	Thomas J. Spencer	May 10, "	June 3, "	Discharged November 18, 1862
Do.	Henry C. Hassey	April 30, "	" 24, "	Resigned May 3, 1863.
Do.	Albert S. Scott	June 8, "	Sept. 1, "	Promoted to 1st Lieutenant.
Do.	John J. Martin	July 13, "	Oct. 13, "	Promoted to 1st Lieut.; resigned Oct. 10, 1863
Do.	Chas. Babbitt	Aug. 10, "	" 17, "	Resigned October 11, 1863.
Do.	Anson B. White	Nov. 18, "	Dec. 17, "	Resigned January 20, 1863.
Do.	Silas Daw	Jan. 20, 1863	Feb. 18, 1863	Promoted to 1st Lieutenant.
Do.	Eli Wilkins	" 18, "	" 23, "	Promoted to 1st Lieutenant.
Do.	Alfred P. Alpin	" 18, "	" 23, "	Promoted to 1st Lieutenant.
Do.	Ludwell M. Cunnard	" 20, "	" 18, "	Resigned August 11, 1863.
Do.	J. J. Miller	Feb. 12, "	" 22, "	Promoted to 1st Lieutenant.
Do.	Wm. Carlisle	" 1, "	" 23, "	Promoted to 1st Lieutenant.
Do.	Chas. H. Hood	May 8, "	June 8, "	Promoted to 1st Lieutenant.
Do.	Wm. H. McArthur	Jan. 11, "	" 17, "	Promoted to 1st Lieutenant.
Do.	John W. Ricketts	Dec. 1, 1862	" 4, "	Promoted to 1st Lieutenant.
Do.	S. A. Pollock	May 14, 1863	" 17, "	Resigned September 14, 1864.
Do.	John H. Colburn	June 6, "	" 17, "	Resigned September 20, 1864.
Do.	Henry S. Byers	July 1, "	July 27, "	Promoted to 1st Lieutenant.
Do.	Columbus L. Williams	Dec. 18, "	Feb. 13, 1864	Promoted to 1st Lieutenant.
Do.	Wm. W. Spurrier	March 11, 1864	March 11, "	Promoted to 1st Lieutenant.
Do.	Emanuel Clark	Dec. 18, 1863	" 10, "	Promoted to 1st Lieutenant.
Do.	Joseph Taylor	March 11, 1864	" 11, "	Promoted to 1st Lieutenant.
Do.	John E. Jones	" 11, "	" 11, "	Resigned September 23, 1864.
Do.	Samuel Southard	" 11, "	" 11, "	Promoted to 1st Lieutenant.
Do.	Wm. Bennett	" 11, "	" 11, "	Promoted to 1st Lieutenant.
Do.	Warren Clark	" 21, "	" 21, "	Promoted to 1st Lieutenant.
Do.	Thompson Gallaher	June 16, 1865	June 16, 1865	Mustered out with regiment.
Do.	Jonathan Culver	" 16, "	" 16, "	Mustered out with regiment.
Do.	Hamilton H. Henry	" 16, "	" 16, "	Promoted to 1st Lieutenant.
Do.	John Stollsmith	" 1, "	" 1, "	Promoted to 1st Lieutenant.
Do.	Nathan V. B. Grist	" 20, "	" 20, "	Mustered out with regiment.

THIRTY-FIRST OHIO VOLUNTEER INFANTRY.

THE THIRTY-FIRST OHIO was organized at Camp Chase between the 4th of August and the 7th of September, 1861. On the 27th of September the regiment received marching orders, and reported to Brigadier-General O. M. Mitchel at Cincinnati. Companies A and B had been detached and sent to Gallipolis to guard Government stores, but they joined the remainder of the regiment at Cincinnati. The regiment quartered at the Orphan Asylum, and received many favors from the citizens. On the 31st it left Cincinnati, and on the 2d of October reached Camp Dick Robinson, Kentucky, where a regular conrse of drill began, which rendered the regiment more efficient. It remained until the 12th of December, when it moved to Somerset, thence on several reconnoissances, and on the 19th of January, 1862, it marched to the assistance of General Thomas at the battle of Mill Springs, but on account of bad roads it arrived too late to participate in the engagement. Here the regiment was assigned to the First Brigade, First Division, Army of the Ohio. Preparations were made to follow the retreating Rebels, but the plans were changed and the troops moved to Lebanon, and from there to Louisville. The regiment embarked on the Magnolia, and proceeding down the Ohio and up the Cumberland landed at Nashville. Owing to the crowded condition of the men, and the difficulty in cooking rations on the transports, much sickness occurred, so that on disembarking there were only five hundred men fit for duty.

After a short rest the health of the men improved greatly, and the regiment moved southward with Buell's army. The brigade halted four miles below Columbia, under orders to collect all the transportation for the army and to act as escort during the remainder of the march. The train was divided into four sections, and one regiment was assigned to each section. The Thirty-First was assigned to the left section, and brought up the rear. By a vast amount of labor the brigade succeeded in reaching Clifton with the train, where the troops and supplies were placed on transports and conveyed to Pittsburg Landing. The regiment advanced with the army toward Corinth, and during the march was engaged frequently in skirmishing with the Rebels. It participated in the siege, and was engaged at times quite warmly. After the evacuation it marched in pursuit of the Rebels about forty miles, and then returned and went into camp near Corinth. On the 22d of June the regiment marched in the direction of Iuka. The weather was intensely warm, and the troops rested during the heat of the day and made up for the lost time by night marches. There was some fighting near Iuka but the troops moved into the town, and on the 26th continued the march toward Tuscumbia, where they arrived on the 28th. The Rebels were recruiting and organizing troops in the vicinity of Tuscumbia, and the regiment was engaged in expeditions against them.

Here the Fourth of July was celebrated. The Declaration of Independence was read, and speeches were made by General Fry, Colonels Walker, Steadman, and Robt. McCook. The regiment was divided into detachments, and two companies were sent to Decatur and one company was sent to Trinity. On the morning of the 19th the brigade marched for Huntsville by way of Decatur. It arrived at the latter place on the 22d, and at once commenced to cross the Tennessee River on a small ferry-boat, which was manned and run by the men of company K. In the regiment were engineers and mechanics of every sort, so that the regiment was always able to perform any kind of duty that might devolve upon it.

After the brigade had crossed the river a messenger arrived with the information that the detachment of the regiment at Trinity, consisting of twenty-eight men, had been attacked by a force of between two and three hundred mounted Rebels. The Rebels were repulsed, but one-half of the detachment was killed or wounded. A train of cars had arrived in Trinity just as the attack began, and after the Rebels were driven off the detachment took the train and came to Decatur, bringing the killed and wounded. It was rumored that Wheeler intended to attack Decatur, and six companies of the Thirty-First were crossed secretly at night and stationed in the town. No attack was made; but at daylight Rebel flags were seen floating from several of the principal dwelling-houses. These houses were searched and arms of every description were found and destroyed.

The regiment moved with the army to Huntsville, and thence to Decherd, Tennessee. From this point the regiment advanced toward the mountains, and was engaged in guarding passes and watching the enemy until the campaign of Buell and Bragg in Kentucky opened, when it moved to Decherd and, with other troops, was placed in charge of the transportation of the army. The regiment marched through Murfreesboro' and Nashville to Louisville. After a short rest the troops again moved southward. At the battle of Perryville the regiment was under fire but was not actively engaged. After the battle the march was continued to Nashville. From this point the army moved toward Murfreesboro', the brigade, of which the Thirty-First was a part, occupying the extreme right. By an accident the brigade became separated from the main army, but it effected a junction on the Murfreesboro' Pike, about half-way between Lavergne and Stewart's Creek. Here the brigade was ordered to remain until further orders, while the remainder of the army moved on to Murfreesboro'. While in camp at this point it was reported that the Rebels were pillaging the train at Lavergne. The Thirty-First and two other regiments marched back rapidly, attacked the Rebels and drove them off, killing, wounding, and capturing quite a number of them. When the battle of Stone River opened the brigade was ordered to the front, and arrived as the right wing of the army was falling back. It was actively engaged during the battle, and the Thirty-First acquitted itself nobly.

The regiment now enjoyed a few months' rest, and on the 23d of June, 1863, it started on the Tullahoma campaign. On the 26th it was engaged at Hoover's Gap, and in connection with the Seventeenth Ohio, it carried a position defended by two Rebel brigades. The next day the Rebels were forced back, and at Fairfield the wounded of the previous day's fight were captured, numbering over three hundred. The advance continued through Tullahoma to Chattanooga. The regiment was engaged on both days at Chickamauga and suffered severely. Its next engagement was Brown's Ferry, and then followed Mission Ridge, where the Thirty-First was among the foremost regiments to bear the loyal standard into the enemy's works. About this time the regiment re-enlisted and received a furlough for thirty days. While in the North three hundred and seventy-four recruits were obtained, thus increasing the regiment's effective strength to about eight hundred men. The regiment returned to the field at the expiration of the furlough, and on the 7th of May, 1864, it marched on the Atlanta campaign. On the 14th it was engaged in an assault on the enemy's line in front of Resaca, and lost heavily. It participated in all the important engagements of the campaign except the battle of Jonesboro'. After the fall of Atlanta the regiment marched in pursuit of Hood, but the chase was abandoned at Gaylesville, Alabama, where the troops rested a few days and then returned to Atlanta.

The Thirty-First moved with Sherman's army toward the sea, leaving Atlanta about noon on the 16th of November. It passed through Decatur and along the Augusta and Atlanta Railroad to Covington, and thence through Monticello to Milledgeville, where the arsenal, with a considerable amount of arms and ammunition, was destroyed. The march was continued without any incident of particular note until the 12th of December, when the works around Savannah were reached. After the surrender of the city the regiment remained quietly in camp until the 20th of February, 1865, when it moved on the campaign of the Carolinas. The route lay through Barnwell to the Augusta and Charleston Railroad at Aiken's Station; across the South and North Edisto to Lexington, and through Winnsboro' to Cheraw; thence to Fayetteville, and on with the movement of the main army until the surrender. After this the regiment moved to Washington City, and participated in the grand review. It was then transferred to Louisville, Kentucky, where it was mustered out on the 20th of July, 1865. With as little delay as possible it was transferred to Camp Chase, Ohio, and the men paid and discharged.

32d REGIMENT OHIO VOLUNTEER INFANTRY.

ROSTER, THREE YEARS' SERVICE.

RANK.	NAME.	DATE OF RANK.	COM. ISSUED.	REMARKS.
Colonel	THOMAS H. FORD	July 26, 1861	Sept. 16, 1861	Discharged November 8, 1862.
Do.	BENJ. F. POTTS	Dec. 25, 1862	Dec. 25, 1862	Appointed Brigadier-General.
Do.	J. J. HIBBITTS	May 18, 1865	May 18, 1865	Mustered out with regiment.
Lt. Colonel	EBENEZER H. SWINNEY	July 26, 1861	Sept. 16, 1861	Honorably Discharged Nov. 21, 1862.
Do.	BENJ. F. POTTS	Nov. 21, 1862	Dec. 21, 1862	Promoted to Colonel, Dec. 25, 1862.
Do.	ROBERT H. BENTLEY	Dec. 25, "	" 25, "	Resigned July 27, 1863.
Do.	J. J. HIBBITTS	July 27, 1863	Aug. 25, 1863	Promoted to Colonel.
Do.	SHELDON GUTHRIE, JR.	May 18, 1865	May 18, 1865	Mustered out with regiment.
Major	SYLVESTER M. HEWETT	July 26, 1861	Sept. 16, 1861	Honorably discharged January 13, 1863.
Do.	A. M. CRUMBACKER	Jan. 13, 1863	Jan. 19, 1863	Resigned September 21, 1864.
Do.	ALEX. R. PATTERSON	May 18, 1865	May 18, 1865	Resigned as Captain January, 1865.
Do.	ISAAC B. POST	June 6, "	June 6, "	Mustered out with regiment.
Surgeon	JOHN COURY	Aug. 21, 1861	Sept. 16, 1861	Resigned January 22, 1862.
Do.	JAMES B. BUCHANAN	Feb. 13, 1862	Feb. 13, 1862	Resigned January 18, 1863.
Do.	ALFRED C. BRUNDAGE	Jan. 18, 1863	Jan. 30, 1863	Resigned September 27, 1864.
Do.	THOMAS P. BOND	Sept. 20, 1864	Sept. 20, 1864	Mustered out with regiment.
Ass't Surgeon	ALFRED C. BRUNDAGE	Aug. 31, 1861	" 16, 1861	Promoted to Surgeon.
Do.	SILAS E. SHELDON	July 4, 1862	July 23, 1862	Honorably discharged March 13, 1863.
Do.	JOHN MORGAN	March 11, 1863	March 11, 1863	Resigned February 29, 1864.
Do.	S. S. GUTHRIE	June 9, "	June 10, "	Died.
Do.	THOMAS P. BOND	April 1, 1864	April 1, 1864	Promoted to Surgeon.
Do.	L. A. GRIMES	" 29, "	" 29, "	Discharged August 9, 1864.
Do.	W. H. PULT	Sept. 8, "	Sept. 8, "	Declined.
Do.	A. J. PATTERSON	" 20, "	" 20, "	Declined.
Do.	JOHN A. SOLIDAY	Oct. 12, "	Oct. 12, "	Died March 27, 1865.
Chaplain	WM. H. NICKERSON	Sept. 5, 1861	Sept. 16, 1861	Resigned March 17, 1862.
Do.	RUSSELL B. BENNETT	March 18, 1862	April 5, 1862	Mustered out at expiration of service.
Captain	Jackson Lacy	Aug. 16, 1861	Sept. 16, 1861	Resigned March 15, 1862.
Do.	Wm. A. Palmer	" 20, "	" 16, "	Discharged December 22, 1862.
Do.	James B. Banning	" 20, "	" 16, "	Discharged May 4, 1863.
Do.	Wm. B. Bowland	" 31, "	" 16, "	Resigned June 17, 1862.
Do.	Milton W. Worden	" 31, "	" 16, "	Honorably discharged June 18, 1863.
Do.	Benj. F. Potts	Sept. 4, "	" 16, "	Promoted to Lieutenant-Colonel Nov. 21, '62.
Do.	Wm. D. Hamilton	" 4, "	" 16, "	Mustered out.
Do.	George M. Baxter	" 5, "	" 16, "	Resigned May 24, 1862.
Do.	Wilson M. Stanley	" 5, "	" 16, "	Resigned February 11, 1862.
Do.	Jay Dyer	" 7, "	" 16, "	Resigned April 10, 1862.
Do.	Clarkson C. Nichols	March 20, 1862	March 20, 1862	Resigned April 10, 1863.
Do.	Abraham M. Crumbacker	" 15, "	May 5, "	Promoted to Major January 13, 1863.
Do.	Joseph Gladden	April "	" 5, "	Discharged May 4, 1864.
Do.	Wm. M. Morris	June 17, "	Dec. 27, "	Resigned September 16, 1864.
Do.	Theobald D. Yost	Nov. 21, "	" 27, "	Appointed Captain 26th Battery Dec. 22, 1863.
Do.	Jefferson J. Hibbitts	April 10, "	" 27, "	Promoted to Lieutenant-Colonel July 27, 1863.
Do.	Samuel R. Breese	May 24, "	" 27, "	Resigned.
Do.	Levi J. Saint	Sept. 15, "	" 27, "	Resigned June 29, 1863.
Do.	Sheldon Guthrie, jr.	Jan. 1, 1863	Jan. 19, 1863	Promoted to Lieutenant-Colonel.
Do.	George Sinclair	Dec. 22, 1862	" 19, "	Mustered out with regiment.
Do.	Elias W. James	Jan. 13, 1863	" 19, "	Resigned September 18, 1864.
Do.	Alex. R. Patterson	May 4, "	" 19, "	Promoted to Major.
Do.	Alfred G. Barnet	June 30, "	July 20, "	Resigned.
Do.	Isaac B. Post	" 18, "	" 27, "	Promoted to Major.
Do.	Wm. A. McCallister	July 27, "	Aug. 25, "	Resigned September 8, 1864.
Do.	Richard H. Fouts	May 25, 1864	May 25, 1864	Declined promotion.
Do.	John Wiley	Aug. 11, "	Aug. 11, "	Mustered out.
Do.	Ebenezer B. Hays	Oct. 12, "	Oct. 12, "	Mustered out at expiration of service.
Do.	Wm. Wise	Nov. 18, "	Nov. 18, "	On detached duty.
Do.	James F. Johnson	" 18, "	" 18, "	Mustered out July 23, 1865.
Do.	Henry Huber	" 26, "	" 26, "	Mustered out May 15, 1865.
Do.	Warren Mills	May 18, 1865	May 18, 1865	Mustered out with regiment.
Do.	Daniel W. Wilson	" 18, "	" 18, "	Mustered out with regiment.
Do.	Richard Blackstone	June 6, "	June 6, "	Mustered out with regiment.
Do.	David R. Potts	" 6, "	" 6, "	Killed at Bentonville, North Carolina.
Do.	Chas. H. Stewart	July 18, "	Sept. 4, "	Complimentary commissions given after mustered out.
Do.	D. Webb	" 18, "	" 4, "	
Do.	Francis E. Hyde	" 18, "	" 4, "	
Do.	George W. Boyd	" 18, "	" 4, "	
1st Lieutenant	Robert H. Bentley	Aug. 10, 1861	" 16, 1861	Promoted to Captain December 25, 1862.
Do.	Abraham M. Crumbacker	" 16, "	" 16, "	Promoted to Captain March 15, 1862.
Do.	Alpheus B. Parmentre	" 20, "	" 16, "	Resigned November 30, 1861.
Do.	Anthony B. Raymond	" 20, "	" 16, "	Discharged October 23, 1862.
Do.	John McLaughlin	" 31, "	" 16, "	Resigned March 13, 1862.
Do.	David N. Stambaugh	" 31, "	" 16, "	Resigned November 25, 1861.
Do.	Charles C. Brandt	Sept. 4, "	" 16, "	Resigned April 5, 1862.
Do.	Albert J. Spaulding	" 4, "	" 16, "	Discharged August 20, 1862.
Do.	Samuel R. Breese	" 5, "	" 16, "	Promoted to Captain May 24, 1862.
Do.	Clarkson C. Nichols	" 5, "	" 16, "	Promoted to Captain March 20, 1862.
Do.	Joseph Gladden	" 7, "	" 16, "	Promoted to Captain April 10, 1862.
Do.	Jerome B. Whelpley	Jan. 9, 1862	Jan. 9, 1862	Resigned January 24, 1861.
Do.	Abraham Norris	" 9, "	" 9, "	Declined.
Do.	Robert F. Jackson	" 9, "	" 14, "	Never in the regiment.
Do.	Francis H. Robbins	Feb. 8, "	Feb. 8, "	Resigned April 27, 1863.
Do.	Alex. R. Patterson	" 8, "	" 8, "	Promoted to Captain.

RANK.	NAME.	DATE OF RANK.	COM. ISSUED.	REMARKS.
1st Lieutenant	George F. Jack	March 20, 1862	March 20, 1862	Resigned April 5, 1862.
Do.	Theobald D. Yost	" 13, "	May 5, "	Promoted to Captain November 21, 1862.
Do.	Ulysses Westerbrook	April 5, "	" 5, "	Discharged August 22, 1862.
Do.	Abraham Norris	" 5, "	" 5, "	Declined promotion.
Do.	David Shellenberger	March 15, "	" 5, "	Resigned January 7, 1864.
Do.	Horatio J. Johnson	April 10, "	" 5, "	Resigned June 15, 1862.
Do.	John Brady Pearce	March 12, "	Sept. 8, "	Resigned April 15, 1863.
Do.	Elijah B. Adams	Oct. 23, "	Dec. 27, "	Honorably discharged January 30, 1864.
Do.	Sheldon Guthrie, jr.	April 5, "	" 27, "	Promoted to Captain January 1, 1863.
Do.	George Sinclair	Aug. 20, "	" 27, "	Promoted to Captain December 22, 1863.
Do.	Elias W. James	Sept. 15, "	" 27, "	Promoted to Captain January 13, 1863.
Do.	Augustus G. Hostetter	Aug. 22, "	" 27, "	Resigned February 18, 1863.
Do.	Levi J. Cox	June 15, "	" 27, "	Appointed 1st Lieut. 26th Battery Dec. 22, '63.
Do.	Richard H. Fouts	Dec. 25, "	" 27, "	Declined promotion; mustered out.
Do.	Cyrus A. Stephens	Jan. 1, 1863	Feb. 18, 1863	Resigned July 27, 1863.
Do.	John Wiley	Dec. 22, 1862	Jan. 19, "	Promoted to Captain.
Do.	Ebenezer B. Hays	Jan. 13, 1863	June 10, "	Promoted to Captain.
Do.	Wm. A. McCallister	Feb. 18, "	" 10, "	Promoted to Captain July 27, 1863.
Do.	Alfred G. Phillips	May 4, "	" 29, "	Killed July 22, 1864.
Do.	John M. Stanton	April 15, "	May 6, "	Resigned August 13, 1863.
Do.	Henry Huber	" 27, "	July 10, "	Promoted to Captain.
Do.	Chas. N. Mowyer	June 30, "	" 20, "	Resigned September 15, 1864.
Do.	Joseph L. Brosius	July 27, "	Aug. 25, "	Honorably discharged September 15, 1864.
Do.	James F. Johnson	April 1, 1864	April 1, 1864	Promoted to Captain.
Do.	Wm. Wise	Nov. 10, 1863	" 6, "	Promoted to Captain.
Do.	John Thompson	April 20, 1864	" 20, "	Discharged.
Do.	Warren Mills	" 20, "	" 20, "	Promoted to Captain.
Do.	Jerome Wells	May 25, "	May 25, "	Declined; no vacancy.
Do.	David H. Lee	" 25, "	" 25, "	Killed October 27, 1864.
Do.	Daniel W. Wilson	Aug. 11, "	Aug. 11, "	Promoted to Captain.
Do.	Richard Blackstone	" 11, "	" 11, "	Promoted to Captain.
Do.	David R. Potts	Oct. 12, "	Oct. 12, "	Promoted to Captain.
Do.	Chas. H. Stewart	" 12, "	" 12, "	Promoted to Captain.
Do.	D. Webb	" 12, "	" 12, "	Promoted to Captain.
Do.	Francis E. Hyde	Nov. 18, "	Nov. 18, "	Promoted to Captain.
Do.	George W. Boyd	" 18, "	" 18, "	Promoted to Captain.
Do.	John Mitchell	" 18, "	" 18, "	Mustered out with regiment.
Do.	John W. Myers	" 26, "	" 26, "	Mustered out with regiment.
Do.	Wm. L. Harrod	" 26, "	" 26, "	Mustered out with regiment.
Do.	Chas. C. Anderron	May 18, 1865	May 18, 1865	Mustered out with regiment.
Do.	Wm. L. Rosegrant	" 18, "	" 18, "	Mustered out with regiment.
Do.	Wm. T. Dallison	June 6, "	June 6, "	Mustered out with regiment as Adjutant.
Do.	Milton Latta	" 6, "	" 6, "	Mustered out with regiment.
Do.	John Porter	July 18, "	Sept. 4, "	Mustered out as 2d Lieutenant.
Do.	James L. Tyler	" 18, "	" 4, "	Mustered out as 2d Lieutenant.
Do.	Michael Adler	" 18, "	" 4, "	Mustered out as 2d Lieutenant.
Do.	Joseph W. Davis	" 18, "	" 4, "	Mustered out as 2d Lieutenant.
Do.	Chas. D. Eoff	" 18, "	" 4, "	Mustered out as 2d Lieutenant.
2d Lieutenant	Robert F. Jackson	Aug. 13, 1861	" 16, 1861	Never in the regiment.
Do.	Abraham Norris	" 16, "	" 16, "	Resigned January 18, 1863.
Do.	Jerome B. Whelpley	" 20, "	" 16, "	Promoted January 9, 1862.
Do.	Chas. B. Church	" 20, "	" 16, "	Resigned January 20, 1862.
Do.	Benj. F. Guck	" 31, "	" 16, "	Resigned October 13, 1861.
Do.	Henry H. Tickel	" 31, "	" 16, "	Resigned April 5, 1862.
Do.	James M. Leith	Sept. 4, "	" 16, "	Resigned October 15, 1861.
Do.	Ulysses Westerbrook	" 4, "	" 16, "	Promoted to 1st Lieutenant April 5, 1862.
Do.	John S. Van Martin	" 5, "	" 16, "	Resigned April 10, 1862.
Do.	George F. Jack	" 5, "	" 16, "	Promoted to 1st Lieutenant March 20, 1862.
Do.	Wm. H. H. Case	" 7, "	" 16, "	Resigned April 5, 1862.
Do.	Francis H. Robbins	Jan. 9, 1862	Jan. 9, 1862	Promoted to 1st Lieutenant February 8, 1862.
Do.	Isaac B. Post	Feb. 8, "	Feb. 8, "	Promoted to 1st Lieutenant.
Do.	Theobald D. Yost	" 8, "	" 8, "	Promoted to 1st Lieutenant March 13, 1862.
Do.	Jefferson J. Hibbitts	" 8, "	" 8, "	Promoted to 1st Lieutenant April 10, 1862.
Do.	Horatio J. Johnson	" 8, "	" 8, "	Promoted to 1st Lieutenant April 10, 1862.
Do.	Elias W. James	March 20, "	March 20, "	Promoted to 1st Lieutenant Sept. 15, 1862.
Do.	Sheldon Guthrie, jr.	" 13, "	May 5, "	Promoted to 1st Lieutenant April 5, 1862.
Do.	Elijah B. Adams	April 5, "	" 5, "	Promoted to 1st Lieutenant October 23, 1862.
Do.	Levi J. Cox	" 5, "	" 5, "	Promoted to 1st Lieutenant June 15, 1862.
Do.	Cerventes Fugate	" 5, "	" 5, "	Died May 13, 1862.
Do.	George Sinclair	" 5, "	" 5, "	Promoted to 1st Lieutenant August 20, 1862.
Do.	Henry Grant	" 10, "	" 5, "	Died April 10, 1864.
Do.	Wm. C. Runyan	Sept. 1, "	Sept. 18, "	
Do.	Calvin A. Bowlaud	April 10, "	Dec. 27, "	Resigned January 17, 1863.
Do.	Alfred G. Barnett	Sept. 15, "	" 27, "	Promoted to 1st Lieutenant June 30, 1863.
Do.	Cyrus A. Stevens	April 5, "	" 27, "	Promoted to 1st Lieutenant January 1, 1863.
Do.	Andrew F. Wedenbacker	Oct. 23, "	" 27, "	Resigned January 30, 1863.
Do.	Omer S. Lee	Aug. 20, "	" 27, "	Appointed 2d Lieutenant 26th Battery.
Do.	Ebenezer B. Hays	June 15, "	" 27, "	Promoted to 1st Lieutenant January 13, 1863.
Do.	Chas. N. Mowyer	May 17, "	" 27, "	Promoted to 1st Lieutenant June 30, 1863.
Do.	James F. Johnson	Dec. 22, "	Jan. 19, 1863	Promoted to 1st Lieutenant.
Do.	Linus R. North	Jan. 18, 1863	Feb. 18, "	Resigned June 24, 1863.
Do.	Wm. A. McCallister	" 17, "	" 18, "	Promoted to 1st Lieutenant February 18, 1863.
Do.	Alfred G. Phillips	" 30, "	" 23, "	Promoted to 1st Lieutenant May 4, 1863.
Do.	Joseph L. Brosius	Feb. 18, "	June 10, "	Promoted to 1st Lieutenant.
Do.	John Thompson	Jan. 13, "	" 10, "	Promoted to 1st Lieutenant.
Do.	Warren Mills	" 14, "	" 10, "	Promoted to 1st Lieutenant.
Do.	Burton Hubble	" 24, "	July 10, "	Deserted.
Do.	Jerome Wells	Nov. 11, "	Jan. 9, "	Resigned.
Do.	Daniel W. Wilson	June 18, "	Aug. 25, "	Promoted to 1st Lieutenant.
Do.	Richard Blackstone	March 16, 1864	March 16, 1864	Promoted to 1st Lieutenant.
Do.	David H. Lee	July 27, 1863	Aug. 25, 1863	Promoted to 1st Lieutenant.
Do.	Samuel B. Rigdon	April 20, 1861	April 20, 1864	Resigned August 20, 1864.
Do.	David R. Potts	" 20, "	" 20, "	Promoted to 1st Lieutenant.
Do.	Chas. H. Stewart	" 20, "	" 20, "	Promoted to 1st Lieutenant.
Do.	Robert F. Smart	May 25, "	May 25, "	Resigned August 20, 1864.
Do.	D. Webb	Feb. 5, "	" 31, "	Promoted to 1st Lieutenant.
Do.	Chas. C. Anderson	April 20, 1865	April 20, 1865	Promoted to 1st Lieutenant.
Do.	Wm. L. Rosegrant	" 20, "	" 20, "	Promoted to 1st Lieutenant.
Do.	Wm. T. Dallison	" 20, "	" 20, "	Promoted to 1st Lieutenant.
Do.	Milton Latta	" 20, "	" 20, "	Promoted to 1st Lieutenant.
Do.	John Porter	" 20, "	" 20, "	Promoted to 1st Lieutenant.
Do.	James L. Tyler	" 20, "	" 20, "	Promoted to 1st Lieutenant.

RANK.	NAME.	DATE OF RANK.	COM. ISSUED.	REMARKS.
2d Lieutenant	Michael Alder	May 18, 1865	May 18, 1865	Promoted to 1st Lieutenant.
Do.	Solomon Kaufman	" 18, "	" 18, "	
Do.	Joseph W. Davis	" 18, "	" 18, "	Promoted to 1st Lieutenant.
Do.	Charles D. Eoff	" 18, "	" 18, "	Promoted to 1st Lieutenant.
Do.	Benj. F. Harris	" 18, "	" 18, "	Mustered out with regiment.
Do.	Jacob Pinnock	July 18, "	Sept. 4, "	Mustered out as 1st Sergeant.
Do.	Joseph H. Eakin	" 18, "	" 4, "	Mustered out as 1st Sergeant.
Do.	Taylor McFadden	" 18, "	" 4, "	Mustered out as 1st Sergeant.
Do.	Wm. G. Snodgrass	" 18, "	" 4, "	Mustered out as 1st Sergeant.
Do.	Artillius V. Norman	" 18, "	" 4, "	Mustered out as 1st Sergeant.
Do.	Francis M. Rider	" 18, "	" 4, "	Mustered out as 1st Sergeant.
Do.	Wm. H. Junkins	" 18, "	" 4, "	Mustered out as 1st Sergeant.
Do.	Wm. Piper	" 18, "	" 4, "	Mustered out as 1st Sergeant.

THIRTY-SECOND OHIO VOLUNTEER INFANTRY.

THIS was one of the first organizations raised in the State on the basis of three years' service. Its rendezvous was Camp Bartley, near Mansfield, but before completion it was transferred to Camp Dennison, where it was completed, organized, equipped, and sent to the field, under the auspices of Colonel Thomas H. Ford, formerly Lieutenant-Governor of Ohio. The date of the commissions of the field-officers was the 26th of July, 1861.

On the 15th of September, 1861, the regiment left Camp Dennison for West Virginia. As was the case with most, if not all, of the first regiments from Ohio, they were poorly equipped and armed with the almost useless old smooth-bore muskets of a by-gone age. The regiment was moved by railroad and arrived at Grafton September 18th, and marched the next day for Beverly, West Virginia, where it arrived on the 22d.

At this point Colonel Ford reported for orders to Brigadier-General Reynolds, then commanding the District of Cheat Mountain, with head-quarters at Huttonsville, and was assigned to the command then stationed on Cheat Mountain Summit, with Colonel Nathan Kimball, of the Fourteenth Indiana Volunteers, commanding the Post.

The Thirty-Second had been hurried to the field without discipline of any kind—in fact it was hardly organized. Here, upon the rugged heights of Cheat Mountain, amid the wild scenery of the Alleghanies, the regiment received its first lesson in the art of war. On the 3d of October, 1861, the Thirty-Second, under orders, made a forward movement, and led the advance of the army against Greenbrier, Virginia, through the mountains and pines of that region by midnight. The regiment remained at Greenbrier during the fall of 1861, engaged in watching the movements of the enemy, then commanded by the afterward renowned Rebel General R. E. Lee.

On the 13th of December the Thirty-Second, under command of Captain Hamilton, accompanied General Milroy in his advance on Camp Alleghany. In his report General Milroy complimented the regiment very highly on its gallantry and good conduct in its charge into the camp of the enemy. The loss of the regiment in this affair was four killed and fourteen wounded, some severely. On the return from this expedition it was ordered to Beverly, where it remained the rest of that severe winter. The time was profitably spent in still further disciplining and organizing the regiment, which made necessary some changes in the roster. The following named officers retired and their places were filled by promotions from the ranks:

Captains J. A. Lacy, company A; W. M. Stanley, company K, and Jay Dyer, of company I; Chaplain Nickerson; First Lieutenants, C. C. Brandt, J. W. McLaughlin, Albert J. Spaulding, and C. C. Nichols; Second Lieutenants, John Vanmeter, H. H. Tickel, J. M. Leith, B. F. Guck,

B. F. Jackson, (Adjutant), Geo. F. Jack, W. H. H. Case, and D. Stambaugh. Surgeon John N. Coury also retired and was succeeded by Dr. Jas. G. Buchanan, of Wellsville, Ohio.

Still retained in General Milroy's command, the regiment took the advance of the expedition under that officer which resulted in the capture of Camp Alleghany, Huntersville, Monterey, and McDowell. About the 1st of May a further advance was made to near Buffalo Gap, seven miles from Staunton, Virginia. The enemy was met at this point, and, after some severe fighting, the National forces fell back on the main army, camped at McDowell, in the Bull Pasture Valley, where Generals Schenck and Milroy had united their forces, numbering about seven thousand men.

The Rebel General Stonewall Jackson advanced against the National force on the 8th day of May, and was met on the side of the Bull Pasture Mountain. A severe battle ensued, which lasted from two P. M. until dark, with varied success on either side. The National forces fell back on Franklin, West Virginia, closely followed by the Rebel army. In this battle the Thirty-Second lost six killed and fifty-three wounded, some mortally. It was the last regiment to leave the field. Lieutenant C. Fugate, of company E, a young officer of fine promise, was among the mortally wounded; he died at Franklin five days after the battle.

On the 12th of May Major-General Fremont, commanding the Mountain Department, effected a junction with Generals Schenck and Milroy, bringing with him about twelve thousand men. Before this junction, however, the Rebel General Jackson had retired from the National front. The combined National forces lay at Franklin inactive until the 25th of May, when they were ordered to the support of General Banks, then operating in the Shenandoah Valley against the Rebel army under Jackson. While the army was in camp at Franklin the Thirty-Second was transferred from Milroy's to Schenck's brigade, composed of the Thirty-Second, Fifty-Fifth. Seventy-Third, Seventy-Fifth, and Eighty-Second Ohio Volunteer Infantry.

In Fremont's pursuit of Jackson up the Shenandoah Valley the Thirty-Second bore its part, and participated in the battles of Cross Keys and Port Republic, on the 8th and 9th days of June, 1862. The regiment returned to Strausburg about the last of June, was transferred to Piatt's brigade, and moved to Winchester, Virginia, July 5th, 1862. It remained at Winchester doing garrison duty until the 1st of September, the day the place was evacuated by General White, when the regiment moved with the brigade to Harper's Ferry and assisted in the defense of that place. After making a hard fight and losing one hundred and fifty of its number, the regiment, with the whole command, was surrendered by the commanding officer of the Post to the enemy as prisoners of war. The history of this unaccountable affair is yet to be written. The Thirty-Second was paroled and sent to Annapolis, Maryland, from whence it was transferred to Chicago, Illinois.

In the defense of Harper's Ferry the regiment lost some gallant officers and brave men. Captain S. R. Breese, company H, who succeeded Captain Baxter, was killed by a musket ball, Captain M. W. Worden lost a leg, Lieutenant A. G. Hostetter was severely wounded in the foot, and Lieutenant E. B. Adams, of company F, lost a hand. Colonel Ford was placed under arrest, and sent to Washington for trial by a Military Commission, on the charge of having neglected his duty in the defense of Maryland Heights. This trial resulted in his dismissal from the service November 8, 1862, by order of the War Department.

At Chicago the regiment became almost completely demoralized. It had not been paid for eight months, and many of the men took "French leave" and went home to look after their families. Captain B. F. Potts was sent to Columbus to ask Governor Tod to procure an order from the War Department transferring the regiment to Camp Taylor, near Cleveland. This application was successful, and the Thirty-Second, or all that was left of it, thirty-five men, arrived at Camp Taylor December 1, 1862. Order came out of chaos, however.

On the 2d of December Captain B. F. Potts was appointed by Governor Tod Lieutenant-Colonel of the regiment, and that energetic officer went immediately to work "reconstructing" the command. Within ten days order prevailed, and eight hundred men had reported for duty. This happy result was not attained, however, without decisive action in the case of several officers who were charged with inciting disaffection and revolt among the men. Secretary Stanton, of the War Office, ordered their instant dismissal, which was consummated on the 23d of December, 1862. The men were paid in full, and on the 12th of January, 1863, declared to be exchanged. On the 18th orders were received to proceed to Memphis, Tennessee, and report to Major-General U. S. Grant, then commanding the Department of the Tennessee. In reorganizing the regiment, Lieutenant-Colonel Potts was made Colonel, Quartermaster R. H. Bentley Lieutenant-Colonel, Captain A. M. Crumbacker Major, Assistant-Surgeon Brundage Surgeon, and Lieutenant George Sinclair Captain. The regiment left Camp Taylor, near Cleveland, January 20th, reached Memphis on the 25th of January, 1863, and was assigned to Logan's division, Seventeenth Army Corps, commanded by Major-General J. B. McPherson. On the 20th of February the Thirty-Second moved with the army to Lake Providence, Louisiana, and during the campaign against Vicksburg took a prominent part in the gallant achievements of the Third Division, Seventeenth Army Corps. At the battle of Champion Hills the Thirty-Second made a bayonet charge and captured the First Mississippi Rebel Battery—men, guns, and horses—with a loss of twenty-four men. For this gallant achievement the captured battery was turned over to the regiment, and manned by company F during the entire siege of Vicksburg. The total loss of the regiment during the campaign and siege of Vicksburg was two hundred and twenty-five, rank and file. It participated in the battles of Port Gibson, Raymond, Jackson, Champion Hills; was in the extreme front of Logan's division when Vicksburg surrendered, and was assigned to post-duty under General Logan.

In August, 1863, the regiment accompanied Stevenson's expedition to Monroe, Louisiana, and McPherson's expedition to Brownsville, Mississippi, in October of the same year. It was also with Sherman in February, 1864, at Meridian, and lost twenty-two men at Boher's Creek, Mississippi, February 5, 1864, in which last affair Captain W. A. McCallister was severely wounded while gallantly leading the advance.

Colonel Potts had been assigned to the command of the Second Brigade, Third Division, Seventeenth Army Corps, in the autumn of 1863, and was thereafter but seldom in command of the regiment. In December and January, 1863–4, more than three-fourths of the regiment re-enlisted as veterans, and on the 4th of March, 1864, it was furloughed home. It rejoined the army at Cairo, Illinois, on the 21st of April, with its ranks largely augmented by recruits. The only change made while at home was the addition of Dr. T. P. Bond, of Champaign County, as Assistant-Surgeon. On the 27th of April the regiment embarked at Cairo, with its division and corps, on transports, landing at Clifton. From thence it marched to Acworth, Georgia, where it joined General Sherman on the 10th of June, 1864. The Thirty-Second was identified with the movements of the Seventeenth Army Corps in Sherman's advance against Atlanta; participated in the assault on Kenesaw Mountain, June 27, 1864, and Nicojack Creek, near Howell's Ferry, on the Chattahoochie River, July 10, 1864. Also in the battles of July 20th, 21st, 22d, and 28th, before Atlanta, and lost more than half its number in killed and wounded. In the affair of the 22d of July Adjutant A. G. Phillips, of Mansfield, Ohio, was killed while encouraging the men, and Captains Huber and Potts were severely wounded. The regiment was commanded in those battles by Lieutenant-Colonel J. J. Hibbetts, Colonel Potts being in command of the First Brigade, Fourth Division, Seventeenth Army Corps. (On the 12th of January, 1865, Colonel Potts was promoted to the rank of Brigadier-General, on the special recommendation of General Sherman, for gallantry before Atlanta, July 22, 1864.)

After the fall of Atlanta the Thirty-Second moved with the army in pursuit of Hood, after which it rejoined General Sherman and accompanied him on his "March to the Sea."

On the 10th of December, 1864, the Thirty-Second was in the advance of the army, and contributed its share toward driving the enemy into his works at Savannah. In this expedition the Savannah and Charleston Railroad was cut, thus destroying the enemy's communications with Charleston. On the 21st of December the regiment entered Savannah with the army, and went into camp near Fort Thunderbolt. After the review by General Sherman of the whole army, the

Seventeenth Army Corps went by transports to Beaufort, South Carolina; thence to Pocotaligo Station, on the Savannah and Charleston Railroad.

On the 1st of February, 1865, the regiment moved with the army through the Carolinas, and, with the Thirteenth Iowa, was the first regiment to enter Columbia. (Colonel Hibbetts, with a mounted detachment of the regiment, entered and captured Fayetteville, North Carolina, March 10, 1865, after a severe fight with Wade Hampton's cavalry.)

On the 20th and 21st of March it was engaged with the enemy at Bentonville, North Carolina, where, on the 21st, Captain D. R. Potts, aide-de-camp to General B. F. Potts, was killed while gallantly leading the skirmish-line of the brigade in an assault on the enemy's works.

The regiment came out of the woods to see their friends at Goldsboro', moved with the army to Raleigh, North Carolina, and was present at the surrender of Johnston's army, May 1, 1865. It marched with the army through Richmond, Virginia, to Washington City, where it participated in the grand review before President Johnston and Cabinet.

The regiment remained in camp, near Washington, until June 8, 1865, when it took the cars for Louisville. It lay there until July 20th, when it was mustered out of the service, and proceeded to Columbus, Ohio, at which place the men received their final discharge, July 26, 1865.

During the stay of the Thirty-Second in Washington, Lieutenant-Colonel Hibbetts was commissioned Colonel, *vice* B. F. Potts promoted; Captain S. Guthrie was made Lieutenant-Colonel, and Captain Isaac B. Post, of company C, promoted to Major, *vice* Crumbacker, resigned.

The Thirty-Second entered the field September 15, 1861, nine hundred and fifty strong, and during the war received more than sixteen hundred recruits. Only five hundred and sixty-five remained at its muster-out. It is believed that the regiment lost and recruited more men than any other from Ohio.

The following extracts give the points of the report by the military commission above mentioned as to Colonel Ford's case:

"The Court is satisfied that Colonel Ford was given a discretionary power to abandon the Heights, as his better judgment might dictate, and it believes from the evidence, circumstantial and direct, that the result did not to any great extent surprise nor in any way displease the officer in command at Harper's Ferry. But . . . the evidence shows conclusively that the force upon the Heights was not well managed; that the point most pressed was weakly defended as to numbers, and, after the wounding of the Colonel of the One Hundred and Twenty-Sixth New York, was left without a competent officer in command, Colonel Ford himself not appearing, nor designating any one who might have restored order and encouraged the men. That the abandonment of the Heights was premature is clearly proved. . . . In so grave a case as this, with such disgraceful consequences, the Court can not permit an officer to shield himself behind the fact that he did as well as he could, if in so doing he exhibits a lack of military capacity. It is clear to the Commission that Colonel Ford should not have been placed in command on Maryland Heights; that he conducted the defense without ability, and abandoned his position without sufficient cause; and that he has shown throughout such a lack of military capacity as to disqualify him for a command in the service."

33d REGIMENT OHIO VOLUNTEER INFANTRY.

ROSTER, THREE YEARS' SERVICE.

RANK.	NAME.	DATE OF RANK.	COM. ISSUED.	REMARKS.
Colonel	JOSHUA W. SILL	July 29, 1861	Aug. 5, 1861	Prom. by Pres't to Brig. Gen. July 16, 1862.
Do.	OSCAR F. MOORE	" 16, "	Nov. 28, 1862	Resigned July 20, 1864.
Do.	JOSEPH HINSON	June 26, 1865	June 26, 1865	Mustered out as Lieutenant-Colonel.
Lt. Colonel	OSCAR F. MOORE	July 31, 1861	Aug. 5, 1861	Promoted to Colonel.
Do.	FREDERICK J. LOCK	" 16, 1862	July 19, 1863	Resigned September 26, 1863.
Do.	JAS. H. MONTGOMERY	Sept. 26, 1863	Jan. 10, 1864	Honorably discharged Jan. 1, 1865.
Do.	BENJ. F. BARGER	Jan. 28, 1865	" 28, 1865	Honorably discharged March 17, 1865.
Do.	JOSEPH HINSON	May 18, "	May 18, "	Promoted to Colonel.
Do.	THOMAS SIKES	June 26, "	June 26, "	Mustered out as Major.
Major	J. V. ROBINSON, JR.	Aug. 1, 1861	Aug. 5, 1861	Died at Portsmouth, Ohio, March 23, 1862.
Do.	FREDERICK J. LOCK	March 23, 1862	May 1, 1862	Promoted to Lieutenant-Colonel.
Do.	EPHRAIM J. ELLIS	Jan. 16, "	Jan. 19, 1863	Killed September 20, 1863.
Do.	BENJ. F. BARGER	Sept. 20, 1863	" 10, 1864	Promoted to Lieutenant-Colonel.
Do.	JOSEPH HINSON	Jan. 28, 1865	" 28, 1865	Promoted to Lieutenant-Colonel.
Do.	THOMAS SIKES	May 18, "	May 18, "	Promoted to Lieutenant-Colonel.
Surgeon	GEORGE W. BROOKS	Feb. 9, 1863	Feb. 9,	Declined.
Do.	DAVID WELSH	April 3, "	April 3,	Resigned September 20, 1864.
Do.	LIONEL J. SMITH	Oct. 12, 1864	Oct. 12, 1864	Mustered out with regiment.
Ass't Surgeon	B. MOSENMEIR	May 26, 1862	May 26, 1862	Resigned October 24, 1863.
Do.	J. H. HAIR	Aug. 21, "	Sept. 1, "	Resigned July 30, 1863.
Do.	WM. T. ROPP	Jan. 4, 1864	Jan. 4, 1864	Mustered out with regiment.
Chaplain	ALBERT G. BOYER	Dec. 23, 1861	" 18, 1862	Resigned September 30, 1862.
Captain	Samuel A. Carrie	Aug. 5, "	Feb. 5, "	Died March 23, 1862.
Do.	Wm. H. Douglass	" 10, "	" 5, "	
Do.	Frederick J. Lock	" 10, "	" 5, "	Promoted to Major March 23, 1862.
Do.	Ephraim J. Ellis	" 10, "	" 5, "	Promoted to Major.
Do.	Jas. H. Montgomery	" 25, "	" 5, "	Promoted to Major.
Do.	Van B. Hibbs	Sept. 3, "	" 5, "	Honorably discharged March 2, 1863.
Do.	Benj. F. Barger	Oct. 11, "	" 5, "	Promoted to Major.
Do.	Thaddeus A. Minshall	" 14, "	March 20, "	Out of service.
Do.	Wm. McKain	Jan. 1, 1862	" 20, "	Killed May 14, 1864, at Resaca.
Do.	Joseph Hinson	March 23, "	May 1, "	Promoted to Major.
Do.	George P. Singer	April 16, "	" 1, "	Honorably discharged January 31, 1863.
Do.	Conduce H. Gatch	Nov. 26, 1861	June 3, "	Resigned June 11, 1862.
Do.	Wm. R. Foster	Oct. 15, "	Dec. 1, "	Honorably discharged March 2, 1863.
Do.	Wm. W. Nixon	June 11, 1862	" 1, "	Resigned May 30, 1863.
Do.	Edward M. De Bruin	Jan. 16, 1863	Feb. 10, 1863	Out of service.
Do.	Van B. Hibbs	June 1, "	June 15, "	Declined.
Do.	Chas. Brooker	March 2, "	" 26, "	Out of service.
Do.	Junius F. Gates	May 30, "	" 26, "	Mustered out with regiment.
Do.	Thomas Sikes	March 2, "	" 26, "	Promoted to Major.
Do.	Francis J. Fitzwilliams	" 15, 1864	March 15, 1864	Declined.
Do.	Robert L. Ramsey	May 25, "	May 25, "	Declined; mustered out as Captain.
Do.	Elias A. Ramsey	" 25, "	" 25, "	Declined.
Do.	A. L. Waddle	Aug. 11, "	Aug. 11, "	Out of service.
Do.	Martin V. B. Morrison	" 11, "	" 11, "	Mustered out as 1st Lieutenant May 8, 1865.
Do.	George C. Winkler	" 11, "	" 11, "	Mustered out with regiment.
Do.	Robert L. Ramsey	Jan. 28, "	Jan. 28, 1865	Mustered out with regiment.
Do.	John J. Gist, jr.	" 28, "	" 28, "	Mustered out as 1st Lieutenant May 8, 1865.
Do.	Wm. B. Dougherty	" 28, "	" 28, "	Mustered out with regiment.
Do.	Ellsworth W. Libby	" 28, "	" 28, "	Mustered out with regiment.
Do.	Archibald W. Rogers	" 28, "	" 28, "	Mustered out July 25, 1865.
Do.	Wm. W. Downing	May 18, "	May 18, "	Mustered out with regiment.
Do.	Samuel Halley	" 18, "	" 18, "	Mustered out with regiment.
Do.	George W. Roby	" 18, "	" 18, "	Mustered out with regiment.
Do.	Daniel R. Shriver	" 18, "	" 18, "	Discharged as 1st Sergeant April 13, 1865.
Do.	Sylvester Keller	" 18, "	" 18, "	Resigned June 27, 1865.
1st Lieutenant	J. Mills Kendrick	Aug. 3, 1861	Aug. 5, 1861	Appointed A. A. G. in the volunteers.
Do.	George P. Singer	" 5, "	Feb. 5, 1862	Promoted to Captain.
Do.	Wm. R. Foster	" 10, "	" 5, "	Promoted to Captain.
Do.	Ezekiel E. Colburn	" 13, "	" 5, "	Resigned May 2, 1863.
Do.	Joseph Hinson	" 17, "	" 5, "	Promoted to Captain.
Do.	Edward M. De Bruin	" 18, "	" 5, "	Promoted to Captain.
Do.	Junius F. Gates	" 25, "	" 5, "	Promoted to Captain.
Do.	Thomas Sikes	Sept. 3, "	" 5, "	Promoted to Captain.
Do.	Francis J. Fitzwilliams	" 11, "	" 5, "	
Do.	Robert L. Ramsey	March 23, 1862	May 1, "	Promoted to Captain.
Do.	John M. Higgins	April 16, "	" 1, "	Dismissed.
Do.	Wm. W. Nixon	Nov. 26, 1861	June 3, "	Promoted to Captain.
Do.	Conduce H. Gatch	Oct. 11, "	" 3, "	Promoted to Captain.
Do.	Charles Brooker	" 15, "	Dec. 1, "	Promoted to Captain.
Do.	Elias A. Ramsey	Jan. 18, 1863	Feb. 10, 1863	Out of Service.
Do.	Martin V. B. Morrison	March 2, "	April 22, "	Promoted to Captain.
Do.	David McCamell	June 11, "	" 22, "	Resigned January 13, 1864.
Do.	W. B. McNeil	April 1, "	Sept. 1, "	Resigned December 15, 1863.
Do.	George G. Winkler	March 2, "	Jan. 21, "	Promoted to Captain.
Do.	Edgar J. Higby	May 30, "	Sept. 1, "	Killed May 28, 1864.
Do.	John J. Gist, jr.	March 2, "	Aug. 28, "	Promoted to Captain.
Do.	A. L. Waddle	Sept. 18, 1861		Promoted to Captain.
Do.	Chas. R. Pomeroy	March 15, 1864	March 15, 1864	Deceased August 13, 1864.
Do.	Wm. Roby	" 15, "	" 15, "	Declined.
Do.	Henry Harrison	May 25, "	May 25, "	Dismissed July 12, 1864.
Do.	Jacob Parrott	" 25, "	" 25, "	Declined.
Do.	Daniel A. Dorsey	" 25, "	" 25, "	Resigned as 2d Lieutenant August 24, 1864.
Do.	Wm. Reddick	" 25, "	" 25, "	Declined.

RANK.	NAME.	DATE OF RANK.	COM. ISSUED.	REMARKS.
1st Lieutenant	Frederick A. Colburn	May 25, 1864	May 25, 1864	Discharged July 2, 1864.
Do.	Joseph H. Cole	" 25, "	" 25, "	Killed in action Sept. 1863; com'sion returned.
Do.	Warren L. Johnson	Aug. 11, "	Aug. 11, "	Mustered out March 22, 1862.
Do.	Wm. H. Myers	" 11, "	" 11, "	Declined.
Do.	Wm. B. Dougherty	" 11, "	" 11, "	Promoted to Captain.
Do.	Ellsworth W. Libby	" 11, "	" 11, "	Promoted to Captain.
Do.	Archibald J. Rogers	" 11, "	" 11, "	Promoted to Captain.
Do.	Wm. W. Downing	" 11, "	" 11, "	Promoted to Captain.
Do.	Samuel Halley	" 11, "	" 11, "	Promoted to Captain.
Do.	George W. Roby	Jan. 28, 1865	Jan. 28, 1865	Promoted to Captain.
Do.	Daniel R. Shriver	" 28, "	" 28, "	Promoted to Captain.
Do.	Sylvester Keller	" 28, "	" 28, "	Promoted to Captain.
Do.	Nelson Purdam	" 28, "	" 28, "	Mustered out with regiment.
Do.	Isaac Jones	" 28, "	" 28, "	Mustered out with regiment.
Do.	John D. Scott	" 28, "	" 28, "	Mustered out with regiment as R. Q. M.
Do.	Rudolph Obrist	" 28, "	" 28, "	Mustered out with regiment as Adjutant.
Do.	Alvah N. Mauk	" 28, "	" 28, "	Mustered out with regiment.
Do.	Alonzo F. Sims	May 18, "	May 18, "	Mustered out with regiment.
Do.	Alex. C. Barcus	" 18, "	" 18, "	Mustered out with regiment.
Do.	Clayton Rogers	" 18, "	" 18, "	Mustered out with regiment.
Do.	Thomas E. Scott	" 18, "	" 18, "	Mustered out with regiment.
Do.	Joab Davis	Jan. 28, "	Jan. 28, "	Mustered out with regiment.
Do.	Perry Gull	" 28, "	" 28, "	Mustered out with regiment.
Do.	Thomas S. Davis	" 31, "	" 31, "	Discharged per General Order No. 77.
2d Lieutenant	John M. Higgins	Aug. 5, 1861	Feb. 11, 1862	Promoted to 1st Lieutenant.
Do.	Robert L. Ramsey	" 17, "	" 11, "	Promoted to 1st Lieutenant.
Do.	Elias A. Ramsey	" 18, "	" 11, "	Promoted to 1st Lieutenant.
Do.	Chas. Brooker	" 24, "	" 11, "	Promoted to 1st Lieutenant October 15, 1862.
Do.	John J. Gist, jr.	" 25, "	" 11, "	Promoted to 1st Lieutenant.
Do.	Milton C. Peters	Sept. 3, "	" 11, "	Resigned December 5, 1861.
Do.	Wm. B. Roby	Oct. 11, "	" 11, "	Out of service.
Do.	Martin V. B. Morrison	" 14, "	March 20, "	Promoted to 1st Lieutenant.
Do.	George G. Winkler	Dec. 8, "	" 20, "	Promoted to 1st Lieutenant.
Do.	Chas. R. Pomeroy	Jan. 1, 1862	" 20, "	Promoted to 1st Lieutenant.
Do.	David McCamell	" 28, "	Jan. 28, "	Promoted to 1st Lieutenant.
Do.	Walter B. McNeil	April 11, "	May 1, "	Promoted to 1st Lieutenant.
Do.	Henry Harrison	March 23, "	June 24, "	Promoted to 1st Lieutenant.
Do.	Wm. S. Baldwin	Jan. 11, 1863	Feb. 10, 1863	Resigned July 13, 1863.
Do.	Jacob Parrott	April 24, "	April 24, "	Out of service.
Do.	Daniel A. Dorsey	March 2, "	" 22, "	Out of service.
Do.	Wm. Reddick	April 28, "	" 28, "	Mustered out with regiment.
Do.	Frederick Colbourn	May 7, "	May 7, "	Out of service.
Do.	Joseph H. Cole	March 2, "	June 26, "	Killed in action September 19, 1863.
Do.	Warren L. Johnson	July 13, "	Sept. 1, "	Promoted to 1st Lieutenant.
Do.	Francis McCampbell	March 2, "	" 1, "	Died July 22, 1864.
Do.	Wm. H. Myers	April 12, 1864	April 12, 1864	Out of service.
Do.	Louis Ferry	May 25, "	May 25, "	Commission returned.
Do.	George W. Roby	Aug. 11, "	Aug. 11, "	Promoted to 1st Lieutenant.
Do.	John E. Sykes	" 11, "	" 11, "	Killed in action September 6, 1864.
Do.	John O. Smith	" 11, "	" 11, "	Declined promotion; commission returned.

THIRTY-THIRD OHIO VOLUNTEER INFANTRY.

THE THIRTY-THIRD OHIO was organized at Camp Morrow, Portsmouth, Ohio, during the latter part of the summer of 1861. It entered the service with an aggregate of eight hundred and thirty-nine men. The Colonel (Joshua W. Sill) spared no pains to render the regiment perfect in drill and discipline, and its future efficiency was in a great measure due to him. Upon entering the field it joined the forces of General Nelson, at Maysville, Kentucky, and accompanied that command in its march to repel an invasion of the Blue Grass Region, by the Rebel Colonel John S. Williams. This campaign lasted about sixty days, in which time the Rebels were driven to Pikeville, and into Virginia. Taking transports at Louisa, on the Big Sandy River, the regiment was landed at Louisville on the 1st of December, 1861. It was there brigaded with the Tenth Wisconsin, Second and Twenty-First Ohio, in General Buell's army, and marched with that army to Bacon Creek, Kentucky, where it remained, with General O. M. Mitchel as division commander, until February, 1862. While lying at Bacon Creek the regiment suffered severely from measles, small-pox, and camp diarrhea.

On February 13th the regiment started with General Mitchel for Bowling Green, driving the enemy before them and occupying his works. On the 21st it marched to Nashville, and encamped in that city on the 26th of February.

On March 18, 1862, the regiment, still under General O. M. Mitchel, advanced along the Chattanooga Railroad to Murfreesboro' and Shelbyville, and thence to Huntsville, Alabama. After the occupation of Huntsville the regiment was on the move constantly, and, in the latter part of the summer, it advanced to Bridgeport. Here the Thirty-Third, with a small detachment of cavalry, were left, in the month of August, to occupy Fort McCook, at the mouth of Battle Creek, while the main force marched back to intercept General Bragg's army. On the 27th of August a detachment of the regiment, guarding a train which had been sent to Bridgeport for forage, was attacked by a party of Rebel cavalry. The cavalry from the fort was sent to the relief of the infantry, and succeeded in driving off the Rebels, and in killing and capturing some. The regiment lost one man killed. During this skirmish a Rebel battery opened on the fort, and for twelve hours the troops were exposed to a severe cannonade, without any opportunity to return the fire. At nightfall the fort was evacuated; all the stores which could not be removed were destroyed, and the troops set out to join the main army at Decherd, Tennessee. The night was fearfully dark, and the rain fell in torrents, but the march was accomplished in safety.

From Decherd the regiment marched, with its brigade and division, to Nashville, and passing through that city joined the main army under General Buell, at Bowling Green. Louisville was reached on the morning of the 26th of September. On October 1st the pursuit of Bragg's Rebel army was again resumed—the National forces marching out of Louisville on the Bardstown Turnpike. Nothing of moment occurred until Perryville was reached. The Thirty-Third Ohio went into this fight with four hundred muskets, and lost one hundred and twenty-nine men killed and wounded, twenty-five of whom were buried on the field. Colonel Oscar F. Moore (who had superseded Colonel Sill, appointed Brigadier-General) was severely wounded and fell into the hands of the enemy. Captains Hibbs and Foster were also severely wounded. This was the first set battle in which the Thirty-Third Ohio had been engaged, and it performed its part so gallantly as to elicit strong commendations from its brigade and division commanders.

The regiment participated in the pursuit of the enemy up to Crab Orchard, and then returned, by easy marches, to Nashville, Tennessee. During this time General Rosecrans had superseded General Buell in the command of the Army of the Ohio, and on assuming command reorganized the whole army, and christened it the Army of the Cumberland. The Thirty-Third Ohio was placed in First Brigade, First Division, of General George H. Thomas's command.

On December 26, 1862, the Thirty-Third Ohio moved out of Nashville, on the Nolin Turnpike, toward Murfreesboro', with General A. M. McCook's column, in the division commanded by General L. H. Rousseau. In the first day's fight at Stone River, the regiment supported Loomis's Michigan Battery, and rendered efficient service in checking the advance of the Rebels after they had broken through the National right. In this battle the regiment lost eight men killed and a number wounded.

The National army lay at Murfreesboro' until June 24, 1863, when it moved on Tullahoma, and made that difficult march to Chattanooga and vicinity. On the first day's march the enemy was met at Hoover's Gap, where a brisk fight ensued. The Thirty-Third Ohio was engaged in this affair, and lost four men wounded. The enemy was driven through the Gap and back toward Tullahoma, which place was abandoned by them on the 29th of June.

About the 1st of September, 1863, the Chickamauga campaign opened. The Thirty-Third Ohio crossed the Tennessee River, just above Bridgeport, marched over Sand and Lookout Mountains, into the valley of Chickamauga, and took part in the battle of Chickamauga on the 19th and 20th of September. It went into action with three hundred and forty-three men, and lost, in killed, wounded, and missing, one hundred and sixty-eight men. Major E. J. Ellis, of Manchester, Ohio, a gallant and beloved officer of the Thirty-Third Ohio, was killed in this battle. Captain (afterwards Colonel) Joseph Hinson also lost his right arm.

The regiment fell back with the main army to Rossville and Chattanooga, and was cooped up in that beleaguered city until the 24th of November, when it participated in the battle of Lookout Mountain, by forming a junction with General Hooker's forces. In this affair the regiment lost heavily. It rejoined its division on the morning of the 25th of November, and took part in carrying Mission Ridge. It lost in this brilliant affair thirty-one men out of two hundred engaged. Lieutenant George W. Roby, of Bainbridge, Ohio, was wounded in this battle. The regiment followed the enemy to Taylor's Ridge, and at that place, on the 27th, had another fight, losing several men wounded. The day previous, at Graysville, it aided in the capture of five pieces of artillery and several hundred prisoners.

Returning to Chattanooga the regiment re-enlisted as veterans, and was sent to Ohio to enjoy its thirty-days' furlough.

On returning to the field the Thirty-Third Ohio reported at Chattanooga, and in May, 1864, joined General Sherman's forces on the Atlanta campaign. During that campaign it participated in the battles of Rocky Face Ridge, Resaca, Pumpkin Vine Creek, Kenesaw Mountain, crossing of the Chattahoochie, Peachtree Creek, in the battles around Atlanta, and Jonesboro'. At Resaca the regiment lost the following-named officers killed: Captain McKain, of Pomeroy, Ohio; Lieutenant Edgar Higbee, of Ross County, and Colonel James H. Montgomery, of Gallipolis. A number of other officers of the regiment were slightly wounded, and about fifty men killed and wounded. The aggregate number of officers and men killed and wounded in this campaign was about one hundred and seventy. The regiment was unfortunate in its loss of officers: Lieutenant Charles R. Pomeroy, of Pomeroy, was killed at Utoy Creek; Colonel Montgomery and Major Benjamin F. Barger were severely wounded in the same battle; Lieutenant Campbell, of Gallipolis, was killed at Peachtree Creek; Lieutenant John E. Sykes, of Kinnickinick, Ross County, Ohio, was killed at Jonesboro'.

The Thirty-Third Ohio followed Hood as far as Villanow, Georgia, in his mad movement toward Nashville, after which it accompanied General Sherman in his march to the sea and in the campaign through the Carolinas. At Bentonville, North Carolina, it suffered severely, paying there its last tribute to the cause of the Union. It then made the triumphant march through the Rebel capital to Washington City, and participated in the grand review. It was then taken to Louisville, Kentucky, and mustered out of the service on the 12th of July, 1865. It was paid off and discharged at Camp Dennison.

34th REGIMENT OHIO VOLUNTEER INFANTRY.

ROSTER, THREE YEARS' SERVICE.

RANK.	NAME.	DATE OF RANK.	COM. ISSUED.	REMARKS.
Colonel	ABRAHAM S. PIATT	Aug. 2, 1861	Sept. 16, 1861	Promoted to Brigadier-General.
Do.	JOHN T. TOLAND	May 14, 1862	May 14, 1862	Killed July 18, 1863.
Do.	F. E. FRANKLIN	July 18, 1863	Aug. 25, 1863	Mustered out.
Lt. Colonel	J. T. TOLAND	Aug. 2, 1861	Sept. 18, 1861	Promoted to Colonel.
Do.	FREEMAN E. FRANKLIN	May 14, 1862	May 14, 1862	Promoted to Colonel.
Do.	JOHN W. SHAW	July 18, 1863	Aug. 25, 1863	Killed July 24, 1864, at Winchester.
Do.	LUTHER FURNEY	Aug. 11, 1864	" 11, 1864	Transf'd to 36th O. V. I.; disch'd Feb. 26, '65.
Major	FREEMAN E. FRANKLIN	" 21, 1861		Promoted to Lieutenant-Colonel.
Do.	THOMAS W. RATHBONE	May 14, 1862	May 14, 1862	Resigned October 10, 1862.
Do.	JOHN W. SHAW	Oct. 10, "	Nov. 14, "	Promoted to Lieutenant-Colonel.
Do.	LUTHER FURNEY	March 21, 1864	March 21, 1864	Promoted to Lieutenant-Colonel.
Do.	S. R. S. WEST	Aug. 11, "	Aug. 11, "	Declined promotion.
Do.	CHAS. W. BOYD	Oct. 1, "	Oct. 1, "	Mustered out at expiration of service.
Do.	BENJ. C. RICKER	Nov. 36, "	Nov. 28, "	Mustered out.
Surgeon	JACOB Y. CANTWELL	Aug. 27, 1861	Sept. 15, 1861	Commission returned January 28, 1862.
Do.	HENRY SPILLMAN	March 20, 1862	March 27, 1862	Commission returned; revoked.
Do.	W. R. S. CLARK	Jan. 11, "	April 30, "	Resigned July 30, 1862.
Do.	JOHN H. AYERS	July 30, "	Oct. 7, "	Mustered out.
Ass't Surgeon	W. R. S. CLARK	Aug. 31, 1861	Sept. 16, 1861	Promoted to Surgeon.
Do.	JOHN H. AYERS	Jan. 16, 1862	Jan. 16, 1862	Promoted to Surgeon.
Do.	WILSON V. COWAN	July 4, "	July 23, "	Mustered out.
Do.	CHAS. A. MILLER	Aug. 27, "	Dec. 5, "	Mustered out.
Do.	J. P. SCHILLING	May 30, 1864	May 30, 1864	Mustered out.
Chaplain	G. W. COLLIER	Aug 30, 1861	Aug. 30, 1861	Transferred to 36th Ohio Volunteer Infantry.
Captain	Thomas W. Rathbone	" 13, "	Sept. 16, "	Promoted to Major.
Do.	J. W. Shaw	" 13, "	" 16, "	Promoted to Major.
Do.	Austin T. Miller	" 14, "	" 16, "	Resigned November 1, 1862.
Do.	Luther Furney	" 16, "	" 16, "	Promoted to Major.
Do.	Herman C. Evans	" 16, "	" 16, "	Discharged August 15, 1863.
Do.	S. R. S. West	" 16, "	" 16, "	Prom. to Major; mustered out at expiration of service.
Do.	Chas. G. Broadwell	" 16, "	" 16, "	Resigned July 7, 1862.
Do.	James A. Anderson	Sept. 2, "	" 16, "	Discharged October 6, 1863.
Do.	Oliver P. Evans	" 6, "	" 16, "	Resigned December 4, 1862.
Do.	Thomas R. Smiley	" 12, "	" 16, "	Resigned August 5, 1862.
Do.	Henry C. Hatfield	May 14, 1862	May 14, 1862	Died of wounds received September 10, 1862.
Do.	Frank B. Helwig	July 17, "	Aug. 14, "	Mustered out.
Do.	John Grace	Aug. 5, "	Oct. 7, "	Mustered out.
Do.	Albert Nesbitt	Sept. 19, "	Nov. 14, "	Mustered out.
Do.	John Cutler	Nov. 1, "	" 28, "	Mustered out March 13, 1865.
Do.	Chas. W. Boyd	Oct. 10, "	" 28, "	Promoted to Major.
Do.	Ezra W. Clark	Dec. 4, "	Dec. 30, "	Declined and returned commission.
Do.	Hiram Peck	" 4, "	Feb. 10, 1863	Mustered out.
Do.	Robert B. Underwood	" 19, 1863	Jan. 8, 1864	Mustered out.
Do.	George W. McKay	March 2, 1864	March 2, "	Deceased.
Do.	Lemuel E. Merry	" 2, "	" 2, "	Discharged August 30, 1864.
Do.	Alfred Butters	Aug. 11, "	Aug. 11, "	Promoted.
Do.	John Cutler	Nov. 1, 1862	Nov. 28, 1862	Mustered out March 13, 1865.
Do.	Benj. C. Ricker	Sept. 30, 1864	Sept. 30, 1864	Promoted to Major 36th O. V. I.
Do.	Asa B. Carter	" 30, "	" 30, "	Killed in action September 19, 1864.
Do.	James P. Donnally	" 30, "	" 30, "	Mustered out.
Do.	Isaac P. Grover	" 30, "	" 30, "	Mustered out.
Do.	John L. Brunson	" 30, "	" 30, "	Mustered out.
Do.	Frank A. Austin	" 30, "	" 30, "	Mustered out.
Do.	Wm. A. Harris	" 30, "	" 30, "	Mustered out.
1st Lieutenant	H. C. Hatfield	Aug. 13, 1861	" 16, 1861	Promoted to Captain May 14, 1862.
Do.	Frank B. Helwig	" 13, "	" 16, "	Promoted to Captain.
Do.	John Grace	" 14, "	" 16, "	Promoted to Captain.
Do.	Hiram Peck	" 16, "	" 16, "	Promoted to Captain.
Do.	Ethan A. Brown	" 16, "	" 16, "	App. Capt. on Gen. Piatt's staff; died of w'nds rec'd Sept. 10, '62.
Do.	Albert Nesbitt	" 16, "	" 16, "	Promoted to Captain September 19, 1862.
Do.	Samuel McCutcheon	" 16, "	" 16, "	Killed September 10, 1862.
Do.	George H. Hart	" 16, "	" 16, "	Resigned April 23, 1862.
Do.	Ezra W. Clark	" 17, "	" 16, "	Assistant Adjutant-General of Volunteers.
Do.	John Cutler	Sept. 2, "	" 16, "	Promoted to Captain.
Do.	Chas. W. Boyd	" 6, "	" 16, "	Promoted to Captain.
Do.	Richard Roe	" 12, "	" 16, "	Resigned July 25, 1862.
Do.	George W. McKay	May 14, 1862	July 29, 1862	Promoted to Captain.
Do.	Wm. H. Carpenter	July 7, "	Aug. 14, "	Discharged August 1, 1863.
Do.	Lemuel E. Merry	April 23, "	Oct. 7, "	Promoted to Captain.
Do.	John Wingett	Aug. 12, "	" 7, "	Resigned September 29, 1863.
Do.	Alfred Butters	" 5, "	" 7, "	Promoted to Captain.
Do.	A. S. Frazer	Oct. 10, "	Nov. 14, "	Honorably discharged June 14, 1864.
Do.	James H. Taylor	Sept. 10, "	" 28, "	Discharged September 1, 1864.
Do.	James Shields	" 19, "	" 28, "	Resigned January 23, 1863.
Do.	Benj. C. Ricker	Oct. 10, "	" 28, "	Promoted to Captain.
Do.	Oliver P. Gotton	Nov. 1, "	" 28, "	Resigned January 8, 1863.
Do.	Robert B. Underwood	Dec. 23, "	Feb. 10, 1863	Promoted to Captain.
Do.	Albany Packham	Jan. 23, "	" 10, "	Discharged November 5, 1863.
Do.	Jeremiah Engle	" 8, "	" 10, "	Mustered out.
Do.	Franklin G. Shaw	March 2, 1864	March 2, 1864	Mustered out.
Do.	Asa B. Carter	" 2, "	" 2, "	Promoted to Captain.
Do.	John Q. A. Fullerton	" 2, "	" 2, "	Mustered out.
Do.	James P. Donnally	" 2, "	" 2, "	Promoted to Captain.
Do.	Frank Millward	" 2, "	" 2, "	Prisoner.
Do.	Isaac P. Grover	" 2, "	" 2, "	Promoted to Captain.

RANK.	NAME.	DATE OF RANK.	COM. ISSUED.	REMARKS.
1st Lieutenant	Nelson W. Hayes	Aug. 11, 1864	Aug. 11, 1864	Prisoner.
Do.	Chas. E. Callahan	" 11, "	" 11, "	Declined promotion.
Do.	Frank Millward	March 2, "	March 2, "	Discharged as 2d Lieutenant Dec. 19, 1864.
Do.	Nelson W. Hayes	Aug. 11, "	Aug. 11, "	Mustered out March 25, 1865.
Do.	John W. Cartwright	Sept. 30, "	Sept. 30, "	Died of wounds November 17, 1864.
Do.	Frank A. Austin	" 30, "	" 30, "	Promoted to Captain.
Do.	Wm. A. Harris	" 30, "	" 30, "	Promoted to Captain.
Do.	Isaac N. Anderson	" 30, "	" 30, "	Transferred to 36th Ohio Volunteer Infantry.
Do.	Thomas H. B. Hopkins	" 30, "	" 30, "	Transferred to 36th Ohio Volunteer Infantry.
Do.	Nathan P. Marvell	Nov. 26, "	Nov. 26, "	Mustered out April 4, 1865.
Do.	James Smith	" 26, "	" 26, "	Transferred to 36th Ohio Volunteer Infantry.
2d Lieutenant	George W. McKay	Aug. 13, 1861	Sept. 16, 1861	Promoted to 1st Lieutenant.
Do.	Wm. H. Carpenter	" 13, "	Dec. 12, "	Promoted to 1st Lieutenant.
Do.	Thomas Lawler	" 14, "	" 12, "	Resigned January 28, 1862.
Do.	Lemuel E. Merry	" 16, "	" 12, "	Promoted to 1st Lieutenant.
Do.	Henry H. Anderson	" 16, "	" 12, "	Resigned December 3, 1862.
Do.	A. S. Frazer	" 16, "	" 12, "	Promoted to 1st Lieutenant.
Do.	Alfred Butters	" 16, "	" 12, "	Promoted to 1st Lieutenant.
Do.	Robert B. Underwood	Sept. 2, "	" 12, "	Promoted to 1st Lieutenant.
Do.	Robert C. Peters	" 6, "	" 12, "	Honorably discharged October 9, 1862.
Do.	John Wingett	" 12, "	" 12, "	Promoted to 1st Lieutenant.
Do.	James Shields	Feb. 19, 1862	Feb. 19, 1862	Promoted to 1st Lieutenant.
Do.	Benj. C. Ricker	May 14, "	July 29, "	Promoted to 1st Lieutenant.
Do.	Oliver P. Gorton	July 7, "	Aug. 14, "	Promoted to 1st Lieutenant.
Do.	James H. Taylor	April 23, "	Oct. 3, "	Promoted to 1st Lieutenant.
Do.	Jeremiah Engle	Aug. 5, "	" 7, "	Promoted to 1st Lieutenant.
Do.	Albany Packham	" 12, "	" 7, "	Promoted to 1st Lieutenant.
Do.	Franklin G. Shaw	Oct. 9, "	" 25, "	Promoted to 1st Lieutenant.
Do.	Asa B. Carter	Sept. 10, "	Nov. 28, "	Promoted to 1st Lieutenant.
Do.	James Cotter	" 19, "	Dec. 16, "	
Do.	John Q. A. Fullerton	Oct. 10, "	" 16, "	Promoted to 1st Lieutenant.
Do.	James P. Donnally	Nov. 1, "	" 16, "	Promoted to 1st Lieutenant.
Do.	Frank Millward	Oct. 10, "	" 16, "	Promoted to 1st Lieutenant.
Do.	Isaac P. Grover	Dec. 3, "	" 16, "	Promoted to 1st Lieutenant.
Do.	Nelson W. Hayes	" 4, "	Feb. 10, 1863	Promoted to 1st Lieutenant.
Do.	Chas. E. Callahan	Jan. 8, 1863	" 10, "	Mustered out.
Do.	Benj. T. Bruce	" 22, "	" 10, "	Discharged September 8, 1863.
Do.	John L. Brunson	March 2, 1864	March 2, 1864	Promoted to 1st Lieutenant.
Do.	Frank A. Austin	Jan. 24, "	" 9, "	Promoted to 1st Lieutenant.
Do.	John W. Cartwright	Oct. 29, 1863	" 15, "	Promoted to 1st Lieutenant.
Do.	Isaiah C. Lindsey	March 15, 1864	" 15, "	Mustered out.
Do.	Wm. C. Sargent	" 15, "	" 15, "	Mustered out.
Do.	Wm. A. Harris	" 15, "	" 15, "	Promoted to 1st Lieutenant.
Do.	Isaac N. Anderson	" 15, "	" 15, "	Promoted to 1st Lieutenant.
Do.	Samuel A. Derr	" 15, "	" 15, "	Deceased.
Do.	Nathan P. Marvell	Sept. 30, "	Sept. 30, "	Promoted to 1st Lieutenant.
Do.	James Smith	" 30, "	" 30, "	Promoted to 1st Lieutenant.
Do.	Samuel Jordan	" 30, "	" 30, "	Declined promotion; commission returned,
Do.	Frederick Billman	" 30, "	" 30, "	Mustered out.
Do.	James K. Agnew	" 30, "	" 30, "	Transferred to 36th Ohio Volunteer Infantry.
Do.	George Watt	" 30, "	" 30, "	Mustered out.
Do.	Morton L. Hawkins	" 30, "	" 30, "	Mustered out.
Do.	John Jordan	Nov. 26, "	Nov. 26, "	Mustered out.
Do.	Andrew J. Temple	" 26, "	" 26, "	Mustered out.
Do.	Chas. A. Metz	" 26, "	" 26, "	Mustered out.

THIRTY-FOURTH OHIO VOLUNTEER INFANTRY.

THIS regiment was organized at Camp Lucas, Clermont County, Ohio, during the months of July and August, 1861; the first detachment entering camp July 15th, and the first regular companies, under Captains Broadwell and Evans, July 21st. On the morning of September 1st it moved to Camp Dennison, and was there prepared for the field, adopting as its uniform (a license allowable at that early period of the war) a light blue Zouave dress. In compliment to their Colonel, the name of "Piatt Zouaves" was adopted.

The regiment left Camp Dennison on the 15th of September, 1861, for Western Virginia, with full ranks, and arrived at Camp Enyart, on the Kanawha River, on the 20th of the same month. On the 25th it fought its first battle in a gap near Chapmanville, Logan County, Virginia, whipping a Virginia regiment, inflicting considerable loss to the Rebels in men, and badly wounding their commander, Colonel Davis. The loss of the Thirty-Fourth was one killed and eight wounded. During the remainder of the autumn and winter the regiment was engaged in the arduous duty of guarding the rear of General Rosecrans's army, and the counties of Cabell, Putnam, Mason, Wayne, and Logan were kept pretty free from guerillas by continual scouting.

In March, 1862, the Thirty-Fourth was ordered to Gauley Bridge to join General Cox in his demonstration on the Virginia and Tennessee Railroad. The regiment participated in the battle of Princeton, on the 17th and 18th of May, losing several men. Lieutenants Peck and Peters were wounded, and Captain O. P. Evans taken prisoner. Humphrey Marshall commanded the Rebels.

When General Cox was ordered to join General McClellan, in August, 1862, there were six regiments left to guard the Kanawha Valley. The Thirty-Fourth and Thirty-Seventh held the outpost at Fayetteville, where, on the morning of September 10th, they were attacked by a Rebel force, under General Loring, ten thousand strong. With the aid of admirable breastworks, previously constructed by General Scammon, two ten-pound brass field pieces and four six-pound mountain howitzers, the position was held until midnight, when the place was evacuated. Part of the time the Thirty-Fourth fought in the open field, and repeatedly charged on the enemy. Its loss was necessarily heavy. Of six companies engaged (the other four, under Major Franklin, being on a scout) the loss was one hundred and thirty, or fully one-third. One-half of the officers were either killed or wounded. Cutting their way out under a heavy fire, the National troops fell back towards the Kanawha river, made a stand at Cotton Mountain the next day, and at Charleston on the 12th, where a severe engagement took place. From this point the entire National force fell back to Point Pleasant, leaving the entire valley in the hands of the Rebels. In October General Cox returned with his command, when another advance was made, and the valley regained.

From this time until May, 1863, nothing of moment occurred to vary the monotony of garrison duty. During May the regiment was furnished with horses and transformed into "Mounted Rifles."

On the 13th of July, 1863, an expedition, consisting of the Thirty-Fourth, two companies of the First, and seven companies of the Second Virginia Cavalry, under command of Colonel Toland, made a demonstration on the Virginia and Tennessee Railroad, striking it, on the evening of the 18th, at Wytheville. A desperate fight ensued, the enemy occupying the houses, barns, yards, etc., on a slight elevation to the rear of the town. About dark the National forces succeeded in capturing the enemy's artillery, and driving him in all directions. Captain Delany, commanding First Virginia, was killed, and Colonel Powell, Second Virginia, badly wounded. The Thirty-Fourth Ohio lost four killed, including Colonel Toland, thirteen wounded and thirty-three missing. (Colonel Toland was shot from a window of a house in his immediate vicinity, while seated on his horse, engaged in giving orders, surrounded by a few of his staff. The ball passed through his left breast. The Colonel did not fall from his horse, but caught the mane with his right hand, when his Orderly, who was about fifty yards distant from him, ran and caught him before he had time to reach the ground. With his last breath he requested that his horse and sword be sent to his mother.)

The brigade left Camp Piatt with nearly one thousand men; marched six hundred and fifty-two miles in eleven days, traversing some of the highest mountains in West Virginia, capturing over two hundred and fifty horses and three hundred and sixty prisoners, two pieces of artillery, and a large amount of commissary stores; destroyed between three and five thousand stand of arms, a bridge of importance, and partially burned one of the wealthiest cities in Virginia.

Upon the fall of Colonel Toland, the command devolved upon Lieutenant-Colonel Franklin, who decided on a retrograde movement. This he found it difficult to execute, from the fact that the Rebel General McCausland had blockaded the roads in the most effectual manner. For several days the command was moving in the mountains, destitute of food for themselves or fodder for their horses, and continually harassed by Rebel cavalry. On the day previous to the arrival of the regiment at Wytheville, company C, acting as rear-guard, was attacked by a superior force of Rebel cavalry. A number was killed and wounded, and Captain Cutter and fifteen men were taken prisoners.

Several expeditions, under General Duffie (who had assumed command of the Kanawha cavalry), to Lewisburg and vicinity, completed this year's campaign.

In January, 1864, about two-thirds of the regiment re-enlisted as veterans. On the 29th of April, 1864, the regiment was divided in two detachments. The mounted portion was to operate with the cavalry, under General Averill; the dismounted, with the Thirty-Sixth Ohio Volunteer Infantry, in General Crook's division of infantry.

On the 1st of May, 1864, the second expedition for the destruction of the Virginia and Tennessee Railroad left Charleston. On the 9th the cavalry arrived at Wytheville, encountered the Rebels under General Morgan, were repulsed, and compelled to fall back, with considerable loss. The infantry, under General Crook, was more successful. On the same day that Averill was defeated, Crook achieved a solid victory over General Jenkins at Cloyd Mountain, near Dublin Depot, which was captured the same evening. On the day following the enemy was again encountered and defeated at the railroad bridge over New River, and the bridge totally destroyed. From this point the command returned to Meadow Bluffs, crossing Salt Pond and Peter's Mountains and the Greenbrier River, arriving at their destination on the 19th of May, completing a distance of four hundred miles marched during the month.

From Meadow Bluffs the Thirty-Fourth started to join General Hunter, at Staunton, in the Shenandoah Valley, passing through White Sulphur Springs, Callahan's Stand, and crossing Panther Gap Mountain, where a skirmish ensued. On the 5th of June the regiment reached Goshen, on the Virginia Central Railroad, and skirmished with a body of cavalry at Cow Pasture River. The day after the Rebels were met at Buffalo Gap, in a position secure from direct attack, but General Hayes's brigade succeeded in flanking and driving them out of it.

Staunton was reached on the 8th of June, where the Thirty-Fourth made its final preparations to join General Hunter on his disastrous raid to Lynchburg. General Hunter, now re-enforced by Generals Crook, Averill, and Duffie, left Staunton on the 9th, and, passing through Brownsburg, reached Lexington on the 11th. The evening of the 14th found the regiment at Buckhannon, on the James River, at which point a few shots were exchanged with a small Rebel force that had been driven out of Lexington. Crossing the Blue Ridge, near the Peaks of Otter, the town of Liberty was reached on the 16th, when another skirmish occurred. From this point

General Crook's command, with whom the dismounted members of the Thirty-Fourth were serving, was sent on a flanking expedition across the James, for the purpose of attacking Lynchburg in the rear, the cavalry, on the left, to make a diversion in their favor. The attack was made late in the afternoon of the 18th of June, was partly successful, and, in the opinion of the Thirty-Fourth, would have been entirely so had General Crook been allowed to occupy the city that night, according to his wish, but orders from his superior officer forbade it. The enemy were re-enforced that night by about twenty thousand men from the vicinity of Richmond, under the command of General Early, which, of course, so strengthened the city that it was impossible, with the small and illy-appointed force under General Hunter, to cope with the Rebels.

The situation was fully developed early the next morning by a fierce cannonade from the Rebels, which was promptly replied to by the National forces. In the afternoon an engagement occurred, in which the Thirty-Fourth suffered severely. The retreat of the National forces commenced at dark on the 19th of June. The rear being heavily pressed by the pursuing enemy, the second skirmish occurred at Liberty. At Salem, on the 21st, while the artillery of Hunter's command was passing through a narrow defile, totally unsupported, a party of Rebels made a sudden descent from the hills, and, dispersing the drivers and gunners, commenced the work of destruction by shooting horses, cutting spokes and harness, and blowing up caissons. The mounted portion of the Thirty-Fourth, being a few miles in the rear, hurried to the scene of action, dismounted, and, with Lieutenant-Colonel Shaw as their leader, encountered the Rebels. After a sharp fight the Rebels were driven off and the artillery regained.

The retreat was continued. Big and Little Sewell Mountains were crossed, and Charleston reached on the 1st of July, where the exhausted, ragged, and starved troops were permitted to rest. Thus ended this most disastrous expedition. The constant skirmishing, the starved bodies, and blistered feet of those who participated in it, made "Hunter's retreat from Lynchburg" an event long to be remembered.

The Thirty-Fourth lay at Charleston on the 10th of July, when it embarked on transports for Parkersburg. (A day or two previous to this move the whole regiment was dismounted and horses and equipments turned over to the cavalry.) From Parkersburg the regiment moved by rail to Martinsburg, arriving there on the 14th of July, 1864.

The regiment was now in the Shenandoah Valley. On the 20th of July, while General Crook, with his main force and the Sixth and Nineteenth Corps, was pressing Early back on Winchester, General Duval's brigade, of which the Thirty-Fourth was a part, attempted to occupy the place in advance of the Rebels, by a forced march from Martinsburg. Early, anticipating the movement, had sent forward his old division, under General Ramseur, to check it. The National force, only twelve hundred strong, met and attacked the Rebels two miles from Winchester, completely routing them, capturing their artillery, and killing and wounding all their brigade commanders. The loss of the Thirty-Fourth was ten killed and twenty wounded. Four days later occurred the fourth battle of Winchester, in which General Early, taking advantage of the absence of the Sixth and Nineteenth Corps, overwhelmed General Crook—the latter, however, effecting an orderly retreat, with the loss of only a few wagons. In this battle General Duval's brigade had the honor of bringing up the rear, and the Thirty-Fourth suffered severely, losing their commander, Lieutenant-Colonel Shaw, a cool, determined soldier, and Christian. He was struck in the abdomen by a musket-ball, and was borne from the field by a few faithful men of his regiment, placed in an ambulance, and carried eleven miles distant, to a place called Bunker Hill, where he died. His last words were, "Welcome, welcome death!" Captain G. W. McKay was wounded about the same time in the leg, and would have fallen into the hands of the enemy but for the heroic devotion of some of his men, who carried him on a litter fifteen miles to Sandy Hook, Maryland, where he died.

The command of the regiment devolved upon Captain S. R. S. West, who fully sustained his reputation as a brave and gallant officer. The next day, July 25th, another stand was made at Martinsburg, the Thirty-Fourth being the last regiment to leave the field, which it did under a galling fire.

The time of the regiment between the 25th of July and the 3d of September was occupied as follows: July 26th, forded the Potomac at Williamsport; 27th, marched to Sandy Hook, Maryland, opposite Harper's Ferry; 28th, crossed the Potomac at Halltown; 30th, recrossed to Sandy Hook; 31st, marched through Middletown toward Pennsylvania State line; August 1st, continued the march to Wolfville, Maryland; 3d, returned by same road to Frederick City, Maryland, and encamped on the Monocacy; 6th, returned to Harper's Ferry; 8th recrossed the Potomac and moved in the direction of Halltown; 10th, reached Berryville, Virginia; 11th, marched in line of battle in the direction of Front Royal—heavy skirmishing with Early, who was falling back on Fisher's Hill; 12th, reached Cedar Creek, found the enemy had burned the bridge, and was intrenched on the south bank of the stream. The Thirty-Fourth lay here until the evening of the 17th (skirmishing heavily in the meantime). It then fell back, marching all night, passing through Winchester, and camping at Berryville early next morning. The 20th of August found the Thirty-Fourth at Charlestown, with the enemy close in its rear. In the expectation of an attack, breastworks were thrown up; but, after waiting in vain until ten o'clock at night, the regiment fell back to Halltown. The enemy still followed, and, taking a position in the immediate front of the regiment, heavy skirmishing ensued until the 27th, when they withdrew to demonstrate on the upper Potomac. On the day following the Thirty-Fourth again occupied Charlestown, where the regimental officers were busily engaged making up the necessary papers for the discharge of the non-veterans, who, on the morning of the 3d of September, proceeded to Columbus, Ohio, in charge of Captain West.

During the few months previous to this time the Thirty-Fourth had been largely re-enforced by new recruits. Counting the veterans and the men of 1862, it still numbered between four and five hundred men, present and absent. (On the evening of the day on which the non-veterans left, the regiment participated in the battle of Berryville. The non-veterans were near enough to hear the booming of cannon.)

The enemy fell back to Winchester and Bunker Hill. The Thirty-Fourth marched to Summit Point, and lay in camp until the morning of the 19th of September, the day on which occurred Sheridan's famous battle of Winchester, it being the third time the regiment had fought over nearly the same ground. It suffered terribly that day, the color-guard having no less than six men, in quick succession, killed and wounded while carrying the flag. It was finally brought through safe by George Rynals, of company A. All know the result of that glorious battle, and remember Sheridan's celebrated dispatch, commencing: "I am moving up the Valley to-night!" In accordance with this announcement, the next evening found the regiment at Cedar Creek, where it lay until the 22d, when occurred the battle of Fisher's Hill. Here again, by the excellent management of General George Crook, the enemy was successfully flanked, which resulted in his total rout and the capture of all his artillery. The loss of the Thirty-Fourth in the last two engagements was sixty-one killed.

The National forces followed the retreating and demoralized enemy to Harrisonburg, where they lay until the 6th of October. In the meantime the cavalry were busily engaged in burning barns filled with grain, driving in stock of all kinds, and otherwise rendering the Valley untenable as a base of supplies, and literally fulfilling Grant's order to Sheridan, to render it so desolate and provisionless that "a crow, in passing over it, would be compelled to carry his rations with him." By the 6th the work of devastation was completed, and the National army again fell back to Cedar Creek; while the enemy, following at a respectful distance, once more resumed his old position at Fisher's Hill.

Of General Early's desperate attempt to regain his lost laurels on the 19th of October, and of his partial success on the morning of "Sheridan's Ride" to the scene of action, and the irretrievable disaster of the Rebels in the afternoon, much has been said and sung. The brunt of the morning's surprise and attack fell on the left flank, composed of General Crook's corps, which, with the Nineteenth Corps occupying the center of the line, was badly shattered. The Sixth Corps, on the right, had time to fall back in good order. The troops were rallied near Middletown, from whence the final advance was made, which swept everything before it. It is sufficient to say that the day was won.

The evening before the battle the regiment, under command of Lieutenant-Colonel L. Furney, was sent on picket. In the morning, before dawn, when the surprise occurred, the Colonel and eighteen of his men were taken prisoners. The Colonel escaped at Mount Jackson, and joined his command a few days thereafter. The loss of the Thirty-Fourth in this affair was two killed, twelve wounded, and eighteen prisoners. From this time until the latter part of December, 1864, the regiment lay in the neighborhood of Kernstown, when it marched to Opequan Crossing, and from thence to Martinsburg.

On the evening of the 22d of December, as the regiment was leaving Martinsburg, on its way to Webster, by rail, the train on which it was being transported came in collision with one loaded with coal, killing two men and wounding fourteen. It reached Webster on the 25th and Beverly on the 28th.

On the 11th of January, 1865, the post of Beverly, garrisoned by the Thirty-Fourth, which, by this time, was reduced to three hundred men present for duty, and the dismounted portion of the Eighth Ohio Cavalry, was attacked by the enemy, under command of General Rosser. So secret and sudden was the attack—no alarm whatever being given until the enemy were in the quarters—that resistance was out of the question, and nearly every man was at one time a prisoner, though subsequently a great many escaped, favored by the darkness and intense excitement of the occasion. Colonel Youart, of the Eighth, commanding post, and Colonel Furney, were both captured, but afterward escaped. The survivors of this most unfortunate and disgraceful affair fell back to Philippi, and from thence were ordered to Cumberland, Maryland, where they were consolidated with the Thirty-Sixth Ohio, (General Crook's old regiment), commanded by Colonel H. F. Duval. The union of the separate organizations dates from the 22d of February, 1865, in which the old Thirty-Fourth loses its identity—the coalition being known as the Thirty-Sixth Ohio Veteran Volunteer Infantry.

35th REGIMENT OHIO VOLUNTEER INFANTRY.

ROSTER, THREE YEARS' SERVICE.

RANK.	NAME.	DATE OF RANK.	COM. ISSUED.	REMARKS.
Colonel	FERD. VANDERVEER	July 26, 1861	July 26, 1861	Brig. Gen. of Vols. and Brvt. Maj. Gen.
Lt. Colonel	CHARLES L'H. LONG	" 27, "	Aug. 15, "	Resigned July 13 1863.
Do.	HENRY V. N. BOYNTON	" 16, 1863	July 20, 1863	Mustered out with regiment.
Major	HENRY V. N. BOYNTON	" 29, 1861	Feb. 4, 1862	Promoted to Lieutenant-Colonel.
Do.	JOSEPH L. BUDD	" 13, 1863	July 20, 1863	Mustered out with regiment.
Surgeon	PERKINS A. GORDON	Sept. 7, 1861	Oct. 15, 1861	Resigned November 2. 1863.
Do.	FRANCIS D. MORRIS	Nov. 1, 1863	Jan. 25, 1864	Resigned August 8, 1862; disability.
Ass't Surgeon	FRANCIS D. MORRIS	Aug. 21, 1861	Aug. 21, 1861	Resigned August 6, 1862.
Do.	CHARLES O. WRIGHT	" 15, 1862	" 29, 1862	Promoted to Surgeon; resigned June 18, 1864.
Do.	A. H. LANDIS	Nov. 13, "	Feb. 16, 1863	Mustered out September 27, 1864.
Chaplain	JOHN WOOD	Sept. 23, 1861	Sept. 30, 1861	Resigned November 19, 1862.
Do.	JOSHUA C. HOULETT	Jan. 13, 1862	Jan. 20, 1862	Resigned February 19, 1863.
Captain	Thomas Stone	Aug. 5, 1861	Feb. 5, "	Resigned June 6, 1862.
Do.	Joseph L. Budd	" 15, "	" 5, "	Promoted to Major.
Do.	John S. Earhart	" 20, "	" 5, "	Died August 10, 1863.
Do.	Nathaniel Reeder	" 26, "	" 5, "	Dismissed August 12, 1863.
Do.	Michael S. Gunckle	" 26, "	" 5, "	Resigned October 21, 1862.
Do.	David M. Gans	Sept. 1, "	" 5, "	Died November 24, 1863.
Do.	Oliver H. Parshall	" 5, "	" 5, "	Killed September 19, 1863.
Do.	Samuel L'Hommedieu	" 7, "	" 5, "	Mustered out with regiment
Do.	Henry Mallary	" 16, "	" 5, "	Resigned February 17, 1862.
Do.	Andrew J. Lewis	Feb. 17, 1862	March 20, "	Resigned January 4, 1864.
Do.	Ransford Smith	June 6, "	June 21, "	Honorably discharged Feb. 18, 1863. [21, '63.
Do.	Samuel Martindale	Oct. 21, "	July 12, 1863	Dismissed July 28,'63; revoked; hon. dis. Aug.
Do.	Jonathan Heninger	Feb. 18, 1863	April 28, "	Resigned September 20, 1864. [20, 1864.
Do.	Lewis F. Dougherty	July 13, "	Aug. 1, "	Killed at battle of Peach-tree Creek, Ga., July
Do.	John G. Vanderveer	March 19, 1864	March 19, 1864	Mustered out with regiment.
Do.	Edward Cottingham	" 19, "	" 19, "	Mustered out March 11, 1865.
Do.	Wm. M. C. Steele	" 19, "	" 19, "	
Do.	Philip Rothenbush	" 19, "	" 19, "	
Do.	Theodore D. Mather	" 19, "	" 19, "	
Do.	Samuel L. Houser	" 19, "	" 19, "	Declined promotion.
Do.	James H. Bone	" 19, "	" 19, "	Mustered out with regiment. [Sep. 13,'63.
Do.	Joel K. Deardorff	Sept. 12, 1861	May 6, "	Died Oct. '63, from wounds at Chickamauga,
Do.	Frederick W. Keil	June 14, "	June 11, "	
1st Lieutenant	George B. Wright	Aug. 2, "	Feb. 4, 1862	Resigned September 18, 1863.
Do.	John G. Vanderveer	" 2, "	" 4, "	Promoted to Captain.
Do.	Ransford Smith	" 9, "	" 4, "	Promoted to Captain June 6, 1862.
Do.	Lewis F. Dougherty	" 15, "	" 4, "	Promoted to Captain.
Do.	Wm. C. Dine	" 26, "	" 4, "	Resigned February 12, 1863.
Do.	Samuel Martindale	" 26, "	" 4, "	Promoted to Captain.
Do.	Edward Cottingham	Sept. 1, "	" 4, "	Promoted to Captain.
Do.	Joseph C. Thomas	" 5, "	" 4, "	Resigned November 3, 1862.
Do.	Wm. M. C. Steele	" 7, "	" 4, "	Promoted to Captain.
Do.	Andrew J. Lewis	" 15, "	" 4, "	Promoted to Captain.
Do.	Philip Rothenbush	Feb. 17, 1862	May 1, "	Promoted to Captain.
Do.	Wm. H. Eacott	June 6, "	June 21, "	Resigned January 30, 1863.
Do.	Theodore D. Mather	Oct. 24, "	Jan. 12, 1863	Promoted to Captain.
Do.	Jonathan Heninger	Jan. 30, "	Feb. 19, "	Promoted to Captain.
Do.	Samuel L. Houser	Feb. 12, "	April 22, "	Declined promotion.
Do.	Thomas M. Harlan	Jan. 1, 1863	June 10, "	Killed September 20, 1863.
Do.	James H. Bone	July 13, "	Aug 1, "	Promoted to Captain.
Do.	Julian R. Fitch	Feb. 18, "	" 8, "	On detached service.
Do.	Frederick W. Keil	Aug. 20, "	Sept. 26, "	Promoted to Captain.
Do.	L. P. Thompson	March 19, 1864	May 19, 1864	Mustered out with regiment.
Do.	John Adams	" 19, "	" 19, "	Resigned as 2d Lieutenant.
Do.	I. F. Sanders	" 19, "	" 19, "	On detached service.
Do.	David W. Schaeffer	" 19, "	" 19, "	
Do.	Robert B. Davidson	" 19, "	" 19, "	
Do.	Joseph H. Taylor	" 19, "	" 19, "	
Do.	James Sabine	" 19, "	" 19, "	Deceased.
Do.	Benj. F. Miller	" 19, "	" 19, "	
Do.	Richard Ford	" 19, "	" 19, "	
Do.	James E. Harris	" 19, "	" 19, "	Mustered out with regiment as Adjutant.
Do.	Lewis Lanebright	Sept. 12, 1861	" 6, "	Absent on fur.; wound. at Mis. Rid. Nov. 23,'63.
Do.	Daniel Stiles	June 8, 1864	June 8, "	
2d Lieutenant	Wm. H. Eacott	Aug. 9, 1861	Feb. 4, 1862	Promoted to 1st Lieutenant.
Do.	James H. Bone	" 15, "	" 4, "	Promoted to 1st Lieutenant.
Do.	Julian R. Fitch	" 26, "	" 4, "	Promoted to 1st Lieutenant.
Do.	Theodore D. Mather	" 26, "	" 4, "	Promoted to 1st Lieutenant.
Do.	L. P. Thompson	Sept. 1, "	" 4, "	Promoted to 1st Lieutenant.
Do.	Thomas M. Harlan	" 5, "	" 4, "	Promoted to 1st Lieutenant.
Do.	George F. Earheart	" 7, "	" 4, "	Resigned October 14, 1862.
Do.	Wm. Andrew	" 15, "	" 4, "	Resigned March 14, 1863.
Do.	Joseph S. Claypoole	June 6, "	June 24, "	Resigned June 20, 1863. [2d Lieut.
Do.	John Adams	Oct. 14, "	Oct. 25, "	Promoted to 1st Lt.; hon. dis. May 28, 1864, as
Do.	Joseph F. Saunders	Nov. 19, "	Nov. 19, "	Promoted to 1st Lieutenant.
Do.	David W. Schaeffer	Oct. 24, "	Jan. 12, 1863	Promoted to 1st Lieutenant.
Do.	Samuel L. Houser	Jan. 20, "	Feb. 19, "	Promoted to 1st Lieutenant.
Do.	John N. Strode	April 27, 1863	April 27, "	Mustered out July 31, 1863.
Do.	Robert B. Davidson	Feb. 12, "	" 22, "	Promoted to 1st Lieutenant.
Do.	Joseph H. Taylor	Jan. 1, "	June 10, "	Promoted to 1st Lieutenant.
Do.	James Sabine	July 13, "	Aug. 1, "	Promoted to 1st Lieutenant.
Do.	Benj. F. Miller	Aug. 20, "	Sept. 26, "	Promoted to 1st Lieutenant.
Do.	David Stiles	Oct. 8, 1861	May 6, 1864	Promoted to 1st Lieutenant.

THIRTY-FIFTH OHIO VOLUNTEER INFANTRY.

THE THIRTY-FIFTH OHIO INFANTRY was organized at Hamilton, Ohio, during the months of August and September, 1861. Companies A and F were recruited in Warren County, H in Montgomery, E and part of G in Preble, and the others in Butler County.

The regiment was composed mostly of young and intelligent men. When organized, it numbered less than nine hundred, rank and file.

On the 26th of September, 1861, the regiment broke camp at Hamilton, and moved to Covington, Kentucky, and on the same night, under orders from General O. M. Mitchel, took a train on the Kentucky Central Railroad, and, placing parties at all the bridges along the road through Harrison and Bourbon Counties, made the head-quarters of the regiment at Cynthiana. It was at this time apprehended that the Rebels would burn these bridges before troops could reach them; but, by seizing the telegraph offices at every point on the way, the movement was a complete surprise, and entirely unsuspected until guards had possession of every bridge.

Afterward the regiment was removed to Paris, where it remained until the first days of December, when it marched to Somerset, and reported for duty to Brigadier-General Schoepff.

At the battle of Mill Springs they were not actively engaged, having been ordered by General Thomas to remain at Somerset. Here they were brigaded with the Eighteenth Regulars, Ninth Ohio, and Second Minnesota, under the command of Brigadier-General Robert L. McCook, remaining with the last two regiments during their whole term of service. This was one of the brigades long composing General George H. Thomas's division. After the battle of Mill Springs the regiment marched to Louisville, and thence took steamer to Nashville. Soon after, Buell having organized the Army of the Ohio, they marched to Pittsburg Landing. Thomas's division being the rear-guard, did not get up in time for the fight at Pittsburg Landing.

The Thirty-Fifth participated in some of the skirmishes during the siege of Corinth, and was among the first to enter the works at that place. Afterward they marched to Tuscumbia, Alabama, and about the last of July, 1862, to Winchester, Tennessee. It was on this last march that General McCook was killed by Rebel guerrillas, near New Market.

Shortly after, commenced that memorable race between Buell and Bragg, the goal being Louisville. From Nashville northward the regiment made about twenty-eight miles per day. In the movement on Bragg, the fight at Perryville, and the pursuit to Crab Orchard, they bore an honorable part. After Buell had been superseded by Rosecrans, the division, then commanded by General Speed S. Fry, marched to Bowling Green, and thence to a camp near Gallatin, Tennessee. In February, 1863, Colonel Vanderveer was assigned to the command of the brigade, and Lieutenant-Colonel Long assumed command of the regiment. All through the campaign, which began at Murfreesboro' and ended at Chattanooga, the Thirty-Fifth was in the front of the marching and fighting. In July of that year Lieutenant-Colonel Long resigned, and Major Boynton was promoted to the vacancy, Captain Budd receiving the Majority. From this time until it quit the service the regiment was under Colonel Boynton's command when he was able for duty.

On the first day of the fight at Chickamauga, the Thirty-Fifth and the other regiments composing Colonel Vanderveer's brigade were stationed on the extreme left of our line, where they engaged, and, after several hours of a fair, stand-up fight, repulsed and beat back three several attacks of Hood's division of Longstreet's corps, the *élite* of the Rebel army. On the next day, September 20th, they were again brought early into action, and, with the rest of the brigade, made a charge upon Breckinridge's division, which at that time had passed entirely around the left of our fortified line. The conflict, like that of the previous day, was severe and desperate, in the open field, and without any protection. Here was presented the uncommon spectacle of two armies charging each other at the same instant. That of the enemy was disorderly and with but little attention to discipline, while our men moved as if on drill, and under complete control. The brigade had been moving through the woods in two lines, the first composed of the Second Minnesota and Eighty-Seventh Indiana; the second, of the Thirty-Fifth and Ninth Ohio. Suddenly emerging into an open field, they found themselves exposed to a murderous fire from artillery and musketry, under which they changed front, and in pursuance of orders laid flat upon the ground. The enemy were then at about one hundred and fifty yards distance, and charging on a run. When the distance was decreased to seventy-five yards, the first line rose and delivered their fire. Immediately the order was given: "Thirty-Fifth and Ninth, pass lines to the front!—Brigade, charge!" The order was executed promptly, and the Rebel line hurled back for almost half a mile at a double-quick, finally making a stand in the woods, where they were protected by their reserves. For more than an hour an obstinate contest was kept up, most effectually ending the attempt to flank the National line upon the left. When the order was given to return to the position occupied by the brigade previous to the charge, it was done in order, by passing lines to the rear, each regiment delivering its fire as it retired.

At half-past two on that day the brigade was reported for duty to General Thomas, who was then holding a ridge to the rear and right of the line of the morning. Here the Thirty-Fifth was placed in the front line, where it built a slight work of wood and stone less than a foot in height. Behind this it remained until the last enemy had retired, repelling repeated charges of the most formidable and desperate character. Line after line of fresh troops of Rebels were sent to the attack, always meeting the same reception, always beaten and crushed. Late in the day anxious inquiry was made for ammunition, but the wagons had been ordered to Chattanooga. Then men and officers could be seen searching the cartridge-boxes of the dead and wounded; and finally, when the brigade commander ordered them to hold their position with the bayonet, these heroes laughed, and promised to stay there. When night came the Thirty-Fifth was formed on and facing the left of the line, and when it was too dark to recognize friend from foe, a force of the enemy appeared before them. Those who had ammunition fired, and the enemy precipitately retreated. These were the last shots fired on the battle-field of Chickamauga by friend or foe. Not a single musket was heard afterward; and the whole army having marched on the road toward Rossville, Vanderveer's brigade, the last to leave the field, under orders from General Thomas, followed.

In the two days' fight at Chickamauga, the Thirty-Fifth Ohio lost just fifty per cent. of those engaged. Scarcely a man was taken by the enemy—they were killed or wounded. Colonel Boynton was conspicuous during the whole fight for his gallantry and the skill with which he managed his men; and the regiment was highly commended in the reports of that action.

During the fall of 1863 they lay with the rest of the army at Chattanooga, and frequently engaged in skirmishes before that place. They were on the front line at Mission Ridge, and were among the first to reach the enemy's works on the crest, from which they drove the Rebel force and captured three pieces of artillery. Early in the fight Colonel Boynton was severely wounded while leading his men up the height, when the command devolved upon Major Budd. Next morning the enemy was pursued to Ringgold, Georgia.

In February, 1864, the regiment was engaged in the first battle at Buzzard's Roost, near Dalton, after which they were stationed at Ringgold until the beginning of the Atlanta campaign. They were with Sherman from the initiation of this movement until the expiration of their term of service, which occurred while lying before Atlanta. They were engaged at Dalton, Resaca, Pine Mountain, Kenesaw, Peachtree Creek, and several other of the fights of that bloody contest.

The Thirty-Fifth was mustered out in August, 1864, at Chattanooga.

In their term of three years the regiment never turned its back upon the enemy, and was never driven from a field.

36th REGIMENT OHIO VOLUNTEER INFANTRY.

ROSTER, THREE YEARS' SERVICE.

RANK.	NAME.	DATE OF RANK.	COM. ISSUED.	REMARKS.
Colonel	GEORGE CROOK	Sept. 12, 1861	Sept. 12, 1861	Appointed Brigadier-General Sept. 7, 1862.
Do.	MELVIN CLARKE	" 7, 1862	" 16, 1862	Killed September 17, 1862.
Do.	E. B. ANDREWS	" 17, "	Oct. 13, "	Resigned April 9, 1863.
Do.	WM. G. JONES	April 13, 1863	April 18, 1863	Killed September 19, 1863.
Do.	HIRAM F. DUVALL	Sept. 19, "	Jan. 10, 1864	Appointed Bvt. Brig. Gen. July 20, 1865.
Lt. Colonel	MELVIN CLARKE	July 30, 1861	July 30, 1861	Promoted to Colonel September 16, 1862.
Do.	E. B. ANDREWS	Sept. 7, 1862	Sept. 16, 1862	Promoted to Colonel September 17, 1862.
Do.	HIRAM F. DUVALL	" 17, "	Oct. 13, "	Promoted to Colonel.
Do.	WM. H. G. ADNEY	May 9, 1864	May 9, 1864	~~Mustered out~~.
Do.	WM. S. WILSON	March 8, 1865	March 8, 1865	Mustered out with regiment.
Major	E. B. ANDREWS	July 28, 1861	July 30, 1861	Promoted to Lieutenant-Colonel Sept. 16, 1862
Do.	HIRAM F. DUVALL	Sept. 7, 1862	Sept. 16, 1862	Promoted to Lieutenant-Colonel.
Do.	WM. H. G. ADNEY	" 17, "	Oct. 13, "	Promoted to Lieutenant-Colonel.
Do.	JEWETT PALMER	May 9, 1864	May 9, 1864	Resigned November 29, 1864.
Do.	WM. S. WILSON	Dec. 30, "	Dec. 30, "	Mustered out.
Do.	BENJ. J. RICKER, JR.	Feb. 3, 1865	Feb. 3, 1865	Transferred from 34th O. V. I.
Surgeon	ROBERT N. BARR	Aug. 22, 1861	Sept. 13, 1861	Resigned February 26, 1862.
Do.	J. H. WHITFORD	March 8, 1862	March 8, 1862	Mustered out with regiment.
Ass't Surgeon	J. H. WHITFORD	Aug. 23, 1861	Dec. 12, 1861	Promoted to Surgeon.
Do.	COLIN MACKENZIE	March 8, 1862	March 8, 1862	Resigned May 19, 1863.
Do.	JOHN DICKERSON	July 4, "	July 23, "	Promoted to Surgeon of new regiment.
Do.	JAMES P. WELCH	" 24, "	" 24, "	Resigned September 18, 1864.
Do.	B. F. HOLCOMB	March 14, 1865	March 14, 1865	Mustered out with regiment.
Do.	A. M. BEERS	June 26, "	June 26, "	Did not accept.
Chaplain	J. G. BLAIR	July 25, 1864	July 25, 1864	Mustered out.
Do.	G. W. COLLIER	Aug. 30, 1861	Aug. 30, 1861	Mustered out.
Captain	Hiram F. Duvall	" 1, "	Sept. 13, "	Promoted to Major September 7, 1862.
Do.	Wm. H. G. Adney	" 14, "	" 13, "	Promoted to Major September 17, 1862.
Do.	John Beckley	" 14, "	" 13, "	Resigned November 26, 1863.
Do.	Wm. H. Dunham	" 22, "	" 13, "	Resigned June 6, 1862.
Do.	Warren Hollister	" 22, "	" 13, "	Resigned January 17, 1863.
Do.	Thomas W. Moore	" 24, "	" 13, "	Resigned March 5, 1862.
Do.	Jewett Palmer	" 24, "	" 13, "	Promoted to Major.
Do.	Wm. S. Wilson	" 24, "	" 13, "	Promoted to Major.
Do.	Wm. S. Taylor	" 24, "	" 13, "	Resigned March 3, 1862.
Do.	Levi M. Stephenson	" 31, "	" 13, "	Resigned March 5, 1862.
Do.	Reuben L. Nye	March 3, 1862	March 20, 1862	Discharged Apr. 26,'63; re-instated Aug. 30,'63.
Do.	Joseph Kelley	" 5, "	" 20, "	Discharged Apr. 26,'63; re-instated Aug. 30,'63.
Do.	Wm. A. Walden	" 5, "	" 20, "	Resigned October 3, 1862.
Do.	James Stanley	June 6, "	Aug. 5, "	Honorably discharged November 25, 1861.
Do.	James G. Barker	Sept. 7, "	Oct. 13, "	Mustered out November 4, 1864.
Do.	Edward P. Henry	" 17, "	" 13, "	Mustered out.
Do.	James C. Selby	Oct. 3, "	" 13, "	Died of wounds September 14, 1864.
Do.	Wm. R. Ford	Jan. 17, 1862	March 30, 1863	Honorably discharged on account wounds.
Do.	Joseph Kelley	Aug. 30, "	Sept. 9, "	Resigned December 9, 1864
Do.	Reuben L. Nye	" 30, "	" 9, "	Mustered out with regiment.
Do.	Benj. F. Stearns	Nov. 26, "	Jan. 18, 1864	Honorably discharged November 25, 1864.
Do.	Homer C. Cherington	May 9, 1864	May 9, "	Appointed Bvt. Maj. by Pres. March 13, 1865.
Do.	Jonathan N. Patton	Dec. 30, "	Dec. 30, "	Resigned.
Do.	John D Mitchell	" 30, "	" 30, "	Mustered out with regiment.
Do.	Thomas M. Turner	" 30, "	" 30, "	Declined promotion.
Do.	Miles A. Stacey	" 30, "	" 30, "	Resigned as 1st Lieutenant Dec. 1, 1864.
Do.	Jesse Morrow	" 30, "	" 30, "	Mustered out with regiment.
Do.	Wallace S. Stanley	" 30, "	" 30, "	Mustered out with regiment.
Do.	Augustus T. Ward	" 30, "	" 30, "	Mustered out with regiment.
Do.	James Haddow	Jan. 20, 1865	Jan. 20, 1865	Mustered out with regiment.
Do.	Jacob Reasoner	" 20, "	" 20, "	Resigned January 10, 1865.
Do.	Isaac C. Phillips	" 20. "	" 20, "	Hon. discharged as 2d Lieut. Jan. 23, 1865.
Do.	Benj. H. Moore	March 8, "	March 8, "	Resigned June 17, 1865.
Do.	Isaac N. Anderson	" 8, "	" 8, "	Mustered out with regiment.
Do.	P. H. B. Hopkins	" 8, "	" 8, "	Mustered out with regiment.
Do.	James W. Smith	" 8, "	" 8, "	
1st Lieutenant	John M. Woodridge	July 31, 1861	July 31, 1861	Resigned.
Do.	James G. Barker	Aug. 13, "	Sept. 13, "	Promoted to Captain.
Do.	Edward P. Henry	" 14, "	" 13, "	Promoted to Captain September 17, 1862.
Do.	Josiah B. Martin	" 14, "	" 13, "	Resigned July 28, 1862.
Do.	Wm. A. Walden	" 22, "	" 13, "	Promoted to Captain.
Do.	Wm. R. Ford	" 22, "	" 13, "	Promoted to Captain.
Do.	Joseph Kelley	" 24, "	" 13, "	Promoted to Captain.
Do.	James Stanley	" 24, "	" 13, "	Promoted to Captain.
Do.	David D. Criss	" 24, "	" 13, "	Discharged July 21, 1862.
Do.	Joshua M. Clark	" 24, "	" 13, "	Resigned September 25, 1862.
Do.	Benj. F. Stearns	" 31, "	" 13, "	Promoted to Captain.
Do.	Levi Barber	" 31, "	" 13, "	Resigned November 29, 1862.
Do.	Benj. H. Moore	March 5, 1862	March 20, 1862	Promoted to Captain.
Do.	James C. Selby	" 5, "	" 20, "	Promoted to Captain.
Do.	Homer C. Cherington	June 6, "	June 21, "	Promoted to Captain.
Do.	Parker Rigg	Sept. 17, "	Oct. 13, "	Resigned August 9, 1863.
Do.	Tertellus E. Dunlap	July 28, "	" 13, "	Resigned February 22, 1863
Do.	John A. Palmer	Sept. 25, "	" 13, "	Resigned January 18, 1863.
Do.	John D. Mitchell	Oct. 3, "	" 13, "	Promoted to Captain.
Do.	Jonathan N. Patton	Sept. 1, "	" 13, "	Promoted to Captain.
Do.	Alphonzo Tiffany	" 17, "	Dec. 1, "	Resigned November 18, 1863.
Do.	O. J. Wood	Nov. 29, "	" 1, "	Resigned August 27, 1863.
Do.	Thomas M. Turner	Dec. 1, "	" 5, "	Mustered out with regiment as R. Q. M.

RANK.	NAME.	DATE OF RANK.			COM. ISSUED.			REMARKS.
1st Lieutenant	James N. De Lay	Jan.	18,	1863	March	30,	1863	Appointed Captain and C. S. Nov. 1, 1864.
Do.	Jesse Morrow	Feb.	22,	"	"	30,	"	Promoted to Captain.
Do.	Miles A. Stacy	Jan.	17,	"	"	30,	"	Promoted to Captain.
Do.	Wallace S. Stanley	April	21,	1864	April	21,	1864	Promoted to Captain.
Do.	Augustus T. Ward	"	21,	"	"	21,	"	Promoted to Captain.
Do.	James Haddow	May	9,	"	May	9,	"	Promoted to Captain.
Do.	Jacob Reasoner	April	21,	"	April	21,	"	Promoted to Captain.
Do.	Isaac C. Phillips	Dec.	30,	"	Dec.	30,	"	Promoted to Captain.
Do.	Samuel S. Grosvenor	"	30,	"	"	30,	"	Hon. discharged as 2d Lieut. Feb. 15, 1865.
Do.	George W. Putnam	"	30,	"	"	30,	"	Hon. discharged as 2d Lieut. Jan. 13, 1865.
Do.	Samuel W. Havery	"	30,	"	"	30,	"	Mustered out with regiment.
Do.	David Montgomery	"	30,	"	"	30,	"	Mustered out with regiment as Adjutant.
Do.	Isaac N. Anderson	"	30,	"	Sept.	30,	"	Promoted to Captain; trans. from 34th O. V. I.
Do.	T. H. B. Hopkins	Sept.	30,	"	"	30,	"	Promoted to Captain; trans. from 34th O. V. I.
Do.	James W. Smith	Nov.	26,	"	Nov.	26,	"	Must'd out with regt; trans. from 34th O. V. I.
Do.	James K. Agnew	March	8,	1865	March	8,	1865	Mustered out with regiment.
Do.	Morton L. Hawkins	"	8,	"	"	8,	"	Mustered out with regiment.
Do.	Charles L. Campbell	"	8,	"	"	8,	"	Mustered out with regiment.
Do.	Henry H. Adney	"	8,	"	"	8,	"	Mustered out with regiment.
Do.	Wm. K. Johnson	"	8,	"	"	8,	"	Mustered out with regiment.
Do.	Frederick S. Wallace	"	8,	"	"	8,	"	Mustered out with regiment.
Do.	Andrew J. Temple	"	8,	"	"	8,	"	Mustered out with regiment.
Do.	George Kress	"	8,	"	"	8,	"	
Do.	George Ebright	"	8,	"	"	8,	"	Declined promotion.
2d Lieutenant	James C. Selby	Aug.	13,	1861	Sept.	13,	1861	Promoted to 1st Lieutenant.
Do.	Robert B. Carter	"	14,	"	"	13,	"	Resigned July 28, 1862.
Do.	Parker Rigg	"	11,	"	"	13,	"	Promoted to 1st Lieutenant.
Do.	Benj. H. Moore	"	22,	"	"	13,	"	Promoted to 1st Lieutenant.
Do.	Jonathan N. Patton	"	22,	"	"	13,	"	Promoted to 1st Lieutenant.
Do.	Alphonzo Tiffany	"	21,	"	"	13,	"	Promoted to 1st Lieutenant.
Do.	Ernest Lindner	"	21,	"	"	13,	"	Resigned June 28, 1862.
Do.	Tartellus E. Dunlap	"	24,	"	"	13,	"	Promoted to 1st Lieutenant.
Do.	Milton Brown	"	31,	"	"	13,	"	Discharged February 5, 1862.
Do.	Homer C. Cherington	"	21,	"	"	13,	"	Promoted to 1st Lieutenant.
Do.	Reuben L. Nye	July	30,	"	"	13,	"	Promoted to 1st Lieutenant.
Do.	Amos Clark	March	3,	1862	March	20,	1862	Resigned March 17, 1863.
Do.	John D. Mitchell	"	5,	"	"	20,	"	Promoted to 1st Lieutenant.
Do.	John A. Palmer	"	5,	"	"	20,	"	Promoted to 1st Lieutenant.
Do.	O. J. Wood	Feb.	5,	"	May	1,	"	Promoted to 1st Lieutenant.
Do.	James N. De Lay	June	6,	"	June	24,	"	Promoted to 1st Lieutenant.
Do.	Miles A. Stacy	"	28,	"	Oct.	13,	"	Promoted to 1st Lieutenant.
Do.	Wallace S. Stanley	July	28,	"	"	13,	"	Promoted to 1st Lieutenant.
Do.	Augustus T. Ward	Sept.	17,	"	"	13,	"	Promoted to 1st Lieutenant.
Do.	Jacob Reasoner	"	25,	"	"	13,	"	Promoted to 1st Lieutenant.
Do.	Wm. A. Rhodes	Oct.	3,	"	"	13,	"	Died October 11, 1863.
Do.	Jesse Morrow	July	28,	"	"	13,	"	Promoted to 1st Lieutenant.
Do.	John B. Holmes	"	29,	"	Dec.	1,	"	Honorably discharged December 30, 1863
Do.	James Haddow	Sept.	17,	"	"	1,	"	Promoted to 1st Lieutenant.
Do.	Abram S. Coe	March	7,	1863	March	30,	1863	Resigned June 7, 1864.
Do.	Isaac C. Phillips	Jan.	18,	"	"	30,	"	Promoted to 1st Lieutenant.
Do.	John M. Hamlin	July	22,	"	"	30,	"	Resigned October 23, 1864.
Do.	Wm. J. Montgomery	Jan.	17,	"	"	30,	"	Resigned July 16, 1863.
Do.	Samuel S. Grosvenor	Oct.	21,	"	Feb.	19,	1864	Promoted to 1st Lieutenant.
Do.	George W. Putnam	"	24,	"	March	1,	"	Promoted to 1st Lieutenant.
Do.	David Montgomery	April	21,	1864	April	21,	"	Promoted to 1st Lieutenant.
Do.	Samuel W. Havery	"	21,	"	"	21,	"	Promoted to 1st Lieutenant.
Do.	James K. Agnew	Sept.	30,	"	Sept.	30,	"	Promoted to 1st Lt.; trans. from 34th O. V. I.
Do.	Morton L. Hawkins	"	30,	"	"	30,	"	Promoted to 1st Lt.; trans. from 34th O. V. I.
Do.	Allen T. Miller	March	8,	1865	March	8,	1865	
Do.	Samuel Buckman	"	8,	"	"	8,	"	Mustered out with regiment.
Do.	Matthew O. Bigger	"	8,	"	"	8,	"	Mustered out with regiment.
Do.	Aaron S. Corbley	"	8,	"	"	8,	"	Mustered out with regiment.
Do.	Silas Shumate	"	8,	"	"	8,	"	Mustered out.
Do.	Ambrose G. King	"	8,	"	"	8,	"	Mustered out with regiment.
Do.	John C. Louthan	"	8,	"	"	8,	"	Mustered out; expiration of service.
Do.	Hugh O. Nibert	"	8,	"	"	8,	"	Mustered out with regiment.
Do.	Benj. Bragg	"	8,	"	"	8,	"	Mustered out with regiment.
Do.	Ransom C. Wyatt	"	8,	"	"	8,	"	Mustered out; expiration of service.
Do.	Hezekiah Sleith	May	2,	"	May	2,	"	Mustered out with regiment.
Do.	Lafayette Hawke	"	2,	"	"	1,	"	Mustered out with regiment.
Do.	Joel E. Stacy	"	31,	"	"	31,	"	

THIRTY-SIXTH OHIO VOLUNTEER INFANTRY.

THIS regiment was organized at Camp Putnam, Marietta, in August, 1861. Its first officers were Melvin Clarke, Esq., a prominent lawyer of Marietta, Lieutenant-Colonel, and E. B. Andrews, Professor of Natural Sciences in Marietta College, Major. For the position of Colonel it was the strong desire of these officers to have a man of thorough military education. After repeated efforts and many failures, such a man was secured in George Crook, of Dayton, then Captain in the Fourth Infantry of the regular army.

Before Colonel Crook assumed command, six companies under the charge of Major A. J. Slemmer, at that time a member of the staff of General Rosecrans, marched through several counties of Western Virginia to clear the country of large bands of guerrillas. Colonel Crook did not join these companies until they had reached Summerville, in Nicholas County. The other four companies, which had rendezvoused and remained at Parkersburg under charge of Lieutenant-Colonel Clarke, were ordered to join the others at Summerville. About this time Major Andrews, aided by Quartermaster Barber, succeeded with much difficulty in securing for the whole regiment Enfield rifles, at that time considered an important success.

The regiment remained at Summerville until the following spring. Under the superintendence of Lieutenant-Colonel Clarke an old saw-mill was refitted, timber in the forest cut and drawn, and a large drill-house seven hundred feet long was erected, in which the regiment was thoroughly drilled. During the winter many expeditions were sent out to destroy guerrillas and obtain supplies of various kinds. These were generally very successful, and served a good purpose in familiarizing and inuring the officers and men to the hardships and dangers of the field. On such an expedition a small force under Major Andrews was attacked by a considerable body of Rebel cavalry, which resulted in the rout of the enemy, and the prisoners and several hundred head of cattle and mules and horses previously captured, were brought safely to camp.

During the winter there was much sickness in the regiment from typhus fever and pneumonia, and nearly fifty deaths occurred. This was a sad era in the history of the Thirty-Sixth Ohio. Frequently two or three funerals in a day would occur. The assiduous care of competent surgeons and the most rigid camp rules did not avail in the least to stay the progress of the fell destroyer, and to be attacked by the prevailing sickness was almost equivalent to a final termination in death. During this time company A, Captain Duvall, was stationed at Cross Lanes, near Carnifex Ferry.

On the 12th of May, 1862, the regiment, excepting company B, which remained to hold the post of Summerville, started south *via* Cold Knob and Frankfort for Lewisburg, Greenbrier County. At that place was met the Forty-Fourth Ohio Volunteer Infantry, Colonel Sam. Gilbert, and a battalion of the Second West Virginia Cavalry, in command of Colonel Bolles, all constituting a brigade, under Colonel Crook. From Lewisburgh Colonel Crook with this small force marched through the mountains to White Sulphur Springs, Covington and Jackson River Depot. Lieutenant-Colonel Clarke being absent on leave, Major Andrews was in command of the Thirty-Sixth Ohio. This movement took the enemy by surprise, and the march was so rapid that the Rebels were not given time to gather force sufficient to attack the expedition in the mountain fastnesses, where they could have inflicted summary punishment upon the National troops.

A few days after the return of this expedition to Lewisburgh, in the early morning of May 23d, General Heth, with from twenty-five hundred to three thousand Rebels, drove in the National pickets, and from a strong position on the hill east of the town began to shell the camp.

The Thirty-Sixth, under Lieutenant-Colonel Clarke, and the Forty-Fourth, containing in the aggregate not more than twelve hundred effective men, were ordered to repel the attack. Disappearing for a few moments among the houses and streets of the town, the National force suddenly emerged upon the open fields occupied by the Rebels. In twenty minutes the Rebels were driven back over the summit of the hill and utterly routed, with a loss of sixty killed and left upon the field, one hundred and seventy-five prisoners, four pieces of artillery, and three hundred stand of small arms, besides a very large number of wounded whom they hurriedly carried off the field. The victory was promptly and gloriously won. The Thirty-Sixth lost seven killed and forty-four wounded, and five captured on picket. The loss of the Forty-Fourth was less. Colonel Crook had no artillery, and his cavalry remained in reserve. This was a fair stand-up fight, in open ground, the enemy having the great advantage in numbers, position, and in the *morale* of the attack. Some fiendish citizens of Lewisburg shot some of our wounded and bleeding soldiers as they were struggling back from the battle-field through the town to the hospital. The next day after the battle the National dead were buried in a beautiful grove near the camp, and a picket-fence placed around their graves.

On the 29th of May the expedition moved back to Meadow Bluffs, in order to be nearer its base of supply. Here it was joined by the Forty-Seventh Ohio. On the 22d of June the brigade moved down to Salt Sulphur Springs, and Union, Monroe County, to return the early morning call received from General Heth at Lewisburg. Although possessing a much superior force, the General reported "not at home," and hastily betook himself to the mountains.

On the 14th of August the regiment, with other forces under General Cox, started for Camp Piatt, on the Kanawha River, to embark on steamers for Parkersburg, and thence to Washington and the Army of the Potomac. At Parkersburg Major Andrews, who had been ordered to Ohio a short time before, joined the regiment, with nearly one hundred recruits, increasing its force to one thousand and twenty men. August 25th the Thirty-Sixth, with a part of the Thirtieth Ohio, reached Warrenton Junction in advance of the rest of General Cox's Kanawha division, and was assigned by General Pope to duty at his head-quarters. General Stonewall Jackson having broken in upon Pope's rear, the National forces moved north with the head-quarter train on the afternoon of the 27th of August, and camped after dark near the battle-ground at Bristow Station. In the succeeding battle of Bull Run the Thirty-Sixth was held in reserve by General Pope, and on the evening of that defeat performed signal service in arresting stragglers and fugitives from the battle, thus preventing thousands from hurrying back to Washington and creating a panic of dismay similar to that after the first battle of Bull Run.

On the 2d of September the regiment fell back to Munson's Hill, near Alexandria, and went into camp for a few days. On the 7th it left Washington with the rest of the Kanawha division for Maryland to repel Lee's invasion. It reached Frederick, Maryland, on the 12th, in advance of the rest of McClellan's army, and had a brisk skirmish with General Stewart's cavalry, the rear-guard of Lee's army. In this little brush Colonel Moore, of the Twenty-Eighth Ohio, the commander of the brigade, was captured. This gave Colonel Crook command of the brigade, and left Lieutenant-Colonel Clarke in command of the Thirty-Sixth. On the 14th of September the regiment and brigade was actively engaged in the battle of South Mountain, and with it made a memorable bayonet charge, by which the enemy were so scattered and routed that they never rallied on that part of the field again. The Thirty-Sixth lost several men, chiefly on the right, where for a short time the enemy obtained an enfilading fire on it. After the charge the regiment was employed to support batteries and other similar work, but was not very actively engaged.

Three days later the Thirty-Sixth was actively engaged in the battle of Antietam. It constituted a part of General Burnside's force on the left. In making a forward movement in the afternoon over open ground, it being a very large and sightly regiment, drew upon itself a heavy artillery fire. In this fire Colonel Clarke was instantly killed by a ten-pound shell while engaged in halting his regiment, and Lieutenant-Colonel Andrews took his place in command. Colonel Clarke was a native of Massachusetts, and was an intelligent and brave officer, a man of great personal purity and worth, a Christian gentleman and soldier. His death was deeply mourned by the regiment. His body was brought home, and now sleeps under a tasteful monument erected by his fellow-officers in the beautiful cemetery in Marietta.

After the fall of Colonel Clarke, Lieutenant-Colonel Andrews moved the regiment forward up the hill a short distance to a stone wall, where it was somewhat subjected to an infantry fire but was sheltered from the Rebel artillery. It being now near night-fall, and General Burnside's troops having failed to gain as much ground as the Thirty-Sixth had gained, and it being thus left without support, at the order of General Crook the regiment was marched back to the hill bordering Antietam Creek, where the men slept on their arms during the night.

During the following day the Thirty-Sixth remained on the front line, its skirmishers exchanging compliments with the Rebel sharpshooters. The enemy had retreated in the night. The loss of the regiment in this battle was small in number, its exposure being chiefly to artillery fire. After the battle the regiment moved down and encamped near the mouth of Antietam Creek, where it remained until October 6th, when the Kanawha division was ordered back to West Virginia. It marched to Hagerstown and thence west to Hancock, where it took the cars on the Baltimore and Ohio Railroad for Clarksburg, West Virginia. The regiment and brigade left Clarksburg toward the close of October for the Kanawha Valley, and reached Charleston on the 16th of November. Its stay at Charleston was for a period of nearly three months.

On the 25th of January, 1863, the Thirty-Sixth embarked on steamers for Nashville, Tennessee, to join the army of General Rosecrans, reaching that place early in February. After remaining a few days in Nashville the regiment, with the Eleventh and Ninety-Second Ohio, all under command of General Crook, was ordered to Carthage, up the Cumberland River. Early in April Colonel Andrews resigned to resume his Professorship in Marietta College, his place having generously been kept vacant for him while serving his country in the army. He was a brave officer and polished gentleman. His successor was William G. Jones, of Cincinnati, a regular army officer.

Early in June the brigade and regiment marched across the country from Carthage to Murfreesboro' to join the main army, and was attached to Major-General Reynolds's division. On the 24th of June it moved southward with the army through a drenching rain, and had a sharp engagement with the enemy the same evening and part of the next day at Hoover's Gap. The enemy were driven so sharply that they were compelled to evacuate Tullahoma and continue their retreat. The pursuit was necessarily and aggravatingly slow, owing to the wretched condition of the roads. At Big Spring the National forces made a halt of several days, and then moved by way of University Place down to and crossed the Tennessee River at Shellmound, thence over Raccoon Mountain to Trenton, Georgia, where another halt of several days was made. They then moved up the valley some ten miles and crossed Lookout Mountain, descending into McLemore's Cove, where a day or two was spent in reconnoitering. They then moved out to Pond Spring, in the neighborhood of which the enemy was discovered in considerable force.

On the 18th of September General Crittenden, then some eighteen or twenty miles to the north-west, being heavily pressed, and it becoming evident that the Rebels meant to make a stand and fight, the National forces were ordered to close up quickly. This order compelled them an all-night march. Soon after sunrise Crawfish Spring was passed, and the line of battle was at once formed near that locality. Soon the low mutterings, as of distant thunder, were heard rolling up the valley, telling that the work of death on the field of Chickamauga had commenced. In the afternoon, while making a charge, the brave and gallant Colonel W. G. Jones fell, mortally wounded, and expired soon after. Lieutenant-Colonel H. F. D[illegible] immediately assumed command, and carried the regiment through the fight. With the Fourteenth Corps, to which the Thirty-Sixth belonged, it assisted into Chattanooga the remnants of the National army. The casualty list of the Thirty-Sixth shows a sad loss in this battle of Chickamauga. Seventy brave and gallant soldiers, officers and men, yielded up their lives for their country.

From the time the National forces entered Chattanooga until the 1st of November, it was in a state of siege and on half rations. Soon after entering the town the Thirty-Sixth made a reconnoissance, in which it lost a dozen men. The regiment participated in the memorable *coup de main* resulting in the capture of Brown's Ferry, on the Tennessee River, below Chattanooga, and on the 25th of November took part in the victory of Mission Ridge, in which it lost eighty-three men.

In February, 1864, the regiment re-enlisted, and on the 10th of March the men were sent home on veteran furlough. At the expiration of the thirty days the regiment was sent to its old familiar camping-ground at Charleston, West Virginia. From thence (General George Crook commanding the brigade) it started on a raid to Dublin Depot, on the Virginia and Tennessee Railroad, a point that had never been reached by the National forces, although several attempts had been made. The expedition moved *via* the Falls of Kanawha, Raleigh, and Princeton. At Princeton a smart skirmish occurred, and at Cloyd's Mountain the enemy was found in position, ready to dispute the further progress of the National forces. A severe engagement ensued, in which the Rebels were driven from their works, two pieces of artillery captured, and the notorious A. G. Jenkins mortally wounded and captured. A large amount of Rebel Government property was destroyed, including locomotives, cars, siege-guns, work-shops, and the railroad bridge across New River. Having accomplished the object of the expedition, and being short of supplies, the National forces moved rapidly back through Union to Meadow Bluff, where a supply train was met. Soon after reaching this point orders were received to join General Hunter in the Shenandoah Valley, and as soon as the necessary supplies could be brought forward the march began. The maiden battle-field of the regiment was passed over going through White and Warm Sulphur Springs and Goshen, on the Virginia Central Railroad. At the latter place a fine bridge, spanning the Calf-Pasture River, was burned, and the railroad track destroyed for the greater part of the way to Cravysville, where the mountain was crossed and a junction effected with General Hunter two days after his victory at Piedmont. Skirmishing was kept up from Warm Springs to Staunton, with a Rebel force under one "Mudwall" Jackson, who took good care to keep well out of the way.

On the 10th of June the National force left Staunton for Lynchburg, skirmishing all the way to Lexington, where "Mudwall" showed the first sign of being in earnest, and delivered himself of a pleasant little fight, which did n't hurt either side much; but snuffing danger from afar, he burned the bridge across the North River, and a couple of flouring-mills, and again showed his heels. On entering Lexington, the National forces burned the Virginia Military Institute, the fine dwelling-houses belonging to it, and the residence of ex-Governor Letcher. The loss of the Thirty-Sixth was three killed and five wounded.

From Lexington General Hunter moved by way of Buckhannon, thence across the Blue Ridge, between the Peaks of Otter, to Liberty. From Liberty, bridges were burned and the railroad destroyed to within a short distance of Lynchburg. At the old Stone Church, on the Liberty Pike, the Rebels were encountered and driven on the run inside of their fortifications. Night coming on, operations were suspended. By morning affairs had assumed a different aspect. The Rebel General Early had arrived from Richmond with a heavy force, and at daylight opened on us with artillery, which soon ceased; but steady skirmishing was kept up till about noon, when the National force was most furiously assailed, but stood its ground, and in turn succeeded in driving the Rebels back inside their works. Meantime it had been decided to fall back, which was done as quietly as possible during the night. Then commenced one of the hardest marches of the war. Supplies were nearly exhausted, and foraging had to be resorted to, with an active enemy hanging upon the rear. The retreat was continued *via* Liberty, Buford's Gap, Salem, Newcastle, Sweet and White Sulphur Springs, and Lewisburg, to Charleston, on the Kanawha. The demoralized, half-starved, and broken-down expedition reached Charleston in sad plight.

On the 12th of July the National troops embarked, including the Thirty-Sixth Ohio, on steamers at Charleston for Parkersburg, and from thence to the Shenandoah Valley by rail, reaching Martinsburg on the 15th. On the 19th a sharp little fight occurred at Cabletown, in which the regiment lost three men killed and four wounded. Again, on the 24th, an engagement was had at Kernstown, four miles from Winchester, in which the division lost one hundred and fifty men killed and wounded. This was the first time the Thirty-Sixth Ohio ever showed its back to the enemy. It is true, it left the field of Chickamauga, and retreated from before Lynchburg, but in both instances the organization was perfect. At this place, however, the regiment and division left the field in disorder. The retreat was made *via* Martinsburg and Williamsport into Maryland, going into camp at Pleasant Valley on the 27th of July.

A body of Rebel cavalry having passed through Maryland into Pennsylvania, the National forces were ordered to move up through Middletown toward the Pennsylvania line to intercept them; but hearing that they had burned Chambersburg and were moving toward Cumberland, the Nationals returned to the Shenandoah Valley *via* Frederick City and Harper's Ferry.

On the 7th of August General Sheridan took command of the Army of the Shenandoah, and the 11th found it at Cedar Creek. After skirmishing three or four days the Nationals fell back again down the Valley to Halltown, four miles from Harper's Ferry. Here fortifications were hastily thrown up and an attack from the Rebels awaited. The brigade of which the Thirty-Sixth Ohio formed a part was, on two occasions, and the division at another, sent out to reconnoiter and develop the strength and position of the enemy, which was successfully accomplished each time, and many prisoners captured, but not without heavy loss in killed and wounded. On the 26th the Rebels fell back and were pursued by the National forces.

On September 3d the little Army of West Virginia, under General George Crook, had a severe engagement of four hours' duration at Berryville. The Thirty-Sixth Ohio distinguished itself as much in this battle, perhaps, as in any other of the war. Its loss in killed and wounded was twenty-five. Captain J. C. Selby, a brave and true soldier, was mortally wounded.

The battle of Opequan occurred on the 19th of September. The Thirty-Sixth Ohio occupied the right of the army. General Crook's little Army of West Virginia, about four thousand strong, made a flank attack, which resulted in a junction with our cavalry, and in the complete rout of the Rebel army. The regiment lost in this battle thirty-three killed and wounded.

The afternoon of September 22d found the National army at Fisher's Hill, making its way over rocks and through gullies and bushes along the base of North Mountain, to strike the enemy again on the flank, a task which was fully accomplished. The movement was a complete surprise to the Rebels, and resulted in an almost bloodless victory to the National forces. The Thirty-Sixth lost four men wounded. Early's fugitive army was followed as far as Harrisonburg, at which place the National forces halted and soon fell back to Cedar Creek, where, on the 19th of October, the Army of West Virginia was surprised by a furious attack at early dawn by the whole Rebel army; and the National army, consisting of the Sixth and Nineteenth Corps and the Army of West Virginia, were sent flying down the Valley some four miles, where the National lines were re-formed and awaited the onset of the enemy.

In the meantime General Phil. Sheridan (who had been absent in Washington) came up. He made some slight changes in the disposition of the troops and awaited the enemy's movements. About two P. M. a portion of the National line was attacked, but the Rebels were handsomely repulsed, and, immediately after, the whole National line was ordered forward, and in an hour's time the Rebel army was flying up the Valley in the utmost confusion. The loss of the Thirty-Sixth was twenty-two killed and wounded. All the National dead were found in the field stripped naked.

The Thirty-Sixth Ohio remained in the Shenandoah Valley until the latter part of December. It was then sent to Cumberland, Maryland, and while there was consolidated with the Thirty-Fourth Ohio. In April, 1865, the consolidated regiment was sent back to Winchester, and from thence to Staunton, where it remained until the middle of June. It was then ordered to Cumberland, Maryland, by way of Winchester and Romney, and from Cumberland to Wheeling, where it was mustered out of the service on the 27th of July, sent to Columbus, Ohio, and paid and disbanded on the 1st of August, 1865.

37th REGIMENT OHIO VOLUNTEER INFANTRY.

ROSTER, THREE YEARS' SERVICE.

RANK.	NAME.	DATE OF RANK.			COM. ISSUED.			REMARKS.
Colonel	EDWARD SIBER	Sept.	12,	1861	Dec.	28,	1861	Resigned March 23, 1864.
Lt. Colonel	L. VON BLESSINGH	Oct.	2,	"	"	28,	"	Mustered out with regiment.
Major	CHARLES ANKELE	Aug.	3,	"	"	28,	"	Resigned June 5, 1863.
Do.	CHARLES HIPP	June	5,	1862	Sept.	25,	1862	Mustered out with regiment.
Surgeon	CONRAD SCHENCK	Oct.	3,	1861	Jan.	15,	"	Resigned November 20, 1862.
Do.	A. C. SWARTZWALDER	Feb.	26,	1863	Feb.	26,	1863	Appointed A. A. G. by the President.
Do.	WM. ARNOLD	Jan.	6,	"	June	26,	"	Mustered out January 6, 1863.
Do.	AUGUSTUS WIEDENBACK	Oct.	5,	"	Oct.	5,	"	Discharged March 28, 1864.
Do.	FREDERICK HOBLY	April	28,	1864	April	28,	1864	Mustered out with regiment.
Ass't Surgeon	JULIUS C. SCHENCK	Sept.	7,	1861	Jan.	15,	1862	Resigned as Surgeon November 28, 1862.
Do.	EUGENE RINGLER	Dec.	5,	1862	Dec.	17,	"	Mustered out for promotion March 10, 1864.
Do.	A. W. BILLHARDT	Jan.	31,	1863	March	30,	1863	Mustered out Oct. 7, '64; expiration of service.
Chaplain	ADOLPH GERWIG	Oct.	2,	18 1	Oct.	2,	1861	Deceased.
Captain	L. Quedenfeld	Sept.	4,	"	Dec.	28,	"	Killed in action at Princeton May 17, 1862.
Do.	L. Von Blessingh	"	6,	"	"	28,	"	Promoted to Lieutenant-Colonel.
Do.	Charles Hipp	"	7,	"	"	28,	"	Promoted to Major.
Do.	John G. Eberhardt	"	19,	"	"	28,	"	Resigned December 29, 1862.
Do.	Frederick H. Rehwinkle	"	19,	"	"	28,	"	Resigned October 8, 1862.
Do.	Anton Valendar	Oct.	3,	"	"	28,	"	Resigned March 31, 1862.
Do.	Frederick Schoening	"	3,	"	"	28,	"	Died of wounds May 18, 1864.
Do.	Charles Messner	"	22,	"	"	28,	"	Resigned November 16, 1862.
Do.	Wm. Krauss	"	22,	"	"	28,	"	Resigned April 19, 1862.
Do.	H. Gœke	"	22,	"	"	28,	"	Killed at Logan, 1861.
Do.	F. M. Sturdlef	Feb.	15,	1862	March	20,	1862	Discharged September 26, 1862.
Do.	Charles Morritz	"	8,	"	Feb.	8,	"	Mustered out December 21, 1864.
Do.	George Bœhm	March	31,	"	May	1,	"	Mustered out January 4, 1865.
Do.	Adolph Von Kissinger	April	19,	"	June	9,	"	Resigned December 20, 1862.
Do.	John Bayer	May	28,	"	Sept.	25,	"	Mustered out January 4, 1865.
Do.	Wm. Weste	June	5,	"	"	25,	"	Resigned March 4, 1863.
Do.	Paul Wittich	Oct.	8,	"	Nov.	18,	"	Killed at Kenesaw July 22, 1864
Do.	Theodore Voges	Sept.	26,	"	Dec.	17,	"	Mustered out.
Do.	Frederick Krumm	Nov.	16,	"	"	30,	"	Resigned as 1st Lieutenant.
Do.	Wm. Schultz	Dec.	20,	"	"	30,	"	Mustered out March 12, 1865.
Do.	Wm. Kœnig	"	29,	"	Feb.	28,	1863	Honorably discharged November 28, 1863.
Do.	John Hamm	"	20,	"	Jan.	20,	"	Honorably discharged November 22, 1864.
Do.	Henry Schmidt	March	4,	"	June	10,	"	Mustered out with regiment.
Do.	Jacob Merry	April	29,	1864	April	29,	1864	Mustered out with regiment.
Do.	Theodore Nieberg	"	29,	"	"	29,	"	Declined promotion; commission returned.
Do.	Herman Rosenbaum	"	29,	"	May	4,	"	Mustered out with regiment.
Do.	Gustav Baither	June	14,	"	June	14,	"	Declined promotion; commission returned.
Do.	John Hamm	Jan.	20,	1865	Jan.	20,	1865	
Do.	Herman Rau	"	20,	"	"	20,	"	Mustered out April 1, 1865, as 1st Lieutenant.
Do.	Diedrich Schmidt	"	20,	"	"	20,	"	Mustered out with regiment.
Do.	Charles Manuel	"	20,	"	"	20,	"	
Do.	Louis Sebastian	"	20,	"	"	20,	"	Mustered out with regiment.
Do.	Louis Lambert	"	20,	"	"	20,	"	Mustered out with regiment.
Do.	Jacob Litter	April	26,	"	April	26,	"	Mustered out with regiment.
Do.	Henry Rentsch	"	26,	"	"	26,	"	Declined.
Do.	Robert Seng	May	31,	"	May	31,	"	Mustered out with regiment.
1st Lieutenant	George Bœhm	Sept.	4,	1861	Dec.	28,	1861	Promoted to Captain March 31, 1862.
Do.	H. Gœke	"	6,	"	"	28,	"	Promoted to Captain.
Do.	Wm. Schultz	"	7,	"	"	28,	"	Resigned December 27, 1861.
Do.	Frederick Krumm	"	19,	"	"	28,	"	Promoted to Captain.
Do.	Adolph Von Kissinger	"	19,	"	"	28,	"	Promoted to Captain.
Do.	Anton Peterson	Oct.	3,	"	"	28,	"	Resigned February 6, 1862.
Do.	Wm. Schultz	"	3,	"	"	28,	"	Promoted to Captain.
Do.	Charles Morritz	"	3,	"	"	28,	"	Promoted to Captain.
Do.	John Bayer	"	22,	"	"	28,	"	Promoted to Captain.
Do.	F. Ingold	"	22,	"	"	28,	"	Discharged April 25, 1862.
Do.	Wm. Weste	"	22,	"	"	28,	"	Promoted to Captain.
Do.	A. Huber	"	22,	"	"	28,	"	Resigned November 9, 1862.
Do.	Theodore Voges	Dec.	28,	"	"	28,	"	Promoted to Captain.
Do.	John Hamm	Aug.	12,	"	Jan.	15,	1862	Promoted to Captain.
Do.	Wm. Kœnig	Feb.	8,	1862	Feb.	8,	"	Promoted to Captain.
Do.	Paul Wittich	"	8,	"	"	8,	"	Promoted to Captain.
Do.	Henry Schmidt	"	28,	"	"	28,	"	Promoted to Captain.
Do.	Magnus W. Blucher	March	31,	"	May	1,	"	Died of wounds May 28, 1862.
Do.	Arthur Stoppel	April	19,	"	June	9,	"	Resigned October 19, 1862.
Do.	Louis Kœppel	May	28,	"	Sept.	25,	"	Resigned May 26, 1863.
Do.	George W. Temme	"	8,	"	"	25,	"	Mustered out with regiment.
Do.	Joseph Langendorfer	"	28,	"	"	25,	"	Resigned February 23, 1864.
Do.	John H. Frenches	June	5,	"	Nov.	18,	"	Resigned September 24, 1864.
Do.	Sebaldus Hassler	Oct.	8,	"	"	18,	"	Killed May 20, 1863.
Do.	Jacob Merry	Nov.	9,	"	Dec.	30,	"	Promoted to Captain.
Do.	Gustav Wintzer	"	18,	"	"	30,	"	Killed May 20, 1863.
Do.	Florentine Finn	Dec.	20,	"	"	30,	"	Died of wounds September 21, 1864
Do.	Theodore Neiberg	"	20,	"	Jan.	20,	1863	Resigned September 20, 1864.
Do.	Herman Rosenbaum	"	29,	"	Feb.	28,	"	Promoted to Captain.
Do.	Louis Wilms	Jan.	1,	1863	June	10,	"	On detached duty at muster out of regiment.
Do.	Herman Rau	April	29,	1864	April	29,	1864	Promoted to Captain.
Do.	Gustav Baither	May	20,	1863	June	10,	1863	Mustered out January 5, 1865.
Do.	Wm. Weiss	"	20,	"	"	10,	"	Killed May 13, 1865.
Do.	Diedrich Schmidt	April	29,	1864	April	29,	1864	Promoted to Captain.
Do.	Charles Manuel	"	29,	"	"	29,	"	Promoted to Captain.
Do.	Louis Sebastian	"	29,	"	"	29,	"	Promoted to Captain.

RANK.	NAME.	DATE OF RANK.	COM. ISSUED.	REMARKS.
1st Lieutenant	Louis Lambert	April 29, 1864	April 29, 1864	Promoted to Captain.
Do.	Jacob Litter	" 29, "	" 29, "	Promoted to Captain.
Do.	Henry Rentsch	June 14, "	June 14, "	Resigned June 21, 1865.
Do.	Robert Seng	Oct. 12, "	Oct. 12, "	Promoted to Captain.
Do.	Herman Borchard	" 20, "	" 20, "	Mustered out with regiment.
Do.	Joseph Seifert	Jan. 20, 1865	Jan. 20, 1865	Mustered out with regiment.
Do.	A. Loesleig	" 20, "	" 20, "	Mustered out with regiment.
Do.	Henry Ponkie	" 20, "	" 20, "	
Do.	G. W. Bader	" 20, "	" 20, "	Mustered out with regiment.
Do.	Louis Eckert	April 26, "	April 26, "	Declined promotion.
Do.	Louis Ritter	" 26, "	" 26, "	Resigned June 15, 1865.
2d Lieutenant	Christian Pfhal	Sept. 4, 1861	Dec. 28, 1861	Resigned December 27, 1861.
Do.	F. Ingold	" 6, "	" 28, "	Promoted to 1st Lieutenant.
Do.	Henry Schmidt	" 7, "	" 28, "	Promoted to 1st Lieutenant March 31, 1862.
Do.	Wm. Weste	" 19, "	" 28, "	Promoted to 1st Lieutenant.
Do.	Paul Wittich	" 19, "	" 28, "	Promoted to 1st Lieutenant.
Do.	Maugus W. Blucher	Oct. 3, "	" 28, "	Promoted to 1st Lieutenant.
Do.	John Hamm	" 3, "	" 28, "	Promoted to 1st Lieutenant.
Do.	Arthur Steppel	" 22, "	" 28, "	Promoted to 1st Lieutenant.
Do.	Moretz Fleischman	" 22, "	" 28, "	Resigned April 19, 1862.
Do.	Louis Kœppel	" 22, "	" 28, "	Promoted to 1st Lieutenant.
Do.	Wm. Kœnig	" 22, "	Jan. 15, 1862	Promoted to 1st Lieutenant.
Do.	George W. Temme	Dec. 28, "	Dec. 28, 1861	Promoted to 1st Lieutenant.
Do.	Frederick Ambrosius	Feb. 8, 1862	Feb. 8, 1862	Resigned July 11, 1862.
Do.	Gustav Wintzer	" 8, "	" 8, "	Promoted to 1st Lieutenant.
Do.	Simon H. Morritz	" 8, "	" 8, "	Resigned.
Do.	Joseph Langenderfer	" 28, "	April 10, "	Promoted to 1st Lieutenant.
Do.	John H. Frenches	May 1, "	May 1, "	Promoted to 1st Lieutenant.
Do.	R. J. Piatt	June 5, "	June 5, "	
Do.	Julius Scheidt	April 19, "	" 9, "	Resigned November 29, 1862.
Do.	Charles B. Ramser	May 28, "	Aug. 20, "	
Do.	Jacob Merry	" 8, "	Sept. 25, "	Promoted to 1st Lieutenant.
Do.	Sebuldus Hassler	April 19, "	" 25, "	Promoted to 1st Lieutenant.
Do.	Christian Humtroch	July 11, "	" 16, "	Resigned December 20, 1862.
Do.	Florentine Finn	June 5, "	Nov. 18, "	Promoted to 1st Lieutenant.
Do.	August Schocke	Oct. 8, "	" 18, "	Resigned March 2, 1863.
Do.	Robert Seng	" 8, "	Dec. 30, "	Promoted to 1st Lieutenant.
Do.	Charles Boesel	Nov. 29, "	" 31, "	Mustered out November 29, 1862.
Do.	Louis Wilms	Sept. 16, "	" 24, "	Promoted to 1st Lieutenant.
Do.	Wm. Weiss	Dec. 20, "	Jan. 20, 1863	Promoted to 1st Lieutenant.
Do.	Herman Rau	" 20, "	Dec. 30, 1862	Promoted to 1st Lieutenant.
Do.	Theodore Seiberg	Nov. 9, "	" 30, "	Promoted to 1st Lieutenant.
Do.	Gustav Baither	" 16, "	" 30, "	Promoted to 1st Lieutenant.
Do.	Diedrich Schmidt	Dec. 20, "	Jan. 20, 1863	Promoted to 1st Lieutenant.
Do.	Herman Rosenbaum	" 29, "	Feb. 20, "	Promoted to 1st Lieutenant.
Do.	Henry Votteler	" 29, "	March 30, "	Resigned May 31, 1864.
Do.	Jacob Litter	Nov. 29, "	June 29, "	Promoted to 1st Lieutenant.
Do.	Charles Manuel	May 20, 1863	" 10, "	Promoted to 1st Lieutenant.
Do.	Louis Sebastian	" 20, "	" 10, "	Promoted to 1st Lieutenant.
Do.	Louis Lambert	" 20, "	" 10, "	Promoted to 1st Lieutenant.

THIRTY-SEVENTH OHIO VOLUNTEER INFANTRY.

THIS was the third German regiment raised in Ohio, and was recruited principally among the patriotic Germans of Cleveland, Toledo, and Chillicothe. The counties of Auglaize, Franklin, Mahoning, and Tuscarawas furnished a number of the men; Erie, Wyandot, and Mercer also contributed liberally. Its organization was commenced under the second call of President Lincoln for three hundred thousand men, in August, 1861. By the latter part of September seven full companies had reported, and on the 1st of October eight hundred men were enrolled. With this number the regiment was placed in Camp Dennison, and on the 2d of October it was mustered into the service, officered, armed, and equipped.

Colonel E. Siber, an accomplished German officer, who had seen active service in Prussia and Brazil, was selected as the commanding officer of the regiment; L. Von Blessingh, of Toledo, Lieutenant-Colonel, and Charles Ankele, of Cleveland, Major. Its line officers were selected from those who had seen service in the preceding three months' campaign.

The regiment moved, *via* Cincinnati, to a point on the Kanawha River, in West Virginia, where it reported to General Rosecrans, then commanding that department. Shortly after its arrival the regiment was sent up the Kanawha, in company with other forces, to the oil-works at Cannelton, with the view of driving the Rebel General Floyd out of that valley. The National forces moved up the valley, marching along Loup Creek, flanked and forced the Rebels to evacuate Cotton Hill, and pursued them to within seven miles of Raleigh C. H.

On its return from this expedition, the regiment went into winter-quarters at Clifton, where it occupied itself in drilling and perfecting its organization, guarding all the principal points in the vicinity, and occasionally sending out scouting parties in all sections of that part of West Virginia. In January, 1862, it went out on an expedition to Logan C. H., east of Guyandotte River, and eighty miles distant from Clifton. After hard marching and brisk skirmishing with the enemy's cavalry, the place was captured and all war material destroyed. This accomplished, the regiment returned to Clifton, having lost one officer and one man killed.

In March, 1862, the Thirty-Seventh Ohio was added to the Third Provisional Brigade of the Kanawha Division, and ordered to accompany that division on a raid to the southern part of West Virginia, with the view of reaching and destroying, if possible, the Virginia and East Tennessee Railroad, near Wytheville, Virginia. But, after severe and unsuccessful fighting at and near Princeton, on East River, in which the regiment lost one officer and thirteen men killed, two officers and forty-six men wounded, and fourteen men missing, the National forces were compelled to retreat to Flat-Top Mountain, where they remained in bivouac until the 1st of August, 1862. On the 1st of August the regiment marched to Raleigh, garrisoned the place, and scouted the country for a circuit of twenty-five miles. In an expedition to Wyoming C. H., a detachment of the regiment fell into an ambuscade, and were surrounded by the enemy, but cut their way out of the difficulty with the loss of two killed, and one officer and seven men taken prisoners. In the latter part of August the regiment marched in detachments to Fayetteville, Virginia, which place was garrisoned by the Thirty-Seventh and Thirty-Fourth Ohio, and a temporary battery, composed of men from the Thirty-Seventh Ohio, detached on temporary duty.

On the 10th of September two companies of the regiment were sent out on the Princeton Road, and, after reaching a spot one and a half miles from their starting point, they encountered the enemy in heavy force, making it necessary to fall back. Shortly after, the whole force was engaged with the enemy, led by General Loring. The fight lasted from twelve M. until dark, when Colonel Siber, the commanding officer of the Thirty-Seventh Ohio, being informed that another force of the enemy was threatening the National rear and line of retreat, the retreat was sounded, and at two o'clock in the morning the regiment moved back on the Gauley Road, taking a position on Cotton Hill, and engaging the enemy for an hour with effective results. The retreat was then resumed, and on the 12th of September the National troops crossed the Kanawha River at Camp Piatt, and arrived at Charleston on the next day. The enemy, who had followed at a respectful distance, was here engaged and kept at bay until dark. This stand was necessary in order to cover the retreat of a valuable train of seven hundred wagons, loaded with the entire supplies of all the troops then in the Kanawha Valley.

After a very exhausting march of three days and nights the Ohio River was reached on the 15th, at a point nearly opposite Ripley, Ohio, and the troops crossed over, but almost immediately thereafter re-crossed the river, and went into camp at Point Pleasant. In this unfortunate retreat the Thirty-Seventh Ohio lost two men killed, three wounded, and sixty-two missing, of which latter a large portion were teamsters and train-guard. All the company wagons, camp equipage, and officers' baggage were lost near Fayetteville by a rear attack of the enemy.

On the 15th of October the regiment again advanced up the Kanawha Valley, under command of Lieutenant-Colonel L. Von Blessingh. Gauley Bridge was reached November 20th, where a camp was formed and occupied up to December 30, 1862, on which day the regiment marched to Camp Piatt, and from thence embarked on steamers for Cincinnati. While lying at the wharf there Colonel Siber assumed command of the regiment, and was fortunate enough to procure new Enfield rifles in exchange for the arm then in use.

Proceeding down the Ohio and Mississippi Rivers, the regiment was landed at Napoleon, Arkansas, on the 16th of January, 1862. Here it was, with other regiments, formed into the Third Brigade, Second Division, of the Fifteenth Army Corps. On the 21st of January the troops moved over to Milliken's Bend, nearly opposite Vicksburg, Mississippi, where they were engaged in the construction of the canal which was to isolate Vicksburg from the river, and make it an inland town. A freshet in the Mississippi River compelled the regiment, with the other troops, to seek higher ground for encampment. Young's Point was selected. From Young's Point a number of expeditions were sent to the east side of the Mississippi, and up the Yazoo River, in all of which the Thirty-Seventh Ohio participated.

On the 29th of April, 1862, the regiment, under the command of Lieutenant-Colonel L. Von Blessingh, with eight other regiments of the division, embarked on steamers, and were taken up the Yazoo River to Haines's Bluff. This movement was made as a feint to cover the movements of General Grant to the south-east of Vicksburg. The regiment returned to the west side of the Mississippi, and again went into camp at Young's Point, performing guard and fatigue duty until the 13th of May, when it was sent down to Grand Gulf. From that place it marched, with the forces under General Grant, to the rear of Vicksburg, where it was assigned as a portion of the front line of the army investing that place. In the bloody but unsuccessful assaults on the enemy's works, May 19th and 22d, and the subsequent siege of Vicksburg, the regiment lost nineteen killed and seventy-five wounded, including among the wounded, Lieutenant-Colonel L. Von Blessingh. This casualty devolved the command of the regiment upon Major C. Hipp until the 18th of June, when Colonel Siber reported from his leave of absence and resumed command.

After the surrender of Vicksburg the Thirty-Seventh participated in the expedition against Jackson, Mississippi, and on its capture, July 17th, it performed provost-guard duty for some days. On the 23d of July it marched to a camp of rest and reorganization, called Camp Sherman, near Big Black River. It remained in this camp up to the 26th of September, 1863, on which day it marched into Vicksburg and embarked on the steamer Nashville for Memphis, Tennessee. From Memphis the regiment marched to Corinth, Mississippi; thence to Cherokee Station, Alabama, reaching the latter place on the 20th of October and remaining in bivouac until the 26th of the same month.

The Rebel General Forrest becoming troublesome, the Thirty-Seventh Ohio marched with its division to drive off his cavalry, who were operating with the view of impeding the march of the National forces toward and for the relief of Chattanooga. On the 21st of November Chattanooga was reached, and on the nights of the 23d and 24th the regiment crossed the Tennessee River opposite Mission Ridge, and held a hill in front of the enemy during the night of the 24th, in order to maintain communication with the First Brigade of the division. On the morning of November 25th the regiment participated in an assault on the enemy's fortified position, in which it lost five men killed and thirty-six wounded, five of the latter being officers. Although not successful in the charge, other points of the Rebel line were broken, and the enemy retreated during the following night, and was pursued as far as Ringgold.

At Gravesville, on the 29th of November, the regiment received orders to march with the division to East Tennessee, to drive the Rebels, under Longstreet, from that part of the State. This campaign lasted for three weeks, and is memorable from the intense suffering endured by the troops. The weather was intensely cold, the men half clad, and numbers of them shoeless, and were compelled to subsist on less than half rations; and yet these brave men endured all these privations without a murmur. On the contrary, unreasonable as it may seem, the men generally were in exuberant spirits, and it was noticed that more humorous jokes were current on that campaign than any that preceded it.

Marching back to Bridgeport, Alabama, the regiment remained there until the 26th of December, when it went into camp at Larkinsville, Alabama.

In the beginning of the month of February, 1864, the Thirty-Seventh formed part of an expedition sent toward Lebanon, Alabama, and on the 15th of the same month it marched to Cleveland, Tennessee, with the Fifteenth Army Corps, on a reconnoissance to the vicinity of Dalton, Georgia, returning to Larkinsville, Alabama, March 2d.

On the 8th of March three-fourths of the men having re-enlisted for another term of three years, they were again mustered into the service, and placed in the Second Brigade, Second Division, of the Fifteenth Army Corps. The usual thirty-days' leave was accorded, and the regiment enjoyed it to the full at their homes in Ohio. At the expiration of the furlough the men promptly rendezvoused at Camp Taylor, near Cleveland, and by the 28th of April were again at the front, ready for duty. On their way to duty a disastrous railroad accident occurred near Munfordsville, Kentucky, by which thirty men were wounded and one killed.

On the arrival of the regiment at Chattanooga it was newly armed and equipped, and was immediately ordered to join its division (May 10th), then operating in Sugar Creek Valley, Georgia. On the 13th of May it participated in the advance on Resaca, in which it lost three killed, two of whom were officers, and ten men wounded. The enemy having been driven out of his strongholds, the division and regiment crossed the Oostenaula River at Lay's Ferry and marched toward Kingston, Georgia, reaching there on the 19th of May. At this time the Thirty-Seventh Ohio was under the command of Major C. Hipp, Lieutenant-Colonel L. Von Blessingh being in Ohio on sick leave.

In the march on Atlanta, Dallas was the next point reached. On the 23d of May the enemy was encountered in strong force at that place sheltered by a strongly-fortified position. In this engagement, and that at New Hope Church (May 28th, 29th, and June 1st) the regiment lost four men wounded. On the retreat of the enemy, the Thirty-Seventh pursued toward Acworth, and went into line of battle in front of Kenesaw Mountain, and participated in the memorable and disastrous assaults made by the National forces against that stronghold, in which the enemy was compelled to fall back and abandon the position. Up to this point (from June 11th to July 2d) the regiment lost four men killed and nineteen wounded.

Again on the march the regiment was next found, with its division, to the extreme right of the army, supporting the Twenty-Third Army Corps in the engagements near the Chattahoochie River and Nicojack Creek. Immediately after it was ordered to the left (July 12th), and marched through Marietta, Rosswell Factories, and across the Chattahoochie River. Strong breastworks were built on the south side of the river, and the regiment moved by a rapid march to the Atlanta and Augusta Railroad, which was destroyed for a considerable distance. It then moved through Decatur on Atlanta, and on the 20th of July, 1864, encamped within two miles of that city.

On the 22d of July the Thirty-Seventh Ohio held a position on the right of its division, in breastworks abandoned by the enemy on the previous night. The enemy, receiving heavy re-enforcements, succeeded in breaking the National lines on the left, whereby the Thirty-Seventh was flanked and compelled to "get out of that." In this reverse movement it lost four men killed, ten wounded, and thirty-eight taken prisoners. The National forces, stung to the quick by the success of the enemy, turned fiercely upon them, and with the help of the Sixteenth Army Corps, re-took the position, and held it. On the 27th of July the Fifteenth Army Corps was moved to the right of the besieging army, thereby threatening the enemy's communications with Macon and the South generally. Perceiving, too late, the advantage that had been gained by the National movement, the enemy made an effort to drive them from their position, and for that purpose the battle of Ezra Chapel was fought (a fierce encounter,) in which the Rebels were severely punished. The Thirty-Seventh Ohio held the extreme right in this engagement, deployed as skirmishers, and completely frustrated an attempt of the enemy to turn the National right. Major C. Hipp commanded the regiment in this affair, and lost his left arm at the commencement of the battle. This devolved the command of the regiment on Captain Morritz, who took it through the remainder of the battle. The regiment lost one man killed and five wounded.

Very nearly a month (from the 28th of July to the 26th of August) was consumed in advancing the National lines toward the fortifications in front of the railroad leading from Atlanta to East Point, during which period the regiment lost five men killed and eight wounded. It then moved with its division over the Atlanta and Montgomery Railroad toward Jonesboro', on the Atlanta and Macon Railroad. The 30th of August found the Thirty-Seventh in line of battle, moving on Jonesboro', in advance of the brigade. Driving the enemy's skirmishers before it, at sundown it had gained a position one-half mile west of the railroad, where, during the night it threw up intrenchments, and participated in the bloody repulse of the enemy's repeated charges on the National position. The loss of the regiment during these two days (August 30th and 31st) was two killed and seven wounded.

Jonesboro' was entered by the National troops on the 1st of September at noon. By night Atlanta was occupied, and the National forces in full pursuit of the Rebel army. The pursuit was abandoned at Lovejoy's Station, and the regiment returned to East Point (September 7th), where it went into camp and rested until the 4th of October, 1864.

The Thirty-Seventh Ohio left its camp, in the pursuit of the Rebel forces under Hood, on the 4th of October. Forced marches were made over Northern Georgia and Alabama, and the enemy's cavalry rear-guard encountered near Gadsden, Alabama, on the Coosa River. On the advance of the brigade in line of battle, the enemy retreated in such haste that it was useless for infantry to attempt the pursuit. The regiment then returned to Ruffin's Station, near the Chattahoochie River, where it remained up to the 13th of November.

Lieutenant-Colonel L. Von Blessingh having recovered from his illness, joined and resumed command of the regiment, relieving Captain G. Boehm, who had taken the place of Captain Morritz, absent on leave.

The great "march to the sea" was forming, and its energetic commander, Major-General W. T. Sherman, had ordered up to Atlanta all the regiments and divisions that could be spared from General Thomas and the other Army Corps. On the 13th of November, 1864, the Thirty-Seventh Ohio marched into Atlanta to draw the necessary outfit for the long march about to be made. On the 15th it took up the line of march. The route of the regiment passed over McDonough's Indian Springs, near which place it crossed the Oemulgee River; thence through the towns of Hillsboro' and Clinton. At the latter place it performed, in company with the Fifteenth Michigan Infantry, valuable guard-duty, in preventing the enemy's cavalry from crossing the road leading to Marion, with the view of capturing and destroying a division train, then parked in the town of Clinton. Covering the rear of the division, the regiment marched the next day toward Griswold, where it joined its division, and having crossed the Georgia Central Railroad, marched through Irvinton. It crossed the Oconee on the 26th of November, and, after marching through extensive swamps, arrived at Summertown November 30th. Continuing its march through the low, swampy lands of Georgia, along the southern side of the Ogeechee River, it crossed the Cannouchee River on the 9th of December; thence to the line of the Savannah and Gulf Railroad, miles of which, with the assistance of other regiments, it destroyed. Recrossing the Cannouchee, it passed the Ogeechee River and advanced to within nine miles of Savannah. On the 13th it again recrossed the Ogeechee at King's Bridge, advanced on Fort McAllister, which was invested by the National forces, and carried by assault on the same day.

After some days' rest the division again marched to the Savannah and Gulf Railroad, and completed its destruction for a distance of thirty miles. On the return of the brigade to Savannah it received orders to report at the head-quarters of the Fifteenth Army Corps to take part in the contemplated general attack on Savannah. In the meantime, however, the enemy evacuated the city, and the Thirty-Seventh Ohio went into bivouac in a camp eleven miles west of that place. It afterward moved in the immediate vicinity of the city, and occupied itself in drilling, perfecting its equipment, and in fortifying against the enemy, who, it was thought, might possibly make an effort to regain possession of Savannah.

On the 19th of January, 1865, the regiment, under orders, marched to Fort Thunderbolt, on the Savannah River, where it embarked for Beaufort, South Carolina, which was reached on the 22d of January. At this point the regiment went into camp until the 27th of January, when it returned to Beaufort and took the division train out of the transports then lying in port at that place. On the 30th it escorted this train to Pocotaligo, and from thence marched to McPhersonville, where it joined the division, and went with it through South Carolina and the southern part of North Carolina. On this march it crossed the Coosawattee, the Big and Little Combahee, the South and North Edisto, often wading through water up to the armpits of the men, and attacking the enemy in fortified positions. After crossing the Congaree the regiment bivouacked on its banks, five miles south of Columbia. On the 16th of February it crossed the Saluda River four miles above Columbia, and guarded the division train into Columbia. It crossed Broad River February 18th, and was engaged for two days in destroying the track of the Columbia and Charleston Railroad. On the 20th of February the regiment continued its march, crossing the Wateree and wading Lynch Creek (which had assumed the dimensions of a river) on the 26th. At this point the regiment was compelled to halt until the 2d of March to allow the balance of the division to come up, freshets and the carrying away of a bridge having retarded the march.

On the 7th of March Cheraw, South Carolina, was entered and the Great Pedee crossed. The next day (March 8th) the State line of North Carolina was crossed. After having passed the head-waters of the Little Pedee, Lumber River, and Little River, the regiment was ordered to escort General Howard's head-quarters and pontoon train of the Army of the Tennessee (right wing). It brought the trains safely into Fayetteville, North Carolina, on the 11th of March. On the 14th Cape Fear River was crossed, the regiment marching on the road leading to Clinton, which was guarded from the enemy's cavalry, then demonstrating in the National front. On the 17th Beaman's Cross-Roads was reached, and the National army drew near Goldsboro', North Carolina.

On the 22d of March the regiment marched toward Goldsboro', crossed the Neuse River on the 24th, and went into camp two miles east of the town. The regiment remained in this camp until the capitulation of Lee and Johnston, when, with the rest of the National army, it marched, *via* Richmond, Virginia, to Washington City; there passed in review before President Johnson and his Cabinet. Thence it was transported by rail to Louisville, Kentucky, where it lay until the latter part of June, when the regiment was sent with the Second Division of the Fifteenth Army Corps to Little Rock, Arkansas, arriving on the 4th of July. The regiment remained in camp there until the 12th of August, when it was mustered out and transported to Cleveland, Ohio, and there discharged—and the men returned to their respective homes.

38th REGIMENT OHIO VOLUNTEER INFANTRY.

ROSTER, THREE YEARS' SERVICE.

RANK.	NAME.	DATE OF RANK.	COM. ISSUED.	REMARKS.
Colonel	EDWIN D. BRADLEY	June 10, 1861	Nov. 20, 1861	Resigned February 8, 1862.
Do.	EDWARD H. PHELPS	Feb. 6, 1862	March 6, 1862	Killed in action November 25, 1863.
Do.	WM. A. CHOATE	Nov. 25, 1863	Feb. 25, 1864	Died of wounds.
Lt. Colonel	EDWARD H. PHELPS	June 10, 1861	Nov. 20, 1861	Promoted to Colonel.
Do.	WM. A. CHOATE	Feb. 6, 1862	March 6, 1862	Promoted to Colonel.
Do.	CHAS. GREENWOOD	Nov. 25, 1863	Feb. 25, 1864	Resigned August 26, 1864.
Do.	WM. IRVING	" 3, 1864	Nov. 3, "	Mustered out with regiment.
Major	EPAPHRAS L. BARBER	June 10, 1861	" 20, 1861	Resigned January 12, 1862.
Do.	MOSES R. BRAILEY	Jan. 28, 1862	Jan. 28, 1862	Resigned February 9, 1862.
Do.	CHAS. GREENWOOD	Feb. 6, "	March 6, "	Promoted to Lieutenant-Colonel.
Do.	WM. IRVING	May 9, 1864	May 9, 1864	Promoted to Lieutenant-Colonel.
Do.	ANDREW NEWMAN	Nov. 3, "	Nov. 3, "	Mustered out with regiment.
Surgeon	ISRAEL COONS	June 10, 1861	" 20, 1861	Resigned July 13, 1863.
Do.	JAMES HALLER	July 13, 1863	Sept. 1, 1863	Mustered out January 4, 1865.
Do.	H. B. POWELL	Jan. 20, 1865	Jan. 20, 1865	Mustered out with regiment.
Ass't Surgeon	JAMES HALLER	June 10, 1861	Nov. 20, 1861	Promoted to Surgeon.
Do.	WALLACE K. HUGHES	Aug. 21, 1862	Sept. 3, 1862	Never reported to reg't; resigned June 31, 1863.
Do.	H. B. POWELL	July 19, "	Oct. 27, "	Promoted to Surgeon.
Do.	THEODORE D. BROOKS	April 29, 1864	April 29, 1864	Mustered out March 30, 1865.
Chaplain	JOHN POUCHER	June 10, 1861	Nov. 20, 1861	Mustered out with regiment.
Captain	Wm. A. Choate	Aug. 12, "	" 20, "	Promoted to Lieutenant-Colonel.
Do.	Benj. Miller	" 15, "	" 20, "	Resigned July 18, 1863.
Do.	John H. Adams	" 17, "	" 20, "	Deceased December 10, 1862.
Do.	Moses R. Brailey	" 21, "	" 20, "	Promoted to Major.
Do.	David S. Tallerday	" 25, "	" 20, "	In gunboat service.
Do.	Chas. Greenwood	" 26, "	" 20, "	Promoted to Major.
Do.	Wm. Stough	Sept. 1, "	" 20, "	Resigned July 13, 1862.
Do.	Resin A. Frank	" 1, "	" 20, "	Resigned April 15, 1863.
Do.	Robert McQuillen	" 3, "	" 20, "	Resigned June 23, 1863.
Do.	Wm. Irving	" 5, "	" 20, "	Promoted to Major.
Do.	Samuel Donaldson	Jan. 28, 1862	Jan. 28, 1862	Declined.
Do.	John Crosson	Feb. 6, "	March 6, "	Declined.
Do.	Wm. E. Kintigh	" 6, "	" 6, "	Resigned March 24, 1863.
Do.	Benj. S. Pindar	March 6, "	May 1, "	Declined.
Do.	Chas. M. Gilbert	" 6, "	Oct. 16, "	Mustered out June 27, 1865.
Do.	Edward D. A. Williams	Jan. 28, "	" 16, "	Resigned April 12, 1864.
Do.	Andrew Newman	" 19, "	" 16, "	Promoted to Major.
Do.	John Crawson	Dec. 10, "	Jan. 24, 1863	Died of wounds.
Do.	Benj. S. Pindar	March 24, 1863	April 22, "	Mustered out.
Do.	Joseph Wagstaff	" 16, "	" 22, "	Mustered out.
Do.	E. M. Feuchar	Jan. 23, "	Sept. 1, "	Died of wounds.
Do.	Samuel Donaldson	July 18, "	" 1, "	Mustered out.
Do.	Chas. U. Gorsuch	May 9, 1864	May 9, 1864	Mustered out with regiment.
Do.	Elias Gleason	" 9, "	" 9, "	Declined.
Do.	Isaiah W. White	" 9, "	" 9, "	Mustered out with regiment.
Do.	Abraham W. Burgoyne	Nov. 3, "	Nov. 3, "	Mustered out with regiment.
Do.	Jacob C. Donaldson	" 3, "	" 3, "	Mustered out with regiment.
Do.	David Renton	" 3, "	" 3, "	Mustered out with regiment.
Do.	Webster Jones	" 3, "	" 3, "	Mustered out with regiment.
Do.	James A. McQuilken	Jan. 20, 1865	Jan. 20, 1865	Died of wounds as 2d Lieutenant.
Do.	John Cameron	" 20, "	" 20, "	Declined promotion.
Do.	John W. Pollock	May 18, "	May 18, "	Mustered out with regiment.
Do.	Joseph D. Coons	" 31, "	" 31, "	Mustered out with regiment.
Do.	E. D. Cantleberry	" 31, "	" 31, "	Mustered out with regiment.
1st Lieutenant	Samuel Donaldson	Aug. 15, 1861	Nov. 20, 1861	Promoted to Captain; declined.
Do.	John Crosson	" 17, "	" 20, "	Promoted to Captain.
Do.	Wm. E. Kintigh	" 19, "	" 20, "	Promoted to Captain February 6, 1862.
Do.	Wm. H. McLayman	" 25, "	" 20, "	Appointed Captain by President Sept. 10, 1862.
Do.	Chas. M. Gilbert	" 26, "	" 20, "	Promoted to Captain March 6, 1862.
Do.	Edward D. A. Williams	" 28, "	" 20, "	Promoted to Captain.
Do.	Andrew Newman	Sept. 1, "	" 20, "	Promoted to Captain.
Do.	Chas. U. Gorsuch	" 1, "	" 20, "	Promoted to Captain.
Do.	E. M. Deuchar	" 3, "	" 20, "	Promoted to Captain.
Do.	Ransom P. Osborn	" 5, "	" 20, "	Resigned March 9, 1862.
Do.	Erastus H. Leland	" 10, "	" 20, "	Resigned February 6, 1862.
Do.	Converse L. Chase	" 10, "	" 20, "	Resigned March 12, 1862.
Do.	Jacob C. Donaldson	Jan. 28, 1862	Jan. 28, 1862	Declined.
Do.	Elias Gleason	Feb. 6, "	March 6, "	Mustered out.
Do.	Benj. S. Pindar	" 6, "	" 6, "	Promoted to Captain.
Do.	Thomas W. Wright	March 9, "	" 20, "	Resigned June 16, 1862; revoked.
Do.	Joseph Wagstaff	" 12, "	" 20, "	Declined.
Do.	Elias Gleason	Feb. 17, "	Oct. 16, "	Promoted to Captain.
Do.	Isaiah W. White	March 10, "	" 16, "	Promoted to Captain.
Do.	Chas. L. Allen	" 21, "	" 16, "	Resigned December 9, 1863.
Do.	Daniel Tresster	" 6, "	" 16, "	Resigned November 13, 1863.
Do.	Elisha Tewlas	June 16, "	" 16, "	Resigned April 20, 1863.
Do.	Peter V. Fulton	July 19, "	" 16, "	Resigned August 2, 1864.
Do.	Joseph Wagstaff	Sept. 10, "	Dec. 19, "	Promoted to Captain.
Do.	Elbright G. Willey	Dec. 10, "	Jan. 24, 1863	Mustered out.
Do.	James Betts	March 16, 1863	" 21, 1864	Died of wounds September 1, 1864.
Do.	Wm. H. Ellis	" 24, "	" 24, "	Resigned February 13, 1865.
Do.	John S. Templeton	April 20, "	" 21, "	Honorably discharged December 29, 1865.
Do.	Abraham W. Burgoyne	June 23, "	Sept. 1, "	Promoted to Captain.
Do.	Jacob C. Donaldson	....	....	Promoted to Captain.
Do.	Brice H. Jay	Dec. 9, 1863	Dec. 31, 1863	Died December, 1863.

RANK.	NAME.	DATE OF RANK.		COM. ISSUED.		REMARKS.
1st Lieutenant	David Renton	April	13, 1864	April	13, 1864	Promoted to Captain.
Do.	Webster Jones	"	13, "	"	13, "	Promoted to Captain.
Do.	Joseph B. Coons	"	13, "	"	13, "	Promoted to Captain.
Do.	Foreman Evans	May	9, "	May	9, "	Resigned November 14, 1864.
Do.	James A. McQuilken	"	9, "	"	9, "	Promoted to Captain.
Do.	John W. Pollock	"	9, "	"	9, "	Promoted to Captain; commission returned.
Do.	E. D. Cantleberry	Nov.	3, "	Nov.	3, "	Promoted to Captain.
Do.	Jacob Lane	"	3, "	"	3, "	Mustered out with regiment.
Do.	Edward Metz	"	3, "	"	3, "	Mustered out with regiment.
Do.	Jacob Kelley	"	3, "	"	3, "	Honorably discharged Dec. 17, 1864, as 2d Lieut.
Do.	James M. Patterson	Jan.	20, 1865	Jan.	20, 1865	Mustered out with regiment.
Do.	George W. Towl	"	20, "	"	20, "	Killed at Jonesboro, 1864.
Do.	Wm. Boyers	"	20, "	"	20, "	Mustered out with regiment.
Do.	Alphonso A. Evans	"	20, "	"	20, "	Mustered out with regiment.
Do.	David W. Lazenby	"	28, "	"	28, "	Mustered out with regiment.
Do.	Edward P. McCutcheon	May	18, "	May	18, "	Mustered out with regiment
Do.	Albert W. Dolph	"	18, "	"	18, "	Mustered out with regiment.
Do.	Jacob Hafer	"	31, "	"	31, "	Mustered out with regiment.
Do.	Simon Waterstone	"	31, "	"	31, "	
Do.	John Cameron	July	13, "	July	13, "	Declined promotion.
Do.	John W. Pollock	Nov.	3, "	Nov.	3, "	Promoted to Captain.
2d Lieutenant	Jacob C. Donaldson	Aug.	15, 1861	"	20, 1861	Promoted to 1st Lieutenant.
Do.	Elias Gleason	"	17, "	"	20, "	Promoted to 1st Lieutenant.
Do.	Benj. S. Pindar	"	19, "	"	20, "	Promoted to 1st Lieutenant.
Do.	Thomas W. Wright	"	21, "	"	20, "	Promoted to 1st Lieutenant.
Do.	Joseph Wagstaff	"	25, "	"	20, "	Promoted to 1st Lieutenant.
Do.	Daniel Tresster	"	26, "	"	20, "	Promoted to 1st Lieutenant.
Do.	Peter V. Fulton	Sept.	1, "	"	20, "	Promoted to 1st Lieutenant.
Do.	Charles L. Allen	"	1, "	"	20, "	Promoted to 1st Lieutenant.
Do.	Abraham W. Burgoyne	"	3, "	"	20, "	Promoted to 1st Lieutenant.
Do.	Alphonso L. Branche	"	3, "	"	20, "	Declined.
Do.	Isaiah W. White	Feb.	5, 1862	Feb.	5, 1862	Promoted to 1st Lieutenant.
Do.	Wm. H. Ellis	"	6, "	June	20, "	Promoted to 1st Lieutenant.
Do.	Elisha Tewlas	March	9, "	"	20, "	Promoted to 1st Lieutenant.
Do.	Thomas B. Hanna	Aug.	12, "	Oct.	1, "	Resigned July 6, 1863.
Do.	James H. Queen	March	16, "	"	16, "	Resigned August 26, 1862.
Do.	Joseph Newman	July	19, "	"	16, "	Died December 12, 1863.
Do.	Wm. Lasure	March	21, "	"	18, "	Resigned September 1, 1863.
Do.	David Renton	"	10, "	"	16, "	Promoted to 1st Lieutenant.
Do.	Webster Jones	Feb.	17, "	"	16, "	Promoted to 1st Lieutenant.
Do.	John S. Templeton	June	16, "	Dec.	19, "	Promoted to 1st Lieutenant.
Do.	James Betts	Sept.	10, "	"	19, "	Promoted to 1st Lieutenant.
Do.	John Lewis	May	6, 1863	May	17, 1863	Killed in action November 25, 1863.
Do.	Joseph B. Coons	March	16, "	April	22, "	Promoted to 1st Lieutenant.
Do.	Foreman Evans	"	24, "	"	22, "	Promoted to 1st Lieutenant
Do.	James A. McQuilken	April	20, "	May	17, "	Promoted to 1st Lieutenant.
Do.	John W. Pollock	Nov.	20, "	Jan.	27, 1864	Promoted to 1st Lieutenant.
Do.	John Cameron	"	21, "	Feb.	25, "	Promoted to 1st Lieutenant.
Do.	E. D. Cantleberry	"	21, "	"	25, "	Promoted to 1st Lieutenant.
Do.	Jacob Lane	"	27, "	"	25, "	Promoted to 1st Lieutenant.
Do.	Edward Metz	Feb.	25, 1864	"	25, "	Promoted to 1st Lieutenant.
Do.	Jacob Kelley	"	25, "	"	25, "	Promoted to 1st Lieutenant.
Do.	James M. Patterson	June	27, "	June	27, "	Promoted to 1st Lieutenant.
Do.	George W. Towl	"	27, "	"	27, "	Promoted to 1st Lieutenant.
Do.	Chas. Hakes	"	27, "	"	27, "	Revoked, special order July 30, 1864.
Do.	Wm. Boyers	"	27, "	"	27, "	Promoted to 1st Lieutenant.
Do.	Alphonso A. Evans	"	27, "	"	27, "	Promoted to 1st Lieutenant.
Do.	David W. Lazenby	"	27, "	"	27, "	Promoted to 1st Lieutenant.
Do.	Jacob Hafer	May	18, 1865	May	18, 1865	Promoted to 1st Lieutenant.
Do.	Simon Waterstone	"	18, "	"	18, "	Promoted to 1st Lieutenant.
Do.	Wm. A. Carnahan	"	18, "	"	18, "	Mustered out with regiment.
Do.	Martin Trowbridge	June	20, "	June	20, "	Mustered out with regiment as Q. M. Sergeant.

THIRTY-EIGHTH OHIO VOLUNTEER INFANTRY.

THIS regiment was organized at Defiance, Ohio, on the 1st of September, 1861, under the President's call for three hundred thousand men for three years. On the 22d of September it was transferred to Camp Dennison, where it was armed, equipped, and, to a considerable extent, drilled and disciplined, and then ordered into active service in Kentucky on the 1st of October.

At sunrise on the morning of the 2d the regiment passed through and encamped near the town of Nicholasville. Remaining here about two weeks, it was ordered to the relief of the garrison at Wild Cat, Kentucky; and, after a forced march of sixty miles, reached its destination on the 19th of October, 1861. Afterward it pursued the enemy to London and Barboursville; marched on all the subsequent campaigns during the fall of 1861; and Christmas found the army encamped near Somerset, Kentucky. During the winter of 1861 and 1862, the men, being almost constantly on duty, and not accustomed to the rough usages of camp life, became sickly; and in a short time, out of nine hundred and ninety men, less than three hundred were fit for duty. The regiment participated in the campaign of Mill Springs, after which it marched to Louisville, where it arrived February 28, 1862.

On March 1st the regiment embarked on transports destined for Nashville, Tennessee, where it arrived on the 5th of the same month, and went into camp to prepare for the coming campaign in the spring of 1862. On the 19th of March it left Nashville with the Army of the Ohio; marched through Middle Tennessee, and, during the month of April, encamped on the battle-field of Pittsburg Landing; marched with the army under Halleck toward Corinth, Mississippi, and took an active part in the siege of that place.

After the evacuation of Corinth, May 27, 1862, the Thirty-Eighth marched with the army in pursuit of Beauregard as far as Booneville, and, on its return, encamped near Corinth until the 20th of June, 1862, when, with the Army of the Ohio, it marched in the direction of Tuscumbia, Alabama, where it arrived on the 28th of June. Remaining there until July 21st, it marched, *via* Decatur and Huntsville, to Winchester, Tennessee, where it arrived August 7, 1862.

During this month several reconnoitering parties made extensive detours through the mountain spurs, in the direction of Chattanooga, then the head-quarters of the Rebel army. In these reconnoissances no regiment took a more active part than the Thirty-Eighth Ohio. A party of eighty men made a forced march of thirty-six miles, captured Tracy City, and, after destroying a large amount of tobacco, whisky, leather, and articles of less value, returned to camp, having marched seventy-two miles and destroyed a large amount of property without losing a man. This march was performed in less than twenty-four hours.

On September 1, 1862, began the retrograde march from the vicinity of Chattanooga, which terminated only when the army reached the Ohio. The Thirty-Eighth Ohio endured all the hardships and shared all the trials of that campaign. Remaining but a short time at Louisville, on the 1st of October the regiment marched southward with the army, and, on the 8th, found the enemy in position at Chaplin Hills, near Perryville, Kentucky. The Thirty-Eighth participated in that battle, and afterward in the campaign in Kentucky, until, on the 27th of October, it went into camp on Rolling Fork, near Lebanon, Kentucky. Remaining here but a short time, during which a detachment of recruits was received, it again took up the line of march in the directior of Nashville, Tennessee. During the months of November and December, 1862, the regiment was guarding railroads between Gallatin and Nashville. In the latter part of December the regiment marched to Nashville, and prepared for the approaching campaign, which terminated with the battle of Stone River. The Thirty-Eighth acted a very conspicuous part in that battle, losing but few men, however; and, after the battle, went into camp near the city, where it remained until March 13th, when it joined the forces then at Triune. While there it built the earth fortress known as Fort Phelps.

On the 23d of June, 1863, the Thirty-Eighth marched with the Army of the Cumberland, and took an active part in the Tullahoma campaign. After resting a short time at Winchester, Tennessee, on the 17th of August the march for Chattanooga began. The Thirty-Eighth moved with the center corps, crossing the Cumberland Mountains, and finally halted on the banks of the Tennessee, opposite Shellmound, where rafts of logs were constructed, preparatory to crossing the river. Crossing the river on the night of September 2, 1863, the march was resumed across Lookout and Raccoon Mountains, and the middle of September found the army in Lookout Valley. Preparations were made for battle by sending everything to the rear that would encumber the army. The large train belonging to the entire army was sent to Chattanooga, and the Thirty-Eighth Ohio, detailed by a special order from General Thomas, was charged with the safe transit of the immense train. Accordingly on the evening of the 18th of September, the train started, and, ere the morning of the 19th of September dawned, the train was within six miles of Chattanooga. The Thirty-Eighth did not participate in the struggle on the field of Chickamauga, but it performed the task which the vicissitudes of war assigned it.

On the 25th of November, 1863, the division to which the Thirty-Eighth belonged assaulted the fortifications at the foot of Mission Ridge, ascended the hill, and carried the works, driving the Rebels from them. The Thirty-Eighth was on the extreme left of the army; and although Bragg had pronounced the slope inaccessible, yet they moved up, up, up, until the summit was reached. The fire from the Rebel batteries was terrific, yet comparatively harmless, and but few were injured. In this charge the regiment lost seven men killed and forty-one wounded.

After pursuing the enemy as far as Ringgold, Georgia, the Thirty-Eighth returned to camp near Chattanooga, where it re-enlisted as a veteran organization, and was furloughed home. At the expiration of the furlough the regiment joined the army then at Ringgold, Georgia. Recruits were sent forward, and when Sherman started for Atlanta the regiment numbered seven hundred and forty-one men.

On the 5th of May, 1864, the regiment broke camp at Ringgold and marched to Buzzard's Roost Gap, where it was brought into action. After skirmishing two days a flank movement was commenced *via* Villanow and Smoke Creek Gap, nearly in rear of Resaca. Here the Thirty-Eighth erected field-works and skirmished continually, and though no general engagement took place, several men were killed and wounded. After the evacuation of that place the regiment participated in the campaign which followed; took an active part in the siege of Kenesaw, fortifying and skirmishing, and, on the 5th of July, 1864, reached the banks of the Chattahoochie River. Remaining here until July 17th, the advance was again sounded and the river was crossed. On the 22d day of July the Thirty-Eighth had the honor of establishing the picket-line of the Fourteenth Army Corps, near the City of Atlanta. It remained there some time holding its place in line, until August 3d, when it moved to Utoy Creek. Here, on the 5th of August, a portion of the regiment (companies A, C, and K) charged the enemy's skirmish-line, and was successful. Out of the one hundred and twenty men who charged, nine were killed and forty-two wounded.

On the night of the 25th of August the regiment marched with the army on a flanking expedition, and, on the 27th, struck the Atlanta and West Point Railroad. Remaining there until the 31st, it again advanced, and that night took possession of the Macon road, near Red Oak Station. Remaining there during the night of September 1st, it was ascertained that the enemy was then fortifying Jonesboro', and the army was put in motion for that place, and about ur o'clock P. M. came upon the pickets of Hardee's corps. Este's brigade (to which the

Thirty-Eighth belonged), of Baird's division was brought forward and assaulted the works. In this charge the regiment lost, out of three hundred and sixty men, forty-two killed and one hundred and eight wounded, making a total loss of one hundred and fifty men.

Corporal O. P. Randall had the colors at the onset. He fell lifeless, pierced by a Minie ball. Corporal Baird next took them, and he too fell dead. Corporal Strawser next took them, and he fell severely wounded. Corporal Donsey then took the flag and bore it to the works. Of the five who had in charge the colors, but one (Corporal H. K. Brookes) escaped unharmed, although not untouched, for five balls passed through his clothing. The dead were buried on a little knoll near the battle-field, and the regiment encamped near the town of Jonesboro'. On the 9th of September the troops fell back to Atlanta, and those who were not veterans were discharged.

On the 3d of October, 1864, the army broke camp and retraced its recent line of operations as far north as Dalton, Georgia—Hood having, in the meantime, marched to the rear of General Sherman. The Thirty-Eighth accompanied the expedition thus far, moved thence *via* Gaylesville, Alabama, to Rome, and, on the 5th of November, marched to Kingston, Georgia. On the 12th of November communication was severed, and the army started for Savannah, marching along the line of the Georgia State Railroad, destroying it as they went, until they reached Atlanta, a second and last time. During the march from Atlanta to Milledgeville there was nothing to mar the progress of the army. Arriving at the capital on the 24th November, the Thirty-Eighth Ohio was ordered into the city as a provost-guard, where it remained until the 25th, when the army moved on in the direction of Louisville. Just before reaching Louisville the army left the road it had been moving on (the Augusta Pike) and marched directly east. It became necessary that the bridge across the Big Ogeechee should be destroyed, and the Thirty-Eighth was designated to perform that duty. This regiment had already marched fifteen miles that day, and it was yet ten miles to the bridge. After marching ten miles and burning the bridge, it was then thirteen miles to where the army went into camp. Misfortune being the guide, the regiment took the wrong road, and marched six miles out of the way, and it was twelve o'clock P. M. when it arrived inside the picket-line, having marched that day forty-four miles and destroyed the bridge.

From Louisville to Savannah the march was an agreeable one, and, on the morning of December 21st, the Thirty-Eighth Ohio went into camp near the conquered city, the enemy having evacuated the night before. During the stay of the Thirty-Eighth here, two hundred drafted men and substitutes were received.

On the 30th of January, 1865, the Thirty-Eighth left Savannah with the army and participated in the "Campaign of the Carolinas," and, after forty days, came to Goldsboro,' North Carolina. From there it followed the retiring army as far as Holly Springs, North Carolina, where it remained until after the surrender of Johnston's army. From Holly Springs the regiment marched back to Raleigh, and thence to Richmond, and finally to Alexandria, Virginia, where it remained until after the grand review at the National Capital, when it encamped near the City of Washington. Remaining there in a state of inactivity until the 15th of June, orders were received to proceed by rail to Louisville, Kentucky. Meantime, a portion of the drafted men were mustered out. On the 15th of June the regiment took the cars for Parkersburg, Virginia, and from there proceeded by boat to Louisville, Kentucky, where it arrived on the 23d of June.

Soon after arriving orders were received for the muster-out of the regiment; and, on the 12th of July, the muster-out was completed, and the regiment proceeded immediately to Cleveland, Ohio, where it was finally discharged on the 22d of July, 1865.

39th REGIMENT OHIO VOLUNTEER INFANTRY.

ROSTER, THREE YEARS' SERVICE.

RANK.	NAME.	DATE OF RANK.	COM. ISSUED.	REMARKS.
Colonel	JOHN GROESBECK	Aug. 24, 1861	Aug. 28, 1861	Resigned July 8, 1862.
Do.	A. W. GILBERT	July 8, 1862	July 11, 1862	Resigned October 1, 1862.
Do.	EDWARD F. NOYES	Oct. 1, "	Oct. 31, "	Honorably discharged April 22, 1865.
Do.	DANIEL WEBER	May 18, 1865	May 18, 1865	Mustered out with regiment.
Lt. Colonel	A. W. GILBERT	July 27, 1861	Aug. 28, 1861	Promoted to Colonel July 8, 1862.
Do.	EDWARD F. NOYES	" 8, 1862	July 11, 1862	Promoted to Colonel October 1, 1862.
Do.	HENRY T. McDOWELL	Oct. 1, "	Oct. 31, "	Mustered out.
Do.	DANIEL WEBER	Feb. 10, 1865	Feb. 10, 1865	Promoted to Colonel.
Do.	WM. C. BUCK	May 18, "	May 18, "	Mustered out as Captain May 15, 1865.
Do.	HENRY A. BABBITT	June 6, "	June 6, "	Mustered out with regiment.
Major	EDWARD F. NOYES	July 27, 1861	Aug. 28, 1861	Promoted to Lieutenant-Colonel.
Do.	HENRY T. McDOWELL	" 8, 1862	July 11, 1862	Promoted to Lieutenant-Colonel.
Do	WM. H. LATHROP	Oct. 1, "	Oct. 31, "	Colonel 3d Alabama col'd reg't April 20, 1864.
Do.	JOHN S. JENKINS	April 25, 1861	May 25, 1861	Mustered out.
Do.	DANIEL WEBER	Jan. 11, 1865	Jan. 11, 1865	Promoted to Lieutenant-Colonel.
Do.	HENRY A. BABBITT	May 18, "	May 18, "	Promoted to Lieutenant-Colonel.
Do.	GEORGE T. RICE	June 6, "	June 6, "	Mustered out with regiment.
Surgeon	OLIVER W. NIXON	Aug. 20, 1861	Nov. 23, 1861	Resigned May 31, 1862.
Do.	THOMAS W. McARTHUR	May 31, 1862	June 17, 1862	Resigned September 3, 1862.
Do.	CHRISTIAN FORESTER	Sept. 3, "	Oct. 31, "	Revoked.
Do.	JOHN A. FOLLETT	" 3, "	March 30, "	Mustered out with regiment.
Ass't Surgeon	THOMAS W. McARTHUR	Aug. 20, 1861	Nov. 23, 1861	Promoted to Surgeon. [Nov. 12, 1862.
Do.	CHRISTIAN FORESTER	May 31, 1862	June 17, 1862	Promoted to Surgeon Sept. 3, 1862; resigned
Do.	JOHN A. FOLLETT	Aug. 13, "	Aug. 15, "	Promoted to Surgeon.
Do.	PIERRE S. STARR	Dec. 13, "	Dec. 13, "	Mustered out with regiment.
Do.	LYONEL J. SMITH	Sept. 5, "	Jan. 6, 1863	
Do.	WM. J. ANDREWS	May 8, 1865	May 8, 1865	Mustered out with regiment.
Chaplain	BENJ. W. CHIDLAW	Aug. 20, 1861	Aug. 30, 1861	Resigned April 9, 1862.
Captain	Henry T. McDowell	July 31, "	" 28, "	Promoted to Major.
Do.	John C. Fill	" 31, "	" 28, "	Resigned April 12, 1862. [26, 1862.
Do.	George W. Baker	" 31, "	" 28, "	Appointed com'y subsistence by Pres't, Nov.
Do.	Christopher A. Morgan	" 31, "	" 28, "	Resigned January 6, 1862.
Do.	John S. Jenkins	" 31, "	" 28, "	Promoted to Major.
Do.	Jacob Koenig	" 31, "	" 28, "	Resigned October 17, 1862.
Do.	Charles W. Pomeroy	" 31, "	" 28, "	Died October 2, 1861.
Do.	Adam Koogle	" 31, "	" 28, "	Died November 30, 1861.
Do.	David C. Benjamin	" 31, "	" 28, "	Resigned July 7, 1862.
Do.	John Rhodes	" 31, "	" 28, "	Resigned February 3, 1862.
Do.	Wm. H. Lathrop	Dec. 28, "	Jan. 1, 1862	Promoted to Major.
Do.	John V. Drake	" 28, "	" 1, "	Killed in action.
Do.	John C. Musser	Feb. 8, 1862	Feb. 8, "	Resigned July 3, 1862.
Do.	Jacob M. Paulk	" 19, "	" 19, "	Mustered out.
Do.	Willard P. Stoms	April 12, "	April 23, "	Resigned June 10, 1862.
Do.	Wm. H. Williams	July 8, "	July 11, "	Resigned September 16, 1864.
Do.	John B. Ryan	June 10, "	" 11, "	Resigned December 19, 1862.
Do.	Ethan O. Hurd	July 3, "	" 11, "	Resigned March 5, 1864.
Do.	Charles G. Knowles	" 7, "	Oct. 31, "	Resigned April 8, 1862.
Do.	Wm. H. Newman	Oct. 1, "	Dec. 8, "	Mustered out.
Do.	John D. White	Nov. 26, "	" 8, "	Resigned April 29, 1864.
Do.	Jacob Koenig	Oct. 18, "	" 31, "	Dead.
Do.	Horace G. Stoms	Dec. 19, "	March 13, 1863	Resigned September 16, 1864.
Do.	John R. Parker	April 8, 1863	May 25, "	Resigned January 7, 1864.
Do.	Wm. C. Buck	May 9, 1864	" 9, 1864	Promoted to Lieutenant-Colonel.
Do.	John W. Orr	" 9, "	" 9, "	Resigned.
Do.	John R. Connell	" 8, "	" 9, "	Mustered out.
Do.	Jacob Broadwell	" 25, "	" 25, "	Mustered out August 9, 1864.
Do.	Jeremiah Hall	" 25, "	" 25, "	Resigned September 28, 1864.
Do.	Daniel Weber	March 2, "	March 2, "	Promoted to Major.
Do.	Henry A. Babbitt	Jan. 11, 1862	Jan. 11, 1865	Promoted to Major.
Do.	George T. Rice	" 11, "	" 11, "	Promoted to Major.
Do.	Wm. Benze	" 11, "	" 11, "	Mustered out.
Do.	Andrew Robinson	" 11, "	" 11, "	Mustered out with regiment.
Do.	Elijah B. Fairchild	" 11, "	" 11, "	Resigned June 28, 1865.
Do.	Wm. H. Minton	" 11, "	" 11, "	Mustered out with regiment.
Do.	Frank Hight	" 11, "	" 11, "	Resigned.
Do.	James Walker	Feb. 10, "	Feb. 10, "	Mustered out with regiment.
Do.	Wm. H. Anshutz	" 10, "	" 10, "	Mustered out with regiment.
Do.	Oscar N. Carr	May 18, "	May 18, "	Mustered out with regiment.
Do.	Wm. H. Pittenger	" 18, "	" 18, "	Mustered out with regiment
Do.	Oliver P. Brown	" 18, "	" 18, "	Mustered out with regiment.
Do.	Robert S. Pomeroy	June 6, "	June 6, "	Mustered out with regiment as Adjutant.
Do.	James Drake	" 6, "	" 6, "	Mustered out with regiment.
Do.	Homer Montgomery	July 10, "	July 10, "	Mustered out with regiment.
1st Lieutenant	John C. Musser	" 31, "	Aug. 28, "	Promoted to Captain.
Do.	Wm. Edgarton	" 31, "	" 28, "	Resigned June 25, 1862.
Do.	John F. Welch	" 31, "	" 28, "	Resigned June 16, 1862.
Do.	Willard P. Stoms	" 31, "	" 28, "	Promoted to Captain.
Do.	John J. Hooker	" 31, "	" 28, "	Discharged November 24, 1862.
Do.	Ethan O. Hurd	" 31, "	" 28, "	Promoted to Captain.
Do.	Wm. H. Lathrop	" 31, "	" 28, "	Promoted to Captain.
Do.	Samuel H. Rulon	" 31, "	" 28, "	Resigned January 10, 1862.
Do.	Fletcher Hypes	" 31, "	" 28, "	Resigned October 1, 1862.
Do.	Jacob M. Paulk	" 31, "	" 28, "	Promoted to Captain.
Do.	Charles F. Sedam	" 31, "	" 28, "	Resigned (or mustered out) February 18,
Do.	Wm. H. Williams	Dec. 28, 1861	Jan. 1, 1862	Promoted to Captain.

RANK.	NAME.	DATE OF RANK.	COM. ISSUED.	REMARKS.
1st Lieutenant	Lewis Sonntag	Feb 8, 1862	Feb. 8, 1862	Resigned February 22, 1862.
Do.	Henry W. Sheppard	" 8, "	" 8, "	Resigned June 10, 1862.
Do.	Charles G. Knowles	" 19, "	" 19, "	Promoted to Captain.
Do.	Thomas D. Minton	" 28, "	" 28, "	Resigned March 26, 1862.
Do.	Daniel Weber	March 26, "	April 14, "	Promoted to Captain.
Do.	Wm. H. Newman	Feb. 28, "	May 1, "	Promoted to Captain.
Do.	John B. Ryan	April 12, "	" 1, "	Promoted to Captain.
Do.	John C. Burnett	June 10, "	July 11, "	Resigned April 13, 1862.
Do.	John D. White	" 18, "	" 11, "	Promoted to Captain.
Do.	Wm. C. Buck	" 25, "	" 11, "	Promoted to Captain.
Do.	August Kropp	July 3, "	" 11, "	Resigned April 1, 1864.
Do.	John W. Orr	" 8, "	" 11, "	Promoted to Captain.
Do.	Horace G. Stoms	June 10, "	" 11, "	Promoted to Captain.
Do.	John R. Parker	Aug. 2, "	Oct. 31, "	Promoted to Captain.
Do.	John R. Connell	July 7, "	" 31, "	Promoted to Captain.
Do.	Bennett N. Davis	Oct. 1, "	Dec. 8, "	Resigned April 1, 1864.
Do.	Uriah D. Hunter	Nov. 26, "	" 8, "	Resigned June 20, 1863.
Do.	Jacob Broadwell	Dec. 19, "	May 13, 1863	Promoted to Captain.
Do.	Jeremiah Hall	" 31, "	" 13, "	Promoted to Captain.
Do.	Wm. R. Babb	April 13, 1863	" 25, "	Resigned September 20, 1864.
Do.	Henry A. Babbitt	" 8, "	" 25, "	Promoted to Captain.
Do.	Frank Fortman	July 20, "	July 20, "	Resigned September 15, 1864.
Do.	George T. Rice	May 9, 1864	May 9, 1864	Promoted to Captain.
Do.	Wm. R. Rabie	" 9, "	" 9, "	Resigned September 15, 1864.
Do.	Silas O. Losel	" 9, "	" 9, "	Mustered out.
Do.	Wm. H. McCurdy	" 9, "	" 9, "	Resigned September 16, 1864.
Do.	Wm. H Williams	" 9, "	" 9, "	Resigned.
Do.	Henry Finger	" 9, "	" 9, "	Resigned September 16, 1864.
Do.	Greenbury Miller	" 25, "	" 25, "	Resigned.
Do.	Wm. Benze	" 25, "	" 25, "	Promoted to Captain.
Do.	Andrew Robinson	July 13, "	July 13, "	Promoted to Captain.
Do.	Elijah B. Fairchild	" 13, "	" 13, "	Promoted to Captain.
Do.	James Walker	Jan. 11, 1865	" 11, 1865	Promoted to Captain.
Do.	Wm. H. Anshutz	" 11, "	" 11, "	Promoted to Captain.
Do.	Oscar N. Carr	" 11, "	" 11, "	Promoted to Captain.
Do.	Wm. H. Pittenger	" 11, "	" 11, "	Promoted to Captain.
Do.	Oliver P. Brown	" 11, "	" 11, "	Promoted to Captain
Do.	Robert S. Pomeroy	" 11, "	" 11, "	Promoted to Captain.
Do.	James Drake	" 11, "	" 11, "	Promoted to Captain.
Do.	John Whetstone	" 11, "	" 11, "	Mustered out with regiment.
Do.	Homer Montgomery	" 11, "	" 11, "	Promoted to Captain.
Do.	Ely Steen	" 11, "	" 11, "	Mustered out with regiment.
Do.	Granville H. Ellis	Feb. 10, "	Feb. 10, "	Mustered out with regiment.
Do.	Alex. McTaggert	" 10, "	" 10, "	Resigned June 20, 1865.
Do.	Barney Shultz	" 10, "	" 10, "	Mustered out with regiment.
Do.	Lucius M. Hubbard	" 14, "	" 14, "	Mustered out with regiment.
Do.	Thomas G. Mears	May 18, "	May 18, "	
Do.	Peter Thompson	" 18, "	" 18, "	Mustered out with regiment.
Do.	Wm. Snodgrass	" 18, "	" 18, "	Discharged July 1, 1865.
Do.	Henry L. Colgrove	June 6, "	June 6, "	Mustered out with regiment.
Do.	Richard A. Taylor	" 6, "	" 6, "	Mustered out with regiment.
Do.	J. L. McClain	July 10, "	July 10, "	
2d Lieutenant	Lewis Sonntag	" 31, 1861	Aug. 28, 1861	Promoted to 1st Lieutenant.
Do.	Henry W. Sheppard	" 31, "	" 28, "	Promoted to 1st Lieutenant.
Do.	Thomas D. Minton	" 31, "	" 28, "	Promoted to 1st Lieutenant.
Do.	Daniel Weber	" 31, "	" 28, "	Promoted to 1st Lieutenant.
Do.	John Davis	" 31, "	" 28, "	Resigned May 23, 1862.
Do.	Chas. Miller	" 31, "	" 28, "	Resigned June 16, 1862.
Do.	Wm. H. Williams	" 31, "	" 28, "	Promoted to 1st Lieutenant.
Do.	John V. Drake	" 31, "	" 28, "	Promoted to Captain.
Do.	Nathan R. Thompson	" 31, "	" 28, "	Resigned October 7, 1861.
Do.	Chas. G. Knowles	" 31, "	" 28, "	Promoted to 1st Lieutenant.
Do.	Harlan A. Edwards	" 31, "	" 28, "	Resigned June 18, 1862.
Do.	Andrew J. Lawell	Oct. 9, "	Oct. 16, "	Resigned June 10, 1862.
Do.	Uriah Hoffman	Dec. 28, "	Jan. 1, 1862	Resigned April 26, 1862.
Do.	John C. Burnett	Jan. 9, 1862	" 9, "	Promoted to 1st Lieutenant.
Do.	John W. Johnson	Feb. 19, "	Feb. 19, "	Resigned December 31, 1862.
Do.	Wm. C. Buck	March 19, "	March 19, "	Promoted to 1st Lieutenant.
Do.	Wm. H. Newman	" 19, "	" 19, "	Promoted to 1st Lieutenant.
Do.	John B. Ryan	" 26, "	April 14, "	Promoted to 1st Lieutenant.
Do.	John D. White	" 26, "	May 14, "	Promoted to 1st Lieutenant.
Do.	Bennett N. Davis	April 26, "	" 1, "	Promoted to 1st Lieutenant.
Do.	Horace G. Stoms	" 12, "	" 1, "	Promoted to 1st Lieutenant.
Do.	John W. Orr	Feb. 28, "	Feb. 24, "	Promoted to 1st Lieutenant.
Do.	Jacob Broadwell	May 23, "	July 11, "	Promoted to 1st Lieutenant.
Do.	John R. Parker	June 10, "	" 11, "	Promoted to 1st Lieutenant.
Do.	Frank Fortman	" 18, "	" 11, "	Promoted to 1st Lieutenant.
Do.	Wyatt H. Hawrick	" 18, "	" 11, "	Declined; discharged.
Do.	Wm. R. Babb	" 10, "	" 11, "	Promoted to 1st Lieutenant.
Do.	George T. Rice	" 25, "	" 11, "	Promoted to 1st Lieutenant.
Do.	Uriah D. Hunter	" 18, "	" 11, "	Promoted to 1st Lieutenant.
Do.	Henry A. Babbitt	" 10, "	" 11, "	Promoted to 1st Lieutenant.
Do.	Wm. M. Chapman	July 8, "	" 11, "	Resigned July 24, 1863.
Do.	Wm. R. Rabie	Aug. 2, "	Oct. 31, "	Promoted to 1st Lieutenant.
Do.	Silas O. Losel	Oct. 1, "	Dec. 8, "	Promoted to 1st Lieutenant.
Do.	Wm. H. McCurdy	Nov. 26, "	" 8, "	Promoted to 1st Lieutenant.
Do.	Wm. H. Williams	Dec. 31, "	March 13, 1863	Promoted to 1st Lieutenant.
Do.	Horace Knowles	" 31, "	" 13, "	Resigned April 9, 1864.
Do.	Henry Finger	April 8, 1863	May 25, "	Promoted to 1st Lieutenant.
Do.	Greenbury Miller	" 13, "	" 25, "	Promoted to 1st Lieutenant Sept. 20, 1864.
Do.	Wm. Benze	June 20, "	July 20, "	Promoted to 1st Lieutenant.
Do.	Andrew Robinson	" 24, "	" 20, "	Promoted to 1st Lieutenant.
Do.	Elijah B. Fairchild	May 9, 1864	May 9, 1864	Promoted to 1st Lieutenant.
Do.	Wm. H. Minton	" 9, "	" 9, "	Promoted to 1st Lieutenant.
Do.	Frank Hight	" 9, "	" 9, "	Promoted to 1st Lieutenant.
Do.	James Walker	" 9, "	" 9, "	Promoted to 1st Lieutenant.
Do.	Wm. H. Anshutz	" 9, "	" 9, "	Promoted to 1st Lieutenant.
Do.	Oscar N. Carr	" 9, "	" 9, "	Promoted to 1st Lieutenant.
Do.	Oliver P. Brown	" 9, "	" 9, "	Promoted to 1st Lieutenant.
Do.	Robert S. Pomeroy	July 13, "	July 13, "	Promoted to 1st Lieutenant.
Do.	Wm. H. Pittenger	" 13, "	" 13, "	Promoted to 1st Lieutenant.
Do.	Granville H. Ellis	" 11, 1865	" 11, 1865	Promoted to 1st Lieutenant.

RANK.	NAME.	DATE OF RANK.	COM. ISSUED.	REMARKS.
2d Lieutenant	Alex. McTaggert	July 11, 1865	July 11, 1865	Promoted to 1st Lieutenant.
Do.	Barney Shultz	" 11, "	" 11, "	Promoted to 1st Lieutenant.
Do.	Henry L. Colgrove	Feb. 14, "	Feb. 14, "	Promoted to 1st Lieutenant.
Do.	Richard A. Taylor	" 14, "	" 14, "	Promoted to 1st Lieutenant.
Do.	Thomas G. Mears	" 14, "	" 14, "	Promoted to 1st Lieutenant.
Do.	Peter Thompson	" 14, "	" 14, "	Promoted to 1st Lieutenant.
Do.	Wm. Snodgrass	" 14, "	" 14, "	Promoted to 1st Lieutenant.
Do.	Allen Easter	May 18, "	May 18, "	Mustered out with regiment.
Do.	J. L. McClain	" 18, "	" 18, "	Promoted to 1st Lieutenant.
Do.	Addison Bowser	" 18, "	" 18, "	Mustered out with regiment.
Do.	Daniel Otterbein	" 18, "	" 18, "	Mustered out with regiment.
Do.	Matthias Kuhn	" 18, "	" 18, "	Mustered out with regiment.
Do.	Buell Congdon	" 18, "	" 18, "	Dismissed.
Do.	Huston Williams	" 18, "	" 18, "	Mustered out with regiment.
Do.	Delmer Stone	" 18, "	" 18, "	Mustered out with regiment.
Do.	Francis M. Wright	June 6, "	June 6, "	Mustered out with regiment.
Do.	Robert H. Campbell	" 6, "	" 6, "	
Do.	John A. Langdon	July 10, "	July 10, "	

THIRTY-NINTH OHIO VOLUNTEER INFANTRY.

THE THIRTY-NINTH OHIO rendezvoused at Camp Colerain, ten miles north of Cincinnati, during the month of July, 1861. On the 31st of July seven companies were mustered into the service; and on the 2d of August, they moved to Camp Dennison, where the remaining three companies and the field and staff officers were mustered in. Being fully armed and equipped, the regiment moved on Sunday, August 18th, by rail to St. Louis, to join the forces organizing under General Fremont. It was the first Ohio regiment to enter the State of Missouri.

It remained in camp near the fair grounds, officers and men perfecting themselves in drill, until the 6th of September, when nine companies were ordered to Macon, on the North Missouri Railroad, to join the forces under General Sturgis. Company K was left in charge of the camp and garrison equipage. On arriving at Macon four companies were ordered to St. Joseph. This separation lasted about five months. The four companies performed guard-duty along the North Missouri Railroad until about the 1st of February, when they were ordered to St. Louis, and rejoined the company left at that place. The other five companies, (C, D, F, G, and H), with the troops under General Sturgis, moved to the relief of Lexington; but before that place was reached, the garrison surrendered, and Sturgis moved to Kansas City, arriving on the 22d of September. This was the first march for the soldiers of the Thirty-Ninth, and, as it was made rapidly and without transportation, they suffered severely. On the 15th of October the command again took up the line of march, and, passing through Pleasant Hill, Osceola, and Greenfield, it arrived at Springfield on the night of November 2d.

On the 9th of November the entire army, under General Hunter, moved toward the Missouri River. It reached Sedalia on the 15th of November, and remained there until the 8th of December, when it moved to Syracuse, where it remained during the months of December and January. On the 2d of February, 1862, the command, crossing the Missouri River at Booneville, moved by way of Columbia, Fulton, Danville, and St. Charles, to St. Louis. The regiment arrived at Benton Barracks on the 19th, when the companies were again united. The march from Syracuse to St. Louis was very severe; the weather was cold; the roads were almost impassable; and the men were compelled frequently to pull the ordnance and supply wagons over the hills by hand.

On the 22d of February the regiment embarked on transports and sailed for Commerce, Mis-

souri, arriving on the 24th. It formed part of the First Brigade, First Division of the army under General Pope. The troops moved upon New Madrid, and arrived in sight of that place on the 3d of March. A movement was made at once upon the defenses, and the enemy's position was developed. The regiment assisted in all the operations that resulted in the capture of New Madrid and Island No. 10; and, on the 13th of April, it embarked on transports and sailed down the Mississippi to within a few miles of Fort Pillow. Here it remained until the 17th of April, when it sailed for Hamburg Landing, on the Tennessee River, and formed part of the army under General Halleck. From this time until the evacuation of Corinth by the Rebels the regiment made numerous reconnoissances, and engaged in a large number of skirmishes, losing many men. It held the advance of Pope's army on entering Corinth, and was one of the first regiments to occupy the place. After pursuing the retreating Rebels as far as Boonville, the regiment returned to within five miles of Corinth and encamped on Clear Creek. Here officers' school, company, and battalion drill was held daily. On the 25th of July the regiment was armed with the Whitney rifle, saber bayonet, instead of the Greenwood rifle, with which it had been previously supplied.

On the 29th of August the Thirty-Ninth moved to Iuka. Here the regiment was again divided. Two companies were ordered to Eastport, four companies were distributed at different points along the railroad, and the remaining four were stationed near Iuka. On the 24th forty-four recruits were received from Ohio.

On the 11th of September the entire command moved toward Corinth, and, leaving all camp and garrison equipage near that place, it marched to Jacinto, to co-operate with other forces in a movement against General Price, then occupying Iuka. The column of which the regiment was a part arrived in advance of the co-operating columns, and, before they could come up, gave battle and defeated the enemy. The command pursued the Rebels for two days, and then returned by a circuitous route to Corinth, arriving in time to participate in the sanguinary conflict of October 3d and 4th, and in the pursuit of the Rebels as far as Baldwin. The regiment then returned to Corinth, and was engaged in constructing the inner line of works for the defense of the place. During these operations sixty-three recruits arrived from Ohio for the regiment.

On the 4th of November the regiment moved to Grand Junction, and joined the army under General Grant. It advanced to Oxford, Mississippi, and was engaged frequently in skirmishes and reconnoissances. On the 18th of December the Thirty-Ninth, with the Twenty-Seventh Ohio, moved by rail to Jackson, Tennessee, to look after General Forrest, who, with a large force, was making raids on the railroads in that vicinity, and was cutting off the supplies for General Grant's army. On the 27th, forming a part of General Sullivan's command, it moved to Trenton, and thence to Parker's Cross Roads, where, on the 31st of December, the force under Forrest was met, defeated, and driven across the Tennessee River. After this the regiment moved to Corinth, arriving on the 9th of January, 1863. The march from Jackson to the Tennessee River and on to Corinth was very severe upon the troops. They moved with but two days' rations, and the country afforded scanty supplies. They subsisted on limited quantities of fresh meat, which could be gathered on the march, and on meal, which the men ground in small and dilapidated mills found in that country. In addition to this many of the men were without shoes, which rendered the march fatiguing and occasioned much suffering from the cold.

The regiment remained at Corinth until the 19th of April, when it moved with the expedition, under General Dodge, to the Tuscumbia Valley, for the purpose of engaging the attention of the Rebels while other forces cut the railroads in the rear of Bragg's army. After an absence of two weeks it returned to Corinth, and from that place it moved, on the 12th of May, to Memphis.

On the 18th of October the regiment moved by way of Corinth, Eastport, Lauderdale, and Pulaski, to Prospect, Tennessee, where it re-enlisted on the 26th of December. On the 27th five hundred and thirty-four men were mustered into the service as veteran volunteers. On the 29th they left for Camp Dennison, Ohio, where they received a furlough for thirty days. Those who did not re-enlist were left at Prospect, in charge of the regiment's camp and equipage. On the

11th of February, 1864, the regiment rendezvoused at Camp Dennison, having gained by enlistment one hundred and twelve men. On the 12th it moved by transports to Nashville, thence by rail to Pulaski, and from there it marched to Athens, Alabama. The regiment moved to Decatur on the 11th of April; and, on the 1st of May, forming part of the Fourth Division of the Sixteenth Corps, under General Dodge, it moved in the direction of Chattanooga.

On the 5th of May the regiment moved on the Atlanta campaign, marching by way of Ship's and Snake Creek Gap to Resaca. It took part in the battle at that place, May 14th and 15th; and, on the 16th, crossed the Oostenaula River at Lay's Ferry, and moved by way of Adairsville to Kingston. On the 23d it crossed the Etowah River and marched to Dallas, taking part in the action there. On the 1st of June it moved to Acworth, and, on the 10th, to Big Shanty, pushing the enemy to the base of Kenesaw Mountain, where the regiment remained under constant fire until July 3d, when the enemy abandoned his line, and took position near the Chattahoochie River.

On the 4th of July the regiment engaged in a successful assault on the enemy's works at Nicojack Creek. On the 5th it moved to Sandtown, and on the 11th crossed the Chattahoochie near Rosswell. On the 19th it marched to Decatur, and on the 22d assisted in repelling the attack of Hardee's corps on the left flank of the Army of the Tennessee. This was the most severe engagement in which the regiment participated during its term of service. It lost one-third of its number in killed and wounded. On the 27th, passing by the rear, it went into position on the right of General Sherman's army; and from this time until the 26th of August was engaged constantly with the enemy, pressing him at last into the main defenses of Atlanta.

The Sixteenth Corps moved to the Montgomery and Atlanta Railroad at Fairburn, where the regiment assisted in destroying the railroad track; and, on the 30th, moved to Jonesboro'. On the 1st of September it pursued the retreating Rebels to Lovejoy's Station, and, on the 5th, it returned and went into camp at East Point, five miles south of Atlanta. During this campaign the regiment lost twenty-four men killed and one hundred and sixty-eight wounded. It was on the march or in battle almost constantly, and scarcely an hour passed during which the sound of a hostile gun could not be heard.

The regiment remained at East Point until the 4th of October, when, forming part of the First Division, Seventeenth Corps, it marched in pursuit of Hood, moving by way of Marietta, Big Shanty, and Kingston, to Resaca, and driving the Rebels down Lookout Valley and across the Coosa River. The pursuit ended at Galesville, Alabama, and the regiment returned to Marietta, where, on the 9th of November, it was paid for the first time in nine months. On the 12th of November, after being thoroughly equipped, the regiment moved three miles north of Marietta, and assisted in destroying the railroad leading to Chattanooga; and the next day it moved to Atlanta.

On the 15th of November the regiment started on the march to the sea. It crossed the Ocmulgee River on pontoons, passed through McDonough, Jackson, Monticello, and Hillsboro', and struck the Macon and Savannah Railroad at Gordon Station on the 22d. The next day was occupied in destroying the railroad. The march was continued along the railroad, the troops destroying a portion of the track each day. The Oconee and Ogeechee Rivers were crossed, and on the 1st of December Millen was reached. On the 10th the regiment approached the fortifications of Savannah, and helped to drive the enemy within his works. On the 11th it moved south of the Ogeechee Canal, and constructed a line of intrenchments; and the next day it moved toward Ossabaw Sound, to open communication with the fleet, and thus procure supplies. Some delay occurred in obtaining supplies from the fleet, and on the 14th the regiment marched as escort to a forage-train. It was necessary to go twenty-five miles before forage could be obtained. The regiment returned to camp on the 16th, and moved immediately with its division toward the Altemaha River, to destroy the Savannah and Florida Railroad. This was accomplished on the 18th, and the command returned to camp. When Savannah was evacuated, the Thirty-Ninth encamped near Thunderbolt, and from there it moved, on the 1st of January, 1865, on transports to Pocotaligo, South Carolina. Here it received two hundred and four recruits from Ohio.

On the 30th of January the regiment entered upon the campaign of the Carolinas. It engaged in the action at Rivers Bridge, on the Salkehatchie, February 3d and 4th; and, on the 7th, struck the Charleston and Augusta Railroad at Midway. It crossed the Edisto at Binaker's Bridge, passed through Orangeburg, crossed the Saluda and Broad Rivers, and on the 17th entered the capital of South Carolina. On the next day the regiment assisted in destroying the tracks around the Columbia and North Carolina Railroad depots, and then resumed the march through Winnsboro' and Liberty Hill to Camden, where the regiment encamped on the 28th.

On the 3d of March the regiment engaged the enemy seven miles from Cheraw, drove him through the town and across the Great Pedee River, and captured large quantities of ordnance and other stores. On the 4th the Thirty-Ninth Ohio, with the Eighteenth Missouri, crossed the river in boats and drove the enemy from the eastern bank. This enabled the pontoons to be laid when the corps crossed, and the march was continued to Fayetteville, North Carolina, which was reached on the 11th. On the 13th the march was continued in the direction of Clinton. On the 17th it was reported that the left wing of the army was confronted by a large force of the enemy near Bentonville. The regiment, after four days and nights hard marching, arrived at that place, and took part in the action there on the 21st of March, with a loss of four killed, seventeen wounded, and three missing. From here the regiment moved to Goldsboro', where it passed in review before General Sherman on the 24th of March. After being clothed and provided, the regiment moved, on the 10th of April, toward Raleigh, where it arrived on the 14th. On the 24th it passed in review before General Grant, and, on the 25th, it moved to Jones's Station, on the North Carolina Railroad. Here the intelligence of the surrender of General Johnston was received, and the command returned to Raleigh.

On the 29th it commenced the march to Washington City. It passed through Petersburg, Richmond, and Fredericksburg, and arrived at Alexandria on the 19th of May. On the 23d the regiment moved to Long Bridge, and the next day passed in review with Sherman's army before the President of the United States, the Heads of Department, the Diplomatic Corps, a large number of distinguished officers of the army and navy, and an immense concourse of citizens. After the review the regiment went into camp on the Bladensburg road.

On the 5th of June the regiment moved by rail to Parkersburg, West Virginia, and thence by transport to Louisville, Kentucky, where it was mustered out of the service on the 9th of July, 1865. It was transferred to Camp Dennison, Ohio, and there was paid and discharged. Few regiments have had a more extensive field of operations than the Thirty-Ninth, and, perhaps, none have rendered more efficient service. It gave to the veteran organization more men than any other regiment from Ohio, and for this it received credit in the Adjutant-General's report; and it has had the good fortune never to turn its back upon the enemy, either in battle or skirmish. It served under Pope, Logan, Howard, McPherson, Sherman, and Grant; and officers and men endeavored continually to reflect the spirit of their distinguished commanders.

During the service of its Chaplain (who has been long known as a minister of the Presbyterian Church and a Sunday School Union Missionary) the religious services of the Thirty-Ninth were a peculiar feature. The Scriptures were read and prayer was offered regularly during dress parade. The demeanor of the soldiers was reverential; nearly all attended preaching on Sundays; and a "Christian Brotherhood" of church members and those religiously inclined was organized. A temperance society was also formed, embracing representatives from all parts of the regiment, and almost every member of Company K. Mr. Chidlaw was compelled by failing health to resign the chaplaincy, in 1862, to the general regret of officers and men.

40th REGIMENT OHIO VOLUNTEER INFANTRY.

ROSTER, THREE YEARS' SERVICE.

RANK.	NAME.	DATE OF RANK.	COM. ISSUED.	REMARKS.
Colonel	JONATHAN CRANOR	Sept. 11, 1861	Dec. 11, 1861	Resigned February 6, 1863.
Do.	JACOB E. TAYLOR	Feb. 5, 1863	Feb. 13, 1863	Mustered out.
Lt. Colonel	JONATHAN CRANOR	Aug. 21, 1861	Dec. 11, 1861	Promoted to Colonel.
Do.	JACOB E. TAYLOR	Sept. 12, "	" 14, "	Dismissed November 21, 1862.
Do.	WM. JONES	Feb. 25, 1863	April 21, 1863	No record in the office.
Do.	JAMES WATSON	March 19, 1864	March 19, 1864	Mustered out.
Major	JACOB E. TAYLOR	Oct. 29, 1861	Dec. 14, 1861	Promoted to Lieutenant-Colonel.
Do.	WM. JONES	Feb. 5, 1863	Feb. 13, 1863	Promoted to Lieutenant-Colonel.
Do.	THOMAS ACTON	" 5, "	April 21, "	No record in the office.
Do.	JOHN L. REEVES	March 19, 1864	March 19, 1864	Mustered out.
Surgeon	ALEX. McBRIDE	Sept. 7, 1861	Dec. 11, 1861	Resigned March 25, 1862.
Do.	JOHN N. BEACH	April 1, 1862	April 14, 1862	Mustered out.
Ass't Surgeon	JOSEPH C. KALB	Oct. 3, 1861	Dec. 14, 1861	Resigned January 6, 1863.
Do.	ALEX. E. ISAMINGER	Aug. 21, 1862	" 5, 1862	Mustered out.
Do.	WM. H. MATCHETT	Feb. 8, 1863	Feb. 8, 1863	Mustered out.
Chaplain	SAMUEL A. BREWSTER	Oct. 15, 1861	Oct. 15, 1861	Resigned October 5, 1862.
Do.	SALEM T. GRISWOLD	Dec. 19, 1862	Dec. 19, 1862	Mustered out.
Captain	Thomas Acton	Aug. 24, 1861	Dec. 14, 1861	Promoted to Major.
Do.	James Watson	" 30, "	" 14, "	Promoted to Lieutenant-Colonel.
Do.	Wm. Jones	Sept. 5, "	" 14, "	Promoted to Lieutenant-Colonel.
Do.	James M. Haworth	" 17, "	" 14, "	Resigned February 7, 1863.
Do.	Wm. Cunningham	" 17, "	" 14, "	Resigned April 25, 1862.
Do.	John D. Jennett	" 18, "	" 14, "	Resigned April 25, 1862.
Do.	John L. Reeves	" 25, "	" 14, "	Promoted to Major.
Do.	Chas. G. Matchett	Oct. 7, "	" 14, "	Mustered out.
Do.	Andrew R. Coldwood	" 15, "	" 11, "	Resigned June 28, 1862.
Do.	Alex. A. Knapp	" 24, "	" 11, "	Resigned March 16, 1864.
Do.	Wm. C. Osgood	April 25, 1862	June 4, 1862	Honorably discharged August 1, 1863.
Do.	John C. Meagher	" 25, "	" 4, "	Deceased.
Do.	Andrew R. Coldwood	Aug. 14, "	Aug. 26, "	Re-instated; resigned January 6, 1863.
Do.	Milton Kemper	Jan. 6, 1863	Jan. 12, 1863	Mustered out.
Do.	Chas. J. Ent	Feb. 7, "	Feb. 10, "	Mustered out.
Do.	Orlando C. Bowles	" 5, "	April 21, "	Resigned June 16, 1863.
Do.	Delamer L. Deland	" 5. "	" 21, "	Mustered out.
Do.	Harmon E. McClure	March 19, 1864	March 19, 1864	Declined promotion; commission returned.
Do.	James Allen	Aug. 1, 1863	Aug. 10, 1863	Transferred to 51st Ohio Volunteer Infantry.
Do.	George D. Stone	March 19, 1864	March 19, 1864	Declined.
Do.	John W. Smith	" 19, "	" 19, "	Mustered out.
Do.	Clement F. Snodgrass	April 1, "	April 1, "	Killed.
Do.	John F. Mahon	March 9, "	May 9, "	Mustered out.
Do.	Chas. Converse	" 9, "	" 9, "	Killed.
1st Lieutenant	Joseph L. Kissinger	Aug. 21, 1861	Dec. 14, 1861	Resigned March 14, 1863.
Do.	Delamer L. Deland	" 26, "	" 14, "	Promoted to Captain.
Do.	Chas. Converse	" 30, "	" 14, "	Resigned—disability—February 17, 1863.
Do.	Orlando C. Bowles	Sept. 5, "	" 14, "	Promoted to Captain.
Do.	James B. Creviston	" 9, "	" 14, "	Resigned March 9.
Do.	Charles J. Ent	" 17, "	" 14, "	Promoted to Captain.
Do.	John C. Meagher	" 17, "	" 14, "	Promoted to Captain.
Do.	Wm. Osgood	" 18, "	" 14, "	Promoted to Captain.
Do.	John T. Frederick	" 25, "	" 14, "	Resigned January.
Do.	Cyrenus Van Mater	Oct. 7, "	" 14, "	Killed at Chickamauga November 20, 1863.
Do.	Milton Kemper	" 20, "	" 14, "	Promoted to Captain.
Do.	David J. Roop	" 25, "	" 14, "	Resigned January 5, 1864.
Do.	Herman E. McClure	May 9, 1862	April 10, 1862	Mustered out.
Do.	James Allen	April 25, "	June 4, "	Promoted to Captain.
Do.	George D. Stone	" 25, "	" 4, "	Mustered out.
Do.	John W. Smith	Jan. 6, 1863	Jan. 12, 1863	Promoted to Captain.
Do.	John F. Mahon	" 31, "	Feb. 10, "	Promoted to Captain.
Do.	John J. Barlow	Feb. 7, "	" 10, "	Resigned October 13, 1863.
Do.	Chas. Converse	" 28, "	March 5, "	Promoted to Captain.
Do.	Laning B. Moody	March 14, "	" 30, "	Resigned March 10, 1864.
Do.	Benj. F. Snodgrass	Feb. 5, "	April 21, "	Promoted to Captain and killed Nov. 20, 1863.
Do.	James C. Peck	" 5, "	" 21, "	Mustered out.
Do.	Isaac N. Edwards	Aug. 5, "	Aug. 10, "	Mustered out.
Do.	Richard B. Cowling	May 9, 1864	May 9, 1864	Mustered out.
Do.	Daniel Cottell, jr.	" 9, "	" 9, "	Died May 30, 1864.
Do.	Matthew P. Simpson	" 9, "	" 9, "	Commission returned.
Do.	Wm. Watson	Jan. 4, "	Jan. 4, "	Mustered out.
Do.	Chas. Cover	March 19, "	March 19, "	Mustered out.
Do.	John M. Wasson	" 19, "	" 19, "	Mustered out.
Do.	James A. Fisher	Jan. 5, "	Jan. 20, "	Transferred to 51st Ohio Volunteer Infantry.
Do.	Wm. Topping	March 19, "	March 19, "	Mustered out.
Do.	Silas Hart	" 19, "	" 19, "	Mustered out.
Do.	Clement F. Snodgrass	Nov. 20, 1863	Jan. 20, "	Promoted to Captain.
Do.	David K. Krouse	March 19, 1864	March 19, "	Captain in 51st, 1865.
Do.	Ezra Tullis	" 19, "	" 19, "	Declined; commission returned.
2d Lieutenant	James C. Peck	Aug. 28, 1861	Dec. 14, 1861	Promoted to 1st Lieutenant.
Do	James M. Dungan	" 30, "	" 14, "	Resigned August 30, 1862.

RANK.	NAME.	DATE OF RANK.	COM. ISSUED.	REMARKS.
2d Lieutenant	Thomas Lilly	Sept. 5, 1861	Dec. 14, 1861	Resigned July 20, 1862.
Do.	John J. Barlow	" 17, "	" 14, "	Promoted to 1st Lieutenant.
Do.	Elisha C. Ward	" 18, "	" 14, "	Resigned April 25, 1862.
Do.	John T. Mahon	Oct. 2, "	" 14, "	Promoted to 1st Lieutenant.
Do.	Wm. Bonner	" 7, "	" 14, "	Resigned November 12, 1862.
Do.	George D. Stone	" 9, "	" 14, "	Promoted to 1st Lieutenant.
Do.	John W. Smith	" 19, "	" 14, "	Promoted to 1st Lieutenant.
Do.	Byron B. Allen	" 26, "	" 14, "	Resigned January 21, 1863.
Do.	Benj. F. Snodgrass	April 25, 1862	June 4, 1862	Promoted to 1st Lieutenant.
Do.	Robert F. McGinnis	" 25, "	" 4, "	Resigned July 12, 1863.
Do.	Wm. Dalton	July 20, "	Nov. 1, "	Resigned January 24, 1863.
Do.	Chas. Cover	Aug. 30, "	" 1, "	Promoted to 1st Lieutenant.
Do.	John M. Wasson	Nov. 29, "	" 29, "	Promoted to 1st Lieutenant.
Do.	Clement F. Snodgrass	Jan. 6, 1863	Jan. 12, 1863	Promoted to 1st Lieutenant.
Do.	Isaac N. Edwards	" 12, "	Feb. 10, "	Promoted to 1st Lieutenant.
Do.	James A. Fisher	" 24, "	" 10, "	Promoted to 1st Lieutenant.
Do.	Wm. Topping	" 31, "	" 10, "	Promoted to 1st Lieutenant.
Do.	Silas Hart	Feb. 7, "	" 10, "	Promoted to 1st Lieutenant.
Do.	David K. Krouse	Jan. 31, "	" 10, "	Promoted to 1st Lieutenant.
Do.	Marvin Simpkins	Feb. 5, "	April 21, "	Resigned January 23, 1864.
Do.	Ezra Tullis	" 5, "	" 21, "	Mustered out.
Do.	Abraham T. Markle	" 5, "	June 17, "	Died November 30, 1863.
Do.	Richard B. Cowling	Aug. 1, "	Aug. 25, "	Promoted to 1st Lieutenant.
Do.	Daniel Collect			Promoted to 1st Lieutenant.

FORTIETH OHIO VOLUNTEER INFANTRY.

THE organization of this regiment was completed at Camp Chase, Ohio, December 7th, 1861, and, on the 11th of the same month, it left camp for Eastern Kentucky, going by railroad to Paris, Kentucky, and marching thence to Paintville, where it formed a junction with Colonel Garfield, who was then moving up Sandy River.

On the 10th of January, 1862, the regiment participated in the battle of Middle Creek, defeating Humphrey Marshall, and after that remained in camp at Paintville, suffering very much from sickness. In February it moved to Piketon, where, in connection with a Kentucky regiment, it remained as an outpost until the 13th of June, when the troops moved to Prestonburg. A month later, Prestonburg was abandoned, the Fortieth going to Louisa, where it remained until September 13th, when it left Louisa and moved to the mouth of the Sandy, and a few days after was ordered to Gallipolis, Ohio. On the 4th of October it moved to Guyandotte, Virginia, and on the 14th of November was again ordered into Eastern Kentucky.

The regiment started for Nashville, Tennessee, February 20, 1863, and on its arrival was assigned to the First Brigade, First Division, Reserve Corps, then at Franklin, which point the regiment reached in the month of March, in time to take part in a forced march after Van Dorn. On the 10th of April, when the Fortieth was on picket south of Franklin, Van Dorn attacked the line with a large mounted force, but was repulsed by the regiment alone.

The Fortieth moved to Triune on the 2d of June, and on the 23d the Reserve Corps moved forward, forming the right of Rosecrans's army in its advance on Shelbyville, Wartrace, and Tullahoma. The regiment was stationed at Wartrace and Tullahoma until the 7th of September, when the Reserve Corps pushed forward rapidly to assist in the movement on Chattanooga. The regiment participated in the battle of Chickamauga, losing quite heavily; and, after falling back to Chattanooga, encamped at Moccasin Point, opposite Lookout Mountain, and finally went into winter-quarters at Shellmound, Tennessee, where four companies re-enlisted.

On the 24th of November the regiment shared in the battle of Lookout Mountain, and behaved with great gallantry. At the close of the campaign the regiment again returned to Shellmound.

On the 20th of January, 1864, the regiment moved, and on the 6th of February went into camp near Cleveland. On the 22d of February it started on a reconnoissance to Dalton, and returned to camp February 28th. On the 2d of May the regiment marched on the Atlanta campaign, participating in many of the battles before that place, and being under fire almost constantly after it reached Dalton. At Pilot Knob, Georgia, on the 7th of October, companies A, B, C, and D were mustered out. The remainder of the regiment shared the fortunes of the Fourth Corps in its chase after Hood, and in its retreat before Hood from Pulaski.

In December, at Nashville, Tennessee, those who were not veterans were mustered out, and the veterans were consolidated with the Fifty-First Ohio Volunteer Infantry.

During the Atlanta campaign, Captains Clement F. Snodgrass and Charles Converse were killed, and Lieutenant-Colonel Watson captured. The death of Major Thomas Acton, in hospital, and resignation of Lieutenant-Colonel Jones, caused the promotion of Captain James Watson to Lieutenant-Colonel, and Captain J. L. Reeves to Major.

Colonel Jonathan Cranor tendered his resignation to the proper authorities in January, but it was not accepted until February 6, 1863. Surgeon Alex. McBride resigned April 1, 1862, and J. N. Beach was promoted to the vacancy. In August, 1862, an additional Assistant-Surgeon (Dr. A. E. Isaminger) was assigned to the regiment. Assistant-Surgeon Kalb resigned January, 1863, and Dr. W. H. Matchett was appointed to the vacancy.

In the battle of Chickamauga the regiment lost two valuable officers killed—Lieutenants Cyreneas Van Mater and Benj. F. Snodgrass.

After the consolidation of the Fortieth Ohio with the Fifty-First Ohio Volunteer Infantry, the combined regiment was transported, with the Fourth Army Corps, to New Orleans, Louisiana, and thence to Texas, where, at the town of Victoria, it performed guard-duty for some months. It was mustered out of the service December 3, 1865, brought home to Camp Chase, Ohio, where it was finally paid and discharged.

41st REGIMENT OHIO VOLUNTEER INFANTRY.

ROSTER, THREE YEARS' SERVICE.

RANK.	NAME.	DATE OF RANK.	COM. ISSUED.	REMARKS.
Colonel	WM. B. HAZEN	Aug. 7, 1861	Nov. 12, 1861	Appointed Brig. Gen. by Pres. Nov. 29, 1862.
Do.	AQUILA WILEY	Nov. 29, 1862	April 8, 1863	Honorably discharged June 7, 1864.
Do.	EPH. S. HOLLOWAY	May 31, 1865	May 31, 1865	Mustered out with regiment.
Lt. Colonel	JOHN J. WIZEMAN	Aug. 7, 1861	Nov. 12, 1861	Resigned March 1, 1862.
Do.	GEORGE S. MYGATT	March 1, 1862	March 20, 1862	Resigned November 20, 1862.
Do.	AQUILA WILEY	Nov. 20, "	Dec. 1, "	Promoted to Colonel.
Do.	ROBERT L. KIMBERLY	Jan. 1, 1863	April 8, 1863	Mustered out to accept promotion March 1, 1865.
Do.	EPHRAIM S. HOLLOWAY	March 18, 1865	March 18, 1865	Promoted to Colonel.
Do.	EZRA DUNHAM	May 31, "	May 31, "	Mustered out with regiment as Major.
Major	GEORGE S. MYGATT	Aug. 7, 1861	Nov. 12, 1861	Promoted to Lieutenant-Colonel.
Do.	WM. R. TOLLARS	March 1, 1862	March 20, 1862	Declined.
Do.	AQUILA WILEY	" 1, "	June 12, "	Promoted to Lieutenant-Colonel.
Do.	ROBERT L. KIMBERLY	Nov. 20, "	Dec. 1, "	Promoted to Lieutenant-Colonel.
Do.	J. H. WILLISTON	Jan. 1, 1863	April 22, 1863	Honorably discharged October 22, 1864.
Do.	EPHRAIM S. HOLLOWAY	Nov. 26, 1864	Nov. 26, 1864	Promoted to Lieutenant-Colonel.
Do.	EZRA DUNHAM	March 18, 1865	March 18, 1865	Promoted to Lieutenant-Colonel.
Do.	JAMES MCCLEARY	Nov. 23, "	Nov. 23, "	Mustered out with regiment.
Surgeon	THOMAS G. CLEVELAND	Aug. 29, 1861	" 12, "	Resigned May 17, 1862.
Do.	JOHN C. HUBBARD	May 12, 1862	May 12, 1862	Resigned August 30, 1862.
Do.	ALBERT G. HART	Aug. 30, "	Oct. 29, "	Resigned November 5, 1864.
Do.	JOHN HILL	Dec. 16, 1864	Dec. 16, 1864	Mustered out with regiment.
Ass't Surgeon	ALBERT G. HART	Sept. 5, 1861	Nov. 12, 1861	Promoted to Surgeon.
Do.	W. C. CATLIN	" 8, 1862	Sept. 22, 1862	Resigned February 18, 1863.
Do.	J. W. BUOH	May 11, 1863	March 11, 1863	Resigned January 5, 1864.
Do.	B. H. CHENEY	Sept. 12, 1862	April 10, "	Resigned August 22, 1864.
Do.	C. E. TUPPER	" 8, 1864	Sept. 8, 1864	Mustered out with regiment.
Chaplain	OSMAN A. LYMAN	Dec. 16, 1861		
Do.	HARVEY E. PROCTOR	March 1, 1862	June 12, 1862	Major in colored regiment.
Do.	JAMES H. WEBSTER	April 20, 1865	April 20, 1865	
Captain	Seth A. Bushnell	Aug. 2, 1861	Nov. 12, 1861	Resigned November 27, 1861.
Do.	Wm. R. Tollars	" 20, "	" 12, "	Mustered out; appointed Lt. Col. 105th O.V.I.
Do.	Daniel S. Leslie	Sept. 2, "	" 12, "	Resigned September 9, 1862.
Do.	Martin H. Hamblin	" 10, "	" 12, "	Resigned January 5, 1862.
Do.	J. H. Williston	" 16, "	" 12, "	Promoted to Major.
Do.	Aquila Wiley	" 19, "	" 12, "	Promoted to Major.
Do.	James H. Cole	" 27, "	" 12, "	Resigned March 17, 1862.
Do.	Frank D. Stone	" 30, "	" 12, "	Resigned January 22, 1862.
Do.	H. Alonzo Pease	Oct. 8, "	" 12, "	Resigned January 5, 1862.
Do.	Wm. Godsell	" 29, "	" 12, "	Resigned January 30, 1862.
Do.	Emerson Opdycke	Jan. 9, 1862	Jan. 9, 1862	Discharged for promotion Sept. 17, 1862.
Do.	Wm. W. Munn	" 9, "	" 8, "	Killed November 23, 1863.
Do.	Wm. J. Morgan	" 9, "	" 8, "	Resigned March 24, 1863.
Do.	John W. Steele	Feb. 3, "	Feb. 3, "	Appointed Major and A. D. C. by President.
Do.	James Horner	" 8, "	" 8, "	Resigned March 30, 1864.
Do.	Wm. Rymes	March 1, "	March 20, "	Resigned September 8, 1862.
Do.	Robert L. Kimberly	" 17, "	April 14, "	Promoted to Major.
Do.	James H. Cole	Aug. 26, "	Sept. 4, "	Resigned March 21, 1864.
Do.	Harvey E. Proctor	Sept. 9, "	Dec. 1, "	Major in colored regiment.
Do.	Ephraim S. Holloway	" 8, "	Oct. 9, "	Promoted to Major.
Do.	James McCleary	" 17, "	" 9, "	Promoted to Major.
Do.	Henry W. Johnson	Nov. 20, "	Dec. 1, "	Mustered out.
Do.	John D. Kirkendall	Jan. 1, 1863	April 22, 1863	Discharged, 1864.
Do.	John Mitchell	March 24, "	May 6, "	Declined.
Do.	Horatio P. Kile	" 21, "	" 24, "	Discharged, 1864.
Do.	Rufus B. Hardy	April 13, 1864	April 13, 1864	Resigned as 1st Lieutenant.
Do.	Wm. M. Bebee	" 13, "	" 13, "	Promoted by President.
Do.	Edwin B. Atwood	" 13, "	" 13, "	Mustered out with regiment.
Do.	Ferdinand D. Cobb	Oct. 12, "	Oct. 12, "	Declined.
Do.	Wm. Hansard	" 12, "	" 12, "	Deceased.
Do.	James N. Clark	Nov. 26, "	Nov. 26, "	Discharged as 1st Lieutenant.
Do.	James McMahan	" 26, "	" 26, "	Resigned February 24, 1865.
Do.	George Dodge	" 26, "	" 26, "	Resigned as 2d Lieutenant December 27, 1864.
Do.	Thomas H. Somers	" 26, "	" 26, "	Mustered out with regiment.
Do.	Ezra Dunham	" 26, "	" 26, "	Promoted to Major.
Do.	R. A. Gault	March 18, 1865	March 18, 1865	Mustered out with regiment.
Do.	Henry G. Delker	" 18, "	" 18, "	Mustered out with regiment.
Do.	Wilson S. Miller	" 18, "	" 18, "	Mustered out with regiment.
Do.	John P. Patterson	" 18, "	" 18, "	Mustered out with regiment.
Do.	Seward S. Palmer	" 18, "	" 18, "	Mustered out with regiment.
Do.	C. C. Huston	July 10, "	July 10, "	Mustered out with regiment as 1st Lieut.
Do.	Alonzo D. Hosmer	" 10, "	" 10, "	Mustered out with regiment.
Do.	James M. Kirkpatrick	Nov. 23, "	Nov. 23, "	Mustered out with regiment as R. Q. M.
1st Lieutenant	Emerson Opdycke	July 26, 1861	" 12, 1861	Promoted to Captain.
Do.	Wm. W. Munn	Aug. 20, "	" 12, "	Promoted to Captain.
Do.	Junius R. Sanford	" 23, "	" 12, "	Resigned January 13, 1862.
Do.	Wm. S. Chamberlin	" 24, "	" 12, "	Resigned December 10, 1861.
Do.	Wm. J. Morgan	" 27, "	" 12, "	Promoted to Captain.
Do.	Zelotus O. Sisson	Sept. 10, "	" 12, "	Resigned January 5, 1862.
Do.	John W. Steele	" 16, "	" 12, "	Promoted to Captain.
Do.	Wm. Rymes	" 16, "	" 12, "	Promoted to Captain.
Do.	Franklin E. Pancoast	" 19, "	" 12, "	Deceased.
Do.	Harvey E. Proctor	" 27, "	" 12, "	Promoted to Captain.
Do.	Ephraim S. Holloway	Oct. 10, "	" 12, "	Promoted to Captain.
Do.	James Horner	" 29, "	" 12, "	Promoted to Captain.
Do.	James McCleary	Jan. 9, 1862	Jan. 9, 1862	Promoted to Captain

RANK.	NAME.	DATE OF RANK.			COM. ISSUED.			REMARKS.
1st Lieutenant	Henry W. Johnson	Jan.	9,	1862	Jan.	9,	1862	Promoted to Captain.
Do.	John D. Kirkendall	"	9,	"	"	9,	"	Promoted to Captain.
Do.	Horatio P. Kile	"	9,	"	"	9,	"	Promoted to Captain.
Do.	Robert L. Kimberly	"	21,	"	"	21,	"	Promoted to Captain.
Do.	Rufus B. Hardy	"	21,	"	"	21,	"	Resigned April 5, 1861.
Do.	C. D. Gaylord	Feb.	3,	"	Feb.	3,	"	Resigned November 24, 1862
Do.	Harry Jones	"	8,	"	"	8,	"	Discharged October 1, 1862.
Do.	Albert McRoberts	March	1,	"	March	20,	"	Resigned May 24, 1862.
Do.	Wm. M. Bebee,	"	17,	"	April	10,	"	Resigned April 15, 1862.
Do.	Wm. M. Bebee	June	7,	"	June	7,	"	Promoted to Captain.
Do.	Calvin Hart	Sept.	9,	"	Dec.	1,	"	Killed December 31, 1862.
Do.	Edwin B. Atwood	"	8,	"	Oct.	9,	"	Promoted to Captain.
Do.	Elias A. Ford	"	17,	"	"	9,	"	Resigned May 29, 1863.
Do.	Truman C. Cutter	May	21,	"	"	13,	"	Revoked.
Do.	James B. Cleveland	"	21,	"	"	13,	"	Resigned March 21, 1863.
Do.	Ferdinand D. Cobb	"	21,	"	Dec.	1,	"	Declined.
Do.	Lester T. Patchin	Sept.	1,	"	"	1,	"	Died January 18, 1863.
Do.	Walter Blythe	Oct.	1,	"	"	1,	"	Mustered out July, 1865.
Do.	Samuel B. Asdell	Nov.	20,	"	"	1,	"	Died November, 1863.
Do.	Timothy D. Brown	"	24,	"	"	30,	"	Revoked.
Do.	John Mitchell	"	21,	"	Jan.	28,	1863	Resigned September 30, 1864.
Do.	Davis C. Fuller	Jan.	1,	1863	"	14,	"	Honorably discharged June 27, 1863.
Do.	Harlan P. Wolcott	"	1,	"	April	22,	"	Mustered out for promotion May 27, 1863.
Do.	Wm. Hansard	March	24,	"	"	22,	"	Promoted to Captain.
Do.	James N. Clark	"	21,	"	May	25,	"	Promoted to Captain.
Do.	Henry S. Dirlam	"	24,	"	April	28,	"	Killed November 23, 1863.
Do.	Wm. E. Boothe	May	29,	"	June	10,	"	Resigned September 22, 1864.
Do.	A. Whittlesey	April	13,	1864	April	13,	1864	Resigned November 26, 1864.
Do.	Wm. H. Pierce	June	27,	1863	Aug.	25,	1863	Mustered out January 27, 1865.
Do.	Lloyd Fisher	April	13,	1864	April	13,	1864	Resigned as 2d Lieutenant.
Do.	Charles W. Hills	"	13,	"	"	13,	"	Resigned as 2d Lieutenant October 24, 1864.
Do.	James McMahan	"	13,	"	"	13,	"	Promoted to Captain.
Do.	George Dodge	Oct.	12,	"	Oct.	12,	"	Promoted to Captain.
Do.	E. R. Eggleston	"	12,	"	"	12,	"	Resigned as 2d Lieutenant Sept. 30, 1864.
Do.	Thomas H. Somers	"	12,	"	"	12,	"	Promoted to Captain.
Do.	Ezra Dunham	"	12,	"	"	12,	"	Promoted to Captain.
Do.	R. A. Gault	Nov.	26,	"	Nov.	26,	"	Promoted to Captain.
Do.	James M. Kirkpatrick	"	26,	"	"	26,	"	Promoted to Captain; declined.
Do.	Henry G. Delker	"	26,	"	"	26,	"	Promoted to Captain.
Do.	Wilson S. Miller	"	26,	"	"	26,	"	Promoted to Captain.
Do.	John P. Patterson	"	26,	"	"	26,	"	Promoted to Captain.
Do.	Seward S. Palmer	"	26,	"	"	26,	"	Promoted to Captain.
Do.	George J. A. Thompon	"	26,	"	"	26,	"	Declined.
Do.	C. C. Huston	March	18,	1865	March	18,	1865	Promoted to Captain.
Do.	Alonzo D. Hosmer	"	18,	"	"	18,	"	Promoted to Captain.
Do.	S. P. Warrener	"	18,	"	"	18,	"	Mustered out with regiment.
Do.	Charles Hammond	"	18,	"	"	18,	"	Mustered out with regiment.
Do.	Philip A. Bowers	"	18,	"	"	18,	"	Mustered out with regiment.
Do.	Philo A. Beardsley	"	18,	"	"	18,	"	Mustered out with regiment.
Do.	John Cronkhite	April	20,	"	April	20,	"	Mustered out with regiment.
Do.	Peter Herriff	May	11,	"	May	11,	"	Mustered out with regiment.
Do.	Lester F. Miller	July	10,	"	July	10,	"	Mustered out with regiment as 2d Lieut.
Do.	Rush Jamison	"	10,	"	"	10,	"	Mustered out with regiment as 2d Lieut.
Do.	Leroy E. Bosley	Nov.	23,	"	Nov.	23,	"	Mustered out with regiment.
Do.	Henry J. Englebeck	"	23,	"	"	23,	"	Mustered out with regiment.
2d Lieutenant	James McCleary	Aug.	20,	1861	"	12,	1861	Promoted to 1st Lieutenant.
Do.	Henry W. Johnson	"	20,	"	"	12,	"	Promoted to 1st Lieutenant
Do.	John D. Kirkendall	Sept.	20,	"	"	12,	"	Promoted to 1st Lieutenant.
Do.	Horatio P. Kile	"	10,	"	"	12,	"	Promoted to 1st Lieutenant.
Do.	Rufus B. Hardy	"	19,	"	"	12,	"	Promoted to 1st Lieutenant.
Do.	Robert L. Kimberly	"	19,	"	"	12,	"	Promoted to 1st Lieutenant.
Do.	Harry W. Jones	"	30,	"	"	12,	"	Promoted to 1st Lieutenant.
Do.	Charles D. Gaylord	Oct.	1,	"	"	12,	"	Promoted to 1st Lieutenant.
Do.	Albert McRoberts	"	8,	"	"	12,	"	Promoted to 1st Lieutenant.
Do.	Wm. M. Bebee	"	29,	"	"	12,	"	Promoted to 1st Lieutenant.
Do.	Calvin Hart	Jan.	9,	1862	Jan.	9,	1862	Promoted to 1st Lieutenant.
Do.	Kenneth Maher	"	9,	"	"	9,	"	Resigned August 17, 1862.
Do.	Charles J. James	"	9,	"	"	9,	"	Resigned March 17, 1862.
Do.	Chauncey H. Talcott	"	21,	"	"	21,	"	Killed at Shiloh.
Do.	Edwin B. Atwood	"	21,	"	"	21,	"	Promoted to 1st Lieutenant Sept. 18, 1862.
Do.	Henry Coon	Feb.	3,	"	Feb.	3,	"	Resigned April 19, 1862.
Do.	Elias A. Ford	"	8,	"	"	8,	"	Promoted to 1st Lieutenant.
Do.	T. C. Cutter	"	8,	"	"	8,	"	Promoted; dismissed November 12, 1862.
Do.	James B. Cleveland	March	1,	"	March	20,	"	Resigned March 24, 1863.
Do.	Ferdinand D. Cobb	"	17,	"	April	10,	"	Promoted to 1st Lieutenant.
Do.	Lester T. Patchin	"	17,	"	"	10,	"	Promoted to 1st Lieutenant.
Do.	Walter Blythe	April	19,	"	June	12,	"	Promoted to 1st Lieutenant.
Do.	Samuel B. Asdell	"	7,	"	Oct.	9,	"	Promoted to 1st Lieutenant.
Do.	Timothy D. Brown	Sept.	5,	"	"	9,	"	Resigned December 21, 1862.
Do.	John Mitchell	March	24,	"	"	9,	"	Promoted to 1st Lieutenant.
Do.	Wm. Hansard	Sept.	8,	"	"	9,	"	Promoted to 1st Lieutenant.
Do.	James N. Clark	"	17,	"	"	9,	"	Promoted to 1st Lieutenant.
Do.	Wm. H. Pierce	March	24,	"	"	13,	"	Promoted to 1st Lieutenant.
Do.	Peter Hitchcock	Aug.	21,	"	"	13,	"	Resigned.
Do.	A. Whittlesey	Nov.	7,	"	Nov.	7,	"	Promoted to 1st Lieutenant.
Do	Davis C. Fuller	May	21,	"	Dec.	3,	"	Promoted to 1st Lieutenant.
Do.	Harlan P. Wolcott	Oct.	1,	"	"	30,	"	Promoted to 1st Lieutenant.
Do.	Wm. E. Boothe	Sept.	9,	"	Jan.	1,	1863	Promoted to 1st Lieutenant.
Do.	Lloyd Fisher	Nov.	20,	"	Dec.	31,	"	Honorably discharged May 27, 1864.
Do.	Charles W. Hills	Jan.	1,	1863	Jan.	14,	"	Promoted to 1st Lieutenant.
Do.	James McMahan	Dec.	21,	1862	"	28,	"	Promoted to 1st Lieutenant.
Do.	Frederick A. McRay	Nov.	24,	"	"	28,	"	Resigned November 22, 1864.
Do.	George Dodge	Jan.	1,	1863	April	8,	"	Promoted to 1st Lieutenant.
Do.	Wm. Watson	May	24,	"	"	8,	"	Killed November 25, 1863.
Do.	E. R. Eggleston	March	24,	"	May	25,	"	Promoted to 1st Lieutenant.
Do.	Thomas H. Somers	May	29,	"	June	10,	"	Promoted to 1st Lieutenant.
Do.	Ezra Dunham	June	27,	"	Aug.	25,	"	Promoted to 1st Lieutenant.
Do.	Peter Herriff	April	20,	1865	April	20,	1865	Promoted to 1st Lieutenant.
Do.	Rush Jamison	"	20,	"	"	20,	"	Promoted to 1st Lieutenant.
Do.	Lester F. Miller	May	11,	"	May	11,	"	Promoted to 1st Lieutenant.
Do.	James J. Mattock	Nov.	23,	"	Nov.	24,	"	Mustered out with regiment.

FORTY-FIRST OHIO VOLUNTEER INFANTRY.

IMMEDIATELY after the battle of Bull Run a number of the citizens of Cleveland, Ohio, set about raising a regiment, and the result of their labors was the Forty-First Ohio Volunteer Infantry, of which Captain William B. Hazen, Eighth United States Infantry, was appointed Colonel.

The camp of rendezvous was established near Cleveland, and the first companies that reported were from Trumbull and Geauga Counties. By the 1st of September a large number of men were in camp, and the work of instruction had commenced. Officers' school was instituted, and the strictest discipline enforced, and by the time the regiment was mustered as complete, on the 31st of October, 1861, the officers and men understood their duties well, and were quite proficient in drill. On the 6th of November the regiment moved by rail to Camp Dennison, where arms were supplied. Two hundred old muskets belonging to the State had sufficed for drill, but these were now exchanged for the "Greenwood Rifle," a weapon nearly useless, and soon discarded by the Government. After a week at Camp Dennison the regiment proceeded to Gallipolis, taking steamer at Cincinnati. A few raiding excursions from this point into Virginia was the only relief from daily drills, and in the latter part of the month the regiment was ordered to Louisville and reported to General Buell, then organizing the Army of the Ohio.

The regiment was encamped near the city limits, and by its neatness and precision attracted crowds of visitors at its guard-mountings and dress-parades. The Forty-First was a part of the Fifteenth Brigade, Nelson's division, and during the winter remained at Camp Wickliffe, Kentucky. Here the Forty-First was made the nucleus of a new brigade (the Nineteenth) to which was assigned the Forty-Sixth and Forty-Seventh Indiana, and the Sixth Kentucky, commanded by Colonel Hazen. On the 14th of February, 1862, Nelson's division marched for West Point, which was reached after a severe march of three days. Upon its arrival at West Point the command embarked on transports for the Tennessee River. Here the two Indiana regiments of Hazen's brigade were sent to Grant, but Nelson ascended the Ohio to the Cumberland and passed up that stream to Nashville, entering the city on the 27th of February, 1862. Here the Ninth Indiana was added to the brigade, and about the middle of March the regiment moved with the army to Savannah, on the Tennessee River, arriving within two miles of that point the Saturday preceding the battle of Pittsburg Landing. Heavy firing was heard on the morning of the 6th of April, and at one o'clock P. M., after being supplied with rations and ammunition, the regiment moved for Pittsburg Landing, one company (G) being left to guard the camp and garrison equipage. At five o'clock the troops arrived opposite the battle-field, and Hazen's brigade was the second to cross the river. The regiment lay that night on the field, in the driving rain, among the dead and wounded, and at daylight moved forward in its first engagement. The Forty-First was on the right of Nelson's division, and when the Rebels were discovered to be advancing Hazen's brigade was ordered to charge. The Forty-First was placed in the front line and advanced steadily through a dense thicket of undergrowth, and emerging in the more open ground was saluted with a murderous fire. The line still advanced, checked the approaching Rebels, drove them back beyond their fortifications, and captured their guns. The brigade, in turn, was driven back to its original line, where it re-formed without difficulty. Three officers and three men, who at different times carried the colors in the charge, were shot down, either killed or wounded, and of the three hundred and seventy-three who entered the engagement, one hundred and forty-one were either killed or wounded in half an hour. The night after the battle Hazen's brigade, as an outlying force, occupied the Tan Bark Road upon the left of the army. The regiment occupied a miserable camp on the field of battle, surrounded by the half buried bodies of men and horses, until the army moved on Corinth. The regiment suffered very much from exposure during the march and in the operations immediately following.

In the siege of Corinth the Forty-First was principally engaged in skirmishing, and after the evacuation marched about forty miles southward from Corinth, joined Pope's forces, then moved eastward to Iuka for supplies and clothing. These being obtained, the march was continued under scorching summer suns, and over roads thick with dust, to Tuscumbia, Florence, and Athens, Alabama. Here the regiment rested two weeks, and to a great extent recovered from the fatigues of the previous four months. In July the regiment was engaged in building a trestle-work on the railroad from Athens to Nashville, in the vicinity of Richland Creek, until it was ordered to Murfreesboro', and, with Hazen's brigade, constituted the garrison at that place. The Forty-First was with Buell's army on its march to Louisville, moving day after day over dusty roads, with short rations and water scarce, until nearly exhausted, ragged and dirty, it entered Louisville on the West Point Road, and sat down for a three days' rest. On the 2d of October the regiment, still in its old brigade and division, and in General Crittenden's corps, marched against Bragg. At the battle of Perryville the regiment was engaged in skirmishing. While Bragg was in position at Camp Dick Robinson, after the battle, Hazen's brigade drove the enemy from Danville, in a brisk running fight of an hour. Crittenden's corps pursued Bragg as far as Wild Cat Mountain, Hazen's brigade having the advance from Mount Vernon, and skirmishing daily with Wheeler's cavalry.

About the 20th of October the brigade commenced its return to Nashville, moving by way of Mount Vernon, Glasgow, Gallatin, and Silver Springs. On the 26th of December the army moved on Murfreesboro', the Forty-First marching on the Murfreesboro' and Nashville Turnpike. On the 27th Hazen's brigade was sent to Stewart's Creek to save a bridge on the Old Jefferson Road. The expedition was successful and returned to the Pike on the 29th, and moved to within two miles of Murfreesboro'. At midnight on the 30th the Forty-First took position in the first line, in an open cotton-field, and facing Cowan's House. A skirmish-line was advanced, and about an hour after daylight Hazen ordered his command forward. At the same time the sound of musketry on the right ceased, and the Rebels having driven back McCook, advanced to crush Crittenden. Hazen's brigade moved out of the cotton-field and received the Rebels with a steady fire, driving them back again and again. When all had fallen back upon the right and Hazen's brigade was attacked on the flank, and almost in the rear, the line slowly withdrew to the slight embankment of the railroad. This position was held during the day against the furious assaults of the Rebels. The Forty-First was afterward posted by General Rosecrans in person to guard a ford, and suffered severely from the enemy's batteries. On Friday the regiment was in reserve, but was moved across the river as the Rebels were sweeping over Van Cleve's division. They were met in their headlong pursuit and driven back almost without effort. A battery still maintained an annoying fire, and Colonel Hazen taking the Forty-First alone, advanced to within three hundred yards of the guns and delivered a volley by battalion. Not another shot was fired. The battery left the field, losing its Captain, several horses, and a caisson. Of the four hundred and ten officers and men of the Forty-First, the largest number it ever took into battle, one hundred and twelve were killed and wounded.

After encamping a day or two on the field the regiment moved to Readyville, about twelve miles from Murfreesboro', on the 10th of January, 1863. Here it enjoyed a season of comparative quiet, being engaged occasionally in excursions against Morgan's cavalry, and against Cluke's brigade, which occupied the town of Woodbury. The camp at Readyville was broken on the 24th of June, and the command moved for Tullahoma; but that place being evacuated before they reached it, the troops returned to Manchester and went into camp. On the 15th of August tents were struck and the regiment moved toward the Tennessee *via* Dunlap, against Chattanooga. After reaching the Valley of the Tennessee, twenty miles above Chattanooga,

Hazen's command was employed until the 9th of September in watching the right bank of the river, making demonstrations against the enemy, and preparing means to cross. At the date mentioned, information of the evacuation of Chattanooga and orders to cross the Tennessee were received. On the 8th the regiment made a night march to the mouth of the West Chickamauga Creek, and on the 10th crossed early in the morning and moved on by Tyner's Station, joining the division next day at Graysville. Ringgold was reached the same day, and the next morning the division moved toward Gordon's Mills. The Forty-First was in the advance, and near Ringgold encountered the Rebel cavalry, driving them back. On the road from Gordon's Mills, toward Lafayette, the enemy's cavalry was again encountered and routed by the Forty-First.

The morning of the 19th of September found the regiment again on the bank of the Chickamauga, near Gordon's Mills. About nine o'clock A. M. the battle commenced, and at one o'clock P. M. Palmer's division (in which the Forty-First was) went into the fight, attacking in echelon by brigades, Hazen's brigade being the first echelon. The regiment advanced rapidly over an open field to a strip of woods. After holding the position two hours, and during the time losing a hundred men, the regiment was withdrawn. Scarcely had they replenished their cartridge-boxes when the brigade was moved to the assistance of General Van Cleve. The brigade formed the second line, and when the first gave way was vigorously assailed. The Forty-First occupied the right of the line, and was rapidly becoming enveloped; and though it kept its front clear by well-directed volleys, it was compelled to retreat while loading to avoid being surrounded. It fell back a hundred yards at a time, until reaching a hill a stand was made, some artillery placed in position, and the Rebel advance checked. The next morning the regiment was lying behind a very slight but very useful barricade of logs and rails, and during the day several fierce assaults were repulsed with little or no loss. There was no communication with the right of the army under General Thomas, and the interval of about a mile which separated it from the left was filled with Rebel sharp-shooters. Ammunition was becoming so scarce that the cartridge-boxes of the killed and wounded were rifled greedily, and all the supplies not captured were with Thomas. General Hazen volunteered to take his brigade across the unexplored interval, which he did successfully, and joined General Thomas in time to participate in the last assault of the day. The Rebels were advancing on the left of Thomas's line, when Hazen formed his brigade in column by regiments, and each advanced, one after the other, and delivered its volley. The dense masses of the enemy reeled and fell back. This was the last fighting on Chickamauga. It was with much sadness that the Forty-First marched off just after dark to Rossville. The next day was spent on Mission Ridge, and the following night the regiment retired to Chattanooga.

In the reorganization of the army, Hazen's brigade was composed of the First, Forty-First, and Ninety-Third Ohio, Fifth Kentucky and Sixth Indiana, and was assigned to the Fourth Army Corps, Major-General Gordon Granger commanding. At three o'clock in the morning of October 27th, fifty-two pontoons, bearing Hazen's brigade, pushed out silently from Chattanooga and floated down the river. In half an hour the leading pontoons were passing in front of the enemy's pickets on the bank, a hundred feet above. The conversation of the Rebels could be distinctly heard, but their attention was not once directed to the twelve hundred silent enemies floating past within pistol-shot. Just as the first pontoon arrived opposite its landing it was discovered; but the landing was effected, the pickets driven in, and the hill gained. When the morning haze cleared away the Rebels on Lookout saw the hills beneath them, commanding two roads to Bridgeport, covered with blue-coats, in a position from which they could not be driven, with a pontoon bridge to connect them with Chattanooga almost completed. At noon on the 23d of November the brigade was ordered to fall in for a reconnoissance. The brigade advanced briskly, driving the enemy's skirmishers into a dense undergrowth on a small ridge between Chattanooga and Mission Ridge. The line followed and received a heavy fire. Nothing could be seen, but it was too hot a fire to bear quietly. Colonel Wiley ordered the regiment to charge, and orders from Hazen at the same time directed the taking of the line on the hill. The Forty-First delivered a volley, trusting to fortune for its effect, then dashed forward through the thicket, through the balls, up to the Rebel works, and into the Rebel works, capturing the colors of the Twenty-Eighth Alabama Regiment. In this, its severest engagement, the Forty-First was associated with the Ninety-Third Ohio, which shared fully the danger and honor of the fight. The position was held without trouble, and was known as Orchard Knob. Soon after the fight, Generals Grant, Thomas, and others passed along the new line, when Thomas, looking at the ground within fifty paces of the Rebel works, where the fight had been fiercest, and where lay the horses of Colonel Wiley and Lieutenant-Colonel Kimberly, called for the officers of the regiment, and said to Colonel Wiley: "Colonel, I want you to express to your men my thanks for their splendid conduct this afternoon. It was a gallant thing, Colonel—*a very gallant thing.*" That from General Thomas was better than an hour's speech from any other man.

On the 25th Hazen's brigade moved across the valley from Orchard Knob to Mission Ridge, under a heavy artillery fire; and, at the foot of the ridge, a dash was made and the enemy's works captured. The troops were here exposed to canister and musketry, and to remain was impossible; so they again advanced up the steep hill, swept by an enfilading fire of artillery; up they went, and, when near the top, the fire of the Forty-First was directed upon the batteries on the right. The Rebels retired, and, with a cheer, the line occupied the works on the ridge. A squad of the Forty-First seized a battery almost before the Rebels were away from it, turned it to the right, and discharged it directly along the summit of the ridge, where the enemy in front of Newton's division still stubbornly held out; and, as the shells went skimming along in front of and among them, the Rebels turned and fled. Eighteen captured pieces of artillery graced General Hazen's head-quarters that night, of which the Forty-First and Ninety-Third could fairly claim six as their trophies, while the former also captured a battle-flag. The losses were severe. One hundred and fifteen of the Forty-First, most of them in the fight of the 23d, had fallen.

After resting scarcely long enough to bury the dead, the regiment moved with its corps for Knoxville. Supplies had been very scarce, and, before the march was half accomplished, two-thirds of the men were walking over the frozen ground barefooted; but, with their feet wrapped up in sheep-skins and cow-hides, they journeyed on, and finally reached Clinch Mountain, twenty miles above Knoxville. Here the regiment re-enlisted, one hundred and eighty out of one hundred and eight-eight becoming veterans, and on the 5th of January, 1864, started for Chattanooga, and reached Cleveland, Ohio, on the 2d of February.

With nearly a hundred recruits, the regiment joined its division, in East Tennessee, on the 26th of March, and was placed in a battalion with the First Ohio, Lieutenant-Colonel Kimberly commanding the battalion.

At Rocky Face Ridge the battalion was complimented for its steadiness under a galling fire, and at Resaca it gained a crest within seventy-five yards of the enemy's main line, and effectually prevented the use of his artillery.

After Johnston retreated from Resaca the battalion drove the enemy from Calhoun to Adairsville in a day's march, keeping the road cleared so as not to delay the column, though it was compelled to maintain a skirmish-line the entire distance. On the 26th of May the regiment went into position before Dallas, but, on the 27th, was withdrawn, and formed part of an expedition to attack the enemy's right. In the afternoon the enemy's position was found, and Kimberly's battalion moved to the top of a ridge covered with underbrush, and there received a murderous volley from the enemy. A brave attempt was made to charge through the brush, but the fire was too severe. Holding the position, and being slightly sheltered by logs, the battalion waited for the second line to come up; but, after remaining forty-five minutes, and no line arriving, being exposed to an enfilading fire of artillery and musketry, the battalion withdrew. The Forty-First lost one hundred and eight men out of two hundred and sixty, one company losing twenty out of twenty-two, and another nine out of eleven. The regiment was again engaged after the evacuation of Johnston's line at Piney Top Mountain, near Kenesaw. The enemy was found strongly posted in a log farm-house and out-buildings, and the Forty-First was ordered to dislodge them, which it did by a rapid charge. On the 6th of July the Chattahoochie River was reached. The battalion struck the river four miles above the main column, endeavoring to cut off some Rebel cavalry. The skirmish-line pushed them so closely that, to save the pontoon bridge, the last man cut it loose, and it swung round to the Rebel side of the river. In this affair the Forty-First lost two men killed and five wounded.

During subsequent movements the regiment was engaged in the passage of Peach Tree Creek, and in various other minor encounters.

On the 28th of July the command being then in front of the enemy's lines at Atlanta, five companies of the Forty-First deployed as skirmishers, dashed upon the Rebel lines, captured a number, and routed the rest completely. This attack was made through a marshy ravine, over an open field, and against a line strongly posted; but there was nothing in the way of a sharp, determined dash which, as skirmishers, the regiment would not attempt. The regiment, though frequently under fire, was not actively engaged during the remainder of the siege, and after the evacuation it encamped east of the city for rest and recuperation. From three hundred and thirty-one men at the beginning of the campaign, the regiment had dwindled to ninety-nine, one hundred and fifty having fallen in fight, and over eighty having succumbed to disease.

When Hood moved to Sherman's rear the regiment marched in pursuit, and when that was abandoned returned to Chattanooga, and embarked in the cars for Athens, Alabama. Here one hundred and sixty-four drafted men and substitutes joined the regiment. Toward the close of November the regiment was at Columbia, and marched from there to Franklin. At Franklin the regiment was not engaged, its division being in reserve, and holding the passage of the river on the morning of the retreat, until the army crossed. Nashville was reached the same day, and here supplies were received and an opportunity for rest afforded.

On the morning of the 15th of December Thomas commenced his movement against Hood. The Forty-First, as it could be efficiently controlled as skirmishers, was designated to attack the enemy's line about a brick house to the right of the Granny White Pike. The regiment, breaking cover of a stone wall, dashed across the intervening field of three hundred yards at a run, and, despite a rattling fire of musketry, speedily mounted the breastworks, drove the enemy to the second line, and captured two pieces of artillery and a number of prisoners. On the morning of the 16th the command moved up to the Rebels' position on Overton Knob. The Forty-First was again selected to cover, as skirmishers, the attacking column, with orders to go as far as possible without the aid of the line of battle. The Rebel works were covered by a strong abattis, at thirty yards' distance, and the regiment approached to within seventy-five yards of this before the enemy appeared. The fire was not severe, and the line advanced at the double-quick. At the same instant two Rebel lines moved into the works and opened a deadly fire. The abattis was, in many places, utterly impassable, and not easily removed; but several of the skirmishers penetrated it in weak places, and private Kleinhaus, of company F, actually leaped the works full in the face of the Rebel lines. Colonel Kimberly, seeing the line of battle could not advance to the support of the skirmishers, withdrew his men. Several of them, however, being inside the abattis, were unable to retreat; and, getting under cover, remained until the enemy, being broken on the right, withdrew. Then they rapidly advanced, captured some prisoners, four pieces of artillery, and two battle-flags. The artillery was marked with the name of the regiment, by order of the Chief of Artillery of the army; and the captors of the flags, Sergeant Garnett, of company G, and private Holcomb, of company A, were afterward sent to Washington with their trophies, by order of General Thomas. The regiment participated in the pursuit of Hood, and finally rested at Huntsville, Alabama.

In June, 1865, the corps was ordered to Texas, and embarked at Nashville, to descend the river. Near Cairo the steamer collided with a gun-boat, and sunk in a few minutes, with all the regimental and company papers and most of the personal property of the officers and men. Fortunately no lives were lost. In Texas the regiment was stationed near San Antonio until November, when it was ordered to be mustered out. It reached Columbus, Ohio, about the middle of the month, and finally was discharged on the 26th of November, 1865, after four years and one month's service.

42d REGIMENT OHIO VOLUNTEER INFANTRY.

ROSTER, THREE YEARS' SERVICE.

RANK.	NAME.	DATE OF RANK.	COM. ISSUED.	REMARKS.
Colonel	JAMES A. GARFIELD	Aug. 14, 1861	Dec. 14, 1861	Appointed Brigadier-General volunteers.
Do.	LIONEL A. SHELDON	March 14, 1862	March 28, 1862	Mustered out.
Lt. Colonel	LIONEL A. SHELDON	Sept. 6, 1861	Dec. 14, 1861	Promoted to Colonel.
Do.	DON A. PARDEE	March 14, 1862	March 28, 1862	Mustered out October 26, 1864.
Major	DON A. PARDEE	Sept. 5, 1861	Dec. 14, 1861	Promoted to Lieutenant-Colonel.
Do.	FREDERICK A. WILLIAMS	March 14, 1862	March 28, 1862	Died July 25, 1862.
Do.	WM. H. WILLIAMS	July 25, "	Oct. 6, "	Mustered out.
Surgeon	JOEL POMERENE	Sept. 7, 1861	Dec. 14, 1861	Resigned July 26, 1863.
Ass't Surgeon	JOSEPH W. HARMON	Oct. 3, "	" 14, "	Resigned November 9, 1862.
Do.	J. N. MINER	Aug. 26, 1862	Aug. 27, 1862	Died December 13, 1862.
Do.	JOSEPH KALB	March 10, 1863	March 10, 1863	Resigned August 27, 1861.
Do.	JOHN W. DRISCOLL	" 21, "	" 30, "	Resigned July 1, 1863.
Do.	H. E. WARNER	Nov. 10, "	Nov. 10, "	Mustered out.
Chaplain	JEFFERSON H. JONES	" 21, 1861	Dec. 14, 1861	Resigned April 18, 1863.
Captain	T. C. Bushnell	Aug. 27, "	March 6, 1862	Resigned October 22, 1862.
Do.	Wm. H. Williams	Sept. 3, "	" 6, "	Promoted to Major July 25, 1862.
Do.	Chas. H. Howe	" 15, "	" 6, "	Resigned May 27, 1863.
Do.	James H. Riggs	" 17, "	" 6, "	Resigned December 31, 1863.
Do.	Chas. P. Jewett	" 19, "	" 6, "	Resigned July 11, 1863.
Do.	Frederick A. Williams	" 20, "	" 6, "	Promoted to Major.
Do.	Andrew Gardner, jr.	" 28, "	" 6, "	Resigned January 28, 1863.
Do.	Seth M. Barber	Nov. 2, "	" 6, "	Honorably discharged March 6, 1864.
Do.	Horace H. Willard	" 18, "	" 6, "	Honorably discharged January 3, 1864.
Do.	Rollin B. Lynch	" 26, "	" 6, "	Resigned March 3, 1863.
Do.	Wm. N. Starr	March 14, "	April 14, "	Revoked.
Do.	Wm. W. Olds	" 14, "	" 14, "	Killed May 1, 1863.
Do.	Horace Potter	July 25, "	Oct. 6, "	Mustered out September 30, 1865.
Do.	Wm. N. Starr	Oct. 22, "	Nov. 17, "	Mustered out September 30, 1865.
Do.	Melvin H. Benham	March 3, "	April 22, 1863	Mustered out.
Do.	Thomas L. Hutchins	Jan. 28, 1863	" 9, "	Mustered out.
Do.	Edward B. Campbell	May 27, "	June 26, "	Transf'd to and must'd out with 96th O. V. I.
Do.	J. S. Ross	" 1, "	" 10, "	Mustered out September 30, 1864.
Do.	Porter S. Foskett	July 11, "	" 10, "	Honorably discharged April 30, 1864.
Do.	David N. Prince	Jan. 1, 1864	Jan. 29, 1864	Mustered out.
Do.	John B. Helman	May 9, "	May 9, "	Mustered out.
Do.	George K. Pardee	" 25, "	" 25, "	Resigned September 24, 1864.
Do.	Alvin J. Dyer	July 25, "	July 25, "	Mustered out.
1st Lieutenant	Wm. W. Olds	Aug. 14, 1861	Aug. 30, 1861	Promoted to Captain.
Do.	Joseph D. Stubbs	" 16, "	Dec. 14, "	App. A. Q. M. of vols.; must'd out Nov. 13, '62.
Do.	Wm. N. Starr	" 31, "	" 14, "	Promoted to Captain.
Do.	Horace Potter	Sept. 3, "	" 14, "	Promoted to Captain.
Do.	George F. Brady	" 15, "	" 14, "	Resigned March 27, 1862.
Do.	Herman Suebedissen	" 17, "	" 14, "	Resigned April 3, 1862.
Do.	David Scott	" 17, "	" 14, "	Resigned January 31, 1862.
Do.	Howard S. Bates	" 20, "	" 14, "	Resigned February 8, 1862.
Do.	Thomas L. Hutchins	" 28, "	" 14, "	Promoted to Captain.
Do.	Orlando C. Risdon	Oct. 7, "	" 14, "	Transferred to colored regiment.
Do.	Wm. S. Spencer	Nov. 9, "	" 14, "	Resigned June 11, 1862.
Do.	Timothy G. Loomis	" 12, "	" 14, "	Resigned June 5, 1862.
Do.	Marion Knight	Feb. 28, 1862	Feb. 28, 1862	Resigned June 6, 1862.
Do.	Edwin D. Saunders	March 17, "	March 17, "	Promoted to regular army.
Do.	John R. Helman	" 14, "	April 14, "	Revoked.
Do.	Melvin H. Benham	" 27, "	" 14, "	Promoted to Captain.
Do.	Wm. H. Clapp	" 14, "	May 5, "	Appointed Capt. A. A. G. May 15, 1863.
Do.	Edward B. Campbell	June 6, "	June 24, "	Promoted to Captain.
Do.	David N. Prince	" 5, "	Oct. 6, "	Promoted to Captain.
Do.	John B. Helman	" 11, "	" 24, "	Promoted to Captain.
Do.	J. S. Ross	July 25, "	" 6, "	Promoted to Captain.
Do.	Porter S. Foskett	" 25, "	" 6, "	Promoted to Captain.
Do.	Chas. B. Howk	Oct. 22, "	Nov. 17, "	Resigned October 23, 1863.
Do.	Alvin J. Dyer	Nov. 13, "	Dec. 31, "	Promoted to Captain.
Do.	George K. Pardee	Jan. 28, 1863	April 9, 1863	Promoted to Captain.
Do.	Chas. P. Goodwin	March 3, "	" 22, "	Resigned August 5, 1863.
Do.	James T. Henry	May 27, "	June 26, "	Resigned June 29, 1861.
Do.	Chas. E. Henry	" 1, "	" 10, "	Mustered out.
Do.	Wm. L. Wilson	" 28, "	" 10, "	Resigned September 21, 1864.
Do.	Henry C. Jennings	Dec. 16, "	Jan. 28, "	Resigned as 2d Lieutenant.
Do.	Albert L. Bowman	July 11, "	Aug. 10, "	Mustered out.
Do.	Joseph D. Moody	Feb. 26, 1864	Feb. 26, 1864	Mustered out.
Do.	Augustus D. Hubbell	" 26, "	" 26, "	Mustered out.
Do.	John F. Flynn	" 26, "	" 26, "	Mustered out.
Do.	Peter Miller	Oct. 23, 1863	Dec. 31, 1863	Mustered out.
Do.	Henry A. Howard	May 9, 1864	May 9, 1864	Mustered out September 30, 1864.
Do.	Matthew Rodecker	" 9, "	" 9, "	Resigned September 24, 1864.
Do.	Calvin Pierce	" 25, "	" 25, "	Mustered out.
Do.	Horace S. Clark	July 25, "	July 25, "	Mustered out.
Do.	Lester K. Lewis	" 25, "	" 25, "	Mustered out.
2d Lieutenant	John R. Helman	Sept. 4, 1861	Dec. 14, 1861	Promoted to 1st Lieutenant June 11, 1862.
Do.	Wm. L. Wilson	" 17, "	" 14, "	Promoted to 1st Lieutenant.
Do.	Andrew J. Stone	" 19, "	" 14, "	Died.
Do.	Wm. H. Clapp	" 20, "	" 14, "	Promoted to 1st Lieutenant.
Do.	Joseph Lackey	" 22, "	" 14, "	Resigned July 5, 1862.
Do.	Horace H. Willard	Oct. 4, "	" 14, "	Promoted to 1st Lieutenant.
Do.	Samuel H. Cole	" 5, "	" 14, "	Resigned May 9, 1862.
Do.	Melvin H. Benham	" 10, "	" 14, "	Promoted to 1st Lieutenant.

RANK.	NAME.	DATE OF RANK.	COM. ISSUED.	REMARKS.
2d Lieutenant	Edwin C. Leach	Nov. 2, 1861	Dec. 14, 1861	Resigned June 5, 1862.
Do.	Porter H. Foskett	" 22, "	" 14, "	Promoted to 1st Lieutenant.
Do.	Marion Knight	" 23, "	" 14, "	Promoted to 1st Lieutenant.
Do.	Wm. L. Steward	Feb. 28, 1862	March 20, 1862	Resigned November 13, 1862.
Do.	Edward B. Campbell	March 20, "	" 20, "	Promoted to 1st Lieutenant.
Do.	Henry C. Jennings	" 9, "	April 11, "	Resigned.
Do.	Chas. P. Goodwin	" 27, "	" 11, "	Promoted to 1st Lieutenant.
Do.	J. S. Ross	" 11, "	May 7, "	Promoted to 1st Lieutenant.
Do.	John F. Robinson	June 6, "	June 24, "	Transferred to colored regiment.
Do.	Peter Miller	July 5, "	Sept. 8, "	Promoted to 1st Lieutenant.
Do.	Calvin C. Marquis	" 25, "	Oct. 6, "	Declined.
Do.	Chas. E. Henry	" 25, "	" 6, "	Promoted to 1st Lieutenant.
Do.	Chas. B. Howk	June 11, "	" 6, "	Promoted to 1st Lieutenant.
Do.	James T. Henry	" 11, "	" 6, "	Promoted to 1st Lieutenant.
Do.	James S. Rowlby	" 5, "	" 6, "	Resigned January 9, 1864.
Do.	George K. Pardee	Oct. 22, "	Nov. 17, "	Promoted to 1st Lieutenant.
Do.	Joseph D. Moody	July 25, "	" 17, "	Promoted to 1st Lieutenant.
Do.	Augustus B. Hubbell	Nov 13, "	Dec. 24, "	Promoted to 1st Lieutenant.
Do.	Albert L. Bowman	Jan. 28, 1863	April 2, 1863	Promoted to 1st Lieutenant.
Do.	Henry Howard	March 3, "	" 22, "	Promoted to 1st Lieutenant.
Do.	John Flynn	April 1, "	July 20, "	Promoted to 1st Lieutenant.
Do.	Matthew Rodecker	May 1, "	June 10, "	Promoted to 1st Lieutenant.
Do.	Calvin Pierce	" 28, "	" 10, "	Promoted to 1st Lieutenant.
Do.	Horace S. Clark	" 25, 1864	May 25, 1864	Promoted to 1st Lieutenant.

FORTY-SECOND OHIO VOLUNTEER INFANTRY.

THE FORTY-SECOND OHIO was organized at Camp Chase, near Columbus, Ohio. Companies A, B, C, and D were mustered into the service September 25, 1861; company E, October 30th; company F, November 12th; and companies G, H, I, and K, November 26th, at which time the organization was completed.

On the 14th of December orders were received to take the field, and on the following day it moved by railroad to Cincinnati, and thence by steamer up the Ohio River to Catlettsburg, Kentucky, where it arrived the morning of December 17th. The regiment, together with the Fourteenth Kentucky Infantry and McLaughlin's squadron of Ohio cavalry, proceeded to Louisa, Kentucky, and moved forward to Green Creek. The whole command advanced December 31st, and by the night of January 7, 1862, encamped within three miles of Paintville, and the next morning five companies, under command of Lieutenant-Colonel Sheldon, took possession of the village. On the evening of the same day Garfield took the Forty-Second and two companies of the Fourteenth Kentucky, and advanced against Marshall's fortified position, about three miles south of the village of Paintville. The infantry reached the works about nine o'clock P. M. found them evacuated, and everything valuable either carried away or destroyed; and, after an all-night march, returned to Paintville a little after daylight.

About noon on the 9th Colonel Garfield, with eleven hundred infantry from the Forty-Second Ohio and other regiments, and about six hundred cavalry, started in pursuit of Marshall, and about nine o'clock in the evening the advance was fired upon by Marshall's pickets, on the summit of Abbott's Hill. Garfield took possession of the hill, bivouacked for the night, and the next morning continued the pursuit, overtaking the enemy at the forks of Middle Creek, three miles south-west of Prestonburg. Marshall's force consisted of about three thousand five hundred men, infantry and cavalry, with three pieces of artillery. Major Pardee, with four hundred men, was sent across Middle Creek to attack Marshall directly in front, and Lieutenant-Colonel Monroe (Twenty-Second Kentucky) was directed to attack on Marshall's right flank. The fight at once opened with considerable spirit, and Pardee and Monroe became hotly engaged with a force four times as large as their own. They held their ground with great obstinacy and bravery until re-enforcements reached the field, when the enemy commenced to fall back. The National forces slept upon their arms, and at early dawn a reconnoissance disclosed the fact that Marshall had burned his stores and had fled, leaving a portion of his dead upon the field.

On the 11th the command took possession of Prestonburg, Kentucky, and on the 12th returned to Paintville, and went into camp until the first of February, when the force moved by boats up the Big Sandy to Pikeville. On the 14th of March the regiment, with other troops, took possession of Pound Gap and destroyed the enemy's camp and stores. The regiment was engaged in several other expeditions against the guerrillas. The arduous nature of the campaign, the exceedingly disagreeable weather, and the want of supplies, were disastrous to the health of the troops, and some eighty-five of the Forty-Second died of disease.

On the 18th of March the regiment received orders to proceed to Louisville, where it arrived and went into camp on the 29th. The Forty-Second was attached to Brigadier-General George W. Morgan's command, and moved by rail to Lexington, Kentucky, and from there marched to Cumberland Ford, with three hundred and fourteen men for duty. At Cumberland Ford the regiment was brigaded with the Sixteenth Ohio, the Fourteenth and Twenty-Second Kentucky, Colonel John F. De Courcey (Sixteenth Ohio) commanding. On the 15th of May the brigade crossed the Cumberland River and encamped at the junction of the roads leading to Cumberland Gap and Rogers's Gap. On the 5th of June Morgan's entire command took up the line of march to cross the mountains into the rear of Cumberland Gap. Moving by way of Rogers's Gap into Powell's Valley, the advance was unopposed until it reached Rogers's Gap, when a series of skirmishes ensued, nearly all of them between the Forty-Second and the enemy. At one o'clock A. M., June 18th, Morgan moved against a force at Big Spring, the Forty-Second leading, but the enemy fled, and Morgan moved toward Cumberland Gap, reaching it at five P. M., and found it had been evacuated a few hours before. The Forty-Second at once moved into the Gap, and was the first regiment to plant its flag on this stronghold. The regiment camped on the extreme right, near Yellow Creek, performing heavy picket-duty, and being frequently on expeditions. It skirmished at Baptist's Gap, at Tazewell, and on the 5th of August engaged and held back the advance of the army with which Kirby Smith invaded Kentucky.

On the morning of the 6th a heavy force attacked the brigade two miles beyond Tazewell, and it fell back leisurely to Cumberland Gap. Company E, of the Forty-Second, escorted a forage-train, and was nearly surrounded, but by shrewdness and gallantry it saved the train and escaped without loss. The Gap was finally evacuated, and the forces fell back through Manchester, crossed the Kentucky River at Proctor, and crossed the Ohio at Greenupsburg. The regiment acted as rear-guard during the march. When the Forty-Second left the Gap it numbered seven hundred and fifty men, and while on the march there were issued to it two hundred and seventy-five pounds of flour, four hundred pounds of bacon, and two rations of fresh pork; the rest of the food consisted of corn, grated down on tin plates and cooked upon them. The distance marched was two hundred and fifty miles, the weather was very dry, and the men suffered for water. They were without shoes, and their clothing was ragged and filthy. The Forty-Second lost but one man on the retreat from all causes, and it was the only regiment that brought through its knapsacks and blankets. These proved of great service, as the men were compelled to camp at Portland, Jackson County, Ohio, two weeks before clothing, camp, and garrison equipage could be furnished them.

On the 21st of October the regiment proceeded to Gallipolis, and thence up the Kanawha to Charlestown, Virginia. It returned to the Ohio November 10th, and embarked for Cincinnati, and moved from there down to Memphis, encamping near the city on the 28th. While at Portland, Ohio, the regiment received one hundred and three recruits, and at Memphis it received sixty-five more. It had from time to time obtained a few, so that the whole number reached two hundred or more, and the regiment could turn out on parade nearly nine hundred men. General Morgan's division was reorganized, and was denominated the Ninth Division, Thirteenth Army Corps.

On the 20th of December the Forty-Second, with other troops, under General W. T. Sherman, embarked at Memphis, and, proceeding down the river, landed at Johnston's plantation on the Yazoo. The Forty-Second led the advance against the defenses of Vicksburg on the 27th of December, and skirmished with the enemy until dark. The next morning the regiment resumed the attack against the enemy thrown out beyond their works, and protected in front by timber and lagoon. The regiment continued to advance, without driving the enemy, until Colonel Pardee ordered a charge, which was made with great spirit, and resulted in gaining possession of the woods and driving the Rebels into their works. About nine o'clock A. M. on the 29th a charge was made, the Forty-Second being on the extreme right of the assaulting column. The storm of shot and shell was terrific, but the regiment maintained its organization, and came off the field in good order. During the remainder of the engagement the regiment held its position in line. The army finally retired, re-embarked, and moved to Milliken's Bend.

On the 4th of January, 1863, the fleet steamed up the river to White River, and up it through a "cut-off" into the Arkansas, and up it to Arkansas Post, where the troops disembarked and invested Fort Hindman, De Courcey's brigade being held in reserve. After four hours of severe cannonading the infantry advanced, and, several unsuccessful charges having been made, De Courcey's brigade was ordered to join Sheldon's brigade in assaulting Fort Hindman. The Forty-Second led the advance, and, soon after getting fairly under fire, the enemy surrendered. Seven thousand prisoners, all the guns and small arms, and a large quantity of stores were captured.

In a few days the troops re-embarked, and on the 24th of January landed at Young's Point. Here the Forty-Second was allotted its proportion of the work on the canal, and was allowed four days to perform it; but, so vigorous was the regiment in the discharge of its duties, that it accomplished its work in seventeen hours. On the 10th of March the division moved to Milliken's Bend, where it was soon joined by the remainder of the corps. Here supplies were received, and four weeks were spent in drilling and fitting for the coming campaign.

The Ninth Division took the advance in the movement toward the rear of Vicksburg. The troops moved to Richmond, Madison Parish, Louisiana, and embarked about thirty miles below Vicksburg, on transports which had run the batteries, and moved down to Grand Gulf. Here they debarked, crossed the point, again took transports, moved down to Bruinsburg, and debarked on the Mississippi side of the river. The division advanced against Port Gibson, and, at twelve o'clock at night, had a slight engagement with the enemy. The whole corps moved up and bivouacked near Magnolia Church. At daybreak the troops were under arms and advancing. The Ninth Division, taking the left of the line, speedily engaged the enemy, and continued in action until four o'clock P. M. The Forty-Second was placed under a heavy fire of artillery at seven o'clock A. M., and continued there until nine o'clock A. M., when it was advanced to the center of the division line and ordered to charge. The order was obeyed with spirit and courage, but, meeting with unexpected obstacles, the division commander ordered it to retire. It continued skirmishing until twelve o'clock, when it joined the Sixteenth Ohio and Twenty-Second Kentucky, and charged a strong position held by the Rebels, but, after a brave effort, failed to dislodge them, and was again ordered to retire. It was moved to the right, and, about three o'clock P. M., made a third charge, and, in conjunction with the Forty-Ninth Indiana and One Hundred and Fourteenth Ohio, carried the enemy's position. In this engagement the regiment sustained a heavier loss than any other one in the corps.

On the 2d of May the corps advanced and took possession of Port Gibson, and moved on by way of Champion Hills and Big Black Bridge to the rear of Vicksburg. The regiment was engaged both at Champion Hills and Big Black, but the loss was comparatively slight. It participated in the charges on the works at Vicksburg on the 19th and 22d of May, the Ninth Division holding an advanced position in the Thirteenth Corps. In these assaults the regiment lost heavily, especially on the 22d. On the 10th of June the Forty-Second was moved toward the right in support of some batteries, where it remained until June 27th, when it moved to Big Black Bridge. After the surrender of Vicksburg the regiment marched to Jackson and participated in the reduction of that place, and then returned to Vicksburg, where it remained until ordered to the Department of the Gulf.

The regiment arrived at Carrollton, near New Orleans, August 15th, and, on the 6th of September, started on the Western Louisiana campaign. At Brashear City the Ninth and Twelfth Divisions of the Thirteenth Corps were consolidated, and Brigadier-General Lawler was assigned to the command of the brigade. The brigade moved up to Vermillion Bayou, and from there to Opelousas, where it remained a few days, and returned with the corps to Berwick Bay. On the 18th of November the brigade crossed to Brashear City, with the intention of going into Texas, but the following night it was ordered to Thibodeaux, and proceeded thence by way of Donaldsonville to Plaquemine, arriving November 21st. The regiment remained here during the winter, and on the 24th of March, 1864, moved to Baton Rouge, and was detailed as provost-guard for the city. On the 1st of May the Forty-Second, with other troops, marched on an expedition toward Clinton, Louisiana, engaged an equal force of the enemy for seven hours, and at last drove the Rebels five miles through canebrakes and over the Comite River. On this expedition the infantry marched fifty-four miles in eighteen hours. The regiment embarked on boats, May 16th, and reported to General Canby at the mouth of Red River, and moved up to Simmsport, on the Atchafalaya River, where a provisional brigade was formed, comprising the Seventh Kentucky, Twenty-Second and Twenty-Third Iowa, Thirty-Seventh Illinois, and Forty-Second Ohio, Colonel Sheldon commanding. Meeting General Banks's army here, the regiment marched to Morganza, Louisiana, with it. The regiment was on several expeditions and in one slight skirmish. Here the Forty-Second was attached to the First Brigade, Third Division, Nineteenth Corps. Here, also, a test-drill was held in the Nineteenth Corps, and company E, of the Forty-Second Ohio, won the first prize.

The brigade moved up the Mississippi, July 15th, and landed at the mouth of White River. While lying here a detachment of the regiment crossed into Mississippi, marched fifteen miles, captured two small parties of Rebels, and returned within ten hours. The brigade moved up to St. Charles, on White River, and, after working ten days on the fortifications, made an expedition of some sixty miles into the country. On the 6th of August the brigade returned to Morganza, and on the 6th of September moved to the mouth of White River again. Companies A, B, C, and D were ordered to Camp Chase, Ohio, September 15th, and were mustered out September 30th. The remaining six companies were ordered to Duvall's Bluff, Arkansas. Companies E and F were mustered out November 25th, and the other four companies were mustered out December 2, 1864. One hundred and one men remained, whose term of service had not expired, and they were organized into a company and assigned to the Ninety-Sixth Ohio.

The regiment bears upon its banners the names of eleven battles, in which it lost one officer and twenty men killed, and eighteen officers and three hundred and twenty-five men wounded.

43d REGIMENT OHIO VOLUNTEER INFANTRY.

ROSTER, THREE YEARS' SERVICE.

RANK.	NAME.	DATE OF RANK.	COM. ISSUED.	REMARKS.
Colonel	J. L. KIRBY SMITH	Sept. 28, 1861	Oct. 9, 1861	Wounded at Corinth, Mississippi, October 4; died October 12, 1862.
Do.	WAGER SWAYNE	Oct. 12, 1862	" 23, 1862	Promoted to Brigadier-General March 8, 1865.
Do.	HORACE PARK	April 20, 1865	April 30, 1865	Mustered out with regiment.
Lt. Colonel	WAGER SWAYNE	Dec. 14, 1861	Feb. 21, 1862	Promoted to Colonel.
Do.	WALTER F. HERRICK	Oct. 12, 1862	Oct. 23, "	Promoted to Brigadier-General.
Do.	HORACE PARK	Feb. 14, 1865	Feb. 15, 1865	Promoted to Colonel.
Do.	JOHN H. RHODES	April 20, "	April 20, "	Mustered out with regiment.
Major	WAGER SWAYNE	Aug. 31, 1861	Feb. 21, 1862	Promoted to Lieutenant-Colonel.
Do.	WALTER F. HERRICK	Jan. 21, 1862	" 21, "	Promoted to Lieutenant-Colonel.
Do.	HARLEY H. SAGE	Oct. 12, "	Oct. 25, "	Resigned March 27, 1863.
Do.	HORACE PARK	March 27, 1863	April. 22, 1863	Promoted to Lieutenant-Colonel.
Do.	ALBERT L. HOWE	April 20, 1865	" 30, 1865	Mustered out with regiment.
Surgeon	CLARK McDERMONT	Sept. 11, 1861	Feb. 21, 1862	
Do.	FRANCIS M. ROSE	April 25, 1862	May 1, "	Mustered out with regiment.
Ass't Surgeon	FRANCIS M. ROSE	Dec. 4, 1861	Feb. 21, "	Promoted to Surgeon.
Do.	D. S. HALL	April 25, 1862	May 1, "	Declined.
Do.	R. L. SWEENEY	May 13, "	" 13, "	Declined.
Do.	WM. S. BELL	June 20, "	June 20, "	Honorably discharged March 29, 1864.
Do.	CORRIDON MORROW	Sept. 5, "	Nov. 19, 1863	Honorably discharged March 29, 1864.
Do.	CHAS. E. POE	April 6, 1861	April 6, 1864	Mustered out with regiment.
Do.	WESLEY ANDERSON	March 10, 1865	March 10, 1865	Mustered out with regiment.
Chaplain	JOHN H. C. BONTE	Jan. 30, 1862	Jan. 30, 1862	Resigned June 1, 1862.
Do.	RICHARD L. CHITTENDEN	Nov. 11, "	Nov. 10, "	Mustered out with regiment.
Captain	Jacob M. Spangler	" 15, 1861	Feb. 21, "	Killed at Corinth October 4, 1862.
Do.	James Marshman	Dec. 6, "	" 21, "	Resigned September 3, 1862.
Do.	Moses J. Urquhart	" 19, "	" 21, "	Resigned April 8, 1862.
Do.	Christian L. Poorman	" 21, "	" 21, "	Promoted to Lt. Col. 98th O. V. I. Aug. 12, '62.
Do.	Harley H. Sage	" 31, "	" 21, "	Promoted to Major October 12, 1862.
Do.	James H. Coulter	" 31, "	" 21, "	Resigned February 8, 1862.
Do.	John Ferguson	" 31, "	" 21, "	Died December 5, 1862.
Do.	Joel A. Dewey	Jan. 10, 1862	" 21, "	Lieutenant-Colonel colored regiment.
Do.	Peter Brown	" 18, "	" 21, "	Resigned June 17, 1862.
Do.	Wm. Walker	Feb. 7, "	" 21, "	Resigned May 15, 1862.
Do.	Horace Park	Jan. 9, "	" 21, "	Promoted to Major.
Do.	Sanford F. Timmons	April 8, "	May 5, "	Discharged September 8, 1863.
Do.	John H. Rhodes	May 15, "	June 6, "	Promoted to Lieutenant-Colonel.
Do.	Peter Hewittson	July 17, "	Aug. 1, "	Mustered out.
Do.	Samuel Martin	Oct. 4, "	Oct. 28, "	Resigned September 20, 1864.
Do.	Moses R. Shalter	Aug. 12, "	Dec. 10, "	Mustered out.
Do.	Isaac Young	Oct. 12, "	" 10, "	Appointed Assistant Surgeon 27th O. V. I. May 11, '62, by permission of War Dep't.
Do.	Dennis H. Williams	Sept. 3, "	" 30, "	Mustered out to receive promotion.
Do.	Hinchman L. Prophet	Dec. 5, "	April 28, "	Resigned May 31, 1863.
Do.	John S. Hamilton	March 27, "	" 28, "	Mustered out.
Do.	Z. A. Connell	....	....	Revoked.
Do.	Albert L. Howe	April 13, 1864	April 13, 1864	Promoted to Major.
Do.	John C. Hamilton	May 31, 1863	Sept. 7, 1863	Mustered out for promotion Sept. 27, 1864.
Do.	John P. Kinney	April 13, 1864	April 13, 1864	Declined.
Do.	Otho W. Rigby	May 9, "	May 9, "	Declined promotion; commission returned.
Do.	George W. Purcell	Nov. 18, "	Nov. 18, "	Declined promotion.
Do.	Martin L. Briner	" 18, "	" 18, "	Declined promotion.
Do.	Thomas G. Harper	" 18, "	" 18, "	Mustered out.
Do.	Jonathan McClaren	" 18, "	" 18, "	Declined promotion.
Do.	Robert McNary	" 18, "	" 18, "	Declined promotion.
Do.	Andrew J. Fitzgerald	Jan. 18, 1865	Jan. 18, 1865	Declined promotion.
Do.	Edward Lybarger	" 18, "	" 18, "	Declined promotion.
Do.	Obadiah M. Davis	" 18, "	" 18, "	Mustered out with regiment.
Do.	Newell E. Carpenter	Feb. 15, "	Feb. 15, "	Mustered out with regiment.
Do.	Jerry O. McDonald	" 15, "	" 15, "	Mustered out with regiment.
Do.	Henry S. Beck	" 15, "	" 15, "	Mustered out with regiment.
Do.	James H. Speakman	" 15, "	" 15, "	Mustered out with regiment.
Do.	Crawford W. Armstrong	" 15, "	" 15, "	Mustered out with regiment.
Do.	J. Alpheus Lautz	" 25, "	" 25, "	Mustered out with regiment.
Do.	Luther Stewart	April 20, "	April 20, "	Mustered out with regiment.
Do.	Hamden Heatherington	" 20, "	" 20, "	Mustered out with regiment.
Do.	Alex. N. Wells	" 20, "	" 20, "	Mustered out with regiment.
1st Lieutenant	Samuel McClaren	Oct. 1, 1861	Feb. 21, 1862	Resigned September 3, 1862.
Do.	Samuel Martin	Nov. 15, "	" 21, "	Promoted to Captain.
Do.	Sanford F. Timmons	Dec. 19, "	" 21, "	Promoted to Captain.
Do.	Dennis H. Williams	" 21, "	" 21, "	Promoted to Captain.
Do.	John P. Kinney	" 31, "	" 21, "	Mustered out.
Do.	Horace Park	" 31, "	" 21, "	Promoted to Captain.
Do.	Edward J. Keller	" 31, "	" 21, "	Resigned June 17, 1862.
Do.	Samuel K. Williams	Jan. 10, 1862	" 21, "	Resigned June 29, 1862.
Do.	Peter Hewittson	" 15, "	" 21, "	Promoted to Captain.
Do.	Moses R. Shalter	Feb. 7, "	" 21, "	Promoted to Captain.
Do.	Sylvester A. Larison	Jan. 9, "	" 21, "	Resigned June 17, 1862.
Do.	Chas. C. Heyl	Oct. 22, 1861	" 21, "	Killed at Corinth October 4, 1862.
Do.	Josiah H. Cochran	Jan. 29, 1862	" 21, "	Resigned November 1, 1862.
Do.	Wm. B. Thornhill	April 8, "	May 5, "	Resigned June 28, 1862.
Do.	Hinchman L. Prophet	June 17, "	Aug. 4, "	Promoted to Captain.
Do.	John S. Hamilton	" 17, "	" 4, "	Promoted to Captain.
Do.	Isaac Young	" 29, "	" 4, "	Promoted to Captain.
Do.	John C. Hamilton	" 25, "	" 4, "	Promoted to Captain.

RANK.	NAME.	DATE OF RANK.			COM. ISSUED.			REMARKS.
1st Lieutenant	John M. Crisswell	June	17,	1862	Aug.	4,	1862	Revoked; resigned as 2d Lieut. Sept. 3, 1862.
Do.	Renick Huston	Aug.	12,	"	Dec.	10,	"	Resigned January 14, 1863.
Do.	Zachariah A. Connell	Sept.	3,	"	"	10,	"	Discharged June 27, 1863.
Do.	Albert L. Howe	Oct.	4,	"	"	10,	"	Promoted to Captain.
Do.	Stacy Taylor	"	12,	"	"	10,	"	Deceased.
Do.	Otho W. Rigby	Nov.	1,	"	"	10,	"	Declined promotion.
Do.	Geo. W. Purcell	Sept.	3,	"	"	30,	"	Promoted to Captain.
Do.	Martin L. Briner	Oct.	4,	"	"	30,	"	Absent.
Do.	Wm. A. Lilley	Sept.	3,	"	"	30,	"	Mustered out November 10, 1864.
Do.	Thomas G. Harper	Dec.	5,	"	April	28,	"	Mustered out.
Do.	Jonathan McClaren	March	27,	"	"	28,	"	Mustered out.
Do.	Samuel Calvin	April	13,	1864	"	13,	1864	Mustered out with regiment.
Do.	Henry J. McFadden	"	13,	"	"	13,	"	Out of service.
Do.	Andrew J. Fitzgerald	"	13,	"	"	13,	"	Out of service; resigned April 6, 1865.
Do.	Cornelius McCaffrey	"	13,	"	"	13,	"	Mustered out.
Do.	Samuel Y. Calvin	May	9,	"	May	9,	"	Void; commission returned.
Do.	Robert McNary	Nov.	18,	"	Nov.	18,	"	Resigned April 6, 1865.
Do.	Edward Lybarger	"	18,	"	"	18,	"	Declined promotion.
Do.	John W. Thompson	"	18,	"	"	18,	"	Declined promotion.
Do.	Samuel S. Snellbaker	"	18,	"	"	18,	"	Declined promotion.
Do.	Obadiah M. Davis	"	18,	"	"	18,	"	Promoted to Captain.
Do.	Newell E. Carpenter	"	18,	"	"	18,	"	Promoted to Captain.
Do.	Luther Stewart	"	18,	"	"	18,	"	Promoted to Captain.
Do.	Tilden Jones	"	18,	"	"	18,	"	Declined promotion.
Do.	George M. Wise	"	18,	"	"	18,	"	Mustered out with regiment as Adjutant.
Do.	Washington G. Irwin	Jan.	18,	1865	Jan.	18,	1865	Revoked.
Do.	Henry H. Adams	"	18,	"	"	18,	"	Declined promotion.
Do.	Hamden Heatherington	Feb.	15,	"	Feb.	15,	"	Promoted to Captain.
Do.	Alex. N. Wells	"	15,	"	"	15,	"	Promoted to Captain.
Do.	Harrison Douglass	"	15,	"	"	15,	"	Killed in action.
Do.	George W. Baughman	"	15,	"	"	15,	"	Mustered out with regiment.
Do.	J. Alphens Lantz	"	15,	"	"	15,	"	Promoted to Captain.
Do.	Adam Williams	April	20,	"	April	20,	"	Mustered out with regiment.
Do.	Thomas Dakin	May	16,	"	May	16,	"	
Do.	Jason Brown	"	16,	"	"	16,	"	Mustered out with regiment.
Do.	Peter Zinn	"	16,	"	"	16,	"	Mustered out with regiment.
Do.	George W. Goodrich	"	16,	"	"	16,	"	Mustered out with regiment.
Do.	James W. Dunn	"	16,	"	"	16,	"	Mustered out with regiment.
Do.	Levi Oman	"	16,	"	"	16,	"	Mustered out with regiment.
2d Lieutenant	Willoughby W. Webb	Oct.	1,	1861	Feb.	21,	1862	Resigned November 24, 1862.
Do.	Sylvester A. Larison	"	29,	"	"	21,	"	Promoted to 1st Lieutenant.
Do.	Hinchman L. Prophet	Nov.	5,	"	"	21,	"	Promoted to 1st Lieutenant.
Do.	David F. Phillips	"	14,	"	"	21,	"	Resigned May 17, 1862.
Do.	John M. Crisswell	"	15,	"	"	21,	"	Promoted to 1st Lieutenant June 17, 1862.
Do.	Wm. B. Thornhill	"	18,	"	"	21,	"	Promoted to 1st Lieutenant.
Do.	Joseph A. Harris	Dec.	21,	"	"	21,	"	Resigned July 7, 1862.
Do.	Edward L. Dunbar	"	31,	"	"	21,	"	Resigned November 1, 1862.
Do.	John A. Pendergast	Jan.	9,	1862	"	21,	"	Resigned June 17.
Do.	Montgomery Close	Feb.	10,	"	"	21,	"	Resigned July 3, 1862.
Do.	Isaac Young	"	7,	"	"	21,	"	Promoted to 1st Lieutenant June 29, 1862.
Do.	John C. Hamilton	April	8,	"	June	5,	"	Promoted to 1st Lieutenant.
Do.	Renick Huston	May	17,	"	"	5,	"	Promoted to 1st Lieutenant.
Do.	Albert L. Howe	July	3,	"	July	18,	"	Promoted to 1st Lieutenant.
Do.	George W. Purcell	June	7,	"	Aug.	1,	"	Promoted to 1st Lieutenant.
Do.	Martin L. Briner	"	29,	"	"	1,	"	Promoted to 1st Lieutenant.
Do.	Otho W. Rigby	July	7,	"	"	1,	"	Promoted to 1st Lieutenant.
Do.	Stacy Taylor	June	28,	"	"	1,	"	Promoted to 1st Lieutenant.
Do.	Zachariah A. Connell	July	17,	"	"	1,	"	Promoted to 1st Lieutenant.
Do.	Wm. A. Lilley	Oct.	4,	"	Oct.	28,	"	Promoted to 1st Lieutenant.
Do.	Thomas G. Harper	Aug.	12,	"	Dec.	10,	"	Promoted to 1st Lieutenant.
Do.	Jonathan McClaren	Sept.	3,	"	"	10,	"	Promoted to 1st Lieutenant.
Do.	Samuel Calvin	Oct.	4,	"	"	10,	"	Promoted to 1st Lieutenant.
Do.	Robert McNary	"	12,	"	"	10,	"	Promoted to 1st Lieutenant.
Do.	Andrew J. Fitzgerald	Nov.	1,	"	Feb.	4,	1863	Promoted to 1st Lieutenant.
Do.	Henry J. McFadden	"	1,	"	Jan.	20,	"	Resigned January 23, 1864.
Do.	Samuel J. Worrell	"	24,	"	Feb.	4,	"	Honorably discharged March 23, 1864.
Do.	Cornelius McCaffrey	Sept.	3,	"	"	4,	"	Promoted to 1st Lieutenant.
Do.	John M. Lindsey	"	3,	"	"	4,	"	Resigned August 2, 1864.
Do.	Edward Lybarger	Dec.	5,	"	April	28,	"	Promoted to 1st Lieutenant.
Do.	John W. Thompson	March	27,	"	"	28,	"	Mustered out.
Do.	Thatcher Vincent	Oct.	4,	"	"	28,	"	Honorably discharged December 12, 1863.
Do.	Samuel S. Snellabaker	Nov.	5,	1863	March	25,	1864	Declined promotion.
Do.	Milo Wilkison	May	9,	1864	May	9,	"	Deceased.
Do.	Obadiah M. Davis	"	9,	"	"	9,	"	Promoted to 1st Lieutenant.
Do.	Washington G. Irwin	Nov.	18,	"	Nov.	18,	"	Promoted to 1st Lieutenant.
Do.	Henry H. Adams	"	18,	"	"	18,	"	Mustered out.
Do.	Jerry O. McDonald	"	18,	"	"	18,	"	Promoted to 1st Lieutenant.
Do.	Basil M. Simpson	May	16,	1865	May	16,	"	Absent on furlough at muster out of reg't.
Do.	Augustus L. Pendergast	"	16,	"	"	16,	"	Mustered out with regiment.
Do.	John R. Campbell	"	16,	"	"	16,	"	Mustered out with regiment.
Do.	George F. Majors	"	16,	"	"	16,	"	Mustered out with regiment.
Do.	Wm. Higgins	"	16,	"	"	16,	"	
Do.	James O'Connell	"	16,	"	"	16,	"	Mustered out with regiment.
Do.	Willoughby Howe	"	16,	"	"	16,	"	Mustered out with regiment.
Do.	James McClain	"	16,	"	"	16,	"	Mustered out with regiment.
Do.	Samuel Pickering	"	16,	"	"	16,	"	

FORTY-THIRD OHIO VOLUNTEER INFANTRY.

THE FORTY-THIRD OHIO was organized at Camp Andrews, Mount Vernon, Ohio, February 7, 1862. It was recruited at a time when men were very difficult to procure, but through the energy and perseverance of Lieutenant-Colonel Wager Swayne the regiment was filled to the minimum number and mustered into the service. After having been well drilled by its Colonel, J. L. Kirby Smith (a nephew of the Rebel General Kirby Smith), it left its rendezvous for the front on the 21st of February, 1862, and reported to Brigadier-General John Pope, commanding the District of Mississippi, on the 26th of February. The regiment was at once assigned to the Ohio Brigade, composed of the Twenty-Seventh, Thirty-Ninth, Forty-Third, and Sixty-Third regiments, First Division, Army of the Mississippi.

It was but a few days before the regiment was introduced to active service, for in March, 1862, it was under fire at New Madrid, Missouri, and in all the operations against that post it bore a prominent part, especially in its final bombardment and capture on the 13th and 14th of March. The loss of the regiment in killed and wounded was quite severe.

In the movements against Island 10, and the crossing of the Mississippi River in the face of the enemy, the Forty-Third Ohio bore a conspicuous part, as it did also in the subsequent capture of the forces of General McCall, at Tiptonville, Tennessee.

The next movement was against Fort Pillow, which was ordered to be abandoned by General Halleck in order that General Pope's troops might assist in the operations against Corinth, Mississippi. In all the operations that distinguished the Army of the Mississippi in that campaign, the Forty-Third bore its part. The actions of the 8th, 9th, and 20th of May, may be particularly mentioned.

The regiment lay in camp at Clear Creek, Mississippi, until the 20th of August, when it moved to Iuka, Mississippi, and soon after to Bear Creek, where it remained on garrison-duty until September 11th, when General Rosecrans began to marshal his forces preparatory to his campaign against Price and Van Dorn. At Iuka the regiment was present and took part in the battle of September 19th, and subsequent pursuit of the enemy as far as Cripple Creek. The Forty-Third Ohio also participated in the arduous marches made by General Rosecrans preceding the battle of Corinth, whereby his entire force was concentrated at the proper hour to meet the attack of Price and Van Dorn, October 3d and 4th. In the battle on the last-named day, the Forty-Third and Sixty-Third Ohio claim to have done more to save the day than any other organizations. These regiments were posted, the Sixty-Third immediately on the right, and the Forty-Third immediately on the left of Battery Robinett, and between that battery and Battery Williams, and were entirely without works or protection of any sort. In descriptions of this battle other regiments have been assigned to this ground, but the regiments above-named occupied and held it during the battle. The grand assault by the Rebels was made at daylight on the 4th. They opened on Battery Robinett with artillery at about three hundred yards, and at ten o'clock A. M., led by Colonel Rogers, of the Second Texas, moved forward to the assault. The Forty-Third and Sixty-Third Ohio stood firmly at their posts, and succeeded in staggering the assaulting column, and in hurling it back, at a time when our lines were broken and our troops were seen flying from every other part of the field. The opposing forces were but a few feet apart, and fought almost hand-to-hand, and men went down on both sides in great numbers. Colonel Smith fell mortally wounded at the first onset, while gallantly discharging his duty. Adjutant Heyl and

Captain Spangler were killed at about the same moment. Captain S. F. Timmons and Lieutenant S. McClaren, A. L. Howe, and H. L. Prophet, received honorable wounds. The casualties among the men were very severe. In a few minutes of fighting over one-fourth of those engaged of the Forty-Third were either killed or wounded. The loss of the Sixty-Third was nearly one-half the number engaged. Colonel Smith died of his wounds on the 12th of October, eight days after the battle. He was a young soldier of great promise, and his death was mourned by every man in his regiment.

The next movements in which the Forty-Third Ohio participated was with Grant's army to Oxford, Mississippi, and in the campaign against Forrest in West Tennessee, in the winter of 1862-3, and in General Dodge's raid in North Alabama in April, 1863. From this time until October, 1863, the Forty-Third was stationed at different points on the railroads of West Tennessee and Memphis, assisting to keep open the communications of General Grant's army, then operating against Vicksburg. And when General Sherman made his memorable march from Memphis for the relief of the Army of the Cumberland, the Forty-Third accompanied him, in General Dodge's column. Reaching Pulaski, Tennessee, General Dodge's command was halted and ordered to occupy and repair the railroad from Columbia, Tennessee, to Decatur, Alabama, the Ohio Brigade going into camp at Prospect, Tennessee.

In December, 1863, the regiment almost unanimously re-enlisted as veterans, and went home on furlough of thirty days, in company with the other regiments of the Ohio Brigade. At the expiration of their furloughs the brigade returned to the field in a body, and immediately thereafter its commander, Colonel John W. Fuller, was directed to cross the Tennessee River and capture the town of Decatur, Alabama, then held by the Rebels under Roddy. For that purpose the Forty-Third and Sixty-Third Ohio regiments were ordered to cross the river in small boats, which was successfully accomplished just at daylight on the 8th. After a slight skirmish the town was captured and occupied by our troops. A long season of inaction was passed in camp at this place. In fact the command lay here until the opening of General Sherman's campaign against Atlanta.

While at Decatur the Ohio Brigade was discontinued and a new brigade was made, composed of the Forty-Third and Sixty-Third Ohio, Twenty-Fifth Wisconsin, and the Thirty-Fifth New Jersey regiments, and placed under the command of Colonel John W. Sprague, of the Sixty-Third Ohio, and designated as the Second Brigade, Fourth Division of the Sixteenth Army Corps.

On the 1st of May, 1864, the command to which the Forty-Third was attached marched from Decatur for Chattanooga, and having taken cars near Huntsville, Alabama, reached Chattanooga May 3d, and immediately took the advance of the Army of the Tennessee in the Atlanta campaign. On the 5th of May a detachment of the regiment, under Captain D. H. Williams, took possession of Mattock's, or Ship's Gap, and held it until the Army of the Tennessee came up and was ready to cross into and take possession of the Valley of Villanow. The march was continued through Snake Creek Gap, and on the evening of the 8th of May the command was in line of battle before Resaca, awaiting the concentration of the army before an advance was made.

The 13th of May was decided on for the advance against Resaca. General Dodge made his preparations accordingly, and at the appointed time was ready with his command. The Forty-Third was in the front line and near the extreme right of the National army. In its advance the National column was irresistible, and swept everything before it. The enemy was sent flying across the Oostenaula. The loss of the Forty-Third was quite severe.

The next day after the battle (the 14th of May) was spent in heavy skirmishing, in which the members of the regiment took an active part; and in the evening of that day Sprague's brigade was sent as a support to General John A. Logan, who was to make an assault on a position commanding the bridge across the Oostenaula. The assault was made about sunset, and it was found necessary to send in Sprague's brigade, in order to hold the advantage gained by Logan. The brigade went forward in gallant style, and not only occupied the ground from whence their comrades were about being driven, but pushed the National lines still further to the front, and held the position thus gained until the night of May 15th, against repeated attempts to dislodge them. All that day was spent in heavy skirmishing with the enemy. The members of the Forty-Third, as was their custom, took the advance in this mode of fighting, and it was made a day memorable in the annals of the regiment. The Rebel skirmish-line was literally annihilated, and the dead found next morning lying where they had fallen, the Rebels having evacuated in the night. Of the Forty-Third, company A, Lieutenant O. M. Davis, and H, Captain A. L. Howe, were the first to enter the enemy's works.

At Dallas the Forty-Third took an important part, and in the advance on the enemy's position near Big Shanty, company D, of the regiment, participated in a most brilliant charge of skirmishers, capturing a strong barricade from the Twenty-Ninth Tennessee, and numerous prisoners. Immediately thereafter came the siege of Kenesaw, with its deadly skirmishing, its grand cannonading, and the disastrous repulse of the National forces on the 29th of June.

The Forty-Third participated in the general movements of its corps until the advance of the Army of the Tennessee from Roswell upon Decatur, Alabama, when it was detached to hold the bridge across the Chattahoochie, at the former place, until the army transportation then loading at Marietta should cross the river. On the morning of July 22d Colonel Swayne, in command of the Forty-Third Ohio and Ninth Illinois Mounted Infantry, started for Decatur, twenty miles distant, with a train of some fifteen hundred wagons. On nearing the town it became evident that a fight was then in progress, and Captain Williams, who had been ordered ahead with two companies early in the day, hurried his detachment forward until he learned that Colonel Sprague, after a most gallant resistance against overwhelming numbers, had been compelled to retreat. This detachment was then placed in position in order to protect the train while it was filing off in rear of the National army. In the meantime Colonel Swayne arrived with the remainder of the Forty-Third, on the double-quick, and a section of artillery. At this time the train was menaced by Iverson's Rebel division of cavalry, assigned to the duty of capturing it, while two other divisions under Wheeler were to capture Sprague and his three small regiments in Decatur. Through the audacity of Colonel Sprague and the fearless spirit of his men, combined with the promptitude of Colonel Swayne, not a wagon was lost, thus averting a calamity that must have been fatal to the success of the National army at that particular time. On entering the town the next day it was ascertained that the enemy had lost over six hundred men in killed and wounded, fully two-thirds of the National force in action. During the remainder of the Atlanta campaign the Forty-Third shared the trials and glories of the Sixteenth Army Corps, and on the 4th and 7th of August particularly, in advancing the National lines, won the thanks of Ransom, the division commander, by splendid and steady fighting.

After the fall of Atlanta the Forty-Third enjoyed General Sherman's "full month's rest." In the reorganization of the army the left wing (Sixteenth Army Corps) was discontinued, and the Forty-Third was assigned to the Second Brigade, First Division, Seventeenth Army Corps.

The "month's rest" had hardly ended before the rash and impetuous Hood disturbed the quiet of the National army by his raids to the rear, in the attempt to destroy General Sherman's communications. The National army was in good trim, and gave immediate chase to the forces under General Hood. That General was chased to Resaca, through Snake Creek Gap, and west as far as Gaylesville, Alabama, where he was left to seek his own destruction by running against the forces of Major-General George H. Thomas.

The Forty-Third Ohio and its brigade hurried back to Atlanta, under orders from General Sherman, to join his great "march to the sea." Of this campaign, the history of one regiment is the history of another. It was a daily succession of easy marches, with little interruption, with plenty of forage for both man and beast, and full of pleasant adventure.

Savannah was reached and besieged. In the operations around that place the Forty-Third performed its full share of duty, and, after the fall of the city, held, with General Sprague's brigade, the important outpost of Dillon's Bridge.

In January, 1865, the regiment moved to Beaufort, and directly afterward upon Pocotaligo, on the Charleston and Savannah Railroad, where it lay until the beginning of Sherman's march through the Carolinas, occupying the interim in demonstrations against the enemy at the crossings of the Salkahatchie.

On the 2d of February the Seventeenth Army Corps marched from Pocotaligo, and having crossed Whippy Swamp were, in due time, confronting the enemy strongly posted at River's Bridge. At this place Colonel Swayne, while engaged in selecting a position for his regiment to camp, lost a leg by a shell. The regiment thus lost a brave and competent leader, who had been with it from the beginning of its organization, in every march and in every fight, and who had always shown the utmost devotion to their interests. For his services during the war he has since been made Brigadier and Brevet Major-General.

The day after the fall of Colonel Swayne at River's Bridge the regiment received a baptism of fire, in a charge on a battery which commanded the bridge and the causeway approaching it. Down this narrow causeway the regiment rushed amid a storm of shot and shell, compelling the Rebels to withdraw the battery and uncover the crossing.

In the South Carolina campaign the Forty-Third stood high, as it always had done, for promptitude, steadiness, and good discipline. The war closing, the regiment went to Washington, took part in the grand review, and from thence to Louisville, Kentucky, with the Army of the Tennessee, whence, in July, 1865, it went to Ohio, and was mustered out of service on the 13th of July, 1865.

44th REGIMENT OHIO VOLUNTEER INFANTRY.

ROSTER, THREE YEARS' SERVICE.

RANK.	NAME.	DATE OF RANK.	COM. ISSUED.	REMARKS.
Colonel	SAMUEL A. GILBERT	Oct. 14, 1861	Oct. 14, 1861	Resigned April 20, 1864.
Lt. Colonel	H. BLAIR WILSON	Sept. 5, "	" 14, "	Resigned April 9, 1863.
Do.	A. O. MITCHELL	April 9, 1863	May 13, 1863	Revoked; resigned as Major January 5, 1863.
Do.	LYSANDER W. TULLEY	" 9, "	July 3, "	Mustered out January 30, 1864.
Major	A. O. MITCHELL	Oct. 10, 1861	Oct. 10, 1861	Resigned June 5, 1863.
Do.	ALPHEUS S. MOORE	April 19, 1863	May 13, 1863	Transferred to 8th Ohio Volunteer Cavalry.
Surgeon	H. K. STEELE	Sept. 23, 1861	Oct. 14, 1861	Mustered out September 9, 1864.
Ass't Surgeon	JOHN H. RODGERS	" 23, "	" 14, "	Appointed Surgeon 104th O. V. I. Feb., 1863.
Do.	DOUGLAS LUCE	July 4, 1862	July 23, 1862	Mustered out January 30, 1864.
Do.	BENJ. F. DAVIS	March 11, 1863	March 11, 1863	Transferred to 8th Ohio Volunteer Cavalry.
Chaplain	THOMAS P. CHILDS	Oct. 10, 1861	Oct. 10, 1861	Mustered out November 4, 1862.
Captain	Alpheus S. Moore	Sept. 10, "	" 14, "	Promoted to Major.
Do.	John C. Langston	" 18, "	" 14, "	Mustered out January 30, 1864.
Do.	Wm. W. Woodward	" 18, "	" 14, "	Resigned July 28, 1864.
Do.	Lysander W. Tulley	" 18, "	" 14, "	Promoted to Lieutenant-Colonel.
Do.	John M. Newkirk	" 23, "	" 14, "	Resigned May 29, 1863.
Do.	Israel Stough	" 25, "	" 14, "	Honorably discharged September 23, 1863.
Do.	Daniel M. Rouzer	" 18, "	" 14, "	Resigned June 30, 1863
Do.	Henry T. Shafer	Oct. 7, "	" 14, "	Resigned June 16, 1862.
Do.	Wilbur F. Cummings	" 9, "	" 14, "	Mustered out January 30, 1864.
Do.	John M. Bell	" 14, "	" 17, "	Drowned November, 1861.
Do.	Robert Youart	Dec. 26, "	Dec. 26, "	Transferred to 8th Ohio Volunteer Cavalry.
Do.	Jacob Souders	June 16, 1862	Sept. 12, 1862	Transferred to 8th Ohio Volunteer Cavalry.
Do.	Nicholas D. Badger	July 28, "	Aug. 5, "	Transferred to 8th Ohio Volunteer Cavalry.
Do.	Jarvis S. Rogers	April 19, 1863	May 13, 1863	Mustered out January 30, 1864.
Do.	James M. Shaw	May 29, "	June 15, "	Transferred to 8th Ohio Volunteer Cavalry.
Do.	Augustus Dotze	June 30, "	July 20, "	Transferred to 8th Ohio Volunteer Cavalry.
Do.	Thomas F. Garlough	April 9, "	" 20, "	Mustered out January 30, 1864.
1st Lieutenant	Gilmer Telford	Aug. 22, 1861	Oct. 14, 1861	App. Capt. by Pres't; hon. disch'd April 6, '64.
Do.	Robert Youart	Sept. 10, "	" 14, "	Promoted to Captain.
Do.	Jacob Souders	" 18, "	" 14, "	Promoted to Captain June 16, 1862.
Do.	George Monroe Shaffer	" 18, "	" 14, "	Resigned April 5, 1862.
Do.	Nicholas D. Badger	" 18, "	" 14, "	Promoted to Captain.
Do.	Jarvis S. Rogers	" 18, "	" 14, "	Promoted to Captain.
Do.	James M. Shaw	" 23, "	" 14, "	Promoted to Captain.
Do.	Jeremiah Klinefelder	" 24, "	" 14, "	Died August 7, 1862.
Do.	Thomas F. Garlough	" 25, "	" 14, "	Promoted to Captain.
Do.	Augustus Dotze	Oct. 7, "	" 14, "	Promoted to Captain.
Do.	Chas. Evans	" 9, "	" 14, "	Transferred to 8th Ohio Volunteer Cavalry.
Do.	Benj. F. Jacobs	" 11, "	" 17, "	Mustered out January 30, 1864.
Do.	Samuel M. Smith	Dec. 26, "	Dec. 26, "	Resigned December 17, 1863.
Do.	Samuel C. Howell	April 5, 1862	May 5, 1862	Mustered out February 12, 1864.
Do.	Wm. H. Banwell	June 16, "	Sept. 12, "	Mustered out January 30, 1864.
Do.	Thomas B. Douglass	Aug. 7, "	Oct. 5, "	
Do.	Hezekiah Winger	July 28, "	" 5, "	Transferred to 8th Ohio Volunteer Cavalry.
Do.	John C. Allen	April 19, 1863	May 13, 1863	Transferred to 8th Ohio Volunteer Cavalry.
Do.	A. N. Thompson	May 29, "	June 15, "	Transferred to 8th Ohio Volunteer Cavalry.
Do.	Wm. W. Knoop	April 9, "	July 20, "	Transferred to 8th Ohio Volunteer Cavalry.
Do.	Samuel F. Todd	June 30, "	" 20, "	Transferred to 8th Ohio Volunteer Cavalry.
Do.	James Lewis Ruley	Nov. 12, "	Nov. 12, "	Transferred to 8th Ohio Volunteer Cavalry.
2d Lieutenant	Samuel M. Smith	Sept. 10, 1861	Oct. 14, 1861	Promoted to 1st Lieutenant.
Do.	Leonard Langston	" 18, "	" 14, "	Resigned March 31, 1862.
Do.	Samuel Billings	" 18, "	" 14, "	Resigned November 17, 1862.
Do.	Samuel C. Howell	" 18, "	" 14, "	Promoted to 1st Lieutenant.
Do.	John Youart	" 18, "	" 14, "	Resigned June 28, 1862.
Do.	Samuel Judy	" 23, "	" 14, "	Resigned March 31, 1862.
Do.	Wm. H. Banwell	" 25, "	" 14, "	Promoted to 1st Lieutenant.
Do.	Edward E. Retter	Oct. 7, "	" 14, "	Resigned March 31, 1862.
Do.	Hezekiah Winger	" 9, "	" 14, "	Promoted to 1st Lieutenant.
Do.	John C. Allen	" 11, "	" 17, "	Promoted to 1st Lieutenant.
Do.	Thomas B. Douglass	Dec. 26, "	Dec. 26, "	Promoted to 1st Lieutenant.
Do.	Dewitt Shellabarger	March 31, 1862	May 15, 1862	Resigned August 19, 1863.
Do.	A. N. Thompson	" 31, "	" 15, "	Promoted to 1st Lieutenant.
Do.	W. H. Simons	" 31, "	" 15, "	Resigned July 21, 1863.
Do.	Edward Rice	April 5, "	" 15, "	Resigned October 5, 1862.
Do.	Wm. W. Knoop	June 28, "	Sept. 12, "	Promoted to 1st Lieutenant.
Do.	Samuel F. Todd	" 16, "	Oct. 5, "	Promoted to 1st Lieutenant.
Do.	George Green	July 28, "	" 5, "	Mustered out January 30, 1864.
Do.	Frank E. Moores	Oct. 5, "	" 5, "	Transferred to 8th Ohio Volunteer Cavalry.
Do.	I. N. Miller	July 28, "	" 5, "	Transferred to 8th Ohio Volunteer Cavalry.
Do.	Joseph Badger	Nov. 17, "	Dec. 8, "	Transferred to 8th Ohio Volunteer Cavalry.
Do.	A. Pettit	April 19, 1863	May 13, 1863	Transferred to 8th Ohio Volunteer Cavalry.
Do.	Alex. McAlpin	May 29, "	June 15, "	Transferred to 8th Ohio Volunteer Cavalry.
Do.	Robert Lyle	April 9, "	July 20, "	Transferred to 8th Ohio Volunteer Cavalry.
Do.	Wm. Sykes	June 30, "	" 20, "	Mustered out June 20, 1864.

FORTY-FOURTH OHIO VOLUNTEER INFANTRY.

THIS regiment rendezvoused at the Fair Grounds near Springfield, Ohio, during the summer and autumn of 1861; and on the 14th of October, being fully organized, it moved, *via* Cincinnati, to Camp Piatt, West Virginia. On the morning of the 19th, having reached its destination, the regiment disembarked and pitched its tents for the first time on disputed ground. Two weeks after its arrival, five companies were ordered to Gauley Bridge, and assisted in driving Floyd from his camp, and engaged in all the skirmishes during his retreat. Before their return two hundred men from the regiment crossed the Kanawha, marched to Platona, captured the place, and moved on against Colonel Jenkins at Logan C. H., but the Colonel decamped before their arrival. After being absent six days they returned, bringing in seven prisoners, some horses, and one hundred head of cattle. After these expeditions the command remained in camp for five months, quietly drilling. Winter-quarters were built and the men were comfortably sheltered. During the month of November Captain John M. Bell, of company K, with an Orderly-Sergeant and six men, were drowned while crossing the river in a skiff to relieve the picket on the opposite side. This sad accident cast a gloom over the whole regiment, and it was felt that a serious loss had been sustained. During the winter the officers of the regiment were ordered before an examining board, and to the credit of the regiment, the great majority of them passed. During the latter part of the winter companies A, B, and K were stationed on the opposite side of the river from Camp Piatt, for the better security of the camp. On the 1st of May, 1862, the regiment moved up the river to Gauley bridge, and was brigaded with the Thirty-Sixth and Forty-Seventh Ohio Volunteer Infantry, under Colonel George Crook. The brigade moved to Lewisburg, and from there the Forty-Fourth and another regiment penetrated as far as Dublin Depot, on the Jackson River Railroad, and destroyed a portion of the track. Hearing that a large force of Rebels were endeavoring to intercept their retreat, the two regiments withdrew to Lewisburg, where the enemy appeared on the 23d of May, and was not only repulsed, but routed, leaving most of their dead and wounded to fall into the hands of our troops, together with three pieces of artillery and many prisoners. The forces occupied the place for a short time after the fight, and then fell back to Meadow Bluffs, where they encamped until the middle of August, engaged in fortifying, scouting, and drilling. On the 15th of August the regiment took up the line of march toward the Kanawha, halting a week at Camp Ewing, and then falling back to Camp Tompkins. A force of six thousand Rebels was advancing against the four regiments in the valley; and, on the 9th of September, the two regiments on the right bank (the Forty-Fourth and another one) were attacked, and fell back on Gauley, where a stand was made until the teams could be removed from danger, when the retreat began in earnest. The Forty-Fourth marched in the rear all day and almost all night, covering the retreating column until it reached Camp Piatt, where it was allowed a short respite. The National forces fell back upon Charleston, and on the 13th the Rebels made the attack, and were firmly met. Superior numbers finally forced the National lines back, but every inch of ground was hotly contested. Our forces withdrew across a deep tributary of the Kanawha, and, with a few blows of an ax, severed the hawsers that held the suspension bridge, and it fell with a crash into the stream. The retreat now continued in safety to Racine, on the Ohio River, and from that place the troops were taken by steamer to Point Pleasant. Transportation was procured, and they were sent forward to Kentucky.

They encamped some time at Covington, watching the movements of Kirby Smith, and on his retreat they pursued as far as Lexington, and were ordered into camp, and assigned to the Second Brigade, Second Division, Army of Kentucky, commanded by General Gordon Granger. The regiment was actively engaged in scouting, taking in its field of operations Richmond and Danville. On the 20th of December the regiment returned to Frankfort and was mounted, and from that time until Burnside's advance into Tennessee there was but little rest for man or beast. The men almost lived in the saddle. It was one continual advance and retreat, with almost constant skirmishing. The regiment partook in the engagement of Dunstan's Hill, charging the Rebels and contributing materially to their rout. The regiment was frequently engaged in chasing John Morgan, with not very satisfactory results, as he generally proved the faster rider.

When General Burnside made his advance into Tennessee, in the fall and winter of 1863, the regiment was dismounted, and accompanied him. It can claim equality with any other regiment in all that took place on this expedition; and finally falling back upon Knoxville and throwing up fortifications, it lay in the wet, chilly ditches day and night. When the Rebels retreated the regiment pursued, and, on its return, went into camp at Strawberry Plains. On the 1st of January, 1864, the proposal to re-enlist was made, accompanied by the promise that they should be armed and mounted as cavalry. Before the 5th, out of six hundred men, five hundred and fifty had re-enlisted. On the 7th they marched for Camp Nelson, Kentucky; on the 21st took cars for Cincinnati, where they arrived next day, and were quartered in the Fifth-Street Bazaar, erected for the Sanitary Fair. Here they were obliged to wait until muster-out and muster-in rolls could be made, which was at last accomplished, and the men were re-mustered by the 29th, and started on a special train for Springfield. Their arrival was heralded by the booming of cannon, and they were received with joyous shouts and enthusiastic greetings.

In a few days the men were paid and furloughed, and when they again re-assembled it was under the name of the Eighth Ohio Cavalry, in the sketch of which organization their further history will be found.

In the sketch, a few pages back, of the Thirty-Sixth Regiment, it is casually mentioned that its loss was much greater than that of the Forty-Fourth at the battle at Lewisburg. The inference must not be drawn from this that the Forty-Fourth was less actively engaged. It was the impetuous charge of the Forty-Fourth that captured the enemy's four-gun battery, threw his left back, and thus began the repulse which really relieved the Thirty-Sixth from check. The guns and prisoners were in the track of the Forty-Fourth.

In the next sketch, that of the Thirty-Seventh, the enemy is spoken of as maintaining a respectful distance after the retreat across the Kanawha from Cotton Hill in September, 1862. This is true, so far as the Thirty-Seventh is concerned; but it might convey a false impression without the further statement here that Colonel Gilbert's brigade, including the Forty-Fourth and Forty-Seventh Ohio, *kept* the enemy at a respectful distance, giving the Thirty-Seventh time to move off, and also securing time for the passage of the immense train, thirteen miles in length. Through that day and the next this brigade continued to skirmish with the enemy and cover the retreat—a service always to be gratefully remembered.

45th REGIMENT OHIO VOLUNTEER INFANTRY.

ROSTER, THREE YEARS' SERVICE.

RANK.	NAME.	DATE OF RANK.	COM. ISSUED.	REMARKS.
Colonel	BENJ. P. RUNKLE	Aug. 14, 1862	Aug. 11, 1862	Hon. dis. July 21, '64, ac't w'nds. rec. in action.
Do.	JOHN H. HUMPHREY	June 16, 1865	June 16, 1865	Mustered out with regiment as Lt. Colonel.
Lt. Colonel	ALEX. S. RAMSEY	Aug. 10, 1862	Oct. 1, 1862	Resigned November 16, 1862.
Do.	JOSEPH HILL	Nov. 16, "	Dec. 4, "	Resigned April 16, 1863.
Do.	GEORGE E. ROSS	April 16, 1863	June 10, 1863	Resigned August 5, 1864.
Do.	JOHN H. HUMPHREY	Oct. 12, 1864	Oct. 12, 1864	Promoted to Colonel.
Do.	JAMES F. JENNINGS	June 16, 1865	June 16, 1865	Mustered out with regiment as Major.
Major	JOSEPH HILL	Aug. 12, 1862	Oct. 1, 1862	Promoted to Lieutenant-Colonel.
Do.	GEORGE E. ROSS	Nov. 16, "	Dec. 11, "	Promoted to Lieutenant-Colonel.
Do.	JAMES E. MARSH	April 16, "	June 23, 1862	Honorably discharged November 25, 1864.
Do.	JAMES F. JENNINGS	Jan. 18, 1865	Jan. 16, 1865	Promoted to Lieutenant-Colonel.
Do.	NELSON G. FRANKLIN	June 16, "	June 16, "	Mustered out with regiment as Captain.
Surgeon	THOMAS H. KEARNEY	July 22, 1862	July 22, 1862	Mustered out with regiment.
Ass't Surgeon	HENRY BESSE	" 7, "	" 7, "	Resigned November 20, 1862.
Do.	JULIUS J. SHELDON	Aug. 15, "	Aug. 15, "	Resigned November 6, 1864.
Do.	R. J. HILL	March 11, 1863	March 11, 1863	Mustered out with regiment.
Chaplain	JACOB V. KOST	Oct. 9, 1862	Oct. 9, 1862	Resigned May 25, 1863.
Do.	JAMES JACKSON	June 1, 1863	July 10, 1863	Resigned August 5, 1864.
Do.	W. J. PECK	Nov. 18, 1861	Nov. 18, 1864	Declined and returned commission.
Do.	JOHN W. LEWIS	Feb. 11, 1865	Feb. 15, 1865	Mustered out with regiment.
Captain	Daniel Amerman	July 9, 1862	Oct. 1, 1862	Resigned November 27, 1862.
Do.	George E. Ross	Aug. 1, "	" 1, "	Promoted to Major.
Do.	James E. Marsh	" 8, "	" 1, "	Promoted to Major.
Do.	James D. Stover	" 10, "	" 1, "	Honorably discharged July 20, 1864.
Do.	Lewis Taylor	" 11, "	" 1, "	Honorably discharged January 4, 1865.
Do.	Miles V. Payne	" 12, "	" 1, "	Resigned March 2, 1863.
Do.	Wm. Rhoads	" 12, "	" 1, "	Deceased.
Do.	Robert Dow	" 14, "	" 1, "	Resigned October 24, 1862.
Do.	John H. Humphrey	" 14, "	" 1, "	Promoted to Lieutenant-Colonel.
Do.	Comfort H. Stanley	" 14, "	" 1, "	Deceased from wounds rec'd at Philadelphia, Tenn.
Do.	James F. Jennings	Oct. 24, "	Nov. 13, "	Promoted to Major.
Do.	Nelson G. Franklin	Nov. 27, "	Dec. 4, "	Promoted to Major.
Do.	Elias F. Scott	" 16, "	" 4, "	Deceased May 13, '64, from wounds received at Resaca, Ga.
Do.	David Sparks	March 2, 1863	June 10, 1863	Mustered out with regiment.
Do.	Adam R. Eglin	April 16, "	July 10, "	Mustered out with regiment.
Do.	David Mitchell	Feb. 1, 1864	Feb. 1, 1864	Resigned April 22, 1864.
Do.	Wm. McBeth	" 1, "	" 1, "	Mustered out with regiment as 1st Lieut.
Do.	Joseph R. Smith	July 13, "	July 13, "	Mustered out with regiment.
Do.	George W. Sparks	" 13, "	" 13, "	Resigned as 1st Lieutenant August 16, 1864.
Do.	Jacob V. Conklin	Oct. 12, "	Oct. 12, "	Resigned March 3, 1865.
Do.	E. B. Crow	" 12, "	" 12, "	Resigned January 21, 1865.
Do.	Wm. H. Allen	" 12, "	" 12, "	Mustered out with regiment.
Do.	Wm. M. Williams	Feb. 10, 1865	Feb. 10, 1865	Mustered out with regiment.
Do.	Joseph W. Wilshire	" 10, "	" 10, "	Mustered out as 2d Lieutenant May 15, 1865.
Do.	Alfred K. Rarey	" 10, "	" 10, "	Mustered out with regiment.
Do.	Thomas W. Hodges	March 20, "	March 20, "	Mustered out with regiment.
Do.	John A. Pickering	June 6, "	June 6, "	
Do.	Frederick L. Dunning	" 16, "	" 16, "	Mustered out with regiment as 1st Lieut.
1st Lieutenant	David Davis	July 2, 1862	Oct. 1, 1862	Resigned June 17, 1863.
Do.	Charles W. Fearns	" 3, "	" 1, "	Declined pro. as Captain; killed in action at Knoxville, Tenn.
Do.	James F. Jennings	" 28, "	" 1, "	Promoted to Captain.
Do.	Elias F. Scott	Aug. 1, "	" 1, "	Promoted to Captain.
Do.	David Sparks	" 6, "	" 1, "	Promoted to Captain.
Do.	Nelson G. Franklin	" 10, "	" 1, "	Promoted to Captain.
Do.	John M. Holloway	" 11, "	" 1, "	Resigned November 20, 1862.
Do.	Samuel H. Cole	" 12, "	" 1, "	Resigned June 17, 1863.
Do.	James I. Miller	" 14, "	" 1, "	Resigned October 5, 1862.
Do.	Joseph P. Bowserman	" 14, "	" 1, "	Resigned October 24, 1862.
Do.	Adam R. Eglin	" 14, "	" 1, "	Promoted to Captain.
Do.	Andrew J. Jordan	" 19, "	" 1, "	Resigned November 20, 1862.
Do.	David Mitchell	Oct. 5, "	Nov. 13, "	Promoted to Captain.
Do.	Wm. McBeth	" 24, "	" 13, "	Promoted to Captain.
Do.	Thomas H. B. Jones	" 24, "	Dec. 4, "	Killed in action near Sweetwater, Tenn.
Do.	David J. Jones	Nov. 20, "	" 4, "	Resigned November 2, 1863.
Do.	George W. Sparks	" 20, "	" 4, "	Promoted to Captain.
Do.	Joseph R. Smith	" 16, "	" 4, "	Promoted to Captain.
Do.	Jacob V. Conklin	" 27, "	" 4, "	Promoted to Captain.
Do.	Orlando F. Lemon	March 21, 1863	June 10, 1863	Resigned April 8, 1864.
Do.	Joseph Kitchen	June 17, "	" 28, "	Promoted to Captain and A. Q. M.
Do.	E. B. Crow	" 17, "	" 10, "	Promoted to Captain.
Do.	Erastus F. Smith	" 16, "	" 10, "	Resigned April 5, 1864.
Do.	Wm. H. Allen	Feb. 1, 1864	Feb. 1, 1864	Promoted to Captain.
Do.	Samuel E. Allman	" 1, "	" 1, "	Resigned September 15, 1864.
Do.	Richard H. Humphreys	" 1, "	" 1, "	Mustered out January 16, 1865.
Do.	Almon Bradford	" 1, "	" 1, "	Resigned September 15, 1864.
Do.	Wm. M. Williams	" 1, "	" 1, "	Promoted to Captain.
Do.	Archibald A. Stewart	July 13, "	July 13, "	Resigned January 21, 1865.
Do.	Joseph W. Wilshire	" 13, "	" 13, "	Promoted to Captain.
Do.	Alfred K. Rarey	" 13, "	" 13, "	Promoted to Captain.
Do.	Thomas W. Hodges	" 13, "	" 13, "	Promoted to Captain.
Do.	John A. Pickering	Oct. 12, "	Oct. 12, "	Promoted to Captain.
Do.	Frederick L. Dunning	" 12, "	" 12, "	Promoted to Captain.
Do.	Hamilton Greer	" 12, "	" 12, "	Mustered out with regiment.
Do.	Robert L. McKean	" 12, "	" 12, "	Resigned May 22, 1865.
Do.	Alex. G. Henderson	" 12, "	" 12, "	Mustered out with regiment.

RANK.	NAME.	DATE OF RANK.	COM. ISSUED.	REMARKS.
1st Lieutenant	James M. Glover	Feb. 10, 1865	Feb. 10, 1865	Mustered out with regiment as Adjutant.
Do.	Henry W. Hitchcock	" 10, "	" 10, "	Mustered out with regiment.
Do.	Philip E. Bush	" 10, "	" 10, "	Mustered out with regiment.
Do.	Joseph A. Walker	" 10, "	" 10, "	Mustered out with regiment.
Do.	Henry N. Bennett	" 10, "	" 10, "	Mustered out with regiment.
Do.	Joseph H. James	March 20, "	March 20, "	Mustered out with regiment as R. Q. M.
Do.	Edward H. Reynolds	May 11, "	May 11, "	Mustered out with regiment.
Do.	Stephen D. Pond	June 6, "	June 6, "	
Do.	Jacob D. Amos	" 6, "	" 6, "	
Do.	John P. Near	" 6, "	" 6, "	
2d Lieutenant	Jacob V. Conklin	July 28, 1862	Oct. 1, 1862	Promoted to 1st Lieutenant.
Do.	Thomas H. B. Jones	" 28, "	" 1, "	Promoted to 1st Lieutenant.
Do.	David Mitchell	Aug. 1, "	" 1, "	Promoted to 1st Lieutenant.
Do.	David J. Jones	" 2, "	" 1, "	Promoted to 1st Lieutenant.
Do.	George W. Sparks	" 6, "	" 1, "	Promoted to 1st Lieutenant.
Do.	Joseph R. Smith	" 11, "	" 1, "	Promoted to 1st Lieutenant.
Do.	Joseph C. Fulton	" 12, "	" 1, "	Resigned October 5, 1862.
Do.	Wm. Gee	" 14, "	" 1, "	Resigned October 24, 1862.
Do.	E. B. Crow	" 11, "	" 1, "	Promoted to 1st Lieutenant.
Do.	Wm. McBeth	" 19, "	" 1, "	Promoted to 1st Lieutenant.
Do.	Orlando F. Lemon	Oct. 5, "	Nov. 13, "	Promoted to 1st Lieutenant.
Do.	Benj. B. Wilson	" 24, "	" 13, "	Resigned July 4, 1863.
Do.	Erastus F. Smith	" 5, "	" 13, "	Promoted to 1st Lieutenant.
Do.	Ezra S. Kimber	" 24, "	" 13, "	Resigned April 8, 1864.
Do.	Wm. H. Allen	" 24, "	Dec. 4, "	Promoted to 1st Lieutenant.
Do.	James T. Lake	Nov. 20, "	" 4, "	Discharged August 19, 1863.
Do.	Robert Young	" 20, "	" 4, "	Declined.
Do.	Samuel E. Allman	" 16, "	" 4, "	Promoted to 1st Lieutenant.
Do.	Hugh O'Harra	" 27, "	" 4, "	Resigned June 14, 1863.
Do.	Richard H. Humphreys	" 20, "	" 31, "	Promoted to 1st Lieutenant.
Do.	Wm. M. Williams	April 8, 1863	June 10, 1863	Promoted to 1st Lieutenant.
Do.	Almond Bradford	March 2, "	" 10, "	Promoted to 1st Lieutenant.
Do.	Joseph W. Wilshire	June 14, "	July 10, "	Promoted to 1st Lieutenant.
Do.	Archibald A. Stewart	April 16, "	" 10, "	Promoted to 1st Lieutenant.
Do.	Charles S. Myers	June 17, "	" 10, "	Resigned February 12, 1864.
Do.	Benj. F. Miller	Feb. 18, 1864	Feb. 18, 1864	Killed June 29, 1864.
Do.	Alfred K. Rarey	Nov. 13, 1863	" 8, "	Promoted to 1st Lieutenant.
Do.	John A. Pickering	Feb. 18, 1864	" 18, "	Promoted to 1st Lieutenant.
Do.	Frederick L. Dunning	" 18, "	" 18, "	Promoted to 1st Lieutenant.
Do.	Hamilton Greer	" 18, "	" 18, "	Promoted to 1st Lieutenant.
Do.	Thomas W. Hodges	Nov. 13, 1863	March 1, "	Promoted to 1st Lieutenant.
Do.	Robert L. McKean	May 23, 1864	May 23, "	Promoted to 1st Lieutenant.
Do.	Alex. G. Henderson	Sept. 8, "	Sept. 8, "	Promoted to 1st Lieutenant.
Do.	James H. Glover	Nov. 26, "	Nov. 26, "	Promoted to 1st Lieutenant.
Do.	Henry W. Hitchcock	" 26, "	" 25, "	Promoted to 1st Lieutenant.
Do.	Philip E. Bush	" 26, "	" 26, "	Promoted to 1st Lieutenant.
Do.	Joseph H. James	Feb. 10, 1865	Feb. 10, 1865	Promoted to 1st Lieutenant.
Do.	Edward H. Reynolds	" 10, "	" 10, "	Promoted to 1st Lieutenant.
Do.	Stephen D. Pond	" 10, "	" 10, "	Promoted to 1st Lieutenant.
Do.	Jacob D. Amos	March 20, "	March 20, "	Promoted to 1st Lieutenant.
Do.	Joseph C. Evart	June 16, "	June 16, "	
Do.	Lyman Means	" 16, "	" 16, "	
Do.	Cyrus L. Holmes	" 16, "	" 16, "	
Do.	James McMillen	" 16, "	" 16, "	
Do.	Benj. F. Humphrey	" 16, "	" 16, "	Mustered out with regiment as Sergeants.
Do.	Stephen L. Dow	" 16, "	" 16, "	
Do.	Daniel D. Bowman	" 16, "	" 16, "	
Do.	Herman L. Holmes	" 16, "	" 16, "	
Do.	Thomas Groves	" 16, "	" 16, "	
Do.	Alonzo Grafton	" 16, "	" 16, "	

FORTY-FIFTH OHIO VOLUNTEER INFANTRY.

THE FORTY-FIFTH REGIMENT was organized at Camp Chase in August, 1862, and mustered into the United States service on the 19th of that month.

The day following its muster-in the regiment was in Kentucky, having been ordered to Cynthiana in that State, where it remained until the advance of General Kirby Smith, after his success at Richmond, compelled it, with the Ninety-Ninth Ohio, to fall back to Covington.

Having participated in the defense of Cincinnati the regiment, in October, advanced to Lexington, reconstructing several of the bridges on the Kentucky Central Railroad. It remained in Lexington until the 25th of January, 1863, when it was ordered to Danville. While in Lexington the Forty-Fifth was brigaded with the Eighteenth and Twenty-Second Michigan Regiments, and One Hundred and Twelfth Illinois, under the command of General Green Clay Smith.

About the middle of February the regiment was mounted at Danville, and brigaded with the Seventh Ohio and Tenth Kentucky Regiments of Cavalry, all under the command of Colonel Runkle. During the end of February and early part of March the regiment performed much arduous service in pursuit of a body of Rebel cavalry, under command of Colonel Cluke, in the region lying between Crab Orchard and Mount Sterling; and at Dutton's Hill, near Somerset, on the 30th of March, a part of the regiment was engaged, for the first time, in the action between the force under General Gillmore and the command of the Rebel General Pegram. In this affair the Forty-Fifth had one man mortally wounded.

From this time until the beginning of July following the regiment was stationed at Somerset, or in that neighboroood, picketing the line of the Cumberland River, and occasionally reconnoitering beyond. These reconnoissances sometimes resulted in skirmishes with the enemy; and in one at Captain West's, between Mill Springs and Monticello, the regiment lost two men killed and several wounded—two of the latter mortally.

On the evening of the 4th of July, 1863, the Forty-Fifth, with Wolford's and the Second Ohio Cavalry, left Jamestown, Kentucky, John Morgan, with his command, having crossed the Cumberland at Burkesville. It constituted a portion of the force under General Hobson which pursued the Rebels in the raid from the Cumberland to the Ohio at Brandenburg, and thence through Indiana and Ohio to Cheshire, where a part of the enemy surrendered on the 20th of July. On that occasion, this regiment being in the advance and pushing the enemy hotly, it had one man mortally and a few others slightly wounded.

Returning to Camp Nelson, Kentucky, toward the end of July, the Forty-Fifth took part in the pursuit of Colonel Scott's force, which had advanced as far as Winchester in that State.

Upon the organization of General Burnside's army in Kentucky, during the month of August, 1863, the Forty-Fifth was included in Byrd's brigade of General Carter's division, with the First Tennessee and One Hundred and Twelfth Illinois Mounted Infantry, and the Eighth Michigan Cavalry. On the 1st of September the army entered Kingston, East Tennessee, and next day the Forty-Fifth was detached and sent to Loudon. It was there ferried across the Tennessee River in advance of all other portions of the army, and was soon after transferred to the cavalry brigade of Colonel Wolford. This brigade, with that of Colonel Byrd, constituting the extreme right of General Burnside's army, occupied the region between Loudon and Charleston, on the Hiawassee River, for some weeks; but after the battle of Chickamauga, in September, the possession of it was disputed by the enemy's cavalry. On the 20th of October Wolford's brigade, then stationed at Philadelphia, was surprised, its direct retreat cut off, and completely routed, with the loss of all its trains, a battery of artillery, and many prisoners. In this affair the Forty-Fifth had three men killed, four mortally wounded, one of whom was an officer, and more than one hundred men captured.

On the 15th of the following month, as the mounted division of General Saunders, to which the Forty-Fifth belonged, was falling back before the enemy's cavalry, the regiment was dismounted and left without any immediate support, while its horses were led to the rear. Being suddenly overpowered by a very spirited attack, and thrown into disorder, one hundred men and officers were taken prisoners, five killed, and several wounded.

After the battle of Campbell's Station General Burnside retired to the defenses of Knoxville with the skeleton Ninth Corps and some raw troops, which afterward constituted a part of the Twenty-Third Corps. On the night of the 16th the mounted division was moved across the river, and next day commenced skirmishing with Longstreet's advance in front of Knoxville. On the following day, November 18th, Saunders's division was hotly engaged, and toward evening driven from the breastworks of rails by which it was partially protected. It was at this juncture that Brigadier-General Saunders, commanding the division, and Adjutant Fearns, of the Forty-Fifth, fell mortally wounded. These troops were again moved across the Holston River and posted in the works on its south bank, where they remained until the siege was abandoned in December. In the fighting of the 18th of November the Forty-Fifth lost five men killed and six mortally wounded, including the Adjutant.

The regiment was next engaged in the action at Bean's Station, on the 14th of December, but without sustaining any loss.

After Longstreet retired toward Virginia the Forty-Fifth, with the Eleventh and Twenty-Seventh Kentucky Mounted Infantry, were sent to Cumberland Gap, and that neighborhood, where they remained until the 8th of February, 1864, when, the animals of the brigade being nearly all worn out, it was marched to Mount Sterling, Kentucky, to be refitted and remounted. This design, however, was never carried out, and the regiment ever after served as infantry proper.

Leaving Mount Sterling April 6th, and Camp Nelson on the 19th of the same month, the Forty-Fifth, with the One Hundred and Twelfth Illinois, and the Eleventh and Sixteenth Kentucky Regiments, marched across the mountains to East Tennessee, reaching Knoxville on the 3d of May. In a few days the regiment was forwarded by rail to Cleveland, Tennessee, whence it marched to Tunnel Hill, Georgia, where it was attached to the Second Brigade, Second Division, Twenty-Third Army Corps, on the 11th. Three days later the battle of Resaca was fought, in which action the Forty-Fifth regiment had two men killed and three mortally wounded; one of whom was Captain Scott, of company A, who commanded the left wing on the occasion, in the absence of the Lieutenant-Colonel and Major. It afterward participated in many of the actions which marked the remarkable Atlanta campaign, which closed with the affair at Lovejoy's Station, having been engaged at New Hope Church, near Dallas, Lost Mountain, and in front of Kenesaw Mountain, besides many other points. Toward the end of June the Forty-Fifth was transferred to the Second Brigade of the First Division, Fourth Corps.

With the Fourth Corps the regiment returned to Middle Tennessee early in November, 1864, and participated in the sanguinary battle of Franklin, and afterward in the two days' fighting in front of Nashville, which resulted so disastrously to the Rebel Army of Tennessee under General Hood.

In the spring of 1865 the Forty-Fifth accompanied the Fourth Corps to East Tennessee; returned with it to Nashville toward the end of April, and was then mustered out of service, on the 15th of the following June, having at that time two months to serve to complete its term of enlistment.

46th REGIMENT OHIO VOLUNTEER INFANTRY.

ROSTER, THREE YEARS' SERVICE.

RANK.	NAME.	DATE OF RANK.	COM. ISSUED.	REMARKS.
Colonel	THOS. WORTHINGTON	July 29, 1861	Jan. 11, 1862	Honorably discharged November 21, 1862.
Do.	CHAS. C. WALCUTT	Sept. 16, 1862	Oct. 9, "	Promoted to Brigadier-General of Vols.
Do.	EDWARD N. UPTON	July 16, 1865	July 16, 1865	Mustered out with regiment as Lieut. Col.
Lt. Colonel	CHARLES C. WALCUTT	Jan. 30, 1862	Feb. 3, 1862	Promoted to Colonel September 16, 1862.
Do.	WILLIAM SMITH	Sept. 16, "	Oct. 9, "	Honorably discharged July 22, 1864.
Do.	ISAAC N. ALEXANDER	Aug. 19, 1864	Aug. 19, 1864	Resigned December 22, 1865.
Do.	EDWARD N. UPTON	Dec. 22, "	Dec. 22, "	Promoted to Colonel.
Do.	JOHN B. NEIL	July 16, 1865	July 16, 1865	Mustered out with regiment as Major.
Major	CHARLES C. WALCUTT	Oct. 1, 1861	Feb. 3, 1862	Promoted to Lieutenant-Colonel.
Do.	WILLIAM SMITH	Jan. 30, 1862	" 3, "	Promoted to Lieutenant-Colonel.
Do.	HENRY H. GIESY	Sept. 16, "	Aug. 9, "	Killed May 28, 1864; buried at Lancaster, Ohio.
Do.	JOSHUA M. HEATH	July 13, 1861	July 13, 1864	Killed July 22, 1864.
Do.	ISAAC N. ALEXANDER	Aug. 11, "	Aug. 11, "	Promoted to Lieutenant-Colonel.
Do.	EDWARD N. UPTON	" 19, "	" 19, "	Promoted to Lieutenant-Colonel.
Do.	JOHN B. NEIL	Jan. 23, 1865	Jan. 23, 1865	Promoted to Lieutenant-Colonel.
Do.	JOHN B. FOSTER	July 16, "	July 16, "	Mustered out with regiment as Captain.
Surgeon	JAMES D. ROBINSON	Sept. 11, 1861	Sept. 11, 1861	Resigned November 21, 1861.
Do.	JAMES McFADDEN	Oct. 11, "	Feb. 7, 1862	Discharged August 19, 1862.
Do.	W. W. BRIDGE	Aug. 26, "	Aug. 27, "	Died August 6, 1864.
Do.	D. P. SMEDLEY	Sept. 19, 1864	Sept. 19, 1864	Resigned December 29, 1864.
Do.	DAVIS HALDERMAN	Jan. 18, 1865	Jan. 18, 1865	Mustered out with regiment.
Ass't Surgeon	GREENLEAF C. NORTON	Oct. 19, 1861	Feb. 7, 1862	Died August 10, 1862.
Do.	D. P. SMEDLEY	" 4, 1862	Oct. 8, "	Promoted to Surgeon.
Do.	J. P. SHAKELFORD	" 8, "	" 8, "	Declined.
Do.	DAVIS HALDERMAN	March 11, 1863	March 11, 1863	Promoted to Surgeon.
Do.	C. J. HAGAN	Feb. 16, 1865	Feb. 16, 1865	Mustered out with regiment.
Chaplain	WM. BAKER	" 1, 1862	" 3, 1862	Died August 25, 1862.
Do.	GEORGE A. EXLINE	Nov. 3, 1864	Nov. 3, 1864	Mustered out with regiment.
Captain	Joshua M. Heath	Sept. 10, 1861	Feb. 7, 1862	Promoted to Major.
Do.	A. G. Sharp	Oct. 16, "	" 7, "	Resigned April 24, 1863.
Do.	Harding C. Geary	" 17, "	" 7, "	Killed at Shiloh April 6, 1862.
Do.	John Wiseman	" 29, "	" 7, "	Resigned May 24, 1864.
Do.	Wm. Pinney	Nov. 8, "	" 7, "	Honorably discharged July 22, 1864.
Do.	Henry H. Giesy	Dec. 16, "	" 7, "	Promoted to Major.
Do.	Philip A. Crow	" 23, "	" 7, "	Discharged December 29, 1862.
Do.	Mitchell C. Lilley	" 31, "	" 7, "	Resigned January 21, 1863.
Do.	Wm. Smith	" 31, "	" 7, "	Promoted to Major.
Do.	Charles Lybrand	Jan. 24, 1862	" 7, "	Resigned January 13, 1863.
Do.	Isaac N. Alexander	" 30, "	" 7, "	Promoted to Major.
Do.	Edward N. Upton	April 6, "	June 16, "	Promoted to Major.
Do.	Emanuel Giesy	Sept. 16, "	Dec. 30, "	Declined; commission returned.
Do.	John J. Carron	" 16, "	Jan. 24, 1863	Resigned May 1, 1864.
Do.	Jacob Lohrer	Dec. 29, "	Feb. 8, "	Resigned September 24, 1864.
Do.	John Ramsey	Jan. 21, 1863	" 7, "	Killed September 5, 1864.
Do.	Lucas A. Bowers	" 13, "	" 8, "	Mustered out.
Do.	John B. Neil	April 14, 1864	April 14, 1864	Promoted to Major.
Do.	Harrison McMichael	July 13, "	July 13, "	Mustered out at expiration of time.
Do.	Joseph Mellen	" 13, "	" 13, "	Returned commission.
Do.	Charles H. Rice	" 13, "	" 13, "	Mustered out with regiment.
Do.	Ebenezer B. Bickett	Aug. 11, "	Aug. 11, "	Died June 27, 1864.
Do.	Wm. W. Watts	" 11, "	" 11, "	Honorably discharged October 20, 1864.
Do.	John Lutz	" 11, "	" 11, "	Killed August 3, 1864.
Do.	John B. Foster	" 19, "	" 19, "	Promoted to Major.
Do.	Elias H. Parsons	" 19, "	" 19, "	Mustered out with regiment.
Do.	Caleb Roberts	" 19, "	" 19, "	Killed at Lovejoy's Station Sept. 5, 1864.
Do.	Marshall B. Wright	Feb. 2, 1865	Feb. 2, 1865	Mustered out with regiment.
Do.	David P. Dunathan	" 2, "	" 2, "	Mustered out with regiment.
Do.	Milton Lochner	" 2, "	" 2, "	Mustered out with regiment.
Do.	Lemuel Grove	" 2, "	" 2, "	Mustered out with regiment.
Do.	Louis Morquart	" 2, "	" 2, "	Mustered out with regiment.
Do.	John A. Murlin	" 2, "	" 2, "	Mustered out with regiment.
Do.	Wm. S. Dalton	April 18, "	April 18, "	Mustered out with regiment.
Do.	John Ackerman	July 18, "	July 16, "	Mustered out with regiment as 1st Lieut.
1st Lieutenant	Isaac N. Alexander	Sept. 10, 1861	Feb. 7, 1862	Promoted to Captain.
Do.	Edward N. Upton	" 10, "	" 7, "	Promoted to Captain.
Do.	Emanuel Giesy	" 27, "	" 7, "	Promoted to Captain by Pres. April 25, 1864.
Do.	John B. Neil	Oct. 1, "	" 7, "	Promoted to Captain.
Do.	Jacob Lohrer	" 16, "	" 7, "	Promoted to Captain.
Do.	Francis M. Lenville	" 29, "	" 7, "	Died July 24.
Do.	Wm. Nessler	Nov. 8, "	" 7, "	Killed September 4, 1862.
Do.	John J. Carron	Dec. 16, "	" 7, "	Promoted to Captain.
Do.	Charles E. Taylor	" 23, "	" 7, "	Resigned December 30, 1862.
Do.	Thomas C. Platt	" 31, "	" 7, "	Mustered out August 18, 1862.
Do.	Charles C. Movers	" 31, "	" 7, "	Resigned August 8, 1863.
Do.	L. A. Bowers	Jan. 24, 1862	" 7, "	Resigned.
Do.	Harrison McMichael	" 30, "	" 17, "	Promoted to Captain.
Do.	Joseph Mellen	April 6, "	June 16, "	Killed September 5, 1862.
Do.	John Ramsey	Aug. 18, "	Oct. 13, "	Promoted to Captain.
Do.	George F. Crarey	Sept. 16, "	Dec. 30, "	Revoked.
Do.	Charles H. Rice	" 18, "	Jan. 24, 1863	Promoted to Captain.
Do.	John Lutz	April 14, 1864	April 14, 1864	Promoted to Captain.
Do.	Ebenezer B. Bickett	Jan. 21, 1863	Feb. 7, 1863	Promoted to Captain.
Do.	John H. Valentine	" 13, "	" 8, "	Resigned July 13, 1864.
Do.	Wm. W. Watts	Sept. 4, 1862	" 7, "	Promoted to Captain.
Do.	David Stewart	Dec. 30, "	" 7, "	Died August 10, 1863.

RANK.	NAME.	DATE OF RANK.	COM. ISSUED.	REMARKS.
1st Lieutenant	John B. Foster	April 14, 1864	April 14, 1864	Promoted to Captain.
Do.	Elias H. Parsons	" 14, "	" 14, "	Promoted to Captain.
Do.	Caleb Roberts	" 14, "	" 14, "	Promoted to Captain.
Do.	Jesse H. Brandt	July 13, "	July 13, "	Honorably discharged November 1, 1864.
Do.	Joseph Amos	" 13, "	" 13, "	Honorably discharged.
Do.	Marshall B. Wright	" 13, "	" 13, "	Promoted to Captain.
Do.	Wm. S. Dalton	Aug. 19, "	Aug. 19, "	Promoted to Captain.
Do.	David P. Dunathan	" 19, "	" 19, "	Promoted to Captain.
Do.	Milton Lochner	" 19, "	" 19, "	Promoted to Captain.
Do.	Lemuel Grove	" 19, "	" 19, "	Promoted to Captain.
Do.	Louis Morquart	" 19, "	" 19, "	Promoted to Captain.
Do.	John A. Murlin	" 19, "	" 19, "	Promoted to Captain.
Do.	John Ackerman	" 19, "	" 19, "	Promoted to Captain.
Do.	Lodwick H. Hopkins	" 19, "	" 19, "	Mustered out August 1, 1865.
Do.	Jacob Schock	" 19, "	" 19, "	Mustered out with regiment.
Do.	Joseph Abright	Feb. 2, 1865	Feb. 2, 1865	Mustered out with regiment.
Do.	George R. Snell	" 2, "	" 2, "	Mustered out with regiment.
Do.	Henry G. Beatty	" 2, "	" 2, "	Mustered out with regiment.
Do.	Wm. De Moss	" 2, "	" 2, "	Mustered out with regiment.
Do.	Lewis F. Ross	" 2, "	" 2, "	Mustered out with regiment.
Do.	Henry H. Brooks	May 31, "	May 31, "	Mustered out with regiment as Adjutant.
Do.	John W. Shaw	" 31, "	" 31, "	Mustered out with regiment.
Do.	Augustus B. Wood	" 31, "	" 31, "	Mustered out with regiment.
Do.	Charles E. Skeels	July 5, "	July 5, "	Mustered out with regiment as Sergt. Maj.
Do.	Noah Dunken	" 16, "	" 16, "	
2d Lieutenant	Harrison McMichael	Feb. 10, 1861	Feb. 7, 1862	Promoted to 1st Lieutenant.
Do.	George F. Crarey	Oct. 5, "	" 7, "	Resigned March 8, 1863.
Do.	Charles H. Rice	" 2, "	" 7, "	Promoted to 1st Lieutenant Sept. 16, 1862.
Do.	Joseph Mellen	" 17, "	" 7, "	Promoted to 1st Lieutenant.
Do.	Wm. W. Watts	" 23, "	" 7, "	Promoted to 1st Lieutenant.
Do.	John Lutz	" 29, "	" 7, "	Promoted to 1st Lieutenant.
Do.	Amos L. Parks	Nov. 13, "	" 7, "	Discharged December 31, 1862.
Do.	Hiram B. Wilson	Dec. 23, "	" 7, "	Killed at Shiloh April 6, 1862.
Do.	John Ramsey	" 31, "	" 7, "	Promoted to 1st Lieutenant.
Do.	Joseph A. Stewart	Jan. 24, 1862	" 7, "	Killed accidentally May 11, 1862.
Do.	Charles B. R. Barker	" 30, "	" 17, "	Resigned September 6, 1862.
Do.	John B. Foster	April 6, "	June 16, "	Promoted to 1st Lieutenant.
Do.	David Stewart	" 6, "	" 16, "	Promoted to 1st Lieutenant.
Do.	Ebenezer B. Bickett	Aug. 18, "	Oct. 14, "	Promoted to 1st Lieutenant.
Do.	Marshall B. Wright	Sept. 16, "	Dec. 30, "	Revoked.
Do.	George Gorman	" 6, "	" 30, "	Killed in action November 25, 1863.
Do.	Elias H. Parsons	" 16, "	Jan. 24, 1863	Promoted to 1st Lieutenant.
Do.	Caleb Roberts	Dec. 26, "	Feb. 7, "	Promoted to 1st Lieutenant.
Do.	John C. Howard	Sept. 4, "	" 7, "	Discharged April 11, 1864.
Do.	John H. Valentine	May 14, "	" 7, "	Promoted to 1st Lieutenant.
Do.	Jesse H. Brandt	Dec. 30, "	" 7, "	Promoted to 1st Lieutenant.
Do.	Joseph Amos	Jan. 21, 1863	" 7, "	Resigned July 13, 1864.
Do.	W. P. Thatcher	" 13, "	" 7, "	Honorably discharged April 29, 1864.
Do.	Marshall B. Wright	March 6, "	April 28, "	Promoted to 1st Lieutenant.
Do.	Noah Dunken	July 16, 1865	July 16, 1865	Promoted to 1st Lieutenant.
Do.	John C. Lilley	" 16, "	" 16, "	Mustered out with regiment as Sergeants; complimentary commissions given after muster out.
Do.	James E. Moore	" 16, "	" 16, "	
Do.	Thomas J. Brellsford	" 16, "	" 16, "	
Do.	Charles W. Kelsey	" 16, "	" 16, "	
Do.	Allen McCutchen	" 16, "	" 16, "	
Do.	John F. McIlvaine	" 16, "	" 16, "	
Do.	Wm. M. Swartz	" 16, "	" 16, "	
Do.	Alexander Mullen	" 16, "	" 16, "	
Do.	John Engle	" 16, "	" 16, "	
Do.	Abraham De Long	" 16, "	" 16, "	

FORTY-SIXTH OHIO VOLUNTEER INFANTRY.

THE FORTY-SIXTH OHIO was recruited at Worthington, Franklin County, Ohio, in the month of September, and was organized on the 16th of October, 1861. It was sent to the field from Camp Chase on the 18th of February, 1862, with an aggregate of nine hundred and seventy-five men, and on the 22d it reported at Paducah, Kentucky. It was brigaded with the Sixth Iowa and the Fortieth Illinois, and was attached to General Sherman's division.

The regiment, with four companies of the Fortieth Illinois, embarked for the Upper Tennessee on the 6th of March, and landed at Savannah on the 8th. Here it remained, within eight miles of the enemy's camp at Pittsburg Landing, for four days, when the grand army arrived, and on the morning of the 14th the fleet reached Pittsburg Landing, which the Rebels had evacuated. A detail from the Forty-Sixth was the first organized body of troops to disembark. The regiment was posted a short distance to the right of Shiloh Church, and there it remained in comparative quiet until the battle. On Saturday, April 5th, companies B and K were on picket. During the night the enemy was feeling the lines constantly, and at daylight his columns could be seen deploying in the distance. At sunrise a Rebel cavalry officer emerged from the woods within thirty yards of the picket-line, and, checking his horse, he stood for a moment in seeming composure, and then inquired: "Are these Union pickets?" He was told they were, and was ordered to come up. He attempted to turn his horse again into the woods, and in an instant the unerring rifle of Sergeant Glenn emptied its deadly contents into his brain; but before the sun had set, the Sergeant, too, lay stark and stiff on the bloody field. The regiment was engaged during the entire battle, with a loss of two hundred and eighty killed and wounded, and fifteen captured. The dead were conveyed to a spot a little to the south of the summit of the ridge overlooking Owl Creek, immediately in front of the first line of battle, and near the Purdy Road, and there they were interred in single graves with the honors of war.

The regiment remained upon the battle-field until the 27th of April, when it moved with the army upon Corinth. The summer and part of the autumn of 1862 were spent in garrisoning the line of the Memphis and Charleston Railroad, and in performing provost-duty in Memphis. In November the regiment started on a campaign through the interior of Mississippi, under General Grant; but, after marching about one hundred miles, the troops were compelled to return to Holly Springs, in consequence of the line of communication having been cut. The regiment was again stationed along the Memphis and Charleston Road; and, being mounted, it was employed principally in raiding and scouting in Northern Mississippi. Early in June, 1863, the regiment was transported to Vicksburg, and it participated in the siege of that place. On the evening of the 4th of July, after the surrender, the regiment took up the line of march in the direction of Jackson, Mississippi, and at eleven o'clock P. M. it halted in the vicinity of Big Black River. Companies E and K were ordered forward to the ford at Birdsong's Ferry, which, after a long search in the darkness, they found; but they had not been there long until unmistakable signs of the enemy were discovered in their immediate front on the opposite bank. It proved to be General Joe Johnston, who, with his army, had reached that point on his way to the relief of Vicksburg. At daybreak the enemy opened fire upon the two companies, and, though they were in a sharp bend of the river, and to a great extent surrounded, they held their position gallantly, but sustained considerable loss. It required several days' severe skirmishing to effect a crossing; and, after gaining the eastern side of the river, the troops moved on upon Jackson, to which point Johnston retreated. After several days' fighting, the enemy was forced to evacuate the city, and the regiment returned to Big Black and went into camp. In this campaign the men suffered greatly from heat and the scarcity of water. On the return march the sick and wounded were carried on the shoulders of fatigue details, on stretchers, exposed to the burning sun, for a distance of thirty miles.

On the 10th of October the regiment, with the Fifteenth Corps, under General Sherman, embarked for Memphis, and from there it marched to the relief of Chattanooga, arriving on the 20th of November. At the battle of Mission Ridge the regiment was engaged severely, and it sustained a heavy loss in killed and wounded. Immediately after this battle the regiment moved on the Knoxville campaign, and, having raised the siege of that place, it marched to Scottsboro', Alabama, for winter-quarters. It arrived on the 31st of December, 1863, having marched over five hundred miles in about two months, exposed to inclement weather, without tents and almost without food and clothing. Here the regiment was armed with Spencer's repeating rifled musket; and here, too, it re-enlisted as veterans. It was furloughed on the 30th of March, 1864, and, after an absence of thirty-eight days, it returned to its camp at Scottsboro'.

On the 1st of May the regiment moved in the direction of Chattanooga, and thence, by way of Snake Creek Gap, to Resaca, where it was actively engaged on the 13th, 14th, and 15th of May, but with small loss. The regiment moved on through Kingston and Van Wert to Dallas, arriving on the 26th. After severe skirmishing, it took position on the Villa Rica Road, on the extreme right of the army, and within five hundred yards of the enemy. On the 27th the Rebels made a bold dash to capture a battery of Parrott guns, but they were repulsed by the brigade of which the regiment was a part. The next day the Rebels made a general attack, but were again repulsed. In these two engagements the Spencer rifles caused such havoc in the charging columns, that ever after the Forty-Sixth was known and dreaded throughout the opposing army. On the 1st of June the regiment, with its division, moved to the left, and relieved the Second and Third Brigades of General Geary's division, Twentieth Corps. Here the regiment participated in the battle of New Hope Church. The command gained a position within one hundred yards of the enemy, and, after severe skirmishing, and by aid of a system of works, the line was advanced to within eighty yards. The enemy's fire harassed the brigade greatly, and Colonel Walcutt, commanding the brigade, determined to gain the Rebel line without loss to his command. His plan succeeded admirably. He arranged the brigade as though a charge was to be made, with flags flying and all the buglers on the line; and he directed his men, who were well covered with works, to stand with their pieces directed along the enemy's parapet. When the bugles sounded the forward, the enemy raised, as had been expected, to repel the anticipated assault, but he received, instead, a very severe fire. The result was that the enemy abandoned his works in confusion, and during the night withdrew from the front of the brigade.

On the 6th of June the brigade passed through Acworth, and went into bivouac until the 9th, when it accompanied General Garrard's cavalry on a reconnoissance to the vicinity of Kenesaw, and there rejoined its division. During the movements on Kenesaw the brigade was in reserve until the 15th of June, when, with the division, it was moved to the extreme left of the army. The Forty-Sixth, with its brigade, supported by the other two brigades of the division, was ordered to charge a line on a ridge a half a mile distant. This was done in gallant style. Twenty-two officers, four hundred men, and six hundred stand of small arms were captured, and many of the enemy were killed and wounded. The division was again placed in reserve until the 25th, when it took position at the base of Kenesaw, and engaged in skirmishing. On the evening of the 26th Walcutt's brigade and two brigades from General Morgan L. Smith's division were detailed as a storming party. The movement took place the next day. Walcutt's brigade led the column, with the Forty-Sixth in advance as skirmishers. The troops moved forward with determination, but it was impossible for them to force their way through the heavy abattis to the enemy's main works, and they were obliged to withdraw. In this assault the Forty-Sixth captured sixty prisoners, but its own loss in killed and wounded was severe. After the evacuation of Kenesaw the regiment moved through Marietta to the junction of the Nickojack with the Chattahoochie. Here it engaged in skirmishing for several days, and then marched to Roswell's Factory, where a crossing of the Chattahoochie was forced on the 15th of July. The regiment remained in bivouac at this point until the 19th, when it moved for Atlanta, and on the evening of the 20th went into line in front of the city.

The regiment was engaged in skirmishing until the 22d, when it assisted in repelling an attack on the Seventeenth Corps. Walcutt's brigade was posted on the left of the Fifteenth Corps, joining the right of the Seventeenth Corps. When the engagement opened the brigade was faced from west to south, partially closing the gap between the two corps. The troops on the right of the brigade gave way, and the enemy gained its rear, while another column was making a direct assault. The column in front was repulsed, and the column in rear was captured. The Forty-Sixth, with its Spencers, did gallant service, and had the honor of retaking a battery of Parrott guns captured by the Rebels during the day. At Ezra Church the regiment was again engaged. When the attack was made the brigade was in reserve, but the regiment was called upon to support the Third Brigade of its division, and it moved into action. While the battle was going on a captured Rebel informed the commanding officer of the regiment that he was of the Thirtieth Louisiana, and that the Forty-Sixth was the regiment that had confronted his at Pittsburg Landing. This was made known to the men, and, remembering their disastrous beginning there, they worked their pieces with redoubled energy. The colors of the Thirtieth Louisiana were captured, and the Colonel, with ten of his officers and fully one-half of his men, were killed. The flag, which was a present from the ladies of New Orleans to the regiment, was presented by General Logan to its immediate captor, Harry Davis, and was contributed by him to the trophies of the State of Ohio, and it can now be seen in the State-House at Columbus.

On the 3d of August the brigade took up an advanced position, and the Forty-Sixth, with details from other regiments, was ordered to drive in or to capture the enemy's outposts. The contest was severe, but it resulted in the capture of about one hundred prisoners. From this time the regiment was constantly engaged in skirmishing until the 26th, when it participated in Sherman's flank movement to Jonesboro'. On the evening of the 28th the division crossed Flint River and went into position near Jonesboro'. On the afternoon of the next day the Rebels made their attack. Three companies of the Forty-Sixth were on the skirmish-line, and the remainder of the regiment was in reserve. The three companies held their ground until the enemy passed their flank, when they retired to the reserve. The regiment received instructions to charge the Rebel line as soon as it wavered. This order was executed, and four officers and fifty men were captured. On the 2d of September the regiment was again engaged, and it succeeded in capturing the enemy's fortified skirmish-line. The regiment followed Hardee's retreating army, and, when near Lovejoy's Station, a halt was made, and the Forty-Sixth was deployed in front of the Fourth Division, Fifteenth Corps, while in front of General Corse's division of the Seventeenth Corps the Sixty-Sixth Illinois was deployed, and preparations were made for an advance. The men of the two regiments challenged each other as to which should first occupy the enemy's line, nearly a mile distant. When the bugles sounded the "forward," they advanced, and for some distance neither seemed to have the advantage. As they neared the line the conflict became hand-to-hand. The enemy was forced to retire, and the Forty-Sixth first occupied its part of the line, capturing about fifty prisoners. After this the army withdrew and went into camp at East Point, near Atlanta. The regiment participated in the campaign against Hood in Northern Georgia and Alabama, and returned to the vicinity of Atlanta on the 5th of November.

On the 15th of November the regiment left Atlanta for Savannah. Nothing extraordinary transpired until in the vicinity of Griswoldsville, when the brigade was ordered to make a reconnoissance in the direction of Macon. The advance soon came upon General Kilpatrick, who was engaging Wheeler's cavalry. An infantry skirmish-line soon dispersed the cavalry, and the brigade pushed on. Wheeler's force was met again soon after, and was again dispersed. The brigade was now withdrawn about a mile, and rude works of logs and stumps were constructed.

While the men were preparing their meal the skirmishers became engaged, and it was discovered that the enemy, about eight thousand strong, was deployed for an assault. The Rebels advanced in three lines, either of which was twice the front of the brigade. The men held their fire until the advancing lines were within one hundred and twenty-five yards, and then they opened with fearful effect. The enemy was broken, but he soon rallied, and again advanced, and was again broken. This was repeated five times. The engagement lasted until near sundown, when the Rebels were forced to retire. In this action the brigade consisted of thirteen hundred muskets and two pieces of artillery, and its loss was less than forty killed and wounded. The regiment shared in the skirmishing around Savannah; and, after the surrender of the city, it embarked, January 10, 1865, on a steamer for Beaufort, South Carolina. On the 27th it started on the march, and moved on without serious interruption until it reached Bentonville. In the battle at that place the Forty-Sixth charged the enemy in his intrenchments, captured and held the works, and was specially complimented for gallantry. The regiment moved on through Goldsboro' to Raleigh, where the news of the surrender of Lee's army was received, and soon after, at the same point, General Johnston surrendered to General Sherman.

The regiment moved by way of Petersburg and Richmond to Washington City. It arrived at Alexandria on the 20th of May, and on the 24th it participated in the grand review, and soon after proceeded to Louisville Kentucky, where it was mustered out on the 22d of July, 1865.

During its term of service, the regiment lost twenty men captured, and seven hundred and five men killed, wounded, and died of disease.

47th REGIMENT OHIO VOLUNTEER INFANTRY

ROSTER, THREE YEARS' SERVICE

RANK.	NAME.	DATE OF RANK.	COM. ISSUED.	REMARKS.
Colonel	FRED'K POSCHNER	Aug. 10, 1861	Aug. 28, 1861	Resigned July 17, 1862.
Do.	L. S. ELLIOTT	July 17, 1862	" 22, 1862	Resigned January 17, 1863.
Do.	AUGUSTUS C. PARRY	Dec. 30, "	Feb. 26, 1863	Mustered out.
Do.	THOMAS T. TAYLOR	Aug. 10, 1865	Sept. 4, 1865	On detached duty at muster out of regiment.
Lt. Colonel	L. S. ELLIOTT	" 23, 1861	Aug. 28, 1861	Promoted to Colonel.
Do.	AUGUSTUS C. PARRY	July 17, 1862	" 22, 1862	Promoted to Colonel.
Do.	FREDERICK HESER	Dec. 30, "	Feb. 26, "	Declined promotion; commission returned.
Do.	JOHN WALLACE	" 30, "	April 14, "	Honorably discharged April 25, 1865.
Do.	THOMAS T. TAYLOR	June 16, 1865	June 16, 1865	Promoted to Colonel.
Major	AUGUSTUS C. PARRY	Aug. 23, 1861	Aug. 28, 1861	Promoted to Lieutenant-Colonel.
Do.	FREDERICK HESER	July 17, 1862	" 22, 1862	Promoted to Lieutenant-Colonel.
Do	JOHN WALLACE	Dec. 30, "	Feb. 26, 1863	Promoted to Lieutenant-Colonel.
Do.	THOMAS T. TAYLOR	" 30, "	April 14, "	Promoted to Lieutenant-Colonel.
Do.	JOSEPH L. PINKERTON	June 26, 1865	June 26, 1865	Resigned as Captain July 3, 1865.
Do.	ALEXANDER CAMPBELL	Aug. 10, "	Aug. 10, "	Mustered out as Captain.
Surgeon	GEORGE A. SPIES	" 27, 1861	" 27, 1861	Resigned April 18, 1862.
Do.	STEPHEN P. BONNER	April 18, 1862	May 10, 1862	Mustered out.
Do.	JACOB HUBER	July 10, 1865	July 10, 1865	Mustered out with regiment.
Ass't Surgeon	AUGUSTUS HOELTGE	Aug. 27, 1861	Aug. 27, 1861	Resigned January 13, 1863.
Do.	AUGUSTUS C. BARLOW	July 4, 1862	July 23, 1862	Resigned November 29, 1862.
Do.	ANDREW DAVIDSON	Jan. 28, 1863	Jan. 28, 1863	Resigned July 26, 1863.
Do.	JACOB HUBER	March 11, "	March 11, "	Promoted to Surgeon.
Chaplain	MICHAEL BITLER	Aug. 28, 1861	Aug. 28, 1861	Resigned November 16, 1861.
Do.	STEPHEN DRAKE SHAFFER	Nov. 14, "	Nov. 20, "	Resigned June 2, 1863.
Captain	Samuel L. Hunter	Aug. 28, "	Aug. 28, "	Resigned December 28, 1862.
Do.	Wm. H. Ward	" 28, "	" 28, "	Mustered out.
Do.	Alex. L. Froelich	" 28, "	" 28, "	Discharged November 12, 1862.
Do.	John Wallace	" 28, "	" 28, "	Promoted to Major.
Do.	Allen S. Bundy	" 28, "	" 28, "	Resigned November 19, 1861.
Do.	Thomas T. Taylor	" 28, "	" 28, "	Promoted to Major.
Do.	Valentine Rapp	" 28, "	" 28, "	Resigned December 15, 1862.
Do.	Chas. N. Helmerick	" 28, "	" 28, "	Mustered out November 24, 1864.
Do.	Hannaniah D. Pugh	" 28, "	" 28, "	Mustered out October 3, 1864.
Do.	Frederick Heser	" 28, "	" 28, "	Promoted to Major.
Do.	Andrew F. Denniston	Jan. 9, 1862	Jan. 9, 1862	Resigned March 17, 1862.
Do.	Webster Thomas	March 17, "	April 21, "	Resigned September 23, 1864.
Do.	John G. Durbeck	July 17, "	Oct. 1, "	Resigned November 29, 1862.
Do.	Lewis D. Graves	Nov. 12, "	Dec. 31, "	Mustered out December 24, 1864.
Do.	Charles Haltenhof	" 29, "	" 31, "	Discharged April 26, 1865.
Do.	Henry H. Sinclair	Dec. 15, "	July 13, 1863	Resigned September 21, 1864.
Do.	George M. Zeigler	" 28, "	" 13, "	Promoted to Colonel 52d U. S. C. T.
Do.	Joseph L. Pinkerton	" 30, "	April 14, "	Promoted to Major.
Do.	Henry Nicholas King	Jan. 1, 1863	July 10, "	Resigned September 27, 1864.
Do.	John W. Duecherman	July 8, 1864	" 8, 1864	Returned commission.
Do.	Alex. Campbell	Aug. 11, "	Aug. 11, "	Promoted to Major.
Do.	Charles P. Dennis	Nov. 26, "	Nov. 26, "	Mustered out at exp'n of service as 1st Lieut.
Do.	Samuel Campbell	" 26, "	" 26, "	Mustered out at exp'n of service as 1st Lieut.
Do.	Obed G. Sherwin	" 26, "	" 26, "	Mustered out at exp'n of service as 1st Lieut.
Do.	Wm. Edward Brachman	Jan. 4, 1865	Jan. 4, 1865	Mustered out with regiment.
Do.	John H. Brown	" 18, "	" 18, "	Mustered out with regiment.
Do.	Henry Bramfoerder	" 18, "	" 18, "	Mustered out with regiment.
Do.	Frederick Seidel	" 18, "	" 18, "	Mustered out with regiment.
Do.	Henry Beckman	June 26, "	June 26, "	Mustered out as 1st Lieutenant June 25, 1865.
1st Lieutenant	Lewis D. Graves	Aug. 28, 1861	Aug. 28, 1861	Promoted to Captain.
Do.	Henry H. Sinclair	" 28, "	" 28, "	Promoted to Captain.
Do.	John G. Durbeck	" 28, "	" 28, "	Promoted to Captain.
Do.	Webster Thomas	" 28, "	" 28, "	Promoted to Captain.
Do.	Andrew F. Denniston	" 28, "	Nov. 19, "	Promoted to Captain.
Do.	Henry Nicholas King	" 28, "	Dec. 12, "	Promoted to Captain.
Do.	Isidora Worms	" 28, "	Aug. 28, "	Resigned November 10, 1861.
Do.	Wm. Durbeck	" 28, "	" 28, "	Resigned (disability removed) October 22, '62.
Do.	Horace A. Egbert	" 28, "	" 28, "	Drowned in West Virginia October 9, 1861.
Do.	Charles Haltenhof	" 28, "	" 28, "	Promoted to Captain.
Do.	John R. Craig	Nov. 25, "	Nov. 25, "	Captain and A. Q. M. General Crook's staff.
Do.	Alonzo Kingsbury	" 27, "	" 27, "	Resigned June 9, 1864.
Do.	George M. Zeigler	Dec. 6, "	Dec. 6, "	Promoted to Captain.
Do.	John W. Duecherman	Jan. 9, 1862	Jan. 9, 1862	Mustered out.
Do.	Joseph L. Pinkerton	March 17, "	April 21, "	Promoted to Captain.
Do.	Abram Wing	July 17, "	Oct. 30, "	Resigned November 16, 1862; revoked.
Do.	Frederick Fisher	Nov. 1, "	Dec. 31, "	Honorably discharged December 15, 1863.
Do.	Wm. C. Wright	" 12, "	" 31, "	Honorably discharged January 19, 1864.
Do.	Isaac N. Walter	" 29, "	" 31, "	Honorably discharged June 22, 1864.
Do.	Alex. Campbell	Dec. 1, "	" 31, "	Promoted to Captain.
Do.	Charles P. Dennis	" 15, "	Jan. 13, 1863	Promoted to Captain.
Do.	Samuel Campbell	" 28, "	" 13, "	Promoted to Captain.
Do.	Wm. H. Kimball	Jan. 24, 1864	" 24, 1864	Honorably discharged November 1, 1864.
Do.	Wm. Durbeck	April 3, "	April 13, "	Revoked.
Do.	Obed G. Sherwin	Jan. 1, "	Jan. 10, "	Promoted to Captain.
Do.	Wm. Edward Brachman	July 8, "	July 8, "	Promoted to Captain.
Do.	Wm. E. Smith	" 8, "	" 8, "	Declined.
Do.	John H. Brown	" 8, "	" 8, "	Promoted to Captain.
Do.	Henry Bramfoerder	" 8, "	" 8, "	Promoted to Captain.
Do.	Frederick Seidel	" 8, "	" 8, "	Promoted to Captain.
Do.	Adolph Ahlers	Nov. 26, "	Nov. 26, "	Honorably discharged Jan. 23, '65 as 2d Lieut
Do.	John W. Wilbur	" 26, "	" 26, "	Honorably discharged Nov. 9, '64, as 2d Lieut

RANK.	NAME.	DATE OF RANK.	COM. ISSUED.	REMARKS.
1st Lieutenant	Henry Beckman	Jan. 18, 1865	Jan. 18, 1865	Promoted to Captain.
Do.	Francis Bickett	" 18, "	" 18, "	Mustered out with regiment.
Do.	Henry Stegeman	" 18, "	" 18, "	Mustered out with regiment.
Do.	George W. Sylvis	" 18, "	" 18, "	Mustered out with regiment.
Do.	Hiram W. Durrell	" 18, "	" 18, "	Mustered out with regiment.
Do.	James H. Bullock	" 18, "	" 18, "	Mustered out May 15, 1865.
Do.	James W. Hallsted	" 18, "	" 18, "	Mustered out.
Do.	George Thompson	" 18, "	" 18, "	Resigned June 20, 1865.
Do.	Wm. B. Everson	" 18, "	" 18, "	Mustered out with regiment.
Do.	Leverett Clendenin	" 18, "	" 18, "	Mustered out with regiment.
Do.	Joseph Rohn	June 26, "	June 26, "	Mustered out with regiment.
Do.	George Wisbey	" 26, "	" 25, "	Mustered out with regiment.
Do.	Rudolph Nell	July 10, "	July 10, "	Mustered out with regiment.
2d Lieutenant	John W. Dueenerman	Aug. 28, 1861	Aug. 28, 1861	Promoted to 1st Lieutenant.
Do.	Abram Wing	" 28, "	" 28, "	Promoted; resigned November 16, 1862.
Do.	Felix Wagner	" 28, "	" 28, "	Resigned February 17, 1862.
Do.	Joseph L. Pinkerton	" 28, "	" 28, "	Promoted to 1st Lieutenant.
Do.	Charles J. Cunningham	" 28, "	" 28, "	Resigned December 21, 1861
Do.	George W. Reeves	" 28, "	" 28, "	Resigned December 6, 1862.
Do.	Wm. H. Koo	" 28, "	" 28, "	Resigned June 16, 1862.
Do.	George M. Zeigler	" 28, "	" 28, "	Promoted to 1st Lieutenant.
Do.	Hubert Stever	" 28, "	Dec. 16, "	Discharged July 29, 1862.
Do.	Frederick Fisher	" 28, "	Aug. 28, "	Promoted to 1st Lieutenant.
Do.	Wm. C. Wright	Jan. 9, 1862	Jan. 9, 1862	Promoted to 1st Lieutenant.
Do.	Theodore Davis	" 9, "	" 9, "	Declined.
Do.	Isaac N. Walter	" 9, "	" 9, "	Promoted to 1st Lieutenant.
Do.	Alex. Campbell	Feb. 3, "	Feb. 3, "	Promoted to 1st Lieutenant.
Do.	Charles P. Dennis	Dec. 21, 1861	April 21, "	Promoted to 1st Lieutenant.
Do.	Obed G. Sherwin	Feb. 17, 1862	" 21, "	Promoted to 1st Lieutenant.
Do.	Philip Schwerer	March 17, "	" 21, "	Resigned August 15, 1864.
Do.	Jacob Wetterer	June 16, "	Oct. 30, "	Resigned Sept., 1864, to date June 14, 1864.
Do.	Wm. H. Kimball	July 29, "	" 30, "	Promoted to 1st Lieutenant.
Do.	Alex. Nasmyth	....	" 30, "	Resigned July 30, 1864.
Do.	Jonathan Casto	Nov. 1, 1862	Dec. 31, "	Died June 20, 1863.
Do.	Adolphus Ahlers	" 12, "	" 31, "	Promoted to 1st Lieutenant.
Do.	John W. Wilbur	Dec. 6, "	" 31, "	Promoted to 1st Lieutenant
Do.	Wm. Edward Brachman	Nov. 29, "	" 31, "	Promoted to 1st Lieutenant.
Do.	Edward Bernard	Dec. 15, "	Jan. 13, 1863	Killed May 19, 1863.
Do.	Frederick Poschner, jr	" 28, "	" 14, "	Resigned August 21, 1863.
Do.	Wm. E. Smith	Jan. 24, 1866	....	Promoted to 1st Lieutenant.
Do.	John H. Brown	April 14, 1864	April 14, 1864	Promoted to 1st Lieutenant.
Do.	Samuel Campbell	Feb. 17, 1862	" 21, 1862	Promoted to 1st Lieutenant.

FORTY-SEVENTH OHIO VOLUNTEER INFANTRY.

THIS was one of the earlier regiments raised in Ohio, at a period when system in recruiting had not been attained. The old rule of the regular army was understood to be in force, requiring a full company to be assembled before a legal muster could be made. This was embarrassing, as it involved delay, tired out the men, and caused many to go home in disgust and remain there.

In spite of these grave disabilities, the regiment, through the perseverance of the Hon. Charles F. Wilstach, now Mayor of Cincinnati, was brought up to the required strength, and thenceforward was known as the "Wilstach Regiment."

Its first rendezvous was at Camp Clay, Pendleton, on the eastern suburbs of Cincinnati, where the men began to assemble on the 15th of June, 1861. July 29th, the rule of muster having been adjusted, companies A and B were mustered into the United States service, and the regiment moved to Camp Dennison, where its organization was completed, August 13th. Thirteen nationalities were represented. Six companies were composed chiefly of Americans and four of Germans.

Frederick Poschner, jr., a native of Hungary, one of the heroes of the Revolution of "Forty-Eight," formerly an officer in the Prussian army, was elected Colonel; Lyman S. Elliott, of Michigan, Lieutenant-Colonel, and Augustus C. Parry, of Cincinnati, Major.

On August 27th orders were received to move to Clarksburg, West Virginia, and report to General W. S. Rosecrans. Arms were issued to the men, and the same day the first dress-parade of the regiment with arms occurred. The day following the regiment left on the cars for Benwood, Western Virginia. Here the first ammunition was distributed, thus impressing the men with the fact that they had reached an enemy's soil, and that they were to commence dealing out war's horrors and punishments to rebellious traitors. This was August 29th.

Upon arriving at Clarksburg the regiment was reported to and reviewed by Brigadier-General Wm. S. Rosecrans. At twelve o'clock M. the order to march was given, and that evening the regiment went into camp at a little place called Jam Loo, after making its first march with knapsacks, a distance of eighteen miles. To say that the men were tired would not express the fact—they were literally exhausted by this first experience of a soldier's life.

Reaching the town of Weston, the regiment camped on the West Fork of the Monongahela River. Two days after, companies A, B, C, D, H, and K, under the Colonel and Major, were ordered to join the main army, leaving companies E, F, G, and I, under Lieutenant-Colonel Elliott, to garrison the village. Colonel Poschner joined the main force of the National army with his regiment at Bulltown, on the Little Kanawha, and was brigaded with the Ninth and Twenty-Eighth Ohio, under command of Colonel Robert L. McCook, whose command was familiarly known, even at that early date, as the "Bully Dutch Brigade."

Arrived at Sutton, company B was left as a re-enforcement to the garrison, while the remainder moved forward and took part in the battle of Carnifex Ferry. Colonel Poschner, with his regiment, was detailed as the storming party, and was awaiting orders to advance, when night put an end to the conflict. Major Parry, in obedience to orders, brought the artillery from the field.

September 24th the brigade crossed Gauley River and advanced on Big Sewell Mountain, encamping on an opposite peak to the Rebel fortifications. While on this mountain the regiment suffered almost beyond description. The heavy and incessant rains inundated the lowlands, swept away the bridges, and converted the roads into a continuous quagmire. It became next to impossible to transport supplies, so that the army was put upon quarter rations. The men had worn out their clothes, were without overcoats or tents, and during this most inclement season of the year were compelled to prosecute a vigorous campaign upon the mountain ranges of Virginia. The troops were at last compelled to retire to Gauley Bridge and vicinity. Colonel McCook's brigade was assigned a camp on the Hamilton farm, about six miles east. While lying here the Forty-Seventh Ohio, in company with the Ninth Ohio, crossed New River to Fayette C. H., and destroyed some Rebel property and placed obstructions in the roads.

The Rebel General Floyd, making his way through and around the obstructions, made his appearance on the banks of New River, opposite the encampment of the Forty-Seventh, and commenced a cannonade, lasting four days, and rendering the National camp almost uninhabitable. A few shots from Captain Mack's ten-pounder Parrotts silenced the Rebel batteries. While Floyd remained the Forty-Seventh was almost constantly engaged in skirmishing with the Rebels on the river bank opposite the mountain. Upon his retreat the regiment went into winter-quarters on the Tompkins farm, Gauley Mountain.

On the 19th of September Lieutenant-Colonel Elliott, with the three companies of the Forty-Seventh left as a garrison at Weston, marched to Cross Lanes to relieve the Thirteenth Ohio and Schneider's battery. That officer took measures to rid the country of the numerous guerrilla bands which infested it. His small force was almost continually engaged on expeditions, generally at night, avoiding roads, and marching with great celerity, surprising the enemy often when in fancied security at home or visiting families scarcely beyond the range of their picket-fires. The country freed of guerrillas, the loyal inhabitants had a chance to organize for their own defense.

The regiment was united at Gauley Mountain, December 5th, and began a line of fortifications covering Gauley Bridge and the Kanawha Valley from an advance on the Lewisburg Road. This occupied the time up to April 23, 1862, excepting the month of January, when, in obedience to orders from General J. D. Cox, Major A. C. Parry led an expedition to Little Sewell Mountain, drove the Rebels from their quarters, destroyed their works, and captured prisoners

BAGGAGE TRAIN ASCENDING THE ALLEGHANIES.

THE ASTOR LIBRARY
NY

On the 23d of April Captain John Wallace, with three companies, was sent on an expedition to Lewisburg, and was alone until the 10th of May, when he was re-enforced by one company of the Forty-Fourth and one from the Forty-Seventh, and the second battalion of the Second Virginia Cavalry, commanded by Major Hoffman. Lieutenant-Colonel Elliott took command of this force and advanced upon Lewisburg the same night. This expedition proved a complete success. The enemy was completely routed and scattered, and his camp equipage, horses, and many prisoners, fell into the hands of the Nationals. In their flight the Rebels threw away arms, clothing, and, in some cases, even their saddles. The cavalry returned to Gauley Bridge, leaving the place in possession of the infantry, under Lieutenant-Colonel Elliott, whose regiment had marched to Meadow Bluffs, where the Forty-Seventh was joined by the Thirty-Sixth and Forty-Fourth Ohio, and with them made up the Third Provisional Brigade of the Kanawha Division, under command of Colonel George Crook, of the Thirty-Sixth. On June 22d the brigade, on an expedition through Monroe County, Virginia, compelled General Loring to retreat to Salt Pond Mountain, and captured a large number of beef-cattle and considerable stores. This march was over ninety miles, occupied three days, and was severe on the men, who suffered from sun-stroke and exhaustion. After a short rest, July 10th, Major Parry commanding, the regiment marched to the relief of two companies of the Forty-Fourth, and to ascertain the enemy's position, and rescue the family of Captain Harris. Crossing Greenbrier River in two columns, he moved upon a camp of the enemy, which was abandoned without a struggle. Making suitable provisions to protect his rear, Major Parry penetrated to Loring's camp, and then fell back to the intersection of the Union and Centerville Roads; but the enemy declined an encounter. On August 6th Major Parry was dispatched with four companies to reconnoiter the country in the northern part of the counties of Greenbrier and Pocahontas, and drive the Moccasin Rangers therefrom. This was successfully done, by many miles of hard marching over the rugged hills of that region. The guerrillas were driven across Greenbrier River to White Sulphur Springs. Similar expeditions were sent out with like success.

Re-enforcements being ordered to General Pope in Eastern Virginia, the regiment retired to the vicinity of Gauley Bridge. Upon arriving within seven miles of that place, two regiments of the brigade, the Forty-Fourth and Forty-Seventh Ohio, were ordered into camp. From this point four companies of the Forty-Seventh, under Lieutenant-Colonel Parry, were sent to hold the country in and around Point Lookout and Locust Lanes. On the 3d of September the remaining six companies, under command of Colonel Elliott, were ordered to Summerville, then threatened by Jenkins. Colonel Elliott assumed command of the garrison and began preparations to receive the attack of the enemy, by throwing up breastworks; but September 10th it was resolved to retreat to Gauley Bridge. The retreat proved disastrous, but was continued almost to Gallipolis, Ohio. The Forty-Seventh, under Lieutenant-Colonel Parry, was largely instrumental in saving the National army from capture.

After maneuvering in the Kanawha Valley for some weeks the Forty-Seventh, on the 30th of December, 1862, embarked on steamers for Louisville, Kentucky, and Memphis, Tennessee. Here the regiment joined the expedition against Vicksburg, in the Third Brigade, Second Division, of the Thirteenth Army Corps. Lieutenant-Colonel Parry was promoted to Colonel, and arrived at Vicksburg and began work on the canal late in January, 1863. The regiment participated in the advance to the rear of Vicksburg, and reached Walnut Hills, behind Vicksburg, May 18, 1863. In this march many prisoners were captured from General Loring's forces.

On May 19th Colonel Parry led in an impetuous assault on Cemetery Hill, gaining a footing close under the works, which was held until nightfall; becoming too hot, it was abandoned. The loss was very severe. Again, on the 22d, Colonel Parry led a charge, with the same result. Until the surrender the regiment was in the front line, and occupied Cemetery Hill Fort. During most of the siege its camp was but three hundred yards from the enemy's main line, and the pickets were in such close proximity that they could bayonet each other by little exertion.

The next day after the city was occupied the Forty-Seventh was dispatched toward Jackson, Mississippi, after Johnston's Rebel forces. It participated in the attack and capture of Jackson.

Colonel A. C. Parry was made Provost-Marshal, and his regiment destroyed the Rebel fortifications and the railroad track about the city. September 27, 1863, the corps returned to Big Black River, and thence to Vicksburg, where it took transports for Memphis, where the Forty-Seventh, with its brigade and division, received orders to march to Germantown.

On October 9th the regiment was sent to Corinth, Mississippi, as guard to the corps train. Corinth was reached October 15th. On the 17th the march was resumed for Iuka; thence to Cherokee Station, Alabama, and, after a halt of five days, to Tuscumbia. While here Colonel Parry successfully forwarded important dispatches to General Sherman at Florence, Alabama. Sergeant Madison Richardson and Corporal William Weber, of company F, Forty-Seventh Ohio, carried them down a portion of the Tennessee River where a Unionist had not sailed for a year.

On October 21, 1863, the Forty-Seventh arrived opposite Chattanooga, and October 23d moved to the mouth of South Chattanooga Creek, and constructed, on the south side of the Tennessee River, rifle-pits for the regiment. By daybreak the pits were finished. At noon, Lieutenant-Colonel Wallace in command of the skirmish-line, the whole army advanced and opened the battle of Chickamauga.

Colonel Parry was ordered to cover Woods's battery, and hold his regiment in reserve. When the summit of Mission Ridge was gained the Forty-Seventh Ohio occupied a point on Mission Ridge adjacent to Tunnel Hill. Without halting, the line was advanced to the southern slope, and met a brigade of the enemy ascending. The Rebels were checked, but again and again advanced, covered by their artillery, and as often driven back. The Rebels then made a demonstration on the left, and were again promptly hurled back. A dense fog now settled over the Ridge and prevented further movements. October 25th the Forty-Seventh was in full pursuit of the enemy. On the 28th it entered Graysville and destroyed a machine-shop, storehouse, and mills, which had been used for manufacturing arms.

The Forty-Seventh marched with the rest of the forces sent to the relief of General Burnside, at Knoxville, and was within four miles of Maryville, November 6th, where information of the retreat of Longstreet's Rebel force was received, causing a return to Chattanooga. This was severe; the men were without shoes, scantily clothed, and almost without rations, and marching left their footprints in blood on the frozen ground. Bellefonte was reached early in January.

On January 25th the regiment, under Major Taylor, marched to Larkin's Landing for the purpose of surprising a force, but through some chance the Rebels were apprised, and escaped.

On January 30th the Forty-Seventh joined a diversion against Rome, Georgia. It crossed the river and marched through the "Narrows," *via* the Sand Mountain Road to Lebanon, Alabama. On February 3d the Rebels appeared in force and a spirited skirmish continued until noon. At one P. M. the regiment marched for Larkin's Landing, arriving February 6th.

While here, by request of Colonel Parry, then in command of the Second Division of the Fifteenth Army Corps, Major Taylor and his officers persuaded one-half of the men to re-enlist as veterans, and at a subsequent meeting, when Colonel Parry was present, the required three-fourths re-enlisted. Thus the Forty-Seventh became a veteran regiment, but was not permitted to enjoy its furlough, so that the men became somewhat soured. Through the officers of the regiment General Thomas promised that it should, after a certain date, enjoy its thirty days' furlough. This calmed the men, and again, March 6th, three-fourths re-enlisted, were mustered, and on the 18th took cars at Bridgeport for Cincinnati, arriving Tuesday, March 22, 1864.

On April 25th, its furlough having expired, the Forty-Seventh re-assembled, to a man, at Camp Dennison, Ohio, and May 3d resumed its proper place in the army, at Stevenson, Alabama.

The Atlanta campaign had been initiated, and the first duty was to march from Chattanooga to Sugar Valley, near Rossville, where it threw up log breastworks. May 11th these were evacuated, and the campaign commenced. Space will not permit a statement of daily marches and encounters with the enemy, the gallant fighting, etc. The enemy was met at Snake Creek Gap, Resaca, Kingston, Dallas, New Hope Church, Big Shanty, Kenesaw, and Ezra Church. At Kenesaw Colonel Parry was severely wounded, and the command devolved upon Lieutenant-Colonel Wallace, who led it until made prisoner in the action before Atlanta. He was succeeded in command by Major Taylor. Colonel Parry recovered from his wound, and resumed command on September 30th.

At Hood's dash to the rear of Sherman's forces, the Forty-Seventh participated up to and beyond Rome, Georgia, almost constantly skirmishing. On the march the regiment was re-enforced by four hundred conscripts and substitutes, who were quickly drilled and disciplined.

On November 15th the Forty-Seventh, with Sherman's army, commenced its "march to the sea." This resembled some gala excursion, so free was it from annoyance. Wild flowers were blooming by the wayside, and in lawns and gardens, with the freshness and fragrance of spring. December 10th the regiment went into camp twelve miles from Savannah, with flooded rice-fields and the enemy in front.

On Monday, December 13th, at seven o'clock A. M., the assault on Fort McAllister commenced, the Forty-Seventh occupying the advance. The ground between the command and the fort was level and open, and about half-way between the line and the fort was a strong plank fence. The order of battle was: the Forty-Seventh Ohio on the extreme left, its flank resting on the river, in the center the Fifty-Fourth Ohio, and on the right the One Hundred and Eleventh Illinois. In the center was the Third, and on the right the First Brigade. The fort numbered twenty guns, which, with the exception of those on the river front, were *en barbette*. Thirteen of them could be brought to bear on the Second Brigade.

At ten minutes to five P. M. the charge was sounded. The enemy opened rapidly with his inland guns: but so effective was the fire of Captain Brachmann's skirmish-fire that, although the regiment was compelled to pass over such a space of cleared ground and climb the fence, very little damage was done. As the regiment approached it was discovered that the enemy had neglected to construct his line of abattis to low-water mark, and it being ebb-tide, there was an unobstructed passage on the beach. Colonel Parry immediately swung the wings of his regiment together and scaled the parapet from that front, taking the land batteries in flank and reverse. It required two volleys from the regiment before the enemy abandoned his guns and retreated to the bomb-proofs. In pursuing them into a bomb-proof Major Taylor was severely wounded in the right hand.

A contest arose between the Forty-Seventh and Seventieth Ohio as to whose colors were first planted on the fort. The witnesses of the assault, while at the fort, inquired into the matter. Several of General Hazen's staff, who were overlooking the entire movement, decided that the colors came up first from the river front, and, as the Forty-Seventh alone assaulted from that front, it was its colors that first reached the fort.

On Christmas Day Savannah was occupied. The troops, after resting a few days, started on the campaign to Raleigh, North Carolina, where the news of Lee's and Johnston's surrender was received. Shortly after the Forty-Seventh marched through the Rebel capital to Washington City, and there participated in the grand review.

When the Forty-Seventh entered the field it numbered eight hundred and thirty men; at the termination of the Atlanta campaign it numbered only one hundred and twenty men, but was subsequently re-enforced by four hundred drafted men and substitutes.

On the surrender of the Confederate forces Lieutenant-Colonel Wallace was paroled, and, under orders from the War Department, May 15, 1865, was mustered out of service. In a short time he died from the effects of starvation while a prisoner of war.

Both Colonel Parry and Colonel Taylor were promoted to the rank of Brigadier-General by brevet toward the close of their services.

From Washington the regiment was carried to Cincinnati, and thence to Little Rock, Arkansas, where it served as a part of the "Army of Occupation" until August 11th, when it was mustered out and ordered to Camp Dennison, Ohio, where it arrived August 22d, and on the 24th was paid off and discharged, having served a period of four years, two months, and nine days, and campaigned through all the slave States except, Texas, Florida, and Missouri.

Of its field-officers, Brigadier-General A. C. Parry, Lieutenant-Colonel L. S. Elliott, and Lieutenant-Colonel John Wallace have died.

48th REGIMENT OHIO VOLUNTEER INFANTRY.

ROSTER, THREE YEARS' SERVICE.

RANK.	NAME.	DATE OF RANK.	COM. ISSUED.	REMARKS.
Colonel	PETER J. SULLIVAN	Jan. 23, 1862	Feb. 28, 1862	Resigned August 7, 1863.
Do.	JOB R. PARKER	March 18, 1864	March 18, 1864	Mustered out January 1, 1865.
Do.	F. W. MOORE	Aug. 22, 1862	Sept. 25, 1862	Transferred from 83d O. V. I.
Lt. Colonel	PETER J. SULLIVAN	Nov. 23, 1861	Feb. 28, "	Promoted to Colonel.
Do.	JOB R. PARKER	Jan. 23, 1862	" 28, "	Promoted to Colonel.
Do.	JOSEPH W. LINDSAY	May 31, 1863	Aug. 20, 1863	Mustered out.
Do.	JAMES R. LYNCH	July 28, 1865	Sept. 4, 1865	Mustered out with regiment.
Major	JAMES S. WISE	Sept. 21, 1861	Feb. 21, 1862	Resigned September 3, 1862.
Do.	SAMUEL G. W. PETERSON	Jan. 11, 1863	" 6, 1863	Revoked; resigned as Captain Feb. 21, 1863.
Do.	VIRGIL H. MOATS	Feb. 21, 1861	March 25, "	Died July 11, 1863.
Do.	JOHN A. BERRING	July 11, 1863	Jan. 27, 1864	
Surgeon	MILTON F. CAREY	Sept. 27, 1861	Feb. 28, 1862	Resigned March 11, 1863.
Do.	PLYN A. WILLIS	March 11, 1863	....	Transferred from 83d O. V. I.
Ass't Surgeon	AARON A. JOHNSON	Oct. 11, 1861	Feb. 28, 1862	Resigned March 8, 1863.
Do.	JOHN K. LEWIS	Aug. 21, 1862	Aug. 25, "	Died October 11, 1862.
Do.	PLYN A. WILLIS	Oct. 15, "	Dec. 2, "	Promoted to Surgeon.
Do.	C. HOMER WILES	April 4, 1863	April 4, 1863	Transferred to 83d O. V. I.
Do.	WM. WATT	" 16, "	" 16, "	Mustered out.
Do.	THOMAS C. BAIRD	July 18, "	July 18, "	Mustered out with regiment.
Chaplain	JOHN F. SPENCE	Nov. 11, 1861	Feb. 28, 1862	Resigned March 18, 1863.
Captain	Job R. Parker	Sept. 9, "	" 28, "	Promoted to Lieutenant-Colonel.
Do.	J. W. Frazer	Oct. 15, "	" 28, "	Resigned January 14, 1863.
Do.	John J. Ireland	Nov. 23, "	" 28, "	Died March 16, 1862.
Do.	Cyrus Elwood	" 25, "	" 28, "	Resigned Sept. 6, '62; hon. disch'd Nov. 1, '62.
Do.	Samuel G. W. Peterson	" 25, "	" 28, "	Promoted; resigned February 21, 1863.
Do.	Wm. L. Warner	Dec. 13, "	....	Killed at Shiloh April 7, 1862.
Do.	Virgil H. Moats	" 13, "	....	Promoted to Major.
Do.	George A. Miller	" 13, "	....	Resigned June 6, 1862.
Do.	J. E. Bond	Jan. 23, 1862	....	Killed April 22, 1862.
Do.	Isaac J. Ross	" 23, "	....	Resigned December 10, 1862.
Do.	Richard A. Robbins	" 23, "	....	Resigned February 14, 1863
Do.	Joseph W. Lindsay	April 7, "	June 24, 1862	Promoted to Lieutenant-Colonel.
Do.	George A. Miller	Sept. 9, "	Sept. 12, "	Resigned June 10, 1863.
Do.	Francis M. Posegate	" 9, "	Oct. 3, "	Resigned June 25, 1863.
Do.	James C. Kelsey	March 17, "	Feb. 6, 1863	Resigned February 20, 1863.
Do.	John A. Berring	Jan. 14, 1863	" 4, "	Promoted to Major.
Do.	Joshua Hussey	" 11, "	" 6, "	Resigned as 1st Lieutenant February 15, 1863.
Do.	Richard T. Wilson	April 12, 1862	" 6, "	Resigned April 12, 1863.
Do.	James Sowrey	Feb. 20, 1863	March 25, "	Mustered out.
Do.	Cyrus Hussey	" 14, "	" 25, "	Mustered out.
Do.	Isaac L. Tice	Dec. 10, 1862	May 28, "	Resigned.
Do.	Robert T. Coverdale	Nov. 1, 1863	Jan. 25, 1861	Captain and A. Q. M.
Do.	Daniel Gunsaullus	Feb. 21, "	March 25, 1863	
Do.	Cyrenus P. Bratt	Nov. 1, "	Jan. 25, 1864	Resigned March 27, 1864; disch'd May 23,'64.
Do.	Andrew M. Cochran	" 1, "	" 25, "	Mustered out with regiment.
Do.	James R. Lynch	" 1, "	" 25, "	Promoted to Lieutenant-Colonel.
Do.	Thomas Montgomery	" 1, "	" 25, "	
Do.	Richard A. South	" 1, "	" 25, "	Revoked; resigned as 1st Lieutenant.
Do.	George W. Mosgrove	" 1, "	" 25, "	Mustered out with regiment.
Do.	Henry H. Eberhart	Jan. 14, "	March 30, 1863	Mustered out with regiment.
Do.	Wesley W. Spear	Aug. 11, 1864	Aug. 11, 1864	Mustered out with regiment.
Do.	Michael McCaffrey	May 2, 1865	May 2, 1865	Mustered out with regiment.
Do.	Wm. H. H. Rike	July 28, "	Sept. 4, "	Mustered out with regiment.
1st Lieutenant	James R. Pollock	Oct. 12, 1864	Oct. 12, 1864	Mustered out with regiment.
Do.	John M. Baer	March 21, "	March 21, "	Mustered out with regiment.
Do.	Benj. W. Ladd	July 28, 1865	Sept. 4, 1865	
Do.	Frank M. Swaney	" 28, "	" 4, "	
Do.	Samuel H. Stevenson	" 28, "	" 4, "	
Do.	Richard A. Robbins	Sept. 9, 1861	Feb. 28, 1862	Promoted to Captain.
Do.	Samuel G. W. Peterson	" 19, "	" 28, "	Promoted to Captain.
Do.	James C. Kelsey	Nov. 23, "	" 28, "	Promoted to Captain.
Do.	Joshua Hussey	" 25, "	" 28, "	Promoted; resigned as 1st. Lt. Feb. 15, 1863.
Do.	John J. Gaer	" 25, "	" 28, "	Resigned March 3, 1863.
Do.	Joseph W. Lindsay	Dec. 13, "	" 28, "	Promoted to Captain.
Do.	Aquilla Coonrod	" 13, "	" 28, "	Resigned July 16, 1862.
Do.	Chas. A. Partridge	" 13, "	" 28, "	Resigned January 23, 1863.
Do.	Wm. A. Quarterman	Jan. 1, 1862	" 28, "	Resigned January 25, 1863.
Do.	Francis M. Posegate	" 23, "	" 28, "	Promoted to Captain September 6, 1862.
Do.	Isaac L. Tice	Feb. 28, "	" 28, "	Discharged December 10, 1862; restored.
Do.	Wm. E. Brayman	Aug. 28, 1861	" 28, "	Resigned February 21, 1863.
Do.	Robert C. McGill	Sept. 19, "	" 28, "	Resigned August 2, 1863.
Do.	Richard T. Wilson	Oct. *25, "	March 20, "	Promoted to Captain.
Do.	David R. Plilfy	April 7, 1862	June 24, "	Resigned October, 1863.
Do.	James Sowrey	Sept. 15, "	Dec. 31, "	Promoted to Captain.
Do.	Robert T. Coverdale	Dec. 10, "	" 31, "	Promoted to Captain.
Do.	Cyrenus P. Bratt	Feb. 1, 1863	Feb. 6, 1863	Promoted to Captain.
Do.	George W. Mosgrove	" 1, "	" 6, "	Promoted to Captain.
Do.	Cyrus Hussey	Sept. 6, 1862	" 6, "	Promoted to Captain.
Do.	Daniel Gunsaullus	Feb. 1, 1863	" 6, "	Promoted to Captain.
Do.	Andrew M. Cochran	June 25, "	March 25, "	Promoted to Captain.
Do.	James R. Lynch	April 12, 1862	Feb. 6, "	Promoted to Captain.
Do.	Cornelius Conrad	March 3, 1863	March 25, "	Resigned September 16, 1862.
Do.	Thomas Montgomery	Feb. 21, "	" 25, "	Promoted to Captain.
Do.	Wm. H. H. Rike	March 1, "	" 25, "	Promoted to Captain.
Do.	Michael McCaffrey	Feb. 21, "	" 25, "	Promoted to Captain.

RANK.	NAME.	DATE OF RANK.	COM. ISSUED.	REMARKS.
1st Lieutenant	Wm. H. Smith	Feb. 20, 1863	March 25, 1863	Honorably discharged May 24, 1864.
Do.	Richard A. South	" 14, "	" 25, "	Resigned January 9, 1864.
Do.	Henry W. Day	Nov. 1, "	Jan. 25, 1864	
Do.	Thomas W. Wright	" 1, "	" 25, "	Revoked ; deceased ; 2d Lieutenant.
Do.	John K. Reed	" 1, "	" 25, "	
Do.	John M. Kendall	" 1, "	" 25, "	Revoked ; resigned as 2d Lieutenant.
Do.	Jesse H. Allison	" 1, "	" 25, "	Revoked ; resigned as 2d Lieutenant.
Do	Wm. J. Srofe	" 1, "	" 25, "	Mustered out with regiment.
Do.	Christian Burkhard	" 1, "	" 25, "	Killed.
Do.	Joseph Stretch	Jan. 1, 1864	" 21, "	
Do.	George L. Byers	Nov. 21, "	Nov. 21, "	Mustered out.
Do.	B. W. Ladd	" 26, "	" 26, "	Mustered out.
Do.	John Wilson	" 26, "	" 26, "	Mustered out.
Do.	John M. Wilson	May 2, 1865	May 2, 1865	Mustered out with regiment.
2d Lieutenant	Francis M. Posegate	Sept. 9, 1861	Feb. 28, 1862	Promoted to 1st Lieutenant.
Do.	John Kean	Oct. 7, "	" 28, "	Discharged September 8, 1862.
Do.	Robert T. Coverdale	" 7, "	" 28, "	Promoted to 1st Lieutenant.
Do.	Theodoric L. Fields	" 28, "	" 28, "	Resigned September 6, 1862.
Do.	Richard T. Wilson	Nov. 11, "	" 28, "	Promoted to 1st Lieutenant.
Do.	James Sowrey	" 23, "	" 28, "	Promoted to 1st Lieutenant.
Do.	George W. Mosgrove	" 25, "	" 28, "	Promoted to 1st Lieutenant.
Do.	Cyreuns P. Bratt	" 25, "	" 28, "	Promoted to 1st Lieutenant.
Do.	Daniel Gunsaullus	Dec. 13, "	" 28, "	Promoted to 1st Lieutenant.
Do.	David R. Philfy	Jan. 20, "	" 28, "	Promoted to 1st Lieutenant
Do.	Cyrus Hussey	" 23, "	" 28, "	Resigned February 15, 1863
Do.	Harvey Goddard	Oct. 25, "	March 20, "	
Do.	John D. Nevins	April 7, 1862	June 24, "	Resigned March 2, 1863.
Do.	Andrew M. Cochran	Sept. 15, "	Dec. 31, "	Promoted to 1st Lieutenant.
Do.	Thomas Montgomery	Jan. 14, 1863	Feb. 4, 1863	Promoted to 1st Lieutenant.
Do.	Wm. H. H. Rike	Feb. 1, "	March 6, "	Promoted to 1st Lieutenant.
Do.	Michael McCaffrey	" 1, "	Feb. 6, "	Promoted to 1st Lieutenant.
Do.	Cornelius Conrad	Sept. 6, 1862	" 6, "	Promoted to 1st Lieutenant.
Do.	Wm. H. Smith	Feb. 1, 1863	March 6, "	Promoted to 1st Lieutenant.
Do.	James R. Lynch	March 1, 1862	Feb. 6, "	Promoted to 1st Lieutenant.
Do.	Richard A. South	Feb. 1, 1863	March 6, "	Promoted to 1st Lieutenant.
Do.	Henry W. Day	Dec. 10, 1862	" 25, "	Promoted to 1st Lieutenant.
Do.	Thomas W. Wright	July 15, "	Feb. 24, "	Promoted to 1st Lieutenant ; deceased.
Do.	John K. Reed	March 2, 1863	March 25, "	Promoted to 1st Lieutenant.
Do.	John M. Kendall	July 25, "	" 25, "	Resigned February 24, 1864.
Do.	Jesse H. Allison	March 3, "	" 25, "	Resigned September, 1863.
Do.	Wm. J. Srofe	" 1, "	" 25, "	Promoted to 1st Lieutenant.
Do.	James Douglass	Sept. 28, 1864	Sept. 4, 1865	Mustered out with regiment.
Do.	Thomas H. Hansell	" 28, "	" 4, "	Mustered out with regiment.
Do.	Asa N. Ballard	" 28, "	" 4, "	Mustered out with regiment.
Do.	John R. Simmons	" 28, "	" 4, "	Mustered out with regiment as Sergeant.
Do.	John M. Crabb	" 28, "	" 4, "	Mustered out with regiment as Sergeant.
Do.	Elihu Hiatt	" 28, "	" 4, "	Mustered out with regiment.

FORTY-EIGHTH OHIO VOLUNTEER INFANTRY.

THIS regiment was organized at Camp Dennison on the 17th of February, 1862, and soon after reported to General W. T. Sherman, at Paducah, Kentucky. After a short rest at Paducah it moved up the Tennessee River, on the steamer Express, and on the 19th of March disembarked at Pittsburg Landing.

On the 4th of April, while the regiment was on drill, firing was heard, and the Forty-Eighth at once moved in the direction of the sound; but the enemy fell back, and at nightfall the regiment returned to its quarters. About seven o'clock on the morning of the 6th the regiment advanced upon the enemy, and was soon warmly engaged. Charge after charge was repulsed, and though the Rebel fire was making fearful gaps in the line the men stood firm. A battery was sent to the regiment's aid, but, after firing four shots, it retired. The Rebels then advanced, confidently expecting to capture the regiment, but they were driven back, and the Forty-Eighth withdrew to its supports, having been ordered three times by General Sherman to fall back. It is claimed that General Johnston, of the Rebel army, was killed in this portion of the battle by some member of the Forty-Eighth. The regiment was actively engaged during the remainder of the day; and, late in the afternoon, in connection with the Twenty-Fourth Ohio and Thirty-Sixth Indiana, it participated in a decisive attack on the Rebel lines. It acted throughout in Buckland's brigade of Sherman's division—a brigade which had no share in the early rout of a part of that division.

On the second day of the battle, about ten o'clock A. M., the regiment went into action across an open field, under a galling fire, and continued constantly exposed until the close of the engagement. The Forty-Eighth lost about one-third of its members in this battle.

From this time until after the close of the rebellion the regiment engaged continually in active duty. In the attack upon Corinth, the Forty-Eighth was among the first organized troops to enter the Rebel works. In General Sherman's first expedition to Vicksburg, it occupied, with credit, a position on the right in the assault; and it was in Sherman's expedition up the Arkansas River, and distinguished itself in the battle of Arkansas Post. It was with Grant during his Vicksburg campaign; fought at Magnolia Hills and Champion Hills; and participated in a general assault on the Rebel works in the rear of Vicksburg, May 23, 1863. On the 25th of June following, another general assault was made upon the same works, and the Forty-Eighth was ordered to cross an open field, exposed to two enfilading batteries, to take position in the advanced line of rifle-pits, and to pick off the enemy's gunners. This order was successfully executed. It took a prominent part in the battle of Jackson, Mississippi, and soon after engaged in the fight at Bayou Teche. At Sabine Cross Roads the Forty-Eighth, then a mere remnant of its former self, severely punished the "Crescent Regiment;" but, in turn, it was overpowered and captured. It was not exchanged until October, 1864. The majority of the men in the regiment re-enlisted, but, on account of the capture, they never received their veteran furlough. After its exchange the regiment shared in the capture of Mobile.

After the surrender of the Rebel armies, the remaining one hundred and sixty-five men of this regiment were ordered to Texas. The regiment was at last mustered out of the service in May, 1866.

49th REGIMENT OHIO VOLUNTEER INFANTRY.

ROSTER, THREE YEARS' SERVICE.

RANK.	NAME.	DATE OF RANK.	COM. ISSUED.	REMARKS.
Colonel	WM. H. GIBSON	July 31, 1861	Sept. 18, 1861	Mustered out.
Do.	JOSEPH R. BARTLETT	June 26, 1865	June 26, 1865	Mustered out with regiment as Lieut. Col.
Lt. Colonel	A. M. BLACKMAN	Aug. 17, 1861	Sept. 18, 1861	Resigned September 30, 1862.
Do.	LEVI DRAKE	Sept. 30, 1862	Oct. 10, 1862	Killed at Stone River January 1, 1863.
Do.	BENJ. S. PORTER	Jan. 1, 1863	Jan. 24, 1863	Appointed Major in Invalid Corps July 2, '63.
Do.	SAMUEL F. GRAY	Oct. 4, "	Dec. 3, "	Resigned October 4, 1864; expiration of term.
Do.	LUTHER M. STRONG	Dec. 5, 1864	" 5, 1864	Resigned March 12, 1865.
Do.	JOSEPH R. BARTLETT	May 29, 1865	May 29, 1865	Promoted to Colonel.
Do.	MILTON F. MILES	June 26, "	June 26, "	Mustered out as Major.
Major	LEVI DRAKE	Aug. 17, 1861	Sept. 18, 1861	Promoted to Lieutenant-Colonel.
Do.	BENJ. S. PORTER	Sept. 30, 1862	Oct. 10, "	Promoted to Lieutenant-Colonel.
Do.	SAMUEL F. GRAY	Jan. 1, 1863	Jan. 24, 1863	Promoted to Lieutenant-Colonel.
Do.	LUTHER M. STRONG	Oct. 4, "	" 10, 1864	Promoted to Lieutenant-Colonel.
Do.	JOSEPH R. BARTLETT	Dec. 5, 1864	Dec. 5, "	Promoted to Lieutenant-Colonel.
Do.	MILTON F. MILES	March 29, 1865	March 29, 1865	Promoted to Lieutenant-Colonel.
Do.	J. KESSLER	June 26, "	June 26, "	Resigned as Captain July 9, 1865.
Do.	GEORGE W. POOL	Sept. 4, "	Sept. 4, "	Mustered out with regiment as Captain.
Surgeon	ROBERT W. THRIFT	Aug. 17, 1861	" 18, 1861	Mustered out.
Do.	WM. H. PARK	Sept. 23, 1864	" 23, 1864	Mustered out with regiment.
Ass't Surgeon	WM. H. PARK	Aug. 17, 1861	" 18, 1861	Promoted to Surgeon.
Do.	H. B. LUNG	" 29, "	Aug. 29, "	Resigned April 27, 1864.
Do.	S. A. SMITH	May 6, 1864	May 6, 1864	Declined; commission returned.
Do.	SAMUEL H. SPENCER	Aug. 19, "	Aug. 19, "	Resigned July 1, 1865.
Chaplain	EUROTUS H. BUSH	" 17, 1861	Oct. 3, 1861	Resigned June 30, 1862.
Do.	GEORGE S. PHILLIPS	May 6, 1863	May 6, 1863	Resigned July 8, 1864.
Captain	A. Langworthy	Aug. 22, 1861	Sept. 18, 1861	Resigned June 22, 1862.
Do.	Benj. S. Porter	" 24, "	" 18, "	Promoted to Major.
Do.	Amos Keller	" 24, "	" 18, "	Killed at Stone River January 1, 1863.
Do.	George W. Culver	" 24, "	" 18, "	Resigned June 9, 1864.
Do.	Wm. Callihan	" 24, "	" 18, "	Resigned January 5, 1862.
Do.	Joseph R. Bartlett	" 26, "	" 18, "	Promoted to Major.
Do.	Luther M. Strong	Sept. 3, "	" 18, "	Promoted to Major.
Do.	Orrin B. Hayes	" 3, "	" 18, "	Resigned June 23, 1863.
Do.	George E. Lovejoy	" 3, "	" 18, "	Discharged February 15, 1862.
Do.	James M. Patterson	" 5, "	" 18, "	Mustered out October 26, 1864.
Do.	Samuel F. Gray	Jan. 9, 1862	Jan. 9, 1862	Promoted to Major.
Do.	Jonas Foster	Feb. 3, "	Feb. 3, "	Commission returned.
Do.	Lyman W. Mow	" 28, "	" 28, "	Resigned July 5, 1862.
Do.	John E. McCormack	June 22, "	Oct. 10, "	Resigned September 15, 1864.
Do.	Morris C. Tyler	July 3, "	" 10, "	Mustered out November 14, 1864.
Do.	Jonas Foster	Sept. 30, "	" 10, "	Resigned April 22, 1864.
Do.	Hiram Chance	Jan. 1, 1863	Jan. 21, 1863	Killed June 24, 1863.
Do.	John Green	" 1, "	" 21, "	Discharged October 22, 1864.
Do.	Daniel Hartsough	June 23, "	July 10, "	Mustered out.
Do.	Samuel M. Harper	" 24, "	" 20, "	Resigned September 13, 1864.
Do.	John L. Hollopeter	May 9, 1864	May 9, 1864	Declined promotion.
Do.	J. Kessler	" 9, "	" 9, "	Promoted to Major.
Do.	George W. Pool	Aug. 11, "	Aug. 11, "	Promoted to Major.
Do.	Thomas J. Ray	" 11, "	" 11, "	Mustered out with regiment.
Do.	Sheppard Green	Oct. 12, "	Oct. 12, "	Mortally wounded November 26, 1864.
Do.	Theodore C. Pero	" 12, "	" 12, "	Died August 25, 1864.
Do.	James Ewing	Nov. 3, "	Nov. 3, "	Mustered out with regiment.
Do.	Jacob Iler	" 3, "	" 3, "	Mustered out with regiment.
Do.	George S. Crawford	Dec. 21, "	Dec. 21, "	Mustered out with regiment.
Do.	Dwight R. Cook	" 21, "	" 21, "	Mustered out with regiment.
Do.	Francis R. Stewart	" 21, "	" 21, "	Mustered out with regiment.
Do.	Milton F. Miles	Oct. 4, 1863	Jan. 10, "	Promoted to Major.
Do.	Nathan L. Lutz	Feb. 10, 1865	Feb. 10, 1865	Mustered out with regiment.
Do.	Anthony W. Adams	March 29, "	March 29, "	Mustered out with regiment.
Do.	Jonathan J. Rapp	Sept. 4, "	Sept. 4, "	Mustered out with regiment.
1st Lieutenant	Charles A. Norton	Aug. 17, 1861	" 18, 1861	
Do.	Samuel F. Gray	" 22, "	" 18, "	Promoted to Captain.
Do.	John E. McCormack	" 21, "	" 18, "	Promoted to Captain.
Do.	Aaron H. Keller	" 24, "	" 18, "	Died of wounds January 26, 1863.
Do.	Jacob Mosier	" 21, "	" 18, "	Resigned April 28, 1862.
Do.	Jonas Foster	" 24, "	" 18, "	Promoted to Captain September 3, 1862.
Do.	Morris C. Tyler	" 26, "	" 18, "	Promoted to Captain.
Do.	Daniel Hartsough	Sept. 3, "	" 18, "	Promoted to Captain.
Do.	Hiram Chance	" 3, "	" 18, "	Promoted to Captain.
Do.	Alonzo F. Prentice	" 3, "	" 18, "	Discharged February 15, 1862.
Do.	Wm. C. Turner	" 5, "	" 18, "	Promoted by President of U. S.
Do.	James W. Davidson	Jan. 9, 1862	Jan. 9, 1862	Resigned July 27, 1863.
Do.	Wm. Martin	Feb. 3, "	Feb. 3, "	Commission returned.
Do.	Moses Abbott	" 8, "	" 8, "	Declined.
Do.	Commodore W. Drake	March 18, "	March 18, "	Resigned July 17, 1862.
Do.	John Green	April 28, "	June 16, "	Promoted to Captain.
Do.	John L. Hollopeter	June 22, "	Oct. 10, "	Resigned September 23, 1864.
Do.	John Kessler	July 5, "	" 10, "	Promoted to Captain.
Do.	Samuel M. Harper	" 18, "	" 10, "	Promoted to Captain.
Do.	Milton F. Miles	Sept. 30, "	" 10, "	Promoted to Captain.
Do.	Henry A. Spaythe	Aug. 1, "	" 10, "	Resigned June 18, 1863.
Do.	James A. Redman	Jan. 1, 1863	Jan. 24, 1863	Resigned January 27, 1863.
Do.	Milton Cowgill	" 1, "	" 24, "	Honorably discharged August 31, 1863.
Do.	Sheppard Green	July 1, 1862	" 24, "	Promoted to Captain.
Do.	Jacob C. Miller	Jan. 26, 1863	Feb. 18, "	Killed November 25, 1863.

RANK.	NAME.	DATE OF RANK.	COM. ISSUED.	REMARKS.
1st Lieutenant	Theodore C. Pero	Jan. 18, 1863	Feb. 26, 1863	Promoted to Captain.
Do.	George W. Pool	June 21, "	July 10, "	Promoted to Captain.
Do.	Thomas J. Ray	" 24, "	" 20, "	Promoted to Captain.
Do.	James Ewing	Nov. 25, "	Jan. 10, 1864	Promoted to Captain.
Do.	Isaac H. White	July 27, "	Aug. 25, 1863	Declined; commission returned.
Do.	John C. Ramsey	Aug. 26, "	Jan. 10, 1864	Killed at Dallas May 27, 1864.
Do.	Jacob Iler	March 10, 1864	March 10, "	Promoted to Captain.
Do.	John Gleck	" 10, "	" 10, "	Resigned June 14, 1865.
Do.	Silas W. Simons	" 10, "	" 10, "	Killed at Dallas May 27, 1864.
Do.	Charles Wallace	May 9, "	May 9, "	Killed at Kenesaw June 21, 1864.
Do.	George S. Crawford	" 9, "	" 9, "	Promoted to Captain.
Do.	Dwight R. Cook	Aug. 11, "	Aug. 11, "	Promoted to Captain.
Do.	Francis R. Stewart	" 11, "	" 11, "	Promoted to Captain.
Do.	John K. Gibson	" 11, "	" 11, "	Died of wounds.
Do.	Nathan L. Lutz	" 11, "	" 11, "	Promoted.
Do.	Daniel M. Fultz	Oct. 12, "	Oct. 12, "	Declined.
Do.	Anthony W. Adams	" 12, "	" 12, "	Promoted to Captain.
Do.	Jonathan J. Rapp	" 12, "	" 12, "	Promoted to Captain.
Do.	John Vandanburg	Dec. 21, "	Dec. 21, "	Mustered out with regiment.
Do.	Edwin P. Dana	" 21, "	" 21, "	Mustered out with regiment.
Do.	Jacob W. Cline	" 21, "	" 21, "	Resigned June 14, 1865.
Do.	John J. Fry	" 21, "	" 21, "	Resigned March 9, 1865.
Do.	Charles W. England	" 21, "	" 21, "	Mustered out with regiment.
Do.	George W. Vail	Feb. 10, 1865	Feb. 10, 1865	Mustered out with regiment.
Do.	Ezra P. Phelps	" 10, "	" 10, "	Discharged March 21, 1865.
Do.	James F. Harper	March 29, "	March 29, "	Mustered out with regiment.
Do.	John H. Yarger	" 29, "	" 29, "	Mustered out with regiment.
Do.	James J. Zint	April 10, "	April 10, "	Mustered out with regiment.
Do.	Conrad Flangher	May 18, "	May 18, "	Declined to accept.
Do.	B. H. Fansey	June 16, "	June 16, "	Mustered out with regiment.
Do.	Casper Snyder	" 26, "	" 26, "	Mustered out with regiment as Sergeant.
Do.	Franklin H. Gibens	" 26, "	" 26, "	Mustered out with regiment as Q. M. Sergeant.
Do.	Wm. Whittaker	Sept. 4, "	Sept. 4, "	Mustered out with regiment as Sergeant.
2d Lieutenant	Henry A. Spaythe	Aug. 17, 1861	" 18, 1861	Promoted to 1st Lieutenant August 1, 1862.
Do.	James W. Davidson	" 22, "	" 18, "	Promoted to 1st Lieutenant.
Do.	Moses Abbott	" 24, "	" 18, "	Resigned.
Do.	Amos B. Charlton	" 24, "	" 18, "	Discharged.
Do.	John Green	" 24, "	" 18, "	Promoted to 1st Lieutenant.
Do.	Wm. Martin	" 24, "	" 18, "	Resigned July 4, 1862.
Do.	Timothy Wilcox	" 26, "	" 18, "	Resigned January 8, 1862.
Do.	Samuel M. Harper	Sept. 3, "	" 18, "	Promoted to 1st Lieutenant.
Do.	John L. Hollopeters	" 3, "	" 18, "	Promoted to 1st Lieutenant.
Do.	Commodore W. Drake	" 3, "	" 18, "	Promoted to 1st Lieutenant.
Do.	John C. Smith	" 5, "	" 18, "	Resigned March 8, 1862.
Do.	Milton F. Miles	Jan. 9, 1862	Jan. 9, 1862	Promoted to 1st Lieutenant.
Do.	John Kessler	Feb. 3, "	Feb. 3, "	Promoted to 1st Lieutenant.
Do.	Jeremiah Bernard	" 3, "	" 3, "	Commission returned.
Do.	Wm. F. Cannon	" 8, "	" 8, "	Commission returned.
Do.	Gilbert S. Blackman	" 19, "	" 19, "	Resigned June 25, 1862.
Do.	Anderson N. Ellis	March 18, "	March 18, "	Resigned September 28, 1863.
Do.	Andrew G. Brown	" 18, "	" 18, "	Resigned May 22, 1863.
Do.	Milton Cowgill	April 28, "	June 16, "	Promoted to 1st Lieutenant.
Do.	James A. Redman	May 23, "	" 24, "	Promoted to 1st Lieutenant.
Do.	John C. Ramsey	Sept. 28, "	Oct. 10, "	Promoted to 1st Lieutenant.
Do.	Jacob C. Miller	July 4, "	" 10, "	Promoted to 1st Lieutenant.
Do.	Israel O. Totten	" 5, "	" 10, "	Honorably discharged August 21, 1863.
Do.	Isaac H. White	" 18, "	" 10, "	Declined.
Do.	Sheppard Green	June 25, "	" 10, "	Promoted to 1st Lieutenant.
Do.	Thomas J. Ray	" 30, "	" 10, "	Promoted to 1st Lieutenant.
Do.	Theodore C. Pero	" 22, "	" 10, "	Promoted to 1st Lieutenant.
Do.	Jacob Iler	Jan. 1, 1863	Jan. 24, 1863	Promoted to 1st Lieutenant.
Do.	John Gleck	" 1, "	" 24, "	Promoted to 1st Lieutenant.
Do.	Harvey Johns	July 1, 1862	" 24, "	Discharged August 14, 1863
Do.	Jacob Woolf	Jan. 26, 1863	Feb. 18, "	Killed November 25, 1863.
Do.	Henry F. Arntt	May 22, "	June 6, "	Killed November 25, 1863.
Do.	Silas W. Simons	June 18, "	" 26, "	Promoted to 1st Lieutenant.
Do.	Charles Wallace	" 24, "	July 20, "	Promoted to 1st Lieutenant.
Do.	George S. Crawford	July 27, "	Aug. 25, "	Promoted to 1st Lieutenant.
Do.	John K. Gibson	March 10, 1864	March 10, 1864	Promoted to 1st Lieutenant.
Do.	Edwin Haff	Oct. 31, 1863	Feb. 25, "	Honorably discharged July 21, 1864.
Do.	Francis R. Stewart	" 31, "	March 10, "	Promoted to 1st Lieutenant.
Do.	Dwight R. Cook	Aug. 21, "	Feb. 25, "	Promoted to 1st Lieutenant.
Do.	Nathan L. Lutz	March 10, 1864	March 10, "	Promoted to 1st Lieutenant.
Do.	Sheldon P. Hare	" 10, "	" 10, "	Discharged October 25, 1864.
Do.	Wm. F. Gibbs	" 10, "	" 10, "	Resigned May 27, 1864.
Do.	Daniel M. Fultz	" 30, "	" 30, "	Promoted to 1st Lieutenant.

FORTY-NINTH OHIO VOLUNTEER INFANTRY.

THE FORTY-NINTH OHIO was organized at Tiffin, Seneca County, under special authority from the Secretary of War. It started from Camp Noble, near Tiffin, to Camp Dennison on the 10th of September, 1861, received its equipment on the 21st of September, and moved for Louisville, Kentucky, where it arrived next day, and reported to Brigadier-General Robert Anderson, who had just assumed command of that place. It was the first organized regiment to enter Kentucky.

The reception of this regiment in Louisville was cordial in the extreme. It was not known outside of military head-quarters that the regiment was on its way from Ohio. As the two boats, lashed together, neared the wharf the regimental band performed National airs, and as the regiment landed the people of the city received it with enthusiasm, formed in its rear and marched with it through the principal streets to the head-quarters of General Anderson. The General appeared on the balcony of the hotel and welcomed the regiment in a short address, to which Colonel Gibson responded. These ceremonies over the people of Louisville turned out *en masse*, improvised a magnificent dinner at the Louisville Hotel, and the members of the regiment had a hilarious time. In the evening the regiment took the cars for Lebanon Junction, with orders to report to General W. T. Sherman, who was at that point in command of Rousseau's Louisville Legion and some Home Guards. The next morning it crossed Rolling Fork, wading the river, and marched to Elizabethtown, and went into camp on Muldraugh's Hill. Lying at this place until the 10th of October it then moved to Nolin Creek and went into Camp Nevin.

In the subsequent organization of the Second Division of the Army of Ohio, the Forty-Ninth was assigned to the Sixth Brigade, General R. W. Johnson commanding. On the 10th of December this division moved to Munfordsville, on Green River, and drove the Rebels to the opposite side of the river, and established Camp Wood, so named in honor of Hon. George Wood, member of the Kentucky Military Board, who lived in Munfordsville. On the 17th of December the National pickets, from the Thirty-Second Indiana Infantry, on the south side of Green River, were attacked by Hinman's Arkansas Brigade and Terry's Texas Rangers. In sending troops to the relief of the pickets, the Forty-Ninth Ohio was the first to cross the river, followed by the Thirty-Ninth Indiana. The enemy was met and repulsed, Colonel Terry, one of the Rebel commanders, being killed.

From the 17th of December to the 14th of February the regiment lay in camp perfecting itself in drill and discipline.

On the 14th of February, 1862, under orders, it left camp and moved on Bowling Green. After some delay in getting across the river it marched toward Nashville, reaching there on the 3d of March, and established Camp Andrew Johnson. On the 16th of March it moved with Buell's army to join Grant's forces at Pittsburg Landing, arriving there on the 6th.

The Forty-Ninth went into battle at eleven o'clock with its brigade, which was commanded by Colonel Gibson, who left his regiment in charge of Lieutenant-Colonel A. M. Blackman. The position of the regiment was on the left of the brigade, connecting on the right with Crittenden's division. Maintaining this position under a hot fire until four o'clock in the afternoon the regiment, with the enemy in full retreat, stacked its arms and lay down to rest. During the battle the regiment twice performed the hazardous movement of changing front under fire.

The Forty-Ninth participated in the succeeding movement on and siege of Corinth, having a sharp fight at Bridge's Creek, and at other points on the way, and entered Corinth with the army on the 30th of May, 1862. It was sent in pursuit of the enemy, passing through Jericho, Iuka, and other points, to Tuscumbia and Florence, Alabama, crossing the river at the latter point. From thence it marched to Battle Creek, Tennessee. Here commenced the movement after Bragg's Rebel army, which was then entering Kentucky, threatening Louisville and Cincinnati. This march was made under terrible sufferings from intense heat, want of water, and short rations.

Reaching Louisville on the 29th of September, and resting for a few days, the army resumed its march in pursuit of the enemy. Moving out on the Frankfort Turnpike, through Shelbyville, driving the enemy before them, Frankfort was reached on the 5th of October, in time to disperse the Rebel troops gathered there to guard the inauguration of Captain Dick Hawes as Rebel Governor of Kentucky.

On the morning of the 7th the march was resumed, under orders to join the main army, the junction being made the day following the battle of Perryville. During the whole of the march from Louisville to Perryville there was daily skirmishing. At Lawrenceburg and Dog Walk brisk engagements were fought, in each of which the Forty-Ninth Ohio was conspicuously engaged, under the command of Lieutenant-Colonel Levi Drake.

Pursuing the enemy to Crab Orchard the Forty-Ninth, with its brigade and division, marched to Bowling Green. From thence it marched toward Nashville, and on the 5th of October was with the advance that raised the siege of that city. It then went into camp at Millcreek, and remained there until the 26th of December.

General Rosecrans, then in command of the Army of the Cumberland, commenced his movement on Murfreesboro' on the 26th of December. The Forty-Ninth moved out of Nashville on the Nolinsville Turnpike with the right wing, under Major-General McCook, and after constant skirmishing found itself in line of battle on the extreme right of the National army before Murfreesboro', on the evening of the 30th. At six o'clock the next morning Kirk's brigade, to the left and front, on the right, was furiously assaulted by the enemy, and, giving way, was thrown back on the Forty-Ninth, which at once became engaged, and was borne back by overwhelming numbers a mile and a half to the Nashville Turnpike, which it reached after an incessant conflict of nine hours.

On the following morning the regiment was sent to reconnoiter on the right and rear of the main army. Returning from this duty it rejoined its brigade, and that day was more or less engaged, operating on the extreme right of the army in connection with Stanley's cavalry. On Friday, January 2d, it occupied a position in reserve, to the center, until late in the afternoon, when, upon the repulse of Van Cleve's division on the left it was ordered, with its brigade, to retrieve the fortunes of the day on that part of the field. It joined in a magnificent bayonet charge, which resulted in recovering the lost ground and a severe defeat to the enemy.

When the battle opened the entire field and staff of the Forty-Ninth were present. At its close it was in command of the junior Captain, S. F. Gray. By the capture of General Willich, Colonel Gibson, of the Forty-Ninth, succeeded to the command of the brigade. Lieutenant-Colonel Drake was killed while bravely cheering his men, Major Porter was wounded, and all the senior Captains present either killed or wounded. The regiment was now engaged in various foraging expeditions, and lost a number of men in encounters with the enemy.

On June 24th the regiment and army moved from Murfreesboro', and at Liberty Gap found the enemy strongly posted to contest an advance of the National forces. The First Brigade, to which the Forty-Ninth was attached, was at once formed in order of battle, and after some maneuvers and hard fighting, the Forty-Ninth assaulted the enemy's right, posted on a high hill. It scaled the heights in the face of a severe fire, drove the enemy from that position, and compelled him to fall back to another but equally strong position, about a mile to his rear.

On the following day the advance was resumed, other troops taking the lead and engaging the enemy until three o'clock P. M., when the Forty-Ninth was brought into action on the enemy's center, which covered the valley, his flanks resting upon the hills. A new and peculiar drill had been introduced into the regiment for formation in four ranks to advance firing. When within range, at the word of command, the regiment opened fire, advancing briskly, and soon the enemy's center was broken, and by the co-operation of other troops his position was occupied. Reaching Tullahoma without further engagement, July 1st, the regiment went into camp.

In August the National army commenced its movement on Chattanooga, and on the 31st the Forty-Ninth crossed the Tennessee River near Bellefonte. The Forty-Ninth, under command of Major S. F. Gray, in the battle of Chickamauga, held a position in the morning of the first day, on the extreme right of the National forces, forming a part of General R. W. Johnson's division. Before being engaged the brigade and division were shifted to the extreme left of the army, and joined with Thomas's corps. At two o'clock P. M. the regiment became engaged with the enemy's right, posted in a dense woods. A charge was made and the enemy driven. In this charge the Forty-Ninth Ohio captured two guns. Three guns, in all, were captured by the brigade. This charge occurred between three and four o'clock P. M. At dusk the enemy, having been re-enforced, made a charge. Moving up silently in the darkness, the Rebels gained a point near to and in front of the National forces, delivered a withering volley, uttered their demoniac yell, and rushed forward with the bayonet. The National forces were on the alert, but the suddenness of the attack staggered and caused them to give ground. They quickly rallied, however, and opening fire the Rebels were repulsed. The Forty-Ninth retired to the rear of other troops and lay down on their arms to rest.

On the second day of this battle the Forty-Ninth Ohio was constantly engaged in various parts of the field, and accomplished a brilliant exploit, in connection with Goodspeed's battery, the Fifteenth Ohio, and other troops, which, it is claimed, saved Thomas's corps from being swept from the field. The enemy had broken through the National left and were exultingly charging for the center, when the Forty-Ninth faced to the rear and poured into the Rebels a withering fire. From the other side of the circle Goodspeed's battery and the Fifteenth Ohio delivered a destructive fire, and the enemy was checked and sent back on his main body.

When the National forces withdrew that night, the Forty-Ninth, with its brigade, was the last to retire. Reaching Rossville it threw up temporary field-works, and awaited the approach of the enemy. On the following night it retired into Chattanooga.

On November 24th the Forty-Ninth, with its brigade, joined in the movement against Mission Ridge. Driving the enemy's advanced line, it reached Orchard Knob, remaining until next day. On the 25th, Hooker having accomplished his brilliant movements on the right, while Sherman was pressing the enemy vigorously on the left, the entire center of the National force was rallied to the charge, and the Forty-Ninth, with conspicuous gallantry, was among the first to plant its colors on the summit of Mission Ridge.

Immediately after this success the regiment moved with Granger's corps to the relief of Burnside's forces at Knoxville. This campaign was one of the most severe that the National forces were called on to endure during the war. The weather was intensely cold, with snow on the ground, the men almost naked, and without shoes, and the rations exhausted. The march of the army was literally tracked by bloody foot-marks. And yet these brave fellows did not grumble, but were eager to be led against the foe. Marching to Strawberry Plains, and hearing that Burnside had repulsed Longstreet, the National troops returned to Chattanooga. In the midst of this severe campaign the men of the Forty-Ninth Ohio were called upon to re-enlist for the war, to which call a prompt response was given.

Returning to Ohio to enjoy its veteran furlough of thirty days, it was warmly received at Tiffin, its place of organization. Judge J. K. Hurd, of Tiffin, delvered a speech of welcome, to which responses were made by Colonel Gibson and other officers of the regiment.

At the expiration of its furlough the regiment reported at the head-quarters of the Fourth Corps at Cleveland, Tennessee, where the National forces were then concentrating and reorganizing for the campaign against Atlanta. In this arduous campaign the history of the regiment was but that of the Fourth Army Corps. It participated in the engagements at Dalton, Resaca, Dallas, Kenesaw Mountain, Chattahoochie River, and Atlanta, exhibiting in every emergency its qualities of courage and discipline, and suffering severely in the loss of men, killed and wounded.

Joining in the movement that forced the enemy from Atlanta, it participated in the battle at Jonesboro' and Lovejoy Station, and, after abandoning the pursuit of the enemy, returned to camp at Atlanta.

When the grand army was divided, and General Sherman commenced his march to the sea, the Army of the Cumberland, under General George H. Thomas, was left to attend to the Rebel General Hood in his mad movement toward Nashville. In the movement of Thomas's forces the Forty-Ninth Ohio, under command of Lieutenant-Colonel Strong, fully sustained its reputation, participating in the various skirmishes, and the battles of Franklin and Nashville. In the battle before Nashville, on the 15th and 16th of December, 1864, the regiment participated in several brilliant charges made by the Fourth Army Corps, and suffered severely in killed and wounded. After the battle it was in the column that pursued Hood's defeated and demoralized forces across the Tennessee River. When the pursuit ceased the regiment, with its corps, went into camp at Huntsville, Alabama, and remained there until about the middle of March, 1865. In that month a movement was made to East Tennessee by rail, going into camp at Greenville. On its return from this expedition to Nashville, it was placed on transports, on the 15th of June, and taken to Texas by way of New Orleans.

Reaching Texas in July, the regiment landed at Victoria, and moved to the interior as far as San Antonio, by way of Green Lake and Gonzales. It suffered the hardships of that service for four months, then returned to Victoria, where it was mustered out of service on the 30th of November, 1865.

The whole number of names upon the rolls of the regiment is fifteen hundred and fifty-two. Nineteen were born in Europe, seven hundred and sixty in Ohio, of whom four hundred and forty were from Seneca County. Eight officers were killed in battle, and twenty wounded (six of these mortally).

Of the privates, one hundred and twenty-seven were killed in battle, seventy-one were mortally wounded, one hundred and sixty-five died from hardships or disease, and seven perished in Rebel prisons at Andersonville and Danville. Six hundred and sixteen were discharged on account of wounds or other disability. Five survive with the loss of an arm and two with the loss of a leg. The killed and mortally wounded of enlisted men were as one to seven and four-fifths, and the entire deaths as one to five and one-sixth. The men of the regiment suffered nine hundred and forty-two gun-shot wounds.

During two-thirds of his term of service Colonel Gibson commanded a brigade by virtue of his rank.

50th REGIMENT OHIO VOLUNTEER INFANTRY.

ROSTER, THREE YEARS' SERVICE.

RANK.	NAME.	DATE OF RANK.	COM. ISSUED.	REMARKS.
Colonel	JONAH R. TAYLOR	Aug. 23, 1862	Sept. 21, 1862	Resigned October 16, 1862.
Do.	SILAS A. STRICKLAND	Oct. 16, "	Oct. 27, "	Mustered out with reg't; brev't Brig. Gen.
Lt. Colonel	S. A. STRICKLAND	Aug. 17, "	Sept. 21, "	Promoted to Colonel.
Do.	THOMAS L. P. DEFRIES	Oct. 16, "	Nov. 1, "	Resigned May 23, 1863.
Do.	GEORGE R. ELSTNER	May 23, 1863	July 29, 1863	Killed August 8, 1864.
Do.	HAMILTON S. GILLESPIE	Aug. 19, 1864	Aug. 19, 1864	Mustered out. [ruary 16, 1865.
Do.	JOHN E. CUMMINGS	" 9, 1862	Sept. 9, 1862	Trans. from 99th O. V. I.; mustered out Feb-
Do.	BENJ F. LEFEVER	Feb. 23, 1865	Feb. 23, 1865	Revoked; commission returned.
Do.	JAMES A. BOPE	April 10, "	April 10, "	Mustered out with regiment.
Major	THOS. L. P. DEFRIES	Aug. 20, 1862	Sept. 26, 1862	Promoted to Lieutenant-Colonel
Do.	THOMAS P. COOK	Oct. 16, "	Nov. 1, "	Resigned May 5, 1863.
Do.	GEORGE R. ELSTNER	May 1, 1863	May 6, 1863	Promoted to Lieutenant-Colonel.
Do.	HAMILTON S. GILLESPIE	" 23, "	Jan. 29, "	Promoted to Lieutenant-Colonel.
Do.	BENJ. F. LEFEVER	Dec. 16, 1862	Feb. 20, "	Mustered out with regiment.
Surgeon	GEORGE KEIFER	July 9, "	....	Mustered out.
Do.	J. F. WOODS	Aug. 19, "	Sept. 9, 1862	Transferred from 99th O. V. I.; mustered out
Ass't Surgeon	SAMUEL K. CRAWFORD	July 9, "	July 9, "	Mustered out.
Do.	NEHEMIAH COLE	Aug. 22, "	Sept. 21, "	Resigned April 25, 1865. [with reg't.
Do.	GEORGE SADLER	June 2, 1864	June 2, 1864	Transferred from 99th O. V. I.; mustered out
Chaplain	GERARD P. RILEY	Sept. 1, 1862	Dec. 3, 1862	Dis. Sept. 7, '63, to accept pos. in 6th U. S. C. T.
Captain	Thomas P. Cook	July 15, "	Sept. 21, "	Promoted to Major.
Do.	Hamilton S. Gillespie	Aug. 1, "	" 21, "	Promoted to Major.
Do.	Patrick McGrew	" 13, "	" 21, "	Resigned May 21, 1863.
Do.	John Carr	" 14, "	" 21, "	Killed October 8, 1862.
Do.	Levi C. Guthrie	" 16, "	" 21, "	Mustered out December 31, 1864.
Do.	Thomas Clark	" 18, "	" 21, "	Resigned June 21, 1864.
Do.	James W. Cahill	" 22, "	" 21, "	Resigned July 9, 1864.
Do.	Lewis C. Simmons	" 20, "	" 21, "	Resigned January 28, 1863.
Do.	Isaac J. Carter	" 21, "	" 21, "	Killed October 8, 1862.
Do.	Leonard A. Hendricks	" 21, "	" 21, "	Resigned June 19, 1863.
Do.	Oscar C. Pratt	Oct. 16, "	Nov. 1, "	Resigned May 15, 1863.
Do.	John S. Conahan	" 8, "	Dec. 8, "	Must'd out with regt.; brvt. Maj. by President.
Do.	Joseph R. Key	" 8, "	" 8, "	Died December 1, 1862.
Do.	Davis J. Thompson	" 1, "	Jan. 30, 1863	Revoked; resigned as 1st Lieutenant.
Do.	Columbus Cones	Jan. 28, 1863	Feb. 19, "	Mustered out.
Do.	Frank A. Crippen	Dec. 1, 1862	March 20, "	Resigned May 16, 1864.
Do.	Thomas M. Gwynne	May 15, 1863	May 25, "	Resigned September 19, 1864.
Do.	David A. Ireland	" 21, "	June 10, "	Resigned August 15, 1864.
Do.	Oliver S. McClure	June 19, "	" 29, "	On detached duty.
Do.	John J. Manker	May 24, "	July 20, "	Resigned March 26, 1864.
Do.	James G. Theaker	April 1, 1864	April 1, 1864	Mustered out with regiment.
Do.	Edwin G. Edgley	Aug. 11, "	Aug. 11, "	Mustered out with regiment.
Do.	James A. Bope	July 23, 1862	Sept. 9, 1862	Trans. from 99th O. V. I.; prom. to Lt. Col.
Do.	John S. Conahan	Oct. 8, "	Dec. 8, "	Mustered out with regiment.
Do.	Wm. Exline	Jan. 5, 1863	March 20, 1863	Mustered out with regiment.
Do.	David L. Anderson	" 8, "	" 29, "	Mustered out with regiment.
Do.	Thomas C. Hunnell	Feb. 2, "	" 29, "	On detached duty.
Do.	Harrison M. Shuey	" 13, "	" 29, "	Mustered out with regiment.
Do.	Samuel Bitler	April 19, "	May 29, "	Mustered out with regiment.
Do.	Elmore W. Williams	Aug. 11, 1864	Aug. 11, 1864	Mustered out with regiment.
Do.	Wm. B. Richards	April 10, 1865	April 10, 1865	Mustered out with regiment.
1st Lieutenant	Oscar C. Pratt	Aug. 23, 1862	Sept. 21, 1862	Promoted to Captain.
Do.	Davis J. Thompson	" 1, "	" 21, "	Promoted to Captain; resigned Dec. 20, 1862.
Do.	David A. Ireland	" 23, "	" 21, "	Promoted to Captain.
Do.	John S. Conahan	" 14, "	" 21, "	Promoted to Captain.
Do.	John J. Manker	" 16, "	" 21, "	Promoted to Captain.
Do.	James G. Theaker	" 18, "	" 21, "	Promoted to Captain.
Do.	Columbus Cones	" 20, "	" 21, "	Promoted to Captain.
Do.	Frederick Buck	" 21, "	" 21, "	Resigned November 9, 1862.
Do.	Oliver S. McClure	" 21, "	" 21, "	Promoted to Captain.
Do.	George R. Elstner	July 12, "	" 21, "	
Do.	Robert Reilly	June 25, "	" 21, "	Resigned November 9, 1862.
Do.	Ellis Moore	Sept. 18, "	Oct. 10, "	Resigned June 14, 1863.
Do.	Thomas M. Gwynne	Oct. 16, "	Nov. 1, "	Promoted to Captain.
Do.	John B. Woodruff	Nov. 9, "	Dec. 8, "	Resigned March 15, 1863.
Do.	Archie V. Steward	" 9, "	" 8, "	Resigned March 22, 1863.
Do.	Elmore W. Williams	Oct. 8, "	" 12, "	Promoted to Captain.
Do.	Anthony Anderson	Jan. 14, 1863	Feb. 7, 1863	Honorably discharged June 21, 1865.
Do.	James Lucas	March 22, "	May 6, "	Killed November 30, 1864, at Franklin Tenn.
Do.	Frank A. Crippen	Jan. 28, "	Feb. 19, "	Promoted to Captain.
Do.	Jerome F. Crowley	March 15, "	March 20, "	Mustered out.
Do.	George W. Garretson jr.	" 22, "	April 9, "	Resigned March 23, 1864.
Do.	Edwin G. Edgely	Dec. 1, 1862	March 30, "	Promoted to Captain.
Do.	John D. McLee	May 11, 1863	May 25, "	Mustered out.
Do.	Nathan A. Ried, jr.	" 15, "	" 25, "	Resigned April 20, 1865.
Do.	Wm. O'Harra	" 21, "	June 10, "	Mustered out. [Tenn., Dec. 15, 1864.
Do.	Edward L. Pyne	June 19, "	" 29, "	Died Feb. 8, '65, of wounds rec'd at Nashville.
Do.	John A. Brown	May 24, "	July 20, "	Resigned June 16, 1864.
Do.	Martin Little	April 1, 1864	April 1, 1864	Resigned as 2d Lieutenant May 17, 1864.
Do.	John Clingman	" 1, "	" 1, "	Reduced to 2d Lieutenant in new organizat'n.
Do.	John H. Haney	Aug. 11, "	Aug. 11, "	Reduced to 2d Lieutenant in new organizat'n.
Do.	Michael Welsh	" 11, "	" 11, "	Resigned May 15, 1865.
Do.	Wm. A. Reed	" 11, "	" 11, "	Resigned March 20, 1861, as 2d Lieutenant.
Do.	Edgar J. Wells	" 11, "	" 11, "	Reduced to 2d Lieutenant in new organizat'n.
Do.	Wm. B. Richards	Nov. 15, 1862	March 30, 1863	Transferred from 99th O. V. I.; prom. to Capt.

RANK.	NAME.	DATE OF RANK.	COM. ISSUED.	REMARKS.
1st Lieutenant	E. B. Walkup	Dec. 26, 1862	March 30, 1863	Transferred from 99th O. V. I.
Do.	Josiah Morehead	Jan. 8, 1863	" 30, "	Mustered out with regiment.
Do.	Wm. H. Shaw	Feb. 2, "	May 29, "	Mustered out with regiment.
Do.	Joseph Tingle	" 13, "	" 29, "	Mustered out with regiment.
Do.	Wm. Zay	Nov. 3, 1864	Nov. 3, 1864	Mustered out with regiment.
Do.	David R. Robinson	" 3, "	" 3, "	Mustered out with regiment.
2d Lieutenant	Thomas M. Gwynne	Aug. 23, 1862	Sept. 21, 1862	Promoted to 1st Lieutenant.
Do.	James Lucas	" 1, "	" 21, "	Killed at Franklin.
Do.	Wm. O'Harra	" 23, "	" 21, "	Promoted to 1st Lieutenant.
Do.	John A. Brown	" 16, "	" 21, "	Promoted to 1st Lieutenant.
Do.	Robert P. Moore	" 18, "	" 21, "	Resigned June 3, 1863.
Do.	Anthony Anderson	" 20, "	" 21, "	Promoted to 1st Lieutenant.
Do.	Frank A. Crippen	" 20, "	" 21, "	Promoted to 1st Lieutenant.
Do.	Joseph R. Keys	" 21, "	" 21, "	Promoted to 1st Lieutenant.
Do.	Edward L. Pyne	" 21, "	" 21, "	Promoted to 1st Lieutenant.
Do.	Elmore W. Williams	" 27, "	Oct. 14, "	Promoted to 1st Lieutenant.
Do.	Nathan A. Ried, jr	Oct. 16, "	Nov. 1, "	Promoted to 1st Lieutenant.
Do.	Jerome F. Crowley	" 8, "	Dec. 8, "	Promoted to 1st Lieutenant.
Do.	George W. Garretson, jr	" 8, "	" 12, "	Promoted to 1st Lieutenant.
Do.	John H. Haney	March 22, 1863	May 6, 1863	Promoted to 1st Lieutenant.
Do.	Martin Little	Jan. 14, "	Feb. 7, "	Promoted to 1st Lieutenant; resigned May 16, 1864.
Do.	Edwin G. Edgely	" 28, "	" 19, "	Promoted to 1st Lieutenant.
Do.	John D. McLee	March 15, "	March 30, "	Promoted to 1st Lieutenant.
Do.	John Clingman	Dec. 1, 1862	" 30, "	Promoted to 1st Lieutenant.
Do.	Michael Welsh	March 28, 1863	April 9, "	Promoted to 1st Lieutenant.
Do.	Wm. A. Reed	May 11, "	May 25, "	Promoted to 1st Lieutenant.
Do.	Edgar J. Wells	" 15, "	" 25, "	Promoted to 1st Lieutenant.
Do.	Chas. H. Ritchey	" 21, "	June 10, "	Mustered out with regiment.
Do.	Chas. A. Van Dersen	June 19, "	" 19, "	
Do.	Levi M. Johnson	May 21, "	July 20, "	
Do.	Thomas C. Tholurn	April 1, 1864	April 1, 1864	Honorably discharged March 10, 1865.
Do.	Aaron W. Aten	" 1, "	" 1, "	Mustered out.
Do.	Sidney H. Cook	May 9, "	May 9, "	Mustered out with regiment.
Do.	Joshua F. Cox	March 23, "	" 29, 1864	Mustered out with regiment.
Do.	Peter F. Pechiney	Jan. 20, 1865	Jan. 20, 1865	Mustered out with regiment.
Do.	Asa M. Weston	April 10, "	April 10, "	Mustered out with regiment.
Do.	John S. Eyler	" 10, "	" 10, "	
Do.	David S. Blakeman	" 10, "	" 10, "	Mustered out with regiment.

FIFTIETH OHIO VOLUNTEER INFANTRY.

THIS regiment, recruited from the State at large, was organized at Camp Dennison, and mustered into the service on the 27th of August, 1862, with an aggregate of nine hundred and sixty-four men. On the 1st of September it moved into Kentucky for the defense of Cincinnati against Kirby Smith's raid, and about the 20th of the same month it went to Louisville.

The Fiftieth was assigned to the Thirty-Fourth Brigade, Tenth Division, McCook's Corps. On the 1st of October the regiment moved out of Louisville, and on the 8th of October went into the battle of Perryville. In this engagement the regiment lost two officers killed and one mortally wounded, and one hundred and sixty-two men killed and wounded. During the advance of the army on Nashville the regiment was stationed at Lebanon, then the base of supplies. After a series of marches and counter-marches in pursuit of John Morgan, the regiment was detached from its brigade, and was stationed at Muldraugh's Hill. Here it remained from February, 1863, until September, 1863, engaged in building fortifications and in constructing trestles over Big Run, and over Sulphur Fork and Rolling Fork of Green River. During this time the regiment built Forts Boyle, Sands, and McAllister. On the 18th of September the Fiftieth moved to Glasgow, Kentucky, and after a few days' rest proceeded to Nashville. Here it remained about two weeks, performing picket-duty, and it was then ordered to Gallatin, Tennessee, and thence to Glasgow, Kentucky. On the 25th of December the regiment was ordered to Knoxville, Tennessee. The route lay eastward to Somerset, Kentucky, and thence southward, crossing the Cumberland River at Point Isabelle. On the 1st of January, 1864, when the weather was so very cold, the regiment was prepared to move across the mountains. In the severest winter weather the men dragged the artillery and wagons over the mountains by hand, slept on the frozen ground, in rain and snow, without shelter, and subsisted on parched corn. Jacksboro', Tennessee, was reached at last, and here the regiment remained until the 22d of February, engaged in building a wagon-road through Wheeler's Gap, along the course of Cove Creek. Upon arriving at Knoxville the Fiftieth camped about two weeks on the south side of the Holston, and then moved to London, Tennessee, where it received orders to join General Sherman's army at Kingston, Georgia.

After forced marches from Cleveland, Tennessee, to Kingston, Georgia, the average distance per day being twenty-seven miles, the regiment reached Kingston on the 23d of May. It was ordered immediately to Cass Station, and arrived that same evening. The next morning the Fiftieth Ohio, the Fourteenth Kentucky Infantry, and the Second Kentucky Cavalry, forming a provisional brigade, were ordered back to Kingston. At half-past seven A. M. the brigade was attacked by three brigades of Wheeler's cavalry. The engagement lasted three hours. The Rebels were driven back and the command marched into Kingston. After two days' stay at Kingston the regiment marched and joined the main army at Burnt Hickory, Georgia. The Fiftieth was assigned to the Third Brigade, Second Division, Twenty-Third Army Corps. From this time until after the siege of Atlanta the regiment was in line of battle almost constantly. It shared in all the movements of the campaign, and participated in the actions at Pumpkin-Vine Creek, Dallas, New Hope Church, Lost Mountain, Pine Mountain, Kenesaw Mountain, Culpe House, Nicojack Creek, Chattahoochie River, Howard House, Atlanta, and Jonesboro'. During this campaign the ranks of the regiment were fearfully thinned.

After the battle of Jonesboro' the regiment remained at Decatur, Georgia, one month, and then started in pursuit of Hood's army. It marched through Marietta, Kingston, Rome, and into Cherokee County, Alabama, and halted for a few days at Cedar Bluffs, on the Coosa River. The regiment moved into Tennessee, and skirmished three days at Columbia. Hood having moved to General Schofield's left, the main army was ordered to Spring Hill. Upon nearing Spring Hill it was found that the Rebels had swung across the main road. The Fiftieth was placed on the left of the road, and, with the remainder of the brigade on the right, it drove the Rebels from their position, and formed a junction with the division of the Fourth Corps which had held Spring Hill during the afternoon against Cheatham's corps. The regimènt arrived at Franklin, Tennessee, at seven o'clock A. M. on the 30th of November, and immediately commenced throwing up fortifications. During the battle in the afternoon the regiment was posted on the right of the Columbia Pike, with its left flank resting on the pike. In this position it received and repelled eleven successive charges. It went into the battle with an aggregate of two hundred and twenty-five men, and came out with one hundred and twelve. It fell back with the army to Nashville, and participated in the battle at that place on the 15th and 16th of December, losing several men. The regiment followed the retreating Rebels as far as Columbia, Tennessee, where it was consolidated with the Ninety-Ninth Ohio Volunteer Infantry. At the time of the consolidation the regiment numbered only about one hundred men. The consolidated regiment was denominated the Fiftieth Ohio Volunteer Infantry.

The regiment accompanied the Twenty-Third Corps to Clifton, Tennessee, and thence to Fort Fisher, moving *via* Cincinnati and Washington City. It moved to Wilmington, North Carolina, and proceeded from there to Kingston, and then to Goldsboro', and then to Raleigh, and then to Greensboro', and at last to Salisbury, North Carolina, where it was mustered out on the 26th of June, 1865. On the 17th of July the regiment arrived at Camp Dennison, Ohio, where it was paid and discharged

51st REGIMENT OHIO VOLUNTEER INFANTRY.

ROSTER, THREE YEARS' SERVICE.

RANK.	NAME.	DATE OF RANK.	COM. ISSUED.	REMARKS.
Colonel	WM. P. N. FITZGERALD	Oct. 14, 1861	Oct. 14, 1861	Resigned.
Do.	STANLEY MATHEWS	" 23, "	" 23, "	Resigned April 11, 1863.
Do.	RICHARD W. McLAIN	April 11, 1863	May 25, 1863	Resigned September 20, 1864.
Do.	CHARLES H. WOODS	Jan. 20, 1865	Jan. 20, 1865	Mustered out with regiment.
Lt. Colonel	RICHARD W. McLAIN	Oct. 15, 1861	Nov. 4, 1861	Promoted.
Do.	CHARLES H. WOODS	April 14, 1863	May 25, 1863	Promoted.
Do.	DAVID W. MARSHALL	Jan. 20, 1865	Jan. 20, 1865	Mustered out with regiment.
Major	RICHARD W. McLAIN	Aug. 28, 1861	Nov. 4, 1861	Promoted.
Do.	NATHANIEL HAYDEN	Oct. 26, "	" 4, "	Resigned March 17, 1863.
Do.	CHARLES H. WOODS	March 17, 1863	March 30, 1863	Promoted.
Do.	DAVID W. MARSHALL	April 14, "	May 25, "	Promoted.
Do.	JAMES McCLINTOCK	Jan. 20, 1865	Jan. 20, 1865	Declined promotion.
Do.	JOHN SERGEANT	April 10, "	April 10, "	Declined promotion.
Do.	JOHN M. FREW	May 2, "	May 2, "	Mustered out with regiment.
Surgeon	M. C. WOODWORTH	Oct. 3, 1861	Nov. 4, 1861	Resigned.
Do.	E. D. W. C. WING	June 27, 1864	June 27, 1864	Mustered out with regiment.
Ass't Surgeon	MARTIN HAGAN	Sept. 28, 1861	Sept. 28, 1861	Resigned November 26, 1862.
Do.	E. D. W. C. WING	" 21, "	Nov. 26, 1862	Promoted.
Do.	R. P. JENNINGS	March 11, 1863	March 11, 1863	Mustered out with regiment.
Do.	L. E. NEAGLEY	" 22, 1865	" 22, 1865	Mustered out with regiment.
Chaplain	NICHOLAS C. WORTHINGTON	Oct. 15, 1861	Nov. 4, 1861	Resigned September 15, 1862.
Captain	Matthias H. Bartilson	Sept. 17, "	" 4, "	Promoted.
Do.	Charles H. Woods	" 17, "	" 4, "	Promoted.
Do.	Benjamin F. Heskitt	" 17, "	" 4, "	Died of wounds January 4, 1863.
Do.	William Patton	" 17, "	" 4, "	Died April 13, 1862.
Do.	David Chalfant	Oct. 3, "	" 4, "	Resigned November 26, 1862.
Do.	David W. Marshall	" 3, "	" 4, "	Promoted.
Do.	James F. Shanter	" 3, "	" 4, "	Discharged February 7, 1863.
Do.	John D. Nicholas	" 4, "	" 4, "	Discharged March 29, 1862.
Do.	James M. Crooks	" 3, "	" 4, "	Resigned March 20, 1862.
Do.	Charles Mueller	" 26, "	" 4, "	Resigned February 6, 1862.
Do.	Alfred K. Robinson	" 28, "	" 4, "	Mustered out November 17, 1864.
Do.	J. D. Cumming	Feb. 19, 1862	Feb. 19, 1862	Resigned January 23, 1863.
Do.	Allen Gaskill	March 20, "	April 14, "	Resigned December 25, 1862.
Do.	John North	June 30, "	Dec. 31, "	Discharged October 10, 1864.
Do.	John Sargent	Nov. 28, "	" 31, "	Detached from reg. to act as Q. M. Dept. of Cumberland.
Do.	Charles B. Harrison	Jan. 23, 1863	Feb. 19, 1863	Resigned December 6, 1864.
Do.	John M. Hodge	" 1, "	" 19, "	Resigned April 21, 1863.
Do.	William Moore	" 4, "	" 19, "	Resigned April 23, 1864.
Do.	Samuel Stephens	Feb. 7, "	April 9, "	Killed June 20, 1864.
Do.	Charles G. Harger	March 17, "	" 9, "	Resigned October 4, 1864.
Do.	John M. Frew	April 21, "	June 10, "	Promoted.
Do.	Samuel Slade	" 14, "	" 10, "	Mustered out with regiment.
Do.	Lewis Crooks	May 25, 1864	May 25, 1864	Resigned November 7, 1864.
Do.	William Nichols	July 13, "	July 13, "	Mustered out with regiment.
Do.	Benjamin F. Croxton	Nov. 3, "	Nov. 3, "	Mustered out with regiment.
Do.	James McClintock	" 26, 1862	Dec. 31, 1862	Mustered out July 7, 1865.
Do.	James Allen	Aug. 6, 1863	Aug. 10, 1863	Mustered out with regiment.
Do.	D. S. Knous	Jan. 6, 1865	Jan. 6, 1865	Mustered out with regiment.
Do.	James A. Fisher	" 6, "	" 6, "	Mustered out with regiment.
Do.	Philip Everhard	" 6, "	" 6, "	Mustered out with regiment.
Do.	William S. Rittelley	" 28, "	" 28, "	Mustered out as 1st Lieutenant.
Do.	John E. Smith	Feb. 16, "	Feb. 16, "	Mustered out with regiment.
Do.	Charles Gentsch	Sept. 29, "	Sept. 29, "	Mustered out as 1st Lieutenant.
1st Lieutenant	John M. Hodge	" 4, 1861	Nov. 4, 1861	Promoted.
Do.	Alfred K. Robinson	" 17, "	" 4, "	Promoted.
Do.	John A. Deihl	" 17, "	" 4, "	Discharged February 25, 1862.
Do.	Allen Gaskill	" 17, "	" 4, "	Promoted.
Do.	John North	" 17, "	" 4, "	Promoted.
Do.	Edward A. Parrish	Oct. 3, "	" 4, "	Resigned June 7, 1862.
Do.	James McClintock	" 3, "	" 4, "	Promoted.
Do.	John D. Cumming	" 3, "	" 4, "	Promoted.
Do.	William Moore	" 3, "	" 4, "	Promoted.
Do.	Charles Donley	" 4, "	" 4, "	Discharged February 28, 1863.
Do.	William S. Hodge	" 26, "	" 4, "	Resigned February 17, 1863.
Do.	C. B. Harrison	" 29, "	" 4, "	Promoted.
Do.	John Sargent	" 28, "	" 4, "	Promoted.
Do.	Charles G. Harger	Feb. 19, 1862	Feb. 10, 1862	Promoted.
Do.	James Stonebocker	" 25, "	March 20, "	Resigned November 16, 1862
Do.	Samuel Stephens	" 25, "	" 20, "	Promoted.
Do.	David M. Jones	March 20, "	April 4, "	Mustered out May 28, 1865.
Do.	Samuel Slade	June 7, "	Oct. 7, "	Promoted.
Do.	John M. Frew	Nov. 26, "	Dec. 31, "	Promoted.
Do.	Noah W. Younders	June 30, "	" 31, "	Resigned July 3, 1863.
Do.	Lewis Crooks	Nov. 26, "	" 31, "	Promoted.
Do.	Philip Everhard	Jan. 1, 1863	April 9, 1863	Promoted.
Do.	Benjamin F. Croxton	" 1, "	" 9, "	Promoted.
Do.	Frank Shrover	" 4, "	" 9, "	Died July 9, 1861.
Do.	Peter Lowe	" 23, "	" 9, "	Honorably discharged December 6, 1864.
Do.	William Nichols	Dec. 25, "	" 9, "	Promoted.
Do.	Thomas H. Morgena	Jan. 31, "	" 13, "	Revoked; resigned as 2d Lieut. May 3, 1863.
Do.	John E. Smith	March 7, "	" 9, "	Promoted.
Do.	William S. Rittelley	April 21, "	" 9, "	Promoted.
Do.	Henry Kaldenbaugh	Jan. 31, "	June 26, "	Mustered out January 23, 1865.
Do.	Josiah D. Lake	April 21, "	" 10, "	Resigned April 22, 1864.

RANK.	NAME.	DATE OF RANK.	COM. ISSUED.	REMARKS.
1st Lieutenant	Charles Geutsch	April 14, 1863	June 10, 1863	Promoted; mustered out October 3, 1865.
Do.	Samson McNeal	Jan. 25, 1864		Mustered out.
Do.	Willis C. Workman	May 25, "	May 25, 1864	Killed June 22, 1864.
Do.	Thomas C. Ayers	" 25, "	" 25, "	Mustered out June 23, 1865.
Do.	John G. Croxton	July 13, "	July 13, "	Mustered out with regiment.
Do.	James Weatherbee	" 13, "	" 13, "	Mustered out April 13, 1865.
Do.	John P. Chapin	Aug. 11, "	Aug. 11, "	Declined promotion.
Do.	George Wood	Nov. 3, "	Nov. 3, "	Mustered out.
Do.	Charles L. Toner	Jan. 5, 1865	Jan. 6, 1865	Mustered out with regiment.
Do.	Nelson White	" 6, "	" 6, "	Mustered out with regiment.
Do.	William Potter	" 6, "	" 6, "	Mustered out with regiment.
Do.	Edward J. Pocock	" 6, "	" 6, "	Resigned June 4, 1865.
Do.	John H. Purvis	" 6, "	" 6, "	Mustered out with regiment.
Do.	John M. Wasson	Feb. 10, "	Feb. 10, "	Mustered out April 13, 1865.
Do.	Thomas J. Staley	" 16, "	" 16, "	Mustered out with regiment.
Do.	John English	" 16, "	" 16, "	Mustered out with regiment.
Do.	Samuel Worthington	May 11, "	May 11, "	Mustered out with regiment.
Do.	Charles C. Welty	" 11, "	" 11, "	Mustered out with regiment.
Do.	George Brainerd	June 6, "	June 6, "	Mustered out with regiment.
Do.	Jacob Wise	" 16, "	" 16, "	Mustered out with regiment.
Do.	John Caruthers	Sept. 29, "	Sept. 29, "	Mustered out with regiment as 2d Lieutenant.
2d Lieutenant	John Sargent	" 17, 1861	Nov. 4, 1861	Promoted.
Do.	Charles G. Harger	" 17, "	" 4, "	Promoted.
Do.	James Stonehocker	" 17, "	" 4, "	Promoted.
Do.	Samuel Stephens	" 17, "	" 4, "	Promoted
Do.	David M. Jones	Oct. 3, "	" 4, "	Promoted.
Do.	John M. Frew	" 3, "	" 4, "	Promoted.
Do.	Noah W. Yonders	" 3, "	" 4, "	Promoted.
Do.	Lewis Crooks	" 3, "	" 4, "	Promoted.
Do.	William Nichols	" 4, "	" 4, "	Promoted.
Do.	Benjamin F. Croxton	" 26, "	" 4, "	Promoted.
Do.	Charles E. Mitchener	" 28, "	" 6, "	Mustered out to accept position as Adjutant of 80th reg. O. V. I.
Do.	Frank Shrorer	Feb. 19, 1862	Feb. 19, 1862	Promoted.
Do.	Peter Lowe	" 28, "	" 28, "	Promoted.
Do.	Philip Everhard	" 25, "	April 14, "	Promoted.
Do.	John E. Smith	" 25, "	" 14, "	Promoted.
Do.	Samuel Slade	March 20, "	May 5, "	Promoted.
Do.	Thomas H. Morgan	June 7, "	Oct. 7, "	Resigned May 3, 1863.
Do.	William S. Ritteley	Nov. 16, "	Dec. 31, "	Promoted.
Do.	Henry Kaldenbaugh	June 30, "	" 31, "	Promoted.
Do.	Samson McNeal	Nov. 26, "	" 31, "	Promoted.
Do.	Willis C. Workman	Dec. 25, "	Feb. 19, 1863	Promoted.
Do.	Charles Geutsch	Jan. 23, 1863	" 13, "	Promoted.
Do.	Thomas C. Ayers	" 4, "	" 19, "	Promoted.
Do.	John G. Croxton	" 23, "	" 19, "	Promoted.
Do.	Albert Dent	" 29, "	" 19, "	Commission revoked.
Do.	Josiah D. Lake	March 17, "	April 9, "	Promoted.
Do.	John P. Chapin	" 17, "	" 9, "	Declined promotion; mustered out Jan. 17, '65.
Do.	James Weatherbee	Jan. 31, "	" 29, "	Promoted.
Do.	Edward J. Pocock	April 21, "	June 10, "	Promoted.
Do.	George Wood	" 14, "	" 10, "	Promoted.
Do.	James Everhard	Feb. 4, 1864	Feb. 20, 1864	Mustered out September, 1861.
Do.	John H. Purvis	Jan. 25, "	" 24, "	Promoted.
Do.	Thomas J. Staley	" 6, 1865	Jan. 6, 1865	Mustered out with regiment.
Do.	Justin L. Robbins	" 6, "	" 6, "	Commission returned.
Do.	John English	" 6, "	" 6, "	Promoted.
Do.	Samuel Worthington	" 6, "	" 6, "	Promoted.
Do.	Charles C. Welty	" 6, "	" 6, "	Promoted.
Do.	George Brainerd	" 6, "	" 6, "	Promoted.
Do.	Jacob Wise	" 6, "	" 6, "	Promoted.
Do.	John Caruthers	Feb. 10, "	Feb. 10, "	Promoted; mustered out with regiment.
Do.	John M. Wasson	Nov. 29, 1862	Nov. 29, 1862	Promoted.
Do.	Robert Hackenson	Feb. 10, 1865	Feb. 10, 1865	Mustered out with regiment.
Do.	Joseph H. Shaw	" 16, "	" 16, "	Mustered out with regiment.
Do.	Robert Carnes	March 25, "	March 25, "	Mustered out with regiment.
Do.	Benjamin F. Jones	" 25, "	" 25, "	Mustered out with regiment.
Do.	Reuben B. Whitaker	" 25, "	" 25, "	Mustered out with regiment.
Do.	David Fisk	May 11, "	May 11, "	Mustered out with regiment.
Do.	Samuel W. Vandevort	" 11, "	" 11, "	Declined promotion.
Do.	Israel Correl	June 6, "	June 6, "	Mustered out with regiment.
Do.	Simon Kail	" 6, "	" 6, "	Mustered out with regiment.
Do.	William P. Baird	" 16, "	" 16, "	Mustered out with regiment.
Do.	Samuel Bartley	Sept. 29, "	Sept. 29, "	

FIFTY-FIRST OHIO VOLUNTEER INFANTRY.

THE FIFTY-FIRST OHIO was organized October 3, 1861, at Camp Meigs, near Canal Dover, Tuscarawas County. On November 3d it left Camp Meigs and went by rail to Wellsville, on the Ohio River. It was there placed on transports and taken to Louisville, Kentucky, remaining, by the way, at Cincinnati and Camp Dennison, some ten days. It arrived at Louisville on the 17th of November, and went into Camp Jenkins, a few miles from the city. It remained in this camp up to the 10th of December, and then, under orders, reported to General Nelson at Camp Wickliffe, near New Haven. This camp was occupied until February 6, 1862, when the regiment moved, with its brigade, to West Point, at the mouth of Salt River, where transports were provided, on which the National army was conveyed to Nashville, Tennessee. It remained at Nashville, on provost-guard duty, until the 9th of July, when it marched, under orders, to Tullahoma, and there joined General Nelson's division of the Army of the Ohio, then on its march from Pittsburg Landing. With this division the regiment returned to Nashville, and there joined the combined movement toward Louisville to checkmate General Bragg in his advance on that place.

After a short rest at Louisville the march in pursuit of the enemy was resumed, the regiment going out on the Bardstown Turnpike. Aside from rear-guard skirmishes, nothing occurred until, on October 8th, the battle of Perryville was fought. The Fifty-First was not engaged, although part of the time in sight of the conflict, and eager to join its hard-pressed comrades.

The Rebel army was pursued up to Crab Orchard, Kentucky, without further results. The National forces were then marched back, by easy stages, to Nashville.

On November 9, 1862, the regiment and brigade, under Colonel Stanley Mathews, were sent out on a foraging expedition, and at Dobson's Ferry, Stone River, met and defeated Wheeler's Rebel cavalry, who had by some means got in their rear. The fight was made by five companies of the Fifty-First, and five companies of the Thirty-Fifth Indiana, led by Colonel Stanley Mathews. The Fifty-First lost thirteen men wounded, three of whom subsequently died; and the Thirty-Fifth Indiana lost its Lieutenant-Colonel (severely wounded), its Adjutant (killed), and a number of men. Colonel Mathews, while in the thickest of the fight, was thrown from his horse and severely injured, but kept the field and command until the troops arrived safely in camp.

On December 26th the regiment moved out on the Murfreesboro' Turnpike, with Brigadier-General Van Cleve's division, of the Twenty-First Army Corps, marching toward Stone River. Nothing of moment occurred until the 31st of December, when the regiment, having been thrown across Stone River on a reconnoissance, found the enemy in force, and returned to its amp. On January 1, 1861, it again crossed the river and took position, four companies being rown out as skirmishers. Advancing half a mile, they met the enemy and skirmished with n all that day and night, and part of the next day. On the afternoon of the 2d of January ckinridge's Rebel division made a charge, and flanking the right, swept it to the west side ne River. The Fifty-First left thirty-two of its number dead on the field, one hundred e wounded, and forty-six captured. It was at this juncture that General Rosecrans massed his artillery, and settled the fortunes of the day by almost literally blowing the Rebel column of attack into and across Stone River.

The enemy retreated during the night of the 2d. On the morning of the 3d the Rebels opened a furious cannonade; but reconnoissances being made, it was discovered that he was drawing off his forces toward Shelbyville. On the morning of the 4th, the enemy having disappeared, the army marched into and took possession of Murfreesboro'.

The army lay at Murfreesboro' until the 24th of June, when it moved on the Tullahoma campaign. The route of the Fifty-First and its division was by the way of McMinnville, crossing the Cumberland Mountains into the Sequatchie Valley; thence to Point Lookout, near Chattanooga, and from there to Ringgold. At the latter place, on September 11th, Wheeler's Rebel cavalry was met, defeated, and driven to Tunnel Hill.

On the 12th the regiment marched to Lee & Gordon's Mills; on the 13th it made a reconnoissance to Shield's Gap, and on the 14th went into position at Crawfish Springs. From that time until the opening of the battle of Chickamauga the members of the regiment feasted on roasting-ears and sweet potatoes.

On the evening of the 18th of September the Fifty-First, being relieved by the Sixth Ohio, marched back to Lee & Gordon's Mills, where it went into position, and lay upon its arms all that night. On the morning of the 19th the regiment met the enemy and drove him back a quarter of a mile; but in doing so lost eight men killed, twenty-five wounded, and as many captured. The enemy, receiving re-enforcements, in turn drove the regiment back to its former position, where it lay on its arms for the night.

On September 20th the regiment was marched to the left to re-enforce General Thomas's column, and on arriving at its position it took part in the effort to stay the enemy in his attempt to get into the rear of the National forces, through a gap left in the lines. The regiment struck the Rebel General Adams's division, wounded and captured its commander, and drove it pell-mell. It was then brought back and again formed on the extreme left of General Thomas's command.

In this battle the Fifty-First lost twelve men and one officer wounded, and thirty captured, including Colonel R. W. McLain, Lieutenants Kittelley, McNeil, and James Weatherbee and Assistant-Surgeon Wing.

On September 21st the army retired behind intrenchments to Chattanooga, and was there besieged by the Rebel forces until the latter part of the following November, when the siege was raised.

On November 24th the regiment participated in the storming of Lookout Mountain, and on the 25th took part in the taking of Rossville Gap, through Mission Ridge. Its loss in these two affairs was one killed and seven wounded.

On January 1, 1864, the Fifty-First re-enlisted, and on February 10th arrived at Columbus on veteran furlough of thirty days. It returned to the front at Blue Springs, near Cleveland, Tennessee. It remained at this place in camp until May 4th, when it marched to Catoosa Springs, and entered on the Atlanta campaign. On May 14th it was engaged at Resaca, and on the 20th of June at Kenesaw. At the first-named place it lost one officer and ten men wounded and one man killed. At Kenesaw it lost two officers (Captain Samuel Stephens and Lieutenant Workman) killed, and ten men killed and thirty wounded. From this time until Atlanta was taken the regiment was almost hourly engaged with the enemy.

On September 1st the regiment was at Jonesboro', and took part in that engagement; and on the 2d pursued the enemy to Lovejoy's Station. Here it lost ten men wounded. It then fell back to Atlanta, and on the 8th of September entered that city. It lay there quietly in camp until the 3d of October, when it marched toward Chattanooga, passing through Cassville, Kingston, Rome, Resaca, and Snake Creek Gap. This march was made in consequence of the Rebel General Hood's movement to the rear of Atlanta, and the consequent return of General Hood's army. At this time a series of arduous marches were made in pursuit of the enemy through Tennessee and Alabama, ending at Pulaski, Tennessee, where it went into camp until November

22, 1864. It then fell back with General Thomas's command to Columbia, Spring Hill, Franklin, and Nashville.

It was engaged at Spring Hill, but in the battle of Franklin it occupied a position not involved in the fight. A number of its men were, however, engaged as skirmishers.

On December 14th and 15th the regiment took part in the battle of Nashville, with a loss of one man killed and fifteen wounded. It joined in the pursuit of the enemy up to Lexington, Alabama. This march was arduous in the extreme, the roads being almost knee-deep in mud and water. The regiment then proceeded to Huntsville, where, on January 5, 1865, it went into camp.

On March 20th it went by rail to Strawberry Plains, and from thence to Bull's Gap, Tennessee. On April 5th it went by rail to Nashville, where it remained until June 16th. It was then taken to Texas, *via* New Orleans, and landed at Indianola, Texas, July 25, 1865. Thence it marched to Blue Lake, and thence to Victoria.

On October 3, 1865, the regiment was mustered out at Victoria by Captain Wm. Nicholas, Commissary of Musters of the Central District of Texas, and on the 4th was on its way to Ohio, where it arrived on November 1, 1865. It was discharged at Camp Chase, near Columbus, Ohio, after a long and faithful term of arduous service honorably performed.

52d REGIMENT OHIO VOLUNTEER INFANTRY.

ROSTER, THREE YEARS' SERVICE.

RANK.	NAME.	DATE OF RANK.	COM. ISSUED.	REMARKS.
Colonel	DANIEL McCOOK	July 15, 1862	Aug. 25, 1862	Died of w'ds rece'd at Kenesaw Mt. July 18, '64.
Do.	CHARLES W. CLANCEY	May 31, 1865	May 31, 1865	Mustered out as Lieutenant-Colonel.
Lt. Colonel	D. D. T. COWAN	Aug. 20, 1862	Aug. 25, 1862	Honorably discharged February 18, 1863.
Do.	CHARLES W. CLANCEY	Feb. 18, 1863	March 30, 1863	Promoted to Colonel.
Do.	J. TAYLOR HOLMES	Jan. 31, 1865	Jan. 31, 1865	Mustered out as Major.
Major	ISRAEL D. CLARK	Oct. 8, 1862	Oct. 27, 1862	Resigned March 8, 1863.
Do.	MATTHEW L. MORROW	May 8, "	March 14, 1863	Revoked; resigned as Captain May 23, 1863.
Do.	J. TAYLOR HOLMES	" 8, "	May 8, "	Promoted to Lieutenant-Colonel.
Do.	WM. H. BUCK	Jan. 31, 1865	Jan 31, 1865	Resigned May 9, 1863.
Surgeon	JOEL MORSE			Resigned September 6, 1864.
Do.	HENRY M. DUFF	May 9, 186[illegible]	May 9, 1862	
Do.	ARTHUR J. ROSA	Oct. 12, 1864	Oct. 12, 1864	Died February 20, 1864.
Do.	NATHAN S. HILL	" 28, "	" 28, "	Mustered out with regiment.
Ass't Surgeon	HENRY M. DUFF	July 7, 1862	July 7, 1862	Promoted to Surgeon.
Do.	ARTHUR J. ROSA	Sept. 5, "	Sept. 5, "	Promoted to Surgeon.
Do.	D. RIDENOUR	July 20, 1863	July 20, 1863	Commission returned.
Do.	S. A. SIMPSON	May 19, 1864	May 19, 1864	Mustered out with regiment.
Chaplain	ASBURY L. PETTY	Sept. 3, 1862	Sept. 3, 1862	Resigned February 2, 1863.
Captain	Charles W. Clancey	Aug. 1, "	Aug. 25, "	Promoted to Lieutenant-Colonel.
Do.	Jacob E. Mottet	" 1, "	" 25, "	Resigned February 1, 1863.
Do.	Israel D. Clark	" 5, "	" 25, "	Promoted to Major.
Do.	Matthew L. Morrow	" 7, "	" 25, "	Resigned May 23, 1863.
Do.	Parker A. Elson	" 8, "	" 25, "	Resigned March 18, 1863.
Do.	James B. Donnelson	" 8, "	" 25, "	Resigned May 19, 1863.
Do.	J. Taylor Holmes	" 11, "	" 25, "	Promoted to Major.
Do.	Joseph A. Culbertson	" 16, "	" 25, "	Resigned December 31, 1862.
Do.	Peter Schneider	" 21, "	" 25, "	Deceased July 19, 1864.
Do.	Andrew S. Bloom	" 21, "	" 25, "	Resigned January 7, 1863.
Do.	Wm. H. Buck	Oct. 8, "	Oct. 27, "	Promoted to Major.
Do.	Charles Swift	Dec. 31, "	Feb. 10, 1863	Resigned April 7, 1865.
Do.	Edward L. Anderson	Jan. 7, 1863	June 26, "	Mustered out with regiment.
Do.	Abisha C. Thomas	Feb. 1, "	Feb. 20, "	Mustered out with regiment.
Do.	Wm. H. Sturgis	" 18, "	April 9, "	Resigned August 25, 1865.
Do.	John H. Collier	March 8, "	March 30, "	Revoked.
Do.	Samuel Rothaker	" 18, "	May 12, "	Resigned January 31, 1865.
Do.	Salathiel M. Neighbor	May 12, "	June 29, "	Died of wounds.
Do.	Samuel C. Hutchinson	" 9, "	" 10, "	Mustered out with regiment.
Do.	Henry O. Mansfield	" 23, "	Aug. 1, "	Honorably discharged November 1, 1864.
Do.	George W. Masury	" 9, 1864	May 9, 1864	Declined promotion.
Do.	Ira H. Pool	Dec. 9, "	Dec. 9, "	Died of wounds received at Peachtree Creek.
Do.	James M. Summers	" 9, "	" 9, "	Died April 16, 1865.
Do.	Wm. H. Lane	" 9, "	" 9, "	Mustered out with regiment.
Do.	Frank B. James	" 9, "	" 9, "	Mustered out with regiment.
Do.	Sylvester L. Brice	June 6, 1865	June 6, 1865	
Do.	Alex. B. McIntyre	" 6, "	" 6, "	
Do.	Christopher W. Grimes	" 6, "	" 6, "	
Do.	Isaac Stokes	" 6, "	" 6, "	Mustered out with regiment as R. Q. M.
Do.	Gasper Rudolph	" 6, "	" 6, "	
1st Lieutenant	Wm. H. Sturgis	Aug. 1, 1862	Aug 25, 1862	Promoted to Captain.
Do.	Abisha C. Thomas	" 1, "	" 25, "	Promoted to Captain.
Do.	Wm. H. Buck	" 5, "	" 25, "	Promoted to Captain.
Do.	John H. Collier	" 7, "	" 25, "	Resigned July 27, 1863.
Do.	Alex. Smith	" 9, "	" 25, "	Resigned July 11, 1862.
Do.	John Irwin	" 8, "	" 25, "	Resigned December 20, 1862.
Do.	Samuel Rothaker	" 11, "	" 25, "	Promoted to Captain.
Do.	Charles Swift	" 16, "	" 25, "	Promoted to Captain.
Do.	George H. Masury	" 21, "	" 25, "	Declined.
Do.	Edward L. Anderson	" 21, "	" 25, "	Promoted to Captain.
Do.	Charles H. Blackburn	May 22, "	" 25, "	Resigned November 26, 1862.
Do.	Israel Fisher	" 29, "	" 25, "	Resigned November 20, 1862.
Do.	Wm. H. Kauffman	Oct. 8, "	Oct. 27, "	Resigned January 21, 1863.
Do.	John J. Troxell	Nov. 20, "	Feb. 20, 1863	Discharged October 23, 1863.
Do.	Ira H. Pool	" 26, "	" 20, "	Promoted to Captain April 24, 1864.
Do.	Samuel C. Hutchinson	Dec. 20, "	" 20, "	Promoted to Captain.
Do.	Henry O. Mansfield	Jan. 11, 1863	" 10, "	Resigned as 2d Lieutenant May 9, 1863.
Do.	Wm. H. Lane	" 21, "	" 20, "	Promoted to Captain.
Do.	James M. Summers	Dec. 31, 1862	" 10, "	Promoted to Captain.
Do.	Wm. P. Shackland	Feb. 1, 1863	" 20, "	Resigned June 8, 1863.
Do.	Wm. A. Judkins	" 18, "	April 9, "	Detached.
Do.	Addison P. Marsh	March 18, "	May 18, "	Resigned October 18, 1863
Do.	Sylvester L. Brice	May 19, "	June 10, "	Promoted to Captain.
Do.	Alex. B. McIntyre	March 24, "	July 29, 1864	Promoted to Captain.
Do.	Frank B. James	Jan. 7, "	Jan. 26, 1863	Promoted to Captain.
Do.	Christopher W. Grimes	June 18, "	July 20, "	Promoted to Captain.
Do.	Isaac Stokes	Nov. 18, 1864	Nov. 18, 1864	Promoted to Captain.
Do.	Samuel J. Brent	Dec. 9, "	Dec. 9, "	2d Lieutenant Signal Corps U. S. A.
Do.	Gasper Rudolph	" 9, "	" 9, "	Promoted to Captain.
Do.	Adam Kneckt	" 9, "	" 9, "	Declined to accept.
Do.	Samuel W. Duff	" 9, "	" 9, "	Mustered out with regiment.
Do.	Julius Armstrong	" 9, "	" 9, "	Mustered out with regiment.
Do.	Wm. H. Ray	" 9, "	" 9, "	Mustered out with regiment.
Do.	Wm. D. Scott	Jan. 28, 1865	Jan. 28, 1865	Mustered out with regiment.
Do.	Wm. D. Scott	June 6, "	June 6, "	Mustered out with regiment.
Do.	Wm. Freeman	" 6, "	" 6, "	No discharge furnished; this man stands as Sergeant-Major on roll.

RANK.	NAME.	DATE OF RANK.	COM. ISSUED.	REMARKS.
1st Lieutenant	Isaac L. Mills	June 6, 1865	June 6, 1865	
Do.	John Seeman	" 6, "	" 6, "	
Do.	Daniel T. Heneroft	" 6, "	" 6, "	
Do.	A. R. Holmes	" 6, "	" 6, "	
Do.	Frank Dull	" 6, "	" 6, "	Mustered out with regiment.
Do.	Thomas Hammond	" 6, "	" 6, "	
2d Lieutenant	Wm. A. Judkins	Aug. 1, 1862	Aug. 25, 1862	Promoted to 1st Lieutenant.
Do.	Ezekiel E. Mills	" 1, "	" 25, "	Promoted; resigned February 13, 1863.
Do.	Wm. H. Kauffman	" 5, "	" 25, "	Promoted to 1st Lieutenant.
Do.	Salathiel Hughbel	" 7, "	" 25, "	Promoted to 1st Lieutenant.
Do.	Henry O. Mansfield	" 9, "	" 25, "	Promoted to 1st Lieutenant.
Do.	Samuel C. Hutchinson	" 8, "	" 25, "	Promoted to 1st Lieutenant.
Do.	Addison P. Marsh	" 11, "	" 25, "	Promoted to 1st Lieutenant.
Do.	James M. Summers	" 16, "	" 25, "	Promoted to 1st Lieutenant.
Do.	Edwin J. Donaldson	" 21, "	" 25, "	Discharged November 1, 1862.
Do.	Samuel J. Brent	" 21, "	" 25, "	Promoted to 1st Lieutenant.
Do.	Lucius F. Dunham	Oct. 8, "	Oct. 27, "	Resigned March 21, 1863.
Do.	Frank H. James	Jan. 20, 1863	Jan. 20, 1863	Promoted to 1st Lieutenant.
Do.	Gasper Rudolph	Dec. 31, 1862	Feb. 20, "	Promoted to 1st Lieutenant.
Do.	James H. Donaldson	July 11, 1863	....	Died July 19, 1864.
Do.	Sylvester L. Brice	Dec. 29, 1862	....	Promoted to 1st Lieutenant.
Do.	Adam Kneckt	Feb. 13, 1863	May 12, 1863	Honorably discharged March 18, 1865.
Do.	Samuel W. Duff	" 18, "	April 9, "	Promoted to 1st Lieutenant.
Do.	David Neighbor	May 12, "	July 10, "	Honorably discharged October 26, 1863.
Do.	David S. Miser	Jan. 10, "	May 18, "	Honorably discharged August 21, 1864.
Do.	Julius Armstrong	May 19, "	June 10, "	Promoted to 1st Lieutenant.
Do.	Wm. H. Ray	Dec. 20, "	April 9, 1864	Promoted to 1st Lieutenant.
Do.	Isaac Stokes	May 9, 1864	May 9, "	Promoted to 1st Lieutenant.

FIFTY-SECOND OHIO VOLUNTEER INFANTRY.

IN the organization of the three-years' regiments, this number (the Fifty-Second) was, for some unexplained reason, left unfilled, notwithstanding repeated efforts had been made to fill it. In May, 1862, Governor Tod called to his aid Captain Dan. McCook, to whom he issued a commission as Colonel. On his arrival at Columbus from the field of Pittsburg Landing, the new Colonel went to work with alacrity and energy in the raising of his new command. During the first month of his labors he was quite successful. After that recruiting for that or any other organization lagged heavily, and almost ceased, and the middle of August was reached before an organization was effected, and then only by a partial consolidation with other straggling organizations.

At sunrise on the 25th of August, 1862, the Fifty-Second Ohio, under orders, left Camp Dennison for Lexington, Kentucky, passing through Cincinnati. While on the wharf, awaiting transportation across the Ohio River, a banner was presented to the regiment by citizens of the "Queen City." The presentation ceremonies concluded, the regiment crossed the river to Covington, and, taking the railroad cars, reached Lexington the following morning. After getting settled in camp, Colonel McCook was placed in command of the post and of all the forces in and about the city.

In the evening of August 30th orders were received to march to the relief of General Nelson, whose troops had met with disaster at Big Hill, near Richmond, Kentucky. Before daylight of the following morning the Fifty-Second Ohio had reached the Kentucky River, fifteen miles from Lexington. Rumors of disaster and defeat were here changed into certainty. The National forces had been completely routed, with great loss in killed, wounded, and prisoners.

Soon after dawn the enemy made his appearance on the opposite side of the river in force, and, after the interchange of a few shots between pickets, a deliberate withdrawal of all the National forces began. After reaching Lexington, and remaining in its vicinity until the evening of September 1st, the regiment moved with the column, acting as rear-guard toward Louisville,

Kentucky. Then commenced a period of hardship and suffering that surely has never been paralleled, or at least surpassed, in the annals of warfare. What was true of the Fifty-Second Ohio was true of nearly every regiment in the retreating column. The men had not been inured to the hardships of the service; and what would have put to the fullest test the powers of endurance of veterans was being suffered by raw recruits. All engaged in that march will ever remember the source from whence came the greatest misery. The parched lips, the blood-shot eyes, the quick, smothered breathings, the uncertain, tottering gait, all proclaimed the thirst that was hourly consuming the very life-blood of those excessively wearied soldiers. The springs were dried up, the heat and dust were terrible, and, added to all these, was the momentary anticipation of an attack from the army under Kirby Smith, flushed with a recent victory. No language can ever portray the tortures of those few days.

The Fifty-Second Ohio, forming, as it did, the rear-guard of the hastily-retreating column, came in for (if possible) an additional share of hardship and suffering. If straggling among the men was possible in the front regiments, it was impossible among those of the rear. Therefore the most exact discipline was absolutely necessary, and was carried out rigidly and to the letter. Men in their agony of suffering would reel out of the ranks and attempt to reach some inviting farm-yard to quench their burning thirst, but were sternly met by the Colonel or his Adjutant and driven back to their places.

The retreat was ended, and the regiment went into camp at Louisville on the 6th of September, 1862. At this date the army under General Buell, in pursuit of the Rebel forces under Bragg, had reached Louisville. The citizens of the city and surrounding country were in the greatest alarm for their safety. Kentucky was overrun by the armies of Generals Bragg and Kirby Smith, and an attack was momentarily expected. Meantime the work of reorganizing and recruiting the National forces steadily progressed. The new regiments were placed in brigades and divisions. The Fifty-Second Ohio, Eighty-Fifth, Eighty-Sixth, and One Hundred and Twenty-Fifth Illinois were thrown into a brigade.

On the 1st of October, 1862, the regiment and brigade moved out of Louisville with the army, then resuming the pursuit of Bragg's retreating forces. The Rebel army was vigorously followed, until, at the little village of Perryville, nestled among what are called the Chaplin Hills, a collision occurred. The brigade in which the Fifty-Second was placed had attacked the enemy about four o'clock on the morning of the same day, and carried Peter's Hill after a sharp conflict. General Bragg ordered the hill retaken, and, as has since been authoritatively learned, informed the division he sent to do the work that they must take the battery (meaning Captain Barnett's Battery I, Second Illinois) attached to the brigade. Bragg said to his troops: "It is supported by green troops, and can easily be captured." His troops made every effort to carry out their commander's orders, but were sent howling back. The regiment and battery, instead of giving way, stood up to their work like veterans. In the general attack several of the new regiments showed signs of demoralization, but as the fight progressed their ranks were closed up, and they stood firm in line until the battle was ended.

The pursuit was resumed the next morning, and on that march the command was much reduced by sickness, and a large number of the members of the Fifty-Second were compelled to go into hospitals along the roads clear up to Nashville.

At Bowling Green, Kentucky, General William S. Rosecrans relieved General Buell and assumed command of the army, and the Fifty-Second Ohio moved with what was then called the Fourteenth Army Corps. On reaching the vicinity of Nashville the Fifty-Second and the other regiments of its brigade were, on the 10th of December, detailed as a part of the garrison of the city of Nashville, and were accordingly sent to that post, where they remained on duty until the 7th day of March, 1863.

The Fifty-Second Ohio was not immediately engaged in the battle of Stone River; but, while that battle was raging, the left wing of the Fifty-Second was detailed as a part of the force to escort an ammunition-train to the front. The enemy's cavalry were swarming in the rear, and the roads were closely watched by them to prevent re-enforcements or aid of any kind reaching Rosecrans's forces. It was, therefore, a responsible and dangerous task to perform. Seven miles from Nashville, near the Lunatic Asylum, on the Murfreesboro' Pike, the train was attacked by a Rebel cavalry force under the command of Pegram and Wheeler. After a brief skirmish, in which the enemy were handsomely repulsed, the train moved on, and reached its destination in safety. The conduct of the troops in this affair called forth the warmest commendation from General Rosecrans.

The battle of Stone River being ended, the regiment returned to Nashville and resumed its former duties. Early in March the brigade was sent over to Franklin to look after Van Dorn's forces, but, after remaining there a few days, returned to its old camp, nothing having transpired to require its services. It will be recollected that about that time Van Dorn was killed by a Dr. Peters, and that his forces were driven out of Franklin by a National column on the 9th of March, 1863.

On the 7th of April the regiment received its first payment since entering the field, and marched with a portion of General James D. Morgan's division to Brentwood Station, eleven miles south of Nashville, where it went into camp and remained up to June 5th, and again returned to Nashville. The brigade remained in General Morgan's division until after the battle of Chickamauga.

On the 28th of June the brigade was ordered to Murfreesboro' to perform garrison-duty, General Rosecrans having commenced his forward movement a few days before. It did not, however, remain long in Murfreesboro', as on the 16th of July it was once more in its old camp at Nashville. During its long stay in Nashville, Murfreesboro', and other stations, discipline and drill had not been neglected, and the regiment had attained to a high degree in both. Its arms (the Springfield musket) were perfect mirrors, and carried the palm for being the neatest, brightest guns on inspection.

Thus, prepared at all points for a vigorous campaign, the regiment and brigade started south at dawn of the morning of the 20th of August, 1863. Their course lay toward Brentwood and Franklin. By the 23d Spring Hill, beyond Franklin, was reached, and on the 24th the camp was pitched at Carter's Creek, six miles from Columbia. The ostensible object of the movement seemed to be the building and repairing of the bridges on the Nashville and Decatur Railroad, and preparations were made accordingly. Before operations were commenced, however, orders were received (August 25th) for the Fifty-Second and One Hundred and Twenty-Fifth Ohio Regiments to march to Columbia, Tennessee, where (on the 29th of August) they were joined by the other regiments of the brigade.

In the evening of the 30th of August Lynnville, Tennessee, was reached, and on the following morning, immediately after reveille, at which call the picket companies had been ordered to rejoin their respective regiments, company E, of the Fifty-Second Ohio, then about leaving its picket-lines, was fired upon by a squad of bushwhackers concealed in the woods near a spring. Two men of the company were wounded by the fire. These cowardly murderers had been heard of the day previous, and the citizens of Lynnville, to which place they belonged, had been notified that for every gun fired by these wretches upon the National troops while they remained in that vicinity, they would be held strictly to account, and an equal number of dwelling-houses burned to the ground. Accordingly, the Colonel commanding directed a detail to fire five buildings in the village, and the order was promptly obeyed. This righteous example was productive of good results, as no further murderous attempts were made upon the forces then stationed there, or to the thousands of other National troops that afterward passed through that portion of Tennessee.

Continuing south by easy marches, the afternoon of September 2d found the regiment in camp at Athens, Alabama. On September 4th it marched from Athens to Huntsville, a distance of twenty-five miles. Keeping close along the line of the Mobile and Charleston Railroad, it reached Stevenson, Alabama, on the 8th of September. During this march, on the morning of the 6th of September, the command passed the house of the murderer of General Robert L. McCook. So soon as the brigade had reached a point beyond the bounds of the farm, Colonel

Dan. McCook selected a detachment from his regiment and sent it back, with instructions to make the place a desert and a desolate waste, leaving only sufficient shelter for some half-dozen negroes who still clung to the doomed place. This order was literally fulfilled. The firebrand and the deadening ax speedily destroyed all save the spot and its accursed memory.

On the 11th of September the Tennessee River was crossed at Bridgeport, and on the 12th the regiment had reached Shellmound. The following night the wagon-road over Lookout Mountain was climbed, and the regiment went into camp in Chattanooga, near the head-quarters of General Rosecrans. Moving six miles out to Rossville, Georgia, it remained quietly in camp at that place until the evening of the 18th, when it, along with the brigade, was moved four or five miles up and to the left of the Lafayette Road. Having reached the position intended after nightfall, the men lay on their arms until dawn the following morning, when the enemy was discovered in heavy force directly in front. A spirited skirmish began, and a brisk strife kept up for some little time as to which party should possess a bubbling spring of water lying between the combatants. This skirmish, it is claimed, was the beginning of the battle of Chickamauga.

From its position on the left of the Lafayette Road, and from the immediate presence of the enemy, the regiment was withdrawn early in the forenoon. The roar of opening battle began on the right and in front of the previous night's position. The brigade then belonged to what was known as the Reserve Corps, and, acting in that capacity, moved to the Rossville Gap about noon, taking position on the Ringgold Road. On Sunday morning, the 20th of September, the regiment and brigade were assigned a new position two miles toward the front, near McAfee's Church, which covered both the Greysville and Ringgold Roads. This position was the extreme left of the National army on that morning. The tide of battle at noon having drifted, owing to an attempt made by the enemy to turn our right flank (which in the end was measurably successful), the brigade was ordered into position about two miles to the right of McAfee's. A few moments before reaching the position, and while the brigade was marching by the flank, the enemy opened upon it with solid shot, shell, grape, and canister at short range, but, by reason of the smoke of burning fences, houses, etc., no great harm was done.

After the brigade had reached its position, a few yards from where the first fire opened, the Rebel artillerists were unable to inflict upon it any serious injury, although their missiles whizzed and hurtled very close to the heads of the men. The Rebels, on the contrary, must have suffered severely from the rapid and precise firing of Barnett's battery.

The fight lasted until dark. At that time the army retreated along the whole line, and that night at eight o'clock the Fifty-Second, one of the last to leave the battle-field, moved into Rossville.

On Monday, the 21st of September, the position of the regiment and brigade was on the right of the Rossville Gap, going south, and was under fire from two o'clock in the afternoon until night, its skirmishers, a few yards in front, being constantly engaged by those of the enemy. At dark the National forces were withdrawn to Chattanooga, and placed in position behind the second line of defenses around that then besieged city. On the 15th of September the regiment crossed the Tennessee and took position at Caldwell's Ford, four miles above Chattanooga. In a few days another movement was made to the mouth of Chickamauga Creek, where the regiment rested after its long march and harassing battle.

On the 29th of September two regiments of the brigade were ordered to report to General Hooker in Lookout Valley. The Fifty-Second Ohio and the Eighty-Sixth Illinois Infantry were detailed, reported to General Hooker, and were temporarily constituted the Third Brigade, Second Division, Eleventh Army Corps. This service proved the most severe of any the regiment had ever performed. For seven days of the most wretched weather it was constantly on duty, without relief, and under the almost incessant fire of the Rebel batteries on Lookout Mountain. It fell to its lot to be stationed in two of the gaps through the range of low hills that skirt the base of the mountain. It was the daily practice of the enemy's gunners stationed on Lookout Mountain to shell troops and trains while passing these gaps. The range was about two miles, yet they would drop their plunging shots through these gaps with the greatest ease.

Although very annoying, no great damage was effected, attributable, as the Rebels said, to the fact that their ammunition was bad. Many of their shells did not burst at all, There were, however, two notable exceptions to this rule, both of which burst in the midst of four companies of the Fifty-Second Ohio, and yet, strange as it may seem, without serious harm to any one. So accustomed did the men become to the programme that the puff of the discharge from the Rebel guns would be followed by the cry: "Lookout!" which would place each individual on the alert to seek shelter. Then would come the scream of the shell, and, immediately after, the explosion, which, if harmless, would call forth lusty cheers.

On the 6th of November the regiment returned to the camp at Chickamauga Creek. In the reorganization of the Army of the Cumberland under General Thomas, early in October, the Reserve Corps was dispensed with, and the brigade to which the Fifty-Second was attached became the Third Brigade, Second Division, Fourteenth Army Corps.

At daylight on the morning of the 24th of November the Fifty-Second Ohio reported at Caldwell's Ford, at which point, under cover of darkness, General Sherman had just finished throwing a bridge across the Tennessee. General Jeff. C. Davis's Second Division had been selected to support General Sherman's corps, both in crossing the river and in attacking the north-eastern extremity of Mission Ridge. At noon on the 24th the Second Division crossed the river, while Sherman moved up Chickamauga Valley and seized the point of the ridge. On the following day Mission Ridge was carried by storm.

At one o'clock in the morning of the 26th of November the troops commenced their movement from the foot of the ridge down the Chickamauga Valley, crossing the mouth of Chickamauga Creek, in pursuit of the flying Rebels. Nothing of moment occurred during the day, but at sunset, the rear of Bragg's forces being hotly pursued, they (the Rebels) made a stand at Shepherd's Run, three miles below Chickamauga Station, near the village of Greysville.

When the fight opened the National troops in the rear began to come up to the front on the double-quick. The Fifty-Second Ohio moving at this gait, passing over logs and through the swamps and bushes, fixed bayonets, and, coming forward into line with a shout, took its place on the left of its brigade. The fight was quickly over, and the troops were directed to bivouac on the spot. On the 27th of November two companies from each of the regiments of the Third Brigade acted as skirmishers on the march between Shepherd's Run and Ringgold, and captured one hundred and fifty prisoners. It was on the 27th that General Hooker gained possession of Ringgold and Ringgold Gap. The Rebel army had been drawn off beyond White Oak Mountains. From this place, passing through McDaniel's Gap in Taylor's Ridge, the regiment and brigade started, on the 29th of November, for East Tennessee or Knoxville. This march was undertaken for the relief of General Burnside's beleaguered forces in and around Knoxville. The march was a forced one, and made at a time when the weather was very inclement, and the men badly off for clothing, shoes, rations, etc. It was an occasion, therefore, of keen suffering. Passing through or near the towns of Cleveland, Charleston, and Loudon, the Fifty-Second crossed the Little Tennessee at Morgantown on the 6th day of December, *en route* for Knoxville. When within fifteen miles of that place it was learned that Longstreet had raised the siege, and was in full retreat in the direction of Richmond, Virginia. The Fifty-Second did not, therefore, proceed any further. Re-crossing the river, it went into camp at some mills near Columbus, Tennessee, for the purpose of providing rations that could not otherwise be obtained.

On the 15th of December the entire division commenced the return march to Chattanooga, and the Fifty-Second reached its old camp on Chickamauga Creek on the night of the 19th of December. The recollections of this arduous march are not very pleasant among the members of the Fifty-Second and of other regiments that participated in it. These men in their early youth, and even in their more mature years, had read with sad and sympathizing hearts of the sufferings of their patriotic forefathers at Valley Forge, under the immortal Washington; but little did they dream that they, too, would be called upon to "repeat history;" that ragged, shivering, hungry, and footsore, they, too, would leave the imprint of their shoeless feet in blood upon the biting snow.

On the 26th of December the regiment moved to McAfee's Church, Georgia, and went into camp near the ground it occupied on the Sunday morning of the battle of Chickamauga. On January 28, 1864, the regiment went on a reconnoissance to Ringgold, returning the following day. On the 14th of February it moved to Chickamauga Station, and on the 23d again returned to Ringgold to witness, on the next day, the flanking and taking of Tunnel Hill. At dusk of that day the regiment bivouacked in front of Buzzard's Roost, four miles from Dalton, Georgia. The enemy's artillery had given warning that the passage of the gap would be warmly disputed. Heavy skirmishing was continued through the 25th and 26th of January. In the afternoon of the 25th the Fifty-Second Ohio was moved to the support of a battery which had been freshly opened on the enemy's works, and lay in range of the Rebel sharpshooters until the night of the 26th, when the entire corps fell back to Ringgold, the main object of its advance having been accomplished.

The Fifty-Second Ohio returned to McAfee's Church on the 27th, and on the 6th day of March received orders to report at Lee & Gordon's Mills, thirteen miles from Chattanooga, where the Lafayette Road strikes Chickamauga River. At this place the regiment lay in camp until the commencement of the Atlanta campaign in May, 1864. At Dalton, the opening struggle of the campaign, it took a marked position, and was skillfully fought. At Resaca, also, on the 14th of May, the Fifty-Second performed a prominent part, making a charge with success, but at a sad cost of life.

At Kenesaw Mountain the brigade was ordered to carry the works opposite it. A terrible struggle ensued. The enemy's position was proof against the assault, and the National column was hurled back with a heavy loss of life. Among the severely wounded was the leader of the brigade and Colonel of the Fifty-Second Ohio. He was borne from the field, and from thence to the residence of kind friends in Cincinnati. At one time it was hoped he would overcome the hurt, but the hope was fallacious, and the soldier went to his rest. On his death-bed his gallantry was fitly acknowledged by the War Department, by conferring upon him the full rank of Brigadier-General of Volunteers.

The Fifty-Second was busily engaged through all the movement up to Atlanta, and maintained throughout its fine reputation for discipline, courage, and endurance.

From Atlanta the Fifty-Second moved with the rest of Sherman's army to Savannah, and thence, with small loss, through Georgia and the Carolinas northward.

Then came the march to Washington, the review before the President and Cabinet, the muster-out at Washington, June 3, 1865; the railroad ride to Columbus, Ohio; the final payment and dispersion of the men to their homes; and the Fifty-Second Ohio ceased to exist as a military organization.

53d REGIMENT OHIO VOLUNTEER INFANTRY.

ROSTER, THREE YEARS' SERVICE.

RANK.	NAME.	DATE OF RANK.	COM. ISSUED.	REMARKS.
Colonel	JESSE J. APPLER	Sept. 16, 1861	Feb. 13, 1862	Mustered out April 18, 1862.
Do.	WELLS S. JONES	April 18, 1862	May 16, "	Mustered out with regiment.
Lt. Colonel	ROBERT A. FULTON	Sept. 16, 1861	Feb. 13, "	Mustered out November 30, 1861.
Do.	JOHN I. FARRELL	Dec. 30, 1864	Dec. 30, 1864	Mustered out.
Do.	PRESTON R. GALLOWAY	June 20, 1865	June 20, 1865	Mustered out with regiment.
Major	HARRISON S. COX	Feb. 16, 1861	Feb. 13, 1862	Honorably discharged November 1, 1862.
Do.	EPHRAIM C. DAWES	Nov. 1, 1862	Jan. 14, 1863	Honorably discharged October 25, 1864.
Do.	PRESTON R. GALLOWAY	March 18, 1865	March 18, 1865	Promoted to Lieutenant-Colonel.
Surgeon	WM. M. CAKE	Oct. 3, 1861	Feb. 13, 1862	Resigned September 20, 1864.
Do.	JOHN A. LAIR	Nov. 17, 1864	Nov. 17, 1864	Mustered out with regiment.
Ass't Surgeon	JAMES P. BING	Oct. 3, 1861	Feb. 13, 1863	Resigned August 31, 1862.
Do.	JOHN A. LAIR	Aug. 19, 1862	Sept. 8, 1862	Promoted to Surgeon.
Do.	ROB'T L. VAN HARLINGEN	Feb. 15, 1863	Feb. 17, 1863	Promoted to Surgeon 70th O. V. I.
Do.	SAMUEL MATHERS	Nov. 17, 1864	Nov. 17, 1864	Mustered out with regiment.
Do.	W. F. HOME	June 26, 1865	June 26, 1865	Mustered out with regiment.
Chaplain	THOMAS MCINTYRE	Dec. 13, 1861	Dec. 18, 1861	Resigned May 23, 1862.
Do.	FREDERICK J. GRIFFITH	July 8, 1862	July 8, 1862	Honorably discharged September 29, 1864.
Captain	Frederick J. Griffith	Oct. 4, 1861	Feb. 13, "	Appointed Chaplain.
Do.	Wells S. Jones	" 4, "	" 13, "	Promoted to Colonel.
Do.	John I. Farrell	Nov. 6, "	" 13, "	Promoted to Lieutenant-Colonel.
Do.	Henry C. Messenger	" 17, "	" 13, "	Died April 28, 1863.
Do.	Samuel W. Baird	" 26, "	" 13, "	Mustered out.
Do.	James R. Percy	Jan. 1, 1862	" 13, "	Killed August 18, 1861.
Do.	Lorenzo Fulton	" 7, "	" 13, "	Resigned February 16, 1862.
Do.	David H. Lasley	" 8, "	" 13, "	Mustered out at exp. of service, Dec. 28, 1864
Do.	George K. Hosford	Feb. 19, "	" 19, "	Discharged August 19, 1862.
Do.	David T. Harkins	" 5, "	" 19, "	Resigned April 17, 1863.
Do.	Preston R. Galloway	Jan. 28, "	" 19, "	Promoted to Major.
Do.	Robert A. Starkey	April 18, "	June 21, "	Resigned May 17, 1861.
Do.	Jacob W. Davis	July 8, "	Sept. 4, "	Killed August 11, 1864.
Do.	Joseph W. Fulton	Aug. 19, "	Feb. 10, 1863	Resigned September 27, 1864.
Do.	Frank M. Lewis	April 17, 1863	Sept. 1, "	Mustered out April 6, 1865.
Do.	Chas. K. Crumit	" 28, "	" 1, "	Mustered out December 31, 1864.
Do.	Eustace H. Ball	March 9, 1864	March 9, 1864	Resigned as 1st Lieutenant April 15, 1864.
Do.	George H. Cake	Sept. 8, "	Sept. 8, "	Declined.
Do.	Robert Curren	" 8, "	" 8, "	Mustered out with regiment.
Do.	James H. Boyce	" 26, "	" 26, "	Killed August 31, 1864, as 1st Lieutenant.
Do.	Joseph M. Long	" 26, "	" 26, "	Mustered out with regiment.
Do.	Wm. W. Gilbert	" 26, "	" 26, "	Mustered out with regiment.
Do.	Thomas J. Bradley	Nov. 18, "	Nov. 18, "	Declined to accept.
Do.	John W. Earles	" 18, "	" 18, "	
Do.	Joshua E. Bailey	Jan. 18, 1865	Jan. 18, 1865	Mustered out with regiment.
Do.	Elias J. Gorby	" 18, "	" 18, "	Mustered out with regiment.
Do.	M. G. McNeal	April 26, "	April 26, "	Mustered out with regiment.
Do.	George W. Eddy	" 26, "	" 26, "	Mustered out with regiment.
Do.	David M. Burchfield	" 26, "	" 26, "	Mustered out with regiment.
1st Lieutenant	Jacob W. Davis	Oct. 4, 1861	Feb. 13, 1862	Promoted to Captain.
Do.	Robert A. Starkey	" 4, "	" 13, "	Promoted to Captain.
Do.	Joseph W. Fulton	" 7, "	" 13, "	Promoted to Captain.
Do.	Calvin D. Brooks	Nov. 17, "	" 13, "	Died September 21, 1862.
Do.	Eustace H. Ball	" 26, "	" 13, "	Promoted to Captain; resigned April 15, 1864.
Do.	Chas. K. Crumit	Jan. 1, 1862	" 13, "	Promoted to Captain.
Do.	George K. Hosford	" 7, "	" 13, "	Promoted to Captain.
Do.	Harvey L. Black	" 8, "	" 13, "	Died May 26, 1862.
Do.	Ephraim C. Dawes	Sept. 26, 1861	" 13, "	Promoted to Major.
Do.	Joseph W. Fulton	" 6, "	" 13, "	Resigned December 11, 1862.
Do.	George E. Cutler	Feb. 19, 1862	" 19, "	Discharged December 31, 1882.
Do.	S. B. Messenger	" 5, "	" 19, "	Honorably discharged September 23, 1862.
Do.	Stafford McMillen	" 24, "	" 19, "	Killed August 3, 1864.
Do.	Robert Curren	April 18, "	June 24, "	Promoted to Captain.
Do.	Kendall D. Lindsay	July 8, "	Sept. 4, "	Died November 1, 1863.
Do.	George H. Cake	May 26, "	....	Mustered out December 24, 1864
Do.	Frank M. Lewis	Sept. 23, "	Feb. 10, 1863	Promoted to Captain.
Do.	Wm. B. Stephenson	Nov. 1, "	" 10, "	Resigned May 14, 1861.
Do.	Edward G. Morrison	Jan. 17, 1863	" 4, "	Died April 25, 1864.
Do.	Robert E. Phillips	Aug. 19, 1862	" 10, "	Colonel colored regiment.
Do.	James H. Boyce	Sept. 21, "	" 10, "	Promoted to Captain.
Do.	George W. Cavett	April 28, "	Sept. 1, "	Mustered out December 31, 1864.
Do.	Samuel P. Gorby	" 17, "	" 1, "	Mustered out December 24, 1864.
Do.	Joseph M. Long	March 1, 1864	March 1, 1864	Promoted to Captain.
Do.	Wm. W. Gilbert	" 9, "	" 9, "	Promoted to Captain.
Do.	Thomas J. Bradley	" 9, "	" 9, "	Mustered out December 24, 1864.
Do.	Frederick Stalder	May 9, "	May 9, "	Mustered out.
Do.	Samuel N. Misner	" 9, "	" 9, "	Declined.
Do.	John W. Earles	Sept. 8, "	Sept. 8, "	Promoted to Captain.
Do.	Joshua E. Bailey	" 8, "	" 8, "	Promoted to Captain.
Do.	Elias J. Gorby	" 8, "	" 8, "	Promoted to Captain.
Do.	M. G. McNeal	" 8, "	" 8, "	Promoted to Captain.
Do.	John D. Moore	" 26, "	" 26, "	Resigned April 4, 1865.
Do.	George W. Eddy	Oct. 12, "	Oct. 12, "	Promoted to Captain.
Do.	David M. Burchfield	" 12, "	" 12, "	Promoted to Captain.
Do.	Samuel R. Betts	Nov. 18, "	Nov. 18, "	Mustered out with regiment.
Do.	Bartlett Boyce	" 18, "	" 18, "	Mustered out with regiment.
Do.	Wm. Worrell	April 26, 1865	April 26, 1865	Mustered out with regiment.
Do.	Wm. B. Irwin	" 26, "	" 26, "	Mustered out with regiment.
Do.	Thomas S. Harkins	" 26, "	" 26, "	Mustered out with regiment.
Do.	Henry Foreman	" 26, "	" 26, "	Mustered out with regiment.
Do.	Patrick L. O'Donnell	" 26, "	" 26, "	Mustered out with regiment.
Do.	James D. Roberts	" 26, "	" 26, "	Mustered out with regiment as Adjutant.
Do.	John W. Pierce	" 26, "	" 26, "	
Do.	Nathan S. Elliott	" 26, "	" 26, "	Mustered out with regiment.

RANK.	NAME.	DATE OF RANK.	COM. ISSUED.	REMARKS.
1st Lieutenant	David H. Lasley	April 26, 1865	April 26, 1865	Mustered out with regiment.
2d Lieutenant	Robert Curren	Oct. 4, 1861	Feb. 13, 1862	Promoted to 1st Lieutenant.
Do.	Robert E. Phillips	" 13, "	" 13, "	Promoted to 1st Lieutenant.
Do.	Spencer McLead	Nov. 6, "	" 13, "	Resigned December 31, 1863.
Do.	Kendall D. Lindsay	" 12, "	" 13, "	Promoted to 1st Lieutenant.
Do.	Francis B. Gilbert	" 20, "	" 13, "	Resigned June 11, 1862.
Do.	George W. Cavett	Jan. 1, 1862	" 13, "	Promoted to 1st Lieutenant.
Do.	George E. Cutler	" 7, "	" 13, "	Promoted to 1st Lieutenant.
Do.	Jonathan H. Lasley	" 8, "	" 13, "	Honorably discharged September 11, 1862.
Do.	Elijah J. Copeland	Feb. 19, "	" 19, "	Resigned January 11, 1863.
Do.	George N. Gray	Jan. 9, "	" 19, "	Resigned January 19, 1863.
Do.	Wm. Shay	Oct. 5, "	" 19, "	Resigned January 22, 1863.
Do.	Frank M. Lewis	April 18, "	June 24, "	Promoted to 1st Lieutenant.
Do.	James H. Boyce	July 11, "	Sept. 4, "	Promoted to 1st Lieutenant.
Do.	Joseph M. Long	" 8, "	" 4, "	Promoted to 1st Lieutenant.
Do.	Thomas J. Bradley	Sept. 11, "	Feb. 10, 1863	Promoted to 1st Lieutenant.
Do.	Wm. W. Gilbert	Aug. 18, "	" 10, "	Promoted to 1st Lieutenant.
Do.	James C. Foster	Sept. 21, "	" 10, "	Captain colored regiment.
Do.	Jesse M. Shoop	" 23, "	" 10, "	Resigned September 28, 1861.
Do.	John W. Earles	Jan. 11, 1863	" 19, "	Promoted to 1st Lieutenant.
Do.	Frederick Stalder	Dec. 31, 1862	" 19, "	Promoted to 1st Lieutenant.
Do.	Samuel N. Misner	Jan. 19, 1863	" 22, "	Honorably discharged December 28, 1864.
Do.	Joshua E. Bailey	" 22, "	March 13, "	Promoted to 1st Lieutenant.

FIFTY-THIRD OHIO VOLUNTEER INFANTRY.

THIS regiment was authorized by Governor Dennison, September 6, 1861, and the rendezvous established at Jackson, Ohio. The organization was completed in January, 1862, and the regiment was ordered to prepare for the field.

On the 16th of February the regiment embarked on a steamboat at Portsmouth, Ohio, and proceeding to Paducah, Kentucky, reported to General W. T. Sherman, and was assigned to the Third Brigade of Sherman's division. The division moved on transports to Savannah, Tennessee, and, remaining a day, started on an expedition to destroy the Memphis and Charleston Railroad, near Inka, Mississippi. Upon their return they disembarked at Pittsburg Landing, and after making reconnoissance of about ten miles and finding no enemy, went into camp near the Landing, and the next day moved near to Shiloh Church. On account of being confined so long on transports, sickness increased very rapidly, and on April 6th the Surgeon's report showed over three hundred men and half the officers of the Fifty-Third unfit for duty.

The regiment maintained itself tolerably during the battle of Pittsburg Landing, several of the companies keeping in almost perfect order all the time. After the close of the struggle, on the morning of the 8th, it pursued the retreating enemy, and when about five miles from camp was deployed to support a battalion of cavalry. The enemy made a charge, routed the cavalry, and captured many prisoners. The Fifty-Third, in turn, charged the enemy, drove them from the field, and rescued most of the prisoners. Here the regiment halted, assisted in destroying the late camp of the enemy, in collecting arms, in carrying off the wounded, and in burying the dead, and then returned to its old camp near Shiloh Church.

The regiment remained in camp, engaged in drilling, until the 29th of April, when it advanced on Corinth. The regiment suffered much from sickness, and the fatigue duty was very heavy. Mile after mile of earthworks and intrenchments were thrown up, and skirmishes between the outposts were constant, occasionally swelling almost to the proportions of a battle. In everything of this kind the regiment bore its full share, and won the confidence and commendation of its commanding officers. About the 15th of May the Third Brigade was reorganized and placed under the command of Brigadier-General J. W. Denver. After the evacuation of Corinth the Fourth and Fifth Divisions of the Army of the Tennessee, under Major-General Sherman, started westward along the Memphis and Charleston Railroad. The march was a very severe one on account of the intense heat and the dusty condition of the roads. The Third

Brigade remained a week at Moscow, then moved to Lafayette, then back to Moscow, then to Holly Springs, and, after a short skirmish, occupied the town on the first of July. Remaining about a week the brigade returned to Moscow, and in a few days received orders to march for Memphis, where it arrived on the 21st.

The regiment camped south of the city, near Fort Pickering, and performed a large amount of fatigue duty on the Fort. On the 26th of November the brigade, with other troops, left Memphis on a tour through Mississippi. Meantime General Denver had assumed command of the division, and Colonel J. R. Cockerill, of the Seventieth Ohio, commanded the brigade. The weather was very unfavorable, as it rained almost continually for ten or twelve days, making the roads nearly impassable, and the creeks and rivers were so swollen that they could not be forded, so that it was necessary to fell and split timber for bridges. They advanced, in spite of all obstacles, as far as Coffeeville, on the Mississippi Central Railroad, where it was learned that Van Dorn had captured Holly Springs, and the command immediately returned to that place (which the enemy evacuated), and then moved to La Grange, Tennessee, which was reached early in January, 1863. The regiment remained here some time and assisted in building a fort. On the night of the 4th of March a fire occurred in the Quartermaster's tent, and several boxes of ammunition exploded, burning four men badly, two of whom died, and the other two recovered after a long and painful illness. On the 7th of March the brigade moved to Moscow, and the Fifty-Third was engaged in guard-duty and drill from day to day. After a few weeks the country was found to be infested with marauding bands, and the Fifty-Third was mounted and succeeded in putting an end to such annoyances. On the 9th of June, 1863, the regiment left camp, and in the afternoon embarked on the steamer Luminary, at Memphis, and proceeded down the river to Young's Point, arriving on the 12th. Hearing here that Joe Johnston was endeavoring to raise the siege of Vicksburg, the regiment at once proceeded up the Yazoo to Snyder's Bluff, and disembarked. The regiment remained here a few days and then moved to Oak Ridge, and on the afternoon of July 4th, 1863, moved against Johnston. The enemy was met at Black River, but after a little skirmishing retired to Jackson. The Fifty-Third assisted in the capture of that city and then returned to Black River on the 20th of July, and went into camp.

About the 1st of October the regiment embarked on transports at Vicksburg and moved to Memphis. About the middle of October the regiment proceeded *via* LaGrange to Iuka, thence to the Tennessee River, which was crossed at Eastport, then to Florence, Alabama, and then to Trenton, Georgia. The Fifty-Third was among the first regiments to enter the town and expel the enemy. From here the regiment moved slowly toward the Tennessee River, and on the 24th was in position before Mission Ridge. The Fifty-Third occupied the second line, but so close was it to the front that it was equally exposed to the enemy's fire. The next day the regiment joined in pursuing the enemy, and on the 26th moved for Knoxville *via* Cleveland Junction, thence to the Holston River, which was crossed at Morgantown, and then on as rapidly as possible to Maryville. Here information of Longstreet's retreat was received, and after a few days' rest the regiment returned, by almost the same route that it advanced, to Chattanooga, arriving late in December. In a few days the regiment was ordered to Scattsboro', Alabama, on the Memphis and Charleston Railroad, which point was reached about the 1st of January, 1863. Here almost every man in the regiment re-enlisted, and by the last of February the entire regiment was on furlough in Ohio, where it remained till April, and then returned to the old camp at Scattsboro', Alabama.

On the 1st of May the Fifty-Third moved *via* Stevenson and Bridgeport to Chattanooga, Tennessee, and about the 5th continued the march through the mountains of Northern Georgia into Sugar Valley, where the enemy was strongly posted, but was soon dislodged. The column then proceeded toward Resaca, and about two miles from town was halted and formed for battle, the Fifty-Third being in the front line. On the afternoon of the 13th of May the advance was made, the Fifty-Third being among the first to draw the enemy's fire. As soon as the enemy's position was ascertained a charge was made and the Rebels driven from hill to hill, till nightfall. The next day was spent in skirmishing till sunset, when a charge was ordered, the Fifty-

Third rushing forward eagerly and assisting in taking the enemy's works. From this point, the enemy having retreated, the regiment moved to Dallas, where, on the 23d, they met the enemy in force. Skirmishing ensued until the 27th, when a general engagement took place and the enemy was completely routed. Skirmishing again continued until the 4th of June, when the enemy withdrew, slowly and stubbornly, to Kenesaw Mountain. The Fifty-Third skirmished day after day till it reached the foot of the mountain, and on the night of the 26th of June moved four miles to the right, fronting Little Kenesaw. The next day at seven o'clock A. M. it took its place in the brigade, with orders to charge the enemy on Little Kenesaw. The regiment moved up in fine order, driving the Rebels from their works, fighting hand-to-hand with *clubbed muskets.* It suffered severely in the engagement, but held the works the remainder of the day under a terrific fire of shot and shell.

On the 2d of July the regiment was moved to the extreme right flank of the army, and the next day was ordered to make a reconnoissance to Ruff's Mills, on the Nicojack, two miles from camp. The regiment had only just cleared the picket-line when it became engaged, and for an hour was exposed to heavy fire of grape and schrapnel. The division moved out, and in two hours the Rebels were driven from Nicojack Creek. The next day was spent in pursuing and skirmishing, and that night Johnson withdrew from Kenesaw. Two days later the Fifty-Third crossed the Chattahoochie and moved to the Atlanta and Augusta Railroad, at Stone Mountain, followed the railroad to Decatur, and then, meeting the enemy, it drove the Rebel forces to Atlanta. The regiment skirmished continually during the siege of Atlanta, and was closely engaged at Ezra Chapel, and again on the Macon Railroad.

After the fall of Atlanta the Fifty-Third pursued Hood across the mountains of Northern Georgia, and some distance into Alabama, and then returned to Atlanta. The regiment marched with Sherman for Savannah, meeting with no opposition, till near Milledgeville a few militia opposed them, but they were scattered. The regiment subsisted off the country, and relied upon the Commissary only for sugar, coffee, and salt. On reaching the Ogeechee they moved down the west bank till near its junction with the Canouchee, and there forced a crossing with little difficulty. The Fifty-Third assisted in surprising the guard on the Gulf Railroad, in destroying about five miles of track, and returned next day to the Ogeechee, and pushed on to Savannah. The regiment shared in the capture of Fort McAllister, and after remaining on duty in Savannah a few weeks, embarked at the mouth of the Savannah for Beaufort, South Carolina.

Early in February, 1865, the Fifty-Third started on the campaign of the Carolinas, doing no fighting until near Columbia, but performing an immense amount of labor in destroying railroads. At the North Edisto the Fifty-Third, exposed to a heavy fire, marched over low ground, covered with water from one to four feet deep, grown up with cypress and briers, a distance of six hundred yards, and assisted in driving the enemy from his intrenchments on the opposite bank of the river. At the Congaree the enemy again made a stand but was soon driven from his position. The day before entering the city of Columbia the regiment was ordered to silence a battery, which it did effectually by approaching it unperceived, and firing volley after volley till the horses of the battery were either killed or disabled, and the men driven from the guns. At night the regiment retired, and joined the brigade at four A. M. next morning. On the afternoon of the 15th of July, 1865, the Fifty-Third entered Columbia. After remaining a few days and utterly destroying everything valuable to the enemy, the command moved toward Goldsboro', North Carolina. At Fayetteville four days were spent in destroying a Rebel arsenal, and in laying a pontoon bridge; and a large amount of provisions which the Rebel authorities had stored here for supplying the army were seized and issued to the citizens.

On the 19th of March, and when within two days' march of Goldsboro', the enemy attacked the advance of the Twentieth Corps. The fight lasted all day, and at night the Fifty-Third was a part of the re-enforcements ordered to them. The regiment marched all night in the mud and darkness, and just before day came upon the beleaguered corps. After twenty-four hours' marching, without sleep, the regiment was placed in position for attack, but at daylight it was found that the enemy had retreated. After resting a day the regiment moved forward and went into camp at Goldsboro' on the 21st of March. The march to Raleigh was resumed on the 10th of April, and after considerable skirmishing the regiment marched into the city on the 13th, and camped on the north-west side, fronting the enemy.

In about ten days after the surrender of Johnston the regiment marched through Virginia to Washington, D. C., and participated in the grand review. Soon after the review the regiment proceeded by railroad to Parkersburg, and thence on the steamer "Sherman" to Louisville. In June the division, of which the Fifty-Third was a part, was ordered to Little Rock, Arkansas. The regiment proceeded down the Ohio and Mississippi, and up White River to Duvall's Bluff, and then by railroad to Little Rock, where it arrived on the 4th of July.

The regiment remained here until the 11th of August, when it was mustered out and ordered to Camp Dennison for discharge; having traveled while in the service six thousand four hundred miles, having been engaged in sixty-seven battles and skirmishes, and having lost in action sixty officers and men killed, and two hundred and sixty-four officers and men wounded, viz.:

ENGAGEMENTS.	OFFICERS.		MEN.		
	Killed......	Wounded	Killed	Wounded	Missing...
Pittsburg Landing	....	1	13	39	
Monterey, April 8, 1862	....	....	....	7	
Actions before Corinth, Siege of Vicksburg, Black River, Jackson, and Mission Ridge,	....	....	....	25	
Resaca, May 13, 1864	....	....	6	41	
Dallas, May 27, 28, 29, 1864	....	3	5	17	
Kenesaw, June 27, 1864	....	3	20	48	
Ruff's Mills, July 3, 1864	....	....	1	24	
Atlanta, July 22, 1864	1	....	4	19	14
Ezra Chapel, July 28, 1864	....	....	3	7	
Before Atlanta	2	....	3	12	
Jonesboro'	1	....	....	7	
Fort McAllister	....	1	....	3	
North Edisto	....	....	1	7	
Total	4	8	56	256	14

The misfortunes of the Fifty-Third in its first action, long influenced both its *morale* and its reputation. Colonel Appler's statement (in his official report which subordinate officers wrote and took to him for signature) was this: "Seeing an overwhelming force of the enemy overlapping the regiment on either flank, I gave the order to retreat, and soon after left the regiment." General Sherman spoke of its conduct as discreditable. The newspapers said the Fifty-Third and Seventy-Seventh ran without firing a gun, leaving Waterhouse's battery to be captured; although, in point of fact, one section of the battery left before its supports, without firing a gun. The officers claim for the regiment that it maintained its organization throughout both days of the fight (which very few of Sherman's regiments did), that it never refused to obey an order, and never made a movement without orders. Sherman praised the Fifty-Third highly the next day in the reconnoissance (when it really saved him from capture), though, with not unusual inconsistency, he subsequently denied it. But he took pains in his letter about Pittsburg Landing to the United States Service Magazine, in 1864, to say: "I also take pleasure in adding, that nearly all the new troops that at Shiloh drew from me official censure, have more than redeemed their good name; among them that very regiment which first broke, the Fifty-Third Ohio, Colonel Appler. Under another leader, Colonel Jones, it has shared every campaign and expedition of mine since, is with me now, and can march, and bivouac, and fight as well as the best regiment in this or any army. Its reputation now is equal to that of any from the State of Ohio."

54th REGIMENT OHIO VOLUNTEER INFANTRY.

ROSTER, THREE YEARS' SERVICE.

RANK.	NAME.	DATE OF RANK.	COM. ISSUED.	REMARKS.
Colonel	THOS. KILBY SMITH	Oct. 31, 1861	March 20, 1862	Brigadier-General volunteers.
Lt. Colonel	J. A. FARDEN	" 31, "	" 20, 1861	Resigned November 27, 1862.
Do.	CYRUS W. FISHER	Nov. 27, 1862	" 30, 1863	Honorably discharged September 29, 1863.
Do.	ROBERT WILLIAMS	Sept. 29, 1863	Jan. 8, 1864	Resigned September 11, 1864.
Do.	ISRAEL T. MOORE	Oct. 12, 1864	Oct. 12, "	Mustered out with regiment.
Major	CYRUS W. FISHER	" 31, 1861	March 20, 1862	Promoted to Lieutenant-Colonel.
Do.	ROBERT WILLIAMS	Nov. 27, 1862	" 30, 1863	Promoted to Lieutenant-Colonel.
Do.	ISRAEL T. MOORE	" 13, 1863	Jan. 8, 1864	Promoted to Lieutenant-Colonel.
Do.	GEORGE KILE	Oct. 12, 1864	Oct. 12, "	Mustered out with regiment.
Surgeon	C. P. BRENT	Sept. 27, 1861	March 20, 1862	Resigned.
Do.	JAMES BAGGS	Feb. 10, 1865	Feb. 10, 1865	Mustered out with regiment.
Ass't Surgeon	THOMAS L. HARPER	Oct. 9, 1861	March 20, 1862	Resigned August 1, 1863.
Do.	JAMES BAGOS	Aug. 28, 1862	Sept. 12, "	Promoted to Surgeon.
Do.	D. H. COWEN	April 8, 1865	April 8, 1865	
Chaplain	JOSEPH MORRIS	Feb. 16, 1862	Feb. 17, 1862	Resigned March 17, 1863.
Captain	Stephen B. Yeoman	Sept. 19, 1861	May 20, "	Resigned June 8, 1863.
Do.	Robert Williams	Nov. 1, "	" 20, "	Promoted to Major.
Do.	Israel T. Moore	" 1, "	" 20, "	Promoted to Major.
Do.	Charles A. White	" 1, "	" 20, "	Deceased May 17, 1862.
Do.	Peter Bertram	" 1, "	" 20, "	Killed April 7, 1862, at Shiloh.
Do.	Jerre Hauser	Jan. 16, 1862	" 20, "	Resigned May 3, 1863.
Do.	Wm. D. Starr	" 21, "	" 20, "	Deceased June 5, 1862.
Do.	Albert Rogall	" 22, "	" 20, "	Resigned January 13, 1863.
Do.	Henry Richardson	Feb. 5, "	" 20, "	Resigned December 11, 1862.
Do.	E. C. Francis	" 16, "	" 20, "	Honorably discharged November 1, 1862.
Do.	Samuel Starr	June 5, "	Dec. 18, "	Resigned March 15, 1863.
Do.	George Kile	May 17, "	" 18, "	Promoted to Major.
Do.	Timothy J. Sullivan	April 7, "	" 18, "	Mustered out.
Do.	Granville M. White	Nov. 1, "	Jan. 12, 1863	Resigned July 13, 1863.
Do.	James C. McCoy	Jan. 13, 1863	Feb. 26, "	Promoted by the President.
Do.	John S. Wells	Nov. 27, "	March 6, "	Mustered out.
Do.	Luther W. Saxton	" 27, "	Jan. 10, 1864	Killed.
Do.	John Bell	" 27, "	" 10, "	Mustered out with regiment.
Do.	Edward B. Moore	" 27, "	" 10, "	Mustered out.
Do.	Samuel W. Ashmead	March 3, 1864	March 3, "	Resigned September 16, 1864.
Do.	Jonathan H. Snyder	" 3, "	" 3, "	Mustered out with regiment.
Do.	Jonathan Doty	" 10, "	" 10, "	Mustered out with regiment.
Do.	Cornelius Neff	" 31, "	April 2, "	Mustered out with regiment.
Do.	Lemuel Carlisle	Oct. 12, "	Oct. 12, "	Mustered out with regiment.
Do.	John W. Shockey	" 12, "	" 12, "	Mustered out.
Do.	Andrew J. Ferguson	Jan. 6, 1865	Jan. 6, 1865	Mustered out as 1st Lieutenant.
Do.	John D. Enoch	" 6, "	" 6, "	Mustered out December 2, 1864.
Do.	Wm. H. Hunt	" 6, "	" 6, "	Mustered out with regiment.
Do.	Thomas H. Bowdel	" 6, "	" 6, "	Mustered out with regiment.
Do.	Silas W. Moore	" 16, "	" 16, "	Mustered out with regiment.
Do.	Abner Haines	Feb. 10, "	Feb. 10, "	Mustered out with regiment.
Do.	Edmund B. Updegrove	May 31, "	May 31, "	Mustered out with regiment.
1st Lieutenant	Benj. W. Goode	Sept. 12, 1861	March 20, 1862	Resigned May 13, 1862.
Do.	George Kile	" 19, "	" 20, "	Promoted to Captain.
Do.	James C. McCoy	" 28, "	" 20, "	Promoted to Captain.
Do.	Granville M. White	Nov. 1, "	" 20, "	Promoted to Captain.
Do.	Daniel Lepley	" 1, "	" 20, "	Resigned February 25, 1863.
Do.	Jerre Hauser	" 1, "	" 20, "	Promoted to Captain.
Do.	Timothy J. Sullivan	" 1, "	" 20, "	Promoted to Captain.
Do.	Henry Richardson	Dec. 17, "	" 20, "	Promoted to Captain.
Do.	Charles Loomis	Jan. 14, 1862	" 20, "	Resigned April 3, 1863.
Do.	John S. Wells	" 14, "	" 20, "	Promoted to Captain.
Do.	Samuel Starr	" 21, "	" 20, "	Promoted to Captain.
Do.	Alfred Morris	" 22, "	" 20, "	Honorably disch'd; re-appointed Nov. 1, 1862.
Do.	Silas W. Potter	Feb. 5, "	" 20, "	Discharged August 19, 1862
Do.	Daniel Taylor	" 16, "	" 20, "	
Do.	James Depoy	May 13, "	June 21, "	Resigned February 19, 1863.
Do.	George W. Browning	Aug. 19, "	Oct. 1, "	Resigned February 13, 1863.
Do.	Samuel W. Ashmead	Nov. 1, "	Jan. 12, 1863	Promoted to Captain.
Do.	Edward B. Moore	June 5, "	Dec. 18, 1862	Promoted to Captain.
Do.	Luther W. Saxton	April 5, "	" 18, "	Promoted to Captain.
Do.	John Bell	May 17, "	" 18, "	Promoted to Captain.
Do.	Jonathan H. Snyder	Nov. 1, "	Jan. 12, 1863	Promoted to Captain.
Do.	Alfred Morris	April 22, 1863	April 22, "	Revoked.
Do.	Lemuel Carlisle	Nov. 13, "	Jan. 8, 1864	Promoted to Captain.
Do.	Andrew J. Ferguson	" 27, "	" 10, "	Promoted to Captain.
Do.	Judson McCoy	" 27, "	" 10, "	Mustered out.
Do.	John F. Cutler	" 27, "	" 10, "	Mustered out.
Do.	John D. Enoch	" 27, "	" 10, "	Promoted to Captain.
Do.	David A. Reese	" 27, "	" 10, "	Deceased June 27, 1864.
Do.	John W. Shockey	" 13, "	" 8, "	Promoted to Captain.
Do.	Henry B. Whetzel	March 16, "	March 16, "	Resigned July 13, 1864.
Do.	Wm. H. Hunt	" 10, 1864	" 10, "	Promoted to Captain.
Do.	David Hinzey	" 31, "	April 2, "	Resigned September 16, 1864.
Do.	Thomas H. Bowdel	July 25, "	July 25, "	Promoted to Captain.
Do.	Silas W. Moore	" 25, "	" 25, "	Promoted to Captain.
Do.	Abner Haines	Oct. 12, "	Oct. 12, "	Promoted to Captain.
Do.	John G. Houck	" 12, "	" 12, "	Declined.
Do.	Edmund B. Updegrove	" 12, "	" 12, "	Promoted to Captain.
Do.	James P. Wiatt	" 12, "	" 12, "	Mustered out with regiment

RANK.	NAME.	DATE OF RANK.		COM. ISSUED.		REMARKS.
1st Lieutenant	James Jardine	Oct.	12, 1861	Oct.	12, 1861	Mustered out with regiment.
Do.	W. H. Nell	Jan.	16, 1865	Jan.	16, 1865	Mustered out with regiment.
Do.	George Marshall	"	16, "	"	16, "	Mustered out with regiment.
Do.	Wm. H. Barringer	"	16, "	"	16, "	Mustered out with regiment.
Do.	Edward McGinn	"	16, "	"	16, "	Mustered out with regiment.
Do.	Philip Weitzel	"	16, "	"	16, "	Mustered out with regiment.
Do.	Miles W. Elliott	Feb.	14, "	Feb.	11, "	Mustered out with regiment.
Do.	David Jones	"	11, "	"	11, "	Mustered out with regiment.
Do.	Norman Shellers	May	31, "	May	31, "	Declined.
Do.	George W. Williams	"	31, "	"	31, "	
Do.	Charles W. Craig	Aug.	10, "	Aug.	10, "	
2d Lieutenant	James Depoy	Sept.	19, 1861	March	20, 1862	Promoted to 1st Lieutenant.
Do.	John Bell	Nov.	1, "	"	20, "	Promoted to 1st Lieutenant.
Do.	Lemuel Carlisle	"	1, "	"	20, "	Promoted to 1st Lieutenant.
Do.	John S. Wells	"	1, "	"	20, "	Promoted to 1st Lieutenant.
Do.	George W. Cosley	"	1, "	"	20, "	Resigned August 3, 1863.
Do.	George De Charms	Dec.	13, "	"	20, "	Killed at Shiloh April 6, 1862.
Do.	S. W. Ashmead	"	21, "	"	20, "	Promoted to 1st Lieutenant.
Do.	Jonathan H. Snyder	"	22, "	"	20, "	Promoted to 1st Lieutenant.
Do.	Thomas M. Darling	Feb.	5, "	"	20, "	Died July 15, 1862.
Do.	George W. Browning	Jan.	11, "	"	20, "	Promoted to 1st Lieutenant.
Do.	Luther W. Saxton	May	13, "	July	10, "	Promoted to 1st Lieutenant.
Do.	Henry B. Whetzel	April	6, "	Sept.	5, "	Promoted to 1st Lieutenant.
Do.	John F. Cutler	Aug.	19, "	Oct.	1, "	Promoted to 1st Lieutenant.
Do.	Seaman M. Bander	July	15, "	Nov.	26, "	Resigned March 20, 1863.
Do.	Andrew J. Ferguson	May	19, "	Dec.	18, "	Promoted to 1st Lieutenant.
Do.	Frank G. Leeds	Nov.	1, "	Jan.	12, 1863	Died March 20, 1863.
Do.	Riley Ashmead	"	1, "	March	30, "	Resigned August 3, 1863.
Do.	John B. Enoch	"	1, "	"	30, "	Promoted to 1st Lieutenant.
Do.	Judson McCoy	March	20, 1863	July	10, "	Promoted to 1st Lieutenant.
Do.	David A. Reese	Nov.	13, "	Jan.	8, 1864	Promoted to 1st Lieutenant.
Do.	Thomas H. Bowdel	March	10, 1864	March	10, "	Promoted to 1st Lieutenant.
Do.	Silas W. Moore	"	31, "	April	2, "	Promoted to 1st Lieutenant.
Do.	Abner Haines	Aug.	26, "	Aug.	26, "	Promoted to 1st Lieutenant.
Do	John G. Houck	"	26, "	"	26, "	Promoted to 1st Lieutenant.

FIFTY-FOURTH OHIO VOLUNTEER INFANTRY.

RECRUITING for this regiment began in the latter part of the summer of 1861, the place of rendezvous being Camp Dennison, where the regiment was organized and drilled during the fall and winter of 1861. The men composing this command were from the counties of Allen, Auglaize, Butler, Cuyahoga, Fayette, Greene, Hamilton, Logan, and Preble.

On the 17th of February, 1862, the regiment went into the field with an aggregate of eight hundred and fifty men. The Fifty-Fourth reached Paducah, Kentucky, February 20, 1862, and was assigned to a brigade in the division commanded by General Sherman. On the 6th of March the command ascended the Tennessee River, disembarked at Pittsburg Landing, and camped near Shiloh Church. On the 6th of April the regiment engaged in the battle of Pittsburg Landing, its position being on the extreme left of the army; but, on the second day, it was assigned a new position near the center of the line.

In the two days' fighting the regiment sustained a loss of one hundred and ninety-eight men killed, wounded, and missing. On the 29th of April the regiment moved upon Corinth, skirmishing severely at Russell House, May 17th, and engaging in the movement upon the works at Corinth May 31st. On the morning of the evacuation the Fifty-Fourth was among the first organized bodies of troops to enter the town. The regimental colors were unfurled from a public building, and the regiment was designated to perform provost-duty, the commanding officer of the regiment being appointed commandant of the post of Corinth.

The regiment moved with the army to La Grange, Tennessee, and from there to Holly Springs, Mississippi, and then returned to Corinth. Soon after it again marched to Holly Springs; from there to Moscow, Tennessee, and thence to Memphis, where it arrived July 21, 1862. During the summer the regiment was engaged in several short expeditions; and on the 26th of November it moved with the army toward Jackson, Mississippi, by way of Holly Springs. The regiment soon returned to Memphis, and with a portion of the army, under General Sherman, moved down the Mississippi, and went into position before the enemy's line at Chickasaw Bayou. It was engaged in the assault on the Rebel works, December 28th and 29th, with a loss of twenty men killed and wounded. On the 1st of January, 1863, the regiment withdrew, ascended the Mississippi and Arkansas Rivers, and engaged in the assault and capture of Arkansas Post. The Fifty-Fourth again descended the Mississippi River and disembarked at Young's Point, Louisiana. Here it was employed in digging a canal, and in other demonstrations connected with the siege of Vicksburg. It was on a severe march among the bayous to the rear of Vicksburg, which resulted in the rescue of the fleet of gun-boats which was about to be abandoned and destroyed.

On the 6th of May the regiment began its march to the rear of Vicksburg, by way of Grand Gulf, and was engaged in the battles of Champion Hills and Big Black Bridge. It was engaged in a general assault on the enemy's works, in the rear of Vicksburg, on the 19th and 22d of June, losing in the two engagements forty-seven killed and wounded. It was continually employed in skirmishing and fatigue-duty during the siege of Vicksburg, except for six days, which were consumed in a march of observation toward Jackson, Mississippi.

After the fall of Vicksburg the Fifty-Fourth moved with the army upon Jackson, Mississippi, and was constantly engaged in skirmishing from the 9th to the 14th of July. After the capture of Jackson the regiment returned to Vicksburg, and remained until October, 1863, when forming a part of the Fifteenth Army Corps, it ascended the Mississippi River to Memphis, and from there proceeded to Chattanooga. It was engaged in the battle of Missionary Ridge, November 26th, and the next day marched to the relief of the garrison at Knoxville, Tennessee. It pursued the enemy's wagon-train from Knoxville through the south-eastern portion of Tennessee and a short distance into North Carolina, and then returned to Chattanooga, and moved thence to Larkinsville, Alabama, where it went into winter-quarters, January 12, 1864.

The regiment was mustered into the service as a veteran organization on the 22d of January, and at once started to Ohio on furlough. It returned to camp in April, with an addition of two hundred recruits, and entered on the Atlanta campaign on the 1st of May. It participated in a general engagement at Resaca, and at Dallas, and in a severe skirmish at New Hope Church, June 6th and 7th. It was in the general assault upon Kenesaw Mountain, June 27th, losing twenty-eight killed and wounded; was engaged in a severe skirmish at Nicojack Creek, July 3d, losing thirteen killed and wounded, and was in a battle on the east side of Atlanta, July 21st and 22d, sustaining a loss of ninety-four killed, wounded, and missing.

The Fifty-Fourth lost eight men killed and wounded at Ezra Chapel on the 28th of July, and from the 29th of July to the 27th of August it was almost continually engaged in skirmishing before the works at Atlanta. It was in a heavy skirmish at Jonesboro', August 30th, and in a general action at the same place the two days immediately following. After resting a few weeks in camp near Atlanta, the regiment started in pursuit of Hood, and followed him within sixty miles of Chattanooga, and from there to Gadsden, Alabama, when it returned to Atlanta, and prepared for the march to Savannah. The Fifty-Fourth started on that wonderful march on the 15th of November, and on the 15th of December was engaged in the assault and capture of Fort McAllister, near Savannah. The regiment assisted in the destruction of the Gulf Railroad toward the Altamaha River, and on the 7th of January, 1865, marched into Savannah. After a rest of several weeks it moved with the army on the march through the Carolinas, skirmishing at the crossing of the South Edisto and North Edisto Rivers, on the 10th and 12th of February, respectively. It was closely engaged in the vicinity of Columbia, and participated in its last battle at Bentonsville, North Carolina, March 21, 1865.

The regiment marched to Richmond, Virginia, and from there to Washington City, where it took part in the grand review of the Western Army. On the 2d of June it was transported by railroad and steamboat to Louisville, Kentucky, and after remaining two weeks there it proceeded to Little Rock, Arkansas, and there performed garrison-duty until August 15, 1865, when it was mustered out. The regiment returned to Camp Dennison, Ohio, where it received final pay, and was disbanded, on the 24th of August, 1865.

The aggregate strength of the regiment at muster-out was two hundred and fifty-five—twenty-four officers and two hundred and thirty-one men. It marched during its term of service a distance of three thousand six hundred and eighty-two miles, participated in four sieges, nine severe skirmishes, fifteen general engagements, and sustained a loss of five hundred and six men killed, wounded, and missing.

55th REGIMENT OHIO VOLUNTEER INFANTRY.

ROSTER, THREE YEARS' SERVICE.

RANK.	NAME.	DATE OF RANK.	COM. ISSUED.	REMARKS.
Colonel	JOHN C. LEE	Nov. 25, 1861	Jan. 20, 1862	Resigned May 8, 1863.
Do.	CHARLES B. GAMBEE	May 8, 1863	May 25, 1863	Killed May 15, 1864.
Do.	EDWIN H. POWERS	June 6, 1865	June 6, 1865	Mustered out with regiment as Lieut. Col.
Lt. Colonel	GEORGE H. SAFFORD	Sept. 11, 1861	Jan. 20, 1862	Resigned March 4, 1863.
Do.	CHARLES B. GAMBEE	March 4, 1863	April 22, 1863	Promoted to Colonel.
Do.	JAMES M. STEVENS	May 8, "	May 25, "	Resigned.
Do.	EDWIN H. POWERS	June 27, 1864	June 27, 1864	Promoted to Colonel.
Do.	CHARLES P. WICKHAM	" 6, "	" 6, "	Mustered out with regiment as Major.
Major	JOHN C. LEE	Sept. 11, 1861	Jan. 20, 1862	Promoted to Colonel.
Do.	DANIEL F. DEWOLF	Nov. 25, "	" 20, "	Resigned October 2, 1861.
Do.	CHARLES B. GAMBEE	Oct. 2, "	Nov. 20, "	Promoted to Lieutenant-Colonel.
Do.	JAMES M. STEVENS	March 4. "	April 22, 1863	Promoted to Lieutenant-Colonel.
Do.	RUDOLPHUS ROBBINS	May 8, "	May 25, "	Killed May 15, 1864.
Do.	CHARLES P. WICKHAM	June 27, 1864	June 27, 1864	Promoted to Lieutenant-Colonel.
Do.	HARTWELL OSBORNE	" 6, 1865	" 6, 1865	Mustered out as Captain.
Surgeon	JAY KLING	Oct. 3, 1861	Jan. 20, 1862	Resigned; expiration of term of service.
Do.	JOSEPH HEBBLE	Nov. 1, 1864	Nov. 1, 1864	Mustered out with regiment.
Ass't Surgeon	HENRY K. SPOONER	Oct. 3, 1861	Jan. 20, 1862	Appointed Surgeon 61st Regt. Nov. 14, 1863.
Do.	J. L. MORRIS	July 4, 1862	July 23, "	Not mustered; did not report to regiment.
Do.	JOSEPH HEBBLE	Feb. 23, 1864	Feb. 23, 1864	Promoted to Surgeon.
Do.	JAMES C. MYERS	Jan. 25, 1865	Jan. 25, 1865	Mustered out.
Chaplain	JOHN G. W. COWLES	Dec. 10, 1861	" 20, 1862	Resigned July 21, 1862.
Do.	ALFRED WHEELER	Sept. 15, 1862	Dec. 19, "	Resigned August 15, 1863.
Captain	Charles B. Gambee	" 30, 1861	Jan. 20, "	Promoted to Major.
Do.	Augustus M. Bement	Oct. 10, "	" 20, "	Resigned March 16, 1863.
Do.	Horatio N. Shipman	" 16, "	" 20, "	Resigned March 10, 1863.
Do.	David S. Brown	" 16, "	" 20, "	Resigned March 6, 1863.
Do.	Frederick A. Wildman	" 20, "	" 20, "	Resigned February 12, 1863.
Do.	James M. Stevens	" 24, "	" 20, "	Promoted to Major March 4, 1863.
Do.	Rudolphus Robbins	Nov. 21, "	" 20, "	Promoted to Major.
Do.	Ira C. Terry	Dec. 7, "	" 20, "	Resigned October 31, 1862.
Do.	Horace Robinson	" 14, "	" 20, "	Killed at Chancellorsville.
Do.	Edwin H. Powers	" 20, "	" 20, "	Promoted to Major.
Do.	Benj. F. Eldridge	Oct. 2, "	Dec. 31, "	Resigned December 28, 1863.
Do.	Charles P. Wickham	" 3, "	" 31, "	Promoted to Major.
Do.	Henry Miller	Feb. 12, 1863	April 22, 1863	Resigned September 28, 1864.
Do.	Albert E. Peck	March 6, "	" 22, "	Killed May 15, 1864.
Do.	Frank W. Martin	" 10, "	" 22, "	Resigned June 6, 1863.
Do.	Robert Bromley	" 16, "	" 22, "	Resigned August 4, 1863.
Do.	Franklin J. Sauter	" 4, "	" 22, "	Killed at Chancellorsville.
Do.	Charles D. Robbins	May 8, "	May 25, "	Resigned March 29, 1864.
Do.	Henry W. Persing	June 6, "	June 29, "	Appointed Captain and A. Q. M.
Do.	Hartwell Osborne	Aug. 4, "	Jan. 10, 1864	Mustered out with regiment.
Do.	Frederick H. Boalt	June 1, "	" 10, "	Resigned September 13, 1864.
Do.	Robert W. Pool	Aug. 1, "	Feb. 17, "	Resigned August 29, 1864.
Do.	Francis H. Morse	March 19, 1864	March 19, "	Resigned April 20, 1864.
Do.	Butler Case	" 19, "	" 19, "	Declined in favor of C. M. Stone.
Do.	Charles M. Stone	April 2, "	April 2, "	Killed in action March 16, 1865.
Do.	Butler Case	" 13, "	" 13, "	Resigned as 1st Lieutenant.
Do.	Charles M. Smith	May 9, "	May 9, "	Mustered out with regiment.
Do.	Augustus M. Wormley	" 9, "	" 9, "	Mustered out with regiment.
Do.	Thomas W. Miller	June 27, "	June 27, "	Commission returned.
Do.	Henry H. Moore	" 27, "	" 27, "	Resigned January 15, 1865.
Do.	John R. Lowe	" 27, "	" 27, "	Mustered out with regiment.
Do.	Jesse Bowsher	July 25, "	July 25, "	Mustered out with regiment.
Do.	Wm. S. Wickham	Sept. 26, "	Sept. 26, "	Mustered out with regiment.
Do.	D. B. Gould	" 26, "	" 26, "	Mustered out with regiment.
Do.	Russell H. Bever	Nov. 3, "	Nov. 3, "	Mustered out with regiment.
Do.	Benj. F. Evans	April 24, 1865	April 24, 1865	Mustered out with regiment.
Do.	Joseph H. Gallup	" 24, "	" 24, "	Mustered out with regiment.
Do.	John H. Boss, jr.	July 10, "	July 10, "	Mustered out as 1st Lieutenant and R. Q. M.
1st Lieutenant	Robert G. Pennington	Aug. 22, 1861	June 22, 1862	Resigned July 23, 1862.
Do.	Benj. F. Eldridge	Sept. 30, "	" 22, "	Promoted to Captain.
Do.	Wm. D. Sherwood	Oct. 11, "	" 22, "	Resigned March 20, 1862.
Do.	Henry W. Persing	" 16, "	" 22, "	Promoted to Captain.
Do.	Jacob Thomas	" 16, "	" 22, "	Resigned July 17, 1862.
Do.	Charles P. Wickham	" 20, "	" 22, "	Promoted to Captain.
Do.	Rudolph Eastman	" 24, "	" 22, "	Resigned December 23, 1862.
Do.	Henry Miller	Nov. 21, "	" 22, "	Promoted to Captain February 12, 1862.
Do.	Albert E. Peck	" 21, "	" 22, "	Promoted to Captain.
Do.	Frank W. Martin	Dec. 1, "	" 22, "	Promoted to Captain.
Do.	Richard F. Patrick	" 7, "	" 22, "	Resigned June 10, 1863.
Do.	Robert Bromley	" 14, "	" 22, "	Promoted to Captain.
Do.	Raymond Burr	April 4, 1862	" 22, "	Appointed A. Q. M.
Do.	Benj. C. Taber	July 17, "	July 28, "	Mustered out.
Do.	Charles D. Robbins	" 23, "	Dec. 31, "	Promoted to Captain.
Do.	Franklin J. Sauter	" 16, "	" 31, "	Promoted to Captain.
Do.	Frederick H. Boalt	Oct. 2, "	" 31, "	Promoted to Captain.
Do.	Robert W. Pool	" 3, "	" 31, "	Promoted to Captain.
Do.	Francis H. Morse	Dec. 23, "	Feb. 10, 1863	Promoted to Captain.
Do.	Hartwell Osborne	Feb. 12, 1863	April 22, "	Promoted to Captain.
Do.	Thomas O'Leary	March 6, "	" 22, "	Resigned December 28, 1863.
Do.	Butler Case	" 10, "	" 22, "	Resigned April 10, 1864.
Do.	Charles M. Smith	" 16, "	" 22, "	Promoted to Captain.
Do.	Charles M. Stone	" 4, "	" 22, "	Promoted to Captain.

RANK.	NAME.	DATE OF RANK.	COM. ISSUED.	REMARKS.
1st Lieutenant	Augustus M. Wormley	May 8, 1863	May 25, 1863	Promoted to Captain.
Do.	Thomas W. Miller	Aug. 21, "	Aug. 21, "	Mustered out at expiration of term, Jan. 4, '65.
Do.	Charles M. Stillman	June 1, 1864	June 10, 1864	Revoked; resigned as 2d Lt.; com. returned.
Do.	Henry H. Moore	" 1, "	" 10, "	Promoted to Captain.
Do.	John R. Lowe	March 19, "	March 19, "	Promoted to Captain.
Do.	Jesse Bowsher	" 19, "	" 19, "	Promoted to Captain.
Do.	Wm. S. Wickham	" 19, "	" 19, "	Promoted to Captain.
Do.	O. B. Gould	" 19, "	" 19, "	Promoted to Captain.
Do.	Russell H. Bever	" 19, "	" 19, "	Promoted to Captain.
Do.	Benj. F. Evans	April 1, "	April 1, "	Promoted to Captain.
Do.	James P. Jones	" 1, "	" 1, "	Mustered out March 12, 1865.
Do.	Philetus C. Lathrop	May 9, "	May 9, "	Honorably discharged October 27, 1864.
Do.	Pliney E. Watson	June 27, "	Jan. 27, "	Mustered out June 8, 1865.
Do.	Thomas T. Pettit	July 25, 1865	July 25, 1865	Declined.
Do.	Adam Cramer	" 25, "	" 25, "	Declined; commission returned.
Do.	Joseph H. Gallup	Aug. 19, "	Aug. 19, "	Promoted to Captain.
Do.	John H. Bass, jr.	" 19, "	" 19, "	Promoted to Captain.
Do.	Lewis Peck	Sept. 26, "	Sept. 26, "	Mustered out May 15, 1865.
Do.	Alvin B. Case	Nov. 3, 1864	Nov. 3, 1864	
Do.	Wm. E. Childs	Jan. 18, 1865	Jan. 18, 1865	Declined; mustered out with regiment.
Do.	Wm. H. Hessinger	" 18, "	" 18, "	Declined; mustered out with regiment.
Do.	Henry B. Warren	April 20, "	April 20, "	Mustered out with regiment.
Do.	Frederick Reser	" 20, "	" 20, "	Mustered out with regiment.
Do.	James T. Boyd	" 24, "	" 21, "	Mustered out with regiment.
Do.	John Bellman	" 21, "	" 21, "	Mustered out with regiment.
Do.	Robert Fewson	" 21, "	" 24, "	Mustered out with regiment.
Do.	Thomas S. Hosler	July 10, "	July 10, "	Mustered out with regiment.
Do.	John Burket	" 10, "	" 10, "	Mustered out with regiment.
Do.	Henry J. Pelton	" 10, "	" 10, "	Mustered out with regiment.
2d Lieutenant	Wm. H. Long	Sept. 30, 1861	Jan. 20, 1862	Resigned August 17, 1862.
Do.	Rudolphus Robbins	Oct. 8, "	" 20, "	Promoted to Captain.
Do.	Franklin J. Sawter	" 10, "	" 20, "	Promoted to 1st Lieutenant.
Do.	Arthur Cranston	" 16, "	" 20, "	Resigned March 15, 1862.
Do.	Charles D. Robbins	" 16, "	" 20, "	Promoted to 1st Lieutenant.
Do.	Frederick H. Boalt	" 20, "	" 20, "	Promoted to 1st Lieutenant.
Do.	Albert E. Peck	" 21, "	" 20, "	Promoted to 1st Lieutenant.
Do.	Ira C. Terry	" 21, "	" 20, "	Promoted to Captain.
Do.	Robert W. Pool	" 21, "	" 20, "	Promoted to 1st Lieutenant.
Do.	Horace Robinson	Nov. 20, "	" 20, "	Promoted to Captain.
Do.	James K. Agnew	" 21, "	" 20, "	Resigned July 16, 1862.
Do.	Francis H. Morse	" 26, "	" 20, "	Promoted to 1st Lieutenant.
Do.	Hartwell Osborne	Dec. 7, "	" 20, "	Promoted to 1st Lieutenant.
Do.	Charles M. Stone	" 11, "	" 20, "	Promoted to 1st Lieutenant.
Do.	Walter W. Thomas	March 15, 1862	April 14, "	Died April 6, 1862.
Do.	Benj. C. Taber	April 6, "	July 23, "	Promoted to 1st Lieutenant.
Do.	Thomas O'Leary	July 17, "	" 28, "	Promoted to 1st Lieutenant.
Do.	Charles M. Smith	Aug. 17, "	Dec. 31, "	Promoted to 1st Lieutenant.
Do.	Augustus M. Wormley	" 19, "	" 31, "	Promoted to 1st Lieutenant.
Do.	Butler Case	July 23, "	" 31, "	Promoted to 1st Lieutenant.
Do.	Nelson Crockett	" 16, "	" 31, "	Resigned.
Do.	Henry H. Regan	Oct. 3, "	" 31, "	Resigned March 24, 1863.
Do.	Charles Stillman	" 2, "	" 31, "	Resigned.
Do.	Henry H. Moore	Dec. 23, "	Feb. 10, 1863	Promoted to 1st Lieutenant.
Do.	Edward Bromley	March 21, 1863	April 22, "	Deceased March 21, 1863.
Do.	O. B. Gould	April 4, "	" 22, "	Promoted to 1st Lieutenant.
Do.	Henry W. Crosby	Feb. 12, "	" 22, "	Revoked.
Do.	John R. Lowe	March 4, "	" 22, "	Promoted to 1st Lieutenant.
Do.	Jesse Bowsher	" 6, "	" 22, "	Promoted to 1st Lieutenant.
Do.	Wm. S. Wickham	" 10, "	" 22, "	Promoted to 1st Lieutenant.
Do.	Russell H. Bever	" 16, "	" 22, "	Promoted to 1st Lieutenant.
Do.	Benj. F. Evans	May 8, "	May 25, "	Promoted to 1st Lieutenant.
Do.	James P. Jones	Feb. 12, "	" 25, "	Promoted to 1st Lieutenant.
Do.	Philetus C. Luthrop	April 1, 1864	April 1, 1864	Honorably discharged October 27, 1864.
Do.	Pliney E. Watson	" 13, "	" 3, "	Promoted to 1st Lieutenant.
Do.	Theodore M. Wood	July 10, 1865	July 10, 1865	Mustered out with regiment as 1st Sergeants; complimentary commissions given after muster out.
Do.	John Lambright	" 10, "	" 10, "	
Do.	David Warren	" 10, "	" 10, "	
Do.	Alpheus J. Peck	" 10, "	" 10, "	
Do.	Moses Pugh	" 10, "	" 10, "	
Do.	George H. Clark	" 10, "	" 10, "	

FIFTY-FIFTH OHIO VOLUNTEER INFANTRY.

THE FIFTY-FIFTH OHIO went into camp at Norwalk, Ohio, on the 17th of October, 1861. On the 25th of January, 1862, it left Norwalk for Grafton, Western Virginia, and after a short stay here it moved to New Creek. From this point it made two severe marches, one to Romney, and the other to Moorefield; at the latter place it participated in a slight skirmish. The regiment returned to Grafton on the 19th of February. Here it suffered greatly from the measles and other diseases, by which more than twenty men lost their lives, and many more were rendered unfit for field-service. At one time over four hundred men in the regiment were unfit for duty. On the 31st of March the regiment was ready for service again. It moved by rail to Green Spring River, near the junction of the North and South Branches of the Potomac, and from thence advanced by slow marches to Romney. Here it joined General Schenck's brigade, moved to Moorefield, and went into camp at a ferry on the Potomac, three or four miles north of the town.

In the latter part of April seven companies of the Fifty-Fifth moved with the brigade to Petersburg, and on through Franklin to McDowell, leaving the three companies D, E, and G, at Moorefield. In the battle of McDowell, or Blue Pasture Mountain, the regiment constituted the reserve, and served as support to a battery, which, owing to the nature of the ground, could not be brought into action. After the battle the troops fell back to Franklin, in order to avoid being cut off by a flank movement. On this march, and during the stay at Franklin, the regiment suffered severely on account of the scarcity of rations. On the 26th of May the army at Franklin broke camp and moved rapidly by the way of Petersburg, Moorefield, and Wardensville, to Strasburg, a distance of ninety miles, a large portion of which had been passed over before Stonewall Jackson knew that the army had left Franklin. Jackson was moving for the Baltimore and Ohio Railroad, but finding his line of communications now seriously threatened, he commenced a retreat, and the National army followed in pursuit. The National advance and the Rebel rear were frequently skirmishing, and many prisoners were captured. The regiment was present at the battle of Cross Keys, but was not engaged. Jackson crossed the Shenandoah at Port Republic and destroyed the bridge. At this point the river was so wide and rapid that it was impracticable, if not impossible, for the National army to cross, and the next morning the troops retraced their steps. About the 20th of June the army arrived at Middletown, near Winchester, where it was allowed a short rest. Here the Army of Virginia was organized. The Fifty-Fifth was brigaded with the Twenty-Fifth, Seventy-Third, and Seventy-Fifth Ohio Regiments, and was attached to General Schenck's division.

On the 7th of July the regiment, with the corps, left Middletown and marched by way of Front Royal and Luray, through a gap in the Blue Ridge, to Sperryville. Here it remained until the 8th of August, when it moved in the direction of Culpepper C. H.; and at three o'clock A. M. on the 10th arrived on the battle-field of Slaughter Mountain. On the morning of the 14th the regiment marched about five miles and encamped on Robertson's River, near the Rapidan. Here the regimental band was mustered out, and a detail of officers, commissioned and non-commissioned, returned to Ohio on recruiting service. On the morning of the 19th the army commenced a retrograde movement. The Fifty-Fifth, with its brigade, covered the retreat, marching in such a manner as to receive an attack either on the flank or in the rear. The march was through Culpepper C. H., and northward toward White Sulphur Springs, at which point the

Rappahannock was crossed. For several days the regiment was engaged in guarding the various fords of the river, in order to prevent the Rebels from crossing. On the night of the 25th the regiment moved by a circuitous route to Warrenton, and thence marched northward to intercept Jackson in his efforts to join Lee's army. Shortly before sunset on the 28th the regiment was pushed forward, partly deployed as skirmishers, to discover Jackson's position. This was upon the old Bull Run battle-ground. On the 29th the two armies were engaged the greater portion of the day, neither party gaining any decided success. The Fifty-Fifth was under severe artillery fire, but was not engaged with the enemy's battle-line. During the 30th the regiment lay in close column, by division, behind a swell of ground, upon which was posted a battery of six steel guns. About an hour before sunset the enemy appeared suddenly on the flank. The regiment deployed under fire, but after giving a few volleys it returned to the main line, which was about one hundred yards in the rear. Here the regiment was re-formed, and it continued to engage the enemy until near dark, when, with the brigade, it gradually moved to the rear, and when night closed it fell back to Centerville.

At midnight on the 1st of September the regiment marched from Centerville to Arlington Heights, and after a few days it encamped on Munson's Hill. On the 22d of September the regiment again returned to Centerville. In the early part of October the Fifty-Fifth, with other regiments, under Colonel Bushbeck, of the Seventy-Ninth Pennsylvania, made a reconnoissance as far as Bristoe Station, and from there, during the forepart of the night, a portion of the regiment went on a quick march to Brentville, with the expectation of surprising a company of Rebel recruits. The recruits were not to be found, so the detachment returned to the Station, and the next morning the troops retraced their steps to Centerville. Immediately upon arriving the regiment resumed the march over the same ground, accompanied by a larger body of troops and a section of artillery. The column proceeded as far south as Catlett's Station, near which there was a skirmish with a small body of Rebels, and then returned to Centerville, where the Fifty-Fifth remained until the 2d of November, when it proceeded to Manassas Junction, and from there, through Hopewell Gap, to Hopewell. The regiment remained here, in camp, until the 20th of November, when it moved *via* Groveton, Bull Run battle-ground, and Centerville, to the neighborhood of Chantilly.

On the 10th of December the regiment broke camp, and after a series of severe marches arrived at Stafford C. H. on the 17th. On the 20th of January, 1863, General Burnside moved his army with the intention of attacking the enemy at Fredericksburg, and the regiment, with the division, was sent to Belle Plain Landing to defend that point. Heavy rains and bad roads arrested the movement of the army, and the regiment marched to Brook's Station and went into winter-quarters. The time was employed in inspections, drills, and picket duty. On the 27th of April the Army of the Potomac commenced its movement upon Fredericksburg, by way of the Wilderness and Chancellorsville. The Eleventh Corps, to which the regiment was attached, marched by way of Hartwood Church, up the Rappahannock to Kelly's Ford where it crossed, and continued the march to the South Branch of the Rappahannock, which was crossed at Germania Ford. From here the regiment moved on the Plank Road to Chancellorsville, arriving on the 30th. The next day the army went into position. The Eleventh Corps occupied the extreme right, and the Fifty-Fifth was in the second brigade from the right. The entire corps was posted either on or parallel to a pike leading westward into the Wilderness, and affording excellent facilities for a flank movement by the enemy. On the 2d of May scouts and skirmishers reported that the enemy was in heavy force upon the right. About five o'clock P. M. the battle opened. It was not preceded by skirmishing or picket-firing, but volleys of musketry and rapid discharges of artillery announced the conflict. The National troops, at the time of the attack, were engaged in preparing and eating supper, and the first regiment on the extreme right fled, leaving three hundred and fifty guns in stack. The next regiment was unable to withstand the shock, and so it fell back. These were the only two regiments that were facing toward the right. The remainder of the brigade, fired into from flank and rear, retreated in confusion toward the left. The Twenty-Fifth Ohio, which constituted a part of the reserve, was deployed, faced to the right, and the Fifty-Fifth formed a few yards in the rear. The Twenty-Fifth was soon compelled to fall back. The Fifty-Fifth stood its ground until the enemy was discovered sweeping around its flank, when it, too, was compelled to fall back. The retreat became general, and was only checked by other troops and darkness. In this engagement the Fifty-Fifth lost one hundred and fifty-three men killed, wounded, and missing. On the morning of the 3d the line was re-formed, and the troops maintained the position until the night of the 5th, when the army retreated, and the regiment went into its old camp near Brook's Station.

About the middle of May the regiment was transferred to the Second Brigade of the Second Division, and it remained in this brigade during the remainder of its term of service. The regiment marched into Pennsylvania with the army, and was present at the battle of Gettysburg. The division was posted first on Cemetery Hill, but was moved subsequently to the left of the Baltimore Pike. The battle-line of the regiment was not engaged, but the skirmish-line was subject, most of the time, to a severe fire. The Fifty-Fifth lost in this battle about fifty men. The regiment followed the retreating enemy, and at last went into camp on the 25th of July in the vicinity of Catlett's Station, on the Orange and Alexandria Railroad. Here the regiment performed very heavy picket-duty.

On the 24th of September the Eleventh and Twelfth Corps broke camp, took cars at Manassas Junction, and moved over the Baltimore and Ohio Railroad, and through Columbus, Indianapolis, Louisville, and Nashville, to Bridgeport, Alabama, arriving on the 30th. On the 25th of October the troops moved for Lookout Valley, and encamped on the 28th near the Tennessee River, in full sight of Lookout Mountain. The enemy attacked the troops in the Valley, but the Fifty-Fifth being on picket was not in the early part of the engagement, and sustained no loss. The regiment moved to Chattanooga on the 22d of November. In the battle of Mission Ridge the corps formed line to the left and front of Fort Hood, and moving forward rapidly, drove the Rebel skirmish-line beyond the East Tennessee Railroad. On the afternoon of the 25th the regiment was posted on the extreme left, and guarded the flank during the remainder of the battle. Immediately after this the regiment entered on the Knoxville campaign, and returned again to Lookout Valley on the 17th of December. This campaign was made in the dead of winter, without tents or blankets.

On the 1st of January, 1864, three hundred and nineteen men in the Fifty-Fifth re-enlisted, and on the 10th the regiment was on the way to Ohio. It arrived at Norwalk on the 20th; on the 22d of February it re-assembled at Cleveland, and on the 4th of March again encamped in Lookout Valley. About this time the Eleventh and Twelfth Corps were consolidated, and denominated the Twentieth, and the regiment formed a part of the Third Brigade of the Third Division.

The regiment started on the Atlanta campaign on the 2d of May, and participated in all the battles in which the Twentieth Corps was engaged. At the battle of Resaca, on the 15th of May, it suffered severely, losing upward of ninety men. It was engaged also at Cassville, Dallas, New Hope Church, Marietta, and Kenesaw. On the 20th of July the regiment crossed Peachtree Creek about five miles north-west of Atlanta, and took position on the right of the Fourth Corps. The enemy attempted a movement on the flank of the Fourth Corps, but in the maneuver exposed his own flank. The Third Brigade of the Third Division of the Twentieth Corps moved upon the exposed point, and the enemy was compelled to fall back with heavy loss. During the siege of Atlanta the Fifty-Fifth occupied its place in the lines, sometimes on the right and sometimes on the left, assisting in the gradual but sure advancement of the parallels toward the city. During the movement of the army against Jonesboro' the Twentieth Corps fell back to the Chattahoochie, and covered several ferries. The Third Brigade was stationed at Turner's Ferry, where earthworks were constructed hastily, in the form of a semicircle, around the ferry. On the 2d of September a reconnoitering party moved in the direction of Atlanta; the fortifications were found deserted, and the troops entered the city without difficulty. The Fifty-Fifth left Lookout Valley with about four hundred men, and during the campaign lost over two hundred. The Twentieth Corps was stationed at Atlanta, and the troops erected comfortable quarters. About the 1st of November the Fifty-Fifth received two hundred drafted men and substitutes, and about the same time those who were not veterans were mustered out. A scarcity of provisions was occasioned by Hood cutting the railroad between Atlanta and Chattanooga. Foraging expeditions were sent out from time to time, and the regiment did its full share of this kind of duty.

The regiment left Atlanta on the 15th of November and moved toward the sea-coast. On the 21st of December it entered Savannah and camped near the city on the north-west. Here it remained until early in January, 1865, when it was thrown across the Savannah River. It marched inland a short distance, and after a few days moved to Hardeesville, on the Charleston and Savannah Railroad. On the 29th of January the regiment started fairly on the campaign of the Carolinas. No incident worthy of particular notice occurred until the 16th of March; when, at the battle of Smith's Farm, the Fifty-Fifth lost thirty-six men killed and wounded; and again on the 19th it was engaged and lost two men killed, one officer and twenty-three men wounded, and seven men missing. On the 24th of March the regiment reached Goldsboro', and with the corps passed in review before General Sherman. The regiment moved from Goldsboro' on the 10th of April, and on the 13th arrived at Raleigh. On the 30th it commenced the march to Washington. It reached Richmond on the 11th of May, and on the 18th camped in the vicinity of Alexandria. On the 24th it crossed Long Bridge, and participated in the grand review, after which it went into camp near Washington. Upon the disbanding of the Twentieth Corps the Ohio regiments belonging to it were organized into a Provisional Brigade, and were assigned to the Fourteenth Corps. On the 10th of June they proceeded to Louisville, Kentucky, where, on the 11th of July, the Fifty-Fifth was mustered out of the service. The regiment was transported to Cleveland, Ohio, where it was paid and discharged on the 19th of July.

During its term of service the regiment enrolled about one thousand three hundred and fifty men, and of these about seven hundred and fifty were either killed or wounded in battle. Ten officers were wounded once or more, and eight officers either died of wounds or were killed in battle.

56th REGIMENT OHIO VOLUNTEER INFANTRY.

ROSTER, THREE YEARS' SERVICE.

RANK.	NAME.	DATE OF RANK.	COM. ISSUED.	REMARKS.
Colonel	PETER KINNEY	Sept. 11, 1861	Jan. 4, 1862	Resigned April 2, 1863.
Do.	WM. H. RAYNOR	April 2, 1863	May 6, 1863	Mustered out.
Do.	HENRY E. JONES	" 20, 1866	April 20, 1866	Mustered out as Lieutenant-Colonel.
Lt. Colonel	WM. H. RAYNOR	Sept. 28, 1861	Feb. 4, 1862	Promoted to Colonel.
Do.	SAMPSON E. VARNER	April 6, 1863	May 6, 1863	Mustered out.
Do.	HENRY E. JONES	Jan. 18, 1865	Jan. 18, 1865	Promoted to Colonel.
Do.	JAMES C. STIMMEL	April 20, 1866	April 20, 1866	Mustered out as Captain.
Major	SAMPSON E. VARNER	Sept. 28, 1861	Feb. 4, 1862	Promoted to Lieutenant-Colonel.
Do.	CHAS. F. REINSIGER	April 2, 1862	....	Mustered out.
Do.	WM. G. SNYDER	" 20, 1866	April 20, 1866	Mustered out as Captain.
Surgeon	W. N. KING	Oct. 3, 1861	Feb. 4, 1862	
Do.	JAMES P. ALCORN	" 29, 1862	Nov. 6, "	Revoked.
Do.	DAVID WILLIAMS	Dec. 23, 1863	Dec. 23, 1863	Mustered out.
Do.	P. M. McFARLAND	April 20, 1866	April 20, 1866	
Ass't Surgeon	W. C. PAYNE	Oct. 3, 1861	Feb. 4, 1862	Resigned April 8, 1862.
Do.	A. F. MARKLE	April 1, 1862	April 21, "	Declined.
Do.	N. H. FISHER	" 1, "	May 26, "	Deceased.
Do.	P. M. McFARLAND	Aug. 21, "	Sept. 4, "	Promoted to Surgeon.
Do.	J. S. POLLOCK	July 24, 1863	July 24, 1863	Declined; commission returned.
Chaplain	JONATHAN S. THOMAS	Sept. 9, 1862	Sept. 9, 1862	Mustered out.
Captain	Maschil Manning	Aug. 8, 1861	Feb. 5, 1866	Mustered out.
Do.	Chas. F. Reinsiger	" 7, "	" 5, "	Promoted to Major.
Do.	Wm. B. Williams	" 7, "	" 5, "	Mustered out.
Do.	Daniel B. Lodwick	" 11, "	" 5, "	Resigned July 27, 1863.
Do.	I. Herbert Evans	" 20, "	....	Mustered out.
Do.	George Willhem	" 21, "	....	Mustered out.
Do.	Isaac Fullerton	" 25, "	....	Resigned February 14, 1863
Do.	Lansing V. Applegate	Dec. 9, "	....	Resigned February 6, 1863.
Do.	Ed. Kinney	" 12, "	....	Resigned October 3, 1862.
Do.	John Cook	" 21, "	....	Died May 22, 1863.
Do.	A. L. Chenoweth	Oct. 3, "	Dec. 24, 1862	Mustered out.
Do.	Henry E. Jones	Feb. 6, 1863	March 13, 1863	Promoted to Lieutenant-Colonel.
Do.	Thomas W. Kinney	" 14, "	May 6, "	Mustered out.
Do.	John Jochem	April 2, "	" 6, "	Mustered out.
Do.	James C. Stimmel	May 16, "	July 10, "	Promoted to Lieutenant-Colonel.
Do.	Wm. D. Wood	" 9, 1864	May 9, 1864	Declined promotion.
Do.	Wm. G. Snyder	Aug. 10, "	Aug. 10, "	Not mustered.
Do.	Levi M. Willetts	Nov. 23, "	Nov. 23, "	Mustered out, exp. of service, December, 1865.
Do.	Moses Rife	Jan. 18, 1865	Jan. 18, 1865	Declined.
Do.	Benj. Roberts	March 29, "	March 29, "	Mustered out with regiment.
Do.	Christian Schaeffer	April 20, 1866	April 20, 1866	Mustered out with regiment.
Do.	Jno. K. Combs	" 20, "	" 20, "	Mustered out with regiment.
1st Lieutenant	Henry E. Jones	Sept. 28, 1861	Feb. 5, 1862	Promoted to Captain.
Do.	W. S. Houston	Oct. 18, "	" 5, "	Resigned December 27, 1863.
Do.	John Jochem	Nov. 7, "	" 5, "	Promoted to Captain.
Do.	Jeremiah P. Woods	" 7, "	" 5, "	Dead.
Do.	Wm. D. Woods	" 8, "	" 5, "	Mustered out.
Do.	Chas. W. Veach	" 11, "	" 5, "	Mustered out June 2, 1862.
Do.	Moses Rife	" 20, "	" 5, "	Declined promotion; mustered out.
Do.	Henry Lantz	" 21, "	" 5, "	Mustered out.
Do.	James C. Stimmel	" 25, "	" 5, "	Promoted to Captain.
Do.	Chas. Soule, jr.	Dec. 9, "	" 5, "	Resigned June 10, 1862.
Do.	Thomas Lowry	" 15, "	" 5, "	Honorably discharged October 3, 1862.
Do.	Martin Owens	" 24, "	" 5, "	Resigned July 22, 1863.
Do.	Thomas Brown	Jan. 10, 1862	June 20, "	Resigned June 18, 1863.
Do.	Wm. L. Porter	Nov. 10, "	Nov. 10, "	Assigned to Gen. Rosecrans' staff at his req'st.
Do.	John D. Neswanger	Oct. 27, "	Dec. 24, "	Mustered out.
Do.	Chas. D. Veach	Feb. 6, 1863	April 9, 1863	Resigned September 10, 1864.
Do.	Thomas W. Kinney	Dec. 27, 1862	" 22, "	Promoted to Captain.
Do.	Erastus Gates	April 2, 1863	May 6, "	Resigned July 22, 1863.
Do.	Joseph Patterson	Feb. 14, "	June 29, "	Promoted.
Do.	Wm. G. Snyder	May 16, "	Sept. 1, 1866	Promoted to Captain.
Do.	Benj. Roberts	June 18, "	" 1, "	Promoted to Captain.
Do.	Oratio De Wolf	May 9, 1864	May 9, 1864	Mustered out.
Do.	Chas. Seiffer	" 16, 1863	Aug. 25, "	Mustered out.
Do.	John J. Markham	" 9, 1864	May 9, "	Mustered out.
Do.	Henry M. Goldsmith	" 9, "	" 9, "	Revoked.
Do.	John K. Combs	Aug. 11, "	Aug. 11, "	Promoted to Captain.
Do.	Orry H. Wadsworth	Nov. 23, "	Nov. 23, "	Honorably discharged May 10, 1865.
Do.	Christian Schaeffer	Jan. 18, 1865	Jan. 18, 1865	Promoted to Captain.
Do.	James Vandervoort	May 31, "	May 31, "	Mustered out December, 1865.
Do.	Thomas J. Williams	Jan. 30, 1866	Jan. 30, 1866	Mustered out with regiment.
Do.	Stephen D. Thoburn	Feb. 24, "	Feb. 24, "	Mustered out with regiment.
Do.	Harvey M. Bidwell	April 20, "	April 20, "	Mustered out with regiment.
2d Lieutenant	Thomas Brown	Oct. 18, 1861	Feb. 5, 1862	Promoted to 1st Lieutenant.
Do.	Chas. Seiffer	Nov. 7, "	" 5, "	Promoted to 1st Lieutenant.
Do.	Benj. Roberts	" 7, "	" 5, "	Promoted to 1st Lieutenant.
Do.	Coleman Gilliland	" 8, "	" 5, "	Honorably discharged July 31, 1862.
Do.	Murty W. Lodwick	" 11, "	" 5, "	Resigned September 5, 1862.
Do.	James K. Campbell	" 20, "	" 5, "	Resigned September 6, 1862.
Do.	John T. Morton	" 21, "	" 5, "	Honorably discharged June 2, 1862.
Do.	Benj. B. Allen	" 25, "	" 5, "	Resigned September 7, 1862.
Do.	A. L. Chenoweth	Dec. 15, "	" 5, "	Promoted to Captain.
Do.	Wm. H. Palmer	" 24, "	" 5, "	Resigned August 31, 1862
Do.	Thomas W. Kinney	June 10, 1862	Aug. 5, "	Promoted to 1st Lieutenant.

RANK.	NAME.	DATE OF RANK.	COM. ISSUED.	REMARKS.
2d Lieutenant	Joseph Patterson	Aug. 31, 1862	Sept. 9, 1862	Promoted to 1st Lieutenant.
Do.	Erastus Gates	Sept. 5, "	" 18, "	Promoted to 1st Lieutenant.
Do.	James L. O. Huston	" 6, "	Oct. 8, "	Honorably discharged March 18, 1863.
Do.	G. W. Manning	July 31, "	Dec. 24, "	Killed May 16, 1863.
Do.	Wm. G. Snyder	Sept. 7, "	" 24, "	Promoted to 1st Lieutenant.
Do.	Oratio D. Wolf	June 2, "	" 24, "	Promoted to 1st Lieutenant.
Do.	A. S. Chute	Oct. 3, "	" 24, "	Killed May 16, 1863.
Do.	John J. Markham	March 18, 1863	April 9, 1863	Promoted to 1st Lieutenant.
Do.	Henry M. Goldsmith	Jan. 1, "	June 15, "	Resigned.
Do.	Henry Schumpe	March 17, "	" 15, "	Mustered out.
Do.	John K. Combs	Feb. 11, "	" 29, "	Promoted to 1st Lieutenant.
Do.	Christian Schaeffer	May 16, "	July 10, "	Promoted to 1st Lieutenant.
Do.	Henry Behrens	" 16, "	Aug. 10, "	Mustered out.
Do.	James Vanderat	June 18, "	Sept. 1, "	Mustered out.
Do.	James Aleshire	May 16, "	" 1, "	Mustered out.
Do.	Thomas J. Williams	Jan. 18, 1865	Jan. 18, 1865	Promoted to 1st Lieutenant.
Do.	Stephen D. Thoburn	" 18, "	" 18, "	Promoted to 1st Lieutenant.
Do.	Harvey M. Bidwell	May 31, "	May 31, "	Promoted to 1st Lieutenant.
Do.	John H. Morris	" 31, "	" 31, "	

FIFTY-SIXTH OHIO VOLUNTEER INFANTRY.

THE organization of this regiment was undertaken at a very unpropitious time for the raising of recruits. The country around Portsmouth (Scioto County) had been well drained of men already, and few seemed left among whom to operate; but the officers, nothing daunted, determined to fill up the ranks. After much solicitation the order was given to organize the regiment. Peter Kinney, of Portsmouth, was appointed Colonel, Wm. H. Raynor, Lieutenant-Colonel, and Sampson E. Varner, Major.

On the 8th day of October, 1861, the camp was organized at Portsmouth, and the officers went vigorously to work raising recruits. Men came in steadily, but not rapidly. By December 12, with the utmost labor, the regiment was filled to the minimum number. The transition from civil life to the soldiers' camp, and the miserable winter weather of that year began to tell upon the health of the men. Measles appeared among the recruits, and some two hundred and fifty cases occurred within a few days, which, although it did not kill at once, rendered them unfit for the spring campaign, and eventually laid many of them in soldiers' graves.

On the 10th of February orders were received to report at Paducah, Kentucky. This was joyful news; and on the 12th the regiment took its departure on transports for its destination. The morning of the 16th of February found the regiment in line of battle before the rifle-pits of the enemy at Fort Donelson, Tennessee, assisting our victorious forces to receive the surrender of thirteen thousand Rebel prisoners of war.

After many changes the Fifty-Sixth was brigaded with the Twentieth, Seventy-Sixth, and Seventy-Eighth Ohio, under their Colonel, Chas. R. Wood, and attached to the Third Division, under Major-General Lew. Wallace. About the middle of March it moved to Pittsburg Landing, where our forces were being concentrated. The Fifty-Sixth arrived there March 17th, and Wallace's division went into camp at Crump's Landing, three miles below Pittsburg Landing. Sickness was rife in the regiment at this point, over sixty being sent to the general hospital at Paducah. Late in March the brigade was ordered to Adamsville, some six miles from the river. On the 6th of April, early in the morning, the booming of artillery and crash of musketry announced that the battle of Pittsburg Landing had commenced. The brigade, in line of battle, waited until two o'clock P. M. for orders to join the strife, but none came. The brigade performed good service, however, in guarding an important road to the river, and picking up stragglers from the National army, sending them back in an organized body of eight hundred men to assist their gallant comrades.

On the advance of our forces toward Corinth the regiment was with the right wing, and participated in most of the warm skirmishing of that advance. After the evacuation of Corinth the division to which the Fifty-Sixth belonged was ordered to Memphis, Tennessee, and marched one hundred and ten miles through the enemy's country. This march was very trying to the men, as they were frequently compelled to make thirty miles a day in order to reach water, and the intense heat caused many to fall in the ranks. On the 13th of June, six days after the capture of the place, the division arrived at Memphis. While at this place, company B, of the regiment, was detailed as a guard to the train engaged in taking out men and material for re-building a bridge burned by the enemy, making daily trips to and from Memphis. Returning from the city on the 24th, the train was thrown from the track, a portion of it having been torn up by the enemy, the cars burned, and a number of company B, with Colonel Kinney, captured.

On the 24th of July the regiment embarked for Helena, Arkansas, under command of Major Varner, Lieutenant-Colonel Raynor being sick in hospital. Colonel Kinney had succeeded in escaping from the enemy, and was at home in Ohio on furlough. The fall and winter were spent in fortifying Helena, the regiment rendering important service in building Fort Curtis and felling timber for abattis, work familiar to the men, most of them being from the furnace region of Southern Ohio. A number of expeditions were made by the regiment from this point up White River into Arkansas, in one of which they routed a force of Rebel cavalry, capturing their arms and camp equipage, and at Eunice Landing, Louisiana, they took possession of a large and valuable wharf-boat and brought it to Helena, where for many months it was of valuable service to Government. While at Helena the regiment suffered severely from disease, some fifty men dying, among them Assistant-Surgeon Fisher, a young man of fine acquirements, and a good officer.

On the 10th of April ill health compelled Colonel Kinney to resign, when Lieutenant-Colonel Raynor was promoted to Colonel, Major S. E. Varner to Lieutenant-Colonel, and Captain C. F. Reinsiger to Major. On the 11th of April the regiment left Helena for the vicinity of Vicksburg to join General Grant's forces, then concentrating for his march on that place. It was here placed in the division commanded by General A. P. Hovey, having for its corps commander Major-General John McClernand. This corps marched across the country from Milliken's Bend to Grand Gulf, and lay in the stream on transports during the bombardment of that place by the gunboats, ready to land and attack the rifle-pits of the enemy as soon as the batteries were silenced. This not being accomplished, the corps landed and marched below, while the gunboats and transports ran past the batteries, and at once began transporting the army across the river to Bruinsburg.

On the last day of April, 1863, General Grant's grand flanking movement on Vicksburg commenced, and at daylight on the 1st of May the battle of Port Gibson was fought. In this battle the Fifty-Sixth Ohio charged and captured two guns and one hundred and twenty-five prisoners in the face of two Rebel regiments, with a loss of forty killed and wounded. On the 16th of May, in the battle of Champion Hills, the regiment again distinguished itself, losing one hundred and thirty-five, killed, wounded, and prisoners. Among the killed were Lieutenants Chute and Manning, two valuable officers. Captain Wilhelm, wounded and a prisoner, turned on his guard, captured and brought him in. At the crossing of Baker Creek, another regiment being ordered to dislodge the enemy, hesitated, when the Fifty-Sixth was called for, and performed the work in a gallant manner, eliciting great praise. After encountering the hardships of that great march, the Fifty-Sixth, with our victorious army, entered Vicksburg on the day of its surrender to General Grant.

But little rest was allowed. The enemy was in force under the Rebel General Jos. Johnston at Jackson. The regiment was ordered there, and, with its brigade and division, took an honorable part in the capture of the capital city of Mississippi and the discomfiture of the Rebel army. On the return of the regiment to Vicksburg, in a violent storm, Color-Sergeant William

Roberts took shelter under a tree, which was struck by lightning, hurling him to the ground, paralyzing his left side, and stripping the flag from its staff as with a knife. Roberts never recovered the use of his side.

The division next moved to Natchez, resting there a few hours, when orders were received to proceed further south, to the Department of the Gulf, under the command of Major-General N. P. Banks. After a few weeks of rest and refitting, they commenced the Teche campaign, leaving New Orleans on the 13th of September, 1863; from New Orleans to Berwick Bay by Opelousas; thence by marches over the beautiful plains of Western Louisiana, through Franklin, New Iberia, Vermilionville, back to Opelousas, having skirmished with the enemy for nearly one hundred miles without bringing them to a stand. During this long march the Fifty-Sixth had not a sick man on its rolls, and many that had but recently left the hospitals were fully restored to vigorous health. Finding it impossible to bring the enemy to a stand, the General commanding ordered a retrograde movement, the Rebels following obstinately in the rear. While General Burbridge's brigade of the Fourth Division was three miles to the rear, encamped on Bayou Cotto, the enemy in force attacked and captured the camp. The Fifty-Sixth Ohio was ordered to his support. The regiment went over the prairie at double-quick, charged through the flying National forces, and came upon the Rebels while in the act of rifling our camp, scattering them in the utmost disorder.

The army next moved back to Vermilionville, offering every inducement to the enemy to give battle, but without avail. Strategy was called into play, and retaliation made for capturing five of the Fifty-Sixth while out foraging, by a night march on one of the Rebel camps at Spanish Lake. The surprise was complete, and one hundred and ten Rebels quietly "bagged," without the loss of a man on the National side.

Without tents, and nearly devoid of clothing, the men suffered very much from the cold, which, in this far southern clime, though not of a very low temperature, had more effect than at the North. This was in November. On the 17th of December orders were received to proceed to New Orleans, a distance of one hundred and seventy-five miles, which was accomplished in six days, bringing in, without loss, a large and valuable train filled with much-needed forage. The regiment went into camp at Algiers, opposite the city, for a few weeks. On the 22d of January the division received orders, and proceeded across Lake Pontchartrain to Madisonville, where they were for some weeks engaged in building fortifications. While at this place more than three-fourths of the men re-enlisted as veterans, thus declaring that they were determined to see the end of the contest.

On the 1st of March the division was ordered to return to New Orleans to prepare for the Red River campaign. After the arrival of the Fifty-Sixth in the city, Lieutenant-Colonel Varner was detached and placed in command of the post of Algiers, with a temporary battalion, composed of the non-veterans of the division, numbering about six hundred men. Major Reinsiger was also detached and put in command of the camp of paroled prisoners, leaving Colonel Raynor in charge of the brigade and Captain Manning of the regiment.

On the 7th of March the Red River campaign commenced by way of Opelousas. After many delays at different points, on the 4th day of April the enemy was encountered, and the battle of Sabine Cross Roads was fought, resulting in a disastrous defeat to the National army. In this battle the Fifty-Sixth lost forty killed, wounded, and missing. Falling back in disorder, harassed at almost every step by the exultant Rebels, the National forces gained the village of Mansfield, threw up breastworks, and prepared to give the enemy battle. On the 8th of April the Rebels arrived in front of the National intrenchments, made a furious attack, and were repulsed with heavy loss. The enemy thus vigorously checked, the National army was able to fall back more leisurely, and took position at Grand Ecore, to enable the National gunboats to descend Red River without being destroyed by Rebel batteries along its banks. In this position it was not unfrequent for regiments, on their own responsibility, to throw up breastworks to protect their camps. The Fifty-Sixth Ohio was so engaged one day as Major-General F—— rode along. The General stopped and said to a member of company G, who was hard at work with the spade: "My man, it is of no use to do that; we can whip the enemy on this ground." The soldier replied: "General, we have been whipped once, and we are now determined to do our own generaling."

The Fifty-Sixth were entitled to return to Ohio on the thirty-days' furlough granted to those who had re-enlisted. While at Alexandria the order was received to return to New Orleans, and there take transport for New York, *en route* for Ohio. The regiment embarked on the steamer John Warner, in which they were to run the terrible gauntlet of Red River. Cotton bales were arranged on the upper deck to protect the sharp-shooters, who were compelled to be constantly on the watch against the enemy. The trip was in truth a fiery ordeal, but the men of the Fifty-Sixth had their thoughts on home, and determined to get through to New Orleans, if possible. The majority of them had not been at home for three years, and had faced the enemy too often to turn back now, when there was a prospect of seeing the loved ones there.

Proceeding down the river, at a certain point the Rebels opened fire on the boat with a battery and two regiments of infantry. An attempt was made to run through, but an unlucky shot disabled the machinery, and the boat swung round to the opposite shore. The enemy still continued their murderous fire, and the crew were afraid to expose themselves to make the boat fast. All was looked upon as lost, as the boat was on fire, and fast swinging out into the stream, when Sergeant Richard Mains and private Samuel Nickels, of company G, seized the line, jumped ashore, rushed up the bank, and made it fast, amid a shower of bullets, miraculously escaping without a scratch. Two tin-clads were seen coming to the rescue, but they soon shared the fate of the John Warner, and were riddled by cannon-balls and burned. Colonel Raynor, of the Fifty-Sixth, was wounded and taken prisoner, the enemy having crossed in small boats and taken possession of the wounded left on the bank. The loss of the Fifty-Sixth in this affair was about fifty, including all the officers but seven. The remainder of the regiment took up the line of march down the river, determined to reach the Mississippi River, even if they had to fight every step of the way. Some twelve miles below the scene of their disaster a gunboat was met; the weary men got on board and were taken to the mouth of the river, and thence by transports to New Orleans, arriving there destitute, having lost almost everything.

Captain James C. Stimmel, of the Fifty-Sixth, who started down the river two days before the regiment, on a steamer, was also captured by the enemy, but before reaching the Rebel prison at Tyler, Texas, he managed, with others, to make his escape, and, after traveling by land and river over seven hundred miles, and enduring almost incredible hardships, reached New Orleans. Lieutenant Ben. Roberts, taken on the John Warner, also made his escape, and ran the gauntlet through to Little Rock, Arkansas. The other prisoners of the regiment were kept confined in Rebel prisons until exchanged, thirteen months afterward.

On the 22d of May, 1864, the Fifty-Sixth sailed from New Orleans to New York on the steamship Cahawba, where they arrived and took the cars for Ohio. On arriving at Columbus the men received individual furloughs for thirty days, with orders to report at Camp Chase at the end of that time.

After enjoying themselves among friends, at the appointed time all reported but two. (They were afterward arrested as deserters and forwarded to New Orleans under guard.)

The regiment was again ordered to the Department of the Gulf, and, on arriving at New Orleans, was attached to the force guarding the defenses of that city, under command of Brigadier-General T. W. Sherman. Lieutenant-Colonel Varner commanded the regiment while it was on this duty. In November, 1864, all the members of the regiment who had not re-enlisted were discharged and sent home. The remainder were consolidated into three companies, and but seven line officers retained, all others being honorably discharged. Later in the season a full company of twelve-months' men were assigned by the Governor of Ohio, which entitled them to a field officer, and the senior Captain, H. E. Jones, was appointed Lieutenant-Colonel.

The rest of the term of the Fifty-Sixth was filled in performing guard-duty in the city of New Orleans, a service full of responsibility and hard work. It was kept on duty there until March, 1866, when the remaining members were honorably mustered out and returned to Ohio.

57th REGIMENT OHIO VOLUNTEER INFANTRY.

ROSTER, THREE YEARS' SERVICE.

RANK.	NAME.	DATE OF RANK.	COM. ISSUED.	REMARKS.
Colonel	WM. MUNGEN	Dec. 16, 1861	Feb. 17, 1862	Resigned April 16, 1863.
Do.	AMERICUS V. RICE	April 16, 1863	May 6, 1863	Appointed Brigadier-General.
Do.	SAMUEL R. MOTT	Aug. 10, 1865	Sept. 4, 1865	Mustered out with regiment.
Lt. Colonel	WM. MUNGEN	Sept. 27, 1861	Feb. 17, 1862	Promoted to Colonel.
Do.	AMERICUS V. RICE	Feb. 8, 1862	" 17, "	Promoted to Colonel.
Do.	SAMUEL R. MOTT	April 16, 1863	May 6, 1863	Promoted to Colonel.
Do.	GEORGE D. McCLURE	Aug. 10, 1865	Sept. 4, 1865	Mustered out with regiment.
Major	SILAS B. WALKER	Oct. 2, 1861	Feb. 7, 1862	Resigned April 26, 1863.
Do.	JOHN McCLURE	April 25, 1863	June 26, 1863	Mustered out December 21, 1864.
Do.	SQUIRE JOHNSON	Aug. 16, 1865	Sept. 4, 1865	Mustered out with regiment.
Surgeon	JOHN P. HAGGETT	Oct. 3, 1861	Feb. 17, 1862	Resigned April 30, 1862.
Do.	WM. D. CARLIN	May 26, 1862	March 26, "	Died December 26, 1862.
Do.	N. C. MESSENGER	Dec. 26, "	Feb. 8, 1863	Honorably discharged November 23, 1864.
Do.	ROBERT H. MILLIKEN	" 14, 1864	Dec. 14, 1864	Mustered out with regiment.
Ass't Surgeon	LAFAYETTE WOODRUFF	Nov. 14, 1861	Feb. 17, 1862	Resigned April 28, 1862.
Do.	N. C. MESSENGER	April 28, 1862	May 13, "	Promoted to Surgeon.
Do.	JACOB W. KNOUFF	May 7, 1863	" 8, 1863	Honorably discharged April 4, 1864.
Do.	S. D. STARR	June 24, "	July 24, "	Never on duty with regiment.
Do.	ROBERT H. MILLIKEN	May 4, 1861	May 4, 1861	Promoted to Surgeon.
Do.	D. M. FRAZER	March 14, 1865	March 14, 1865	Mustered out with regiment.
Chaplain	JOSEPH HAWKINS	Nov. 12, 1864	Nov. 12, 1864	Mustered out with regiment.
Captain	Americus V. Rice	Sept. 2, 1861	Feb. 17, 1862	Promoted to Lieutenant-Colonel.
Do.	Philip Faulhaber	Oct. 4, "	" 17, "	Killed at Vicksburg, Miss., Dec. 31, 1862.
Do.	Samuel R. Mott	" 20, "	" 17, "	Promoted to Lieutenant-Colonel.
Do.	Patrick Kilkenny	Dec. 1, "	" 17, "	Resigned April 22, 1862.
Do.	Samuel Morrison	" 14, "	" 17, "	Deceased.
Do.	James Wilson	Jan. 4, 1862	" 17, "	Honorably discharged April 12, 1865.
Do.	John B. May	" 10, "	" 17, "	Resigned January 30, 1863.
Do.	Charles A. Junghans	" 21, 1862	" 17, "	Killed at Pittsburg Landing April 6, 1862.
Do.	James C. Gribben	Feb. 8, "	" 17, "	Killed at Pittsburg Landing April 6, 1862.
Do.	Daniel N. Strayer	" 10, "	" 17, "	Mustered out August 19, 1862.
Do.	Alva S. Skilton	" 10, "	" 17, "	Honorably discharged April 13, 1865.
Do.	Abner J. Sennett	April 6, "	May 24, "	Honorably discharged March 29, 1865.
Do.	John McClure	" 6, "	" 20, "	Promoted to Major.
Do.	Hiram E. Henderson	" 22, "	" 24, "	Honorably discharged August 31, 1863.
Do.	John A. Smith	Aug. 19, "	Feb. 17, 1863	Mustered out with regiment.
Do.	John W. Underwood	April 16, 1863	May 6, "	Mustered out with regiment.
Do.	John W. Wheeler	Dec. 31, 1862	Feb. 17, "	Honorably discharged March 28, 1864.
Do.	Daniel Gilbert	Jan. 30, 1863	March 13, "	Honorably discharged November 14, 1863.
Do.	George D. McClure	April 26, "	Jan. 29, 1864	Promoted to Lieutenant-Colonel.
Do.	Robert W. Smith	May 9, 1864	May 9, "	Mustered out with regiment.
Do.	Wm. M. Newell	" 9, "	" 9, "	Honorably discharged as 1st Lt. Nov. 18, 1864.
Do.	Jacob A. Tussing	" 9, "	" 9, "	Declined; returned commission.
Do	Edmund W. Firmin	Aug. 16, "	Aug. 16, "	Declined; returned commission.
Do	Hubbard D. Stone	" 16, "	" 16, "	Honorably discharged as 1st Lt. Oct. 26, 1864.
Do.				
Do.	James A. Dixon	Feb. 10, 1865	Feb. 10, 1865	Mustered out with regiment.
Do.	Squire Johnson	" 10, "	" 10, "	Promoted to Major.
Do.	John D. Marshall	March 18, "	March 18, "	Mustered out with regiment.
Do.	Edward E. Root	April 8, "	April 8, "	Mustered out with regiment.
Do.	Edward A. Gordon	June 16, "	June 16, "	Mustered out with regiment.
Do.	David Baker	" 16, "	" 16, "	Mustered out with regiment.
Do.	Benj. B. Heaton	" 16, "	" 16, "	Mustered out with regiment.
Do.	George Trichler	Aug. 10, "	Sept. 4, "	Mustered out with regiment.
Do.	James McCauley	" 10, "	" 4, "	Mustered out with regiment.
Do.	David Ayres	" 10, "	" 4, "	Mustered out with regiment.
Do.	Wm. H. Kellison	" 10, "	" 4, "	Mustered out with regiment.
1st Lieutenant	James C. Gribben	Sept. 2, 1861	Feb. 17, 1862	Promoted to Captain.
Do.	Daniel S. Price	" 21, "	" 17, "	Died April 6, 1862.
Do.	John McClure	" 27, "	" 17, "	Promoted to Captain.
Do.	Samson Switzer	Oct. 4, "	" 17, "	Resigned April 27, 1864.
Do.	John W. Underwood	" 20, "	" 17, "	Promoted to Captain.
Do.	Hiram E. Henderson	Dec. 1, "	" 17, "	Promoted to Captain.
Do.	Andrew J. Banks	" 14, "	" 17, "	Resigned April 27, 1864.
Do.	John W. Wheeler	Jan. 4, 1862	" 17, "	Promoted to Captain.
Do.	Daniel Gilbert	" 10, "	" 17, "	Promoted to Captain.
Do.	Abner J. Sennett	" 24, "	" 17, "	Promoted to Captain.
Do.	George D. McClure	Feb. 8, "	" 17, "	Promoted to Captain.
Do.	John A. Smith	" 10, "	" 17, "	Promoted to Captain.
Do.	George P. Blystone	" 10, "	" 17, "	Resigned April 6, 1863.
Do	Ogden Meader	March 29, "	May 9, "	Resigned February 3, 1863.
Do.	Robert W. Smith	April 6, "	" 24, "	Promoted to Captain.
Do.	Oliver Mungen	" 22, "	" 24, "	Resigned February 9, 1863.
Do.	Wm. S. Bonnell	" 6, "	June 20, "	Revoked.
Do.	John A. Hardy	" 6, "	Dec. 24, "	Resigned August 3, 1863.
Do.	Wm. M. Newell	Aug. 19, "	Feb. 17, 1863	Promoted to Captain.
Do.	Jacob A. Tussing	Dec. 31, "	May 12, "	Mustered out.
Do.	Edmund W. Firmin	Jan. 30, 1863	" 12, "	Mustered out.
Do.	Hubbard D. Stone	Feb. 3, "	June 29, "	Promoted to Captain.
Do.	George M. Rogers	Aug. 20, "	Aug. 29, "	Resigned July 12, 1864.
Do.	Edward E. Root	April 6, "	May 12, "	Promoted to Captain.
Do.	John Doneyson	" 16, "	" 12, "	Declined.
Do.	James A. Dixon	" 26, "	June 29, "	Promoted to Captain.
Do.		Aug. 3, "	Aug. 25, "	
Do.	Squire Johnson	May 9, 1864	May 9, 1864	Promoted to Captain.

RANK.	NAME.	DATE OF RANK.	COM. ISSUED.	REMARKS.
1st Lieutenant	Stephen H. Carey	May 9, 1864	May 9, 1864	Honorably discharged December 2, 1864.
Do.	John M. Jordan	" 9, "	" 9, "	Mustered out.
Do.	John D. Marshall	" 9, "	" 9, "	Promoted to Captain.
Do.	W. Cramer Good	" 9, "	" 9, "	Commission returned; declined.
Do.	George M. Patton	" 9, "	" 9, "	Commission returned; declined.
Do.	David Ayres	Aug. 16, "	Aug. 16, "	Honorably discharged January 4, 1865.
Do.	Edward A. Gordon	" 16, "	" 16, "	Promoted to Captain.
Do.	Lewis L. Parker	" 16, "	" 16, "	Declined.
Do.	Owen Francis	" 19, "	" 19, "	Mustered out May 15, 1865.
Do.	David Baker	Jan. 18, 1865	Jan. 18, 1865	Promoted to Captain.
Do.	Benjamin B. Heaton	" 18, "	" 18, "	Promoted to Captain.
Do.	George Berger	" 18, "	" 18, "	Mustered out with regiment.
Do.	James McCauley	" 18, "	" 18, "	Promoted to Captain.
Do.	George Trichler	" 18, "	" 18, "	Promoted to Captain.
Do.	Wm. A. Armstrong	Feb. 10, "	Feb. 10, "	Declined.
Do.	Wm. Dalzell	" 10, "	" 10, "	Declined.
Do.	David Ayres	April 15, "	April 15, "	Promoted to Captain.
Do.	John N. Ricketts	June 16, "	June 16, "	Mustered out with regiment.
Do.	Wm. H. Kellison	" 16, "	" 16, "	Promoted to Captain.
Do.	Israel L. Cramer	" 16, "	" 16, "	Mustered out with regiment.
Do.	Daniel R. Miller	" 16, "	" 16, "	Mustered out with regiment.
Do.	Joseph McCrate	" 16, "	" 16, "	Mustered out with regiment.
Do.	Andrew Dieffenbacher	" 16, "	" 16, "	Mustered out with regiment.
Do.	Charles L. Brown	Aug. 10, "	Sept. 4, "	Mustered out with regiment.
Do.	Jasper T. Rickets	" 10, "	" 4, "	Mustered out with regiment.
Do.	Charles M. Hathaway	" 10, "	" 4, "	Mustered out with regiment.
Do.	Charles Wessinger	" 10, "	" 4, "	Mustered out with regiment.
Do.	Solomon Good	" 10, "	" 4, "	Mustered out with regiment.
2d Lieutenant	George D. McClure	Sept. 2, 1861	Feb. 17, 1862	Promoted to 1st Lieutenant.
Do.	Wm. S. Bonnell	Oct. 4, "	" 17, "	Promoted to 1st Lieut.; resigned March 27, 62.
Do.	Oliver Mungen	" 9, "	" 17, "	Promoted to 1st Lieutenant.
Do.	John Doneyson	" 15, "	" 17, "	Promoted to 1st Lieutenant.
Do.	Ogden Meader	Dec. 14, "	" 17, "	Promoted to 1st Lieutenant.
Do.	John Adams	Jan. 4, 1862	" 17, "	Resigned April 27, 1864.
Do.	Edmund W. Firmin	" 10, "	" 17, "	Promoted to 1st Lieutenant.
Do.	John Steinmets	" 21, "	" 17, "	Honorably discharged December 12, 1863.
Do.	James A. Dixon	Feb. 8, "	" 17, "	Promoted to 1st Lieutenant.
Do.	Lucius Cane	" 16, "	" 17, "	Honorably discharged September 11, 1862.
Do.	Edward E. Root	" 10, "	" 17, "	Promoted to 1st Lieutenant.
Do.	Hubbard D. Stone	March 29, "	May 9, "	Promoted to 1st Lieutenant.
Do.	John A. Hardy	April 22, "	" 24, "	Promoted to 1st Lieutenant.
Do.	Wm. M. Newell	Aug. 19, "	Dec. 24, "	Promoted to 1st Lieutenant.
Do.	Squire Johnson	" 19, "	" 24, "	Promoted to 1st Lieutenant.
Do.	Stephen H. Carey	Sept. 11, "	" 24, "	Promoted to 1st Lieutenant.
Do.	John M. Jordan	Nov. 27, "	Jan. 12, 1863	Promoted to 1st Lieutenant.
Do.	David Ayres	Feb. 3, 1863	Aug. 10, "	Re-entered below.
Do.	John D. Marshall	April 16, "	May 11, "	Promoted to 1st Lieutenant.
Do.	Marcellus B. Dickey	" 6, "	" 12, "	Resigned April 27, 1864.
Do.	W. Cramer Good	Jan. 30, "	" 12, "	Mustered out.
Do.	George M. Patton	April 26, "	June 29, "	Mustered out.
Do.	David Ayres	Feb. 3, "	" 29, "	Promoted to 1st Lieutenant.
Do.	John A. Plumb	Aug. 3, "	Aug. 25, "	Killed at Resaca, Ga.
Do.	Lewis L. Parker	Feb. 20, 1864	Feb. 20, 1864	Promoted to 1st Lieutenant.
Do.	Edward A. Gordon	Dec. 29, 1863	" 27, "	Promoted to 1st Lieutenant.
Do.	Owen Francis	Aug. 16, 1864	Aug. 16, "	Promoted to 1st Lieutenant.
Do.	David Baker	" 16, "	" 16, "	Promoted to 1st Lieutenant.
Do.	Joshua Collar	" 10, 1865	Sept 4, 1865	Mustered out with regiment.
Do.	Jacob Baker	" 10, "	" 4, "	Mustered out with regiment.
Do.	John Woosley	" 10, "	" 4, "	Mustered out with regiment.
Do.	David W. Martin	" 10, "	" 4, "	Mustered out with regiment.
Do.	Samuel T. Winegardner	" 10, "	" 4, "	Mustered out with regiment
Do.	Marion Beemer	" 10, "	" 4, "	Mustered out with regiment.
Do.	John J. Thompson	" 10, "	" 4, "	Mustered out with regiment.
Do.	Ezra Hipsher	" 10, "	" 4, "	Mustered out with regiment.
Do.	Aaron Glottheart	" 10, "	" 4, "	Mustered out with regiment.
Do.	Albert Woodruff	" 10, "	" 4, "	Mustered out with regiment.

FIFTY-SEVENTH OHIO VOLUNTEER INFANTRY.

ON the 14th day of September, 1861, Governor Dennison gave authority to recruit a regiment of infantry, to be designated the Fifty-Seventh Regiment, and to rendezvous at Camp Vance, Findlay, Hancock County, Ohio. Recruiting commenced on the 16th day of September, and was pushed forward rapidly. The regiment was partially organized at Camp Vance, from where it moved on the 22d of January, 1862, to Camp Chase, where it was completed on the 10th of February, numbering nine hundred and fifty-six men and thirty-eight commissioned officers. The localities in which the different companies were recruited are as follows: Company A, in Putnam County; B, in Hancock, Seneca, and Wood; C, in Auglaize, Mercer, and Sandusky; D, in Hamilton; E, in Hamilton, Allen, and Van Wert; F and G, in Hancock; H, in Hancock and Seneca; I, in Crawford, Shelby, and Sandusky; K, in Logan and Sandusky.

The regiment left Camp Chase on the 18th of February, 1862, under orders to report at Fort Donelson. When it arrived at Smithland, Kentucky, the order was changed, and it reported at Paducah, Kentucky. Here the regiment was assigned to the Third Brigade, Fifth Division of the Army of the Tennessee. On the 8th of March, 1862, the regiment left Paducah, on the steamer Continental, and arrived at Fort Henry, on the Tennessee River, on the 9th. From here it proceeded to Savannah, Tennessee, where it arrived on the 11th. On the 14th six gunboats and sixty-five transports went up the river to the mouth of Yellow Creek, where the troops disembarked, and attempted to strike the Memphis and Charleston Railroad, at Iuka, Mississippi, nine miles distant, but failed in consequence of exceedingly high water. They returned to the transports, embarked, and went to Pittsburg Landing, where they arrived on the 16th. On the following day the Fifth Division made a reconnoissance to Pea Ridge, toward Corinth, about nine miles from the Landing. On the 19th it went into camp at Shiloh Chapel, three miles southwest of the Landing. The 22d and 24th of March were spent in making reconnoissances in the direction of Corinth. On the 1st of April the regiment, in company with other troops and two gunboats, went to Eastport, Mississippi, about thirty miles distant. The Fifty-Seventh was on the foremost transport. The gunboats threw a number of shells into the town of Eastport, but elicited no reply. The boats moved up the river to Chickasaw, Alabama, and shelled both the Rebel works and the town. The Rebels having left, the Fifty-Seventh was ordered ashore to scout the hills surrounding the village. It captured a few prisoners, men and boys, and then returned to camp.

The regiment suffered much from sickness, and on the morning of the 6th of April there were but four hundred and fifty men for duty. The regiment was posted with its right resting on the Corinth Road, immediately south of the Shiloh Church. About six o'clock on the morning of the 6th the Fifty-Seventh formed and advanced until it reached the little eminence upon which the Shiloh Church stood. The regiment held this position until ten o'clock, and successfully withstood three Rebel regiments—the Mississippi Rifles, the Crescent Guards, from New Orleans, and the Fourteenth Tennessee, from Memphis. These regiments left seventy-eight dead in front of the Fifty-Seventh. The regiment was ordered to fall back upon the Hamburg and Purdy Road, and it executed the movement in good order. The battle continued with great fury, and the line was pressed back three-quarters of a mile further. Here the fighting was terrific, but the enemy was forced to give way a little, and by five o'clock in the afternoon the firing had almost ceased in front of the Fifty-Seventh. The regiment lay on its arms in a drenching rain all night, and at daybreak again went into action. The enemy was driven back, and by four o'clock in the afternoon the regiment occupied its old position. Everything was destroyed except the sutler's tent, which General Beauregard had used as his head-quarters, and in which he had written his dispatches to the Rebel Secretary of War. The regiment lay on its arms another night in the rain and mud, and on the morning of the 8th moved about seven miles toward Corinth, and near to Pea Ridge, where it encountered Forrest's cavalry and about fifteen hundred Rebel infantry. Two companies of the Fifty-Seventh and Seventy-Seventh Ohio were thrown out as skirmishers. Forrest's cavalry charged, the National cavalry gave way, and the four companies of skirmishers were captured. The Fifty-Seventh did not dare to fire into the Rebels lest it should kill its own men. It fixed bayonets and charged on the double-quick against the cavalry. As it advanced it received a volley, but at the command, "Guide center—steady, boys!" it closed up, and pressed forward. The cavalry gave way. The captured companies rushed to their comrades or laid down, and the regiment halted and poured a volley into the retreating Rebels. The enemy's stores were burned, and then the troops returned to camp, arriving about ten o'clock P. M. The men in the Fifty-Seventh had eaten scarcely anything since the evening of the 5th, but that night there was some mule steak broiled on the coals, and it was pronounced "tolerably good." In these three days the regiment lost twenty-seven killed, one hundred and fifty wounded (sixteen mortally), and ten captured.

From this time until the 29th of April, the regiment remained in camp near Shiloh Church, engaged in drilling and preparing for the coming campaign. On the 29th it began the advance to Corinth, and until the evacuation of that place the regiment, day, and night, was marching, picketing, skirmishing, or building breastworks. At Camps Six and Seven and at the Russell House it was warmly engaged. During the advance the regiment was assigned to the First Brigade of the Fifth Division. After the evacuation the regiment was engaged in repairing the Memphis and Charleston Railroad, and in making reconnoissances. On one of these, from La Grange to Holly Springs, the men suffered intensely for water. While the regiment lay at Moscow, near the Mississippi line, a detachment of two hundred and twenty men were ordered to accompany a train to Memphis for supplies. The detachment marched through Macon, and struck the Memphis and Nashville Road near Morning Sun. Here the train was attacked by about six hundred Rebel cavalry. They charged the train three times, but were repulsed each time, and at last were driven off, with a loss of eleven killed, twenty-six wounded, and some prisoners, horses, and arms captured. The detachment lost four men wounded. The trip was completed successfully. The regiment moved to Memphis on the 18th of July, and on the 29th of August it was ordered to Raleigh to look after Burrows's Rebel cavalry. The cavalry fled after exchanging a few shots, but the regiment captured a number of horses. Again, on the 8th of September, the regiment was ordered on a scout into Mississippi. It was absent four days, was engaged with the enemy six different times, and marched one hundred and ten miles. The regiment was ordered into camp on the Randolph road, north of Memphis, and was placed in charge of the road, and especially of the bridge over Wolf Creek. On the 23d of September a detachment of Burrows's cavalry attacked the post, with the view of burning it. The Rebels were repulsed with a loss of one killed and six wounded; two horses were captured. The regiment sustained no loss. On the 12th of November it was assigned to the First Brigade, First Division, Fifteenth Army Corps. During the stay at Memphis the regiment was drilled very thoroughly in the skirmish-drill and the bayonet exercise.

On the 26th of November the regiment, with quite a large force, moved against General Price, on the Tallahatchie River, near Wyatt, Mississippi. The Rebels delayed the march by obstructing the roads, and Wyatt was not reached until the 2d of December. The Rebels evacuated and the march was continued toward Grenada. The regiment camped near Bowls's Mills, Little Hurricane Creek, in Lafayette County, until the 9th of December, when the Fifteenth Corps returned to Memphis, arriving on the 13th. Here the regiment received one hundred and eighteen volunteers and two hundred and five drafted men, which made the aggregate force of the regiment six hundred and fifty men. Soon after this the regiment embarked on the Omaha, and, with the Fifteenth Corps, moved down the Mississippi. Young's Point was reached on the 26th of December. From here the troops moved up the Yazoo, and disembarked on Sidney Johnston's plantation. The next day they marched to Chickasaw Bayou; where, for five days, the Fifteenth Corps, in trying to effect a crossing, was engaged with the enemy. The Fifty-Seventh was engaged all the time, and brought up the rear when the troops returned to the transports. In this action the regiment lost thirty-seven killed and wounded. On the 2d of January, 1863, the corps moved down the Yazoo to the Mississippi, up the Mississippi to White River, up White River to the "cut-off," through the "cut-off" into the Arkansas, and up the Arkansas to within two miles of Arkansas Post, disembarking on the 10th. The First Brigade was ordered to attack the Rebel pickets, which it did, and drove them within six hundred yards of Fort Hindman. The Fifty-Seventh Ohio and Sixth Missouri were ordered to drive the Rebels from their barracks, in front of their lines, and about half a mile further to the west. This also was done, and by twelve o'clock M. on the next day preparations were completed for the assault. The Fifty-Seventh led the brigade in the charge on the works, and after a desperate battle of three hours, during two hours of which time the regiment was within ninety yards of the Rebel parapet, the enemy surrendered. It lost in this action thirty-seven killed and wounded.

On the 13th the regiment was ordered on an expedition to the Clay Plantation. Here it engaged and defeated some Rebel cavalry, burned forty thousand bushels of corn, a large amount of fodder, a splendid residence and all its furniture, and then returned to the fleet and moved for Vicksburg. It disembarked at Young's Point on the 21st of January, and went to work in the canal. It continued digging for about two weeks, exposed to the shot and shell from a Rebel gun known as Whistling Dick. On the 12th of February it moved up the river on the Chancellor on a foraging expedition. It returned on the 15th with one hundred and seventy-five head of cattle, twelve thousand bushels of corn, and numerous chickens. The latter were not turned over to the Government, but were appropriated to private use. On the 17th of March the regiment started on the expedition to Haines's Bluff. The march was very laborious; and navigating, swimming, and wading, the brigade came up with two of the gunboats, in a bayou near the Sunflower, completely hemmed in by fallen trees, and exposed to the fire of the Rebel sharpshooters. The Fifty-Seventh being in the advance, became engaged in a severe fight, in which the Rebels were driven off. The gunboats were unable to advance, and so the expedition returned to Young's Point.

On the 29th of April the regiment, with a large body of troops, moved upon Snyder's Bluff, to engage the attention of the Rebels, while General Grant attacked Grand Gulf. On the 30th the regiment participated in a severe battle, which lasted until noon the next day, when the troops retired and moved down the Mississippi to Grand Gulf, which had been captured by General Grant. The regiment advanced upon Vicksburg, participating in the battles of Raymond, Champion Hills, and Black River. At Champion Hills it suffered severely. The regiment reached the works around Vicksburg on the 18th of May. It participated in a general assault on the 19th, and advanced, under a terrific fire, to within seventy yards of the Rebel line. It held this position until two o'clock of the morning of the 20th, when the entire brigade was withdrawn to a position three hundred yards in rear of the line of fortifications. At nine o'clock on the 22d the bugle again sounded the advance, and the Fifty-Seventh moved forward in the front line. The attempt was more stubborn, the fighting more desperate, and the casualties greater than on the 19th; but the assault was no more successful. The regiment advanced to within sixty yards of the enemy's works; but on the evening of the 23d it fell back to its old position and commenced fortifying. On the 26th of May it accompanied the division on a reconnoissance between the Big Black and Yazoo Rivers. It had an engagement with the enemy at Mechanicsburg, and routed him. The expedition returned to Vicksburg by way of Haines's Bluff, on the 3d of June, having marched seventy-eight miles. From this time until the surrender it was continually engaged, either on the picket-line or in the trenches.

On the 5th of July the regiment marched upon Jackson, which was then held by the Rebels under Johnston. The troops reached Jackson on the 8th, and drove the Rebels into their works. The National forces intrenched, and skirmishing continued until the 17th, when the Rebels evacuated. The Rebels were pursued to Pearl River. Here the Fifty-Seventh had one man killed and several severely wounded by torpedoes. After this the regiment moved toward Vicksburg, and on the 25th it pitched its tents four miles west of Big Black River, at Camp Sherman. Here it remained until the 27th of September, when it moved to Vicksburg, embarked on the steamer Commercial, and proceeded up the Mississippi to Memphis, where it arrived on the 4th of October. On the 8th it marched for Chattanooga, and on the 22d of November it arrived at the mouth of North Chickamauga Creek, ten miles north-east of Chattanooga. The march was long and fatiguing, and skirmishing with the enemy's cavalry was frequent. The regiment now formed a part of the First Brigade, Second Division, Fifteenth Corps. On the night of the 23d of November the Brigade embarked in boats on the North Chickamauga Creek, floated down the creek into the Tennessee, crossed the river with muffled oars, landed, captured the Rebel pickets, secured their countersign, and with it relieved the whole line. By daylight a line of rifle-pits was thrown up, and the position was secured. On the 24th a pontoon was laid, and Sherman's army crossed the Tennessee, and drove the Rebels two miles. On the 25th the regiment participated in the battle of Mission Ridge, with heavy loss. It pursued the Rebels to within two miles of Ringgold, and rested there one day, and on the 29th it started with the corps to the relief of Burnside, at Knoxville. The corps marched one hundred and four miles in four days, over bad roads, and arrived within striking distance, when Longstreet raised the siege and retired with his forces into Virginia. On the 7th of December the corps returned to Chattanooga, where it arrived on the 18th, and drew "hard tack" for the first time in fifteen days. On the 19th it was again on the march, and on the 29th of December it arrived at Bellefonte, Alabama. By this time the regiment was almost exhausted by fatigue, privation, hunger, and exposure. The men were hatless, shoeless, and half naked; yet, notwithstanding all this, the regiment re-enlisted on the 1st of January, 1864, being the first regiment to re-enlist as veterans in the Fifteenth Army Corps.

The regiment started for Cincinnati on the 4th of February, and on arriving received a furlough for thirty days. On the 16th of March the regiment, with two hundred and seven recruits, rendezvoused at Camp Chase. It arrived at Nashville on the 29th of March, and was detained there until the 4th of April, when it marched through to Larkinsville, Alabama, and at that point rejoined its brigade on the 17th. On the 1st of May it moved on the Atlanta campaign. It arrived in the vicinity of Chattanooga on the 6th, and advanced through Snake Creek Gap to Resaca. The Fifty-Seventh participated in the battle of this place, May 13th and 14th. On the 14th it was posted in an important position, and received three successive charges from an overwhelming force of the enemy, but it held its ground firmly. This was one of the most severe contests in which the regiment ever engaged, and its loss was fifty-seven killed and wounded. The regiment pursued the retreating foe, crossed the Oostenaula, and advanced through Kingston to Dallas. Here the enemy made a stand, and fighting continued for three days. The regiment lost fifteen men.

On the 1st of June the regiment moved to New Hope Church, where it engaged the enemy, with a loss of four men. The Rebels were driven back on Kenesaw Mountain, and the regiment followed through Acworth and Big Shanty, skirmishing and fighting almost every day. On the 27th it participated in an assault on the enemy's lines at Kenesaw. The regiment gained a position very near the Rebel works, but was compelled to abandon it. In this engagement it lost fifty-seven killed and wounded. On the 5th of July it reached the Chattahoochie, and skirmishing continued almost incessantly until the 9th, when the enemy crossed the river. The regiment moved on through Marietta, Rosswell, and Decatur to Atlanta, where it arrived on the 20th, and drove the Rebels inside their fortifications.

On the 22d the Rebels attacked the line furiously. The fighting was desperate, and the works in the immediate front of the Fifty-Seventh were captured by the enemy and recaptured by the regiment three times. The Rebels were forced back at last, and the regiment held its position. The Fifty-Seventh was in the heat of the engagement, and lost ninety-two men. On the 24th the regiment moved to the extreme right of the army, and on the morning of the 28th again met the enemy. The engagement lasted seven hours, and the Rebels were repulsed. At this time the Fifty-Seventh belonged to the First Brigade, Second Division, Fifteenth Army Corps; and in this battle the enemy left on the field, in front of the brigade, four hundred and fifty-eight of their number dead. The regiment lost twelve men killed and fifty-five wounded. The regiment continued to press the enemy until the 26th, when it again moved to the right, and struck the Augusta and Atlanta Railroad ten miles from East Point. A portion of the road was destroyed, and on the 30th the regiment moved for the Macon Road, and, after marching all day, reached it at eight o'clock, P. M. The battle of Jonesboro' was fought on the 31st. The Rebels massed and advanced in four lines of battle upon the Second Division. They were protected by the ground until within sixty or seventy yards of the division, and they advanced steadily and well closed up; but when the division opened fire their line was shattered. They advanced three times, but to no purpose. They were driven back with fearful slaughter. The number of killed and wounded in front of the Fifty-Seventh nearly equaled the number of men in the regiment. On the 2d of September the Rebels evacuated Jonesboro'. It was occupied by the National troops, and the regiment advanced about eight miles and found the enemy in position. The division was ordered to destroy the railroad, and the regiment assisted in the work all night and until ten o'clock of the next day. On the 6th the Fifty-Seventh was ordered to Jonesboro', and on the 7th it marched toward Eastport, where it arrived and went into camp on the 8th.

Here it was engaged in drilling most of the time until the 4th of October, when it started after Hood. It moved by way of Kenesaw, Marietta, Kingston, Centerville, and Resaca, and on the 15th attacked the Rebels at Snake Creek Gap. The Rebels were repulsed, and the regiment followed to Taylor's Ridge, where another fight occurred, and the Rebels were defeated. The regiment moved on through Lafayette, Somersville, Gaylesville, Little River, Cedar Bluff, Cave Spring, and Cedartown, skirmishing and fighting, marching and counter-marching, and tearing up railroad track, until the 13th of November, when it arrived at Atlanta.

The regiment left Atlanta with Sherman's army on the 15th of November on the march to the sea. On the 21st it was engaged with the Rebel cavalry near Clinton, and on the 25th it participated in quite a severe fight at the crossing of the Oconee River. On the 3d of December some of the regiment's foragers were captured, and on the 4th it engaged the Rebels at Statesboro' and lost heavily. It engaged in the assault on Fort McAllister on the 13th. The fort was carried at the point of the bayonet, and in the attack the regiment lost ten killed and eighty wounded. On the 17th it moved with its division on an expedition to the Gulf Railroad, and, after destroying about fifty miles of track, returned to camp.

On the 1st of January, 1865, the regiment moved two miles south-west of Savannah, and went into camp until the 14th, when it started by land for Beaufort, South Carolina. The regiment was detained by high water, and on the 25th was compelled to embark on the steamer George Leary. It arrived at Beaufort on the same day, and overtook the remainder of the forces on the next day, three miles from town. Here it remained until the 30th, when it started on the campaign of the Carolinas. It passed through Pocotaligo, and on the 3d of February fought the Rebels at Duall's Creek. It passed through Bramburg, on the Charleston Railroad; crossed the South and North Edisto, skirmishing with the Rebels at both crossings; crossed the Saluda and Broad Rivers, and, after heavy skirmishing, entered Columbia on the 17th. It also assisted in the destruction of the railroad buildings, and again took up the line of march. It crossed the Wateree River on the 22d, and on the 23d recrossed the river near Liberty Hill, passed two miles to the left of Camden, and struck Lynch's Creek twenty-two miles from Camden.

The Fifty-Seventh moved five miles down the creek to a bridge, but could not cross on account of the high water. It remained here until the 2d of March, when the march was resumed, and on the 12th the regiment arrived at Fayetteville. Pontoons were laid over the Cape Fear River on the 13th, and on the 14th the regiment was on the march again. It skirmished heavily on the 15th at Black River, which it crossed at Mickey Bridge. When within about twenty-five miles of Goldsboro' it was ordered back to re-enforce the left wing of the army, then menaced by General Joseph E. Johnston. The regiment was engaged severely on the 19th, and on the 20th and 21st there was sharp skirmishing. On the 22d the enemy retired across Mill Creek, and, after passing a short distance, it was ordered toward Goldsboro'. The regiment moved on to Raleigh, and, after the surrender of General Johnston, the march was continued through Petersburg and Richmond to Washington City.

The Fifty-Seventh participated in the grand review, May 24th; and on the 2d of June it was ordered to Louisville, Kentucky, where it arrived on the 7th. On the 25th of June the regiment started for Little Rock, Arkansas, and arrived at that place on the 6th of August. On the 14th it was mustered out of the service, and on the 25th was paid and discharged at Camp Chase, Ohio.

The Fifty-Seventh traveled by railroad, steamboat, and on foot, more than twenty-eight thousand miles.

The names of one thousand five hundred and ninety-four men had been on its muster-rolls, and of that number only four hundred and eighty-one were alive at its muster out.

58th REGIMENT OHIO VOLUNTEER INFANTRY.

ROSTER, THREE YEARS' SERVICE.

RANK.	NAME.	DATE OF RANK.		COM. ISSUED.		REMARKS.
Colonel	VAL. BAUSENWEIN	Oct.	1, 1861	Jan.	8, 1862	Discharged.
Lt. Colonel	FERDINAND F. REMPEL	Dec.	5, ''	''	8, ''	Resigned August 11, 1862.
Do.	PETER DISTER	Oct.	2, 1862	Oct.	2, ''	Killed December 29, 1862.
Do.	EZRA P. JACKSON	Dec.	29, ''	Aug.	8, 1863	Mustered out.
Do.	WM. S. FRIESNER	May	3, 1865	May	3, 1865	Mustered out with regiment.
Major	VAL. BAUSENWEIN	Sept.	21, 1861	Sept.	21, 1861	Promoted to Colonel.
Do.	PETER DISTER	Aug.	11, 1862	''	30, ''	Promoted to Lieutenant-Colonel.
Do.	EZRA P. JACKSON	Oct.	2, ''	Oct.	2, ''	Promoted to Lieutenant-Colonel.
Do.	SAMUEL M. MORRISON	Jan.	1, 1864	Feb.	2, 1864	Discharged as Captain August 26, 1864.
Do.	ANDREW GALLFY	Oct.	20, ''	Oct.	20, ''	Mustered out.
Surgeon	RAINER SCHALLERN	''	7, 1861	Feb.	8, 1862	Resigned April 6, 1862.
Do.	CHRISTIAN FORSTER	Nov.	18, 1862	''	10, 1863	Mustered out.
Ass't Surgeon	EUGENE RINGLER	Jan.	9, ''	''	8, 1862	Resigned May 30, 1862.
Do.	A. M. MCELWEE	Oct.	26, ''	Oct.	31, ''	Resigned December 8, 1862.
Do.	NATHAN J. BARBER	Jan.	31, 1863	Jan.	31, 1863	Mustered out.
Do.	ELI DAYTON	Dec.	23, 1862	Feb.	10, ''	Mustered out.
Do.	E. C. DEFORREST	June	26, 1865	June	26, 1865	
Chaplain	FRED. W. RICHMAN	May	5, 1862	May	5, 1862	Honorably discharged October 3, 1862.
Captain	Andrew Gallfy	Jan.	8, ''	Jan.	8, ''	Promoted to Major.
Do.	Joseph N. Brown	''	8, ''	''	8, ''	Cancelled; commission returned.
Do.	Launtz Barentzen	''	8, ''	''	8, ''	Resigned April 19, 1862.
Do.	Andrew Huber	''	8, ''	''	8, ''	Resigned September 4, 1862.
Do.	Albert Stepley	''	8, ''	''	8, ''	Resigned October 3, 1862.
Do.	John Bunz	''	8, ''	''	8, ''	Resigned March 27, 1862.
Do.	Oscar Brabender	Feb.	7, ''	Feb.	7, ''	Resigned April 22, 1862.
Do.	Ezra P. Jackson	Nov.	26, 1861	''	8, ''	Promoted to Major.
Do.	Samuel M. Morrison	Dec.	13, ''	''	8, ''	Promoted to Major.
Do.	Charles A. Barker	''	16, ''	''	8, ''	Discharged October 3, 1862.
Do.	Wilford Steirs	March	27, 1862	May	1, ''	Resigned.
Do.	John C. Anderegg	April	19, ''	''	10, ''	Mustered out.
Do.	Ferdinand Fix	''	22, ''	''	10, ''	Honorably discharged September 30, 1862.
Do.	Baptist Benkler	Sept.	4, ''	Sept.	19, ''	Resigned January 30, 1863.
Do.	Alexander Miller	Oct.	3, ''	Oct.	3, ''	Resigned September 21, 1862.
Do.	E. J. Brunnis	Sept.	21, ''	''	2, ''	Resigned March 30, 1864.
Do.	Christopher Kinser	Oct.	2, ''	''	2, ''	Killed December 27, 1862.
Do.	Wm. S. Friesner	''	3, ''	Nov.	29, ''	Promoted to Lieutenant-Colonel.
Do.	Peter Kaufman	''	3, ''	Dec.	31, ''	Killed at Fort Morgan, Miss., Dec. 29, 1862.
Do.	Jacob Haering	Jan.	1, 1863	Aug.	8, 1863	Mustered out as 1st Lieut. Dec. 22, 1863.
Do.	Wm. Rode	March	15, 1861	March	15, 1864	Mustered out.
Do.	Joseph Dister	Jan.	1, ''	Feb.	2, ''	Mustered out.
Do.	Charles Kette	''	1, ''	''	2, ''	Mustered out.
Do.	Wm. H. Hulls	''	1, ''	''	2, ''	Mustered out.
Do.	Henry Oderfeld	March	15, ''	March	15, ''	Mustered out.
Do.	Joseph S. Krause	''	29, ''	''	29, ''	Mustered out January 10, 1865.
Do.	Wm. Roby	Jan.	1, ''	Feb.	2, ''	Mustered out.
Do.	Lewis Keller	Nov.	18, ''	Nov.	18, ''	Mustered out with regiment.
Do.	John T. Morrison	May	3, 1865	May	3, 1865	Mustered out with regiment.
Do.	Wm. Geilhausen	''	3, ''	''	3, ''	Mustered out with regiment.
Do.	Philip Frœbe	''	3, ''	''	3, ''	Mustered out with regiment.
1st Lieutenant	Oscar Brabender	Sept.	21, 1861	Sept.	21, 1861	Promoted to Captain.
Do.	Launtz Barentzen	Oct.	7, ''	Oct.	21, ''	Promoted to Captain.
Do.	Theodore Dichmen	Jan.	8, 1862	Jan.	8, 1862	Resigned December 8, 1862.
Do.	Charles Strœdeter	''	8, ''	''	8, ''	Discharged on account of wounds, Dec. 4,'62.
Do.	E. J. Brunnis	''	8, ''	''	8, ''	Promoted to Captain.
Do.	Henry Buehl	''	8, ''	''	8, ''	Resigned November 28, 1862.
Do.	August Brisworth	''	8, ''	''	8, ''	Resigned March 15, 1862.
Do.	Wilford Steirs	''	8, ''	''	8, ''	Promoted to Captain March 27, 1862.
Do.	Romaine Lujeane	Dec.	14, 1861			Resigned February 7, 1862.
Do.	Peter A. Bishop	Oct.	1, ''			Discharged April 9, 1863.
Do.	Jacob Haering	Jan.	10, 1862	Feb.	6, 1862	Promoted to Captain.
Do.	Christopher Kinser	Nov.	28, 1861	''	8, ''	Promoted to Captain.
Do.	Wm. Roby	Dec.	13, ''	''	8, ''	Promoted to Captain.
Do.	Wm. S. Friesner	''	16, ''	''	8, ''	Promoted to Captain.
Do.	Harlan P. Christie	Feb.	7, 1862	''	10, ''	Discharged November 13, 1862.
Do.	Peter Kaufman	March	15, ''	April	14, ''	Promoted to Captain.
Do.	Frederick Teuscher	''	27, ''	May	1, ''	Resigned.
Do.	Theodore Schied	Sept.	21, ''	Oct.	2, ''	Honorably discharged.
Do.	Wm. H. Hulls	Oct.	2, ''	''	2, ''	Promoted to Captain.
Do.	Wm. Rode	Nov.	13, ''	Nov.	29, ''	Promoted to Captain.
Do.	Henry Oderfeld	Oct.	3, ''	Dec.	31, ''	Resigned February 8, 1863.
Do.	Harlan P. Christie	Nov.	28, ''	Jan.	21, 1863	Resigned April 27, 1863.
Do.	Joseph Dister	Jan.	1, ''	Sept.	1, ''	Promoted to Captain.
Do.	Henry Oderfeld	Sept.	9, ''	''	9, ''	Promoted to Captain.
Do.	John T. Morrison	Jan.	1, 1864	Feb.	2, 1864	Promoted to Captain.
Do.	Charles Stoppel	May	25, ''	May	25, ''	Mustered out.
Do.	Stephen Miller	''	25, ''	''	25, ''	Mustered out.
Do.	Henry H. Sibert	Jan.	1, ''	Feb.	2, ''	Mustered out.
Do.	Wm. Geilhausen	May	25, ''	May	25, ''	Promoted to Captain.
Do.	Frederick Riegelman	''	25, ''	''	25, ''	Mustered out.
Do.	Philip Frœbe	''	25, ''	''	25, ''	Promoted to Captain.
Do.	Henry Buehring	''	25, ''	''	25, ''	Mustered out.
Do.	Lewis Keller	Jan.	1, ''	Feb.	2, ''	Promoted to Captain.
Do.	Charles Kette	April	9, 1863			Promoted to Captain.
Do.	John Schmidt	Jan.	1, 1864	Feb.	2, 1864	Mustered out.
Do.	John Hanson	''	1, ''	''	2, ''	Mustered out.

RANK.	NAME.	DATE OF RANK.	COM. ISSUED.	REMARKS.
1st Lieutenant	Stephen Defenbaugh	Jan. 1, 1864	Feb. 2, 1864	Mustered out.
Do.	John H. Price	May 3, 1865	May 3, 1865	Mustered out with regiment.
Do.	David Jenkins	" 3, "	" 3, "	Mustered out with regiment.
Do.	Leonard Krimm	" 3, "	" 3, "	Mustered out with regiment.
Do.	Jacob Kinser	" 3, "	" 3, "	Mustered out with regiment.
Do.	Enoch E. Parish	" 3, "	" 3, "	Mustered out with regiment.
2d Lieutenant	Michael Muller	Jan. 8, 1862	Jan. 8, 1862	Resigned.
Do.	Henry Oderfeld	" 8, "	" 8, "	Promoted to 1st Lieutenant.
Do.	Ehrhard Goehl	" 8, "	" 8, "	Honorably discharged February 8, 1863.
Do.	Wm. Rode	" 8, "	" 8, "	Promoted to 1st Lieutenant.
Do.	Peter Kaufman	" 8, "	" 8, "	Promoted to 1st Lieutenant.
Do.	Fred. Teuscher	" 8, "	" 8, "	Promoted to 1st Lieutenant.
Do.	Conrad B. Krause	" 10, "	Feb. 6, "	Resigned March 4, 1863.
Do.	Wm. H. Hulls	Nov. 26, 1861	" 8, "	Promoted to 1st Lieutenant.
Do.	Stephen Defenbaugh	Dec. 13, "	" 8, "	Promoted to 1st Lieutenant.
Do.	Leander E. Hodges	" 16, "	" 8, "	Honorably discharged December 29, 1862.
Do.	Joseph Dister	March 8, "	March 8, "	Promoted to 1st Lieutenant.
Do.	Theodore Schied	" 15, "	April 14, "	Promoted to 1st Lieutenant.
Do.	Peter Leonhardt	" 27, "	May 1, "	Revoked.
Do.	Charles Kette	" 27, "	July 8, "	Promoted to 1st Lieutenant.
Do.	Thaddeus H. Ream	Oct. 3, "	Dec. 31, "	Resigned January 17, 1863.
Do.	Robert Specht	Sept. 21, "	" 31, "	Resigned December 26, 1863.
Do.	Elias L. Dodrow	Oct. 3, "	" 31, "	Killed December 29, 1862.
Do.	Lewis Keller	Nov. 13, "	" 31, "	Promoted to 1st Lieutenant.
Do.	Charles Stoppel	" 14, 1863	Feb. 11, 1864	Promoted to 1st Lieutenant.
Do.	Ehrhard Goehl	Sept. 9, "	Sept. 9, 1863	Declined promotion.
Do.	Fred. Riegelman	Jan. 16, 1865	Jan. 16, 1865	Revoked May 3, 1865.
Do.	John H. Price	" 18, "	" 18, "	Promoted to 1st Lieutenant.
Do.	Wm. Larimer	May 3, "	May 3, "	Mustered out with regiment.
Do.	George W. Sherlock	" 3, "	" 3, "	Mustered out with regiment.
Do.	John Stuber	" 3, "	" 3, "	Mustered out with regiment.
Do.	John Krinn	" 3, "	" 3, "	Mustered out with regiment.

FIFTY-EIGHTH OHIO VOLUNTEER INFANTRY.

RECOGNIZING the urgent necessity for an increase of the National forces in the field, in order to cope successfully with the armies raised by the Rebel authorities, the President called on the different States for an additional contingent of three hundred thousand men. Ohio, always foremost in responding to the calls of the Government, took hold of the matter with energy. Among a number of regiments projected at that time was the Fifty-Eighth Ohio. Under authority from the Governor, the regiment was organized by the appointment of Colonel Valentine Bausenwein as Colonel, and the full complement of line and field officers.

The regiment remained at Camp Chase, near Columbus, perfecting itself in the "school of the soldier," until February 10, 1862, when, an urgent call being made for troops, the Fifty-Eighth was at once placed under orders, and transported by rail to Cincinnati, arriving in that city on the 11th of February. Embarking on the steamers Tigress and Dictator, the regiment left on the same day, *en route* for Fort Donnelson, Tennessee, and arrived there on the morning of the 13th of February.

Tarrying only long enough to prepare their coffee, the regiment, then within four miles of the fort, pushed on with energy, impelled by the sounds of the conflict resounding through the woods. After making a fatiguing march of twelve miles over rough and circuitous roads, in order to get into a proper position, it went into camp late in the evening in sight of the fort. Tired and exhausted by the excessive fatigue of the day, the men threw themselves on the ground and were soon sound asleep, utterly oblivious of what might befall them the next day. They awoke in the morning surprised to find themselves covered by a fall of snow three inches in depth. The regiment was assigned to Thayer's brigade of Lew. Wallace's division.

Preparations were at once made to take part in the assault on the fort. The Colonel (V. Bausenwein) being ill, the second officer, Lieutenant-Colonel Ferd. Rempel, took command. This officer led the regiment at once toward the enemy. After moving a short distance a furious attack was made by the enemy, but the shock was met with coolness, and ended in the Rebels being hurled back into their intrenchments. This ended the active work of the day, although the regiment remained in line of battle until late in the evening, when it returned to camp. Early on the morning of the 16th the regiment was marched to the center of the line, where it remained until the announcement of the surrender of the fort. The Fifty-Eighth was immediately marched into the fort, and Lieutenant-Colonel Rempel, with his own hands, hauled down the first Rebel flag the members of the regiment had ever gazed upon.

At the battle of Fort Donelson the Fifty-Eighth supported Taylor's Illinois Battery, placed on the Nashville Road, and successfully held that important position against the Rebel division under Bushrod Johnston. The Rebels, on their repulse, reported to Johnston that it was impossible to take the Nashville Road, as it was filled with regular soldiers. This mistake occurred from the fact that the men of the Fifty-Eighth Ohio wore hats with the regulation feather and dark blue uniforms.

Remaining near Fort Donelson until the 7th of March, the regiment left for Fort Henry, and arrived there the same day. On the 15th of March it moved up the Tennessee River to Crump's Landing and went into camp.

The Fifty-Eighth went into the battle of Pittsburg Landing on the morning of the 7th of April, its position being on the right, in Taylor's brigade, General Lew. Wallace's division, and was under fire until four P. M., at which time the enemy retreated. The Fifty-Eighth was highly complimented for its conduct in the battle by General Lew. Wallace and other officers in command. Its loss was nine killed and forty-three wounded.

After the battle Lieutenant-Colonel Rempel was detailed as Provost-Marshal of the army, in post at Pittsburg Landing.

Then came the tedious, exhausting march on Corinth, creeping with snail-like pace toward that miserable town. On May 8th Corinth was evacuated by the Rebels, and the Fifty-Eighth, with the rest of the army, took possession. Our forces lay quiet here until the 1st of June, when a portion of them were ordered to different quarters. The Fifty-Eighth received orders for Memphis, where it arrived on the 17th of June. It remained but a short time at Memphis, orders being received to move down the river to Helena, Arkansas. It arrived there on the 27th of July, and remained until the 5th of October. During the time the regiment was at this place several reconnoissances were made down the Mississippi on transports, convoyed by gunboats, for the purpose of attacking and dispersing the guerrillas along the shores of that river. In one of these expeditions a Rebel steamer, the Fair Play, with five thousand stand of arms and two pieces of artillery, was captured near Milliken's Bend, Louisiana. A brisk skirmish was also had with the Thirty-First Louisiana Regiment, capturing forty of their number and all their camp equipage.

The next expedition was up the Yazoo River, a detachment of the Fifty-Eighth acting as sharp-shooters on the steamers Monarch, Sampson, and Lioness. On reaching Haines's Bluff a few shots were exchanged with the enemy, who soon retreated, leaving three heavy siege-guns, two brass field-pieces, one thirty-pound Parrott, and a large amount of ordnance stores, which were destroyed by being thrown into the river. This occurred on the 20th of August. At Greenville, on the Mississippi, returning, another skirmish was had with the enemy, and several prisoners and some horses captured. At Bolivar Landing the Rebels were met a third time, and, after a spirited little fight, scattered into the woods. On the 27th of August the expedition reached the camp at Helena, and remained there until October 6th. Orders were then received for the regiment to embark on the steamers Lacrosse and Conway for St. Genevieve, Missouri, where it arrived October 6th. On the 22d the regiment marched to Pilot Knob, but returned to St. Genevieve again on the 18th of November, and, embarking on the steamers War Eagle and White Cloud, the regiment moved to Camp Steele, Mississippi.

The Fifty-Eighth remained at Camp Steele until the 22d of December, when it again embarked on the steamers Polar Star and Adriatic for Johnston's Landing, on the Yazoo River. On the 27th of December there was heavy skirmishing, in which the regiment took the lead, losing several men, among them Captain Christopher Kinser, of company K, a gallant and meritorious officer. The Fifty-Eighth continued on the skirmish-line all night. The next day it was ordered to charge the enemy's works, which it performed in gallant style, being the first to reach the works. After pressing the enemy back and gaining the first line of rifle-pits, it became evident that further efforts would prove unsuccessful. The regiment, therefore, fell back. In this affair the Fifty-Eighth lost forty-seven per cent. of the whole number engaged. Among the killed were three officers, including the brave and efficient Lieutenant-Colonel Peter Dister. Among the wounded were Captains Morrison and Fix, and Lieutenants Defenbaugh, Kette, and Oderfeld. Captains Gallfy and Anderegg were captured.

The regiment remained in this vicinity until January 2, 1863, when it re-embarked on transports and sailed down the Yazoo River to its mouth; thence up the Mississippi and White Rivers to Arkansas Post, where it arrived late on the evening of the 9th of January, and took a prominent part in the capture of that place. With the rest of the National forces the Fifty-Eighth embarked for Young's Point, Louisiana, and went into camp, and remained until the 8th of February, 1863.

The Fifty-Eighth at this time received an order to serve on board the iron-clads of the Mississippi flotilla, and was distributed by companies to the different steamers. In this line of duty it performed valuable service.

On the 15th of March an expedition was ordered up the Yazoo River into Deer Creek, which resulted in a three days' fight at "long-taw." Although quite a spirited affair, the regiment lost but few men. The expedition returned to the mouth of the Yazoo and remained there until the night of the 16th of April. On that memorable night the iron-clads and transports ran the gauntlet of the Vicksburg batteries, losing but one man of those belonging to the Fifty-Eighth.

On the 29th of April the battle of Grand Gulf was fought. In this battle the Fifty-Eighth lost heavily. The expedition marched up the river to Alexandria; thence up the Wachita as far as Trinity, where it captured and destroyed a large amount of goods belonging to the enemy; thence up to Harrisonburg, where the Rebels were found strongly fortified, so much so as to stand a heavy bombardment of two days without results, and to compel our forces to abandon the attack and return down the river to Bayou Sara, on the Mississippi River. Remaining here but a few days, the mouth of the Red River was again visited, and made the base of the flotilla until the 1st of September, 1863. From this point scouting expeditions were occasionally sent into the interior, with, however, little result.

At this date the Fifty-Eighth was ordered to join the land-forces at Vicksburg, and was assigned to the First Brigade, First Division, Seventeenth Army Corps. The regiment remained at Vicksburg, performing provost-duty, until December 24, 1864, when it was ordered to report at Columbus, Ohio, for discharge and muster-out of the service. This was consummated on the 14th of January, 1865, and the members of the Fifty-Eighth returned to civil life.

59th REGIMENT OHIO VOLUNTEER INFANTRY.

ROSTER, THREE YEARS' SERVICE.

RANK.	NAME.	DATE OF RANK.	COM. ISSUED.	REMARKS.
Colonel	JAMES P. FYFFE	Sept. 26, 1861	Oct. 16, 1861	Resigned October 6, 1863.
Lt. Colonel	F. OLMSTED	" 26, "	" 16, "	Resigned August 11, 1862.
Do.	WM. HOWARD	Aug. 11, 1862	Sept. 10, 1862	Resigned February 24, 1863.
Do.	GRANVILLE A. FRAMBERS	Feb. 24, 1863	March 9, 1863	Mustered out October 29, 1864.
Major	WM. HOWARD	Oct. 9, 1861	Oct. 16, 1861	Promoted to Lieutenant-Colonel.
Do.	GRANVILLE A. FRAMBERS	Aug. 11, 1862	Nov. 4, 1862	Promoted to Lieutenant-Colonel.
Do.	R. J. VANAUSDOL	Feb. 25, 1863	March 9, 1863	Resigned March 8, 1864.
Do.	THOMAS M. LEWIS	May 9, 1864	May 9, 1864	Mustered out October 29, 1864.
Surgeon	ABRAM C. MCCHESNEY	Oct. 24, 1861	Nov. 26, 1861	Mustered out October 29, 1864.
Ass't Surgeon	CHARLES F. WILBUR	Nov. 7, "	" 7, "	Resigned June 22, 1862.
Do.	FREDERICK SWINGLEY	June 22, 1862	July 22, 1862	Resigned November 26, 1862.
Do.	S. C. GORDON	Aug. 25, "	Aug. 25, "	Mustered out October 29, 1864.
Do.	NATHANIEL J. BARBER	Feb. 21, 1863	Nov. 10, 1863	Mustered out October 29, 1864.
Chaplain	JAMES SARGENT	Oct. 15, 1861	....	Resigned July 17, 1862.
Do.	JOHN W. CHAFFEN	March 1, 1863	March 4, 1863	Resigned October 13, 1863.
Captain	Robert L. McKinlay	Sept. 12, 1861	Oct. 16, 1861	Resigned May 26, 1862.
Do.	Granville A. Frambers	" 21, "	" 16, "	Promoted to Major.
Do.	R. J. Vanausdol	" 27, "	" 16, "	Promoted to Major.
Do.	Thomas M. Lewis	" 27, "	" 16, "	Promoted to Major.
Do.	Lewis J. Egbert	" 29, "	" 16, "	Resigned February 9, 1863.
Do.	Wm. A. Watkins	" 30, "	" 16, "	Resigned July 11, 1862.
Do.	Robert H. Higgins	Oct. 11, "	" 16, "	Discharged February 29, 1864; restored.
Do.	J. W. Hill	" 15, "	Jan. 9, 1862	Resigned May 10, 1863.
Do.	Charles A. Sheafe	Jan. 26, 1862	May 15, "	Mustered out.
Do.	Orlando J. Hopkins	May 26, "	June 20, "	Revoked.
Do.	John S. Watson	" 26, "	Dec. 31, "	Revoked.
Do.	Frederick R. Kautz	Oct. 9, "	" 22, "	Mustered out October 29, 1864.
Do.	C. F. King	July 11, "	" 31, "	Mustered out October 29, 1864.
Do.	Andrew B. McKee	Aug. 11, "	" 31, "	Mustered out October 29, 1864.
Do.	Marcellus J. W. Holton	" 11, "	May 9, 1863	Revoked.
Do.	Nelson Stevens	Feb. 24, 1863	" 9, "	Mustered out October 29, 1864.
Do.	Elbert M. Sargent	Aug. 14, 1862	Nov. 25, 1862	Mustered out January 28, 1865.
Do.	James S. Riley	May 10, 1863	May 22, 1863	Mustered out October 29, 1864.
Do.	Lowell H. Smith	March 9, 1864	March 9, 1864	Mustered out October 29, 1864.
Do.	Marcellus J. W. Holton	May 9, "	May 9, "	Mustered out October 29, 1864.
Do.	Edward S. Sinks	" 9, "	" 9, "	Mustered out October 29, 1864.
Do.	Wm. A. Bartlow	Feb. 14, 1865	Feb. 14, 1865	Mustered out with regiment.
1st Lieutenant	Orlando J. Hopkins	Sept. 12, 1861	Oct. 16, 1861	Promoted by President.
Do.	Andrew B. McKee	" 21, "	" 16, "	Honorably discharged January 31, 1863.
Do.	C. F. King	" 28, "	" 16, "	Promoted to Captain.
Do.	H. F. Leggett	" 26, "	" 16, "	Resigned April 1, 1862.
Do.	Lowell H. Smith	" 27, "	" 16, "	Promoted to Captain.
Do.	Marcellus J. W. Holton	" 27, "	" 16, "	Promoted to Captain August 11, 1862.
Do.	Wm. H. Lawrence	" 29, "	" 16, "	Resigned December 21, 1863.
Do.	Firman C. Warner	" 30, "	" 16, "	Resigned January 21, 1863.
Do.	James W. Hill	" 30, "	" 16, "	Promoted to Captain.
Do.	Wm. T. Trout	Oct. 15, "	Jan. 9, 1862	
Do.	James R. Semple	Jan. 26, 1862	" 26, "	Resigned January 31, 1862.
Do.	John S. Watson	April 1, "	May 5, "	Promoted to Captain.
Do.	Wm. Johnson	May 26, "	June 20, "	Revoked.
Do.	Edward S. Sinks	Aug. 1, "	Nov. 4, "	Promoted to Captain.
Do.	George P. Tyler	Oct. 9, "	Dec. 22, "	Resigned October 14, 1863.
Do.	James Jennings	May 26, "	" 31, "	Resigned January 21, 1863.
Do.	Clifford Lindsey	Aug. 11, "	" 31, "	Mustered out October 29, 1864.
Do.	Francis F. Kibler	Jan. 11, "	" 31, "	Discharged, expiration of term, Oct. 19, 1864
Do.	Nelson Stevens	Dec. 21, "	Feb. 25, 1863	Promoted to Captain.
Do.	Wm. A. Bartlow	Jan. 10, 1863	March 9, "	Promoted to Captain.
Do.	John O. Connor	Oct. 11, 1861	Oct. 16, 1861	Mustered out October 29, 1864.
Do.	Russell F. Smith	Jan. 21, 1863	March 9, 1863	Commission returned.
Do.	Jesse Ellis	" 31, "	" 9, "	Commission returned.
Do.	Michael Sells	March 1, "	" 9, "	Commission returned.
Do.	Leonidas Molen	Jan. 31, "	" 9, "	Mustered out October 29, 1864.
Do.	Frank H. Wood	Aug. 14, "	....	Killed September 19, 1863.
Do.	Michael Lynch	Dec. 12, 1862	April 16, 1863	Resigned November 4, 1864.
Do.	Edward Perkins	Nov. 1, 1863	Nov. 13, "	Mustered out October 29, 1864.
Do.	Michael Sells	March 9, 1864	March 9, 1864	Mustered out October 29, 1864.
Do.	David A. Bannister	" 9, "	" 9, "	Resigned as 2d Lieutenant Sept. 15, 1864.
Do.	Russell F. Smith	" 9, "	" 9, "	Mustered out October 29, 1864.
Do.	Elisha Hawkins	May 9, "	May 9, "	Mustered out October 29, 1864.
Do.	Wm. McCalgin	" 9, "	" 9, "	Resigned as 2d Lieutenant October 26, 1864.
Do.	John P. Purden	Nov. 29, "	Nov. 29, 1864	Discharged May 27, 1865.
Do.	George W. McElfresh	Feb. 14, 1865	Feb. 14, 1865	Declined to accept.
Do.	Daniel F. Molen	March 18, "	March 18, "	Resigned June 26, 1865.
Do.	George W. McElfresh	June 16, "	June 16, "	Mustered out with regiment as 2d Lieut.
2d Lieutenant	John S. Watson	Sept. 12, 1861	Oct. 16, 1861	Promoted to 1st Lieutenant.
Do.	Wm. Hamilton	" 21, "	" 16, 1861	Resigned March 14, 1862.
Do.	Wm. Johnson	" 27, "	" 16, "	Promoted; resigned July 25, 1862.
Do.	Edward S. Sinks	" 27, "	" 16, "	Promoted to 1st Lieutenant.
Do.	James Jennings	" 29, "	" 16, "	Promoted to 1st Lieutenant.
Do.	Clifford Lindsey	" 30, "	" 16, "	Promoted to 1st Lieutenant.
Do.	Wm. T. Trout	" 30, "	" 16, "	Promoted to 1st Lieutenant.
Do.	Wm. A. Bartlow	Jan. 9, 1862	Jan. 9, 1862	Commission returned.
Do.	Francis F. Kibler	" 26, "	" 26, "	Promoted to 1st Lieutenant.
Do.	Nelson Stevens	March 14, "	April 14, "	Promoted to 1st Lieutenant.
Do.	Oliver P. Elliott	Jan. 9, "	May 5, "	Resigned August 7, 1862.

RANK.	NAME.	DATE OF RANK.	COM. ISSUED.	REMARKS.
2d Lieutenant	Wm. H. Bartlow	April 1, 1862	June 20, 1862	Promoted to 1st Lieutenant.
Do.	Russell F. Smith	May 26, "	Dec. 31, "	Promoted to 1st Lieutenant.
Do.	Jesse Ellis	Aug. 1, "	" 31, "	Killed September 19, 1863.
Do.	Michael Sells	Feb. 1, 1863	Feb. 24, 1863	Promoted to 1st Lieutenant.
Do.	Leonidas Molen	Dec. 21, 1862	" 25, "	Promoted to 1st Lieutenant.
Do.	James S. Riley	Aug. 7, "	March 4, "	Promoted to Captain.
Do.	Elisha Hawkins	Jan. 1, 1863	" 9, "	Promoted to 1st Lieutenant.
Do.	Henderson Smith	" 10, "	" 9, "	Commission returned.
Do.	Richard Cochran	" 1, "	" 9, "	Commission returned.
Do.	Charles M. Grant	" 31, "	" 9, "	Commission returned.
Do.	Wm. McCalgan	March 1, "	" 9, "	Promoted to 1st Lieutenant.
Do.	Edward Perkins	Jan. 31, "	" 11, "	Promoted to 1st Lieutenant.
Do.	David A. Bannister	Aug. 14, 1862	" 11, "	Promoted to 1st Lieutenant.
Do.	John W. Shinn	April 1, 1863	April 3, "	Died June 17, 1864.
Do.	Tobias R. Larkin	May 10, 1862	May 23, "	Honorably discharged March 14, 1864.
Do.	John P. Purden	June 1, "	July 10, "	Promoted to 1st Lieutenant.
Do.	George W. McElfresh	Nov. 29, 1864	Nov. 29, 1864	Mustered out June 28, 1865.
Do.	Daniel F. Molen	" 29, "	" 29, "	Promoted to 1st Lieutenant.
Do.	Robert C. Drake	Feb. 14, 1865	Feb. 14, 1865	Mustered out with regiment.
Do.	Samuel Bolander	June 16, "	June 16, "	Mustered out with regiment.

FIFTY-NINTH OHIO VOLUNTEER INFANTRY.

THIS regiment was organized at Camp Ammen, in Ripley, Ohio, October 1, 1861, and on that day was taken by steamer to Maysville, Kentucky, for the purpose of quelling an anticipated outbreak in that place, caused by the arrest of a number of prominent Rebel sympathizers. After the trouble was over, the regiment went into Camp Kenton, a short distance in the rear of Maysville.

On the 23d the regiment moved from Camp Kenton, with other regiments, under General William Nelson, on a campaign to Eastern Kentucky, passing through Mount Sterling, Hazel Green, and Prestonburg, to Ivy Mountain, where the enemy was met and defeated. Pursuit was made as far as Piketon, where the regiment went into camp. After the lapse of a week it was compelled by lack of rations, to return to Louisa, Kentucky, where it took steamers for Louisville. At that place it joined the forces of General Buell, who was then organizing the Army of the Ohio.

On December 11th the regiment left Louisville, arrived at Columbia, Kentucky, on the 13th, and reported to General Boyle, commanding at that place. It remained here in winter-quarters until February 13, 1862.

On February 25th the regiment joined the main army at Bowling Green, and marched with it to Nashville, Tennessee, which it reached on the 8th of March, going into Camp Andrew Jackson, three miles from the city, on the Murfreesboro' Turnpike. Here it was brigaded with the Fifth Division, General Thomas L. Crittenden commanding. The brigade consisted of the Fifty-Ninth and Nineteenth Ohio, the Ninth and Thirteenth Kentucky, and Bradley's Sixth Ohio Battery.

On the 18th the regiment left Nashville with General Buell's forces for Pittsburg Landing, passing through Columbia, and fording Duck River on the night of the 30th. Savannah, on the Tennessee River, was reached April 6th, at eight o'clock P. M.; at ten o'clock it was placed on board the steamer John J. Roe, and at twelve was in line on the battle-field. April 7th, the second day of the battle, the regiment was engaged with the enemy during the whole day. Sergeant James C. Sargent, Corporal Obed Bishop, privates Daniel W. Kirby and James A. Buchanan were killed, and fifty-three men wounded. Of the wounded, Sergeant Edwin B. Ham, privates David Howell, Joseph G. Harris, Jacob Aultman, and Joseph Hines died from the effects of their wounds.

After the battle of Shiloh the regiment moved with the army on Corinth, and participated in all the skirmishes and severe marches of that approach. May 29th, the day before the evacuation of Corinth, Lieutenant A. B. McKee, of company B, was severely wounded. The Fifty-Ninth Ohio, being in the front line of the National army, was among the first to enter the town; and, in the pursuit, followed the enemy to a point six miles beyond Rienzi. Thence it marched with Buell's forces to Stevenson, Alabama, passing through Iuka, Tuscumbia, Florence, Huntsville, and Athens, crossing the Tennessee River on steamers at General Jackson's old ford, near Florence.

On July 24th the regiment passed through Stevenson and went into camp one mile from Battle Creek, where it remained up to the 20th of August, engaged in watching the movements of General Bragg, who was then preparing to invade Kentucky.

On August 20th the regiment began its march, or race, through Tennessee and Kentucky, for the purpose of checkmating Bragg, who had headed his forces toward Louisville, Kentucky. The Cumberland Mountains were crossed near Tracy City; thence passing through Hillsboro', Manchester, Murfreesboro', Nashville, and thence through Bowling Green and Munfordsville, the regiment reached Louisville on the night of the 25th of September.

At Louisville the whole army rested and recruited for one week, and on the 1st of October resumed the pursuit of the enemy. The regiment on that day marched out the Bardstown Turnpike, and on the 8th of October reached a point three miles from Perryville, while the battle at that place was in progress. The cannonading and musketry were distinctly heard; yet the division was not permitted to re-enforce McCook's hard-pressed corps.

The enemy was pursued, after the battle, up to London, Kentucky, passing through Danville, Mount Vernon, Crab Orchard, and Wild Cat. From London the regiment and army returned to Bowling Green *via* Columbia, Kentucky. Reaching Bowling Green the army was reorganized under its new commander, General W. S. Rosecrans, and shortly thereafter marched into Nashville. At Nashville, on the 1st of December, Colonel James P. Fyffe, of the Fifty-Ninth, was ordered to take command of the Fourteenth Brigade, Fifth Division, and Major G. A. Frambers was placed in command of the regiment.

On December 26th the regiment marched with the Twenty-First Army Corps on the Murfreesboro' Turnpike, on its approach to the battle-field of Stone River. Sharp skirmishing was had with the enemy during the whole day, with some loss. On the 27th it had a heavy skirmish at Lavergne. On the 28th it lay in camp; 29th, it crossed Stewart's Creek and went into bivouac within three miles of Murfreesboro'; on the 30th, the regiment was placed in column of division as a reserve, and remained so all day; 31st, the regiment was sent back on the Nashville Turnpike to recapture from the Rebels a valuable army train. It was then ordered, with its division, to stay, if possible, the surging columns of McCook's army corps, then being driven back to the Nashville Turnpike. This duty was effectually and bravely accomplished, but not without serious loss. Sergeant Wm. P. English, Corporal W. C. Owen, and private A. L. Penn were killed, and forty men wounded, of whom privates Aaron Leach, Benj. F. Slye, Wm. Hutchinson, John Howe, Marcellus South, and Sergeant W. B. King (who had just received his commission as Second-Lieutenant) died.

About the time of this movement private Wm. F. Brown, of company B, while on duty with the advanced skirmish-line, discovered a number of Rebel soldiers hidden in a fissure of the rocks lining the turnpike, and succeeded in capturing, singly, a Lieutenant and twenty-seven men, for which he was recommended by General Rosecrans to the War Department for a medal.

Thursday, January 1, 1863, the regiment moved across Stone River and formed line of battle on the left, and remained in that position the entire day. Friday, 2d, it was placed in line of battle at one o'clock A. M., threw out skirmishers, and remained so until half-past three o'clock P. M., when it participated in the counter-charge against Breckinridge's Rebel corps, driving the Rebels back with great slaughter.

On the 3d the regiment crossed over Stone River but was not engaged. At night, however, there was a fierce fight in the center, the Rebels having attempted to retrieve their misfortunes

BRIDGE AT BRIDGEPORT, ALABAMA.

This was but the prelude to their retreat; for at daylight of the 4th they had disappeared, and Murfreesboro' was occupied by the National army. The regiment went into camp one mile out on the Lebanon Turnpike, from which it moved to a point, on the 19th, about six miles out, to guard the Stone River Ford. It remained at this place until June 24th, the day on which the army under General Rosecrans made its initial movement in the Tullahoma campaign.

On this campaign the regiment marched through Manchester to McMinnville, and remained there from July 10th to September 3d. It then crossed the mountains with its brigade into Sequatchie Valley. Going down that valley to Bridgeport, there crossing the Tennessee River, and then moving up the valley, it rejoined its corps at Squirrel Town Creek, near Chattanooga.

On the 8th of September Chattanooga was evacuated by Bragg's forces, and Crittenden's corps marched into and took possession of the place. Leaving a garrison there, the regiment, with its corps, followed in pursuit, and had some heavy skirmishes with the enemy.

On September 13th, the regiment and brigade made a reconnoissance toward Lafayette, by which the enemy was discovered in force. On the 15th it moved to Crawfish Springs; from thence, on the 18th, it marched to Lee & Gordon's Mills to support General Woods's division. That night, at ten o'clock, the Fifty-Ninth had the honor of opening the battle of Chickamauga.

On September 19th, in the morning, the fight became general, and raged fiercely all day. The Fifty-Ninth Ohio went into the battle at twelve o'clock M., and, after hotly contesting the ground, was compelled to fall back to Mission Ridge, where a new line of battle was formed. Lieutenants Frank H. Woods and Jesse Ellis were killed in this battle; also privates John L. Downing, Alfred H. E. Eckland, John M. Ferre, and Hezekiah L. Laycock. Thirty-five men were wounded.

On the 20th the fighting was continued, the regiment operating on the left, with General Thomas's command. The Rebels had the advantage in numbers, and drove the National forces behind the intrenchments at Chattanooga. At this time the army was reorganized, and the Fifty-Ninth Ohio was placed in the Fourth Corps, General Howard commanding.

The regiment next day was sent out on the Harrison Road to prevent the enemy from crossing the bridge over Chickamauga Creek, where it lost two officers and fifteen men captured.

The National army was then besieged by the Rebel forces, and kept within the limits of Chattanooga until the 25th of November, when the battle of Mission Ridge was fought. Color-bearer Wm. C. Thompson was killed while planting the colors on a Rebel battery. Thirty-three men were wounded.

Immediately after the battle of Chattanooga the regiment was ordered, with others, to Knoxville to relieve General Burnside, where, and in the vicinity of Strawberry Plains, it spent the winter, enduring terrible privations from want of clothing and rations.

On April 7, 1864, the regiment left Powder Spring Gap, East Tennessee, and went into camp at Cleveland, Tennessee. It remained here until May 2d. May 8th it had a fight at Rocky Face Ridge, and lost one man killed and six wounded. It was also engaged at Resaca, Adairsville, Cassville, Dallas (or New Hope Church), Kenesaw, Peachtree Creek, Atlanta, and Jonesboro'. At Dallas Lieutenant-Colonel Frambers, Adjutant M. J. W. Holter, and nine men were captured.

The regiment reached Atlanta September 8th, at which time its three-year term was nearly finished. While at Atlanta it was transferred to the Twenty-Third Corps, and ordered to report to General Milroy at Tullahoma. October 24th orders were received to proceed to Nashville, where the regiment was mustered out of the service, October 31, 1864. It was then sent to Louisville and paid. Thence it was taken to Cincinnati and there finally discharged.

60th REGIMENT OHIO VOLUNTEER INFANTRY.

ROSTER, ONE YEAR'S SERVICE.

RANK.	NAME.	DATE OF RANK.	COM. ISSUED.	REMARKS.
Colonel	WM. H. TRIMBLE	Sept. 28, 1861	March 3, 1862	Resigned November 12, 1862.
Lt. Colonel	NOAH H. HIXON	" 27, "	" 20, "	
Major	JOSEPH K. MARLAY	" 28, "	" 3, "	[No muster-out rolls of one year men and
Surgeon	DAVID NOBLE	" 28, "	" 3, "	nothing to show what became of them.]
Ass't Surgeon	R. A. DWYER	Jan. 9, 1862	" 3, "	Resigned May 7, 1862.
Do.	HENRY T. GREER	May 3, "	May 3, "	
Chaplain	WM. M. MCREYNOLDS	March 21, "	March 24, "	
Captain	John S. Hill	Oct. 24, 1861	Feb. 13, "	
Do.	Philip Rothrock	Nov. 26, "	" 13, "	
Do.	George B. Gardner	Dec. 7, "	" 13, "	
Do.	Robert Harry	" 12, "	" 13, "	
Do.	Milton Cowgill	" 12, "	" 13, "	
Do.	Michael Lynch	Nov. 8, "	March 3, "	
Do.	Wm. S. Irwin	" 21, "	" 3, "	
Do.	Manford Willard	Feb. 25, 1862	" 3, "	
Do.	Richard L. Parker	" 25, "	" 3, "	
Do.	Joshua Gore	" 25, "	" 3, "	
1st Lieutenant	George M. Barrere	Oct. 24, 1861	Feb. 13, "	
Do.	Wm. O. Donaho	Nov. 27, "	" 13, "	
Do.	Robert Stewart	Dec. 7, "	" 13, "	
Do.	Samuel Coleman	" 12, "	" 13, "	
Do.	Obadiah Demise	" 12, "	" 13, "	
Do.	E. J. Blount	Sept. 28, "	March 4, "	
Do.	John M. Barrere	Oct. 1, "	" 4, "	
Do.	Asher Curles	Feb. 8, 1862	" 4, "	
Do.	James W. Vance	" 25, "	" 4, "	Killed at battle of Cross Keys June 8, 1862
Do.	Joseph Richards	" 25, "	" 4, "	Discharged April 12, 1862.
Do.	Wm. C. Blair	" 25, "	" 6, "	
Do.	Thomas M. Platter	Nov. 21, 1861	" 6, "	
Do.	James W. Gamble	April 2, 1862	June 20, "	Declined.
Do.	Finley O. Cummings	" 2, "	July 24, "	
Do.	Edward S. Young	June 8, "	" 24, "	
2d Lieutenant	James W. Gamble	Oct. 24, 1861	Feb. 13, "	
Do.	A. S. Witherington	Nov. 26, "	" 13, "	
Do.	Frank C. Ankeny	Dec. 7, "	" 13, "	Died May 25, 1862.
Do.	George W. Davis	" 12, "	" 13, "	Died.
Do.	Cary T. Pope	" 12, "	" 13, "	
Do.	James P. Elliott	" 21, "	March 4, "	
Do.	Bowen Dunham	Feb. 8, 1862	" 4, "	
Do.	Wm. Pearce	" 21, "	" 4, "	
Do.	Edmond S. Young	" 25, "	" 4, "	
Do.	Levi Monroe Rienhart	" 25, "	" 4, "	
Do.	Jacob Lindsey	Jan. 26, "	" 4, "	
Do.	John J. Myers	June 8, "	July 24, "	Revoked.
Do.	Samuel P. Trumper	May 25, "	" 24, "	

ROSTER, THREE YEARS' SERVICE.

RANK.	NAME.	DATE OF RANK.	COM. ISSUED.	REMARKS.
Lt. Colonel	JAMES N. MCELROY	April 6, 1864	April 13, 1864	Resigned.
Do.	MARTIN P. AVERY	Aug. 16, "	Aug. 16, "	Discharged July 31, 1865.
Major	MARTIN P. AVERY	April 20, "	April 20, "	Promoted to Lieutenant-Colonel.
Do.	WM. L. STEARNS	Aug. 16, "	Aug. 16, "	Resigned April 18, 1865.
Do.	HENRY R. STEVENS	June 26, 1865	June 26, 1865	Mustered out with regiment.
Surgeon	CHAS. E. AMES	April 18, 1864	April 18, 1864	Mustered out with regiment.
Ass't Surgeon	JOHN M. EVANS	" 20, "	" 20, "	Discharged.
Do.	J. F. THOMPSON	March 22, 1865	March 22, 1865	Mustered out with regiment.
Captain	Wm. L. Stearns	" 1, 1864	" 12, 1864	Promoted to Major.
Do.	Elisha D. House	" 2, "	" 21, "	Honorably discharged March 2, 1865.
Do.	Thomas B. Kyle	April 4, "	April 4, "	Resigned September 12, 1864.
Do.	Robert Eddy	" 2, "	" 5, "	Mustered out with regiment. [dria, Va.
Do.	Wm. W. Robbins	" 5, "	" 6, "	On det'd duty by G. O. Soldiers Rest, Alexan-
Do.	A. G. Quintrelle	" 18, "	" 18, "	
Do.	Earl A. Cranston	" 18, "	" 18, "	Resigned June 7, 1864.
Do.	Henry R. Stevens	March 31, "	March 31, "	Promoted to Major.
Do.	Wesley L. Patterson	May 19, "	May 19, "	Disch'd on acc't of physical debility Oct. 19, '64.
Do.	Albert P. Merkel	Nov. 3, "	Nov. 3, "	Mustered out with regiment.
Do.	Norman D. Meacham	" 3, "	" 3, "	Resigned July 3, 1865.
Do.	S. S. Blackford	Dec. 30, "	Dec. 30, "	Honorably discharged March 20, 1865.
Do.	George W. Little	March 18, 1865	March 18, 1865	Declined.
Do.	Phocion R. Way	Dec. 16, 1864	Dec. 16, 1864	Mustered out with regiment.
Do.	John M. Underwood	July 25, 1865	Sept. 4, 1865	Mustered out with regiment as 1st Lieut.
Do.	James Smith	" 25, "	" 4, "	Mustered out with regiment as 1st Lieut.
Do.	Joshua Roof	" 25, "	" 4, "	Mustered out with regiment as 1st Lieut.
Do.	Franklin Paine, jr.	" 25, "	" 4, "	Mustered out with regiment as 1st Lieut.
Do.	Wm. S. Matthews	" 25, "	" 4, "	Mustered out with regiment as 1st Lieut
1st Lieutenant	Norman D. Meacham	Feb. 26, 1864	March 12, 1864	Promoted to Captain.

RANK.	NAME.	DATE OF RANK.	COM. ISSUED.	REMARKS.
1st Lieutenant	George W. Campbell	March 2, 1864	March 2, 1864	Honorab~ discharged November 25, 1864.
Do.	S. S. Blackford	" 31, "	" 31, "	Promoted to Captain.
Do.	Albert P. Merkel	April 2, "	April 5, "	Promoted to Captain.
Do.	John C. Bolen	" 4, "	" 6, "	Honorably discharged November 22, 1864.
Do.	Samuel J. Evans	" 5, "	" 6, "	Killed June 7, 1864.
Do.	Joseph F. Curren	" 13, "	" 13, "	Honorably discharged November 27, 1864.
Do.	George W. Little	" 13, "	" 13, "	Declined promotion.
Do.	Lorenzo D. Bullard	" 18, "	" 18, "	Honorably discharged November 15, 1864.
Do.	John M. Underwood	" 18, "	" 18, "	Promoted to Captain.
Do.	John Long	May 19, "	May 19, "	Resigned July 18, 1864.
Do.	James B. McCormick	July 18, "	July 18, "	Declined; commission returned.
Do.	Henry J. Weiny	Nov. 3, "	Nov. 3, "	Hon. disch'd as 2d Lieut. November 28, 1864.
Do.	James Smith	" 3, "	" 3, "	Promoted to Captain.
Do.	Wm. H. Lawrence	" 3, "	" 3, "	Hon. disch'd as 2d Lieut. November 18, 1864.
Do.	Joshua Roof	" 3, "	" 3, "	Promoted to Captain.
Do.	John D. Halsey	Dec. 30, "	Dec. 30, "	Honorably discharged February 20, 1865
Do.	James B. McKisson	" 30, "	" 30, "	Honorably discharged March 18, 1865.
Do.	Franklin Paine, jr.	" 30, "	" 30, "	Promoted to Captain.
Do.	Isaac Shotwell	" 30, "	" 30, "	Mustered out with regiment.
Do.	Wm. S. Matthews	" 30, "	" 30, "	Promoted to Captain.
Do.	Samuel M. Hudson	" 30, "	" 30, "	On det'ched duty, G. C. M., Washington, D. C.
Do.	Andrew R. Kirshner	" 30, "	" 30, "	
Do.	Willis W. Cox	March 18, 1865	March 18, 1865	Mustered out with regiment.
Do.	Thomas Hall	" 18, "	" 18, "	Mustered out with regiment as 2d Lieut.
Do.	Wm. H. Farrand	July 25, "	Sept. 4, "	Mustered out with regiment as 2d Lieut.
Do.	Edwin Cress	" 25, "	" 4, "	Mustered out with regiment as 2d Lieut.
Do.	Orlando W. Haynes	" 25, "	" 4, "	Mustered out with regiment as 2d Lieut.
Do.	Willis W. Cox	" 25, "	" 4, "	Mustered out with regiment.
Do.	F. Murray Swingley	" 25, "	" 4, "	Mustered out with regiment as Serg't-Major.
2d Lieutenant	Henry J. Weiny	Feb. 5, 1864	March 2, 1864	Promoted to 1st Lieutenant.
Do.	Wm. H. Lawrence	Jan. 16, "	" 12, "	Promoted to 1st Lieutenant.
Do.	James Smith	Feb. 9, "	April 5, "	Promoted to 1st Lieutenant.
Do.	Joshua Roof	March 22, "	March 22, "	Promoted to 1st Lieutenant.
Do.	John D. Halsey	" 31, "	" 31, "	Promoted to 1st Lieutenant.
Do.	Charles E. Austin	April 4, "	April 4, "	Died May 28, 1864.
Do.	James B. McKisson	" 5, "	" 6, "	Promoted to 1st Lieutenant.
Do.	Wm. H. Farrand	March 18, 1865	March 18, 1865	Promoted to 1st Lieutenant.
Do.	Edwin Cress	" 18, "	" 18, "	Promoted to 1st Lieutenant.
Do.	Orlando W. Haynes	" 18, "	" 18, "	Promoted to 1st Lieutenant.
Do.	Wm. Miller	July 25, "	Sept. 4, "	Mustered out with regiment as 1st Sergeant.
Do.	Thomas Hall	" 25, "	" 4, "	Promoted to 1st Lieutenant.
Do.	G. B. Davis	" 25, "	" 4, "	Mustered out with regiment as 1st Sergeant.
Do.	Ira W. Wallace	" 25, "	" 4, "	Mustered out with regiment as 1st Sergeant.
Do.	Willis W. Cox	Dec. 16, 1864	Dec. 16, 1864	Promoted to 1st Lieutenant.
Do.	Francis Bowman	July 25, 1865	Sept. 4, 1865	Mustered out with regiment as 1st Sergeant.
Do.	H. F. Hunt	" 25, "	" 4, "	Mustered out with regiment as 1st Sergeant.
Do.	Fernando Gitchell	" 25, "	" 4, "	Mustered out with regiment as 1st Sergeant.
Do.	George E. Kountz	" 25, "	" 4, "	Mustered out with regiment as 1st Sergeant.
Do.	Levi Strader	" 25, "	" 4, "	Mustered out with regiment as 1st Sergeant.
Do.	Joseph E. Lewis	" 28, "	" 4, "	Mustered out with regiment as 1st Sergeant.

SIXTIETH OHIO VOLUNTEER INFANTRY.

ONE-YEAR REGIMENT.

THERE were two regiments of this number—the first raised for a term of one year, and the second for three years. The one now under consideration is that raised for the one-year term. It was recruited in Highland, Fayette, Ross, Clark, Brown, Clermont, Adams, Gallia, and Noble Counties, by Colonel William Trimble, and was intended specially for the defense of the border counties of Ohio.

The regiment being ready for the field was ordered, on the 8th of February, 1862, to Gallipolis, to guard military stores, and during the three months it was on duty at this point paid such special attention to drill and discipline as to eminently fit it for field-service. On the 25th of February, 1862, the regiment was fully mustered into the United States service, and sent to the field on the 27th of April, 1862. It joined General Fremont's forces at New Creek, in Western Virginia, about that time.

The Sixtieth was placed in a brigade with the Eighth Virginia Infantry, and with Fremont's forces, marched to McDowell, to the relief of Schenck's and Milroy's troops, then threatened by the enemy at that point. The march was a forced one, and from the indiscretion of the commanding-officer of the brigade, Colonel Cluseret, a French officer, many men of the Sixtieth, and other regiments, were totally disabled from further service for months. The enemy was met, after many skirmishes, near Strasburg, and a brisk engagement ensued. In this affair the Sixtieth Ohio behaved like veterans and won reputation.

The march up the Shenandoah Valley, in pursuit of Jackson, was one of the most terrible ever endured by men, yet the brave soldiers of the Sixtieth, and other regiments, bore it without a murmur. At Port Republic the enemy was again overtaken and engaged. The Sixtieth Ohio once more displayed its good discipline and fine fighting qualities. Ashby's Rebel cavalry figured in this battle, and was almost directly opposed by the Sixtieth Ohio. Ashby was killed, confusion ensued in the Rebel ranks, and in a few minutes all signs of the enemy disappeared.

The pursuit was continued, with more or less skirmishing, and occasionally a determined stand by the enemy. At Cross Keys the Rebel General Stonewall Jackson made overtures for battle. He was at once resolutely met by General Fremont's army, and after a fierce engagement, lasting some hours, both parties withdrew. The battle commenced at an early hour in the morning and lasted until four o'clock P. M. It was a well-contested affair, in which both the National and Rebel troops displayed the most determined bravery. The Sixtieth Ohio was highly complimented on the field for its firmness and coolness under fire. Its loss in men killed and wounded was severe.

Early on the morning of the 9th of June the Sixtieth and Eighth Virginia, forming an extended skirmish-line, swept over the battle-field of the previous day, but without encountering the enemy. He had fled during the night, and escaped across the Shenandoah River near Port Republic, burning the bridge after him. Shield's forces had failed to intercept him. Colonel Carroll's brigade, of Shield's division, did get into position on the opposite side of the river, but after making a gallant fight was overpowered and driven off.

The National forces did not pursue Jackson's Rebel army. The morning of the 12th of June found Fremont's army at Mount Jackson, it having fallen back to that position to prevent the Rebel army from getting into its rear and endangering its communications. Here, for the first time during the campaign, the officers and men of the Sixtieth slept in tents. At this point the Sixtieth Ohio and Eighth Virginia parted, the Thirty-Second Ohio taking the place of the Eighth Virginia. Both of the last-named regiments were assigned to General Piatt's brigade, and made part of General Schenck's division.

The National army moved from Mount Jackson on the 19th of June, and reached Strasburg on the 22d. The illness of General Piatt placed Colonel Trimble, of the Sixtieth, in command of the brigade. Leaving General Milroy's brigade at Strasburg, General Fremont moved to Middletown on the 24th, at which point the army, with the exception of Piatt's brigade, remained until July 8th. At this point General Fremont and staff left the army, leaving it in command of General Schenck until General Sigel, the successor of Fremont, should report.

The National forces moved from Middletown on the 8th of July, by Front Royal, to join General Pope, leaving a large amount of military stores in and around Middletown, guarded by a force of infantry, cavalry, and artillery. While lying at this place news was received that the Rebel General Jackson had again penetrated into the Shenandoah Valley with five thousand cavalry, and was menacing Winchester. Colonel Trimble, of the Sixtieth, was ordered to take a force from his regiment, and assume command on reaching other National forces near Strasburg, the point where Jackson was maneuvering. Two hundred and fifty volunteers were selected from the Sixtieth, many of the line-officers serving as privates. Thirty mule-teams were taken with the expedition for the purpose of expediting the movement and transporting supplies. Middletown was reached before daylight. The enemy still threatening this point all the Government stores were removed to Front Royal, and the National forces marched into Winchester.

Winchester was held until the night of the 2d of September, when it was evacuated by order of the War Department; the defeat of the Army of the Potomac, under General Pope, rendering the move necessary. The Sixtieth Ohio led the column on the night march from Winchester, reaching Harper's Ferry on the 3d of September. General White was ordered by Major-General Wool to Martinsburg, and his Winchester command was added to that of Colonel Miles at Harper's Ferry. Then came the disaster to the National forces at Harper's Ferry. It would be useless to go into a detailed statement of that affair. The Sixtieth Ohio, under command of Colonel Trimble, resisted successfully the attack of General A. P. Hill's Rebel division on the left flank, in an infantry and artillery engagement lasting from three o'clock P. M. on Sunday, September 14th until after dark. It endured, with the balance of Colonel Trimble's command, on the morning of the 15th, till near nine o'clock, the concentrated fire of over fifty guns, which enfiladed the position, making a dangerous cross-fire over every portion of the command. The anxiety of the Rebels to silence Rigby's battery, supported on the right by the Sixtieth, caused a continuous front, flank, and rear fire upon this point. The Sixtieth Ohio remained firm under this severe fire, protected only by a slight breastwork thrown up hastily on Sunday morning. The enemy, though constantly feeling for the regiment, failed to get its range until near the time of surrender. If the men had risen to their feet they would have been swept from the ground. The Adjutant of the regiment lost his hand by a solid shot early in the engagement. Twelve privates were killed and wounded. None felt more keenly the mortification of surrender than the men of the Sixtieth Ohio.

After the surrender it marched in the same brigade-organization to Annapolis. General Tyler being placed in command of the paroled troops, re-organized them, with several regiments, including the Sixtieth and some artillery companies, under Colonel Trimble. The Colonel was, shortly after this, badly crippled by being thrown from his horse, and did not join the regiment before its honorable discharge by the Secretary of War, October 10, 1862, at Camp Douglas, Chicago.

Almost immediately after the discharge of the regiment the great majority of its members re-enlisted into other organizations for three years, and served gallantly until the close of the war, many of them laying down their lives in the cause of their country.

The failure, by General White, to provide in the capitulation for the free colored servants in the command came near proving disastrous to them. Colonel Trimble's anxiety upon this subject, and a sense of duty to those whose freedom was imperiled by the surrender, caused him to bring the subject to the attention of General Jackson, on his entering the lines with his staff. He was told no provision had been made for them. The appeal in their behalf was met in a generous manner. General Jackson informed him that General Hill would remain in command at Harper's Ferry, and would have control of such questions; but added: "If you have any difficulty with General Hill you can appeal to me." Thanking him, and instructing the servants to keep in close quarters with the regiment, and the officers to protect them till his return, he rode to Harper's Ferry and called on General Hill at his head-quarters. Waiting patiently till D'Utassy finished discussing a claim for five surplus horses, which General Hill very properly refused to allow, he told the General he, too, had lost horses, but had called to present a matter of much more importance. He had learned from General Jackson that no provision had been made in the capitulation for the free colored servants. There was a number in his regiment who had accompanied it from Ohio, and perhaps others in the command. General Jackson had referred the matter to him. General Hill said: "As great numbers had fled from the surrounding country to Harper's Ferry, it would be difficult to decide who was free and who was not; he would, therefore, leave it to the Colonel's honor, and give him passes for whoever he said was free." Thanking the General for his courtesy and confidence, he returned to camp to communicate the glad tidings to men, whose fears for their own safety had been increased by seeing hundreds of men, women, and children, bond and free, driven past; their bowed heads and sad countenances telling the tale of their disappointed hopes. When marching out next day he was detained at General Hill's head-quarters in getting the passes for thirteen colored men connected with the Sixtieth Ohio, by another horse-claim of D'Utassy. On reaching the river he found the regiment halted, a Rebel guard, with crossed bayonets, in front, several countrymen, and a Rebel Major on horseback near the lines, and others on foot, dragging the colored boys from their positions near the officers. He asked what all this meant. Was told in fierce tones, "he was a d——d nigger thief, stealing their slaves, and his command should n't pass till every d——d nigger was taken out." He told them they were free—he had passes for them from General Hill. "They swore they would n't regard the order of General Hill in such case." A citizen said: "General Hill's pass ought to be sufficient." The Rebel Major told him to "shut his d——d mouth and attend to his own business." The moment for action had come. The quick, sharp, decisive words: "*My men are unarmed—I am not. I'll sell my life for these free boys. Unhand them! Guards, give way! Regiment, march!*" unloosed the grasp of these man-stealers, sent the guards from the front, and the regiment forward over the pontoon-bridge with quick and steady tread. When safe on the Maryland side of the Potomac these men, some of whom had families in Ohio, felt like a new birth of freedom had been vouchsafed them, and every officer and soldier sympathized with them in the joy of their deliverance.

The surrender of Harper's Ferry was investigated by an able Military Commission, of which Major-General D. Hunter was President. It was very severe in some of its findings, but it reported that no blame attached to Colonel Trimble.

SIXTIETH OHIO VOLUNTEER INFANTRY.

THREE YEARS' ORGANIZATION.

THIS regiment was organized early in the spring of 1864, under command of Lieutenant-Colonel J. N. McElroy. Upon the completion of six companies it was ordered to the field. Two companies of Independent Sh' rp-shooters, rendezvousing at Camp Taylor, near Cleveland, were assigned to duty with the battalion; and the command reported to Major-General Burnside, commanding the Ninth Army Corps, at Alexandria, Virginia, 24th of April, 1864, and was assigned to the Second Brigade, Third Division.

The Sixtieth marched with the corps on the 27th of April, to join the Army of the Potomac, on the Rapidan. On the 5th of May it crossed that stream, and took part in the actions in the Wilderness. On the 9th of May the battalion led the advance of a column of two divisions of the Ninth Corps, in the attack at Mary's Bridge, Nye River, and was specially distinguished in orders by the General commanding, for the gallantry with which it crossed the stream and carried the position of the enemy. In all the actions about Spottsylvania in which the corps was engaged, the Sixtieth took an honorable part, suffering very much in that series of engagements. It would be a work of supererogation to detail in the history of this regiment the movements of an army already so well known.

It is sufficient to say that this regiment took an honorable part in the engagements at the North Anna, Tolopotomoy, Bethesda Church, 2d and 3d of June; at Cold Harbor until the 12th of June, and the siege of Petersburg, and the actions about Richmond, which brought the Rebel army of Northern Virginia to pass under the Caudine Forks, on the 9th of April, 1865, and the Army of the Potomac turned its face homeward.

Two additional companies joined the regiment—one at Cold Harbor in June, the other in January before Petersburg. It, however, never became a maximum regiment, as its losses far exceeded the additions. The muster-out rolls, in the office of the Adjutant-General of Ohio, show the casualties to be *five hundred and five*, with but *seventeen* missing.

Few regiments have had so eventful and brilliant a career in less than one year's active service. The Sixtieth was mustered out of service on the 25th of July, 1865.

61st REGIMENT OHIO VOLUNTEER INFANTRY.

ROSTER, THREE YEARS' SERVICE.

RANK.	NAME.	DATE OF RANK.	COM. ISSUED.	REMARKS.
Colonel	NEWTON SCHLEICH	April 1, 1862	May 26, 1862	Resigned September 23, 1862
Do.	S. J. McGROARTY	Sept. 23, "	Dec. 2, "	Transferred to 82d O. V. I.
Lt. Colonel	STEPHEN J. McGROARTY	April 23, "	May 26, "	Promoted to Colonel.
Do.	WM. H. H. BROWN	Sept. 23, "	Dec. 2, "	Died.
Major	WM. H. H. BROWN	April 23, "	May 26, "	Promoted to Lieutenant-Colonel Sept. 23, '62
Do.	DAVID C. BECKET	Sept. 23, "	Dec. 2, "	Died from wounds, June 22,'64. (March 13,'65.
Surgeon	ENOCH PEARCE	Oct. 15, 1861	May 26, "	App. Lieut. Colonel for meritorious services,
Do.	H. K. SPOONER	Nov. 14, 1863	Nov. 14, 1863	Mustered out.
Ass't Surgeon	WM. S. MOORE	Oct. 16, 1861	May 26, 1862	Killed at Gettysburg July 3, 1863.
Do.	J. J. CONLAN	Aug. 15, 1862	Aug. 15, "	Honorably discharged Sept. 14, 1864.
Do.	L. P. CULVER	Nov. 10, 1863	Nov. 10, 1863	Transferred to 82d O. V. I.
Chaplain	E. P. CORCORAN	Dec. 14, 1861	May 12, 1862	Mustered out.
Captain	Frederick S. Wallace	April 23, 1862	" 26, "	Mustered out with regiment.
Do.	Daniel J. Schleich	" 23, "	" 26, "	Resigned October 6, 1862.
Do.	Daniel W. Crouse	" 23, "	" 26, "	Resigned October 9, 1862.
Do.	John D. Bothwell	" 23, "	" 26, "	Resigned December 23, 1863.
Do.	Charles A. Leiter	" 23, "	" 26, "	Resigned October 9, 1862.
Do.	David C. Becket	" 23, "	" 26, "	Promoted to Major.
Do.	Silas J. McMillen	" 23, "	" 26, "	Discharged July 30, 1862.
Do.	John Garrett	" 23, "	" 26, "	Mustered out.
Do.	Wm. H. McGroarty	" 23, "	" 26, "	Died November 17, 1863.
Do.	Joseph McCutcheon	" 23, "	" 26, "	Resigned January 11, 1863.
Do.	Henry R. Bending	July 30, "	Aug. 26, "	Transferred to 82d O. V. I.
Do.	James M. Reynolds	Oct. 6, "	Nov. 28, "	Died July 4, 1863.
Do.	James Armstrong	" 9, "	Dec. 31, "	Commission returned.
Do.	John M. Fallis	Sept. 23, "	" 31, "	Resigned January 25, 1863.
Do.	Leonidas J. Jewett	Jan. 11, 1863	Feb. 1, 1863	Honorably discharged March 17, 1865.
Do.	Edward H. Newcomb	Sept. 23, 1862	" 5, "	Killed.
Do.	Peter Duffey	April 29, 1864	April 29, 1864	Mustered out.
Do.	John Elbert	" 29, "	" 29, "	Mustered out.
Do.	Anton Grodzicki	" 29, "	" 29, "	Transferred to 82d O. V. I.
Do.	Jacob F. Meader, jr.	" 29, "	" 29, "	Mustered out.
Do.	Robert Patterson	" 29, "	" 29, "	Transferred to 82d O. V. I.
1st Lieutenant	Henry R. Bending	" 21, 1862	May 26, 1862	Promoted to Captain.
Do.	James M. Reynolds	" 21, "	" 26, "	Promoted to Captain.
Do.	Alonzo Miller	" 21, "	" 26, "	Discharged July 30, 1862.
Do.	James Armstrong	" 21, "	" 26, "	Resigned December 23, 1863.
Do.	John M. Fallis	" 21, "	" 26, "	Promoted to Captain.
Do.	Charles A. Dietrick	" 21, "	" 26, "	Appointed Captain by Pres. Oct. 17, 1863.
Do.	Philip F. Theis	" 21, "	" 26, "	Resigned September 19, 1862.
Do.	David Rankin	" 21, "	" 26, "	Resigned September 21, 1862.
Do.	Stephen Hayes	" 21, "	" 26, "	Resigned February 3, 1863.
Do.	Samuel B. Givens	" 21, "	" 26, "	Resigned September 14, 1862.
Do.	George J. Wygum	Oct. 2, 1861	" 26, "	Honorably discharged October 21, 1863.
Do.	Leonidas J. Jewett	" 24, "	" 26, "	Promoted to Captain.
Do.	George J. Leininger	July 30, 1862	Aug. 26, "	Resigned September 21, 1862.
Do.	Milton M. Junkin	" 30, "	" 26, "	Resigned October 6, 1862.
Do.	Wm. Kirkwood	Oct. 6, "	Nov. 10, "	
Do.	John L. Young	Sept. 14, "	Dec. 2, "	Mustered out.
Do.	Peter Duffey	" 19, "	" 2, "	Promoted to Captain.
Do.	Rufus Aurand	" 21, "	" 2, "	Resigned February 10, 1863.
Do.	John Elbert	" 21, "	" 2, "	Promoted to Captain.
Do.	Anton Grodzicki	Oct. 17, "	" 31, "	Promoted to Captain.
Do.	Edward Brent	" 6, "	" 31, "	Honorably discharged September 14, 1863.
Do.	Jacob F. Meader, jr.	" 9, "	" 31, "	Promoted to Captain.
Do.	Samuel Mottinger	Sept. 23, "	Jan. 25, 1863	Honorably discharged August 25, 1863.
Do.	Robert Patterson	Jan. 11, 1863	Feb. 5, "	Promoted to Captain.
Do.	Daniel Williams	Feb. 3, "	Jan. 10, "	Died.
Do.	Theodore J. Palmer	" 10, "	" 29, "	Resigned April 15, 1864.
Do.	Charles Tinckler	April 29, 1864	April 29, 1864	Transferred to 82d O. V. I.
Do.	John Bell	" 29, "	" 29, "	Honorably discharged December 15, 1864.
Do.	L. F. Rankin	" 29, "	" 29, "	Resigned as 2d Lieutenant September 1, 1864.
Do.	T. Frampton	" 29, "	" 29, "	Mustered out.
Do.	Wm. A. Smith	" 29, "	" 29, "	Mustered out.
Do.	Joseph R. Mell	" 29, "	" 29, "	Transferred to 82d O. V. I.
Do.	John P. Arbuckle	" 29, "	" 29, "	Resigned November 2, 1864.
Do.	Robert S. McMains	May 25, "	May 25, "	Killed.
Do.	John Thorp	" 25, "	" 25, "	Mustered out.
2d Lieutenant	George J. Leininger	April 23, 1862	" 26, 1862	Promoted to 1st Lieutenant.
Do.	John C. Edmonson	" 23, "	" 26, "	Discharged July 30, 1862.
Do.	John Hess	" 23, "	" 26, "	Discharged July 30, 1862.
Do.	Charles W. Reeves	" 23, "	" 26, "	Resigned September 14, 1862.
Do.	James H. Bird	" 23, "	" 26, "	Resigned September 21, 1862.
Do.	Henry Riff	" 23, "	" 26, "	Honorably discharged October 15, 1862.
Do.	Wm. Meyer	" 23, "	" 26, "	Resigned July 27, 1862.
Do.	Milton M. Junkin	" 23, "	" 26, "	Promoted to 1st Lieutenant.
Do.	John L. Young	" 23, "	" 26, "	Promoted to 1st Lieutenant.
Do.	John P. McDougal	" 23, "	" 26, "	Resigned October 2, 1862.
Do.	Anton Grodzicki	July 30, "	Aug. 30, "	Promoted to 1st Lieutenant.
Do.	Edward R. Hay	" 30, "	" 30, "	Resigned October 2, 1862.
Do.	Creed Ritchie	" 30, "	" 30, "	Resigned October 2, 1862.
Do.	Edward Brent	" 27, "	Dec. 2, "	Promoted to 1st Lieutenant.
Do.	Jacob F. Meader, jr.	Oct. 2, "	Nov. 10, "	Promoted to 1st Lieutenant.
Do.	Samuel Mottinger	Sept. 21, "	Jan. 20, 1863	Promoted to 1st Lieutenant.
Do.	Isaiah Grafton	July 30, "	Dec. 2, 1862	Mustered out April 5, 1865.

RANK.	NAME.	DATE OF RANK.	COM. ISSUED.	REMARKS.
2d Lieutenant	Charles Tinckler	Oct. 15, 1862	Dec. 2, 1862	Promoted to 1st Lieutenant.
Do.	John Bell	Sept. 14, "	" 2, "	Promoted to 1st Lieutenant.
Do.	Magnus W. Stribling	Oct. 9, "	" 31, "	Promoted to 1st Lieutenant.
Do.	Daniel W. Williams	Sept. 14, "	Jan. 20, 1863	Killed July 3, 1863.
Do.	D. O. Sullivan	Oct. 17, "	" 20, "	Resigned November 2, 1862.
Do.	L. F. Raukin	" 6, "	Feb. 5, "	Promoted to 1st Lieutenant.
Do.	T. Frampton	" 9, "	" 5, "	Promoted to 1st Lieutenant.
Do.	Wm. A. Smith	" 9, "	" 5, "	Promoted to 1st Lieutenant.
Do.	Joseph R. Mell	Jan. 1, 1863	April 9, "	Promoted to 1st Lieutenant.
Do.	John P. Arbuckle	Aug. 5, "	Aug. 5, "	Promoted to 1st Lieutenant.
Do.	Robert S. McMains	" 5, "	" 5, "	Promoted to 1st Lieutenant.
Do.	John Thorp	May 9, 1864	May 9, 1864	Promoted to 1st Lieutenant.

SIXTY-FIRST OHIO VOLUNTEER INFANTRY.

THIS regiment was made up of citizens from almost every county in the State. It was organized at Camp Chase, April 23, 1862, and left that camp for the field in Western Virginia, May 27, 1862. It joined Major-General Fremont's army, June 23d, at Strasburg, and marched with it across the Blue Ridge to Sperryville, Virginia. At this point General Fremont was relieved and succeeded by Major-General Pope. From Sperryville the regiment, with its brigade and division, marched to the vicinity of Cedar Mountain, but did not reach the field in time to participate in the battle at that point. It then retreated to the Rappahannock River, and at Freeman's Ford, on that river, had its first fight with the enemy—a part of Longstreet's corps.

On August 23d and 24th it had another fight with Longstreet's corps at Sulphur Springs, Virginia, in which it lost some men. On the 25th it had a brisk skirmish at Waterloo Bridge. On the same night it fell back to Warrenton, and remained there until the 27th. From Warrenton it fell back with the National army, and took part in the second Bull Run battle, and covered the retreat of the National forces on the Centerville Turnpike toward Washington. In the battle at Bull Run the regiment lost twenty-five men killed and wounded.

On September 2d the regiment was engaged in a skirmish with the enemy at Fairfax C. H., or Chantilly. It again fell back to the Chain Bridge, and lay between Washington and Centerville until the 2d of October, 1862. It formed part of the grand reserve force for the protection of Washington, under command of General Sigel.

On November 1st the Sixty-First moved through Thoroughfare Gap to the Rappahannock and to Warrenton; then returned to Centerville. On December 10th it started, under orders, for Fredericksburg, but arrived too late to participate in Burnside's first attack on that place. From Falmouth it fell back to Aquia Creek and went into winter-quarters.

The regiment marched to Hartwood Church January 20, 1863, and built winter-quarters; but, after sleeping in them only one night, was ordered to abandon them and march to Stafford C. H. At that place it again speculated in winter-quarters, and retained them till April 27, 1863.

The Sixty-First then crossed the Rappahannock at Kelly's Ford, and moved to the rear of the Rebel position at Fredericksburg, where it formed a connection with that portion of the National army which crossed the Rappahannock at United States Ford. It took position on the right preparatory to the battle of Chancellorsville, which was opened at six o'clock in the evening of May 2d. The Sixty-First was engaged on the 2d, 3d, 4th, and 5th. It lost four officers wounded, besides a large number of men wounded, and five killed.

On May 6th the regiment fell back to its old quarters at Stafford C. H., and remained there until June 12th. It then joined in the pursuit of Lee's Rebel army, which was at that time making its way into Pennsylvania. At Gettysburg, on the 1st of July, it opened the battle, being thrown out as skirmishers, and was so roughly handled as to be compelled to fall back to Cemetery Hill. In this action the regiment suffered severely, losing heavily in killed, wounded, and prisoners. Captain Bending and Lieutenant Mell were captured and kept in Rebel prisons until the close of the war.

The Sixty-First Ohio held its position on Cemetery Hill until the close of the fight, and then joined in the pursuit of the Rebel army. On July 12th it had a skirmish with the Rebel rear-guard near Hagerstown, Maryland.

From July 26th to September 25th the regiment guarded the Orange and Alexandria Railroad from incursions of the Rebel cavalry. On the 26th of September it was transported to the Army of the Cumberland, along with the Twelfth Corps, reaching Bridgeport, Alabama, on the 1st of October.

On October 27th it started for Chattanooga to aid in opening communications, by way of the Tennessee River, with that beleaguered city. On the night of the 28th it was engaged in a fierce fight at Wauhatchie Valley, defeating and driving the Rebels across Lookout Creek. In this fight Captain William McGroarty and two men were killed and a number wounded.

On November 22d the Sixty-First crossed the Tennessee River and marched to Chattanooga, where it joined the main army. On the 23d, 24th, and 25th of November the regiment was engaged in the Mission Ridge fight, moving round on the third day to the extreme left of the National lines, to prevent a flanking movement on the part of the enemy.

On November 29th it marched with the National forces to the relief of Knoxville. Reaching a point within ten miles of Knoxville, it received orders to return to Chattanooga. The regiment stopped and went into winter-quarters in Wauhatchie Valley, but did not remain at this point over two weeks. It then returned to Bridgeport, Tennessee, and there went into winter-quarters.

In the month of March, 1864, the Sixty-First re-enlisted, and was ordered to Ohio on its veteran furlough of thirty days.

On April 28, 1864, the regiment re-assembled at Camp Dennison, Ohio, and on the same day started for the front, reaching Chattanooga on the 5th of May. It joined the main forces of the National army at Rocky Face Ridge on the 7th. This was the commencement of the Atlanta campaign. In this campaign the Sixty-First was brigaded with the Third Brigade, First Division, of the Twentieth Corps, under Major-General Hooker. Marching from Rocky Face Ridge through Snake Creek Gap to the vicinity of Resaca, the regiment, on the 14th of May, was ordered to aid General Howard in preventing a flank movement of the enemy on his left. On the evening of that day the Sixty-First had an engagement with the enemy, in which it drove them and rescued the Fifth Indiana Battery, which had been abandoned by its support. Several men were wounded in this affair.

On Sunday, May 15th, the regiment participated in the bloody action at Resaca, losing several men. The retreating Rebels were pursued for two or three days. On May 19th it caught up with the enemy and again drove them about two miles, to Cassville, Georgia. The regiment then went into camp and remained until the 23d of May. On that day it crossed the Etowah River and resumed the march. On the 25th the army again found the enemy near Dallas, Georgia. At this point the Sixty-First, then occupying the extreme rear of the First Division, was ordered to the front of the division and deployed as skirmishers. While engaged in this duty the regiment lost six men killed and seventeen wounded.

On May 28th the regiment was ordered to return to Kingston to guard an ammunition-train, and did not again reach the main army until the 31st of May. On June 1st it moved around to the left of the Fourth Corps, which position it retained until the 2d of June. During this time it was frequently engaged with the enemy.

On the 3d the regiment moved further to the left and skirmished with the enemy. These flanking movements were continued up to the 15th of June, when the regiment had reached the vicinity of Lost Mountain. On the morning of the 16th it had five men wounded while lying behind temporary breastworks.

On June 17th the enemy was driven and skirmished with, and on the 19th and 21st the regiment reached and moved around the base of Kenesaw Mountain. On June 22d it moved up still further and built works at Culp's Farm. While building these works the enemy made a dash on the National lines, and for a few minutes had things all their own way, but the troops rallied and drove them back. In this affair the Major was killed, and one officer and five men wounded. While this fight was in progress a curious incident occurred. Colonel McGroarty was ordered to advance his regiment to a certain point, but in executing the order he placed it far beyond the line intended, and in the dark became almost isolated from his brigade. An attempt was made by a Rebel regiment to capture them; but in moving through the dense woods in the dark the men of the Rebel regiment were detached from their officers, and, becoming alarmed, attempted to hide themselves in the thickets. The Sixty-First, in falling back to its proper line, stumbled across these fellows and captured a large number of them. Colonel McGroarty, with his own hands, brought in seventeen of the scared Rebels.

The Chattahoochie River was crossed at four o'clock in the afternoon of the 17th of June and the regiment went into camp on its banks. June 18th and 19th were consumed in marching to Peachtree Creek. On July 20th the regiment crossed Peachtree Creek and skirmished with the enemy until four o'clock in the afternoon, when the Rebels made a desperate attempt to drive the National forces back across the Chattahoochie. This fight was one of the most desperate of the war. At one time the Rebels were in the full tide of success, but the Twentieth Corps, under Major-General Hooker, stood firm and drove them back to their main works.

In the battle of Peachtree Creek five officers were wounded—one fatally. Over seventy men were wounded, and eighteen or twenty killed.

On July 27th the regiment and corps were sent back to the Chattahoochie to guard the bridge. The Sixty-First remained in the rear till the 5th of August. Atlanta having been captured the corps moved up and went into camp on the east side of the city.

The regiment lay at Atlanta until the 15th of November, when it started with General Sherman's army on its "march to the sea." In this great march the regiment had but one skirmish with the enemy—at Sandersonville, Georgia.

While lying at Savannah the Sixty-First was detached from its brigade and assigned to a Provisional Brigade, on duty in the city. About the middle of January, 1865, it moved with the Second Brigade of the Twentieth Corps, under General Geary, to Sister's Ferry, on the Savannah River. Crossing the river, after a week's detention, it marched to the vicinity of Robertsville, South Carolina, and there joined its proper command.

Aside from hard marches through the swamps of South Carolina nothing of interest occurred until Bentonville was reached. At this point the last real battle of the march was fought. The Sixty-First Ohio performed its part in this battle, and lost some men wounded and captured.

Marching with the army the regiment reached Goldsboro', North Carolina, and there went into camp. Here the Sixty-First was consolidated with the Eighty-Second Ohio, the combined regiment taking the name of the latter-named organization.

This act blotted from the rolls of the army the name of the Sixty-First Ohio, but its deeds remain on record. It was always a reliable regiment, and was ever found where duty called it. Its losses by the casualties of the field were so numerous that at the close of its service a little band of only about sixty men and officers remained to answer to its last roll-call.

The consolidated regiment, now the Eighty-Second Ohio, joined in the march through the Rebel capital to Washington City, where it participated in the grand review, and after a slight detention was sent home to Columbus, and there mustered out of the service about the 1st of September, 1865.

62d REGIMENT OHIO VOLUNTEER INFANTRY.

ROSTER, THREE YEARS' SERVICE.

RANK.	NAME.	DATE OF RANK.	COM. ISSUED.	REMARKS.
Colonel	FRANCIS B. POND	Oct. 31, 1862	Jan. 20, 1862	Resigned November 5, 1864.
Do.	HENRY R. WEST	June 16, 1865	June 16, 1865	Transferred to 67th O. V. I. as Lieut. Col.
Lt. Colonel	FRANCIS B. POND	Sept. 28, 1861	Jan. 20, 1862	Promoted to Colonel.
Do.	CLEMENS F. STEELE	Oct. 31, "	" 20, "	Honorably discharged October 24, 1863.
Do.	SAMUEL B. TAYLOR	March 23, 1864	March 23, 1864	Died of wounds.
Do.	HENRY R. WEST	Nov. 18, "	Nov. 18, "	Promoted to Colonel.
Do.	THOMAS J. PLATT	June 16, 1865	June 16, 1865	Transferred to 67th O. V. I. as Major.
Major	CLEMENS F. STEELE	Sept. 28, 1861	Jan. 20, 1862	Promoted to Lieutenant-Colonel.
Do.	DETARFIELD DUBOIS	Oct. 31, "	" 20, "	Resigned December 16, 1862.
Do.	WM. EDWARDS	Dec. 16, 1862	May 14, 1863	Killed July 31, 1863.
Do.	SAMUEL B. TAYLOR	Aug. 1, 1863	Sept. 4, "	Promoted to Lieutenant-Colonel.
Do.	FRANCIS M. KAHLER	March 23, 1864	March 23, 1864	Mustered out October 16, 1864.
Do.	THOMAS J. PLATT	Dec. 9, "	Dec. 9, "	Promoted to Lieutenant-Colonel.
Do.	JOHN C. EDWARDS	June 16, 1865	June 16, 1865	Transferred to 67th O. V. I. as Captain.
Surgeon	CHARLES H. HOOD	Oct. 28, 1861	Jan. 20, 1862	Resigned January 27, 1863.
Do.	AUGUSTUS C. BARLOW	March 10, 1863	March 10, 1863	Mustered out by consolidat'n with 67th O.V.I
Ass't Surgeon	THOMAS J. HAYNES	Nov. 25, 1861	Jan. 20, 1862	Resigned June 13, 1862.
Do.	WM. J. WOLFLEY	Aug. 26, 1862	Aug. 27, "	Honorably discharged May 30, 1864.
Do.	JOHN TRUMAN	" 27, "	" 27, "	Resigned June 26, 1863
Do.	JOHN A. SAYLOR	Feb. 10, 1864	Feb. 10, 1864	Discharged September 25, 1865.
Chaplain	ANDREW J. LANE	Dec. 28, 1861	Jan. 30, 1862	Resigned June 17, 1863.
Do.	JOHN C. GREGG	" 8, 1863	Dec. 8, 1863	Resigned October 23, 1865.
Captain	Wm. Edwards	Oct. 11, 1861	Jan. 20, 1862	Promoted to Major.
Do.	Wm. H. Floyd	" 24, "	" 20, "	Discharged February 15, 1864.
Do.	Patterson Hirst	Nov. 14, "	" 20, "	Resigned June 24, 1863.
Do.	Alexander M. Poundstone	" 18, "	" 20, "	Resigned December 25, 1862.
Do.	Benj. A. Thomas	" 18, "	" 20, "	Resigned June 28, 1863.
Do.	Henry G. Jackson	Dec. 7, "	" 20, "	Resigned May 26, 1862.
Do.	Milton Barnes	" 7, "	" 20, "	Resigned May 26, 1862.
Do.	Wm. Doherty	" 18, "	" 20, "	Discharged September 18, 1862.
Do.	Bazel Rogers	" 19, "	" 20, "	Killed at Folly Island April 13, 1862.
Do.	Nicodemus D. Hofford	" 30, "	" 20, "	Resigned September 11, 1862.
Do.	Edward S. Converse	May 26, 1862	June 20, "	Declined.
Do.	Daniel C. Leggett	" 26, "	" 20, "	Declined.
Do.	Samuel B. Taylor	" 26, "	....	Promoted to Major.
Do.	James Adair	" 26, "	Sept. 22, 1862	Killed.
Do.	Francis M. Kahler	Sept. 11, "	" 22, "	Promoted to Major.
Do.	Henry R. West	" 18, "	Dec. 31, "	Promoted to Lieutenant-Colonel.
Do.	James Johnston	Oct. 26, "	" 31, "	Mustered out.
Do.	Samuel B. Larimer	Dec. 25, "	May 18, 1863	Mustered out October 17, 1864.
Do.	Joseph M. Paul	" 16, "	March 1, "	Killed July 18, 1863.
Do.	John W. Pinkerton	May 1, 1863	May 1, "	Mustered out October 16, 1864.
Do.	Norman H. Chamberlain	June 24, "	Oct. 15, "	Mustered out November 16, 1864.
Do.	Thomas J. Platt	" 28, "	" 15, "	Promoted to Major.
Do.	Samuel D. Hopper	Aug. 1, "	" 15, "	Mustered out November 10, 1864.
Do.	Henry S. Williams	July 18, "	" 15, "	Resigned August 20, 1864.
Do.	Josiah G. Hatcher	March 23, 1864	March 23, 1864	Resigned July 18, 1864.
Do.	Thomas H. Combs	" 23, "	" 23, "	Mustered out November —, 1864.
Do.	John C. Edwards	Nov. 18, "	Nov. 18, "	Promoted to Major.
Do.	John B. Larimer	" 18, "	" 18, "	Mustered out October —, 1864.
Do.	James Shoop	" 18, "	" 18, "	Mustered out as 1st Lieutenant Nov. —, 1864.
Do.	Crawford W. Clowe	" 18, "	" 18, "	Mustered out as 1st Lieutenant Nov. —, 1864.
Do.	Rufus P. Stokely	" 18, "	" 18, "	Declined.
Do.	Daniel W. Welsch	" 26, "	" 26, "	Mustered out by reason of consolidation.
Do.	Wm. B. Lowrey	" 26, "	" 26, "	Resigned as 1st Lieutenant July 31, 1865.
Do.	Henry H. Hitchcock	Dec. 9, "	Dec. 9, "	Transferred to 67th Ohio Volunteer Infantry.
Do.	John S. Smith	" 9, "	" 9, "	Transferred to 67th Ohio Volunteer Infantry.
Do.	Franklin Whitmer	" 9, "	" 9, "	Mustered out May 15, 1865.
Do.	John D. Kennedy	" 9, "	" 9, "	Transferred to 67th Ohio Volunteer Infantry.
Do.	Wm. Hedges	" 9, "	" 9, "	Transferred to 67th Ohio Volunteer Infantry.
Do.	Robert B. Denny	Jan. 18, 1865	Jan. 18, 1865	Mustered out by reason of consolidation.
Do.	Joseph Shaw	" 18, "	" 18, "	Declined promotion.
Do.	Thomas Wilson	June 16, "	June 16, "	Transferred to 67th O. V. I. as 1st Lieut.
Do.	John R. Murray	" 16, "	" 16, "	Transferred to 67th O. V. I. as 1st Lieut.
1st Lieutenant	Edward S. Converse	Oct. 5, 1861	Jan. 20, 1862	Appointed Captain by President.
Do.	Daniel C. Leggett	" 10, "	" 20, "	Died July 18, 1863.
Do.	Henry Dilts	" 11, "	" 20, "	Resigned June 13, 1862.
Do.	Francis M. Kahler	" 24, "	" 20, "	Promoted to Captain.
Do.	Jacob K. Skinner	" 30, "	" 20, "	Resigned August 11, 1862.
Do.	Jesse Rowick	Nov. 14, "	" 20, "	Resigned May 9, 1862.
Do.	Henry L. Harbaugh	" 18, "	" 20, "	Resigned September 17, 1862.
Do.	John M. Davis	" 18, "	" 20, "	Died July 10, 1862.
Do.	Samuel B. Taylor	Dec. 7, "	" 20, "	Promoted to Captain May 26, 1862.
Do.	James Adair	" 7, "	" 20, "	Promoted to Captain May 26, 1862.
Do.	Joseph M. Paul	" 19, "	" 20, "	Died July 18, 1863.
Do.	Henry R. West	" 18, "	" 20, "	Promoted to Captain.
Do.	John W. Pinkerton	May 26, 1862	June 20, "	Promoted to Captain.
Do.	Perley B. Johnson	" 26, "	" 20, "	Died July 18, 1863.
Do.	Henry Hazeltine	Aug. 11, "	Sept. 18, "	Honorably discharged February 10, 1864.
Do.	Coulson D. Ripler	July 10, "	" 18, "	Resigned June 24, 1863.
Do.	James Johnston	May 26, "	" 22, "	Promoted to Captain.
Do.	Samuel B. Larimer	Sept. 17, "	" 22, "	Promoted to Captain.
Do.	Henry S. Williams	" 11, "	Dec. 31, "	Promoted to Captain.
Do.	Andrew J. Foutz	June 3, "	" 31, "	Killed July 18, 1863.
Do.	Thomas Showers	May 26, "	" 31, "	Resigned January 27, 1863.

RANK.	NAME.	DATE OF RANK.			COM. ISSUED.			REMARKS.
1st Lieutenant	James Palmer	Sept.	18,	1862	Dec.	31,	1862	Resigned January 24, 1863.
Do.	Wilson Berdling	Oct.	26,	"	"	31,	"	Died July 18, 1863.
Do.	Norman H. Chamberlain	Jan.	27,	1863	May	25,	1863	Promoted to Captain.
Do.	Josiah G. Hatcher	Dec.	25,	1862	"	20,	"	Promoted to Captain.
Do.	Samuel D. Hopper	"	16,	"	"	25,	"	Promoted to Captain.
Do.	Thomas J. Platt	May	1,	1863	July	13,	"	Promoted to Captain.
Do.	Thomas H. Combs	June	24,	"	Oct.	15,	"	Promoted to Captain.
Do.	John B. Larimer	July	24,	"	"	15,	"	Promoted to Captain.
Do.	James Shoop	Aug.	1,	"	"	15,	"	Promoted to Captain.
Do.	James C. Morrison	July	18,	"	"	15,	"	Promoted to Captain.
Do.	John N. Starr	March	23,	1864	March	23,	1864	Discharged as 2d Lieutenant August 9, 1864.
Do.	John B. Powell	Aug.	1,	1863	Oct.	15,	1863	Honorably discharged November 20, 1863.
Do.	George W. Hirst	June	21,	"	"	15,	"	Resigned October 12, 1864.
Do.	John C. Edwards	July	18,	"	"	15,	"	Promoted to Captain.
Do.	Daniel W. Welsch	May	9,	1864	May	9,	1864	Promoted to Captain.
Do.	Wm. B. Lowrey	"	9,	"	"	9,	"	Promoted to Captain.
Do.	Crawford W. Clowe	March	23,	"	March	23,	"	Promoted to Captain.
Do.	Henry H. Hitchcock	Nov.	18,	"	Nov.	18,	"	Promoted to Captain.
Do.	Rufus P. Stockley	March	23,	"	March	23,	"	Mustered out.
Do.	John S. Smith	Nov.	18,	"	Nov.	18,	"	Promoted to Captain.
Do.	Franklin Whitmer	"	18,	"	"	18,	"	Promoted to Captain.
Do.	Francis M. Bradshaw	"	18,	"	"	18,	"	Mustered out at expiration of service.
Do.	John D. Kennedy	"	18,	"	"	18,	"	Promoted to Captain.
Do.	Wm. Hedges	"	18,	"	"	18,	"	Promoted to Captain.
Do.	Robert H. Denny	"	18,	"	"	18,	"	Promoted to Captain.
Do.	Joseph Shaw	"	18,	"	"	18,	"	Declined promot'n; mustered out by reason of consolidation.
Do.	Silas D. Kain	"	18,	"	"	18,	"	Discharged March 17, 1865.
Do.	Thomas Wilson	"	26,	"	"	26,	"	Promoted to Captain.
Do.	John R. Murray	"	26,	"	"	26,	"	Promoted to Captain.
Do.	Robert Davidson	Dec.	9,	"	Dec.	9,	"	Transferred to 67th O. V. I.
Do.	Calvin Woodruff	"	14,	"	"	14,	"	Mustered out May 15, 1865.
Do.	Aaron D. Yocum	"	14,	"	"	14,	"	Transferred to 67th O. V. I.
Do.	Absalom Craig	"	14,	"	"	14,	"	Transferred to 67th O. V. I.
Do.	Joseph C. Tomlinson	"	30,	"	"	30,	"	Mustered out May 15, 1865.
Do.	Gardner Howe	Jan.	18,	1865	Jan.	18,	1865	Transferred to 67th O. V. I.
Do.	Frank M. Lauk	June	16,	"	June	16,	"	Never mustered; prisoner of war.
Do.	Wilson Fouts	"	16,	"	"	16,	"	Never mustered.
Do.	Alfred Bugh	"	16,	"	"	16,	"	Mustered out as 1st Sergeant.
Do.	Wilson Strahl	"	16,	"	"	16,	"	Transferred to the 67th O. V. I. as 1st Sergt.
Do.	John W. Storer	"	16,	"	"	16,	"	Mustered out as principal musician.
Do.	George G. Sopher	"	16,	"	"	16,	"	Prisoner of war; never mustered.
Do.	David Dougherty	"	16,	"	"	16,	"	Prisoner of war; never mustered.
2d Lieutenant	John W. Pinkerton	Oct.	3,	1861	Jan.	20,	1862	Promoted to 1st Lieutenant.
Do.	Perley B. Johnson	"	4,	"	"	20,	"	Promoted to 1st Lieutenant.
Do.	Jackson Thorpe	"	11,	"	"	20,	"	Resigned July 15, 1862.
Do.	James Palmer	"	15,	"	"	20,	"	Promoted to 1st Lieutenant.
Do.	Henry Hazeltine	"	30,	"	"	20,	"	Promoted to 1st Lieutenant.
Do.	Wm. McLaren	Nov.	4,	"	"	20,	"	Resigned July 25, 1862.
Do.	Samuel B. Larimer	"	18,	"	"	20,	"	Promoted to 1st Lieutenant.
Do.	Coulson D. Ripler	"	18,	"	"	20,	"	Promoted to 1st Lieutenant.
Do.	Joel M. Merring	Dec.	7,	"	"	20,	"	Resigned August 11, 1862.
Do.	James Johnston	"	7,	"	"	20,	"	Promoted to 1st Lieutenant.
Do.	Henry S. Williams	May	26,	1862	June	20,	"	Promoted to 1st Lieutenant.
Do.	Andrew J. Foutz	"	26,	"	Sept.	18,	"	Promoted to 1st Lieutenant.
Do.	Thomas Showers	July	15,	"	"	18,	"	Promoted to 1st Lieutenant.
Do.	Samuel D. Hopper	Aug.	11,	"	"	18,	"	Promoted to 1st Lieutenant.
Do.	Thomas J. Platt	July	10,	"	"	18,	"	Promoted to 1st Lieutenant.
Do.	George S. Brownell	Aug.	14,	"	"	18,	"	Killed July 18, 1863.
Do.	Wm. Beidling	May	26,	"	"	22,	"	
Do.	Henry C. Knoop	Sept.	17,	"	"	22,	"	Killed July 18, 1863.
Do.	John W. Hendricks	"	18,	"	Dec.	31,	"	Resigned June 28, 1863.
Do.	John N. Starr	Oct.	26,	"	"	31,	"	Promoted to 1st Lieutenant.
Do.	Norman H. Chamberlain	July	25,	"	"	31,	"	Promoted to 1st Lieutenant.
Do.	Daniel W. Welsch	Feb.	1,	1863	Feb.	19,	1863	Promoted to 1st Lieutenant.
Do.	John C. Edwards, jr.	Jan.	1,	"	April	22,	"	Promoted to 1st Lieutenant.
Do.	John B. Powell	Dec.	16,	1862	May	1,	"	Promoted to 1st Lieutenant.
Do.	George W. Hirst	Jan.	27,	1863	"	1,	"	Promoted to 1st Lieutenant.
Do.	Crawford W. Clowe	Feb.	1,	"	March	1,	"	Promoted to 1st Lieutenant.
Do.	Rufus P. Stockley	May	1,	"	July	1,	"	Promoted to 1st Lieutenant.
Do.	Wm. B. Lowrey	March	23,	1864	March	23,	1864	Promoted to 1st Lieutenant.
Do.	Henry H. Hitchcock	May	9,	"	May	9,	"	Promoted to 1st Lieutenant.

SIXTY-SECOND OHIO VOLUNTEER INFANTRY.

THE SIXTY-SECOND OHIO was organized at Camp Goddard, near Zanesville, in November, 1861. Unavoidable delay kept the regiment in camp through November and December, and a part of January, 1862.

On January 17th orders were received from the Governor of Ohio to report to General Rosecrans, then commanding in Western Virginia. On the same day the regiment was placed on board the cars of the Ohio Central Railroad, and Bellair (on the Ohio River opposite the terminus of the Baltimore and Ohio Railroad) was reached on the 18th. The regiment continued by rail to Cumberland, Maryland, and there joined the forces under command of Brigadier-General Lander, then in camp at Patterson's Creek.

On February 3d the Sixty-Second proceeded eastward, on the Baltimore and Ohio Railroad, to Paw-paw Tunnel, and thence to Great Cacapon Creek, Virginia, where it remained in camp until March 10, 1862. On that day it moved forward to Martinsburg, and thence to Winchester and Strasburg. It bivouacked over night at the last-named place, returning to Winchester the next morning.

On March 22d the regiment was placed on picket; but on the next morning was ordered to the front again. The battle of Winchester was impending. The Rebel forces under General Jackson had attacked the army, now under General James Shields (General Lander having suddenly died). The Sixty-Second arrived on the field just as the battle had fairly commenced, and took position on the center of the line in support of a battery. This position was occupied until near nightfall, when the regiment was ordered forward on the double-quick, in time to witness the enemy defeated and flying, leaving their wounded and dead upon the field. On the following day the army marched in pursuit, passing through Strasburg. The Sixty-Second went into camp three miles south of that place. The next morning (the 25th) it moved to Mount Jackson, near which it had a skirmish with the enemy. The regiment then returned to Edinburg, Virginia, and remained there in camp until April 17th. It then moved forward again, through Mount Jackson, arriving at New Market on the 18th.

On May 2d the regiment left New Market, and marched up the Valley as far as Harrisonburg, Virginia, and on the 4th again fell back to a point within five miles of New Market.

On May 12th the regiment commenced one of its hardest marches. Passing through New Market it crossed the first range of mountains east of the Shenandoah (*via* Swift's Gap), and, fording the eastern branch of the Shenandoah, ended its first day's march at Luray. On May 13th and 14th it made Cheat Gap and Great Cross Roads. At the last-named point it had a slight skirmish, the enemy retreating.

On May 16th the march was resumed, the route leading through Warrenton on the 17th, and Catlett's Station on the 18th. The regiment then marched to Falmouth, where, on the 25th, it was reviewed by the President of the United States, General Shields, and General McDowell.

On May 24th the regiment received orders to return to Western Virginia. It started toward the Shenandoah on the 24th, and passed through Catlett's Station, Manassas Junction,

Hay Market, Rectortown, Front Royal, Luray, and Columbia Bridge, reaching the last-named place June 5th. On that day it made a forced march to within five miles of Port Republic, where the two advance brigades of the army met the enemy under Stonewall Jackson, and, after a fierce struggle, lasting some hours, were compelled to retreat, with heavy loss, to Columbia Bridge and Luray. The regiment arrived at the last-named place on June 10th.

On June 15th and 16th it marched to Front Royal, encamped there until the 20th, and then resumed its march across the mountains *via* Manassas Gap. It reached White Plains on the 24th, and Bristol Station on the 28th of June. It left Bristol Station on the same day, and arrived at Alexandria in the evening.

On June 30th the Sixty-Second went on board of transports and sailed for Fortress Monroe. Thence it was taken to Harrison's Landing, and sent to the front on picket-duty. On the 4th of July it had a skirmish with the enemy, and continued on picket-duty until August 15th. The regiment occupied the extreme left of the army under General McClellan.

On the 16th of August it moved in the famous retreat down the Peninsula to Yorktown and Fortress Monroe. From Fortress Monroe the regiment was taken to Suffolk, from which point, on the 21st of September, it made a reconnoissance to Black Water. A second and third reconnoissance was made from this place. On October 24th the regiment had a skirmish, in which it succeeded in killing and wounding several of the enemy, captured some prisoners and two pieces of artillery. A fourth and last reconnoissance was made on December 12th, during which the regiment had a heavy skirmish with the enemy.

On December 31st the regiment moved from Suffolk to Norfolk, and on January 4, 1863, went by transports to Beaufort, North Carolina, and from there by rail to Newbern, North Carolina. On January 25th it sailed to Port Royal, South Carolina, and disembarked on the 8th of February, on St. Helena Island. Lying in camp here for some weeks, it again embarked on transports and went to Coal Island.

On April 3d the regiment crossed over to Folly Island, and on April 7th to Morris Island, where, after two hours of desperate fighting, the enemy was driven into their intrenchments with great loss. The force captured fourteen siege guns, and the camp and garrison equipage, and some prisoners from the Rebels.

On July 18th, 1863, Fort Wagner was assaulted. In this desperate affair the Sixty-Second lost one hundred and fifty men killed, wounded, and missing. In this charge Lieutenant-Colonel C. F. Steele and Adjutant Daniel C. Liggett were wounded, as also were Captain William Edwards of company A; Lieutenants A. J. Fouts of company B; S. B. Larimer and G. S. Brownell of company C; Lieutenants S. D. Hopper of company E, and P. B. Johnson of company F. Lieutenants William Brading of company C, and J. M. Paul of company I, were killed. A scene during the charge is thus described by a person who participated in the assault:

"The rear division of the Seventh New Hampshire and a portion of the One Hundredth New York, massed together, crossed the ditch, and essayed to get a footing from one point, while the Sixty-Second and Sixty-Seventh Ohio made an assault on another. One corner of the Fort only was occupied by the National forces, and that was swept by grape and canister, and exposed to musketry. The troops looked back, saw they were alone, and began to falter. No relief came; and, sad and disappointed, they fell back, and left the field and their dead and wounded in the hands of the enemy."

The regiment also took part in the siege of Charleston, which lasted from the 10th of July to the 31st of October, when it returned to Folly Island. On November 5th it went to Hilton Head.

In January, 1864, the Sixty-Second re-enlisted and received the usual thirty days' veteran furlough.

On March 3d, 1864, the regiment rendezvoused at Washington City, and was immediately sent to the front near Petersburg, Virginia. From this time onward the Sixty-Second participated in the contest that raged about the lines of the Rebel capital. It was hotly engaged on the 9th and 10th of May, and lost heavily in killed and wounded.

On May 20th a portion of the lines fell into the hands of the enemy. The Sixty-Second was one of the regiments designated to retake the ground. A desperate charge was made, in which many men were killed and wounded. The enemy's rifle-pits were taken, and his men driven out. During October it had repeated engagements and lost heavily.

During the spring, summer, and fall of 1864 the Sixty-Second was almost continually under fire—not a movement could be made without encountering the enemy. The men of the regiment were compelled to keep an incessant vigil, and, for weeks at a time, dared not throw off their accouterments.

In the spring of 1865 the Sixty-Second took part in the assault on the Rebel works below Petersburg. On the 2d of April it was one of the foremost regiments in the assault on Fort Gregg. It also participated in the action at Appomattox C. H.

About the 1st of September, 1865, the Sixty-Second was consolidated with the Sixty-Seventh Ohio, and thereafter lost its identity—the name of the Sixty-Seventh being retained.

63d REGIMENT OHIO VOLUNTEER INFANTRY.

ROSTER, THREE YEARS' SERVICE.

RANK.	NAME.	DATE OF RANK.	COM. ISSUED.	REMARKS.
Colonel	JOHN W. SPRAGUE	Jan. 23, 1862	March 3, 1862	Promoted to Brigadier-General volunteers.
Do.	CHAS E. BROWN	June 6, 1865	June 6, 1865	On detached duty at muster out of regiment.
Lt. Colonel	WM. E. GILMORE	Oct. 17, 1861	Oct. 17, 1861	Resigned July 17, 1862.
Do.	ALEX. L. HASKINS	July 17, 1862	Aug 5, 1862	Revoked.
Do.	J. HUNTER ODLIN	March 20, 1863	April 10, 1863	Declined.
Do.	CHAS. E. BROWN	" 20, "	May 11, "	Promoted to Colonel.
Do.	OSCAR L. JACKSON	June 6, 1865	June 6, 1865	Mustered out with regiment as Major.
Major	ALEX. L. HASKINS	Oct. 1, 1861	March 3, 1862	Promoted; honorably disch'ed March 20, '63.
Do.	J. HUNTER ODLIN	" 1, 1862	" 17, "	Resigned January 3, 1863.
Do.	JOHN W. FOUTS	Jan. 1, 1863	Jan. 17, 1863	Mustered out.
Do.	OSCAR L. JACKSON	" 28, 1865	" 28, 1865	Promoted to Lieutenant-Colonel.
Surgeon	ISAAC L. CRANE	Oct. 7, 1861	March 3, 1862	Resigned January 28, 1863.
Do.	JOEL MORSE	April 26, 1862	April 26, "	Said to be a mistake; name not on the roll.
Do.	ARTHUR B. MONOHAN	Jan. 28, 1863	March 11, 1863	Mustered out July 21, 1865.
Ass't Surgeon	ARTHUR B. MONOHAN	Nov. 7, 1861	" 3, 1862	Promoted to Surgeon.
Do.	J. O. MARSH	Aug. 21, 1862	Sept. 1, "	Resigned October 2, 1862.
Do.	JOHN B. McDELL	March 11, 1863	March 11, 1863	Resigned May 31, 1865.
Do.	JOHN G. BINGHAM	Jan. 28, "	" 11, "	Revoked; refused to muster.
Chaplain	BENJAMIN ST. JAMES FRY	Feb. 13, 1862	July 1, 1862	Mustered out September 27, 1864; exp. of time.
Captain	Nathan Pickett	Sept. 28, 1861	March 3, "	Resigned July 11, 1862.
Do.	Charles E. Brown	Oct. 23, "	" 3, "	Promoted to Lieutenant-Colonel.
Do.	John W. Fouts	" 28, "	" 3, "	Promoted to Major.
Do.	Christopher E. Smith	" 28, "	" 3, "	Resigned December 22, 1862.
Do.	Thomas McCord	Dec. 16, "	" 3, "	Resigned September 3, 1862.
Do.	Rodney K. Shaw	" 20, "	" 3, "	Resigned August 31, 1862.
Do.	Chas. J. Titus	" 20, "	" 3, "	Resigned June 18, 1862.
Do.	Chas. W. McGinnis	Jan. 1, 1862	" 3, "	Resigned September 3, 1862.
Do.	Oscar L. Jackson	" 16, "	" 3, "	Promoted to Major.
Do.	James Taggart	" 17, "	" 3, "	Resigned June 23, 1862.
Do.	Otis W. Pollock	June 18, "	July 1, "	Mustered out with regiment.
Do.	Frank T. Gilmore	" 23, "	" 1, "	Mustered out; expiration of time.
Do.	Daniel T. Thorne	Aug. 11, "	Dec. 31, "	Died October 5, 1864, in prison, S. C.
Do.	George Wightman	" 11, "	" 31, "	Discharged October 19, 1864.
Do.	Wm. J. Collinower	" 11, "	" 31, "	Resigned August 6, 1864.
Do.	G. W. Fitzsimmons	Sept. 24, "	" 31, "	Resigned September 17, 1864.
Do.	Winslow L. Bay	Jan. 1, 1863	Jan. 17, 1863	Mustered out with regiment.
Do.	Charles J. McGinnis	March 20, "	May 14, "	Resigned September 26, 1864.
Do.	Wm. Cornell	June 1, "	June 17, "	Mustered out.
Do.	John L. Antrim	Sept 26, 1864	Sept. 26, 1864	Declined promotion.
Do.	A. C. Fenner	Oct. 4, "	Oct. 4, "	Mustered out with regiment.
Do.	James A. Gilmore	" 4, "	" 4, "	Declined promotion.
Do.	George B. Bartlett	Nov. 12, "	Nov. 12, "	Mustered out with regiment.
Do.	Marvin A. Stewart	" 12, "	" 12, "	Declined promotion; commission returned.
Do.	Thomas J. McCord	Jan. 20, 1865	Jan. 20, 1865	Mustered out with regiment.
Do.	Angus McDonald	" 20, "	" 20, "	Detached in Pioneer Corps.
Do.	Charles M. Harrison	" 20, "	" 20, "	Mustered out with regiment.
Do.	J. W. Jenkins	" 20, "	" 20, "	Mustered out with regiment.
Do.	Madison Hoon	" 28, "	" 28, "	Mustered out with regiment.
Do.	Andrew Smith	" 28, "	" 28, "	Mustered out with regiment.
1st Lieutenant	Clark Huchinson	Sept. 28, 1861	March 3, 1862	Declined.
Do.	Thomas A. P. Champlin	Oct. 1, "	" 3, "	Resigned April 26, 1862.
Do.	Frank T. Gilmore	" 1, "	" 3, "	Promoted to Captain.
Do.	Wesley J. Tucker	" 28, "	" 3, "	Resigned June 18, 1862.
Do.	Wm. S. Bradshaw	" 28, "	" 3, "	Resigned June 28, 1862.
Do.	Mahlon P. Davis	Dec. 14, "	" 3, "	Resigned May 29, 1862.
Do.	Elias V. Cherry	" 16, "	" 3, "	Resigned February 16, 1863.
Do.	Henry S. Burt	" 20, "	" 3, "	Detailed on staff duty at own request.
Do.	Otis W. Pollock	" 20, "	" 3, "	Promoted to Captain.
Do.	Francis A. Gibbons	Jan. 16, 1862	" 3, "	Resigned September 3, 1862.
Do.	Wm. Cornell	" 17, "	" 3, "	Promoted to Captain.
Do.	Louis Schmidt	Feb. 13, "	" 3, "	Resigned August 24, 1864.
Do.	Holly Skinner	April 26, "	June 20, "	Promoted to Captain and A. Q. M.
Do.	Solomon H. Johnson	Feb. 13, "	March 3, "	Resigned September 2, 1862.
Do.	Richard B. Cheatham	June 18, "	July 1, "	Died July 18, 1863.
Do.	Nesbit Comley	May 29, "	" 1, "	Resigned November 18, 1862.
Do.	John W. Browning	June 18, "	" 1, "	Resigned September 16, 1864.
Do.	Chas. J. McGinnis	" 23, "	" 1, "	Promoted to Captain.
Do.	Howard Forrer	Nov. 5, "	Nov. 8, "	Killed July 22, 1864.
Do.	John L. Antrim	Aug. 11, "	Dec. 31, "	Mustered out May 3, 1865.
Do.	A. C. Fenner	" 11, "		Promoted to Captain.
Do.	John R. Shirley	" 19, "		Resigned February 13, 1863.
Do.	James A. Gilmore	Feb. 13, 1863	May 14, 1863	Mustered out.
Do.	Wm. H. Cherry	June 1, "	June 17, "	Accidentally killed June 23, 1864.
Do.	Giles Hinson	" 1, "	" 17, "	Resigned October 14, 1864.
Do.	Reuben G. Clark	" 1, "	July 17, "	Declined.
Do.	George B. Bartlett	July 18, "	" 20, "	Promoted to Captain.
Do.	Edward B. Boyd	May 25, 1864	May 25, 1864	Captain and A. Q. M.
Do.	Andrew J. Howard	Aug. 11, "	Aug. 11, "	Declined; returned commission.
Do.	Wm. C. Thomas	" 19, "	" 19, "	Declined.
Do.	Marvin A. Stewart	Sept. 26, "	Sept. 26, "	Returned commission; mustered out.
Do.	Thomas J. McCord	" 26, "	" 26, "	Promoted to Captain.
Do.	Angus McDonald	" 26, "	" 26, "	Promoted to Captain.
Do.	Wallace S. Roach	" 26, "	" 26, "	Returned commission.
Do.	Chas. M. Harrison	Oct. 4, "	Oct. 4, "	Promoted to Captain.
Do.	J. W. Jenkins	" 4, "	" 4, "	Promoted to Captain.

RANK.	NAME.	DATE OF RANK.	COM. ISSUED.	REMARKS.
1st Lieutenant	Madison Hoon	Oct. 4, 1861	Oct. 4, 1861	Promoted to Captain.
Do.	Andrew Smith	Nov. 3, "	Nov. 3, "	Promoted to Captain.
Do.	Alex. H. Brill	Jan. 20, 1865	Jan. 20, 1865	Mustered out with regiment.
Do.	Wallace C. Bay	" 20, "	" 20, "	Resigned May 23, 1865.
Do.	David E. Hisey	" 20, "	" 20, "	Mustered out with regiment.
Do.	John C. Lowry	" 20, "	" 20, "	Mustered out with regiment.
Do.	Wm. R. Boughner	" 20, "	" 20, "	
Do.	Obadiah P. Hill	" 20, "	" 20, "	Mustered out with regiment.
Do.	Wm. C. Dugan	" 28, "	" 28, "	Discharged.
Do.	Augustus C. Hall	" 28, "	" 28, "	Mustered out with regiment.
Do.	Robert A. Pollock	Feb. 10, "	Feb. 10, "	Mustered out with regiment as A. Q. M.
Do.	Wm. J. Johnson	April 26, "	April 26, "	Mustered out with regiment.
Do.	Joseph P. Studebaker	June 16, "	June 26, "	Mustered out with regiment.
Do.	Wm. S. Appleteo	" 26, "	" 26, "	
2d Lieutenant	John M. Wisehart	Aug. 15, 1861	March 3, 1862	Resigned April 12, 1862.
Do.	Solomon H. Johnson	Sept. 28, "	" 3, "	Promoted to 1st Lieutenant.
Do.	Robert Booth	Oct. 1, "	" 3, "	Resigned June 28, 1862.
Do.	George W. Fitzsimmons	" 15, "	" 3, "	Promoted to Captain.
Do.	Chas. J. McGinnis	" 23, "	" 3, "	Promoted to 1st Lieutenant.
Do.	John B. Hageman	" 24, "	" 3, "	Resigned January 1, 1862.
Do.	Wm. W. Mason	" 28, "	" 3, "	Resigned November 18, 1862.
Do.	Benj. Knight	Nov. 12, "	" 3, "	Resigned September 3, 1862.
Do.	Wm. Pickett	Jan. 16, 1862	" 3, "	Resigned July 12, 1862.
Do.	James A. Gilmore	" 17, "	" 3, "	Promoted to 1st Lieutenant.
Do.	Lewis L. Grubb	Feb. 13, "	" 3, "	Resigned May 26, 1862.
Do.	Silas W. Cunningham	April 12, "	June 20, "	Died June 30, 1863.
Do.	Elisha B. Pickett	Feb. 13, "	March 3, "	Resigned August 31, 1862.
Do.	George B. Bartlett	May 25, "	Dec 23, "	Promoted to 1st Lieutenant.
Do.	David J. Comley	June 23, "	July 1, "	Declined.
Do.	Wm. G. Renner	Oct. 7, "	Oct. 7, "	Resigned April 1, 1864.
Do.	R. G. Clark	Aug. 11, "	Dec. 31, "	Promoted to 1st Lieutenant.
Do.	Levi Emrick	" 11, "	" 31, "	Resigned March 20, 1863.
Do.	Giles Hinson	Oct. 4, "	" 31, "	Promoted to 1st Lieutenant.
Do.	Winslow L. Bay	Jan. 30, "	" 31, "	Promoted to Captain.
Do.	Wm. H. Cherry	Sept. 21, "	" 31, "	Promoted to 1st Lieutenant.
Do.	Edward B. Boyd	Feb. 1, 1863	Feb. 20, 1863	Promoted to 1st Lieutenant.
Do.	Andrew J. Howard	Jan. 1, "	Jan. 17, "	Honorably discharged November 9, 1864.
Do.	Wm. C. Thomas	" 1, "	" 17, "	Promoted to 1st Lieutenant.
Do.	Lorin B. Matheny	" 1, "	" 17, "	Mustered out.
Do.	Marvin A. Stewart	" 1, "	" 17, "	Mustered out.
Do.	Thomas J. McCord	" 1, "	" 17, "	Promoted to 1st Lieutenant.
Do.	James C. Matheny	" 1, "	July 17, "	Mustered out.
Do.	Angus McDonald	July 18, "	" 30, "	Promoted to 1st Lieutenant.
Do.	Wallace S. Roach	June 30, "	" 30, "	Mustered out.
Do.	Charles M. Harrison	May 25, 1864	May 25, 1864	Promoted to 1st Lieutenant.
Do.	J. W. Jenkins	June 27, "	June 27, "	Promoted to 1st Lieutenant.
Do.	Andrew Smith	Oct. 4, "	Oct. 4, "	Promoted to 1st Lieutenant.
Do.	Alex. H. Brill	Nov. 12, "	Nov. 12, "	Promoted to 1st Lieutenant.
Do.	Wm. C. Dugan	Jan. 20, 1865	Jan. 20, 1865	Promoted to 1st Lieutenant.
Do.	Augustus C. Hall	" 20, "	" 20, "	Promoted to 1st Lieutenant.

SIXTY-THIRD OHIO VOLUNTEER INFANTRY.

THE SIXTY-THIRD OHIO was organized by the consolidation of two battalions of recruits, known as the Twenty-Second and Sixty-Third Regiments Ohio Volunteer Infantry. The battalion of the Twenty-Second was recruited at Camp Worthington, Chillicothe, Ohio, and furnished for the new organization six companies, A, B, E, H, I, and K. The battalion of the Sixty-Third was recruited at Marietta, Ohio.

The consolidation was occasioned by the earnest call of the General Government upon the State authorities for troops, directing that recruits be pushed into the field as rapidly as possible. The order for the consolidation was issued at Columbus, on the 18th of January, 1862, and the organization was completed on the 23d of the same month, the Twenty-Second having been ordered to report at Marietta.

The regiment moved from Marietta on February 18th, under orders to report at Paducah, Kentucky. From this place it was ordered to join the Army of the Mississippi, which was then being organized at Commerce, Missouri, by Major-General John Pope. The regiment reached Commerce February 23d, and encamped near the town. The army took up the march for New Madrid on the 28th, and reached the town on the 3d of March. The regiment took part in the reconnoissance on the day of its arrival, and was under fire for the first time. In the permanent organization of the army at New Madrid, the regiment was brigaded with the Twenty-Seventh, Thirty-Ninth, and Forty-Third Ohio Regiments, commanded by Brigadier-General David S. Stanley. The organization was known as the Ohio Brigade. The regiment shared in a reconnoissance on the 7th of March, and its services on the 13th were officially recognized in an order from General Pope's head-quarters. The regiment was present in all the movements which resulted in the surrender of Island No. 10, and on the 12th of April embarked on the transport Silver Wave, and moved with the army to the vicinity of Fort Pillow. Later in the month it was ordered to join Halleck in the siege of Corinth, and landed at Hamburg, Tennessee, on the 23d of April.

The regiment took part in all the operations on the left of Halleck's forces; was in the reconnoissance beyond Farmington on the 8th of May, and in the engagement at Farmington on the 28th of the same month, sustaining severe loss. After the evacuation of Corinth the regiment joined in the pursuit as far as Boonville Station, on the Mobile and Ohio Railroad, and returning to Corinth on the 11th of June, took up quarters on Clear Creek. On the 20th of August the regiment with the brigade, moved first to Iuka and then to Bear Creek. When Price's army advanced toward Iuka, on September 12th, the troops fell back to Clear Creek again, but when Rosecrans advanced to Jacinto the regiment again marched for Iuka on the 19th, and was the reserve at the battle of that name and date. The next day the regiment pursued the Rebels, and returning the day after camped at Jacinto.

From the 28th of September till the 3d of October Stanley's division, of which the Sixty-Third was a part, acted as a corps of observation, watching the combined armies of the Rebel Generals Van Dorn, Price, and Lovell. The regiment took part in all the movements of the division marching to Rienzi, making a reconnoissance toward Ripley, and marching to the Tuscumbia River.

On the morning of October 3d the regiment moved into Corinth, forming line in rear of the outer works on the extreme left. During the night it was placed on the right of Battery Robinett, which position it held during the battle on the following day. Before daylight on the morning of the 4th a picket force from the regiment, moving out the Chevalla Road, met the enemy advancing to place a battery. The picket drove the Rebels back, capturing the Captain of the battery and one gun. During the engagement which immediately followed the regiment was much exposed, losing, in killed and wounded, forty-eight per cent. of the officers and men in action. There were but three line-officers who were not killed or wounded, and some of them were wounded more than once. The next day the regiment commenced pursuing the Rebels, and continued until it reached Ripley, when it returned to Corinth and encamped.

On the 2d of November the regiment left Corinth to join General Grant in Mississippi. On the 5th, near Grand Junction, it was joined by the battalion of the One Hundred and Twelfth Ohio which had been consolidated with it, and added materially to its strength in both officers and men. The regiment moved with General Grant and went into camp near Oxford, Mississippi, on December 11th. On the 17th it accompanied the brigade to Jackson, Tennessee, to defend the communications of the army against Von Dorn and Forrest. By order of General Grant the regiment was detached and left at Bolivar, Tennessee. On the 27th it joined the command of General Sullivan; on the 31st moved to the relief of Colonel Lanman's Brigade and engaged in battle with Forrest, at Parker's Cross Roads. After repulsing the enemy and pursuing as far as the Tennessee River, the regiment marched for Corinth, where it arrived January 9, 1863. Here the regiment went into winter-quarters and built barracks.

On the 20th of April the regiment moved, with the forces under General Dodge, beyond Tuscumbia, Alabama, and returned to Corinth May 2d. On the 16th of May the regiment moved to Memphis, and performed garrison-duty with the brigade. The Sixty-Third joined Sherman's movement for the support of the Army of the Cumberland, and marched from Memphis October 18th, to Eastport, Tennessee; crossed the Tennessee River November 4th, marching to Pulaski, and then to Prospect, Tennessee, on Elk River, arriving November 13th.

The regiment, having re-enlisted, left Prospect on the 2d of January, 1864, marching to Columbia, and proceeding thence by rail to Cincinnati, Ohio, where furloughs were issued on the 15th. The regiment re-assembled at Columbus, Ohio, and on the 18th of February left for the front, reported to General Dodge at Pulaski, and was ordered to Decatur Junction, Alabama, where it went into camp on the 28th. The regiment took an active part in the movements which resulted in the possession of Decatur by our forces. On the 10th of March the Sixty-Third was assigned to the Second Brigade, Fourth Division, Sixteenth Army Corps. The regiment marched east from Decatur, May 1st, *via* Huntsville to Woodville, and thence proceeded to Chattanooga by railroad. From Chattanooga the regiment moved through Rossville, across Mission Ridge and Chickamauga Creek, to Snake Creek Gap. The Sixty-Third shared in the battle of Resaca, May 14th, and companies C, H, and A, being on the skirmish-line, were among the first troops, on the morning of the 14th, to reach the river near the village. On the 16th the regiment crossed the Oostenaula, moved to Adairsville, and afterward to Dallas; participating in all the actions before that place, and losing heavily in killed and wounded. The regiment was next under fire at Kenesaw Mountain, and sustained its part in all the operations at that point, being well up to the front the whole time. It was engaged in the battle of Decatur, Georgia, losing three officers killed and wounded. On the 30th of August it assisted in taking possession of the Macon Railroad, south of Atlanta, and on the 1st of September engaged in the battle of Jonesboro'.

After the fall of Atlanta the regiment pursued a short distance, returned and went into camp at Eastpoint, Georgia, September 10, 1864. From the time the regiment left Chattanooga in May, until it went into camp at Eastpoint, it lost in action one hundred and fifty-eight men. While in camp at this place the Fourth Division, Sixteenth Army Corps, was transferred, and became the First Division, Seventeenth Army Corps. On the 4th of October the Regiment moved north across the Chattahoochie, and was engaged in the action at Snake Creek Gap. After crossing the Chattahoochie the campaigning was of the most severe kind. The men were on half-rations of bread and fresh beef, and the animals were entirely without forage. A halt was made at Gaylesville, Alabama, for a few days' rest, and from this point twenty-three members of the regiment who had not re-enlisted were sent to Chattanooga for muster-out.

The regiment moved with Sherman on his march from Atlanta to Savannah, participating in all the dangers and pleasures of that great campaign. Soon after leaving Atlanta an abundance of provisions was found, and the formality of issuing rations was dispensed with almost entirely. The army moved at the rate of fifteen miles per day, easy marching for the most of the troops; but the regiments guarding the trains would frequently get into camp just as the others were starting out. The Seventeenth Army Corps moved *via* McDonough, Gordon's Junction, and Millen; took part in a slight skirmish at Oliver Station, and on the 10th of December the regiment waded the Ogeechee Canal in line, under a brisk fire, and secured a good position near to the forts defending the city of Savannah. The regiment moved into Savannah on the 21st of December, and resting until the 5th of January, 1865, embarked at Thunderbolt Landing and proceeded to Beaufort, South Carolina. Soon after their arrival they moved to Pocotaligo, and again prepared for campaigning.

On the 1st of February the regiment started northward, moving along the Salkahatchie, and met the enemy, February 3d, at River's Bridge, and in the engagement lost twelve men killed and wounded. Continuing the march, the regiment occupied and destroyed the Savannah and Charleston Railroad at Midway, crossed the South Edisto at Pelican's Bridge, and occupied Columbia on the 17th. The movement was continued in a north-easterly direction. Chiroa, South Carolina, was occupied March 4th, the Pedee crossed on the 6th, and Fayetteville reached on the 11th. The regiment was engaged at Bentonville, and moved on to Goldsboro'. From this point a detachment of the regiment was sent to Newbern, with several hundred animals, captured by the Seventeenth Army Corps. On the 31st of March, while escorting a forage-train, the regiment skirmished with the enemy, and lost one man killed and one captured. The regiment occupied Raleigh on the 14th of April, and on the 20th was detailed to escort the teams of the Seventeenth Army Corps to Goldsboro', for supplies. The regiment returned to Raleigh with a train of several hundred wagons, having marched over one hundred miles in five days. After the surrender of Johnston the regiment again took the northern route, crossing the Roanoke River at Robinson's Ferry, and striking the Boydtown Plank Road forty miles west of Petersburg, Virginia. On the 8th of May the regiment passed through Petersburg, and the next evening camped at Mansfield, opposite Richmond. The Sixty-Third crossed the James, May 12th, marched through Richmond, crossed the Rappahannock at Fredericksburg, and went into camp near Alexandria, on the 19th of May. On the 24th of May the regiment passed in review before the President, General Grant, and others, and in the evening went into camp at Crystal Springs.

Here the records were completed and everything prepared for a muster-out. One officer and sixteen men, whose term of service would have expired before October 1st, were sent to Columbus, Ohio, for discharge; and one hundred and ninety-six drafted men and substitutes that had been assigned to the regiment, but never had an opportunity of joining it, were mustered out at New York, in accordance with orders from the War Department. The regiment took the cars on the Baltimore and Ohio Railroad on the 5th of June, and proceeded to Parkersburg, and thence by boat to Louisville. Here the regiment spent a month, waiting impatiently for the order to muster-out. The muster-out took place on the 8th of July, in accordance with General Orders No. 24, of 1865, from head-quarters Army of the Tennessee. On the 10th the regiment embarked for Camp Dennison, where it arrived safely, and on the 17th and 18th of July, 1865, was paid and discharged.

During its term of service it had enrolled an aggregate of ninety commissioned officers and over fifteen hundred men; and at its discharge from the service mustered twenty-two commissioned officers and five hundred and thirty-seven men. By authority of General Orders it was entitled to inscribe upon its banners the names of the following battles: New Madrid, Island No. 10, Iuka, Corinth, October 4th, Atlanta, and Savannah.

64th REGIMENT OHIO VOLUNTEER INFANTRY.

ROSTER, THREE YEARS' SERVICE.

RANK.	NAME.	DATE OF RANK.	COM. ISSUED.	REMARKS.
Colonel	JAMES W. FORSYTH	Nov. 11, 1861	Dec. 18, 1861	Declined.
Do.	JOHN FERGUSON	Jan. 21, 1862	Jan. 21, 1862	Dismissed March 11, 1863.
Do.	ALEX. McILVANE	March 11, 1863	March 31, 1863	Killed May 9, 1864, at Rocky Face Ridge.
Do.	ROBERT C. BROWN	June 24, 1864	June 24, 1864	Mustered out as Lieutenant-Colonel.
Do.	SAMUEL M. WOLFF	Dec. 15, 1865	Dec. 15, 1865	Mustered out as Lieutenant-Colonel.
Lt. Colonel	ISAAC GASS	Nov. 30, 1861	" 18, 1861	Resigned June 30, 1862.
Do.	JOHN J. WILLIAMS	June 30, 1862	July 29, 1862	Resigned August 10, 1862.
Do.	ALEX. McILVANE	Aug. 19, "	Nov. 19, "	Promoted to Colonel.
Do.	ROBERT C. BROWN	March 11, 1863	March 31, 1863	Promoted to Colonel.
Do.	SAMUEL L. COULTER	June 27, 1864	June 27, 1864	Mustered out Feb. 16, 1865.
Do.	SAMUEL M. WOLFF	March 18, 1865	March 18, 1865	Promoted to Colonel.
Do.	NORMAN K. BROWN	Dec. 15, "	Dec. 15, "	Mustered out with regiment as Major.
Major	JOHN J. WILLIAMS	Nov. 30, 1861	" 18, 1861	Promoted to Lieutenant-Colonel.
Do.	ALEX. McILVANE	June 30, 1862	July 29, 1862	Promoted to Lieutenant-Colonel.
Do.	WM. W. SMITH	Aug. 10, "	Nov. 19, "	Resigned July 15, 1863.
Do.	SAMUEL L. COULTER	March 11, 1863	March 31, 1863	Promoted to Lieutenant-Colonel.
Do.	SAMUEL M. WOLFF	Feb. 23, 1865	Feb. 23, 1865	Promoted to Lieutenant-Colonel.
Do.	NORMAN K. BROWN	March 18, "	March 18, "	Promoted to Lieutenant-Colonel.
Do.	GEORGE HALL	Dec. 15, "	Dec. 15, "	Mustered out with regiment as Captain.
Surgeon	HENRY O. MACK	Oct. 3, 1861	" 18, 1861	Resigned August 2, 1862.
Do.	ABRAHAM McMAHAN	Aug. 2, 1862	Aug. 25, 1862	Mustered out July 14, 1864.
Do.	HUGH P. ANDERSON	July 21, 1864	July 21, 1864	Mustered out with regiment.
Ass't Surgeon	HUGH P. ANDERSON	Nov. 27, 1861	Dec. 18, 1861	Promoted to Surgeon.
Do.	V. G. MILLER	Aug. 21, 1862	Aug. 29, 1862	Resigned May 16, 1863.
Do.	A. POTTER	June 29, 1863	June 29, 1863	Resigned Nov. 9, 1863.
Do.	MOSES H. QUINN	July 25, 1864	July 25, 1864	Mustered out with regiment.
Chaplain	A. R. BROWN	Nov. 26, 1861	Dec. 18, 1863	Resigned July 13, 1862.
Do.	R. G. THOMPSON	July 1, 1863	July 20, "	Mustered out with regiment.
Captain	Alex. McIlvane	Oct. 15, 1861	Dec. 18, 1861	Promoted to Major.
Do.	Hugh P. Anderson	" 21, "	" 18, "	Promoted to Assistant Surgeon.
Do.	James B. Brown	" 21, "	" 18, "	Resigned May 4, 1862.
Do.	Wm. W. Smith	" 24, "	" 18, "	Promoted to Major.
Do.	Samuel Nepper	" 31, "	" 18, "	Honorably discharged May 17, 1864.
Do.	Isaac Gass	Nov. 1, "	" 18, "	Promoted to Lieutenant-Colonel.
Do.	Furenne C. Myers	" 6, "	" 18, "	Dismissed December 6, 1862.
Do.	John H. Finfrock	" 12, "	" 18, "	Discharged November 5, 1862.
Do.	Robert C. Brown	" 27, "	" 18, "	Promoted to Lieutenant-Colonel.
Do.	Charles R. Lord	" 30, "	" 18, "	Resigned January 31, 1863.
Do.	Joseph B. Sweet	" 30, "	" 18, "	Killed at Murfreesboro.
Do.	Samuel L. Coulter	Dec. 1, "	" 18, "	Promoted to Major.
Do.	Michael Keiser	May 4, 1862	June 20, 1862	Resigned June 28, 1861.
Do.	David A. Scott	June 30, "	July 29, "	Resigned March 23, 1863.
Do.	Warner Young	Nov. 19, "	Dec. 9, "	Honorably discharged October 1, 1863.
Do.	Wm. O. Starr	Dec. 6, "	March 31, 1863	Mustered out August 26, 1864.
Do.	Aaron S. Campbell	Nov. 5, "	" 31, "	Resigned August 5, 1863.
Do.	Joseph B. Ferguson	Jan. 31, "	April 2, "	Resigned May 18, 1863.
Do.	Samuel M. Wolff	" 3, 1863	March 31, "	Promoted to Major.
Do.	Norman K. Brown	March 11, "	April 12, "	Promoted to Major.
Do.	Bryant Grafton	" 11, "	" 22, "	Mustered out.
Do.	Henry H. King	" 23, "	" 22, "	Killed November 25, 1863.
Do.	John W. Zeigler	May 18, "	May 29, "	Killed September 20, 1863.
Do.	Robert S. Chamberlain	Aug. 5, "	Aug. 25, "	Honorably discharged September 23, 1864.
Do.	Tip. S. Marvin	July 13, 1864	July 13, 1864	Declined.
Do.	Chauncy Woodruff	" 13, "	" 13, "	Declined promotion.
Do.	George Hall	" 13, "	" 13, "	Promoted to Major.
Do.	Dudley C. Carr	Aug. 11, "	Aug. 11, "	Declined to accept.
Do.	Thomas E. Tillottson	" 11, "	" 11, "	Mustered out with regiment.
Do.	John K. Shellenbarger	Sept. 26, "	Sept. 26, "	Declined.
Do.	Thomas R. Smith	Nov. 3, "	Nov. 3, "	Declined promotion.
Do.	David Cummins	" 3, "	" 3, "	Resigned as 1st Lieutenant October 29, 1864.
Do.	James D. Herbert	" 3, "	" 3, "	Resigned as 2d Lieutenant January 3, 1866.
Do.	Alonzo Hancock	Dec. 9, "	Dec. 9, "	Mustered out with regiment.
Do.	Jacob G. Bittinger	" 9, "	" 9, "	Mustered out with regiment.
Do.	Alfred A. Reed	" 9, "	" 9, "	Mustered out with regiment.
Do.	Wm. G. Patterson	Jan. 28, 1865	Jan. 28, 1865	Mustered out with regiment.
Do.	Charles E. Baker	" 28, "	" 28, "	Mustered out with regiment.
Do.	Harrison Lawrence	Feb. 23, "	Feb. 23, "	Declined to accept.
Do.	Christian M. Gowing	March 18, "	March 18, "	Mustered out with regiment.
Do.	Wm. H. Faber	April 26, "	April 26, "	Mustered out with regiment.
Do.	Wm. J. Holden	June 16, "	June 16, "	Mustered out with regiment.
Do.	John F. Couter	Dec. 15, "	Dec. 15, "	Mustered out with regiment as 1st Lieutenant.
1st Lieutenant	Roeliff Brinkerhoff	Sept. 28, 1861	Sept. 28, 1861	R. Q. M.; appointed by Pres. Capt. and A. Q. M. [Nov. 4, '61.
Do.	Michael Keiser	Oct. 15, "	Dec. 18, "	Promoted to Captain.
Do.	David A. Scott	" 21, "		Promoted to Captain.
Do.	Cornelius C. White	" 28, "		Resigned November 21, 1862.
Do.	Robert C. Brown	" 31, "		Promoted to Captain.
Do.	Augustus N. Goldwood	" 31, "		Resigned August 12, 1861.
Do.	Samuel L. Coulter	Nov. 1, "		Promoted to Captain.
Do.	Ebenezer B. Finley	" 5, "		Mustered out July 11, 1862.
Do.	Simeon B. Conn	" 12, "		Dismissed February 2, 1863.
Do.	Marcus T. Myer	" 25, "		Resigned November 3, 1862.
Do.	Warner Young	" 27, "		Promoted to Captain November 19, 1862.
Do.	Aaron S. Campbell	" 27, "		Promoted to Captain.
Do.	Wilbur F. Sanders	" 30, "		Resigned August 10, 1862.
Do.	Lorenzo D. Myers	" 30, "		Appointed Captain by President of U. S.

RANK.	NAME.	DATE OF RANK.	COM. ISSUED.	REMARKS.
1st Lieutenant	Tip. S. Marvin	Nov. 30, 1861	....	Mustered out at expiration of time.
Do.	Wm. O. Starr	May 4, 1862	June 20, 1862	Promoted to Captain.
Do.	Ebenezer B. Finley	July 12, "	July 22, "	Resigned August 11, 1862.
Do.	Samuel M. Wolff	June 20, "	" 29, "	Promoted to Captain.
Do.	Bryant Grafton	Aug. 10, "	Oct. 18, "	Promoted to Captain.
Do.	Chauncey Woodruff	" 11, "	Nov. 26, "	Resigned October 2, 1864.
Do.	Dudley C. Carr	" 12, "	Dec. 9, "	Mustered out under Order 75.
Do.	Henry H. King	Nov. 19, "	" 9, "	Promoted to Captain.
Do.	Joseph B. Ferguson	" 21, "	" 9, "	Promoted to Captain.
Do.	Cyrus Y. Freeman	" 3, "	" 9, "	Revoked.
Do.	John L. Smith	Feb. 2, "	April 22, "	Revoked.
Do.	Thomas H. Ehlers	July 3, "	March 31, 1863	Killed.
Do.	George Hall	Dec. 6, "	" 30, "	Promoted to Captain.
Do.	Norman K. Brown	Nov. 3, "	" 31, "	Promoted to Captain.
Do.	Thomas E. Tillottson	April 1, 1863	April 29, "	Promoted to Captain.
Do.	John K. Shellenbarger	" 1, "	" 29, "	Mustered out February 6, 1865.
Do.	Thomas R. Smith	" 1, "	" 29, "	Mustered out.
Do.	Robert S. Chamberlain	" 1, "	" 29, "	Promoted to Captain.
Do.	Frank H. Killinger	" 1, "	" 29, "	Dismissed June 21, 1864.
Do.	David Cummins	" 1, "	" 29, "	Promoted to Captain.
Do.	John W. Zeigler	" 1, "	" 29, "	Promoted to Captain.
Do.	John C. Marshall	May 18, "	May 29, "	Killed May 27, 1864.
Do.	Riley Albach	Aug. 5, "	Aug. 25, "	Resigned May 7, 1864.
Do.	James D. Herbert	July 13, 1864	July 13, 1864	Promoted to Captain.
Do.	John Q. McIlvane	" 13, "	" 13, "	Resigned as 2d Lieutenant July 26, 1864.
Do.	Daniel Howe	" 13, "	" 13, "	Commission returned.
Do.	Alonzo Hancock	" 13, "	" 13, "	Promoted to Captain.
Do.	Jacob G. Bittinger	" 13, "	" 13, "	Promoted to Captain.
Do.	Lewis High	Aug. 11, "	Aug. 11, "	Declined promotion; commission returned.
Do.	Alfred A. Reed	" 11, "	" 11, "	Promoted to Captain.
Do.	Samuel B. Barker	Sept. 8, "	Sept. 18, "	Declined.
Do.	Wm. G. Patterson	" 26, "	" 26, "	Promoted to Captain.
Do.	Charles E. Baker	" 26, "	" 26, "	Promoted to Captain.
Do.	Harrison Lawrence	Nov. 3, "	Nov. 3, "	Resigned May 11, 1865.
Do.	Christian M. Gowing	" 3, "	" 3, "	Promoted to Captain.
Do.	Wm. H. Faber	Dec. 9, "	Dec. 9, "	Promoted to Captain.
Do.	Wm. J. Holden	" 9, "	" 9, "	Promoted to Captain.
Do.	John F. Conter	March 18, 1865	March 18, 1865	Promoted to Captain.
Do.	Andrew Lybold	" 18, "	" 18, "	Mustered out with regiment.
Do.	Stephen A. McCollum	" 18, "	" 18, "	Mustered out with regiment as Adjutant.
Do.	Albert Thomas	" 18, "	" 18, "	Mustered out with regiment.
Do.	John W. McChesney	" 18, "	" 18, "	Mustered out with regiment.
Do.	Samuel Garrett	" 18, "	" 18, "	Mustered out with regiment as R. Q. M.
Do.	Thomas L. Thompson	April 26, "	April 26, "	Mustered out with regiment.
Do.	Joseph Andrews	" 26, "	" 26, "	Mustered out with regiment as 1st Sergeant.
Do.	Samuel E. Smith	" 26, "	" 26, "	Resigned October 16, 1865.
Do.	David B. Leiter	May 31, "	May 31, "	Mustered out with regiment.
Do.	Wm. A. Dillon	" 31, "	" 31, "	Mustered out with regiment.
Do.	John A. Gillis	Sept. 4, "	Sept. 4, "	Honorably discharged January 2, 1866.
Do.	Joseph Andrews	Dec. 15, "	Dec. 15, "	Mustered out with regiment as 1st Sergeant.
Do.	Andrew Andrews	" 15, "	" 15, "	Mustered out with regiment as 1st Sergeant.
2d Lieutenant	Wm. O. Starr	Oct. 1, 1861	" 18, 1861	Promoted to 1st Lieutenant.
Do.	John L. Smith	" 3, "	" 18, "	Resigned May 31, 1862.
Do.	Thomas McGill	" 8, "	" 18, "	Deceased.
Do.	Samuel M. Wolff	" 26, "	" 18, "	Promoted to 1st Lieutenant.
Do.	Bryant Grafton	" 30, "	" 18, "	Promoted to 1st Lieutenant.
Do.	Isaac F. Biggerstaff	Nov. 25, "	" 18, "	Resigned February 23.
Do.	Cyrus Y. Freeman	" 27, "	" 18, "	Promoted; dismissed March 20, 1863.
Do.	Wm. McDowell	" 30, "	" 18, "	Resigned September 7, 1862.
Do.	Norman K. Brown	" 30, "	" 18, "	Promoted to 1st Lieutenant.
Do.	Chauncey Woodruff	Dec. 1, "	" 18, "	Promoted to 1st Lieutenant.
Do.	Henry H. King	Feb. 23, 1862	March 20, 1862	Promoted to 1st Lieutenant.
Do.	Dudley C. Carr	May 31, "	June 24, "	Promoted to 1st Lieutenant.
Do.	George Hall	" 4, "	July 29, "	Promoted to 1st Lieutenant.
Do.	Thomas H. Ehlers	June 30, "	" 29, "	Promoted to 1st Lieutenant.
Do.	John L. Smith	July 24, "	Aug. 18, "	Dismissed July 31, 1863.
Do.	Thomas E. Tillottson	Aug. 10, "	Oct. 16, "	Promoted to 1st Lieutenant.
Do.	Joseph B. Ferguson	" 11, "	Nov. 26, "	Promoted to 1st Lieutenant.
Do.	Thomas R. Smith	Sept. 7, "	Dec. 9, "	Promoted to 1st Lieutenant.
Do.	Frank H. Killinger	Aug. 12, "	" 31, "	Promoted to 1st Lieutenant.
Do.	Alex. Maffitt	April 1, 1863	April 29, 1863	Resigned October 15, 1863.
Do.	John K. Shellenbarger	Nov. 26, "	March 6, "	Promoted to 1st Lieutenant.
Do.	John Blecker	" 3, "	" 31, "	Resigned July 9, 1864.
Do.	James D. Herbert	Dec. 6, "	" 31, "	Promoted to 1st Lieutenant.
Do.	David Cummins	Nov. 5, "	" 31, "	Promoted to 1st Lieutenant.
Do.	John Q. McIlvane	April 1, "	April 29, "	Resigned July 26, 1864.
Do.	Riley Albach	" 1, "	" 29, "	Promoted to 1st Lieutenant.
Do.	Daniel Howe	" 1, "	" 29, "	Mustered out.
Do.	Alonzo Hancock	" 1, "	" 29, "	Promoted to 1st Lieutenant.
Do.	Jacob G. Bittinger	" 1, "	" 29, "	Promoted to 1st Lieutenant.
Do.	Lewis High	" 1, "	" 29, "	Mustered out April 4, 1865.
Do.	Addison M. Bloom	July 31, "	Aug. 20, "	Transferred to 128th O. V. I.
Do.	Alfred A. Reed	Aug. 5, "	" 25, "	Promoted to 1st Lieutenant.
Do.	Augustus Noeltnor	Dec. 15, 1865	Dec. 15, 1865	Mustered out as 1st Sergeants; complimentary commissions given after they were mustered out.
Do.	David E. Barrett	" 15, "	" 15, "	
Do.	Robert Fisher	" 15, "	" 15, "	
Do.	John Rhodes	" 15, "	" 15, "	
Do.	John W. Leidigh	" 15, "	" 15, "	
Do.	Alfred G. Anderson	" 15, "	" 15, "	
Do.	Samuel Campbell	" 15, "	" 15, "	
Do.	Silas S. Mallory	" 15, "	" 15, "	
Do.	Josiah Galbraith	" 15, "	" 15, "	
Do.	George Davy	" 15, "	" 15, "	

SIXTY-FOURTH OHIO VOLUNTEER INFANTRY.

THE SIXTY-FOURTH OHIO was organized and recruited at Mansfield, Ohio, and went into Camp Buckingham, Mansfield, November 9, 1861. About the middle of December it moved by rail to Cincinnati; thence by steamer to Louisville, Kentucky. Under orders, moved from Louisville December 26th, and marched to Bardstown, Kentucky. It was brigaded there, and moved to Danville and Hall's Gap. Here the regiment engaged in building corduroy roads to facilitate the movement of supplies to General Thomas's forces at Somerset, Kentucky. The battle of Mill Springs having been won, the Sixty-Fourth Ohio was ordered up to Bowling Green, and reaching Munfordsville, joined the National forces and marched with them to Nashville, Tennessee.

At Nashville one week, it moved with General T. J. Wood's division for Pittsburg Landing, by way of Columbia. It reached Savannah, seven miles below Pittsburg Landing, at nine o'clock on the morning of the 7th of April, and taking steamers, arrived on the battle-field of Shiloh at eleven o'clock A. M. The regiment, with its brigade, commanded by General Garfield, disembarked on the battle-field, and was moved up on the double-quick to the scene of conflict. The brunt of the battle was over, however, and but one company of the regiment (company A, Captain Alexander McIlvaine) succeeded in getting into action.

After the battle the regiment was chiefly engaged in burying the dead, getting up supplies, and performing picket-duty. It participated in the movement on and siege of Corinth, and was thereafter sent to Iuka, Tuscumbia, Decatur, Huntsville, and Stevenson. Here it erected Fort Harker, in honor of its brave and talented brigade commander.

About the 1st of August, 1862, the regiment and its brigade moved with the National forces toward Nashville, and from there pushed on in a race with Bragg's Rebel forces to Louisville, Kentucky. At Munfordsville a sharp skirmish was had with the enemy, who was driven out of the place and across Green River.

After remaining at Louisville about ten days the regiment, with the National forces, moved out on the Bardstown Turnpike to the vicinity of Perryville, and had the mortification of witnessing the battle at that place without the permission to help their hard-pressed comrades. Much feeling existed at the time concerning this battle, and many slanderous stories about General Buell were circulated by the partisans of the General who brought it on.

Following the enemy beyond Wild Cat, the retrograde movement of the National forces commenced. The Sixty-Fourth moved, with its brigade, through Stamford, Scottsville, Gallatin, and on to Nashville, and there went into camp out on the Nolinsville Turnpike, three miles.

The next important event in the history of the regiment was the battle of Stone River. In this the Sixty-Fourth was in Crittenden's corps and Wood's division, on the left wing. On Tuesday evening, just at dusk, the regiment was thrown across Stone River, but, meeting with overwhelming opposition, it was recalled, and returned to its former position in line, after sustaining slight loss. Lying on its arms that night, the next morning at seven o'clock it received orders to double-quick to the relief of the right wing; General R. W. Johnson's line having been forced. Immediately on arrival it became engaged, and held the enemy in check until the scattered National forces were rallied. It then fell back on the main line, drawing the Rebels, until within reach of a prepared line of Nationals, who poured into the exultant Rebels a murderous fire, which staggered and drove them back to the point they started from.

The regiment then returned to its former line of 30th of December on the left. On the last day of the battle (Friday, January 2, 1863), the regiment was in all the movements of its brigade. Of about three hundred engaged it lost, in this battle, seventy-five men killed and wounded.

At Murfreesboro' until June 7, 1863, the Sixty-Fourth moved with the National army under General Wm. S. Rosecrans, on the Tullahoma campaign, up to Chattanooga; stopped over night and marched out to Chickamauga Creek. On September 11th the regiment, brigade, and division moved toward Lee & Gordon's Mills, and skirmished with the enemy, driving them beyond the mills. On Friday, September 18th, had another skirmish without loss. The 19th, the first day of the battle of Chickamauga, the Sixty-Fourth was closely engaged during the whole day; also on Sunday, the 20th, until after dark. Loss in this battle, in killed, wounded, and missing, over one hundred men.

Falling back into Chattanooga, the regiment was employed building fortifications and performing picket-duty until the movement of Hooker's corps and the relief of the National forces. Moving out on the 25th of November the Sixty-Fourth, with its brigade, participated in the taking of Mission Ridge, losing few men. Captain King and private George Cropp were killed.

Immediately following the battle of Chickamauga the regiment was sent up with the expedition for the relief of Knoxville, and marched as far as Strawberry Plains. The siege of Knoxville being raised, the regiment returned to Chattanooga. About January, 1864, the subject of re-enlistment was agitated. Three-fourths of the Sixty-Fourth expressed a willingness to enlist again for three years, and the men were sent to Ohio furloughed for thirty days.

At Mansfield they were warmly received by the citizens, and honored with a grand supper at Miller's Hall.

On March 14th the regiment again left Mansfield "for the front," and arrived at Chattanooga about the 1st of April, being compelled to march by land from Nashville to Cleveland, Tennessee, resting ten days at Chattanooga.

On May 3d General Sherman ordered his army to take the initiative on Atlanta. On the 9th the regiment, with its brigade, participated in the charge on Rocky Face Ridge. Colonel Alex. McIlvaine, then in command, and Lieutenant Thomas H. Ehlers were killed, with nineteen men, and sixty-five wounded. Captain Chamberlain, of Summit County, commanding company C, was severely wounded in the face.

At Resaca, on the 14th of June, the Sixty-Fourth lost several men killed and wounded. At Muddy Creek, June 18th, the regiment again participated, but its loss was slight. During this whole campaign it was daily skirmishing with the enemy up to the 20th of July, when it went into the battle of Peachtree Creek, in which it lost Sergeant Marion Trage, of company H, shot through the head.

On June 21st, with its brigade and division, it moved to the front of Atlanta, where a line of strong works was thrown up. From this date until August 26th the regiment was daily, almost hourly, under fire.

At midnight of that day the flanking movement on Jonesboro' was commenced by General Sherman. September 3d the fight of Jonesboro' took place, in which the regiment was engaged, with but slight loss. September 6th, in the evening, the regiment was engaged in a skirmish at Lovejoy's Station, losing one man (Sergeant Towsley, of company G), shot through the bowels, who died in the ambulance before reaching the hospital.

Atlanta taken, the regiment, with its brigade and division, marched back to that place and went into camp. Remaining there two weeks it was dispatched by rail, with the Fourth Army Corps, in pursuit of Hood and his Rebel forces, to Chattanooga. It remained there a few days, during which it was paid off. Receiving four hundred new recruits from Ohio, the regiment was sent on a reconnoissance in pursuit of Hood's forces to Alpine, Georgia, fifty miles south of Chattanooga.

Returning to Chattanooga the regiment was almost immediately thereafter sent by cars to Athens, Alabama. From thence it marched to Pulaski, Tennessee, and to Spring Hill, passing through Columbia. At Spring Hill the regiment was engaged with the enemy, and lost a few men killed and wounded.

From Spring Hill the Sixty-Fourth moved to Franklin, Tennessee, and was in the battle at that place, with severe loss in killed, wounded, and missing.

After this battle the regiment marched to Nashville, and was engaged in the sorties and battles before that city, with but slight loss.

Following this the regiment was in the pursuit of Hood's scattered and demoralized forces across the Tennessee River, and then marched to Huntsville and went into camp. From there it moved to Decatur and Athens, where it remained two months, and then returned to Huntsville. From Huntsville it was sent into East Tennessee as far as Strawberry Plains, remained there a week, and returned to Nashville.

From Nashville the Sixty-Fourth was taken by transports to New Orleans, where it lay three months. While in that city the regiment lost heavily by sickness.

About the middle of September it was sent to Victoria, Texas, and remained there until the 3d of December, 1865.

It was mustered out at Victoria, and sent to Camp Chase, Ohio, and was there paid off and discharged.

65th REGIMENT OHIO VOLUNTEER INFANTRY.

ROSTER, THREE YEARS' SERVICE.

RANK.	NAME.	DATE OF RANK.	COM. ISSUED.	REMARKS.
Colonel	CHARLES G. HARKER	Nov. 11, 1861	Dec. 18, 1861	Promoted Brigadier-General; killed in action.
Do.	ORLOW SMITH	" 21, 1865	Nov. 21, 1865	Mustered out with regiment as Lieut. Col.
Lt. Colonel	DANIEL FRENCH	" 30, 1861	Dec. 18, 1861	Resigned August 8, 1862.
Do.	ALEX. CASSIL	Aug. 8, 1862	Oct. 28, 1862	Resigned March 22, 1863.
Do.	HORATIO N. WHITBECK	March 22, 1863	March 27, 1863	Resigned August 16, 1865.
Do.	ORLOW SMITH	Oct. 10, 1865	Oct. 10, 1865	Promoted to Colonel.
Do.	WILBUR F. HINMAN	Nov. 21, "	Nov. 21, "	Mustered out with regiment as Captain.
Major	JAMES OLDS	" 30, 1861	Dec. 18, 1861	Resigned October 7, 1862.
Do.	HORATIO N. WHITBECK	Oct. 7, 1862	Nov. 29, 1862	Promoted to Lieutenant-Colonel.
Do.	SAMUEL C. BROWN	March 22, 1863	March 22, 1863	Killed September 22, 1863.
Do.	ORLOW SMITH	Sept. 22, "	Oct. 29, "	Promoted to Lieutenant-Colonel.
Do.	WILBUR F. HINMAN	Oct. 10, 1865	" 10, 1865	Promoted to Lieutenant-Colonel.
Do.	J. F. SONNESTINE, jr.	Nov. 21, "	Nov. 24, "	Mustered out with regiment as Captain.
Surgeon	JOHN G. KYLE	Oct. 3, 1861	Dec. 18, 1861	Resigned August 20, 1862.
Do.	J. W. TODD	" 20, 1862	Jan. 22, 1863	Resigned December 7, 1864.
Do.	J. H. CRUTHERS	Jan. 4, 1865	" 4, 1865	Mustered out with regiment.
Ass't Surgeon	JOHN C. GILL	Nov. 11, 1861	Dec. 18, 1861	Resigned June 24, 1862.
Do.	WM. M. MCCULLEY	Aug. 21, 1862	Sept. 21, 1862	Resigned November 3, 1863.
Do.	W. S. PATTERSON	Oct. 7, "	Feb. 10, 1863	Resigned.
Do.	CHAS. J. HAGAN	July 13, 1864	July 13, 1864	Declined; commission returned.
Do.	W. E. PATTERSON	Feb. 15, 1865	Feb. 15, 1865	Discharged for disability August 25, 1865.
Chaplain	ANDREW BARNES	Nov. 30, 1861	Dec. 18, 1861	Resigned February 16, 1863.
Do.	THOMAS POWELL	July 1, 1864	July 1, 1864	Mustered out with regiment.
Captain	Alex. Cassil	Oct. 24, 1861	Dec. 18, 1861	Promoted to Lieutenant-Colonel.
Do.	Horatio N. Whitbeck	Nov. 2, "	" 18, "	Promoted to Major.
Do.	Henry Camp	" 4, "	" 18, "	Resigned August 16, 1862.
Do.	Daniel French	" 6, "	" 18, "	Promoted to Lieutenant-Colonel.
Do.	Edward L. Austin	" 4, "	" 18, "	Resigned November 4, 1862.
Do.	James Olds	" 7, "	" 18, "	Promoted to Major.
Do.	Samuel C. Brown	" 7, "	" 18, "	Promoted to Major.
Do.	Joshua S. Preble	" 17, "	" 18, "	Resigned April 14, 1862.
Do.	Jacob Christophel	" 22, "	" 18, "	Killed December 31, 1862.
Do.	Orlow Smith	" 25, "	" 18, "	Promoted to Major.
Do.	John C. Baxter	" 30, "	" 18, "	Resigned February 26, 1862.
Do.	Richard M. Voorhis	" 30, "	" 18, "	Honorably discharged March 28, 1864.
Do.	Albert Ellis	Feb. 26, 1862	March 20, 1862	Revoked; resigned as 1st Lieut. Nov. 13, 1863.
Do.	Samuel L. Bowlby	April 14, "	May 5, "	Resigned May 24, 1863.
Do.	Thomas Powell	Aug. 8, "	Nov. 25, "	Appointed Chaplain July 1, 1864.
Do.	Francis M. Graham	" 16, "	" 25, "	Resigned February 20, 1863.
Do.	Joseph M. Randall	Oct. 7, "	" 25, "	Mustered out January 19, 1865.
Do.	Lucien B. Eaton	May 26, "	Dec. 31, "	Promoted to Lieut. Col. colored regiment.
Do.	N. L. Williams	Nov. 4, "	" 31, "	Killed June 27, 1864.
Do.	John C. Matthias	Feb. 20, "	April 19, 1863	Resigned November 17, 1864.
Do.	Charles O. Tannehill	Dec. 31, "	March 6, "	Resigned September 16, 1864.
Do.	Andrew Howenstein	March 20, 1863	" 27, "	Honorably discharged March 10, 1865.
Do.	Wm. M. Farrar	May 24, "	June 10, "	Resigned October 14, 1863.
Do.	Wilbur F. Hinman	June 14, 1864	" 14, 1864	Promoted to Major.
Do.	Asa A. Gardner	Oct. 14, 1863	Jan. 12, "	Mustered out May 15, 1865.
Do.	Asa M. Trimble	June 14, 1864	June 14, "	Declined; commission returned.
Do.	Joel P. Brown	July 13, "	July 13, "	Declined.
Do.	Franklin Pealer	" 13, "	" 13, "	Resigned December 12, 1864.
Do.	J. F. Sonnestine, jr.	" 13, "	" 13, "	Promoted to Major. [no discharge.
Do.	Brewer Smith	Aug. 29, "	Aug. 29, "	On detach serv. as A.D.C. to Brig Gen. Elliott,
Do.	Joseph H. Wilsey	Sept. 26, "	Sept. 26, "	On detached duty at muster out of regiment.
Do.	Otho M. Shipley	Nov. 1, "	Nov. 1, "	Mustered out with regiment.
Do.	P. P. McCune	Dec. 7, "	Dec. 7, "	Mustered out with regiment.
Do.	Christian M. Bush	" 9, "	" 9, "	Mustered out with regiment.
Do.	Benj. Trescott	Feb. 10, 1865	Feb. 10, 1865	Mustered out with regiment.
Do.	John C. Zollinger	" 10, "	" 10, "	Declined promotion as Captain.
Do.	E. E. Scranton	April 8, "	April 8, "	Mustered out with regiment.
Do.	Ezekiel Moore	Oct. 10, "	Oct. 10, "	Mustered out with regiment as 1st Lieutenant.
Do.	Wm. A. Bell	" 10, "	" 10, "	Mustered out with regiment as 1st Lieutenant.
Do.	James P. Mills	Nov. 24, "	Nov. 24, "	Mustered out with regiment as Q. M. Serg't.
Do.	Edward G. Powell	" 24, "	" 24, "	Mustered out with regiment as Q. M.
1st Lieutenant	Albert Ellis	Oct. 24, 1861	Dec. 18, 1861	Promoted; resigned November 13, 1863.
Do.	Horace H. Justice	Nov. 1, "	" 18, "	Died February 11, 1862.
Do.	Daniel G. Swain	" 4, "	" 18, "	Resigned.
Do.	Samuel L. Bowlby	" 4, "	" 18, "	Promoted to Captain.
Do.	Richard M. Voorhis	" 6, "	" 18, "	Promoted to Captain.
Do.	John C. Baxter	" 7, "	" 18, "	Promoted to Captain.
Do.	Thomas Powell	" 7, "	" 18, "	Promoted to Captain.
Do.	Francis M. Graham	" 12, "	" 18, "	Promoted to Captain.
Do.	Joseph M. Randall	" 17, "	" 18, "	Promoted to Captain.
Do.	Lucien B. Eaton	" 22, "	" 18, "	Promoted to Captain.
Do.	Clark S. Gregg	" 28, "	" 18, "	Died May 11, 1862.
Do.	Wm. M. Farrar	" 30, "	" 18, "	Promoted to Captain.
Do.	D. H. Rowland	" 30, "	" 18, "	Resigned June 16, 1862.
Do.	N. L. Williams	" 30, "	" 18, "	Promoted to Captain.
Do.	John M. Palmer	Feb. 26, 1862	March 20, 1862	Declined.
Do.	Johnson Armstrong	April 14, "	May 5, "	Resigned August 12, 1862.
Do.	George W. Huckins	Feb. 26, "	June 24, "	Deceased.
Do.	Frank B. Hunt	Aug. 8, "	Nov. 26, "	Resigned November 29, 1863.
Do.	Charles O. Tannehill	" 12, "	" 26, "	Promoted to Captain.
Do.	Andrew Howenstein	" 16, "	" 26, "	Promoted to Captain.
Do.	Asa A. Gardner	Oct. 7, "	" 26, "	Promoted to Captain.

RANK.	NAME.	DATE OF RANK.	COM. ISSUED.	REMARKS.
1st Lieutenant	Oscar D. Walker	Nov. 13, 1862	Nov. 26, 1862	Resigned February 13, 1863.
Do.	W. F. Hinman	June 16, "	Dec. 31, "	Promoted to Captain.
Do.	Wm. H. Massey	July 1, "	" 31, "	Deceased.
Do.	Asa M. Trimble	May 26, "	" 31, "	Declined promotion.
Do.	Peter Markle	Nov. 4, "	" 31, "	Resigned November 20, 1863.
Do.	John C. Matthias	May 11, "	Feb. 22, 1863	Promoted to Captain.
Do.	Franklin Pealer	Feb. 13, 1863	" 21, "	Promoted to Captain.
Do.	Joel P. Brown	Dec. 31, 1862	March 6, "	Resigned November 20, 1864.
Do.	J. F. Sonnestine, jr.	March 22, 1863	April 9, "	Promoted to Captain.
Do.	Brewer Smith	" 23, "	" 9, "	Promoted to Captain.
Do.	R. S. Rook	April 5, "	June 18, "	Resigned December 11, 1863.
Do.	Nelson Smith	May 21, "	" 18, "	Resigned December 19, 1863.
Do.	Joseph H. Wilsey	June 11, 1864	" 11, 1864	Promoted to Captain.
Do.	John S. Talmadge	" 11, "	" 11, "	Resigned as 2d Lieutenant.
Do.	John Body	" 11, "	" 11, "	Honorably discharged as 2d Lieut. Aug. 7, 1864.
Do.	Otho M. Shipley	" 14, "	" 11, "	Promoted to Captain.
Do.	Culbertson Henwood	" 11, "	" 14, "	Killed.
Do.	P. P. McCune	" 11, "	" 14, "	Promoted to Captain.
Do.	Christian M. Bush	" 11, "	" 11, "	Promoted to Captain.
Do.	Benj. Trescott	July 13, "	July 13, "	Promoted to Captain. [as R. Q. M.
Do.	John C. Zollinger	" 13, "	" 13, "	Declined promotion; mustered out with reg't.
Do.	E. E. Scranton	" 13, "	" 13, "	Promoted to Captain.
Do.	Ezekiel Moore	" 13, "	" 13, "	Promoted to Captain.
Do.	Jonas Smith	" 13, "	" 13, "	Died June 10, 1865.
Do.	Wm. A. Bell	Aug. 29, "	Aug. 29, "	Promoted to Captain.
Do.	Edward G. Powell	Sept. 28, "	Sept. 28, "	Promoted to Captain.
Do.	John Kanel	Nov. 26, "	Nov. 26, "	Mustered out with regiment.
Do.	George S. Pope	Dec. 9, "	Dec. 9, "	Mustered out December, 14, 1864.
Do.	Wm. H. H. Smith	March 29, 1865	March 29, 1865	Mustered out with regiment.
Do.	George W. Carpenter	" 29, "	" 29, "	Mustered out with regiment.
Do.	George W. McFadden	" 29, "	" 29, "	Mustered out with regiment.
Do.	Joseph S. Covert	" 29, "	" 29, "	Mustered out with regiment.
Do.	Joseph Crow	" 29, "	" 29, "	Mustered out with regiment.
Do.	James P. Miller	Nov. 21, "	Nov. 21, "	Mustered out with regiment.
Do.	Alex. C. Copeland	" 21, "	" 24, "	Mustered out with regiment as Sergeant.
Do.	John S. Goshorn	" 21, "	" 24, "	
Do.	Horace W. Curtis	" 21, "	" 24, "	Mustered out with regiment as Sergeant.
Do.	Wm. H. Mozier	" 21, "	" 24, "	
2d Lieutenant	John M. Palmer	Oct. 10, 1861	Dec. 18, 1861	Promoted by President, February 19, 1862.
Do.	Johnson Armstrong	Nov. 4, "		Promoted to 1st Lieutenant.
Do.	George W. Huckins	" 15, "		Promoted to 1st Lieutenant.
Do.	Frank B. Hunt	" 18, "		Promoted to 1st Lieutenant.
Do.	Jacob Hammond	" 19, "		Resigned April 1, 1862.
Do.	Charles O. Tannehill	" 26, "		Promoted to 1st Lieutenant.
Do.	Samuel McKinney	" 28, "		Resigned June 3, 1862.
Do.	John T. Hyatt	" 30, "		Deceased.
Do.	Andrew Howenstein	" 30, "		Promoted to 1st Lieutenant.
Do.	Joseph P. Bradley	" 30, "		Resigned March 30, 1862.
Do.	Asa A. Gardner	Feb. 8, 1862	Feb. 8, 1862	Promoted to 1st Lieutenant.
Do.	Francis H. Kline	March 30, "	June 20, "	Resigned November 4, 1862.
Do.	Oscar D. Walker	April 1, "	" 20, "	Promoted to 1st Lieutenant.
Do.	Wm. H. Massey	June 3, "	Aug. 18, "	Promoted to 1st Lieutenant.
Do.	J. F. Sonnestine, jr.	" 16, "	Oct. 9, "	Promoted to 1st Lieutenant.
Do.	Asa M. Trimble	Feb. 26, "	" 9, "	Promoted to 1st Lieutenant.
Do.	Peter Markle	Aug. 8, "	Nov. 26, "	Promoted to 1st Lieutenant.
Do.	Dolsen Vankirk	" 12, "	" 26, "	Killed December 31, 1862.
Do.	Joel P. Brown	" 16, "	" 26, "	Promoted to 1st Lieutenant.
Do.	Franklin Pealer	Nov. 13, "	" 26, "	Promoted to 1st Lieutenant.
Do.	Samuel H. Young	" 4, "		Resigned March 30, 1862.
Do.	R. S. Rook	April 14, "	Dec. 31, "	Promoted to 1st Lieutenant.
Do.	John C. Matthias	Feb. 19, 1863	Feb. 21, 1863	Promoted to 1st Lieutenant.
Do.	Brewer Smith	Jan. 1, "	" 22, "	Promoted to 1st Lieutenant.
Do.	Joseph H. Wilsey	" 1, "	" 22, "	Promoted to 1st Lieutenant.
Do.	John S. Talmadge	Feb. 1, "	" 22, "	Resigned July 20, 1864.
Do.	John Body	" 13, "	" 24, "	Promoted to 1st Lieutenant.
Do.	Nelson Smith	Dec. 31, 1862	March 6, "	Promoted to 1st Lieutenant.
Do.	Charles Schroder	" 31, "	" 6, "	Dismissed June 9, 1863.
Do.	Otho M. Shipley	" 31, "	" 27, "	Promoted to 1st Lieutenant.
Do.	Culbertson Henwood	March 22, 1863	April 9, "	Killed September 19, 1863.
Do.	P. P. McCune	" 23, "	" 9, "	Promoted to 1st Lieutenant.
Do.	Christian M. Bush	" 30, "	" 28, "	Promoted to 1st Lieutenant.
Do.	Benj. Trescott	April 5, "	June 18, "	Promoted to 1st Lieutenant.
Do.	Eben. Bingham	May 24, "	" 18, "	Killed June 15, 1864.
Do.	Wm. A. Bell	July 13, 1864	July 13, 1864	Promoted to 1st Lieutenant.
Do.	Roland Critchfield	Nov. 21, 1865	Nov. 24, 1865	Mustered out as 1st Sergeants; complimentary commissions given after they were mustered out.
Do.	Christopher Bushert	" 24, "	" 24, "	
Do.	Joel Wright	" 21, "	" 21, "	
Do.	Thomas Clague	" 21, "	" 24, "	
Do.	Hugh Woods	" 24, "	" 24, "	
Do.	David Walter	" 24, "	" 21, "	
Do.	Silas T. Wagner	" 24, "	" 24, "	
Do.	Melville C. Porter	" 24, "	" 24, "	
Do.	Joseph Meredith	" 21, "	" 24, "	
Do.	Joseph Critchfield	" 21, "	" 24, "	

SIXTY-FIFTH OHIO VOLUNTEER INFANTRY.

THE SIXTY-FIFTH was one of the regiments included in the brigade raised at Mansfield, Ohio, by the Hon. John Sherman. It was organized at Camp Buckingham, near Mansfield, on the 3d of October, 1861, and was mustered into service on the 1st of December.

The regiment left Mansfield for active duty on the 18th of December, and moved, by way of Cincinnati, to Louisville, Kentucky, where it remained for a week, and then marched to Camp Morton, four miles east of Bardstown, arriving on the 30th of December. The Sixty-Fifth was assigned to a brigade composed of the Sixty-Fourth and Sixty-Fifth Ohio, the Fifty-First Indiana, and Ninth Kentucky. Colonel Harker, of the Sixty-Fifth, commanded the brigade, and General Wood the division.

On the 13th of January, 1862, the brigade broke camp, and passing through Bardstown, Springfield, Lebanon, Haysville, Danville, and Stanford, Kentucky, arrived at Hall's Gap on the 24th. The regiment was ordered to corduroy the roads. The labor was severe, the country being swampy; and the miasma engendered disease to such degree that many of the men died. On the 7th of February the regiment marched to Lebanon, and on the 12th embarked on cars for Green River. It arrived at Camp Wood, near Munfordsville, on the 13th, where it remained until the 23d, when it crossed Green River on the railroad bridge, and passing Bowling Green, Franklin, Tyree Springs, and Goodlettsville, arrived at Nashville on the 13th of March, and went into camp two and a half miles south-east of the city. On this march the troops were forced, at times, to march through woods and on by-roads, as the Rebels had destroyed the turnpike in places. The men were compelled frequently to transport the contents of the baggage wagons on their backs over steep hills; and in one instance, after marching three days, the regiment had advanced only twelve miles.

On the 29th of March, the regiment, with General Garfield in command of the brigade, marched by way of Columbia to Savannah, where it arrived on the 6th of April, and on the morning of the 7th it moved on steamer to Pittsburg Landing. At four o'clock P. M. it was on the battle-field, but it did not become actively engaged. It lost two men wounded. The regiment next participated in the movements against Corinth, and during the siege was under fire almost hourly. After the evacuation it moved through Eastport, Iuka, Tuscumbia, Decatur, and Huntsville to Bridgeport, where it was engaged in guarding the Tennessee River until the 29th of August, when it marched northward in pursuit of Bragg's army, passing through Murfreesboro', Nashville, and Bowling Green, arriving at Louisville on the 24th of September. After resting about a week it moved to the vicinity of Perryville, and from there marched to Nashville.

In the reorganization of the army at Nashville, under General Rosecrans, the regiment remained in its old brigade, with Colonel Harker commanding. On the 26th of December the brigade moved on the Nashville Pike, in Crittenden's corps, fighting its way into Lavergne, across Stewart's Creek, and up to Stone River. On the night of the 29th the brigade crossed Stone River under orders, the men wading in water to their armpits, in the face of a murderous fire. The opposite bank was gained, and a line was formed, but the supports failed to come up and the brigade was ordered to retire, which it did in good order. Crittenden's corps lay on its arms all that night and during the whole of the next day; it was waiting for McCook to move on the right. Early on the morning of the 31st, McCook's corps was driven back, and Harker's brigade was ordered to its support. The brigade met a storm of bullets, and a solid column of exultant Rebels. For eight hours the brigade was engaged heavily, and at last succeeded in checking the Rebel army. In this engagement the Sixty-Fifth lost two officers killed and eight wounded (one mortally), and thirty-eight men killed, one hundred and six wounded, nineteen missing, and three deserted in the face of the enemy. All the commissioned officers of Company A were either killed or wounded; but Sergeant Culbertson Henwood bravely took command of the company and led it through the battle. He was promoted to Second-Lieutenant by Governor Tod. The regiment was under fire throughout the entire engagement.

The regiment remained at Murfreesboro' until the 7th of June, 1863, when it moved to the vicinity of Chattanooga, and on the 7th of September, skirmished with the enemy, losing one man. During the first day of the battle of Chickamauga, the regiment was held in reserve at Lee & Gordon's Mills until five o'clock in the afternoon, when it became briskly engaged. It moved to the left center, and lay on its arms all night. On the next morning at 10 o'clock it advanced about a mile but was driven back to a ridge, on which it re-formed. Fighting continued all day with alternate success and reverse. On the night of the 20th the entire army fell back to Mission Ridge, and from there to Chattanooga. In this engagement the regiment lost three officers killed and five wounded, and thirteen men killed, sixty wounded, and twenty-four missing. During the siege of Chattanooga supplies became exceedingly scarce, and men and animals suffered greatly. The regiment participated in the battle of Mission Ridge, with a loss of one officer wounded, one man killed, and thirteen wounded.

In the Atlanta campaign the Sixty-Fifth was under fire almost constantly. At Lookout Mountain it lost three men wounded and one missing. At Resaca it lost one officer wounded, two men killed and twenty-five wounded. At Dallas it lost one officer wounded, one man killed and four wounded. At Marietta it lost one officer killed, one man killed and ten wounded. In a skirmish near Kenesaw it lost two men wounded; and in a charge on Kenesaw it lost one officer killed and one wounded, and two men killed and six wounded. In this charge Brigadier-General Harker, formerly Colonel of the Sixty-Fifth, was killed. At Peachtree Creek it lost four men wounded and one missing; and at Atlanta, on the 22d of July, it lost one man killed and one wounded. The regiment participated in the flanking movement to Jonesboro', and from there advanced to Lovejoy. After the evacuation of Atlanta it fell back to that place, and went into camp.

The Sixty-Fifth remained at Atlanta about three weeks, and then moved in pursuit of Hood. It marched to Mission Ridge, and was sent from there, on cars, to Alpine, Georgia; but after remaining there four days it moved to Chattanooga, and was engaged in guarding the railroad near the Tennessee River. On the 29th of November the regiment participated in the battle of Springfield, losing two officers wounded (one of whom was captured), and five men killed, twenty wounded, and fourteen missing. On the 30th of November it was engaged in the battle of Franklin, with a loss of one man killed, twenty-two wounded, and twenty-one missing. The non-veterans were discharged on the 3d of October, 1864, leaving the regiment with an aggregate of one hundred and thirty men. The regiment was engaged in the battle of Nashville, and in the pursuit of the Rebel army across the Tennessee. When the pursuit was abandoned the regiment returned to Nashville and went into camp.

In June, 1865, the regiment moved from Nashville to Johnsonville, on the Tennessee River, where it embarked on transports for New Orleans. It remained at New Orleans for several weeks, and was then ordered to Texas. It performed garrison duty at San Antonio until December, 1865, when it was ordered to Camp Chase, Columbus, Ohio, where it was mustered out, paid, and discharged, on the 2d of January, 1866.

66th REGIMENT OHIO VOLUNTEER INFANTRY.

ROSTER, THREE YEARS' SERVICE.

RANK.	NAME.	DATE OF RANK.	COM. ISSUED.	REMARKS.
Colonel	CHARLES CANDY	Nov. 25, 1861	Jan. 17, 1863	Honorably discharged December 16, 1864.
Do.	JOHN T. MITCHELL, JR.	July 13, 1865	July 13, 1865	Mustered out with regiment as Lieut. Col.
Lt. Colonel	JAMES H. DYE	Sept. 28, 1861	Jan. 17, 1862	Resigned May 24, 1862.
Do.	EUGENE POWELL	May 24, 1862	June 20, "	Discharged for pro. in new reg't March 12, '65.
Do.	JOHN T. MITCHELL, JR.	April 12, 1865	April 12, 1865	Promoted to Colonel.
Do.	SAMUEL H. HEDGES	July 13, "	July 13, "	Mustered out as Major August 9, 1865.
Major	EUGENE POWELL	Oct. 22, 1861	Jan. 17, 1862	Promoted to Lieutenant-Colonel.
Do.	CHARLES E. FELTON	May 24, 1862	June 20, "	Resigned December 5, 1865.
Do.	JOSIAH G. PALMER	Dec. 5, "	Dec. 26, "	Killed July 3, 1863, at Gettysburg.
Do.	THOMAS MCCONNELL	July 20, "	Aug. 1, 1863	Honorably discharged as Captain Oct. 22, '64.
Do.	JOHN T. MITCHELL, JR.	April 8, 1865	April 8, 1865	Promoted to Lieutenant-Colonel.
Do.	SAMUEL H. HEDGES	" 12, "	" 12, "	Promoted to Lieutenant-Colonel.
Do.	CHARLES E. BUTTS	July 13, "	July 13, "	Mustered out as Captain.
Surgeon	THOMAS P. BOND	Sept. 26, 1861	Jan. 17, 1862	Discharged September 12, 1863.
Do.	JESSE W. BROCK	" 13, "	Nov. 19, "	Mustered out with regiment.
Ass't Surgeon	JESSE W. BROCK	Nov. 5, "	Jan. 17, "	Promoted to Surgeon.
Do.	SOLOMON F. CRUTCHFIELD	Aug. 21, 1862	Aug. 29, "	Failed to report.
Do.	JAMES P. BING	March 11, 1863	March 11, 1863	Declined.
Do.	B. F. LUDLUM	" 12, "	" 12, "	Mustered out with regiment.
Chaplain	W. R. PARSONS	Dec. 12, 1861	Dec. 27, 1861	Honorably discharged August 13, 1864.
Captain	J. G. Palmer	Nov. 9, "	Jan. 17, 1862	Promoted to Major.
Do.	Charles E. Felton	" 7, "	" 17, "	Promoted to Major.
Do.	Samuel F. McMorran	" 19, "	" 17, "	Resigned January 27, 1863.
Do.	Alvin Clark	" 22, "	" 17, "	Resigned December 10, 1862.
Do.	Thomas J. Buxton	" 30, "	" 17, "	Resigned June 5, 1863.
Do.	John Cassill	Dec. 11, "	" 17, "	Resigned June 21, 1862.
Do.	James Q. Baird	" 14, "	" 17, "	Resigned May 31, 1863.
Do.	Wm. McAdams	" 17, "	" 17, "	Resigned April 16, 1863.
Do.	Versalius Horr	" 17, "	" 17, "	Resigned October 27, 1862.
Do.	J. H. Van Deman	" 17, "	" 17, "	Resigned January 27, 1863.
Do.	Wm. M. Gwynne	May 24, 1862	June 20, "	Declined.
Do.	Thomas McConnell	" 24, "	July 28, "	Promoted to Major.
Do.	Wm. M. Gwynne	June 21, "	Oct. 16, "	Honorably discharged December 16, 1864.
Do.	John O. Dye	Nov. 10, "	Jan. 12, 1863	Resigned August 13, 1864.
Do.	Lemuel W. Smith	Dec. 5, "	" 12, "	Mustered out.
Do.	A. H. Yeazell	Nov. 1, "	" 12, "	Resigned May 26, 1863.
Do.	Martin R. Wright	Jan. 27, 1863	Feb. 21, "	Resigned July 31, 1863.
Do.	Wm. A. Sampson	" 27, "	" 10, "	Honorably discharged December 16, 1864.
Do.	B. F. Ganson	April 16, "	May 12, "	Mustered out.
Do.	Robert H. Russell	May 31, "	June 10, "	Mustered out.
Do.	John W. Watkins	" 27, "	" 15, "	Mustered out.
Do.	John F. Morgan	July 30, "	Aug. 1, "	Resigned July 26, 1864.
Do.	John N. Rathbone	March 3, 1864	March 3, 1864	Resigned October 17, 1864.
Do.	Joseph C. Brand	April 2, "	April 2, "	Declined; commission returned.
Do.	John T. Mitchell, jr.	May 9, "	May 9, "	Promoted to Major.
Do.	Samuel H. Hedges	Aug. 11, "	Aug. 11, "	Promoted to Major.
Do.	Archie Houston	" 19, "	" 19, "	Resigned September 30, 1864, as 1st Lieut.
Do.	T. G. Keller	Nov. 12, "	Nov. 12, "	Resigned.
Do.	James McIlroy	" 12, "	" 12, "	Resigned April 3, 1865.
Do.	Charles E. Butts	April 12, 1865	April 12, 1865	Promoted to Major.
Do.	James P. Conn	" 12, "	" 12, "	Mustered out with regiment.
Do.	W. Wallace Cranston	" 12, "	" 12, "	Mustered out under G. O. 24, June 28, 1865.
Do.	James C. Bowe	" 12, "	" 12, "	Mustered out as 1st Lieutenant May 15, 1865.
Do.	John H. Diltz	" 12, "	" 12, "	Mustered out with regiment.
Do.	Charles A. Poffenberger	" 12, "	" 12, "	Resigned June 2, 1865.
Do.	Richard E. Plunkett	" 12, "	" 12, "	Resigned June 2, 1865.
Do.	Wm. W. Jackson	" 12, "	" 12, "	Mustered out with regiment.
Do.	C. Warren Guy	May 31, "	May 31, "	Mustered out under G. O. 24, June 28, 1865.
Do.	Ridgely P. Wilkins	June 14, "	June 14, "	Mustered out with regiment.
Do.	Robert Simpson	" 14, "	" 14, "	Mustered out with regiment.
Do.	Henry Fraley	" 14, "	" 14, "	Mustered out with regiment.
Do.	James A. McClain	" 14, "	" 14, "	Mustered out with regiment.
Do.	John R. Clayton	July 13, "	July 13, "	Mustered out with regiment as Adjutant.
1st Lieutenant	Wm. M. Gwynne	Sept. 5, 1861	" 17, 1862	Promoted to Captain.
Do.	Joseph C. Brand	" 28, "	" 17, "	Promoted to Captain by President April 11, '64.
Do.	B. F. Ganson	Nov. 15, "	" 17, "	Promoted to Captain.
Do.	Martin R. Wright	" 19, "	" 17, "	Promoted to Captain.
Do.	Thomas McConnell	" 20, "	" 17, "	Promoted to Captain.
Do.	Robert Crockett	" 22, "	" 17, "	Resigned May 26, 1862.
Do.	L. L. Powell	" 30, "	" 17, "	Resigned March 1, 1863.
Do.	Lemuel W. Smith	Dec. 11, "	" 17, "	Promoted to Captain.
Do.	James W. Christie	" 14, "	" 17, "	Resigned February 3, 1863.
Do.	Wm. Hamilton	" 17, "	" 17, "	Resigned February 19, 1863.
Do.	A. H. Yeazell	" 17, "	" 17, "	Promoted to Captain.
Do.	Wilson Martin	" 17, "	" 17, "	Appointed Captain 121st O. V. I. Aug. 11, 1862.
Do.	John O. Dye	May 24, 1862	June 20, "	Revoked.
Do.	Wm. A. Sampson	" 26, "	" 20, "	Promoted to Captain.
Do.	Marshall L. Dempsey	" 24, "	July 28, "	Resigned March 23, 1863.
Do.	John N. Rathbone	Dec. 5, "	Jan. 12, 1863	Promoted to Captain.
Do.	A. L. Sheppard	Nov. 1, "	" 12, "	Revoked.
Do.	John F. Morgan	" 1, "	Feb. 10, "	Promoted to Captain.
Do.	Watson N. Clark	Jan. 27, 1863	" 10, "	Resigned April 14, 1863.
Do.	Robert H. Russell	Feb. 3, "	" 25, "	Promoted to Captain.
Do.	John T. Mitchell, jr.	Jan. 27, "	April 9, "	Promoted to Captain.
Do.	John W. Watkins	March 1, "	March 10, "	Promoted to Captain.

RANK.	NAME.	DATE OF RANK.	COM. ISSUED.	REMARKS.
1st Lieutenant	Harrison Davis	Feb. 19, 1863	April 22, 1863	Killed.
Do.	Samuel H. Hedges	April 16, "	May 12, "	Promoted to Captain.
Do.	James Jacoby	" 16, "	" 12, "	Resigned May 5, 1864.
Do.	Joseph W. Hitt	" 16, "	" 12, "	Killed at Dallas May 25, 1864.
Do.	Archie Houston	May 27, "	June 15, "	Promoted to Captain.
Do.	Elhannan W. Zook	" 31, "	" 10, "	Resigned July 27, 1864.
Do.	T. G. Keller	July 20, "	Aug. 1, "	Promoted to Captain.
Do.	Charles E. Butts	April 2, 1864	April 2, 1864	Promoted to Captain.
Do.	John R. Organ	Jan. 1, "	Jan. 28, "	Killed July 20, 1864.
Do.	James P. Conn	April 2, "	April 2, "	Promoted to Captain.
Do.	James McIlroy	Jan. 1, "	Jan. 8, "	Promoted to Captain.
Do.	Nelson Card	" 1, "	" 28, "	Discharged August 29, 1864.
Do.	Wm. V. Taylor	May 9, "	May 9, "	Mustered out as Sergeant.
Do.	Wm. A. Brand	June 27, "	June 27, "	Resigned May 30, 1865.
Do.	W. Wallace Cranston	Aug. 11, "	Aug. 11, "	Promoted to Captain.
Do.	Wm. A. Cavis	" 11, "	" 11, "	Resigned October 20, 1864.
Do.	James C. Bowe	" 11, "	" 11, "	Promoted to Captain.
Do.	John H. Diltz	" 11, "	" 11, "	Promoted to Captain.
Do.	Charles A. Poffenberger	" 19, "	" 19, "	Promoted to Captain.
Do.	Richard E. Plunkett	Nov. 12, "	Nov. 12, "	Promoted to Captain.
Do.	Wm. W. Jackson	" 12, "	" 12, "	Promoted to Captain.
Do.	C. Warren Guy	" 12, "	" 12, "	Promoted to Captain.
Do.	Ridgely P. Wilkins	April 6, 1865	April 6, 1865	Promoted to Captain.
Do.	Robert Simpson	" 8, "	" 8, "	Promoted to Captain.
Do.	Joseph H. Cas-	" 12, "	" 12, "	Mustered out with regiment.
Do.	Silas C. Shastall	" 12, "	" 12, "	Mustered out with regiment.
Do.	John R. Clayton	" 12, "	" 12, "	Promoted to Captain.
Do.	Aaron Riker	" 12, "	" 12, "	Mustered out with regiment.
Do.	Henry Fraley	" 12, "	" 12, "	Promoted to Captain.
Do.	James T. Maggs	" 12, "	" 12, "	Revoked.
Do.	Frank Baldwin	" 12, "	" 12, "	Mustered out with regiment.
Do.	James A. McClain	" 12, "	" 12, "	Promoted to Captain.
Do.	Daniel D. Davisson	May 31, "	May 31, "	Mustered out under G. O. 24, June 28, 1865.
Do.	Wm. Scott	" 31, "	" 31, "	Mustered out under G. O. 24, June 28, 1865.
Do.	Samuel Croxton	June 14, "	June 14, "	Mustered out with regiment.
Do.	James H. Corbin	" 14, "	" 14, "	Mustered out with regiment.
Do.	John F. Morgan	" 20, "	" 20, "	Mustered out with regiment as Sergeant.
Do.	J. M. Mitchell	July 13, "	July 13, "	Mustered out with regiment as Sergeant.
Do.	Calvin Gibson	" 13, "	" 13, "	Mustered out with regiment as Sergeant.
Do.	Elijah E. Weaver	" 13, "	" 13, "	Mustered out with regiment as Sergeant.
2d Lieutenant	John O. Dye	Oct. 1, 1861	Jan. 17, 1862	Promoted to 1st Lieutenant Nov. 10, 1862.
Do.	Wm. A. Sampson	" 1, "		Promoted to 1st Lieutenant May 26, 1862.
Do.	D. A. McDonald	" 14, "		Died August 15, 1862.
Do.	John W. Watkins	" 19, "		Promoted to 1st Lieutenant.
Do.	James K. Hurley	Nov. 19, "		Resigned April 26, 1862.
Do.	Marshall L. Dempsey	" 20, "		Promoted to 1st Lieutenant.
Do.	James O. Carter	Dec. 11, "		Resigned April 21, 1862.
Do.	Charles H. Rhodes	" 14, "		Resigned February 28, 1862.
Do.	A. L. Sheppard	" 17, "		Promoted; resigned January 19, 1863.
Do.	Monroe Elliott	" 21, "		Resigned November 27, 1862.
Do.	Robert Murdock	Feb. 28, 1862	April 14, 1862	Died August 25, 1862.
Do.	John N. Rathbone	April 21, "	June 2, "	Promoted to 1st Lieutenant.
Do.	Watson N. Clark	May 26, "	" 26, "	Promoted to 1st Lieutenant.
Do.	John T. Mitchell, jr.	" 24, "	July 28, "	Promoted to 1st Lieutenant.
Do.	Archie Houston	Aug. 15, "	Oct. 3, "	Promoted to 1st Lieutenant.
Do.	John T. Northcutt	Sept. 1, "	Jan. 12, 1863	
Do.	Samuel H. Hedges	Nov. 27, "	Dec. 31, "	Promoted to 1st Lieutenant.
Do.	Joseph W. Hitt	Dec. 5, "	" 31, 1862	Promoted to 1st Lieutenant.
Do.	John F. Morgan	Nov. 1, "	Jan. 13, 1863	Promoted to 1st Lieutenant.
Do.	Robert H. Russell	Aug. 25, "	Dec. 31, 1862	Promoted to 1st Lieutenant.
Do.	Harrison Davis	Nov. 10, "	Jan. 14, 1863	Promoted to 1st Lieutenant.
Do.	James Jacoby	Jan. 27, 1863	Feb. 10, "	Promoted to 1st Lieutenant.
Do.	Henry S. Swisher	Nov. 1, 1862	" 10, "	Promoted.
Do.	Elhannan W. Zook	Feb. 3, 1863	" 25, "	Promoted to 1st Lieutenant.
Do.	Nelson Card	March 1, "	March 10, "	Promoted to 1st Lieutenant.
Do.	John R. Organ	Jan. 27, "	April 9, "	Promoted to 1st Lieutenant.
Do.	T. G. Keller	Feb. 19, "	" 22, "	Promoted to 1st Lieutenant.
Do.	Wm. Overs	April 16, "	May 12, "	
Do.	Charles E. Butts	" 16, "	" 12, "	Promoted to 1st Lieutenant.
Do.	Wm. C. Flage	" 16, "	" 12, "	Killed May 3, 1863.
Do.	James P. Conn	May 27, "	June 15, "	Promoted to 1st Lieutenant.
Do.	Wm. V. Taylor	" 31, "	" 10, "	Promoted to 1st Lieutenant.
Do.	Wm. A. Brand	" 9, 1864	May 9, 1864	Promoted to 1st Lieutenant.
Do.	W. Wallace Cranston	July 13, "	July 13, "	Promoted to 1st Lieutenant.
Do.	Wm. A. Cavis	" 30, "	" 30, "	Promoted to 1st Lieutenant.
Do.	John L. Davis	" 13, 1865	" 13, 1865	Mustered out with regiment as Sergeants; complimentary commissions given after muster out.
Do.	O. Fairchild	" 13, "	" 13, "	
Do.	Wm. McCorkle	" 13, "	" 13, "	
Do.	Francis M. Williams	" 13, "	" 13, "	
Do.	Thomas Thompson	" 13, "	" 13, "	
Do.	Sylvester Rook	" 13, "	" 13, "	
Do.	Orville Stokes	" 13, "	" 13, "	
Do.	Jacob Houts	" 13, "	" 13, "	
Do.	Jacob Ulwine	" 13, "	" 13, "	
Do.	Daniel Griffin	" 13, "	" 13, "	

SIXTY-SIXTH OHIO VOLUNTEER INFANTRY.

UNDER the President's second call for troops an order was obtained from Governor Dennison to raise a regiment of infantry in Champaign County. The order was dated October 1, 1861. On the 17th day of December following the regiment was mustered into the United States service, numbering eight hundred and fifty men. Six companies and about fifty men of other companies were from Champaign County, two from Delaware, one from Union, and one from Logan. From the day of muster until the day of departure for the field the regiment received additions to the number of one hundred and thirty.

On the 17th of January, 1862, tents were struck at Camp McArthur, near Urbana, and the regiment proceeded to join the forces of General Lander on the Baltimore and Ohio Railroad, in West Virginia. Colonel Candy reported to General Lander at New Creek, where the first field-camp was made. The first active service of the regiment was the campaign against Romney. In the early part of February, 1862, General Lander concentrated his troops at two points on the railroad, commencing his movements at nightfall. The troops marched all night, forded a deep and rapid stream, and by daylight were fifteen miles from their starting points. General Jackson, however, had evacuated Romney, and retreated through the mountains upon Winchester, while our army fell back toward the railroad and encamped on the Highlands, without tents or blankets. The first night snow fell to the depth of twelve inches.

General Shields succeeded General Lander, and the Sixty-Sixth regiment was led along the railroad to Martinsburg, where it was stationed as provost-guard for the space of about three weeks. Again, at Winchester and Strasburg, it performed the duties of provost and general guard for the immediate vicinities. Following the victorious division of General Shields to New Market it was assigned to the Second Brigade, commanded by Brigadier-General O. S. Terry. After a short but rapid march to Harrisonburg the division received orders to make a long and tedious march across the Blue Ridge to Fredericksburg, on the Rappahannock. The march occupied ten days. At Fredericksburg the Sixty-Sixth, the Fifth, Seventh, and Twenty-Ninth Ohio regiments formed the Third Brigade, under command of General E. B. Tyler. Remaining one day at Fredericksburg the division received orders to counter-march for the relief of General Banks in the Shenandoah Valley, and for the protection of Washington. General Jackson was in possession of nearly the whole Valley, and was making demonstrations against the capital. The division marched back by way of Manassas to Front Royal, in Warren County. From Front Royal the regiment accompanied General Shields up the right bank of the Shenandoah until arriving at the bridge across that river at Port Republic.

On the morning of June 9th General Tyler's brigade, with two regiments of the Fourth Brigade, were in line of battle awaiting the attack of the enemy, numbering thirty-two thousand, under General Stonewall Jackson. At sunrise the enemy opened with artillery, and soon made a general attack with heavy columns of infantry. In this battle the Sixty-Sixth acted a conspicuous part in defending a battery of seven guns on the left of the line. The enemy had possession of these guns three times and as many times were driven from them by the regiment. So quickly was the enemy compelled to abandon its ground that it had no time to turn the artillery upon the National lines. The retreat being ordered on the right, the whole line was compelled to pass a few rods behind the Sixty-Sixth. As the Fifth Ohio approached it deployed upon the right, and the enemy was driven about two hundred yards. The force immediately in front of the regiment consisted of a full brigade of Virginians and Wheat's battalion of Louisianians. The force under General Tyler, numbering about twenty-seven hundred men, held General Jackson's army in complete check for five hours and a half, not moving a rod, until an order for retreat was sent by General Shields. The regiment lost one hundred and nine men of the four hundred engaged. The division fell back to the Orange and Alexandria Railroad by way of Front Royal, and at this pl ice was broken up.

In July the Sixty-Sixth regiment, with its brigade, was ordered to join General Pope, and reported at Sperryville, where it was re-enforced by the Twenty-Eighth Pennsylvania. General John W. Geary was placed in command of the brigade, which was assigned to the Second Division (General Augur's), of what was afterward known as the Twelfth Corps. General Banks commanded the corps at Cedar Mountain, where the Second Division opened the ball. After nightfall the First Brigade was ordered to move forward, and, with a handful of men, Colonel Candy, who assumed command after General Geary had been carried from the field badly wounded, proceeded some distance in the direction of the mountain whereon the enemy was securely perched. In a dense wood, through which the brigade was passing, an ambuscade of the enemy was discovered, but too late to retreat. In the manly fight which ensued one-half of the National troops were killed outright and many wounded. The loss to the regiment was eighty-seven killed and wounded of two hundred in arms. After the defeat at Cedar Mountain the regiment pursued its way with the corps to Antietam, and was actively engaged in that battle.

On the 27th of December, 1862, General J. E. B. Stuart, with two thousand Rebel cavalry, made an attack upon Dumfries, a small town on the Potomac, which was garrisoned by the Fifth, Seventh, and Sixty-Sixth Ohio regiments. The garrison consisted of less than seven hundred muskets. After a sharp and determined fight, lasting several hours, the enemy was driven off. This battle was remarkable on account of the disparity of forces. In the battle of Chancellorsville the regiment held a position on the right of the plank road and in front of General Hooker's head-quarters. The repeated attacks made upon the whole corps were repelled with coolness and courage. When the Eleventh Corps was driven from its works, on the right of the Twelfth Corps, the "White Star Division" received the charges of General Jackson upon the flank, but stood manfully to the post of duty, and checked the Rebel army.

At Gettysburg the Sixty-Sixth regiment held a position near the right of the line. After the battle of Gettysburg the pursuit of Lee brought the regiment again to the Rappahannock. At this time trouble occurred in New York in enforcing the draft, and the Sixty-Sixth was one of the regiments ordered to that city to protect the Government officers in enforcing the laws. On the 29th of August the regiment and brigade disembarked from the steamship Baltic, and encamped on Governor's Island, in New York Harbor. On the 8th of September they commenced the return trip, and reached the Rapidan River on the 17th. A few days' duty, and the Eleventh and Twelfth Corps bade adieu to Virginia and the Army of the Potomac.

Under General Hooker they were transferred to the Army of the Cumberland, in the vicinity of Chattanooga, a distance of twelve hundred miles, which they traveled in seven days. November 24th the regiment proceeded with the division across the creek at the western foot of Lookout Mountain. The stronghold of the enemy was attacked, and a foothold was obtained near the crest of the mountain. After remaining in bivouac all night another advance was made, and the Stars and Stripes were planted on Lookout Mountain at sunrise, November 25th. The resistance of the enemy was not so great a difficulty to be surmounted as the rough ground and ponderous rocks over which the troops had to pass. The battles of Mission Ridge and Ringgold followed. The Sixty-Sixth Ohio participated in both battles. In the latter engagement the First Brigade of the Second Division charged up a steep and rough mountain in the face of a strong force of Rebels, who were posted behind formidable works. Every officer save one of the Seventh Ohio was killed or wounded. The Sixty-Sixth, under command of Major Thomas McConnell, carried the crest of the mountain and held it against the forces on the summit. Major McConnell sent for ammunition, but received an order to fall back to the railroad.

Returning to their camp in Wauhatchie Valley, near Chattanooga, the men of this regiment became enthusiastic on the subject of re-enlistment. On the 15th of December, 1863, the rolls were completed, and the old organization was changed into the Sixty-Sixth Regiment Ohio Veteran Volunteer Infantry. The Sixty-Sixth was among the first regimental organizations in the whole army to which the term "Veteran Volunteer" was applied. A month of joys and pleasures, a day of leave-taking and tears, and it was again on the road to the field. It was sent to Bridgeport, Alabama, where it remained in camp about three months. Besides an excursion down the Tennessee River on an old steamer, the regiment experienced little active service until the advance on Atlanta commenced. On the 3d of May, 1864, tents were struck at Bridgeport, and the troops in the vicinity moved forward to Chattanooga and joined the corps, which had been consolidated with the Eleventh, and was now called the Twentieth, under command of Major-General Joseph Hooker. The first fight of the long campaign then opening was at Rocky Face Ridge, where the First Brigade, Second Division, Twentieth Corps, charged the enemy's works on the summit, and were repulsed with great slaughter. At Resaca the regiment was kept well to the front, but was fortunate in having no losses beyond a few wounded. In passing around the Alatoona Mountains the Twentieth Corps traveled the Burnt Hickory Road, which crosses Pumpkin Vine Creek a few miles north of Dallas, and leads to New Hope Church.

In the afternoon of May 25th the First Brigade was in the advance, and marched beyond Pumpkin Vine Creek two miles, when it was suddenly attacked by a strong force of the enemy. Deploying rapidly, it held the enemy in check until the whole division had taken position. An advance was made, and the enemy was driven one and a half miles. The Sixty-Sixth at this point lost several men—among them Lieutenant Joseph W. Hitt, who had been selected as a brigade staff-officer on account of his courage. For eight days the two armies occupied works within a stone's throw of each other, and both lost heavily in the continuous musketry and cannonading. On the night of June 15th the regiment was in the advance of a movement against Pine Mountain. While moving up a ravine the enemy opened upon it with grape and canister from heavy works. Under a galling fire of musketry and four pieces of artillery the regiment approached to within a hundred feet of the works, and each man built for himself a little rifle-pit. This position gave them control of the enemy's artillery at that point; and there the regiment remained until the next day, when it was relieved by a new regiment. At Culp's farm, at Kenesaw, and at Marietta, at which places battles were fought in quick succession, the regiment acted its part, and also in the important battle of Peachtree Creek.

After the capture of Atlanta the Sixty-Sixth was placed on duty in that city, and remained there until the army of General Sherman took up its line of march to the sea-board. The country knows the history of the pleasant march to Savannah. Reaching the city, the regiment took its position near the left of the line on the Savannah River, within sight of the city. The position was not a favorable one, as the Rebel gunboats on the river could reach the line with enfilading shot. General Geary's division entered Savannah and carried the "white-star" flag through the streets, and received possession of the public and government buildings and the property belonging to them. Following General Sherman the regiment proceeded northward through South Carolina; thence to Goldsboro' and to Raleigh, it being at the latter place at the end of the war. After the surrender of General Johnston the march was prolonged until the regiment arrived at Washington by way of Richmond. In the march from Richmond to Washington the Twentieth Corps passed over the Chancellorsville battle-field, and had the proud satisfaction of knowing that it had made the entire circuit of the Southern States. The regiment was finally mustered out and paid off at Columbus, July 19, 1865.

The regiment received recruits at various times to the number of three hundred and seventy, and the number of men mustered out at the end of its term of service was two hundred and seventy-two. It lost in killed one hundred and ten, and in wounded over three hundred and fifty. It served in twelve States, marched more than eleven thousand miles, and participated in eighteen battles.

67th REGIMENT OHIO VOLUNTEER INFANTRY.

ROSTER, THREE YEARS' SERVICE.

RANK.	NAME.	DATE OF RANK.	COM. ISSUED.	REMARKS.
Colonel	OTTO BURSTENBINDER	Oct. 17, 1861	Jan. 16, 1862	Dismissed July 29, 1862.
Do.	ALVIN C. VORIS			Mustered out with regiment; brvt. Brig. Gen
Lt. Colonel	ALVIN C. VORIS	Oct. 2, 1861	Jan. 16, 1862	Promoted to Colonel.
Do.	JOHN R. BOND	July 29, 1862	Aug. 8, "	Mustered out August 28, 1862.
Do.	HENRY S. COMMAGER	Aug. 28, "	Sept. 4, "	Mustered out for promotion Feb. 17, 1865.
Do.	LEWIS CASS HUNT	March 18, 1865	March 18, 1865	Mustered out September 1, 1865. [Brig.Gen.
Do.	HENRY R. WEST			Mustered out with regiment; brvt. Col.; brvt.
Major	JOHN R. BOND	Oct. 1, 1861	Jan. 16, 1862	Promoted to Lieutenant-Colonel.
Do.	HENRY S. COMMAGER	July 29, 1862	Aug. 8, "	Promoted to Lieutenant-Colonel.
Do.	EDWIN S. PLATT	Aug. 28, "	Sept. 4, "	Resigned January 13, 1863.
Do.	LEWIS BUTLER	Jan. 13, 1863	April 22, 1862	Discharged for promotion October 10, 1864.
Do.	THOMAS J. PLATT			Mustered out with regiment.
Surgeon	SAMUEL F. FORBES	Oct. 10, 1861	Jan. 16, 1862	Resigned October 7, 1863.
Do.	JAMES WESTFALL	" 7, 1863	Oct. 23, 1863	Mustered out with regiment.
Ass't Surgeon	JAMES WESTFALL	Jan. 9, 1862	Jan. 16, 1862	Promoted to Surgeon.
Do.	C. COSTAN	April 24, "	Feb. 10, 1863	Resigned March 6, 1863.
Do.	JOSEPH H. VAN DEMAN	May 9, 1863	May 9, "	Commission returned.
Do.	A. S. COMBS	Nov. 3, "	Nov. 3, "	Mustered out May 15, 1865.
Chaplain	JOHN CRABBS	Jan. 15, 1862	Jan. 16, 1862	Resigned July 7, 1864.
Captain	Henry S. Commager	Nov. 10, 1861	" 16, "	Promoted to Major.
Do.	Hyatt G. Ford	Dec. 18, "	" 16, "	Killed at Winchester March 23, 1862.
Do.	Marcess M. Speigle	" 18, "	" 16, "	Discharged for promotion October 2, 1863.
Do.	Charles A. Rowsey	" 18, "	" 16, "	Resigned May 26, 1862.
Do.	Edwin S. Platt	" 18, "	" 16, "	Promoted to Major.
Do.	E. D. Mason	" 18, "	" 16, "	Mustered out October 5, 1862.
Do.	Valentine Hickman	" 18, "	" 16, "	Died at Strasburg May 13, 1862.
Do.	John B. Spafford	" 18, "	" 16, "	Resigned February 3, 1863.
Do.	Lewis Butler	" 18, "	" 16, "	Promoted to Major.
Do.	Charles C. Lewis	" 18, "	" 16, "	Dismissed July 14, 1863.
Do.	Henry J. Crane	March 23, 1862	April 30, "	Mustered out January 17, 1865.
Do.	Charles F. Handy	May 26, "	June 20, "	Revoked.
Do.	Alfred P. Girty	" 13, "	Aug. 28, "	Honorably discharged April 25, 1864.
Do.	Charles Hennessey	" 26, "	Oct. 14, "	Resigned December 27, 1862.
Do.	R. Rudolph	Aug. 28, "	" 14, "	Resigned June 28, 1863.
Do.	Lewis Cass Hunt	Sept. 1, "	" 14, "	Promoted to Lieutenant-Colonel.
Do.	Sidney G. Brock	Oct. 2, "	" 14, "	Mustered out January 2, 1865.
Do.	Dewitt C. Dewey	" 5, "	Dec. 31, "	Resigned June 24, 1863.
Do.	John B. Chapman	Dec. 27, "	Feb. 10, 1863	Resigned June 7, 1864.
Do.	Charles P. Schafer	Jan. 13, 1863	May 9, "	Mustered out January 17.
Do.	John C. Albert	Feb. 3, "	" 9, "	Killed July 18, 1863.
Do.	George Emmerson	July 1, "	Aug. 21, "	Killed May 10, 1864.
Do.	Hugh Shields	Feb. 18, 1864	Feb. 18, 1864	Mustered out October 16, 1864; time expired.
Do.	Charles L. Stevens	" 18, "	" 18, "	Absent at Richmond, Va.; no discharge given.
Do.	Wm. Nixon	May 25, "	May 25, "	Mustered out September 1, 1865.
Do.	George L. Childs	" 25, "	" 25, "	Mustered out with regiment.
Do.	Grove L. Heaton	Aug. 11, "	Aug. 11, "	Captain and A. Q. M. United States Vols.
Do.	Theodore J. Curtiss	Sept. 26, "	Sept. 26, "	Mustered out with regiment.
Do.	Thomas Ward	" 26, "	" 26, "	Died October 24, 1864.
Do.	Wm. Kief	Dec. 9, "	Dec. 9, "	Mustered out September 1, 1865.
Do.	Florence J. O'Sullivan	" 9, "	" 9, "	Mustered out June 23, 1865, as 2d Lieutenant.
Do.	Charles E. Minor	March 18, 1865	March 18, 1865	Mustered out with regiment as 1st Lieut.
Do.	George Ansell	" 18, "	" 18, "	Mustered out with regiment.
Do.	Robert McMurray	" 18, "	" 18, "	Mustered out with regiment.
Do.	Orville Eddy	" 18, "	" 18, "	Mustered out September 1, 1865.
Do.	John C. Edwards			Trans. from 62d O.V.I.; must'd out with regt.
Do.	Henry H. Hitchcock			Trans. from 62d O.V.I.; must'd out with regt.
Do.	John S. Smith			Trans. from 62d O.V.I.; must'd out with regt.
Do.	John D. Kennedy			Trans. from 62d O.V.I.; must'd out with regt.
Do.	Wm. Hedges			Trans. from 62d O.V.I.; must'd out with regt.
1st Lieutenant	John Faskin	Oct. 4, 1861	Jan. 16, 1862	Resigned May 26, 1862.
Do.	Henry S. Wood	Dec. 4, "	" 16, "	Resigned April 17, 1863.
Do.	Charles F. Handy	" 18, "	" 16, "	Promoted; resigned August 2, 1862.
Do.	Joseph Jacobs	" 18, "	" 16, "	Resigned April 28, 1862.
Do.	John B. Chapman	" 18, "	" 16, "	Promoted to Captain.
Do.	Charles Hennessey	" 18, "	" 16, "	Promoted to Captain.
Do	R. Rudolph	" 18, "	" 16, "	Promoted to Captain.
Do.	Dewitt C. Dewey	" 18, "	" 16, "	Promoted to Captain.
Do.	Alfred P. Girty	" 18, "	" 16, "	Promoted to Captain.
Do.	Sidney G. Brock	" 18, "	" 16, "	Promoted to Captain.
Do.	Charles P. Schafer	" 18, "	" 16, "	Promoted to Captain. [Va., March 23, '62,
Do.	Sheldon Colton	" 18, "	" 16, "	Hon. dis. Oct. 9, '62; wounded at Winchester.
Do.	Gustavius Takrion	May 26, 1862	Oct. 14, "	Revoked.
Do.	George Emmerson	" 26, "	" 14, "	Promoted to Captain.
Do.	Alvin W. Howe	Aug. 2, "	" 14, "	Honorably discharged December 8, 1862.
Do.	Hugh Shields	" 28, "	" 14, "	Promoted to Captain.
Do.	John C. Albert	" 28, "	" 14, "	Promoted to Captain.
Do.	Charles L. Stevens	Sept. 1, "	" 14, "	Promoted to Captain.
Do.	Wm. Nixon	Oct. 2, "	" 14, "	Promoted to Captain.
Do.	George L. Childs	" 9, "	" 14, "	Promoted to Captain.
Do.	Henry Bredt	Dec. 8, "	Dec. 31, "	Resigned July 7, 1863.
Do.	John C. Cochran	Oct. 8, "	" 31, "	Died of wounds.
Do.	Theodore J. Curtiss	Dec. 27, "	Feb. 10, 1863	Promoted to Captain.
Do.	Grove L. Heaton	" 8, "	May 9, "	Promoted to Captain.
Do.	Thomas Ward	Jan. 12, 1863	" 9, "	Promoted to Captain.
Do.	George M. Ballard	Feb. 3, "	" 9, "	Killed.

RANK.	NAME.	DATE OF RANK.	COM. ISSUED.	REMARKS.
1st Lieutenant	Wm. Kief	Feb. 18, 1864	Feb. 18, 1864	Promoted to Captain.
Do.	Florence J. O'Sullivan	" 18, "	" 18, "	Promoted to Captain.
Do.	Carey D. Lindsey	" 18, "	" 18, "	Declined promotion.
Do.	Franklin Briggs	" 18, "	" 18, "	Mustered out October 16, 1864.
Do.	Rodney J. Hathaway	" 18, "	" 18, "	Mustered out November 11, 1864.
Do.	Charles E. Minor	" 18, "	" 18, "	Promoted to Captain.
Do.	Henry M. Wallack	" 18, "	" 18, "	Killed May 10, 1864.
Do.	George Ansel	May 25, "	May 25, "	Promoted to Captain.
Do.	Henry L. Aldrich	" 25, "	" 25, "	Mustered out January 17.
Do.	John J. Parsons	Aug. 11, "	Aug. 11, "	Killed in action August 16, 1864.
Do.	Herman H. Hausenn	" 11, "	" 11, "	Killed October 28, 1864.
Do.	Emil Rampano	Sept. 26, "	Sept. 26, "	Died of wounds.
Do.	Henry J. Carter	" 26, "	" 26, "	Deceased.
Do.	Robert McMurray	" 26, "	" 26, "	Promoted to Captain.
Do.	Orville Eddy	Dec. 9, "	Dec. 9, "	Promoted to Captain.
Do.	Louis Helenthall	March 18, 1865	March 18, 1865	Mustered out September 1, 1865.
Do.	Charles Autenraith	" 18, "	" 18, "	Resigned November 27, 1865.
Do.	Wm. Terry	" 18, "	" 18, "	Never mustered.
Do.	Alfred N. Briggs	" 18, "	" 18, "	Never mustered.
Do.	George G. Tappan	" 18, "	" 18, "	Mustered out with regiment.
Do.	Wellington Smith	" 18, "	" 18, "	Mustered out September 1, 1865.
Do.	Francis L. Vosburg	" 18, "	" 18, "	Mustered out September 1, 1865.
Do.	Edward C. Jeffries	" 18, "	" 18, "	Mustered out with regiment.
Do.	Andrew J. Bowman	" 18, "	" 18, "	Mustered out with regiment.
Do.	Oscar F. Nicholas	" 18, "	" 18, "	Never mustered.
Do.	John H. Whitehead	" 18, "	" 18, "	Mustered out September 1, 1865.
Do.	Thomas Wilson			Trans. from 62d O.V.I.; must'd out with regt.
Do.	Robert Davison			Trans. from 62d O.V.I.; must'd out with regt.
Do.	John R. Murray			Trans. from 62d O.V.I.; must'd out with regt.
Do.	Absalom Craig			Trans. from 62d O.V.I.; must'd out with regt.
Do.	Gardner Howe			Trans. from 62d O.V.I.; must'd out with regt.
2d Lieutenant	Gustavius W. Fahrion	Oct. 4, 1861	Jan. 16, 1862	Mustered out March 30, 1862.
Do.	George Worts	" 8, "		Resigned June 20, 1862.
Do.	George Emmerson	" 25, "		Promoted to 1st Lieutenant.
Do.	Joseph Pool	Nov. 7, "		Resigned December 18, 1861.
Do.	Alvin W. Howe	Dec. 4, "		Promoted to 1st Lieutenant.
Do.	Henry J. Crane	" 18, "		Promoted to 1st Lieutenant.
Do.	Hugh Shields	" 18, "		Promoted to 1st Lieutenant
Do.	Marquis E. Woodruff	" 18, "		Resigned August 6, 1862.
Do.	John C. Albert	" 18, "		Promoted to 1st Lieutenant.
Do.	Joseph Seiter	" 18, "		Resigned April 15, 1862.
Do.	George L. Childs	Oct. 15, "		Promoted to 1st Lieutenant.
Do.	Louis Miller	Dec. 31, "		Void; commission revoked.
Do.	Gustavius W. Fahrion	March 30, 1862	April 22, 1862	Reinstated; promoted; resigned Jan. 13, '63.
Do.	Wm. Nixon	" 23, "	May 5, "	Promoted to 1st Lieutenant.
Do.	John C. Cochran	April 15, "	" 5, "	Promoted to 1st Lieutenant.
Do.	Henry Bredt	May 26, "	June 20, "	Promoted to 1st Lieutenant.
Do.	Grove L. Heaton	Aug. 19, "	Sept. 8, "	Promoted to 1st Lieutenant.
Do.	Thomas Ward	" 25, "	Oct. 7, "	Promoted to 1st Lieutenant.
Do.	Florence J. O'Sullivan	May 26, "	" 14, "	Promoted to 1st Lieutenant.
Do.	Theodore J. Curtiss	Aug. 6, "	" 14, "	Promoted to 1st Lieutenant
Do.	George M. Ballard	" 28, "	" 14, "	Promoted to 1st Lieutenant.
Do.	John P. Hoffman	" 28, "	" 14, "	Resigned June 24, 1863.
Do.	Elijah Whitmore	Oct. 2, "	" 14, "	Resigned January 28, 1864.
Do.	Peter Bell	" 9, "	" 28, "	Resigned November 20, 1863.
Do.	Franklin Briggs	" 5, "	Dec. 31, "	Promoted to 1st Lieutenant
Do.	George W. Parsons	" 8, "	" 31, "	Resigned December 3, 1863.
Do.	Wm. Kief	Dec. 27, "	Feb. 10, 1863	Promoted to 1st Lieutenant.
Do.	Rodney J. Hathaway	" 8, "	May 9, "	Promoted to 1st Lieutenant.
Do.	Henry M. Wallack	Jan. 13, 1863	" 9, "	Promoted to 1st Lieutenant.
Do.	James Baxter	Feb. 3, "	" 9, "	Killed July 18, 1863.
Do.	Carey D. Lindsey	June 24, "	Aug. 1, "	Promoted to 1st Lieutenant.
Do.	Henry L. Aldrich	Nov. 19, 1863	Feb. 12, 1864	Promoted to 1st Lieutenant.
Do.	John J. Parsons	Feb. 18, 1864	" 24, "	Promoted to 1st Lieutenant.
Do.	George Ansel	Nov. 19, 1863	Jan. 20, "	Promoted to 1st Lieutenant.
Do.	Herman H. Hausenn	March 11, 1864	March 11, "	Promoted to 1st Lieutenant.
Do.	Emil Rampano	May 25, "	May 25, "	Promoted to 1st Lieutenant.
Do.	Charles E. Minor	Nov. 19, 1863	Jan. 15, "	Promoted to 1st Lieutenant.
Do.	James Shoemaker	May 25, 1864	May 25, "	Declined promotion; never mustered.
Do.	Henry J. Carter	" 25, "	" 25, "	Promoted to 1st Lieutenant.
Do.	James E. Bruce	" 25, "	" 25, "	Declined promotion; never mustered.
Do.	Robert McMurray	" 25, "	" 25, "	Promoted to 1st Lieutenant.
Do.	Orville Eddy	" 25, "	" 25, "	Promoted to 1st Lieutenant.
Do.	Wm. Sorge	Aug. 20, 1865	Sept. 4, 1865	Never mustered.
Do.	Homer Sawyer	" 20, "	" 4, "	Never mustered.
Do.	Christian Gets	" 20, "	" 4, "	Mustered out with regiment
Do.	George W. Baker	" 20, "	" 4, "	Mustered out with regiment.
Do.	Joseph L. Walcott	" 20, "	" 4, "	Mustered out with regiment.

SIXTY-SEVENTH OHIO VOLUNTEER INFANTRY.

THIS regiment had its rise in the consolidation of two partly organized regiments—the Forty-Fifth and the Sixty-Seventh. The regiment left Columbus, Ohio, for the field January 19, 1862, going into Western Virginia, under General Lander. With the exception of a march to Bloomrey Gap, the greater portion of the month of February was spent at Paw Paw Tunnel. On the 5th of March the regiment moved to Winchester, General Shields commanding the division, where skirmishing was frequent, on the picket-line, with Ashby's cavalry.

On the afternoon of March 22d the regiment reported to General Banks in Winchester, and soon engaged the enemy, driving them till past nightfall, as far south as Kearnstown. The regiment lay on their arms all night, and on the next morning were the first to engage the enemy. After the infantry fighting had been fairly opened the Sixty-Seventh was ordered to re-enforce General Tyler's brigade; to do which it was necessary to pass over an open field for three-fourths of a mile, exposed to the enemy's fire. The regiment executed the movement on the double-quick, and came into action in splendid order. The regiment lost in this action fifteen killed and thirty-two wounded. Until the last of the next June the Sixty-Seventh endured the hardships of marches up and down the valley, over the mountains and back again, from the Potomac to Harrisonburg, from Front Royal to Fredericksburg, from Fredericksburg to Manassas, from Manassas to Port Republic, and from Port Republic to Alexandria.

On the 29th of June the regiment embarked on steamer Herald and barge Delaware and started for the James to re-enforce General McClellan. In the night of the 30th, when near the mouth of Chesapeake Bay, in a heavy gale, the hawser by which the barge was towed parted, leaving the barge to toss about in the trough of the sea. Men, horses, arms, and camp and garrison equipage, were carried overboard and lost, and it was nearly an hour before the steamer was able to return to the barge. At Harrison's Landing the regiment campaigned with the Army of the Potomac till the evacuation of the Peninsula, when it went to Suffolk, Virginia, with only three hundred men for duty out of the eight hundred and fifty which composed the regiment at the organization. While here the regiment enjoyed its first opportunity for rest and drill; and in the last of December was transferred to North Carolina, and then to Hilton Head, where it arrived February 1, 1863. The regiment shared in the Charleston expedition, landing on Cole's Island on the 2d of April. For seven months the regiment heroically endured all the hardships, privations, and dangers of the siege, taking part in the attack on Fort Wagner, and sustaining a heavy loss. It was at last relieved and allowed a few days' rest preparatory to an expedition into Florida.

The regiment re-enlisted, and returned to Ohio February, 1864. At the expiration of their furloughs the soldiers of the Sixty-Seventh returned to the field, reaching Bermuda Hundred, Virginia, under General Butler, on the 6th of May, 1864. On the 9th of May the Sixty-Seventh was detached to guard the right flank of the Tenth Corps, that had gone to the railroad at Chester Station to destroy it from there to Petersburg. A section of artillery was sent with the regiment, and they were placed on the turnpike from Richmond to Petersburg, about eleven miles from the former place, with orders to hold the position at all hazards. During the night re-enforcements arrived, and next morning the Rebels made a general attack upon them. The Sixty-Seventh maintained its position from first to last, presenting an unbroken front to four successive charges.

A section of our artillery, for a short time, fell into the hands of the enemy, but was recaptured by a portion of company F. The 10th of May, 1864, will always be remembered, as a sad but glorious day, by the Sixty-Seventh. Seventy-six officers and men were killed and wounded in that battle.

On the 20th of May, a portion of our lines having fallen into the hands of the Rebels, the Sixty-Seventh, with other regiments, was designated to recapture it, which they did by a charge, in which the regiment lost sixty-nine officers and men killed and wounded. The Rebel General W. H. S. Walker was wounded and captured, his sword passing into the hands of Colonel Voris as a trophy. On the 16th of August four companies of the Sixty-Seventh charged the rifle-pits of the enemy at Deep River, and at the first volley lost a third of their men; but before the Rebels could reload the rifle-pits were in our possession. On the 7th, 13th, 27th, and 28th of October the regiment engaged the enemy, with a loss of over one hundred men. During the spring, summer, and fall of 1864 the Sixty-Seventh confronted the enemy, at all times within range of their guns; and it is said, by officers competent to judge, that during the year it was under fire two hundred times. No movement was without danger; firing was kept up for days, and men wore their accouterments for weeks at a time. Out of over six hundred muskets taken to the front in the spring, three-fifths were laid aside during the year on account of casualties.

In the spring of 1865 the Sixty-Seventh participated in the assault on the Rebel works below Petersburg; on the 2d of April was foremost in the charge on Fort Gregg, and at Appomattox C. H. was in at the death, bearing her battle-flag proudly in the last fight our forces made against the Army of Northern Virginia.

On the 5th of May the regiment reported to General Voris, commanding the District of South Anna, Virginia, and garrisoned that portion of the State till December, 1865. In the meantime the Sixty-Second Ohio was consolidated with the Sixty-Seventh, the latter regiment retaining its organization. The Sixty-Seventh was mustered out of the service on the 12th of December, 1865, wanting but six days of having been recognized as a regiment for four years.

68th REGIMENT OHIO VOLUNTEER INFANTRY.

ROSTER, THREE YEARS' SERVICE.

RANK.	NAME.	DATE OF RANK.			COM. ISSUED.			REMARKS.
Colonel	SAMUEL H. STEEDMAN	Nov.	29,	1861	Jan.	28,	1862	Mustered out July 5, 1862.
Do.	ROBERT K. SCOTT	July	5,	1862	July	25,	"	Brigadier-General volunteers, Feb. 14, 1865.
Do.	GEORGE E. WELLES	Jan.	16,	1865	June	16,	1865	Brevet Brigadier General March 15, 1865.
Lt. Colonel	SAMUEL H. STEEDMAN	Oct.	1,	1861	Jan.	21,	1862	Promoted to Colonel.
Do.	ROBERT K. SCOTT	Nov.	30,	"	"	21,	"	Promoted to Colonel.
Do.	JOHN S. SNOOK	July	5,	1862	Nov.	17,	"	Killed May 16, 1863.
Do.	GEORGE E. WELLES	May	16,	1863	Jan.	10,	1864	Promoted to Colonel.
Do.	ARTHUR C. CROCKETT	June	16,	1865	June	16,	1865	Mustered out with regiment as Major.
Major	ROBERT K. SCOTT	Oct.	1,	1861	Jan.	21,	1862	Promoted to Lieutenant-Colonel.
Do.	JOHN S. SNOOK	Nov.	29,	"	"	21,	"	Promoted to Lieutenant-Colonel.
Do.	GEORGE E. WELLES	July	5,	1862	Dec.	3,	"	Promoted to Lieutenant-Colonel.
Do.	ARTHUR C. CROCKETT	Feb.	26,	1861	Feb.	26,	1864	Promoted to Lieutenant-Colonel.
Do.	ROBERT MASTERS	June	16,	1865	June	16,	1866	Mustered out with regiment as Captain.
Surgeon	EUGENE B. HARRISON	Nov.	6,	1861	Jan.	21,	1862	Honorably discharged June 9, 1864.
Do.	WM. MASSIE	July	13,	1861	July	13,	1864	Declined; commission returned.
Do.	M. A. BROWN	Sept.	26,	"	Sept.	26,	"	Returned commission.
Do.	JOHN G. BINGHAM	Dec.	7,	"	Dec.	7,	"	Mustered out with regiment.
Ass't Surgeon	BENJ. F. BERKLEY	Oct.	21,	1861	Jan.	21,	1862	Resigned December 31, 1862.
Do.	S. C. CHASE	Aug.	19,	1862	Sept.	1,	"	Resigned October 31, 1862.
Do.	DAVID C. RATHBURNE	Feb.	3,	1863	Feb.	3,	1863	Declined; commission returned.
Do.	W. E. CATLIN	April	28,	"	April	28,	"	Declined.
Do.	WM. MASSIE	July	20,	"	July	20,	"	Promoted to Surgeon.
Do.	L. B. VOORHEES	"	13,	1864	"	13,	1864	Declined; commission returned.
Do.	E. C. DE FOREST	Oct.	25,	"	Oct.	25,	"	Declined; commission returned.
Chaplain	MARTIN PERKLEY	Dec.	24,	1861	Jan.	21,	1862	Resigned September 17, 1863.
Captain	Lewis Y. Richards	Nov.	5,	"	"	21,	"	Mustered out October 25, 1864.
Do.	Sidney S. Sprague	"	13,	"	"	21,	"	Resigned July 22, 1863.
Do.	Arthur C. Crockett	"	21,	"	"	21,	"	Promoted to Major.
Do.	Patrick H. Mooney	"	27,	"	"	21,	"	Mustered out.
Do.	Edwin J. Evans	"	27,	"	"	21,	"	Resigned August 9, 1863.
Do.	Nelson A. Skeels	Dec.	1,	"	"	21,	"	Killed in action July 22, 1864.
Do.	Wesley W. Bowen	"	17,	"	"	21,	"	Mustered out.
Do.	James J. Vorhees	"	17,	"	"	21,	"	Resigned December 29, 1862.
Do.	Wm. C. Comstock	"	18,	"	"	21,	"	Resigned November 21, 1862.
Do.	Hiram H. Poe	"	18,	"	"	21,	"	Mustered out October 22, 1864.
Do.	John C. Harmon	Nov.	21,	1862	Dec.	31,	"	Mustered out October 22, 1864.
Do.	Abram C. Urquhart	Dec.	29,	"	Jan.	10,	1864	Declined Lieutenant-Colonel.
Do.	Jedediah C. Banks	May	16,	1863	"	10,	"	Declined Lieutenant-Colonel.
Do.	James H. Long	Nov.	25,	"	Feb.	26,	"	Honorably discharged November 8, 1864.
Do.	James Lannen	Feb.	26,	1864	"	26,	"	Mustered out with regiment.
Do.	Robert Masters	May	9,	"	May	9,	"	Promoted to Major.
Do.	Thomas T. Cowen	"	9,	"	"	9,	"	Declined promotion; commission returned.
Do.	Wm. F. Williams	"	9,	"	"	9,	"	Mustered out with regiment.
Do.	Chas. Bates	Nov.	26,	"	Nov.	26,	"	Declined promotion.
Do.	Henry Welty	"	26,	"	"	26,	"	Declined promotion.
Do.	Samuel R. Adams	"	26,	"	"	26,	"	Promoted to A. A. G. volunteers April 27, '65.
Do.	Isaac McCoy	"	26,	"	"	26,	"	Mustered out with regiment.
Do.	Joseph Ice	"	26,	"	"	26,	"	Mustered out with regiment.
Do.	Elias J. Ottinger	"	26,	"	"	26,	"	Mustered out with regiment.
Do.	Jacob A. Dorshimer	Jan.	11,	1865	Jan.	11,	1865	Mustered out with regiment.
Do.	W. H. Doering	"	11,	"	"	11,	"	Mustered out with regiment.
Do.	Milton Stout	"	11,	"	"	11,	"	Mustered out with regiment.
Do.	John D. Travis	"	11,	"	"	11,	"	Mustered out with regiment.
Do.	George W. Kniss	June	16,	"	June	16,	"	Mustered out with regiment.
1st Lieutenant	James G. Haley	Oct.	26,	1861	Jan.	21,	1862	Resigned October 26, 1862.
Do.	Georg E. Welles	"	29,	"	"	21,	"	Promoted to Major.
Do.	John C. Harmon	Nov.	12,	"	"	21,	"	Promoted to Captain.
Do.	Abram C. Urquhart	"	21,	"	"	21,	"	Mustered out.
Do.	Leverett G. Randall	"	21,	"	"	21,	"	Mustered out.
Do.	Jedediah C. Banks	"	25,	"	"	21,	"	Mustered out.
Do.	James H. Long	"	27,	"	"	21,	"	Promoted to Captain.
Do.	Thomas H. Lambert	Dec.	1,	"	"	21,	"	Declined promotion.
Do.	James Lannen	"	17,	"	"	21,	"	Mustered out.
Do.	Thomas Quigley	"	17,	"	"	21,	"	Resigned April 1, 1862.
Do.	Robert Masters	"	18,	"	"	21,	"	Promoted to Captain.
Do.	Ira M. Kelsey	"	18,	"	"	21,	"	Mustered out.
Do.	Thomas T. Cowen	April	1,	1862	April	14,	"	Declined promotion; mustered out.
Do.	Andrew Jackson	July	5,	"	Dec.	5,	"	Resigned February 24, 1863.
Do.	Wm. F. Williams	Oct.	26,	"	"	31,	"	Promoted to Captain.
Do.	Levi Coffman	Nov.	21,	"	"	31,	"	Resigned September 20, 1864.
Do.	James Cosgro	Dec.	29,	"	Jan.	10,	1864	Declined.
Do.	Chas. Bates	May	16,	1863	"	10,	"	Mustered out.
Do.	Henry Welty	Feb.	26,	1864	Feb.	26,	"	Declined promotion.
Do.	Samuel R. Adams	"	26,	"	"	26,	"	Promoted to Captain.
Do.	George W. Kniss	"	24,	1863	Jan.	10,	"	Promoted to Captain.
Do.	Lay W. Richardson	May	9,	1864	May	9,	"	Mustered out.
Do.	Jacob A. Dorshimer	Nov.	26,	"	Nov.	26,	"	Promoted to Captain.
Do.	Willoughby H. Doering	"	26,	"	"	26,	"	Promoted to Captain.
Do.	Wm. H. Highshew	"	26,	"	"	26,	"	Mustered out.
Do.	Upton Spurgeon	"	26,	"	"	26,	"	Mustered out with regiment.
Do.	Wm. Gilson	Jan.	11,	1865	Jan.	11,	1865	Mustered out with regiment.
Do.	Jasper H. Smith	"	11,	"	"	11,	"	Mustered out with regiment.
Do.	Wm. Palmer	"	11,	"	"	11,	"	Mustered out with regiment.
Do.	Wm. A. Ward	"	11,	"	"	11,	"	Mustered out with regiment.
Do.	Jacob Wolff	"	11,	"	"	11,	"	Mustered out with regiment.

RANK.	NAME	DATE OF RANK.	COM. ISSUED.	REMARKS.
1st Lieutenant	Mortimer Belding	Jan. 11, 1865	Jan. 11, 1865	Mustered out with regiment.
Do.	Elmor Y. Smutz	" 11, "	" 11, "	Mustered out with regiment as Adjutant.
Do.	Joseph Hoy	" 11, "	" 11, "	Mustered out with regiment.
Do.	Edwin J. Nason	June 16, "	June 16, "	
2d Lieutenant	Thomas T. Cowen	Oct. 4, 1861	Jan. 21, 1862	Promoted to 1st Lieutenant.
Do.	Lewis Dubbs	" 8, "	" 21, "	Resigned April 14, 1863.
Do.	John Dwyer	" 8, "	" 21, "	Died March 28, 1862.
Do.	Andrew Jackson	" 10, "	" 21, "	Promoted to 1st Lieutenant.
Do.	James G. Harley	" 10, "	" 21, "	Promoted to 1st Lieutenant.
Do.	Wm. F. Williams	Nov. 21, "	" 21, "	Promoted to 1st Lieutenant.
Do.	Levi Coffman	" 21, "	" 21, "	Promoted to 1st Lieutenant.
Do.	George W. Kniss	" 25, "	" 21, "	Promoted to 1st Lieutenant.
Do.	James Cosgro	" 27, "	" 21, "	Mustered out.
Do.	Jacob Bartlett	Dec. 1, "	" 21, "	Resigned February 14, 1863.
Do.	Alex. Boyd	" 18, "	" 21, "	Resigned August 15, 1862.
Do.	Chas. Bates	April 1, 1862	April 14, "	Promoted to 1st Lieutenant.
Do.	Webster C. Sheppard	March 27, "	June 20, "	Killed in action.
Do.	Henry Welty	July 5, "	Dec. 31, "	Promoted to 1st Lieutenant.
Do.	Samuel R. Adams	Oct. 26, "	March 13, 1863	Promoted to 1st Lieutenant.
Do.	Robert B. Mead	Nov. 2, "	" 13, "	Mustered out.
Do.	Henderson J. Hunter	April 14, 1863	April 14, "	Mustered out.
Do.	Lay W. Richardson	Aug. 15, 1862	March 24, "	Promoted to 1st Lieutenant.
Do.	Isaac McCoy	Nov. 10, 1863	" 2, 1864	Promoted to 1st Lieutenant.
Do.	Joseph Ice	Jan. 15, 1864	" 11, "	Promoted to 1st Lieutenant.
Do.	Elias J. Ottinger	April 1, "	April 1, "	Promoted to 1st Lieutenant.
Do.	Edward J. Nason	Jan. 11, 1865	Jan. 11, 1865	Promoted to 1st Lieutenant.
Do.	Carey E. McCann	" 11, "	" 11, "	
Do.	George W. Scott	" 11, "	" 11, "	

SIXTY-EIGHTH OHIO VOLUNTEER INFANTRY.

THIS regiment commenced to rendezvous at Camp Latta, Napoleon, Henry County, on the 21st of November, 1861. Defiance, Paulding, Williams, and Fulton Counties, each furnished one company, and Henry County furnished the majority of the men in the other companies. The regiment was quartered in Sibley tents and furnished with stoves, and the men were rendered very comfortable. Rations were abundant and of an excellent quality; and supplies of poultry, vegetables, fruit, and cakes, from home were received frequently. All these things made the campaign in the winter of 1861–2, in Henry County, the most pleasant campaign through which the regiment ever passed.

On the 21st of January, 1862, the regiment moved to Camp Chase, where it remained until the 7th of February, when it moved to Fort Donelson, Tennessee, arriving on the 14th. The regiment was assigned to General Charles F. Smith's division, and was constantly engaged in skirmishing on the left of the lines during both days' operations. After the surrender the regiment encamped near Dover until the 15th of March, when it moved to Metal Landing, on the Tennessee, and from there by boat to Pittsburg Landing. The health of the regiment until this time had been remarkably good; but now bad weather, bad water, and bad rations, reduced the regiment's strength from one thousand to less than two hundred and fifty men. The regiment was assigned to General Lew. Wallace's division, and during the battle of Pittsburg Landing was engaged in guarding ordnance and supply trains. Lieutenant-Colonel Scott and Captain Richards, finding that the regiment was not likely to be engaged, went as volunteer aids to General Thayer, and in his official report were mentioned for gallant and efficient service. During the operations around Corinth the regiment was constantly engaged in building roads, bridges, and intrenchments. After the evacuation the Sixty-Eighth, with the Twenty-Third Indiana, was stationed at Bolivar, where they rebuilt the bridge across the Hatchie, and formed the guards along the railroad for a number of miles.

The regiment participated in the battles of Iuka and Matamora, and for gallantry in the latter engagement was complimented in general orders. It closed the campaign of 1862 by forming the advance of an expedition which attempted to penetrate the interior of Mississippi to Vicksburg. The design was frustrated by the surrender of Holly Springs, and the regiment returned to Memphis. Disasters in different portions of the army, and the influence of the traitorous press North, tended to depress the spirits of the Western army, and some regiments lost heavily by desertion; but, during this time, only one man in the Sixty-Eighth was reported as a deserter. During the campaign in Mississippi the regiment was assigned to the Second Brigade, Third Division, Seventeenth Army Corps, and it continued to serve with the same until the close of the war.

The spring campaign of 1863 found the regiment at Lake Providence, Louisiana, where it worked hard on the Lake Providence Canal, and in a fruitless attempt to clear a passage for boats through Bayou Tensas. It was engaged, also, on a similar work at Walnut Bayou, in the vicinity of Eagle Bend. About the 10th of April, 1863, the regiment moved down to Milliken's Bend, and was for some time engaged in working on the military road toward Richmond, Louisiana. While here Lieutenant J. C. Banks, of company C, and privates John Snyder, of company A, Joseph Longberry and William Barnhart, of company C, volunteered to take one of the transports, a common river steamer, past the Vicksburg batteries. They accomplished their undertaking successfully on the night of the 21st of April. On the 23d of April the regiment began its march for the rear of Vicksburg. It marched more than seventy miles over low bottom lands, still partly submerged, crossed innumerable bayous on bridges hastily constructed of timber from neighboring houses and cotton-gins, and reached the Mississippi at Grand Gulf. The regiment moved down to Bruinsburg, where it crossed the river, and by a forced march was able to participate in the battle of Thompson's Hill, May 1, 1863. The regiment followed closely after the retreating Rebels, and was engaged in the battles of Raymond, Jackson, May 14th, Champion Hills, and Big Black. The regiment sustained considerable loss in all these engagements, and especially at Champion Hills.

The regiment engaged in an attack on the Rebel works in the rear of Vicksburg on the 18th of May, and it participated in the assault on Fort Hill on the 22d. During the early part of the siege the regiment was almost constantly in the trenches, and it also furnished large details of sharpshooters; but during the latter part of the siege it was placed in the Army of Observation, near Big Black. It was on the reconnoissance toward Yazoo City, in the latter part of June, and it participated in the engagement at Jackson on the 12th of July. After the battle it guarded about six hundred prisoners into Vicksburg. The regiment was quartered comfortably in the suburbs of Vicksburg until the middle of August, when it moved on an expedition to Monroe, Louisiana, and returned with one-third of its men either in the hospital or on the sick list. In October the regiment moved on a reconnoissance with the Seventeenth Corps, and was engaged in a skirmish at Bogue Chitta Creek, and on the 5th of February, 1864, it participated in the fight at Baker's Creek, while moving on the Meridian raid. This expedition prevented the regiment from going North on veteran furlough as promptly as it otherwise would have gone. It was one of the first regiments in the Seventeenth Corps to report three-fourths of its men re-enlisted, it having done so on the 15th of December, 1863. Upon its return from the Meridian raid the men were supplied with clothing, and the regiment embarked for the North, leaving one hundred and seventy recruits at Vicksburg, who arrived just as the regiment was moving down to the landing. The regiment arrived at Cairo on the 23d of March, and embarked on the cars, moved by way of Indianapolis, Bellefontaine, and Columbus, to Cleveland, where it arrived on the 26th. Through Illinois and Indiana the regiment was welcomed everywhere with banners and flags. It was entertained substantially at the Soldiers' Home in Indianapolis on the morning of the 24th, and was feasted bountifully by the citizens of Muncie, Indiana, on the evening of the same. The regiment was detained ten days at Cleveland before a paymaster could be obtained, and soon after payment the regiment started for Toledo, where it arrived at three o'clock P. M. on the 6th of April. It was met by a delegation of citizens, headed by the Mayor of the city, with bands of music, and after marching through the principal streets it was escorted to the Island House, where a splendid dinner was in waiting. This was the first welcome the regiment had received since entering the State. Special trains were made up on the different roads, and by night all the men were where they felt sure of a welcome—at home.

On the 7th of May the regiment again took the cars at Cleveland, and proceeded to Cairo by way of Cincinnati. At Cairo it was joined by the recruits left at Vicksburg, and these, with those obtained during furlough, numbered over three hundred. Here, too, the regiment turned over its old arms and drew new Springfield muskets. On the 12th of May the regiment, with more than seven hundred men for duty, embarked for Clifton, Tennessee, and thence it marched by way of Huntsville, Decatur, and Rome, to Acworth, Georgia, where it joined the main army under Sherman on the 10th of June. During the remainder of the Atlanta campaign the Sixty-Eighth was under fire almost constantly. It was on the advance line for sixty-five days and nights, and it was engaged at Kenesaw, Nicojack, Atlanta, July 22d and 28th; Jonesboro', and Lovejoy. On the 22d of July the regiment was engaged very heavily. It had been selected to go to the rear, and to picket the roads in the vicinity of army and corps head-quarters; but upon reaching its position it discovered in its front, instead of cavalry, a corps of Rebel infantry; while, at the same time, another line of Rebel troops was forming across the road in its rear. Thus the Sixty-Eighth was sandwiched between the enemy's advance and rear lines. The Rebels were totally unaware of the position of this little Buckeye band. The commands of the Rebel officers could be heard distinctly, and prisoners were captured almost from the Rebel line of file-closers. As the Rebel line moved forward the Sixty-Eighth advanced, cheering, on the double-quick, and, dropping behind a fence, poured a volley into the Rebels, who were in the open field. The batteries of Fuller's brigade, Sixteenth Corps, responded to the alarm thus given, and the fight opened in earnest. The Sixteenth Corps engaged the enemy so promptly that the regiment was enabled by a rapid movement by the flank, and a wide detour, to pass around the enemy's right, and to rejoin its brigade, which it found warmly engaged. The attack came from front and rear, and the men fought first on one side of the works and then on the other. At one time a portion of the brigade was on one side of the works, firing heavily in one direction, while a little way lower down the line the remainder of the brigade was on the other side of the works, firing heavily in the other direction. The left of the brigade swung back to the crest of a small hill, the right still resting on the old works, and a few rails were thrown together, forming a barricade, perhaps a foot high, when the last charge of the day was made by two Rebel divisions. On they came in splendid style, not firing a shot, arms at "right shoulder shift," officers in front, lines well dressed, following each other in quick succession. The brigade held firm until the first line had crossed a ravine in its front, and the second line of reserves could be seen coming down the opposite slope. Then came a terrific crash of musketry, and then volley after volley. The Rebels fell back, leaving the ground thickly strewn with the dead and dying.

After the engagement at Lovejoy the regiment was stationed on the Rough and Ready Road, near Eastpoint, for two weeks, when it moved in pursuit of Hood. The regiment advanced as far as Gaylesville, Alabama, and here quite a number of men were mustered out by reason of expiration of term of service. The regiment commenced its return march about the 1st of November, and moved by way of Cave Springs and Lost Mountain to Smyrna Camp-meeting Ground, where the men were supplied with clothing, and everything was thoroughly overhauled. The railroad was destroyed, and on the 14th the regiment moved to Atlanta, and at daylight on the 15th commenced the march to the sea. With the exception of an engagement with the Georgia militia at the crossing of the Oconee, and the destruction of the railroad buildings at Millen, the regiment experienced no variation from the easy marches and pleasant bivouacs which all enjoyed. On the 10th of December the regiment reached the works around Savannah. On the 12th the Seventeenth Corps moved well around to the right of the main road running from the city to King's Bridge. Here the regiment assisted in throwing up a heavy line of works, and furnished two companies daily as sharpshooters. During the operations around Savannah the regiment subsisted almost entirely upon rice, which was found in large quantities near camp, and which the men hulled and ground in rude hand-mills. Upon the occupation of the city the regiment was ordered on guard-duty in the town, and was quartered comfortably in Warren and Oglethorpe Parks. Here, too, the regiment lost some valuable men who were mustered out by reason of expiration of term of service. A large number of commissions were received, and the regiment was supplied with a fine corps of young and enthusiastic officers.

On the 5th of January, 1865, the regiment embarked at Thunderbolt Bay for Beaufort, and from there it formed the advance of the corps for the most of the way to Pocotaligo. Here some heavy works were thrown up, and after resting about two weeks the troops moved on the campaign of the Carolinas. The regiment marched by way of Orangeburg, Columbia, Winnsboro', and Cheraw, destroying property, both public and private; but upon entering the State of North Carolina this destruction of property was forbidden by orders from superior head-quarters. The march was continued through Fayetteville to Goldsboro', where the regiment arrived ragged, barefooted, and bareheaded, and blackened and begrimed with the smoke of pine-knots. On the morning after its arrival the Adjutant's report showed forty-two men barefooted, thirty-six bareheaded, and two hundred and sixty wearing some article of citizens' clothes. The regiment rested ten days and then moved out to Raleigh.

After the surrender of Johnston the regiment marched by way of Dinwiddie C. H., Petersburg, Richmond, Fredericksburg, and Alexandria, to Washington City, where it participated in the grand review on the 24th of May. After the review the Sixty-Eighth camped at Tenallytown for a week, when it was ordered to Louisville, Kentucky. It went into camp about two miles from the city, and a regular system of drill and discipline was maintained until the 10th of July, when the muster-out rolls were signed, and the regiment was ordered to report to Camp Taylor, near Cleveland, for payment and discharge. Upon arriving at Cleveland the Sixty-Eighth was met at the depot by a delegation of citizens, and was escorted to Monument Square, where a splendid breakfast was served. After this the regiment marched to camp, where it remained until the 18th of July, 1865, when it was paid and discharged.

During its term of service the regiment was on the "sacred soil" of every Rebel State except Florida and Texas. It marched over seven thousand miles, and traveled by railroad and steamboat over six thousand miles. Between nineteen hundred and two thousand men belonged to the regiment, and of these ninety per centum were native Americans, the others being Germans, Irish, or English—the Germans predominating. Colonel R. K. Scott commanded the regiment in all its engagements except Metamora, when Lieutenant-Colonel J. S. Snook commanded, until after the Vicksburg campaign, when the command devolved upon Lieutenant-Colonel George E. Welles, and he continued to hold the command in all the subsequent engagements, skirmishes, and marches until the close of the war. The regiment was presented with a beautiful banner by the citizens of Henry County just before its muster-out; it having been impracticable to send the flag to the regiment at Atlanta as was intended. The flag was returned by Colonel Welles, on behalf of the regiment, to the citizens of Henry County, and it is now in the possession of Mr. Joseph Stout, of Napoleon, one of the principal donors, and always a staunch friend to the Sixty-Eighth. The regimental colors were turned over to the Adjutant-General of the State, and were deposited in the archives. Upon these flags, by authority from corps and department head-quarters, were inscribed the names of the following battles: Fort Donelson, Pittsburg Landing, Siege of Corinth, Iuka, Metamora, Thompson's Hills, Raymond, Jackson, Champion Hills, Big Black, Vicksburg, May 22d, and siege; Jackson, July 12th; Monroe Raid, Bogue Chitta, Meridian Raid, Kenesaw, June 27th, and siege; Nicojack, Atlanta, July 21st, 22d, and 28th, and siege; Jonesboro', Lovejoy, Oconee, Savannah, Pocotaligo, Salkehatchie, Orangeburg, Columbia, Cheraw, Bentonville, and Raleigh.

69th REGIMENT OHIO VOLUNTEER INFANTRY.

ROSTER, THREE YEARS' SERVICE.

RANK.	NAME.	DATE OF RANK.	COM. ISSUED.	REMARKS.
Colonel	LEWIS D. CAMPBELL	Oct. 2, 1861	April 17, 1862	Resigned August 9, 1862.
Do.	WM. B. CASSILLY	Aug. 9, 1862	Sept. 9, "	Dismissed December 31, 1862.
Do.	MARSHALL T. MOORE.	Dec. 31, "	Feb. 23, "	Honorably discharged November 7, 1864.
Do.	JOS. H. BRIGHAM	July 10, 1865	July 10, 1865	Mustered out with regiment as Lieut.-Colonel.
Lt. Colonel	Wm. B. Cassilly	April 17, 1862	April 17, 1862	Promoted to Colonel August 9, 1862.
Do.	Chas. L. Gano	Aug. 9, "	Sept. 9, "	Resigned October 24, 1862.
Do.	George F. Elliott	Oct. 24, "	Nov. 1, "	Resigned February 2, 1863.
Do.	Joseph H. Brigham	Dec. 31, "	Feb. 23, 1863	Promoted to Colonel.
Do.	Lewis E. Hicks	July 10, 1865	July 10, 1865	Mustered out with regiment as Major.
Major	Chas. L. Gano	Nov. 5, 1861	April 17, 1862	Promoted to Lieutenant-Colonel.
Do.	George F. Elliott	Aug. 9, 1862	Sept. 9, "	Promoted to Lieutenant-Colonel.
Do.	Eli J. Hickox	Oct. 24, "	Nov. 1, "	Resigned May 23, 1863.
Do.	James J. Hanna	May 23, 1863	June 10, 1863	Mustered out.
Do.	Alex. Lemon	July 14, 1865	July 14, 1865	Mustered out with regiment as Captain.
Do.	Lewis E. Hicks	May 31, "	May 31, "	Promoted to Lieutenant-Colonel.
Surgeon	Lewis Slusser	Feb. 12, 1862	April 17, 1862	Mustered out April 10, 1865; time out.
Do.	Robert A. Stephenson	April 24, 1865	" 24, 1865	Mustered out with regiment.
Ass't Surgeon	Moses H. Haynes	Oct. 3, 1861	April 17, 1862	Resigned September 10, 1862.
Do.	M. A. Frost	Aug. 15, 1862	Aug. 29, "	Resigned April 25, 1863.
Do.	James M. Kuhn	Dec. 18, "	Feb. 10, 1863	Declined.
Do.	Robert A. Stephenson	April 4, 1863	April 4, "	Promoted to Surgeon.
Do.	H. H. Ford	Aug. 4, "	Aug. 4, "	Commission returned.
Do.	Levi B. Northrop	June 26, 1865	June 26, 1865	Mustered out with regiment.
Chaplain	Wm. G. Brownlow	April 15, 1862	April 15, 1862	Mustered out April 16, 1862.
Do.	Wm. H. Rogers	Jan. 24, 1863	Feb. 25, 1863	
Captain	Joseph H. Brigham	Oct. 17, 1861	April 17, 1862	Promoted to Lieutenant-Colonel.
Do.	Chas. N. Gibbs	Dec. 9 "	" 17, "	Resigned August 13, 1862.
Do.	George F. Elliott	" 9, "	" 17, "	Promoted to Major.
Do.	Eli J. Hickox	" 16, "	" 17, "	Promoted to Major.
Do.	David Putman	" 16, "	" 17, "	Resigned June 20, 1863.
Do.	Robert Clements	" 16, "	" 17, "	Discharged November 3, 1863.
Do.	Wm. Patton	" 29, 1862	" 17, "	Resigned July 25, 1863.
Do.	Leonard C. Councellor	March 3, "	" 17, "	Killed January 22, 1863.
Do.	John V. Heslip	" 21, "	" 17, "	Resigned April 11, 1863.
Do.	James J. Hanna	" 25, "	" 17, "	Promoted to Major.
Do.	George B. Hubbard	Aug. 9, "	Sept. 9, "	Resigned March 7, 1863.
Do.	Marmaduke D. Welpley	" 13, "	Nov. 1, "	Resigned April 11, 1863.
Do.	James Devor	Oct. 24, "	Dec. 31, "	Resigned May 15, 1863.
Do.	Jacob J. Rarick	Jan. 2, 1863	June 10, 1863	Mustered out.
Do.	Richard Cunningham	Dec. 31, 1862	May 6, "	Declined.
Do.	Ross J. Hazeltine	March 7, 1863	April 28, "	Resigned December 18, 1863.
Do.	Alex. Lemon	April 11, "	June 10, "	Promoted to Major.
Do.	Edward R. Black	May 15, "	" 10, "	
Do.	Lewis E. Hicks	" 23, "	" 11, "	Promoted to Major.
Do.	David P. Reed	Jan. 1, "	" 26, "	Mustered out.
Do.	Wm. Lazalier	July 25, "	Sept. 1, "	Mustered out; time expired.
Do.	George W. Moore	Jan. 1, "	" 1, "	Mustered out.
Do.	Alex. Mahood	June 20, "	" 1, "	Resigned November 5, 1864.
Do.	Frank Sweeney	Aug. 11, 1864	Aug. 11, 1864	Resigned as 1st Lieutenant September 1, 1864.
Do.	Wm. H. Mead	" 11, "	" 11, "	Dismissed January 7 1865.
Do.	Jacob S. Pearson	Nov. 26, "	Nov. 26, "	Killed September 1, 1864.
Do.	Timothy Hubbard	Jan. 18, 1865	Jan. 18, 1865	Mustered out.
Do.	Nelson E. Chenoweth	" 18, "	" 18, "	Mustered out with regiment.
Do.	F. D. Louthan	" 18, "	" 18, "	Declined to accept.
Do.	Thomas B. Hofman	" 18, "	" 18, "	Declined to accept.
Do.	Samuel E. Murray	May 31, "	May 31, "	Mustered out with regiment.
Do.	James Wharey	" 31, "	" 31, "	Mustered out with regiment.
Do.	Wm. W. Benedict	" 31, "	" 31, "	Mustered out with regiment.
Do.	Levi C. Chenoweth	" 31, "	" 31, "	Mustered out with regiment.
Do.	Jacob Leas	" 31, "	" 31, "	Mustered out with regiment.
Do.	Jacob Shaffer	" 31, "	" 31, "	Mustered out with regiment.
Do.	Zenas S. Poulson	" 31, "	" 31, "	Mustered out with regiment.
1st Lieutenant	Joseph W. Boynton	Oct. 5, 1861	April 17, 1862	Died from w'ds rec'd at battle of Stone River.
Do.	Fred. B. Landis	" 6, "	" 17, "	Mustered out; promoted to Capt. and A.Q.M.
Do.	Richard H. Cunningham	" 17, "	" 17, "	Mustered out December 3, 1864; time out.
Do.	Marmaduke D. Welpley	" 9, "	" 17, "	Promoted to Captain.
Do.	George B. Hubbard	" 9, "	" 17, "	Promoted to Captain.
Do.	James Devor	" 16, "	" 17, "	Promoted to Captain.
Do.	John M. Boatman	" 16, "	" 17, "	Resigned April 30, 1862.
Do.	Clement D. Smith	" 16, "	" 17, "	Resigned May 21, 1863.
Do.	Wm. Van Dorn	Jan. 29, 1862	" 17, "	Resigned August 1, 1863.
Do.	Edward R. Black	March 3, "	" 17, "	Promoted to Captain.
Do.	James G. Elrick	" 21, "	" 17, "	Resigned September 18, 1862.
Do.	Wm. Cady	" 25, "	" 17, "	Mustered out December 25, 1862.
Do.	Frank Sweeney	April 30, "	June 20, "	Revoked.
Do.	Jacob J. Rarick	" 30, "	July 12, "	Promoted to Captain.
Do.	Ross J. Hazeltine	Aug. 9, "	Sept. 9, "	Promoted to Captain.
Do.	Alex Lemon	" 13, "	Nov. 1, "	Promoted to Captain
Do.	Wm. H. Mead	Sept. 18, "	Dec. 31, "	Promoted to Captain.
Do.	Frank Sweeney	Aug. 31, "	" 31, "	Promoted to Captain.
Do.	Timothy Hubbard	Feb. 31, 1863	Feb. 10, 1863	Promoted to Captain.
Do.	Wm. Lazalier	Jan. 1, "	June 10, "	Promoted to Captain.
Do.	George W. Moore	March 7, "	" 10, "	Promoted to Captain.
Do.	David P. Reed	May 21, "	" 10, "	Promoted to Captain.
Do	Jacob S. Pearson	Jan. 2, "	" 10, "	Promoted to Captain.

RANK.	NAME.	DATE OF RANK.	COM. ISSUED.	REMARKS.
1st Lieutenant	Joseph E. Tucker	April 11, 1863	June 10, 1863	Resigned November 10, 1863.
Do.	John S. Scott	May 15, "	Sept. 1, "	Killed in action November 25, 1863.
Do.	Frederick E. Wilson	Jan. 1, "	" 1, "	Resigned September 13, 1864.
Do.	Nelson E. Chenoweth	Aug. 1, "	" 1, "	Promoted to Captain.
Do.	F. D. Louthan	July 25, "	" 1, "	Mustered out.
Do.	Martin Bailey	Jan. 1, "	" 1, "	Killed in battle September 1, 1864.
Do.	Thomas B. Hoffman	March 3, 1864	March 3, 1864	Declined promotion.
Do.	Wm. C. Barnett	" 3, "	" 3, "	Mustered out.
Do.	Samuel E. Murray	Aug. 9, "	Aug. 11, "	Promoted to Captain.
Do.	James Wharey	" 11, "	" 11, "	Promoted to Captain.
Do.	Thurston C. Challen	Jan. 18, 1865	Jan. 18, 1865	Honorably discharged March 20, 1864.
Do.	Wm. W. Benedict	" 18, "	" 18, "	Promoted to Captain.
Do.	Levi C. Chenoweth	" 18, "	" 18, "	Promoted to Captain.
Do.	Jacob Leas	" 18, "	" 18, "	Promoted to Captain.
Do.	Jacob Shaffer	" 18, "	" 18, "	Promoted to Captain.
Do.	Zenas S. Poulson	" 18, "	" 18, "	Promoted to Captain.
Do.	James T. King	May 31, "	May 31, "	Mustered out with regiment.
Do.	Wm. J. Porter	" 31, "	" 31, "	Mustered out with regiment
Do.	Thomas B. White	" 31, "	" 31, "	Mustered out with regiment.
Do.	Oscar F. Smith	" 31, "	" 31, "	Killed by accident
Do.	Danforth B. Thompson	" 31, "	" 31, "	Mustered out with regiment.
Do.	Augustus Mizner	" 31, "	" 31, "	Mustered out with regiment.
Do.	Jeremiah S. Heck	July 10, "	July 10, "	
Do.	Levi E. Bysel	" 10, "	" 10, "	
Do.	G. W. Hamilton	" 10, "	" 10, "	
2d Lieutenant	Frank Sweeney	Oct. 17, 1861	April 7, 1862	Promoted to 1st Lieutenant.
Do.	Alex. Lemon	Dec. 9, "	" 7, "	Promoted to 1st Lieutenant.
Do.	Ross J. Hazeltine	" 9, "	" 7, "	Promoted to 1st Lieutenant.
Do.	Jacob W. Shively	" 16, "	" 7, "	Resigned June 21, 1862.
Do.	George W. Moore	" 16, "	" 7, "	Promoted to 1st Lieutenant.
Do.	Wm. Lazalier	" 16, "	" 7, "	Promoted to 1st Lieutenant.
Do.	David P. Reed	Jan. 29, 1862	" 7, "	Promoted to 1st Lieutenant.
Do.	Frederick Pickering	March 3, "	" 7, "	Dismissed May 7, 1863.
Do.	Thomas B. Hoffman	" 21, "	" 7, "	Promoted to 1st Lieutenant.
Do.	Patrick H. Ludditt	" 25, "	" 7, "	Resigned September 18, 1862.
Do.	Abram P. Cox	Aug. 9, "	Sept. 19, "	App. Capt. Miss. Marine Brig. by President.
Do.	Wm. J. Faulkner	June 21, "	Oct. 7, "	Resigned May 17, 1863.
Do.	Joseph Tucker	Aug. 3, "	Nov. 1, "	Promoted to 1st Lieutenant.
Do.	Alex. Mahood	Sept. 18, "	Dec. 31, "	Promoted to 1st Lieutenant.
Do.	Lewis E. Hicks	Aug. 31, "	" 31, "	Promoted to 1st Lieutenant.
Do.	Jacob S. Pierson	March 15, "	April 28, "	Promoted to 1st Lieutenant.
Do.	John S. Scott	May 17, "	June 10, "	Killed November 25, 1863.
Do.	Wm. C. Barnett	Jan. 1, "	" 10, "	Promoted to 1st Lieutenant.
Do.	F. E. Wilson	March 7, "	" 10, "	Promoted to 1st Lieutenant.
Do.	N. E. Chenoweth	April 11, "	" 10, "	Promoted to 1st Lieutenant.
Do.	James Wharey	May 21, "	" 10, "	Promoted to 1st Lieutenant.
Do.	Samuel E. Murray	Jan. 2, "	" 10, "	Promoted to 1st Lieutenant.
Do.	Thurston C. Challen	May 23, "	July 10, "	Promoted to 1st Lieutenant.
Do.	Wm. W. Benedict	Aug. 11, 1864	Aug. 11, 1864	Promoted to 1st Lieutenant.

SIXTY-NINTH OHIO VOLUNTEER INFANTRY.

THIS regiment was recruited in Butler, Darke, Montgomery, Preble, Harrison, and Fairfield Counties. On the 19th of February, 1862, seven companies, which had been organized in camp near Hamilton, moved by rail to Camp Chase, Ohio. While here three companies, recruited in Harrison County, were added, thus completing the regiment.

On April 19, 1862, the Sixty-Ninth received orders to report for duty at Nashville, Tennessee, at which place it arrived on the 22d. It went into camp on Major Lewis's grounds, near the city, and was reviewed by Andrew Johnson, then Military Governor of Tennessee. Remaining here until the 1st of May it then went to Franklin, Tennessee, and was there detailed to guard forty miles of the Tennessee and Alabama Railroad. Aside from frequent alarms, nothing of moment occurred while the regiment was performing this duty. The Rebel women of Franklin were especially bitter, and on one occasion evinced their venom against the National dead buried in the cemetery, by dancing on their graves. Colonel Campbell, of the Sixty-Ninth, issued an order commenting in severe terms on this indignity, and warning the people of Franklin against a repetition of such dastardly insults.

On June 8th the regiment left Franklin and returned to Nashville. From thence it went by rail to Murfreesboro', where it joined an expedition under General Dumont, of Indiana, to

McMinnville, and thence marched across the Cumberland Mountains to Pikeville. Its object having been effected the expedition returned to Murfreesboro'. This march and counter-march was very severe, and the suffering was much aggravated by the fact that the rations were almost completely exhausted.

June 20th found the Sixty-Ninth at Nashville again, where it remained, performing provost and guard-duty, until the last of July. Its Colonel, Honorable Lewis D. Campbell (since Minister to Mexico) was appointed Provost-Marshal of Nashville, which position he held until his resignation, in the following August. During the stay of the regiment here the Rebel General Morgan made a raid on the town of Gallatin. The Sixty-Ninth Ohio and Eleventh Michigan were ordered there, and drove the enemy from the place, the Sixty-Ninth losing one man killed, Isaac Repp, of Dayton. This was the first loss of the regiment in battle.

When Bragg's army attempted a flank movement toward Louisville, the Sixty-Ninth and other regiments were left at Nashville as garrison for the city. From the scarcity of troops this duty was rendered quite severe. Hardly a day passed without some fight or skirmish with the enemy, who were continually making demonstrations on the Nashville and other turnpikes. This duty was performed until the 20th of December, when the regiment went into a camp about five miles from the city.

On December 26, 1862, the Sixty-Ninth moved, with the army under General Rosecrans, toward Murfreesboro'. It was brigaded in the Fourteenth Corps, which marched on the Franklin Turnpike. On the 31st, the first day of the battle of Stone River, the regiment, with its brigade, was engaged with the enemy, taking position in the advance line of General George H. Thomas's Fourteenth Corps. It became involved in the disaster on the right, and was compelled to fight its way back to the Nashville Turnpike. On this day the regiment suffered severely both in killed and wounded. It was not engaged in the movements on the 1st of January, 1863.

On Friday, January 2d, the Sixty-Ninth took part in the brilliant and desperate charge across Stone River against Breckinridge's Rebel corps, in which the Rebels were driven back with heavy loss. In this charge it captured a section of the famous Washington Battery from New Orleans. Sergeant Frederick Wilson, of company E, captured the flag of the battery. This fight lasted until after dark, and proved the termination of the battle, as on the next day the Rebel army was not to be seen. Captain L. C. Counsellor, of company H, Sergeant McGillam, of company B, Corporal D. P. Albright and private Stopher, of company E, were killed in the charge. Many others were wounded.

On June 24, 1863, the Tullahoma campaign was commenced. The regiment moved with the Fourteenth Corps, under General George W. Thomas, on the Manchester Road. No opposition was met with until in the passage through Hoover's Gap the enemy's rear-guard was engaged in a brisk fight. At Elk River, also, the enemy made a stand, but was quickly driven. Reaching Cowan's Station, on the Nashville and Chattanooga Railroad, the army went into camp, it being impossible to make further progress through the deep mud and terrible roads of that region.

When the army moved again the Sixty-Ninth was left at Cowan's Station, as guard to the General Hospital, and it remained at that point until the 8th of September. It was then detailed as guard to an ammunition train of four hundred and fifty wagons, going to Bridgeport, on the Tennessee River. It then marched to Chattanooga.

Preparatory to the battle of Chickamauga, the Sixty-Ninth Ohio, with the Reserve Corps under General Gordon Granger, marched from Rossville to Chickamauga Creek. At this point, in obedience to an order from Colonel Dan McCook, commanding the brigade, the regiment advanced, under Colonel Brigham, and burned Reed's Bridge, thus preventing the enemy from coming in on the rear of the National army. The regiment then fell back to Rossville, and immediately thereafter took charge of the division trains. For this reason it did not participate in the battle of Chickamauga.

On September 20th, in the afternoon, the Sixty-Ninth was ordered to report at the front, near Rossville, where it performed picket-duty and aided in covering the retreat of the Fourteenth Corps toward Chattanooga.

The regiment participated in the battle of Mission Ridge, and was among the first to reach the top of the mountain. In this charge it was commanded by Major J. J. Hanna, who was highly complimented for his bravery and efficiency. In ascending the Ridge, Lieutenant J. S. Scott, Color-Sergeant Jacob Wetzell, Color-Corporals D. W. Leach and John Meredith, Corporal E. J. Manche, privates Kluger, Elsom, Vankirk, Sewers, and Hefling were killed, and a large number wounded, many of whom subsequently died.

On March 16, 1864, the regiment, after having re-enlisted as veterans, started for Ohio, on a furlough of thirty days. At the end of their furlough the men reported promptly at Camp Dennison, and on the 22d of April again started for the field. Arriving at Nashville the regiment was compelled, for lack of transportation, to march to Cowan's Station. It joined Sherman's forces at Buzzard's Roost on the 11th of May.

On May 14th the regiment, with the army, moved through Snake Creek Gap to a point near Resaca, where the enemy was met and engaged. At this place Color-Sergeant John A. Compton and four others were killed and twenty-six men wounded. At Pumpkin-Vine Creek and at Dallas the enemy was again engaged. In these affairs the regiment lost five killed and nineteen wounded. Kenesaw Mountain was reached in the evening of June 14th. During this siege two men were killed. At Marietta, July 4th another engagement was had with the enemy, in which the regiment lost one man killed and seven wounded. The next stand was at the crossing of the Chattahoochie River. In this affair the regiment escaped without loss. On the 21st the regiment lost one man killed and ten wounded. July 22d brought the regiment and the army before Atlanta. During the siege nine men were wounded, two of whom subsequently died.

On September 1st the Sixty-Ninth took part in the fight at Jonesboro', and lost Lieutenants Jacob S. Pierson, Martin V. Bailey, Color-Sergeant Allen L. Jobes, of company D, and five men killed, and thirty-six wounded, some of whom died in a few hours after the fight. This battle caused the evacuation of Atlanta, and the National forces occupied that city.

The regiment participated in the subsequent chase after Hood, through the upper part of Georgia and into Alabama. It then returned to Atlanta and joined Sherman's march to the sea. On that march it lost one man by disease and four captured. Arriving in front of Savannah it took position in the front line.

In the campaign through the Carolinas the regiment was engaged with the enemy near Goldsboro', North Carolina, March 19, 1865, and lost two killed and eight wounded. This was the last affair in which it participated.

Then came the march through Richmond, the review at Washington, the transfer to Louisville, and lastly the final muster-out of the service, on the 17th of July, 1865.

70th REGIMENT OHIO VOLUNTEER INFANTRY.

ROSTER, THREE YEARS' SERVICE.

RANK.	NAME.	DATE OF RANK.	COM. ISSUED.	REMARKS.
Colonel	JOSEPH R. COCKERILL	Oct. 2, 1861	March 4, 1862	Resigned April 13, 1864.
Do.	DEWITT C. LOUDEN	April 26, 1864	April 26, 1864	Discharged as Lieutenant-Colonel Aug. 9, '64.
Lt. Colonel	DEWITT C. LOUDEN	Oct. 2, 1861	March 4, 1862	Promoted to Colonel.
Do.	WM. B. BROWN	April 26, 1864	April 26, 1864	Deceased.
Do.	H. L. PHILLIPS	Sept. 30, "	Sept. 30, "	Mustered out with regiment.
Major	J. W. MCFARREN	Oct. 2, 1861	March 4, 1862	Died October 3, 1862.
Do.	WM. B. BROWN	" 3, 1862	Oct. 13, "	Promoted to Lieutenant-Colonel.
Do.	LEWIS LOVE	Sept. 30, 1864	Sept. 30, 1864	Mustered out.
Do.	JAMES BROWN	Nov. 18, "	Nov. 18, "	Mustered out with regiment.
Surgeon	C. H. SWAIN	Oct. 21, 1861	March 4, 1862	Resigned August 3, 1863.
Do.	ROB'T L. VAN HARLINGEN	" 1, 1863	Oct. 1, 1863	Mustered out with regiment.
Ass't Surgeon	T. J. FARRILL	Dec. 11, 1861	March 4, 1862	Mustered out.
Do.	F. JAEGER	Sept. 17, 1862	Feb. 10, 1863	Resigned January 29, 1864.
Do.	J. M. SHOEMAKER	June 7, 1864	June 7, 1864	Never mustered in.
Chaplain	JOSEPH BLACKBURN	April 14, 1862	April 21, 1862	Resigned August 28, 1862.
Do.	JOHN M. SULLIVAN	Sept. 11, "	Oct. 3, "	Resigned June 10, 1864.
Captain	Wm. B. Brown	Oct. 16, 1861	March 4, "	Promoted to Major.
Do.	Reason T. Naylor	Nov. 18, "	" 4, "	Resigned June 2, 1863.
Do.	Chas. Johnson	" 20, "	" 4, "	Honorably discharged May 11, 1864.
Do.	Joseph Blackburn	" 26, "	" 4, "	Appointed Chaplain April 14, 1863.
Do.	John T. Wilson	" 26, "	" 4, "	Resigned November 27, 1862.
Do.	Watson Foster	Dec. 10, "	" 4, "	Honorably discharged December 13, 1864.
Do.	James F. Summers	" 23, "	" 4, "	Killed July 28, 1864.
Do.	Benj. T. Willis	" 28, "	" 4, "	Resigned June 3, 1863.
Do.	Daniel B. Carter	Jan. 28, 1862	" 4, "	Dismissed.
Do.	Felix G. Stone	Feb. 11, "	" 27, "	Resigned August 4, 1863.
Do.	James H. De Bruin	April 14, "	May 5, "	Declined.
Do.	H. L. Phillips	Oct. 3, "	Oct. 13, "	Promoted to Lieutenant-Colonel.
Do.	Lewis Love	July 1, "	Dec. 31, "	Promoted to Lieutenant-Colonel.
Do.	Valentine Zimmerman	Nov. 27, "	" 31, "	Resigned June 2, 1863.
Do.	James Brown	March 11, 1864	March 11, 1864	Promoted to Major.
Do.	James Drennin	June 2, 1863	Jan. 10, "	Dismissed.
Do.	Brice Cooper	" 3, "	" 10, "	Resigned October 28, 1864.
Do.	John Campbell	" 2, "	" 10, "	Mustered out.
Do.	John C. Nelson	March 11, "	March 11, "	Mustered out with regiment.
Do.	Townsend Heaton	Sept. 20, "	Sept. 20, "	Mustered out.
Do.	Walter S. Cox	" 20, "	" 20, "	Mustered out.
Do.	Wm. C. Marlatt	Oct. 1, 1864	Oct. 1, "	Mustered out with regiment.
Do.	Wm. McDaniel	" 1, "	" 1, "	Honorably discharged October 29, 1864.
Do.	Richard McKee	Nov. 18, "	Nov. 18, "	Mustered out as 1st Lieut. January 18, 1865.
Do.	Marquis De Lafayette Hare	" 18, "	" 18, "	Killed March 21, 1865.
Do.	David Dodd	" 18, "	" 18, "	Mustered out with regiment.
Do.	L. L. Edginton	" 18, "	" 18, "	Mustered out with regiment.
Do.	Wm. H. H. Hooper	" 18, "	" 18, "	Mustered out with regiment.
Do.	Chas. H. Ebert	Jan. 6, 1865	Jan. 6, 1865	Mustered out with regiment.
Do.	Wilson Foster	" 6, "	" 6, "	Mustered out with regiment.
Do.	Harvey Hughes	" 18, "	" 18, "	Mustered out with regiment.
Do.	John T. Brady	Feb. 6, "	Feb. 6, "	Mustered out with regiment.
Do.	Benj. F. Everton	April 10, "	April 10, "	Mustered out with regiment.
1st Lieutenant	J. H. De Bruin	Oct. 11, 1861	March 4, 1862	Resigned June 2, 1863.
Do.	Lewis Love	" 16, "	" 4, "	Promoted to Captain.
Do.	H. L. Phillips	" 28, "	" 4, "	Promoted to Captain.
Do.	Valentine Zimmerman	Nov. 18, "	" 4, "	Promoted to Captain.
Do.	Samuel W. Woodruff	" 20, "	" 4, "	Died January 9, 1863.
Do.	John Campbell	" 26, "	" 4, "	Promoted to Captain.
Do.	James Drennin	" 26, "	" 4, "	Promoted to Captain.
Do.	John K. Truitt	Dec. 10, "	" 4, "	Honorably discharged February 14, 1863.
Do.	Samuel B. Richards	" 23, "	" 4, "	Dismissed December 18, 1862.
Do.	Wm. Herbert	" 28, "	" 4, "	Honorably discharged November 1, 1862.
Do.	Reif Joinville	June 28, 1862	" 4, "	Cashiered February 2, 1863.
Do.	Wm. R. Harmon	Feb. 11, "	" 27, "	Resigned September 31, 1862.
Do.	Brice Cooper	April 14, "	May 5, "	Promoted to Captain.
Do.	Wm. R. Stewart	Oct. 3, "	Oct. 13, "	Resigned August 3, 1863.
Do.	Joseph Spurgeon	Sept. 3, "	Dec. 31, "	Revoked.
Do.	Isaac W. Adams	Nov. 1, "	" 31, "	Resigned January 20, 1863.
Do.	John C. Nelson	Oct. 4, "	" 31, "	Promoted to Captain.
Do.	George A. Foster	Nov. 27, "	" 31, "	Dismissed June 8, 1863.
Do.	Andrew Urban	Dec. 21, 1862	Feb. 7, 1863	Killed in action at Jonesboro'
Do.	Townsend Heaton	Jan. 22, 1863	" 7, "	Promoted to Captain.
Do.	Walter S. Cox	" 23, "	" 7, "	Promoted to Captain.
Do.	James Brown	Nov. 28, 1862	" 7, "	Promoted to Captain.
Do.	Alfred Louden	May 14, 1863	May 11, "	Not in regiment; never mustered.
Do.	C. A. Grimes	June 2, "	Jan. 10, 1864	Resigned January 26, 1865.
Do.	Wm. C. Marlatt	" 8, "	" 10, "	Promoted to Captain.
Do.	Thomas Scott	Aug. 3, "	" 10, "	Dismissed June 21, 1864.
Do.	John Krepps	June 2, "	" 10, "	Killed July 28, 1864.
Do.	Wm. McDaniel	March 11, 1864	March 11, "	Promoted to Captain.
Do.	Richard McKee	" 11, "	" 11, "	Promoted to Captain.
Do.	Marquis De Lafayette Hare	" 11, "	" 11, "	Promoted to Captain.
Do.	David Dodd	" 11, "	" 11, "	Promoted to Captain.
Do.	Jamuel J. Mutticks	Sept. 20, "	Sept. 20, "	Declined.
Do.	L. L. Edington	" 20, "	" 20, "	Promoted to Captain.
Do.	Wm. H. H. Hooper	Oct. 1, "	Oct. 1, "	Promoted to Captain.
Do.	Chas. H. Ebert	" 1, "	" 1, "	Promoted to Captain.
Do.	Wilson Foster	" 1, "	" 1, "	Promoted to Captain.

RANK.	NAME.	DATE OF RANK.	COM. ISSUED.	REMARKS.
1st Lieutenant	Harvey Hughes	Oct. 1, 1864	Oct. 1, 1864	Promoted to Captain.
Do.	John T. Brady	" 1, "	" 1, "	Promoted to Captain.
Do.	Benj. F. Everton	" 1, "	" 1, "	Promoted to Captain.
Do.	Thomas B. Stiles	Jan. 6, 1865	Jan. 6, 1865	Mustered out with regiment.
Do.	Wm. R. Harmon	" 6, "	" 6, "	Mustered out with regiment.
Do.	Jonas P. Nixon	" 6, "	" 6, "	Mustered out with regiment.
Do.	Thomas E. Grier	" 18, "	" 18, "	Died from disease.
Do.	Andrew J. Sebberal	" 18, "	" 18, "	Mustered out with regiment.
Do.	Robert C. Monnaugh	" 18, "	" 18,	Mustered out with regiment.
Do.	Jesse McKinley	" 18, "	" 18, "	Mustered out with regiment.
Do.	Francis M. Rickards	April 10, "	April 10, "	
Do.	Wm. H. McGinnis	" 10, "	" 10, "	Mustered out with regiment.
Do.	Isaac Washburn	" 10, "	" 10, "	Mustered out with regiment.
Do.	Franklin Harding	" 10, "	" 19, "	Mustered out with regiment.
Do.	Fred'k Autenreith	" 10, "	" 10, "	Dismissed.
Do.	Nelson H. Edgerington	" 10, "	" 10, "	
2d Lieutenant	Brice Cooper	Oct. 16, 1861	March 4, 1862	Promoted to 1st Lieutenant.
Do.	Wm. R. Stewart	Nov. 18, "	" 4, "	Promoted to 1st Lieutenant.
Do.	Josiah W. Denham	" 20, "	" 4, "	Discharged September 29, 1862.
Do.	Joseph Spurgeon	" 26, "	" 4, "	Honorably discharged November 1, 1862.
Do.	Isaac W. Adams	" 26, "	" 4, "	Resigned January 20, 1863.
Do.	John C. Nelson	Dec. 10, "	" 4, "	Promoted to 1st Lieutenant.
Do.	Wm. P. Spurgeon	" 23, "	" 4, "	Resigned February 14, 1863.
Do.	John Taylor	" 28, "	" 4, "	Honorably discharged November 1, 1862.
Do.	George A. Foster	Jan. 28, 1862	" 4, "	Promoted to 1st Lieutenant.
Do.	Amos F. Ellis	Feb. 21, "	" 27, "	Resigned January 10, 1863.
Do.	James Brown	April 11, "	July 11, "	Promoted to 1st Lieutenant.
Do.	Andrew Urban	Oct. 3, "	Oct. 13, "	Promoted to 1st Lieutenant.
Do.	W. C. Marlatt	Jan. 22, 1863	Feb. 7, 1863	Promoted to 1st Lieutenant.
Do.	Thomas Scott	" 23, "	" 7, "	Promoted to 1st Lieutenant.
Do.	John Krepps	" 24, "	" 7, "	Promoted to 1st Lieutenant.
Do.	Wm. Mc. Daniel	" 25, "	" 7, "	Promoted to 1st Lieutenant.
Do.	Richard McKee	" 26, "	" 7, "	Promoted to 1st Lieutenant.
Do.	Marquis De Lafayette Hare	" 27, "	" 7, "	Promoted to 1st Lieutenant.
Do.	David Dodd	" 28, "	" 7, "	Promoted to 1st Lieutenant.
Do.	Samuel J. Matticks	" 29, "	" 7, "	Mustered out.
Do.	Henry H. Johnson	" 30, "	" 7, "	Resigned February 25, 1863.
Do.	G. W. Buesart	" 31, "	" 7, "	Mustered out.

SEVENTIETH OHIO VOLUNTEER INFANTRY.

WHEN the rebellion began to assume its gigantic proportions, in the fall of 1861, the President made his second call for men in numbers commensurate with the serious work on hand. Ohio, as ever, was equal to the occasion, and every effort was put forth to raise her quota.

Upon application in person, J. R. Cockerill, of Adams County, was appointed, by the Governor, to the rank of Colonel, with authority to raise the Seventieth Ohio Volunteer Infantry. On the 14th day of October a camp was established at West Union, and in the course of a few days four hundred men had reported, including one full company, commanded by Captain Brown. Owing to the unprepared state of the General and State Governments, arms and equipments were not furnished to the regiment until at least a full month after they went into camp. Necessarily, therefore, the officers and men experienced at the outset some of the hardships of a soldier life, the officers sleeping in the large hall on the County Fair Grounds, the citizens furnishing supplies of bed-clothes for both officers and men.

By the 25th of December seven full companies were organized and the other three in process of formation; at which time the regiment was ordered to Ripley to repel an anticipated raid from Kentucky. While at Ripley two companies, originally intended for the Fifty-Second Ohio, were sent from Camp Dennison and attached to the Seventieth, thus completing the regiment.

The regiment, during its stay in camp, was thoroughly drilled and fitted for the field. On the 17th of February it was ordered to Paducah, Kentucky, and, on its arrival, reported to General W. T. Sherman, and was incorporated into his division, (Fifth), then organizing. In brigading this division the Seventieth was placed in the Third Brigade, with the Forty-Eighth and Seventy-Second Ohio, Colonel Buckland, of the Seventy-Second, commanding.

On the 10th day of March the division moved up the Tennessee River in transports, and disembarked at Pittsburg Landing. On the 17th it went into camp near Shiloh Church, on the Corinth Road, three miles from the Landing. At this point three brigades of Sherman's division were encamped in partial line of battle, facing south, the Third Brigade in the center, and left of the Seventieth resting directly upon the Shiloh Church, with a narrow road between the left company and the church; a small creek three or four hundred yards in their front, forming a depression of forty or fifty feet on the table-land.

Orders were received on the 3d day of April, from General Sherman, sending the Third Brigade to reconnoiter to the front. No enemy in force was found within five miles. On the next day the Rebel cavalry made a dash, and carried off one officer and seven men of the Seventieth from the picket-post on the Corinth Road, about three-fourths of a mile in front of the camp. On the 5th the enemy's cavalry and the National pickets were exchanging shots all the afternoon. On Sunday morning, the 6th, the picket-line was driven in upon the line of battle, which was formed about one hundred yards in front of the color-line of the camp, and here it was that the storm struck it. The enemy withdrew his skirmishers, developed his advancing lines on the opposite slope, and opened a fierce fire with artillery and musketry, and the bloody battle of Pittsburg Landing had begun. The Seventieth stood its ground for about two hours, and only fell back to the color-line of the camp. After the entire line to the left of the Shiloh Church had been completely turned, and not a soldier of any other regiment was to be seen on the original line of battle, the regiment fell slowly back, fighting every inch of ground during the entire day, and lay in front of the enemy at night over half way from Shiloh Church to the Landing. On Monday the regiment took part in the action during the whole day, and established an enduring name for bravery and endurance. General Sherman, under whose eye they fought, spoke of the conduct of the regiment to every one in the most flattering terms, and in the report of the battle said: "Colonel Cockerill behaved with great gallantry, and held together the largest regiment of any Colonel in my division; and stood by me from first to last."

In common with the rest of the army the Seventieth took part in the advance on Corinth, sharing in the reconnoissances and skirmishes of that movement. After the fall of Corinth Sherman's division moved westward, arrived at Memphis in July, and remained on duty there until the following autumn. A large number of new troops having arrived from the North, General Sherman was put in command of an army corps, General Denver of the division, and Colonel Cockerill of a brigade, consisting of the Seventieth, with the Fifty-Third Ohio, Ninety-Seventh and Ninety-Ninth Indiana, and two batteries of artillery. [While at Memphis, Major J. W. McFerrin died of congestive fever, much regretted by the regiment. Captain Brown was promoted to fill the vacancy.] After November 25, 1862, Colonel Cockerill never commanded the Seventieth, being continued in charge of the brigade until April, 1864, when he resigned.

The army left Memphis in November, 1862, and, concentrating upon the banks of the Tallahatchie River, prepared to march southward, through Mississippi, and invest Vicksburg. General Sherman was sent back to Memphis from Oxford, with General M. L. Smith's division, and with the other troops then concentrating at Memphis, moved down the river to attack the Bluffs, while the main army was to march *via* Jackson and invest the city from that side. The loss of the entire stores and subsistence at Holly Springs compelled the army to fall back to the Memphis and Charleston Railroad, and the troops were sent to Vicksburg during the winter and spring of 1863, by the river, the division, now commanded by W. S. Smith, arriving *via* Yazoo Bluffs about the 1st of June.

The command of the Seventieth now devolved on Major Brown, Lieutenant-Colonel Louden having been sent home from Memphis on sick leave. The division was placed in the line commanded by General W. T. Sherman, formed in the rear of Vicksburg, to prevent the advance of the enemy under General Joseph E. Johnston.

After the fall of Vicksburg General Sherman moved upon Jackson, the capital of the State, and during the siege the Seventieth and the entire brigade behaved in a gallant manner. The army returned to Black River, where the Forty-Eighth Illinois was added to the Brigade. Also company F, First Illinois Light Artillery, Captain Cheney.

A few days after the battle of Chickamauga the Fifteenth Army Corps, General Sherman, to which the brigade belonged, moved up the river to Memphis, and the corps marched through Northern Mississippi, Alabama, and Southern Tennessee, and took part in the battle of Chattanooga on the 25th and 26th of November.

The enemy was pursued to Ringgold, Georgia, from where the Fifteenth Army Corps was sent to Knoxville to re-enforce General Burnside. It returned about the 1st of January to the vicinity of Huntsville, Alabama. The division, which, during this campaign had been commanded by General Hugh Ewing, went into winter-quarters at Scottsboro', Alabama.

The march from Memphis to Knoxville *via* Chattanooga and back was over seven hundred miles, and is worthy of mention from the fact that almost incredible hardships were endured without a murmur. Many of the men of the Seventieth were without shoes, and the snowy, frozen earth retained their bloody footprints. Starvation also stared them in the face, as thirty thousand men were compelled to forage for subsistence from a belt of country but a few miles in width.

In January, 1864, the Seventieth re-enlisted as veterans, every company in the regiment carrying on the rolls the proper number of men to retain its organization. Every eligible company in the brigade did the same thing.

In May, 1864, the entire army of General Sherman was put in motion, and commenced the grand advance upon Atlanta. During this memorable march the Seventieth participated in all the battles on the way and around Atlanta, and maintained in each and all its high reputation. The regiment suffered a severe loss at Atlanta, in the death of its commanding officers, Major Brown and Captain Summers, both of whom fell at their post. Lieutenant Krepps and Adjutant Urban, both of the city of Cincinnati, were also killed in this campaign, and were much regretted as gallant and meritorious soldiers. To fill the vacancies occasioned by these losses the following promotions were made: Captain H. L. Phillips, who had acted as Assistant Adjutant-General for the brigade since its organization in 1862, at Memphis, was commissioned as Lieutenant-Colonel, and took command; Captain Brown, (brother of the late Major Brown), was commissioned Major; and these two officers served in their respective capacities until the end of the war.

During the autumn and winter months the regiment marched through Georgia to the sea. On the 13th of December, 1864, Fort McAllister was taken by storm, in which the Seventieth participated and suffered severely. It was the first regiment to enter the work through the abattis and ditch, sweeping over the plain and through the works without a halt.

The Seventieth was with Sherman in his march through the Carolinas, and at Bentonville North Carolina, lost a valuable officer in Captain Hare, killed in that action. Marching through Richmond to Washington City it participated in the grand review before the President and his Cabinet. Thence it was sent to Louisville, Kentucky. Thence to Little Rock, Arkansas, where it was finally mustered out of the service and discharged August 14, 1865, having been nearly four years in the field. It returned home without a blemish upon its reputation, and was greeted by the citizens of the State and its peculiar locality with distinguished marks of approbation. It lost many valuable officers and men, whose memory will be forever cherished.

"How sleep the brave who sink to rest
With all their country's honor blest."

It is somewhat remarkable that every officer who from first to last had a command in the regiment, was a member of it in its original organization before it left Ohio.

71st REGIMENT OHIO VOLUNTEER INFANTRY.

ROSTER, THREE YEARS' SERVICE.

RANK.	NAME.	DATE OF RANK.	COM. ISSUED.	REMARKS.
Colonel	RODNEY MASON	Oct. 15, 1861	June 5, 1862	Cashiered Aug. 22, '62; ord. rev. March 22,'64.
Do.	HENRY K. McCONNELL	May 30, 1863	May 30, 1863	Brevet Brigadier-General of Volunteers.
Do.	JAMES H. HART	Nov. 29, 1865	Nov. 29, 1865	Mustered out as Lieutenant-Colonel.
Lt. Colonel	BARTON S. KYLE	Oct. 2, 1861	April 1, 1862	Killed at Shiloh April 6, 1862.
Do.	GEORGE W. ANDREWS	April 6, 1862	June 5, "	Resigned June 3, 1863.
Do.	JAMES H. HART	" 2, 1864	April 2, 1864	Promoted to Colonel.
Major	GEORGE W. ANDREWS	Oct. 29, 1861	June 5, 1862	Promoted to Lieutenant-Colonel.
Do.	JAMES H. HART	April 6, 1862	" 5, "	Promoted to Lieutenant-Colonel.
Do.	JAMES W. CARLIN	" 2, 1864	April 2, 1864	Killed in Sultana disaster, April 27, 1865.
Do.	AMOS H. BRANDON	Nov. 29, 1865	Nov. 29, 1865	
Do.	SAMUEL J. McCONNELL	" 29, "	" 29, "	Mustered out as Captain.
Surgeon	CORNELIUS N. HOAGLAND	Oct. 28, 1861	June 5, 1862	Resigned September 7, 1863.
Do.	CORNELIUS N. HOAGLAND	Nov. 11, 1863	Nov. 11, 1863	Re-appointed November 11, 1863.
Ass't Surgeon	WM. H. CRANE	Jan. 9, 1862	June 5, 1862	Mustered out January 9, 1865; time out.
Do.	M. J. BOWLAND	Aug. 28, "	Dec. 1, "	Assigned to McLaughlin's Squadron.
Do.	SIDNEY R. WAKEFIELD	Sept. 7, "	Nov. 1, 1863	Mustered out June 12, 1865.
Do.	AMOS BRACHLER	Nov. 29, 1865	" 29, 1865	
Chaplain	A. L. McKINNEY	March 23, 1862	April 4, 1862	Mustered out March 22, 1865.
Captain	Henry K. McConnell	Nov. 13, 1861	Feb. 14, 1862	Promoted to Colonel.
Do.	James W. Carlin	" 27, "	" 14, "	Promoted to Major.
Do.	Wm. H. Callinder	" 29, "	" 14, "	Discharged August 29, 1862.
Do.	John R. Woodward	Dec. 1, "	" 14, "	Discharged August 29, 1862.
Do.	Smith H. Clark	" 14, "	" 14, "	Discharged August 29, 1862.
Do.	Charles H. Cramer	" 24, "	" 14, "	Discharged August 29, 1862.
Do.	Gideon L. Blonde	Jan. 25, 1862	" 14, "	Resigned November 16, 1862.
Do.	J. W. Moody	" 10, "	June 5, "	Resigned September 1, 1865.
Do.	Thomas W. Brown	" 28, "	" 5, "	Discharged August 29, 1862.
Do.	Solomon J. Howk	Feb. 7, "	" 5, "	Mustered out February 25, 1865.
Do.	John G. Taylor	Oct. 14, "	Oct. 14, "	Resigned April 11, 1861.
Do.	Wm. L. Avery	" 19, "	" 19, "	Mustered out September 16, 1863.
Do.	Charles E. Lewis	Nov. 1, "	Dec. 3, "	Resigned April 17, 1863.
Do.	George O. Toms	Oct. 1, "	Feb. 22, 1863	Resigned June 5, 1863.
Do.	Wm. H. McDevitt	Dec. 6, "	Dec. 6, 1862	Honorably discharged May 9, 1865.
Do.	Joseph R. Goodwin	Aug. 3, 1863	Aug. 3, 1863	Mustered out May 15, 1865.
Do.	Elisha S. Williams	" 3, "	" 3, "	Resigned April 21, 1864.
Do.	Amos H. Brandon	April 2, 1864	April 2, 1864	Promoted to Major.
Do.	Samuel J. McConnell	" 2, "	" 2, "	Promoted to Major.
Do.	Alexander Gable	" 2, "	" 2, "	Resigned September 22, 1864.
Do.	Wm. H. McClure	May 9, "	May 9, "	Mustered out with regiment.
Do.	Joshua L. Babb	Oct. 12, "	Oct. 12, "	Resigned November 28, 1864.
Do.	Wm. S. Wilson	Nov. 3, "	Nov. 3, "	Resigned October 3, 1865.
Do.	Charles T. Riley	Dec. 14, "	Dec. 14, "	Declined promotion.
Do.	Jesse C. Nichols	April 8, 1865	April 8, 1865	Mustered out with regiment.
Do.	Potterfield H. Troxell	May 11, "	May —, "	Mustered out with regiment.
Do.	James Johnson	Nov. 29, "	Nov. 29, "	Mustered out with regiment.
Do.	Lewis Cooper	" 29, "	" 29, "	Mustered out with regiment.
Do.	Harvey McGowen	" 29, "	" 29, "	
Do.	Robert G. Dinsmore	" 29, "	" 29, "	
Do.	Sidney A. Smith	" 29, "	" 29, "	
Do.	Daniel A. Bright	" 29, "	" 29, "	
1st Lieutenant	Elisha S. Williams	Oct. 5, 1861	Feb. 14, 1862	Promoted to Captain.
Do.	John M. Hill	Nov. 25, "	" 14, "	Resigned July 14, 1862.
Do.	George O. Toms	" 29, "	" 14, "	Promoted to Captain.
Do.	Ira L. Morris	Dec. 11, "	" 14, "	Honorably discharged August 29, 1863.
Do.	Joseph R. Goodwin	" 14, "	" 14, "	Promoted; resigned November 10, 1863.
Do.	Nickols Eidemeller	" 21, "	" 14, "	Died May 16, 1862.
Do.	Joseph N. Hetzler	Jan. 25, 1862	" 14, "	Resigned December 29 1862.
Do.	Newton J. Harter	Feb. 7, "	May 27, "	Discharged August 29, 1862.
Do.	James H. Hart	Oct. 7, 1861	June 5, "	Promoted to Captain.
Do.	Amour Nickols	Jan. 10, 1862	" 5, "	Resigned June 8, 1863.
Do.	Wm. H. McDevitt	" 28, "	" 5, "	Promoted to Captain.
Do.	Edward P. Ransom	Oct. 12, 1861	" 5, "	Discharged October 11, 1862.
Do.	Thomas F. Moore	April 6, 1862	" 5, "	Discharged August 29, 1862.
Do.	Amos H. Brandon	May 16, "	" 20, "	Promoted to Captain.
Do.	A. J. Douglass	Sept. 18, "	Sept. 18, "	Resigned November 24, 1864.
Do.	Willard S. Hickox	Oct. 3, "	Oct. 3, "	Major 10th cavalry.
Do.	Thomas C. Chase	" 22, "	" 22, "	Mustered out November 27, 1863.
Do.	Joseph J. Ennis	" 25, "	" 25, "	Reduced to ranks Oct. 27, '63, to serve 3 years.
Do.	Samuel A. Bonsall	Nov. 3, "	Nov. 3, "	Honorably mustered out November 21, 1863.
Do.	Alexander Gable	Dec. 29, "	Feb. 10, 1863	Promoted to Captain.
Do.	Samuel J. McConnell	Nov. 16, 1863	" 10, "	Promoted to Captain.
Do.	Wm. H. McClure	Aug. 3, "	Aug. 3, "	Promoted to Captain.
Do.	Wm. S. Wilson	" 3, "	" 3, "	Promoted to Captain.
Do.	Charles T. Riley	" 3, "	" 3, "	Resigned January 1, 1865.
Do.	Joshua L. Babb	" 3, "	" 3, "	Promoted to Captain.
Do.	Jesse C. Nichols	April 2, 1864	April 2, 1864	Promoted to Captain.
Do.	Potterfield H. Troxell	" 2, "	" 2, "	Promoted to Captain.
Do.	George B. Frye	" 2, "	" 2, "	Resigned November 22, 1864.
Do.	Benj. A. Hamilton	" 2, "	" 2, "	Resigned February 24, 1865.
Do.	Samuel H. Brandon	" 2, "	" 2, "	Resigned March 12, 1865.
Do.	George W. Gunder	" 2, "	" 2, "	Resigned September 28, 1864.
Do.	James Johnson	" 2, "	" 2, "	Promoted to Captain.
Do.	Elijah A. Widener	" 2, "	" 2, "	Killed in action December 16, 1862.
Do.	Lewis Cooper	" 2, "	" 2, "	Promoted to Captain.
Do.	Augustus A. Brown	May 9, "	May 9, "	Dismissed September 12, 1864.

RANK.	NAME.	DATE OF RANK.	COM. ISSUED.	REMARKS.
1st Lieutenant	John W. Davis	Oct. 12, 1864	Oct. 12, 1864	Mustered out May 15, 1865.
Do.	Harvey McGowen	" 12, "	" 12, "	Promoted to Captain.
Do.	Robert G. Dinsmore	Dec. 14, "	Dec. 14, "	Promoted to Captain.
Do.	John A. Pittman	" 14, "	" 14, "	Resigned July 7, 1865.
Do.	J. W. Wright	" 14, "	" 14, "	Died September 18, ——.
Do.	Charles H. Rollins	Jan. 20, 1865	Jan. 20, 1865	Mustered out with regiment.
Do.	Jacob Zangline	" 20, "	" 20 "	Mustered out with regiment.
Do.	Sidney A. Smith	" 30, "	" 20, "	Promoted to Captain.
Do.	Daniel A. Bright	March 18, "	March 18, "	Promoted to Captain.
Do.	Wm. McConnell	April 8, "	April 8, "	Resigned August 31, 1865.
Do.	Charles J. Bryant	" 8, "	" 8, "	
Do.	Wilbur F. McCue	" 8, "	" 8, "	Mustered out with regiment.
Do.	George T. Fuller	May 11, "	May 11, "	Mustered out with regiment.
Do.	Simon W. Kittering	Sept. 4, "	Sept. 4, "	Mustered out with regiment.
Do.	Sylvester Brock	" 4, "	" 4, "	Mustered out with regiment.
Do.	N. M. Palmer	Nov. 29, "	Nov. 29, "	
Do.	Enos Pemberton	" 29, "	" 29, "	
Do.	Frank Beaver	" 29, "	" 29, "	
Do.	John B. McDevitt	" 29, "	" 29, "	
Do.	Elijah Martz	" 29, "	" 29, "	
2d Lieutenant	Thomas F. Moore	Oct. 5, 1861	Feb. 14, 1862	Promoted to 1st Lieutenant.
Do.	Amos H. Brandon	Nov. 25, "	" 14, "	Promoted to 1st Lieutenant.
Do.	Ezekiel Z. Hitchens	" 27, "	" 14, "	Resigned April 11, 1862.
Do.	Isaac Mann	Dec. 11, "	" 14, "	Discharged August 29, 1862.
Do.	Horace M. Drury	" 11, "	" 14, "	Discharged August 29, 1862.
Do.	Stephen W. Beman	" 21, "	" 14, "	Discharged August 29, 1862.
Do.	Alexander Gable	Jan. 25, 1862	" 14, "	Promoted to 1st Lieutenant.
Do.	John H. Hunter	Nov. 27, 1861	May 6, "	Resigned September 3, 1862.
Do.	Wm. S. Hamilton	Jan. 28, 1862	June 5, "	Deceased August 20, 1862.
Do.	Charles Lewis	April 6, "	" 5, "	Promoted to 1st Lieutenant.
Do.	Wm. H. McClure	May 16, "	Aug. 12, "	Promoted to 1st Lieutenant.
Do.	Samuel J. McConnell	April 1, "	" 20, "	Promoted to 1st Lieutenant.
Do.	Charles T. Riley	Oct. 8, "	Oct. 8, "	Promoted to 1st Lieutenant.
Do.	Daniel W. Brown	" 22, "	" 22, "	Resigned January 1, 1863.
Do.	Joshua L. Babb	" 8, "	Nov. 25, "	Promoted to 1st Lieutenant.
Do.	Jesse C. Nichols	Nov. 26, "	" 26, "	Promoted to 1st Lieutenant.
Do.	J. B. Rollins	Aug. 29, "	" 28, "	Resigned June 5, 1863.
Do.	E. C. Le Blonde	Nov. 28, "	" 28, "	Resigned January 1, 1865.
Do.	Potterfield H. Troxell	" 1, "	Dec. 3, "	Promoted to 1st Lieutenant.
Do.	Wm. S. Wilson	Aug. 20, "	Jan. 14, 1863	Promoted to 1st Lieutenant.
Do.	George B. Frye	Nov. 16, "	Feb. 11, "	Promoted to 1st Lieutenant.
Do.	John M. Simmons	Dec. 29, "	" 21, "	Deceased —— 24, 1863.
Do.	Benj. A. Hamilton	March 1, 1863	May 9, "	Promoted to 1st Lieutenant.
Do.	Wm. G. Nichols	June 5, "	June 26, "	Commission returned.
Do.	Augustus A. Brown	Aug. 3, "	Aug. 3, "	Promoted to 1st Lieutenant.
Do.	Samuel H. Brandon	" 3, "	" 3, "	Promoted to 1st Lieutenant.
Do.	George W. Gander	" 3, "	" 3, "	Promoted to 1st Lieutenant.
Do.	John A. Pittman	Nov. 26, 1864	Nov. 26, 1864	Promoted to 1st Lieutenant.
Do.	Charles H. Rollins	" 26, "	" 26, "	Promoted to 1st Lieutenant.
Do.	Jacob Zangline	" 26, "	" 26, "	Promoted to 1st Lieutenant.
Do.	Sidney A. Smith	" 26, "	" 26, "	Promoted to 1st Lieutenant.
Do.	Daniel A. Bright	" 26, "	" 26, "	Promoted to 1st Lieutenant.
Do.	Wm. McConnell	" 26, "	" 26, "	Promoted to 1st Lieutenant.
Do.	Charles T. Bryant	Jan. 20, 1865	Jan. 20, 1865	Promoted to 1st Lieutenant.
Do.	Wilbur F. McCue	" 20, "	" 20, "	Promoted to 1st Lieutenant.
Do.	Daniel W. Ellis	Nov. 29, "	Nov. 29, "	
Do.	John Fike	" 29, "	" 29, "	
Do.	Wm. M. Johnson	" 29, "	" 29, "	
Do.	A. M. Pearson	" 29, "	" 29, "	
Do.	S. H. Wilson	" 29, "	" 29, "	
Do.	J. D. Richey	" 29, "	" 29, "	
Do.	John E. Reed	" 29, "	" 29, "	
Do.	David L. Lee	" 29, "	" 29, "	
Do.	Frank Vitt	" 29, "	" 29, "	
Do.	M. H. Davis	" 29, "	" 29, "	

SEVENTY-FIRST OHIO VOLUNTEER INFANTRY.

THE SEVENTY-FIRST OHIO was recruited mainly in the counties of Miami, Auglaize, and Mercer, under the superintendence of B. S. Kyle, of Troy, and G. W. Andrews, of Wapakonetta. Recruits began to rendezvous at Troy in the latter part of October, 1861, and about the 1st of February, 1862, the organization was complete. It was recruited and organized with as little expense to the Government as any regiment sent into the service from Ohio to serve for three years. Rodney Mason, of Springfield, a gentleman who possessed something of a military education, and had passed through the three-months' service as Lieutenant-Colonel of the Second Ohio, was appointed Colonel of the regiment by Governor Dennison, Messrs. Kyle and Andrews concurring in the appointment, and being commissioned respectively Lieutenant-Colonel and Major.

The regiment received marching orders on the 10th of February, and four days later reported to General Sherman at Paducah, Kentucky, and encamped at the outskirts of the town. Though the weather was very inclement, the regiment was drilled frequently; and, by the superior skill of Colonel Mason, considerable proficiency was attained in a very short time. About the 25th of February General Sherman determined to make a reconnoissance toward Columbus; and taking one-half of the Seventy-First Ohio and one-half of the Fifty-Fifth Illinois, embarked on one of the largest Mississippi steamers, and, passing down to Cairo, was joined by two large mortar-boats and three gunboats. When the force approached within two miles of Columbus the Rebels were discovered to be evacuating. The troops disembarked as soon as possible, and the Seventy-First immediately occupied the summit of the bluff overlooking the town and river. Here it remained three days, and then returned to Paducah to join the general advance up the Tennessee River. The regiment moved up the Tennessee on two steamers, the Ocean and the Hazel Dell, and was among the first troops at Pittsburg Landing. Colonel Mason drilled the regiment as constantly as the health of the men and the proximity of the enemy would admit, his military education and his skill in imparting it to those under his command being found to far excel that of some West Pointers. The regiment was brigaded with the Fifty-Fourth Ohio and the Fifty-Fifth Illinois, and the brigade was commanded by Colonel Stewart.

About seven o'clock on the morning of the 6th of April, 1862, while Colonel Mason was giving some instructions to the line-officers, an orderly rode up with a written notice that the line had been attacked at the center. In less than five minutes the regiment was in line of battle; and just then Colonel Stewart galloped up and asked Colonel Mason's advice in regard to dispositions and positions. General Sherman, the division commander, had located the brigade on the extreme left of the army, and was himself with the remainder of the command near the right and center, two miles away, where the battle was raging. Some of the bullets whistled over the brigade, and Colonel Mason suggested to Colonel Stewart that the line be formed immediately. Colonel S. seemed undecided, and Colonel Mason advised that the brigade be moved to the left, where the enemy seemed to be concentrating. The suggestion was immediately carried into effect by the brigade commander, and the three regiments went into position without any assistance from artillery. The Fifty-Fifth Illinois was placed on the left of the line, formed in a hollow square; the Fifty-Fourth Ohio took the center, and the Seventy-First was posted on the right of the line, along a road, in such a way that the enemy approaching had the advantage, as the undulations of the ground were decidedly in their favor. A heavy cannonade was opened upon the line, and Colonel Mason, seeing the enemy about to advance in overwhelming numbers, directed the regiment to retire two or three hundred yards, where it was sheltered by a slight elevation, and where a better connection was formed with the regiments on the left. The enemy soon approached the former position of the Seventy-First with two batteries of artillery. The attack was terrible; and had not the new position been well chosen, half an hour would not have elapsed before every man would have been killed or captured; but a depression like a wide ravine intervened between the two lines, and the regiment held its ground bravely. About two P. M., after every regiment in the brigade had retired, the Seventy-First also fell back. In this retrograde movement the regiment became separated, but it re-formed at the landing under Colonel Mason, and, at the last rally of the army at sunset, it fought with good effect, and received the commendations of its superior officers. On Monday the Seventy-First was actively engaged, some of the line-officers behaving with great gallantry. In this battle it lost one hundred and thirty men killed and wounded. On the 16th of April the regiment was ordered on the Cumberland River to hold the posts of Fort Donelson and Clarksville. The district of country garrisoned by the Seventy-First comprised a large part of Northern Middle Tennessee, and it relieved two regiments of infantry and one of cavalry, a fact which shows that the highest confidence was reposed in its efficiency and bravery.

During the spring and summer of 1862 strenuous efforts were made by the Rebels in Southern Kentucky and Middle Tennessee in behalf of their cause. Almost the entire male population were members of some kind of military organization. The regiment was actively engaged in suppressing these organizations, and a good degree of order was maintained until the middle of August. Colonel Woodward, a graduate of West Point, secretly raised a force, with head-quarters at Hopkinsville, Kentucky, and Colonel A. R. Johnson raised a force between Clarksville and Nashville. On Sunday, August 17th, these forces united, about ten miles east of Clarksville, and the next morning Colonel Woodward took command and led an attack on the garrison at Clarksville. Colonel Mason had less than two hundred effective men, having been obliged to send guards to Harpeth Shoals, Clarksville Landing, and to the railroad west of the city. A surrender was demanded by Colonel Woodward, and Colonel Mason summoned a council of war to decide on the demand. It was agreed in the council, from indubitable evidence, that the Rebel force was four times as large as the National force, and it was voted unanimously to accede to the demand. A few days after all the line-officers were dismissed the service, and Colonel Mason was cashiered; but the facts connected with the surrender becoming fully known, the War Department finally revoked the order, and the officers were all *honorably discharged*.

After the regiment was exchanged, four companies, on the 25th of August, 1862, engaged and completely defeated Woodward's force at Fort Donelson. It went into winter-quarters at Fort Henry, there joining the forces under General Lowe. On the 3d of February, 1863, the regiment was on an expedition to Fort Donelson against the combined force of Wheeler and Forrest, but the enemy retreated, and the Seventy-First was not brought into action. During the latter part of the year 1863 the regiment was stationed along the Louisville and Nashville Railroad, with head-quarters at Gallatin, and was actively engaged in dispersing guerrillas.

In the early part of the campaign of 1864 the Seventy-First moved south, and was engaged in some skirmishes, in all of which both officers and men behaved gallantly. It took an active and effective part in the battle of Nashville, displaying great bravery and courage, and losing one-third of its number in killed and wounded—among them several valuable officers.

The regiment, decimated as it was, still retained its zeal and energy, and shortly after the battle was ordered to Texas, whither it took its way; and there, through all the summer of 1865, the officers and men did their duty, and thought it harder than on the battle-field; for patriotism alone had taken them into the army; and now that the fighting was over, they were anxious to return to their homes. At length the order directing their return to Camp Chase, Ohio, was received, and there the regiment was mustered out and discharged in January, 1866.

The death of its Lieutenant-Colonel in its first battle, and the dismissal of the rest of its officers not long afterward, had a dispiriting effect upon the regiment; and it came to be talked of as one of the unlucky regiments of the State. The injustice of the dismissals, however, was subsequently confessed by the Government, and on more than one bloody field the rank and file attested their devotion and their courage.

72d REGIMENT OHIO VOLUNTEER INFANTRY.

ROSTER, THREE YEARS' SERVICE.

RANK.	NAME.	DATE OF RANK.	COM. ISSUED.	REMARKS.
Colonel	RALPH P. BUCKLAND	Oct. 31, 1861	Jan. 11, 1862	Brevetted Major General.
Do.	LEROY CROCKETT	Nov. 29, 1862	July 23, 1863	Died December 10, 1863.
Do.	CHAS. G. EATON	April 9, 1864	April 9, 1864	Mustered out as Lieutenant Colonel.
Lt. Colonel	HERMAN CANFIELD	Oct. 30, 1861	Jan. 11, 1862	Killed at Shiloh, April 6, 1862.
Do.	LEROY CROCKETT	April 6, 1862	June 20, "	Promoted to Colonel.
Do.	CHAS. G. EATON	Nov. 29, "	July 23, 1863	Promoted to Colonel.
Do.	EUGENE A. RAWSON	April 9, 1864	April 9, 1864	Killed in action July 22, 1864.
Do.	SAMUEL A. J. SNYDER	Sept. 4, 1865	Sept. 4, 1865	Mustered out as Major.
Major	LEROY CROCKETT	Nov. 26, 1861	Jan. 11, 1862	Promoted to Lieutenant-Colonel.
Do.	CHAS. G. EATON	April 6, 1862	June 20, "	Promoted to Lieutenant Colonel.
Do.	EUGENE A. RAWSON	Nov. 29, "	July 23, 1863	Promoted to Lieutenant-Colonel.
Do.	SAMUEL A. J. SNYDER	April 9, 1864	April 9, 1864	Promoted to Lieutenant-Colonel.
Do.	JAMES C. FERNALD	Sept. 4, 1865	Sept. 4, 1865	Mustered out as Captain.
Surgeon	J. B. RICE	Nov. 25, 1861	Jan. 11, 1862	
Do.	C. B. RICHARDS	Jan. 31, 1865	Jan. 31, 1865	
Do.	WM. S. GAINES	May 31, "	May 31, "	Mustered out as Ass't-Surgeon 95th O. V. I.
Do.	WM. H. WILSON	Aug. 3, "	Sept. 4, "	
Ass't Surgeon	WM. M. KAULL	Nov. 5, 1861	July 11, 1862	Resigned June 4, 1863.
Do.	JOHN W. GOODWIN	Aug. 21, 1862	Aug. 22, "	Dismissed March 30, 1863.
Do.	WM. CALDWELL	April 11, 186	April 11, 1863	Honorably discharged January 4, 1865.
Do.	JACOB STAMP	Jan. 31, 1865	Jan. 31, 1865	Declined; returned commission.
Do.	W. W. FOUNTAIN	March 11, "	March 11, "	Declined; returned commission.
Do.	FRED'K F. FLAK	" 28, "	" 28, "	
Chaplain	A. B. POE	Jan. 11, 1862	Jan. 11, 1862	Resigned January 15, 1863.
Captain	Chas. G. Eaton	Nov. 30, 1861	Jan. 11, 1862	Promoted to Major.
Do.	George Raymond	Dec. 2, "	" 11, "	Resigned May 23, 1862.
Do.	Samuel A. J. Snyder	" 8, "	" 11, "	Promoted to Major.
Do.	Andrew Nuhler	" 12, "	" 11, "	Mustered out May 15, 1865.
Do.	John H. Blinn	" 28, "	" 11, "	Resigned January 15, 1863.
Do.	Leroy Moore	Jan. 4, 1862	" 11, "	Mustered out March 12, 1865.
Do.	James C. Fernald	" 7, "	" 11, "	Promoted to Major.
Do.	Michael Wegstein	" 10, "	" 11, "	Killed at Shiloh April 6, 1862.
Do.	Jacob Fickes	" 10, "	" 11, "	Resigned February 4, 1863.
Do.	Stephen A. Baron	" 12, "	" 11, "	Revoked.
Do.	Theodore M. Thompson	" 11, "	March 13, "	Mustered out, expiration of service.
Do.	Henry W. Gifford	April 6, "	June 20, "	Mortally wounded.
Do.	Anthony Young	" 6, "	" 20, "	Resigned July 23, 1863.
Do.	Henry W. Buckland	May 23, "	" 20, "	Mustered out.
Do.	Spencer Russell	July 15, "	Nov 20, "	Resigned August 21, 1863.
Do.	Charles Dennis	Jan. 15, 1863	Feb. 26, 1863	Resigned August 3, 1863.
Do.	Manning A. Fowler	Feb. 4, "	March 5, "	Resigned July 23, 1863.
Do.	Milton F. Williamson	July 21, "	Jan. 10, 1864	Mustered out, expiration of service.
Do.	John M. Lemon	" 23, "	" 10, "	Mustered out June 24, 1865.
Do.	W. C. Biddle	April 9, 1864	April 9, "	Mustered out.
Do.	Chas. Derlam	" 9, "	" 9, "	Mustered out March 19, 1865.
Do.	Wm. A. Strong	" 9, "	" 9, "	Resigned as 1st Lieutenant, Aug. 16, 1864.
Do.	Orrin O. England	Nov. 16, "	Nov. 16, "	
Do.	Lorenzo Dick	" 16, "	" 16, "	Mustered out as 1st Lieutenant May 15, 1865.
Do.	Alpheus R. Putnam	" 16, "	" 16, "	Revoked.
Do.	Daniel W. Hoffman	March 18, 1865	March 18, 1865	Mustered out as 1st Lieutenant, May 15, 1865.
Do.	Merritt Sexton	" 18, "	" 18, "	Mustered out with regiment.
Do.	Morris Reese	" 18, "	" 18, "	Mustered out April 24, 1865.
Do.	John F. Harrington	May 2, "	May 2, "	Mustered out with regiment.
Do.	Joseph Seaford	" 2, "	" 2, "	Mustered out with regiment.
Do.	Josiah Fairbanks	" 31, "	" 31, "	Mustered out with regiment.
Do.	Charles A. McCleary	" 31, "	" 31, "	Mustered out with regiment.
Do.	Edward McMahan	" 31, "	" 31, "	Mustered out with regiment.
Do.	Charles H. Hudson	Aug. 10, "	Sept. 4, "	Mustered out as 1st Lieutenant.
Do.	John G. Nuhler	Sept. 4, "	" 4, "	Mustered out as 1st Lieutenant.
Do.	Christian Edwards	" 4, "	" 4, "	Mustered out as 1st Lieutenant.
1st Lieutenant	Daniel W. M. Harkness	Oct. 5, 1861	Jan. 11, 1862	Resigned January 16, 1863.
Do.	Henry W. Gifford	Nov. 30, "	" 11, "	Promoted to Captain.
Do.	Henry W. Buckland	Dec. 2, "	" 11, "	Promoted to Captain.
Do.	Eugene A. Rawson	" 4, "	" 11, "	Promoted to Captain.
Do.	Jacob Snyder	" 8, "	" 11, "	Cancelled.
Do.	Manning A. Fowler	Dec. 12, 1861	" 11, "	Promoted to Captain
Do.	Charles Dennis	" 28, "	" 11, "	Promoted to Captain.
Do.	Alfred H. Rice	Jan. 14, 1862	" 11, "	Mustered out August 8, 1863.
Do.	James Fernald	" 7, "	" 11, "	Promoted to Captain.
Do.	Anthony Young	" 10, "	" 11, "	Promoted to Captain.
Do.	Albert Bates	" 10, "	" 11, "	Resigned August 8, 1863.
Do.	Wm. C. Biddle	" 10, "	" 11, "	Revoked.
Do.	Wm. H. Skerrett	" 11, "	March 13, "	Mustered out January 11, 1865.
Do.	Milton F. Williamson	Feb. 13, "	April 24, "	Promoted to Captain.
Do.	Spencer Russell	April 6, "	June 20, "	Promoted to Captain.
Do.	Wm. T. Fisher	May 23, "	" 20, "	Resigned July 22, 1863.
Do.	Andrew Kline	April 6, "	" 20, "	Honorably discharged November 1, 1862.
Do.	Alfred H. Rice	Sept. 1, "	Oct. 24, "	Resigned August 8, 1863.
Do.	John H. Power	Nov. 11, "	Dec. 31, "	Revoked.
Do.	Charles Darlem	July 15, "	" 31, "	Promoted to Captain.
Do.	Joshua W. Waterman	Jan. 16, "	Feb. 4, 1863	Mustered out.
Do.	Orrin O. England	Feb. 4, "	March 5, "	Promoted to Captain.
Do.	Wm. A. Strong	Jan. 15, 1863	Feb. 26, "	Promoted to Captain.
Do.	Lorenzo Dick	Nov. 1, 1862	" 26, "	Promoted to Captain.
Do.	Alonzo V. Johnson	" 29, "	July 23, "	Resigned August 1, 1864.

RANK.	NAME.	DATE OF RANK.		COM. ISSUED.		REMARKS.
1st Lieutenant	Alphens R. Putnam	Feb.	18, 1864	Feb.	18, 1864	
Do.	Daniel W. Hoffman	"	18, "	"	18, "	Promoted to Captain.
Do.	John B. Gilmore	"	18, "	"	18, "	Died in Charleston prison October 9, 1864.
Do.	Merritt Sexton	April	9, "	April	9, "	Promoted to Captain.
Do.	Morris Reese	"	9, "	"	9, "	Promoted to Captain.
Do.	John F. Harrington	"	9, "	"	9, "	Promoted to Captain.
Do.	Rollin Edgerton	"	9, "	"	9, "	Resigned as 2d Lieutenant September 28, 1864.
Do.	Joseph Seafford	Nov.	16, "	Nov.	16, "	Promoted to Captain.
Do.	Joy Winters	"	16, "	"	16, "	Mustered out as 2d Lieutenant May 15, 1865.
Do.	Josiah Fairbanks	"	16, "	"	16, "	Promoted to Captain.
Do.	Charles A. McCleary	"	16, "	"	16, "	Promoted to Captain.
Do.	Zelotus Perrin	"	16, "	"	16, "	Mustered out May 15, 1865.
Do.	Edward McMahan	March	18, 1865	March	18, 1865	Promoted to Captain.
Do.	David Van Doren	"	18, "	"	18, "	Mustered out as 2d Lieutenant May 15, 1865.
Do.	John Carbaugh	"	18, "	"	18, "	Died in hospital March 11, 1865.
Do.	Sherman Jackson	"	18, "	"	18, "	Died at Annapolis, Maryland.
Do.	Charles H. Hudson	"	18, "	"	18, "	Promoted to Captain.
Do.	John G. Nahler	"	18, "	"	18, "	Promoted to Captain.
Do.	Christian Edwards	May	2, "	May	2, "	Promoted to Captain.
Do.	Corwin Ensminger	"	31, "	"	31, "	Mustered out with regiment.
Do.	Abraham Elredge	Sept.	4, "	Sept.	4, "	
Do.	Mathias Lavartzlander	"	4, "	"	4, "	
Do.	Martin Houpragle	"	4, "	"	4, "	
Do.	Benjamin Ohlinger	"	4, "	"	4, "	
Do.	Louis Ruppert	"	4, "	"	4, "	
Do.	Elihu Fenald	"	4, "	"	4, "	
Do.	Jefferson Russell	"	4, "	"	4, "	
Do.	Jonas M. Stanbery	"	4, "	"	4, "	
Do.	Philip Fertig	"	4, "	"	4, "	
Do.	Samuel Roush	"	4, "	"	4, "	
2d Lieutenant	John H. Poyer	Oct.	19, 1861	Jan.	11, 1862	Resigned December 3, 1862.
Do.	Thomas W. Egbert	"	30, "	"	11, "	Revoked.
Do.	Spencer Russell	Nov.	30, "	"	11, "	Promoted to 1st Lieutenant.
Do.	Wm. T. Fisher	Dec.	2, "	"	11, "	Promoted to 1st Lieutenant.
Do.	Daniel W. Hoffman	"	8, "	"	11, "	Promoted to 1st Lieutenant.
Do.	Jesse J. Cook	"	12, "	"	11, "	Resigned June 6, 1862.
Do.	Wm. A. Strong	"	28, "	"	11, "	Promoted to 1st Lieutenant.
Do.	John B. Gilmore	Jan.	4, 1862	"	11, "	Promoted to 1st Lieutenant.
Do.	Andrew Kline	"	10, "	"	11, "	Promoted to 1st Lieutenant.
Do.	James Donnell	"	10, "	"	11, "	Resigned September 3, 1863.
Do.	Caleb F. Goshorn	Feb.	13, "	May	13, "	Resigned January 15, 1863.
Do.	Charles Darlem	April	6, "	June	20, "	Promoted to 1st Lieutenant.
Do.	John M. Lemon	May	23, "	"	20, "	Promoted to 1st Lieutenant.
Do.	George Dick	April	6, "	"	20, "	Promoted to 1st Lieutenant.
Do.	Alphens R. Putnam	Sept.	1, "	Sept.	16, "	Promoted to 1st Lieutenant.
Do.	Morris Reese	"	3, "	Feb.	26, 1863	Promoted to 1st Lieutenant.
Do.	John F. Harrington	Jan.	1, 1863	"	26, "	Promoted to 1st Lieutenant.
Do.	Merritt Sexton	Nov.	1, 1862	Jan.	19, "	Promoted to 1st Lieutenant.
Do.	James H. Stewart	Jan.	15, 1863	Feb.	26, "	Resigned May 3, 1863.
Do.	Rollin Edgerton	"	15, "	"	28, "	Promoted to 1st Lieutenant.
Do.	Joseph Seafford	"	1, "	"	28, "	Promoted to 1st Lieutenant.
Do.	D. L. Goodrich	March	3, "	July	20, "	Revoked.
Do.	Joy Winters	April	9, 1864	April	9, 1864	Promoted to 1st Lieutenant.
Do.	Josiah Fairbanks	"	9, "	"	9, "	Promoted to 1st Lieutenant.
Do.	Charles A. McCleary	"	9, "	"	9, "	Promoted to 1st Lieutenant.
Do.	Zelotus Perrin	"	9, "	"	9, "	Promoted to 1st Lieutenant.
Do.	Edward McMahan	"	9, "	"	9, "	Promoted to 1st Lieutenant.
Do.	David Van Doren	"	9, "	"	9, "	Promoted to 1st Lieutenant.
Do.	John Carbaugh	"	9, "	"	9, "	Promoted to 1st Lieutenant.
Do.	Andrew Unkle	"	9, "	"	9, "	Mustered out December 10, 1864.
Do.	Sherman Jackson	"	9, "	"	9, "	Promoted to 1st Lieutenant.
Do.	Charles H. Hudson	Nov.	16, "	Nov.	16, "	Promoted to 1st Lieutenant.
Do.	John Engle	Sept.	4, 1865	Sept.	4, 1865	Mustered out as Sergeants, complimentary commissions issued after muster out.
Do.	Enoch F. Jones	"	4, "	"	4, "	
Do.	Wm. Meyers	"	4, "	"	4, "	
Do.	George Albert	"	4, "	"	4, "	
Do.	George Dowing	"	4, "	"	4, "	
Do.	Charles Haws	"	4, "	"	4, "	
Do.	G. A. Gessner	"	4, "	"	4, "	
Do.	Add. Blair	"	4, "	"	4, "	
Do.	John K. Moses	"	4, "	"	4, "	
Do.	Lafayette Cornell	"	4, "	"	4, "	

SEVENTY-SECOND OHIO VOLUNTEER INFANTRY.

THIS regiment was organized at Fremont, Ohio, during the months of October, November, and December, 1861. Companies, A, B, C, D, E, F, H, and I were recruited principally in Sandusky County. Company G, with a small portion of H and A, was recruited in Erie County. Company K was recruited mostly in Medina County, and portions of C and E were from Wood.

On the 24th of January, 1862, the regiment, numbering about nine hundred men, left Fremont for Camp Chase. As the regiment had not the maximum number of men, company K was broken up and distributed among the other companies. The officers rendered supernumary were discharged, and a company, originally recruited for the Fifty-Second Ohio, was assigned to the Seventy-Second, and designated company K. The regiment was equipped fully, and in February was ordered to report to General W. T. Sherman, at Paducah. Here the regiment was assigned to a brigade, composed of the Forty-Eighth, Seventieth, and Seventy-Second Ohio Regiments; Colonel Buckland commanded the brigade. Early in March, 1862, Sherman's division proceeded up the Tennessee to Fort Henry, where the main army was concentrated. The Seventy-Second was on the steamer Baltic. From here the main army proceeded to Savannah, but Sherman's division was ordered up to Eastport, Mississippi, in order to cut the Memphis and Charleston Railroad, and thus to prevent General J. S. Johnston from re-enforcing Beauregard. Heavy rains and consequent high waters defeated the plan, and after a confinement of sixteen days on board the boats, Buckland's brigade disembarked at Pittsburg Landing, and encamped near Shiloh Church. The long confinement on the transports, and bad water at Pittsburg Landing, proved disastrous to the health of the troops, and the Seventy-Second was very much reduced in numbers. On the 3d of April Buckland's brigade was engaged in a reconnoissance, in which the Seventy-Second met the Rebel pickets and exchanged shots. On the next day companies B and H were ordered to reconnoiter the front of the picket-line. The companies became engaged, separately, with the Rebel cavalry, and Major Crockett and two or three men of company H were captured and several were wounded. Company B was surrounded, but it fought for an hour against great odds, and was saved by the arrival of companies A, D, and F. Company B lost four men wounded.

Buckland's brigade met the enemy about seven o'clock on the morning of April 6th and withstood the onset of three successive Rebel lines; and, notwithstanding the defection of the brigade on the left, held its position for two hours, when Sherman ordered it to retire. The Rebels had advanced on the left and threatened to cut off the retreat, but the brigade made a rapid detour to the right, through a dense woods, and at eleven o'clock was in position on the right of the National line. The regiment was at the front constantly, and on the 7th it participated in the final charge, which swept the enemy from the field, and that night rested in the camp which it had abandoned the day before. The regiment lost two officers killed, three wounded, and one missing; and thirteen men killed, seventy wounded, and forty-five missing. The regiment participated in the pursuit as far as Monterey.

In the siege of Corinth the Seventy-Second bore a conspicuous part. Its losses were trifling in action but terrible by disease. During the siege General J. W. Denver assumed command of Buckland's brigade, and Colonel Buckland returned to the regiment. After the evacuation Sherman's division moved westward along the Memphis and Charleston Railroad, and on the 21st of

July the regiment entered Memphis. No clothes had been drawn since the battle of Pittsburg Landing, and the men were covered with rags. The Seventy-Second was posted at Fort Pickering, and was engaged in the ordinary camp and garrison duties. The regiment was brigaded with the Thirty-Second Wisconsin, Ninety-Third Indiana, Ninety-Third Illinois, and One Hundred and Fourteenth Illinois. The brigade was designated the First Brigade of the Third Division. General Lanman commanded the division and Colonel Buckland the brigade.

On the 26th of November the regiment marched toward Wyatt, on the Tallahatchie. The Rebels retreated, and Sherman's forces were ordered back to Memphis. When the Memphis and Charleston Railroad was reached, the regiment was ordered to Moscow to hold the bridge over Wolf River. Here the regiment fell in with Richardson's guerrillas, but experienced no loss. The regiment remained at Moscow about two weeks, performing picket-duty, and on the 9th of January, 1863, it was ordered to Corinth. It made the march in seven days, by way of Bolivar and Purdy. On the night after arriving the weather turned intensely cold and the men suffered severely. Buckland's brigade was assigned to the Sixteenth Corps, and was concentrated near Memphis. The Seventy-Second reached White's Station, nine miles east of Memphis, on the 31st of January, and was engaged in picket-duty and in work on the fortifications.

On the 13th of March the regiment moved to Memphis, embarked on steamer Champion, and on the 14th proceeded down stream. The regiment had been re-enforced by about forty nine-months recruits, and these, with the addition of some returned convalescents, increased somewhat its effective strength. On the 2d of April the regiment went into camp four miles above Young's Point. It engaged in work on the canal, and in preparations for the coming campaign. The regiment commenced the march for the rear of Vicksburg on the 2d of May. It moved seventy miles southward through Louisiana, and struck the Mississippi opposite Grand Gulf. It crossed the river on the 7th, and the next day moved for Jackson, Mississippi. It participated in the battle at Jackson on the 14th, and on the next day continued the march toward Vicksburg, where it arrived on the 18th. It participated in the assault on the Rebel works on the 19th and 22d of May, and after that came the labor of the siege. It occupied a position on the right of Tuttle's division, and within half a mile of the Mississippi, on the north of Vicksburg. On the 22d of June the regiment formed part of the force ordered to Big Black River to intercept General Joe Johnston, who was attempting the relief of Vicksburg. The Seventy-Second was thrown out on the advance picket-line, and continued to hold that position until the surrender of Vicksburg. The regiment then moved against General Johnston at Jackson, and, after the battle, pursued the Rebels to Brandon, where it had an engagement. After destroying a portion of the railroad, it returned to Big Black to rest and refit.

The regiment moved to Oak Ridge, twenty-one miles from Vicksburg, and near Yazoo River, in the latter part of the summer, and in September it participated in a four days' scout to Mechanicsville, in which it experienced some severe marching and lively skirmishing. On the 15th of October the regiment moved on General McPherson's expedition to Canton, and on its return went into camp eight miles in the rear of Vicksburg. About the middle of November the regiment was ordered with its division to Memphis, to guard the Memphis and Charleston Railroad. It was stationed at Germantown, fourteen miles east of Memphis. On the 2d of January, 1864, the regiment re-enlisted and soon after moved to Memphis, and in February it took part in the expedition under Colonel McMillan to the Tallahatchie River, to create a diversion in favor of General W. S. Smith's cavalry expedition; all being a part of General Sherman's Meridian expedition. This lasted thirteen days, and the regiment marched one hundred and fifty miles.

On the 23d of February it received its veteran furlough and proceeded North. It arrived at Fremont, Ohio, on the 28th of February, and received a cordial welcome from the citizens of Sandusky County. On the 5th of April the regiment re-assembled at Fremont and moved to Cleveland. During the furlough recruiting had been brisk, and the regiment returned to the front numbering nearly five hundred men.

On the 8th of April the Seventy-Second moved by rail to Cairo, where it arrived on the 10th, and while awaiting river transportation it was ordered to Paducah, Kentucky, to assist in the defense of that place against Forrest. On the 14th the Rebels made a slight attack, but it was nothing more than a skirmish. The regiment remained at Paducah until the 22d, when it embarked for Memphis, where it arrived the next day. The regiment remained quietly in camp, drilling the new recruits, until the 30th of April, when it joined an expedition under General Sturgis against Forrest. The infantry moved by rail nearly to Wolf River, thirty-eight miles east of Memphis, and from there marched to Bolivar, arriving just in time to find the place evacuated. From here the expedition marched southward toward Ripley, Mississippi, but finding no enemy it turned back, and on the 9th of May reached Memphis.

On the 1st of June the regiment formed part of an expedition, consisting of twelve regiments of infantry and a division of cavalry, against Forrest. At one o'clock P. M., on the 10th of June, Forrest was encountered at Brice's Cross Roads, Mississippi, and the cavalry commenced skirmishing. The enemy was in a well-chosen position, behind Tishomingo Creek. The infantry was brought up on the double-quick for several miles, and at once thrown into action. No attempt was made to establish a line, and the regiments were hurled against the enemy, one at a time; and thus each regiment was subjected to great odds, and was badly cut up. To make matters worse, an attempt was made to advance the wagon-train across the creek, directly under the enemy's fire. Great confusion ensued. A retreat was ordered and the retreat became a panic. A portion of the train had been destroyed, and the rest fell into the hands of the Rebels; so the National troops were without ammunition and without rations. No attempt was made to cover the rear and to secure an orderly retreat. It was a regular stampede; and on the same day of the fight the expedition fell back twenty-three miles to Ripley. Here an attempt was made to reorganize, but to no purpose. The officer in command of the expedition surrounded himself with cavalry and started for Memphis, leaving the infantry, as he expressively remarked, "to go to the devil." The only safety to the infantry from death or Rebel prisons lay in reaching Memphis, and to do this it must outmarch the Rebel cavalry. Incredible as it may seem, nine officers and one hundred and forty men of the Seventy-Second reached Germantown on the morning of the 12th, thus marching at the close of a battle, and without a morsel of food, one hundred miles in forty-one hours. Eleven officers and two hundred and thirty-seven men of the Seventy-Second were killed, wounded, or captured—the greater portion were captured—and of these very few ever returned to the regiment. Many of those who reached Germantown were broken down completely, and upon reaching Memphis, where the regiment was transported by rail, many of the men were utterly helpless, and could neither walk nor stand.

The regiment was assigned to the First Brigade (General McMillan commanding) of Mower's division, Sixteenth Corps; and on the 22d of June it was ordered on an expedition, moving in the direction of Tupelo, Mississippi. On the 11th of July the Rebels were found in position near Pontotoc. The corps made a feint against the enemy, and then moved rapidly eastward toward the Mobile and Ohio Railroad at Tupelo. In this movement McMillan's brigade, barely nine hundred strong, was in rear of the infantry column, and just in advance of the wagon-train. When about two miles west of Tupelo Bell's brigade of N. B. Forrest's command, which was in ambush, attacked the column. The attack fell mainly upon the Seventy-Second. The regiment at once charged the enemy. The remainder of the brigade was brought into action, and within twenty minutes the Rebels were driven from the field, utterly routed. On the return march, McMillan's brigade again marched in rear of the infantry column; and just as it was going into bivouac for the night, at Tishomingo Creek, Bell's brigade fell upon the cavalry rear-guard and drove it into camp. McMillan's brigade formed rapidly and advanced. A volley checked the enemy and a charge drove him from the field. In this charge Major E. A. Ransom, a gallant officer, who was in command of the Seventy-Second, was mortally wounded. The expedition reached Memphis without further molestation. During this expedition the casualties in the Seventy-Second were two officers and nineteen men wounded, and of these one officer and four men mortally.

About the 27th of July the regiment moved with the corps in the direction of Oxford, Mississippi, but the Third Division of the corps was ordered to Atlanta, and the troops returned to

Memphis. On the 1st of September Mower's division was ordered to Arkansas to resist Price. On the 2d the regiment embarked on a steamer for Duvall's Bluff, but it did not reach its destination until Price had passed north; thus it failed to intercept him. After a short delay at Duvall's Bluff Mower's division moved northward. The march was continued for eighteen days; and in that time the troops traveled three hundred and fifty miles, forded four rivers, and reached the Mississippi at Cape Girardeau, Missouri. The weather was very warm, and the men were on less than half rations. At Cape Girardeau the division took transports for St. Louis, and, after a short halt there, moved to Jefferson City. From this point the division moved against Price. The troops marched from early in the morning till late at night, making every day from thirty to forty-five miles. But Price's force was well mounted, and it was impossible to overtake him. The pursuit continued as far as Little Santa Fe, on the Kansas line, and there the infantry turned back to St. Louis. The weather became intensely cold. The men had only the clothing which was on their backs and a rubber blanket. Wood was not to be found, and snow fell to the depth of twelve inches. After enduring many hardships the Seventy-Second reached St. Louis on the 16th of November.

The rest was brief. The division was ordered up the Cumberland, and on the 30th of November it joined the forces under General Thomas at Nashville, and was posted on the right of the line. General J. A. McArthur now commanded the division, General Mower having been ordered to join General Sherman in October. On the 7th of December the Seventy-Second was on a reconnoissance, and became warmly engaged, losing eleven men killed and wounded. During the first day of the battle of Nashville the regiment participated in a charge, in which three hundred and fifty prisoners and six pieces of artillery were captured. At night it was sent to Nashville with prisoners, but it returned in time to take part in the fight on the 16th, and was engaged in the charge on Walnut Hills. In this battle McMillan's brigade, numbering less than twelve hundred men, captured two thousand prisoners and thirteen pieces of artillery, while its total loss was only one hundred and sixty. The division moved to Eastport, Mississippi, and went into camp. Supplies were scarce, and the troops subsisted for some days on parched corn.

In February, 1865, it moved to New Orleans and camped on the old battle-ground. On the 28th of February it embarked on the ocean steamer Empire City, and on the 3d of March it landed at Fort Gaines, on Dauphin Island. On the 19th it crossed the east side of Mobile Bay, moved up Fish River, and landed about thirty miles east of Spanish Fort. A short time was allowed for bringing up supplies, and on the 27th Spanish Fort was invested. The siege lasted until the 8th of April, when the fort was evacuated. In these operations the Seventy-Second lost one man killed and three wounded. On the 9th of April the regiment moved against Fort Blakely, which was captured on that same day. On the 13th of April it marched for Montgomery, Alabama, and, after thirteen days, reached its destination. On the 10th of May the division moved to Selma, arriving on the 14th, and on the following day McMillan's brigade was ordered to Meridian, Mississippi. Here the regiment remained on garrison duty until June, when it was placed along the line of the railroad west of Meridian. About the same time orders were received to muster out all men in the regiment whose term of service would expire before October 1, 1865. Under this order forty-one men were discharged. In September the Seventy-Second moved to Corinth, but it was soon ordered to Vicksburg, where it was mustered out on the 11th of September, 1865. It at once embarked for Ohio, and was paid and discharged at Camp Chase.

73d REGIMENT OHIO VOLUNTEER INFANTRY.

ROSTER, THREE YEARS' SERVICE.

RANK.	NAME.	DATE OF RANK.	COM. ISSUED.	REMARKS.
Colonel	ORLANDO SMITH	Oct. 3, 1861	Jan. 15, 1862	Resigned February 17, 1864.
Do.	RICHARD LONG	Feb. 17, 1864	Feb. 24, 1864	Resigned June 27, 1864.
Do.	SAMUEL H. HURST	July 13, "	July 13, "	Not mustered.
Lt. Colonel	JACOB HYER	Oct. 3, 1861	Jan. 15, 1862	Resigned June 21, 1862.
Do.	RICHARD LONG	June 21, 1862	July 30, "	Promoted to Colonel.
Do.	SAMUEL H. HURST	Feb. 17, 1864	Feb. 24, 1864	Promoted to Colonel.
Do.	THOMAS W. HIGGINS	July 13, "	July 13, "	Mustered out as Major.
Major	RICHARD LONG	Dec. 20, 1861	Jan. 15, 1862	Promoted to Lieutenant-Colonel.
Do.	SAMUEL H. HURST	June 21, 1862	July 30, "	Promoted to Lieutenant-Colonel.
Do.	THOMAS W. HIGGINS	Nov. 5, "	Nov. 5, "	Revoked.
Do.	THOMAS W. HIGGINS	Feb. 17, 1864	Feb. 24, 1864	Promoted to Lieutenant-Colonel.
Do.	THOMAS LUCAS	July 13, "	July 13, "	Resigned as Captain September 11, 1864.
Do.	ABISHA DOWNING	" 17, 1865	" 17, 1865	Mustered out as Captain.
Surgeon	JONAS P. SAFFORD	Oct. 26, 1861	Jan. 15, 1862	Dismissed February 18, 1863.
Do.	ISAAC N. HINES	Dec. 31, 1862	Feb. 26, 1863	Mustered out at expiration of service.
Do.	JOHN C. PRESTON	Feb. 1, 1865	" 5, 1865	Mustered out with regiment.
Ass't Surgeon	ISAAC N. HINES	Oct. 26, 1861	Jan. 15, 1862	Promoted to Surgeon February 1, 1863.
Do.	JAMES SEGAFOOR	Aug. 15, 1862	Aug. 15, "	Resigned October 21, 1862.
Do.	WM. RICHARDSON	March 18, 1863	March 30, 1863	Resigned June 27, 1864.
Do.	JOHN C. PRESTON	" 19, "	" 30, "	Promoted to Surgeon.
Do.	SMITH D. STEER	Feb. 1, 1865	Feb. 1, 1865	Mustered out with regiment.
Chaplain	C. A. VANANDA	Jan. 16, 1862	Jan. 17, 1862	Declined.
Do.	C. E. FELTON	March 13, "	March 13, "	Declined.
Do.	JOSEPH HILL	" 13, "	June 20, "	Resigned December 17, 1862.
Do.	JAMES R. STILWELL	June 20, 1865	" 20, 1865	
Captain	Samuel H. Hurst	Nov. 7, 1861	Jan. 15, 1862	Promoted to Major.
Do.	Thomas W. Higgins	" 20, "	" 15, "	Promoted to Major.
Do.	Thomas Beach	" 20, "	" 15, "	Honorably discharged December 24, 1862.
Do.	Thomas Lucas	" 20, "	" 15, "	Resigned September 11, 1864.
Do.	Silas Irwin	Dec. 13, "	" 15, "	Resigned July 17, 1863.
Do.	John Earhart	" 23, "	" 15, "	Resigned March 27, 1862.
Do.	Edward H. Allen	" 30, "	" 15, "	Resigned February 28, 1863.
Do.	Justus G. McShooler	" 30, "	" 15, "	Honorably discharged December 24, 1862.
Do.	Lewis W. Burkett	" 30, "	" 15, "	Died of wounds.
Do.	John V. Patten	" 30, "	" 15, "	Resigned March 9, 1864.
Do.	Luther M. Buckwalter	June 21, 1862	July 30, "	Killed October 29, 1863.
Do.	John D. Madeira	March 27, "	" 30, "	Mustered out December 29, 1864.
Do.	James Q. Barnes	Sept. 15, "	Nov. 20, "	Mustered out December 29, 1864.
Do.	George M. Doherty	Dec. 24, "	Jan. 27, "	Died July 13, 1863.
Do.	Archibald Lybrand	" 24, "	" 27, "	Resigned October 28, 1864.
Do.	Benj. F. Stone	Feb. 28, "	March 30, "	Mustered out December 29, 1864.
Do.	John Kinney	July 13, 1863	Jan. 10, 1864	Declined.
Do.	Henry Hinson	Aug. 29, "	" 10, "	Resigned October 20, 1864.
Do.	James F. McCommon	March 19, "	March 19, "	Honorably discharged October 23, 1864.
Do.	James C. McKell	" 19, "	" 19, "	Resigned January 1, 1865.
Do.	Abisha Downing	" 19, "	" 19, "	Promoted to Major.
Do.	Presley Talbott	April 16, "	April 16, "	Resigned as 1st Lieutenant.
Do.	Rufus Hosler	Aug. 11, "	Aug. 11, "	Resigned as 1st Lieutenant November 25, 1864.
Do.	David P. Ranney	" 11, "	" 11, "	Mustered out with regiment.
Do.	Joshua Davis	Nov. 3, "	Nov. 3, "	Declined promotion.
Do.	J. E. F. Jackson	" 18, "	" 18, "	Declined promotion; mustered out.
Do.	Samuel R. Peters	" 18, "	" 18, "	Resigned May 28, 1865.
Do.	Isaac N. Hawkins	Feb. 10, 1865	Feb. 10, 1865	Declined promotion.
Do.	Wm. H. Eckman	" 10, "	" 10, "	Resigned as 1st Lieutenant March 30, 1865.
Do.	John W. Adams	" 10, "	" 10, "	Resigned May 30, 1865.
Do.	Wm. A. Pontius	" 10, "	" 10, "	Mustered out May 19, 1865.
Do.	Wm. B. Davis	" 10, "	" 10, "	Mustered out with regiment.
Do.	Samuel Ambrose	" 10, "	" 10, "	Mustered out with regiment.
Do.	David A. Lamb	" 10, "	" 10, "	
Do.	Albert H. Sanders	May 11, "	May 11, "	Mustered out with regiment.
Do.	Martin L. Bookwalter	" 11, "	" 11, "	Mustered out with regiment.
Do.	John W. Martin	June 16, "	June 16, "	
Do.	Asa F. Couch	" 16, "	" 16, "	Mustered out with regiment.
1st Lieutenant	Wm. D. Wesson	Oct. 9, 1861	Jan. 15, 1862	Appointed Captain by President July 11, 1862.
Do.	Luther M. Buckwalter	Nov. 9, "	" 15, "	Promoted to Captain; resigned April 4, 1862.
Do.	George M. Lanman	" 20, "	" 15, "	Resigned May 21, 1862.
Do.	James Q. Barnes	" 20, "	" 15, "	Promoted to Captain.
Do.	George M. Doherty	" 20, "	" 15, "	Promoted to Captain.
Do.	Richard Long	" 26, "	" 15, "	Promoted to Major.
Do.	James H. Dwyer	Dec. 13, "	" 15, "	Resigned March 8, 1862.
Do.	Thomas M. Gray	" 26, "	" 15, "	Resigned March 19, 1862.
Do.	Frederick Smith	" 26, "	" 15, "	Died April 16, 1862.
Do.	Benj. F. Stone	" 30, "	" 15, "	Promoted to Captain.
Do.	Archibald Lybrand	" 30, "	" 15, "	Promoted to Captain.
Do.	John D. Madeira	" 30, "	" 15, "	Promoted to Captain.
Do.	John Kinney	" 30, "	" 15, "	Promoted to Captain.
Do.	Samuel Fellers	March 8, 1862	April 14, "	Resigned August 15, 1863.
Do.	John F. Martin	" 19, "	July 30, "	Honorably discharged December 24, 1862.
Do.	James F. McCommon	April 16, "	" 30, "	Promoted to Captain.
Do.	Thos. J. Throckmorton	June 21, "	" 30, "	Resigned November 23, 1862.
Do.	Henry Hinson	May 21, "	" 30, "	Promoted to Captain.
Do.	J. W. J. Stephenson	March 27, "	" 30, "	Resigned September 18, 1862.
Do.	James C. McKell	Sept. 18, "	Nov. 20, "	Promoted to Captain.
Do.	Abisha Downing	" 15, "	" 20, "	Promoted to Captain.
Do.	Robert M. Rogers	Nov. 20, "	" 20, "	Appointed Cadet West Point November 5, 1863.

RANK.	NAME.	DATE OF RANK.	COM. ISSUED.	REMARKS.
1st Lieutenant	Rufus Hosler	Nov. 23, 1862	Dec. 31, 1862	Promoted to Captain.
Do.	John Spence	Jan. 21, 1863	Feb. 26, 1863	Resigned March 6, 1864.
Do.	David P. Ranney	Dec. 24, 1862	" 26, "	Promoted to Captain.
Do.	Horace J. Clark	" 21, "	" 26, "	Honorably discharged October 23, 1863.
Do.	David L. Greine	Feb. 28, 1863	March 30, "	Resigned January 22, 1863.
Do.	Chas. W. Stone	June 22, "	Aug. 1, "	Resigned July 5, 1864.
Do.	Joseph P. Talbott	Dec. 13, "	Jan. 10, "	Resigned June 18, 1864.
Do.	Joshua Davis	Oct. 29, "	" 10, "	Honorably discharged July 25, 1864.
Do.	J. E. F. Jackson	March 19, "	March 19, "	Promoted to Captain.
Do.	Samuel P. Peters	" 19, "	" 19, "	Promoted to Captain.
Do.	Isaac N. Hawkins	" 19, "	" 19, "	Mustered out May 15, 1865.
Do.	Wm. L. Eckman	" 19, "	" 19, "	Promoted to Captain.
Do.	John W. Martin	April 1, "	April 1, "	Promoted to Captain.
Do.	John W. Adams	" 1, "	" 1, "	Promoted to Captain.
Do.	Wm. A. Pontius	May 9, "	May 9, "	Promoted to Captain.
Do.	Samuel C. Glover	April 16, "	April 16, "	Promoted to Captain C. S., U. S. Vols.
Do.	Wm. B. Davis	Sept. 8, "	Sept. 8, "	Promoted to Captain.
Do.	Samuel Ambrose	" 8, "	" 8, "	Promoted to Captain.
Do.	David A. Lamb	" 8, "	" 8, "	Promoted to Captain.
Do.	Albert H. Sanders	" 8, "	" 8, "	Promoted to Captain.
Do.	Martin L. Bookwalter	Nov. 18, "	Nov. 18, "	Promoted to Captain.
Do.	Asa F. Couch	" 18, "	" 18, "	Promoted to Captain.
Do.	Thomas F. Hamilton	Feb. 10, 1865	Feb. 10, 1865	Mustered out with regiment.
Do.	James Earl	" 10, "	" 10, "	
Do.	James Ferguson	" 10, "	" 10, "	Mustered out with regiment.
Do.	John Burke	" 10, "	" 10, "	Mustered out with regiment.
Do.	John Hildenbrand	" 10, "	" 10, "	Mustered out with regiment.
Do.	David M. Lyons	" 10, "	" 10, "	
Do.	James Ross	May 11, "	May 11, "	Mustered out with regiment.
Do.	John B. Smith	" 18, "	" 18, "	
Do.	John C. Alton	June 16, "	June 16, "	On detached duty.
Do.	Michael S. Mackerly	" 16, "	" 16, "	Mustered out with regiment.
2d Lieutenant	J. W. J. Stephenson	Oct. 3, 1861	Jan. 15, 1862	Promoted to 1st Lieutenant.
Do.	Richard Long	" 4, "	" 15, "	Promoted to 1st Lieutenant.
Do.	Abisha Downing	Nov. 4, "	" 15, "	Promoted to 1st Lieutenant.
Do.	Thos. J. Throckmorton	" 9, "	" 15, "	Promoted to 1st Lieutenant.
Do.	Henry Hinson	" 20, "	" 15, "	Promoted to 1st Lieutenant.
Do.	John Mitchell	" 20, "	" 15, "	Resigned December 23, 1863.
Do.	Samuel Fellers	Dec. 13, "	" 15, "	Promoted to 1st Lieutenant.
Do.	John F. Martin	" 26, "	" 15, "	Promoted to 1st Lieutenant.
Do.	James F. McCommon	" 30, "	" 15, "	Promoted to 1st Lieutenant.
Do.	Chas. W. Trimble	" 30, "	" 15, "	Killed at Bull Run, August 30, 1862.
Do.	David P. Ranney	" 30, "	" 15, "	Promoted to 1st Lieutenant.
Do.	David L. Greiner	March 8, 1862	April 14, "	Promoted to 1st Lieutenant.
Do.	Edward H. Miller	" 19, "	July 30, "	Resigned February 1, 1863.
Do.	Dayton Morgan	June 21, "	" 30, "	Resigned September 25, 1862.
Do.	Joshua Davis	May 21, "	" 30, "	Promoted to 1st Lieutenant.
Do.	James C. McKell	April 16, "	" 30, "	Promoted to 1st Lieutenant.
Do.	John B. Eckman	March 27, "	" 30, "	Revoked.
Do.	Horace L. Clark	Aug. 30, "	Nov. 20, "	Honorably discharged.
Do.	Rufus Hosler	Sept. 25, "	" 20, "	Promoted to 1st Lieutenant.
Do.	John Spence	" 15, "	" 26, "	Promoted to 1st Lieutenant.
Do.	Robert E. Beecher	Sept. 18, "	" 20, "	Appointed Captain A. A. G.
Do.	J. E. F. Jackson	" 20, "	Dec. 31, "	Promoted to 1st Lieutenant.
Do.	J. B. Dresbach	Nov. 23, "	" 31, "	Resigned August 12, 1863.
Do.	Joseph P. Talbott	" 25, "	Feb. 10, 1863	Promoted to 1st Lieutenant.
Do.	John B. Ira	Jan. 21, 1863	" 26, "	Honorably discharged October 23, 1863.
Do.	Samuel P. Peters	Dec. 24, 1862	" 26, "	Promoted to 1st Lieutenant.
Do.	Isaac N. Hawkins	Feb. 28, 1863	March 30, "	Promoted to 1st Lieutenant.
Do.	Chas. W. Stone	Dec. 23, 1862	" 6, "	Promoted to 1st Lieutenant.
Do.	Wm. H. Eckman	Feb. 1, 1863	" 30, "	Promoted to 1st Lieutenant.
Do.	John W. Martin	June 22, "	Aug. 1, "	Promoted to 1st Lieutenant.
Do.	John W. Adams	Nov. 1, "	March 15, 1864	Promoted to 1st Lieutenant.
Do.	Wm. A. Pontius	April 16, 1864	April 16, "	Promoted to 1st Lieutenant.

SEVENTY-THIRD OHIO VOLUNTEER INFANTRY.

ON the 6th of October, 1861, Governor Dennison authorized Orlando Smith, of Chillicothe, to raise a regiment which, when completed, he should command. Camp Logan, near Chillicothe, was selected as the place of rendezvous. Recruiting commissions were secured for the prospective commanders of companies—mostly young men of Chillicothe and vicinity.

The work of recruiting progressed with energy; and on the 30th of December, 1861, the regiment having attained the maximum, was regularly mustered into the service. The majority of the men composing it were recruited in Ross County, though parts of several companies came from the counties of Pike, Highland, Pickaway, Athens, and Hocking.

The Seventy-Third remained in camp, perfecting its drill, until the 24th of January, 1862, when it moved, *via* Parkersburg, to Grafton and Fetterman, West Virginia, and thence, a few days later, to New Creek. On the 6th of February it formed part of an expedition against Romney, the Rebels evacuating the place on the approach of the National troops. The expedition returned to New Creek. A few days later the regiment marched on a similar expedition against Moorefield, and at that place had its first experience of fighting. After a few hours' skirmishing they crossed the river under fire and captured the town. These two expeditions were arduous in the extreme, being forced marches of eighty miles over wretched mountain-roads in stormy winter weather. The hardships and fatigue of this brief campaign exceeded in severity any which the regiment ever encountered, all unused as the men were to campaigning, and ignorant of the many appliances by which the veterans of after years knew how to shield themselves from the most inclement seasons, and to alleviate the hardships of the most extended and severe marches. It is not surprising, then, that the seeds of disease were thickly sown among them, and that numbers went to their graves early in the campaign.

On the return of the regiment to New Creek the measles and camp-fever began to appear. In a few days the regiment was ordered to Clarksburg, arriving there on the 19th of February. Amid sleet and snow it laid out its camp and entered upon a month's campaign of disease. Wm. Pearce, of company A, died on the 24th of February; and for nearly a month thereafter one, two, or more died each day, and near three hundred men were placed in hospital. On the 20th of March, the sickness having considerably abated, the regiment was moved to the town of Weston. At this place the health of the men was measurably restored, and after a fortnight's rest it marched to join General Milroy's command at Cheat Mountain. To reach General Milroy the mountain was to be crossed. The regiment, unaccustomed as yet to move without baggage, after reducing its equipage and turning over the surplus as far as was thought possible, marched with a train of forty wagons, a number that would have excited the amusement of an old campaigner. Halting on the way for a day or two at Buckhannon, Rich Mountain, and Beverly; passing through Huttonsville and over the Cheat and Alleghany Ridges, the regiment reached General Milroy at Monterey. The whole command, including the Seventy-Third, soon moved forward to McDowell. Meanwhile a small foraging party of the regiment had been sent out toward Williamsville. On its return-trip it was attacked by guerrillas, the train burned, and the guard nearly all wounded or captured. A force of picked men, under Major Long, was immediately sent out, and coming up with the scoundrels, ample vengeance was taken, and the expedition returned to camp laden with supplies.

On the 7th of May the enemy, under Stonewall Jackson, attacked General Milroy's advanced forces at Shenandoah Mountain, driving them back to McDowell. On the next day a spirited engagement occurred at McDowell, in which the Seventy-Third was engaged, and met with slight loss. On the night succeeding, the National army began its retreat toward Franklin, reaching that place on the 10th of May. General Fremont now took command in person, and reorganized the force preparatory to an offensive campaign.

An Ohio brigade was formed, consisting of the Seventy-Third, Fifty-Fifth, Seventy-Fifth, Twenty-Fifth, and Eighty-Second, General Schenck commanding. Here, owing to the wretched transportation, supplies became scarce, and for some days the regiment really suffered from hunger.

On the 25th of May the command moved to encounter Jackson again. Passing through Petersburg, where the sick, baggage, and transportation were left, they reached Moorefield, the scene of the regiment's first essay at fighting, and overtook the enemy at Strasburg. Then followed the pursuit up the Shenandoah Valley, through Woodstock, Edinburg, Mount Jackson, New Market, and Harrisonburg, pressing upon the rear of Jackson. Beyond hard marching and some skirmishing, nothing was effected.

On June 8, 1862, the regiment was engaged in the battle of Cross Keys, and lost eight men killed and wounded.

After the escape of Jackson the troops retired slowly down the valley and encamped near Middleton. At this place General Schenck took command of the division, and Colonel McLean of the Seventy-Third Ohio, of the brigade. Nothing of note occurred until July 7th, when the regiment, with the rest of the army, now under command of General Sigel, started for Eastern Virginia. Moving through Front Royal and Luray, it crossed the Blue Ridge at Luray Gap, and encamped at Sperryville. While lying at this place a number of changes and promotions occurred.

The Seventy-Third passed a delightful month at Sperryville. The long-needed rest, after the severe campaign it had passed through, was most grateful; the fruits and vegetables in which the valley abounded made army life, for once, seem like home; and the men, recruited and refreshed, were soon ready for another campaign.

On August 8th the command took up its line of march for Culpepper, where it arrived next evening in time to relieve General Banks's corps on the battle-field of Cedar Mountain. The following day was occupied in skirmishing, and the next in pursuit of Stonewall Jackson to the Rapidan. Here the regiment encamped until August 18th, when, the entire army of General Lee having come up and passed the flank of General Pope, the latter began his retreat toward Washington City. Thenceforward until the 1st of September the regiment, with occasional brief intervals, had no rest. Night and day it fought, marched, skirmished, picketed, and maneuvered in the face of the enemy, scarce ever out of the range of hostile cannon and musketry.

Passing through Culpepper, the Seventy-Third crossed the Rappahannock at White Sulphur Springs, moved down the river to Rappahannock Station, and thence up to Freeman's Ford, where it engaged the enemy; thence back to White Sulphur and Waterloo, to prevent the enemy from crossing.

The Rebels, baffled thus far, having at length flanked General Pope's right, the whole army drew back toward Manassas. Passing through Warrenton, New Baltimore, and Gainesville, the Seventy-Third reached the battle-ground the evening of August 27th. The next day was occupied in skirmishing and maneuvering, without any severe fighting. The next morning the regiment was held in reserve until afternoon, when the brigade was ordered to occupy Bald Hill, a prominent eminence on the left of the main road, where it formed the extreme left of the line of battle. The enemy having pressed back General Pope's right and center, came sweeping down upon the front and flank of the left wing. Everything was falling back except Milroy's division, posted immediately on the right of the brigade of Schenck's division in which the Seventy-Third was acting. The retreat was rapidly becoming a rout. Milroy's right began to give way. At this juncture the conduct of the Seventy-Third and its brigade undoubtedly saved the army from destruction. Its conspicuous position on the hill enabled the whole line to witness its gallant behavior.

Flushed with success and yelling like demons, the enemy rushed to the very muzzles of the National muskets, but the brigade stood firm and repulsed them with great slaughter. With loud cheers the National brigade announced its success. Milroy was thus enabled to rally his broken line. The enemy made another dash, only to meet the fate of the former. They fell back in confusion, leaving a winrow of dead and wounded behind them. The victorious shouts of the Nationals resounded to the extreme right of the line. The retreating columns were halted. Milroy stood firm. Meade, next on the right, rallied his division to a strong position, which he held for hours thereafter, punishing Longstreet, who assailed him, with fearful slaughter. This enabled the commanders still further to the right to rally their troops. The entire line was restored and held until nightfall, though too late to win a victory.

Meanwhile the enemy had returned to the charge on the left; and, having largely the advantage in numbers, his column pressed, not only upon the National front, but upon its exposed and unprotected flank. Changing front, the Ohio Brigade, now greatly exhausted, vainly endeavored to stay the last onset. Slowly, in good order, it fell back to the woods in the rear, fighting as it retreated. Flanked again and again, it retreated, fighting as before, across the run. It was now nightfall, and the enemy having suffered severely, did not follow. During the night the Ohio Brigade fell back across Bull Run and went into camp at Centerville. After a day's rest it moved through Fairfax C. H. to the defense of Washington.

The service rendered by the Seventy-Third and its brigade on this occasion can hardly be overestimated. Its firm stand and desperate fighting at a critical juncture, in the sight of the entire army, enabled General Pope to rally his broken lines, re-form, and hold the enemy in check until nightfall. But for this, the defeat would have been an utter rout. General Pope, in his official report, gave it due credit.

The loss of the regiment was very severe. Out of three hundred and ten men present for duty, one hundred and forty-four were killed or wounded, and twenty captured. Lieutenant Trimble was killed, Captain Burkett mortally wounded, Lieutenant McKell wounded, and Lieutenant Martin captured.

The regiment remained in the defenses of Washington, at Fairfax, and Centerville, until November, engaged in picketing and reconnoissances. About the last of October it received one hundred and twenty new recruits. While near Washington a new brigade was formed, consisting of the Seventy-Third Ohio, One Hundred and Thirty-Sixth and One Hundred and Thirty-Fourth New York, and the Thirty-Third Massachusetts Regiments, Colonel Smith, of the Seventy-Third, in command.

The new brigade participated in a reconnoissance to Thoroughfare Gap and New Baltimore early in November. Aside from this nothing of note occurred till December 12th, when the corps (now numbered as the Eleventh) moved to join General Burnside at Fredericksburg, which place it reached just as the battle ended. The regiment did its share of marching and exposure in the second attempt for the capture of Fredericksburg. Thereafter it went into camp at Aquia Creek until April 27, 1863, when the Chancellorsville campaign began. While lying here a number of changes and promotions occurred.

In the Chancellorsville campaign the regiment formed part of the column which turned the left of Lee's Army, crossing the Rappahannock at Kelly's Ford and the Rapidan at Germania; and, passing through the Wilderness, encamped on the plankroad, two miles from Chancellorsville, on the night of May 1st. The next day the brigade was ordered to join General Birney in a reconnoissance to the front, which occupied it until midnight. This saved it from participation in the terrible fight and rout of the Eleventh Corps which occurred that day. With the rest of the army, after the battle, it returned to its old camping-ground.

Nothing noteworthy occurred until June 12th, when the army entered upon the Gettysburg campaign. Passing through Catlett's and Manassas, it crossed the Potomac at Edward's Ferry, and pushing through Middletown, occupied South Mountain. Thence the brigade made a forced march of thirty-eight miles in twenty-four hours, through rain and mud, to Emmettsburg. Delaying there but a short time, it hurried on toward Gettysburg, the sound of cannon giving assurance that fighting had already begun. It reached the battle-field late in the afternoon, just as the broken remnants of the First Corps and the remaining brigades of the Eleventh came streaming back in disorder. Immediately the command was deployed upon Cemetery Hill to check the enemy and cover the retreat of its defeated comrades. At that moment, and until midnight, it was the only organized force in good condition for fight on the battle-field, and in the face of nearly the whole of Lee's army, flushed with victory. The bold front which the brigade assumed, and its promptness in checking the Rebel pursuit, aided by the now approaching darkness, which concealed its numbers, deceived the enemy, who supposed a fresh corps had arrived, and induced him to defer further operations until daybreak. This saved the Cemetery Hill, and insured the subsequent victory at Gettysburg.

Displayed into one great picket-line, this little band of four regiments stood around the hill until midnight, when the advance of the other corps brought relief from the terrible suspense. By morning the National army was in position. Thenceforward until the end of the battle the regiment, with its brigade, held the line in front of Cemetery Hill, to the left of the town, and was almost incessantly engaged on the ground in its front. Its losses during the fight amounted to one hundred and forty-three officers and men out of about three hundred.

After the battle the regiment was engaged in the pursuit of Lee, moving *via* Emmettsburg, Middletown, and South Mountain, to Hagerstown, and thence to Falling Water. No fighting of any note occurred. After Lee's retreat over the Potomac the regiment, retracing its steps, crossed the river with the rest of the army at Berlin, and marching *via* White Plains, New Baltimore, and Catlett's, finally went into camp at Bristow's Station, where it remained until September 24th, and was then transferred, as part of General Hooker's command, to the Army of the Cumberland.

The regiment reached Bridgeport, Alabama, in five days from starting. It remained here and at Stevenson until October 24th, when, as the advance of General Hooker's army, it moved to the relief of Chattanooga. Crossing the Tennessee River, it marched to Lookout Valley *via* Shellmound and Wauhatchie. At the latter place the enemy made a stand, but was speedily driven over Lookout Creek, and the National army, under the fire of Rebel batteries on the mountain, pushed down the valley and formed a junction with the Army of the Cumberland at Brown's Ferry, General Geary's division only being left at Wauhatchie, five miles in the rear.

During the night following the enemy recrossed Lookout Creek, occupied the hills between Wauhatchie and the main body of the army, and made a furious attack upon General Geary. The Eleventh Corps, aroused at midnight by the firing, moved at once to re-establish communication and succor him. Colonel Smith's brigade was ordered to charge the most important of the hills on which the enemy was posted. Supposing the enemy's force to be small, Colonel Smith placed the Seventy-Third Ohio and a part of the Eighty-Third Massachusetts (in all less than five hundred muskets) in line, and directed them to move up the slope. Nothing was known of the ground, and the night was very dark. Scrambling up the steep acclivity through underbrush, the men sometimes pulling themselves up by hand, as the little column approached the summit it was saluted by a terrible fire of musketry from what afterward proved to be an entire brigade of Longstreet's corps, over two thousand strong, and covered by breastworks. Nothing dismayed, the column fixed bayonets, and, climbing to the top, drove the Rebels out of their trenches and down the opposite slope in great confusion. This decided the battle. The entire Rebel line gave way and fled precipitately across Lookout Creek.

The conduct of the Seventy-Third on this occasion called forth high praise and especial notice from Generals Hooker, Thomas, and Grant, who visited the scene on the following day. The latter, in his official dispatches, named it "one of the most daring feats of arms of the war." In this action the regiment lost sixty-five men and officers out of two hundred.

Encamping near the scene of its late victory, the Seventy-Third Ohio was occupied by picket-duty and building earthworks until November 22d, when, with the rest of the corps, it crossed the river and was engaged in the battle of Mission Ridge. Its position was in the left center, and subsequently on the extreme left, with General Sherman. After the fight it formed part of the pursuing column, and immediately thereafter marched with General Sherman to the relief of Knoxville. Returning, it reached Chattanooga December 17th, and shortly thereafter re-enlisted as veterans.

On January 4, 1864, the regiment joyfully set out for home on veteran furlough. It reached Chillicothe on the 15th of January, and was welcomed with music, banners, and feasting.

The month of furlough expired only too soon, and, with one hundred and twenty recruits, the Seventy-Third returned to its old camping-ground in Lookout Valley. While at home Colonel Orlando Smith resigned, which led to several changes and promotions.

In the army as now reorganized the regiment was assigned to the Third Brigade (Wood's), Third Division (Butterfield's), Twentieth Corps (Hooker's), Army of the Cumberland.

On the morning of May 2d the Seventy-Third, now numbering three hundred and eighteen muskets, marched out of its camp in Lookout Valley to take its part in the coming great campaign. Passing over the Chickamauga battle-ground, moving by the way of Gordon's Mills and Ringgold, it took its place in the line in front of Rocky Face Ridge, near Buzzard's Roost. After a few days of skirmishing and reconnoitering here, it moved with the corps through Snake Creek Gap and confronted the enemy at Resaca. At the opening of the battle the regiment, with its brigade, charged the hill in its front, driving the enemy back to their works. After holding the position for some time the regiment was ordered to the left of the brigade. It moved thither across an open field, in good order, under fire; then advanced its line over a recreant regiment lying in its way, to the exposed crest of the hill in front, which position it maintained firmly, under constant fire, until nightfall. By morning the enemy had retreated, and the regiment joined in the pursuit. It was highly complimented by its brigade and division commanders for brilliant conduct in this action.

Pressing hard upon the enemy in his retreat, the brigade narrowly escaped capture near Ringgold by its daring advance. With the exception of severe skirmishing near Casswell, it had no fighting of consequence to do. The enemy having retreated across the Etowah River, the command rested on its northern bank for three days. It then marched toward Dallas. Within five miles of Dallas, near Pumpkin-Vine Creek, it met the Rebel foe once more. Pressing forward and driving back the hostile skirmishers, the regiment brought up at length in front of the main body of Johnston's army, securely positioned near New Hope Church, behind breastworks, with tangled woods and marshes in front. A severe battle followed. The Seventy-Third was posted on the extreme left, on an open slope, which descended toward the enemy, who were concealed behind thick underbrush and breastworks.

Though badly exposed and suffering severely every moment, the regiment stood firm and fought till nightfall, when it was relieved. In this engagement three officers and seventy-two men were killed and wounded. This battle was followed by some days of inaction, varied only by skirmishing and fatigue-duty. The latter occupation had become a daily and hourly one; the spade was as familiar as the musket. At this place Colonel Long, whose health had been failing for some months, tendered his resignation, which was accepted, and Lieutenant-Colonel Hurst, Major Higgins, and Captain Lucas were each commissioned to the next higher rank, but, owing to the reduced number of the regiment, could not be mustered.

For the next few weeks the regiment participated in the common work of the army, viz.: successive movements by the flank, each one being followed by the retreat of the enemy to a new position, each one bringing us nearer to the objective of the campaign—Atlanta. At every step, skirmishing, picketing, and fortifying formed the daily and nightly duty of the soldier. Scarce ever was the regiment out of range of the enemy's guns, and almost each day some one was killed or wounded.

Pine Mountain, then the railroad, with Acworth and Allatoona, then Lost Mountain were gained; and the army confronted the enemy strongly intrenched upon Kenesaw and around Marietta. In front of the latter position the Seventy-Third and its division made a gallant fight. Pushing to the front without support or connections, it charged the enemy and drove them from their advanced line. The regiment lost sixteen men killed and wounded.

On the 24th of May the brigade was similarly engaged. The enemy's advanced works were taken and re-taken several times, and finally held; and the Seventy-Third again lost nineteen men in the action. On the 6th of June the Chattahoochie was reached, and the spires of Atlanta loomed in sight. After a few days of rest the river was crossed, and, in line with the rest of the army, the regiment moved on the devoted city.

On June 20th the regiment reached Peachtree Creek. Crossing this creek, impeded only by some scattering skirmishers, the troops halted for dinner. Suddenly sharp firing by the pickets gave evidence that the enemy were coming. Springing to arms and moving up the slope, they found that the Rebels, in heavy columns, at double-quick, were driving in our pickets with all possible speed, hoping to take the National army by surprise. For once in this long campaign they were to meet the enemy in the open field, and not behind formidable breastworks. At last they were to repel an attack, not make one. Almost without waiting for the word of command, as the attacking column drew near, they rushed at them in a counter-charge of resistless fury, firing and fixing bayonets as they ran. In less than thirty minutes the tide of battle was turned, and they were driving the foe before them. A halt was made to re-form ranks. The Rebels rallying, renewed the fight, only to be repulsed repeatedly with great loss. At nightfall the Rebels retreated to the inner defenses of the city. In this engagement the Seventy-Third lost eighteen men. The next day the National army closed around the city.

During the month which followed, the regiment was constantly in the front line of works, and day and night under fire, and continually at work skirmishing and fortifying. Each day one or more men were killed or wounded.

At length the great flank movement toward Jonesboro' was made, the Twentieth Corps being left to hold the line of the Chattahoochie. The Seventy-Third was stationed at Turner's Ferry, where the enemy attacked it, but were repulsed.

At length Atlanta was evacuated, and two companies of the Seventy-Third, forming part of a reconnoissance, were the first troops to enter the city. Thus this long and terrible campaign was ended. Out of one hundred and twenty days' campaigning, the regiment had been under fire one hundred and three days, and most of the remainder had been occupied in marching and hard work. It had lost two hundred and ten men and eight officers out of less than three hundred and fifty; had been repeatedly engaged with the enemy, and had never retreated before him. The regiment now encamped near the city, recruiting and working upon the defenses of Atlanta, until November 15th, when it started with Sherman on his "march to the sea."

The incidents of this famous expedition—the marching, foraging, destruction of railroads, cotton, and whatever else could cripple the enemy's resources; the plentiful provisions; the crowd of contrabands following; the humors and festivities of the camp and march, being so much the same with all parts of the army—need not be repeated here. The line of march of the Seventy-Third was through Decatur, Roxbury, and Social Circle, Madison and Eaton, to Milledgeville, where the regiment halted and ate bountiful thanksgiving dinners. Thence through Sandersville, Davisboro', and Louisville; past the horrible prison-house at Millen; on through Sylvania and Springfield to the magnificent live-oaks and rice-fields in the suburbs of Savannah. The regiment traversed the State without firing a shot at a foe or meeting an armed enemy.

Here the non-veterans of the regiment, eighty-five in number, and three officers—Captains Stone, Barnes, and Madeira—were mustered out and sent home. Captain McKell and Lieutenant Jackson resigned.

On January 2, 1865, the regiment crossed the Savannah River into South Carolina, and entered upon its last campaign.

The army corps crossed Cape Fear River on the 12th, and were opposed by a considerable force of Rebel cavalry. Early on the morning of March 16th Kilpatrick skirmished heavily with the enemy under General Hardee, who seemed determined to dispute the advance of the

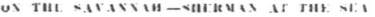

ON THE SAVANNAH—SHERMAN AT THE SEA

National forces, at least until his trains could get into a safe retreat. The battle of Averysboro' was fought. The National soldiers waded up to their knees in the swamps and bravely attacked the Rebel works. The enemy gave way and retreated through Averysboro' in the direction of Smithfield. In this affair the Seventy-Third lost fifteen men wounded.

On Sunday, March 19th, the last battle of the war was fought—that of Bentonville. It was fiercely contested on both sides, but the Rebels were compelled to succumb. The loss of the Seventy-Third in this battle was five men killed and four officers and twenty-one men wounded.

Little was left to do after this engagement. Sherman's army went into camp around Goldsboro', North Carolina. On the 10th of April, while moving out from Goldsboro', the news of Lee's surrender was received; and, with shouts of gladness, the National army crossed the Neuse River, and on the 13th took possession of Raleigh without opposition. On the 22d the Rebel army under General Joe Johnston was surrendered to General Sherman, and the agreement sent to Washington for ratification. On the 22d the Twentieth Corps (in which was brigaded the Seventy-Third) was reviewed by General Sherman in the streets of Raleigh. General Grant arrived with the President's rejection of the Sherman-Johnston treaty, and on the 25th the National troops moved against the enemy. The Twentieth Corps marched ten miles on the road to Holly Springs, while Grant and Sherman held a conference with the Rebel commander, which resulted in the surrender of Johnston's entire army. On the 28th the National army marched back to Raleigh, filled with gladness that at last the Great Rebellion was ended.

Then came the march to Washington, passing through the Rebel capital, Richmond, Virginia; the grand review; the transfer to Louisville, Kentucky; and finally the muster-out. On the 20th of July, 1865, the rolls of the Seventy-Third Ohio were ready, and on that day the regiment was mustered out of the service, and started for Camp Dennison, Ohio, where, on the 24th of July, it was paid off and finally discharged.

Colonel Smith and Colonel Hurst subsequently were brevetted Brigadier-Generals for gallant and faithful service.

The history and character of the Seventy-Third may be summed up briefly. It served three years and eight months, and was always in active service, never at posts or guarding communications. It marched several thousand miles, participated in twenty battles, not to speak of numberless skirmishes and minor affairs. On three occasions, in connection with its brigade, its behavior in battle decided the fortunes of the day. Its conduct was frequently commended in general orders, and never reproached. Its discipline and drill were uniformly the subject of remark in its brigade and division. As proof of its gallantry and services, out of a little more than twelve hundred members, including recruits, two hundred and eighty-five sleep beneath the sod, and five hundred and sixty-eight are now bearing about the scars of honorable combat, many of them crippled for life.

74th REGIMENT OHIO VOLUNTEER INFANTRY.

ROSTER, THREE YEARS' SERVICE.

RANK.	NAME	DATE OF RANK.	COM. ISSUED.	REMARKS.
Colonel	GRANVILLE MOODY	Dec. 10, 1861	March 28, 1862	Resigned May 16, 1863.
Do.	A. VON SCHRAEDER	May 16, 1863	May 22, 1863	Declined.
Do.	JOSIAH GIVEN	" 16, "	June 2, "	Resigned September 29, 1864.
Do.	R. P. FINDLEY	July 12, 1865	July 12, 1865	Mustered out as Lieutenant-Colonel.
Lt. Colonel	ALEX. VON SCHRAEDER	Dec. 10, 1861	March 28, 1862	Resigned April 8, 1863.
Do.	THOMAS C. BELL	May 16, 1863	May 25, 1863	Revoked.
Do.	ROBERT P. FINDLEY	" 18, 1865	" 18, 1865	Promoted to Colonel.
Do.	CORNELIUS MCGREAVY	July 12, "	July 12, "	Mustered out as Major.
Major	ALEX. S. BALLARD	Oct. 5, 1861	March 28, 1862	Resigned November 22, 1862.
Do.	THOMAS C. BELL	Nov. 22, 1862	Nov. 27, "	Resigned June 7, 1863.
Do.	JOSEPH FISHER	May 16, "	May 26, 1863	Revoked.
Do.	ROBERT P. FINDLEY	June 7, "	Sept. 9, "	Promoted to Lieutenant-Colonel.
Do.	CORNELIUS MCGREAVY	Nov. 12, "	Nov. 12, "	Promoted to Lieutenant-Colonel.
Do.	M. H. PETERS	May 18, 1865	May 18, 1865	Mustered out with reg't as Adj't, rank Capt.
Do.	JOSEPH FISHER	July 12, "	July 12, "	Mustered out.
Surgeon	J. R. BELLSFORD	Nov. 5, 1861	March 28, 1862	
Do.	MATTHEW W. DICKSON	Dec. 7, 1864	Dec. 7, 1864	Mustered out with regiment.
Ass't Surgeon	E. W. STEELE	Jan. 9, 1862	March 28, 1862	Resigned June 4, 1862.
Do.	WM. ARNOLD	June 4, "	June 17, "	Resigned November 22, 1862.
Do.	A. L. WILLIAMS	July 4, "	July 23, "	Discharged December 31, 1862.
Do.	MATTHEW W. DICKSON	Dec. 23, "	Dec. 31, "	Promoted to Surgeon
Do.	WM. HAYES	June 9, 1863	June 10, 1863	
Do.	C. A. MOORE	" 8, 1865	" 8, 1865	
Chaplain	SAMUEL MARSHALL	March 12, 1862	March 18, 1862	Resigned September 8, 1862.
Captain	Thomas C. Bell	Nov. 2, 1861	" 28, "	Promoted to Major.
Do.	Stephen A. Bassford	Dec. 5, "	" 28, "	Resigned July 28, 1862.
Do.	Samuel T. Owens	" 23, "	" 28, "	Resigned December 22, 1862.
Do.	Austin McDowell	" 28, "	" 28, "	Resigned February 10, 1863.
Do.	Joseph Fisher	" 31, "	" 28, "	Promoted to Major.
Do.	Walter Crook	Jan. 7, 1862	" 28, "	Mustered out.
Do.	Albion W. Bostwick	Feb. 18, "	April 2, "	Resigned November 19, 1862.
Do.	Robert P. Findley	" 27, "	" 2, "	Promoted to Major.
Do.	Joseph H. Ballard	" 20, "	" 4, "	Resigned February 20, 1862.
Do.	Patrick Dwyer	Dec. 31, 1861	" 17, "	Resigned February 17, 1863.
Do.	Wm. Mills	Sept. 1, 1862	Dec. 20, "	On detached service.
Do.	Wm. McGinnis	Nov. 22, "	" 27, "	Resigned April 26, 1864.
Do.	Wm. T. Armstrong	Dec. 22, "	Jan. 11, 1863	Resigned November 6, 1864.
Do.	Franklin J. Tedford	Nov. 19, "	" 16, "	Mustered out June 11, 1865.
Do.	Thomas C. McIlravy	Feb. 10, 1863	Feb. 17, "	Resigned September 20, 1864.
Do.	Robert Cullen	" 17, "	March 6, "	Revoked.
Do.	David Snodgrass	" 20, "	April 9, "	Resigned April 28, 1864.
Do.	Henry H. Herring	Feb. 1, 1864	Feb. 13, 1864	Resigned November 8, 1864.
Do.	Cornelius McGreavy	" 17, 1862	Jan. 10, 1864	Promoted to Major.
Do.	John W. McMillen	June 14, 1864	June 14, "	Mustered out with regiment.
Do.	Robert Hunter	" 14, "	" 14, "	Declined.
Do.	Matthew H. Peters	July 13, "	July 13, "	Promoted to Major.
Do.	John Q. Hutchinson	Nov. 12, "	Nov. 12, "	
Do.	Perry A. Weaver	" 12, "	" 12, "	Declined promotion.
Do.	Robert Hunter	" 10, "	" 10, "	Mustered out with regiment.
Do.	Joseph Hammill	" 18, "	" 18, "	Resigned as 1st Lieutenant.
Do.	Thomas Kirby	Jan. 28, 1865	Jan. 18, 1865	Mustered out with regiment.
Do.	Wm. T. Drummond	May 18, "	May 18, "	Mustered out with regiment.
Do.	Matthew K. McFadden	" 18, "	" 18, "	Mustered out with regiment.
Do.	Wm. C. Galloway	June 6, "	June 6, "	Mustered out as 1st Lieutenant.
Do.	Philip W. Stumm	" 6, "	" 6, "	Mustered out as Q. M.
Do.	Martin Ryan	" 16, "	" 16, "	Mustered out as 1st Lieutenant.
Do.	John N. Haynes	July 12, "	July 12, "	Mustered out as 1st Lieutenant.
1st Lieutenant	Thomas C. Bell	Oct. 24, 1861	March 28, 1862	Promoted to Captain.
Do.	Wm. McGinnis	Nov. 8, "	" 28, "	Promoted to Captain.
Do.	Franklin J. Tedford	Dec. 5, "	" 28, "	Promoted to Captain.
Do.	Wm. T. Armstrong	" 23, "	" 28, "	Promoted to Captain.
Do.	John W. McClung	" 28, "	" 28, "	Resigned November 25, 1862.
Do.	Henry H. Herring	" 31, "	" 28, "	Promoted to Captain.
Do.	Matthew H. Peters	Jan. 7, 1862	" 28, "	Promoted to Captain.
Do.	James H. Cochnower	Dec. 21, 1861	April 2, "	Discharged.
Do.	Thomas C. McIlravy	Feb. 18, 1862	" 2, "	Promoted to Captain.
Do.	David Snodgrass	" 20, "	" 4, "	Promoted to Captain.
Do.	Henry M. Cist	Oct. 22, 1861	" 17, "	Promoted to Captain and A. A. G.
Do.	Wm. Mills	" 5, "	" 17, "	Promoted to Captain.
Do.	Robert Cullen	Dec. 31, "	" 17, "	Honorably discharged October 26, 1863.
Do.	Robert Hunter	Nov. 25, 1862	Dec. 4, "	Promoted to Captain.
Do.	John. W. McMillen	" 22, "	" 27, "	Promoted to Captain.
Do.	Robert Stevenson	Dec. 22, "	Jan. 14, 1863	Resigned as 2d Lieutenant February 10, 1863.
Do.	Benj. A. Weaver	Jan. 13, 1863	Feb. 11, "	Discharged April 6, 1865; time out.
Do.	John Q. Hutchinson	Dec. 22, 1862	March 6, "	Promoted to Captain.
Do.	George W. Bricker	Feb. 10, 1863	Feb. 17, "	Died Sept. 12, 1864, of wounds rec'd at Jonesboro'.
Do.	Cornelius McGreavy	Dec. 31, 1862	March 6, "	Promoted to Captain.
Do.	Wm. H. H. Moody	Feb. 20, 1863	April 9, "	Died September 28, 1864
Do.	Joseph Hammill	March 21, 1864	March 21, 1864	Promoted to Captain.
Do.	Thomas Kirby	June 14, "	June 14, "	Promoted to Captain.
Do.	Thomas H. Adams	" 14, "	" 14, "	Mustered out October 17, 1864.
Do.	Wm. T. Drummond	" 14, "	" 14, "	Promoted to Captain.
Do.	John Scott	" 14, "	" 14, "	Killed at Jonesboro' September 1, 1864.
Do.	Matthew K. McFadden	July 27, "	July 27, "	Promoted to Captain.
Do.	Michael McGreavy	Oct. 12, "	Oct. 12, "	Declined promotion.

RANK.	NAME.	DATE OF RANK.	COM. ISSUED.	REMARKS.
1st Lieutenant	John W. Baldwin	Oct. 12, 1861	Oct. 12, 1861	Declined promotion.
Do.	Richard Powell	" 12, "	" 12, "	Mustered out May 15, 1865.
Do.	Wm. C. Galloway	Nov. 12, "	Nov. 12, "	Promoted to Captain.
Do.	Philip W. Stumm	" 12, "	" 12, "	Promoted to Captain.
Do.	Martin Ryan	" 12, "	" 12, "	Promoted to Captain.
Do.	John N. Haynes	" 18, "	" 18, "	Promoted to Captain.
Do.	Chas. C. Dodson	Jan. 6, 1865	Jan. 6, 1865	Mustered out with regiment.
Do.	Wm. M. Snyder	" 6, "	" 6, "	Mustered out with regiment as Adjutant.
Do.	John B. Gundy	May 11, "	May 11, "	Mustered out with regiment as Q. M. Serg't.
Do.	James McCann	" 11, "	" 11, "	Mustered out with regiment.
Do.	Chas. L. Gallsher	" 18, "	" 18, "	
Do.	Robert C. Finley	" 18, "	" 18, "	Mustered out with regiment.
Do.	Edward R. Barnett	" 31, "	" 31, "	Mustered out with regiment.
Do.	Isaac Miller	June 6, "	June 6, "	Mustered out with regiment.
Do.	Andrew Flannigan	" 6, "	" 6, "	
Do.	Thomas C. Hook	" 4, "	" 4, "	Mustered out as Sergeant-Major.
Do.	Samuel Poland	July 12, "	July 12, "	
2d Lieutenant	Robert Stevenson	Oct. 10, 1861	March 10, 1862	Promoted to 1st. Lieut.; resigned Feb. 10, '63.
Do.	John W. McMillen	" 24, "	" 28, "	Promoted to 1st Lieutenant.
Do.	Benj. F. Sickley	Nov. 11, "	" 28, "	Resigned September 25, 1862.
Do.	Richard A. King	Dec. 5, "	" 28, "	Resigned January 23, 1863.
Do.	John R. Hitesman	" 16, "	" 28, "	Resigned June 6, 1863.
Do.	Robert Hunter	" 28, "	" 28, "	Promoted to 1st Lieutenant.
Do.	Wm. H. Reed	" 2, "	April 2, "	Resigned April 28, 1863.
Do.	George W. Bricker	Feb. 18, 1862	" 2, "	Promoted to 1st Lieutenant.
Do.	Wm. H. H. Moody	Jan. 4, "	" 4, "	Promoted to 1st Lieutenant.
Do.	Bernard J. Connaughtin	Dec. 31, 1861	" 17, "	Resigned June 24, 1862.
Do.	Wm. T. Drummond	Nov. 25, 1862	Dec. 4, "	Promoted to 1st Lieutenant.
Do.	Michael McGreavy	June 21, "	" 8, "	Revoked; mustered out January 12, 1865.
Do.	Joseph Hammill	Dec. 15, "	" 15, "	Promoted to 1st Lieutenant.
Do.	Thomas H. Adams	Nov. 22, "	" 27, "	Promoted to 1st Lieutenant.
Do.	Thomas Kirby	Sept. 25, "	" 27, "	Promoted to 1st Lieutenant.
Do.	John Q. Hutchinson	Dec. 22, "	Jan. 11, 1863	Promoted to 1st Lieutenant.
Do.	John Scott	Jan. 23, 1863	Feb. 11, "	Promoted to 1st Lieutenant.
Do.	Cornelius McGreavy	June 21, 1862	" 16, "	Promoted to 1st Lieutenant.
Do.	James A. Worden	Feb. 10, 1863	" 18, "	Resigned May 21, 1863.
Do.	John B. Burrows	Dec. 22, 1862	March 6, "	Resigned August 5, 1863.
Do.	Edwin Ballard	Feb. 20, 1863	May 1, "	Resigned December 16, 1863.
Do.	John A. McKee	April 28, "	" 19, "	Drowned.
Do.	Matthew K. McFadden	May 21, "	June 26, "	Promoted to 1st Lieutenant.
Do.	Michael McGreavy	Jan. "	" 10, "	Declined promotion.
Do.	John W. Baldwin	March 19, 1864	March 19, 1864	Declined promotion.
Do.	Richard Powell	" 21, "	" 21, "	Promoted to 1st Lieutenant.
Do.	John W. Devoe	July 9, 1865	July 9, 1865	Mustered out with regiment as 1st Sergeant.

SEVENTY-FOURTH OHIO VOLUNTEER INFANTRY.

THIS regiment was organized in camp at Xenia, Ohio, in October, 1861, to the extent of seven companies. On the 24th of February, 1862, it was ordered to Camp Chase, where three full companies were added, making the complement, and aggregating nine hundred and seventy-eight men.

The regiment was ordered to the field on the 20th of April, 1862, reported at Nashville, Tennessee, on the 24th of the same month, and went into camp near that city. While here it was thoroughly drilled, and portions of it detailed for provost-duty in Nashville. The first real service performed by the regiment was on its march over the Cumberland Mountains with General Dumont, in June. Immediately thereafter it was detailed as guard to the railroad between Nashville and Columbia, and continued to perform that duty during the month of August. It returned to Nashville September 3d, and remained there during the blockade of September, October, and November, 1862. During this period the regiment was engaged in several skirmishes in the vicinity of the city.

In December it was placed in the Seventh Brigade (Miller's), Eighth Division (Negley's), formerly part of the center, (Thomas's), Fourteenth Army Corps, Department of the Cumberland.

When General Rosecrans made his movement on Bragg's army lying at Murfreesboro', the Seventy-Fourth marched with its division and corps. On the 29th of December it went into the battle of Stone River, and remained in it until nightfall of January 3, 1863; was hotly engaged December 31st, and was one of the regiments selected to charge across Stone River, January 2d, against Breckinridge's Rebel corps. The Seventy-Fourth went into this battle with three hundred and eighty effective men, of whom it lost, in killed and wounded, one hundred and nine, and in prisoners, forty-six.

On the reorganization of the army at Murfreesboro', Tennessee, in February, 1863, the Seventy-Fourth was assigned to the Third Brigade (Miller's), Second Division (Negley's), Fourteenth Army Corps (Thomas's), and during the stay of the army at that place assisted in guard-duty on the fortifications. At this place several changes took place among the officers. Colonel Moody, Major Bell, and Captains Owens, McDowell, and Ballard, resigned, which made necessary the following promotions: To Colonel, Josiah Given, (late Lieutenant-Colonel of the Eighteenth Ohio); to Captains, Mills, Armstrong, McGinnis, Tedford, and McIlravy; to First-Lieutenants, McMillen, Hunter, Hutchison, Weaver, and Bricker; to Second-Lieutenants Adams, Scott, Drummond, and McGreavy.

On the movement toward Chattanooga, June 23, 1863, the Seventy-Fourth was in the column, and participated in the battles of Hoover's Gap, June 24th; Dog Gap, Georgia, September 11th, and Chickamauga, September 19th and 20th, arriving at Chattanooga September 22, 1863. The regiment also participated in the battles of Lookout Mountain and Missionary Ridge, November 23, 24, and 25, 1863.

While at Chattanooga a majority of the men of the regiment re-enlisted as veteran volunteers from January 1, 1864. About the same time Captain Fisher was promoted to Major.

Entitled, as they were, to thirty days' furlough at home, the regiment left Chattanooga on the 25th of January, 1864, and arrived at Xenia, Ohio, where it was received with the greatest honors, kindness, and hospitality, in the power of the loyal and patriotic ladies of that beautiful city to bestow. On their way home, everywhere in Ohio, the members of the regiment were the recipients of the most marked kindness and consideration.

The regiment reassembled at Xenia on the 17th of March, and before leaving for the field passed resolutions returning their hearty thanks for the unbounded kindness with which they had been treated, and making the utterance of the word "Xenia," by visitors to their camp in the field, a talismanic passport to their hearts and hospitality.

The regiment being reorganized numbered, with the addition of one hundred new recruits, six hundred and nineteen men.

The Seventy-Fourth, once more ready for the field, started for "the front" on the 23d of March, 1864, and on the 12th of April rejoined its brigade, at Graysville, Georgia. Remaining in this camp until the 7th of May it started with the army on the Atlanta campaign—that long and arduous march, so famous in the history of the rebellion. One day's history of this campaign was that of the next. For over one hundred days the regiment was under an almost continuous fire of Rebel musketry and artillery. At Buzzard's Roost it was specially engaged, and in an attempt to storm that stronghold, on the 9th of May, lost sixteen men killed and wounded; and, at Resaca, May 15th, nine men killed and wounded. In the engagement of the 27th of May the conduct of the Seventy-Fourth, and other regiments of the Third Brigade, elicited from the division commander the following commendatory notice:

"HEAD-QUARTERS FIRST DIVISION, FOURTEENTH ARMY CORPS,
"NEAR DALLAS, GEORGIA, MAY 28, 1864.

"*Colonel:* General Johnson desires to express to you his high appreciation of the gallantry exhibited by the noble troops of your brigade in the night-engagement of the 27th instant. The admirable spirit displayed by them on that occasion is, above all things, desirable and commendable. Soldiers animated by such courage and fortitude are capable of the very highest achievements. * * * * * * * * *

(Signed) "E. F. WELLS, A. A. G."

At Kenesaw Mountain the regiment had a most arduous and perilous duty to perform. Fotwo weeks it was under a constant fire of musketry and shells. It was also engaged at the Chattahoochie River, Peachtree Creek, and in front of Atlanta. At the battle of Jonesboro' it made three distinct charges on the afternoon of September 1st, and lost two Lieutenants and twelve non-commissioned officers and privates killed, and twenty-five privates wounded. For which gallant achievement the regiment was included in the following complimentary notice:

"HEAD-QUARTERS FIRST DIVISION, FOURTEENTH ARMY CORPS,
"JONESBORO', SEPTEMBER 2, 1864.

"CIRCULAR.

"The General commanding the division congratulates the officers and enlisted men of the Second and Third Brigades on the success of their splendid assault on the enemy, September 1, 1864. They charged a strongly intrenched double line, passing over swamps and through thickets under a murderous fire of musketry, dragged the enemy out of his works at some points, and drove him from them at others. The troops opposed to them were the most celebrated for obstinate fighting of any division of the Rebel army. * * * * The conduct of all was gratifying to our commanding General, and the day should be remembered and celebrated by every soldier engaged in the battle.

"By order of Brigadier-General W. P. Carlin.

(Signed) "G. W. SMITH, A. A. G."

The aggregate loss of the Seventy-Fourth in this campaign was eighteen killed and eighty-eight wounded. The battle of Jonesboro' ended the Atlanta campaign. The Rebel General Hood's unexpected dash for the rear of General Sherman's army, for the purpose of cutting his communications, rendered it necessary for a movement of the National army to counteract it, and the Seventy-Fourth, with its brigade and division, counter-marched to Kingston, Georgia.

By this time several of the officers resigned and were mustered out, viz.: Colonel Given, Captains McMillen, Armstrong, and Baldwin, and Lieutenants Adams and Baldwin. The Seventy-Fourth was the last regiment to leave Kingston on the new campaign through Georgia. Thus it severed the link that connected it with the North on the 12th of November, and moved with Sherman through Georgia, arriving at Savannah without casualties, December 21, 1864. It left Savannah with the army on the 20th of January, 1865, on what was called the South Carolina campaign.

The spirits of the men of the Seventy-Fourth were buoyant. They were about to realize a long-cherished desire to bear in triumph the "Old Flag" over the "sacred soil" of South Carolina, the hot-bed and originator of all the bloody scenes through which they had passed in the preceding four years of the war. It struck its tents in the camp near Savannah, loaded the one wagon allotted to each regiment, and moved out with its corps toward Sister's Ferry. Recent heavy rains had flooded the swamps through which the road lay, making it almost impassable, and rendering it necessary to corduroy the greater part of it. The labor of so doing was so great that the corps did not reach their destination until the last day of the month. The point reached was about forty-five miles above Savannah, where the river was much swollen and nearly three miles wide. Laying pontoons, and corduroying Black Swamp on the Carolina shore, occupied to the 5th of February, on which day the Fourteenth Corps was over the river, and across the first great swamp of South Carolina.

The Seventy-Fourth was at this time detailed as train-guard, a post of danger and responsibility, as the enemy were watching eagerly for a chance to capture it. Aside from the constant skirmishing, toiling through swamps, destroying railroads, etc., nothing of special interest occurred in passing through South Carolina. The North Carolina line was crossed, and the Fourteenth Corps pushed directly and rapidly toward Fayetteville, which place it entered in advance of the army on the 11th of March, driving the enemy, under Hardee, over the Cape Fear River in confusion. At this point, for the first time since leaving the Savannah River, news from the outside world was received, brought by two Government transports laden with supplies. The Rebel arsenals and work-shops at Fayetteville were destroyed; and once more the National forces turned their faces northward, again cut off from all communication. The Rebel Capital was rapidly approached, and opposition from the enemy grew stronger every day. Heavy skirmishing was encountered at Averysboro', and at Bentonville the last battle of the army was fought, March 22, 1865.

In coming up to this point the First Division of the Fourteenth Corps led the column. It kept well in advance, driving back a strong force of Rebel cavalry, until confronted by the whole Rebel army under Johnston, and within fifty yards of his intrenchments. A desperate fight ensued. The Rebels came out of their works *en masse*, to attack the audacious little band, but the veterans of the "Red Acorn" were equal to the emergency. Although driven back by overwhelming numbers, they were able to hold the Rebels in check until the main column came up and formed its line, and then advanced with it, driving the Rebels back into their works. The Rebel General, finding himself pressed on all sides, made a hasty retreat toward Raleigh, leaving his dead and wounded in our hands. From this field of victory the National army moved directly to Goldsboro', arriving at that place on the 23d day of March. Making a halt of ten days, for clothing, rations, ammunition, etc., the regiment and division again moved in pursuit of the enemy, who were then rapidly retreating. On the morning of the 13th of April the First Division, Brigadier-General C. C. Wolcott, being in the advance, took peaceable possession of Raleigh, the Capital of North Carolina. Before this time the glorious news of Lee's surrender had been received, and now the Rebel General Johnston begged permission to surrender his army to Sherman.

The Twenty-Third Corps was left in North Carolina, and the Fourteenth, Fifteenth, and Twentieth Corps were at once started toward home *via* Richmond and Washington, by two routes. The Fifteenth and Seventeenth were to march to Richmond *via* Petersburg; the Fourteenth and Twentieth on a route farther to the west, *via* Oxford, Boydton, and Nottoway C. H. These two corps were to march on parallel roads. On the 30th of April the friendly race to Richmond began. The First Division, under Brigadier-General C. C. Wolcott, was the victor, arriving on the bank of the James River at Manchester, opposite Richmond, on the morning of May 7th, having averaged thirty-two miles per day. The Seventy-Fourth was the third regiment to arrive on the bank of the river, where they stacked arms, with but *one* man absent from the ranks. Thus ended what, in the language of Major-General Hitchcock, "is the most wonderful march on record, and exhibited in these veterans of many battles unparalleled powers of endurance in marching." On the arrival of all the troops, on the 11th of May, the march to Washington began. In passing through the Rebel Capital the men of the Seventy-Fourth who had been prisoners in Libby, Castle Thunder, and Belle Isle, pointed out to their comrades the places they occupied. Washington was reached on the 23d of May, 1865.

This was the first time the Seventy-Fourth had been at Washington as a regiment, and but few of its members had ever been there before. The soldiers were tired, and the three days before the review were spent in cleaning their guns and accouterments, and in necessary rest. Before nine A. M. of the 24th of May the regiment had marched five miles, and was in its place in the column for review. This was a proud day to the veterans of the Seventy-Fourth. They had seen the rebellion crushed—their record during the war was without a stain. They could look back upon Kentucky, Tennessee, Georgia, South and North Carolina, with all their cities and towns, brought back into the Union by the prowess of themselves and their comrades of the armies of the Cumberland and Tennessee.

A few days after the review the soldiers of the Fourteenth Corps were formed in line to meet their old commander, Major-General George H. Thomas, whose duties had called him on a visit to the Capital. The men of this corps had learned, under his long and faithful leadership, to love and trust him. As the brave old veteran rode through their serried lines he betrayed the emotions of a warm and tender heart, and received their heartiest cheers.

The Western troops were sent to Louisville, Kentucky, under command of Major-General John A. Logan, for muster-out. The Seventy-Fourth traveled by railroad to Parkersburg, and from thence by boat down the Ohio River to Louisville, where it arrived on the 20th day of

June. On the 4th day of July the troops were formed by brigade for the last time, to meet and receive the final farewell of their trusted and honored chief, Major-General Wm. T. Sherman, whose fortunes they had followed to the very end with firm and unshaken confidence.

The muster-out rolls of the Seventy-Fourth were made out, bearing date July 10, 1865, and signed by the mustering-officer of the First Division, and on the 11th of July the regiment received the farewell addresses and thanks of their corps, division, and brigade commanders, and the warm and affectionate good-by's of the members of the regiments with which they had served so long, and started for Camp Dennison, Ohio, on the 11th of July. The friends of the regiment at home wished to give it a reception before the men were disbanded, and permission was granted them to go to Xenia on the 16th of July for that purpose. An immense crowd was gathered in the little city. Congratulatory addresses were delivered, and tables loaded with all the choicest delicacies were spread by the fair daughters of Xenia. Boquets and wreaths of flowers were profusely showered through the ranks. Everything was done that could in any way express the unbounded joy and gratitude of fathers, mothers, wives, sisters, and friends.

On the 17th of July the regiment returned to Camp Dennison, and on the 18th received pay and final discharge-papers. That evening the veteran Seventy-Fourth Ohio Regiment was no more. The parting of these veterans was a sad one. Nearly four years' service had made them as brothers, and as they turned toward their homes it was no slight sorrow that was mingled with their joy. At the closing scene the thoughts of many naturally reverted to those comrades who did not return—whose bones were left to bleach on the far-off battle-fields of the South. The remains of some have since been carefully gathered up and deposited in the different National Cemeteries, while others have been brought by loving hands and buried with their people at home:

"Rest on, embalmed and sainted dead,
Dear as the blood ye gave;
No traitor's footsteps e'er shall tread
The herbage o'er your grave:
Nor shall your glory be forgot
While Fame her record keeps,
For Honor mourns the hallowed spot
Where loyal valor sleeps."

At the outset the Seventy-Fourth was noted for being commanded by a well-known Methodist minister and popular orator. Between him and the Lieutenant-Colonel a coolness sprang up, which promised to lead to injurious results. So handsome, however, was Colonel Moody's conduct at Stone River, that, on the field, the Lieutenant-Colonel dashed up to him and held out his hand, saying he could not remain at variance with so gallant an officer.

75th REGIMENT OHIO VOLUNTEER INFANTRY.

ROSTER. THREE YEARS' SERVICE.

RANK.	NAME.	DATE OF RANK.	COM. ISSUED.	REMARKS.
Colonel	NAT. C. McLEAN	Sept. 18, 1861	Jan. 11, 1862	Appointed Brig. Gen. by Pres't. Nov. 29, 1862.
Do.	R. A. CONSTABLE	Dec. 3, 1862	Dec. 31, "	Resigned January 12, 1863.
Do.	ROBERT REILY	Jan. 12, 1863	March 11, 1863	Died May 5, 1863.
Do.	ANDREW L. HARRIS	May 3, "	June 10, "	Mustered out January 15, 1865.
Lt. Colonel	R. A. CONSTABLE	Dec. 18, 1861	Jan. 11, 1862	Promoted to Colonel.
Do.	ROBERT REILY	" 3, 1862	Dec. 31, "	Promoted to Colonel.
Do.	CHARLES W. FRIEND	Jan. 12, 1863	March 13, 1863	Resigned January 9, 1863.
Do.	BENJ. MORGAN	June 11, "	June 15, "	Mustered out March 15, 1865.
Major	ROBERT REILY	Sept. 18, 1861	Jan. 11, 1862	Promoted to Lieutenant-Colonel.
Do.	CHARLES W. FRIEND	Dec. 3, "	Dec. 31, "	Promoted to Lieutenant-Colonel.
Do.	ANDREW L. HARRIS	Jan. 12, 1863	March 13, 1863	Promoted to Colonel.
Do.	BENJ. MORGAN	May 3, "	June 10, "	Promoted to Lieutenant-Colonel.
Do.	GEORGE B. FOX	June 11, "	Aug. 25, "	Mustered out March 19, 1865.
Surgeon	SAMUEL HART	Jan. 11, 1862	March 24, 1862	Appointed by President May 15, 1863.
Do.	CHARLES L. WILSON	May 15, 1863	June 5, 1863	Resigned October 2, 1863.
Do.	JOHN INGRAM	Nov. 23, "	Nov. 23, "	Mustered out.
Ass't Surgeon	CHARLES L. WILSON	Dec. 28, 1861	March 24, 1862	Promoted to Surgeon.
Do.	HENRY W. OWEN	July 4, 1862	July 24, "	Honorably discharged November 28, 1862.
Do.	JOHN HILL	Nov. 5, "	Nov. 28, "	Resigned in 1863.
Do.	D. B. WREN	June 29, 1863	June 29, 1863	Resigned July 29, 1864.
Do.	JOHN A. JAYNE	Aug. 29, 1864	Aug. 29, 1864	Never mustered.
Chaplain	JOHN W. WEAKLY	Oct. 14, 1861	Oct. 14, 1861	Resigned March 24, 1863.
Captain	Charles W. Friend	Sept. 23, 1861	Jan. 11, 1862	Promoted to Major.
Do.	Horace W. Deshler	Dec. 14, "	March 24, "	Resigned January 11, 1863.
Do.	Ben Morgan	" 14, "	" 24, "	Promoted to Major.
Do.	James W. Swope	" 14, "	" 24, "	Resigned September 21, 1862.
Do.	Wm. S. Metcalf	" 16, "	" 24, "	Resigned January 11, 1863.
Do.	George Fry	" 22, "	" 24, "	Resigned June 10, 1863.
Do.	James D. Foster	" 25, "	" 24, "	Resigned December 19, 1862.
Do	Thomas M. D. Pilcher	" 25, "	" 21, "	Resigned May 15, 1862.
Do.	James A. Johnson	Dec. 30, "	June 24, "	Died September 7, 1862.
Do.	Oscar Minor	Sept. 21, "	Dec. 2, "	Appointed Captain by the President.
Do.	Theodore K. Keckeler	" 7, 1862	Nov. 12, "	Resigned January 2, 1863.
Do.	Andrew L. Harris	Nov. 9, 1861	" 14, "	Promoted to Major.
Do.	Oscar Deshler	May 15, 1862	" 14, "	Honorably discharged January 18, 1863.
Do.	George B. Fox	Dec. 3, "	Jan. 20, 1863	Promoted to Major.
Do.	John C. S. Miller	" 19, "	" 20, "	Resigned February 19, 1863.
Do.	Jasper N. Watkins	Jan. 12, 1863	" 20, "	Honorably discharged October 2, 1863.
Do.	Henry L. Morey	" 11, "	March 13, "	Mustered out.
Do.	Mahlon Briggs	" 18, "	" 13, "	Killed July 4, 1863.
Do.	James Mulharen	Feb. 19	June 10, "	Killed July 1, 1863.
Do.	Elias R. Monfort	Jan. 12, "	July 10, "	Honorably discharged December 29, 1863.
Do.	Phineas B. Hascall	June 2, "	Aug. 25, "	Mustered out.
Do.	Thomas Wheeler	" 11, "	" 25, "	Deceased.
Do.	Wm. J. Rannells	" 10, "	" 25, "	
Do.	David McCully	July 1, "	" 25, "	Deceased June 15, 1864.
Do.	Joseph H. Potts	April 13, 1864	April 13, 1864	Mustered out as 2d Lieut. January 17, 1865.
Do.	David B. Caldwell	" 13, "	" 13, "	Mustered out as 2d Lieut. January 17, 1865.
Do.	Joseph B. Alters	" 13, "	" 13, "	Mustered out March 16, 1865.
Do.	Thomas H. Davenport	" 13, "	" 13, "	Mustered out March 12, 1865.
Do.	David C. Ballentine	Jan. 10, "	Jan. 10, "	Mustered out.
Do.	Oscar D. Ladley	April 13, "	April 13, "	Mustered out.
Do.	Alonzo Ford	Oct. 12, "	Oct. 12, "	Mustered out.
Do.	James Stover	Feb. 6, 1865	Feb. 6, 1865	Declined promotion.
Do.	Daniel J. Flemming	July 10, "	Sept. 4, "	Mustered out as 1st Lieut. Sept. 22, 1864.
1st Lieutenant	James A. Johnson	Oct. 10, 1861	Oct. 10, 1861	Promoted to Captain.
Do.	Oscar Deshler	Dec. 14, "	March 24, 1862	Promoted to Captain.
Do.	Harvey Crampton	" 14, "	" 24, "	Resigned.
Do.	Franklin J. Raikes	" 14, "	" 24, "	Resigned October 31, 1862.
Do.	Ephraim C. Wayman	" 14, "	" 24, "	Resigned March 24, 1862.
Do.	Judson W. Caldwell	" 14, "	" 24, "	Resigned October 6, 1862.
Do.	Abraham W. Thomas	" 14, "	" 24, "	Resigned October 6, 1862.
Do.	Joseph M. Goodspeed	" 14, "	" 24, "	Resigned October 6, 1862.
Do.	Wm. G. Ross	" 14, "	" 24, "	Resigned September 21, 1862.
Do.	Henry B. Lucy	Oct. 20, "	" 24, "	Promoted by President September 12, 1863.
Do.	George W. Hopper	Dec. 18, "	" 24, "	Resigned February 9, 1863.
Do.	Benj. F. Metcalf	March 24, 1862	May 5, "	Resigned January 11, 1863.
Do.	Henry L. Morey	May 15, "	June 24, "	Promoted to Captain.
Do.	Elias R. Monfort	" 15, "	" 24, "	Promoted to Captain.
Do.	Theodore K. Keckeler	Dec. 30, 1861	Nov. 12, "	Promoted to Captain.
Do.	Oscar Minor	Nov. 9, "	" 14, "	Promoted to Captain.
Do.	George B. Fox	Sept. 21, 1862	" 14, "	Promoted to Captain.
Do.	Jasper N. Watkins	May 15, "	Dec. 31, "	Promoted to Captain.
Do.	Wm. J. Rannells	Sept. 21, "	" 31, "	Promoted to Captain.
Do.	John C. S. Miller	Oct. 6, "	" 31, "	Promoted to Captain.
Do.	Mahlon Briggs	" 6, "	" 31, "	Promoted to Captain.
Do.	Oscar D. Ladley	" 6, "	" 31, "	Promoted to Captain.
Do.	Samuel C. Ruckman	" 31, "	" 31, "	Resigned May 23, 1863.
Do.	James Mulharen	Dec. 3, "	Jan. 20, 1863	Promoted to Captain.
Do.	George A. Russell	Jan. 12, 1863	" 20, "	Discharged as 2d Lieutenant December 18, 1863
Do.	Phineas B. Hascall	Dec. 19, 1862	Feb. 10, "	Promoted to Captain.
Do.	Thomas Wheeler	Jan. 11, 1863	March 13, "	Promoted to Captain.
Do.	Jacob W. Gano	Feb. 9, "	" 6, "	Honorably discharged November 6, 1863.
Do.	Thomas H. Davenport	Sept. 12, "	" 13, "	Promoted to Captain.
Do.	David McCully	Jan. 11, "	" 13, "	Promoted to Captain.

RANK.	NAME.	DATE OF RANK.	COM. ISSUED.	REMARKS.
1st Lieutenant	Wm. H. H. Dumont	Jan. 12, 1863	June 15, 1863	Revoked.
Do.	Joseph H. Potts	" 12, "	Aug. 25, "	Promoted to Captain.
Do.	David H. Miller	May 21, "	" 25, "	Honorably discharged January 22, 1864.
Do.	David C. Ballentine	June 10, "	" 25, "	Promoted to Captain.
Do.	David B. Caldwell	" 10, "	" 25, "	Promoted to Captain.
Do.	Joseph B. Alters	" 11, "	" 25, "	Promoted to Captain.
Do.	James A. Crezett	" 2, "	" 25, "	Mustered out.
Do.	James A. Mendenhall	April 13, 1864	April 13, 1864	Mustered out March 11, 1865.
Do.	Resin F. Hall	" 13, "	" 13, "	Mustered out March 12, 1865.
Do.	James F. Kempton	" 13, "	" 13, "	Mustered out March 11, 1865.
Do.	Isaiah C. Price	" 13, "	" 13, "	Mustered out.
Do.	Barney Sprung	" 13, "	" 13, "	Mustered out March 12, 1865.
Do.	Conrad Bryant	" 13, "	" 13, "	Discharged April 16, 1864.
Do.	Mark A. Knowlton	" 13, "	" 13, "	Mustered out.
Do.	Daniel J. Cline	June 27, "	June 27, "	Mustered out March 17, 1865.
Do.	Martin V. Strader	" 27, "	" 27, "	Died July, 1864.
Do.	James M. Malambra	" 27, "	" 27, "	Mustered out.
Do.	James Stover	" 27, "	" 27, "	Promoted to Captain.
Do.	Daniel J. Flemming	" 27, "	" 27, "	Promoted to Captain.
Do.	Alphonso C. Davis	Feb. 6, 1865	Feb. 6, 1865	
2d Lieutenant	Elias R. Monfort	Oct. 8, 1861	March 24, 1862	Promoted to 1st Lieutenant.
Do.	Henry L. Morey	" 18, "	" 24, "	Promoted to 1st Lieutenant.
Do.	James W. Whaley	" 23, "	" 24, "	Dismissed November 26, 1862.
Do.	George B. Fox	Nov. 5, "	" 24, "	Promoted to 1st Lieutenant.
Do.	Jasper N. Watkins	Dec. 14, "	" 24, "	Promoted to 1st Lieutenant.
Do.	Benj. F. Metcalf	" 16, "	" 24, "	Promoted to 1st Lieutenant.
Do.	Wm. J. Rannells	" 22, "	" 24, "	Promoted to 1st Lieutenant.
Do.	John C. S. Miller	" 25, "	" 24, "	Promoted to 1st Lieutenant.
Do.	Mahlon Briggs	March 24, "	May 5, "	Promoted to 1st Lieutenant.
Do.	Oscar D. Ladley	May 15, "	Oct. 22, "	Promoted to 1st Lieutenant.
Do.	John H. Fessenden	Oct. 4, "	Nov. 12, "	Honorably discharged November 22, 1862.
Do.	James Mulharen	Nov. 9, "	" 11, "	Promoted to 1st Lieutenant.
Do.	Samuel C. Ruckman	May 15, "	" 14, "	Promoted to 1st Lieutenant.
Do.	Thomas Wheeler	Sept. 21, "	" 14, "	Promoted to 1st Lieutenant.
Do.	David B. Caldwell	Oct. 6, "	" 14, "	Promoted to 1st Lieutenant.
Do.	Thomas H. Davenport	Nov. 26, "	Dec. 31, "	Promoted to 1st Lieutenant.
Do.	Wm. H. H. Dumont	Aug. 1, "	" 31, "	Resigned May 25, 1863.
Do.	Phineas B. Hascall	Sept. 21, "	" 31, "	Promoted to 1st Lieutenant.
Do.	David McCully	Oct. 6, 1862	Jan. 20, 1863	Promoted to 1st Lieutenant.
Do.	Alonzo Ford	" 6, "	" 20, "	Promoted to 1st Lieutenant.
Do.	Caleb Parent	Jan. 1, 1863	June 10, "	Commission returned.
Do.	George A. Russell	" 31, "	" 10, "	Promoted to 1st Lieutenant.
Do.	Joseph H. Potts	Dec. 3, 1862	March 13, "	Promoted to 1st Lieutenant.
Do.	David C. Ballentine	March 30, 1863	May 12, "	Promoted to 1st Lieutenant.
Do.	James A. Crezett	Dec. 18, 1862	Feb. 10, "	Promoted to 1st Lieutenant.
Do.	David H. Miller	Sept. 12, 1863	March 13, "	Promoted to 1st Lieutenant.
Do.	James A. Mendenhall	Jan. 11, "	" 13, "	Promoted to 1st Lieutenant.
Do.	Resin F. Hall	" 12, "	June 10, "	Promoted to 1st Lieutenant.
Do.	Emmanuel M. Shultz	" 12, "	Aug. 25, "	Deceased.
Do.	James F. Kempton	" 12, "	" 25, "	Promoted to 1st Lieutenant.
Do.	Isaiah C. Price	Feb. 19, "	" 25, "	Promoted to 1st Lieutenant.
Do.	Barney Sprung	Jan. 12, "	" 25, "	Promoted to 1st Lieutenant.
Do.	Conrad Bryant	May 23, "	" 25, "	Promoted to 1st Lieutenant
Do.	Mark A. Knowlton	June 2, "	" 23, "	Promoted to 1st Lieutenant.
Do.	Daniel J. Cline	Nov. 17, "	April 20, 1864	Promoted to 1st Lieutenant.
Do.	Martin V. Strader	July 13, 1864	July 13, "	Promoted to 1st Lieutenant.
Do.	James O. James	Aug. 19, "	Aug. 19, "	Mustered out.
Do.	James M. Townsend	Feb. 6, 1865	Feb. 6, 1865	

SEVENTY-FIFTH OHIO VOLUNTEER INFANTRY.

THE SEVENTY-FIFTH OHIO was organized at Camp John McLean, near Cincinnati, on the 18th day of December, 1861. N. C. McLean, son of the late Judge John McLean (afterward promoted to Brigadier-General), was commissioned Colonel; R. A. Constable, of Athens, Ohio, Lieutenant-Colonel, and Robert Reilly, of Cincinnati, Major.

Western Virginia was its first field of duty. The regiment arrived at Grafton on the 29th day of January, 1862, and immediately went into camp. On the 17th day of February it left the Baltimore and Ohio Railroad, and on the 1st day of March joined General Milroy's brigade at Huttonsville, at the foot of Cheat Mountain. This march fairly initiated the men into the hardships and privations of a soldier's life, as it was made over the most wretched roads and in the most wretched weather.

On the 6th day of April, 1862, General Milroy put his brigade in motion toward Staunton. Owing to the terrible condition of the roads over Cheat and Alleghany Mountains, the march was slow, and the advance was finally compelled to halt at Monterey C. H. until the rear regiments and transportation could be extricated from the deep and sticky mud of the mountain roads. While at this point, on the 12th of April, 1862, the enemy made a spirited attack with the purpose of driving Milroy back to Huttonsville. The Seventy-Fifth being in the advance, received the Rebels in gallant style, and punished them so severely that they seemed to be fully convinced that General Milroy meant to hold his ground. For full two hours the fighting was very severe, and the enemy, finding that Milroy was constantly gaining ground, concluded to give way and leave the road clear to the "Old War Eagle," as the men styled General Milroy. In this engagement the Seventy-Fifth displayed bravery, and gave evidence of the fine discipline to which it had attained under the teachings of the officers of the regiment.

A few days thereafter General Milroy led his forces over the Shenandoah Mountains, near Buffalo Gap, with his rear threatening Staunton. Stonewall Jackson, who was then in front of Banks, immediately turned his attention to Milroy, compelling that General to fall back over the Shenandoah Mountains to McDowell, a little village at the foot of Bull Pasture Mountain, where he established his head-quarters resolving to protect the stores accumulated at that place. It was a desperate resolve, as his combined force did not amount to quite three thousand men, while Jackson had near twenty thousand under his command.

On the morning of the 8th of May, 1862, Jackson appeared in force on the high grounds overlooking McDowell, exulting in his supposed ability to crush Milroy's small force before that General could retreat to a place of safety, or receive re-enforcements from General Schenck, who was then at the town of Franklin, thirty-five miles distant. General Milroy awaited the attack of the enemy until three o'clock P. M., but it was sullenly refused as the Rebels had everything to gain by the delay, while Milroy's forces had all to lose; for, if Jackson should succeed in surrounding Milroy's position, surrender would be compelled. Without hesitation, therefore, Milroy took the offensive and attacked Jackson with the Seventy-Fifth and Twenty-Fifth Ohio Infantry, opposing with them a whole division of the enemy, and persistently held their ground until dark, when, under cover of the night, Milroy retreated in the direction of Franklin. This battle was very severe for the number of National troops engaged in it. The Rebels made charge after charge, but each time were met and cut down by the continued and destructive fire of the National troops. So severe was the loss of the enemy that he reported it as the "bloodiest of the war for the number engaged, and that no prisoners were taken on either side."

The Seventy-Fifth added new laurels to its former good name, under the immediate eye of Milroy, who warmly congratulated Colonel McLean on the gallantry of his regiment.

Captain A. L. Harris was severely wounded, and eighty-seven men killed and wounded. Among the killed were Color-Sergeant E. M. Gordon, and Sergeant-Major L. L. Stewart, two brave and noble young men. The last named was a printer, and like so many others had volunteered from the purest patriotism, having left a comfortable home and a young wife whom he wedded immediately before joining the ranks.

General Milroy fell back to Franklin closely followed by Jackson. The National force, under General Schenck at Franklin, was soon joined by a division from the Army of the Potomac, and General Fremont the commander of the Mountain Department. For ten days the enemy tried Fremont's lines in force, each attack resulting in brisk skirmishing, but slight loss. Finally Jackson left Franklin and returned to the Shenandoah Valley, encountering and driving General Bank's forces before him in the direction of Harper's Ferry.

General Fremont was ordered to get, if possible, in the rear of Jackson's army, and prevent him from returning up the Valley. With that purpose General Fremont crossed the Shenandoah at Strasburg, but Jackson was too fleet for him and had already passed that point. Fremont pursued and overtook him at Cross Keys, on the 10th of June, 1862, when Jackson stood at bay, and a brisk but decisive battle was fought. General Schenck's Ohio Brigade, consisting of the Fifty-Fifth, Seventy-Third, Seventy-Fifth, and Eighty-Second Ohio Infantry Regiments were, during a portion of the day, in reserve, and were not called into action until late in the afternoon.

A change of commanders occurred immediately after this battle. General Fremont was relieved, his army reorganized and named Army of Virginia, Major-General Pope commanding. In this organization General Schenck was assigned to a division, and Colonel McLean, of the Seventy-Fifth, to his brigade.

The next affair in which the Seventy-Fifth faced the enemy was at Cedar Mountain, Virginia, on the 8th of August, 1862, but as Bank's corps did nearly all the fighting before General Sigel's forces arrived on the ground, the loss of the Seventy-Fifth was slight. Jackson fell back beyond the Rapidan, where he remained until Lee withdrew his forces from Richmond and opened the campaign which closed with the battle of Antietam. As soon as the advance of Lee's army reached Jackson he again took the offensive. General Pope fell back beyond the Rappahannock and took position to prevent Jackson from crossing. For a week the north bank of the river was closely watched, and at every point that Jackson attempted to cross he found himself too strongly opposed to succeed. During this week the Seventy-Fifth was frequently engaged, and at Freeman's Ford lost heavily. Jackson finally flanked Pope, got in his rear, burnt his wagon-trains and three trains of cars, and was again attacked by General Pope at Groveton, near the old Bull Run battle-field on the evening of the 28th of August, 1862. The fighting was very severe. The Seventy-Fifth was hotly pressed by the enemy on the afternoon of the 30th of August, when Longstreet hurled his whole corps against the left, made weak by the withdrawal of Porter's corps. For a time the fighting was bloody in the extreme, and the Seventy-Fifth lost heavily, having one color-bearer killed and another mortally wounded, and twenty-one men killed and ninety-two wounded. All the killed, and a portion of the wounded, were left on the field where they fell in the hands of the enemy, when the National army fell back on Centerville. It was observed, as an evidence of the severity of the fire, that ninety odd shots took effect on the colors of the Seventy-Fifth during this battle.

The National army fell back to Washington, and from thence was led by General McClellan in pursuit of the Rebel army in the direction of Maryland. General Sigel's corps (in which was the Seventy-Fifth) was left encamped on Arlington Hights, for the protection of the Capital from any sudden dash that might be made from the direction of Richmond.

When the Army of the Potomac returned from the battle-fields of South Mountain and Antietam, Sigel's corps again joined it, and was present, but not engaged, at Fredericksburg. At that place, it will be recollected, the Eleventh and Twelfth Corps formed the grand reserve division of the army under Siegel. After the second attempt on Fredericksburg, the Eleventh Corps went into camp at Brook's Station, Virginia, and spent their time in drills and reviews. President Lincoln reviewed it while there in the spring of 1863.

Nothing of importance occurred in the history of the Seventy-Fifth, until the 2d of May, 1863, at Chancellorsville. The Eleventh Corps (now under command of General Howard) broke camp on the 27th of April, and, on the 30th, took up its position on the extreme right flank of the Army of the Potomac at Chancellorsville. The history of that battle is well known. The Eleventh Corps surprised and overwhelmed by the impetuous Rebels, fell back in almost complete demoralization. Yet McLean's Ohio Brigade, a part of that corps, merited the highest praise for the bravery of its officers and men, and the cool, steady manner in which it received the enemy under the most trying circumstances. Owing to the peculiar formation of the line and nature of the ground at the point of the attack, but few troops could open on the enemy at a time. The Seventy-Fifth changed front under this severe fire, and received the enemy in the most gallant manner. But the odds were too great, and to keep from being surrounded and captured, the brigade fell back in the direction of the Chancellorsville House. In the short space of half an hour the Seventy-Fifth lost one hundred and fifty men killed and wounded. It was in this battle that the brave and patriotic officer, Colonel Robert Reilly, of Cincinnati, fell mortally wounded and died on the field. At the same time fell Adjutant Jacob Gano and Captain Mathias, both dangerously wounded.

After this battle the Seventy-Fifth returned to its old camp near Brooks's Station, where it remained until about the 12th June following, when it again took the field with its brigade and division, and formed a part of the forces confronting the enemy at Gettysburg on the 1st of July, 1863. The regiment was again placed in the reserve division, but when the battle became general it was thrown to the front, and, under command of Colonel Harris, made a successful charge upon a ledge of rock held by the enemy. This position was not gained, however, without serious loss. Just at this time the head of Ewell's corps arrived from York, and made an effort to get in the rear of Howard, who was now commanding the First and Eleventh Corps, all of the National army that were then on the ground. This caused Howard to fall back hastily to the town of Gettysburg, rendering the situation of the Seventy-Fifth very embarrassing, as all connection with the brigade was severed and no chance left to receive orders. As a dernier resort the regiment fell back, though not without adding greatly to its list of killed and wounded.

The regiment was under fire every day of the battle until its termination. Of sixteen officers that went into the engagement, Captains Mulhaner and Briggs, and Lieutenant Wheeler were killed; Lieutenant-Colonel Benjamin Morgan, Captains W. J. Rannells and L. R. Montfort, and Lieutenants D. Miller and George Russell dangerously, and Colonel A. L. Harris and Alonzo Force severely wounded; and Lieutenants W. D. McCaulley, Caldwell, Potts, and Mendenhall, taken prisoners; and out of two hundred and ninety-two enlisted men, sixty-three were killed, one hundred and six wounded, and thirty-four prisoners. The loss in other regiments of the brigade was about equal in proportion to that of the Seventy-Fifth.

On the 6th of August, 1863, the Ohio Brigade was sent to Charleston, South Carolina, where it arrived on the 12th, and on the 18th went into the trenches on Morris Island, and remained there until after the fall of Forts Wagner and Gregg, which took place on the morning of the 7th of September following. The duty on this Island was terribly severe, owing to the extreme heat and the impossibility of even temporary relief; the hot sun beating pitilessly on the heads and bodies of the devoted troops. Large numbers died from this cause. Disease killed more than the enemy's shells. In fact, only two men were killed and five wounded of the Seventy-Fifth during the siege.

Soon after the fall of Morris Island the Seventy-Fifth, together with its brigade, was sent down to Folly Island, where it remained until the 22d of February, 1864 (just after the battle of Olustee). It was then sent to Jacksonville, Florida, and shortly thereafter mounted. From that time the regiment was designated in orders as the Seventy-Fifth Mounted Infantry, and performed all the duties of a regular cavalry regiment.

On the 25th of April, 1864, General Birney, commanding the District of Florida, sent Colonel Harris with the Seventy-Fifth on a raid to the head-waters of the St. John and Kissinnee Rivers, for the purpose of breaking up a system of blockade-running carried on in the Rebel cause along the Indian River. The regiment proceeded as far as Lake Harmer when it was divided into two parts; one division was sent to Smyrna, on the coast, where it captured two schooners loaded with cotton, and sent them, together with their crew, safely to St. Augustine. The remainder of the regiment continued their march southward, captured and destroyed five hundred bales of cotton, destroyed three salt furnaces and burned a large lot of resin, tar, and turpentine stored by the Rebels at Sand Point, on the Indian River, from which place blockade-runners received and carried it to Nassau, New Providence. From this point the detachment made its way to the head-waters of the Kissinnee River, and captured a large lot of cattle driven there by the Rebel owners to prevent them from falling into the hands of the National army. The detachment brought in about five thousand head of fine beef cattle, an article just then much needed by the National forces in Florida. This was accomplished without the loss of a man.

The regiment had scarcely time to rest and recruit its horses, when it was again dispatched to the head-waters of the St. John, for the purpose of protecting the Unionists of that locality from the barbarous cruelty of the Rebel cavalry. This expedition, though made with great rapidity, was only partially successful. Rapidly following this, the Seventy-Fifth was ordered to Jacksonville to assist in repelling a threatened attack of the enemy. On its arrival, the regiment was placed on outpost duty, and hardly a day passed without a skirmish with the enemy—the Second Florida Cavalry—from whom a number of prisoners were taken, but not without loss on the part of the Seventy-Fifth.

On the 12th of July, 1864, General Birney, tired of the constant and, in the main, fruitless skirmishes with the enemy, determined to get in their rear, and, if possible, force them to abandon their strong position at Baldwin Crossing of the Florida Railroad by the Cedar Keys Railroad. The Seventy-Fifth was detached to do the work. It was sent up the St. John's River in steamboats to Black River, and there secretly disembarked and marched across the country to a point where the Florida Railroad crosses the St. Mary's River. Here it burned the railroad bridge and a long range of trestle-work, and on the night of the 16th of July, 1864, burned two thousand barrels of resin, near the enemy's lines. The flanking movement proved entirely successful. The Rebels abandoned their works, and on the 17th of July the Seventy-Fifth took undisputed possession. This point being of great importance to the enemy, General Birney determined to hold it, and accordingly brought up his infantry force, while the enemy took up his position on the bank of the St. Mary's, a distance of only eight miles. Here, again, the Second Florida Rebel Cavalry tried its strength with the Seventy-Fifth in almost daily skirmishes, with slight loss to either side, excepting in the expenditure of horseflesh and excessive fatigue of constant duty night and day.

On the 10th of August, 1864, General Birney was relieved as commander of the District of Florida, by General Hatch. That General, as it turned out unfortunately for the Seventy-Fifth, sent it on an expedition to the rear of the enemy and into the interior of Florida. The horses of the Seventy-Fifth, by constant duty, without proper feed, were in bad condition for such service—so much so that but two hundred of the command could be mounted at all. With this little band Colonel Harris started from Baldwin on the morning of the 14th of August, 1864; at daylight succeeded in getting in the rear of the enemy's right flank, took a few prisoners, but was met by a much superior force, compelling him to ride night and day in order to keep out of the enemy's hands. On the morning of the 17th of August the regiment halted at Gainesville to rest, thinking it had distanced the enemy by several miles during the night. Before the regiment was ready to move the enemy attacked with a force of about fourteen hundred men. No chance was left but to fight, as retreat was impossible. The fight was kept up for two hours and a half, until the ammunition of the Seventy-Fifth giving out, no alternative was left but to surrender or cut their way through the enemy. The latter was tried, and partially succeeded, about half of the command getting through, and by swift marches reached Jacksonville. The Seventy-Fifth lost in this affair fourteen men killed, and two commissioned officers and about thirty men wounded, who, together with about sixty men and twelve officers, were taken prisoners, nearly all of whom were held by the enemy until the spring of 1865.

On the 26th of September, 1864, the Seventy-Fifth was dispatched on a secret expedition to the head-waters of the St. John's River, and, on the night of the 29th, captured an entire company of the Second Florida Cavalry, together with their horses, arms, etc., and returned with them to St. Augustine, without the loss of a man.

In October, 1864, companies A, B, and C, were sent to Columbus, Ohio, for muster-out, and in November companies D, G, and F, were also sent to the same place for the same purpose, their term of service having expired.

On the 8th of December, 1864, Colonel Harris, with the four remaining companies of his regiment and the One Hundred and Seventh, was sent from Jacksonville, Florida, to Hilton Head, South Carolina; and from thence to join General Hatch's forces, then essaying to make a diversion in favor of General Sherman by threatening the Charleston and Savannah Railroad.

After the fall of Savannah the Seventy-Fifth was sent to Jacksonville, Florida, to prepare the muster-out rolls and organize the veterans and recruits into a Veteran detachment. This was accomplished on the 15th of January, 1865, and thereafter the Seventy-Fifth Ohio was known as the Veteran Battalion, under the command of Captain W. J. Rannells. This battalion performed valuable and arduous service at District Head-quarters, Jacksonville, Florida; and during the summer of 1865 it was stationed at Tallahassa. In August of 1865 it was mustered out of the service, thus ending the career of the Seventy-Fifth Ohio, and completing a record alike honorable to its members and to their State.

76th REGIMENT OHIO VOLUNTEER INFANTRY.

ROSTER, THREE YEARS' SERVICE.

RANK.	NAME.	DATE OF RANK.	COM. ISSUED.	REMARKS.
Colonel	CHARLES R. WOODS	Oct. 12, 1861	Oct. 12, 1861	Promoted to Brig. Gen. August 22, 1863.
Do.	WM. B. WOODS	Aug. 22, 1863	Sept. 9, 1863	Promoted to Brigadier-General.
Do.	EDWARD BRIGGS	July 13, 1865	July 13, 1865	Mustered out as Lieut. Col. with regiment.
Lt. Colonel	WM. B. WOODS	Nov. 4, 1861	March 22, 1862	Promoted to Colonel.
Do.	WILLARD WARNER	Sept. 10, 1863	Dec. 14, 1863	Discharged for promotion October 12, 1864.
Do.	EDWARD BRIGGS	Oct. 12, 1864	Oct. 12, 1864	Promoted to Colonel.
Do.	REASON C. STRONG	July 13, 1865	July 13, 1865	Mustered out with regiment as Major.
Major	WILLARD WARNER	Dec. 28, 1861	March 24, 1862	Promoted to Lieutenant-Colonel.
Do.	EDWARD BRIGGS	March 10, 1864	" 10, 1864	Promoted to Lieutenant-Colonel.
Do.	REASON C. STRONG	June 16, 1865	June 16, 1865	Promoted to Lieutenant-Colonel.
Do.	JEHIEL F. WINTRODE	July 13, "	July 13, "	Declined; commission returned.
Surgeon	CHARLES R. PIERCE	Jan. 9, 1862	March 24, 1862	Died January 28, 1863.
Do.	ANDREW SABIN	Feb. 16, 1863	Feb. 16, 1863	Mustered out with regiment.
Ass't Surgeon	THOMAS B. HOOD	Nov. 6, 1861	March 24, 1862	Resigned January 26, 1863.
Do.	ROBERT P. MUENCHER	Aug. 21, 1862	Sept. 4, "	Died October 2, 1862.
Do.	GEORGE E. SMITH	Dec. 23, "	Feb. 10, 1863	Resigned January 4, 1863.
Do.	S. C. MENDENHALL	Feb. 16, 1863	" 16, "	Absent with leave at muster out of regiment.
Do.	RALPH E. FORTE	June 18, "	June 18, "	
Chaplain	JOHN W. McCARTY	Dec. 17, 1861	Dec. 18, 1861	Resigned October 3, 1862.
Captain	Thadeus Lemert	Nov. 1, "	Feb. 6, 1862	Killed January 11, 1863.
Do.	James M. Scott	" 12, "	" 6, "	Resigned September 30, 1862.
Do.	Levi P. Coman	Dec. 4, "	" 6, "	Resigned January 21, 1863. [War.
Do.	Charles H. Kibler	" 18, "	" 6, "	Resigned May 23,'63; dis. removed by Sec'y of
Do.	Joseph C. Wehrle	" 16, "	" 6, "	Mustered out.
Do.	Strew. M. Emmons	" 18, "	" 6, "	Resigned January 21, 1863.
Do.	James Stewart	Jan. 7, 1862	" 6, "	Mustered out December 23, 1865.
Do.	Jerome N. Rappleyed	" 24, "	" 6, "	Resigned October 1, 1862.
Do.	Edward Briggs	Nov. 27, 1861	" 6, "	Promoted to Major.
Do.	James M. Jay	Feb. 7, 1862	March 24, "	Honorably discharged March 21, 1864.
Do.	Charles H. Kibler	July 22, "	July 22, "	Re-instated; promoted.
Do.	Ira B. French	Sept. 30, "	Nov. 28, "	Killed November 27, 1863.
Do.	Beverly W. Lemert	Oct. 1, "	Dec. 31, "	Mustered out.
Do.	James M. Blackburn	Jan. 11, 1863	Feb. 19, 1863	Honorably discharged October 11, 1864.
Do.	Jehiel F. Wintrode	March 10, 1864	March 10, 1864	Pro. to Maj.; declined; must. out with regt.
Do.	Freeman Morrison	" 10, "	" 10, "	Murdered at Nashville. [1864.
Do.	Charles D. Miller	" 10, "	" 10, "	Mustered out at expiration of service Nov. 18,
Do.	Reason C. Strong	" 10, "	" 10, "	Promoted to Major.
Do.	Richard W. Burt	" 11, "	" 11, "	Mustered out with regiment.
Do.	Frederick H. Wilson	April 13, "	April 13, "	Resigned May 31, 1865.
Do.	Zebulon P. Evans	Jan. 18, 1865	Jan. 18, 1865	Mustered out with regiment.
Do.	John J. Metzgar	" 18, "	" 18, "	Mustered out with regiment.
Do.	George W. Jeremy	" 18, "	" 18, "	Mustered out with regiment.
Do.	Jacob A. Jury	" 18, "	" 18, "	Mustered out with regiment.
Do.	John Hiser	Feb. 10, "	Feb. 10, "	Mustered out with regiment.
Do.	Carey M. Marriott	June 16, "	June 16, "	Mustered out with regiment.
Do.	Frank Brackett	" 15, "	" 15, "	Mustered out with regiment as 1st Lieut.
Do.	Jarius G. Evans	July 13, "	July 13, "	Mustered out with regiment as 1st Lieut.
Do.	Robert B. Williamson	" 13, "	" 13, "	Mustered out with regiment as 1st Lieut.
1st Lieutenant	Beverly W. Lemert	Nov. 1, 1861	Feb. 6, 1862	Promoted to Captain.
Do.	Ira B. French	" 12, "	" 6, "	Promoted to Captain.
Do.	John S. Anderson	Dec. 4, "	" 6, "	Died January 24, 1863.
Do.	Newton Hempstead	" 16, "	" 6, "	Resigned March 27, 1862.
Do.	Michael P. Maher	" 16, "	" 6, "	Honorably discharged August 7, 1862.
Do.	James H. H. Hunter	" 18, "	" 6, "	Resigned January 30, 1863.
Do.	Jehiel F. Wintrode	Jan. 7, 1862	" 6, "	Promoted to Captain.
Do.	Jerome N. Rappleyed	Nov. 25, 1861	" 6, "	Promoted to Captain.
Do.	John A. Dill	Jan. 24, 1862	" 6, "	Deceased.
Do.	James M. Blackburn	Nov. 27, 1861	" 12, "	Promoted to Captain.
Do.	Henry D. Wright	Oct. 14, "	March 24, "	Resigned February 22, 1864.
Do.	S. Sylvester Wells	Jan. 21, 1862	" 24, "	Resigned May 30, 1863.
Do.	David R. Kelley	Feb. 7, "	" 24, "	Dismissed.
Do.	John R. Miller	March 27, "	April 14, "	Killed November 27, 1863.
Do.	Charles D. Miller	May 30, "	June 24, "	Promoted to Captain.
Do.	Simeon B. Wall	" 31, "	Sept. 16, "	Killed November 27, 1863.
Do.	Charles Luther	Aug. 7, "	Nov. 28, "	Died May 24, 1863.
Do.	John H. Hardgrove	Sept. 30, "	" 28, "	Declined; commission returned.
Do.	Reason C. Strong	" 30, "	Dec. 31, "	Promoted to Captain.
Do.	Freeman Morrison	Oct. 1, "	" 31, "	Promoted to Captain.
Do.	Richard W. Burt	Jan. 11, 1863	Feb. 19, 1863	Promoted to Captain.
Do.	Frederick H. Wilson	March 10, 1864	March 10, 1864	Promoted to Captain.
Do.	Zebulon P. Evans	" 10, "	" 10, "	Promoted to Captain.
Do.	Wm. H. Darlington	" 10, "	" 10, "	Discharged December 29, 1864.
Do.	John J. Metzgar	" 10, "	" 10, "	Promoted to Captain.
Do.	George W. Jeremy	" 10, "	" 10, "	Promoted to Captain.
Do.	Jacob A. Jury	" 10, "	" 10, "	Promoted to Captain.
Do.	John Hiser	" 10, "	" 10, "	Promoted to Captain.
Do.	Carey M. Marriott	" 10, "	" 10, "	Promoted to Captain.
Do.	Jarius G. Evans	" 10, "	" 10, "	Promoted to Captain.
Do.	Miles Arnold	" 10, "	" 10, "	Discharged November 4, 1864.
Do.	Frank Brackett	" 11, "	" 11, "	Promoted to Captain.
Do.	Norman H. Steffa	April 13, "	April 13, "	Killed July 22, 1862.
Do.	Robert B. Williamson	Jan. 6, 1865	Jan. 6, 1865	Promoted to Captain.
Do.	L. W. Humphrey	" 6, "	" 6, "	Mustered out with regiment.
Do.	Wm. Held	" 18, "	" 18, "	Mustered out with regiment.
Do.	Edwin Freeman	" 18, "	" 18, "	Mustered out with regiment.

RANK.	NAME.	DATE OF RANK.	COM. ISSUED.	REMARKS.
1st Lieutenant	Lewis Follett	Jan. 18, 1865	Jan. 18, 1865	Mustered out with regiment as Adjutant.
Do.	Wm. H. Gale	" 18, "	" 18, "	Mustered out with regiment.
Do.	Samuel Hupp	" 18, "	" 18, "	Mustered out with regiment.
Do.	Alcenas Richardson	" 18, "	" 18, "	Honorably discharged.
Do.	Virgil W. Graves	Feb. 10, "	Feb. 10, "	Mustered out with regiment.
Do.	Wm. F. Focke	June 16, "	June 16, "	Mustered out with regiment.
Do.	Jabez L. Rhodeback	" 16, "	" 16, "	Mustered out with regiment.
Do.	James Kelley	July 10, "	July 10, "	
Do.	Leonard Holloway	" 10, "	" 10, "	Mustered out as Sergeant-Major.
2d Lieutenant	John R. Miller	Oct. 10, 1861	Feb. 5, 1862	Promoted to 1st Lieutenant.
Do.	Simeon B. Wall	Nov. 1, "	" 5, "	Promoted to 1st Lieutenant.
Do.	John W. Gray	Dec. 4, "	" 5, "	Honorably discharged October 14, 1862.
Do.	Reason C. Strong	" 16, "	" 5, "	Promoted to 1st Lieutenant.
Do.	Charles Luther	" 18, "	" 5, "	Promoted to 1st Lieutenant.
Do.	Freeman Morrison	" 18, "	" 5, "	Promoted to 1st Lieutenant.
Do.	Richard W. Burt	Jan. 7, 1862	" 5, "	Promoted to 1st Lieutenant.
Do.	Lucian B. Wright	Oct. 9, 1861	" 5, "	Resigned February 26, 1862.
Do.	John H. Hardgrove	Nov. 27, "	" 12, "	Promoted; honorably discharged Dec. 12, 63.
Do.	Calvin G. Wells	Feb. 26, 1862	March 20, "	Deceased May 28, 1862.
Do.	Mark Sperry	" 7, "	" 21, "	Resigned February 26, 1863.
Do.	M. S. Moore	March 27, "	April 14, "	Resigned October 31, 1862.
Do.	Frederick H. Wilson	Aug. 11, "	Sept. 4, "	Promoted to 1st Lieutenant.
Do.	John A. Lemert			Promoted to 1st Lieutenant.
Do.	Wm. B. Darlington	Oct. 14, 1862	Nov. 28, 1862	Promoted to 1st Lieutenant.
Do.	John M. Hart	Aug. 7, "	" 28, "	Died December 15, 1862.
Do.	John J. Metzgar	Sept. 30, "	" 28, "	Promoted to 1st Lieutenant.
Do.	Joseph M. Ward	Oct. 31, "	Dec. 31, "	Dismissed March 5, 1863.
Do.	A. A. Batter	Sept. 30, "	" 31, "	Died July 30, 1863.
Do.	George W. Jeremy	Oct. 1, "	" 31, "	Promoted to 1st Lieutenant.
Do.	Jacob A. Jury	Jan. 11, 1863	Feb. 19, 1863	Promoted to 1st Lieutenant.
Do.	John Hiser	" 1, "	Aug. 25, "	Promoted to 1st Lieutenant.
Do.	Carey M. Marriott	Nov. 24, "	Feb. 26, 1864	Promoted to 1st Lieutenant.
Do.	Jarius G. Evans	" 24, "	" 26, "	Promoted to 1st Lieutenant.
Do.	Frank Brackett	" 24, "	" 26, "	Promoted to 1st Lieutenant.
Do.	Miles Arnold	" 24, "	March 7, "	Promoted to 1st Lieutenant.
Do.	Lyman W. Humphrey	" 24, "	" 7, "	Promoted to 1st Lieutenant.
Do.	Norman H. Stella	" 24, "	" 7, "	Promoted to 1st Lieutenant.
Do.	Zebulon P. Evans	" 24, "	" 7, "	Promoted to 1st Lieutenant.
Do.	Lyman W. Humphrey	May 25, "	May 25, "	Promoted to 1st Lieutenant.

SEVENTY-SIXTH OHIO VOLUNTEER INFANTRY.

CAPTAIN CHARLES R. WOODS, of the Ninth United States Infantry, having been authorized to raise a regiment for the three-years' service, recruited and organized the Seventy-Sixth Ohio Volunteer Infantry at Newark, Ohio, on the 9th of February, 1862. The regiment left Newark, and, proceeding *via* Paducah, Kentucky, to Fort Donelson, took an active part in the engagement at that place. On the 6th of March it moved to the Tennessee River, and then up the river to Crump's Landing, where it remained until the 31st, when it marched to Adamsville, and took position in General Lew. Wallace's division, in the right wing of General Grant's army. The division made a forced march to Pittsburg Landing on the 6th of April, and was in line of battle by dark, and during the entire engagement was constantly exposed to the enemy's fire. In the latter part of April the regiment formed a part of a reconnoitering party toward Corinth, charging the Rebels, driving them from their position, and destroying their camp equipage. It formed a part of the grand reserve during the advance on Corinth, and, after the evacuation, moved to Memphis, arriving on the 17th of June, having marched one hundred and thirty miles with wagon supplies. The Seventy-Sixth moved down the river on the 24th of July, and encamped near Helena, Arkansas.

In the reorganization of the Army of the South-West the Seventy-Sixth was placed in the Second Brigade, commanded by Colonel C. R. Woods, and in the Third Division, commanded by General P. J. Osterhaus. On the 16th of August the regiment, forming a part of an expedition of observation, moved down the Mississippi, landed at Milliken's Bend on the 18th, surprised the Thirty-First Louisiana Regiment, and captured all its camp and garrison equipage.

The enemy was followed nine miles, and forty prisoners were captured. The fleet dropped down to the mouth of the Yazoo, and a detachment, comprising a portion of the Seventy-Sixth, proceeded up the Yazoo, surprised Haines's Bluff, and captured four siege-guns, two field-pieces, and a large quantity of fixed ammunition. The expedition returned to Helena on the 27th. The regiment embarked for St. Genevieve, Missouri, early in October, and, remaining a week, moved with the division to Pilot Knob, where it encamped for rest and reorganization. It became very healthy and efficient during its stay here, and on the 12th of November returned to St. Genevieve and embarked for Camp Steele, Mississippi. On the 21st of December it formed a part of General Sherman's expedition for Vicksburg. The fleet arrived at Johnson's Landing, on the Yazoo, on the 26th, and the division, then commanded by General Steele, disembarked; and Hovey's brigade, of which the Seventy-Sixth was a part, made a feint on Haines's Bluff, and then took position on the extreme left of the army. On the 29th the division moved to the main army at Chickasaw Bayou; and, during the battle, the regiment was held in reserve.

General Sherman having abandoned the assault on Vicksburg, the troops re-embarked and proceeded up the Mississippi, landing at Arkansas Post on the evening of the 10th of January, 1863. That night the regiment marched six miles through mud and water, and by two o'clock next morning the troops occupied the cantonments of the enemy. Shortly after daylight they moved upon the enemy's works, and about one o'clock the Seventy-Sixth charged within one hundred yards of the rifle-pits, halted, opened fire, and held the position for three hours, when the enemy surrendered. On the 14th, after burning the cantonments of the enemy, it returned to the river, and, embarking on the 23d, the troops landed at Young's Point, Louisiana. On the night of the 14th of February two non-commissioned officers of company B were killed and four disabled by lightning. During the entire month heavy details were made from the regiment to work upon the canal then in progress across the neck of land opposite Vicksburg. On the 2d of April the regiment, with Steele's division, proceeded on transports up the river to Greenville, Mississippi. The command marched down Deer Creek after the Rebel force under Colonel Ferguson, and on the 7th made an attack and routed them. The command returned to Greenville after destroying a million dollars' worth of corn and cotton, and bringing off a large number of cattle, horses, and mules. About three hundred negroes followed the troops on their return, and were enlisted in colored regiments.

On the 24th the Seventy-Sixth returned to Young's Point, and on the 26th moved to Milliken's Bend, and prepared to march with the grand army southward. On the 2d of May the Fifteenth Corps started for Hard Times Landing, where it arrived on the 6th, and crossed to Grand Gulf. The Seventy-Sixth moved eastward, and, at Fourteen-Mile Creek, the division was attacked by a mounted force of the enemy. Colonel Woods's brigade pushed across the creek in the face of a sharp fire and drove the enemy back. At Jackson the regiment charged the works on the enemy's left. The works were evacuated and the city surrendered. On the 16th the corps marched for Vicksburg, and on the 18th took position in the line of investment. The next day the regiment pushed along the foot of the bluffs near the river, and established itself in position six hundred yards from the main lines of the enemy. The batteries of the enemy in front of the Seventy-Sixth were silenced, and none of his guns could be manned except those of the water-batteries. Heavy details were constantly made for strengthening the works. In the course of several nights eight guns were taken off the sunken gunboat Cincinnati and placed in position with telling effect. After the surrender of Vicksburg the regiment marched in pursuit of Johnston, and arrived at Jackson on the 10th of July. While here it was chiefly employed in foraging and making reconnoissances. On the 23d the regiment marched for Big Black Bridge, where the corps went into camp for rest and reorganization.

On the 23d of September the division (General Osterhaus in command) embarked at Vicksburg for Memphis; and on the 30th moved from the latter place by railroad to Corinth. During the months of October and November the regiment marched and skirmished in Northern Alabama and Tennessee, arriving at Chattanooga in time to join General Hooker in the assault on Lookout Mountain; was engaged at Mission Ridge; and on the 27th of November charged up Taylor's Ridge under a heavy fire, suffering a fearful loss. In one company of twenty men eight were killed and eight wounded, and seven men were shot down while carrying the regimental colors. After marching and bivouacking in various places, on the 1st of January, 1864, the regiment went into camp for the winter at Paint Rock, Alabama.

On the 4th of January about two-thirds of the regiment re-enlisted as veterans, and leave was granted to proceed to Ohio. On the 30th it moved, *via* Nashville, Louisville, and Cincinnati, to Columbus, Ohio, and on the 8th of February took the train for Newark. The regiment disembarked one mile from the city, and moved into town in column by company. It was enthusiastically welcomed by a large concourse of the citizens; speeches were made and a sumptuous repast was partaken of at the City Hall. The members were furloughed to their homes. The Seventy-Sixth went away nine hundred and sixty-two strong, and returned in two years with less than three hundred. The regiment returned to Cincinnati on the 15th of March, and proceeded, *via* Louisville, Nashville, and Huntsville, to the old camp at Paint Rock. On the 1st of May it broke camp and marched with the division for Chattanooga. At Bridgeport it was presented with a new stand of colors from the citizens of Newark. The troops arrived at Chattanooga on the 6th, and pushed forward twelve miles. On the 9th the regiment moved through Snake Creek Gap, and continued moving forward, skirmishing and fortifying, until the 14th, at six o'clock in the evening, when the regiment, with the brigade, charged across the fields under a hot fire, and gained a footing on the first line of hills west of Resaca. On the 16th, the enemy having evacuated, the Seventy-Sixth moved through Resaca and Adairsville to Dallas. Hardee's corps assaulted the lines of the Fifteenth Corps on the 28th, and was repulsed, leaving many dead on the field, some of them within fifty yards of the works in front of the Seventy-Sixth Ohio.

On the 1st of June the corps moved to the left, near New Hope Church, then to Acworth, then south, and so on, each day advancing and fortifying, until, on the 22d, it occupied a position near the railroad at the foot of Kenesaw Mountain. The regiment remained in the rifle-pits until after the Rebels evacuated it; then moved to Rossville; thence across the Chattahoochie, through Decatur, to within four miles of Atlanta, on the 20th of July. On the 22d the Rebels captured four twenty-pound Parrott guns, and the Seventy-Sixth Ohio and the Thirtieth Iowa, of the First Brigade, were the first to drive the enemy from the works and to recapture the guns. About noon on the 28th the enemy attacked the whole line of the Fifteenth Corps; and three successive charges being made, each one proved unavailing. One thousand of the Rebel dead were found in front of the Fifteenth Corps. On the 13th of August the skirmish-line in front of the division was advanced, and the Seventy-Sixth captured fifty prisoners. On the 26th the regiment moved out of the works, with the division, to the West Point and Montgomery Railroad, which they destroyed, marched southward toward Jonesboro'; and on the night of the 30th formed in line across Flint River. The next day the Rebels charged the line and were repulsed, the Seventy-Sixth taking an active share in the engagement, without the protection of rifle-pits.

On the 8th of September the division moved to East Point and encamped for rest and reorganization. On the 4th of October the regiment crossed the Chattahoochie, marched through Marietta, north of Kenesaw Mountain, near Adairsville; through Resaca; through Snake Creek Gap; and on the 16th skirmished with the enemy at Ship's Gap. On the next day the regiment marched through Lafayette, and on the 18th moved south through Summerville and bivouacked. Here the non-veterans were mustered out. The regiment moved with the army to Little River, Cave Springs, and near to Atlanta. On the 15th of November the Fifteenth Corps cut loose from Atlanta and moved southward with the right wing of the army, averaging fifteen miles per day, and foraging off the country.

The route of the Fifteenth Corps was *via* McDonough, Indian Springs, Clinton, and Irwintown, crossing the Macon and Augusta Railroad twenty miles east of Macon; thence eastward across the Oconee River to the Ogeechee, and down the west bank of that stream to the mouth of the Cannouchee; thence across the Ogeechee eastward to Savannah, where it formed on the 18th of December, being twenty-six days out from Atlanta.

After the evacuation the regiment performed provost-guard duty in the city until the 9th of January, 1865, when it embarked on the gunboat Winona for Beaufort, South Carolina. From Beaufort it marched to Gardner's Corners, where preparations were made for the march northward; and on the 31st the command broke camp and started on the "Campaign of the Carolinas." On the 16th of February the troops formed on the outskirts of Columbia, and the Seventy-Sixth was engaged in skirmishing until the evacuation of the city, when it again performed provost-guard duty for four days. The troops arrived at Fayetteville on the 12th of March; crossed Cape Fear and Black Rivers; moved to Bentonville, where they engaged the enemy; and thence *via* Goldsboro' to Raleigh, where the Seventy-Sixth remained until Johnston's surrender.

On the 30th of April the army broke camp and marched, *via* Richmond and Hanover C. H., to Washington, reaching the capital on the 23d of May, 1865. The Seventy-Sixth shared in the grand review, and shortly after moved to Louisville, Kentucky, where it was mustered out. It then proceeded to Columbus, Ohio, and was discharged on the 24th of July, 1865.

This regiment participated in forty-four battles; moved nine thousand six hundred and twenty-five miles on foot, by rail, and by water; passed through the rebellious States of Kentucky, Missouri, Arkansas, Tennessee, Louisiana, Mississippi, Alabama, Georgia, South Carolina, North Carolina, and Virginia. Two hundred and forty-one men were wounded in battle; three hundred and fifty-one died on the field or in hospitals; two hundred and twenty-two carry scars as evidence of their struggle with the enemy, and two hundred and eighty-two have the seeds of disease contracted in the line of duty. It is a sad, but noble record, and the survivors may well be proud of the part they have taken in establishing the greatness and permanence of the American Union.

77th REGIMENT OHIO VOLUNTEER INFANTRY.

ROSTER, THREE YEARS' SERVICE.

RANK.	NAME.	DATE OF RANK.	COM. ISSUED.	REMARKS.
Colonel	JESSE HILDEBRAND	Oct. 5, 1861	Feb. 12, 1862	Died April 18, 1863.
Do.	WM. B. MASON	April 18, 1863	April 28, 1863	Mustered out.
Do.	WM. E. STEVENS	March 7, 1866	March 7, 1866	Mustered out as Lieutenant-Colonel.
Lt. Colonel	WILLIS DE HASS	Oct. 5, 1861	Feb. 12, 1862	Dismissed February 16, 1864.
Do.	WM. E. STEVENS	March 19, 1864	March 19, 1864	Promoted to Colonel.
Do.	CHAS. H. MORRIS	" 7, 1866	" 7, 1866	Mustered out as Captain.
Major	BENJ. D. FEARING	Dec. 17, 1861	Feb. 12, 1862	Appointed Lieut. Col. of 92d, August 26, 1862.
Do.	WM. B. MASON	Aug. 26, 1862	Oct. 8, "	Promoted to Colonel.
Do.	WM. E. STEVENS	April 18, "	May 16, "	Promoted to Lieutenant-Colonel.
Do.	LEWIS E. SISSON	March 19, 1864	March 19, 1864	Mustered out.
Do.	CHAS. H. MORRIS	Nov. 14, 1865	Nov. 14, 1865	Promoted to Lieutenant-Colonel.
Do.	ROBERT E. SMITHSON	March 7, 1866	March 7, 1866	Mustered out as Captain.
Surgeon	JAMES W. WARFIELD	Feb. 3, 1862	Feb. 12, 1862	Honorably discharged May 15, 1864.
Do.	ANDREW WALL	Aug. 11, 1864	Aug. 11, 1864	Mustered out with regiment.
Ass't Surgeon	PARDON COOK	Oct. 29, 1861	Feb. 12, 1862	Died August 31, 1863.
Do.	ANDREW WALL	Sept. 8, 1862	" 10, 1862	Promoted to Surgeon.
Do.	F. H. ARMSTRONG	Aug. 11, 1864	Aug. 11, 1864	Mustered out.
Do.	MILTON VALENTINE	" 29, "	" 29, "	Declined.
Do.	F. H. JONES	Sept. 17, "	Sept. 7, "	Mustered out.
Chaplain	WM. PIERCE	Jan. 4, 1862	Feb. 12, 1862	Resigned August 31, 1862.
Do.	JAMES T. HOLLIDAY	July 13, 1864	July 13, 1864	Mustered out.
Captain	Wm. E. Stevens	Nov. 23, 1861	Feb. 12, 1862	Promoted to Major.
Do.	Wm. B. Mason	Dec. 2, "	" 12, "	Promoted to Major.
Do.	Lewis E. Sisson	" 10, "	" 12, "	Promoted to Major.
Do.	Enoch W. Blasdell	" 12, "	" 12, "	Resigned February 23, 1863.
Do.	Andrew Smith	" 12, "	" 12, "	Resigned February 5, 1863.
Do.	James H. Luigen	" 31, "	" 12, "	Resigned March 13, 1864.
Do.	Andrew W. McCormick	" 31, "	" 12, "	
Do.	Richard Fourakre	" 31, "	" 12, "	Resigned September 2, 1862.
Do.	Wm. T. Robinson	" 31, "	" 12, "	Mustered out.
Do.	Albert Chandler	Jan. 4, 1862	" 12, "	Mustered out.
Do.	Isaac B. Kinkaid	April 8, "	May 9, "	Revoked October 31, 1862; mustered out as [supernumerary.
Do.	Robert H. McKitrick	Aug. 26, "	Oct. 8, "	Mustered out.
Do.	Thomas Ross	Sept. 2, "	Dec. 23, "	Dismissed September 29, 1863.
Do.	Thomas Garrett	Feb. 5, 1863	Feb. 19, 1863	Mustered out.
Do.	Sam'l. S. McNaughton	" 25, "	May 12, "	Mustered out.
Do.	Charles H. Morris	April 18, "	" 25, "	Promoted to Major.
Do.	Thomas Mitchell	March 19, 1864	" 19, 1864	Resigned December 9, 1864.
Do.	Wm. H. Fisher	" 29, 1865	March 29, 1865	Mustered out.
Do.	Wm. W. Scott	" 29, "	" 29, "	Resigned December 1, 1865.
Do.	Robert E. Smithson	" 29, "	" 29, "	Promoted to Major.
Do.	Samuel Fulton	" 29, "	" 29, "	Mustered out with regiment.
Do.	Robert H. Flemming	" 29, "	" 29, "	Mustered out with regiment.
Do.	Henry L. Pugh	Sept. 29, "	Sept. 29, "	Mustered out with regiment.
Do.	John L. McIntyre	Nov. 14, "	Nov. 14, "	Mustered out with regiment as 1st Lieutenant.
Do.	Leonard A. Marlow	Dec. 30, "	Dec. 30, "	Mustered out with regiment.
Do.	Gordon B. West	March 7, 1866	March 7, 1866	Mustered out as 1st Lieutenant and R. Q. M.
1st Lieutenant	Harvey Anderson	Nov. 23, 1861	Feb. 12, 1862	Resigned February 12, 1863.
Do.	Robert H. McKitrick	Dec. 2, "	" 12, "	Promoted to Captain.
Do.	Thomas Mitchell	" 2, "	" 12, "	Promoted to Captain.
Do.	John Henrick	" 2, "	" 12, "	Resigned September 20, 1862.
Do.	Thomas Garrett	" 2, "	" 12, "	Promoted to Captain.
Do.	Herschel B. White	" 2, "	" 12, "	Honorably discharged October 20, 1862.
Do.	Sam'l. S. McNaughton	" 2, "	" 12, "	Promoted to Captain.
Do.	Wm. W. Scott	" 2, "	" 12, "	Honorably discharged August 31, 1862.
Do.	Horatio W. Mason	Jan. 4, 1862	" 12, "	Resigned March 6, 1862.
Do.	Wm. West	Oct. 15, 1861	" 12, "	Resigned June 5, 1862.
Do.	Thomas J. Cochran	Nov. 25, "	" 12, "	Resigned October 6, 1862.
Do.	Wm. H. Fisher	March 6, 1862	April 14, "	Promoted to Captain.
Do.	Thomas Ross	" 27, "	" 14, "	Promoted to Captain.
Do.	Edgar B. Pearce	June 5, "	June 24, "	Mustered out.
Do.	David F. Jones	Aug. 26, "	Oct. 8, "	Mustered out.
Do.	Wm. P. Richener	Sept. 20, "	" 17, "	Mustered out.
Do.	Marion N. Burris	Oct. 8, "	" 29, "	Resigned July 15, 1863.
Do.	Edward R. Moore	Aug. 31, "	Dec. 31, "	Honorably discharged August 1, 1863.
Do.	Hanson Criswell	" 2, "	" 31, "	
Do.	David A. Henry	Oct. 31, "	" 31, "	Resigned December 9, 1864.
Do.	Wm. W. Scott	Feb. 5, 1863	Feb. 19, 1863	Promoted to Captain.
Do.	Charles H. Morris	" 13, "	" 23, "	Promoted to Captain.
Do.	Robert E. Smithson	" 25, "	March 6, "	Promoted to Captain.
Do.	Samuel Fulton	April 18, "	May 25, "	Promoted to Captain.
Do.	Charles J. Eagler	March 19, 1864	March 19, 1864	Resigned December 9, 1864.
Do.	Henry L. Pugh	" 19, "	" 19, "	Promoted to Captain.
Do.	Robert H. Flemming	Aug. 1, 1863	Nov. 27, 1863	Promoted to Captain.
Do.	Nathan B. Smith	March 19, 1864	March 19, 1864	Not mustered as 1st Lieutenant.
Do.	John L. McIntyre	" 29, 1865	" 29, 1865	Promoted to Captain.
Do.	Leonard A. Marlow	" 29, "	" 29, "	Promoted to Captain.
Do.	Gordon B. West	" 29, "	" 29, "	Promoted to Captain.
Do.	Robert C. Berry	" 29, "	" 29, "	Mustered out.
Do.	Augustus McCarty	" 29, "	" 29, "	Discharged.
Do.	Wm. W. Burris	" 29, "	" 29, "	Mustered out with regiment.
Do.	Joseph M. Mitchell	" 29, "	" 29, "	Mustered out with regiment.
Do.	Wm. M. Atkinson	" 29, "	" 29, "	Mustered out with regiment.
Do.	Benj. T. Hill	Sept. 29, "	Sept. 29, "	Mustered out with regiment as 1st Lieut. and [Adjutant.
Do.	Henry H. Dye	Nov. 14, "	Nov. 14, "	Resigned October 10, 1865, as 2d Lieutenant.

RANK.	NAME.	DATE OF RANK.	COM. ISSUED.	REMARKS.
1st Lieutenant	Wm. A. Day	Nov. 16, 1865	Nov. 16, 1865	Mustered out with regiment as 2d Lieutenant.
Do.	John Smith	Dec. 30, "	Dec. 30, "	Mustered out with regiment as 2d Lieutenant.
Do.	Thomas Wiseman	" 30, "	" 30, "	Mustered out with regiment.
Do.	James P. Daugherty	March 7, 1866	March 7, 1866	Mustered out with regiment as 2d Lieutenant.
2d Lieutenant	Joseph S. Steenrod	Nov. 23, 1861	Feb. 12, 1862	Killed April 8, 1862.
Do.	David F. Jones	Dec. 2, "	" 12, "	Promoted to 1st Lieutenant.
Do.	Marion N. Harris	" 10, "	" 12, "	Promoted to 1st Lieutenant.
Do.	Edward R. Moore	" 12, "	" 12, "	Promoted to 1st Lieutenant.
Do.	Hansen Criswell	" 12, "	" 12, "	Promoted to 1st Lieutenant.
Do.	Oliphant S. Thomas	" 10, "	" 12, "	Died May 13, 1862.
Do.	David A. Henery	" 31, "	" 12, "	Promoted to 1st Lieutenant.
Do.	Levi J. Fourakre	" 31, "	" 12, "	Honorably discharged October 21, 1862.
Do.	Henry Hoblitzell	" 31, "	" 12, "	Discharged January 8, 1863.
Do.	Wm. H. Fisher	Nov. 5, "	" 12, "	Promoted to 1st Lieutenant.
Do.	Robert B. Greggs	March 6, 1862	May 9, "	Discharged October 10, 1862.
Do.	Charles H. Morris	April 8, "	April 8, "	Promoted to 1st Lieutenant.
Do.	Thomas R. Campbell	Aug. 26, "	" 8, "	Died September 25, 1862.
Do.	Robert E. Smithson	May 31, "	" 20, "	Promoted to 1st Lieutenant.
Do.	Charles J. Eagler	Aug. 26, "	Aug. 29, "	Promoted to 1st Lieutenant.
Do.	Jesse Hildebrand, jr.	Oct. 21, "	Nov. 25, "	Mustered out January 23, 1864.
Do.	Henry L. Pugh	Aug. 26, "	Dec. 31, "	Promoted to 1st Lieutenant.
Do.	Nathan B. Smith	Oct. 21, "	" 31, "	Promoted to 1st Lieutenant.
Do.	Gordon B. West	Feb. 11, 1863	Feb. 5, 1863	Promoted to 1st Lieutenant.
Do.	John L. McIntyre	Jan. 1, "	March 5, "	Promoted to 1st Lieutenant.
Do.	Jesse Province	May 1, 1862	Feb. 10, "	Mustered out.
Do.	Isaac B. Kinkaid	Nov. 1, "	March 6, "	Mustered out.
Do.	Samuel Fulton	Feb. 13, 1863	Feb. 13, "	Promoted to 1st Lieutenant.
Do.	Robert H. Flemming	" 25, "	March 6, "	Promoted to 1st Lieutenant.
Do.	Leonard A. Marlow	Jan. 1, "	May 21, "	Promoted to 1st Lieutenant.
Do.	Robert C. Berry	April 18, "	" 21, "	Promoted to 1st Lieutenant.
Do.	Wm. E. Smithson	Nov. 1, "	March 7, 1864	Resigned December 9, 1864.
Do.	Benj. T. Hill	March 29, 1864	" 29, "	Promoted to 1st Lieutenant.
Do.	Henry H. Dye	" 29, "	" 29, "	Resigned October 10, 1865.
Do.	Wm. A. Day	" 29, "	" 29, "	Promoted to 1st Lieutenant.
Do.	John Smith	" 29, "	" 29, "	Promoted to 1st Lieutenant.
Do.	Thomas Wiseman	May 31, "	May 31, "	Promoted to 1st Lieutenant.
Do.	Joseph M. Mitchell	March 29, "	June 6, "	Promoted to 1st Lieutenant.
Do.	Wm. W. Burris	June 29, "	" 6, "	Promoted to 1st Lieutenant.
Do.	Henry H. Chudeust	Sept. 29, "	Sept. 29, "	Never mustered.
Do.	Gamaliel J. Lund	Nov. 14, "	Nov. 14, "	Mustered out with regiment as Sergeant.
Do.	Jeremiah Fish	" 14, "	" 14, "	Mustered out with regiment as Sergeant.
Do.	James P. Daugherty	" 14, "	" 14, "	Promoted to 1st Lieutenant.
Do.	Wm. H. Hose	" 14, "	" 14, "	Mustered out with regiment.
Do.	Wm. H. Hanson	" 16, "	" 16, "	Mustered out with regiment as Sergeant.
Do.	Christopher Black	Dec. 30, "	Dec. 30, "	Mustered out with regiment as Sergeant.
Do.	Wm. H. Bingham	March 7, 1866	March 7, 1866	Mustered out with regiment as Sergeant.

SEVENTY-SEVENTH OHIO VOLUNTEER INFANTRY.

THIS regiment was organized at Marietta, Ohio, in the fall of 1861, with Jesse Hildebrand as its Colonel. Colonel Hildebrand was well qualified to accomplish the work assigned him by the Governor of the State, being well known as the most active militia General in Southern Ohio for many years. At the time of his appointment recruiting was very difficult, his territory was already well drained of men, as five regiments of infantry, a battalion of cavalry, and several independent companies of artillery had been raised there, yet so well directed were his energies, that his regiment almost reached its maximum in sixty days.

Immediately upon the organization of the regiment, and before equipment, it was ordered from the place of rendezvous, at Marietta, Ohio, to Camp Dennison. From thence it was ordered on the 17th of February following, to report to General W. T. Sherman, at Paducah, Kentucky.

Reporting on the 20th of February, it was assigned to Sherman's division of Grant's army, and with the Fifty-Third and Fifty-Seventh Ohio, and two battalions of the Fifth Ohio Cavalry, formed the Third Brigade, with Colonel Hildebrand commanding.

On the 9th of March the regiment with the brigade embarked on transports, joining the expeditionary corps under the command of Major-General C. F. Smith, at the mouth of the Tennessee River. With the division it took part in the attempt to break the Memphis and Charleston Railroad, landing at Yellow Creek for that purpose on the 14th of March; re-embarked on the 15th; passing down the river disembarked at Pittsburg Landing on the 16th.; made a reconnoissance to Monterey, on the main road to Corinth, on the 17th; on the 18th moved out some two miles from the Landing and went into camp, the right of the regiment resting on the Corinth road—Shiloh Church being in the midst of the camp.

The regiment took part in the operations of the division from this point toward Corinth and Purdy. On the 1st of April it embarked on transports, and passed up the river to Eastport, Mississippi; disembarked and had a spirited skirmish with the enemy between Eastport and Iuka, Mississippi, to which point it had been ordered to ascertain the strength and position of the enemy about Iuka; re-embarked and returned to Pittsburg Landing in time to take part in the affair on the 5th with the enemy's advance. At this time Sherman's division occupied the advance toward Corinth, the Third Brigade posted in the left-center of his line.

On Sunday morning, April 6th, the Seventy-Seventh moved from its camp, in accordance with orders received from General Sherman the previous evening: "That the regiment would be posted covering the open fields to the right of the See House" (three-quarters of a mile in our front, where the reserves of the picket were stationed), in anticipation of a movement of our cavalry that morning by our left. The order was repeated to the commandant of the regiment by the General in person in the morning, when he learned that our picket lines were heavily pressed by the enemy. In the execution of this movement the advance of the Rebel infantry was encountered in the open woods beyond the creek (flowing along our front to the north). Our skirmishers gathering up and steadying the retiring picket details, held the enemy in check until the regiment was disposed, in conjunction with the Fifty-Seventh Ohio, covering the Corinth road and the approaches to the creek. The regiment was strongly favored in its position, and engaged the enemy at once in his efforts to gain a footing on our side of the ravine, and break this our center. A struggle was maintained by the Seventy-Seventh and Fifty-Seventh Ohio, and Taylor's Battery (Battery A, of Chicago). Our left flank, much exposed, compelled the Fifty-Seventh to retire, and the Seventy-Seventh to withdraw on a line with the battery on the right of the Corinth Road, the left resting on Shiloh Meeting-House, still having the Rebels at disadvantage in their efforts to pass the creek and carry our position and the battery by storm. The Seventy-Seventh remained the immediate support of "Battery A," until it was ordered into the new line, then forming under the eye of Sherman. It covered this perilous movement of the battery, then yielded its camps and the church, the last position of the first line of battle. Here fell Thomas, Bruce, Booth, Wyss, Wright. Lipple, Book, Batton, Burries, Brabham, Cline, Devol, Davis, Marlow, and Fleming, besides the many brave fellows in the ranks. The regiment, driven from the old line, took position in the new one, participated in its struggle, and was actively engaged till night ended the contest. It took part with the brigade in its operations and engagements during the day of the 7th, and marched into its old camp at four o'clock P. M.

On Tuesday, the 8th instant, the regiment moved with the advance in pursuit of the retreating army. Finding the enemy, it was ordered forward to ascertain their strength and position. So reduced was the regiment by the losses in the two days' fighting, by sickness, details, and straggling, that it numbered but a little over two hundred men, with thirteen officers.

With a strong line of skirmishers, the enemy were forced through their camps, developing their line of battle in the rear. This proved to be a brigade of Kentucky, Mississippi, and Texan cavalry, led by General Forrest. Before squares were formed, or any disposition made to guard against cavalry, Forrest had charged. It was faring ill with them in this unequal contest until the Fifty-Third Ohio came into the fight, when the enemy were driven from the field. In this short affair the regiment lost many of its best and bravest. Lieutenant Steenrod was killed here, with Porterfield, Kimberly, Hepburn, Easley, Hankey, and eighteen from the ranks. Lieutenants Mitchell, Garrett, White, Fischer, Fouraker, Scott, and the Sergeant-Major, West, were severely wounded. Captains McCormick and Chandler and Lieutenant Creswell were captured.

The loss of the regiment in the battle, and this subsequent affair, was one officer and forty-nine rank and file killed; seven officers and one hundred and seven men wounded; three officers and fifty-three men missing. Total killed, wounded, and missing, two hundred and twenty.

General Sherman commended the conduct of this regiment in its determined and protracted struggle for the position at the church, and in baffling the enemy in all his attempts to capture Taylor's battery. The brigade commander, Colonel Hildebrand, says in his official report: "With regard to the officers and men who participated in the affair at 'Fallen Timbers,' and at Shiloh, I am happy to bear testimony to the fidelity, bravery, and devotion of all. Major B. D. Fearing, who was in immediate command of the Seventy-Seventh Regiment Ohio Volunteer Infantry, was cool and brave, and acquitted himself with as much skill as an old officer of larger experience, and was not excelled by any other field-officer who came under my observation." *

From the 9th to the 29th of April the Seventy-Seventh was in camp preparing for the advance. It took part in all the active operations of Sherman's division during the siege of Corinth, constructing field-works, roads, and bridges; picketing, skirmishing, and fighting, until the division rested beyond Corinth, returning from pursuit of the enemy. From June 1st to July 21st it was on an expedition into Northern Mississippi, and repairing the Memphis and Charleston Railroad as the division moved westward. It reached Memphis, Tennessee, July 21st, and encamped in Fort Pickering. On the 27th of August it was ordered to Alton, Illinois, to relieve the Thirteenth United States Infantry, in charge of the military prisons at that station. It left Alton July 31, 1863, with a full complement of men. The regiment reached Helena, Arkansas, August 5, 1863—the men in splendid condition. It was assigned to the Third Brigade, Third Division, Arkansas Expedition, under command of General Fred. Steele.

It participated in all the movements of Steele's army, until December 20, 1863, when the

* Justice compels us to add that General Sherman made severe complaints, at the time, concerning the conduct of this whole brigade, and that subsequently, in his official report, he said: "My Third Brigade did break much too soon, and I am not yet advised where they were Sunday afternoon and Monday morning."

regiment re-enlisted as veterans; was relieved from duty, December 22d, and started for Columbus, Ohio. At that point it was mustered into service on the 22d of January, 1864, and furloughed for thirty days, to rendezvous at Camp Dennison. It left Camp Dennison for Little Rock with full ranks, on March 3d, and moved with the army thence to Shreveport, Louisiana, March 23d. It was actively engaged in the many skirmishes and fights of the army between Arkadelphia and Camden, enduring patiently and without a murmur the hardships and privations of this campaign.

On the 22d of April, 1864, the Seventy-Seventh, with the Forty-Third Indiana and Thirty-Sixth Iowa, started from Camden to escort a large train to Pine Bluff after supplies, the whole commanded by Lieutenant Colonel Drake, of the Thirty-Sixth Iowa. General Fagan's Rebel division attacked these regiments in detail while they were encumbered with the train, on the 25th, at Marks's Mills. Colonel Drake fought desperately with the Forty-Third and Thirty-Sixth, but being overpowered, was unable to hold out till the Seventy-Seventh could make a junction from the rear of the train, some four miles away. The Seventy-Seventh, under Captain McCormick, came on to the field at the moment Colonel Drake was overwhelmed. They went into the fight at once, but no effort of their's could rescue the train or their captured comrades, and after an unequal contest of two hours, being surrounded, they were compelled to accept the enemy's terms. The portion of the regiment captured, after marching until May 15th, reached the Rebel prison-pens known as Camp Ford, near Tyler, Texas, where they were kept ten months.

Those of the Seventy-Seventh not captured at Marks's Mills, together with many left at Camden, were formed into a company and took part in the struggle at "Jenkins's Ferry," on Sabine River, during the retreat of General Steele, losing, in killed and wounded, more than one-half the number engaged.

When the Seventy-Seventh was exchanged, in February, 1865, at the request of General Steele, it was transferred with him to the Army of the Gulf, and with General Steele, under General Canby, they took part in the campaign that resulted in the capture of Mobile. It then went to the Rio Grande, marching from Brazos de Santiago to Clarksville, and then to Brownsville, Texas, and encamped near that city, and were on duty there from August 1, 1865 until March 8, 1866. It was mustered out of service March 8th, and left on the same day for Columbus, Ohio.

The regiment reached Columbus, Ohio, March 23d, and received its payment and final discharge March 25, 1866, at which time its strength was seventeen commissioned officers and three hundred and forty-eight men.

Their work was done, and they who had been in the advance of the grand army in its struggle for universal freedom and enduring Nationality, became the rear-guard as they turned their faces toward home and peace.

Inscribed on the scarred and tattered banners they bore to the capitol, were Shiloh, Corinth, Little Rock, Camden, Okalona, Prairie de Ann, Marks's Mills, Jenkins's Ferry, Fort Spanish, Blakely, and Mobile; and then they, the last but one of Ohio's many noble regiments, passed back into the repose of civil life.

Organizing in 1861, reorganizing as a veteran regiment in 1863, having enlisted and on its rolls, during the four years of its service, one thousand and nine hundred men. They returned to their homes the heroes of two distinct periods of the war.

78th REGIMENT OHIO VOLUNTEER INFANTRY.

ROSTER, THREE YEARS' SERVICE.

RANK.	NAME.	DATE OF RANK.	COM. ISSUED.	REMARKS.
Colonel	MORTIM'R D. LEGGETT	Jan. 21, 1862	Feb. 6, 1862	Appointed Brigadier-General Nov. 29, 1862.
Do.	ZAC. M. CHANDLER	Nov. 29, "	May 1, 1863	Declined.
Do.	GREENBE'RY F. WILES	July 23, 1863	Sept. 1, "	Promoted Brevet Brig. General March 13, 1865.
Lt. Colonel	MORTIMER D. LEGGETT	Dec. 18, 1861	Jan. 20, 1862	Promoted to Colonel.
Do.	BENJ. F. HAWKES	Feb. 6, 1862	Feb. 6, "	Mustered out September 3, 1862.
Do.	ZACHARIAH M. CHANDLER	Oct. 1, "	Oct. 1, "	Resigned July 23, 1863.
Do.	GREENBERRY F. WILES	Nov. 29, "	May 1, 1863	Promoted to Colonel.
Do.	JOHN F. RAINEY	July 23, 1863	Jan. 10, 1864	Mustered out.
Do.	HENRY L. WALLER	Jan. 11, 1865	" 11, 1865	Declined; mustered out December 31, 1864.
Do.	ISRAEL C. ROBINSON	" 18, "	" 18, "	Revoked; special order 38, 1865.
Do.	GILBERT D. MUNSON	" 12, "	" 12, "	Mustered out with regiment.
Major	DAVID F. CARNAHAN	Dec. 26, 1861	" 20, 1862	Resigned September 7, 1862.
Do.	ZACHARIAH M. CHANDLER	Sept. 7, "	Oct. 1, "	Promoted to Lieutenant-Colonel.
Do.	JOHN F. RAINEY	Oct. 1, "	Dec. 4, "	Promoted to Lieutenant-Colonel.
Do.	HENRY L. WALLER	Dec. 21, 1864	" 21, 1864	Promoted to Lieutenant-Colonel.
Do.	ISRAEL C. ROBINSON	Jan. 11, 1865	Jan. 11, 1865	
Do.	JOHN B. MILLS	" 18, "	" 18, "	Revoked; special order 38, 1865.
Surgeon	JAMES S. REEVES	Nov. 21, 1861	" 20, 1862	Mustered out with regiment.
Ass't Surgeon	SAMUEL C. MENDENHALL	" 26, "	" 20, "	Resigned April 20, 1862.
Do.	W. MORROW BEACH			Promoted to Surgeon 118th O. V. I.
Do.	J. D. WIRTMAN	Aug. 26, 1862	Aug. 27, 1862	Resigned February 14, 1863.
Do.	E. C. DEFORREST	" 26, "	" 27, "	Discharged November 4, 1863.
Do.	GEORGE F. PECKHAM	May 25, 1864	May 25, 1864	Mustered out with regiment.
Do.	RALPH D. WEBB	March 31, 1865	March 31, 1865	Mustered out with regiment.
Chaplain	OLIPHANT M. TODD	Jan. 11, 1862	Jan. 20, 1862	Resigned November 14, 1862.
Do.	THOMAS M. STEVENSON	Feb. 20, 1863	April 16, 1863	Mustered out with regiment.
Captain	Horace D. Munson	Nov. 25, 1861	Jan. 20, 1862	Resigned February 22, 1863.
Do.	Zachariah M. Chandler	Dec. 13, "	" 20, "	Promoted to Major.
Do.	Samuel W. Spencer	" 14, "	" 20, "	Resigned April 16, 1862.
Do.	E. Hilles Talley	" 14, "	" 20, "	Died April 4, —.
Do.	Thomas M. Stevenson	" 23, "	" 20, "	Resigned February 14, 1863.
Do.	Avery L. Waller	" 26, "	" 20, "	Promoted to Major; declined.
Do.	Peter Gebhart	Jan. 8, 1862	" 20, "	Resigned September 3, 1863.
Do.	John F. Rainey	" 8, "	" 20, "	Promoted to Major.
Do.	Andrew Scott	" 11, "	" 20, "	Mustered out December 26, 1864.
Do.	John W. Cornyn	" 11, "	" 20, "	Appointed Com. of Subsistence April 23, 1863.
Do.	Thomas P. Wilson	March 27, "	May 9, "	Declined.
Do.	Wm. S. Harlan	April 4, "	June 24, "	Resigned February 13, 1863.
Do.	Greenberry F. Wiles	" 16, "	Oct. 1, "	Promoted to Lieutenant-Colonel.
Do.	Gilbert D. Munson	Sept. 7, "	" 1, "	Promoted to Lieutenant-Colonel.
Do.	John W. A. Gillespie	" 3, "	" 1, "	Mustered out.
Do.	John Orr	Oct. 1, "	May 1, 1863	Mustered out.
Do.	W. W. McCarty	Feb. 14, "	March 7, "	Mustered out May 15, 1865.
Do.	Israel C. Robinson	" 13, "	May 11, "	Promoted to Major.
Do.	Thomas P. Wilson	" 22, "	March 30, "	Mustered out December 26, 1864.
Do.	Alexander Scales	Nov. 29, "	Aug. 10, "	Resigned December 26, 1863.
Do.	John B. Mills	May 2, 1864	May 2, 1864	Mustered out with regiment.
Do.	Hugh Dunne	Feb. 1, "	Feb. 8, "	Honorably discharged September 15, 1864.
Do.	George W. Porter	Nov. 18, "	Nov. 18, "	On det. duty; A.D.C. to Maj. Gen. Leggett.
Do.	Cyrus M. Roberts	Dec. 25, "	Dec. 25, "	Detached at head-quarters 17th A. C.
Do.	Adolphus Search	Jan. 11, 1865	Jan. 11, 1865	Mustered out with regiment.
Do.	Addison A. Adair	" 11, "	" 11, "	Revoked; special order 38, 1865.
Do.	Andrew McDaniels	" 11, "	" 11, "	Revoked; special order 38, 1865.
Do.	John P. Ross	" 11, "	" 11, "	Revoked; special order 38, 1865.
Do.	James H. Gander	" 11, "	" 11, "	Revoked; special order 38, 1865.
Do.	Henry Bigalow	" 12, "	" 12, "	Declined to accept.
Do.	Wm. H. Hessin	" 12, "	" 12, "	Detached at head-quarters 17th A. C.
Do.	Jacob P. Springer	" 12, "	" 12, "	Detached as A.A.Q.M. head-quarters 17th A.C.
Do.	James T. Story	" 12, "	" 12, "	Resigned April 1, 1865.
Do.	Addison A. Adair	" 12, "	" 12, "	Mustered out with regiment.
Do.	Iret Rhinehart	April 20, "	April 20, "	On detached duty at head-quarters 17th A. C.
Do.	Andrew McDaniels	" 26, "	" 26, "	Absent on duty.
1st Lieutenant	John C. Douglass	Oct. 22, 1861	Jan. 20, 1862	Appointed Captain and A. A. G.
Do.	John E. Jewett	Nov. 1, "	" 20, "	Resigned June 13, 1862.
Do.	Thomas P. Wilson	" 25, "	" 20, "	Promoted to Captain.
Do.	Greenberry F. Wiles	Dec. 13, "	" 20, "	Promoted to Captain.
Do.	Wm. C. Godfrey	" 14, "	" 20, "	Resigned April 20, 1862.
Do.	Benj. A. Blandy	" 14, "	" 20, "	Resigned June 1, 1862.
Do.	W. W. McCarty	" 23, "	" 20, "	Promoted to Captain.
Do.	Hugh Dunne	" 26, "	" 20, "	Promoted to Captain.
Do.	John W. A. Gillespie	Jan. 11, 1862	" 20, "	Promoted to Captain.
Do.	John F. Grimes	" 8, "	" 20, "	Resigned April 20, 1862.
Do.	John B. Mills	" 11, "	" 20, "	Promoted to Captain.
Do.	John Hamilton	" 11, "	" 20, "	Resigned August 31, 1862.
Do.	Lewis M. Dayton	April 20, "	May 1, "	Appointed Captain by President.
Do.	John Orr	March 27, "	" 9, "	Promoted to Captain.
Do.	Wm. S. Harlan	April 20, "	" 9, "	Promoted to Captain.
Do.	James T. Caldwell	" 4, "	June 24, "	Killed.
Do.	Israel C. Robinson	June 1, "	Aug. 11, "	Promoted to Captain.
Do.	Gilbert D. Munson	April 16, "	Oct. 1, "	Promoted to Captain.
Do.	Jesse Patterson	Sept. 3, "	" 1, "	Dismissed April 2, 1863.
Do.	George W. Porter	" 7, "		Promoted to Captain.
Do.	Howard S. Abbott	June 13, "	Oct. 27, 1862	Honorably discharged October 14, 1863.
Do.	A. C. Cassidy	Aug. 31, "	Dec. 20, "	Resigned March 24, 1863.
Do.	Cyrus M. Roberts	Feb. 14, 1863	March 7, 1863	Promoted to Captain.

RANK.	NAME.	DATE OF RANK.	COM. ISSUED.	REMARKS.
1st Lieutenant	James T. Caldwell	Feb. 22, 1863	March 30, 1863	Died of wounds May 22, 1863.
Do.	James C. Harris	March 24, "	May 11, "	Mustered out December 26, 1864.
Do.	Henry Bigalow	April 2, "	June 10, "	Quartermaster; declined promotion.
Do.	Josiah Scott	May 1, "	May 9, "	Died April 18, 1864.
Do.	James Carothers	Feb. 13, "	" 11, "	Mustered out.
Do.	Wm. H. Hessin	Aug. 1, "	Aug. 8, "	Promoted to Captain.
Do.	Jacob P. Springer	Oct. 14, "	Nov. 12, "	Promoted to Captain.
Do.	Adolphus Search	July 10, "	Jan. 6, 1864	Promoted to Captain.
Do.	James T. Story	Feb. 1, 1864	Feb. 8, "	Promoted to Captain.
Do.	Iret Rhinehart	Dec. 19, 1863	March 3, "	Promoted to Captain.
Do.	Howard S. Abbott	Oct. 27, 1862	May 2, "	Honorably discharged October 14, 1863.
Do.	Addison A. Adair	Jan. 6, 1865	Jan. 6, 1865	Promoted to Captain.
Do.	Andrew McDaniels	" 6, "	" 6, "	Promoted to Captain.
Do.	John P. Ross	" 6, "	" 6, "	Promoted to Captain.
Do.	James H. Gander	" 6, "	" 6, "	Promoted to Captain.
Do.	Russell Bethel	" 11, "	" 11, "	Revoked; special order 38, 1865.
Do.	Arthur W. McCarty	" 11, "	" 11, "	Revoked; special order 38, 1865.
Do.	Joseph Miller	" 11, "	" 11, "	Revoked; special order 38, 1865.
Do.	David M. Watson	" 11, "	" 11, "	Revoked; special order 38, 1865.
Do.	Meander Mott	" 11, "	" 11, "	Revoked; special order 38, 1865.
Do.	Charles C. Wiles	" 11, "	" 11, "	Revoked; special order 38, 1865.
Do.	Alfred Wymer	" 11, "	" 11, "	Revoked; special order 38, 1865.
Do.	John R. Edgar	" 11, "	" 11, "	Revoked; special order 38, 1865.
Do.	Humphrey A. McDonald	" 12, "	" 12, "	Mustered out April 6, 1865.
Do.	Archibald W. Stewart	" 12, "	" 12, "	A. A. C. to Major-General Leggett.
Do.	Wm. M. Sleith	" 12, "	" 12, "	Mustered out as Adjutant.
Do.	Russell Bethel	" 12, "	" 12, "	A. A. D. to General R. K. Scott.
Do.	Arthur W. McCarty	" 12, "	" 12, "	Mustered out with regiment.
Do.	Joseph Miller	" 12, "	" 12, "	Mustered out with regiment.
Do.	David M. Watson	" 12, "	" 12, "	Mustered out with regiment.
Do.	Meander Mott	" 12, "	" 12, "	Mustered out January 12, 1865.
Do.	Charles C. Wiles	" 12, "	" 12, "	Mustered out with regiment.
Do.	Alfred Wymer	April 22, "	April 22, "	Mustered out with regiment.
Do.	John R. Edgar	May 1, "	May 1, "	On leave of absence.
2d Lieutenant	John Orr	Nov. 13, 1861	Jan. 20, 1862	Promoted to 1st Lieutenant.
Do.	James T. Caldwell	" 25, "	" 20, "	Promoted to 1st Lieutenant.
Do.	Thomas E. Ross	Dec. 14, "	" 20, "	Resigned March 27, 1862.
Do.	Wm. S. Harlan	" 14, "	" 20, "	Promoted to 1st Lieutenant.
Do.	Cyrus M. Roberts	" 23, "	" 20, "	Promoted to 1st Lieutenant.
Do.	Gilbert D. Munson	" 26, "	" 20, "	Promoted to 1st Lieutenant.
Do.	James T. Story	" 26, "	" 20, "	Promoted to 1st Lieutenant.
Do.	Joseph C. Jenkins	Jan. 11, 1862	" 20, "	Dismissed September 11, 1862.
Do.	Samuel A. De Wolff	" 11, "	" 20, "	Resigned August 31, 1862.
Do.	James Carothers	" 11, "	" 20, "	Promoted to 1st Lieutenant.
Do.	Alexander Seale	March 27, "	June 24, "	Promoted to 1st Lieutenant.
Do.	Wm. A. Dodds	" 27, "	" 24, "	Resigned January 28, 1863.
Do.	Israel Robinson	April 20, "	" 24, "	Promoted to 1st Lieutenant.
Do.	James C. Harris	June 1, "	Aug. 11, "	Promoted to 1st Lieutenant.
Do.	Iret Rhinehart	Sept. 11, "	Oct. 1, "	Promoted to 1st Lieutenant.
Do.	Joseph R. Miller	" 7, "	" 1, "	Resigned September 21, 1864.
Do.	George W. Porter	April 16, "	" 1, "	Promoted to 1st Lieutenant.
Do.	Humphrey A. McDonald	Jan. 1, 1863	Feb. 26, 1863	Promoted to 1st Lieutenant.
Do.	Josiah Scott	" 28, "	April 3, "	Promoted to 1st Lieutenant.
Do.	Archibald W. Stewart	Feb. 14, "	March 7, "	Promoted to 1st Lieutenant.
Do.	Wm. M. Sleith	" 22, "	" 30, "	Promoted to 1st Lieutenant.
Do.	James Brewnan	" 13, "	May 11, "	Dismissed April 8, 1864.
Do.	Wm. H. Hessin	March 24, "	July 10, "	Promoted to 1st Lieutenant.
Do.	Jacob P. Springer	May 1, "	" 10, "	Promoted to 1st Lieutenant.
Do.	Wm. M. Laughlin	Nov. 29, 1862	Sept. 1, "	Killed July 22, 1864.
Do.	Henry Spear	" 17, 1863	March 2, 1864	Died August 28, 1864, of wounds.
Do.	Addison A. Adair	" 17, "	" 9, "	Promoted to 1st Lieutenant.
Do.	Albert G. Gault	" 18, "	" 10, "	Resigned September 27, 1864.
Do.	Andrew McDaniels	March 31, 1864	March 31, "	Promoted to 1st Lieutenant.
Do.	John P. Ross	Nov. 18, "	Nov. 18, "	Promoted to 1st Lieutenant.
Do.	James H. Gander	" 18, "	" 18, "	Promoted to 1st Lieutenant.
Do.	Russell Bethel	" 18, "	" 18, "	Promoted to 1st Lieutenant.
Do.	Robert H. Brown	Jan. 11, 1865	Jan. 11, 1865	Declined to accept; revoked; special order 38, 1865.
Do.	Alexander V. P. Hager	" 11, "	" 11, "	
Do.	James R. Earich	" 11, "	" 11, "	
Do.	James H. Echelberry	" 11, "	" 11, "	
Do.	Milton Ward	" 11, "	" 11, "	
Do.	Simon P. Joy	Feb. 10, "	Feb. 10, "	
Do.	Amos Norman	" 10, "	" 10, "	
Do.	Alfred Wymer	Jan. 12, "	Jan. 12, "	Promoted to 1st Lieutenant.
Do.	John R. Edgar	" 12, "	" 12, "	Promoted to 1st Lieutenant.
Do.	Robert H. Brown	" 12, "	" 12, "	Mustered out with regiment.
Do.	A. V. P. Hager	" 12, "	" 12, "	Mustered out with regiment.
Do.	James H. Echelberry	" 12, "	" 12, "	Mustered out with regiment.
Do.	Milton Ward	" 12, "	" 12, "	On leave of absence.
Do.	Simon P. Joy	Feb. 10, "	Feb. 10, "	Mustered out with regiment.
Do.	Amos Norman	" 10, "	" 10, "	Mustered out with regiment.
Do.	John R. Kennedy	April 22, "	April 22, "	Mustered out with regiment.
Do.	Wm. H. Cockins	" 22, "	" 22, "	Resigned July 6, 1865.
Do.	Cyrus H. Gardner	" 22, "	" 22, "	Mustered out with regiment.
Do.	Martin Durant	May 1, "	May 1, "	Mustered out with regiment.

Those whose commissions were revoked signed a request to the Governor asking them to be so revoked because of a mistake in the order of promotion.

SEVENTY-EIGHTH OHIO VOLUNTEER INFANTRY.

THE SEVENTY-EIGHTH OHIO was raised under special authority from Governor Dennison, issued to M. D. Leggett, Esq., of Zanesville, Ohio. The first man of the regiment was enlisted on the 30th day of October, 1861. The organization was completed on the 11th day of January, 1862, and the regiment left by cars for Cincinnati on the 11th of February, where steamers were found on which it embarked for Fort Donelson, on the Tennessee River. This point was reached on the 16th of February, and the regiment went into position on the battle-field, but too late to take part in the action. Immediately after this battle the regiment saw its first field-duty—that of taking care of the Rebel prisoners and stores.

On the first of March the regiment marched across the country to Metal Landing, on the Tennessee River, where it went into camp awaiting transportation. About the 10th of March it moved with the National forces to Crump's Landing, and thence to Adamsville, on the road to Purdy, to guard an exposed flank of the army at Pittsburg Landing. Nothing of interest transpired here excepting a few slight skirmishes with the enemy.

Early on the morning of the 6th of April picket-firing was heard by the troops stationed at Adamsville. The whole command was immediately drawn up in line awaiting orders. Receiving orders at twelve o'clock M., the Seventy-Eighth, with its brigade, marched to the battle-field, a distance of fourteen miles, and reached Pittsburg Landing at eight o'clock in the evening, in company with the whole of General Lew. Wallace's division. The fight being over for the day the regiment went into camp for the night on the extreme right of the National army.

At daylight on the morning of the 7th the regiment went into the battle on the right, and was under fire throughout the day, with, however, but slight loss. Only one man was killed and nine wounded. Retaining its position on the right, the Seventy-Eighth shared in the movement on Corinth. In guarding the right flank of the army the regiment was frequently engaged in reconnoissances and skirmishes with the enemy.

On the evacuation of Corinth the regiment marched with Lew. Wallace's division to Bethel, where it was detached and sent with the Thirtieth Illinois, under command of Colonel Leggett, to Jackson, Tennessee. The town was found in possession of a small Rebel force, which was driven off and the place occupied. At this place the regiment had the honor to raise a National flag on the pole where the first Rebel flag was raised in Tennessee.

At Jackson the Seventy-Eighth was transferred from Lew. Wallace's to General Logan's division. From Jackson the Seventy-Eighth, with the Thirtieth Illinois, were again sent, under Colonel Leggett, to Grand Junction. It remained at this point one month, and then returned to Bolivar. While there the regiment made several important and arduous reconnoissances, in which a number of skirmishes were had with the enemy. On the 30th of August the Seventy-Eighth and Twentieth Ohio, one company of the Eleventh Illinois Cavalry, and a section of the Ninth Indiana Artillery had a brisk engagement at Spring Creek, six miles from Bolivar. While this engagement was in progress, four companies of the Second Illinois Cavalry, under Colonel Hogg, reported and took part in the fight. Colonel Hogg was killed. On the day before the fight a force of mounted infantry was improvised from the Seventy-Eighth and Twentieth Ohio, by selecting three tried men from each company. This force, under command of Lieutenants G. D. Munson, of the Seventy-Eighth, and Ayers, of the Twentieth Ohio, was sent on a reconnoissance the night previous, and discovered the enemy in force. After capturing the Rebel outposts it fell back to its main body. On the next day in the battle this "Mule Cavalry" performed excellent service, and to them was attributed largely the successful result of the fight. In this affair the loss of the regiment was slight.

When the Rebel army under Price and Van Dorn moved on Iuka, the Seventy-Eighth marched with Logan's division to that point, but did not participate in the battle. Returning to Bolivar it joined Grant's forces in the movement toward Grenada, Mississippi, and was near Grenada in advance of the whole army, when, in consequence of the destruction by the enemy of Holly Springs, it fell back with the National army on that place. Immediately thereafter it accompanied Grant's forces to Memphis, Tennessee, and thence by steamer to Lake Providence, where it was employed in cutting the bank of the Mississippi, and opening Bayou Jackson for the purpose of overflowing the country below. While lying at this point the regiment, with its brigade, went to Eagle Point and up Mud Bayou to aid in saving some gunboats surrounded by the enemy.

Millikin's Bend was the next point to which the Seventy-Eighth was sent, where it joined the National army under General Grant, then concentrating for the march on Vicksburg. On the occasion of running the blockade of Vicksburg with transports, twelve members of the Seventy-Eighth Ohio were selected as part of the crew of one of the boats. Of this detail Sergeant James McLaughlin and Private Huffman occupied themselves during the trip in playing cards by the light of the enemy's guns!

Crossing the Mississippi River at Bruinsburg, the regiment marched with the army to the rear of Vicksburg. On this march it participated in the battle of Raymond, on the 12th of May, 1863, and lost, in killed and wounded, about eighty men. On the 16th of May it was engaged in the battle of Champion Hills, where it lost one hundred and sixteen men killed and wounded. During these battles General Leggett was commanding the brigade, having received his commission as Brigadier-General on the 29th of November, 1862.

On the 17th, 18th, and 19th of May the investment of Vicksburg was completed. On the 22d of May the Seventy-Eighth participated in the general charge of that day on the enemy's works with slight loss. About the 25th of May the regiment was joined to a force sent up the Yazoo River, under General Frank P. Blair, to look after a Rebel force reported to be moving to the relief of Vicksburg, under General Joseph E. Johnston. Johnston having changed his line of march to a point further south toward Jackson, the command returned to Vicksburg, and the Seventy-Eighth Ohio resumed its position before the city. At this point General Leggett was transferred to the command of the First Brigade of General Logan's division.

On the 22d of June the Seventy-Eighth was again sent with a force to prevent the Rebels, under Johnston, from crossing the Black River at Bovina. The regiment remained at Bovina until after the surrender of Vicksburg.

On the 4th of July the Seventy-Eighth joined General Sherman in his march on Jackson, Mississippi. It was left at Clinton, where, on the 7th of July, it was attacked by Rebel cavalry, which attack it handsomely repulsed. On the return of the National forces to Vicksburg, the regiment accompanied them and remained there until the latter part of August. It then marched with McPherson's expedition to destroy the Rebel mills near Canton. Coming back to Vicksburg, it went with General Logan's division to Monroeville, Louisiana, on the Washita River, to look after a force of Rebels reported to be in that vicinity.

On the 5th of January, 1864, the Seventy-Eighth re-enlisted for the war. Immediately thereafter the regiment marched with General Sherman on the Meridian expedition, and on its return was sent home on veteran furlough.

The regiment returned on the 1st of May, and rendezvoused at Cairo, Illinois. The division was reorganized at this point, and moved by steamers up the Tennessee River to Clifton. From Clifton it marched over the Blue Mountain Ridge, and joined General Sherman's army at Acworth, Georgia. It was immediately placed in position on the left, and commenced its part of the campaign against Atlanta.

On the 17th of June the regiment took part in the attack on and capture of Bushy Mountain. About the time the order was given to move on the mountain a heavy rain-storm commenced.

General M. D. Leggett, commanding the Third Division of Logan's corps, dashed up the slope and captured the Rebel works, turning its guns on the Rebels as they fled. By reason of the driving rain the other divisions that were to co-operate in the affair did not perceive General Leggett's movement, and supposing the Rebels still held the mountain and were firing on the National cavalry, directed their batteries on Leggett's division, and shelled the mountain until a staff-officer was sent to undeceive them.

On the 27th of June the regiment participated in the battle of Kenesaw Mountain. The regiment, with the Army of the Tennessee, then swung around the mountain to the extreme right of Sherman's line, extending to the Chattahoochie, at the mouth of the Nicojack Creek, thus flanking the Rebel forces and causing them to evacuate the mountain. From the 5th to the 16th of July the regiment was engaged in an almost continuous skirmishing and artillery duel. During this time, at intervals, it was almost impossible to prevent the privates of the two armies from affiliating. On one occasion a large boat was procured and placed in the middle of the Chattahoochie River, in each end of which a hostage was seated, and a squad of either party placed on the banks to shoot the hostage if treachery was practiced. Brisk trade and card playing then commenced, and continued until discovered and stopped by some of the officers.

On the night of the 15th of July the Rebels evacuated the north side of the Chattahoochie River, and on the 16th the regiment with its brigade and division marched to Rosswell Factories, and crossed the Chattahoochie at that place. While the Seventy-Eighth was on its march to this point, an affecting incident occurred. Major James Reeves, the Surgeon of the regiment, while walking through a clump of bushes was accosted by a citizen of the country with a request for a National Surgeon to administer medical aid to his sick daughter. The doctor at first demurred, but on reflection concluded to go with the man, who took him down in a valley and into a cave. In this secluded spot were congregated about two hundred Union refugees hiding from the persecution of the Rebel authorities.

From Rosswell the regiment moved directly on Atlanta. On the 21st of July the regiment participated in the attack on and capture of Bald Knob, a position commanding the city of Atlanta. The Rebels occupied it in force behind strong works. In carrying it the division suffered severely. This position being carried, shells were at once thrown into Atlanta by the National artillery. This position was considered so important by the Rebel commander that, in his anxiety to retake it, he, on the next day, threw his whole army on the left flank of the National lines and a terrible battle was the result, costing the life of the brave McPherson. The Seventy-Eighth Ohio suffered severely. It lost two hundred and three officers and men killed and wounded. At a critical moment the Seventy-Eighth and Sixty-Eighth Ohio held a line near Bald Knob, on which the Rebels made a determined attack. A hand-to-hand fight ensued in which desperate valor was displayed by both sides. Of thirteen flag and color-bearers of the Seventy-Eighth Ohio all were either killed or wounded. On one occasion a Rebel was about to capture the flag, when Captain John Orr, of company H, seized a short sword from the ground and almost completely decapitated him. For this the Captain received a gold medal from the Board of Honor of the Army of the Tennessee.

The Seventy-Eighth participated in the subsequent movements of the Army of the Tennessee till the fall of Atlanta. It then went into camp near Atlanta, and remained there until about the middle of October, when it was sent up the Atlanta Railroad to the vicinity of Chattanooga, to guard that line of supply against Hood. When Hood left the railroad and marched toward Decatur, the Seventy-Eighth returned to Atlanta by the way of Lost Mountain, reaching that place on the 13th of November. On the 15th it started with General Sherman's forces on the march to the sea.

After the taking of Savannah, and the march through the Carolinas, up to the surrender of Johnston's Rebel army, the regiment accompanied the National forces through Richmond, Virginia, to Washington City, and there participated in the grand review.

From Washington it was sent by rail and river to Louisville, Kentucky. On the 9th day of July it started for Columbus, Ohio, and on the 11th was paid off and mustered out of service.

79th REGIMENT OHIO VOLUNTEER INFANTRY.

ROSTER, THREE YEARS' SERVICE.

RANK.	NAME.	DATE OF RANK.	COM. ISSUED.	REMARKS.
Colonel	HENRY G. KENNETT	Nov. 1, 1862	Nov. 1, 1862	Resigned August 1, 1864.
Do.	AZARIAH W. DOANE	June 8, 1865	June 8, 1865	Mustered out as Lieutenant-Colonel.
Lt. Colonel	AZARIAH W. DOANE	Aug. 19, 1862	Nov. 12, 1862	Promoted to Colonel.
Do.	SAMUEL A. WEST	June 8, 1865	June 8, 1865	Mustered out as Major.
Major	HENRY S. CLEMENT	Aug. 30, 1862	Nov. 12, 1862	Resigned April 9, 1864.
Do.	WM. W. WILSON	May 9, 1864	May 9, 1864	Honorably discharged November 8, 1864.
Do.	SAMUEL A. WEST	Nov. 29, "	Nov. 29, "	Promoted to Lieutenant-Colonel.
Surgeon	W. P. ELSTUN	Aug. 19, 1862	" 12, 1862	Resigned February 5, 1863.
Do.	HENRY A. LANGDON	Feb. 5, 1863	Feb. 23, 1863	Mustered out with regiment.
Ass't Surgeon	HENRY A. LANGDON	Aug. 13, 1862	Nov. 12, 1862	Promoted to Surgeon.
Do.	WM. H. SWANDER	" 25, "	" 12, "	Resigned December 2, 1863.
Do.	JOHN E. JONES	May 7, 1863	May 7, 1863	Mustered out with regiment.
Chaplain	JAMES R. STILLWELL	Jan. 19, "	Feb. 19, "	Mustered out with regiment.
Captain	Wm. W. Wilson	July 19, 1862	Nov. 12, 186_	Promoted to Major.
Do.	John Cretors	" 20, "	" 12, "	Resigned December 20, 1862.
Do.	Isaac B. Allen	" 21, "	" 12, "	Resigned April 14, 1863.
Do.	George H. Hicks	" 21, "	" 12, "	Resigned December 29, 1863.
Do.	James Thompson	" 21, "	" 12, "	Resigned September 10, 1864.
Do.	John W. Kilbreth	" 21, "	" 12, "	Resigned April 25, 1863.
Do.	Ethan A. Spencer	" 26, "	" 12, "	Resigned March 15, 1863.
Do.	Joshua Smith	Aug. 5, "	" 12, "	Resigned June 7, 1864.
Do.	James R. Stillwell	" 17, "	" 12, "	Resigned January 19, 1863.
Do.	Jacob Flegle	Sept. 26, "	" 12, "	Resigned May 10, 1863.
Do.	Samuel A. West	Dec. 20, "	Dec. 25, "	Promoted to Major.
Do.	Ira N. Snell	Jan. 29, 1863	Jan. 29, 1863	Mustered out with regiment.
Do.	Howard Dunlevy	March 15, "	March 21, "	Honorably discharged August 7, 1864.
Do.	Abraham H. Bodkin	April 14, "	May 6, "	Honorably discharged April 17, 1865.
Do.	Benton Halstead	" 25, "	April 25, "	Mustered out May 29, 1865.
Do.	Robert C. Williamson	May 10, "	June 23, "	Mustered out with regiment.
Do.	Rodney Foos	" 9, 1864	May 9, 1864	Declined promotion.
Do.	Edward L. Patterson	Dec. 29, 1863	Jan. 20, "	Mustered out with regiment.
Do.	Bryant Robinson	July 25, 1864	July 25, "	Declined promotion to Captain.
Do.	David Giffin	Aug. 19, "	Aug. 19, "	Resigned as 1st Lieutenant August 24, 1864.
Do.	John Cretors	Sept. 26, "	Sept. 26, "	Mustered out with regiment.
Do.	Thomas E. Smith	" 26, "	" 26, "	Mustered out with regiment.
Do.	Wm. N. Wilkerson	" 26, "	" 26, "	Mustered out with regiment.
Do.	Joseph A. Hill	Jan. 20, 1865	Jan. 20, 1865	Mustered out with regiment.
Do.	Thomas Van Tress	" 20, "	" 20, "	Mustered out with regiment.
1st Lieutenant	Ira N. Snell	July 19, 1862	Nov. 2, 1862	Promoted to Captain.
Do.	Samuel A. West	" 19, "	" 12, "	Promoted to Captain.
Do.	Rodney Foos	" 21, "	" 12, "	Prom.; decl'd prom.; hon. disch'd Oct. 26,'64.
Do.	Howard Dunlevy	" 21, "	" 12, "	Promoted to Captain.
Do.	Abraham H. Bodkin	" 21, "	" 12, "	Promoted to Captain.
Do.	Bryant Robinson	" 23, "	" 12, "	Resigned January 7, 1865.
Do.	Benton Halstead	" 25, "	" 12, "	Promoted to Captain.
Do.	David Giffin	" 26, "	" 12, "	Promoted to Captain.
Do.	Israel D. Compton	Aug. 5, "	" 12, "	Died December 31, 1862.
Do.	Collin J. Ford	" 17, "	" 12, "	Mustered out Major colored regiment.
Do.	Edward L. Patterson	July 19, "	" 12, "	Promoted to Captain.
Do.	Isaiah Dougham	Sept. 26, "	" 12, "	Resigned April 20, 1863.
Do.	John Cretors	Dec. 20, "	" 25, "	Promoted to Captain.
Do.	Thomas E. Smith	" 31, "	Jan. 20, 1863	Promoted to Captain.
Do.	Wm. N. Wilkerson	Jan. 19, 1863	" 24, "	Promoted to Captain.
Do.	John W. Morris	March 15, "	April 3, "	Mustered out with regiment.
Do.	Henry W. Reading	April 25, "	" 25, "	Honorably discharged July 9, 1864.
Do.	Thornton Thompson	" 14, "	May 6, "	Honorably discharged December 15, 1864.
Do.	Henry C. Corbin	" 25, "	" 6, "	Resigned November 15, 1863.
Do.	Thomas Van Tress	May 9, 1864	" 9, "	Promoted to Captain.
Do.	Nathan Cleaver	" 9, "	" 9, "	Resigned as 2d Lieutenant October 7, 1864.
Do.	Joseph A. Hill	Dec. 29, 1863	Jan. 20, 1864	Promoted to Captain.
Do.	Joseph W. Slack	July 25, 1864	July 25, "	Mustered out with regiment.
Do.	Sylvester Snyder	" 25, "	" 23, "	Discharged November 26, 1864.
Do.	Wm. H. Wells	Aug. 19, "	Aug. 19, "	Declined promotion to 1st Lieutenant.
Do.	George F. Reed	Sept. 26, "	Sept. 26, "	Mustered out as 2d Lieutenant May 15, 1865.
Do.	Stephen Janney	" 26, "	" 26, "	Mustered out May 15, 1865.
Do.	James O. Redman	" 26, "	" 26, "	Mustered out with regiment.
Do.	Chas. G. Hallam	Jan. 20, 1865	Jan. 20, 1865	Mustered out with regiment as Adjutant.
Do.	Cyrus E. Custis	" 20, "	" 20, "	Mustered out with regiment.
Do.	Richard H. Parcell	" 20, "	" 20, "	Mustered out with regiment.
Do.	John W. Collett	" 20, "	" 20, "	Mustered out with regiment.
Do.	John D. Clements	" 20, "	" 20, "	Mustered out with regiment.
Do.	Robert A. Wherry	" 20, "	" 20, "	Mustered out with regiment.
Do.	Wm. P. Juday	Feb. 10, "	Feb. 10, "	Mustered out with regiment.
2d Lieutenant	Wm. N. Wilkerson	July 19, 1862	Nov. 12, 1862	Promoted to 1st Lieutenant.
Do.	Thornton Thompson	" 19, "	" 12, "	Promoted to 1st Lieutenant.
Do.	Henry S. Doane	" 21, "	" 12, "	Resigned February 22, 1863.
Do.	John Reese	" 21, "	" 12, "	Resigned February 18, 1863.
Do.	Henry S. Corbin	" 25, "	" 12, "	Promoted to 1st Lieutenant.
Do.	John Harrison	" 26, "	" 12, "	Resigned February 26, 1863.
Do.	Thomas E. Smith	Aug. 5, "	" 12, "	Promoted to 1st Lieutenant.
Do.	Joseph W. Slack	" 17, "	" 12, "	Promoted to 1st Lieutenant.
Do.	Joseph A. Hill	July 19, "	" 12, "	Promoted to 1st Lieutenant.
Do.	Robert C. Williamson	Sept. 26, "	" 12, "	Promoted to 1st Lieutenant.
Do.	Nathan D. Cleaver	Dec. 31, "	Jan. 20, 1863	Promoted to 1st Lieutenant.
Do.	Thomas Van Tress	Jan. 19, 1863	" 26, "	Promoted to 1st Lieutenant.

RANK.	NAME.	DATE OF RANK.	COM. ISSUED.	REMARKS.
2d Lieutenant	George Travilla	Feb. 18, 1863	April 3, 1863	Deceased.
Do.	Sylvester Snyder	" 22, "	" 3, "	Promoted to 1st Lieutenant.
Do.	Wm. H. Wells	" 26, "	" 3, "	Declined promotion.
Do.	Henry Barlow	" 18, "	May 6, "	Discharged November 3, 1863.
Do.	George F. Reed	April 25, "	" 6, "	Promoted to 1st Lieutenant.
Do.	Stephen Janney	" 25, "	" 6, "	Promoted to 1st Lieutenant.
Do.	James O. Redman	May 10, "	June 23, "	Promoted to 1st Lieutenant.
Do.	Chas. G. Hallam	April 5, 1864	April 5, 1864	Promoted to 1st Lieutenant.
Do.	Cyrus E. Custis	Aug. 19, "	Aug. 19, "	Promoted to 1st Lieutenant.

SEVENTY-NINTH OHIO VOLUNTEER INFANTRY.

THIS regiment was organized under the call of July, 1862, in the military district composed of the counties of Warren, Clinton, and Hamilton. One company was raised in Hamilton County, four in Warren, and four in Clinton. Clermont County organized one company of sharpshooters, which was assigned to the regiment, but did not join it until June, 1863. Though recruiting commenced on the 22d of July, before the 1st of September, 1862, nine companies had reported in Camp Dennison, and had been mustered into the service.

On the 3d day of September, 1862, the regiment received marching orders. It crossed the Ohio River at Cincinnati into Kentucky, that city being menaced by the Rebel army, concentrated at Lexington. After remaining near the Ohio River a few days, awaiting re-enforcements, an advance was made into the State as far as Crittenden, driving straggling parties of Rebels beyond that point. Returning from this fatiguing march, in which the troops suffered severely from heat, dust, and scarcity of water, the Seventy-Ninth was ordered to Louisville. On its arrival it reported to General Nelson, and was assigned to General W. T. Ward's brigade. Early in the month of October General Buell made an advance. The Seventy-Ninth accompanied General Dumont's division on the pike to Frankfort, which place was occupied with but little fighting, being defended by a small force of the enemy. The regiment remained at Frankfort until the 1st day of November, engaged in various expeditions against General Morgan's forces, and other roaming bands of guerrillas, in which much hard labor was performed. From Frankfort the regiment marched to Bowling Green, reporting to General Rosecrans, who was in command of General Buell's army. Great suffering attended the march. The part of Kentucky which it traversed was dependent on pools for water, and these the Rebels had attempted to destroy by killing animals and throwing their carcasses into them. The soldiers had to drink from these pools or perish. After a few days' rest the regiment marched to Scottsville, thence to Gallatin, Tennessee, without incident of note, save that the measles broke out in the regiment, causing the loss of many lives.

Arriving at Gallatin the regiment was much reduced by sickness and hardships, having marched, in bad weather, a distance of five hundred and fifty miles, not including many expeditions of limited distances. From 1st December, 1863, to the 24th of February, 1864, the Seventy-Ninth was stationed at Gallatin, Buck's Lodge, Lavergne, Edgefield, and Nashville, engaged in guarding railroads, supplies, and breaking up bands of guerrillas on the Cumberland and Stone Rivers. At Nashville company F joined the regiment, having marched from Knoxville, Tennessee, where it was acting as head-quarter guard for General Burnside. At Lavergne company K (sharpshooters) joined the command, armed with Spencer rifles, and was a great acquisition to the regiment. On the 24th day of February the Seventy-Ninth, having been transferred from the Army of the Cumberland to the Eleventh Army Corps, then stationed in Lookout Valley, marched over the Cumberland Mountains, in bad weather, over miserable roads, and reached the Valley on the 10th day of March, having lost but one man. Active measures were at once inaugurated for the coming campaign, and all detailed men were ordered to rejoin the regiment. On the 2d day of May, 1864, the regiment numbered six hundred effective men; but the strength was reduced by detailing company I to division head-quarters, where it remained on duty until the close of the war. In the reorganization of the army previous to the Atlanta campaign, the Seventy-Ninth was assigned to the First Brigade, Third Division, Twentieth Army Corps, under General Hooker, an assignment that continued uninterrupted during the war.

On the 2d day of May the armies in Lookout Valley moved from their encampments on the enemy, concentrated in force at Dalton, Georgia. The Seventy-Ninth was not engaged in the demonstrations at Buzzard's Roost and Dug Gap, being in the reserve line, but after passing through Snake Creek Gap, on the 13th and 14th, near Resaca, it skirmished with the enemy, with considerable loss in killed and wounded. On the 18th day of May the Seventy-Ninth was one of five regiments that were ordered to assault a strong position held by the enemy on the road leading from Dalton to Resaca. The position was defended by artillery and infantry. The assaulting party was composed of about twenty-five hundred men, under General W. T. Ward. It approached within four hundred yards of the enemy's position under cover of a dense forest of pine. At a given signal the troops rushed forward, amid a storm of grape, canister, and musket-balls, and, after hard fighting, carried the works, with a loss to the enemy of a number of prisoners, four pieces of artillery, and fifteen hundred stand of small arms. This was the introduction of the regiment to a hand-to-hand fight with the foe; and the dead and wounded that lay thick before the face of the enemy's works, on the parapet and within, indicated as landmarks where the regiment had struggled for victory. The loss in this engagement fell most severely on the enlisted men. There were no officers killed, but five were wounded. The enemy retreated during the night, and was found the following day at "Gravelly Plateaux," from which it was driven back early on Cassville. Here it made a more stubborn resistance, and again the Seventy-Ninth was engaged, but with small loss. At Dallas, on the 25th of May, the enemy was brought to bay, and the whole Twentieth Corps was hurled again and again against the lines, until sixteen hundred men were lost by the corps. On the 27th day of May an advance was ordered, and the Seventy-Ninth was one of the first to march. The movement was a success, but cost the regiment many lives. On the 28th the enemy opened on the position of the regiment with artillery. On the same night an attack was made along the whole line, but was repulsed.

The Twentieth Army Corps was moved to the enemy's flank, and an attack was made on the 3d day of June. This engagement was a severe test of firmness, as the regiment was exposed to the shell of the enemy in an open field, without an opportunity of returning the fire. Another retreat by the enemy, and fighting was resumed at Pine Mountain. Skirmishing continued for some days, ascertaining the enemy's true position, and on the 15th an advance by the Twentieth Corps was ordered. On the evening of that day the Seventy-Ninth Ohio and the Seventieth Indiana were detached from the other troops, a swamp cutting off these two regiments from the main line. These regiments came upon the enemy, a desperate conflict ensued, and the enemy was driven at the point of the bayonet within seventy yards of its main works. These two regiments attempted to carry the works of the enemy, but failed; yet they held, at heavy cost, the advantage they had gained until night, when re-enforcements came to the rescue. All night was occupied in strengthening the position of the National army. The 16th day of June was occupied in an artillery duel and skirmishing. In the night the enemy retreated, and the following day was employed in skirmishing near Kenesaw Mountain.

On the 22d an assault was ordered, and in the charging party was the Seventy-Ninth, which lost several men. On the morning of the 3d of July the enemy evacuated, and the regiment was in the pursuing column, on the Marietta Railroad, being engaged with the enemy's rear-guard for about four miles. From this time until the 20th of July skirmishing and fighting was of daily occurrence.

At Peachtree Creek the Seventy-Ninth was in the front line, being the second regiment engaged. From three o'clock until seven o'clock the battle raged terribly, and the regiment lost one-half its men. The enemy made assault after assault, but was each time repulsed. The regiment had seven color-bearers killed and wounded. At the commencement of the battle it had but four or five officers, and several companies were commanded by non-commissioned officers. After this battle, and until after the capture of Atlanta, where the regiment received recruits, it was only a regiment in name not in numbers. The labor in the trenches and on the skirmish-line, the attempted surprise by day and by night, the charge and the counter-charge, go to make up the history of the siege of Atlanta. The regiment commenced the campaign with six hundred men, and at its close had one hundred and eighty-two. Fifteen recruits were received during the campaign, of whom seven were lost, thus making the loss in about one hundred days four hundred and twenty-five men. Of this number many were slightly wounded, and rejoined the regiment; so that with the recruits received on the 15th day of November, when General Sherman commenced his march to the sea, it numbered about four hundred men. The Seventy-Ninth was never engaged during the march to the sea except as details for foraging, in which it lost two men. It took part in the siege of Savannah, and it was the sharpshooters of this regiment that silenced the guns of the fort commanding the entrance to Savannah, on the Springfield Road. Here no loss was sustained.

In the march through South Carolina the Seventy-Ninth took part in the affairs of Langtonville and Columbia. The loss was small, not exceeding thirty men killed, wounded, and prisoners. In North Carolina the regiment, at the battle of Averysburg, took an active part, assaulting and carrying that part of the enemy's lines where its artillery was posted. It captured three pieces of artillery, one hundred stand of small arms, and thirty-one prisoners. In this charge the regiment received many encomiums. The loss in killed and wounded was severe, being one-fourth of its men engaged. At Bentonville, on the 19th day of March, 1865, the regiment performed its part in contributing to the final overthrow of General Johnston's forces. This was the last action in which it was engaged. After sixteen days it reported at Goldsboro', and thence marched to Raleigh. About the first day of May it turned homeward by way of Richmond, and was mustered out at Washington, June 9, 1865.

The loss of the regiment, from all causes, was about one thousand men—more than its original number. On the 17th day of June, at Camp Dennison, it was paid off and discharged.

80th REGIMENT OHIO VOLUNTEER INFANTRY.

ROSTER, THREE YEARS' SERVICE.

RANK.	NAME	DATE OF RANK.	COM. ISSUED.	REMARKS.
Colonel	EPHRIAM R. ECKLEY	Dec. 29, 1861	Feb. 19, 1862	Resigned February 14, 1863.
Do.	M. H. BARTLESON	Feb. 14, 1863	March 5, 1863	Died August 11, 1863.
Do.	JAMES E. PHILPOT	Aug. 15, "	Aug. 31, "	Revoked.
Do.	PREN. METHAM	Jan. 4, 1864	Jan. 4, 1864	Mustered out as Lt. Colonel April 8, 1865.
Do.	THOMAS C. MORRIS	June 16, 1865	June 16, 1865	Mustered out with regiment as Lt. Col.
Lt. Colonel	MATTHEW H. BARTLESON	Dec. 23, 1861	Feb. 19, 1862	Promoted to Colonel.
Do.	WM. MARSHALL	Feb. 11, 1863	March 2[illegible], 1863	Resigned July 23, 1863.
Do.	PREN. METHAM	July 23, "	Aug. 21, "	Promoted to Colonel.
Do.	DAVID SKEELS	Jan. 4, 1864	Jan. 4, 1864	Mustered out December 20, 1864.
Do.	THOMAS C. MORRIS	May 11, 1865	May 11, 1865	Promoted to Colonel.
Do.	HENRY C. ROBINSON	June 16, "	June 16, "	Mustered out with regiment as Major.
Major	RICHARD LANNING	Dec. 23, 1861	Feb. 19, 1862	Killed at Corinth October 4, 1862.
Do.	CHAS. H. MATTHEWS	Oct. 4, 1862	Dec. 31, "	Resigned as Captain January 15, 1863.
Do.	PREN. METHAM	Jan. 15, 1863	Feb. 20, 1863	Promoted to Lieutenant-Colonel.
Do.	DAVID SKEELS	" 23, "	Aug. 21, "	Promoted to Lieutenant-Colonel.
Do.	THOMAS C. MORRIS	" 28, 1865	Jan. 28, 1865	Promoted to Lieutenant-Colonel.
Do.	HENRY C. ROBINSON	May 11, "	May 11, "	Promoted to Lieutenant-Colonel.
Do.	JAMES M. SCOTT	June 16, "	June 16, "	Mustered out with regiment.
Surgeon	EZEKIEL P. BUELL	Jan. 8, 1862	Feb. 19, 1862	Mustered out.
Do.	C. W. BUVINGER	" 28, 1865	Jan. 28, 1865	Mustered out with regiment.
Ass't Surgeon	SAMUEL H. LEE	Jan. 8, 1862	Feb. 9, 1862	Resigned September 3, 1862.
Do.	G. BAMBACK	Aug. 19, "	Sept. 8, "	Resigned July 26, 1862.
Do.	E. G. CLARK	Oct. 9, "	Oct. 9, "	Declined.
Do.	C. W. BUVINGER	May 12, "	May 12, "	Promoted to Surgeon.
Do.	THOMAS B. EAGLE	March 10, 18'5	March 10, 1865	
Do.	H. G. TOPE	June 26, "	June 26, "	Mustered out with regiment.
Chaplain	GEORGE W. PEPPER	Dec. 3, 1863	Dec. 3, 1863	Absent per Special Order.
Captain	Isaac Ulman	Nov. 5, 1861	Feb. 19, 1862	Resigned May 21, 1862.
Do.	Chas. H. Matthews	" 26, "	" 19, "	Promoted; resigned January 15, 1863.
Do.	John J. Robinson	Dec. 9, "	" 19, "	Resigned April 27, 1863.
Do.	David Skeels	" 21, "	" 19, "	Promoted to Major.
Do.	Emmerson Goodrich	" 23, "	" 19, "	Resigned March 8, 1863.
Do.	Wm. Marshall	" 27, "	" 19, "	Promoted to Lieutenant-Colonel.
Do.	Pren. Metham	" 31, "	" 19, "	Promoted to Major.
Do.	Joseph H. Anderson	Jan. 6, 1862	" 19, "	Mustered out January 5, 1865.
Do.	George W. Pepper	" 7, "	" 19, "	Resigned June 13, 1862.
Do.	John H. Gardner	" 11, "	" 19, "	Resigned.
Do.	Thomas C. Morris	March 12, "	March 12, "	Promoted to Major.
Do.	Michael C. West	June 13, "	June 24, "	
Do.	Isaac Ulman	" 30, "	July 3, "	Declined.
Do.	Sylvester Wallace	May 24, "	Sept. 12, "	Resigned July 22, 1863.
Do.	James Carnes	Oct. 31, "	Dec. 31, "	Honorably discharged September 21, 1864.
Do.	Wm. Wagstaff	Jan. 15, 1863	Feb. 19, 1863	Mustered out January 12, 1865.
Do.	John Kinney	Feb. 14, "	March 27, "	Died November 25, 1863.
Do.	Daniel Korn	March 8, "	April 9, "	Resigned July 30, 1864.
Do.	James E. Philpot	April 27, "	July 10, "	Revoked.
Do.	Wm. J. Eckley	" 27, "	Aug. 21, "	Honorably discharged September 21, 1864.
Do.	Daniel G. Hildt	July 12, "	" 21, "	Mustered out December 22, 1864.
Do.	Frank. Farmer	" 23, "	" 25, "	Mustered out December 20, 1864.
Do.	George F. Robinson	" 22, "	Jan. 10, 1864	Mustered out March 12, 1865.
Do.	John W. Summons	April 29, 1864	April 29, "	Resigned as 1st Lieutenant July 30, 1864.
Do.	Henry C. Robinson	Sept. 8, "	Sept. 8, "	Promoted to Major.
Do.	Oliver C. Bowleson	" 8, "	" 8, "	Detached at own request.
Do.	Robert G. Hill	Oct. 12, "	Oct. 12, "	Resigned January 3, 1865.
Do.	Thomas W. Collier	" 12, "	" 12, "	Detached at own request.
Do.	James E. Graham	Feb. 10, 1865	Feb. 10, 1865	Detached at own request.
Do.	James M. Scott	" 10, "	" 10, "	Promoted to Major.
Do.	Peter Hack	" 10, "	" 10, "	Mustered out with regiment.
Do.	Sylvester Baldwin	" 10, "	" 10, "	Resigned January 31, 1865, as 1st Lieutenant.
Do.	Milton B. Culter	" 10, "	" 10, "	Mustered out with regiment.
Do.	James M. Cochran	" 14, "	" 14, "	Mustered out with regiment.
Do.	Christian Deis	May 11, "	May 11, "	Mustered out with regiment.
Do.	Freeman Davis	June 16, "	June 16, "	Mustered out with regiment.
Do.	Cyrus W. Borton	" 16, "	" 16, "	Mustered out with regiment.
Do.	Othello M. Everett	Aug. 10, "	Aug. 10, "	Mustered out with regiment as R. Q. M.
1st Lieutenant	Clark H. Robinson	Oct. 23, 1861	Feb. 19, 1862	Resigned June 29, 1863.
Do.	Sylvester Wallace	Nov. 5, "	" 19, "	Promoted to Captain.
Do.	Chas F. Davis	" 26, "	" 19, "	Resigned September 2, 1862.
Do.	George W. Ecker	Dec. 9, "	" 19, "	Resigned March 21, 1862.
Do.	Michael C. West	" 21, "	" 19, "	Promoted to Captain.
Do.	John Orme	" 23, "	" 19, "	Mustered out May 31, 1862.
Do.	Peter Hack	" 27, "	" 19, "	Resigned June 26, 1862.
Do.	James Carnes	" 31, "	" 19, "	Promoted to Captain.
Do.	Wm. Wagstaff	Jan. 6, 1862	" 19, "	Promoted to Captain.
Do.	John Kinney	" 7, "	" 19, "	Promoted to Captain.
Do.	Daniel Korn	" 11, "	" 19, "	Promoted to Captain.
Do.	Chas. E. Mitchener	Feb. 21, "	" 21, "	Declined.
Do.	James E. Philpot	March 21, "	April 14, "	Resigned July 12, 1863.
Do.	John McLaughlin	June 13, "	June 13, "	Resigned February 25, 1863.
Do.	Wm. J. Eckley	" 24, "	" 24, "	Promoted to Captain.
Do.	John J. Robinson, Jr.	" 25, "	July 31, "	Killed October 4, 1862.
Do.	Daniel G. Hildt	May 24, "	Sept. 12, "	Promoted to Captain.
Do.	John W. Summons	Sept. 2, "	Nov. 17, "	Promoted to Captain.
Do.	Henry C. Robinson	Oct. 4, "	Dec. 31, "	Promoted to Captain.
Do.	Frank. Farmer	" 4, "	" 31, "	Promoted to Captain.

RANK.	NAME.	DATE OF RANK.	COM. ISSUED.	REMARKS.
1st Lieutenant	Oliver C. Dowleson	Oct. 4, 1862	Dec. 31, 1862	Promoted to Captain.
Do.	George F. Robinson	Jan. 15, 1863	Feb. 19, 1863	Promoted to Captain.
Do.	Robert G. Hill	Feb. 11, "	April 9, "	Promoted to Captain.
Do.	John Beatty	March 8, "	" 9, "	Honorably discharged January 7, 1865.
Do.	Henry W. Kirby	April 27, "	July 10, "	Mustered out January 13, 1865.
Do.	Wm. Hay	" 27, "	" 10, "	Resigned July 30, 1864.
Do.	Frank. M. Ross	" 29, "	" 28, "	Killed November 25, 1863.
Do.	Frederick Buell	" 27, "	Aug. 21, "	Mustered out December 21, 1864.
Do.	Thomas W. Collier	July 12, "	" 21, "	Promoted to Captain.
Do.	Nicholas R Tidball	" 23, "	" 25, "	Revoked; resigned as 2d Lieutenant.
Do.	John Bidwell	April 29, 1864	April 29, 1864	Honorably discharged June 1, 1862.
Do.	James E. Graham	" 29, "	" 29, "	Promoted to Captain.
Do.	James M. Scott	May 9, "	May 9, "	Promoted to Captain.
Do.	John Wilson	" 9, "	" 9, "	Honorably discharged September 21, 1864.
Do.	Peter Hack	" 7, "	" 7, "	Promoted to Captain.
Do.	George W. Maw	Sept. 8, "	Sept. 8, "	Mustered out.
Do.	Sylvester Baldwin	" 8, "	" 8, "	Promoted to Captain.
Do.	Milton B. Culter	" 8, "	" 8, "	Promoted to Captain.
Do.	James M. Cochran	Oct. 12, "	Oct. 12, "	Promoted to Captain.
Do.	Christian Deis	" 12, "	" 12, "	Promoted to Captain.
Do.	Freeman Davis	" 12, "	" 12, "	Promoted to Captain.
Do.	Sylvester S. West	Feb. 10, 1865	Feb. 10, 1865	Mustered out.
Do.	Othello M. Everett	" 10, "	" 10, "	Promoted to Captain.
Do.	Alpheus B. Davis	" 10, "	" 10, "	Insane; sick in hospital at Newbern, N. C.
Do.	Frank R. Price	" 10, "	" 10, "	Mustered out.
Do.	Cyrus W. Borton	" 10, "	" 10, "	Promoted to Captain.
Do.	Wilson M. Courtwright	" 10, "	" 10, "	Mustered out.
Do.	John Isenogle	April 20, "	April 20, "	Mustered out with regiment.
Do.	Ebenezer H. McCall	" 20, "	" 20, "	Mustered out with regiment.
Do.	Zaven Lanning	" 20, "	" 20, "	Mustered out with regiment.
Do.	George B. Wilson	" 20, "	" 20, "	Mustered out with regiment.
Do.	Samuel Clark	" 20, "	" 20, "	Mustered out with regiment.
Do.	James McBain	June 16, "	June 16, "	Mustered out with regiment.
Do.	J. H. Cateral	" 16, "	" 16, "	Mustered out with regiment.
Do.	Wm. H. Anderson	" 16, "	" 16, "	Mustered out with regiment.
Do.	Otis W. Hoiles	" 16, "	" 16, "	Mustered out with regiment.
Do.	Solomon Murphey	" 16, "	" 16, "	Mustered out with regiment.
Do.	James McBair	Sept. 4, "	Sept. 4, "	Mustered out with regiment as Serg't Major.
2d Lieutenant	James E. Philpot	Nov. 5, 1861	Feb. 19, 1862	Promoted to 1st Lieutenant.
Do.	John J. Robinson, jr.	Dec. 9, "	" 19, "	Promoted to 1st Lieutenant.
Do.	John McLaughlin	" 21, "	" 19, "	Promoted to 1st Lieutenant.
Do.	Daniel G. Hildt	" 23, "	" 19, "	Promoted to 1st Lieutenant.
Do.	John D. Ross	" 27, "	" 19, "	Resigned August 31, 1862.
Do.	Frank, Farmer	" 31, "	" 19, "	Promoted to 1st Lieutenant.
Do.	Chas. F. Espy	Jan. 6, 1862	" 19, "	Mustered out May 31, 1862.
Do.	Jacob W. Doyle	" 7, "	" 19, "	Resigned August 22, 1862.
Do.	Oliver C. Bowleson	" 11, "	" 19, "	Promoted to 1st Lieutenant.
Do.	Henry C. Robinson	" 11, "	" 19, "	Promoted to 1st Lieutenant.
Do.	George F. Robinson	March 21, "	June 10, "	Promoted to 1st Lieutenant.
Do.	Robert G. Hill	June 13, "	Jan. 24, "	Promoted to 1st Lieutenant.
Do.	John Beatty	" 26, "	July 31, "	Promoted to 1st Lieutenant.
Do.	Thomas L. Patton	Sept. 10, "	Sept. 12, "	Resigned February 22, 1862.
Do.	Henry W. Kirby	Aug. 22, "	Oct. 7, "	Promoted to 1st Lieutenant.
Do.	John Bidwell	" 19, "	Nov. 19, "	Promoted to 1st Lieutenant.
Do.	Wm. Hay	" 31, "	Dec. 4, "	Promoted to 1st Lieutenant.
Do.	Thomas W. Collier	Oct. 4, "	" 31, "	Promoted to 1st Lieutenant.
Do.	James M. Scott	" 4, "	" 31, "	Promoted to 1st Lieutenant.
Do.	James E. Graham	" 4, "	" 31, "	Promoted to 1st Lieutenant.
Do.	Frederick Buell	Jan. 15, 1863	March 11, 1863	Promoted to 1st Lieutenant.
Do.	Nicholas R. Tidball	Feb. 22, "	" 27, "	Promoted; resigned July 27, 1863.
Do.	John Wilson	" 14, "	April 9, "	Promoted to 1st Lieutenant.
Do.	George W. Maw	March 8, "	" 9, "	Promoted to 1st Lieutenant.
Do.	Sylvester Baldwin	April 27, "	July 10, "	Promoted to 1st Lieutenant.
Do.	Milton B. Culter	" 27, "	" 10, "	Promoted to 1st Lieutenant.
Do.	James M. Cochran	July 27, "	Aug. 21, "	Promoted to 1st Lieutenant.
Do.	Frank H. Price	April 27, "	" 21, "	On detached service at own request.
Do.	Christian Deis	July 23, "	" 25, "	Promoted to 1st Lieutenant.
Do.	Freeman Davis	May 9, 1864	May 9, 1864	Promoted to 1st Lieutenant.
Do.	Daniel Suiter	Aug. 10, 1865	Sept. 4, 1865	
Do.	James B. Wilson	" 10, "	" 4, "	
Do.	Adam Walters	" 10, "	" 4, "	
Do.	David A. Mulvane	" 10, "	" 4, "	Mustered out with regiment as Sergeants; complimentary commissions given after they were mustered out.
Do.	George W. Cox	" 10, "	" 4, "	
Do.	John C. Miller	" 10, "	" 4, "	
Do.	Joseph Pershing	" 10, "	" 4, "	
Do.	John M. Potts	" 10, "	" 4, "	
Do.	Joseph Finley	" 10, "	" 4, "	
Do.	Isaac R. Alter	" 10, "	" 4, "	

EIGHTIETH OHIO VOLUNTEER INFANTRY.

THE EIGHTIETH OHIO was recruited principally in the counties of Tuscarawas, Coshocton, and Carroll, and was organized at Camp Meigs, near Canal Dover, in Tuscarawas County. It left Camp Meigs with nine hundred and nineteen men, in February, 1862, and was taken by rail to Columbus, and thence by rail and river to Paducah, Kentucky. The regiment was not armed until it reached Paducah.

On April 20, 1862, it left Paducah, and was taken up the Tennessee River on transports to Hamburg Landing. Here it was assigned to General Pope's command, and it operated with that army throughout the siege of Corinth. On the 9th of May the regiment was ordered to the support of a Missouri Battery in front of Farmington, and in performing that duty was for the first time under fire. Thereafter during the siege it was frequently under fire in skirmishes and reconnoissances.

On the evacuation of Corinth it pursued the enemy as far as Booneville, Mississippi, and then returned to Corinth. On June 22d the regiment made a forced march to Ripley, Mississippi, a distance of forty-six miles, during which it suffered intensely from the dust and heat, and a number of the men died from the effects of sun-stroke.

On September 19th the regiment took part in the battle of Iuka, and lost forty-five men killed and wounded. Lieutenant-Colonel M. H. Bartleson commanded the regiment in this battle, and was severely wounded in the thigh. His horse was killed under him at the same time. Adjutant James E. Philpot was also wounded.

The Eightieth was now ordered to Jacinto for the purpose of watching the movements of the Rebels under General Price. It remained there some days scouting and drilling; then moved to Corinth. It took a prominent part in the battle that ensued and lost heavily. Major Richard Lanning, in command of the regiment, was killed, as also was First Lieutenant John J. Robinson of company C. Lieutenants Oliver C. Bowleson and George F. Robinson were both severely wounded. The total loss of the regiment in this battle was eighty officers and men killed and wounded. Lieutenant-Colonel Bartleson, although yet suffering severely from his wound, hearing of Major Lanning's death, mounted his horse and commanded the regiment through the remainder of the battle. It joined in the pursuit of the Rebels, and made some very severe marches. Returning to Corinth it remained there but a few days, and then marched with Grant's army through Central Mississippi. On this march the Eightieth, in company with General Sullivan's brigade, took part in a reconnoissance from Davis's Mills to Cold Water. General Sullivan, in pressing forward, went into Holly Springs, Mississippi, surprised the Rebels, and took a number of prisoners. Holly Springs was beyond the point to which General Sullivan was ordered, and he was immediately ordered back to Davis's Mills. In executing that order a forced march of twenty-two miles was made. For several miles on this march the Rebels in heavy force were in plain view, but for some cause they failed to attack.

The march toward Vicksburg was resumed, but owing to the destruction by the Rebels of the National stores at Holly Springs, the whole army abandoned the movement, and returned to Holly Springs. The Eightieth, with General Quinby's division, was ordered as guard of a provision train to Memphis, Tennessee, there to load with rations and return to the remainder of the army, then making its way toward Memphis, repairing the railroad as it marched.

The regiment remained in camp at Forrest Hill, eighteen miles east of Memphis, until about the middle of February. Marching into Memphis, it went into camp in the suburbs of the city, preparatory to the Vicksburg expedition. While at Memphis Colonel Eckly resigned his commission and returned to Ohio.

On March 1, 1863, the regiment embarked on the steamer Ed. Walsh and was taken to Woodruff's Landing. From this point it was ordered back to Helena, and in a few days thereafter it went with Quinby's division on the Yazoo Pass expedition. This was one of the wildest the regiment participated in during its whole service.

Returning to Helena it almost immediately moved to Milliken's Bend. It there disembarked and marched around through Richmond, Louisiana, and crossed the Mississippi River at Bruinsburg, with Grant's forces, on the 1st of May, 1863. The battle of Port Gibson was fought on that day, but the regiment did not get up in time to participate. It marched, however, in line of battle, and skirmished with the enemy almost the whole way to Little Black River.

On May 12th the regiment participated in the battle of Raymond, but did not lose any men. Two days later, at Jackson, the Eighteenth with its brigade had a desperate fight, and in a charge made by the brigade lost about one-third of its number killed and wounded. Captain Wallace and Lieutenant Tidball were wounded. Just after the charge was ended, General McPherson, in command of the Seventeenth Corps, rode up to the regiment, and lifting his hat, exclaimed, "God Almighty bless the Eightieth Ohio." Its loss was ninety killed and wounded.

At Champion Hills, May 16th, the Eightieth occupied the rear as train-guard, and did not actively participate in the battle. The next morning it was detailed as guard to one thousand five hundred Rebel prisoners, and ordered to take them to Memphis. This duty performed it returned to Vicksburg and took part in the entire siege and capture of that Rebel stronghold.

About a month after the capture of Vicksburg, the regiment went to Helena to re-enforce General Steele, who was moving on Little Rock. But before it reached General Steele information was received of the repulse at Chickamauga, and it was immediately ordered to Memphis, there to join General Sherman's forces in their march to Chattanooga, a distance of nearly four hundred miles. It reached the bank of the Tennessee River, opposite the mouth of Chickamauga Creek, and the regiment with other troops crossed in pontoon boats soon after midnight of the 22d of November. By daylight strong earthworks were thrown up to cover the men until the pontoon bridge was laid over the river.

On the evening of the 23d the regiment with its division marched out and took the east end of Mission Ridge. That night the regiment was on the skirmish-line for seven hours without relief. Next day the regiment, in entering the battle, was compelled to pass around a point of rocks covered by three Rebel batteries, and was exposed to a most terrific artillery fire. Singular to relate, not a man was hit. It entered the fight just east of the tunnel, was hotly engaged until near nightfall, and lost several commissioned officers and nearly one hundred men. Captain John Kinney was shot through the heart and killed. Lieutenant F. M. Ross was also killed. Lieutenant F. Robinson was wounded and captured. Lieutenant George Maw was captured.

After the battle the regiment pursued the Rebels to Graysville, Georgia, and then returned to its old camp near Chattanooga. From thence it went to Bridgeport. While here the regiment and division were permanently transferred from the Seventeenth to the Fifteenth Corps.

January 6, 1864, found the regiment at Huntsville, Alabama. Shortly after this it re-enlisted for another term. After wintering near Huntsville, the regiment started, on the 1st of April, to enjoy its veteran furlough of thirty days at home, in Ohio.

At the expiration of its furlough the Eightieth returned to Larkinsville, Alabama, where it performed guard-duty on the line of the Memphis and Charleston Railroad.

In June, 1864, the regiment went from Huntsville to Charleston, Georgia, a long and tedious March. From Kingston it went to Alatoona, and remained two weeks, and was then ordered back to Resaca to relieve the Tenth Missouri. While at Resaca the Rebel General Hood made his dash to the rear of General Sherman's army. On the 12th of October twenty-eight thousand Rebels appeared before Resaca, invested the place, and demanded its surrender. Colonel Weaver of the Seventeenth Iowa, in command of Resaca, replied that "he was there to defend the post, and if the Rebel Commander wanted it he might come and take it." They immediately opened on the garrison with artillery and musketry from the entire line. The National force numbered barely one thousand men, but by a ruse, in displaying numerous flags, and placing the entire force on the picket-line, the Rebels were made to believe that it consisted of at least ten thousand men, and that it would cost too much loss of life to risk an assault. After annoying the little garrison for two days the enemy withdrew, and swept up the railroad toward Chattanooga, destroying the road as they marched.

From Resaca the Eightieth marched back to Atlanta, and joined General Sherman's "march to the sea." It went through to Savannah without meeting or performing anything of special interest. After the capture of Savannah the regiment was quartered near the city, and remained in camp until the 19th of January, 1865. It was then, with its division, ordered to Pocotaligo, and from that point made its way through to Goldsboro', participating on the way in a brisk skirmish with the enemy at Salkahatchie River.

On March 19th, at Cox's Bridge, over the Neuse River, the regiment performed an important flank movement, under Colonel Morris, for the purpose of preventing the Rebels from burning the bridge. The movement was successful, the Rebels being compelled to withdraw and leave the way open to Goldsboro'.

The Eightieth Ohio then marched to Bentonville, and reached that place in time to participate in the closing scenes of that battle. It then marched to Goldsboro', where, after being refitted, it went to Raleigh, North Carolina. On this march the Eightieth Ohio held the advance of the whole army the day it crossed the Neuse River. It was ordered to make a forced march to an important bridge over that river, and, if possible, prevent the Rebels from destroying it. In four hours' time it made seventeen miles, and accomplished its order to the letter. As it came in sight of the bridge several Rebel wagons were in the act of crossing it. When the regiment reached it one end was on fire, but it was easily extinguished.

Raleigh was reached on the day it was first occupied by Federal troops. After the surrender of Johnston's Rebel army to General Sherman, the Eightieth Ohio marched, with the rest of the National forces, through Richmond to Washington City, and there participated in the grand review. A few days thereafter it was taken by rail and river to Louisville, Kentucky, and from thence to Little Rock, Arkansas, where, for some months, it performed guard and garrison-duty.

The last-named duty closed its military career. It was mustered out of the service at Little Rock, August 15, 1865, arrived at Columbus, Ohio, in a few days thereafter, and was finally discharged August 25, 1865.

81st REGIMENT OHIO VOLUNTEER INFANTRY.

ROSTER, THREE YEARS' SERVICE.

RANK.	NAME.	DATE OF RANK.	COM. ISSUED.	REMARKS.
Colonel	THOMAS MORTON	Aug. 19, 1861	April 23, 1862	Resigned July 30, 1864.
Do.	ROBERT N. ADAMS	" 8, 1861	Aug. 8, 1864	Appointed Brevet Brigadier-General.
Lt. Colonel	JOHN A. TURLEY	" 19, 1861	April 23, 1862	Resigned December 1, 1861.
Do.	ROBERT N. ADAMS	Dec. 1, "	May 7, "	Promoted to Colonel.
Do.	JAMES W. TITUS	Aug. 8, 1864	Aug. 8, 1864	Resigned September 8, 1864.
Do.	WM. H. HILL	Oct. 10, "	Oct. 10, "	Mustered out with regiment.
Major	CHAS. N. LAMISON	Aug. 19, 1861	April 23, 1862	Resigned April 6, 1862.
Do.	ROBERT N. ADAMS	Dec. 1, "	May 7, "	Never commissioned.
Do.	FRANKL'N EVANS	April 16, 1862	" 7, "	Resigned June 27, 1864.
Do.	JAMES W. TITUS	Aug. 8, 1864	Aug. 8, 1864	Promoted to Lieutenant-Colonel.
Do.	WM. H. CHAMBERLAIN	" 9, "	" 9, "	Resigned.
Do.	WM. C. HENRY	Oct. 10, "	Oct. 10, "	Mustered out with regiment.
Surgeon	WM. H. LAMME	Nov. 27, 1861	April 23, 1862	Resigned March 31, 1862.
Do.	R. G. McLEAN	April 1, 1862	" 14, "	Resigned November 6, 1862.
Do.	WM. C. JACOBS	Dec. 23, "	Feb. 10, 1863	Mustered out with regiment.
Ass't Surgeon	R. G. McLEAN	Nov. 20, 1861	April 23, 1862	Promoted to Surgeon.
Do.	J. T. REED	April 1, 1862	" 14, "	Resigned.
Do.	JOHN W. GREEN	" 24, "	" 24, "	Resigned.
Do.	C. R. REED	June 6, "	June 23, "	Never reported.
Do.	JOHN WHITTAKER	Aug. 19, "	Sept. 1, "	Resigned November 11, 1864.
Do.	HIRAM M. SHAFFER	March 19, 1863	March 19, 1863	Mustered out August 24, 1864.
Chaplain	JAMES YOUNG	Feb. 11, "	April 6, "	Resigned December 26, 1863.
Captain	Peter O. Kane	Aug. 30, 1861	" 23, 1862	In 22d Regiment.
Do.	Martin Armstrong	" 30, "	" 23, "	Killed at Pittsburg Landing April 7, 1862.
Do.	Robert N. Adams	" 30, "	" 23, "	Promoted to Major.
Do.	Peter A. Tyler	" 30, "	" 23, "	Discharged February 20, 1863.
Do.	George A. Taylor	" 30, "	" 23, "	Resigned December 7, 1861.
Do.	Ozro J. Dodds	Sept. 1, "	" 23, "	Promoted to Lieutenant-Col. 1st Ala. Col Reg.
Do.	Chas. M. Hughes	" 3, "	" 23, "	Resigned September 3, 1862.
Do.	R. B. Kinsell	Oct. 2, "	" 23, "	Resigned August 15, 1862.
Do.	R. T. Lanins	Dec. 12, "	" 23, "	Resigned February 13, 1863.
Do.	James W. Titus	April 7, 1862	" 27, "	Promoted to Major.
Do.	Samuel E. Adams	Dec. 1, 1861	" 25, "	Declined.
Do.	Wm. H. Hill	July 12, 1862	" 15, "	Promoted to Lieutenant-Colonel.
Do.	Wm. C. Henry	" 24, "	" 15, "	Promoted to Major.
Do.	James Gibson	" 31, "	" 15, "	Honorably discharged March 27, 1865.
Do.	George W. Overmyer	Aug. 9, "	" 15, "	Honorably discharged November 6, 1864.
Do.	Benj. F. Matthews	" 15, "	" 15, "	Resigned December 31, 1862.
Do.	Wm. H. Chamberlain	May 7, "	Dec. 31, "	Promoted to Major.
Do.	Chas. Lane	Dec. 31, "	Feb. 11, 1863	Killed July 22, 1864.
Do.	James H. Conns	Feb. 20, 1863	April 20, "	Honorably discharged November 28, 1863.
Do.	George L. Hughes	" 13, "	March 30, "	Honorably discharged March 11, 1864.
Do.	Noah Stoker	Nov. 28, 1863	Jan. 10, 1864	Mustered out.
Do.	David S. Van Pelt	May 9, 1864	May 9, "	Mustered out with regiment.
Do.	Wesley B. Guthrie	" 9, "	" 9, "	Mustered out July 25, 1865.
Do.	Hugh K. S. Robinson	Aug. 9, "	Aug. 9, "	Declined promotion; commission returned.
Do.	Chas. W. Lockwood	" 9, "	" 9, "	Resigned January 3, 1865.
Do.	Oliver P. Irion	" 9, "	" 9, "	Honorably disch'd as 1st Lieut. Aug. 22, 1864.
Do.	Jonathan McCain	Sept. 8, "	Sept. 8, "	Mustered out with regiment.
Do.	George W. Dixon	Oct. 10, "	Oct. 10, "	Mustered out.
Do.	Robert E. Roney	" 10, "	" 10, "	Discharged October 28, 1864.
Do.	Wm. A. Johnson	Feb. 14, 1865	Feb. 14, 1865	Mustered out with regiment.
Do.	James C. Crawford	" 14, "	" 14, "	Mustered out with regiment.
Do.	Benj. R. Howell	" 11, "	" 14, "	Mustered out July 26, 1865.
Do.	C. C. Platter	" 14, "	" 14, "	Mustered out with regiment.
Do.	Rufus K. Darling	March 24, "	March 21, "	Mustered out with regiment.
Do.	Ira Pfoutz	" 24, "	" 24, "	Mustered out with regiment.
Do.	John Allaback	May 18, "	May 18, "	Mustered out with regiment.
1st Lieutenant	Samuel E. Adams	Aug. 19, 1861	April 23, 1862	Declined promotion; mustered out.
Do.	Frank Evans	" 19, "	" 23, "	Promoted to Captain.
Do.	Daniel Sherman	" 30, "	" 23, "	In 22d Regiment.
Do.	James W. Titus	" 30, "	" 23, "	Promoted to Captain.
Do.	Wm. H. Chamberlain	" 30, "	" 23, "	Promoted to Captain.
Do.	F. Agerter	" 30, "	" 23, "	Resigned November 14, 1862.
Do.	Wm. C. Henry	Sept. 1, "	" 23, "	Promoted to Captain.
Do.	John L. Hughes	" 3, "	" 23, "	Promoted to Captain.
Do.	Eli A. James	Oct. 2, "	" 23, "	Dropped from Rolls.
Do.	Wm. F. Wilcox	April 16, 1862	June 24, "	Resigned April 2, 1862.
Do.	James H. Conns	" 7, "	" 24, "	Promoted to Captain.
Do.	David S. Van Pelt	July 31, "	Oct. 15, "	Promoted to Captain.
Do.	John R. Hunt	Sept. 9, "	Sept. 9, "	Resigned September 20, 1864.
Do.	Wesley B. Guthrie	Aug. 5, "	Oct. 15, "	Promoted to Captain.
Do.	Hugh K. S. Robinson	" 7, "	" 15, "	Honorably discharged November 11, 1864.
Do.	Caleb J. Sprague	" 14, "	" 15, "	Honorably discharged January 10, 1865.
Do.	Chas. Lane	" 15, "	" 15, "	Promoted to Captain.
Do.	Chas. W. Lockwood	" 20, "	" 15, "	Promoted to Captain.
Do.	Oliver P. Irion	May 7, "	Dec. 31, "	Promoted to Captain.
Do.	Noah Stoker	Nov. 14, "	....	Promoted to Captain.
Do.	Hezekiah Hoover	Dec. 31, "	Feb. 11, 1863	Killed in action July 22, 1864.
Do.	Jonathan McCain	Feb. 13, 1863	March 31, "	Promoted to Captain.
Do.	Timothy Shaffer	" 20, "	April 20, "	Declined; commission returned.
Do.	George W. Dixon	" 20, "	June 20, "	Promoted to Captain.
Do.	James C. Crawford	May 9, 1864	May 9, 1864	Declined; commission returned.
Do.	Robert E. Roney	" 9, "	" 9, "	Promoted to Captain.
Do.	Wm. A. Johnson	June 14, "	June 14, "	Promoted to Captain.

RANK.	NAME.	DATE OF RANK.	COM. ISSUED.	REMARKS.
1st Lieutenant	Wm. D. Tyler	June 14, 1864	June 14, 1864	Resigned January 31, 1865.
Do.	James C. Crawford	Aug. 9, "	Aug. 9, "	Promoted to Captain.
Do.	Benj. R. Howell	" 9, "	" 9, "	Promoted to Captain.
Do.	George W. Miller	" 9, "	" 9, "	Declined promotion; commission returned.
Do.	John Allaback	" 9, "	" 9, "	Promoted to Captain.
Do.	Thomas Harpster	Sept. 26, "	Sept. 26, "	Mustered out.
Do.	C. C. Platter	Oct. 10, "	Oct. 10, "	Promoted to Captain.
Do.	Wm. Pittman	" 10, "	" 10, "	Mustered out.
Do.	Adam C. Post	Feb. 14, 1865	Feb. 14, 1865	Mustered out with regiment.
Do.	Thomas M. Sellers	" 14, "	" 14, "	Mustered out with regiment.
Do.	Wm. M. Murphey	" 14, "	" 14, "	Mustered out May 15, 1865.
Do.	Thomas C. Harbaugh	" 14, "	" 14, "	Mustered out with regiment.
Do.	Thomas H. Imes	" 14, "	" 14, "	Mustered out with regiment.
Do.	Wm. B. Rush	" 14, "	" 14, "	Mustered out with regiment as Adjutant.
Do.	John W. Hays	" 14, "	" 14, "	Mustered out with regiment as Q. M.
Do.	Price J. Jones	March 24, "	March 24, "	Mustered out with regiment.
Do	David Kinsey	" 24, "	" 24, "	Sick at Newbern, N. C.
Do.	Gideon Howe	May 18, "	May 18, "	Mustered out with regiment.
Do.	Seth Dixon	" 18, "	" 18, "	Mustered out with regiment.
Do.	Harry C. Doldridge	" 18, "	" 18, "	Mustered out.
Do.	Sumner F. Mason	July 5, "	July 5, "	Mustered out with regiment.
Do.	Corwin B. Van Pelt	" 5, "	....	Mustered out with regiment as 2d Lieut.
2d Lieutenant	Wm. E. Lockwood	Aug. 19, 1861	April 23, 1862	In 22d Regiment.
Do.	Wm. F. Wilcox	" 30, "	" 23, "	Promoted to 1st Lieutenant
Do.	O. P. Irion	" 30, "	" 23, "	Promoted to 1st Lieutenant.
Do.	James W. Post	" 30, "	" 23, "	Killed at Pittsburg Landing April 7, 1862.
Do.	Anthony Bowsher	Oct. 1, "	" 23, "	Resigned July 13, 1862.
Do.	Caleb Ayers	" 2, "	" 23, "	Resigned September 30, 1862.
Do.	Mahlon G. Bailey	Dec. 3, "	May 2, "	Resigned September 5, 1862.
Do.	Noah Stoker	April 7, 1862	" 7, "	Promoted to 1st Lieutenant.
Do.	Timothy Shaffer	July 15, "	Oct. 15, "	Discharged August 21, 1864.
Do.	James C. Crawford	Aug. 7, "	" 15, "	Promoted to 1st Lieutenant.
Do.	Hezekiah Hoover	" 15, "	" 15, "	Promoted to 1st Lieutenant.
Do.	Robert E. Roney	" 20, "	" 15, "	Promoted to 1st Lieutenant.
Do.	Matthew A. Ferguson	" 23, "	" 15, "	Resigned July 30, 1863.
Do.	Wm. A. Johnson	May 7, "	Dec. 31, "	Promoted to 1st Lieutenant.
Do.	Wm. D. Tyler	Nov. 14, "	" 31, "	Promoted to 1st Lieutenant.
Do.	John Allaback	Dec. 31, "	Feb. 11, 1863	Promoted to 1st Lieutenant.
Do.	George W. Miller	Sept. 8, "	March 31, "	Mustered out.
Do.	Thomas Harpster	Feb. 13, 1863	" 31, "	Promoted to 1st Lieutenant.
Do.	Benj. R. Howell	Sept. 5, 1862	" 31, "	Promoted to 1st Lieutenant.
Do.	John R. Chamberlain	Feb. 20, 1863	April 20, "	Honorably discharged April 6, 1864.
Do.	C. C. Platter	June 14, 1864	June 14, 1864	Promoted to 1st Lieutenant.
Do.	Wm. Pittman	" 14, "	" 14, "	Promoted to 1st Lieutenant.
Do.	Adam C. Post	" 14, "	" 14, "	Promoted to 1st Lieutenant.
Do.	Thomas M. Sellers	" 14, "	" 14, "	Promoted to 1st Lieutenant.
Do.	Wm. M. Murphey	Aug. 9, "	Aug. 9, "	Promoted to 1st Lieutenant.
Do.	Thomas C. Harbaugh	" 9, "	" 9, "	Promoted to 1st Lieutenant.
Do.	Thomas H. Imes	" 9, "	" 9, "	Promoted to 1st Lieutenant.
Do.	Gideon Ditto	" 9, "	" 9, "	Declined promotion.
Do.	Gideon Howe	March 24, 1865	March 24, 1865	Promoted to 1st Lieutenant.
Do.	Seth Dixon	" 24, "	" 24, "	Promoted to 1st Lieutenant.
Do.	Sumner F. Mason	May 18, "	May 18, "	Promoted to 1st Lieutenant.
Do.	Corwin B. Van Pelt	" 18, "	" 18, "	Promoted to 1st Lieutenant.
Do.	Joseph H. Harbison	" 18, "	" 18, "	Mustered out as Sergeant.
Do.	Samuel Dotson	" 18, "	" 18, "	Mustered out as Sergeant.
Do.	John T. Collier	" 18, "	" 18, "	Mustered out as Sergeant.
Do.	Jacob Young	" 18, "	" 18, "	Mustered out with regiment.
Do.	John M. Henness	" 18, "	" 18, "	Mustered out as Sergeant.
Do.	Daniel Worley	" 18, "	" 18, "	Mustered out as Sergeant.
Do.	Chas. Brennan	" 18, "	" 18, "	Mustered out as Sergeant.
Do.	Joseph S. Campbell	" 18, "	" 18, "	Mustered out as Sergeant.
Do.	John D. Neiswanger	July 5, "	July 5, "	Mustered out as Sergeant.
Do.	James Tucker	" 5, "	" 5, "	Mustered out as Sergeant.

EIGHTY-FIRST OHIO VOLUNTEER INFANTRY.

DURING the summer of 1861 it was allowable, by order from the War Department, for any one to enlist men for General Fremont's command, and to have them mustered either singly, or in squads, or companies, and forwarded to his head-quarters at St. Louis. Under these orders Colonel Morton, formerly Colonel of the Twentieth Ohio, contracted to raise a full regiment, which was to be armed with the best of rifles, and was to be known as "Morton's Independent Rifle Regiment." By some bad management one company, after having been sent to St. Louis, was incorporated into another regiment, and this loss, together with the loss of one or two other companies, which were expected to join Morton's regiment, but were prevailed upon to go elsewhere, delayed the filling up of the regiment, so that it did not seem likely that the Colonel would fulfill his promise in the time allowed. At this juncture the State took the independent regiment into its fold. It was denominated the Eighty-First Ohio Volunteer Infantry, and it was agreed that the officers already appointed should be commissioned by the Governor, and that the State authorities should use every endeavor to have the regiment filled to the maximum.

Benton Barracks was the rendezvous of all the troops sent to Fremont's department; and in the ample grounds of that well-known camp the regiment entered upon its first military duties. On the 24th of September, 1861, the detachment received marching orders, and on the following day was taken to Franklin, Missouri, and a day or two after to Herman. Here the regiment went into camp, and attained a tolerable degree of skill in the evolutions. It had now reached its maximum, not the legal, but the possible, and it numbered eight companies, with an aggregate of nearly six hundred men. In November the regiment moved against a Rebel force in Calloway County, but the Rebel camp was found deserted. In December the guerrillas destroyed a portion of the Northern Missouri Railroad, and orders came for the force at Herman to march to the railroad and drive off the troublesome bands. The troops moved in extremely cold weather, with snow on the ground; and the advance reached Danville, the county-seat of Montgomery County, just as the Rebel rear left. Pursuit was in vain, as the Rebels were mounted.

During the next two weeks the regiment was marching through Northern Missouri, sleeping on the ground, in rain, sleet, and snow, with no covering but blankets. At the end of that time it was stationed at Wellsville, Montgomery City, Florence, and Danville, on the Northern Missouri Railroad, with head-quarters at the latter place. While thus stationed the regiment did an enormous amount of work, in scouting, arresting accomplices and principals in the work of destroying the railroad, and in restoring peace and quiet in the whole country round about.

About the 1st of March, 1862, the regiment was ordered to St. Louis. It was armed with short Enfields, was placed on board the steamer Meteor, and about midnight on the 17th it disembarked at Pittsburg Landing. In a few days the Eighty-First was assigned to the Second Brigade, Second Division, Army of the Tennessee. The brigade was commanded by Colonel McArthur, and the division by General C. F. Smith. The regiment went to drilling earnestly, under the direction mostly of Adjutant Evans, and attained a proficiency that was valuable in the coming contest. The battle of Pittsburg Landing opened on Sabbath morning, April 6th, while the regiment was undergoing the usual morning inspection. It was ordered across Snake Creek, and was placed in position until nearly noon, when it was withdrawn to its own color-line. It was almost one o'clock when the Eighty-First saw the enemy approaching its front, but there was only a small cavalry force, and a volley from the two right companies put them to flight. About two o'clock there was a lull; and General Grant ordered Colonel Morton to move toward the center of the line of battle and then forward until he found the enemy. Starting up a ravine in rear of the line, he proceeded thus until he could go unperceived to the front. He passed through the line of battle at a point where General Sherman was watching the movements of the enemy, and advancing toward the front and left, the Colonel soon found his little regiment alone far ahead of the main line, and out of sight of it. The regiment was marching by the flank, left in front, and as the left emerged into a clear piece of ground it was greeted with a discharge of canister from a battery not more than two hundred yards away. The regiment formed line, faced to the rear, and lying down, delivered a volley or two, which silenced the enemy's fire. Not liking the position, Colonel Morton ordered a movement to a ravine a little further to the left. To reach this, a road, swept by the enemy's battery at short range, had to be passed. A company at a time ran the gauntlet, and the whole regiment was safely re-formed in the ravine. While in this position some Rebel cavalry commenced a movement to the regiment's rear, but before it was completed General Grant ordered the regiment back to the main lines. Just as Captain Armstrong, commanding the right company, gave the command, "By file right, march!" a grape shot struck him on the head and killed him instantly. The regiment was extricated without further loss, and upon reporting to General Grant, Colonel Morton was complimented for having held the enemy in check until the main line could be firmly established. The regiment was then ordered to take place in line near the right, where it remained during the rest of the day.

In the fighting on the 6th the regular brigades and divisions had in many cases become scattered. On the morning of the 7th there was no time for organization, and provisional brigades were appointed, to one of which the Eighty-First was assigned. The regiment advanced and after crossing an open field came upon a rude breastwork of logs, manned by the enemy, and raking the regiment from left to right. The shot and shell from two opposite batteries were also flying through the ranks, and it was determined to withdraw. Owing to the favorable nature of the ground this was done with but small loss. It was but a short time until the Eighty-First found itself again alone, and closely confronting a Rebel force. Lying down, the eager boys opened a brisk fire, which was hotly returned by the enemy, but so furiously did the regiment ply the Enfields that at last the Rebels broke and fled. No sooner was this perceived than the Eighty-First rose, and with yells followed the vanquished foe. So wild was the enthusiasm of the men that they never halted until they found themselves far in advance of any support and flanked both by infantry and artillery; even then it was with difficulty that they were withdrawn. In this charge the regiment captured a number of prisoners, also a battery; and it was here, too, that its principal loss was sustained. Resting and caring for the wounded occupied the next day, and then followed a month of inactivity.

On the 29th of May the Second Division started toward Corinth. There was nothing of importance in this advance, except that on the 31st of May the Eighty-First participated in a very considerable skirmish, and lost several wounded. After the evacuation of Corinth the Second Division pursued as far as Boonville. Taking into consideration the condition of the troops and the intense heat, the march to Boonville and back to Corinth was the most severe the regiment ever made. For some time the regiment was employed in picketing and fortifying. In July a recruiting party was sent to Ohio with authority to obtain a sufficient number of recruits to fill up the regiment. Companies H and G were consolidated with other companies, and this made five minimum companies in the regiment. About the middle of August, the Eighty-First was ordered to Hamburg, on the Tennessee River, where it remained in charge of public stores and performing post-duty, until the middle of September, when it returned to Corinth. In a few days marching orders were received and the regiment moved, under General Ord, against Iuka. General Rosecrans also moved upon Iuka from the rear. General Ord waited at Burnsville for Rosecrans to come up before he pressed the attack, but he waited too long, as Rosecrans pushed on and fought the battle of Iuka alone. General Ord's column returned to Corinth, and the Second Brigade took up camp in its old position, two miles south of Corinth, on the Mobile Railroad.

On the morning of the 3d of October the regiment moved toward Corinth, the brigade commanded by General Oglesby, and the division by General Davis. General Davis's division marched out by Battery Robinett, and going a short distance into the woods was halted. The Third Brigade went into the old Rebel works to the left, the Second (Oglesby's) moved a half mile further to the right, with the First Brigade on its right. The Eighty-First was on the left of its brigade, and was prolonged to its utmost capacity. The troops were hardly in position before the Rebels opened fire and with great impetuosity rushed upon the weak line. It gave way, but was speedily re-formed in front of the White House, and being now more compact than at first, it held its position during the remainder of the day. The brunt of battle had fallen upon Davis's division, and the Tishomingo Hotel, which had been converted into a hospital, gave sad evidence of the severity of the fighting. Every room was filled with the wounded, and the porches were crowded with men, mostly from Davis's division. In the ladies' parlor were General Davis's three brigade commanders—Colonel Baldwin, slightly wounded; General Oglesby, suffering intensely from a wound, which the surgeons hardly dared to say was not mortal; and General Heckelman dying. During the night General Davis's division was posted facing northwardly, its left resting on Battery Powell and its right covering Battery Richardson. About nine or ten o'clock in the morning the Rebels rushed on Davis's division, stretched in a single line, without reserves or intrenchments. The troops gave way, but the Rebels were checked by Hamilton's artillery and Batteries Williams and Robinett, and the division rallied and killed or captured the greater portion of the assaulting column. This was the end of the battle in front of the Eighty-First. The regiment lost eleven men killed, forty-four wounded, and three missing. When the regiment advanced, on the 4th, Sergeant David McCall, the color-bearer, was the first to fall. At Pittsburg Landing, though unable for duty, he left his bed and carried the flag through that battle. He had but just recovered from his sickness and joined the regiment a short time before he fell.

The regiment moved in pursuit of the Rebels to a point on the Tuscumbia River, near Chewalla. It remained here a week, and then returned to Corinth. The remainder of October, and the month of December were spent in garrison-duty. On the 19th of October five new companies arrived, which had been organized in Ohio by the recruiting party. This made the Eighty-First a full regiment. The reception of these recruits was made a formal matter. They slept all night at the depot, having arrived late, and the next morning the old troops were formed and started to Corinth, with drums beating and colors flying. When they had proceeded far enough they halted, and formed in line in open order, and faced inward. The recruits approached by the right flank, and when the head of the column entered the lines the old troops came to a "present arms." When the new companies had passed through they were formed as the old troops had been, and the latter passed through their lines, in turn receiving the salute. When this was done the regiment formed on the color-line and stacked arms. On the 1st of November the regiment moved within the inner defenses of Corinth, and erected winter-quarters. About the middle of December the regiment moved on a reconnoissance through Rienzi, Blackland, Guntown, and Saltillo to Tripoli. No enemy was found and the troops returned, bringing in numbers of mules, horses, and contrabands, and a large quantity of cotton. Forrest's raid cut communications, and on the 22d of December the garrison at Corinth was placed on half rations. This lasted about three weeks, though it occasioned less suffering than many would suppose. Foraging parties were sent out which obtained food for the animals, and limited supplies for the men. After the battle of Parker's Cross Roads, the Eighty-First, with other troops, moved to intercept Forrest at Clifton, but learning that he had crossed the river, they returned to Corinth. On the 26th of January, 1863, the regiment with the Twenty-Seventh Ohio, two Illinois regiments, and a battery, started to Hamburg for supplies. Upon reaching Hamburg the force was placed on transports, with the intention of capturing the forces under Roddy, encamped near Florence. About three miles from Hamburg it was discovered that one of the boats had injured her wheel, and the expedition was compelled to return. The Eighty-First marched immediately for Corinth, and reached its camp, a distance of twenty miles, in seven hours.

On the 15th of April the regiment moved, with almost the entire force of General Dodge, on an expedition to Tuscumbia, to co-operate with Colonel Streight in his movement upon the Southern Railroads. General Dodge remained at and near Tuscumbia several days in order to engage the attention of the Rebels. On the 28th of April there was an extensive skirmish at Town Creek, in which the Eighty-First had a few men wounded. After keeping the enemy engaged for two days and nights General Dodge returned to Corinth as expeditiously as possible. This march was one of eighteen days' duration, yet it was the best the regiment had yet made; and when it marched into camp at Corinth every man was in his place. On the 3d of June the Eighty-First moved to Pocahontas, where it spent the next few months in garrison-duty. It left Pocahontas about the last of October, expecting to join the army at Chattanooga. Upon reaching Pulaski, Tennessee, the regiment was halted, and distributed to different posts, again to perform garrison-duty. Wales, Pulaski, Sam's Mills, and Nance's Mills, were thus garrisoned. Regimental head-quarters were at Pulaski, where Major Evans had a few of his men mounted, and spent a great portion of the time in scouring the country in pursuit of guerrillas.

In January, 1864, three-fourths of the men in the regiment were willing to re-enlist, but the Secretary of War decided that the five companies lately recruited were not entitled to the privilege of re-enlisting. This prevented the regiment from going North as a veteran organization. The old companies furnished quite a number of veterans, and these went home on furlough in two squads, each in charge of a Sergeant. On the 26th of April the regiment concentrated at Pulaski, and on the 29th it moved for Chattanooga, by way of Huntsville and Larkinsville. On arriving it went into bivouac at the foot of Lookout Mountain. On the 5th of May the regiment moved southward to Lee & Gordon's Mills, and entered fairly on the Atlanta campaign. During the fight at Resaca the regiment was brought into line several times, but was not engaged. On the 14th the Eighty-First was withdrawn from the main battle-field, and was ordered to Lay's Ferry, to lay a pontoon across the Oostenaula. The enemy was found in force on the opposite bank, but the boats were launched and manned in Snake Creek, and then they floated into the Oostenaula, and were pulled rapidly to the opposite shore. The men landed, and soon captured a portion of the enemy and dispersed the remainder. Three men of company C, Eighty-First Ohio, took eleven prisoners in one squad, including a Captain and two Lieutenants. The order for laying the pontoon was countermanded, and it was not put down until the evacuation of Atlanta, when the regiment crossed and again had a slight engagement with the Rebels. On the 16th of May the regiment fought at the battle of Rome Cross Roads. The regiment cleared its front of Rebels, and held its position until the Second Division was relieved by the Fourth. The regiment moved by way of Kingston and Van Wert to Dallas, where, on the 28th of May, an effort was made to draw General McPherson's corps to the left, in order to join it more closely to the rest of the army. While the movement was in progress the Rebels made seven assaults, but they were every time repulsed. The Eighty-First contributed its full share toward the result.

The regiment pressed on, with continuous skirmishing, to Kenesaw. During the movement around that place the Eighty-First was in the front line almost all the time, and was often on picket-duty; yet it was not called on to make an assault. The regiment advanced with the army, and on the 21st of July closed around Atlanta. In the battle on the 22d the Eighty-First, with three companies in reserve, was the second regiment from the right of Sweeney's division. The command stood like a rock, and never was there made a more daring or more effective resistance. At an opportune moment the Eighty-First Ohio and Twelfth Illinois moved forward in a resistless charge, carrying everything before them. The Eighty-First captured a number of prisoners and three battle-flags. Later in the day General Logan called on General Dodge for re-enforcements to assist the Fifteenth Corps in recovering its works. Mersey's brigade, which included the Eighty-First, was sent. It marched on the double-quick nearly two miles, and joined in a charge by which the lost line was recovered. The Eighty-First furnished a detail to assist Captain DeGres in serving his guns on the retreating Rebels. Late at night Mersey's brigade was moved to Bald Hill, and there the Eighty-First Ohio and Twelfth Illinois built a perfect labyrinth of works. On the 28th of July, while a portion of the army was moving toward the right, Hood made another assault. The Eighty-First, with other regiments, were hurried to the assistance of the Fifteenth Corps. These regiments arrived in time to take an active part in repelling the enemy. The regiment now settled down into the regular duties of a siege. It marched on the flanking movement to Jonesboro', and participated in the engagement at that place, and in the skirmish at Lovejoy, after which it withdrew to the vicinity of Atlanta. Here the few men of the five old companies who had served three years and had not re-enlisted, were mustered out. They numbered about one hundred and fifty, and their withdrawal did not change the organization of the regiment. It was not until late in December that official notice of their muster-out was received, and even then only two companies (B and C) lost their existence. The remaining members of those companies, veterans and recruits, were assigned to the other companies of the regiment.

In September the Eighty-First was ordered to Rome, and was assigned to the Fourth Division of the Fifteenth Corps. On the 11th of November the regiment set out for Atlanta. It arrived on the 15th, and on the 16th it continued the march toward Savannah. It made the march without any notable incident, and on the 13th of December it commenced to fortify around Savannah. On the 21st the brigade entered Savannah, and on the 23d the regiment went into camp on the Thunderbolt Road, near the city. On the 19th of January, 1865, the Eighty-First crossed the Savannah River to Hutchinson's Island, but, owing to the unprecedented rain, it was found impossible to proceed in that direction, and the regiment returned to its old quarters. However, on the 28th, it marched northward to Sisters' Ferry, and there crossed the Savannah into South Carolina. The regiment participated in all the labors and dangers of the campaign of the Carolinas, and was engaged in the battle of Bentonville. Upon reaching Goldsboro' the Army of the Tennessee passed in review. The men were just off a five hundred-mile march, were in all kinds of uniform, and some were without any uniform. In the Eighty-First all the shoeless and hatless men were placed in one company, and so they passed in review before Sherman, Schofield, Terry, Howard, and Logan, with more pride than their more fortunate companions who wore shoes and hats. In the brief rest which followed a number of absentees and recruits joined the regiment. The Eighty-First, though but a fraction of a regiment for more than a year at first, in 1862 received more recruits than any other regiment in the service. Again in 1864 enough of recruits were received to supply all deficiencies, and now in 1865 such a large number was obtained that two entire companies were formed, besides giving some men to the old companies. The two new companies were designated B and C, and they filled the gap which had existed since the muster-out of these companies in 1864. The regiment marched on through Raleigh to Morrisville, where it lay while Sherman was negotiating with Johnston, after which it marched back to Raleigh.

On the 29th of April the regiment started on its homeward march. It reached Washington City on the 20th of May, and on the 24th it passed in review. Early in June it started to Louisville, going by the Baltimore and Ohio Railroad to Parkersburg, and thence by the Ohio River. Encamping at Woodlawn, near the city, the boys enjoyed themselves as best they could, until at last came the welcome order to muster out. This was done on the 13th of July, and the regiment immediately started to Camp Dennison, Ohio, where it was paid and discharged, July 21, 1865.

Thus we have followed the fortunes of this regiment from its first scouting over the prairies of Missouri; through its bloody baptism at Pittsburg Landing; its march into Mississippi; its participation in the battle of Corinth; its garrison-duty at that place; its march into Northern Alabama; its brief stay at Pocahontas; its march to Pulaski, and duty there; its deeds and privations in the Atlanta campaign; its march to Rome; its journey to the sea; and finally its march from Savannah to Raleigh, Washington, Louisville, and Camp Dennison. It may be truly said that in all these scenes and actions the Eighty-First ever bore an honorable part. During the regiment's term of service thirty-four men were killed in action; twenty-four died of wounds; one hundred and twenty-one died of disease; and one hundred and thirty-six were discharged for disability.

82d REGIMENT OHIO VOLUNTEER INFANTRY.

ROSTER, THREE YEARS' SERVICE.

RANK.	NAME.	DATE OF RANK.			COM. ISSUED.			REMARKS.
Colonel	JAMES CANTWELL	Dec.	31,	1861	Jan.	24,	1862	Killed August 29, 1862.
Do.	JAMES S. ROBINSON	Aug.	29,	1862	Oct.	5,	"	Promoted to Brigadier-General of Vols.
Do.	STEPH. J. McGROARTY	Sept.	23,	"	Dec.	2,	"	Mustered out with regiment.
Lt. Colonel	Bradford R. Durfee	Jan.	1,	"	Jan.	21,	"	Resigned April 9, 1862.
Do.	James S. Robinson	April	9,	"	May	1,	"	Promoted to Colonel.
Do.	David Thompson	Aug.	29,	"	Oct.	5,	"	Brevetted Brigadier-General March 13, 1865.
Do.	James S. Crall	Jan.	11,	1865	Jan.	11,	1865	Mustered out with regiment.
Major	James S. Robinson	Dec.	31,	1861	July	24,	1862	Promoted to Lieutenant-Colonel
Do.	David Thompson	April	9,	1862	May	1,	"	Promoted to Lieutenant-Colonel.
Do.	James S. Crall	Aug.	29,	"	Oct.	5,	"	Promoted to Lieutenant-Colonel.
Do.	F. S. Wallace	July	11,	1865	July	11,	1865	Mustered out with regiment.
Surgeon	Jacob Y. Cantwell	Jan.	1,	1862	Jan.	24,	1862	Appointed to U. S. service by Pres. April 17, 1864.
Do.	C. W. Myers	April	26,	1864	April	28,	1864	Mustered out; resigned May 28, 1865.
Do.	L. P. Culver	June	13,	1865	June	13,	1865	Mustered out with regiment.
Ass't Surgeon	Augustus W. Munson	Dec.	26,	1861	Jan.	21,	1862	Resigned April 4, 1863.
Do.	C. W. Myers	July	4,	1862	July	23,	"	Promoted to Surgeon.
Do.	L. P. Culver	"	23,	1863	"	21,	1863	Refused to muster; commission returned.
Do.	Wm. B. Hedges	April	27,	1864	April	27,	1864	Mustered out with regiment.
Chaplain	Henry B. Fry	Jan.	21,	1862	May	30,	1862	Resigned July 18, 1862.
Do.	John Burke	"	14,	1863	Jan.	14,	1863	Resigned June 28, 1864.
Captain	David Thompson	Nov.	11,	1861	"	24,	1862	Promoted to Major.
Do.	Lemon S. Powell	"	25,	"	"	24,	"	Discharged July 30, 1862.
Do.	Peter C. Boslow	"	28,	"	"	24,	"	Resigned May 6, 1862.
Do.	James Ewing	Dec.	11,	"	"	24,	"	Resigned May 18, 1862.
Do.	James S. Crall	"	19,	"	"	24,	"	Promoted to Major.
Do.	Charles Mains	"	20,	"	"	24,	"	Resigned July 23, 1862.
Do.	John S. Reig	"	20,	"	"	24,	"	Resigned May 10, 1863.
Do.	Nicholas Jerolaman	"	20,	"	"	24,	"	Resigned July 7, 1862.
Do.	George H. Purdy	"	21,	"	"	24,	"	Killed at Chancellorsville, May 3, 1863.
Do.	David S. Sampsell	"	21,	"	March	20,	"	Resigned July 30, 1862.
Do.	Wm. E. Schofield	April	9,	1862	May	1,	"	Mustered out October 31, 1864.
Do.	John Campbell	March	6,	"	July	31,	"	Mustered out December 9, 1864; time expired.
Do.	Solomon L. Hoge	"	18,	"	Aug.	5,	"	Resigned April 24, 1863.
Do.	Wm. D. W. Mitchell	Jan.	1,	"	"	5,	"	Mortally wounded at Gettysburg July 1, 1863.
Do.	David J. Mentzer	"	30,	"	"	10,	"	Resigned November 6, 1862.
Do.	John Costin	"	23,	"	Sept.	15,	"	Mortally wounded at Gettysburg July 1, 1863.
Do.	Alfred E. Lee	"	30,	"	"	15,	"	Mustered out with regiment.
Do.	Francis S. Jacobs	Aug.	29,	"	Dec.	18,	"	Resigned.
Do.	Wm. J. Dickson	Nov.	6,	"	"	18,	"	Killed at Resaca.
Do.	James B. McConnell	April	21,	1863	June	10,	1863	Mustered out with regiment.
Do.	Cyrus Herrick	May	3,	"	"	10,	"	Mustered out.
Do.	Joseph Gutzwiller	"	10,	"	"	10,	"	Mustered out with regiment.
Do.	James Cricket	Nov.	2,	"	April	12,	1864	Mustered out with regiment.
Do.	John A. Mitchell	Aug.	11,	1864	Aug.	11,	"	Honorably discharged March 6, 1865.
Do.	John P. Drennan	"	11,	"	"	11,	"	Ap. Capt. and A. Q. M.; must'd out as 1st Lt.
Do.	Robert C. Wiley	Sept.	6,	"	Sept.	6,	"	Mustered out as 1st Lieut. Nov. 11, 1864.
Do.	Wm. Ballentine	"	6,	"	"	6,	"	Killed in action.
Do.	Alanson P. Cutting	Dec.	30,	"	Dec.	30,	"	Mustered out as 1st Lieutenant April 4, 1865.
Do.	Milton Marsh	Jan.	28,	1865	Jan.	28,	1865	Mustered out with regiment.
Do.	J. E. Criswell	"	28,	"	"	28,	"	Mustered out as 1st Lieutenant April 8, 1865.
Do.	F. S. Wallace	April	23,	1862	May	28,	1862	Promoted to Major.
Do.	Henry B. Bending	July	31,	"	Aug.	26,	"	Mustered out June 29, 1865.
Do.	Anthony Gradyiski	April	29,	1864	April	29,	1864	Mustered out with regiment.
Do.	Robert Patterson	"	29,	"	"	29,	"	Mustered out with regiment.
Do.	Wm. H. Kirkwood	July	20,	1865	Sept.	4,	1865	Mustered out with regiment.
Do.	Charles Tinckler	"	20,	"	"	4,	"	Mustered out with regiment as 1st Lieut.
1st Lieutenant	Wm. E. Schofield	Oct.	30,	1861	Jan.	24,	1862	Promoted to Captain.
Do.	Alexander S. Ramsey	Nov.	4,	"				Resigned May 15, 1862.
Do.	Solomon L. Hoge	"	14,	"				Promoted to Captain.
Do.	David J. Mentzer	"	25,	"				Promoted to Captain.
Do.	John Campbell	"	28,	"				Promoted to Captain.
Do.	Wm. Porterfield	Dec.	6,	"				Resigned May 16, 1862
Do.	John Costin	"	19,	"				Promoted to Captain.
Do.	Samuel R. Smith	"	20,	"				Discharged August 13, 1862.
Do.	Samuel H. Berry	"	20,	"				Mustered out August 19, 1862.
Do.	Alfred E. Lee	"	21,	"				Promoted to Captain.
Do.	Wm. D. W. Mitchell	"	20,	"	June	7,	1862	Promoted to Captain.
Do.	John S. Fulton	"	31,	"	March	20,	"	Died April 17, 1862.
Do.	Preston Faught	April	9,	1862	May	1,	"	Resigned October 30, 1862.
Do.	Francis S. Jacobs	"	17,	"	"	1,	"	Promoted to Captain.
Do.	John P. Drennan	May	16,	"	July	3,	"	Promoted to Captain.
Do.	Cyrus Herrick	July	31,	"	"	31,	"	Promoted to Captain.
Do.	James B. McConnell	March	18,	"	Aug.	5,	"	Promoted to Captain.
Do.	Wm. M. Brown	"	15,	"	"	19,	"	Resigned September 12, 1862.
Do.	Wm. J. Dickson	July	30,	"	"	19,	"	Promoted to Captain.
Do.	Andrew H. Nickell	Aug.	13,	"	"	22,	"	Resigned October 24, 1862.
Do.	Henry Litzenberg	July	23,	"	Sept.	15,	"	Killed August 29, 1862.
Do.	Wm. Cessna	"	30,	"	"	15,	"	Resigned May 13, 1863.
Do.	John T. Carlin	Aug.	19,	"	"	15,	"	Resigned January 20, 1863.
Do.	John A. McClasky	Sept.	12,	"	Nov.	20,	"	Resigned.
Do.	Joseph Gutzwiller	Nov.	1,	"	"	29,	"	Promoted to Captain.
Do.	Nelson M. Carroll	Aug.	29,	"	Dec.	18,	"	Killed May 3, 1863.
Do.	Wm. F. Scott	Oct.	24,	"	"	18,	"	Resigned April 13, 1863.
Do.	James J. Beer	"	29,	"	"	18,	"	Killed May 3, 1863.
Do.	Stowell L. Burnham	"	30,	"	"	18,	"	Killed July 1, 1863.

RANK.	NAME.	DATE OF RANK.	COM. ISSUED.	REMARKS.
1st Lieutenant	John H. Ballard	Nov. 6, 1862	Dec. 18, 1862	Resigned July 19, 1864.
Do.	James Cricket	March 1, 1863	March 7, 1863	Promoted to Captain.
Do.	John A. Mitchell	April 13, "	May 28, "	Promoted to Captain.
Do.	George W. Blackburn	May 3, "	June 10, "	Discharged October 2, 1864.
Do.	Philander C. Meredith	April 24, "	" 10, "	Killed July 1, 1863.
Do.	Robert C. Wiley	May 3, "	" 10, "	Promoted to Captain.
Do.	Alfred Goodin	" 10, "	" 10, "	Mustered out March 12, 1865
Do.	George B. Fry	July 1, "	Aug. 25, "	Mustered out.
Do.	Wm. Ballentine	June 1, "	Dec. 21, "	Promoted to Captain.
Do.	Alanson P. Cutting	July 5, "	" 21, "	Promoted to Captain.
Do.	Wm. S. Mahan	" 6, "	" 21, "	Mustered out.
Do.	Milton Marsh	" 7, "	" 21, "	Promoted to Captain.
Do.	Henry Jacoby	Aug. 11, 1864	Aug. 11, 1864	Killed at Gettysburg.
Do.	J. E. Criswell	" 11, "	" 11, "	Promoted to Captain.
Do.	Warren H. Wasson	" 11, "	" 11, "	Resigned October 27, 1864.
Do.	Jeff. P. Davis	" 11, "	" 11, "	Mustered out with regiment.
Do.	Wm. Brant	Sept. 6, "	Sept. 6, "	Resigned June 2, 1865.
Do.	George W. Youngblood	" 6, "	" 6, "	Mustered out with regiment.
Do.	Erwin Barnhart	" 6, "	" 6, "	Mustered out with regiment.
Do.	B. Dickerson	Dec. 30, "	Dec. 30, "	Mustered out.
Do.	Jasper S. Snow	" 30, "	" 30, "	Mustered out with regiment as Adjutant.
Do.	James O. Lacy	" 30, "	" 30, "	Mustered out with regiment.
Do.	Amos Wheeler	Jan. 28, 1865	Jan. 28, 1865	Mustered out; resigned June 3, 1866.
Do.	Benj. S. Reilly	" 28, "	" 28, "	Mustered out.
Do.	Wm. H. Thompson	" 28, "	" 28, "	Mustered out with regiment.
Do.	Nathan B. Phillips	" 28, "	" 28, "	Mustered out with regiment.
Do.	Wm. H. Kirkwood	Oct. 6, 1862	Nov. 10, 1862	Promoted to Captain.
Do.	Charles Tinckler	April 29, 1864	April 29, 1864	Promoted to Captain.
Do.	Joseph R. Mell	" 29, "	" 29, "	Mustered out with regiment.
Do.	Leonard G. Burns	June 24, 1865	June 24, 1865	Mustered out with regiment.
Do.	John Conoway	July 20, "	Sept. 4, "	Mustered out with regiment.
Do.	George M. McPeek	" 20, "	" 4, "	
Do.	Jacob Bush	" 20, "	" 4, "	Mustered out with regiment as Serg't-Major.
Do.	Henry Harmon	" 20, "	" 4, "	
2d Lieutenant	Preston Faught	Nov. 6, 1861	Jan. 24, 1862	Promoted to 1st Lieutenant.
Do.	John P. Drennan	" 9, "	....	Promoted to 1st Lieutenant.
Do.	James B. McConnell	" 14, "	....	Promoted to 1st Lieutenant.
Do.	Wm. J. Dickson	" 25, "	....	Promoted to 1st Lieutenant.
Do.	Morgan Simonson	" 28, "	....	Resigned July 17, 1862.
Do.	Andrew H. Nickell	Dec. 20, "	....	Promoted to 1st Lieutenant.
Do.	Charles Diebold	" 30, "	....	Mortally wounded May 8, 1862.
Do.	Loyd B. Lippitt	" 30, "	....	Resigned July 17, 1862.
Do.	Henry Litzenberg	" 21, "	....	Promoted to 1st Lieutenant.
Do.	Francis S. Jacobs	Nov. 12, "	March 20, 1862	Promoted to 1st Lieutenant.
Do.	Wm. M. Brown	April 17, 1862	May 1, "	Promoted to 1st Lieutenant.
Do.	Wm. Cessna	" 9, "	" 1, "	Promoted to 1st Lieutenant.
Do.	John T. Carlin	May 16, "	July 3, "	Promoted to 1st Lieutenant.
Do.	Cyrus Herrick	July 17, "	" 31, "	Promoted to 1st Lieutenant.
Do.	Nelson M. Carroll	" 30, "	Aug. 19, "	Promoted to 1st Lieutenant.
Do.	James J. Beer	May 15, "	" 19, "	Promoted to 1st Lieutenant.
Do.	Stowell L. Burnham	" 18, "	" 19, "	Promoted to 1st Lieutenant.
Do.	John H. Ballard	Aug. 13, "	" 22, "	Promoted to 1st Lieutenant.
Do.	Joseph Gutzwiller	" 19, "	Sept. 15, "	Promoted to 1st Lieutenant.
Do.	James Cricket	" 19, "	" 12, "	Promoted to 1st Lieutenant.
Do.	John A. Mitchell	July 7, "	Nov. 17, "	Promoted to 1st Lieutenant.
Do.	George W. Blackburn	" 25, "	" 26, "	Promoted to 1st Lieutenant.
Do.	Philander C. Meredith	" 30, "	" 26, "	Promoted to 1st Lieutenant.
Do.	Robert C. Wiley	" 31, "	Dec. 2, "	Promoted to 1st Lieutenant.
Do.	Alfred Goodin	Aug. 29, "	" 18, "	Promoted to 1st Lieutenant.
Do.	George B. Fry	" 29, "	" 18, "	Promoted to 1st Lieutenant.
Do.	Peter W. Lee	Oct. 30, "	" 18, "	Resigned March 12, 1862,
Do.	Thomas Abrell	Nov. 6, "	" 18, "	Killed May 3, 1863.
Do.	Hyman M. Howard	" 1, "	Jan. 16, 1863	Resigned January 8, 1864.
Do.	Henry Jacoby	March 1, 1863	March 7, "	Promoted to 1st Lieutenant.
Do.	J. E. Criswell	" 12, "	" 27, "	Promoted to 1st Lieutenant.
Do.	Wm. Ballentine	May 3, "	May 25, "	Promoted to 1st Lieutenant.
Do.	Conrad Lue	April 13, "	" 25, "	Resigned August 5, 1863.
Do.	Alanson P. Cutting	May 3, "	June 10, "	Promoted to 1st Lieutenant.
Do.	George W. McGeary	April 24, "	" 10, "	Killed at Gettysburg July 4, 1863.
Do.	Wm. S. Mahan	May 3, "	" 10, "	Promoted to 1st Lieutenant.
Do.	Milton Marsh	" 10, "	" 10, "	Promoted to 1st Lieutenant.
Do.	Warren H. Wasson	July 1, "	July "	Promoted to 1st Lieutenant.
Do.	Asa H. Geary	Oct. 23, "	Feb. 24, 1864	Killed July 20, 1864.
Do.	Wm. Brant	Nov. 2, "	" 24, "	Promoted to 1st Lieutenant.
Do.	Jeff. P. Davis	Oct. 10, "	" 29, "	Promoted to 1st Lieutenant.
Do.	George W. Youngblood	Dec. 1, "	March 16, "	Promoted to 1st Lieutenant.
Do.	Erwin Barnhart	March 19, "	" 19, "	Promoted to 1st Lieutenant.
Do.	B. Dickerson	Dec. 1, "	April 12, "	Promoted to 1st Lieutenant.
Do.	Jasper S. Snow	Aug. 11, 1864	Aug. 11, "	Promoted to 1st Lieutenant.
Do.	James O. Lacy	Sept. 6, "	Sept. 6, "	Promoted to 1st Lieutenant.
Do.	Amos Wheeler	" 6, "	" 6, "	Promoted to 1st Lieutenant.
Do.	Benj. S. Reilly	" 6, "	" 6, "	Promoted to 1st Lieutenant.
Do.	Wm. C. Layton	" 6, "	" 6, "	Declined.
Do.	Wm. H. Thompson	" 6, "	" 6, "	Promoted to 1st Lieutenant.
Do.	Nathan B. Phillips	" 6, "	" 6, "	Promoted to 1st Lieutenant.
Do.	Wm. A. Gray	July 20, 1865	" 4, 1865	Mustered out with regiment as Sergeant.
Do.	Christopher W. Denig	" 20, "	" 4, "	Mustered out with regiment as Sergeant.
Do.	Samuel Armstrong	" 20, "	" 4, "	Mustered out with regiment as Sergeant.
Do.	Ephraim Shellenbarger	" 20, "	" 4, "	Mustered out with regiment as Sergeant.
Do.	James Wallace	" 20, "	" 4, "	Mustered out with regiment as Sergeant.
Do.	John S. Delamater	" 20, "	" 4, "	Mustered out with regiment as Sergeant.
Do.	John Dunn	" 20, "	" 4, "	Mustered out with regiment as Sergeant
Do.	Thomas H. Bushong	" 20, "	" 4, "	Mustered out with regiment as Sergeant.
Do.	Daniel C. Sieter	" 20, "	" 4, "	Mustered out with regiment as Sergeant.
Do.	James C. Erb	" 20, "	" 4, "	Mustered out with regiment as Sergeant.

EIGHTY-SECOND OHIO VOLUNTEER INFANTRY.

THE EIGHTY-SECOND was composed of men from the counties of Logan, Richland, Ashland, Union, and Marion. Recruiting began on the 5th of November, 1861. The regiment rendezvoused at Kenton, Ohio, and was mustered into the service on the 31st of December, with an aggregate of nine hundred and sixty-eight men.

On the 25th of January, 1862, the regiment moved for Western Virginia. It crossed the Ohio River at Benwood, and on the 27th arrived at Grafton. On the 28th it went into camp near the village of Fetterman, where a regular system of instruction was instituted. On the 16th of March the Eighty-Second was assigned to General Schenck's command. It was transported by railroad from Grafton to New Creek, and from there it marched to Moorefield, arriving on the 23d. The regiment was ordered by General Schenck to explore the Lost River region, and to capture, if possible, a noted guerrilla named Harness; but Harness made his escape. The Eighty-Second moved with Schenck's brigade up the South Branch Valley, and on the 3d of May crossed the Potomac at Petersburg. Franklin was reached on the 5th. Here the troops halted two days, and then moved in the direction of Monterey. On the 6th a courier arrived with the information that Stonewall Jackson was threatening the force under Milroy. Schenck hastened to his relief, and by noon the next day joined the troops under Milroy near McDowell. The Rebels were posted on Bull-Pasture Mountain, and were well sheltered by natural obstacles. At three o'clock P. M. the National troops moved to the assault, and the fight continued until after dark. During the night the troops under Schenck and Milroy withdrew, and arrived at Franklin on the 10th. The Rebel army followed, but did not molest the retreat. On the 12th the enemy moved apparently to attack the lines at Franklin. He threw out his skirmishers, but these were repulsed, and on the night of the 13th the Rebels retired.

Schenck's brigade left Franklin with the army under Fremont on the 25th of May. On the 26th it passed through Petersburg, where knapsacks and all other baggage which could not be carried on the person were left. On the 29th the Potomac was crossed near Moorefield, and the next day the troops entered the defiles of Branch Mountain. On the 1st of June the advance of the army became engaged at Strasburg. Schenck's brigade hastened forward and deployed, but a tremendous storm put an end to the battle. During the night the Rebels, under Jackson, withdrew. The pursuit commenced at early dawn, and many Rebels who had given out on the march were captured. The column passed through Woodstock and Harrisonburg, and on the 8th fought the battle of Cross Keys. Schenck's brigade, though in season, and participating but little in the actual fighting, was exposed throughout the battle to the enemy's artillery and musketry. The next day the Rebels were in retreat and the National army in pursuit; but the destruction of the bridge over the Shenandoah stopped the chase. The troops moved back through New Market, Mount Jackson and Strasburg to Middletown, where General Sigel took command of the army.

In the organization of the Army of Virginia, under General Pope, Sigel's command was denominated the First Corps; and the Eighty-Second was assigned to an independent brigade, under Milroy. Severe campaigning had fearfully thinned the regiment's ranks, and it now mustered only about three hundred men, and additions to the sick-list were made daily. On the night of the 7th of August Sigel's corps moved toward Culpepper, and on the following morning halted in the woods south of the village. At seven o'clock P. M. the corps moved toward Cedar

Mountain, where fighting had been going on nearly all day. It arrived on the field at ten o'clock P. M.; and Milroy's brigade moved to the front and relieved a portion of the exhausted forces. The troops remained under arms all night. On the 9th there was some skirmishing, but no general engagement, and on the night of the 10th the Rebels retreated. In the pursuit Milroy's brigade led the advance of Sigel's corps. On the 11th the brigade crossed Robertson's River, and went into camp on the south bank.

On the 15th of August the Army of Virginia began to withdraw from Robertson's River. Milroy's brigade covered the movement. On the 16th Sigel's corps arrived at Warrenton Sulphur Springs; but on the next day it reversed its course and marched southward along the left bank of the Rappahannock River to Rappahannock Station. Here the two armies met on opposite banks of the river. Sigel's corps was at the front constantly, and on the 18th participated in a sharp skirmish at Freeman's Ford. For ten successive days Milroy's brigade was within hearing, and most of the time under fire of the enemy's guns. On the 21st Sigel's corps moved northward, hugging closely to the river. Milroy's brigade was charged with the defense of Waterloo Bridge. The Rebels made a persistent effort to gain the bridge, but with no avail. The destruction of the bridge was ordered finally, and the work was intrusted to the Eighty-Second. A select party dashed forward under a brisk fire, ignited the timbers, and in a few moments the work of destruction was complete.

On the evening of the 21st McDowell engaged the enemy in a short but severe conflict five miles east of Gainesville. Sigel's corps hastened to his assistance, but darkness prevented a general engagement. At early dawn the next morning the battle opened, and Milroy's brigade was pushed forward to reconnoiter the enemy's line. At nine o'clock A. M. Sigel's corps began a general advance. Milroy's brigade preceded the main body in battle order. The Eighty-Second and Third Virginia were deployed, and supported by the other regiments of the brigade in column. The Rebel skirmishers were driven back through a dense timber to their main force, which was posted behind a railroad embankment. When Milroy's brigade had approached within a few yards of the embankment some of the troops sprang from behind it, and crying, "Don't fire on your friends," threw down their arms, while at the same time the remainder of the force opened a heavy volley. The ruse did not have its expected effect. The firing was returned vigorously. The Eighty-Second pressed forward and commenced scaling the embankment, a portion of the regiment passing it through an opening for a culvert. Just at this moment a large force of Rebels appeared on the regiment's right flank. The Eighty-Second was now unsupported, and it was necessary to change front in order to repel the new attack. The movement was executed successfully, under a galling cross-fire; but during the evolution Colonel Cantwell fell from his horse dead, with the words of command and encouragement upon his lips. The brigade had already retired, and the regiment, under orders from Milroy, now withdrew. Under the personal direction of General Milroy the Eighty-Second, consisting of only a handful of men, was re-formed and assigned to the support of a battery. The advancing Rebels were met resolutely and repulsed, and an opportunity was afforded for the regiment and battery to retire to a safe position. In this engagement the Eighty-Second lost heavily. At dawn on the 30th it was in line, and by two o'clock P. M. it had advanced to the position so fiercely contested on the day before. At four o'clock P. M. the Rebels massed in front of McDowell's corps, and a portion of Sigel's corps, including Milroy's brigade, was sent to his assistance. The brigade was in position in time to receive the enemy's advance. The formation was slightly concave, the Eighty-Second being in the center. The Rebels advanced repeatedly, but were driven back, and Milroy's brigade maintained its position. The fighting ceased when night came on, and, under cover of darkness, the National army withdrew to Centerville.

On the 3d of September Sigel's corps arrived at Fairfax C. H. Here the Eighty-Second was detailed as provost-guard for the corps, and was attached to General Sigel's head-quarters. On the 9th of September Sigel moved his head-quarters to Fort De Kalb. The corps about this time, by orders from the War Department, was denominated the Eleventh, and was assigned to the Army of the Potomac. On the 25th the corps advanced to Fairfax C. H., and on the 4th of November it moved to Gainesville; but on the 18th it was again withdrawn to Fairfax. Here the corps remained until General Burnside's advance on Fredericksburg, when it marched to join the Army of the Potomac at that point. On the 17th of December General Sigel established his head-quarters at Stafford C. H., and the corps went into winter-quarters, the campaign having closed with the attempted capture of the Heights of Fredericksburg. General Howard succeeded General Sigel in command of the Eleventh Corps; and, at the request of Colonel Robinson, the Eighty-Second was relieved from duty at head-quarters, and was ordered to report to its division commander, General Schurz. By him it was designated as a battalion of sharpshooters for the division, and was not assigned to any brigade, but was held subject to his personal direction.

The Eleventh Corps broke camp at Stafford on the 27th of April, 1863, and moved on the Chancellorsville campaign. It crossed the Rappahannock at Kelly's Ford and the Rapidan at Ely's Mills; and on the evening of the 30th it halted within three miles of Chancellorsville. At nine o'clock A. M. on the following day the corps took up a defensive position and began to intrench. When the battle opened, on the afternoon of the 2d, the regiment stood to arms and awaited the orders of General Schurz. By his direction it was deployed with fixed bayonets to repel the attack. It was ordered very soon to fall back to the rifle-pits. The movement was executed in good order. The men moved steadily into the intrenchments, and opened a rapid fire upon the advancing foe. Disorganized bodies of troops were falling back through the Eighty-Second, and the regiment was left unsupported. The enemy swept around the flanks of the Eighty-Second, but the regiment stood to its post until retreat or capture became inevitable. The order was reluctantly given, and the regiment fell back in good order; and when the new position was reached one hundred and thirty-four men were with the colors. It remained in this position until ordered by General Howard to retire to Chancellorsville. On the morning of the 3d the Eleventh Corps was transferred to the extreme left of the army, and was charged with the defense of the approaches to the river and the pontoons. The regiment was on duty in the trenches or on the picket-line until the morning of the 7th, when the army commenced to retire; and at seven o'clock P. M. the Eighty-Second reached its old camp near Stafford.

The regiment was assigned to the Second Brigade of the Third Division, and was engaged in ordinary camp duties until the 10th of June, when it moved on the Gettysburg campaign. The Eleventh Corps marched by way of Catlett's, Manassas Junction, Centerville, Goose Creek, Edwards's Ferry, Middletown, and Frederick to Emmettsburg, where it arrived on the 29th. On the 1st of July the march was resumed, and at twelve o'clock M. the corps came in sight of Gettysburg. Without any halt the troops were formed in order of battle, and the Eighty-Second was placed in support of a battery. In about an hour the battery was withdrawn, and the regiment prepared to join in a general advance. It moved over an open plain swept by the Rebel artillery, and before the regiment fired a shot it lost twenty men killed and wounded. The gaps were filled promptly, and the Eighty-Second advanced to within seventy-five yards of the Rebel lines. The Rebels were in force in overwhelming numbers, and the Eighty-Second was compelled to retire. It was assigned a position near the entrance of the now famous Gettysburg cemetery. It went into this action with twenty-two commissioned officers and two hundred and thirty-six men; and of these, nineteen officers and one hundred and forty-seven men were killed, wounded, and captured, leaving only three officers and eighty-nine men. This little band brought off the colors safely. It was not engaged seriously during the remainder of the battle.

On the evening of the 5th the Eleventh Corps moved in pursuit of the Rebels, passing through Emmettsburg, Middletown, Boonsboro', and Sharpsburg to within a few miles of Hagerstown, where it arrived on the 11th. At this point the Eighty-Second was assigned to a new brigade, which was denominated the First Brigade of the Third Division. The brigade was commanded by General Tyndal. The Eleventh Corps continued the pursuit as far as Warrenton Junction; and soon after arriving there the Third Division was assigned to the duty of guarding the Orange and Alexandria Railroad. The Eighty-Second was ordered to Catlett's

Station, and there it performed very arduous guard and patrol duty until the 25th of September, when the Eleventh Corps left Catlett's Station to join the Army of the Cumberland.

On the 1st of October Tyndal's brigade arrived at Bridgeport, Alabama. On the 3d it crossed the Tennessee River, and was engaged in patrolling the adjacent country. On the 27th the Eleventh Corps, under Hooker, moved up the left bank of the Tennessee, and on the afternoon of the next day, as the column emerged from the defiles of Raccoon Mountain, it drew the fire from a Rebel battery on Lookout Mountain. After a lively skirmish the Rebel outposts were driven in, and by five o'clock the troops were encamped quietly in Lookout Valley. About ten o'clock P. M. firing was heard in the rear, and it was found that Longstreet had occupied Wauhatchie Heights, and had descended into the valley. Detachments were at once sent out from the Eleventh Corps, and Tyndal's brigade was directed to recapture Wauhatchie Heights. The brigade moved out on the double-quick; and, upon reaching the point where the assault was to be made, the Eighty-Second deployed two companies as skirmishers, and the remainder of the regiment supporting them, led the advance up the steep and rugged slope, and drove the Rebels from the summit without difficulty. The position thus gained was held by the Eleventh Corps until the 22d of November, when the corps moved down the valley, crossed the Tennessee twice, passed through Chattanooga, and bivouacked under the guns of Battery Wood. The corps was held in reserve during the engagement at Orchard Knob, but it moved up under a heavy fire from the batteries on Mission Ridge, to the left of the Fourteenth Corps, and assisted in the skirmishing which followed the engagement, and in building the intrenchments. On the 25th the Eleventh Corps marched to join Sherman's forces. The movement was completed by ten o'clock P. M. Sherman was still engaged on Mission Ridge, and the Eleventh Corps was ordered to support the assaulting column. The Third Division took position on the southern face of the ridge, and there proceeded to intrench. A party from the different regiments of the First Brigade reconnoitered the front and drove in the enemy's flankers. By night the intrenchments were complete and the position secure. The Eleventh Corps moved in pursuit of Bragg's army as it fell back from Chattanooga, to within seven miles of Ringgold. From this point an expedition was sent from the corps to destroy the railroad connecting Cleveland and Dalton. The enterprise was entirely successful.

On the 28th of November the corps moved to the relief of Knoxville. When it arrived near the town of Louisville, only eighteen miles from Knoxville, a courier arrived from General Burnside with the information that Longstreet had raised the siege. Then commenced the return march; and, after many hardships, the troops half naked and half starved, arrived at their old encampments in Lookout Valley on the 17th of December. The Eighty-Second had scarcely recovered from the effects of the Knoxville campaign, when it declared anew its devotion to the country by veteranizing. Out of three hundred and forty-nine enlisted men present, three hundred and twenty-one were mustered into the service as veteran volunteers on the 1st of January, 1864. On the 10th of the same month the regiment started to Ohio on veteran furlough. It arrived at Columbus on the 21st, and was furloughed for thirty days from the 24th. It rendezvoused on the 23d of February with two hundred recruits. It started for the front on the 26th, and on the 3d of March joined its brigade at Bridgeport, Alabama.

The Eleventh and Twelfth Corps were consolidated, forming the Twentieth, and the Eighty-Second was assigned to the Third Brigade of the First Division of this corps. On the 30th of April marching orders were received, and the regiment entered upon the Atlanta campaign. It marched by way of Whitesides, Lookout Valley, Gordon's Mills, Grove Church, Nicojack Gap, and Snake Creek Gap, to Resaca. Toward evening, on the 14th of May, the Twentieth Corps, under Hooker, was shifted to the left, in order to envelop the enemy's right. Robinson's brigade (the third), of Williams's division (the first), reached the Dalton Road just as a division of the Fourth Corps was being forced back in great confusion. Robinson's brigade at once charged and drove back the Rebels in gallant style. The Eighty-Second participated in the charge, but sustained little loss, as the enemy was too much surprised and embarrassed to fire effectively. On the next day Butterfield's and Geary's divisions advanced and captured the enemy's first line. Williams's division was then thrown forward, and took position on the left, with Robinson's brigade on the left of the division, constituting the extreme left of the army. The flank "hung in air," and, being without breastworks, was much exposed. The enemy seeing this, moved two divisions into position for an attack. Robinson's brigade was posted behind a low rise of ground, with an open field in front. The enemy charged gallantly across the open space, and advanced to within fifty yards of Robinson's position, but a terrible fire forced him to retire. In twenty minutes the enemy renewed the attack, but with the same result; again he advanced, and again was forced back with fearful slaughter. Throughout the engagement the Eighty-Second held an important position, but had a slight advantage in being protected by a breastwork. It lost one officer killed. Darkness ended the conflict; and during the night parties were employed caring for the Rebel wounded.

The Rebels withdrew by night, and in the morning the National army started in pursuit; and on the evening of the 19th the enemy was found in position near Cassville. The enemy evacuated without a battle, and the National army was allowed a few days to rest. On the 23d the march was resumed. Hooker's corps crossed the Etowah, and marched by way of Stilesboro' to Burnt Hickory. On the 25th, while the three divisions of the Twentieth Corps were advancing by different roads, General Geary encountered the enemy on a high wooded ridge, four miles north-east of Dallas. Williams's division, which had arrived within three miles of Dallas by another road, at once about-faced and marched to the support of Geary. Upon arriving it was determined to attack the Rebels, and Williams's division was formed in column of brigade, with Robinson's in front. At the sound of the bugle the column advanced, and fire was opened immediately. The troops moved with great steadiness and in almost perfect order, sometimes, even in the midst of the firing, halting for a moment and dressing the line. General Hooker accompanied the column, and, turning to Colonel Robinson, said: "Your movement is splendid, Colonel—splendid." The Eighty-Second held the center of the line, and behaved with conspicuous gallantry. After advancing about half a mile Robinson's brigade was relieved and Ruger's brigade took the lead. General Ruger advanced within two hundred yards of the Rebel parapet, and maintained his position until the ammunition failed, and then Robinson's brigade again moved to the front. The brigade was exposed to a severe canister fire, and by sunset almost every cartridge was gone. The cartridge-boxes of the dead and wounded were searched, and a straggling fire was kept up until night, when Robinson's brigade was relieved.

During the 26th and 27th Williams's division was in reserve. About midnight on the 27th Robinson's brigade was detailed to escort a supply-train for ammunition to Kingston and back. This duty was performed successfully. On the 1st of June the army began to move toward the left. On the 6th Robinson's brigade arrived at a position near Pine Knob, where it remained until the 15th, when the line was advanced about two miles and to within a stone-throw of the Rebel parapet. The enemy was forced back upon Kenesaw, and in the operations around that place Robinson's brigade was held in reserve, and only engaged the enemy in skirmishes. After the evacuation of Kenesaw the Twentieth Corps went into position near Nicojack Creek. The corps crossed the Chattahoochie at Pace's Ferry on the 17th of July, and pressed forward toward Atlanta. On the 20th it crossed Peachtree Creek and found the Rebels in their works four miles from Atlanta. About ten o'clock P. M. the Rebels made a determined attack. Williams hurried his brigades into position. While Robinson's brigade was forming it received a volley which would have disconcerted any but veteran troops. The Eighty-Second was the second regiment in position, and it was hardly formed before the Rebels were upon it. The combatants became mingled with each other, and for some time the issue seemed doubtful; but at last the Rebels were forced to yield. In this engagement the Eighty-Second lost not less than seventy-five in killed and wounded. Lieutenant-Colonel Thompson was struck by a bullet, but it was turned aside by a pen-knife in his pocket, and only inflicted a slight wound.

During the siege of Atlanta the Eighty-Second held an important and an exposed position on a hill adjoining Marietta street. It was within range both of artillery and musketry, and on one occasion a cannon shot carried away the regimental colors and tore them to shreds. On the night of the 25th of August the Twentieth Corps withdrew from the intrenchments, and before daylight it was fortifying a new position along the Chattahoochie. At this point General Slocum assumed command of the corps. The rest of the army in the meantime moved southward. During the night of September 1st loud explosions and a bright light were seen in the direction of Atlanta. Early on the next morning a reconnoitering party was sent toward Atlanta. About noon the Eighty-Second joined another party moving in the same direction. The city was found evacuated. The entire corps moved up, and the regiment went into camp in the suburbs, near Peachtree street.

The regiment remained in camp at Atlanta, engaged in work on the fortifications and occasionally moving on a foraging expedition, until the 15th of November, when it started with Sherman's army for Savannah. The Eighty-Second met with nothing worthy of particular note until the 25th, when Wheeler's cavalry was encountered at Buffalo Creek. One company from the Eighty-Second Ohio, with one company from the Thirty-First Wisconsin, was sent forward to dislodge the enemy. The work was well done. Wheeler was forced from his position and driven back about a mile. Robinson's brigade was on the front line about Savannah, for a time, but it was moved to the rear, and was formed, facing outward, in order to cover the trains. Here it remained until the city was occupied by the National army.

On the 17th of January, 1865, the Third Division, commanded since leaving Atlanta by General N. J. Jackson, crossed the Savannah, and on the 19th arrived at Pureysville, South Carolina. Here the command was detained by high water until the 27th, when the march was resumed, and on the 29th Robertsville was reached. Here again the column was delayed until the 2d of February, when communications were abandoned and the march through the Carolinas commenced. The Eighty-Second performed its full share of marching, foraging, and corduroying. Upon one occasion three "bummers" from the Eighty-Second, with only a carbine, unexpectedly encountered a Rebel patrol of twelve cavalry fully equipped; the bummers put on a bold front, and calling out "forward, boys, here they are!" started for the Rebels, who betook themselves to flight. A swamp impeded their progress, and accordingly they dismounted and fled on foot, leaving their horses and equipments to the bummers.

On the 18th of February the Twentieth Corps crossed the Saluda four miles above Columbia; Broad River was crossed near Alston on the 20th, and on the 21st Winnsboro' was reached. On the 23d Wateree River was crossed near Rocky Mount Post-office, and on the 27th some foragers from the Eighty-Second captured, at Lancaster, a beautiful silk banner, inscribed upon one side, "Our cause is just: We will defend it with our lives;" and upon the other side, "Presented by the ladies to the Lancaster Invincibles." The march was continued by way of Chesterfield and Cheraw, and on the 11th of March the Twentieth Corps reached Fayetteville. On the 14th the march was resumed up the left bank of the Cape Fear River, and on the 16th the enemy was encountered three miles below Averysboro'. Robinson's brigade arrived on the field about ten o'clock A. M. The Rebels were gradually forced back, and toward evening they occupied a fortified line at the junction of the roads leading to Averysboro' and Bentonville. Here they made an obstinate stand and held the position until nightfall, when they withdrew. In this affair the Eighty-Second lost two officers and eight men wounded.

On the 18th the column crossed Black River and advanced twelve miles toward Cox's Bridge. At ten o'clock A. M. on the 19th cannonading was heard in front, and at one o'clock P. M. orders were received for the troops in the rear to hasten to the front. As soon as Robinson's brigade arrived it was thrown forward to fill the vacancy in Carlin's division, of the Fourteenth Corps. The men were without intrenching tools, but with their hatchets they at once commenced building a breastwork. Skirmishers were thrown out, and an effort was made to gain possession of some buildings, but the skirmishers were driven back by a murderous fire, and the enemy moved forward to the attack. The assault was made on Carlin's left, and in five minutes all the troops to the left of Robinson's brigade were swept away, and the enemy was coming down upon the flank in irresistible masses. The brigade immediately changed front but it was now enveloped both on front and flank, and orders were given to withdraw. The line was re-formed and again Robinson's brigade was enveloped on front and flank, but with the aid of artillery the Rebels were repulsed. No less than six assaults were made on this line during the afternoon, and every time the enemy was repulsed handsomely. The firing ceased shortly after nightfall, and Robinson's brigade was relieved and permitted to drop to the rear. The next day the enemy was content to assume the defensive, and on the 21st he retired. In the battle of Bentonville the Eighty-Second lost two officers and nine men wounded and fourteen men missing.

The whole army now turned toward Goldsboro', where it arrived on the 24th. On the 9th of April, and while still at Goldsboro', the Eighty-Second and Sixty-First Ohio were consolidated. The new regiment was denominated the Eighty-Second, and a few surplus officers were mustered out. On the 10th the troops moved to Raleigh, where they remained until after the surrender of Johnston's army. On the 30th of April the corps marched for Washington City, by way of Richmond, and on the 19th of May arrived at Alexandria. The regiment participated in the grand review in Washington on the 24th of May, and then went into camp near Fort Lincoln. When the Twentieth Corps was dissolved the Eighty-Second was assigned to a provisional division which was attached to the Fourteenth Corps. On the 15th of June the corps moved to Louisville, Kentucky. At Parkersburg the troops embarked on transports. Upon reaching Cincinnati the boats carrying Robinson's brigade, of which the Eighty-Second was still a part, stopped a short time, and General Hooker came down to the wharf. He was greeted enthusiastically by his old soldiers, and in return made a brief speech. On arriving at Louisville the regiment went into camp on Speed's plantation, five miles south of the city. Here it remained until the 25th of July, when it proceeded to Columbus, Ohio, where it was paid and discharged on the 29th.

www.ingramcontent.com/pod-product-compliance
Lightning Source LLC
Chambersburg PA
CBHW021415300426
44114CB00010B/505

* 9 7 8 3 3 3 7 1 3 3 8 4 9 *